THE OXFORD HANDBOOK OF

CORPORATE LAW AND GOVERNANCE

THE OXFORD HANDBOOK OF

CORPORATE LAW AND GOVERNANCE

Edited by

JEFFREY N. GORDON

and

WOLF-GEORG RINGE

OXFORD
UNIVERSITY PRESS

OXFORD

UNIVERSITY PRESS

Great Clarendon Street, Oxford, OX2 6DP,
United Kingdom

Oxford University Press is a department of the University of Oxford.
It furthers the University's objective of excellence in research, scholarship,
and education by publishing worldwide. Oxford is a registered trade mark of
Oxford University Press in the UK and in certain other countries

Published in the United States of America by Oxford University Press
198 Madison Avenue, New York, NY 10016, United States of America

British Library Cataloguing in Publication Data

Data available

Library of Congress Cataloging in Publication Data

Data available

ISBN 978-0-19-874368-2 (Hbk.)
ISBN 978-0-19-874369-9 (Pbk.)

Printed and bound by
CPI Group (UK) Ltd, Croydon, CR0 4YY

For Jessica
J.G.

For Dorothea
G.R.

Preface

CORPORATE law and corporate governance have been at the forefront of regulatory activities and scholarly attention across the world for several decades, but the field has drawn increased public attention in light of the alleged role of corporate governance in the 2007–2009 Global Financial Crisis. There is a growing need for a global framework through which to understand the aims and methods of legal research in this field. The aim of this *Oxford Handbook of Corporate Law and Governance* is to supply scholars, students, and the educated layperson with a comprehensive resource, a common point of entry into cutting edge work in corporate law and governance while not giving priority to a particular view. The approach is cross-jurisdictional, interdisciplinary, and functional. In doing so, we are proud to say, this handbook is unique; a comparable resource for corporate governance and law does not exist.

Experts and leading scholars on corporate law and governance from across the globe were given the mandate to contribute a critical reflection on scholarship in their respective subfields. It turned out that the approaches used by the various contributors are as diverse as their substance: We are happy to assemble contributions that develop ground-breaking new insights, provide critical literature reviews, explain scholarly developments and methodological controversies, and make policy contributions. In sum, the fruit of this approach is an extremely rich resource of the current state of play of scholarship in the field across a broad range of topics.

The task of putting together a volume of this ambition has been challenging. Our contributors come from different disciplines and many different jurisdictions around the globe. They bring a broad variety of approaches and methodologies to corporate law and governance, and they come with divergent cultural and historical traditions. That in itself poses a number of formidable challenges for the editors. But the greatest trial has been to cope with the dynamics and the internationalization of the field. Corporate law, as seen through an economic lens, is not anymore the simple, bi-polar conflict over power in the corporation as epitomized by the principal-agency conflict between managers and owners. Research is mushrooming on different patterns of ownership, of different legal approaches that are tested and dismissed, of competition between firms and between regulators, of standard-setting by international agencies, of trade integration and disintegration, of different negotiations of the gap between sovereigns and the firm. Globalization is penetrating into the forays of the law with an unprecedented force. Non-legal issues, practices, and mechanisms are becoming more important for both scholarship and corporate practice. This brings up a number of new challenges and poses questions of legitimacy, of law enforcement, and of market pressure.

We can make advances on these questions only with a common canon of scholarship that is grounded in international and interdisciplinary dialogue. Only by listening to each other, by understanding each other's economic problems and legal solutions, will we learn from each other. The contributors to this volume are all leading scholars in their fields and provide an international, non-parochial approach to research that is indispensable for deep dialogue. During the genesis of this Handbook, we held an authors' conference under the auspices of the Ira M. Millstein Center for Global Markets and Corporate Ownership at Columbia Law School, funding for which we acknowledge gratefully. This conference facilitated exchange and dialogue between the authors and helped to create a joint effort with a coherent trajectory.

We hope that this *Oxford Handbook* will provide a valuable resource for scholarship and research, but also for practitioners or students who seek to familiarize themselves with the latest findings from a particular field of interest. The consequence of our ambition has been a very hefty book of more than 1000 pages. But the book is also available on-line on a chapter-by-chapter basis at www.oxfordhandbooks.com.

New York and Hamburg, October 2017
Jeffrey N. Gordon
Wolf-Georg Ringe

Contents

PART II SUBSTANTIVE TOPICS

PART III NEW CHALLENGES IN CORPORATE GOVERNANCE

PART IV ENFORCEMENT

PART V ADJACENT AREAS

LIST OF CONTRIBUTORS

Zoe Adams is a Ph.D. student at the Faculty of Law, University of Cambridge.

John Armour is the Hogan Lovells Professor of Law and Finance at the University of Oxford.

Stephen M. Bainbridge is the William D. Warren Distinguished Professor of Law at UCLA Law School.

John C. Coates Jr. is the John F. Cogan, Jr. Professor of Law and Economics at Harvard Law School.

James D. Cox is the Brainerd Currie Professor of Law at Duke University School of Law.

Lawrence A. Cunningham is the Henry St. George Tucker III Research Professor of Law at George Washington Law School.

Paul Davies is a senior research fellow and a fellow of the Commercial Law Centre at Harris Manchester College, University of Oxford.

Simon Deakin is Professor of Law at the University of Cambridge.

Horst Eidenmüller is the Freshfields Professor of Commercial Law at the University of Oxford.

Luca Enriques is the Allen & Overy Professor of Corporate Law at the University of Oxford.

Guido Ferrarini is Professor Emeritus of Business Law at the University of Genoa.

Allen Ferrell is the Harvey Greenfield Professor of Securities Law at Harvard Law School.

Holger Fleischer is Director of the Max Planck Institute for Comparative and International Private Law, Hamburg.

Merritt B. Fox is the Michael E. Patterson Professor of Law and NASDAQ Professor for the Law and Economics of Capital Markets at Columbia Law School.

Ronald J. Gilson is the Charles J. Meyers Professor of Law and Business at Stanford Law School and Marc and Eva Stern Professor of Law and Business at Columbia Law School.

Jeffrey N. Gordon is Richard Paul Richman Professor of Law at Columbia Law School.

Zohar Goshen is the Alfred W. Bressler Professor of Law at Columbia Law School.

Assaf Hamdani is Professor of Law at the Buchmann Faculty of Law, Tel Aviv University.

Henry Hansmann is the Oscar M. Ruebhausen Professor of Law at Yale Law School.

Gerard Hertig is Professor of Law at the Swiss Federal Institute of Technology, Zurich.

Klaus J. Hopt is former director of the Max Planck Institute for Comparative and International Private Law, Hamburg.

Howell E. Jackson is the James S. Reid, Jr. Professor of Law at Harvard Law School.

Marcel Kahan is the George T. Lowy Professor of Law at NYU Law School.

Hideki Kanda is Emeritus Professor at the University of Tokyo and Professor at Gakushuin University.

David Kershaw is Professor of Law at the London School of Economics.

Michael Klausner is the Nancy and Charles Munger Professor of Business and Professor of Law at Stanford Law School.

Amir N. Licht is Professor of Law at the Interdisciplinary Center Herzliya.

Jonathan R. Macey is the Sam Harris Professor of Corporate Law, Corporate Finance and Securities Law at Yale Law School.

Joseph A. McCahery is Professor of International Economic Law at Tilburg University.

Curtis J. Milhaupt is Professor of Law at Stanford Law School.

Geoffrey Parsons Miller is the Stuyvesant P. Comfort Professor of Law at NYU Law School.

Maureen O'Hara is the Robert W. Purcell Professorship of Management and Adjunct Professor of Law at Cornell Law School.

Mariana Pargendler is Professor of Law at Fundação Getulio Vargas Law School, São Paulo.

Adam C. Pritchard is the Frances and Georges Skestos Professor of Law at the University of Michigan School of Law.

Wolf-Georg Ringe is Professor of Law and Director of the Institute of Law & Economics at the University of Hamburg.

Edward B. Rock is the Martin Lipton Professor of Law at NYU Law School.

Mark J. Roe is the David Berg Professor of Law at Harvard Law School.

Alexander de Roode is a researcher at the Quantitative Research department of Robeco.

Amanda M. Rose is Professor of Law at Vanderbilt School of Law.

David M. Schizer is Dean Emeritus and the Harvey R. Miller Professor of Law and Economics at Columbia Law School.

Mathias M. Siems is Professor of Commercial Law at Durham University.

Richard Squire is the Alpin J. Cameron Chair in Law at Fordham Law School.

Randall S. Thomas is the John S. Beasley II Professor of Law and Business at Vanderbilt Law School.

Maria Cristina Ungureanu is Head of Corporate Governance at Eurizon.

Massimiliano Vatiero is the Brenno Galli Chair of Law and Economics at the Law Institute (IDUSI) of the Università della Svizzera Italiana.

Erik P.M. Vermeulen is Professor of Business and Financial Law at Tilburg University.

Charles K. Whitehead is the Myron C. Taylor Alumni Professor of Business Law at Cornell Law School and Professor and Director of the Law, Technology, and Entrepreneurship Program at Cornell Tech.

Cynthia A. Williams is the Osler Chair in Business Law at Osgoode Hall Law School.

Jaap Winter is President of the Executive Board at VU University Amsterdam.

Jeffery Y. Zhang is an economist at the Board of Governors of the Federal Reserve System.

PART I

THEORETICAL APPROACHES, TOOLS, AND METHODS

CHAPTER 1

....

FROM CORPORATE LAW TO CORPORATE GOVERNANCE

....

RONALD J. GILSON

1 INTRODUCTION
....

IN 1962, Bayless Manning, the Yale Law School corporate law scholar and later Stanford Law School dean, announced the death of corporate law. Writing evocatively about a subject that was at the time deadly boring, Manning wrote:

> [C]orporation law, as a field of intellectual effort, is dead in the United States. When American law ceased to take the "corporation" seriously, the entire body of law that had been built upon that intellectual construct slowly perforated and rotted away. We have nothing left but our great empty corporation statutes—towering skyscrapers of rusted girders, internally welded together and containing nothing but wind.[1]

Manning bemoaned that the corporate statute—the rusted girders of his metaphor that provided the formal structure of the enterprise—no longer was enough to understand what really mattered: how the corporation performed. Once the formalism of the statute was recognized as insufficient itself to explain the true matter of concern, the conclusion followed: nothing was left but wind.

Manning's lament could be written off as just a law professor's realization that his discipline no longer explained enough about actual corporation behavior. But the concern was not limited to legal scholars; the same realization was coming to the surface in financial economics. In 1976, Jensen and Meckling provided what became the canonical account of the corporation in "Theory of the Firm: Managerial Behavior, Agency Costs and the Theory of

---

[1] Bayless Manning, "The Shareholders' Appraisal Remedy: An Essay for Frank Coker", 72 Yale L. J. 223, 245 n. 37 (1962). Manning's dirge for corporate law was hardly limited to the US. Speaking in broader geographic terms, Manning expanded his point. "Those of us in academic life who have specialized in corporation law face technological unemployment, or at least substantial retooling. There is still a good bit of work to be done to persuade someone to give a decent burial to the shivering skeletons. And there will be plenty of work overseas for a long time to come, for in Latin America, and to a lesser extent on the Continent, the 'corporation' yet thrives and breeds as it did in this country eighty years ago" (id.).

the Firm."[2] Addressing a different literature, Jensen and Meckling educed a metaphor similar to Manning's: the theory of the firm in economics was an "empty box."[3]

> While the literature of economics is replete with references to the 'theory of the firm,' the material generally subsumed under that heading is not a theory of the firm but actually a theory of markets in which firms are important actors. The firm is a "black box" operated so as to meet the relevant marginal conditions . . . Except for a few recent and tentative steps, however, we have no theory which explains how the conflicting objectives of the individual participants are brought into equilibrium so as to yield this result.[4]

Jensen and Meckling focused centrally on the concept of agency costs—the cost of techniques to align the incentives of the different participants necessary to conducting the corporation's business. From their perspective, the corporation was a "form of legal fiction which serves as a nexus for contracting relationships and which is also characterized by the existence of divisible residual claims on the assets and cash flows of the organization which can generally be sold without permission of the other contracting individuals."[5] Reframed in current Silicon Valley terminology, the corporation is a multi-sided platform that integrates inputs on the one hand and customers on the other.

The intellectual impact of the agency cost characterization is hard to overstate: for the last 40 years, the mission of American corporate law, and of corporate scholarship more broadly, has taken the form of a search for the organizational Holy Grail, a technique that bridges the separation of ownership and control by aligning the interests of shareholders and managers through a series of techniques, over time highlighting the role of independent directors, hostile takeovers, and activist shareholders in this effort.[6] This coalescence around corporate law as a vehicle to produce shareholder profits hit its high point when Henry Hansmann and Reinier Kraakman, in an article confidently titled "The End of History for Corporate Law," concluded that "in key commercial jurisdictions . . . there is no longer any serious competitor to the view that corporate law should principally strive to increase long-term shareholder value."[7]

The result of Jensen and Meckling's seminal reframing of corporate law into something far broader than disputes over statutory language was that both Manning's empty skyscrapers and Jensen and Meckling's empty box began to be filled. And it was no coincidence that the term "corporate governance" appeared at about this time.[8] Over a reasonably

---

[2] Michael C. Jensen & William H. Meckling, "Theory of the Firm: Managerial Behavior, Agency Costs and the Theory of the Firm", 3 J. Fin. Econ. 305 (1976).

[3] Id. at 306.   [4] Id. at 306–07.   [5] Id. at 311 (emphasis omitted).

[6] Ronald J. Gilson, "Corporate Governance and Economic Efficiency: When do Institutions Matter?", 74 Wash. U. L. Q. 327, 330 (1996). The literature and the courts are now beginning to address what happens to this theory and the case law derived from it when corporations have increasingly concentrated ownership, albeit in the form of institutions as record holders for their beneficiaries, what Jeffrey Gordon and I have called "Agency Capitalism." See Ronald J. Gilson & Jeffrey N. Gordon, "The Agency Costs of Agency Capitalism: Activist Investors and the Revaluation of Governance Rights", 113 Colum. L. Rev. 883 (2013); Ronald J. Gilson & Jeffrey N. Gordon, Agency Capitalism: Further Implications of Equity Intermediation, in Research Handbook on Shareholder Power 32 (Jennifer Hill & Randall Thomas eds., 2015).

[7] Henry Hansmann & Reinier Kraakman, "The End of History for Corporate Law", 89 Geo. L. J. 745 (2001).

[8] Brian R. Cheffins, The History of Corporate Governance, in The Oxford Handbook of Corporate Governance (2013), nicely tracks the emergence of the term corporate governance. He notes that the

short period, corporate governance codes appeared, like that of the OECD,[9] which ranged much more broadly than the limited coverage of a particular national (or state) corporate statute. Perhaps most aggressively, in 1997 during the East Asian financial crisis the International Monetary Fund and the World Bank included corporate governance reform as a condition to assistance alongside traditional macroeconomic restraints such as deficit reduction.[10] Academic attention followed the same growth pattern. For example, more than a quarter of all articles published in the Journal of Financial Economics, one of the two leading finance journals, from 1995 through August 29, 2013 were related to corporate governance.[11]

But with what have the empty skyscrapers and boxes been filled? The short answer is that the new content has addressed the variety and interaction of contracts—formal contracts, implicit contracts,[12] and the braiding of the two[13]—that Jensen and Meckling's treatment of the corporation as a nexus of platforms invites. In the remainder of this chapter, I will address three somewhat idiosyncratically chosen but nonetheless related examples of the implications of the shift from corporate law to corporate governance, from legal rules standing alone to legal rules interacting with non-legal corporate processes and institutions. Of course, the point is not to be exhaustive, nor even to provide a taxonomy covering the categories of the new content that is filling empty skyscrapers and boxes; the number and breadth of the chapters in this book make obvious that either effort necessarily exceeds my ambition here. Rather, my more limited goal is to provide examples of how this shift from

term only came into vogue in the 1970s in a single country—the United States. One outcome of this shift was that the "technological unemployment" that Manning feared did not arise. Hostile takeovers, a response to agency costs made broadly possible by the development of junk bonds, generated enormous amounts of work and profits for fancy law firms. Lincoln Caplan, Skadden: Power, Money, and the Rise of a Legal Empire chap. 5 (1993) captures the phenomenon.

[9] A current compilation of current country and NGO corporate governance codes can be found at the European Corporate Governance Institute website: http://www.ecgi.org/codes/index.php. For examples of the governance codes of large public and private institutional investors, see, e.g., "Cal. Pub. Employees' Ret. Sys., Global Principles of Accountable Corporate Governance" (2015), https://www.calpers.ca.gov/docs/forms-publications/global-principles-corporate-governance.pdf; "BlackRock, Proxy Voting Guidelines for U.S. Securities," available at http://www.blackrock.com/corporate/en-no/literature/fact-sheet/blk-responsible-investment-guidelines-us.pdf.

[10] See, e.g., Timothy Lane, et al., "IMF-Supported Programs in Indonesia, Korea, and Thailand," 72–73 (Int'l. Monetary Fund Occasional Paper No. 178, 1999); Asia Pacific Talks Vow Tough Action on Economic Crisis, N.Y. Times, Nov. 26, 1997, at A1.

[11] Out of a total of 1,533 articles published by the Journal of Financial Economics between January 1, 1995 and August 29, 2013, 414 (27%) dealt with corporate governance. Author's calculation.

[12] The term "implicit contract" comes out of the labor economics literature. The critical point is that, from a legal perspective, an implicit contract is not a contract at all: it has neither formal terms nor formal enforcement. Rather, it is a description of patterns of behavior that are enforced by reputation markets. See Sherwin T. Rosen, "Implicit Contracts: A Survey", 23 J. Econ. Lit. 1144 (1985).

[13] Ronald J. Gilson, Charles Sabel, & Robert E. Scott, "Braiding: The Interaction of Formal and Informal Contracting in Theory, Practice and Doctrine", 110 Colum. L. Rev. 1377 (2010). The term "braiding" reflects the potential for complementarity between formal law and explicit contracts on the one hand, and implicit contracts on the other. In this account formal law and explicit contracts facilitate the development and maintenance of implicit contracts; in effect, the formal components of the braid endogenize trust, the foundation for sustainable implicit contracts. Id. at 1384.

corporate law to corporate governance—from a largely legal focus to one that focuses on the corporation's inputs, outputs and how they are managed and, ultimately, the manner in which governance interfaces with other institutional elements that make up a capitalist system—complicates the problem corporate scholars, of whatever mix of disciplines, have to confront.[14]

The chapter proceeds by tracking how corporate law became corporate governance through three examples of how we have come to usefully complicate the inquiry into the structures that bear on corporate decision making and performance. Section 2 frames the first level of complication in moving from law to governance by defining governance broadly as the company's operating system, a braided framework encompassing legal and non-legal elements. Section 3 then adds a second level of complication by treating corporate governance dynamically: corporate governance becomes a path-dependent outcome of the tools available when a national governance system begins taking shape, and the process by which elements are added to the governance system going forward—driven by what Paul Milgrom and John Roberts call "supermodularity."[15] That characteristic reads importantly on both the difficulty of corporate governance, as opposed to corporate law, reform, and the non-intuitive pattern of the results of reform: significant reform leads to things getting worse before they get better. Section 3 then further complicates corporate governance by expanding it beyond the boundaries of the corporation, treating particular governance regimes as complementary to other social structures—for example, the labor market, the capital market, and the political structure—that together define different varieties of capitalism.

Section 4 then considers commonplace, but I will suggest misguided, efforts to take a different tack from sections 2 and 3: to simplify rather than complicate corporate governance analysis by recourse to now familiar single-factor analytic models in academic corporate law and governance: stakeholder theory, team production, director primacy, and shareholder primacy. Section 4 suggests that these reductions are neither models nor particularly helpful; they neither bridge the contextual specificity of most corporate governance analysis nor address the necessary interaction in allocating responsibilities among shareholders, teams, and directors. In addition, these "models" are static rather than dynamic, a serious failing in an era in which the second derivative of change is positive in many business environments and Schumpeter seems to be getting the better of Burke. Section 5 concludes by examining the importance of a corporate governance system's capacity to respond to changes in the business environment: the greater the rate of change, the more important is a governance system's capacity to adapt and the less important its ability to support long-term, firm-specific investment.

---

[14] Like Manning, I have a personal concern about the role of corporate law academics. On this front, the shift from corporate law to corporate governance and to the role of corporate governance in the larger structure of a capitalist economy, has had the desirable result of forcing corporate law academics to become interdisciplinary.

[15] Paul Milgrom & John Roberts, "Complementarities and Systems: Understanding Japanese Economic Organization", 9 Estudios Economicos 3 (1994).

2 CORPORATE GOVERNANCE AS THE CORPORATION'S OPERATING SYSTEM

In teaching corporations, I ask at the beginning of the first class a seemingly simple question: what is a corporation? After a predictable series of ever more complicated and sophisticated responses from very smart students, I dramatically display[16] a copy of a California corporation's articles of incorporation together with the Secretary of State's certifying cover page, on which appear attractive pictures of the California state animal (the grizzly bear) and state flower (the California poppy).[17] The corporation is nothing but a few pieces of paper I say, leading up to a point similar to that made by Jensen and Meckling: corporations are best understood not as a single thing but as the intersection of different things—recall that Jensen and Meckling describe then as "legal fictions."[18] To be sure, the formalities are thin and incomplete, but they are nonetheless important. For example, the corporate statute gives the entity limited liability and unlimited life, features that caused the Economist in 1926 to equate the corporation's invention with the industrial revolution's most important technological innovations.[19] But these are passive characteristics. Something more is necessary to bring the golem to life.

This sets the stage for my real point. A corporation should be defined functionally by reference to the structure that allows a legal fiction to operate a business and makes it possible for third parties to confidently do business with it. Some of these structures are legal rules that, in specified circumstances, allow the corporation to be treated, like Pinocchio, as if a real boy. However, the mass of the business operation, both in importance and in bulk, is not legal at all. It is processes of information flow, decision making, decision implementation, and decision monitoring: how people operating the corporation (1) obtain the information they need to make, implement, and monitor the results of business decisions (including information relevant to regulatory compliance); (2) distribute information from information originators to managers with sufficient expertise and experience to evaluate it; and (3) make decisions, communicate decisions to the employees who implement them, and then gather information about the consequences, for the next round.

It is obvious that the formal corporate legal skeleton covers only a very small part of how the corporation actually operates to carry out its business and continually adapts to its business environment. In Bernard Black's terms, most of the legal rules concerning the corporation's operations are "trivial,"[20] in the sense that the rules are important only if

---

[16] At least I imagine that the students have that assessment of the gesture rather than a variety of less flattering characterizations ranging from showboating to simply strange.

[17] This was how the document looked at the time my class exemplar was issued. California, as of 2014 the world's 8th largest economy (Samanta Masunaga, We're Number 8: California Near the Top of World's Largest Economies, Los Angeles Times, July 25, 2015), has statutorily designated not only a state animal and state flower, but also a state bird, a state amphibian, a state fossil, a state insect, and 28 other categories of designated state symbols. See California Governance Code Sections 420–429.8.

[18] Jensen & Meckling, *supra* note 2, at 310.   [19] Economist, Dec. 18, 1926.

[20] Bernard Black, "Is Corporate Law Trivial? A Political and Economic Analysis", 24 Nw. U. L. Rev. 542 (1990).

they are ignored despite how easy they are to satisfy. The rest and obviously most important part of the governance structure—the dark matter of corporate governance—is the realm of reporting relationships, organizational charts, compensation arrangements, information gathering, and internal controls and monitoring, all largely non-legally dictated policies, practices, and procedures that do not appear in the corporate statute or the corporation's charter or bylaws. To be sure, non-legal governance processes can morph into the "legal" when legislatures conclude that self-generated governance is less effective than social welfare demands. A familiar example: after the Enron/WorldCom accounting scandals, Sarbanes–Oxley imposed a set of governance requirements over financial reporting, which included external monitoring of internal controls, a specified board committee structure and composition, and mandatory officer responsibilities. But, in general, even where the board has compliance responsibilities, the implementation is for the firm to work out.

Put differently, corporate governance is the corporation's operating system. This characterization of governance in operational terms is reflected in the description of corporate governance offered by the Business Roundtable, an organization composed of the CEOs of many of the largest US corporations:

> A good corporate governance structure is a working system for principled goal setting, effective decision making, and appropriate monitoring of compliance and performance. Through this vibrant and responsive structure, the CEO, the senior management team and the board of directors can interact effectively and respond quickly and appropriately to changing circumstances, within a framework of solid corporate values, to provide enduring value to the shareholders who invest in the enterprise.[21]

The end of the odd journey from corporate law to a more complex corporate governance system would give Dean Manning solace. His skyscrapers have been filled to overflowing, but formal law—the corporate statute and cases interpreting it—occupy far fewer floors in the building. The outcome of this integration of law and managerial mechanisms puts law in an important but plainly subordinate role in the corporation's operating system:

> Investors provide to a corporation the funds with which it acquires real assets. The investors receive in return financial claims (securities) on the corporation's future cash flows. The size of these future cash flows then depends importantly on management's choice of what real assets to acquire and how well these assets are managed over time. The capital market's pricing of the financial claims acquired by investors is in effect a valuation of these future cash flows. Corporate law provides a framework within which a firm's managers make these investment and operating decisions. Properly designed, this legal framework helps spur management to choose and deploy assets in ways that maximize the value of the firm's expected future cash flows . . . The better corporate and securities law perform these tasks, the more valuable the corporation's underlying business and correspondingly, the financial claims that the corporation issues.[22]

---

[21] "Principles of Corporate Governance 2005," Business Roundtable, November 2005, at 6.
[22] Edward G. Fox, Merritt B. Fox, & Ronald J. Gilson, "Economic Crisis and the Integration of Law and Finance", 116 Colum. L. Rev. 325, 327–28 (2016).

3 PATH DEPENDENCE: CORPORATE GOVERNANCE, COMPLEMENTARITY, AND SUPERMODULARITY

The second effort to complicate corporate governance adds a dynamic dimension. Corporate governance is path dependent—history matters significantly.[23] In a path-dependent environment with factors such as increasing returns and network externalities, an observed equilibrium may be inefficient compared to arrangements possible at the time of the comparison that were not available when the arrangements arose. Initial conditions, determined by fortuitous events or non-economic factors such as culture, politics, or geography, can start the system down a specific path. For example, Silicon Valley's development near to the San Francisco Bay next to Stanford University, as opposed to the shores of Lake Michigan where Northwestern and the University of Chicago are about the same distance from each other as Stanford and the University of California at Berkeley, depended importantly on initial conditions. These included, importantly, Stanford's hiring Frederick Terman as dean of the engineering school shortly after World War II. Terman had directed one of the Cambridge, Massachusetts wartime labs that sought to bring cutting-edge science to bear in support of the war effort and so recognized the value of translational research, that is, the link between university research and its practical application.[24] Put simply, "history matters."[25]

That history matters influences the dynamics of the system to be understood. In particular, history's shadow can make it difficult to reform existing institutions or adjust to changes in a company's product market even if current alternatives exist that, absent transition costs, would be more efficient. In the context of corporate governance as defined here, the role of complementarities drives the system down a path from which it is difficult later to depart. By "complementarities" I have in mind governance elements that create value because they make the existing system work better as a whole, and the fact that the "efficiency" of an element cannot be separated from the question of "fit."

One of the major corporate governance questions to which path dependence and complementarity gives rise can be usefully framed in terms of the operating system metaphor: in a world of increasingly global product and capital markets, is there room for multiple corporate operating systems? Do particular corporate governance systems give rise to sustainable competitive advantage in particular product markets? What happens if a particular

---

[23] Among the efforts to apply path dependency to corporate governance, see Lucian A. Bebchuk & Mark J. Roe, "A Theory of Path Dependence in Corporate Governance and Ownership", 52 Stan. L. Rev. 127 (1999); Marcel Kahan & Michael Klausner, "Path Dependence in Corporate Contracting: Increasing Returns, Herd Behavior and Cognitive Biases", 74 Wash. U. L. Q. 347 (1996); See Ronald J. Gilson, "Corporate Governance and Economic Efficiency: When do Institutions Matter?", 74 Wash. U. L. Q. 327 (1996).

[24] "[I]ndustrial districts are path dependent—an industrial district's location may result not from the invisible hand of efficiency, but from 'the details of the seemingly transient and adventitious circumstance.'" Ronald J. Gilson, "The Legal Infrastructure of High Technology Industrial Districts: Silicon Valley, Route 128 and Covenants not to Compete", 74 N. Y. U. L. Rev. 575, 577 (1999), quoting Paul A. David & Joshua L. Rosenboom, "Marshallian Factor Market Externalities and the Dynamics of Industrial Localization", 28 J. Urban Econ. 349, 368 (1990).

[25] Masahisa Fujita & Jacques-François Thisse, "Economics of Agglomeration", 10 J. Japanese & Int'l. Econ. 339, 341 (1996); Paul Krugman, "Space: The Final Frontier", 12 J. Econ. Perspect. 161 (1998).

governance system is efficient until a change in the market renders it less efficient than that of new competitors and path dependency slows adjustment?[26]

3.1 The Japanese Example

The development of Japanese corporate governance exemplifies the influence of complementarities on the persistence of corporate governance structure as broadly defined in section 2. Suppose one begins with an initial condition of a commitment to lifetime employment for a large number of employees, as was the case in the development of postwar Japanese corporate governance.[27] The next question relates to the influence of that initial condition on a corporation's production process. Because the norm of lifetime employment makes human capital a long-term asset, the company will sensibly make substantial firm-specific human capital investments in its employees, thus developing a work force that supports team and horizontal coordination.[28]

In turn, the need to protect this long-term investment in human capital fits best with bank, as opposed to stock market-based, financing, to prevent the stock market from upsetting the company's implicit commitments to labor. Bank-based finance elevates the role of the bank as the monitor of managerial performance, rather than the public shareholders; this means suppressing public shareholders' rights and expectations relative to those of the bank. The need to monitor the performance of a management freed from stock market oversight thus led to the post-World War II Japanese main bank system. A single bank (typically leading a syndicate of banks) directly monitored a company's investment choice through the company's need to borrow to fund new projects, and through the information about the company's cash flow and performance that came to the bank through its provision of the company's general banking services.[29] Commonly, the main bank and the other banks that participated in providing loans to the company also held significant amounts of the company's equity, again out of a concern that a hostile takeover might upset the company's labor and financing arrangements.

---

[26] An early article, Rebecca M. Henderson & Kim M. Clark, "The Reorganization of Existing Product Technologies and the Failure of Established firms", 35 Admin. Sci. Qtly. 9 (1990), illustrates this point by demonstrating that the market leader in one generation of product architecture loses out in the next, weighed down by having to unlearn all of the capabilities that made it succeed in the prior generation. For more recent analysis, see Steven Blader, Claudine Gartenberg, Rebecca Henderson & Andrea Prat, "The Real Effects of Relational Contracts", 105 Am. Econ. Rev. 452 (2015, Papers and Proceedings).

The same analysis applies when the question is posed with respect to competition between national governance systems. For the application of this analysis to the effect of changes in product markets on competition between national governance systems, see Gilson, *supra* note 23, at 329–34.

[27] A commitment to lifetime employment was itself a response to labor conditions in post-World War II occupied Japan manifested by labor occupation of factories and the belief that it was needed to constrain the communist movement in Japan. See Ronald J. Gilson & Mark Roe, "Lifetime Employment: Labor Peace and the Evolution of Japanese Corporate Governance", 99 Colum. L. Rev. 508 (1999).

[28] See Masahiko Aoki, "Toward an Economic Model of the Japanese Firm", 28 J. Econ. Lit. 1 (1990).

[29] The collection of articles in The Japanese Main Bank System: Its Relevance for Developing and Transforming Economies (M. Aoki & H. Patrick eds., 1995) depicts the main bank system at its apogee.

Should the company fall on hard times, the main bank was expected to bail it out, through the provision of additional funds, but at the price of displacement of management with bank employees. The main bank bailout expectation was understood to be "an institutional arrangement complementary to the system of permanent employment." Bailout "helps to preserve the firm-specific human assets accumulated in the framework of the lifetime employment system and hence provides incentives for them to be generated in the first place."[30] In turn, this package of attributes and the related internal production methods are complementary to particular kinds of activity. The Japanese governance system, with its large investment in firm-specific employee human capital, is very effective when innovation is linear, and depends importantly on team work, but it is much less effective when innovation is discontinuous—the Japanese structure does not lend itself to Schumpetarian (or Christensen-like[31]) disruption.[32] The overall result has been a tightly integrated system of production that has been difficult to change in response to changing business conditions and opportunities for innovation.

In Milgrom and Roberts' terms, the relationship between these governance and associated organizational characteristics is supermodular. By that term they mean that at each decision node where a new governance or characteristics must be added to the existing system, the corporation will choose from among the alternatives that which best "fits" with the already present elements. That fit, in turn, is a function not just of the efficiency of the new element standing alone—the increased productivity that results simply from its addition—but also of the new element's capacity to improve the performance of the existing elements—the extent to which it is supermodular.[33]

The complementarity among elements of the system, then, is a barrier to reform of the system because changing one element in the system results in degrading the performance of all other system elements to which that element was complementary. Just as adding a complementary element increased system performance by more than its own contribution, removing an element, by regulatory design or voluntarily in response to changed economic conditions, reduces performance of all elements. Like financial leverage, supermodularity steepens the performance curve both on the upside and on the downside: short of changing all elements of the system at once, reform will result in reduced system performance until enough of the system changes to recreate complementarities among the new and remaining elements.

Continuing the Japanese example, the combination of allowing Japanese companies to access non-Japanese sources of capital through the Eurodollar market and the enormous success of Japanese companies such that projects could be financed through cash flow rather than bank-provided project finance, eroded the role of the main bank. The contemporaneous drop in the value of the Nikkei reduced the value of the banks' cross-holdings in its

---

[30] Masahiko Aoki, Hugh Patrick, & Paul Sheard, The Japanese Main Bank System: An Introductory Overview 3, 18, in Aoki & Patrick, *supra* note 29.

[31] See Clayton M. Christensen, The Innovator's Dilemma: When New Technologies Cause Great Firms to Fail (1997).

[32] See Peter A. Hall & David Soskice, An Introduction to Varieties of Capitalism, in Varieties Of Capitalism: The Institutional Foundations of Comparative Advantage 35 (Peter A. Hall & David Soskice eds., 2001); Aoki & Patrick, *supra* note 29.

[33] Milgrom & Roberts, *supra* note 15.

customer companies, which necessitated sales of significant amounts of those holdings to maintain bank compliance with capital requirements.[34] At the same time, conditions in many product markets came to favor discontinuous innovation rather than linear innovation. Reduced performance of any part of a governance system built on complementarities reduced the performance of the entire Japanese governance system, yet the previously efficient complementarities create a barrier to reform.

This analysis provides background to understanding why the recent corporate governance reform proposals of Prime Minister Shinzo Abe represent more than tinkering with the formal relationships between shareholders and managers. The main bank system has not functioned for years, cross-shareholdings are of lesser significance, and Companies' Act revisions provide a better framework for activist investors and reflect a conscious effort to use government intervention to overcome path dependencies that sustain a no longer advantageous system of governance and production. Nonetheless, there has been little change in the labor market, including especially the continued absence of an external market for managerial talent and the actual operation of Japanese corporate governance—the Japanese corporation's operating system—remains familiar.

3.2 Expanding the Complementarity Concept: Varieties of Capitalism

The transformation of corporate law into corporate governance discussed in section 2 and the recognition of the impact of complementarities within a single country's governance system were importantly expanded through a literature that has been styled "the varieties of capitalism."[35] A governance system experiences path-dependent complementarities, not only internally among a company's factors of production, but also among a country's corporate governance system and other social and economic institutions including, importantly, the state. Simplifying the more complex yet elegant structure of the literature, different countries have different varieties of capitalism. A capitalist system necessarily has more or less coordination among labor markets, corporate governance arrangements, capital markets, and the educational system that provides worker training both outside and inside the firm consistent with the skill sets associated with firm organization and production. The state's political and social system—for example, the government's role in the economy both directly through state ownership and also more indirectly through the regulatory structure—must fit with the overall structure dictated by the interaction of the other elements. In turn, the institutions through which government and social influences operate are both forged through the relationships among the various inputs to the particular form of capitalism, and serve as the field on which those controlling the input strategically interact.[36]

---

[34] See Hideaki Miyajima & Fumiaki Kuroki, The Unwinding of Cross-Shareholding in Japan: Causes, Effects, and Implications, in Corporate Governance in Japan: Institutional Change and Organizational Diversity 79 (Masahiko Aoki, Gregory Jackson, and Hideaki Miyajima eds., 2007).

[35] See generally, Varieties of Capitalism: The Institutional Foundations of Comparative Advantage (Peter A. Hall & David Soskice eds., 2001).

[36] Peter A. Hall & David Soskice, An Introduction to Varieties of Capitalism 3, in Hall & Soskice, *supra* note 35.

The result is a stylized typology of two general forms of economic and political organ-ization. Each displays, although the term is not used, supermodularity—the pieces evolve to facilitate the variety's functioning and to reinforce each of its elements. In this account, the two rough forms of political economy are called "liberal market economies" (LME) and "coordinated market economies" (CME). In LMEs, firms coordinate their activities largely through hierarchies within the firm and through competitive markets outside the firm.[37] The basic tools are said to be contracts and arm's-length arrangements.[38] In CMEs, firm activities operate importantly through non-market arrangements, relying on relational arrangements supported by reputation and, more generally, through incomplete contracting supported by public and private regulatory institutions. Firms and markets are organized through strategic interaction among firms and other institutions. "In some nations, for in-stance, firms rely primarily on formal contracts and highly competitive markets to organize relationships with their employees and suppliers of finance, while, in others, firms coord-inate these endeavors differently."[39] It will be obvious, for example, into which category the Japanese main bank system falls.

The last element in the analysis is dynamic: each system's political, social, and corpor-ate governance institutions evolve in a path-dependent fashion from an initial condi-tion to a coordinated structure of complementary institutions driven by choices based on supermodularity and complementarities: "nations with a particular kind of coordination in one sphere of the economy should tend to develop complementary practices in other spheres as well."[40] For example, a stock-market-based capital market implies market-based institutions in the financial sector consistent with the development of a vibrant venture capital market not generally present in countries with a bank-centered capital market[41] and a labor market characterized by employment at will, while extensive employment pro-tection is associated with non-market coordination of industrial relations.[42] Similarly, stock-market-based capital markets are associated with market monitoring of company per-formance through control contests, while bank-centered capital markets are associated with bank-mediated monitoring and the absence of stockholder-driven control contests. On this account, the United States and the United Kingdom exemplify LME nations while Germany and Japan are CME nations.

My goal in this section was to further complicate our understanding of corporate law and corporate governance by embedding governance in a broader framework whose components are complementary and by highlighting the dynamics of that broader system. The "varieties of capitalism" approach takes us part of the way. On the one hand, it stresses how different systems came to their present form. On the other, however, it does not fully

---

[37] Id. at 8.

[38] Later developments in contract theory complicate this formulation somewhat. In LMEs, formal and informal contracts can be complementary, supporting relational arrangements. See Gilson, Sabel, & Scott, *supra* note 13.

[39] Hall & Soskice, *supra* note 35, at 9.

[40] Id. at 18. Mark Roe, for example, explores in detail the interaction between a country's political institutions and its corporate governance practices. See Mark J. Roe, Political Determinants of Corporate Governance (2006).

[41] See Ronald J. Gilson & Bernard Black, "Venture Capital and the Structure of Capital Markets: Banks versus Stock Markets", 47 J. Fin. Econ. 243 (1998).

[42] Hall & Soskice, Introduction, *supra* note 36.

address the tension between path dependency and the need for a particular variety to respond to changes in markets and products. For example, the capacity of globalization and technology to disrupt existing industry and employment patterns highlights the importance of the extent to which particular varieties (and sub-varieties) of capitalism are adaptively efficient.[43] The US system is said to be adaptively efficient but at the same time criticized for being too "short-term" oriented, while the Japanese system was praised for its capacity to credibly commit to long-term investment horizons, but appears to be slow in adapting to significant changes in markets and technologies.[44]

This poses what now may be the most interesting question—can a single system be both adaptive and committed? To close with a speculation, corporate governance serves to support risk transfer. As capital markets become more complete, additional mechanisms of transfer become available. The ability to transfer risk in slices through derivatives, in contrast to a broadband risk-bearing instrument like common stock, creates the option of a company remaining privately held as a commitment device to a particular investment horizon that matches its markets and skills.[45] From this perspective, adaption takes place through self-selection at the company level, rather than at the system level.

A final qualification remains. The "varieties of capitalism" approach dates from the turn of the millennium. We now observe new governance patterns evolving from scratch where there is no prior path. Chinese state capitalism offers a form of coordinated system, but one in which the resolution of tensions among stakeholders more directly flows through the state and party apparatus rather than through the interaction between the company and other relational institutions, and where a question remains whether corporate governance and its formal components serve the same function in the Chinese system that they do in other varieties of capitalism.[46]

4 ANALYTIC MODELS IN CORPORATE GOVERNANCE

To this point, I have broadly summarized the evolution of corporate law into corporate governance and then from corporate governance as a stand-alone concept into a component of

---

[43] See Douglas C. North, Institutions, Institutional Change and Economic Performance 36 (1990).

[44] This is a debate that goes back at least 25 years. See Gilson & Gordon, *supra* note 6, at 332–33.

[45] Ronald J. Gilson & Charles Whitehead, Deconstructing Equity, discusses the potential for this method of adaptive efficiency. See Ronald J. Gilson & Charles Whitehead, "Deconstructing Equity: Public Ownership, Agency Costs and Complete Capital Markets", 108 Colum. L. Rev. 231 (2008).

[46] Curtis Milhaupt raises the question of whether corporate governance in China serves the same function as in other systems, and so whether familiar comparative analysis is helpful. Curtis J. Milhaupt, "Chinese Corporate Capitalism in Comparative Context" (October 13, 2015). Columbia Law and Economics Working Paper No. 522. Available at SSRN: http://ssrn.com/abstract=2673797. Elsewhere, Milhaupt helpfully describes the existing pattern and structures of Chinese government ownership of large companies, posing the question of whether the challenge is not the particular elements of Chinese corporate governance, but whether there is a span of control problem that suggests a conglomerate on steroids. See Li-Wen Lin & Curtis J. Milhaupt, "We Are the (National) Champions: Understanding the Mechanisms of State Capitalism in China", 67 Stan. L. Rev. 697 (2013).

a particular capitalist system made up of complementary subsystems and whose path dependency defines the characteristics of the broader system's adaptive dynamics. Like evolutionary systems more generally, the movement was towards greater complexity. Section 4 now further emphasizes complexity by critically assessing recent efforts to simplify, rather than complicate, our understanding of corporate governance through single-factor governance models. As can be predicted by my account in sections 2 and 3, I view these models as interesting and intriguing, but inevitably partial, the equivalent of a painter's studies for a larger work. For the kind of analytic non-formal models used by legal academics, the right methodological move is to complicate, not simplify. Perhaps most important, these single-factor models are largely static, immune in their positive and normative analysis to the influence of the broader concept of governance addressed in section 3.

4.1 Models in Corporate Law

Some 40 years after economics began making important inroads into corporate law scholarship, a significant amount of academic, but not judicial, attention is still directed at devising the right "model" of corporate law and governance.[47] The "shareholder primacy" model contests with the "stakeholders" model, which in turn confronts the "team production" model and the "director primacy" model. In section 4 I argue that this debate, as engaging, interesting, and extended as it has been, is ultimately a blind alley, both theoretically and practically. The reasons are not complicated, although as I have suggested in sections 2 and 3, we have come to understand that the behavior that this dialogue has sought to explain is quite complicated. Indeed, it is the very complexity of the phenomenon to be explained that allows a simple critique of singular static explanations.

Each of these "models" seeks to explain the structure and performance of complex business organizations—law is relevant only to the extent that it interacts with other factors in shaping the corporation's operating system—by reference to a single explanatory variable. The single variable character of the contending accounts has resulted in an oddly driven circular debate that is prolonged because those proffering each model defend it by emphasizing the limits of the others—something like an academic perpetual motion machine. In fact, each of the models is part of a more complicated description of a very complex phenomenon.

Stephen Bainbridge, whose entry into the single factor horse race I will address later in this section, invokes the fable of the blind men and the elephant in arguing that an overarching concept of the corporation is needed.[48] An account of corporate organization that does not feature prominently each of the contending model's central features—shareholders, managers, and employees, stakeholders and directors—is limited to explaining only

---

[47] It is interesting that the Delaware judiciary appears to be more sensitive to the dynamics of corporate governance. While the broad claim of the adaptive character of Delaware corporate law dates to the Supreme Court's approval of an early variety of the poison pill in *Unocal Corp. v. Mesa Petroleum*, 493 A.2d 946 (Del. 1985), the Delaware courts appear to recognize the impact on governance of the intermediation of equity. See Gilson & Gordon, *supra* note 6.

[48] Stephan M. Bainbridge, "Competing Concepts of the Corporation (a.k.a. Criteria—Just Say No)", 2 Berkeley Bus. L. J. 79, 83 (2005). Lynn Stout, whose competing model is also addressed in section 4, invokes the parable as well. Lynn A. Stout, "On the Nature of Corporations", 9 Deakin L. Rev. 775 (2004).

part of the phenomenon. Elephants have trunks, tails, ears, and legs; corporations have shareholders, managers, and employees, stakeholders and directors. Making the elephant walk and the corporation function effectively requires that all of these parts work together— the task is organizational intelligent design or, as I have called the exercise more generally, transaction cost engineering.[49] And that requires an explanation that focuses on more than one factor, however overarching. The problem of understanding corporate organization is interesting and hard because it requires explaining the interaction of multiple inputs in a dynamic setting, a problem that vexes both formal and informal modelers.

I should pause for a moment to clarify what I mean by a model. Of course, none of the accounts I address here involves a formal mathematical model of the sort familiar from the economic and finance literatures. They are more in the style of an informal analytic narrative,[50] which persuades because its explanation rings true rather than because the equations balance.[51] This technique is a kind of verbal regression that restricts the degrees of freedom in explaining a phenomenon by complicating rather than simplifying. A real regression first simplifies the problem as the interaction of two variables, and then measures the power of the explanation by the closeness of the data point—the dots—to the least square line.[52] An analytic regression operates in exactly the opposite fashion: by increasing the number of dots that must be connected, but now by a narrative rather than by a regression line. A workshop question that asks "what about" a particular fact challenges the verbal regression with a dot the presenter's explanation of a phenomenon cannot explain, and so limits the degrees of freedom in constructing a narrative explanation.

In the remainder of this section I will briefly survey the contending models—stakeholders, team production, director primacy, and shareholder primacy—highlighting both why each model's animating factor is important and why it is partial. In doing so I will not do justice either to the extensive literature associated with each model or the sophistication of some of the debate.[53] My point is simply that, standing alone, none of the single-factor models explain the complex phenomenon of the governance of corporations in a dynamic context.

4.1.1 *Stakeholder Model*

A stakeholder model of corporation law or governance recognizes that the corporation is a major social institution that is at the core of a capitalist system. In the United States, large public corporations produce the bulk of GDP, employ vast numbers of workers and so support the stability of families and communities, and pay taxes at every level of the nation— local, state, and federal. It has become commonplace to credit the corporate form with a

---

[49] See Ronald J. Gilson, "Value Creation by Business Lawyers: Legal Skills and Asset Pricing", 93 Yale L. J. 239 (1984).

[50] See Robert H. Bates, Avner Grief, Margaret Levi, Jean-Laurent Rosenthal, & Barry R. Weingast, Analytic Narratives 3–23 (1998). Robert H. Bates, Beyond the Miracle of the Market: The Political Economy of Agrarian Development in Kenya (2005), provides an excellent example of this approach.

[51] This genre characterizes most of my own work as well, with the exception of occasional efforts with more formally oriented colleagues. See, e.g., Ronald J. Gilson & Alan Schwartz, "Corporate Control and Credible Commitment", 43 Int'l. Rev. L. & Econ. 115 (2015).

[52] For present purposes, I do not address multiple variable analysis.

[53] In particular, I will keep the number of references in the footnotes limited to illustrative examples. Otherwise, I fear, the references will get in the way of the argument.

significant role in economic productivity. For example, writing in 1926, the Economist magazine trumpeted this role:

> Economic historians of the future may assign to the nameless inventor of the principle of limited liability, as applied to trading corporations, a place of honor with Watt and Stephenson, and other pioneers of the industrial revolution. The genius of these men produced the means by which man's command of natural resources has multiplied many times over; the limited liability company the means by which huger aggregations of capital required to give effect to their discoveries were collected, organized and efficiently administered.[54]

It then follows simply enough that all those affected by the performance of the corporation have an interest in its operation, which leads in turn to an economic measure of social welfare against which a corporation's performance can be measured: as framed by economists Patrick Bolton, Marco Becht, and Alicia Roell, the net gain to all those doing business with the company, thereby requiring a netting of gains and losses among, for example, customers, suppliers, employees, and shareholders.[55]

Intertwined with this measure of overall productivity, however, is a distributional concern. If the gains arising from the corporation's activity are not shared among stakeholders in a fashion perceived as equitable, the social legitimacy necessary to support efficient production breaks down, a framing that resonates with the current income equality debate and the populist themes now current in US politics across both the Democratic and Republican parties.[56] In the more recent governance debate, the stakeholder model is situated as a response to the position Hansmann and Kraakman describe as now dominant: that the corporation should be run to maximize shareholder value.[57]

What is missing in the stakeholder account, however, is the link between the stakeholder model and production. While production may depend on a broad perception that the fruits of production are equitably distributed, in the absence of efficient production, that task is made more difficult because there is less to distribute. A fair criticism is that too little attention is given to the governance mechanisms through which stakeholder interests can be taken into account consistent with efficient production. To be sure, stakeholder board representation has been a matter of debate but hardly implementation in the United States, and co-determination is a familiar but narrow European phenomenon.[58] And as Henry

---

[54] Economist, *supra* note 19.

[55] Patrick Bolton, Marco Becht, & Alicia Roell, Corporate Governance and Control, Handbook of the Economics of Finance, vol. 1, 1–109 (2003). See Michael Magill, Martine Quinzil, & Jean-Charles Rochet, "A Theory of the Stakeholder Corporation", 83 Econometrica 1685 (2015). Roberta Romano traces recognition in the United States of corporations' need to orchestrate the competing demands of suppliers, customers, employees, and the community to Adolf Berle in Power Without Property (1959). Roberta Romano, "Metapolitics and Corporate Law Reform", 36 Stan. L. Rev. 923 (1984).

[56] Mark J. Roe, "Backlash", 98 Colum. L. Rev. 222 (1998), provides an interesting account of the intersection of these forces in early twentieth-century Argentina.

[57] Hansmann & Kraakman, *supra* note 7. To be fair, Hansmann and Kraakman are typically used as a trope for a position—all that matters is shareholders—that they explicitly do not take. See *infra* note 62.

[58] See, e.g., Romano, *supra* note 55 at 963–971. A flurry of US state statutes that allowed or obligated boards of directors to take stakeholders into account have been largely without substance. Most important, these statutes, as well as corporate charter provisions that mirrored the statutes, were not enforceable by their putative beneficiaries.

Hansmann pointed out some years ago, there is no legal reason why large corporations are capital rather than labor cooperatives.[59]

Yet the problem with a stakeholder model remains: it is a one-factor model, largely concerned with distributional issues as a counterpoint but not as an alternative to shareholder primacy. To be sure, behavioral economics provides evidence that perceptions of fairness may in some circumstances be complementary to, rather than in tension with, maximizing production[60] and that framing the corporate purpose only in terms of shareholder value may dissuade boards of directors from taking action that increases the size of the pie if it reduces the piece shareholders receive. However, what remains largely unaddressed in the stakeholder discussion is how to hold accountable the corporate decision makers, composed largely of white, older men and, almost without exception, wealthy people, whatever their ethnicity or gender, for the size of the pie the corporation creates or for its distribution.

4.1.2 *Team Production*

A team production theory of corporate governance, energetically advanced by Margaret Blair and Lynn Stout, seeks to fill the gap in stakeholder theory by directly linking a concern with non-shareholder constituencies, especially employees, to firm productivity.[61] The model, stated simply, is that efficient production is a function of firm-specific investment by a wide range of stakeholders—a team, rather than a hierarchy. However, if the stakeholder's firm-specific investment is subject to opportunistic grabbing by a different stakeholder—for example, the shareholders—the stakeholder will be less willing to make the efficient level of investment. For example, employees may be reluctant to make firm-specific human capital investments if shareholders can subsequently renege on the firm's promise to pay the employee a return on that investment.[62]

---

[59] Henry Hansmann, The Ownership of Enterprise (1996).

[60] The empirical evidence is collected in Gilson, Sabel, & Scott, *supra* note 13, at 1384–86.

[61] The original statement of the model is found in Margaret M. Blair & Lynn A. Stout, "A Team Production Theory of Corporate Law", 85 Va. L. Rev. 247 (1990).

[62] The converse will also be true. While shareholders can sell their shares if they are treated poorly, the sale price will reflect that treatment, in effect capitalizing the expected reduced returns associated with other stakeholders' opportunism. The drop in share price then will reflect the stakeholders' opportunism. The usual reference for the argument to how shareholders can opportunistically shift returns from other stakeholders to themselves is Andrei Shleifer & Lawrence Summers, Breach of Trust in Hostile Takeovers, in Hostile Takeovers: Causes and Consequences 33 (A. Auerbach ed., 1988). For present purposes I note only that the analysis does not parse. In short form, Shleifer & Summers use post-airline deregulation as an examination of shareholder opportunism. The effect of deregulation was to allow entry of low-cost airlines with the result that the loss of the regulatory rents that had accrued to capital and labor resulted in losses to both. From this perspective, the takeovers that hit the industry were a process of allocating that loss between labor and capital. While Shleifer and Summers argue that the resulting allocation violated an implicit contract between airline and management, they do not explain how one would identify the terms of an implicit contract concerning an event—deregulation—that was not anticipated. They do suggest that the reallocation was only possible because post-takeover management did not value the prior management's reputation and the resulting ability to enter into implicit contracts. However, they do not explain why an asset that is valuable to prior management is not equally valuable to post-takeover management. See Ronald J. Gilson & Bernard S. Black, The Law and Finance of Corporate Acquisitions 620–22 (1995).

The need to protect all stakeholders' firm-specific investments gives rise to the team production model's governance implications. The model calls for a decision maker who will coordinate the contributions of different stakeholders to protect their expectations of a return on their investments, i.e., to see that the stakeholders play well together and so increase the size of the pie rather than squabble over the efforts of one stakeholder group to expropriate a different group's piece. Blair and Stout assign this function to the board of directors who operate, in their somewhat awkward term, as "mediating hierarchs," balancing the various stakeholders' interaction, and so facilitating the right ex ante level of specific investment by all parties.

The reader will recognize that the team production model closely tracks the efficiency analysis of the Japanese main bank governance model considered in section 3; Japanese horizontal organization of production is framed, as is the team production model, in contrast to US vertical organization. In the Japanese governance model, lifetime employment, protected by limited reliance on equity financing and main bank monitoring, encourages employees to make firm-specific human capital investment by protecting them from opportunistic behavior by shareholders, and so provides a foundation for a very efficient manufacturing system that is built around horizontal planning, decision-making, and production processes. But the reader will also recall that the advantage of Japanese horizontal organization of production is contextual. First, it is more effective than US-style hierarchical organization when innovation is linear, as in precision manufacturing, but inferior to the US style when innovation is discontinuous. Second, team production's stability depends on conditions in the capital and product markets—increasing alternative sources of capital, for example, degraded the critical role of the main bank, as did the success of the companies themselves, who then could avoid main bank monitoring by financing projects through internally generated funds.

Unlike Aoki's development of "J form governance,"[63] Blair and Stout's claim for team production is largely acontextual. The problem is that, as analysis of Japanese governance shows, team production is a strategy, not the "right" way to organize governance or production; it fits some industries, some production techniques, and some clusters of complementary elements of one variety of capitalism at particular times, but not others. Indeed, in some contexts, horizontal teams and vertical non-teams both may work. The difference in strategies between Costco and Sam's Club, both US big-box-membership grocery and sundries stores, is a good example. They are direct competitors but they treat their workers quite differently. Costco pays higher wages, provides healthcare, etc. Costco's position is that company profits are higher if their workers like their jobs and want to keep them (a business person's account of an efficiency wage story). Sam's Club (owned by Walmart) treats its workers materially worse than Costco, but nonetheless performs adequately.[64]

A second problem is more directly governance related: who polices the behavior of the mediating hierarchs even in a team production context? In the US governance model, the only formal source of constraint is the right of only one stakeholder—the shareholders—to vote. However, as Blair and Stout stress, so long as the corporation resembles the Berle and Means pattern of widely distributed ownership, the right to vote and so the power to monitor the hierarchs, is dramatically diluted by coordination costs: proxy contests are expensive

---

[63] Aoki, *supra* note 28.

[64] This assessment is examined in Liza Featherstone, "Wage Against the Machine", Slate (June 27, 2008), http://www.slate.com/articles/business/moneybox/2008/06/wage_against_the_machine.html.

and while their costs are borne by the proponent of the fight, the gains are shared by all shareholders. This leaves the hierarchs on a very long leash indeed.

The problem with hierarchs, then, is that strategy and governance follow changes in the capital market rather than lead it.[65] The wide discretion Blair and Stout claim for the hierarchs was first challenged by the development of junk bonds in the 1980s.[66] The availability of financing to corporate outsiders allowed a large increase in hostile takeovers that were used to take apart the residue of the failure of the 1970s conglomerate experiment. The result was to significantly shorten management's leash. Non-statutory monitoring techniques, like tender offers, provided a shortcut around the coordination costs associated with widely distributed shareholdings: Even small shareholders could recognize a large premium when one was offered, although the need to secure financing to purchase the target limited the size of the companies that were potential targets. The debate over efforts to constrain capital market monitoring though target company defensive tactics—the extent to which mediating hierarchs could prevent shareholders from accepting a hostile bid—then raged on for 30 years.

More recently, the capital market fault line shifted again—ownership of equity became increasingly intermediated through institutional investors holding stock as record owners for widely dispersed beneficial owners. Shareholdings in US public corporations are now quite concentrated as a result of equity intermediation—a number of institutions whose representatives could be seated around a large boardroom table collectively hold voting rights that effectively control most corporations—ushering in what Jeff Gordon and I have called "Agency Capitalism."[67] At this point, activist hedge funds and other specialized shareholder activists entered the fray as complements to the new ownership concentration. Rather than buying targets themselves, such activists tee up strategic business choices for decision by "reticent" rather than passive institutional shareholders and in that way serve as a catalyst for the expression of institutional shareholder voice. This further erodes the coordination costs barrier to monitoring mediating hierarchs. Because an activist's own stock purchase need be only large enough to credibly signal its conviction in its proposals, even the largest public corporations are potentially "in play." Put differently, the activist shareholders differ from the raiders of the 1980s in that instead of leveraging the target's balance sheet to finance a takeover, they leverage the equity holdings of institutional investors to win a proxy contest conditional on convincing the institutional investors that the activist's proposal is sound.[68] And here context is again central. If the mediating hierarchs are largely walled off from capital market monitoring, now through proxy fights rather than takeovers, companies' responses to changes in the business environment are slowed down, a very undesirable result if, as appears to be the case, the rate of change in the business environment is increasing. Bad governance then leads to bad strategy.

---

[65] Gilson & Gordon, *supra* note 6.

[66] See Ronald J. Gilson, "Catalyzing Corporate Governance: The Evolution of the United States' System in the 1980s and 1990s", 24 Corp. & Sec. L. J. 143 (2006).

[67] Gilson & Gordon, *supra* note 6.

[68] Ronald J. Gilson & Jeffrey N. Gordon, Agency Capitalism: Further Implications of Equity Intermediation, in Research Handbook on Shareholder Power 32 (Jennifer Hill & Randall Thomas eds., 2015).

4.1.3 Director Primacy

Stephen Bainbridge proffers a director primacy model as a counterpoint to both the stakeholder and the team production models on the one hand, and as an element of a shareholder primacy model on the other.[69] The differences among those models are nicely organized around two simple concepts proffered by Bainbridge: the corporation's ends and the means by which those ends are achieved. Director primacy differs sharply from the stakeholder model and somewhat more obliquely from team production on the ends sought. It includes an undiluted commitment to "shareholder wealth maximization"[70] as the measuring rod of a corporation's performance. The significant difference between director primacy and team production, conceptually but not necessarily operationally, concerns the means by which shareholder wealth maximization is achieved. Both team production and director primacy share a commitment to a very long leash for boards of directors, relegating shareholders to a limited role as a vehicle for constrained capital market intervention. The shareholders' cameo role is expected to be limited to those unusual circumstances when the shortfall in corporate performance, whether in its use of existing assets or in its failure to reach out for new opportunities, exceeds the coordination costs of energizing shareholders either directly through a takeover or indirectly through elections. In this important respect, team production and director primacy share a central feature of Aoki's description of Japanese corporate governance discussed in section 3:[71] capital market intervention, in Japan through main bank intercession and in the US through the stock market, should be triggered only by very poor performance.[72]

Thus, central to both models is the limited role of shareholders; under both team production and director primacy, management and directors are on a very long leash. Team production and director primacy differ, however, not only in the intellectual foundation of their respective models—Blair and Stout channeling Alchian and Demsetz[73] and

[69] Stephen M. Bainbridge, "Director Primacy: The Means and Ends of Corporate Governance", 97 Nw. U. L. Rev. 547 (2002).

[70] Id. at 580.

[71] Japan may actually illustrate how the stakeholder model, team production, and director primacy can all co-exist in one system (suggesting that they need not be distinct "models" at all). That is, the Japanese firm in its heyday favored employees over shareholders. Those employees engaged in a tournament to become directors, whereupon they would reap the largest rewards (partly through tenure) and play the role of Blair & Stout's (*supra* note 61) mediating hierarchs. Because these senior managers were largely insulated from capital market pressures, and due to the absence of a lateral market for managerial talent, the system was one of director primacy in the extreme. I am grateful to Curtis Milhaupt for making this connection.

[72] In the 1980s, when hostile takeovers were dismantling the failed conglomerate experiment, firms representing 1–3% of total stock market value underwent leveraged buyouts each year from 1985 to 1988. Bengt Holstrom & Steven Kaplan, "Corporate Governance and Merger Activity in the U.S.: Making Sense of the 1980s and 1990s", 15 J. Econ. Persp. 121 (2001). This volume of takeovers led to a report by the Council on Competiveness, headed by Harvard Business School strategy professor Michael Porter, extolling the Japanese governance system: "In general, the U.S. system is geared to optimize short-term returns, the Japanese and German systems optimize long-term returns." Michael E. Porter, "Capital Choices: Changing the Way America Invests in Industry", 5 J. Appl. Corp. Fin. 4 (1992). The phenomenon generalizes: However long management and the board's leash, when the capital market begins to tug on it, those being tugged don't like it. See section 4.1.4.

[73] See Armen Alchian & Harold Demsetz, "Production, Information Costs, and Economic Organization", 67 Am. Econ. Rev. 777 (1972), discussed in Blair & Stout, *supra* note 61, at 266–68.

Holstrom[74], and Bainbridge building on Coase[75] and Arrow[76]—but also in the breadth of their claim. Fairly assessed, team production is a particular production strategy, not a governance model for all seasons. Director primacy makes the broader claim: it purports to be a generally applicable governance structure. In striking the governance balance between, in Arrow's terms, "authority" and "responsibility," it plainly favors authority—management over shareholders. But this broader claim founders on the same rock that scuppered team production's broader claim.

Japan's main bank primacy model, like director primacy protecting management save in dire circumstances, no longer worked when the structure of the Japanese economy changed as a result of Japanese corporations' success and the contemporaneous opening of the Japanese capital market. Director primacy's stability and its normative appeal depend on circumstances in the capital market: the cost of shareholder coordination sets the limit on director discretion, in Arrow's terms again, setting the efficient trade-off between authority and responsibility. The reconcentrated ownership of large public US corporations as catalyzed by activist investors dramatically reduced the shareholder coordination costs in challenging managements and boards; this shortened the leash. But the critical new feature of "coordination" was the activists' role as credible information intermediaries. Insofar as the board's claim to "authority" rested on both a purported informational advantage and the cost of informing widely dispersed shareholders, the activists' information-based counterview shifted the balance, as evidenced by the voting behavior of sophisticated institutional investors. Arrow himself anticipated that if smaller groups could assess specific claims of error on the part of those in authority, responsibility could be achieved without so general a scope of review that authority was dissipated and information costs multiplied.[77]

Stated most simply, the "right" governance model is contextual. It depends on what the particular company does and on conditions in the capital market; in other words, a governance model must be dynamic. One-factor models that cannot accommodate changes in either the product market or the capital market are too simple to accommodate the complexity of the business environment in which corporations function.[78]

---

[74] See Bengt Holstrom, "Moral Hazard in Teams", 13 Bell J. Econ. 324 (1982), discussed in Blair and Scott, *supra* note 61, at 268–69.

[75] See Ronald Coase, The Nature of the Firm, 386 (1937), discussed in Bainbridge, *supra* note 69, at 547.

[76] Kenneth J. Arrow, The Limits of Organization (1974), discussed in Bainbridge, *supra* note 69, at 57–59.

[77] Arrow, *supra* note 76, at 78–79.

[78] As a style of proof that their model is right (and that others are wrong), both Blair & Stout and Bainbridge offer extended arguments that current and historical corporate law is consistent with their respective models. I do not discuss these efforts here for two reasons. First, they necessarily depend on some version of an older argument that the common law, in this case corporate law, is efficient; without needing to rely on Alchian & Demsetz, Holstrom, Coase and Arrow, the process of case selection (and the structure of other lawmaking institutions) will result in efficient rules. This claim, whose intuition was understandable when first made, has not fared well. Absent a mechanism that leads to efficient outcomes based on distributed incentives, the claim devolves into a belief that judges can be expected to get the answer right. My task here is instrumental, intelligent design rather than a blind belief in the operation of the judicial system. Put differently, a claim of survivorship in favor of an observable structure is a weak proof of efficiency. Second, invocation of the consistency of statutory rules and judicial decisions with the proffered models is an "inside baseball" argument. The authors discussed in the text (and I) are, with the exception of one economist whose appointment is in a law school, lawyers.

4.1.4 Shareholder Primacy

Setting out the shareholder primacy model is somewhat more complicated than the description of the stakeholder, team production, and director primacy models. In Bainbridge's nice dichotomy, shareholder primacy is used as a label for both an end and a means; it is at once the corporation's goal but also how that goal should be achieved. Thus, there is a need to be precise about the subject under examination. With respect to the end of corporate governance, I start with a broad definition of social welfare in the organization of public corporations: the net impact on all those effected by the company, thereby requiring a netting of gains and losses among, for example, customers, suppliers, employees, communities, and shareholders, in effect Kaldor–Hicks efficiency with a broad reach of whose utility counts.[79]

With respect to means, my focus in this section is the role assigned to shareholders. For this purpose, we have to bring in another literature, beginning in the early 1980s and continued to date by the energy of Lucian Bebchuk among others, who argues for a much broader role for shareholders than contemplated by either Blair and Stout or Bainbridge.

In important but unfortunate respects, the debate over shareholder primacy was clouded by some of its early framing. Two characterizations are particularly regrettable: that the allocation of authority through the corporate governance system turns on shareholder ownership or, alternatively, on the specificity of different stakeholders' contribution to the corporation. The ownership claim—that the corporation should maximize shareholder wealth because shareholders "owned" the corporation—was straightforward but far too simple. In fact, we have known better than that from the beginning of the debate. Ownership is a bundle of rights; which elements of the bundle we give to a particular party depends on what we want to accomplish; the inquiry is instrumental not normative. That distinction was drawn sharply in the corporate governance context as early as 1981. The shareholder's governance role depends on the organizational design needed to give residual claimants the power to assess management and the board's performance. "[I]ndeed, if the statute did not provide for shareholders we would have to invent them."[80] Debates about the specificity of different stakeholders' contributions to the corporation were also little help; the relative character of those contributions depended on the particular and changing character of the corporation's business environment, so it was difficult to generalize based on this characteristic.

Thus, tying a claim for a particular model back to legal arguments is understandable but backwards: In an intelligent design context, existing legal institutions and rules are a tool, not evidence of efficiency.

[79] See Bolton et al., *supra* note 55. Henry Hansmann and Reinier Kraakman point out that even this broad measure of social welfare is contestable. "For many individuals, increasing social stability may be worth sacrificing a meaningful amount of productivity as measured—as it conventionally is—in terms of the net value of market transactions . . . It is not crazy to feel that a leisurely daily walk to a dependable workplace in the well-preserved medieval city of one's birth is preferable to lower prices on smartphones." Henry Hansmann & Reinier Kraakman, Reflections on the End of History for Corporate Law, in Convergence of Corporate Governance: Promise and Prospects (Abdul Rasheed & Toru Yoshikawa eds., 2012). Of course, this trade-off is hardly limited to corporate governance, as a moment's reflection on the current debate over the desirability of lowering trade barriers reminds. Addressing the broader issue is beyond my ambitions here other than to note that there is nothing in a Kaldor–Hicks analysis that counsels against redistribution of gains and losses.

[80] Ronald J. Gilson, "A Structural Approach to Corporations: The Case Against Defensive Tactics in Tender Offers", 33 Stan. L. Rev. 819, 834 n. 56 (1981). Easterbrook and Fischel made the same point in "Voting in Corporate Law", 26 J. L. & Econ. 395 (1983).

Table 1.1 A Stakeholder Income Statement

Line item	Amount	Stakeholder
Sales	XXXXX	Customers
Wages	XXXXX	Employees
Cost of goods sold	XXXXX	Suppliers
Taxes	XXXXX	Community
Net Income	XXXXX	Shareholders

Once we recognize that the problem with the firm specificity branch of the shareholder primacy argument is that all stakeholders make contributions and the character of those contributions, and hence the various stakeholders' investment in the corporation, depend on the firm's strategy, the second characterization problem appears: it follows that the right governance structure is also going to depend on context. Sometimes the contributions, driven by the nature of the business and the corporation's strategic response support horizontal team production; sometimes they support vertical hierarchical organization and sometimes a mix. This appears from Table 1.1 above, a stylized income statement. The figure illustrates that each line item in an income statement reflects the participation of a different category of stakeholders. And it requires little imagination to think of how all but the shareholders' interests are conditional on circumstances. Different events will differentially affect the value of different stakeholders' inputs. Only the shareholders have an incentive to adjust the returns other shareholders receive for their inputs, because the residual returns will depend on the success of that adjustment. Put differently, one could substitute for the term "shareholder primacy" that of "Kaldor–Hicks efficiency" as a description of the operative governance model, and so match the label to the measure of social welfare.[81]

It is apparent that, as the reference to the blind men and the elephant fable reveals, corporate performance depends on the complex coordination of all stakeholder groups, taking into account the particular context of the company's business. We return to where we started this part: the corporate elephant needs customers, employees, suppliers, communities, and shareholders to perform. That implies a basic structure of management monitored by directors, with shareholders in the position of residual owners and having the vote—the right to disrupt existing management through their influence on the identity of the directors. It is at this point that the issue around shareholder primacy takes form. The team production and director primacy models, for different reasons, share the view that shareholders' role in changing management should be formally limited—management's leash must always be long. As we've seen, the two positions as so framed share a more than passing relation to Aoki's description of Japanese management. The main bank in Japan (during its

---

[81] I recognize the difficulty of specifying and then operationalizing a fully developed measure of Kaldor–Hicks efficiency. However, I am concerned here with a real corporation's operating system, where the measure is pragmatic: does it work to manage the stakeholders competing for the corporation's revenues?

prominence) and shareholders in the US can replace management, but only when things get very bad.

But the Japanese experience also teaches that the efficient length of the leash depends on history, strategy, and conditions in the capital market. The evolution of complexity in our understanding of corporate governance highlights that the role of shareholders—and so the length of management's leash—depends on the circumstances. In the 1970s, management and directors experimented with conglomerate strategies. Consistent with the team production and director primacy models, management and directors had the autonomy to carry out the experiment. In the end, the experiment failed and changes in the capital market—Michael Milken and Drexel Burnham's development of junk bonds—shortened management's leash by facilitating shareholder-dependent bust-up hostile takeovers. The length of management's leash was shortened again in the new century by the growing intermediation of equities and the rise of activist shareholders who levered institutional investors' equity holdings to extend capital market oversight to firms that were too big to take over in the 1980s.

The lesson of this section is that one-factor corporate governance models are too simple to explain the real-world dynamics we observe. Hansmann and Kraakman are descriptively correct that there seems to be convergence around a governance structure that generally contemplates shareholders as the residual owner. In equilibrium, directors oversee management's efforts to coordinate the inputs of all stakeholders and their competing claims on corporate revenues, with the particular resolution depending on the corporation's product market and strategy; shareholders have a limited function. When performance is lacking, management's leash shortens based on the techniques available to shareholders through the capital market. Corporate governance matters when the leash shortening is triggered by changes in the product market in which the company participates, in the instruments the capital market provides, and in the pattern of shareholdings that results from conditions in the capital market.

5 CONCLUSION

In the end, governance is messy, complicated, and contextual because that is the character of dynamic markets. And that is the point of this chapter. The move from corporate law to corporate governance reflects a move from a simple legal view of the corporation to one that became increasingly complex and dynamic, hand in hand with the increased complexity and dynamics of the capital market, input markets, and product markets that corporations inhabit. And therein lies the problem with corporate governance models: at best they are snapshots, stills of a moment in a motion picture. Corporate governance is part of the structure of an economy whose behavior, and hence whose architecture, is dictated by the interaction among all of the markets in which the corporation operates, each of which is itself in motion. In a sense we are confronted with a corporate governance version of the physicist three-body problem: the interaction of the bodies that influence the structure of corporate governance are too complex to allow a prediction of the optimal governance structure going forward.[82]

---

[82] I understand the standard reference is to Henri Poincaire, New Methods of Celestial Mechanics (1892).

Is there a lesson from recognizing the complexity of real world corporate governance? I think so. It is the centrality of change. As discussed in section 2, there is a trade-off between a governance system that encourages long-term firm-specific investment and one that is mutable, quickly adapting to changes in the business environment.[83] This tension between stability and change is baked into a capitalist system, Change is a source of progress, but it is always risky since the established order more or less works, sometimes seemingly well.[84] Reinier Kraakman and I characterized the tension as a debate across the years between Burke and Schumpeter:[85] should we preserve what is working against a potentially disruptive innovation?

Burke cast this tension in terms that anticipate today's tendentious long-term versus short-term debate. Remarking on the leaders of the French revolution, Burke stressed their short-term orientation: "Their attachment to their country itself is only so far as it agrees with some of their fleeting projects; it begins and ends with that scheme of polity which falls in with their momentary opinion."[86] In contrast, Burke has a great respect for the French aristocracy who were threatened by the purported short-termists: "Of my best observation, compared with my best inquiries, I found [the French] nobility for the greater part composed of men of high spirit, and of a delicate sense of honor, both with regard to themselves individually, and with regard to their whole corps, over who they kept, beyond what is common in other countries, a censorial eye."[87]

Schumpeter's riposte to the Burkean fear of chaos has become familiar:

> The opening up of new markets—and the organizational development from the craft shop to such concerns as U.S. Steel illustrate the same process of industrial mutation— . . . that incessantly revolutionizes the economic structure from within, incessantly destroying the old one, incessantly creating a new one. This process of Creative Destruction is the essential fact about capitalism.[88]

---

[83]   Ronald J. Gilson, "The Political Ecology of Takeovers: Thoughts on Harmonizing the European Corporate Governance Environment", 61 Ford. L. Rev. 161 (1992), emphasizes the importance of a corporation's mutability—its capacity to respond quickly to changes in its business environment.

[84]   Clayton Christensen, The Innovator's Dilemma (2002), focuses on the dangers to market leaders from staying with what seems to work and what they are good at: why industry leaders fail to anticipate an innovation that devalues their skills and products, and as a result dilutes their dominant position—in Christensen's terms, a "disruptive" technology. The problem is not that the leaders are poorly managed; rather they are attentive to their customers, continually improve the quality of and reduce the prices for their product, and usually anticipate what their customers will want before their customers know it themselves. Instead of merely extending the existing product architecture, a disruptive technology reflects so sharp a break with existing strategies that neither a market leader nor its customers initially see the new technology's potential. When the disruptive technology develops so that it is generalized to the industry core, the dominant firms are then displaced because they cannot respond quickly enough to the change in the architecture of production. More recently, the concept has been extended to any change in technology that severely degrades market leaders' capabilities and opens the door to new entrants. See Rebecca Henderson: "The Innovator's Dilemma as a Problem of Organizational Competence", 23 J. Prod. Innovat. Manag. 5 (2006).

[85]   Ronald J. Gilson & Reinier Kraakman, "Takeovers in the Target Boardroom: Burke versus Schumpeter", 50 Bus. Law. 1419 (2005).

[86]   Edmund Burke, Reflections on the Revolution in France 75 (Frank M. Turner ed., 2003)(originally published in 1790).

[87]   Id. at 115.   [88]   Joseph Schumpeter, Capitalism, Socialism and Democracy 82–83 (1942).

From this perspective, the governance trade-off—between stability and mobility—depends on the predicted range of future change in a particular industry and company. If the second derivative of change is positive but whose direction is difficult to predict, then a governance system that privileges mutability over stability will outperform. And here path dependency raises its head a final, pessimistic time. In a governance system characterized by supermodularity, shifts from a commitment-based governance system to one that facilitates adaptation to changing conditions will be hard to accomplish. Again, Japan's slow progress at reforming the operation of its corporate governance system despite dramatic changes in its formal corporate law stands witness to the problem.

This is an appropriate point to conclude. The move from corporate law to corporate governance, and the resulting increase in complexity, allows us both to understand the problems we need to solve and the difficulty of doing so.

CHAPTER 2

....

CONVERGENCE AND PERSISTENCE IN CORPORATE LAW AND GOVERNANCE

....

JEFFREY N. GORDON

1 INTRODUCTION

....

ALMOST 15 years ago Jeff Gordon and Mark Roe co-edited a book, *Convergence and Persistence in Corporate Governance*[1]. In their introductory essay, Gordon and Roe ("G&R") linked the convergence-persistence question to globalization in two distinct senses. The first is whether corporate governance is an element of comparative advantage in global *product* markets, which would imply that the corporate governance norms that tend toward efficient production would disseminate widely. The second sense is whether corporate governance is an element of comparative advantage in global *capital* markets, either because (1) acquirers in cross-border mergers and acquisitions would want to use a standardized "currency" or (2) equity capital suppliers such as institutional investors would push for a standardized corporate governance model. This source of comparative advantage would suggest a convergence toward an international standard of corporate governance because of its appeal to international capital markets and, generally, a lower cost of equity capital.

G&R also observed that a key feature of corporate governance is its embeddedness in national legal systems and in particular in patterns of ownership, control, and monitoring that have national origin. In consequence, notwithstanding the impact of globalization, the rate and extent of convergence will be constrained by the forces of path-dependency, along two distinct dimensions. First, from an efficiency perspective, a particular national system might well be linked to a set of complementary institutions, so that a governance change to conform to the "international" model might well reduce the value of the firm and, indeed, its global competitiveness. For example, imagine a governance regime dominated by blockholders that included "affiliated" directors placed by the large bank that provided debt

[1] Cambridge University Press (2004).

finance and the lead underwriters of the company's public equity. These affiliated directors would have institutional backing for their efforts to check private benefit extraction and the misrepresentation of performance. Adoption of the convergent governance standard in favor of "independent" directors rather than affiliated directors would likely undercut the monitoring capacity of the particular national system. Independent directors would be an efficient substitute only if the domestic court system became robust enough to control private benefit extraction and the domestic securities regulation system became robust enough to protect against fraud. Substitution of the convergent standard without regard for these institutional complements could result in companies that are less efficient and compete less well in global markets.[2] In consequence, national elites may defend the domestic corporate governance regime.

Second, an existing governance setup will inevitably create rents that incumbents will fight to preserve. Controllers in a blockholder regime may well resist a move toward convergent governance institutions that could impede various sorts of "tunneling"[3] (as from genuinely independent directors) or that could facilitate the growth of public capital markets that could finance rivals (as from an increase in minority shareholder protection). Unions may resist convergent measures that "empower" shareholders because of the concern that shareholder pressure could increase the likelihood of employee layoffs. The point is that even if corporate governance convergence was "efficient" in a macro-sense, important local actors might be disadvantaged and use their political tools to resist convergent legal and institutional change.

G&R conjectured that globalization could also affect the pace of convergence through its effect on complementarities. For example, if global competitive pressure forced banks away from a relationship model towards a transactional model, the mutual gains from "delegated monitoring" might well disappear. Alternately, global capital markets might give rise to large institutional investors that pursued a monitoring strategy that exploited different complementarities.

One convergent trend noted by G&R was the decline of state ownership, in light of the privatization waves of the 1990s and 1980s. These privatizations often catalyzed the strengthening of investor protection measures in service of the state's goal of maximizing the proceeds on the privatization.[4] But the consequence was to strengthen public stock markets more generally.

The question is, what is the state of convergence versus persistence as of 2017? The not particularly informative answer is that there has been considerable convergence, and also considerable persistence. There has been convergence in many of the formal governance rules but local applications reveal considerable divergence. Substantial differences in ownership structure persist. Even with improvements in minority shareholder protection, the Anglo-American model of the diffusely-owned firm does not predominate. Instead we see

---

[2] See, e.g., Carola Frydman & Eric Hilt, "Investment Banks as Corporate Monitors in the Early Twentieth Century United States", 107 Am. Econ. Rev. 1938 (2017) (removal of investment bank designees from railroad boards increased their cost of external capital).

[3] See Vladimir Atanasov, Bernard Black, & Conrad Ciccotello, "Unbundling and Measuring Tunneling", 2014 Univ. of Illinois L. Rev. 1697 (2014).

[4] Jeffrey Gordon, "Deutsche Telekom, German Corporate Governance, and the Transition Costs of Capitalism", 1998 Colum. Bus. L. Rev. 185 (1998).

a proliferation of forms of ownership concentration, including family ownership, foundation ownership, and entrepreneur ownership. The rise of China in the post-2000 period has brought prominence to a new form of concentrated ownership, the state-owned enterprise, which has now taken on a pyramidal form.[5] The success of this organizational form in spearheading China's rapid economic growth has provided counter-evidence to the privatization trend.

G&R, writing in 2003, emphasized the role of global competition in promoting convergence. In 2017, it would also be right to add the role of "global governance," the effort to set standards flowing from supranational public institutions. This has been propelled through three separate channels. First is the World Bank's insistence on corporate governance reform as a condition for receipt of financial assistance, particularly following the East Asian financial crisis but also part of its "development" agenda. Second is the formulation by the OECD of governance "principles" first in 1999 and then in subsequent versions, most recently in 2015 (helpfully available on the OECD website in 10 languages). This in turn has led to the adoption of governance codes by dozens of countries. Third is the push for governance reforms as part of the post-financial crisis agenda of the G-20 group of leading countries, with the Financial Stability Board both shaping the agenda and also providing for follow-up auditing of national adoption of appropriate measures.

From another perspective, it has become hard to separate out the convergence/persistence question from "financial globalization"—the development of worldwide capital markets and a set of complementary actors that make it possible for firms from countries with persistently weak governance institutions to opt into higher governance regimes.[6] Firms can issue stock in a "global" offering: cross-listing on an exchange with higher governance standards; submitting to a more rigorous, better policed disclosure system of the "borrowed" jurisdiction; making use of an international network of credible investment intermediaries, such as underwriters and accounting firms (applying globally accepted International Accounting Standards)[7]; enlisting high-reputation foreigners as independent directors,[8] and selling into the portfolios of global asset managers who will bring a certain level of monitoring.[9] More specifically, careful examination of "what matters" in corporate governance suggests that

---

[5] See, e.g., Keun Lee & Young-Sam Kang, Business Groups in China, in The Oxford Handbook of Business Groups (Aslim Colpan, Takashi Hikino, & James R. Lincoln eds., 2010); Curtis Milhaupt, The Governance Ecology of China's State-Owned Enterprises (2017), in Oxford Handbook of Corporate Law and Governance (Jeffrey Gordon & Georg Ringe eds., 2018) (hereinafter "Gordon and Ringe"). Singapore's state-owned enterprises also provide a directional model. See Cheng-Han Tan, Dan W. Puchniak, & Umakanth Varottil, "State-Owned Enterprises in Singapore: Historical Insights into a Potential Model for Reform", 28 Colum. J. Asian Law 61 (2015).

[6] Craig Doidge, G. Andrew Karolyi, & Rene Stulz, "The U.S. Left Behind? Financial Globalization and the Rise of IPOs Outside the U.S.", 110 J. Fin. Econ. 546 (2013).

[7] See, e.g., Vivian W. Fang, Mark Maffett, & Bohui Zhang, "Foreign Institutional Ownership and the Global Convergence of Financial Reporting Practices", 53 J. Acct. Research 593 (2015).

[8] Mihail Miletkov, Annette Poulsen, & M. Banajide Wintoki, "Foreign Independent Directors and the Quality of Legal Institutions", 48(2) J. Int'l. Bus. Stud. 267 (2017).

[9] Reena Aggarwal, Isil Erel, Miguel Ferreira, & Pedros Matos, "Does Governance Travel Around the World? Evidence from Institutional Investors", 100 J. Fin. Econ. 154 (2011) (foreign institutional investors from countries with strong shareholder protection improve governance of firms in weak-governance jurisdictions); Miguel A. Ferreira & Pedro Matos, "The Colors of Investors' Money: The Role of Institutional Investors Around the World", 88 J. Fin. Econ. 499 (2008).

the quality of the national disclosure regime is a critical variable.[10] High-quality disclosure facilitates better monitoring internally and externally. Yet this is also the governance feature that is most readily borrowed through a global offering. The US disclosure pattern sets the general template because of the desire to include US institutional investors as offerees. The reputations of global intermediaries as well as legal enforcement play a role in making the disclosure credible.[11]

Local complementarities may have eroded as cross-holdings unwind (e.g., in Germany[12] and Japan[13]), but global complementarities have become stronger. The pace of strictly national convergence may be slowed by the ability of local issuers to opt into the global governance system.

The "convergence" question also operates on what might be thought of as the teleological level. Have governance systems converged on "shareholder control" and "shareholder value" to the exclusion of stakeholder concerns? The assertion that we had reached the "End of History" in favor of shareholders[14] produced an intense debate. Where are we now?

A final introductory thought: When the G&R book was put together, the questions about "convergence and persistence" related principally to developed market economies. Attention was focused on differences among developed countries: The two-board/codetermination structure of Germany and the main bank/keiretsu structure of Japan were signature preoccupations. More generally, the main difference was framed as between "outsider" and "insider" forms of corporate governance. Were these differences political, relating to the relative power of employees versus shareholders;[15] functional, optimizing for certain forms of production, investment, and adaptability to changing conditions;[16] or rather the result of strong path dependencies?[17]

---

[10] Bernard Black, Antonio Gledson De Carvalho, Vikramaditya Khanna, Woochan Kim, & B. Burcin Yurtoglu, "Which Aspects of Corporate Governance Matter in Emerging Markets: Evidence from Brazil, India, Korea, and Turkey" (May 2015), available at http://ssrn.com/abstract=2601107.

[11] See generally Alan Dignam & Michael Galanis, The Globalization of Corporate Governance (2009).

[12] See, e.g., Wolf-Georg Ringe, "Changing Law and Ownership Patterns in Germany: Corporate Governance and the Erosion of Deutschland AG", 63 Am. J. Comp. Law 493 (2015).

[13] Ronald J. Gilson, "Reflections in a Distant Mirror: Japanese Corporate Governance through American Eyes", 1998 Colum. Bus. L. Rev. 203 (1998).

[14] Henry Hansmann & Reinier Kraakman, "The End of History for Corporate Law", 89 Geo. L. J. 439 (2001), reprinted in Convergence and Persistence in Corporate Governance (Jeffrey Gordon and Mark Roe eds., 2004) (hereinafter "Gordon and Roe"); H. Hansmann & R. Kraakman, "Reflections on the End of History for Corporate Law, in Convergence of Corporate Governance: Promise and Prospects" (Abdul Rasheed & Toru Yoshikawa eds., 2012), available at http://ssrn.com/abstract=2095419.

[15] E.g., Mark J. Roe, "Political Preconditions to Separating Ownership from Corporate Control", 53 Stan. L. Rev. 1463 (2000).

[16] Varieties of Capitalism: The Institutional Foundations of Comparative Advantage (Peter Hall & David Soskice eds., 2001); Ronald J. Gilson, "Globalizing Corporate Governance: Convergence of Form and Function", 49 Am. J. Comp. Law 329 (2001), reprinted in Gordon and Roe; Ronald Gilson & Mark J. Roe, "Understanding Japanese Keiretsu: Overlaps Between Corporate Governance and Industrial Organization", 102 Yale L. J. 871 (1993). For a more recent summary, see Thomas Clarke, "The Continuing Diversity of Corporate Governance: Theories of Convergence and Variety", 16(1) Ephemera 19 (2016).

[17] Mark J. Roe & Lucian Bebchuk, "A Theory of Path Dependence in Corporate Ownership and Governance", 52 Stan. L. Rev. 127 (1999), reprinted in Gordon & Roe.

The corporate governance convergence debate today focuses much more on emerging market economies. There are three reasons. First, the East Asian financial crisis of 1997–1998 was taken as showing that the corporate governance failures in such countries could produce financial instability with sharply negative consequences for developed economies. The global externalities of poor corporate governance meant that countries could not be left to internalize costs and benefits. Thus corporate governance reform immediately rose to the top of the global governance agenda through the concerted efforts of the IMF and World Bank. Indeed, a 2016 IMF report reaffirms the financial stability connection, developing the case that emerging market economies with better corporate governance were better positioned to bear the financial shocks of the Global Financial Crisis of 2007–2008.[18]

Second, a group of scholars became convinced that better corporate governance would accelerate financial market development and that this in turn would produce faster economic development in emerging market economies.[19] So improved corporate governance became part of the development agenda, also promoted by the World Bank. Third, institutional investors came to believe in both the portfolio value of international diversification and the possibilities in emerging market economies of a higher growth rate than in OECD countries. Corporate governance reform would facilitate pricing, cabin the risks of sudden losses because of insider opportunism, and thus produce superior risk-adjusted returns. Institutional investors became advocates for corporate governance reform,[20] operating through private organizations like the International Corporate Governance Network and important quasi-official bodies like the OECD.

The debate about convergence within developed countries is still interesting. For example, given the robust governance of the European Union, why is it that the corporate governance regimes of the EU Member States still exhibit significant divergence? Why isn't there a fully harmonized company law after more than 20 years of trying?

This chapter explores the "convergence or persistence" question as follows: Section 2 explores the efforts to measure convergence directly by observing the evolution of law-on-the-books governance provisions. Section 3 looks at convergence through some capital market indicators: (1) the reduced incidence of "cross-listings" onto US stock exchanges by firms from jurisdictions with weaker investor protection; (2) the increase in IPOs on emerging market stock exchanges; and (3) the increase in cross-border mergers involving a US party in which the survivor is not a US corporation, a so-called "inversion."

Section 4 looks at evidence of divergence, particularly "divergence within convergence," which seems to describe the general state of play. In this regard, a 2017 compilation by the OECD of various national corporate governance provisions, the OECD Corporate Governance Factbook, is a valuable resource. One element that has driven measures of convergence over the past 20 years has been the increasing employment of independent

---

[18] Corporate Governance, Investor Protection, and Financial Stability in Emerging Markets, in IMF, Global Financial Stability Report: Fostering Stability in a Low Growth, Low-Rate Era 93–102 (Oct. 2016).

[19] See *infra* notes 23–25 (work of La Porta et al.). Ross Levine, "Financial Development and Economic Growth: Views and Agenda", 65 J. Econ. Lit. 688 (1997).

[20] Reena Aggarwal, *supra* note 9; Stuart Gillian & Laura Starks, "Corporate Governance, Corporate Ownership, and the Role of Institutional Investors: A Global Perspective", 13 J. Applied Fin. 4 (2003).

directors across many countries. This section looks at divergent practices regarding the role and selection of the independents. It also looks at the divergent takeup of a governance innovation, shareholder votes on remuneration, "Say on Pay Policy" and "Say on Pay." Metering convergence/divergence is methodologically challenging. Without detailed country analyses, we may be at risk of assuming "convergence" on the basis of formal similarities that mask important functional differences. In this spirit, a recent set of case studies on independent directors in Asia argues for "varieties" of independent directors rather than a unitary institution.[21] Do we emphasize the divergences, which may fade over time as the convergent features assert themselves, or will the divergences attain their own functional legitimacy?

Section 5 discusses the role of global governance in corporate governance convergence, focusing particularly on the role, post-East Asian financial crisis, of the IMF, World Bank, and OECD, and the additional impact of the global financial crisis in enlisting the G-20 world leaders and the Financial Stability Board in promoting corporate governance convergence. One conclusion is that the convergence push through global governance is motivated by financial stability concerns perhaps at least as much as by efficiency and productivity.

Section 6 asks why the EU, a supranational body empowered with governance authority, has not produced more convergent corporate governance. The asserted answer is not so much the efficiencies of local adaptations and institutions but the desire of the member states to throw sand in the gears of economic and political integration. Divergence makes it harder to accomplish cross-border merger and acquisition activity, which otherwise would produce much tighter integration.

Section 7 briefly addresses the "End of History" debate: whether corporate governance indeed has converged on a "shareholder value" model. The terms of the debate have shifted, however. It's not shareholders versus stakeholder in a straightforward sense. We may all be shareholder value proponents now. The current question is, *which* shareholders: the ones who will pursue "efficiency only" or others who may include "stability" within their maximizing function? Stakeholders may fare differently depending on which shareholder objective function is predominant. Family shareholding groups that need political buy-in to protect their economic stakes are likely to see value in stability; large institutional investors that are subject to government regulation, or see themselves as permanent investors locked into the systemic risk of instability, may well have a similar perspective. Global governance institutions, which are accountable to governments, are also likely to have "stability" objectives. One important piece of evidence is the growing movement for "Stewardship Codes" and the concerted campaign against the purported "short-termism" of hedge funds, all designed to add stability to the shareholder maximizing function. The chapter concludes by asking whether "stability" will become a general objective of corporate governance convergence.

---

[21] Independent Directors in Asia: A Historical, Contextual and Comparative Approach (Dan W. Puchniak, Harold Baums, & Luke Nottage eds., 2017).

2 THE EFFORT TO MEASURE CONVERGENCE DIRECTLY

How do we know if corporate governance systems are in fact converging? Can we break a corporate governance regime into discrete elements and measure them, and then sum them up in a reliable way?[22] The first effort to do this is associated with the decade-long series of "legal origins" papers of Rafael La Porta et al., which devised various measures of investor protection that were in turn presented as explanatory elements of different ownership patterns and levels of financial development. The project initially focused on an "anti-director rights" index,[23] which was effectively dismantled as a flawed coding exercise by Holger Spamann,[24] but then reclaimed through a more accurately coded "self-dealing" index.[25] The project was at its core "anti-convergence," since it was heavily invested in the thesis of transnational "families" of corporate law, locked into their paths through their "legal origins." But the data that fueled this argument was cross-sectional, not time series, so actually the "legal origins" project was not sufficiently powered to test its most interesting conjecture.

An alternative way to measure a critical dimension of corporate law and governance, "shareholder protection," has been devised by a group of scholars associated with Mathias Siems, developing "leximetric" measures and evidence.[26] The most recent entry states its punchline in the title: "Disappearing Paradigms in Shareholder Protection, 1990–2013."[27] The general strategy is similar to the La Porta et al. approach, devising a "shareholder protection" index with a somewhat different set of variables focused on shareholder powers only. Subjectivity and some arbitrariness are inevitable, as they acknowledge. Coding requires quantification and an index requires summing, for which there is only questionable theoretical justification.[28] With these inevitable caveats, the special contribution of Katelouzou

---

[22] For the intellectual history with detailed citations, see David Cabrelli & Mathias Siems, "Convergence, Legal Origins, and Transplants in Comparative Corporate Law: A Case-Based and Quantitative Analysis", 63 Am. J. Comp. Law 109, 117–24 (2015).

[23] Rafael La Porta, Florencio Lopez-de-Silanes, Andrei Shleifer, & Robert W. Vishny, "Legal Determinants of External Finance", 52(3) J. Fin. 1131–50 (1997); Rafael La Porta, Florencio Lopez-de-Silanes, Andrei Shleifer, & Robert W. Vishny, "Law and Finance", 106(6) J. Pol. Econ. 1113–55 (1998).

[24] Holger Spamann, "The 'Antidirector Rights Index' Revisited", 23 Rev. Fin. Stud. (2010).

[25] Simeon Djankov, Rafael La Porta, Florencio Lopez-de-Silanes, & Andrei Shleifer, "The Law and Economics of Self-Dealing", 88 J. Fin. Econ. 430 (2008).

[26] The most recent entry is Dionysia Katelouzou and Mathias Siems, "Disappearing Paradigms in Shareholder Protection: Leximetric Evidence for 30 Countries, 1990–2013", 15 J. Corp. L. Stud. 127 (2015) (hereinafter "Katelouzou and Siems"). The article contains a history of the project including citations. For a useful theoretical discussion of corporate governance indices and empirical results that link changes in shareholder protection to securities markets development, see Simon Deakin, Prabirjit Sarkar, & Mathias Siems, "Is There a Relationship Between Shareholder Protection and Stock Market Development?", J. Law, Finance and Accounting (forthcoming). See also Mathias Siems, Taxonomies and Leximetrics (2017), in Gordon and Ringe.

[27] Id.

[28] See Michael Klausner, Empirical Studies in Corporate Law and Governance (2017), in Gordon and Ringe.

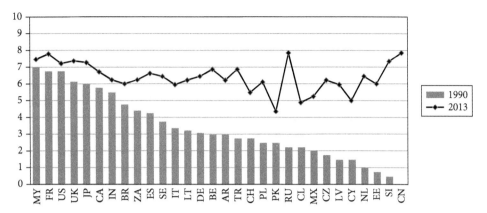

FIGURE 2.1   Katelouzou and Siems, p. 133, fig. 1.

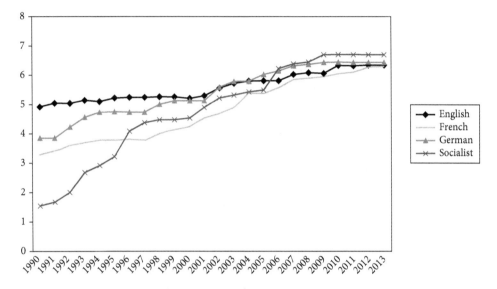

FIGURE 2.2   Katelouzou and Siems, p. 148, fig. 7.

and Siems is the coverage: 10 elements, 30 countries, and 24 years of data; and the use of network analysis to assess country clusters. The authors also divide the variables into "enabling"—those that empower shareholders to take self-protective action—and "paternalistic"—mandatory features.[29]

Their results come through in two charts (see Figures 2.1 and 2.2). Figure 2.1 shows significant convergence across the 30 countries over the period. The average level of shareholder protection as measured by their index advances in every country from the beginning of the period (1990) to the end (2013), and the countries that were lowest at the beginning of the

---

[29]   For an early effort at this distinction see Jeffrey N. Gordon, "The Mandatory Structure of Corporate Law", 89 Colum. L. Rev. 1549 (1989).

period have made the biggest changes. Further analysis shows that the convergence occurs over roughly the same elements of shareholder protection, consistent with the evolution of a normative model of corporate governance that has international acceptance.[30] Figure 2.2 puts paid to the La Porta et al. idea that "origins" are "destiny" by showing great convergence in shareholder protection among the purportedly distinct legal families. More controversially, Katelouzou and Siems seem to think that their results disprove the emergence of a paradigm based on the "American" model, since many of the convergent protections are mandatory rather than enabling.[31] But the US has adopted many mandatory corporate governance elements over the time period. Indeed, adjustments in mandatory legal rules to reset the accountability of managers and shareholders have constituted an essential part of the American model.[32]

There are three important limitations on such direct convergence measures. First, they are based on law-on-the-books coding. Explicit and implicit enforcement mechanisms can vary significantly. For example, the value of the right to bring a shareholder derivative suit for a breach of directors' fiduciary duties will importantly depend upon the functional capacity of the local judicial system.

Second, nominally similar governance elements measures may function quite differently across national regimes, depending on ownership patterns and other complementary institutions. For example, director "independence" in jurisdictions characterized by family and blockholder ownership ought to be defined differently than in the case of jurisdictions characterized principally by diffuse share ownership, in light of the different agency problems to be solved.[33] Directors who are "independent" from management may help constrain managerial agency costs for the typical American firm, but independence from the controlling shareholders is crucial elsewhere for "good governance." Moreover, correctly-framed definitions of "independence" from controllers may be inadequate without public minority shareholders' selection (or veto) rights. To take another example, government ownership presents distinct challenges to the value of "independence." China's state-owned enterprises are populated with "independent directors," but their role presumably is to advance rather than constrain the state's employment of ownership prerogatives. Thus some would argue that a coding methodology is inadequate and even misleading in its capturing

---

[30] Katelouzou and Siems, at 155.   [31] Id., at 151–53.

[32] For example, the mandatory director independence rules found in Sarbanes–Oxley and the stock exchange listing rules, the limits on loans to insiders in Sarbanes–Oxley, and "Say on Pay" in the Dodd–Frank Act. A similar effort to code and quantify shareholder protections is found in Mauro F. Guillen & Laurence Capron, "State Capacity, Minority Shareholder Protections, and Stock Market Development", 61(1) Admin. Sci. Q. 125 (2016). The Guillen & Capron index, which covers 78 countries over the 1970–2011 period, shows a similar pattern of convergence, both generally across countries and across legal "families." The IMF has done similar work in creating coded measures of corporate governance change, focusing on emerging market economies. This work also shows convergence. See Corporate Governance, Investor Protection, and Financial Stability in Emerging Markets, in IMF, Global Financial Stability Report 88–93 (2016). For further work focusing on emerging markets, see Stijn Claessens & B. Burcin Yurtogly, "Corporate Governance in Emerging Markets: A Survey", 15(C) Emerging Markets Review 1 (2013).

[33] This point is forcefully argued in Dan W. Puchniak & Kon Sik Kim, "Varieties of Independent Directors in Asia: A Taxonomy", available at https://papers.ssrn.com/sol3/papers.cfm?abstract_id=2930785.

of governance features, advocating instead for thick accounts of local governance evolution.[34] The convergence picture becomes much more complex through this lens.

Third, direct convergence measures are often incomplete as a measure of a country's corporate governance system. As is explained in Section 3.1, the separate elements of mandatory disclosure found in securities regulation may play a crucial governance role. Yet disclosure regimes and practices can vary widely, quite separate from formal shareholder protection. More generally, even if particular elements of governance are concededly important, such as board structure and disclosure, valid measures of these governance elements may vary significantly across countries.[35]

3 CAPITAL MARKET EVIDENCE ON CONVERGENCE

One important measure of the extent of corporate governance convergence is the behavior of firms seeking to raise equity capital in a globally competitive capital market. Evidence of convergence comes in (1) the decline of cross-listings by firms from purportedly lower investor protection jurisdictions onto US stock exchanges; (2) the increasing capacity of firms in emerging market economies to raise equity capital through IPOs; and (3) an increase in "inversion" transactions in which issuers switch their domicile from the US to a foreign jurisdiction. None of these developments suggest that investor protection is less robust in the US than previously; rather, that the gap between the highest and lowest investor protection regimes has diminished so that countervailing factors might dominate the listing or domicile choice. This is consistent with the convergence pattern reflected in the Katelouzou and Siems study.

3.1 The Decline in Cross-Listings

A substantial literature documents the existence of a valuation premium for foreign firms that cross-list on US stock markets, and the effect is strongest for firms whose primary listing is in a jurisdiction with weaker investor protection.[36] One component of valuation creation

---

[34] Independent Directors in Asia: A Historical, Contextual and Comparative Approach (Dan W. Puchniak, Harold Baums, & Luke Nottage eds., 2017).

[35] See Bernard Black, Antonio Gledson De Carvalho, Vikramaditya Khanna, & Woochan Kim, "Corporate Governance Indices and Construct Validity", 25(6) Corporate Governance: An International Review 397 (2017); Bernard Black, Antonio Gledson De Carvalho, Vikramaditya Khanna, Woochan Kim, & B. Burcin Yurtoglu, "Methods for Multicountry Studies of Corporate Governance (and Evidence from the BRIKIT Countries)", 183 J. Econometrics 230 (2014).

[36] See Nicholas C. Howson & Vikramaditya S. Khanna, "Reverse Cross-Listings—the Coming Race to List in Emerging Markets and an Enhanced Understanding of Classical Bonding", 47 Cornell Int'l. L. J. 607, 611–14 (2015). A more detailed literature survey is found in G. Andrew Karolyi, "Corporate Governance, Agency Problems and International Cross-Listings: A Defense of the Bonding Hypothesis", 13 Emerging Markets Review 516 (2012). Additional literature discussion is found in Chinmoy Ghosh & Fan He, "The Diminishing Effect of U.S. Cross-Listing: Economic Consequences of SEC Rule 12h-6", 52 J. Fin. Quant. Anal. 1143 (2017).

is how the listing "bonds" the foreign issuer to the higher quality US regime, in particular the disclosure requirements of the federal securities laws, as enforced by public and private litigation, and the stock exchange listing rules.[37] This bonding effect shows the limits of efforts to measure governance convergence through coding corporate law, since a national regime of investor protection can be improved by opting into a more credible disclosure regime.[38] The number of cross-listings began to decline in the mid-2000s, and various US business and political leaders claimed that the toughening US regulatory regime, reflected in the Sarbanes–Oxley law that followed the post-Enron/WorldCom scandals, had undercut the value proposition.[39] In consequence, the SEC liberalized the "delisting" rules in the hope that easier exit would encourage more firms to cross-list.[40] Recent papers suggest that the consequence was to reduce the cross-listing premium, especially for firms with weaker corporate governance, because the new rule undercut the credibility of the cross-listing bond.[41] This would reduce the appeal of the US as a "bonding" regime.

But what accounts for the previous decline in cross-listings? It's not that the US regime is so onerous; rather, the need for bonding has declined. As shown in the prior discussion of "convergence," corporate governance has leveled up in many jurisdictions. Imperfect coding may still reflect an underlying phenomenon. Firms can also credibly engage in governance self-help through adoption of strong internal governance arrangements (such as credibly independent directors[42]) and through measures that make disclosure robust and reliable, such as reporting on international accounting standards and retention of high-reputation external accountants. Firms can also hire internationally reputed underwriters in their IPO. Cross-listing may still be valuable for weakly governed firms (even if diminished by the easier US exit), but the decline in cross-listings reflects reduced demand because of reduced need. The willingness of foreign issuers to go public on foreign exchanges rather than the US suggests that the governance-quality advantage of the US has dissipated. Leveling up means

---

[37] John C. Coffee, Jr., "Racing Towards the Top? The Impact of Cross-Listings and Stock Market Competition on International Corporate Governance", 102 Colum. L. Rev. 1757 (2002).

[38] The importance of disclosure in assessing a corporate governance regime is demonstrated in Bernard Black, Antonio Gledson De Carvalho, Vikramaditya Khanna, Woochan Kim, & B. Burcin Yurtoglu, "Which Aspects of Corporate Governance Matter in Emerging Markets: Evidence from Brazil, India, Korea, and Turkey" (May 2015), available at https://papers.ssrn.com/sol3/papers.cfm?abstract_id=2601107.

[39] See, e.g., Interim Report of the Committee on Capital Markets Regulation (2006), available at http://www.capmktsreg.org/wp-content/uploads/2014/08/Committees-November-2006-Interim-Report.pdf; Michael R. Bloomberg & Charles Schumer, Sustaining New York's and the US' Global Financial Services Leadership (2007); Craig Doidge, G. Andrew Karolyi, & Rene Stulz, "Why Do Foreign Firms Leave U.S. Equity Markets?", 65 J. Fin. 1507 (2010).

[40] This was through the SEC's adoption of Rule 12h-6 under the 1934 Securities and Exchange Act.

[41] E.g., Chinmoy Ghosh & Fan He, "The Diminishing Effect of U.S. Cross-Listing: Economic Consequences of SEC Rule 12h-6", 52 J. Fin. Quant. Anal. 1143 (2017).

[42] See Jay Dahya, Orlin Dimitrov, & John J. McConnell, "Dominant Shareholders, Corporate Boards, and Corporate Value: A Cross-Country Analysis", 87 J. Fin. Econ. 73 (2008) (independent boards create value in countries with weak investor protection); Miguel A. Ferreira & Pedro Matos, "The Color of Investors' Money: The Role of Institutional Investors Around the World", 88 J. Fin. Econ. 499 (2008).

2015 USD, billion

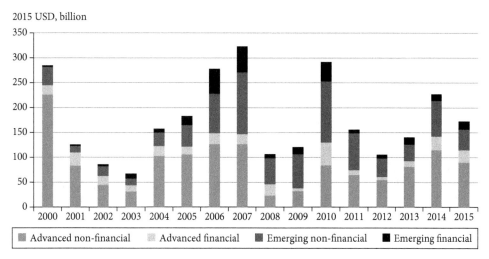

FIGURE 2.3 OECD Business and Finance Scorecard (2016), fig. 6.

that issuers obtain an insufficient cost-of-capital discount for bonding the firm to the US governance regime, given the costs.[43]

3.2 Increased Emerging-Market IPOs

Another indication of "convergence" is provided by the ability of firms in emerging market economies to access capital markets through IPOs, whether on local exchanges or through cross-listing on an exchange at a global financial center. The OECD Business and Finance 2016 Scoreboard has a graphic, reproduced in Figure 2.3, that shows this, covering the 2000–2015 period.[44] Firms in emerging markets are able to raise an increasing amount of equity capital over the period, in dollar amount (correcting for the immediate run-up prior to the crisis) and as a percentage of the total amount raised. As shown by the graphic in Figure 2.4 from OECD researchers Mats Isaakson and Serdar Çelik, "advanced economies" dominated the IPO market early in the period; more recently the split with emerging economies has been 50:50.[45] Moreover, most equity raising by non-OECD firms occurs in non-OECD capital markets. To a significant extent, of course, these changes reflect the economic rise of

---

[43] For recent contrasting empirical claims on the current value of the US "bond," *compare* Louis Gagnon & G. Andrew Karolyi, "The Economic Consequences of the U.S. Supreme Court's *Morrison v. National Australia Bank* Decision for Foreign Stocks Cross-Listed in US Markets" https://papers.ssrn.com/sol3/papers.cfm?abstract_id=1961178 (titled as "An Unexpected Test of the Bonding Hypothesis") *with* Amir N. Licht, Chris Poliquin, Jordan Siegel & Xi Li, "What Makes the Bonding Stick? A Natural Experiment Testing the Legal Bonding Hypothesis", J. Fin. Econ. (forthcoming), available at http://ssrn.com/abstract=1744905.

[44] OECD Business and Finance Scoreboard 2017, available at www.oecd.org/daf/oecd-business-and-finance-scoreboard.htm.

[45] See Mats Isaksson & Serdar Çelik, "Adapting Global Standards to a Changing World" (p. 3, fig. 1) (2016), www.law.columbia.edu/millstein-center/press/10th-anniversary-essays. See also Mats Isaksson & Serdar Çelik, "Who Cares? Corporate Governance in Today's Equity Markets, OECD Corporate

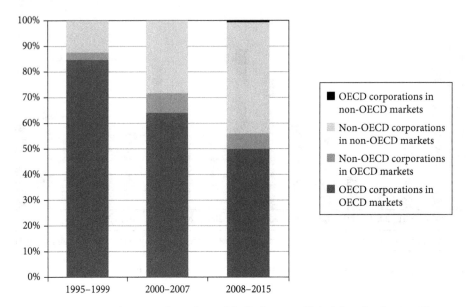

FIGURE 2.4 Mats Isaksson and Serdar Çelik, "Adapting Global Standards to a Changing World", p. 3, fig. 1.

China,[46] but such changes do carry evidentiary weight on the governance setup, since public shareholders are directly exposed to frailties in governance.[47]

3.3 "Inversions"

An "inversion" is a merger in which the target is the formal corporate survivor of the transaction, which is so structured to shift the corporate domicile of the ongoing enterprise. Often this is to take advantage of the more desirable governance regime of the new domicile. In the current mergers and acquisition environment, the term most particularly refers to transactions in which a US issuer, typically organized in Delaware, merges into a foreign

Governance W.P". No. 8 (2013) (fig. 2.3), available at http://www.oecd.org/naec/Who%20Cares_Corporate%20Governance%20in%20Today%27s%20Equity%20Markets.pdf.

[46] A recent OECD report describes China's relative importance as follows: "Since the 2008 financial crisis, Asian non-financial companies have raised a total amount of USD 539 billion through initial public offerings. The single largest group was companies from China who raised 63% of the total proceeds. China has traditionally been the largest IPO venue among emerging markets. Moreover, in eight out of the last ten years Chinese non-financial companies have also ranked first in the world in terms of the total amount of money raised through IPOs. In this context it may also be noted that IPOs in China were suspended during two periods in the last five years." "OECD Equity Markets Review: Asia" 2017, www.oecd.org/corporate/OECD-Equity-Markets-Review-Asia-2017.pdf, at 16.

[47] An alternative explanation is that shareholders in China companies, many of which have substantial state ownership, are relying on an implicit state guarantee against losses. Evidence for this is provided by the extensive state intervention that halted the sharp Chinese stock market decline in summer 2015, leading to a recovery of prices by year end.

target, choosing a non-US domicile for the ongoing enterprise. The motivation is tax min-imization: US-domiciled firms are subject to US corporate income tax on their worldwide earnings; non-US-domiciliaries are subject to US tax only on their US activities.[48] Favorite destinations have been Ireland, the Netherlands, and the UK, but Bermuda, Switzerland, and Canada have been chosen as well. The firms retain their US stock-exchange listings and thus remain subject to the US federal securities laws. There are two messages relevant to the convergence debate. First, even though the governance regimes of these particular jurisdictions differ, at least formally, in most respects they are convergent. Or rather, if there is a decrement to governance quality, it is swamped by the immediate tax savings. Second, in considering what "counts" as corporate governance, the content of securities regulation and the exchange's listing rules also must be included. The "inverted" firms were in the same position as any other cross-listed firm. Their US listing bonded themselves to the disclosure and other regulatory elements of the US federal securities laws and to the exchanges' own rules, including the implicit and explicit enforcement mechanisms.

4 EVIDENCE OF NON-CONVERGENCE OR DIVERGENCE-WITHIN-CONVERGENCE

Notwithstanding indications of some convergence, there is also ample evidence of signifi-cant divergence. Indeed, the continuing (if reduced) cross-listing premium indicates this. Surveys of institutional investors indicate wariness about foreign firms in countries with relatively weak corporate governance, especially for firms whose ownership structure (such as family control) and internal governance indicate vulnerability.[49] Empirical evidence on institutional investor investment behavior bears out the reliability of the surveys.[50]

Divergence takes two forms: The first is a non-following of the convergent norm—for ex-ample, not requiring independent directors. The second, far more common, is divergence within the convergent norm: "divergent convergence." Evidence of both forms of divergence is found in the OECD Corporate Governance Factbook (2017), a readily accessible current guide to worldwide corporate law and governance.

For example, the OECD describes a divergent practice on board structure: One-tier boards are most common (19 jurisdictions), two-tier boards are also common (10 jurisdictions), but the optional choice between one-tier or two-tier boards is growing (12 jurisdictions, given the development of the Societas Europaea (SE) in the EU. And there are still other variants in three important jurisdictions: Italy, Japan, and Portugal.[51] The maximum term for board

---

[48] See Eric L. Talley, "Corporate Inversions and the Unbundling of Regulatory Competition", 101 Va. L. Rev. 1649 (2015). Tax-minimizing inversions became particularly popular in 2010–2014 but were slowed by the adoption of US Treasury regulations that narrowed the qualifications. See generally Anton Babkin, Brent Glover, & Oliver Levine, "Are Corporate Inversions Good for Shareholders?", 126 J. Fin. Econ. 227 (2017).

[49] E.g., McKinsey & Co., Global Investor Opinion Survey (July 2002).

[50] E.g., Christian Leuz, Karl V. Lins, & Francis E. Warnock, "Do Foreigners Invest Less in Poorly Governed Firms?", 22 Rev. Fin. Stud. 3245 (2009) (effect is most pronounced in countries with weak disclosure and poor shareholder protection).

[51] OECD 2017 Corporate Governance Factbook, at 93, 101–05.

members varies from one year to indefinite terms, though the most common maximum term is three years.[52]

There is a convergent practice on the presence of independent directors on the board, whether in a two-tier board structure (for the supervisory board) or a one-tier structure.[53] Yet the number of independent directors diverges: most common is two or three by law and 50% by voluntary measures (via a "comply or explain" Code). Jurisdictions vary on the numbers and ratios. Moreover, "national approaches on the definition of independence for independent directors vary considerably, particularly with regard to maximum tenure and independence from a significant shareholder."[54] These differences would predictably result in divergence on the independence-in-fact of nominally "independent" directors and, indeed, their putative function.

Similarly, there is convergence on "independent" audit committees, formally required for listed companies by 89% of jurisdictions; covered by Code in the rest.[55] Yet there is divergence on whether this means "majority" independent directors or 100%.[56] And there appears to be no convergent practice on the relationship between the audit committee and the external auditors.

One fundamental divergence relates to the function of independent directors deriving from the divergent patterns of ownership.[57] The stylized division is between diffuse ownership (or ownership that is reconcentrated in institutional owners that represent diffuse beneficial owners) and family or blockholder ownership. Independent directors of diffusely owned firms are called to protect the interests of shareholders vis-à-vis the management teams. In family-dominated firms, the controllers monitor management; independent directors are called to protect minority shareholders. This aims to monitor insider dealings of various types. On a count-the-countries basis, family ownership dominates throughout the world.[58]

Nevertheless, in a substantial fraction of jurisdictions (19 jurisdictions of 46), board approval is not required for important related-party transactions, and, where required, independent directors' review is not necessary (13 jurisdictions), nor is an opinion from an outside specialist (9 jurisdictions).[59] Moreover, only seven of 46 jurisdictions have special arrangements designed to facilitate minority representation on the board.[60] Within this group of seven, only Israel gives the public minority the right to veto the reelection of independent directors. How genuinely convergent is the practice of director independence if

---

[52] Id. at 94, 106–07.   [53] Id. at 95–96.   [54] Id. at 98–100, 108–11.   [55] Id. at 114.

[56] Id. at 115, 117–19.

[57] For a current analysis of such ownership patterns, see Gur Aminadav & Elias Papaioannou, "Corporate Control around the World", NBER W.P. No. 23101 (Dec. 2016) (figs. 4a, 4b: Type of Control in 2012, 2007 (approx. 26,000 Companies; Market Cap approx. $4 trillion)) available at http://www.nber.org/papers/w23010; Julian Franks & Colin Mayer, "Evolution of Ownership and Control Around the World: The Changing Face of Capitalism, ECGI W.P. No. 503/207" (Apr. 2017), available at http://ssrn.com/abstract_id=2954589.

[58] See sources in preceding note.

[59] OECD 2017 Corporate Governance Factbook, at 67–69. For further discussion of cross-country differences in the treatment of related party transactions, see Anatasia Kossov & Dimitri Lovyrev, "Related Party Transactions: International Experience and Russian Challenges, OECD Russian Corporate Governance Roundtable" (2014), at 3–16, available at http://www.oecd.org/daf/ca/RPTsInternationalExperienceandRussianChallenges.pdf.

[60] Id. at 123, 126.

(1) independent directors will not necessarily review important related-party transactions and (2) formally independent directors are elected by the controllers whose potential self-dealing they are supposed to monitor?[61]

Do these divergent elements within a convergent practice matter? The evidence is "yes, they should." First, the particulars of a reform can determine whether it is "high impact" or not. In the case of the move to independent directors, for example, whether the fraction of independent directors is relatively high or low and whether they are given key governance roles predictably should affect investor protection. The importance of these variations is borne out in a recent (2017) detailed cross-country analysis of board reforms.[62] The study finds that "high impact" measures that markedly change the fraction of independent directors, particularly if implemented quickly, will increase the value of the firm (measured by Tobin's q), as will measures that assure audit committee and auditor independence.[63]

Second, governance elements commonly have country-specific effects because of country-specific positive and negative complementarities, as well as substitution effects. For example, the level of enforcement resources available to a market regulator will affect the quality of disclosure. The efficiency of a court system will affect the impact of legal rules on investor protection. Independent boards staffed by high-quality directors may substitute for weaknesses in the formal legal system.[64] The importance of country-specific analysis of "good corporate governance" is argued most forcefully in Bernard Black et al., which builds country-specific corporate governance indices for four emerging market economies covering critical governance variables such as board structure and disclosure.[65] The index elements that measure "good disclosure" or "better board structure," for example, vary within each country; the divergences matter.

A good example of partial convergence and divergence-within-convergence is the experience with "Say on Pay," a shareholder vote on the company's remuneration practices. The concept has had remarkably quick takeup as an element of global governance best practice since its legislative adoption in the UK in 2002.[66] Rapid diffusion shows convergence, yet the convergence has been partial. First, jurisdictions have divided on whether to require

---

[61] See María Gutiérrez Urtiag & Maribel Sáez, "Deconstructing Independent Directors", 13 J. Corp. L. Stud. 63 (2013); see also Donald C. Clarke, "The Independent Director in Chinese Corporate Governance", 31 Del. J. Corp. L. 125, 170 (2006). See generally Guido Ferrarini & Marilena Filippelli, "Independent Directors and Controlling Shareholders Around the World", available at https://papers.ssrn.com/sol3/papers.cfm?abstract_id=2443786, published in Research Handbook on Shareholder Power (Randall Thomas & Jennifer Hill eds., 2015).

[62] See Larry Fauver, Mingyi Hung, Xi Li, & Alvaro Taboada, "Board Reforms and Firm Value: Worldwide Evidence", 125 J. Fin. Econ. 120 (2017).

[63] Id. at 133–38.

[64] Dominic Barton & Simon C.Y. Wong, "Improving Board Performance in Emerging Markets", 2006(1) McKinsey Quarterly 36 (2006).

[65] Bernard Black, Antonio Gledson De Carvalho, Vikramaditya Khanna, Woochan Kim, & B. Burcin Yurtoglu, "Which Aspects of Corporate Governance Matter in Emerging Markets: Evidence from Brazil, India, Korea, and Turkey" (May 2015), http://ssrn.com/abstract=2601107.

[66] For a distillation of the UK legislative history, see Jeffrey N. Gordon, " 'Say on Pay': Cautionary Notes on the U.K. Experience and the Case for Shareholder Opt-In", 46 Harvard J. Legislation 323, 341 (2009). For discussion on differences among national takeups, see, e.g., Guido Ferrarini & Maria Cristina Ungureanu, Executive Remumeration, in Gordon and Ringe; Randall Thomas and Christoph Van Der Elst, "Say on Pay Around the World", 92 Wash. Univ. Law Rev. 653 (2015).

(or recommend) shareholder votes on remuneration *policy*, a general ex ante view on the company's pay strategy. As of the OECD's 2017 survey, 29 of 46 countries (63%) had adopted such "Say on Pay *Policy*."[67] Yet a significant number still do not require even *disclosure* of individualized pay and thus are far from empowering shareholders in this way. The division is even sharper on shareholder votes on the level/amount of remuneration, "Say on Pay." Only 24 countries (52%) require (or recommend) such a shareholder vote. Is the vote binding or advisory? For "Say on Pay *Policy*,"19 countries (41%) adopt the "binding approval" variant, making that the most widespread. For "Say on Pay," 17 countries (37%) adopt the binding approval variant (versus seven, advisory only). Takeup of shareholder voting on remuneration policy and practices appears to be far more widespread in the OECD countries, especially the US and the EU member states, than emerging market economies. The EU, for example, promoted shareholder voting on remuneration in the 2017 Shareholder Rights Directive.[68] As an innovation on a core corporate governance question, there is more convergence on the thesis than on the implementation.

A more radical version of "divergence within convergence" is advanced in a recent volume on independent directors in Asia,[69] which argues both that (1) independent directors are "ubiquitous" in Asia, found in higher proportion across more firms than in the "West," *and* that (2), functionally, there are "varieties" of independent directors in Asia, differing substantially from the US variant and differing even within Asia.[70] Adoption of a transplant, particularly under pressure of foreign investors or global governance institutions, does not determine how the new institution will function. That emerges over time, as the transplant is contextualized within the local ecology, and can lead to significant divergence in practice.

5 GLOBAL GOVERNANCE AS PROMOTING CONVERGENCE

5.1 Origins

Reform of corporate governance has been on the global development agenda for nearly 25 years. Nearly every country seeking access to external finance has undertaken major reform, as documented by Katelouzou and Siems (30 countries) and also by Fauver et al. (40 countries).[71] This wave of activity is not simply the result of independent action by different countries responding to the imperatives of the global capital market or acceding to letter-writing campaigns by institutional investors. Rather, this widespread adoption of corporate

---

[67] OECD 2017 Corporate Governance Factbook, at 131–38.

[68] Directive (EU) 2017/828 (May 17, 2017).

[69] Independent Directors in Asia: A Historical, Contextual and Comparative Approach (Dan W. Puchniak, Harold Baums, & Luke Nottage eds., 2017).

[70] Dan W. Puchniak & Kon Sik Kim, Varieties of Independent Directors in Asia: Diversity Revealed, in id., ch. 3.

[71] Larry Fauver, Mingyi Hung, Xi Li, & Alvaro Taboada, "Board Reforms and Firm Value: Worldwide Evidence", 125 J. Fin. Econ. 120 (2017); E. Han Kim & Yao Lu, "Corporate Governance Reforms Around the World And Cross-Border Acquisitions", 22 J. Corp. Fin. 236 (2013) (26 countries).

governance reforms has been stimulated through what might be thought of as global governance, in which the main actors have been the IMF, the World Bank, and the OECD. In the aftermath of the global financial crisis of 2007–2009, the G-20 group of national leaders and the Financial Stability Board have joined the project.

Probably the origin of the global corporate governance reform movement was the Cadbury Committee Report issued in 1992.[72] Although aimed at the governance of UK firms, particularly the "control and reporting functions of boards, and on the role of auditors," the Report became internationally influential both for the substance of its recommendations and for the form that they took: a "Code of Best Practice" enforced on the "comply or explain" model. The recommendations were not mandatory, but, as a condition of listing on the London Stock Exchange, firms were required to state whether they "complied" with a recommendation, and if not, to "explain" why not. Codes of corporate governance best practice are now a common feature of stock-exchange listing rules or national corporate law, generally following the "comply or explain" pattern, and have provided a channel for convergence.[73]

5.2 East Asian crisis

The East Asian financial crisis of 1997–1998 propelled corporate governance to the realm of global governance. The Asian "Tigers" flourished in the 1990s, which led to a massive influx of Western finance, generally in the form of dollar-denominated credit to private companies whose earnings were principally in local currencies. This mismatch left these firms seriously exposed to exchange rate risk; depreciation in the value of the local currency would undercut the firms' ability to repay foreign creditors. Insofar as the entanglement of these firms with the government gave rise to an implicit government credit guarantee, sovereign creditworthiness was also at risk. A devaluation of the Thai baht triggered competitive currency devaluations across many countries in the region and a "run on the bank" by Western lenders who anticipated default. The crisis exploded, threatening the economic stability of many countries and the region as a whole. Indeed, except for the Great Depression, it was "the crisis of the century." The IMF stepped in with multi-billion dollar rescue packages.

The IMF imposed many conditions on countries accepting aid ("conditionality"), including corporate governance reform. Financial crises are generally assumed to arise principally from macroeconomic considerations and policy mistakes and have been ubiquitous over time.[74] The structure of many East Asian enterprises raised problematic governance concerns, however. Family groups owned vast business enterprises through control

---

[72] More formally styled Report of the Committee on the Financial Aspects of Corporate Governance. The chair was Sir Adrian Cadbury, scion of the Cadbury–Schweppes confectionary firm. The report may be found at http://www.ecgi.org/codes/documents/cadbury.pdf.

[73] On the adoption and spread of corporate governance codes, which generally operate on the Cadbury-inspired "comply or explain model," see, e.g., Ruth Aguilera & Alvaro Cuervo-Cazurra, "Codes of Good Governance Worldwide: What Is the Trigger?", 25(3) Org. Stud. 415 (2004); Ruth Aguilera & Alvaro Cuervo-Cazurra, "Codes of Good Governance", 17 Corporate Governance: An International Review 376 (2009). The European Corporate Governance Institute maintains a database of codes. See http://www.ecgi.org/codes/all_codes.php.

[74] See Carmen M. Reinhart & Kenneth S. Rogoff, This Time Is Different: Eight Centuries of Financial Folly (2009).

mechanisms that separated cash flows from control rights, and commonly received preferred access to credit in coordination with the economic growth plans of government elites.
This setup provided many opportunities for private benefit extraction at the expense of
public shareholders and external creditors. An influential article by Simon Johnson, later the
chief economist of the IMF, described the importance of the corporate governance channel
as follows:

> The theoretical explanation is simple and quite complementary to the usual macroeconomic
> arguments. If expropriation by managers increases when the expected rate of return on invest-
> ment falls, then an adverse shock to investor confidence will lead to increased expropriation as
> well as lower capital inflow and greater attempted capital outflow for a country. These, in turn,
> will translate into lower stock prices and a depreciated exchange rate. In the case of the Asian
> crisis, we find that corporate governance provides at least as convincing an explanation for the
> extent of exchange rate depreciation and stock market decline as any or all of the usual macro-
> economic arguments.[75]

Without sufficient protections for public shareholders and creditors:

> [M]anagement [in firms that failed] was able to transfer cash and other assets out of com-
> pany with outside investors, perhaps to pay management's personal debts, to shore up another
> company with different shareholders, or to go straight into a foreign bank account. The fact
> that management in most emerging markets is also the controlling shareholder makes these
> transfers easier to achieve. The downturns in these countries have been associated with signif-
> icantly more expropriation of cash and tangible assets by managers.[76]

To elaborate some on the channel: Poor corporate governance enhanced the risks of private benefit extraction. One safeguard was for external credit providers to insist on short
maturities. This increased the run risk (from non-rollovers) as creditors would anticipate an
increased likelihood of default from (1) the exchange rate mismatch and (2) extra extractions
by controllers to protect their positions.

In its report on the crisis, the World Bank concluded that:

> The poor system of corporate governance has contributed to the present financial crisis by
> shielding banks, financial companies, and corporations from market discipline. Rather than
> ensuring internal oversight and allowing external monitoring, corporate governance has been
> characterized by ineffective boards of directors, weak internal control, unreliable financial re-
> porting, lack of adequate disclosure, lax enforcement to ensure compliance and poor audit.[77]

Hence significant corporate governance reform became part of the IMF's conditionality
program and then, subsequently, associated with lending and more general development
activity by the World Bank. Not to demean the development motives, but the impetus for
this insistence on corporate governance came from "first world" concerns: In a regime of

---

[75] Simon Johnson, Peter Boone, Alasdair Breach, & Eric Friedman, "Corporate Governance in the
Asian Financial Crisis", 58 J. Fin. Econ. 141, 142 (2000).

[76] Id. The connection between good institutions and local financial stability received a full exposition
in Daron Acemoglu, Simon Johnson, James Robinson, & Yunyong Thaicharoen, "Institutional Causes,
Macroeconomic Symptoms: Volatility, Crises and Growth", 50 J. Monetary Econ. 49 (2003).

[77] The World Bank, "East Asia: The Road to Recovery" (1998) at 67–68, http://documents.worldbank.
org/curated/en/364021468770639382/East-Asia-the-road-to-recovery.

robust cross-border capital mobility, weak corporate governance in emerging market economies was a threat to global financial stability. A country's corporate governance setup that internalized *local* economic and political costs and benefits could nevertheless produce *global* externalities. Thus corporate governance reform had a new imperative.

5.3 OECD Principles

But what "reforms" exactly? The Asian crisis prompted a call for the OECD to develop "a set of corporate governance standards and guidelines,"[78] which resulted in the OECD Principles of Corporate Governance, issued in 1999.[79] The Principles relied heavily upon the work of the business and legal community in the US that had been focusing on corporate governance matters since the 1970s, including the American Law Institute project on corporate governance, as well as the insights and further discussion stirred by the Cadbury Committee Report.[80] The OECD Principles identified five specific elements: shareholder rights, equitable treatment of shareholders, the role of stakeholders, disclosure and transparency, and the responsibilities of the board. The Principles were somewhat elaborated, both in the text, and in a set of "annotations." The investor protection thesis was supported by the work of economists pursuing the "law and finance" research program,[81] but the Principles had both broader and more specific reach.

5.4 Promoting Governance Reforms

After the East Asian crisis, the World Bank and the IMF established the "Financial Sector Assessment Program," which entailed a country-specific assessment of the soundness of the financial system, the "infrastructure, institutions and markets" needed for development, and the country's adherence to "selected financial sector standards and codes."[82] The OECD Principles were immediately wrapped into this global governance project of the World Bank and the IMF. The Principles "underpin the corporate governance component of the World Bank/IMF Reports on the Observance of Standards and Codes" (ROSC) and were designated by the Financial Stability Forum (established in 1999, in the crisis aftermath) as "one of the 12 key standards for sound financial systems."[83] The Principles were intended to serve as a "reference point," but, between the Principles and the Annotations, there was significant basis for a prescriptive agenda of corporate governance reform and comparative evaluation.

---

[78] OECD Principles of Corporate Governance (1999) (frontispiece).   [79] Id.

[80] For alternative accounts of the intellectual history of the OECD Principles, see Mathias Siems & Oscar Alvarez-Macotela, "The G20/OECD Principles of Corporate Governance 2015: A Critical Assessment of Their Operation and Impact", J. Bus. 310, 312 (2017).

[81] See the papers cited *supra* notes 23–25.

[82] "Financial Sector Assessment Program (FASP)", http://www.worldbank.org/en/programs/financial-sector-assessment-program.

[83] OECD Principles, 2d version (2004), at 3. Corporate governance assessments under the ROSC initiative are at the invitation of country authorities and in general have been requested only by emerging market economies, not developed economies.

As part of its ROSC program, the World Bank prepares country "assessments" that highlight changes and "improvements," make policy recommendations, and "provide investors with a benchmark against which to measure corporate governance" in the studied country. In the case of non-OECD countries, the recommendations can be rather detailed.[84] The corporate governance indicators also became important in the World Bank's "Doing Business" measures of country-specific business-relevant factors. These indicators, presented in index form, are presumably relevant for foreign director investment and portfolio investment, which becomes the reason that governments may pursue reform. The World Bank also prepares thematic reports arguing for particular "Doing Business" improvements in corporate governance; for example, enhancing investor protection.[85]

In the aftermath of the Asian financial crisis, the World Bank, in cooperation with the Asian Development Bank and the OECD, embarked on a campaign to proselytize for higher corporate governance standards in Asian economies.[86] Among the tools were "roundtables" of business, government, and academic elites.[87] Most notable has been the OECD-Asian Roundtable on Corporate Governance, hosting its 18th meeting, October 2017, in Tokyo. Convergence onto an international standard was plainly the agenda. The 2003 Roundtable produced agreement on an "action plan for improving corporate governance," viz., "The White Paper on Corporate Governance in Asia" (published in English, Chinese, and Japanese). The 2011 Roundtable updated the White Paper with specific reform recommendations; it included an overview of corporate governance frameworks in 13 Asian countries. The OECD Principles were used as the benchmark for developing the ASEAN Corporate Governance Scorecard in 2012, which ranks the top listed companies in six countries.

More generally, the OECD has recently (2017) produced a new OECD Corporate Governance Factbook, a comparative report on 47 jurisdictions "hosting 95% of all publicly traded corporations in the world as measured by market value," which is presented as "a unique source for monitoring the implementation" of the latest OECD Principles.[88] The

---

[84] See, e.g., World Bank, Report on the Observance of Standards and Codes, Corporate Governance Country Assessment: Vietnam (2013).

[85] World Bank, Doing Business: Protecting Minority Investors—Achieving Sound Corporate Governance (2017) (tracking countries that adopt measures that strengthen minority investor protection).

[86] The IMF has recently used evidence from the global financial crisis of 2007–2009 to re-emphasize the connection between corporate governance and financial stability, especially in emerging market economies, presenting evidence that "stronger corporate governance and investor protection frameworks enhance the resilience of emerging market economies to global financial shocks." Corporate governance improvements "foster deeper and more liquid capital markets, allowing them to absorb shocks better" and more efficient stock markets, less prone to crashes. Better corporate governance and investor protection is associated with stronger corporate balance sheets, less reliant on short-term (runnable) funding. These findings, argues the IMF, should lead to further, deeper corporate governance reform, especially on the dimensions of minority shareholder protection and disclosure. See IMF, Global Financial Stability Report: Fostering Stability in a Low Growth, Low-Rate Era (Oct. 2016) (ch. 3, Corporate Governance, Investor Protection, and Financial Stability in Emerging Markets, at 93–102).

[87] "OECD-Asian Roundtable on Corporate Governance", http://www.oecd.org/daf/ca/oecd-asianroundtableoncorporategovernance.htm.

[88] OECD 2017 Corporate Governance Factbook, at 5.

goal of this OECD venture is to promote, through the "soft law" of global governance,[89] a movement toward a convergent best practice.[90]

5.5 Global Financial Crisis: the Focus on Financial Firms

The global financial crisis of 2007–2009 produced another crisis in corporate governance, in particular the corporate governance of financial institutions. The prevailing governance model was found to encourage excessive risk taking. The deficiencies included misaligned compensation schemes, insufficient board monitoring of the risk taking by the firm, and overly complex organizational structures that made it difficult to manage (or monitor) the business and which greatly complicated resolution planning. This led to revision of the convergent corporate governance prescription for banks, undertaken by the Basel Committee on Banking Supervision. In "Principles for Enhancing Corporate Governance in 2010" (revised in 2014), the Basel Committee's additions focused on risk monitoring, including internal controls, compensation, and complexity.

With greater confidence in pursuing a distinctive governance agenda, the Basel Committee revisited bank governance in 2015, with "*Guidelines*: Corporate Governance Principles for Banks" (emphasis added). These "Guidelines/Principles" give considerable specificity to the board's role in a banking institution, especially the board's role in risk monitoring and assuring adequate internal controls. Moreover, the board is tasked with additional attention to compliance monitoring in light of other issues that emerged about bank behavior before and after the crisis. The Guidelines/Principles are not meant to be regulatory, but to guide supervisors in assessing corporate governance regimes; nevertheless, the degree of specificity is much greater than in the OECD Principles.

5.6 The G-20 and the FSB

The most important post-crisis global financial governance vehicle was a series of G-20 Leader Summits which brought together presidents and prime ministers of a self-organized group of 20 leading countries to deal with the crisis and its aftermath across a broad range of economic and regulatory items. In turn the G-20 empowered a recharged "Financial Stability Board," which was tasked with charting out a common regulatory agenda to guard against a crisis recurrence.[91] Obviously neither the G-20 nor the FSB has compulsory authority, but the relevant international organizations have pursued a compliance strategy of "peer assessment" of whether particular countries are pursuing agreed-upon reforms.

---

[89] See Chris Brummer, Soft Law and the Global Financial System (2012).

[90] Another important source of "principles" designed to guide governance choices and expectations has been produced by International Corporate Governance Network, "an investor led group of governance professionals." The 4th edition is found at http://icgn.flpbks.com/icgn_global_governance_principles/#p=5.

[91] For more detail see John Armour, Dan Awrey, Paul Davies, Luca Enriques, Jeffrey Gordon, Colin Mayer, & Jennifer Payne, Principles of Financial Regulation (2016), at 623–25.

Corporate governance made its way to the G-20 agenda in 2015. The OECD examined its Principles in the wake of the financial crisis and decided that the application rather than the Principles themselves were the flaw in the governance of financial firms.[92] The ongoing second revision of the Principles focused mostly on the expanding significance of institutional investor ownership. The 2015 version of the Principles was submitted to the G-20 Leaders Summit in November 2015 and adopted there. They are now known as the G20/OECD Principles of Corporate Governance. In addition to the additional weight they carry because of the G-20 imprimatur, country-specific compliance with the Principles will now become part of the FSB's peer assessment process.[93] This is important because it will permit the FSB to focus on the country-specific implementation of appropriate governance norms for financial firms.

5.7 Basel Committee and the FSB

Thus it appears that the corporate governance of financial firms will be subject to scrutiny through two elements of the global financial regulatory system: the board focus of the Basel Committee, as transmitted through national supervisors, and the broader governance elements that emanate from the national governance setup, per the FSB's scrutiny. Yes, the Guidelines/Principles of the Basel Committee admit of diversity, as do the G20/OECD Principles, but convergence pressure seems likely.

The general point is this: To an extent that might surprise academics focused on the political economy of races to the top or bottom driven by local conditions, convergence on a common set of corporate governance principles and practices has been driven by various forms of global governance. One conclusion is that the convergence push through global governance is motivated by financial stability concerns at least as much as by efficiency and productivity. The global governance push has particularly affected less developed countries—"emerging market economies"—that are more sensitive to the certification of the World Bank and other development organizations. But it has affected OECD countries as well, as reflected in the quite common adoption of corporate governance "codes" as well as various elements of prescriptive reform.[94] Moreover, after the financial crisis of 2007–2009

---

[92] OECD Steering Group on Corporate Governance, Corporate Governance and the Financial Crisis (February 2010).

[93] See FSB, Thematic Peer Review on Corporate Governance—Summary Terms of Reference (Aug. 2016): "The overarching objective of the review is to take stock of how FSB member jurisdictions have applied the Principles to publicly listed, regulated financial institutions, identifying effective practices and areas where good progress has been made while noting gaps and areas of weakness. It will also inform work that is underway to revise the OECD's Assessment Methodology that is used by the World Bank as the basis for country assessments undertaken as part of its Corporate Governance Report of Standards and Codes initiative and will provide input to governance-related aspects of the FSB's broader work on conduct for financial institutions."

[94] On the adoption and spread of corporate governance codes, see sources cited *supra* in note 73. Although the "codes" movement seems principally driven by global governance actors, investors have played a significant role as well. For example, the International Corporate Governance Network, founded in 1995, which claims affiliation of major institutional investors and asset managers holding over $20 trillion in assets, has been a major promoter of codes, most recently Stewardship Codes. See https://www.icgn.org//global-stewardship-codes-network.

the corporate governance of large banking organizations has become a particular global governance target.

6 Supranational Governance—the EU

When the G&R book was put together in 2002, the most salient questions of "convergence and persistence" related to the EU countries, Japan, and the United States. The main EU-specific questions were (1) the durability of codetermination in Germany and elsewhere in the EU and (2) the appeal of bank and blockholder monitoring, both elements in opposition to the movement toward the diffuse shareholder-centric model associated with the UK and the United States. As noted in the introduction to this chapter (Section 1), the debate focused, structurally, on "outsider" versus "insider" governance, and whether the governance differences resulted from political stories, functional sorting, or simply strong path dependencies that had perhaps an internal efficiency dimension even if not global efficiency. In any event, the divergent EU countries were member states in a transnational federation with legislative and executive authority, which on many dimensions sought to "harmonize" local regimes. Company law and corporate governance practices seemed a natural target.

So what happened? A recent analysis by Martin Gelter, which reviews the relevant history in some detail, reports that "there is no uniform assessment of company law harmonization in the European Union; views vary between characterizing company law as a 'success story of European efforts to regulate' and the claim that EU Company law is 'trivial.'"[95] From one perspective, the countries of the EU have converged on a high level of minority shareholder protection and robust disclosure, even if the particulars of such protections are not "harmonized." Within that convergence, lawmaking on company law in the EU generally has provided significant latitude for national variations, with the rare exception of some prescriptive post-financial crisis limits on executive compensation in banking organizations, which were linked to other financial stability regulation.[96]

An EU path to greater convergence seems stalled for three fundamental reasons. First, "top-down" harmonization applying to all firms in all Member States would produce significant inefficiencies because of diverse initial conditions, particularly diverse ownership patterns that produce different core agency problems. Provisions for shareholder empowerment that may be desirable where ownership is diffuse would have negative consequences for minority public shareholders where ownership is concentrated. Moreover, the complex

---

[95] Martin Gelter, "EU Company Law Harmonization between Convergence and Varieties of Capitalism", available at https://papers.ssrn.com/sol3/papers.cfm?abstract_id=2977500, published in Research Handbook on the History of Corporate Law (Harwell Wells ed., forthcoming 2018). When it comes to "the board," that critical governance institution, the judgment of two experienced corporate analysts is unequivocally equivocal: "The overall result is an unstable balance between convergence and divergence, shareholder and stakeholder influence, as well as European v. national rulemaking." Paul L. Davies & Klaus J. Hopt, "Boards in Europe: Accountability and Convergence", 61 Am. J. Comp. Law 301 (2013).

[96] See the Capital Requirements Directive IV (CRD IV), 2013/36/EU, Article 94(1)(g), and the implementing Capital Requirements Regulation (CRR), 575/2013.

EU politics of lawmaking would also conduce to significant inefficiencies in a top-down approach.[97]

Second, "bottom-up" harmonization in which *companies* could choose the corporate governance model most suited to their objectives would upset national decisions about the balance of power between shareholders and employees. For example, "regulatory competition" on the US model could permit a German firm to shuck codetermination and its two-tiered board via a simple merger with a UK shell set up for purposes of the merger (assuming approval of such a transaction is for shareholders). There is also general concern among EU parties that permitting firms freely to move their "seats" to pursue the optimal company law would lead to a "race to the bottom," though of course some would claim that Delaware, the winner of the US race, has produced a package of corporate law and judicial machinery that has many positive attributes.

The third factor that has produced corporate governance divergence in the EU is the profound ambivalence about the project of transnational economic and political integration that a convergent system would facilitate. The place where this is clearest is the discord over the 13th Company Law Directive, the Takeover Directive, a debate that raged in the late 1990s and early 2000s.[98] A key sticking point was the "level playing field": the need to avoid protectionist national company law that heightened defensive barriers for local firms while permitting acquisition of foreign targets. Firms needed to be mutually contestable to guard against mercantilist behavior.

In the effort to break a deadlock, a representative group of "High Level Company Law Experts" was convened in 2001. The Experts called for a "board neutrality" rule in the face of a hostile bid, a "breakthrough" rule that would permit the holder of at least 75% of the cash flow interest in a target to succeed in the bid, and an overcoming of "Golden Share" vetoes by governments in privatized former state-owned enterprises. The goal of the Experts was to foster the EU's project of transnational economic integration, which they understood to be advanced by cross-border mergers in order to create companies of EU-wide scale:

> An important goal of the European Union is to create an integrated capital market in the Union by 2005. The regulation of takeover bids is a key element of such an integrated market.
>
> ...
>
> Many European companies will need to grow to an optimal scale to make effective use of the integrating internal market. The same is true for companies which compete on global markets. Takeover bids are a means to achieve this for those engaged in the business of both bidder and target.
>
> ...
>
> In many parts of Europe on the other hand, takeover barriers existing in various Member States more often tend to result in control over listed companies being incontestable. In the view of the Group, this is undesirable in the European context, as an integrated capital market has to be built up in order for business to fully benefit from and make effective use of the integrating internal market in Europe.[99]

---

[97] See European Company Law Experts, Response to the European Commission's Consultation on the Future of European Company Law (May 2012).

[98] See generally Jeffrey Gordon, "The International Relations Wedge in the Corporate Convergence Debate in Gordon & Roe", at 202–08, available at https://papers.ssrn.com/sol3/papers.cfm?abstract_id=374620.

[99] "Report of the High Level Group of Company Law Experts on Issues Related to Takeover Bids", Jan 10, 2002, available at www.ecgi.org/publications/winter.htm.

There were various technical objections to the Experts' proposal and the proposed follow-on directive from the European Commission, but the rejection came from a deeper source. Strong form convergence, which truly would have brought about free mobility of capital, people, and products—genuine transnational economic integration—was actually not what the Member States wanted, at least not the relevant business and political elites. Too much autonomy and national identity would be sacrificed. The barrier to adoption of the proposed Takeover Directive was not so much the efficiencies of local adaptations and institutions but the desire of the Member States to throw sand in the gears of economic and political integration. Divergence makes it harder to accomplish cross-border merger and acquisition activity, which otherwise would produce much tighter integration. The strength of national identity and the comparative weakness of European identity is the ultimate hindrance to corporate law convergence in the EU.

7 CONVERGENCE ON "SHAREHOLDER VALUE," BUT WHICH SHAREHOLDERS?

Twenty years (1997) ago Henry Hansmann and Reinier Kraakman wrote an essay for a Columbia Law School conference to address the question, "Are Corporate Systems Converging?" Their answer, "The End of History for Corporate Law,"[100] identified a particular governance modality for large economic enterprises, the "standard shareholder-oriented model," organized on these principles:

> [First, t]he ultimate control over the corporation should rest with the shareholder class; the managers of the corporation should be charged with the obligation to manage the corporation in the interests of its shareholders; [second] other corporate constituencies, such as creditors, employees, suppliers, and customers, should have their interests protected by contractual and regulatory means rather than through participation in corporate governance; [third] noncontrolling shareholders should receive strong protection from exploitation at the hands of controlling shareholders; and [fourth] the market value of the publicly-traded corporation's shares is the principal measure of its shareholders' interests.[101]

They claimed that this model was superior to a state-oriented model, a labor- (or stakeholder-) oriented model, or a manager-oriented model. Subsequently, they would claim superiority to a model oriented around a powerful family tied to the state and largely free of regulation. The measures for superiority were all of: ideological (normative) appeal, comparative efficiency, and dominance as an empirical matter. The essay spawned a literature with many interesting objections,[102] some seeing the essay as a polemic and responding in kind.

---

[100] Henry Hansmann & Reinier Kraakman, "The End of History for Corporate Law", 89 Geo. L. J. 439 (2001), reprinted in Gordon and Roe. For the sequel, see Henry Hansmann & Reinier Kraakman, Reflections on the End of History for Corporate Law, in Convergence of Corporate Governance: Promise and Prospects (Abdul Rasheed & Toru Yoshikawa eds., 2012), available at http://ssrn.com/abstract=2095419.

[101] End of History, 89 Geo. L. J. at 440–41.

[102] See, e.g., Adam Winkler, "Corporate Law or the Law of Business?: Stakeholder and Corporate Governance at the End of History", 67 L. & Contemp. Probs. 109 (2004); Cynthia Williams

It seems to me that the current deep question of corporate governance teleology is not "shall the firm be run for the interest of shareholders?" but "which shareholders?" And the end pursued by many shareholders as well as global governance actors (including many governments) is not just "efficiency" but "stability."

Around the same time as the Hansmann and Kraakman essay, Gordon argued that the linked regimes of trade liberalization, capital market liberalization, and a newly flexible labor market constituted a "new economic order," and the interaction would produce an unprecedented level of economic adjustment costs.[103] In particular, the interaction between globalized trade, which heightens product market competition, and liberalized capital markets, which provide additional ways for shareholder insurgents to pressure managements to cut costs, improve margins, and become more efficient, was likely to increase layoffs and flatten wage growth. Finding a new job is costly, and for a meaningful fraction of employees, wage loss after re-employment will be significant.

If adjustment costs are large, widespread, and persistent, social and political stability may be put at risk. "Which shareholders" will affect adjustment costs in important ways. Let us posit that there will be two types of shareholders, overlapping in most respects, but one type that is purely efficiency-minded, and the other, stability-minded as well. First, efficiency-only shareholders may push firms to respond quickly to a changed competitive environment, heedless of adjustment cost issues (to the extent not required by law). A rapid response by one firm in a competitive environment will evoke rapid responses from its competitors, leading to a change in the rate of economic change, an increase in the second derivative, which will much increase the realization rate of adjustment costs. Thus change driven by efficiency-only shareholders will have a redoubling effect on adjustment costs and thereby heighten stability concerns.

Governments are certainly likely to see strong reasons for concern about stability, because of electoral consequences in some countries or simply to retain popular support. But some shareholders will be stability-minded as well, because their interests require attending to stability-preserving objectives. Family shareholding groups that need political buy-in to protect their economic stakes are likely to see value in social and political stability, particularly if their planning horizon is multi-generational. Large institutional investors may well have a similar perspective. First, they are subject to the regulation of stability-preferring governments. But further: a large institutional investor that is diversified across the economy and is a permanent investor will have stability concerns irrespective of implicit government pressure. An efficiency-only investor can opt out of instability by holding cash or gold. A large institutional investor cannot and therefore must internalize instability costs. Global governance institutions, which are accountable to governments, are also likely to have stability objectives. This is demonstrated by the growing global governance movement for "Stewardship Codes" and the concerted campaign against the purported "short-termism" of hedge funds.

& John M. Conley, "An Emerging Third Way? The Erosion of the Anglo-American Shareholder Value Construct", 38 Cornell Int'l. L. J. 493 (2005); Franklin A. Gevurtz, "The Globalization of Corporate Law: The End of History or a Never-Ending Story?", 86 Washington Law Review 475 (2011).

[103] Jeffrey N. Gordon, "Employees, Pensions, and the New Economic Order", 97 Colum. L. Rev. 1519 (1997).

The irony, of course, in the "which shareholder" question, is that stakeholder concerns enter through the side door. Worrying about downsizing and depressed wages thus reframed through the stability channel is still about maximizing shareholder value, but for "which shareholder?" To say that we are at "the end of history" only begins the analysis.

8 CONCLUSION: CONVERGENCE AND STABILITY

Corporate governance "convergence" first entered the agenda as a growth and development question. At a time of worry about performance of the US corporate governance model, would "strong monitors" of insider systems prove superior to "weak owners"? The East Asian financial crisis injected corporate governance into the machinery of global financial stability as well as economic development. Perhaps the reconcentration of weak owners in outsider systems into institutional investors will produce another sort of convergence: special attention to the interests of stability-minded shareholders, including the social implications of corporate governance. Stability concerns already exist where family ownership is high. Will stability be added as a first-order element in corporate governance convergence?

CHAPTER 3

....

CORPORATE GOVERNANCE AND ITS POLITICAL ECONOMY

....

MARK J. ROE AND MASSIMILIANO VATIERO

1 INTRODUCTION

....

IN this chapter, we analyze three instances that illustrate the political economy of corporate governance. First, we examine how the politics of organizing financial institutions affects, and often determines, the flow of capital into the large firm, thereby affecting, and often determining, the power and authority of shareholder-owners. Second, we show how continental European nations have been slow in developing diffusely owned public firms in the years after World War II. The third political economy example deals with management in diffusely owned firms. The chapter also looks at the historical organization of capital ownership in the United States, noting how the country's fragmented financial system limited the institutional blockholders and increased managerial autonomy over the years. Finally, it discusses the power of labor in postwar Europe, political explanations for the continuing power of the American executive and the board in recent decades, other political economy channels for corporate governance, and the limits of a political economy analysis.

To fully understand the modern corporation's ownership, shape, and distribution of authority, one must attend to politics. Because basic dimensions of corporate organization can affect the interests of voters, because powerful concentrated interest groups seek particular outcomes that deeply affect large corporations, because those deploying corporate and financial resources from within the corporation to buttress their own interests can affect policy outcomes, and because the structure of some democratic governments fits better with some corporate ownership structures than with others, politics can and does determine core structures of the large corporation.

Douglass North captures something close to the idea we use in this chapter: "institutions [for us here, the institutions of corporate governance] are not necessarily or even usually created to be socially efficient, rather they . . . are created to serve the interests of those with the bargaining power to devise [the] new rule."[1] Interest groups often seek to obtain via politics both immediate results and enduring institutions that promote their own current interests and preferences. They do so generally and they do so in ways that can determine corporate governance. The results may be economically efficient, inefficient, or neutral.[2]

Figures 3.1 and 3.2 illustrate the first generality of our argument here: the firm is embedded in financial, labor, and product markets, each of which affects the shape of the large firm and each of which attracts considerable political attention. The polity shapes the firm directly and, through these three markets, indirectly, as Figure 3.1 illustrates.

Moreover, the principal players inside the firm—corporate owners, executives, and employees—can themselves project power into the polity. Owners seek mechanisms that minimize agency costs, managers seek autonomy and prestige, and workers seek job stability and good wages; each group seeks rules that favor themselves in contested transactions. They are at the three vertices in the triangle in Figure 3.2, with each side of the triangle representing a potential coalition between two of these actors. These three actors interact inside the firm[3] and in the economy, and contend or coalesce in the political arena. Corporate governance arrangements inside the firm among these three main corporate actors interact deeply with a nation's politics through party systems, political institutions, political orientations of governments and coalitions, ideologies, and interest groups.[4]

A major part of the differences among corporate governance regimes in advanced industrial countries is determined by policies concerning labor protection, orientation to shareholder value, and product market conditions. How a polity decides to organize capital, labor, and product markets can deeply affect the firm's corporate governance structure.

Complications abound. A simple map from politics to economics to corporate governance cannot be drawn because causation is bidirectional, as the dotted arrows in Figure 3.2 illustrate. Sometimes causation is circular, with several economic, institutional, and political features determined simultaneously. Sometimes there are multiple equilibria due to path-dependence phenomena, making the original conditions—which may result from chance, contestable events—determinative. Thus, the present corporate governance

---

[1] Douglass C. North, "Institutions", Institutional Change and Economic Performance 16 (1990).

[2] Cf. Daron Acemoglu, "Why Not a Political Coase Theorem? Social Conflict, Commitment, and Politics", 31 J. Comp. Econ. 620 (2003).

[3] One of the first works on interactions among corporate owners, managers, and workers is Masahiko Aoki, The Co-operative Game Theory of the Firm 33, 61–91, 119–28 (1984) ("it seems reasonable to characterize the firm as a field of bargaining among firm-specific resource-holders including the body of employees . . . There does not seem to exist, therefore, a single objective of the firm such as the maximization of residual (profits); rather, the firm internalizes a bargaining process in which the conflicting objectives of the firm-specific resource-holders are brought into [an organizational] equilibrium within a framework of the co-operative relations"). Aoki did not investigate the influence of politics on these interactions inside the firm.

[4] See Mark J. Roe, "Political Determinants of Corporate Governance". Political Context, Corporate Impact 4 (2003); Peter A. Gourevitch & James J. Shinn, Political Power and Corporate Control: The New Global Politics of Corporate Governance 59–67, esp. tbl. 4.1 at 60 (2005).

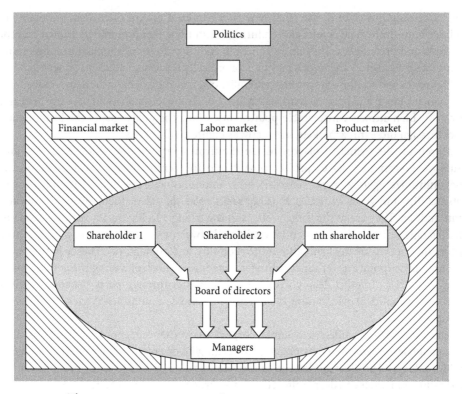

FIGURE 3.1 The corporate governance environment.

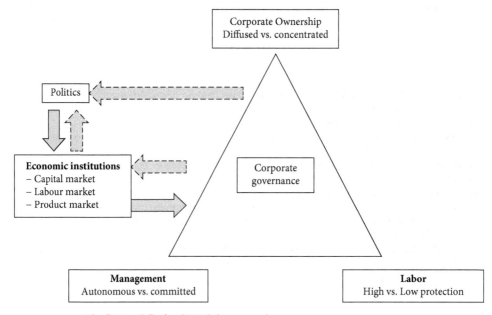

FIGURE 3.2 The "triangle" of political theory and corporate governance.

structure is the consequence of past politics and is also a cause of future politics and eco-nomic institutions.

* * *

Corporate structures around the world[5] and over time[6] have been heterogeneous, with the differences seen as most important being "the structure of rights and responsibilities among the parties with a stake in the firm."[7] We focus on the large, usually public, firm, partly be-cause the largest firms are the "most politically salient firms in every jurisdiction"[8] and the institutional differences in corporate governance are more evident in the largest business firms than in medium or small firms. "The different connotations of capitalism that spice political debates in different countries so differently are mainly due to differences in who controls countries' large corporations."[9]

In this chapter, we examine three instances of vital intersections between politics and the organization of the modern corporation. In the first, we look at how the politics of organizing financial institutions affects the flow of capital into the large firm and, hence, the power and authority of shareholder-owners. The channels through which capital flows into the large firm can determine ownership structure and, hence, the distribution of governance authority in the large firm. If financial institutions are barred from owning stock or from operating on a large, national scale, to take an extreme example, then they will be unable to serve as a counterweight to managerial and board authority. Concentrated ownership with institu-tional blockholding will be difficult or impossible. Its opposite, diffuse ownership with strong managerial control, can readily become the only alternative if the polity prevents financial institutions from growing large or having a role in stock ownership and corporate govern-ance. Powerful financial institutions will produce more of the former—blockholding—than of the latter—diffuse ownership with strong managerial control.[10]

[5] The literature distinguishes between (at least) two modern models of corporate governance; some call the two a neoliberal model and a Rhenish–Alpine–Japanese model, Michael Albert, Capitalism against Capitalism (1993); others call them an insider model and outsider model, Julian Franks & Colin Mayer, Ownership and Control, in Trends in Business Organization: Do Participation and Cooperation Increase Competitiveness? 174 (Horst Siebert ed., 1995); others a market-system and hierarchical-control system, Franklin Allen & Douglas Gale, Comparing Financial Systems (2000); and others call them Anglo-American corporate governance and continental European corporate governance, Ruth V. Aguilera & Gregory Jackson, "The Cross-National Diversity of Corporate Governance: Dimensions and Determinants", 28 Acad. Mgmt. Rev. 447 (2003).

[6] See Julian Franks, Colin Mayer, & Stefano Rossi, "Ownership: Evolution and Regulation", 22 Rev. Fin. Stud. 4009, 4034 (2009) (evolution of corporate ownership in the United Kingdom over the twentieth century, with "the rate[] of dispersion in the first half of the century [being] generally higher than in the second half"); Julian Franks, Colin Mayer, & Hideaki Miyajima, "Equity Markets and Institutions: The Case of Japan (Am. Finance Ass'n 2010 Atlanta Meeting Paper)", available at http://ssrn.com/abstract=1362613 (surprisingly high level of ownership dispersion in Japan in the first half of the twentieth century).

[7] Masahiko Aoki, Information, Corporate Governance, and Institutional Diversity: Competitiveness in Japan, the USA, and the Transnational Economies 11 (2000).

[8] Paul Davies, Luca Enriques, Gerard Hertig, Klaus J. Hopt, & Reiner Kraakman, Beyond the Anatomy, in The Anatomy of Corporate Law: A Comparative and Functional Approach 306 (Reiner Kraakman et al. eds., 2009).

[9] Randall K. Morck & Lloyd Steier, The Global History of Corporate Governance, in A History of Corporate Governance around the World: Family Business Groups to Professional Managers 8 (Randall K. Morck ed., 2005).

[10] Marco Becht & Colin Mayer, Introduction, in The Control of Corporate Europe 1 (Fabrizio Barca & Marco Becht eds., 2001), call this the over-regulation thesis.

Because the flow and organization of capital attracts political attention, corporate structure can be, and often has been, a consequence of politics. The United States historically kept financial institutions small and without authority to own stock and influence large firms, coming close to the extreme instance just mentioned. As a consequence, when American industry went national at the end of the nineteenth century, the continent-spanning industrial firms could not raise capital from a nation-spanning financial market. Capital had to come from disparate institutions and individuals. In other nations tight relationships between large-scale industry and large-scale finance were possible. As a result, in the United States, the large public firm with diffuse ownership and powerful managers became more important, more widespread, and more persistent earlier than in other nations with more concentrated financial institutions and more concentrated ownership. Some of these patterns persisted to the end of the twentieth century. Only in recent years have we seen the rise of stockholding financial firms with noticeable corporate governance authority.

In the second instance, we examine the slowness of continental European nations to develop diffusely-owned public firms in the decades after World War II. While the decades-long persistence of concentrated ownership was surely due in important part to economic forces,[11] micro- and macro-politics strongly shaped the structure of the European firm. In particular, during the reconstruction after World War II, powerful labor movements in Western Europe made strong claims on firms' cash flows. Diffuse ownership in a strongly social democratic political environment was dangerous for dispersed shareholders. When labor made these strong claims on firm value, shareholders needed more and stronger mechanisms to keep executives loyal to shareholders. But because the polity would not provide such mechanisms readily, or at all, owners had reason to stay close to the firm to handle managerial agents themselves—either by directly running the firm's day-to-day operations or by keeping a close eye on the managers who did. Shareholders could contain labor's claims on large firms' cash flows better if stock was in the hands of a close owner than with diffuse owners, which would lead to independent managers and an independent board running a diffusely held firm. Hence, to keep the firm's operating managers more loyal to shareholders, close ownership persisted.[12]

The third example concerns management in diffusely owned firms. Managers wield considerable political influence, which they use to shape the rules governing corporate finance and capital markets. In the 1980s, for example, American capital markets created the hostile takeover, by which an investor or another firm bought enough dispersed stock to control the targeted firm. Managers and directors sought to disrupt those hostile takeovers transactionally and legislatively, with poison pills, staggered boards, antitakeover legislation, and court rulings, all of which made takeovers harder to accomplish.

The first two instances of the politics of corporate governance have the firm (or players inside the firm) reacting to the political environment. If the polity keeps capital channels fragmented, such as they were in the United States for the nineteenth and much of the twentieth centuries, then the firm learns how to deal with diffuse ownership. In the second instance, when labor

---

[11] Cf. Peter A. Hall & David Soskice, An Introduction to Varieties of Capitalism, in Varieties of Capitalism: The Institutional Foundations of Comparative Advantage 1–68 (Peter A. Hall & David Soskice eds., 2001), who contrast liberal and coordinated market economies, with concentrated ownership playing a more important role in the latter—common in postwar Europe—than in the former.

[12] Cf. Harold Demsetz & Kenneth Lehn, "The Structure of Corporate Ownership: Causes and Consequences", 93 J. Pol. Econ. 1155, 1158–60 (1985) (corporate ownership concentration provides scale economies in collecting information and monitoring managers).

makes particularly powerful claims on the firm's value, executives and owners of the firm learn how to create countervailing power inside the firm. In contrast, in the final example that we investigate here, we see players inside the firm—executives and boards—proactively seeking public policies that favor themselves. Those in command of the firm can project power into the polity and will use that power to maintain, and sometimes to obtain, corporate law and other supports that favor them and maintain their authority inside the firm.

In section 2, we examine how the fragmented financial system in the United States historically limited the institutional blockholders and heightened managerial autonomy. In section 3, we analyze the relationships between owners and labor in polities where labor is strong—a corporate governance result well exemplified by German codetermination. In section 4, we examine political explanations for the continuing power of the American executive and the American board during recent decades. In section 5, we briefly look at other political economy channels for corporate governance. And in section 6, we consider the limits of a political economy analysis before we conclude.

We do not assert that these three political channels exhaust all important political channels of corporate governance and, for completeness, we describe at the end of this chapter several other channels, including some that need further research. Nor do we assert that analysis of economics, law, finance, contracts, institutional capacity, and lawmakers' sensibility of what is right and appropriate should be abandoned—i.e., we do not assert that behind each such perspective is a political economy story. Our aim is rather to develop the perspective that corporate governance often reflects political choice and that this channel can complement other efforts to explain the shape of the modern public corporation in the United States and around the world. More sharply, we claim that without political economy analytics, the shape, structure, and extent of the corporation, its ownership, and its place in an economy, cannot be understood.

2 THE HISTORICAL ORGANIZATION OF CAPITAL OWNERSHIP IN THE UNITED STATES

When the large firm became technologically possible at the end of the nineteenth century, the types of capital providers were few: banks, insurers, governments, and individuals. There were no institutional investors such as modern-day hedge funds, mutual funds, or pension funds. Individuals were major capital providers to, and owners of, the large firm, but the largest firms in the United States outstripped the financial capacity of even the richest individuals. John D. Rockefeller, the richest person in the United States at the time, owned only a fraction of Standard Oil's stock.

The question to consider here is why deposit-gathering banks (and large life insurers), which were the major financial players of the time, were not then major players in American corporate governance. The answer seems on the surface simple—banks were barred from stock ownership throughout the era (and the insurers were barred eventually as well). Equally or more importantly, American banks were too small to play a role in major firm ownership anyway.[13]

---

[13] See generally Eugene Nelson White, "The Political Economy of Banking Regulation, 1864–1933", 42 J. Econ. Hist. 33, 34 (1982).

A political economy explanation underlies the organization of American capital markets at the end of the nineteenth century.[14] The United States had its unusual, fragmented financial system largely because the small banks were politically dominant in the United States and made sure that Congress would not disrupt their local monopolies. That history begins with Andrew Jackson's 1830s destruction of the Second Bank of the United States, a large, nation-spanning bank that could have been the model for a continent-spanning financial system. Alexander Hamilton had sought in the 1790s to create a truly national banking system. Several Congresses chartered, at Hamilton's urging at first, and then re-chartered a Bank of the United States, with branches in the major American cities of the time. But the smaller banks found themselves stressed and pressed by the Second Bank's quasi-regulatory efforts.[15] In a Congress that was organized locally, district by district, the small, local bankers could be quite influential and they wanted Congress to rein in the Bank of the United States. Voter sentiment favored the small banks, making it easier for them to prevail. Jackson's famous veto message tapped into populist sentiment that wanted finance small, local, and weak.[16]

Those forces—local banker power, American congressional structure, and American anti-big-bank populism—combined to keep the financial system weak (as compared to what was possible and to what emerged in other nations) for well over a century.[17] The United States during the nineteenth century and much of the twentieth had the most unusual banking system in the industrialized world: banking rules barred banks from operating on a national scale—and sometimes even a state-wide scale.[18] Thus, by the end of the nineteenth century, although American industry spanned the continent, banks were small and local. Hence, industry could not gather capital from one or a few large deposit-gathering banks that provided one-stop financing. There was a major mismatch between the scale of American industry and the scale of American banking.

Insurers sought to fill the financing gap left by fragmented, local banking. And life insurers, whose obligations were long-term, were even better suited structurally for long-term big stockholdings than banks. The life insurers moved to fill the gap that American banking regulation created by taking large stock positions, initially in railroads and utilities. But the then-famous Armstrong investigation (which nearly propelled Charles Evans

---

[14]   See generally Mark J. Roe, Strong Managers, Weak Owners: The Political Roots of American Corporate Finance (1994) ("Strong Managers, Weak Owners"); Mark J. Roe, "A Political Theory of American Corporate Finance", 91 Colum. L. Rev. 10 (1991).

[15]   Roe, Strong Managers, Weak Owners, *supra* note 14, at 54–59.

[16]   Bray Hammond, "Jackson, Biddle, and the Bank of the United States", 76 J. Econ. Hist. 1 (1947); Bray Hammond, Banks and Politics in America from the Revolution to the Civil War 149–55 (1957); Arthur Schlesinger, Jr., The Age of Jackson (1945).

[17]   By populism we mean "a widespread attitude that large institutions and accumulations of centralized power are inherently undesirable and should be reduced, even if concentration is productive [because] . . . concentrated private groups can capture government." Roe, Strong Managers, Weak Owners, *supra* note 14, at 29.

[18]   Daniel C. Giedeman, "Branch Banking Restrictions and Finance Constraints in Early-Twentieth-Century America", 65 J. Econ. Hist. 129, 129 (2005) ("For most of the early twentieth century the American banking system was more severely restricted by regulations than the system of almost every other developed nation. A particularly important set of these banking regulations prevented the formation of widespread branching networks. Banking laws prohibited nationally chartered banks from opening branches, and most state-chartered banks faced similar limitations. The result of these restrictions was a nationwide banking system composed mostly of individual unit banks").

Hughes, its protagonist, to the presidency) culminated by barring life insurers from stock ownership.[19] The consequence was that the weak and local structure of American banking, combined with barring large life insurers from owning equity, raised the demand and need for securities markets.

Although regulators intermittently sought to permit nation-wide banking, the small local bankers and their allies in Congress blocked their efforts. The National Bank Act, for example, passed to help finance the Civil War, created entities called "national" banks, but they were national only in the sense that Washington provided the charter and legal basis for them to operate. Their operations were largely local, as they were barred from operating from more than a single location. At the end of the nineteenth century, when industry was becoming national, the Treasury Department sought to allow banks to operate more widely geographically. Congress, presumably under the influence of the local bankers (and perhaps with public opinion still moved by an anti-big-bank animus) blocked these changes.[20]

Banks and insurers were the core financial institutions when industry went national and continued to be core for much of the twentieth century. With banks and insurers restricted in size and from stock ownership, financial institutions could thus not play a strong role in corporate governance. But with money to be made in industry by achieving large-scale economies or sufficient market power to raise prices, firms found ways to raise money from bondholders and stockholders in diffuse securities markets. That result then created groups—small-town bankers with local monopolies—that wanted to preserve that status quo. Consequently, as the founders of nation-spanning industrial firms left their positions, with no blockholder or influential financial institution replacing the founders, diffuse ownership shifted power from capital providers to executives and boards, and these managerial players then also became interests that wished to preserve their authority relative to others inside the firm. With the firm lacking concentrated owners, these managers became freer to act in the policy-making environment than close owners would have allowed them to be.

True, banks' and insurers' capacity to improve firm value is limited. Such financial institutions are not entrepreneurs or CEOs. For some industrial firms, financial blockholders may do little of value, and the costs to the financial firm of holding big concentrated blocks may induce even legally authorized, large financial institutions to choose their blocks carefully. Yet, with the rise in recent years of blockholding hedge funds, we know that *some* investors will find blocks to be worth acquiring.[21] The only question is one of extent. Overall the normative idea is that corporate governance value is probably lost if an organizational form is barred. The normative question then is (1) the size of the value lost and (2) whether better rules could have channeled institutions to the most value-enhancing results and away from value-diminishing channels.

If the corporate governance consequences here had limited impact on firm value, then the normative story becomes less important but the explanatory story more important. If not

---

[19] Cf. Roe, Strong Managers, Weak Owners, *supra* note 14, at 60–93.

[20] This political economy of fragmented American banking is set forth in id. at 51–145.

[21] See generally Marcel Kahan & Edward B. Rock, "Hedge Funds in Corporate Governance and Corporate Control", 155 U. Pa. L. Rev. 1021 (discussing impact of hedge fund blockholding); Stuart Gillan & Laura T. Starks, "The Evolution of Shareholder Activism in the United States", J. Appl. Corp. Fin. 55 (2007); and Alon Brav, Wei Jiang, Frank Partnoy, & Randall S. Thomas, "Hedge Fund Activism, Corporate Governance, and Firm Performance", 63 J. Fin. 1729 (2008) (for an empirical analysis of the influence of hedge funds on the corporate governance).

much operational value separated the various corporate governance choices, then even small political restraints could sharply shift power inside the firm. That is, if concentrated ownership and diffuse ownership are value-neutral choices for all firms, then political choices are easier for the polity to make, because the economic cost of the choice would be low, or zero. The political choices may be serendipitous or depend on ephemeral political alignments. But if little value is lost from a modest political push, then the explanatory power of politics even more strongly explains the shape of authority inside the firm.[22]

The bottom line here in terms of the structural outcome, apart from any normative economic story, is that these interest group and popular configurations left the United States with severe limits to national financial operations: The United States long lacked a national banking system, American banks lacked the power to engage in commerce and, generally, to own any stock at all, and insurance companies lacked the authority to own common stock for most of the twentieth century.

Although other nations have had some of these limits on banks and insurers, few have had them all. Banks and insurers in other countries historically played a role in corporate governance that was more vigorous than the role they played in the United States. Britain, for example, has had powerful insurers that owned or controlled significant stock positions, and continues to have such influential institutional stockholders.[23] Germany has had universal banks with substantial stock ownership and even more powerful control of their brokerage customers' votes.[24] Japan has had nation-spanning banks with significant stock ownership.[25] The latter two channels of universal banks and main banks have narrowed in importance in the past several decades, although they have not disappeared.

---

[22] Bradford J. DeLong, Did J.P. Morgan's Men Add Value?, in Inside the Business Enterprise (Peter Temin ed., 1991) provides some of the better-known evidence that the costs of barring financial institutions from substantial governance roles were not small: In end-of-nineteenth-century America, the Morgan firm put its partners on firms' boards, thereby offering the firm's own reputation to protect shareholders from scurrilous or incompetent management. Pernicious insider dealings, or undiscovered managerial incompetence, would cost the Morgan firm dearly, so it warranted (albeit weakly) that such nefarious or incompetent results would be unlikely to occur in the firms on whose boards its partners sat. Outside investors might mistrust the firm and its inside managers, but they had more reason to trust the Morgan directors.

[23] Insurance companies are currently important investors in British equities, having owned approximately 20% of the market since the early 1980s. Bernard S. Black & John C. Coffee, "Hail Britannia?: Institutional Investor Behavior Under Limited Regulation", 92 Mich. L. Rev. 1997, at 2008–2010 (1994). As Cheffins notes, unlike in the United States, there was no legislation in the United Kingdom during the twentieth century explicitly discouraging concentrations of shareholdings. Brian Cheffins, Putting Britain on the Roe Map: The Emergence of the Berle–Means Corporation in the United Kingdom, in Corporate Governance Regimes: Convergence and Diversity 147–72 (Joseph A. McCahery et al. eds., 2002). And in the modern era, other institutional investors have played a major role in large British firms.

[24] A universal bank not only takes demand deposits and makes loans, but can also underwrite, hold, and trade all other securities. Alexander Gerschenkron, Economic Backwardness in Historical Perspective: A Book of Essays (1962) argued that universal banking was critical to Germany's industrialization and that it is critically useful when countries catch up in industrial development. His thesis relates to the radical vs. incremental innovation discussion *infra*, in section 3.

[25] See Masahiko Aoki, Hugh Patrick, & Paul Sheard, The Japanese Main Bank System: An Introductory Overview, in Japanese Main Bank System—Its Relevance for Developing and Transforming Economies 3 (Masahiko Aoki & Hugh Patrick eds., 1995).

3 The Power of Labor in Postwar Europe

If labor makes powerful claims on large firms' cash flows, such that how the firms handle these pressures deeply affects shareholder value, then that labor power will affect corporate governance players' choices as to structure, ownership, and power allocations. Moreover, if labor is powerful across the polity, then its power can even more directly determine corporate governance. German codetermination, by which labor gets about half of the seats on public firms' boards, is an explicit instance. And more generally, labor power in Germany and elsewhere in social democratic countries affects ownership structure by making diffuse ownership considerably less valuable for stockholders than close ownership. There is good reason to think that in the immediate postwar decades in Western Europe this impact of labor's power was a large determinant of corporate governance.[26]

The general principle here is this: if labor makes strong claims on large firms' cash flows, then shareholders have reason to limit those claims. But executives who are not subject to strong shareholder control can readily "defect" from shareholder value, as the executives' preferred agenda for the firm often overlaps with labor's. Thus, labor and management of a diffusely held firm may have similar agendas in polities with strong labor pressures, and that combined agenda may more sharply differ from that of owners in strong labor environments than in weak labor environments. That difference makes the diffusely owned firm costlier for owners in strong labor environments.

For diffuse stock markets to arise and persist, the diffuse capital owners must see their firms as managed well enough for stockholders, as compared to close ownership's value for stockholders. The public firm provides liquidity and diversification for the original investors and brings in professional managers to run the firm. But for the original dominant shareholders to turn their firm's ownership over to liquid stock markets and, hence, to managerial control, they must expect value from turning over control. If the benefits to stockholders of shareholder liquidity and professional management are exceeded by the costs of turnover due to increased managerial disloyalty because the polity will not support the institutions and rules that facilitate managerial loyalty to shareholders, then fewer dominant stockholders will turn their firms over to managers than otherwise.

3.1 Labor Power and Managerial Agency Costs

Consider the range of agency costs that explained widespread hostile takeovers in the United States in the 1980s: a managerial tendency to expand the firm beyond its efficient boundaries, a managerial tendency to spend the firm's free cash flow instead of returning it to shareholders, a managerial preference for low-risk operations that do not threaten the firm and managers' positions, and a managerial tendency to use up capital in place even when the firm no longer was profitable rather than move the capital elsewhere. Michael Jensen's 1986 analytic is the

---

[26]   See Mark J. Roe, "Legal Origins, Politics and Modern Stock Markets", 120 Harv. L. Rev. 462 (2006) ("Legal Origins").

iconic one of the time.[27] These managerial agency costs (if one considers the managers to be working primarily for shareholders) map closely onto the goals of powerful labor: to avoid risky operations that threaten jobs and factories, and to avoid closing down factories even if they are no longer profitable. In such a pro-labor environment, shareholders would have a high demand for the tools that would keep managers pro-shareholder. Their demand for such tools presumably would exceed shareholders' demand for such tools in the United States in the 1980s, as the United States lacked such strong labor pressures. That is, even without such labor pressures, managerial agency costs in diffusely owned firms have been sufficiently important that shareholders sought tools to reduce those costs. Labor pressures like those in Germany would have made those costs even higher in the United States.

For shareholders to count on executives being satisfactorily loyal to shareholder goals, shareholders need institutions and norms that reward that loyalty and that give them means to detect and punish disloyalty. But if a polity will not provide those institutions, or if it denigrates such shareholder-value norms, then dominant stockholders can obtain more shareholder value for themselves by keeping control of the firm. Managerial control will not ordinarily appear in such a political environment and will be unstable if it does. Stock markets will not be strong in such nations, because managerial agency costs will be too high and too hard to lower to levels that stockholders would find acceptable.[28]

More texture: A polity in which labor was often the decisive political player would not facilitate managerial shareholder-loyalty mechanisms, such as takeovers, incentive compensation, and corporate transparency for shareholders, as these tools would not be in labor's interest. Without shareholders having those tools, the costs to shareholders of labor power could be large. Consider a firm that contemplates a major expansion into a new market or contemplates whether to take advantage of a new technology to re-orient its production. If the expansion fails or the technology backfires in a weak labor environment, the firm contracts and reverses the expansion. The contraction and reversal are costly, but achievable, limiting the losses to shareholders. Such expansions and, if needed, contractions are common in the United States. But if a pro-labor environment makes contraction and reversal even more costly because it would trigger government inquiry and costs, or if contraction is functionally impossible because the polity and its labor rules will not allow layoffs or make them very costly, then the downside costs to shareholders of misdirected expansion rise.[29] Yet, a basic agency managerial cost is posited to be that managers seek larger firms for prestige, power, and often compensation. In a pro-labor environment, shareholders would be especially wary of the firm expanding and would therefore want the upside to be particularly strong and the probability of the downside low. Shareholders with weak corporate governance tools could readily find that the best way to prevent unwarranted expansion is for them to keep a close eye on managers. For them to keep a close eye on managers, they would have to keep close ownership of the firm. And that is approximately what we saw in Western Europe in the immediate postwar decades.

---

[27] Michael Jensen, "Agency Costs of Free Cash Flow, Corporate Finance and Takeover", 76 Am. Econ. Rev. 323 (1986). Cf. Michael Jensen & William Meckling, "Theory of the Firm: Managerial Behavior, Agency Costs and Ownership Structure", 3 J. Fin. Econ. 305 (1976).

[28] See Roe, Political Determinants, *supra* note 4, at 29–37.   [29] Id.

3.2 German Codetermination

German codetermination, as noted above, provides the most direct labor-oriented corporate governance mechanism here, with German law requiring that half of the seats on the supervisory board be reserved for employees. It resulted from political compromises: Codetermination of labor and shareholders arose just after World War II in the coal and steel industry. In one rendition of the postwar explanation, labor's presence in the boardroom would weaken the wartime industrialists' influence and, hence, the victorious Allies would not need to dismantle the steel and coal industry so as to demilitarize Germany.[30] Later political events, such as labor unrest, led to settlements to have the rest of German industry codetermined.[31]

Codetermination is best seen as an amalgam of political objectives, like the goal of industrial and political leaders for labor peace, and the realpolitik that labor had considerable voting power in the polity. Either way—whether by compromise or power play—codetermination directly determines core aspects of German corporate governance, namely the composition of the board of directors, and it is a political economy result. The German supervisory board has a major labor presence and, because the supervisory board appoints the management board (which runs the firm day to day), there is a major difference in power and governance in the German firm as compared to, say, the American firm. German senior managers typically need some level of labor support, or acquiescence.[32]

The logic of the incentives that codetermination creates should foster concentrated ownership as well, in the manner suggested above for pro-labor polities. With employees wielding power in the supervisory board, shareholders would typically do better for themselves overall if they maintained strong countervailing power in the boardroom, as well as having the means to monitor managers directly outside of the boardroom. The obvious way to do both would be to maintain concentrated ownership.

3.3 Data on Correlation of Labor Power and Close Ownership: Bidirectional Causation

Figure 3.3 illustrates the relationship between labor power (quantified by union and job security rules[33]) and the degree to which large firms had large blockholders in the year 1995. Greater labor power coincides with greater ownership concentration, weaker labor power

---

[30] In Italy, the Allies also preferred to preserve incumbent large firms. Cf. Fabrizio Barca, Katsuhito Iwai, Ugo Pagano, & Sandro Trento, "The Divergence of the Italian and Japanese Corporate Governance Models: The Role of Institutional Shocks", 23 Econ. System 25 (1999).

[31] See Katharina Pistor, Codetermination: A Sociopolitical Model with Governance Externalities, in Employees and Corporate Governance 163 (Margaret Blair & Mark J. Roe eds., 1999). For a recent analysis of the changes in German corporate law that facilitated ownership dispersion (but without a political interpretation), see Wolf-Georg Ringe, "Changing Law and Ownership Patterns in Germany: Corporate Governance and the Erosion of Deutschland AG", 63 Am. J. Comp. L. 493 (2015).

[32] Cf. Pistor, *supra* note 31, at 191; and Roe, Political Determinants, *supra* note 4, at 29–33.

[33] Roe, Legal Origins, *supra* note 26, at 497 (tbl. 7).

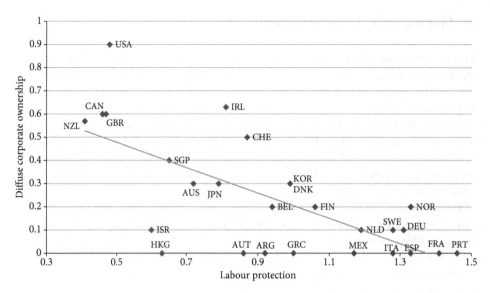

FIGURE 3.3 Correlation between labor protection and corporate ownership diffusion.

The 27 countries represented are Argentina (ARG), Australia (AUS), Austria (AUT), Belgium (BEL), Canada (CAN), Denmark (DNK), Finland (FIN), France (FRA), Germany (DEU), Greece (GRC), Hong-Kong (HKG), Ireland (IRL), Israel (ISR), Italy (ITA), Japan (JPN), Mexico (MEX), the Netherlands (NLD), New Zealand (NZL), Norway (NOR), Portugal (PRT), South Korea (KOR), Singapore (SGP), Spain (ESP), Sweden (SWE), Switzerland (CHE), the United Kingdom (GBR), and the United States (USA). y = −0.55x + 0.75; R-squared= 0.47; p-value <.02; n=27. We include here all nations for which the ownership data is available. One sees that the sample includes a handful of less developed nations, whose inclusion would not change the relationship. Sources and background to the figure can be found in Roe, Legal Origins, *supra* note 26, at 497, tbl. 7.

with more diffuse ownership.[34] Wealthy nations with high employment protection and high labor power lack diffuse stock markets; conversely, nations with high stock market diffusion and fewer large controlled firms do not vigorously protect employees with jobs in place. Essen, Oosterhout, and Heugens bring forward evidence that relational blockholders are better than other owner types at handling powerful labor pressures.[35]

The negative correlation between labor power and shareholder power is striking, making this a good spot to raise the possibility, indeed the likelihood, of bidirectional causation. Thus far, the thesis of this part has been that blockholding persistence is a reaction to labor power. It's of course possible, indeed even likely, that some of labor's power comes from the polity reacting negatively to blockholding.

---

[34] See Mark J. Roe, Political Determinants, *supra* note 4, at 52; Marco Pagano & Paolo F. Volpin, "The Political Economy of Corporate Governance", 95 Am. Econ. Rev. 1005 (2005); Beth Ahlering & Simon Deakin, "Labor Regulation, Corporate Governance, and Legal Origin: A Case of Institutional Complementarity?", 41 L. & Society Rev. 865 (2007); Marianna Belloc & Ugo Pagano, "Co-evolution of Politics and Corporate Governance", 29 Int'l. Rev. L. & Econ. 106 (2009): Marianna Belloc & Ugo Pagano, "Politics–Business Co-evolution Paths: Workers' Organization and Capital Concentration", 33 Int'l. Rev. L. & Econ. 23 (2013).

[35] Marc van Essen, J. Hans van Oosterhout, & Pursey Heugens, "Competition and Cooperation in Corporate Governance: The Effects of Labor Institutions on Blockholder Effectiveness in 23 European Countries", 24 Org. Sci. 530 (2014).

Concentrated ownership may induce workers to seek employment protection privately via unions and contracting, as well as publicly via employment and anti-layoff rules; that is, ownership concentration may induce employees to call for protection *via* politics:

> [E]arly in the twentieth century, the visible power of Germany's large banks, people's envy and resentment of rich industrialists, and the disorientation and anomie induced by Germany's rapid transformation from an agricultural nation into an industrial one helped to call forth codetermination to tame the bankers and industrialists, and to give the workers a voice in the strange new industrial enterprises.[36]

3.4 Institutional Complementarity

This reverse causation between corporate ownership and labor protection corresponds to the literature on institutional complementarity.[37] Briefly, in some economies labor training and skills better complement ownership structures that facilitate labor stability than other ownership systems. Choices in one domain, such as labor protection, act as exogenous parameters in other domains (e.g., the corporate ownership), and vice versa.

Similarly, innovation systems are complementary to ownership systems,[38] and determining one economic piece of the corporate governance structure via politics can lock in other elements of the large firm. Corporate governance with large shareholders and highly protected workers supports incremental innovation that requires more cooperation among stakeholders than sharp, radical innovation, as noted above, whereas diffuse ownership and weak employee protection facilitate radical innovation by allowing new production technologies and new products to quickly disrupt labor arrangements.[39] Whatever innovation system is in place then interacts with political demands for corporate governance, as noted in section 5. Incremental innovation systems call forth labor

---

[36] Roe, Political Determinants, *supra* note 4, at 112–13.

[37] See Hall & Soskice, *supra* note 11. Cf. Masahiko Aoki, Towards a Comparative Institutional Analysis (2001); Bruno Amable, "Institutional Complementarity and Diversity of Social Systems of Innovation and Production", 7 Rev. Int'l. Pol. Econ. 645 (2002); Martin Gelter, "The Dark Side of Shareholder Influence: Managerial Autonomy and Stakeholder Orientation in Comparative Corporate Governance", 50 Harv. Int'l. L. J. 129 (2009); Ugo Pagano, "The Evolution of the American Corporation and Global Organizational Biodiversity", 35 Seattle U.L. Rev. 1271 (2012); Ugo Pagano & Massimiliano Vatiero, "Costly Institutions as Substitutes: Novelty and Limits of the Coasian Approach", 11 J. Inst. Econ. 265 (2015). Griffith and Macartney provide empirical evidence on these theoretical issues. Rachel Griffith & Gareth Macartney, "Employment Protection Legislation, Multinational Firms, and Innovation", 96 Rev. Econ. & Stat. 135 (2014).

[38] Wendy Carlin & Colin Mayer, "Finance, Investment, and Growth", 69 J. Fin. Econ. 191, 193 (2003) ("financial and ownership systems are associated with different *types* of corporate activities and investments") (emphasis in original). See generally Hall & Soskice, *supra* note 11. Puca and Vatiero provide evidence from Swiss listed firms. Marcello Puca & Massimiliano Vatiero, "Ownership and innovation: Evidence from Switzerland" (Working Paper, Università della Svizzera italiana 2017), available at https://papers.ssrn.com/sol3/papers.cfm?abstract_id=2739880.

[39] Gilson and Roe advance a different explanation for the Japanese case. They see Japanese managers' ability to close down parts of the inter-firm labor market as more important for developing firm-specific human capital than firms' commitment to keep the employees working. Ronald J. Gilson & Mark J. Roe, "Lifetime Employment: Labor Peace and the Evolution of Japanese Corporate Governance", 99 Colum. L. Rev. 508 (1999).

protection and, consequently or directly, blockholder ownership. Radical innovation fits best with corporate governance systems with limited commitments to labor and ongoing trading partners.

Overall, as long as institutional complementarities are deep and strong, they can affect, or conceivably determine, the institutional equilibrium, and that system will differ depending on which local complement dominates.

3.5 Coalitions and Rents

Thus far in this section, we have considered the possibility that owners seek to keep managers loyal in high-labor-power environments. This roughly corresponds to the line linking employees and owners in the triangle in Figure 3.2. Next, we consider another such linkage between owners and employees.

Consider first Rajan and Zingales's showing that blockholders will often want to suppress financial market development, particularly if product market competition is weak, because easier access to financing for upstarts would more likely erode blockholders' monopoly rents.[40] Hence, poor shareholder protection should correlate with trade protectionism.[41]

Although this is not prima facie a labor-oriented explanation, it could become so. Indeed, since in a functioning democracy the blockholders do not necessarily get their way with the polity if voters do not agree,[42] labor can play a role in buttressing the incumbent blockholders.[43] If labor obtains a portion of the rents that accrue to firms that lacks sharp competition, then this sector of labor also disfavors financial development, which would threaten their rents. They ally with the blockholders, either directly or more likely via coalition voting in parliament to defeat financial liberalization. In this way Rajan and Zingales's blockholder interest explanation can be deepened and extended with labor power in the postwar European democracies. In this amendment to the blockholder power theory, labor at established firms allies with incumbent blockholders to influence in the polity to protect their mutual interests.[44]

---

[40] Blockholder power can be magnified if it's a function of what the blockholder controls rather than the monetary value of what it owns. Consistently, Morck, Wolfenzon and Yeung show that family control via pyramids amplifies the owners' political influence relative to their actual stakes. Randall Morck, Daniel Wolfenzon, & Bernard Yeung, "Corporate Governance, Economic Entrenchment, and Growth", 43 J. Econ. Lit. 655 (2005).

[41] Raghuram Rajan & Luigi Zingales, "The Great Reversals: The Politics of Financial Development in the Twentieth Century", 69 J. Fin. Econ. 5 (2003). A related generalized version is advanced by Enrico Perotti & Paolo F. Volpin, "Lobbying on Entry" (Working Paper, London Business School 2004), available at http://ssrn.com/abstract=558588. For the regular influence of families in dominant businesses on politics, often in developing nations, see Randall Morck & Bernard Yeung, "Family Control and the Rent-Seeking Society", 28 Entrepreneurship: Theory and Practice 391 (2003).

[42] Anonymous, disparate, especially individual (as opposed to institutional) shareholders seem to be a classic instance of Mancur Olson's "inchoate group," namely a group that, although large, is too scattered and poorly organized to influence political decisions than smaller, but organized, groups such as corporate executives. Mancur Olson, The Logic of Collective Action: Public Goods and the Theory of Groups (1965).

[43] See Roe, Political Determinants, *supra* note 4, at 134–49.

[44] That is, labor is not a unified block, but divided between labor at core industries (which allies directly or through their parliamentary representatives) with blockholders, on the one hand, and labor in outside or

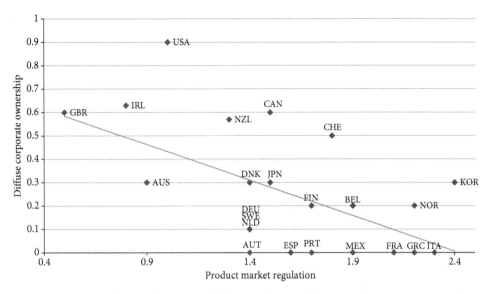

FIGURE 3.4 Correlation between product market regulation and corporate ownership diffusion.

The 23 countries are Australia (AUS), Austria (AUT), Belgium (BEL), Canada (CAN), Denmark (DNK), Finland (FIN), France (FRA), Germany (DEU), Greece (GRC), Ireland (IRL), Italy (ITA), Japan (JPN), Mexico (MEX), the Netherlands (NLD), New Zealand (NZL), Norway (NOR), Portugal (PRT), South Korea (KOR), Spain (ESP), Sweden (SWE), Switzerland (CHE), the United Kingdom (GBR), and the United States (USA). $y = -0.3047x + 0.7374$; R-squared= 0.33; p-value <.02; n=23. Sources: product market regulation comes from Giuseppe Nicoletti, Stefano Scarpetta, & Oliver Boylaud, "Summary Indicators of Product Market Regulation with an Extension to Employment Protection Legislation", OECD Econ. Dep't Working Paper no. 226, at 79, tbl. A3.6 (2000). Nicoletti, Scarpetta and Boylaud measure how deeply product markets are regulated, which presumably causes or is correlated with weaker product market competition. Diffuse ownership is from Rafael La Porta, Florencio Lopez-de-Silanes & Andrei Shleifer, Corporate Ownership around the World, 54 J. Fin. 471, 494 tbl. 3 (1999), which tabulates the portion of the 10 firms with a December 1995 stock market capitalization of common equity of just above $500 million that lack a 20% blockholder.

Blockholders and incumbent workers may ally to create or maintain monopoly rents, which can be split between them; the two can influence the polity to keep trade barriers high and financial competition weak:

> [W]ith the monopolies in place in a democracy, the benefited owners have to get other players' political support. Union and employee benefits, instead of being "grabs", could be "pay-offs" from owners, to keep political and internal support strong for hampering competitors. Or, slightly differently, employees and owners can coalesce politically, aiming to weaken competitors, both domestic and foreign, via blocking rules, subsidies, and trade barriers.[45]

Figure 3.4 provides evidence of the negative correlation between product market competition and the diffusion of corporate ownership.

less-influential industries, on the other hand. See David Rueda, Social Democracy Inside Out: Partisanship and Labor Market Policy in Advanced Industrialized Democracies 2, 6, 12–22 (2008) (analyzing Spain, Britain, and the Netherlands in such terms); Assar Lindbeck & Dennis J. Snower, "The Insider-Outsider Theory: A Survey" (IZA Discussion Paper No. 534 2002), available at http://ssrn.com/abstract=325323.

[45] Roe, Political Determinants, *supra* note 4, at 139.

Weaker product markets and the concomitant monopoly rents can affect corporate governance by loosening constraints on managers and/or by setting up a fertile field where shareholders can cooperatively split rents with incumbent workers.[46] Large owners and incumbent workers can ally politically in order to frustrate competition policy and its related financial market policy.

* * *

Related but differing political economy explanations for corporate governance have emerged, which we discuss further in section 5.

In this section, we have argued that the structure of markets that the large firm faces, the power of labor in the polity overall, and the power of labor vis-à-vis the large firm all deeply affect the large firm. Some ownership structures can do better than others in the face of muscular labor. When labor is powerful, it can determine corporate structures directly, as is the case for German codetermination. The degree of labor power also affects structures pervasively. Managerial agency costs need to be contained, or so shareholder interests demand, and those managerial agency costs in public firms are harder to contain in pro-labor environments. Hence, shareholders have less reason to favor diffuse ownership when labor is powerful. The postwar European evidence suggests that they in fact disfavored diffuse ownership and preferred concentrated ownership.

4 THE CONTINUING POWER OF THE AMERICAN CORPORATE EXECUTIVE

Managers of large diffusely owned firms have reason to disrupt their shareholders' capacity to aggregate their stock ownership in ways that would project more shareholder power into the firm's boardroom. The executives may not own much of the firm's capital themselves, but they control the firm and they seek to maintain their control; powerful stockholders would limit executive autonomy. Managers thus seek laws that impede or bar hostile takeovers and that make large, active shareholder positions costly for shareholders. They oppose voting rules that would make it easier for shareholders to elect directors other than those whom incumbent managers support. Such rules are more likely to arise and persist in countries like the United States, where diffuse ownership prevents blockholders from vetoing managerial influence in lawmaking, because there are fewer blockholders. In countries in which concentrated blockholders tightly control the firm, managers could not readily seek such rules, because the powerful stockholder would be unhappy with such managerial lobbying.

These managerial efforts to affect the terms of basic corporate and securities law have been significant in the United States historically and continue today. Managers successfully opposed the strongest proposals in this past decade to allow shareholders easy access to the firm's proxy statement, which would allow dissidents to more easily elect directors.[47] Prior

---

[46] See Roe, Political Determinants, *supra* note 4, at 125–49; Peter A. Gourevitch, "The Politics of Corporate Governance Regulation", 112 Yale L. J. 1829, 1841 et seq., 1871 et seq. (2003).

[47] Mark J. Roe, "The Corporate Shareholder's Vote and Its Political Economy, in Delaware and in Washington", 2 Harv. Bus. L. Rev. 1 (2012).

outbreaks of the shareholder voting reform efforts in the United States, starting in the 1940s, also died after managers successfully opposed the proposals. The literature on the spillover of managerial preferences and authority into the political sphere is thinner.[48]

The economic circumstances of the 1980s presented a powerful twin challenge to senior American executives' autonomy. Large manufacturers were challenged by the rise of international competition, mostly from Germany and Japan. Simultaneously, the hostile takeover rose to prominence: a takeover entrepreneur would acquire the funding to buy a target firm's stock and then appeal over the heads of executives and the board to the firm's shareholders. If the shareholders sold their stock to the takeover entrepreneur—often a person, investor group, or another large firm—the takeover entrepreneur would own the company and, often enough, replace the firm's managers.

Managers reacted swiftly and ferociously, building up antitakeover transactional tactics and, when those failed—several were barred by courts in early decisions—the managers sought changes in the law to strengthen their ability to fend off hostile takeovers. The typical antitakeover transactional tool became the poison pill, which would dilute the value of the takeover entrepreneur's stake. The tactic needed validation from courts and legislatures that it was a permitted managerial tool. Eventually, the managers got that authorization and (along with other antitakeover tools) beat back the hostile takeover wave.[49] As a consequence of the political battles over takeovers, power shifted further to the board of directors in large American firms by the 1990s.[50]

Some of the managers' success in beating back hostile takeovers was due to the strength of their lobbying organizations (such as Chambers of Commerce and the Business Roundtable) in influencing state legislatures to validate antitakeover tools and leave court decisions in place that permitted poison pills. Two political economy aspects ought to be noted. First, the managers' lobbying organizations did well on their own, but acquired even more heft by the fact that employees and voter opinion were mostly on their side in seeking stability and slowing corporate change. This roughly corresponds to an alliance between employees and managers, one side of the Figure 3.2 triangle. Moreover, public opinion was against the hostile takeover, even if it wasn't for the manager.[51]

One can see a managerial–labor coalition as decisive in making for some state antitakeover law.[52] When a Pennsylvania corporation was targeted for a hostile takeover, it sought strong

---

[48] Efforts can be found in Mark J. Roe, Takeover Politics, in The Deal Decade 321–52 (Margaret Blair ed., 1993); Joseph A. Grundfest, "Subordination of American Capital", 27 J. Fin. Econ. 89 (1990); and Lucian A. Bebchuk & Zvika Neeman, "Investor Protection and Interest Group Politics", 23 Rev. Fin. Stud. 1089 (2010).

[49] Cf. Emiliano Catan & Marcel Kahan, "The Law and Finance of Anti-Takeover Statutes", 68 Stan. L. Rev. 629 (2016).

[50] Stephen M. Bainbridge, The New Corporate Governance and Practice (2008).

[51] Roberta Romano, "The Future of Hostile Takeovers: Legislation and Public Opinion", 57 U. Cincinnati L. Rev. 457 (1988). Cf. Roe, Strong Managers, Weak Owners, *supra* note 14, at 152–53.

[52] John C. Coffee Jr., "Shareholders versus Managers: The Strain in the Corporate Web", 85 Mich. L. Rev. 1, 70 (1986) ("Employees and managers constitute the best example of a class that has had to accept the imposition of higher risk. Many recent instances can be identified where corporations first leveraged up as a takeover defence and then followed this action with subsequent massive dismissals or compelled retirements of employees"); Geoffrey Miller, "Political Structure and Corporate Governance: Some Points of Contrast between the United States and England", 2 Colum. Bus. L. Rev. 51 (1998). Cf. Martin F. Hellwig, On the Economics and Politics of Corporate Finance and Corporate Control, in Corporate

antitakeover law from the state's legislature. For many Pennsylvania legislators, voting for the legislation was easy, as both the Chamber of Commerce and the AFL-CIO supported the legislation. Consider a contemporary comment: "[The] lobbying effort is the product of teamwork between . . . Pennsylvania labor unions and a coalition of over two dozen corporations working for the passage of the bill under the well-organized direction of the Pennsylvania Chamber of Business and Industry."[53]

Many states also contemporaneously enacted constituency statutes, which formally authorized boards to weight the impact of hostile takeovers on corporate constituencies, such as employees, when deciding whether to reject or accept an outside bid. In time, boards successfully defeated hostile takeovers when the poison pill was fully validated. When they did, constituency statutes played a limited role thereafter in takeovers.

True, economic circumstances eventually undercut the hostile takeover in that the 1980s hostile takeover was most efficacious for breaking up the conglomerates of the 1960s. Once most were broken up and their separate businesses spun off, there were fewer sweet spots for easy money takeovers. And in time, the takeover machinery monetized incumbent managers' positional advantage, with hostile takeovers ceasing but "friendly" takeovers proceeding. Nominally, these takeovers were "friendly" and the managers, who often departed, departed very rich.[54]

We can combine this section's focus on managerial political power with section 2's focus on the historical weakness of nation-spanning financial institutions in the United States. With managers historically controlling large firms early on in the twentieth century, due to the lack of a strong financial counterweight to managerial authority, they were freer to use political levers to maintain their authority. By weakening proxy fights in the 1950s, by beating back takeovers in the 1980s, and by more generally reducing or reversing reformers' success in creating rules that would strengthen shareholders and weaken managers, managers maintained their position of authority. If blockholders had been in place, managers could not as readily have lobbied for rules that extend or maintain managerial autonomy and authority.

That is, path dependence affects the corporation and some of that path dependence operates through political channels.[55] Once there is diffuse ownership and managerial autonomy, for whatever reason, those with power in the firm can project that power into the polity to resist new laws that would reduce their autonomy. That chain of events makes a first- and second-order, path-dependent political economy explanation plausible: autonomy first developed because American politics independently made banks and insurers, the institutional investors of their time, too weak to play a corporate governance role. Diffuse ownership ensued, without controlling institutional shareholders. If there had been controlling shareholders, one assumes they would have looked askance at their CEOs and

---

Governance: Theoretical and Empirical Perspectives 95, 134 (Xavier Vives ed., 2000) (showing how the convergence of interests between managers and workers at the corporate level may induce them to converge on a common platform at the political level); Marco Pagano & Paolo F. Volpin, "Managers, Workers, and Corporate Control", 60 J. Fin. 841 (2005); Marco Pagano & Paolo F. Volpin, "Shareholder Protection, Stock Market Development, and Politics", 4 J. Eur. Econ. Ass'n 315 (2006).

[53]   As quoted in Roe, Takeover Politics, *supra* note 48, at 393.

[54]   Marcel Kahan & Edward B. Rock, "How I Learned to Stop Worrying and Love the Pill: Adaptive Responses to Takeover Law", 69 U. Chi. L. Rev. 871 (2002) (incumbent managers bought off).

[55]   See Mark J. Roe, "Chaos and Evolution in Law and Economics", 109 Harv. L. Rev. 641 (1996); Lucian R. Bebchuk & Mark J. Roe, "A Theory of Path Dependence in Corporate Ownership and Governance", 52 Stan. L. Rev. 127 (1999); Massimiliano Vatiero, "On the (Political) Origin of 'Corporate Governance' Species", 31 J. Econ. Surv. 393 (2017).

senior executives seeking to cut back on shareholder power. Managers thus had substantial power to operate in the political arena independently of shareholders, and they used that freedom to act in that political arena (a freedom that came from an absence of controlling shareholders) to bolster their autonomy. As in other path-dependent settings, an early decision and structure affect a later decision, tending to preserve the earlier structure.

Moreover, one can see the ongoing importance of political economy explanations for corporate governance through another political channel. Substantial managerial power may simply originate from the baseline efficiency of separating ownership from control. That separation then gives managers authority in the firm, which they can project into the political sphere, *further enhancing* their authority beyond that which would have prevailed in an efficient, politically neutral setting.

The converse is also true. Once controlling shareholders are dominant across most firms in a given polity, they will tend to use their resulting political power to maintain their controlling positions. For example, in some polities, controlling shareholders can shift value to themselves more easily than in other jurisdictions. Reformers might want to change these rules, lowering the private benefits of control to controllers—by devising rules and processes by which small shareholders can reverse related-party transactions between the firm and the controlling insiders, and restricting the ease with which controlling shareholders can squeeze out minority stockholders at an unfair price. But once a player controls a public firm, it has an interest in maintaining (or expanding) its capacity to shift value to itself.[56] When many controlling shareholders are in place in an economy, they become influential in the polity. This feature seems to have been important in recent decades in several Western European nations.[57]

5 FURTHER POLITICAL CHANNELS

In this section, we examine further interactions between politics and corporate governance in developed countries.

5.1 The Median Voter and the Elites

Politicians seek out the median, pivotal voter, who determines elections in a democracy.[58] In particular, Perotti and von Thadden show how the preferences of the pivotal voter can depend on the size and form of the returns to human capital relative to the voter's return from financial assets.[59] If the median voter has substantial financial assets, then she will support financial development and securities markets. But if the median voter has relatively low financial savings and relatively high human capital, then she will prefer low-risk,

---

[56] Bebchuk & Roe, *supra* note 55, at 149–50, 158–60.
[57] See *infra* section 5; Randall Morck, ed., Concentrated Corporate Ownership (2000).
[58] Anthony Downs, An Economic Theory of Democracy (1957).
[59] Enrico C. Perotti & Ernst-Ludwig von Thadden, "The Political Economy of Corporate Control and Labor Rents", 114 J. Pol. Econ. 145 (2006). Cf. Hans Degryse, Thomas Lambert, & Armin Schwienbacher, "The Political Economy of Financial Systems: Evidence from Suffrage Reforms in the last two centuries", Econ. J. (forthcoming).

go-slow economic policies overall and will have little personal interest in supporting securities markets. That preference arises because a financially weakened middle class is largely concerned about the labor income risk associated with freer markets and supports a more corporatist financial system characterized by dominant banks. Banks are dominant because they profit from low-risk loans and their strong presence in corporate governance keeps firms less risky, which is what employees want. In Germany, firms with stronger labor have more bank debt, with the explanation being "that both employees and debt providers have a strong interest in the long-term survival and stability of the firm,"[60] with other profit-maximizing goals presumably subordinate.

This median voter thesis relates to the idea that labor, if powerful, prefers block ownership to diffuse ownership.[61] True, workers might well prefer weakened, dispersed shareholders to strong blockholders. Indeed, if the shareholder side becomes weaker, then the corporation is more likely to follow more of labor's preferences. But, workers, particularly if they own only small financial stakes, would prefer risk-reducing banks or large family shareholders to diffused shareholders *if* they believe that the former will typically choose safer, incremental operational strategies. In contrast, a strong equity market would presumably lead to more pro-equity, risky ventures that disrupt workers' lives and jobs. This abstraction largely describes Western Europe in the latter part of the twentieth century.

Culpepper analyses how corporate actors have been able to influence the development of corporate governance law in France, Germany, the Netherlands, and Japan.[62] When an issue has low political salience to the median voter, then it will likely be decided through "quiet politics," in which corporate actors are preeminent. This is particularly so for those issues that strongly affect corporate actors' interests, such as laws on hostile takeovers. In contrast, where political salience is high, companies are not able to rely on quiet politics, and must instead seek partisan political protection more directly, and try to counter or change public opinion. "Business [elites] frequently lose . . . political battles when the general public pays attention to them [regulatory politics], because when the public pays attention to issues, political parties start paying attention to the opinion of the median voter and stop paying attention to powerful interest groups."[63]

In this perspective, median voter theory explains the corporate governance outcomes for issues that are salient for the average voter, but fails when the issue is not salient for voters. When it is not salient, the institutions of corporate governance will follow the elite's preferences. Rajan and Zingales argued that controlling shareholders had little reason to

---

[60] Chen Lin, Thomas Schmid, & Yuhai Xuan, "Employee Representation and Financial Leverage", J. Fin. Econ. (forthcoming).

[61] However, the populist movement in the United States that fragmented the financial system included also the labor class.

[62] Pepper D. Culpepper, Quiet Politics and Business Power: Corporate Control in Europe and Japan 3–4, 177 (2011) ("the more the public cares about an issue, the less managerial organizations will be able to exercise disproportionate influence over the rules governing that issue. In other words, business power goes down as political salience goes up").

[63] Id. at 6. Rhodes and van Adeldoorn structure a similar argument: If corporate elites see their authority challenged, they will resist corporate governance reforms strongly, often strongly enough to overcome general voter sentiment. Martin Rhodes & Bastiaan van Apeldoorn, "Capital Unbound? The Transformation of European Corporate Governance", 5 J. Eur. Public Policy 406 (1998).

support corporate governance reform that would undermine their interests, particularly if the reform would foment better access to funding for upstart competitors of incumbent elites.[64]

5.2 Geopolitics

A related, geopolitical conceptualization may be also in play. The looming presence of the Soviet Union in the second half of the twentieth century was the central geopolitical fact for continental Europe. In the initial postwar elections, the Communist Party did well in France (about 20% of votes from the 1950s to 1970s) and Italy (about 25% of the vote from the 1950s to 1980s), making it important for centrist and conservative parties to co-opt the communist program, which they did. The result was policy that favored incumbent labor and incumbent owners.[65]

5.3 Ideology

We should not ignore the power of ideas and ideologies (or culture in a broad sense). For instance, Aguilera and Jackson report that cross-national differences in managerial behavior depend on differences in managers' world-views, with the differences in world-view highly influenced by education. Specifically, managers in the United States are typically well educated in finance and socialized in business schools to have a shareholder-value orientation. In contrast, German managers more typically hold advanced degrees in technical fields such as engineering, and thus tend to adopt a corporatist view of the firm as serving multiple interests and constituents.[66] Finally, Allen documents that in Japan even junior-high-school textbooks stress that companies should be managed in the interests of all stakeholders.[67]

Ideology can affect corporate governance in ways that go beyond the ideas and training patterns for senior managers, because ideology, whether or not tied tightly to material interests, can affect the organization of finance and the rules that govern the large firm. As we saw above, anti-power populism in the United States favored the fragmentation of the banking system, while in Europe social democratic ideologies[68] supported empowering employees more and pressured managers to side with employees instead of owners, thereby creating conditions conducive to the concentration of corporate ownership in response.

While ideologies surely often correspond to material interests, we should not discount the possibility that some societies and some polities conceptualize how to handle problems

---

[64] Rajan & Zingales, *supra* note 41.

[65] For analysis of such a result in Italy, see Fabrizio Barca, Katsuhito Iwai, Ugo Pagano, & Sandro Trento, "The Divergence of the Italian and Japanese Corporate Governance Models: The Role of Institutional Shocks", 23 Econ. System 25 (1999).

[66] Aguilera & Jackson, *supra* note 5, at 458–59.

[67] Franklin Allen, "Corporate Governance in Emerging Economies", 21 Oxford Rev. Econ. Policy 164, 173 (2005).

[68] By social democracy we mean a nation committed to private property, but where distributional considerations are vital, where labor is typically powerful, and where government action to foster economic equality is central to the political agenda. See Adam Przeworski, Capitalism and Social Democracy 8 (1985); Shannon C. Stimson, Social Democracy, in The New Palgrave: A Dictionary of Economics 395–96 (John Eatwell et al. eds., 1987).

and conflicts and that some of these conceptualizations have a life independent of material interests. For example, the widespread belief in social democracy prevailing in Europe for several decades after World War II was partly due to the shared experience of the world war and the economic devastation it had wrought.[69]

The strength of these European social democratic views has diminished in recent decades. Presumably, underlying interests have changed—basic manufacturing has shifted to a service-oriented economy, reducing the size of the blue-collar vote. Savings have increased, altering the median voter's interests.[70] Moreover, other influences can affect ideas without necessarily being based only or primarily on narrow self-centered interest. Until the 2008–2009 financial crisis, market-oriented economies performed well; European communism collapsed with the Berlin Wall in 1989, making socialist policies less likely to be seen as successful.

Whatever the underlying explanations, the broad shift in the polity toward a market orientation, at least until the financial crisis, and a weakening of social democratic thinking has been recently measured and documented.[71]

That political shift in opinion and interests allows for more complex political configurations in recent years. Left parties that once opposed financial market development came to promote it.[72] The left of the 1990s did not have the same policy views as the left of the 1960s or 1970s. That shift can be seen in the data of mutating party ideologies[73] and can be grasped intuitively by comparing Tony Blair's market-friendly Labour Party to Callaghan's hard-left Labour Party of the 1970s.

Unstated is the possibility that as the economy shifted from basic manufacturing to services, there were simply fewer labor voters for the left parties to appeal to. More generally, when the power of the left subsided, corporate owners and executives could more readily obtain their policy preferences. Culpepper so argues for recent decades.[74]

5.4 The Nature of Political Representation

Pagano and Volpin show that corporate governance regimes may be the result of the political mechanisms of preference aggregation rather than of political preferences.[75] They suggest

[69] Cf. Roe, Legal Origins, *supra* note 26, at 498–501; Massimiliano Vatiero, "Learning from Swiss Corporate Governance Exception", 70 Kyklos 330 (2017) (governance evolution of Swiss firms and its interaction with legal origin).

[70] Enrico C. Perotti & Armin Schwienbacher, "The Political Origin of Pension Funding", 18 J. Fin. Econ. 384, 387, 402 (2009).

[71] Mark J. Roe & Travis G. Coan, "Financial Markets and Political Center Gravity", 2 J.L. Fin. & Accounting 125 (2017).

[72] Helen Callaghan, "Insiders, Outsiders, and the Politics of Corporate Governance, How Ownership Structure Shapes Party Position in Britain, Germany, and France", 42 Comp. Pol. Stud. 733 (2009); John W. Cioffi, Public Law and Private Power: Corporate Governance Reform in the Age of Finance Capitalism (2010); John Cioffi & Martin Höpner, "The Political Paradox of Finance Capitalism: Interests, Preferences, and Center-Left Party Politics in Corporate Governance Reform", 34 Politics and Society 463 (2006); Pablo M. Pinto, Stephen Weymouth, & Peter Gourevitch, "The Politics of Stock Market Development", 17 Rev. Int'l. Pol. Econ. 378 (2010).

[73] Roe & Coan, *supra* note 71.   [74] Culpepper, *supra* note 62, at 3–4.

[75] Marco Pagano & Paulo F. Volpin, "The Political Economy of Corporate Governance", 94 Am. Econ. Rev. 1005, 1007, 1009–11 (2005).

that a proportional system predicts weak shareholder protection and strong employment protection, while a majoritarian system predicts the opposite: strong shareholder protection and weak employment protection. The intuition behind these results is that proportional voting pushes political parties to cater more to the preferences of social groups with homogeneous interests such as one party for managers and another for employees, whose party representatives can ally and make deals in the parliament.[76]

Mueller shows further how first-past-the-post electoral systems, such as those in the United States, can affect corporate governance outcomes.[77] In such political systems, a national interest group, such as labor, needs to persistently recapture a working majority in the legislature, working district by district, legislator by legislator. This process is costly for interest groups. But in a party-list system, the identity of the particular legislator is not vital to the interest group getting that legislator's vote: the legislator follows party discipline, thereby facilitating national deal-making in which national labor institutions can be quite influential. First-past-the-post territorial elections make national coalitions harder to create and maintain. It's thus no accident that Tip O'Neill's famous aphorism—that all politics is local—came from an American national politician, the locally elected leader of the House of Representatives, a legislative body that is a collection of locally elected representatives who make national policy.

Persson and Tabellini have developed an analogous argument.[78] The state sector will be smaller in majoritarian than in proportional representation systems because competition for votes is in marginal districts rather than nationwide. Politicians accordingly will make smaller commitments in majoritarian systems, because they only need support from voters in the marginal districts. Broader interest groups will therefore get larger support in proportional than majoritarian systems.

5.5 Government Authority

A basic political economy feature is the allocation of authority between the government itself and private sector players who command capital. Government often seeks to obtain for itself capital that it lacks, or seeks to command its use in the private sector, often in ways that favor a dominant governing coalition. In extreme form, a non-democratic, dictatorial government could prefer directly to allocate capital itself, stifling the development of a private sector in general, which might become a counterweight to that dictatorial government, and determining corporate results.

Governmental authority can be a mask for private interests. But we mean something more. Governmental authorities can build, shape, or destroy capital markets and economic institutions for their own reasons and not just as tools of other interests or ideologies. One

---

[76] Gourevitch & Shinn, *supra* note 4, nicely develop this perspective further.

[77] Dennis C. Mueller, The Economics and Politics of Corporate Governance in the European Union, in Investor Protection in Europe: Corporate Law Making, the MiFID and Beyond 3–30 (Guido Ferrarini & Eddy Wymeersch eds., 2006). Cf. Torben Iversen & David Soskice, "Electoral Institutions, Parties and the Politics of Coalitions: Why Some Democracies Redistribute More than Others", 100 Am. Pol. Sci. Rev. 165 (2006) (proportional representation facilitates center-left redistributive coalitions, as compared to majoritarian and presidential systems).

[78] Torsen Persson & Guido Tabellini, "The Size and Scope of Government: Comparative Politics with Rational Politicians", 43 Eur. Econ. Rev. 699 (1999).

can recast the concept as a variant of Weingast's dilemma under which a government that is "strong enough to protect property rights . . . is also strong enough to confiscate the wealth of its citizens."[79] Governmental authorities may denigrate a rival power center.

Moreover, governmental authorities could be susceptible to beliefs that capital markets will not produce social welfare and that government needs to direct and control capital flows to better produce wealth or justice.[80] In this conceptualization, governmental authorities are themselves an interest, seeking power and enhanced authority.

Finally, governmental authorities may see government action as the vanguard of economic and social development; in pursuing policies to implement their goals, they can crowd out private capital markets and thereby prevent them from developing nicely.[81] As an example, consider the following statement from William O. Douglas, the well-known 1930s chair of the Securities and Exchange Commission (SEC): people who dominate financial markets, he said, have "tremendous power . . . Such [people] become virtual governments in the power at their disposal. [Sometimes it is] the dut[y] of government to police them, at times to break them up."[82] True, Douglas's view on governmental power may simply reflect that he favored the underlying interests that such a policy would favor. But one should not neglect the possibility that government authorities are themselves an interest group seeking to forward its own interests and ideology, with its own interests distinct from those in the civil, nongovernmental society. Their own direct interests and beliefs can motivate their actions vis-à-vis capital markets. This sub-category may be more vivid in authoritarian nations, but one should not assume its absence in the governments of the rich democracies.

5.6 Cross-Class Coalitions

We have seen conflicts and coalitions among different classes. Here, we describe sectoral and cross-class divisions, which have captured the attention of political scientists who consider corporate and related issues. Hall and Soskice, as well as Iversen and Soskice, emphasize that preferences and interests may follow the production technologies and, hence, can be dissimilar for owners in different sectors and for labor in different sectors.[83] Blockholding and employment protection fit well with incremental innovation, they argue, and accordingly owners, managers, and employees in incremental sectors prefer political and corporate institutions that protect employees and facilitate blockholding, each of which supports incremental technical improvement. Owners, workers, and employees are all committed in

---

[79] Barry R. Weingast, "The Economic Role of Political Institutions: Market-Preserving Federalism and Economic Growth", 11 J.L. Econ. & Org. 1 (1995).

[80] To see an extreme instance of political leaders' belief systems affecting economic results, of which corporate governance and ownership would be a part, consider the case of South and North Korea. The current economic differences are largely due to "Rhee, Park, and other South Korean leaders believ[ing] in the superiority of capitalist institutions and private property, while Kim Il Sung and Communist Party members in the North believed that communist policies would be better for the country." Acemoglu, *supra* note 2, at 632.

[81] Cf. Roe, Strong Managers, Weak Owners, *supra* note 14, at 36–42.

[82] William O. Douglas, Democracy and Finance 11, 14 (1940).

[83] See Hall & Soskice, *supra* note 11; Torben Iversen & David Soskice, "An Asset Theory of Social Policy Preferences", 95 Am. Pol. Sci. Rev. 875 (2001). Cf. Gourevitch, *supra* note 46, at 1854–57.

such sectors to working with specific assets.[84] The German economy represents an example of this system.

In contrast, corporate governance with dispersed owners and weak employee protection fits well with radical innovation, limited commitments, and flexible assets. Assets are more likely to be general-purpose. The American economy exemplifies this system.

5.7 Democratic versus Aristocratic Roots

Ugo Pagano argues that the diversity of corporate governance systems rests on political conditions existing when "big business" emerged in a country.[85] If a robust democratic system had already developed when large firms emerged, then democratic politics would likely have challenged the concentration of economic power. With democratic politics limiting the power of large firms and their owners, there was less intensity in the demand from employees for counterbalancing, powerful unions. These democratic roots, hence, supported the public company with diffused corporate ownership, because neither side in the corporate power balance needed to concentrate excessively.

In contrast, if a robust democratic system had not emerged before large firms developed, then social democratic power and unions were more likely to have arisen as a counterbalance to owners' political and economic power. These non-democratic roots explain a pattern different from the one illustrated for democratic roots.[86] In this perspective, the United States and Switzerland are two modern economies that had democratic systems at the time of industrialization and, hence, had diffused corporate ownership as a byproduct. Most continental European countries, in contrast, are generally economies that were not democracies when they industrialized and, hence, they did not limit concentrated corporate ownership.

6 THE LIMITS OF A POLITICAL ANALYTIC

Without a political economy analytic, one can neither fully understand the structure of the modern corporation nor account for international differences. The way capital is organized and how those with authority in the firm project their power into the political sphere to maintain their internal authority are both basic determinants of the modern corporation.

But there are limits to the political economy analytic. First off, while it gives us insight into the broad patterns, it does not give us granularity and precision in understanding

---

[84] Oliver E. Williamson, The Economic Institutions of Capitalism 30–34, 52–56, 60–62, 95, 96, 301 (1985). Specific investments have little or no value outside a relationship but great value inside.

[85] Ugo Pagano, "The Evolution of the American Corporation and Global Organizational Biodiversity", 35 Seattle L. Rev. 1271, 1272–73 (2012).

[86] Cf. Barrington Moore, Jr., Social Origins of Dictatorship and Democracy 20–22 (1966). Moore points out that the landed aristocracy was stronger in some nations that industrialized and weaker in others. Its strength varied in Europe, but was typically much stronger there than the landed elite was in the United States. Cf. Pagano, *supra* note 85, at 1270–71.

specifics. It is not a substitute for the practice of law, for comprehending judicial opinions, and constructing the corporate statutes. It is big picture, not transactional.

Second, even the broad patterns are sometimes applicable only to subsets of nations. The social democratic analytic set forth above broadly explains the situation in the wealthy West in the decades after World War II, but is less good at explaining corporate structures and the (lack of) public markets in less developed and/or more authoritarian polities. But even here, a political economy analytic is needed to fully explain the financial and corporate phenomena. Financial markets and ownership separation cannot and do not develop well in politically unstable environments, with that political instability having economic inequality as a primary determinant (because the unequal have much to contest). Such politicized explanations have been brought forward and hold promise.[87]

Third, political economy explanations often lack predictability,[88] because the political process is often dominated by local,[89] geographic, and historical specifics. Some aspects that seem unpredictable, when properly analyzed, strongly fit with a political theory. For example, some have raised the idea that European social democratic parties, particularly in the 1990s, promoted investor protection, calling this shift a political paradox.[90] However, the European polity had shifted sharply from the 1950s, moving from polities that were not attuned to markets to polities that grudgingly accepted market-oriented policies. Data is consistent. Again, a comparison illustrates: Tony Blair's Labour Party was much more market-oriented than, say, the 1970s Labour Party of James Callaghan and Harold Wilson. To equate the 1990s Labour Party with that of the 1960s in order to conclude that politics is unpredictable is a comparison that risks conceptual error. Data is broadly consistent: polities moved pro-market as financial markets deepened.[91]

Fourth, the political economy analytic lacks strong normative content. It does not tell us what the best corporate policies are, other than perhaps to warn one off policy initiatives that would lack political support.

Lastly, and importantly from an academic perspective, some—perhaps too many—political explanations are susceptible to a narrative but not a test and regression. In

---

[87] Mark J. Roe & Jordan Siegel, "Political Stability's Impact on Financial Development", 39 J. Comp. Econ. 279 (2011); Mark J. Roe & Jordan Siegel, "Finance and Politics: A Review Essay", 47 J. Econ. Lit. 782 (2009). Cf. Sibylle Lehmann-Haemeyer et al., "The Political Stock Market in the German Kaiserreich—Do Markets Punish the Extension of the Benefit of the Working Class? Evidence from Saxony", 74 J. Econ. Hist. 1140, 1163 (2014) ("investors [in turn of twentieth century Saxony] feared a revolution . . . [I]nvestors supported more participation of the middle and working class, possibly for reasons of political stability, but opposed it if they felt this influence became too large.").

[88] Kenneth Shepsle, "Institutional Arrangements and Equilibrium in Multidimensional Voting Models", 32 Am. J. Pol. Sci. 27 (1979); Donald P. Green & Ian Shapiro, Pathologies of Rational Choice Theory 99–120 (1994); Richard D. McKelvey, "Intransitivities in Multidimensional Models and Some Implications for Agenda Control", 12 Econ. Theory 472 (1976).

[89] For instance Mark Freeman, Robin Pearson, & James Taylor, "Law, Politics and the Governance of English and Scottish Joint-Stock Companies, 1600–1850", 55 Bus. Hist. 633 (2013), examine joint-stock firms in England and Scotland before 1850 and present evidence that local political institutions played a bigger role in shaping organizational forms and business practice than the legal system. (The Scottish legal system differs from England's.)

[90] Cioffi & Höpner, *supra* note 72, at 502. See also Pinto, Weymouth, & Gourevitch, *supra* note 72.

[91] See Roe & Coan, *supra* note 71.

econometric terms, political events are often low-frequency occurrences—one nation, one era, one political deal. Some political processes happen once, in one nation, and then become embedded in institutions, politics, and corporations. One cannot readily test how important the one-off decision was and what would have happened if contingent decisions came out differently.

The American history of banking is one such instance. The impact of social democracy on the corporation is more susceptible to testing since multiple nations went through the experience.

7 Conclusion

We have here pushed forward a main thesis with three subsidiary examples. The main thesis is that the shape of the public corporation will attract political attention in wealthy democracies, and democratic politics will accordingly affect the allocation of authority in the large public corporation in a major way. First, politics can determine and indeed has determined the ways in which capital flows into the large firm, shattering financial channels into weak tributaries in the United States for the nineteenth and much of the twentieth century. The consequence of shattered financial channels is that the large public firm could not readily have major and powerful shareholders. Boards and executives had more autonomy than they otherwise would have had. The Berle–Means corporation with diffuse ownership and powerful managers was a political construct as much as it was an economic one.

Second, when labor makes powerful claims on a large firm's cash flow, shareholders have reason to keep large offsetting blocks to reduce the strength of those claims. Postwar European polities had such a setting, and one major reason that blockholding by financial institutions like banks and insurers and by stockholding families persisted in the postwar decades seems to have been because they offset labor's claims.

And third, once a corporate governance system is in place, corporate players can project power into the polity and can use that political power to maintain their corporate authority. Managers in the United States fit that example, as they have repeatedly blocked transactions and legal changes that would confine their authority and shift power from themselves to others, typically shareholders, in the large public firm.

CHAPTER 4

··

THE "CORPORATE CONTRACT" TODAY

··

MICHAEL KLAUSNER[1]

1 INTRODUCTION

LED largely by the work of Frank Easterbrook and Daniel Fischel in the 1980s, a "contractarian" theory of corporate governance and corporate law dominated thinking among US corporate law scholars for many years.[2] The notion was that a public company's shareholders and managers enter into a relationship with one another voluntarily on terms that are reflected in the company's share price, and that managers, as agents in the relationship, have incentives to adopt governance arrangements that minimize agency costs and maximize firm value. The contractarian theory was a positive theory, positing that market forces would lead to optimal governance arrangements in firms. It also had a clear

[1] Nancy and Charles Munger Professor of Business and Professor of Law, Stanford Law School. I would like to thank Michal Barzuza, Marcel Kahan, Jeff Gordon, and Georg Ringe for helpful comments on earlier drafts on this chapter.

[2] Frank H. Easterbrook & Daniel R. Fischel, The Economic Structure of Corporate Law 15 (1991). The contractarian theory originated in the context of US corporate law and was developed and debated primarily by US scholars. Corporate law scholars outside the US, in the past and to some extent today, tend to begin with a more regulatory perspective. This chapter, therefore, focuses on the US context and on the contractarian debate in the US. The following are some of the early articles that contributed to the contractarian theory: Oliver E. Williamson, The Economic Institutions of Capitalism: Firms, Markets, Relational Contracting (1985); Armen A. Alchian & Harold Demsetz, "Production, Information Costs, and Economic Organization", 62 Am. Econ. Rev. 777 (1972); Eugene F. Fama & Michael C. Jensen, "Separation of Ownership and Control", 26 J. L. & Econ. 301 (1983); Sanford J. Grossman & Oliver D. Hart, "The Costs and Benefits of Ownership: A Theory of Vertical and Lateral Integration", 94 J. Pol. Econ. 691 (1986); Henry Hansmann, "Ownership of the Firm", 4 J. L. Econ. & Org. 267 (1988); Benjamin Klein et al., "Vertical Integration, Appropriable Rents, and the Competitive Contracting Process", 21 J. L. & Econ. 297 (1978); Michael C. Jensen & William H. Meckling, "Theory of the Firm: Managerial Behavior, Agency Costs and Ownership Structure", 3 J. Fin. Econ. 305 (1976); Ronald Coase, "The Nature of the Firm", 4 Economica 386 (1937). The following are some articles that applied and further developed the theory: Barry Baysinger & Henry Butler, "Race for the Bottom v. Climb to the Top: The ALI Project

normative implication, which was that there is little, if any, need for law to impose rules on the manager–shareholder relationship.[3]

Today, the status of the contractarian theory is unclear. Few would deny that when investors buy shares in a public company, they enter into a relationship with management that can reasonably be conceptualized as "contractual." The key question, however, is whether the "corporate contract" is socially optimal, as the contractarian theory holds?[4] Theoretical and empirical doubts have been raised over the years regarding the theory's validity. We no longer hear the contractarian refrain in opposition to any and all corporate law reform proposals—that any particular proposal cannot possibly be value enhancing, because if it were, firms would have already adopted it in their charters, at least at the IPO stage. We do, however, hear a weaker variant of the contractarian claim, largely from advocates for management opposing legal rules that would shift power to shareholders. This modern-day variant of the contractarian theory is more of a slogan than a theory—that "one size does not fit all."[5]

This chapter will evaluate the substantive validity of the contractarian theory in light of theoretical and empirical developments since the 1980s. As I explain in the remainder of this chapter, the contractarian theory was really two theories: one of the IPO stage and one of the "mid-stream" stage, when a company is publicly held.

The theory of the IPO stage suffered from a few theoretical flaws, but most fundamentally it assumed that the relationship between shareholders and managers was captured by the neoclassical model of atomistic contracting, with no interdependencies across firms in the terms adopted. This was the basis of the theory that market equilibria must be socially optimal—and therefore the basis of the theory's non-intervention prescription.[6] The IPO theory also depended on the validity of the mid-stream theory, since any arrangement put in place at the IPO stage could be undone at the mid-stream stage. With respect to empirical

and Uniformity in Corporate Law", 10 J. Corp. L. 431, 457 (1985) (hereinafter Race); Barry D. Baysinger & Henry N. Butler, "The Role of Corporate Law in the Theory of the Firm", 28 J. L. & Econ. 179, 182–83 (1985) (hereinafter Role of Corporate Law); Barry D. Baysinger & Henry N. Butler, "Antitakeover Amendments, Managerial Entrenchment, and the Contractual Theory of the Corporation", 71 Va. L. Rev. 1257 (1985); Jonathan Macey, David D. Haddock & Fred S. McChesney, "Property Rights in Assets and Resistance to Tender Offers", 73 Va. L. Rev. 701 (1987); Jonathan Macey, "Corporate Law and Corporate Governance: A Contractual Perspective", 18 J. Corp. L. 185 (1993).

[3] Easterbrook & Fischel, *supra* note 2, at 15. Although I will refer to corporate law throughout this chapter, the points that I make apply broadly to corporate law, securities law, and listing requirements—any rules that govern the shareholder–manager relationship.

[4] Id. at 7.

[5] See, e.g., Letter from Cravath, Swaine & "Moore LLP et al. to Elizabeth Murphy, Secretary, US Securities and Exchange Commission" (Aug. 17, 2009), available at http://www.sec.gov/comments/s7-10-09/s71009-212.pdf; Letter from Wachtell, Lipton, Rosen, & Katz to Elizabeth M. Murphy, "Secretary, US Securities and Exchange Commission" (Aug. 17, 2009), available at http://www.sec.gov/comments/s7-10-09/s71009-263.pdf; letter from Business Roundtable to Elizabeth Murphy, "Sec'y, US Securities and Exchange Commission", available at http://businessroundtable.org/resources/business-roundtable-statement-on-the-presidents-remarks-on-financial-regula.

[6] Michael Klausner, "Corporations, Corporate Law, and Networks of Contracts", 81 Va. L. Rev. 757, 826–29 (1995).

validity, contractarian theorists never attempted to investigate their claims empirically, and when some of us did later on, we discovered that the facts did not fit.[7]

The contractarian theory of the mid-stream stage was recognized from the start as weak. It relied on the existence of market forces to drive managers to adopt and maintain governance arrangements that promote shareholder interests. No proponent of the theory, however, convincingly explained how this would occur, and experience with management resistance of shareholder demands casts serious doubt on the theory as an empirical matter.

Beginning roughly in the mid-2000s, however, legal and nonlegal institutional changes have occurred in the US that one could characterize as a new contract between shareholders and managers. Today's contract is not an explicit contract written into a corporate charter, as the contractarian theory envisioned. It is instead an implicit contract in the sense that economists use that term—a contract that is not legally enforceable, but that is self-enforcing as a result of carrots and sticks that the parties hold. This new implicit contract reflects a shift in power from managers to shareholders compared to earlier decades. While one can make judgments regarding whether the current balance of power is better or worse than alternatives, there is no analytic basis on which to claim that the current equilibrium is either optimal or suboptimal.

2 The Contractarian Theory

Built on the work of Jensen and Meckling and ultimately that of Ronald Coase, the original contractarian theory of the corporation characterized the relationship between managers and shareholders of a public company as one of contract mediated through the securities market. The implication of conceptualizing the shareholder–manager relationship as contractual was that, in the absence of transaction costs, externalities, or other market imperfections, market forces could be relied upon to create governance arrangements that minimize agency costs and thereby maximize firm value.

The theory was clearest and most promising at the point a company goes public. When a company goes public, its charter is in effect a contract between its management and its public shareholders. The charter confers legally binding rights on shareholders and obligations on managers. It can commit the company to separate the positions of CEO and board chair, to forgo a poison pill, to have a staggered board, to limit directors' exposure to liability risk, to require managers to hold a certain amount of stock, to compensate management in a certain way, and so on. There are few, if any, legal limits to this freedom.[8] Pre-IPO managers

---

[7] Michael Klausner, "Fact and Fiction in Corporate Law and Governance", 65 Stan. L. Rev. 1325 (2013) (hereinafter Fact and Fiction); Robert Daines & Michael Klausner, "Do IPO Charters Maximize Firm Value? Antitakeover Provisions in IPOs", 17 J. L. Econ. & Org. 83, 87 (2001); John C. Coates IV, "Explaining Variation in Takeover Defenses: Blame the Lawyers", 89 Cal. L. Rev. 1301 (2001); Laura Casares Field & Jonathan M. Karpoff, "Takeover Defenses of IPO Firms", 57 J. Fin. 1857 (2002).

[8] The legal limit to the corporate governance commitments a company can include in its charter is that it cannot violate federal law or the law of the state in which the firm is incorporated—which, as discussed below, is itself a matter of contract. For example, the Delaware General Corporation Law provides: "(T)he certificate of incorporation may also contain any or all of the following matters: (1) Any provision for the management of the business and for the conduct of the affairs of the corporation, and any

and shareholders write the firm's post-IPO charter and sell shares to the public. As public investors purchase those shares, the market sets their price, and that price is expected to reflect the effectiveness of the firm's governance structure in reducing agency costs. Pre-IPO shareholders—venture capitalists, angel investors, managers, employees, and others—reap the benefit of a high share price and the detriment of a low share price. Hence, the contractarian theory posits, pre-IPO shareholders reap the benefit and detriment of good or bad governance structures. Consequently, the contractarian theory posited that pre-IPO shareholders would design governance mechanisms that maximize the value of their firm, given the particular circumstances of each firm, and that pre-IPO shareholders would make legally enforceable commitments to those mechanisms by drafting them into their charters—the document that reflects the "corporate contract."[9] This is the simple, yet compelling, contractarian logic of how governance arrangements formed at the IPO stage.

Once shares of a company are dispersed among public shareholders, the concern became whether management could take advantage of its control to loosen the constraints adopted at the IPO stage or to decline to adopt new contractual constraints in response to agency cost-increasing changes in the business environment.[10] Here, the contractarian theory held that market forces would induce management to maintain and update optimal governance arrangements, proposing charter amendments to shareholders where appropriate.[11] The claim was that managers would ultimately reap rewards—through higher compensation or longer-term career success—for increasing firm value by adopting good governance arrangements. This post-IPO or "mid-stream" element of the contractarian theory was viewed as its weakest, even by advocates of the theory.[12]

The contractarian theory's normative claim followed from its positive claim that market forces would drive firms to adopt optimal, legally enforceable governance arrangements. If this were true, and there were no costs externalized on parties other than a firm's managers and shareholders, then it would follow that corporate law should stay out of the way and impose no mandatory legal rules on the shareholder–manager relationship. Advocates of the theory viewed contractual governance as superior to legally imposed governance because firms vary along numerous dimensions, and market forces were expected to induce firms to customize their own governance arrangements in ways that suited their particular circumstances. In addition, market pressure was expected to spur innovation in governance mechanisms over time. In the contractarian view, mandatory legal intervention would prevent customization, and state legislatures (let alone Congress) would be a weak source of innovation compared to the governance ingenuity present in individual firms.[13]

The proper role of corporate law in the original contractarian view was fairly minor. It was to provide default rules that firms could take "off the rack" and incorporate into their

---

provision creating, defining, limiting and regulating the powers of the corporation, the directors, and the stockholders . . . if such provisions are not contrary to the laws of this State." Del. Code Ann. tit. 8, § 102(b) (1). Regardless of the state of incorporation, the legal constraint on charter terms is not a strong one.

  [9] Easterbrook & Fischel, *supra* note 2, at 6.

  [10] For an overview of this issue, see Lucian Arye Bebchuk, "The Debate on Contractual Freedom in Corporate Law", 89 Colum. L. Rev. 1395 (1989).

  [11] Easterbrook & Fischel, *supra* note 2, at 32–34.   [12] Id.

  [13] Easterbrook & Fischel, *supra* note 2, at 15; Jonathan Macey, "Corporate Law and Corporate Governance: A Contractual Perspective", 18 J. Corp. L. 185, 198 (1993).

governance arrangements, and to enforce whatever terms firms adopted.[14] Furthermore, in the United States, choice of corporate law is itself a matter of contract. When a firm goes public, its pre-IPO managers and shareholders select the state in which to incorporate, and in so doing, opt into that state's body of corporate law. Once public, the firm can reincorporate with the approval of the firm's board and its shareholders. Consequently, the contractarian expectation was that firms would initially incorporate, and later re-incorporate, in states whose corporate law best reduce agency costs in each particular firm.[15]

The conceptualization of the shareholder–manager relationship as "contractual" is relatively uncontroversial. Shareholders voluntarily enter into the relationship and in doing so they accept the terms of the deal. The securities markets price securities, so it is reasonable to expect that governance terms will be priced—though whether they are or not is an empirical question. But the fact that shareholders and managers come together voluntarily—even if we call the relationship "contractual"—does not mean that the terms of the contract will be socially optimal, as the contractarian theory maintains. There could be a market imperfection that breaks the neoclassical connection between market equilibrium and social optimality.

If the original contractarian theory had been valid, we would expect to see the following:

- firms, at least at the IPO stage, adopting diverse and innovative governance arrangements in their charters;
- governance arrangements tending to maximize firm value; and
- once firms are publicly held, managers proposing value-increasing charter amendments for shareholder approval.

As discussed in the remainder of this chapter, we observe none of the above. In section 3, I explain how the contractarian theory's claim about the IPO stage are invalid, and in section 4, I address its invalidity with respect to the mid-stream stage—once companies are publicly held. Finally, in section 5, I discuss what appears to be a newly emergent unwritten implicit contract that reflects a shift in power from managers to shareholders.

3 The Contractarian Theory of the IPO Stage Does Not Hold Up to the Facts

In the discussion below, I first report the results of empirical studies of two questions. First, do firms customize and innovate governance-related charter terms when they go public? Second, do IPO charters appear to maximize firm value? The contractarian theory of the IPO implies a positive answer to both questions. The data, however, answer the questions primarily in the negative. After discussing these empirical findings, I explain how the contractarians went wrong as a theoretical matter.

---

[14] Easterbrook & Fischel, *supra* note 2, at 34.
[15] Id. at 218; Baysinger & Butler, Race, *supra* note 2, at 556.

3.1 Customization and Innovation, or Plain Vanilla IPO Charters?

The contractarian theory implied that firms would customize and innovate governance arrangements that minimize agency costs to suit their particular business environments, and that firms would make legally binding commitments to those arrangements in their charters. Describing the "corporate contract," a term they coined, Easterbrook and Fischel stated: "Agreements that have arisen are wonderfully diverse, matching the diversity of economic activity carried on within corporations."[16] But is this true? Do corporate charters contain customized and innovative governance terms?

In a study published in 2013, I investigated this question by collecting data from a random sample of 373 companies that went public during the period from 2000 through 2012.[17] I searched their charters (and bylaws) for examples of governance customization and innovation.[18] I searched for any nonstandard governance mechanism. In order to structure the search, however, I specifically looked for arrangements that have been the focus of corporate governance debates since the 1980s. Some of these governance arrangements became mandatory under the Sarbanes–Oxley Act or the Dodd–Frank Act: majority independent board, independent board committees, and say on pay. One mechanism, proxy access, was briefly mandated by the SEC and is now explicitly permitted but not mandated. A fifth innovation, majority voting in shareholder elections of directors, has been widely adopted by publicly held firms, and has been shown in some studies to be value enhancing. For each governance innovation that ultimately became legally required, I investigated whether the innovation had previously appeared in IPO charters (or bylaws).[19] For purposes of this chapter, I supplemented these data on these governance innovations with data on a sixth innovation—exclusive forum provisions for shareholder litigation. I obtained these data from Roberta Romano and Sarath Sanga, who have studied the diffusion of these provisions in IPO charters. Exclusive forum provisions require that all corporate-law-related disputes be brought in a single forum—typically the forum of the state in which the company is incorporated, which for companies adopting these provisions is nearly always Delaware. Romano and Sanga found that these

---

[16] Easterbrook & Fischel, *supra* note 2, at 12.

[17] Klausner, Fact and Fiction, *supra* note 7. The sample included 30 companies per year, except for 2008, when there were fewer than 30 IPOs. I omitted spin-offs, carve-outs, blank-check companies, regulated financial institutions, and real estate investment trusts.

[18] Bylaws are not part of a binding contract in the way a charter is. Whereas a charter can be amended only with the approval of the board and the shareholders, bylaws can be amended unilaterally by shareholders, and more importantly for the immediate discussion, by the board so long as the charter allows the board to amend the bylaws, which is universally the case. Nonetheless, I collected data from bylaws as well.

[19] On November 4, 2003, the SEC approved New York Stock Exchange and NASDAQ rules requiring that firms have compensation, nominating/corporate governance, and audit committees consisting entirely of independent directors. Those rules were effective beginning with a company's first annual meeting after January 15, 2004 (or no later than October 31, 2004 if there was not an earlier annual meeting). NASD and NYSE Rulemaking: Relating to Corporate Governance, Exchange Act Release No.

provisions appear in IPO charters beginning in 2010, when they were endorsed in an opinion of the Delaware Chancery court.[20]

A finding that these six innovations commonly appear in IPO charters would support the contractarian theory that the economics of the IPO stage promotes governance innovation and customization. Conversely, a finding that they never or rarely appear in IPO charters would cast substantial doubt on the theory. Although it is possible that the particular innovations for which I searched are not value enhancing for *any* firm, this would be a far-fetched interpretation.[21]

Table 4.1 presents my findings. Of the innovations described above, only exclusive forum provisions were adopted to any significant extent. Of 373 firms sampled, no firm had any of the five other provisions in their charters, and only nine firms had bylaws containing one or more of the five arrangements. Because management could amend these bylaws unilaterally, this handful of provisions are not contractual in the contractarians' sense of the term.[22]

Where do these data leave us regarding the contractarian claim that IPO charters are a locus of innovation and customization in corporate governance? The claim is largely inconsistent with the data. The experience with exclusive forum provisions is unique and, at best, can be generalized only to charter terms that are directly beneficial to management—presumably along with shareholders. Unlike the other provisions that potentially enhance firm value by enhancing shareholder rights, exclusive forum provisions potentially do so by protecting directors and officers from burdensome litigation in multiple jurisdictions. Whether or not they enhance share value, they are attractive to management and could well be adopted for that reason alone. Protecting directors and officers from litigation risk is in the wheelhouse of the lawyers advising management of firms going public. A lawyer

---

48,745, 68 Fed. Reg. 64,154 (Nov. 12, 2003). In Table 4.1, I use April 1, 2004 as the relevant starting date for this rule. The SEC's proxy access rule, which was later vacated by the United States Court of Appeals for the District of Columbia Circuit, see *Bus. Roundtable v. SEC*, 647 F.3d 1144 (D.C. Cir. 2011), was effective as of November 15, 2010. Facilitating Shareholder Director Nominations, Securities Act Release No. 9136, Exchange Act Release No. 62,764, Investment Company Act Release No. 29,384, 75 Fed. Reg. 56,668 (Sept. 16, 2010). The SEC's say-on-pay rule became effective on April 4, 2011. Shareholder Approval of Executive Compensation and Golden Parachute Compensation, Securities Act Release No. 9178, Exchange Act Release No. 63,768, 76 Fed. Reg. 6010 (Feb. 2, 2010). It became salient as a governance issue in 2006, when the American Federation of State, County, and Municipal Employees (AFSCME) filed the first shareholder proposal seeking a say-on-pay vote. See Challie Dunn & Carol Bowie, RiskMetrics Grp., "Evaluating US Company Management Say on Pay Proposals: Four Steps for Investors" 4–5 (2009), available at http://www.shareholderforum.com/sop/Library/20090316_RiskMetrics.pdf.

[20] Roberta Romano & Sarath Sanga, "The Private Ordering Solution to Multiforum Shareholder Litigation", (Dec. 1, 2015), available at http://ssrn.com/abstract=2624951. The Chancery Court decision was *In re Revlon Shareholders Litigation*, 990 A. 2d 940, 960 (Del. Ch. 2010).

[21] This would be the classic (if circular) contractarian inference: If it is not adopted by firms going public, then it is not value enhancing (and should not be legally required). For example, Easterbrook & Fischel argue that if holding an auction among bidders were the value-maximizing response to a hostile offer, then charter terms would require management or the board to hold an auction. Easterbrook & Fischel, *supra* note 2, at 204–05. Haddock et al. similarly argued that, if management passivity in response to a hostile bid were value maximizing, then provisions mandating passivity would be included in IPO charters. Haddock et al., *supra* note 2, at 728.

[22] The reported results would not change if I were to use the time period 2000 to 2012 for all provisions. That is, outside the restricted periods used in Table 4.1, there were no additional charters or bylaws that contained these provisions.

Table 4.1 Incidence of governance innovations or customization in IPO bylaws
(2000–2012)

	Relevant Period	Yes	No	Total
Majority Independent Board	1/1/2000 to 4/1/2004*	0	127	128
Independent Compensation Committee	1/1/2000 to 4/1/2004*	1	127	128
Independent Nominating Committee	1/1/2000 to 4/1/2004*	0	128	128
Independent Governance Committee	1/1/2000 to 4/1/2004*	0	128	128
Proxy Access	1/1/2000 to 12/31/2012	0	224	373
Majority Vote	1/1/2000 to 12/31/2012	4	220	373
Say on Pay	1/1/2000 to 1/21/2011**	0	143	314
Separation of CEO and Board Chair	1/1/2000 to 12/31/2012	4	369	373
Exclusive Forum	1/1/2000 to 12/31/2012	30***	373	373

* These periods end when the independence requirements of the Sarbanes–Oxley Act became effective.
** This period ends when the SEC adopted its mandatory say-on-pay rule. Differences in totals reflect shorter and longer time periods relevant for each mechanism.
*** All 30 of these IPOs occurred after the Delaware Chancery Court decision endorsing these provisions.

would readily understand the provision and how it could benefit management and perhaps increase firm value. This is not necessarily true of innovations that increase firm value by enhancing shareholder rights.

The lack of governance diversity evident in charters is also evident in firms' incorporation choices. A large and increasing majority of firms incorporate in Delaware, and nearly all others incorporate in their home states for reasons apparently unrelated to value-maximizing choices of corporate.[23]

The most plausible explanation for these findings is that the contractarian claims about the IPO stage are incorrect or at least drastically overstated. But how could the theory be incorrect when it is undeniable that shareholders enter into a relationship with managers voluntarily, and that they do so in a setting that can be reasonably described as contractual? I address that question in section 3.3.

3.2 Are IPO Charters Suboptimal?

The near absence of customization and innovation in IPO charters poses a serious challenge to the contractarian claim that the economics of the IPO stage promotes value-maximizing

---

[23] Robert Daines, "The Incorporation Choices of IPO Firms", 77 N.Y.U. L. Rev. 1559 (2002); Lucian A. Bebchuk & Alma Cohen, "Firms' Decisions Where to Incorporate", 46 J. L. & Econ. 383 (2003); Lucian A. Bebchuk et al., "Does the Evidence Favor State Competition in Corporate Law?" 90 Cal. L. Rev. 1775, 1820 (2002); Marcel Kahan & Ehud Kamar, "The Myth of State Competition in Corporate Law", 55 Stan. L. Rev. 679 (2002).

contracting. Additional evidence weighing against this claim is the presence of staggered boards in the charters of many firms going public. Although some recent studies have found that staggered boards are associated with higher firm value in certain situations,[24] the bulk of the research finds that staggered boards are value-reducing mechanisms that management uses to protect itself from the market for corporate control.[25] This was certainly the prevailing view when the contractarian theory was developed. The contractarian theory, therefore, implied that staggered boards would not appear in IPO charters. Easterbrook and Fischel expressed this expectation as a statement of fact: "[Takeover defenses] are not included [in IPO charters]. Instead firms go public in easy-to-acquire form: no poison pill securities, no supermajority rules or staggered boards. Defensive measures are added later, a sequence that reveals much."[26]

Whether IPO charters contain takeover defenses was an empirical question that was not investigated for another decade. Easterbrook and Fischel apparently made the factual statement above based on theory alone, and for the next decade, no one thought it was worth reading actual charters to validate the theory empirically or even anecdotally.

Three articles published in 2001 and 2002 presented data on the charters of firms going public. Each found that IPO charters commonly contain takeover defenses, including staggered boards.[27] The studies covered different sample periods between 1988 and 1999 and found that between 34% and 82% of sample firms had staggered boards, with higher frequencies in later years.

Two of these articles analyzed whether there were efficiency explanations for the presence of staggered boards in IPO charters. Both Laura Field and Jonathan Karpoff and Robert Daines and I analyzed whether the adoption of staggered boards was explained by the need for extra bargaining power in the event of a hostile bid.[28] Neither study found support for this explanation. Daines and I also tested whether staggered boards were explained by asymmetric information regarding firm value, which would create the possibility of undervaluation by the market and hence a vulnerability to bids lower than true value. We found no support for this explanation either. In fact, Daines and I found that staggered boards tended to be present when both these efficiency theories suggested that they would be *least* needed. We concluded that, contrary to the contractarian theory, management entrenchment was the best explanation for staggered boards in IPOs.[29]

---

[24] William C. Johnson et al., "The Bonding Hypothesis of Takeover Defenses: Evidence from IPO Firms", available at http://ssrn.com/abstract=1923667; Martijn Cremers, Lubomir P. Litov, & Simone M. Sepe, "Staggered Boards and Firm Value, Revisited" (2014), available at http://ssrn.com/abstract=2364165; Weili Ge, Lloyd Tanlu, & Jenny Li Zhang, "Board Destaggering: Corporate Governance Out of Focus?" (2014), available at http://ssrn.com/abstract=2312565.

[25] Klausner, Fact and Fiction, *supra* note 7, at 352–55.

[26] Easterbrook & Fischel, *supra* note 2, at 204–05.

[27] John C. Coates IV, "Explaining Variation in Takeover Defenses: Blame the Lawyers", 89 Cal. L. Rev. 1301, 1353 tbl.3, 1377 fig. 3 (2001) (summarizing the results of four sample periods and noting that defenses became more common in the late 1990s); Daines & Klausner, *supra* note 7, at 96 tbl.2; Field & Karpoff, *supra* note 7, at 1861. When Rob Daines and I presented a draft of our article at the American Law and Economics Association annual meeting in 2000, the first response in the discussion that followed was from a dyed-in-the-wool contractarian who began by saying: "Well, this is certainly disconcerting."

[28] Daines & Klausner, *supra* note 7, at 98–99; Field & Karpoff, *supra* note 7, at 1857–58.

[29] Daines & Klausner, *supra* note 7, at 102.

John Coates investigated the influence of lawyers in the adoption of staggered boards. He found that firms that were advised in their IPOs by law firms with extensive M&A transactional or litigation work tended to adopt staggered boards more frequently than did other firms. He inferred that those law firms instill in their lawyers, or in the form charters that their lawyers use, a preference for takeover defenses. As Coates explains, this is hardly evidence of value maximization at work.

There is, however, some recent research supporting the proposition that staggered boards can enhance firm value for a subset of firms under limited circumstances.[30] I therefore cannot rule out the possibility that some day we will have a satisfactory efficiency-based explanation for staggered boards in IPO charters. At this point, however, their presence certainly appears to further undermine the contractarian theory of the IPO stage.

3.3 Where Did the Contractarian Theory Go Wrong Regarding the IPO Stage?

The contractarian theory's application to the IPO stage was its most convincing. Neoclassical theory, coupled with the undeniable fact that shareholders and managers enter into their relationship voluntarily, seemed unequivocally to imply that market forces would produce socially optimal governance arrangements. Yet the facts do not fit the theory. With the exception of exclusive forum provisions, there has been no governance innovation or customization at the IPO stage, and the common use of staggered boards raises serious doubts about the theory's optimality claims, independent of the lack of customization or innovation. What was the flaw in the logic? Theoretical developments and some further thought have yielded at least two theoretical explanations for the failure of the IPO stage to conform to contractarian expectations. This section provides those explanations.

3.3.1 Customization and Innovation

Two explanations have emerged to explain why the IPO stage does not generate customized or innovative governance arrangements. The first explanation is well grounded in economic theory, but not the neoclassical model on which the contractarian theory was based. Consistent with neoclassical economics, the contractarian theory assumed that each firm's decision to adopt a particular governance arrangement is independent of other firms' decisions—that firms were atomistic actors in that one firm's choice of a governance structure has no effect on another firm's choice. For at least some corporate governance arrangements, however, this assumption is not valid. There are interdependencies among firms' choices of governance arrangements. The value of a governance mechanism can be dependent on the number of firms that use the mechanism. If few firms use a governance mechanism, the mechanism will not be as valuable as if many firms use it. The underlying dynamic is the same dynamic that is present in product markets with network externalities, such as the market for computer operating systems, word processing and spreadsheet applications, and social network platforms such as Facebook. In each of these markets, the

---

[30] See sources cited at note 27.

value of a product increases with the volume of use. (Imagine Facebook with one user or even 1,000.)

When network benefits are present, market forces will not necessarily yield socially optimal equilibria. In this type of market, theory shows that there are multiple, socially suboptimal equilibria. In one suboptimal equilibrium, excess uniformity emerges in the products produced. Note that there are very few computer operating systems, word processing and spreadsheet applications, and social network platforms and that each has a large number of users—in contrast, say, to the markets for office supplies, skis, and restaurants. This appears to be the case with respect to corporate governance—there is little variety in the corporate governance arrangements; firms' governance arrangements are fairly uniform.[31]

Corporate governance arrangements have some of the same qualities as network products. The more firms there are that use a governance mechanism or that operate under the same legal or contractual rule, the more valuable the arrangement becomes. One source of these network benefits stems from judicial precedents that interpret the arrangement in varied settings, thereby reducing legal uncertainty. One can think of each new judicial opinion in a new setting as analogous to a software update for Windows or Word. The more firms there are that operate under, say, a particular state's fiduciary duty standard, the more precedents there will be—today and into the future. Firms will therefore be attracted to incorporate in that state, and to adopt its default fiduciary duty rule.

Judicial precedents are especially valuable when a governance arrangement entails a legal or contractual rule that is framed as an open-ended legal standard, as opposed to a detailed, specific rule. Open-ended standards are pervasive in corporate law and governance. Fiduciary duties are classic, open-ended legal standards, as are concepts of director disinterestedness and materiality in the disclosure context. They are given content as courts interpret them in a variety of contexts. A firm that adopts, for example, its own unique fiduciary duty, definition of director disinterestedness, or disclosure rule would not have the benefit of ongoing judicial interpretations. The customized arrangement would remain static, unless it is amended (which entails a separate set of problems discussed below). In contrast, a commonly used arrangement will evolve with judicial interpretations. As a result, a firm with a customized arrangement will face greater uncertainty regarding how its own arrangement will apply in unanticipated settings.

Other network benefits associated with corporate governance arrangements are familiarity among lawyers advising firms and familiarity among investors. A lawyer who is familiar with a legal rule can provide advice based on his or her experience, independently of legal precedents. That advice will be more valuable in reducing legal uncertainty than advice regarding a governance arrangement the lawyer has never seen before. Similarly, all other factors being equal, familiarity among investors will be a benefit for a firm. Investors considering the securities of a firm with a unique governance arrangement will have to figure out what the arrangement means in terms of value to the investor. All other factors being

---

[31] This discussion is based on Michael Klausner, "Corporations, Corporate Law, and Networks of Contracts", 81 Va. L. Rev. 757, 826–29 (1995). Marcel Kahan and I suggested additional attractions of commonly used terms. One is based on a herding dynamic associated with principal–agent relationships—in this context the relationship between a firm's lawyers and the firm. Another is based on cognitive biases. See Kahan & Klausner, "Path Dependence in Corporate Contracting: Increasing Returns, Herd Behavior and Cognitive Biases", 74 Wash. U. L. Q. 347 (1996).

equal, this will deter investment and could drive down the liquidity and value of a company's securities.

Network benefits associated with corporate governance arrangements tend to make default rules attractive. It is not that default rules are inherently more attractive from the start than alternatives, but rather that they typically are expected to be widely adopted in the future. This may be due to a focal quality that default rules have or to the state legislature's endorsement. Governance rules and structures provided by statute as menu options—such as staggered boards, voting by written consent, shareholders calling a special meeting, exculpatory charter provisions, and more—have a similar quality. Once statutory terms, whether default or menu, have been used and litigated, their attraction to new firms is even greater.

Delaware corporate law, specifically its default rules and statutory menu options, has benefited from network effects. The large installed base of firms incorporated in Delaware ensures a constant supply of judicial decisions applying Delaware law to many situations. There also is a large supply of lawyers with expertise in Delaware law and an investment community familiar with the workings of key governance arrangements.[32] The expertise of Delaware judges is certainly a major attraction as well, but that too is a result of the large number of firms incorporated in Delaware, which produce a large volume of corporate litigation. This volume of litigation has both made the job of the Delaware judge attractive to talented Delaware corporate lawyers and enhanced their expertise while in the job.

Network benefits do not necessarily preclude customization, innovation, or incorporation in a state other than Delaware. If the inherent value of an innovative or customized governance arrangement outweighs the network benefit of a widely used arrangement, a firm could well adopt the former. This would tend to occur with respect to governance arrangements that do not entail open-ended standards, like Delaware fiduciary duties, or a high degree of complexity, like that of disclosure rules under the securities laws. An example of a governance term the attraction of which is not significantly affected by network benefits might be a charter provision that separates the CEO and board chair. This is clear and simple, with no great need for interpretation by courts or expertise in application by lawyers. The network quality of many corporate governance arrangements, however, creates a bias—and apparently a very large bias—in favor of conformity along many dimensions of corporate governance.[33]

Accordingly, the theory of network externalities tells us that while a firm going public may maximize its own value by adopting Delaware default rules, all other factors being equal, this does not mean that it is socially optimal for large numbers of firms to adopt Delaware default rules. Accordingly, from a societal point of view, there could well be a suboptimal level of innovation and customization. Moreover, any given default rule may be inherently

---

[32] The quality of the Delaware judges can be viewed as a complementary service that developed as a result of the widespread use of Delaware law.

[33] Two firms whose particular governance needs were very different from those of the typical public company are Visa and Mastercard, each of which went public with highly customized governance arrangements. In each case, banks had ownership and interests and governance rights that were different from those of public shareholders. Visa, Inc., Registration Statement (Form S-1) (Mar. 19, 2008) (allocating separate classes of stock with limited voting rights to bank shareholders with pre-IPO ownership rights); Mastercard Inc., Registration Statement (Form S-1) (May 25, 2006) (similar to Visa's arrangement but also giving bank shareholders with pre-IPO ownership power to elect up to three directors).

suboptimal in the sense that an alternative rule might increase aggregate firm value across all firms *if* it were widely adopted. Similarly, greater heterogeneity in incorporation choices could be socially beneficial. Thus, network externalities inherent in corporate governance arrangements may explain why there is so much uniformity in corporate governance and further explain that, contrary to the contractarian theory, there is no reason to believe this market outcome is socially optimal.

A second explanation for the lack of governance customization or innovation at the IPO stage lies in the acknowledged weakness of the contractarian theory of the mid-stream stage. The dependence of the IPO leg of the theory on the weaker "mid-stream" leg was overlooked by the original contractarians, but there is an important link. Optimal governance arrangements for a firm can change over time. Moreover, as a firm lives with a particular governance arrangement for a period of time, problems may become apparent. If the pre-IPO shareholders and investors can be sure that a suboptimal arrangement will be modified later on, perhaps they would be more inventive at the IPO stage. But if such a change would impair management's discretion or reduce its perqs, there can be no assurance that management will agree to modify the arrangement when it becomes optimal to do so. That is, shareholders cannot count on a midcourse correction. Consequently, an innovative or customized arrangement adopted at the IPO stage could last as long as the firm exists, which could well make it inherently unattractive at the IPO stage.

3.3.2 *Staggered Boards at the IPO Stage*

Network benefits do not explain why firms adopt staggered boards at the time they go public. Both annually elected and staggered boards are well defined by statute, commonly used, and addressed by a large body of case law ruling on board conduct with each type of board. No-one has come up with a satisfying explanation for the widespread, but not universal, adoption of staggered boards among companies going public, but there are a few candidates.

First, while the bulk of the research suggests that staggered boards tend to reduce firm value, it may be that staggered boards increase shareholder value for some firms. Second, while staggered boards may reduce share value, they could provide more than offsetting private benefits to managers, in which case they could increase the total value of a firm. Perhaps the managers of firms that go public with staggered boards enjoy especially high private benefits and perhaps the cost to shareholders is low.[34] Daines and I tested this hypothesis and found no support, but private benefits are not directly observable and proxies for their presence are imperfect. Therefore, we could not exclude this explanation of the data. Either of these explanations, if borne out, would eliminate the inconsistency between the contractarian theory and the common use of staggered boards.

A third potential explanation that would pose a moderate threat to the contractarian theory is that, even if pre-IPO managers and shareholders incur costs by having their firms go public with staggered boards, they can recoup those costs later by having their boards de-stagger before they selling their shares. So long as pre-IPO shareholders can coordinate with

---

[34] If the market for management talent is perfect, staggered boards would increase shareholder value under these conditions because managers with high private benefits would accept lower compensation. But there are reasons to believe the market for management talent is not so perfect.

one another and control the firm's board before any wants to sell, a staggered board provides an implicit option on an annually elected board in the future. Public shareholders will gladly vote to de-stagger a board if the incumbent board gives them the opportunity. On the other hand, an annually elected board is permanent. Public shareholders cannot be expected to adopt a staggered board later on. Thus while this interpretation of staggered boards at the IPO stage is plausible in the abstract, it has no empirical support. Until recent years, firms did not de-stagger their boards after going public, and many firms' pre-IPO shareholders sold shares not long after their IPO. Moreover, even in recent years, the de-staggering that has occurred has been in response to public shareholder demands, not the interest of insiders who want to sell their shares.

A fourth explanation that does call into question the contractarian theory—indeed one that amounts to heresy among economics-oriented scholars—is that governance arrangements adopted at the IPO stage may not be priced. John Coates raised this possibility in his study of staggered boards at the IPO stage, stating: "A lack of pricing penalty is also consistent with anecdotal reports from IPO participants, including investment bankers, venture capitalists, and lawyers from Wilson Sonsini (among other lawyers), who all uniformly report in conversations that conventional defenses do not affect IPO pricing."[35] A difficulty with this explanation is that since most pre-IPO shareholders, including venture capitalists, continue to own shares after the IPO, the pricing explanation for the presence of takeover defenses would have to extend to pricing in secondary market trading after the IPO as well. This is more difficult to believe, especially in light of studies showing that staggered boards have an impact on price.[36]

In sum, the weight of the evidence suggests that the widespread adoption of staggered boards at the IPO stage is inconsistent with the contractarian theory. But we still lack a satisfying explanation for why a large number of firms would adopt an apparently suboptimal governance arrangement when they go public.

4 The Contractarian Theory of the Mid-stream Stage also Misses the Mark

In the foreword to a widely read issue of the *Columbia Law Review* in 1989, Lucian Bebchuk stated: "The debate on contractual freedom in corporate law should be viewed as two debates, not one. The questions of contractual freedom in the initial charter and in mid-stream (that is, after the corporation is publicly held) are different and require separate examination."[37] In

---

[35] Coates, *supra* note 7, at 1381–82. I too have heard many market participants express this view.

[36] Ron Gilson and Bernie Black, extending an argument they made regarding implicit contracting between VCs and entrepreneurs, might argue that VCs will incur this cost as part of an implicit deal they have with entrepreneurs to return control to them if they are successful. See Ronald Gilson & Bernard Black, 47 J. Fin. Econ. 243 (1998). Evidence against this explanation is that only some VC-backed companies go public with staggered boards.

[37] Bebchuk, *supra* note 10, at 1399.

the same issue, Easterbrook and Fischel acknowledged that "[t]he difference between governance provisions established at the beginning and provisions added later suggests some caution in treating the two categories alike."[38]

Once a company goes public, the conceptualization of the manager–shareholder relationship as "contractual" is less accurate than at the IPO stage. The board can make substantial changes to a company's governance structure unilaterally—for example, it can adopt a poison pill or change executive compensation. It can also decline to accede to a value-enhancing charter amendment that disfavors management.

Contractarians nonetheless had faith that market forces would yield optimal governance arrangements once a company is publicly held. They supported their position in two ways. First, they expected that IPO charters would contain provisions that constrain management from changing corporate governance arrangements to the disadvantage of shareholders—limits on management's freedom to adopt a poison pill, for example.[39] Second, they believed that market forces would pressure boards to initiate value-increasing governance arrangements. Their logic was that poor governance structures would lead to high costs of capital, which in turn would lead to a lack of competitiveness in the product market, which ultimately would lead to a takeover or bankruptcy and the loss of managers' jobs.[40] There was a division in the ranks of the contractarians with respect to mid-stream adoption of governance arrangements related to takeover defenses—for example, a charter provision that disallowed the adoption of poison pills. Easterbrook and Fischel believed that boards should pre-commit to remain passive in response to a takeover bid and allow shareholders to tender their shares. They were doubtful, however, that boards would actually initiate charter amendments imposing such a restriction on themselves, and were thus inclined toward a mandatory legal rule requiring passivity.[41] This sole instance of a lack of faith in their own contractarian logic in such an important area of corporate governance was surprising. David Haddock, Jonathan Macey, and Fred McChesney cried foul. Market forces, they believed, would indeed induce management to adopt value-maximizing charter amendments, including arrangements that limited management's defense against hostile bids. Although Haddock et al. did not explain what market mechanisms would provide such

---

[38]   Frank H. Easterbrook & Daniel R. Fischel, "The Corporate Contract", 89 Colum. L. Rev. 1416, 1443 (1989). In their book, they say "It is important, however, to keep the latecomer term (a contract term added unilaterally by management) in mind as a potential problem in a contractual approach to corporate law." Id. at 34. In other articles, many of which were included in the *Columbia Law Review* symposium issue, legal scholars spelled out the weaknesses of the contractarian arguments at the mid-stream stage. Robert C. Clark, "Contracts, Elites, and Traditions in the Making of Corporate Law", 89 Colum. L. Rev. 1703 (1989); John C. Coffee, Jr., "The Mandatory/Enabling Balance in Corporate Law: An Essay on the Judicial Role", 89 Colum. L. Rev. 1618 (1989); Melvin Aron Eisenberg, "The Structure of Corporation Law", 89 Colum. L. Rev. 1461 (1989); Jeffrey N. Gordon, "The Mandatory Structure of Corporate Law", 89 Colum. L. Rev. 1549 (1989); see also Lucian Arye Bebchuk, "Limiting Contractual Freedom in Corporate Law: The Desirable Constraints on Charter Amendments", 102 Harv. L. Rev. 1820, 1848 (1989).

[39]   Easterbrook & Fischel, *supra* note 2, at 33; Haddock et al., *supra* note 2, at 727–30; Macey, *supra* note 2, at 193.

[40]   See e.g., Easterbrook & Fischel, *supra* note 2, at 32–33; Baysinger & Butler, Role of Corporate Law, *supra* note 2, at 182; Baysinger & Butler, Race, *supra* note 2, at 448–51.

[41]   Easterbrook & Fischel, *supra* note 2, at 167–74.

discipline, and they did not provide any examples of managers whom the market punished for failing to promote shareholder interests in this way, they nonetheless expressed this faith based on "overwhelming [though uncited] empirical evidence from various aspects of corporate governance suggest[ing] that faithful managers are rewarded while the faithless are punished."[42]

The contractarian claims for the mid-stream stage raise two empirical questions: First, do IPO charters constrain management-initiated mid-stream governance changes, as the contractarians expected? Second, after a company goes public, do managers tend to initiate value-enhancing charter amendments to improve governance—regarding takeover defenses or otherwise?

Empirical studies of IPO charters address the first question unequivocally: IPO charters do not constrain management's initiation of mid-stream governance changes.[43] Indeed, in contrast to the contractarian expectation, IPO charters commonly restrict *shareholders* from initiating governance changes by requiring supermajority shareholder votes to amend bylaws—particularly bylaw provisions that protect management.[44]

Regarding the second question—whether management initiates value-enhancing charter amendments—there is no evidence of such a contractarian invisible hand driving management to initiate such charter amendments. On the contrary, until recent years, when shareholders have exerted pressure on management to improve governance, management resisted. From the late 1980s to the mid-2000s, shareholders and managers battled over takeover defenses.[45] Shareholder proposals to redeem poison pills or to subject them to shareholder approval received substantial and increasing support throughout this period, as did shareholder proposals to destagger boards.[46] Nonetheless, management declined to accede to either demand.[47]

In sum, the experience of the period from the mid-1980s to the mid-2000s does not support the contractarian expectation that management would initiate agency cost-reducing charter amendments.

---

[42] Haddock et al., *supra* note 2, at 737. In another article, Macey and McChesney state: "The 'market for managers' penalizes management teams who try to advance their own interest at shareholders' expense." Jonathan R. Macey & Fred S. McChesney, "A Theoretical Analysis of Corporate Greenmail", 95 Yale L. J. 13, 40 (1985). As was true of other legal scholarship at the time, they offered no empirical support for this statement. In their original article on management responses to hostile takeovers, Easterbrook & Fischel advocated a mandatory legal rule of passivity. Easterbrook & Fischel, *supra* note 2, at 1164. In their book, ten years later, they remained doubtful that a contractual approach would work, but changed their position to one in which the default rule would require passivity. Easterbrook & Fischel, *supra* note 2, at 174 ("[T]he optimal legal rule prevents resistance unless expressly authorized by contract ex ante.").

[43] Daines & Klausner, *supra* note 7, at 95; Coates, *supra* note 7, at 1357. The sample of charters on which I report above also contain no limitations on charter amendments favoring management.

[44] For example, among firms whose bylaws provided for a staggered board, half required a supermajority vote as high as 80% to amend the bylaws to get rid of the staggered board.

[45] Georgeson, a provider of strategic shareholder consulting services, has made available online a series of annual reports that provide a useful chronology of shareholder proposals. See Annual Corporate Governance Review, Georgeson, http://www.georgeson.com/us/resource/Pages/acgr.aspx (last visited May 11, 2013).

[46] Klausner, Fact and Fiction, *supra* note 7, at 757–62.   [47] Id. at 758 & n.7, 759 tbl.2.

5 CORPORATE GOVERNANCE SINCE THE MID-2000S: A NEW (IMPLICIT) CORPORATE CONTRACT?

In the wake of the Enron and WorldCom scandals of the early 2000s and the passage of the Sarbanes–Oxley Act in 2002,[48] dramatic changes occurred in the US that shifted power from management to shareholders. Some of these were changes in the law. Others were nonlegal institutional changes. Still others were norms that directors appear to have adopted.

These changes have created a new *implicit* contract in the economists' sense of that term—a self-enforcing arrangement in which parties have carrots and sticks that keep their interests aligned. The central weakness of the contractarian theory of the mid-stream stage was that the market mechanisms envisioned as aligning shareholder and management interests were largely just that—envisioned, with little if any theoretical or empirical support. The ultimate connection between weak governance structures and market forces leading to managers being fired was conceivable, but the connection needed to be proved. It wasn't. Beginning in the mid-2000s, however, new mechanisms emerged that have induced managers of public companies to act in the interest of shareholders. The new implicit contract thus turns the contractarian theory on its head. It works at the mid-stream stage, while the IPO stage remains largely moribund from a contracting perspective.

There is no basis for claiming that the new implicit contract is optimal. To the extent that agency costs were a significant concern in the past, the shift in power toward shareholders could well be a change for the good. On the other hand, critics of the new regime correctly point out that the newly powerful institutional shareholders are run by agents, and that the proxy advisers on which they rely may well offer ungrounded judgments.[49]

5.1 Legal Changes

The Sarbanes–Oxley Act and the stock exchange rules issued in the aftermath of the Enron and WorldCom scandals imposed several requirements on firms regarding the independence and role of outside directors. A majority of directors must satisfy the stock exchanges' criteria for independence.[50] Independent directors must meet at least once a year in executive session without members of management present, and they must name a director to lead those meetings.[51] In many companies, the result has been the establishment of an ongoing position of lead director.[52] In addition, Sarbanes–Oxley expanded the role

---

[48] Sarbanes–Oxley Act of 2002, Pub. L. 107–204, 116 Stat. 745 (codified as amended in scattered sections of 11, 15, 18, 28, and 29 U.S.C.).

[49] See Robert Daines, Ian Gow, & Robert F. Larcker, "Rating the Ratings: How Good Are Commercial Governance Ratings?", 98 J. Fin. Econ. 439 (2010).

[50] See Order Approving NYSE and NASDAQ Proposed Rule Changes Relating to Equity Compensation Plans, Exchange Act Release No. 48,108, 68 Fed. Reg. 39,995 (July 3, 2003).

[51] See NASDAQ Stock Market Rules § 5605(b)(2) (2013); NYSE, Listed Company Manual § 303A.03 (2013).

[52] David Larcker & Brian Tayan, Corporate Governance Matters: A Closer Look at Organizational Choices and their Consequences 136–39 (2011).

of the audit committee and strengthened its independence requirements.[53] The New York Stock Exchange required that boards create compensation, nominating, and governance committees, each comprised entirely of independent directors.[54] The NASDAQ did not require firms to form those committees, but it required that CEO pay and other executives' pay be approved by either a majority of independent directors or a compensation committee comprised of independent directors. The NASDAQ imposed a similar requirement for the nomination of directors.[55] These requirements imposed formal independence on boards. But how independently directors would actually conduct themselves remained to be seen, and of course would necessarily vary across firms.

5.2 Nonlegal Changes

Heading into the mid-2000s, non-legal changes were also developing in the US governance environment. These changes involved executive pay, the composition and attitude of shareholders, and the ability of shareholders to overcome the collective action problem that shareholders had faced in the past. In combination with the legal changes that had occurred, the result appears to be a greater alignment of management interests with shareholder interests.[56]

From the 1980s to the 2000s, executive pay became increasingly stock-based. John Core and Wayne Guay found that, between 2004 and 2008, the median holdings of company stock by CEOs ranged from $59 to $79 million (accounting for stock options by converting them into stock equivalents).[57] This was ten times the amount of stock CEOs held in 1993. CEOs' increased share ownership is the carrot that is expected to lead them to act in the interests of shareholders.

Institutional shareholdings also increased dramatically from the 1990s to the 2000s. Total institutional stock ownership increased from 37% in 1990 to 50% in 2008.[58] This increased concentration of shareholdings created an inchoate stick in the new implicit corporate contract. In order for shareholders to wield that stick effectively, however, additional forces would be helpful.

One development that enhanced the power of institutional shareholders was the advent of the proxy advisory services—Institutional Shareholder Services (ISS) and Glass Lewis. ISS and Glass Lewis emerged well before the 2000s, but their power grew as institutional shareholdings grew. These organizations communicate information and substantive judgments to institutional shareholders and, in effect, coordinate voting on everything from board elections to merger approvals to approvals of stock option plans. A second

---

[53] See Sarbanes–Oxley Act § 301; NASDAQ, *supra* note 51, § 5605(c)–(e); NYSE, *supra* note 51 § 303A.04-.07. Prior to Sarbanes–Oxley, the stock exchanges imposed some independence requirements in audit committees.

[54] NYSE, Inc., Listed Company Manual § 303A.04-.05.

[55] NASDAQ, Inc. Rule 5605(d)–(e).

[56] Some argue that shareholders have too much power and that they wield it in ways inconsistent with their long-term interest. I take no position on that issue.

[57] John E. Core & Wayne R. Guay, "Is Pay Too High and Are Incentives Too Low: A Wealth-Based Contracting Framework", 24 Acad. Mgmt. Persp. 5–19 (2010).

[58] Marcel Kahan & Edward Rock, "Embattled CEOs", 88 Tex. L. Rev. 987, 996–1001 (2010).

development in the mid-2000s was the emergence of the activist hedge fund. Although the shareholdings of hedge fund activists are relatively small, traditional institutions have supported their challenges of management.[59] As a result of these developments, the collective action problem long associated with shareholder voting is not an impediment to shareholders exerting power over management. Institutions are able to use the stick that their increased shareholdings gave them.

The stick was arguably enhanced further in the mid-2000s by firms' adoption of majority voting in place of plurality voting. Under majority voting, a director running unopposed needs to garner a majority of votes in order to keep his or her board seat.[60] From the beginning of 2006 through 2007, the percentage of S&P 500 firms that adopted majority voting rose from 16% to 66%,[61] and from 2003 to 2009, the number of S&P 100 firms that adopted majority voting rose from ten to 90.[62] This rapid adoption of majority voting both reflected the growing power of shareholders and potentially increased their power. Although few directors have lost their seats by failing to receive a majority of votes,[63] majority voting and "just vote no" campaigns seem to augment the power of the shareholders' stick. A recent study found that majority voting increases firms' responsiveness to shareholder concerns, and that the adoption of majority voting was associated with an increase in share price.[64]

At least as dramatic as the rapid spread of majority voting was the de-staggering of boards in the mid-2000s—after two decades in which boards refused shareholder demands to de-stagger. According to one study of the period from 2003 to 2010, approximately 60 firms per year de-staggered their boards—compared to an average of four firms per year from 1987 and 2002.[65] Like majority voting, the de-staggering of a board both reflects increased shareholder power and further adds to their power. Not only does a de-staggered board mean a lower barrier to a takeover, it also exposes all directors every year to the danger of becoming the target of a "just vote no" campaign, especially in combination with majority voting.

---

[59] Kahan & Rock, *supra* note 58; Ronald Gilson & Jeffrey Gordon, "The Agency Costs of Agency Capitalism: Activist Investors and the Revaluation of Governance Rights", 113 Colum. L. Rev. 883 (2013); Ronald Gilson & Jeffrey Gordon, Agency Capitalism: Further Implications of Equity Intermediation, in Research Handbook on Shareholder Power (J. Hill & R. Thomas eds., 2015).

[60] In some forms of majority voting, a director may not take his seat if he or she does not get a majority of votes, and in others the director must tender a resignation, which the board is free to accept or reject.

[61] Claudia H. Allen, "Study of Majority Voting in Director Elections" (2007), available at http://www.ngelaw.com/files/Uploads/Documents/majoritystudy111207.pdf.

[62] Kahan & Rock, *supra* note 58, at 1011 tbl.3.

[63] Yonca Ertimur, Fabrizio Ferri, & David Oesch, "Does The Director Election System Matter? Evidence from Majority Voting", 29–31 available at http://ssrn.com/abstract=1880974.

[64] Firms with majority voting tend to implement successful shareholder proposals more than firms with plurality voting. In addition, when shareholders withhold votes as a means of expressing dissatisfaction with a general governance matter, as opposed to dissatisfaction with a particular director, firms with majority voting are more likely to address the matter than firms with plurality voting. Id. at 15, 20–22, 25–27; see also Jay Cai, Jacqueline L. Garner, & Ralph L. Walkling, "A Paper Tiger? An Empirical Analysis of Majority Voting", 21 J. Corp. Fin. 119, 129–30 (2013) (finding a positive price reaction to the announcement of a proposal to adopt majority voting).

[65] See Re-Jin Guo et al., "Undoing the Powerful Anti-Takeover Force of Staggered Boards", 14 J. Corp. Fin. 274, 278 fig. 1 (2008); Re-Jin Guo, Timothy A. Kruse, & Tom Nohel, Activism and the Shift to Annual Director Elections 30 fig. 1 (CELS Version, Nov. 2012) (on file with author).

Marcel Kahan and Edward Rock, who have reported on these changes in a series of articles,[66] conclude that the consequence of these legal and institutional developments has been a change in directors' conception of their role: independent directors became not just nominally independent but "substantively" independent.[67] As Kahan and Rock explain, this substantive independence is evident in surveys regarding how much time directors devote to their board responsibilities, how directors spend their time, and how they view their roles.[68]

In sum, by roughly the mid-2000s a system of carrots and sticks arose that created what economists would call an implicit contract between management and shareholders. Greater stock-based pay and stock holdings shifted CEOs' interests more toward shareholder interests, and the potential for collective action among institutional shareholders has kept CEOs' feet to the fire in terms of satisfying shareholder demands.

Is this the contract the contractarians originally had in mind? No. First, it took two decades to come together, and even then only after key legal changes occurred. Moreover, it happened at the mid-stream stage, which was the weakest leg of the contractarian theory. The IPO stage, which was the core of the contractarian claims and which relied on legally enforceable commitments, remains largely moribund as a source of innovation or customization.

Moroever, as legal and nonlegal institutional changes in the 2000s have increased shareholder power, there has been a mild resurgence of contractarian-like rhetoric *against* the changes. This opposition has come from advocates for management, most visibly Wachtell, Lipton, Rosen & Katz and the Business Roundtable, and from some academics, with Professor Stephen Bainbridge providing the most sweeping criticism of these changes. The battle cry of these opponents is "one size does not fit all." They leveled this rhetorical weapon at Sarbanes–Oxley's requirements concerning independent directors, Dodd–Frank's requirements regarding executive compensation, the SEC's proxy access proposal, and ISS's approach to some governance issues.[69]

With respect to proxy access, the Business Roundtable and Wachtell Lipton took the position that the proposed mandatory rules should instead be default rules, and that *shareholders* should be permitted to vote to have their corporations opt out of them. This is quite different from the approach of the original contractarians, who believed that *management* would have incentives to do right by the shareholders. Bainbridge, however, has maintained the original contractarian line, advocating "board-centric" corporate governance.[70]

---

[66] Edward Rock, "Adapting to the New Shareholder Centric Reality", 161 U. Pa. L. Rev. 1907 (2013); Kahan & Rock, *supra* note 58; Marcel Kahan & Edward Rock, "Hedge Funds in Corporate Governance and Corporate Control", 155 U. Pa. L. Rev. 1021 (2007).

[67] See id. at 1022.   [68] Id. at 1022–32.

[69] See, e.g., Business Roundtable, "Letter to SEC on Proxy Access", Sept. 14, 2009, available at http:// businessroundtable.org/resources/business-roundtable-statement-on-the-presidents-remarks-on-financial-regula; Martin Lipton, Steven A. Rosenblum, & Karessa L. Cain, "Proxy Access Revisited", 44 Bank & Corp. Gov. L. Rep. 499 (2010); Letter from Wachtell, Lipton, Rosen, & Katz to Elizabeth M. Murphy, "Secretary, Securities and Exchange Commission" (Aug. 17, 2009), available at http://www.sec.gov/comments/s7-10-09/s71009-263.pdf; Stephen Bainbridge, Corporate Governance after the Financial Crisis (2012); Stephen Bainbridge, "Dodd–Frank: Quack Federal Corporate Governance Round II", 95 Minn. L. Rev. 179 (2011).

[70] Stephen Bainbridge, ProfessorBainbridge.com, Gut Proxy Access, available at http://www.professorbainbridge.com/professorbainbridgecom/2010/06/gut-proxy-access.html (last visited Feb. 25, 2018). Professor Michal Barzuza has responded with an adverse selection theory of governance choice that undermines the "one size does not fit all" argument. Michael Barzuza,

6 Conclusion

This chapter has addressed two questions. The primary question is whether the contractarian theory is a valid positive theory of corporate governance. The answer to that question is no. The theory does not fit the facts uncovered in empirical studies of the content of corporate charters at the IPO stage—the primary focus of the contractarian theory. Corporate charters at the IPO stage are not the fount of innovation and customization that the contractarian theorists imagined them to be, and there is no reason to believe that pre-IPO shareholders customize their charters to maximize firm value. With the exception of the sui generis case of exclusive forum provisions, essentially no innovation or customization occurs in charters. On the contrary, charters are boilerplate documents that overwhelmingly adopt default rules or statutory menu options. Furthermore, the primary menu option that has been adopted is the staggered board, which the weight of evidence suggests reduces firm value. The essentially uniform adoption of default rules and menu options—primarily those of Delaware—is instead consistent with the theory that network economics drive the adoption of corporate governance arrangements. The implication of this alternative theory is that legal rules are important to maintaining effective corporate governance. In contrast to the claims of the contractarian view, decentralized contracting between management and shareholders will not get us there.

The contractarian theory was always viewed as weak with respect to the mid-stream stage. Are managers of public companies truly subject to strong incentives to adopt governance structures that enhance firm value? The contractarians of the 1980s and 1990s did not make a convincing case that they were, and the mid-stream theory was not supportable. But by the mid-2000s, a set of legal and institutional changes had led management to respond to shareholder interests as never before. Firms have de-staggered their boards, adopted majority voting, faced withhold-the-vote campaigns, responded to activist demands, and increased stock-based pay for management so that management's financial interests have shifted toward shareholder interests. This is not a result of any sort of charter-based, legally enforceable contract that the contractarians imagined. Nor is it the result of managers simply responding to market forces as the contractarians envisioned. It is instead the result of legal and nonlegal changes that occurred over twenty years. These institutional changes have created a new implicit contract in the economists' sense of that term—a self-enforcing set of legal and nonlegal carrots and sticks that has emerged to shift managements' interests toward (but not necessarily into perfect alignment with) shareholders' interests. Of course, one does not have to use the term "contract" to describe the system of carrots and sticks that shapes corporate governance. I use that term here simply to draw at least a linguistic connection with the original theory of market-driven corporate governance. One could instead describe the relationship simply as one in which legal rules and market forces have engendered a set of institutions and norms that constrain management to be responsive to shareholder interests to an extent that may or may not enhance firm value.

No-Size-Fits-None: Adverse-Selection and Inefficient Self-Selection in Private Ordering of Corporate Law and Governance (draft, Aug. 12, 2015).

CHAPTER 5

....

THE STATE OF STATE COMPETITION FOR INCORPORATIONS

....

MARCEL KAHAN[1]

1 INTRODUCTION

....

THE competition by states for incorporations has long been the subject of extensive scholarship.[2] Views of this competition differ radically. While some commentators regard it as "the genius of American corporate law,"[3] others believe it leads to a "race to the bottom,"[4] and still others have taken the position that it barely exists.[5] Despite this lack of consensus among corporate law scholars, scholars in other fields have treated state competition for incorporations as a paradigm case of regulatory competition.[6]

[1] George T. Lowy Professor of Law, New York University School of Law. I would like to thank Ryan Bubb, Emiliano Catan, Mike Klausner, Shmuel Leschem, and Wolf-Georg Ringe for helpful comments and the Milton and Miriam Handler Foundation for financial support.

[2] See, e.g., Lucian Arye Bebchuk & Allen Ferrell, "Federalism and Takeover Law: The Race to Protect Managers from Takeovers", 99 Colum. L. Rev. 1168 (1999); Michael Klausner, "Corporations, Corporate Law, and Networks of Contracts", 81 Va. L. Rev. 757 (1995); Lucian Arye Bebchuk, "Federalism and the Corporation: The Desirable Limits on State Competition in Corporate Law", 105 Harv. L. Rev. 1435, 1461–70 (1992); Frank H. Easterbrook & Daniel R. Fischel, The Economic Structure of Corporate Law (Harvard, 1991); Melvin A. Eisenberg, "The Structure of Corporation Law", 89 Colum. L. Rev. 1461, 1512–13 (1989); Roberta Romano, "Law as a Product: Some Pieces of the Incorporation Puzzle", 1 J.L. Econ. & Org. 225 (1989); Daniel R. Fischel, "The 'Race to the Bottom' Revisited: Reflections on Recent Developments in Delaware's Corporation Law", 76 Nw. U. L. Rev. 913 (1982); Ralph K. Winter, Jr., "State Law, Shareholder Protection, and the Theory of the Corporation", 6 J. Leg. Stud. 251, 256 (1977); William L. Cary, "Federalism and Corporate Law: Reflections upon Delaware", 83 Yale L. J. 663, 666 (1974).

[3] Roberta Romano, The Genius of American Corporate Law (American Enterprise Institute, 1993).

[4] Cary, *supra* note 2, at 666.

[5] Marcel Kahan & Ehud Kamar, "The Myth of State Competition in Corporate Law", 55 Stan. L. Rev. 679 (2002).

[6] See, e.g., Richard L. Revesz, "Rehabilitating Interstate Competition: Rethinking the 'Race to the Bottom' Rationale for Federal Environmental Regulation", 67 N.Y.U. L. Rev. 1210 (1992) (arguing

In this chapter, I will try to deconstruct the state competition debates by showing that, in fact, scholars are engaged in three separate debates that are only loosely connected to each other. The first, "directional" debate concerns whether firms, if given a choice, will choose corporate law rules that maximize shareholder value, maximize managerial benefits, something in between,[7] or something else entirely.[8] Resolution of this question is relevant regardless of whether states "compete." All it takes to make this question important is for firms to have a meaningful choice among legal rules.

In the US, a firm can incorporate in any state (or, for that matter, in a foreign country) regardless of where it is headquartered and have its "internal affairs" governed by the laws of its state of incorporation. An existing firm can also change its state of incorporation with the approval of the board and its shareholders without triggering major consequences other than the change in governing law.

As a result, even in the absence of state competition, firms have a choice among legal regimes as long as states offer different legal rules. For that matter, firms can have meaningful choices even if they have no choice of where to incorporate as long as the state's legal regime offers firms flexibility in devising their governance rules.

The second "competition" debate concerns whether, how, and which states compete for incorporations. Depending on what is meant by "competition," competition can exist even in a regime where firms have no choice over where they incorporate[9] and may not exist in a regime where firms have free choice.

The third "federalism" debate concerns the desirability of federal corporate law as an alternative to the present regime, where many corporate law rules are determined by the law of the firm's state of incorporation. How such a law would stack up in absolute terms along various dimensions—pro-shareholder versus pro-manager, concern for other constituents such as creditors and employees, speed of adopting innovations, and so on—is a question that is entirely separate from the earlier two debates.

that, unlike in corporate law, state regulation of environmental law will not result in a race to the bottom); Lynn M. LoPucki & Sara D. Kalin, "The Failure of Public Companies in Delaware and New York: Empirical Evidence of a 'Race to the Bottom'", 54 Vand. L. Rev. 231, 232–37 (2001) (analogizing state competition for incorporations to bankruptcy venue choices); Robert K. Rasmussen & Randall S. Thomas, "Timing Matters: Promoting Forum Shopping by Insolvent Corporations", 94 Nw. U. L. Rev. 1357, 1382–1406 (2000) (drawing on the competition-for-incorporations literature to propose reforms in bankruptcy venue rules); Edward J. Janger, "Predicting When the Uniform Law Process Will Fail: Article 9, Capture, and the Race to the Bottom", 83 Iowa L. Rev. 569, 588–92 (1998) (drawing on state-competition-for-incorporations literature to argue that uniform law drafters may facilitate the adoption of inefficient rules); David Charny, "Competition among Jurisdictions in Formulating Corporate Law Rules: An American Perspective on the 'Race to the Bottom' in the European Communities", 32 Harv. Int'l. L. J. 423 (1991) (using the state-competition paradigm to analyze whether corporate law in the European Union should be harmonized).

[7] Brett H. McDonnell, "Getting Stuck Between Bottom and Top: State Competition for Corporate Charters in the Presence of Network Effects", 31 Hofstra L. Rev. 681 (2003).

[8] William W. Bratton, "Corporate Law's Race to Nowhere in Particular", 44 U. Toronto L. J. 401 (1994).

[9] Ehud Kamar, "Beyond Competition for Incorporations", 94 Geo. L. J. 1725 (2006).

2 The Directional Debate: To the Bottom or to the Top?

The issue in the state competition debate that has been the subject of the fiercest controversy is whether the "race" that state competition supposedly engenders leads to the "bottom"—to laws favoring managers at the expense of shareholders[10]—or to the "top"—to laws that maximize firm value.[11] That this is the issue most analyzed by commentators is, on the one hand, not surprising: the direction of the "race" is clearly very important from a policy perspective.[12] On the other hand, however, the factors that determine whether the "race" is to the top or to the bottom have virtually nothing to do with state competition. Rather, these factors are internal to the firm.

"Race to the bottom" theorists, in effect, posit that, when given a choice between laws favoring managers that reduce overall value and laws disfavoring managers that increase overall value, firms will choose the former. "Race to the top" theorists posit that firms will choose the latter. Viewed from this perspective, the theoretical debate about direction is more closely connected to the debate about the need for mandatory rules than it is to state competition more generally.[13]

As I will discuss here, the positions taken by the partisans, properly understood, are much closer to each other than the literature lets on. At the same time, the theoretical underpinnings make the question of firm choice significantly more complex than the "to the top" and "to the bottom" monikers suggest.

2.1 Extreme versus Nuanced Versions in the Directional Debate

The extreme claim that state competition has resulted in a race to the bottom is clearly false and was probably never seriously asserted. At the very bottom, managers have appropriated all shareholder wealth. The combined market capitalization of stock in US publicly traded companies is (and the returns that investors have earned from stock ownership are) sufficiently high that it is safe to conclude that we have not arrived at the very bottom. Indeed, Lucian Bebchuk, the contemporary scholar most identified with the "race to the bottom" view, argues that firms will choose a law favoring managers which reduces firm value over a

---

[10] See, e.g., Bebchuk, *supra* note 2 (arguing that state competition leads to rules biased toward managerial interests); Cary, *supra* note 2 (arguing that state competition results in a race to the bottom).

[11] See, e.g., Winter, *supra* note 2 (arguing that state competition results in a race to the top); Fischel, *supra* note 2 (challenging Cary's analysis); Romano, *supra* note 2 (adducing evidence that state competition results in a race to the top).

[12] Even if firms chose legal rules that maximize firm value, the result may not be optimal due to the presence of network and other types of externalities, see Klausner, *supra* note 2.

[13] See, e.g., Lucian A. Bebchuk, "The Debate on Contractual Freedom in Corporate Law", 89 Colum. L. Rev. 1395 (1989); Jeffrey N. Gordon, "The Mandatory Structure of Corporate Law", 89 Colum. L. Rev. 1549 (1989).

law favoring shareholders which increases firm value only if the reduction in firm value, relative to the benefit to the managers, is not excessive.[14]

The extreme "race to the top" claim is also difficult to maintain. If firms, when given a choice, always choose the law that maximizes value, it must be either that managers have no power over that decision or that the interests of managers and shareholders regarding the choice coincide perfectly.

A more nuanced version of the "race to the top" claim would admit that firms may sometimes choose a law that reduces firm value and benefits managers. This more nuanced "race to the top" claim differs from Bebchuk's more nuanced version of the "race to the bottom" claim only in degree (and perhaps not at all). For example, Easterbrook and Fischel, among the most prominent early "to the top" scholars, share Bebchuk's view[15] that managers regularly choose rules that entrench them against hostile bids even though they lower firm value.[16] So, possibly, the main difference between the two camps has less to do with their views on the directional debate and more to do with their (less well-argued and articulated) views on the federalism debate: how good (or bad) would a federal corporate law be.

2.2 The Multiplicity of Settings for Choice

Firms chose their domicile, and thereby the legal rules that govern them, in a multiplicity of settings. Specifically, firms can make this choice prior to an IPO or mid-stream; they can make it explicitly (by reincorporating) or implicitly (by failing to reincorporate); and managers, at the time of the choice, can hold a small fraction ("outside managers") or a significant fraction ("large shareholder managers") of the firm's voting power. But the direction of firm choice depends on the power and incentives of managers and of shareholders. Because these factors will vary systematically among the settings for choice, there is no a priori reason why the directions of firm choices in different settings should be identical.

2.2.1 The Power to Effect Mid-Stream Incorporation Decisions

To change its state of incorporation, a firm typically merges with a wholly-owned subsidiary incorporated in a different state, with the subsidiary surviving the merger. Mergers generally require a recommendation by the board of directors and the approval of at least a majority of the shares entitled to vote.[17] According to Guhan Subramanian, 373 firms effected mid-stream reincorporations over the 1991 to 2001 period.[18]

To effect a mid-stream reincorporation that benefits them at the expense of shareholder value, manager thus need to *both* dominate the board of directors sufficiently to get the board to recommend the merger *and* either own sufficient shares to approve a merger or

---

[14] Bebchuk, *supra* note 2, at 1461.   [15] See Bebchuk & Ferrell, *supra* note 2.

[16] Frank H. Easterbrook & Daniel R. Fischel, "The Proper Role of a Target's Management in Responding to a Tender Offer", 94 Harv. L. Rev. 1161 (1981).

[17] See, e.g., Delaware General Corporation Law, Section 251.

[18] See Guhan Subramanian, "The Influence of Antitakeover Statutes on Incorporation Choice: Evidence on the 'Race' Debate and Antitakeover Overreaching", 150 U. Pa. L. Rev. 1795, 1820 (2002).

induce sufficient other shareholders to vote for the merger. To block a reincorporation that benefits shareholders at the expense of managers, managers merely need to dominate the board of director sufficiently to get the board *not to* recommend a reincorporation merger *or* have sufficient shares to block the merger. Obviously, large shareholder managers will have greater power than outside managers to effect or block a reincorporation as they own a greater fraction of shares and as they are more likely to dominate the board.

2.2.1.1 Board Domination

"Race to the bottom" scholars have generally assumed that even outside managers have sufficient influence over board decisions to block a reincorporation that runs counter to their interests and "race to the top" scholars have not directly challenged this assumption.[19] While this assumption may be justified for many companies, the degree to which managers control boards is not uniform and has declined over the years.[20] As Ed Rock and I have shown elsewhere, the percentage and the relative power of outside directors on corporate boards have increased substantially over the last 40 years.[21] Thus, at least in some companies, managers may not have the power to block a reincorporation on the board level.

Whether outside managers in many companies have sufficient sway over their boards to get them to recommend a reincorporation that favors managerial interest at the expense of shareholder interest is questionable. The fact that there is no widespread shareholder opposition to reincorporation recommendations (unlike, say, to board decisions to adopt a poison pill and retain a staggered board) suggests that managerial power in this regard is limited.

2.2.1.2 Shareholder Approval

That shareholders must vote in favor of a reincorporation would seem to indicate that reincorporations ought to benefit shareholders as long as managers do not control the shareholder vote. "To the bottom" theorists have countered that shareholders have imperfect information about the effect of a reincorporation on the value of the firm and may vote in favor of reincorporations that run counter to their interest.[22]

Whatever the merits of this argument may have been[23] in the past, it has lost much of its currency in light of the increased power of institutional investors. Institutional investors (such as mutual funds and pension funds) hold much larger stakes in specific firms than

---

[19] See, e.g., Winter, *supra* note 2. An exception is Romano, who points out that, when Pennsylvania enacted a disgorgement anti-takeover statute in 1990, the boards of almost three-quarters of all exchange-traded Pennsylvania companies decided to opt out. Roberta Romano, "Competition for Corporate Charters and the Lesson of Takeover Statutes", 61 Fordham L. Rev. 843, 859 (1993).

[20] Marcel Kahan & Edward Rock, "Embattled CEOs", 88 Tex. L. Rev. 987 (2010).

[21] Kahan & Rock, *supra* note 20; Marcel Kahan & Edward Rock, "How I learned to Stop Worrying and Love the Pill: Adaptive Responses to Takeover Law", 69 U. Chi. L. Rev. 871, 881–84 (2002).

[22] Bebchuk, *supra* note 2, at 1470–76.

[23] The argument that some shareholders are imperfectly informed is clearly valid. But it does not necessarily follow that they will tend to vote for value-reducing mergers. It may be more rational for rationally uninformed shareholders to abstain, split their votes, vote randomly, or even systematically vote against board proposals (if they believe that most proposals are adverse to shareholder interests). These strategies would be particularly effective if there are other, better informed, shareholders whose votes would become more likely to carry the day. Whether uninformed shareholders ever followed these more sophisticated strategies, however, is unclear.

the individual investors of lore.[24] They also hold shares in many more different companies. This generates economies of scope to the extent that they vote on recurring issues that have similar effects on companies (such as decisions to reincorporate). Moreover, institutional investors can pool their resources by hiring proxy advisory firms to give them voting advice.[25] It is thus highly doubtful that institutional investors have significantly less information about the effect of a reincorporation than managers do and regularly approve of reincorporations that reduce company value.

A second argument put forth by "to the bottom" scholars is that firms will propose reincorporations that maximize managerial benefits, but subject to the constraint that they do not reduce shareholder value.[26] The result of such a process could be characterized as a "crawl upwards," as firm value increases whenever a firm reincorporates (if only by a little). As discussed in greater detail below, the "crawl upwards" model has significant implication for the optimal competitive strategy of states trying to attract reincorporations.

2.2.2 Conflicts of Interest in Mid-Stream Decisions

Mid-stream, various forces outside of legal rules (e.g., incentive compensation, the managerial labor market, the product market, etc.) align the interests of managers with those of shareholders.[27] Some "race to the top" scholars have suggested that these forces are sufficient to induce managers to prefer rules than maximize firm value.[28] But since these market forces do not work perfectly, residual conflicts of interest are likely to persist. Indeed, if outside market forces worked to align shareholder and managerial interests perfectly, there would not be much need for corporate law.

Individual managers, however, will have incentives to seek pro-manager rules only to the extent that they themselves profit from these rules. The ability of outside managers to profit from pro-manager rules is a function of their expected tenure. The longer their expected tenure, the larger the benefits they derive, for example, from rules insulating managers from hostile takeovers.[29]

This has two significant implications. First, since expected managerial tenure is limited,[30] incumbent managers will obtain only a fraction of the aggregate managerial benefit of a pro-management rule. Second, because managers differ in their expected remaining tenure, they

---

[24] See Kahan & Rock, *supra* note 20, at 996 (institutional shareholders have increased from 14% in 1965 to 50% in 2008).

[25] Id. at 1005–07.

[26] Bebchuk, *supra* note 2, at 1471–72. A more elaborate version of the basic argument is presented in Oren Bar-Gill, Michal Barzuza, & Lucian A. Bebchuk, "The Market for Corporate Law", 172 J. Institutional and Theoretical Econ. 134 (2006).

[27] The extent to which legal rules (e.g., rules on hostile takeover defenses) align interests is not relevant here since these rules can, in principle, be changed through reincorporation. See, e.g., Bebchuk, *supra* note 2, 1467–70.

[28] See, e.g., Winter, *supra* note 2, at 256–66; Fischel, *supra* note 2, at 919.

[29] With respect to other types of rules, for example those permitting blatant forms of self-dealing, even a manager with short tenure may be able to extract the bulk of the value from the company. However, such rules are not really at issue in the state competition debate. See Bebchuk, *supra* note 2; Bebchuk & Ferrell, *supra* note 2.

[30] See, e.g., Steven N. Kaplan & Bernadette A. Minton, "How Has CEO Turnover Changed?", 12 Int'l. Rev. Fin. 57 (2012) (estimating an average CEO tenure of six years).

will differ in their incentives to favor a pro-management rule. Indeed, the incentives of a CEO close to retirement to seek rules that maximize share value (and thereby the value of her stock and stock options) through reincorporations are likely to exceed the incentives to seek pro-management rules.

Large shareholder managers, however, may reasonably expect to sell their shares as a block. If such blocks sell for a higher price as a result of pro-manager legal rules, large shareholder managers can appropriate to themselves the benefits generated by such rules beyond the duration of their managerial tenure.[31] At the same time, large equity holdings by large shareholder managers reduce conflicts of interests.

2.2.3 The Power over Pre-IPO Incorporation Decisions

Pre-IPO firms generally have few shareholders. It is thus likely that pre-IPO boards will reflect the wishes of the pre-IPO shareholders. Pre-IPO, the power to change (and not to change) the state of incorporation therefore effectively rests with the pre-IPO owners of the firm.

The extent to which the pre-IPO owners are identical to the post-IPO managers of the firm varies from firm to firm. At one extreme, there may be a firm where the founding entrepreneur owns or controls most of the stock and plans to continue managing the firm post-IPO. At the other extreme, the pre-IPO owners may plan not to be involved in the management at all. In between are firms where both the managers and other pre-IPO investors (such as venture capitalists) own substantial shares and jointly exercise the power to make the pre-IPO incorporation decision.

2.2.4 Conflicts of Interest in Pre-IPO Incorporation Decision

In the IPO, the pre-IPO owners will sell a significant fraction of the equity in the firm. The pre-IPO owners—including pre-IPO managers to the extent they are owners—will thus have an incentive to make an incorporation decision that increases the price at which the firm shares can be sold at the IPO. To the extent that the market accurately values the effect of the incorporation state, this gives pre-IPO owners strong incentives to choose a domicile that maximizes firm value.

"Race to the bottom" theorists have made two retorts to this argument. First, they suggest that the market may not value the effect of the incorporation state correctly.[32] Second, they argue that, whatever the incentives for pre-IPO incorporation decisions, it will be post-IPO decisions that will drive the direction of state competition.[33] The second retort relates to the competition debate, rather than the directional debate, and will be taken up in the next section.

Whether incorporation decisions are accurately priced in the IPO is essentially a debate about stock market efficiency. Since the firm's state of incorporation and its laws are public information, believers in market efficiency would argue, their import is reflected in the stock price. "To the bottom" theorists, by contrast, would have to argue that the market

---

[31] Barzuza makes a similar argument in the context of cross-listings. See Michal Barzuza, *Lemon Signaling in Cross-Listing*, Virginia Law and Economics Research Paper No. 2012-03.
[32] Bebchuk, *supra* note 2, at 1479.   [33] Id. at 1481.

systematically undervalues features of the incorporation law that protect shareholders against various forms of entrenchment and overreaching by managers.[34]

"To the bottom" theorists, however, have failed to present a cogent argument as to why the market would systematically mis-value companies in that fashion.[35] Indeed, theoretically, the market should be likely to price standard terms like the incorporation regime reasonably well. While small pricing inaccuracies may persist, it is unlikely that prices would fail to reflect legal rules that had a significant effect on company value.

2.2.5 *Summary*

Because of these systematic differences related to the multiplicity of settings, and because firms and managers will differ in less systematic ways (e.g., with respect to the degree of influence managers have over the board), it is unlikely that all firm choices follow the same paradigm. Rather, both across settings and, to a lesser extent, within settings, firms may choose different sets of rules.

2.3 Empirical Evidence on the Directional Debate

I now turn to some of the empirical evidence relevant to the directional debate. At the outset, it is important to note that this evidence is almost necessarily inconclusive. It is virtually impossible to distinguish the nuanced versions of the "to the top" and "to the bottom" positions empirically. Heterogeneity among settings and firms further complicates the empirical analysis.

The earliest empirical studies related to the directional debate are event studies that examine the effect of mid-stream decisions to reincorporate on firm value. There have been several such event studies and they generally find a slight (in the range of 1%) statistically significant positive effect on the stock price upon the announcement of a reincorporation.[36] "To the top" scholars point to these reincorporation studies as evidence for their hypothesis.[37] Alas, these event studies at most show that mid-stream reincorporations tend to benefit shareholders. This result would be consistent with the view by "race to the bottom" scholars that the requirement for shareholder approval constrains managers in this setting and would have no direct implications for pre-IPO incorporation decisions or mid-stream failures to reincorporate. Moreover, the event studies do not distinguish between companies with outside and large shareholder managers.

---

[34] Bebchuk, *supra* note 2, at 1478–81.

[35] See, e.g., Bebchuk, *supra* note 2, at 1478–81 (noting generic belief of some commentators that markets may not price corporate law rules efficiently). Later on, Bebchuk argues that pro-shareholder rules are likely to be innovative and that innovative rules may not be accurately priced. Id. at 1482. But innovative rules (like rules permitting poison pills, anti-takeover laws, or the set of legal decisions originally attacked by Cary) may also often be pro-management.

[36] The studies are summarized in Sanjai Bhagat and Roberta Romano, "Event Studies and the Law: Part II: Empirical Studies of Corporate Law", 4 Jam. L. & Econ. Rev. 424 (2002). As the authors note, some of the studies find significant results only for certain subsamples.

[37] See Romano, *supra* note 3, at 16–22.

Another set of studies looks directly at the factors influencing incorporation decisions of firms. In separate studies, Guhan Subramanian[38] and Lucian Bebchuk and Alma Cohen[39] present evidence that firms are more likely to be incorporated in their home state than in Delaware if their home state has adopted anti-takeover statutes. If these statutes reduce firm value, this result would be consistent with the "to the bottom" view in the directional debate. However, most anti-takeover statutes are rendered redundant by poison pills, so it is unclear why these statutes should matter at all. Indeed, in a different study, I have shown that judicial quality and state law flexibility significantly affect IPO decisions and that, if one controls for these variables, anti-takeover provisions are insignificant.[40]

Another set of studies looks at anti-takeover charter provisions (ATPs) of IPO firms. The selection of charter provisions and the selection of domicile represent similar decisions of firms choosing among legal rules (or sets of legal rules). The first of these studies, by Robert Daines and Michael Klausner,[41] compares IPOs by firms that went public with venture capital backing, firms controlled by LBO specialists, and other firms. Daines and Klausner found that many IPO charters contained ATPs, with about 43% of the firm charters providing for staggered boards and 6% opting for dual-class voting stock. Dual-class stock was less common in firms with VC or LBO fund backing, but the incidence of staggered boards did not vary significantly between the three groups of companies.

The results found by Daines and Klausner pose questions for both camps. If staggered boards reduce firm value, as believed by several (though not all) "to the top" commentators, IPO charters should not provide for them and should instead (but do not) contain provisions limiting the board's authority to adopt takeover defenses. But if ATPs reflect managerial self-interest, as "to the bottom" scholars tend to believe, why are they not more universal? In particular, the small percentage of firms with a dual-class share structure is consistent with strong entrenchment provisions being priced at the IPO and being avoided by most firms for that reason. However, the fact that VC and LBO fund backed IPOs are as likely to adopt staggered boards as other firms (even though managers in these firms wield less power),[42] as well as anecdotal evidence, suggests that these weaker provisions may not affect the IPO price, arguably because their effect on firm value is not clear cut.[43]

---

[38] Guhan Subramanian, "The Influence of Antitakeover Statutes on Incorporation Choice: Evidence on the 'Race' Debate and Antitakeover Overreaching", 150 U. Pa. L. Rev. 1795 (2002).

[39] Lucian A. Bebchuk & Alma Cohen, "Firms' Decisions Where to Incorporate", 46 J. L. & Econ. 383–425 (2003).

[40] Marcel Kahan, "The Demand for Corporate Law: Statutory Flexibility, Judicial Quality, or Takeover Protection?", 22 J. L. Econ. & Org. 340 (2006); see also Robert Daines, "The Incorporation Choices of IPO Firms", 77 N.Y.U. L. Rev. 1559 (2002) (anti-takeover provisions are not significant if one controls for the law firm advising the firm at the IPO).

[41] Robert Daines & Michael Klausner, "Do IPO Charters Maximize Firm Value? Antitakeover Protection in IPOs", 17 J. L. Econ. & Org. 83 (2001). Other studies include John C. Coates IV, "Explaining Variation in Takeover Defenses: Blame the Lawyers", 89 Cal. L. Rev. 1301 (2001) (arguing that variation in defenses can be explained by characteristics of law firms advising owner-managers) and Laura C. Field & Jonathan M. Karpoff, "Takeover Defenses of IPO Firms", 57 J. Fin. (2002).

[42] Daines and Klausner report that pre-IPO CEOs own on average 34% of the stock of "other" firms, compared to 15% and 8% respectively of the stock of VC and LBO fund backed firms. The pre-IPO holdings of VCs and LBO funds are, on average, 54% and 75%.

[43] Marcel Kahan & Edward Rock, "Corporate Constitutionalism: Anti-Takeover Provisions as Precommitment", 152 U. Pa. L. Rev. 473 (2003).

3 THE COMPETITION DEBATE: WHO COMPETES AND HOW?

The second debate concerns the actions of states: do they in fact compete for incorporations and, if they do, what is their competitive strategy? I refer to this prong as the competition debate.

Until recently, most state competition scholars have regarded the notion that many states compete for incorporations as a premise for their other arguments, without bothering to inquire much into whether this premise is correct.[44] Starting with Bill Cary, state competition scholars have asserted that states stand to earn substantial franchise taxes by firms incorporated in them, which provides an incentive for many states (especially the smaller ones) to actively seek incorporations.[45] Other scholars have noted that incorporations generate business for local lawyers, which enhances the incentives provided by the franchise tax.[46]

Whether states in fact compete has only recently become a focus of the academic debate. In two articles from 2001 and 2002, Ehud Kamar and I have argued that only Delaware actively competes for incorporations.[47] Since our articles, three different positions on whether states compete have emerged. Kamar and I attribute the failure of states other than Delaware to compete to political as well as economic factors. Lucian Bebchuk and Assaf Hamdani basically agree that only Delaware competes for incorporations, but they attribute the failure of other states to do so to other states having realized that competition with Delaware would be futile.[48] Romano maintains that several states are trying to attract incorporations. Notably, all camps in this debate agree that Delaware competes; the debate only concerns states other than Delaware.

3.1 Do States Compete?

The claim by Kamar and me that states other than Delaware do not actively compete for incorporations rests on two grounds: their lack of meaningful incentives to compete and their failure to take meaningful measures to compete. At the time our article was written, most states either charged a low, flat franchise tax on in-state firms or a tax based on the amount of business conducted in the state that was also charged on firms incorporated in other states. Other than Delaware, no state stood to derive substantial revenues, even if it attracted a large portion of all public companies. Therefore, contrary to the claims in the

---

[44] The most notable exceptions are Romano, *supra* note 2, and William J. Carney, "The Production of Corporate Law", 71 S. Cal. L. Rev. 715 (1998).

[45] See Kahan & Kamar, *supra* note 5, at 687, note 31 (citing literature).

[46] See Jonathan R. Macey & Geoffrey P. Miller, "Toward an Interest-Group Theory of Delaware Corporate Law", 65 Tex. L. Rev. 469 (1987); Bebchuk *supra* note 2, at 1443; Romano, *supra* note 2, at 240–41.

[47] See Kahan & Kamar, *supra* note 5; see also Marcel Kahan & Ehud Kamar, "Price Discrimination in the Market for Corporate Law", 86 Cornell L. Rev. 1205 (2002).

[48] Lucian A. Bebchuk & Assaf Hamdani, "Vigorous Race or Leisurely Walk: Reconsidering the Debate on State Competition over Corporate Charters", 112 Yale L. J. 553 (2002).

earlier state competition literature, franchise tax revenues do not drive competition by other states.[49]

Kamar and I further show that the benefits states stand to gain from attracting (or retaining) legal business through incorporations are modest.[50] These modest benefits may account for the fact that states periodically revise their corporation law or take other low-cost measures.[51] States, however, have not taken any more substantial—and possibly more effective—measures to compete, such as replicating Delaware's highly regarded Chancery Court which specializes in resolving corporate disputes.[52] Given the at best modest economic incentives to compete and the at best half-hearted measures to compete, Kamar and I conclude that only Delaware makes significant efforts to attract incorporations.

Consistent with our argument, Rob Daines has shown that most firms incorporate either in Delaware or in their headquarter state.[53] If states competed, Daines's findings would imply that states other than Delaware either do not try, or do not succeed, in attracting firms headquartered elsewhere. It is, however, unclear what competitive strategy other states would follow to produce such a result. It is more likely, as Daines argues, that the pre-existing relationships between managers and (locally-based) lawyers account for the "Delaware or headquarter state" incorporation pattern.

More recently, Michal Barzuza has presented evidence that Nevada competes for, and attracts, some firms who seek extremely lax laws.[54] Nevada, which had raised its maximum franchise tax from \$85 to \$11,100 in 2003, accounts for about 6–7% of incorporations by firms not incorporated in their home state and could be seen as a niche competitor.[55] Barzuza's argument supports our notion, discussed in the next section, that competition (and the lack thereof) is politically contingent, rather than futile, and hence may emerge.

3.2 Why Don't States Compete?

The prevailing franchise tax structure, which accounts for the fact that only Delaware (and perhaps Nevada) stand to gain substantial revenues from attracting incorporations, is endogenous. States can revise their franchise tax structure, as Nevada did, to give them greater incentives to compete. Why have states not done so?

Bebchuk and Hamdani argue that unerodable economic entry barriers account for the lack of competition. Drawing on Michael Klausner's prior work,[56] they argue that Delaware has competitive advantages over any other state attributable principally to "network benefits" (more on that later) derived from the fact that a large percentage of public companies are incorporated in the state. No competing states could compensate for these advantages because

---

[49] Kahan & Kamar, *supra* note 5, at 687–94.   [50] Id. at 694–99.

[51] See also Carney, *supra* note 44, at 722–28, 737–41 (discussing the role of lawyers in corporate law production).

[52] Kahan & Kamar, *supra* note 5, at 708–15.

[53] Robert Daines, "The Incorporation Choices of IPO Firms", 77 N.Y.U. L. Rev. (2002).

[54] Michal Barzuza, "Market Segmentation: The Rise of Nevada as a Liability-Free Jurisdiction", 99 Va. L. Rev. 935 (2012).

[55] Id. at 949.   [56] See Klausner, *supra* note 2.

Delaware would quickly copy any "improvement" in the law offered by that state. Other states, understanding this dynamic, have realized that competition would be futile.[57]

For Bebchuk and Hamdani's argument to work, the entry barriers generated by network benefits must be steep. Delaware earns profit margins from the incorporation business that are, in economic terms, of a stupendous magnitude.[58]

As Michael Klausner, on his own and with me, has argued, legal rules in general (and Delaware corporate law in particular) generate possible network benefits since the market is more familiar with Delaware law (making the law easier to price); lawyers are more familiar with Delaware law (and it is therefore easier to obtain legal advice); and there are more judicial precedents (clarifying Delaware law). Importantly, because Delaware is expected to continue to have a large market share, network benefits derive from the expectation that market familiarity and lawyer familiarity will continue in the future and that additional judicial precedents will be generated.[59] Given their somewhat intangible nature, it is difficult to estimate the magnitude of these benefits with precision. But it seems a stretch to suggest that the entry barriers generated by these benefits are so high as to make competition futile.[60]

Moreover, Bebchuk and Hamdani's argument that competition is futile because Delaware would copy any innovation is premised on the notion that all firms are attracted to the same legal regime. But as discussed before, due to the multiplicity of settings and the heterogeneity of firms, different firms may be attracted to differing regimes. Furthermore, outside managers and large shareholder managers will differ in the kind of legal rules that bestow benefits on them. Outside managers will be interested in rules that entrench them vis-à-vis shareholders (such as rules on takeover defenses), while large shareholder managers will be interested in rules that make it difficult to sue them for breaches of fiduciary duties (e.g., if they engage in self-dealing transactions). Even if Delaware enjoys substantial network benefits, it would thus seem feasible for states to offer a differentiated product attractive to a subset of public corporations, as Nevada does according to Barzuza, and as Maryland does for regulated investment companies.[61]

Rather than purely economic factors, Kamar and I argue that political ones account for the lack of more significant competition. For one, states are not firms. Entry is limited (one cannot form a new state) and the notion that existing states will generally try to maximize their profits in designing their corporate law is unsupported. Indeed, both Romano, and

---

[57] Bebchuk & Hamdani, *supra* note 48, at 586.

[58] Kahan & Kamar, *supra* note 47, at 1211 (estimating that Delaware's margin is several thousand percent).

[59] Klausner, *supra* note 2; Marcel Kahan & Michael Klausner, "Corporate Contracting: Standardization, Innovation and the Role of Contracting Agents (or 'The Economics of Boilerplate')", 83 Va. L. Rev. 713 (1997).

[60] There is further reason to doubt that it is network benefits that immunize Delaware from attack. To maximize its profits, Delaware should set its franchise taxes at a level where demand for Delaware incorporations is elastic (i.e., where a change in price will induce a change in the number of firms that decide to incorporate in Delaware). That about half of all public corporations incorporate outside Delaware, and that franchise tax savings are a frequently stated reason for why they do so, is consistent with such a pricing regime. So is the fact that Delaware charges higher franchise taxes to large public firms (which are likely to attribute a greater dollar value to a Delaware incorporation) than to small public firms, but still has a larger market share among large corporations. But if demand for Delaware incorporations is elastic, it follows that a state *could* attract incorporations by improving its products.

[61] Kahan & Kamar, *supra* note 5, at 721–22.

Bebchuk and Hamdani acknowledge that economic benefits from attracting incorporations are unlikely to induce larger states to compete. But even most smaller states have probably never given serious thought to competing for incorporations or taken actions like hiring a consultant to explore whether competition would be profitable.

Moreover, seriously competing for incorporations entails substantial *political* costs. For example, in most states, establishing a court modeled after Delaware's Chancery Court would require a constitutional amendment and attract political opposition, e.g., from the plaintiffs' bar worried about undermining the right to a jury trial. If established, the most qualified potential judges would probably not be residents of the state. Small-firm lawyers, who would stand to gain little from attracting public incorporations, may oppose a wholesale change in the state's corporate law. And so on.[62]

While more costly reform is difficult, states still revise their law. But as Bill Carney has argued, in some states these revisions are driven by the influence of political interest groups—lawyers and management—rather than by a desire to attract incorporations, while other states try to reduce the cost of lawmaking by adopting the Model Business Corporation Act.[63]

Whether it is just economic or whether it is also political factors that explain the present state of (non-)competition bears on the stability of that state. For Bebchuk and Hamdani, it would take a significant economic upheaval to permit states to compete effectively. For Kamar and me, competition may emerge spontaneously, more states may start pursuing niche strategies, and some niche players may start aiming at a greater market share, as the political dynamics in a state change.

3.3 Competitive Strategy

Though the directional debate and the competition debate are in many ways separate, they are linked with respect to one issue: what competitive strategy should Delaware (and other competing states) adopt?

The discussion of the competitive strategies for Delaware in this section will be somewhat stylized. In reality, it is of course difficult for anyone—and surely for amorphous political entities like states—to devise and implement a strategy. One important aspect of this difficulty is that a significant portion of Delaware corporate law is judge made. And while the judiciary may not be oblivious to a state's goals in attracting incorporations, it is also not the stooge of the state budget and economic development office. Moreover, the interests of lawyers, an important interest group even in Delaware,[64] may lead to deviations from the profit-maximizing strategy. Thus, whatever a state's maximizing strategy is in theory, in practice it will be implemented imperfectly.

A starting point to the analysis of Delaware's optimal strategy is to determine the forces that shape the law of other states. One possibility is that states will neglect their corporate laws. This is indeed what several very large and very small states seem to be doing. The laws of states like New York, California, Alaska, and West Virginia and the District of Columbia

---

[62] Kahan & Kamar, *supra* note 5.   [63] See Carney, *supra* note 44.
[64] See Cary, *supra* note 2; Macey & Miller, *supra* note 46.

contain, or did until recently, antiquated provisions requiring, for example, a supermajority to approve a merger or cumulative voting for directors. One can speculate that, in these states, corporate laws are not regularly updated either because the corporate bar takes no interest (because it is small or because it is dominated by firms specializing in Delaware law) or because the state legislature has bigger fish to fry.

Another possibility is that managers of in-state public firms will lobby for pro-managerial laws. Bill Carney, among others, has argued that such lobbying accounts for the adoption of anti-takeover laws.[65] In addition, labor groups may sometimes affect corporate law provisions, as is the case with the notorious section in New York's law imposing personal liability on the ten largest shareholders for unpaid wages.

Third, the local corporate bar may induce states to adopt a relatively decent, and relatively up-to-date, statutory law, either by adopting the Model Business Corporation Act (and updating it regularly) or by devising and updating their own code.[66] Members of the local bar may do so for a variety of reasons, such as benefiting closely-held companies incorporated in the state or enhancing their reputation. Such updating could also reflect a low-cost attempt to retain and attract incorporations by public firms.

Finally, some states may pursue a niche competition strategy. Such a strategy would not be designed to replicate Delaware's high-quality judiciary and would not significantly erode Delaware's network benefits, but might attract a significant share of firms in a certain market segment.[67]

The resulting laws of states other than Delaware can be mapped along two dimensions. The first dimension concerns the degree to which the law contains pro-management or pro-shareholder rules. The second dimension concerns the overall quality (including the content of rules where shareholder and manager interest do not conflict, judicial quality, and network benefits). The laws of states other than Delaware will differ along both dimensions, because states will differ in their susceptibility to managerial lobbying, in the degree of attention the corporate bar devotes to updating the law, in the influence of the local bar on the political process, in the niche strategy they may pursue, etc.[68]

Delaware's problem then becomes one of positioning its product optimally relative to both the demand by firms and to the products offered by its competitors. If all firms preferred the same position on the pro-management/pro-shareholder dimension, as posited by the more extreme "race to the top" and "race to the bottom" positions, Delaware's strategy would be simple. But if, as argued above, firm choices are heterogeneous, Delaware's positioning choice becomes more complex. To position its law optimally, Delaware would have to take account of the effect on whether existing Delaware corporations migrate out of the state, whether non-Delaware corporations move to Delaware, where companies incorporate at the IPO stage, and how high a franchise tax it could charge.[69] Moreover, to the extent that it does not reduce network benefits, Delaware would want to provide firms with a choice of rules along the pro-management/pro-shareholder dimension.

Return now to the argument that firms will try to maximize shareholder value at the IPO stage (to the extent that the rules of the state of incorporation are priced). "To the bottom"

---

[65] See Carney, *supra* note 44, at 750.   [66] Id.   [67] See Barzuza, *supra* note 54.

[68] See Barzuza et al., *supra* note 26, for a formal model making similar points.

[69] See also Michal Barzuza, "Price Considerations in the market for Corporate Law", 26 Cardozo L. Rev. 127 (2004) (highlighting interaction of positioning and maximum franchise tax).

theorists have argued in response that, since the stock of already existing companies is larger than the flow of IPOs, a state trying to compete for incorporations will focus on the latter rather than the former segment of the market.[70] But if Delaware caters to existing companies (which prefer relatively pro-management rules), why does Delaware attract a high percentage of companies at the IPO stage (which prefer rules that maximize company value)?[71] The answer presumably is that Delaware is superior from the company value perspective, despite its hypothesized pro-management rules.

But such a conclusion raises questions for "race to the bottom" theorists. If states compete, at least some of them should have adopted a niche strategy of catering to IPO firm demand for pro-shareholder rules. And if states do not compete, it must be that, however distorted Delaware law allegedly is by the dynamics of state competition, the product of non-competing states is even worse for shareholders.

Rather, it is more plausible that Delaware positions its law to appeal to both IPO firms and existing companies by pursuing a middle ground on the pro-manager/pro-shareholder dimension and otherwise focusing on maximizing quality (by having an up-to-date law, a good court system, quickly correcting court decisions that reduce firm value, etc.). Since no other state offers a product that is superior for both shareholders and managers, few firms would migrate out of Delaware (and firms from some other states may migrate in). And because the combination of balanced rules and high general quality results in relatively high firm value (possibly higher, or at least not significantly lower, than the rules of any other state), many IPO firms will choose Delaware law.

3.4 Refinements

The preceding discussion of Delaware's competitive strategy can be refined in several ways. First, whether or not other states are actively competing with Delaware, Delaware has market power. The presence of such market power is suggested by Delaware's substantial market share and confirmed by the supra-competitive profits Delaware earns from its chartering business.[72]

Commentators have examined several ways in which market power may affect Delaware's strategy. Most notably, Ehud Kamar has suggested that Delaware's use of fact-intensive standards serves to protect its competitive advantages. A competing state can easily copy Delaware's law. But without an expert judiciary to interpret that law, a law based on fact-intensive standards is less valuable. By using standards, in conjunction with an expert court, it becomes harder for other states to replicate Delaware.[73]

---

[70] Bebchuk, *supra* note 2, at 1459. In particular, Bebchuk argues, both states that already have a large stock of companies incorporated in them (like Delaware) and states with presently few domiciled corporations that become successful in attracting IPO firms will (the latter ultimately) focus on reincorporation decisions.

[71] See Daines, *supra* note 53.

[72] A high market share is not necessarily indicative of market power as the market may be "contestable." However, a contestable market does not offer more than a normal rate of profit. William J. Baumol, "Contestable Markets: An Uprising in the Theory of Industry Structure", Am. Econ. Rev. 1 (1982).

[73] Ehud Kamar, "A Regulatory Competition Theory of Indeterminacy in Corporate Law", 98 Colum. L. Rev. 1908 (1998). Although Kamar, when writing the article, assumed that other states competed with

A relationship between federal lawmaking and Delaware corporate law has given rise to other refinements to the competition debate. Congress has the power, and to some extent has exercised the power, to adopt corporate law rules. Thus, federal law governs issues like insider trading, the right to have shareholder proposals included in the company's proxy statement, and whether a company can make loans to officers. In theory, federal law could completely supplant the present regime of state-based corporate law. Such a move would be harmful to Delaware, which derives substantial revenues from the franchising business.[74]

Commentators have taken different positions on how the threat of federal intervention affects Delaware law. On one extreme, Mark Roe has argued in a 2003 article that Delaware either mimics the rules favored by federal lawmakers or gets preempted by federal law.[75] In Roe's world, Delaware is basically a federal implementation agent that enjoys little autonomy. Put in our earlier terms, the threat of federal intervention forces Delaware to place its law at a certain position along the pro-management/pro-shareholder dimension.

On the other extreme, Roberta Romano has argued that states compete largely unimpeded by federal threats because states correlatively exercise power over Congress. As evidence, Romano points out that the key components of state corporate law—fiduciary duties and the allocation of authority between managers and shareholders—are largely governed by state law.[76]

Ed Rock and I have taken an intermediate position.[77] We argue that the possibility of federal preemption constitutes a threat to Delaware, but that this threat is significant only in times when systemic change can generate a significant populist payoff. At other times, as long as the interest groups representing managers and investors are reasonably satisfied, the built-in inertia of federal legislation makes federal intervention unlikely.[78]

To minimize its exposure to a populist attack, Rock and I argue, Delaware has adopted a classical or nineteenth-century common law model of lawmaking that makes Delaware law less overtly political. Specifically, most important and controversial legal rules are the product of judge-made law. Delaware's judiciary has technocratic expertise on corporate law and is appointed on a non-partisan basis. Its opinions are filled with quasi-deterministic reasoning. Statutory amendments to the corporation law are initially drafted by a bar committee, are adopted without debate or change by the legislature, and address largely technical matters.[79]

Delaware, his argument requires only that Delaware is concerned about potential competition emerging in the future. In another article, Kamar and I have argued that Delaware engages in price discrimination. In particular, Delaware's franchise tax effectively discriminates between publicly traded firms (who attribute a greater value to a Delaware incorporation) and closely held firms (who attribute a lower value), as well as, among publicly traded firms, between larger and smaller firms. Kahan & Kamar, *supra* note 47.

[74] See Kahan & Kamar, *supra* note 47, at 1251 (revenues of $425 million in 1999).

[75] Mark J. Roe, "Delaware's Competition", 117 Harv. L. Rev. 588, 591–92 (2003).

[76] Roberta Romano, "Is Regulatory Competition a Problem or Irrelevant for Corporate Governance?", 21 Oxford Rev. Econ. Pol. 212 (2005).

[77] Another intermediate position, taken by Cary, *supra* note 2, and Bratton, *supra* note 8, at 418–25, is that Delaware, in some instances but not always, adjusts its law to ward off federal intervention.

[78] Marcel Kahan & Edward Rock, "Symbiotic Federalism and the Structure of Corporate Law", 58 Vand. L. Rev. 1573 (2005).

[79] Id. at 1590–1615. In a subsequent 2005 article, Roe seems to depart from his earlier claim that the threat of federal intervention is highly constraining and adopts an intermediate position similar to

3.5 Empirical Evidence

There is relatively little statistical evidence as to whether states compete. In an early, seminal article on state competition, Roberta Romano found that there is a statistically significant correlation between the percentage of a state's total tax collections derived from franchise taxes and the speed at which the state enacts corporate law innovations.[80] However, since most states do not stand to gain material franchise tax revenues from attracting incorporations, this correlation does not provide evidence that states adopt innovations to increase revenue.

Another approach in the competition debate is to examine the law of Delaware, the state that is clearly most successful in attracting incorporations. Indeed, several commentators have also tried to resolve the directional debate based on Delaware's actions. For example, Bill Cary, who wrote the first significant modern article on state competition in corporate law, examined several then-recent decisions by the Delaware Supreme Court, found that they were unduly pro-management, and concluded that the race must be heading "to the bottom."[81] Cary's conclusion, of course, depends on knowing how the optimal law compares to Delaware law.

A more systematic and elaborate study in a similar vein by Brian Cheffins, Steven Bank, and Harwell Wells (CBW) tracks the development of shareholder rights under Delaware law, Illinois law, and the Model Business Corporations Act (MBCA) from 1899 to the present using three different rights indexes.[82] CBW reason that, if competition has resulted in an erosion of shareholder rights, the index scores they study should decline. They find a modest downward trend for two of the three indexes and a mixed trend for the third index for each of the three bodies of law.

There are some inherent limitations in the CBW approach: reasonable minds can differ as to what items to include in a rights index and how to score an item. In particular, one may question whether the shareholder rights score should be based on a state's default rules, the approach taken by CBW, or only on mandatory rules.[83]

It is also unclear how CBW's results should be interpreted. For much of the period of analysis, Illinois and the drafters of the MBCA did not compete intensely, if at all, for

---

the one taken by Rock and myself. Roe observes that the set of groups that are influential in Delaware (e.g., managers, shareholders, lawyers) is narrower than those that wield power in Washington. As a result, the major state-level players want to minimize federal intervention, at least as long as Delaware does not adopt a lopsided law. This creates space where Delaware has room to maneuver in fashioning its law. Mark J. Roe, "Delaware's Politics", 118 Harv. L. Rev. 2493 (2005).

[80] Romano, *supra* note 2. Romano, *supra* note 76, at 218, argues that the S-shaped pattern of adoption of innovations and the movement of firms from non-responsive states to responsive states are additional evidence that states compete. An S-shaped adoption pattern, however, does not show that diffusion is due to competition (see Kahan & Kamar, *supra* note 5, at 715–16) and the action of firms relate to the directional debate, not to whether states compete.

[81] Cary, *supra* note 2.

[82] Brian R. Cheffins, Steven A. Bank, & Harwell Wells, "The Race to the Bottom Recalculated: Scoring Corporate Law over Time", Working Paper (2014).

[83] The same arguments that "to the bottom" commentators have advanced to argue that firm choice will trend "to the bottom" also imply that default rules do not offer protection. This suggests that erosion of rights could take the form of a state adopting a default rule offering protection (instead of a mandatory rule) with firms opting out of the rule.

incorporations. The impact of competition would then be reflected in *differential* trends in the index for Delaware compared to Illinois, and the MBCA. If the Delaware indices show a similar trend to the ones for Illinois and the MBCA, as found by CBW, this could indicate that competition did not drive the index changes.

The most significant statistical analysis of Delaware law is a study by Robert Daines. Daines shows that firms incorporated in Delaware have a higher value (as measured by Tobin's Q) than similar firms incorporated elsewhere, and argues that this Delaware premium is due to Delaware's relatively takeover-friendly corporate law.[84] In a follow-up study employing a different methodology, Guhan Subramanian confirms the results reported by Daines, but finds no statistically significant Delaware premium after 1996.[85]

That Delaware firms have higher value is consistent with the notion that Delaware is competing for incorporations. That Delaware is trying to attract incorporations is, of course, undisputed. So the noteworthy result in Daines is that he was able to show that Delaware law contributes sufficient value to be reflected in a statistically significant difference in Tobin's Q.

Daines's results have also become enmeshed in the directional debate. While "to the top" scholars have embraced Daines's findings as confirmation of their view,[86] "to the bottom" scholars have pointed to the disappearance of a significant Delaware premium after 1996.[87] This controversy illustrates once again the conceptual confusion engendered by the failure to separate the various strands within the state competition debate. About half of all firms are *not* incorporated in Delaware. Thus, it is hard to see how a Delaware premium can be proof that *firms* chose a legal regime that maximizes firm value.

Rather, the results by Daines suggest that other states either do not try to compete (or do not compete effectively). In the presence of effective competition, neither the "to the top" nor the "to the bottom" theories would predict a sizeable Delaware premium. If states raced "to the top," it would be hard to see how Delaware could have earned such a significant lead. And if states raced "to the bottom," then Delaware would, at most, have to be as good as or slightly better on the shareholder value front than other states. But if other states do not compete and thus offer an inferior product, Delaware becomes able to design its law to appeal to both managers and shareholders.

4 THE FEDERALISM DEBATE: WHAT WOULD FEDERAL LAW LOOK LIKE?

Although the arguments are least well worked out, the federalism debate lurks in the background of many disagreements among state competition scholars. If we had a mandatory federal corporate law that replaced the current regime that gives corporations a choice

---

[84] See Robert Daines, "Does Delaware Law Improve Firm Value?", 62 J. Fin. Econ. 525 (2001).

[85] Guhan Subramanian, "The Disappearing Delaware Effect", 20 J. L. Econ. & Org. 32 (2004).

[86] See, e.g., Jonathan R. Macey, "Displacing Delaware: Can the Feds Do a Better Job than the States in Regulating Takeovers?", 57 Bus. Law. 1025 (2002); Roberta Romano, "The Need for Competition in International Securities Regulation", 2 Theoretical Inq. L. 387 (2001).

[87] See, e.g., Lucian Bebchuk, Alma Cohen, & Allen Ferrell, "Does the Evidence Favor State Competition in Corporate Law?", 90 Cal. L. Rev. 1775, 1784–90 (2002).

among different bodies of state law, what would it look like and how would it compare to state corporate law?

For adherents to the more extreme positions in the directional debate, it is not necessary to devote much energy to this issue. However, for proponents of the more nuanced versions, the quality they expect federal corporate law to take may be a key determinant of their normative views of the present regime.

But even though one can make some sensible predictions on how federal law would differ from state law, it is hard to arrive at firm conclusions on whether a mandatory federal law, on the whole, would be better or worse than the current regime. This difficulty is compounded by the fact that, in the current regime, only about half of the public companies are incorporated in Delaware, and governed by Delaware law, while the other half are incorporated in other states with a hodge-podge of different laws.

4.1 The Pro-Management/Pro-Shareholder Dimension

As several commentators have noted, federal law would be influenced by political factors, rather than by the desire to attract incorporations.[88] "Race to the bottom" theorists have acknowledged that federal law may have a pro-management bias as a result of lobbying of managerial interest groups. But they argue that at least such lobbying would be made against a neutral baseline. By contrast, the argument goes, in a state competition regime, pro-management lobbying may also take place, but would occur against a baseline that is already excessively pro-management as a result of states' interests in attracting incorporations.[89] Therefore, they claim, federal law would be less pro-management than current state law.

This argument is problematic in two respects. First, unlike federal lawmakers, Delaware lawmakers would have strong incentives to resist lobbying for laws that would reduce Delaware's attractiveness as an incorporation domicile. As a result, in Delaware (and any other state that is actively competing), lobbying would be *less* influential than it would be in a system where attracting incorporations would not be a countervailing objective for lawmakers. If both lobbying and competition introduce a pro-managerial bias, it is a priori unclear when the bias is stronger. At least under some versions of the nuanced "to the bottom" theory (that takes account of the fact that shareholders also have power over incorporation decisions), it is possible that the pro-management bias resulting from lobbying is the stronger one.

Second, not all states actively compete for incorporations. The law of non-competing states, like federal law, would be determined by political factors.[90] To be sure, the political

---

[88] See, e.g., Roe, *supra* note 79; Kahan & Rock, *supra* note 78; Kahan & Kamar, *supra* note 5; Roberta Romano, "Empowering Investors: A Market Approach to Securities Regulation", 107 Yale L. J. 2359 (1998) (arguing that the federal government would be subject to significant managerial lobbying); Roberta Romano, "The Sarbanes-Oxley Act and the Making of Quack Corporate Governance", 114 Yale L. J. 1521, 1568–94 (2005).

[89] See, e.g., Bebchuk, *supra* note 2, at 1503–04.

[90] Carney, *supra* note 44; Kahan & Kamar, *supra* note 5, at 736–38; Bebchuk & Hamdani, *supra* note 48, at V.B.2.

dynamic on the federal level may work differently than on the state level. In particular, interest groups would have very different incentives to lobby at the federal level, where they would be dealing with a large, monopolistic rulemaker,[91] than they presently do at the state level, where they are dealing with a much smaller lawmaker and may be able to escape any laws by reincorporating.[92] But it is not evident whether federal law would therefore be more or less pro-management than the laws of non-competing states.

On the other side, commentators have suggested that federal law may impose excessive regulations that are purportedly in the interest of shareholders, but in fact reduce company value. In particular, such overregulation may be the political response to corporate scandals.[93] Thus, Roberta Romano has analyzed various corporate governance mandates in the Sarbanes–Oxley Act (SOX) and concluded that the empirical literature does not support the view that they enhance corporate value.[94]

However, many of the studies cited by Romano also do not show that SOX mandates reduce company value. In any case, it would be possible that federal law overreacts to corporate scandals, but at other times provides reasonably efficient regulation. Thus, SOX may not be emblematic of a wholesale federal corporate law. In sum, neither "to the top" nor "to the bottom" scholars have succeeded in establishing that federal law would be, respectively, inferior or superior to state laws on the pro-management/pro-shareholder dimension.

4.2 Other Considerations

4.2.1 *Other Interest Groups*

Several commentators have argued that groups representing labor, creditor, and similar interests may be more influential on the federal level than they are in Delaware.[95] To the extent that federal law will cater to such other interest groups, it may result in lower benefits to shareholders or managers (or both). This may, or may not, enhance overall welfare.[96]

One particular interest group—lawyers—requires differentiation. According to Bill Carney, lawyers have a significant effect on the corporate law of states other than Delaware,[97] and even Delaware law probably caters significantly to the interest of the bar.[98] Unlike other interest groups, lawyers may thus have less influence in a federal regime than they do presently.

---

[91] Cf. Bratton, *supra* note 8, at 432 (noting the presence of economies in federal lobbying).

[92] See also Kahan & Kamar, *supra* note 5, at 743.

[93] See Romano, *supra* note 88; see also Kahan & Rock, *supra* note 78.

[94] Romano, *supra* note 88, at 1529–43.

[95] See, e.g., Roe, *supra* note 79; Kahan & Rock, *supra* note 78.

[96] See, e.g., Bebchuk, *supra* note 2, at 1505. Even at present, other interest groups may have influence over the corporate law of non-competing states. See, e.g., Kahan & Kamar, *supra* note 5, at 732 (noting the influence of labor groups on certain provisions of New York law).

[97] See Carney, *supra* note 44.

[98] See, e.g., Cary, *supra* note 2, Macey & Miller, *supra* note 46; Douglas M. Branson, "Indeterminacy: The Final Ingredient in an Interest Group Analysis of Corporate Law", 43 Vand. L. Rev. 85 (1990).

4.2.2 Judicial Quality and Network Effects

Delaware has an expert corporate law judiciary and, according to many commentators, Delaware law generates network benefits. A federal corporate law would presumably be adjudicated to a large extent by federal courts. Although federal judges are generally highly regarded, they would lack the specialized expertise of Delaware's judiciary. However, companies incorporated in states other than Delaware may see a benefit in a greater opportunity to have corporate law disputes resolved by federal courts rather than state courts.

A uniform federal corporate law is also likely to generate network benefits. However, to the extent that the network benefits generated by Delaware law are dependent on the fact that Delaware corporate law disputes are resolved by Delaware's small judiciary, they may exceed the network benefits arising under federal law.

4.2.3 Innovation

A federal lawmaker would lack incentives to update its law and adopt useful innovations in order to attract incorporations. As a result, the speed of innovation may be lower than it currently is for Delaware.[99] This is likely true regardless of whether Delaware's market power generates monopoly's slack, as argued by some commentators,[100] or increases its incentives to develop innovations, as argued by others.[101] Other states, of course, presently adopt innovations at a lesser pace than Delaware does, and federal law may compare favorably to at least some of such other states.

4.2.4 Rules versus Standards

To the extent that a regulatory agency would have authority to promulgate federal corporate law, federal law may be substantially rule based. Some commentators have suggested that Delaware law relies on open-ended standards more than is optimal.[102] To the extent that this is correct, a more rule-based approach may be superior at the margin. There is, however, no particular reason to believe that federal law would be optimally rule-based or, for that matter, that it would be superior in this respect to the law of Delaware and other states.

4.3 Summary

While the specific parameters of federal law are unclear, there are some weak reasons to believe that federal law would be superior to the laws of non-competing states. Federal law would likely be superior in some respects—like the generation of network benefits and judicial quality—and there are no particular reasons to predict how it would differ in others.

---

[99] See Romano, *supra* note 2.   [100] Bebchuk & Hamdani, *supra* note 48, at V.A.3.
[101] Kahan & Kamar, *supra* note 5, at 742.
[102] See Kamar, *supra* note 73; Branson, *supra* note 98; see also Kahan & Rock, *supra* note 78.

Whether federal law would be superior or inferior to Delaware law is not clear. Moreover, unlike in the present regime, firms would have no alternative to monopolistic federalist regulation if federal law turns out to be substantially suboptimal.[103]

5 A Note on Competition for Incorporations Elsewhere

The notion that jurisdictions may compete for incorporations is not confined to the United States. There is a significant literature and debate about jurisdictional competition in the European Union[104] and, to a lesser extent, in Canada.[105] If there is one take-away point from this chapter, it is that the dynamics of how firms chose rules, whether and how jurisdictions compete, and how the resulting product would compare with a mandatory regime can play out differently, depending not only on the formal requirements for choosing the corporate domicile, but also the institutional and economic context.

As to firm choice, the factors that will affect whether it will trend to the top or the bottom, and by how much, include the extent to which firms have controlling shareholders; whether shareholdings among non-controlling shareholders are highly dispersed or more concentrated; the presence of information intermediaries; the prevalence of non-law-based devices that align the interests of managers and shareholders; and the degree to which legal rules are reflected in the IPO price.

Predicting whether and how jurisdictions will compete is even harder. We do not have a good model that explains when jurisdictions will act as profit maximizers rather than as political actors. Perhaps the only factor one can identify with reasonable confidence is size: smaller jurisdictions are more likely to compete actively than larger ones. The extent to which jurisdictions will face political costs can also not be generalized. Finally, geographic and language barriers may impede competition. Thus, for example, some of the smallest countries in the European Union, such as Cyprus and Estonia, may make unlikely competitors.

Finally, multi-jurisdictional bodies can differ in the power and the political economy of the central government. Even just considering the constitutional structure, there are major differences. Thus, for example, Canada, like the United States, is a federal state; but as a parliamentary democracy with a weak upper house, it is much easier to pass legislation than it is in the US. The European Union is a treaty-based union of sovereign member states, where the governments of member states have much more influence over EU-wide

---

[103] Romano, *supra* note 88, at 2387.

[104] See, e.g., David Charny, "Competition Among Jurisdictions in Formulating Corporate Law Rules: An American Perspective on the 'Race to the Bottom' in the European Communities", 32 Harv. Int'l. L. J. 423 (1991); Karsten Engsig Sorenson & Mette Neville, "Corporate Migration in the European Union", 6 Colum. J. Eur. L. 181, 186–87 (2000).

[105] See, e.g., Douglas J. Cumming & Jeffrey G. MacIntosh, "The Role of Interjurisdictional Competition in Shaping Canadian Corporate Law", 20 Int'l. Rev. L. & Econ. 141–86 (2000).

legislation than state or provincial governments have over federal legislation in the US or Canada.

Thus, the main lesson that other jurisdictions should draw from the US experience is that it is difficult to draw any lessons. It is not only that different scholars have come to widely different conclusions regarding the three debates that make up the larger state competition debate. More importantly, however one views the dynamics that evolved in the United States, they may evolve differently elsewhere.

6 Conclusion

Absent clear evidence that federal law would be superior to the current system, one may be inclined not to advocate any major changes. For one, the devil we know may be better than the devil we don't know. Delaware law works at least tolerably well, so why take a chance and replace it with some unknown federal rules. Moreover, the current system has at least the feature that, if the political process for some reason produces a deficient law, companies can opt into a different regime.

This suggests that commentators should focus on how to improve the present regime of state competition, rather than on how to replace it. To the extent that firm choice has features that cause firms to choose suboptimal law, can these features be changed? To the extent that states do not compete (and more competition would be desirable), can more states be induced to compete?

Perhaps the most interesting proposal in this vein has been advanced by Lucian Bebchuk, writing with various co-authors. They suggest that, as a matter of federal law, shareholders should be permitted to initiate and approve a reincorporation from one state to another *without* board approval.[106] Although their premise is that the current system trends to the bottom, their proposal should also appeal to commentators who take a nuanced "to the top" position.

There are various complications and details with Bebchuk et al.'s suggestion that would still need to be worked out. Should large shareholders have a fiduciary duty to minority shareholders in pushing for a reincorporation? Should there be a built-in delay between the time shareholders first vote for a reincorporation and the time the reincorporation becomes effective? What would be the status of charter provisions that are invalid in the state that a company migrates to? Should shareholder power to initiate reincorporations be mandatory or should companies have the ability to opt out?

On the other hand, the proposal has some intriguing elements. The present requirement that boards recommend a reincorporation, together with the possibility that managers at least sometimes use their position on and relationship with the board to advance their personal interest, will bias firm choice at the margin downwards. This, in turn, will induce Delaware to position its law to cater more to managerial interests than it would if managers had less power over incorporation decisions. A shake-up in the rules on reincorporation may

---

[106] See Lucian A. Bebchuk & Allen Ferrell, "A New Approach to Takeover Law and Regulatory Competition", 87 Va. L. Rev. 111, 161–63 (2001); Bebchuk & Hamdani, *supra* note 48, at 611–12.

also induce other states to enter the competitive fray. Finally, even for "to the top" scholars, it is easy to think of reasons why Delaware would not, on its own, change its law to permit this option.[107] Thus, even though at present it looks as if shareholders would not avail themselves of a power to initiate reincorporations on a regular basis,[108] giving shareholders this power could improve the competitive dynamic and make the present regime more attractive.

[107] For example, Delaware, as the state with the largest market share, may not want to adopt a rule that makes it easier for firms to change their state of incorporation.

[108] At present, precatory shareholder resolutions requesting the board to propose a reincorporation are scarce and gain little shareholder support. For example, in 2013, there were two such proposals among S&P 1500 companies (each requesting a reincorporation from Oklahoma to Delaware) with neither gathering more than 5% shareholder support. See, Georgeson, *Annual Corporate Governance Review* (2013).

CHAPTER 6

....

CULTURE AND LAW IN
CORPORATE GOVERNANCE

....

AMIR N. LICHT[1]

1 INTRODUCTION

UNDERSTANDING the role of culture in corporate governance has been a subject of growing importance since the latter concept emerged in the late 1980s and even more so since the advent of research on comparative corporate governance during the 1990s.[2] In the beginning, references to culture—when they were made—tended to be impressionistic. Even those references, however, evinced a newly found awareness of the idea that corporate governance is a complex system whose structure and functioning depend on more than law and economics. Today, no institutional analysis of corporate governance systems would be complete without considering the potential role of the cultural environment in which such systems are embedded. This sea change is largely due to the adoption of dimensional models of culture—an analytical framework developed primarily in social psychology. This chapter provides an overview of the different accounts of how culture interacts with the law (especially corporate law) to shape corporate governance and of how this may help explain diversity and persistence in corporate governance.

To motivate the discussion, consider the People's Republic of China. Better yet, consider China together with its Hong Kong SAR, and then Taiwan, South Korea, Japan, and Vietnam for good measure. These countries, on whose significance in today's world economy one need not elaborate, share a deepseated Confucian tradition which goes back up to twenty-five hundred years ago. With inevitable differences and to various degrees, Confucian values and beliefs—namely, culture—permeate all aspects of life in this region of the world. Notwithstanding past attempts to suppress Confucian traditions in China, Confucianism is

[1] Professor of Law, Radzyner Law School, Interdisciplinary Center Herzliya, Israel. alicht@idc.ac.il. For helpful comments, I would like to thank the participants of the Handbook authors' conference held at Columbia Law School.

[2] See Edward B. Rock, "America's Shifting Fascination with Comparative Corporate Governance", 74 Wash. U. L.Q. 367 (1996); Donald C. Clarke, "'Nothing but Wind'? The Past and Future of Comparative Corporate Governance", 59 Am. J. Comp. L. 75 (2011).

on the rise and is taken pride in.[3] Numerous questions thus may warrant analysis. First, are Confucian values also liable to affect the working of corporate governance?[4] Does the all-important concept of guanxi ("relationship" is an imprecise translation) entail implications similar to those that director networks have in US and UK firms?[5] What to make of the fact that both Korea and China have introduced US-inspired "fiduciary duties" of board members into their corporate laws?[6] Should one expect legally mandated independent directors in these countries to resemble their American counterparts—if not now then after some period of adjustment?[7]

The list of questions could go on. In addressing such issues of culture, law, and corporate governance, two kinds of responses are helpful only to a degree. On the one hand, one may point out that "even Confucian managers respond to incentives," as Bernard Black has noted with regard to Korea.[8] On the other hand, a common admonition emphasizes "the need to adapt implementation to varying legal economic and cultural circumstances," as the OECD does with regard to its Principles of Corporate Governance.[9] Both points are well taken, but they do not inform policy- and law-makers how to take culture into account short of ignoring it or just paying it some lip service. What is needed for a meaningful consideration of cultural factors in corporate governance analysis is a tractable framework for comparing cultures. Such an analytical framework could indicate, for instance, whether board members' affiliation with a social network of school alumni may entail similar implications for deeming them independent directors in different countries.[10] Without such a framework, cultural analysis of corporate law and governance runs the risk of being little more than mere hand waving or telling "just-so stories."[11]

---

[3] See generally, Ruiping Fan, ed., The Renaissance of Confucianism in Contemporary China (2011); Daniel A. Bell, China's New Confucianism: Politics and Everyday Life in a Changing Society (2008).

[4] For recent brief discussions with good references, see Kun L.A. Lau & Angus Young, "Why China Shall Not Completely Transit from a Relation Based to a Rule Based Governance Regime: A Chinese Perspective", 21 Corp. Governance: Int'l. Rev. 577 (2013); Lilian Miles & Say Hak Goo, "Corporate Governance in Asian Countries: Has Confucianism Anything to Offer?", 118 Bus. & Soc'y Rev. 23 (2013).

[5] See, e.g., Chao C. Chen, Xiao-Ping Chen, & Shengsheng Huang, "Chinese *Guanxi*: An Integrative Review and New Directions for Future Research", 9 Mgmt. & Org. Rev. 167 (2013). For further discussion, see note 143 and accompanying text.

[6] See Rebecca Lee, "Fiduciary Duty Without Equity: 'Fiduciary Duties' of Directors Under the Revised Company Law of the PRC", 47 Va. J. Int'l. L. 897 (2007); Hwa-Jin Kim, "Living With the IMF: A New Approach to Corporate Governance and Regulation of Financial Institutions in Korea", 17 Berkeley J. Int'l. L. 61 (1999); see also Hideki Kanda & Curtis J. Milhaupt, "Re-examining Legal Transplants: The Director's Fiduciary Duty in Japanese Corporate Law", 51 Am. J. Comp. L. 887 (2003).

[7] See Donald C. Clarke, "The Independent Director in Chinese Corporate Governance", 31 Del. J. Corp. L. 125 (2006).

[8] Bernard S. Black et al., "Corporate Governance in Korea at the Millennium: Enhancing International Competitiveness", 26 J. Corp. L. 199, 545 (2000).

[9] Organisation for Economic Co-operation and Development, OECD Principles of Corporate Governance 10 (2004).

[10] Compare Jordan Siegel, "Contingent Political Capital and International Alliances: Evidence from South Korea", 52 Admin. Sci. Q. 621 (2007); Kelly Shue, "Executive Networks and Firm Policies: Evidence from the Random Assignment of MBA Peers", 26 Rev. Fin. Stud. 1401 (2013).

[11] Amir N. Licht, "Social Norms and the Law: Why Peoples Obey the Law", 4 Rev. L. & Econ. 715 (2008); compare Rudyard Kipling, Just So Stories (1902).

2   WHAT IS CULTURE AND HOW DO WE KNOW IT?

2.1   Basic Concepts

Social scientist Raymond Williams has noted that "[c]ulture is one of the two or three most complicated words in the English language."[12] A definition proposed by the pioneering scholar Geert Hofstede considers culture as "the collective level of mental programming that is shared with some but not all other people" or the "software of the mind."[13] Another simple yet insightful definition of culture would hold that culture defines "what goes with what." This definition reflects the fact that culture refers to implicit knowledge that people have about a wide variety of social practices, ranging from the conduct of leaders and lay people to clothing and food. Only rarely can one find reliable advice on "what goes with what" in guidebooks or in other formal sources.[14] What is "not done" ("faux pas") belongs in the unwritten and unspoken but still widely known in the society.

These definitions may suggest intuitions about what culture is, yet they do not provide an analytical framework for cross-cultural analysis of law and governance. According to a definition by the preeminent anthropologist Clifford Geertz, culture "denotes an historically transmitted pattern of meaning embodied in symbols, a system of inherited conceptions expressed in symbolic forms by means of which men communicate, perpetuate, and develop their knowledge about and attitudes toward life."[15] But what are these "symbolic forms"? Social scientists usually mention values, beliefs, and norms as the major components that constitute culture. Shalom Schwartz thus defines culture as "the latent, normative value system, external to the individual, which underlies and justifies the functioning of societal institutions."[16]

With a meaningful definition of culture at hand, the next step is to identify the ways in which culture may influence individual conduct and social structure. The literature has pointed out two major mechanisms: constraints and motivations. The view of culture as a source of constraints is shared by economists and psychologists. The economic approach deserves some elaboration.[17]

---

[12]   Raymond Williams, Keywords: A Vocabulary of Culture and Society 76 (rev. ed. 1985).

[13]   See, respectively, Geert H. Hofstede, Culture's Consequences: Comparing Values, Behaviors, Institutions and Organizations Across Nations 2 (2d ed., 2001) (hereinafter "Hofstede 2001"); Geert H. Hofstede, Cultures and Organizations: Software of the Mind (3d ed. 2010) (hereinafter "Hofstede 2010").

[14]   Compare top chef Thomas Keller, What Goes with What, Esquire (Feb. 28, 2013) (six tips on how to pair your food).

[15]   Clifford Geertz, The Interpretation of Cultures: Selected Essays 89 (1973).

[16]   Florence R. Kluckhohn & Fred L. Strodtbeck, Variations in Value Orientations (1973).

[17]   For an insightful survey, see Sjoerd Beugelsdijk & Robbert Maseland, Culture in Economics: History, Methodological Reflections, and Contemporary Applications (2011); see also Licht, *supra* note 11. In psychology, see, e.g., Michael Harris Bond & Peter B. Smith, "Cross-Cultural Social and Organizational Psychology", 47 Ann. Rev. Psychol. 205, 209 (1996) (Culture is "shared constraints that limit the behavior repertoire available to members of a certain . . . group."); see also Clifford Geertz, The Interpretation of Cultures: Selected Essays 89 (1973) (defining culture as the values, orientations, and underlying assumptions that are prevalent among the members of a society).

Culture became an issue of central interest with the advent of New Institutional Economics.[18] In a canonical definition of social institutions, Douglas North states: "Institutions are the rules of the game in a society or, more formally, are the humanly devised constraints that shape human interaction."[19] Oliver Williamson has elaborated this notion with a model of stratified social institutions.[20] The analysis of culture and law deals with the informal institutions (culture) located at Level 1 and their relations with formal institutions (law) at Level 2 in his model. According to Williamson, "Level 1 is taken as given by most institutional economists." He further postulates that Level 1 informal institutions are "pervasively linked with complementary institutions," both formal and informal. The resulting institutions "have a lasting grip on the way a society conducts itself."[21]

In this view, the constraining effect of informal institutions is exogenous. Alternatively, informal institutions are modeled as endogenously appearing self-enforcing rules that are the equilibrium of a repeated game, in which the content of such institutions is common knowledge.[22] Social players thus interact with partners assumed to share the same priors (beliefs) and to be guided by a similar set of motivational goals (values). The constraining effect of culture as societal common knowledge in equilibrium stems from the shared conviction that it is in everybody's self-interest to adhere to these values and beliefs unless and until an exogenous shock upsets the equilibrium.

2.2 Cultural Value Dimensions

The thorniest challenge perhaps in introducing culture into institutional analysis stems from its complexity, which makes it difficult to derive tractable, and testable, hypotheses about its role. Cultures are rich, multi-faceted institutions with protracted histories. On the one hand, this richness enables everyone to find, in a particular culture, something to their liking and to tell a just-so story about it. On the other hand, culture's complexity may lead an observer to avoid the details and treat culture as a "black box" but such an approach is, at bottom, similar to the former. A meaningful, rigorous analysis of informal institutions requires a methodology for operationalizing culture, i.e., identifying factors with which cultures could be represented and compared.

---

[18]   A line of scholarship on institutional theory, infused with insights from sociology, has evolved largely in parallel, though there is some recent convergence. I abstract from it for scope limits. See Paul J. DiMaggio & Walter W. Powell, "The Iron Cage Revisited: Institutional Isomorphism and Collective Rationality in Organizational Fields", 48 Am. Soc. Rev. 147 (1983); W. Richard Scott, Institutions and Organizations (2d ed. 2001); W. Richard Scott, "Approaching Adulthood: The Maturing of Institutional Theory", 37 Theory & Soc. 427 (2008).

[19]   Douglass C. North, Institutions, Institutional Change, and Economic Performance 3 (1990).

[20]   Oliver E. Williamson, "The New Institutional Economics: Taking Stock, Looking Ahead", 38 J. Econ. Lit. 595 (2000).

[21]   Williamson, *supra* note 20, at 597.

[22]   See Gérard Roland, "Understanding Institutional Change: Fast-Moving and Slow-Moving Institutions", 38 Stud. Comp. Int'l. Dev. 109 (2004); Masahiko Aoki, Towards a Comparative Institutional Analysis (2001); Avner Greif & David D. Laitin, "A Theory of Endogenous Institutional Change", 98 Am. Pol. Sci. Rev. 633 (2004).

Cross-cultural psychology has made considerable progress toward developing an analytical framework for comparing cultures. A common postulate in cross-cultural psychology is that all societies confront similar basic issues or problems when they come to regulate human activity. The cultural responses to the basic problems that societies face are reflected, among other things, in prevailing value emphases of individuals.[23] Because values vary in importance, it is possible to characterize societies by the relative importance attributed to these values in society using dimensional models. This yields unique cultural profiles for societies or countries.[24]

Among the dimensional models for cross-cultural analysis, by far the more important ones are the models advanced by Hofstede and by Schwartz. Hofstede's pioneering and still influential dimensional framework for characterizing cultures was first published in 1980 using data that were collected from IBM employees around the world during 1968–1973.[25] Hofstede identified four, and later five, value dimensions: individualism/collectivism, power distance, uncertainty avoidance, masculinity/femininity,[26] and long-term orientation.[27] His framework has been used in hundreds of studies; it is widely used in studies on management and accounting and, in recent years, it has gained traction in economics. Table 6.1 provides definitions of the cultural value dimensions distinguished by Hofstede.

Schwartz developed a cultural-level theory during the 1990s and validated it in survey data that covered some 67 nations.[28] Schwartz derives three bipolar cultural value dimensions from three basic issues he identifies as confronting all societies: embeddedness/autonomy, hierarchy/egalitarianism, and mastery/harmony. In coping with these issues, societies exhibit greater or lesser emphasis on the values at one or the other pole of each dimension.

---

[23] See, e.g., Milton Rokeach, The Nature of Human Values (1973); Kluckhohn & Strodtbeck, *supra* note 16.

[24] I use "cultural" and "societal" interchangeably because the present focus is on national societies. However, it is possible to implement the value dimension framework to study sub-national groups. See Heather M. Coon & Markus Kemmelmeier, "Cultural Orientations in the United States: (Re-)examining Differences Among Ethnic Groups", 32 J. Cross-Cultural Psychol. 348 (2001); compare Andriy Boytsun, Marc Deloof, & Paul Matthyssens, "Social Norms, Social Cohesion, and Corporate Governance", 19 Corp. Governance: Int'l. Rev. 41 (2011).

[25] Geert H. Hofstede, Culture's Consequences: International Differences in Work-Related Values (1980); Hofstede 2001, *supra* note 13.

[26] This label has elicited negative responses. Writing originally in 1980, Hofstede nonetheless kept this term, arguing that it reflects a positive reality that is independent of its normative implications. Hofstede 1980, *supra* note 25, at 189–90. In the 2001 edition, Hofstede follows the modern distinction between sex and gender and uses the latter term when referring to social function. Hofstede 2001, *supra* note 13, at 280; see also Geert H. Hofstede & Willem A. Arrindell, Masculinity and Femininity: The Taboo Dimension of National Cultures (1998).

[27] Hofstede added this dimension in 1991 in the first edition of Hofstede 2010, *supra* note 13, in light of a study led by Michael Bond. There, it was named "Confucian work dynamism." See Chinese Cultural Connection, "Chinese Values and the Search for Culture-Free Dimensions of Culture", 18 J. Cross-Cultural Psychol. 143 (1987).

[28] See Shalom H. Schwartz, "Cultural Value Differences: Some Implications for Work", 48 Appl'd Psychol. Int'l. Rev. 23 (1999); Shalom H. Schwartz, "A Theory of Cultural Value Orientations: Explication and Applications", 5 Comp. Soc. 137 (2006) (hereinafter "Schwartz 2006"); Shalom H. Schwartz, Culture Matters: National Value Cultures, Sources and Consequences, in Understanding Culture: Theory, Research and Application 157 (Chi-Yue Chiu et al. eds., 2009).

Table 6.1 The Hofstede Cultural Value Dimensions

Individualism/Collectivism	Valuing loosely knit social relations in which individuals are expected to care only for themselves and their immediate families versus tightly knit relations in which they can expect their wider in-group (e.g., extended family, clan) to look after them in exchange for unquestioning loyalty
Power Distance	Accepting an unequal distribution of power in institutions as legitimate or illegitimate
Uncertainty Avoidance	Feeling uncomfortable or comfortable with uncertainty and ambiguity and therefore valuing or devaluing beliefs and institutions that provide certainty and conformity
Masculinity/Femininity	Valuing achievement, heroism, assertiveness, and material success versus relationships, modesty, caring for the weak, and interpersonal harmony
Long-Term Orientation	Having a long-term time orientation; emphasizing traits of Confucian work ethic, such as thrift and persistence

Seven value orientations on which cultures can be compared derive from the analysis of the bipolar dimensions (due to a distinction between intellectual autonomy and affective autonomy). The theory also specifies the structure of relations among these types of values. Table 6.2 provides definitions of the cultural value dimensions distinguished by Schwartz. Figure 6.1 presents graphically the relations among the value dimensions and orientations as well as values that are prominent in each orientation.

Both the Hofstede and Schwartz models retain their usefulness notwithstanding a generation gap between them. The dimensions of each model bear some conceptual similarity and empirical convergence yet they do not fully overlap. Individualism might exhibit significant relations in a particular study while autonomy would not, whereas in another study egalitarianism may feature highly while power distance would not.[29] Each dimension thus likely captures a somewhat different social institutional feature. Between the two models, Schwartz's model is currently considered more advanced for a number of reasons. First, the model is theory-drive; its central elements having been derived from earlier work in the social sciences. Second, and most important, the model uses value measures shown to have cross-culturally equivalent meanings at the individual level to operationalize the cultural dimensions. Finally, validating data for this model were collected more recently.[30] In addition to the Hofstede and Schwartz frameworks, a handful of other dimensional models

---

[29] See, e.g., Yuriy Gorodnichenko & Gerard Roland, "Which Dimensions of Culture Matter for Long Run Growth?", 101 Am. Econ. Rev. 492 (2011); Mariko J. Klasing, "Cultural Dimensions, Collective Values and their Importance for Institutions", 41 J. Comp. Econ. 447 (2013); Jordan I. Siegel, Amir N. Licht, & Shalom H. Schwartz, "Egalitarianism and International Investment", 102 J. Fin. Econ. 621 (2011).

[30] See Peter B. Smith, Michael Harris Bond, & Cigdem Kagitcibasi, Understanding Social Psychology across Cultures: Living and Working in a Changing World (2006); Beugelsdijk & Maseland, *supra* note 17. Hofstede's framework has met a series of criticisms. For a review and responses to these criticisms, see Hofstede 2001, *supra* note 13.

Table 6.2 The Schwartz Cultural Value Dimensions

Embeddedness/Autonomy	This dimension concerns the desirable relationship between the individual and the group. Embeddedness represents a cultural emphasis on maintenance of the status quo, propriety, and restraint of actions or inclinations that might disrupt the solidary group or the traditional order. The opposite pole describes cultures in which the person is viewed as an autonomous, bounded entity who finds meaning in his or her own uniqueness.
Hierarchy/Egalitarianism	This dimension refers to guaranteeing responsible behavior that will preserve the social fabric. Hierarchy represents a cultural emphasis on obeying role obligations within a legitimately unequal distribution of power, roles, and resources. Egalitarianism represents an emphasis on transcendence of selfish interests in favor of voluntary commitment to promoting the welfare of others.
Mastery/Harmony	This dimension refers to the relation of humankind to the natural and social world. Mastery stands for a cultural emphasis on getting ahead through active self-assertion whereas Harmony represents an emphasis on fitting harmoniously into the environment.

and datasets that share a similar impetus also allow for cross-cultural analysis. Because they are less frequently used and suffer from various limitations that cannot be discussed in the present scope, I abstract from them here.[31]

2.2.1 *Social Capital*

A different vantage point for considering culture and corporate governance draws on social capital theory. While there is no agreed upon definition of social capital, much of the discourse about it is dominated by the views of James Coleman and Robert Putnam.[32] Social

[31] See, in particular, Ronald Inglehart & Wayne E. Baker, "Modernization, Cultural Change, and the Persistence of Traditional Values", 65 Am. Soc. Rev. 19, 24 tbl. 1 (2000); for details and data, see World Values Survey, available at http://www.worldvaluessurvey.org (last visited Feb. 13, 2014). For a comparative discussion, see Schwartz 2006, *supra* note 28; see also Global Leadership & Organizational Behavior Effectiveness (GLOBE), Project, Culture, Leadership, and Organizations: The GLOBE Study of 62 Societies (Robert J. House et al. eds., 2004); Charles M. Hampden-Turner & Fons Trompenaars, Building Cross-Cultural Competence: How to Create Wealth from Conflicting Values (2000); Michael Harris Bond et al., "Culture-Level Dimensions of Social Axioms and Their Correlates Across 41 Cultures", 35 J. Cross-Cultural Psychol. 548 (2004); Michele J. Gelfrand, Lisa H. Nishii, & Jana L. Rayer, "On the Nature and Importance of Cultural Tightness-Looseness", 91 J. Applied Psychol. 1225 (2006); Michele J. Gelfrand, et al., "Differences between Tight and Loose Cultures: A 33-Nation Study", 332 Sci. 1100 (2011).

[32] James S. Coleman, "Social Capital in the Creation of Human Capital", 94 Am. J. Soc. S95 (1988); Robert D. Putnam, Making Democracy Work: Civic Traditions in Modern Italy (1993); Robert D. Putnam, Bowling Alone: The Collapse and Revival of American Community (2000); see also Pierre Bourdieu, The Forms of Capital, in The Handbook of Theory: Research for the Sociology of Education 241 (John G. Richardson ed., 1986). For a historical survey, see James Farr, "Social Capital: A Conceptual History", 32 Pol. Theory 6 (2004).

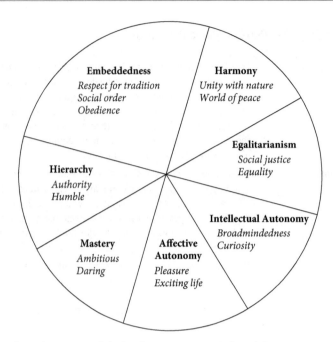

FIGURE 6.1 The Schwartz Model of Relations among Cultural Orientations.

capital consists of shared values, beliefs, and norms—hence the conceptual proximity to culture. The most prominent norm is a norm of generalized trust, defined as the shared belief that most others are trustworthy and therefore have benign intentions or, more technically, the probability that two randomly chosen people will trust each other in a one-time interaction. According to Coleman, a group within which there is extensive trustworthiness and extensive trust is able to accomplish much more than a comparable group that lacks them. A social norm of generalized trust entails wide-ranging implications, including implications for corporate governance, as this norm implies lesser concern with, and perhaps lesser incidence of, opportunistic behavior in firms. This, in turn, may be conducive to economic growth and other beneficial effects.[33]

Operationalizing and measuring generalized trust—especially with the "generally speaking question" in Inglehart's World Values Survey and in similar surveys in Europe and the United States—is not free of issues, however.[34] Indeed, the very notion of trust is currently debated and is anything but stable even as a concept.[35] Nevertheless, social capital theory goes beyond theories of cultural value dimensions in pointing out the centrality of

[33] See Stephen Knack & Philip Keefer, "Does Social Capital Have an Economic Payoff? A Cross-Country Investigation", 112 Q. J. Econ. 1251 (1997); Paul J. Zak & Stephen Knack, "Trust and Growth", 111 Econ. J. 295 (2001); Roman Horváth, "Does Trust Promote Growth?", 41 J. Comp. Econ. 777 (2013).

[34] Specifically, the question is: "Generally speaking, would you say that most people can be trusted, or that you cannot be too careful in dealing with people?" See Benjamin Volland, "Trust, Confidence, and Economic Growth: An Evaluation of the Beugelsdijk Hypothesis", Working Paper (2010).

[35] See Ken Newton & Sonja Zmerli, "Three Forms of Trust and their Association", 3 Eur. Pol. Sci. Rev. 169 (2011).

social networks, in which social relationships and interactions are embedded.[36] Ties in social networks function as information channels for observing, monitoring, advising, and consulting with others, etc.

These observations point to various structural features of social networks as factors that may affect their functioning, including in corporate governance. For example, a network's density, defined as the number of ties between actors in a network, may positively affect the flow of information. Dense networks thus may discourage opportunistic behavior within the network because defection is more likely to be observed due to lower information asymmetry. A separate line of social network scholarship initiated by Ronald Burt emphasizes a structural feature dubbed "structural holes." A structural hole denotes weaker connections between groups that impede the flow of information between them, while providing those who can bridge a hole with opportunities to derive private benefits from such brokerage.[37]

2.2.2 Causality

Culture used to have a bad name among economists. It was not particularly popular among lawyers either. One reason probably was that culture is very difficult to observe. One may therefore fear that people would resort to cultural explanations when they run out of good ones, as the former would be impossible to disprove—what was referred to above as "just-so stories." This problem can be addressed by using data on cultural dimensions that derive from rigorous operationalization methodologies. Integrating cultural factors into institutional analyses faces another challenge, however—of showing causality. Because culture comprises values and beliefs and these factors are usually assessed using survey data, one might fear that cultural observations might be either merely epiphenomenal—namely, reflections of more fundamental factors—or endogenous with other institutional factors or policy outcomes. These concerns are well taken.

To argue that "culture matters" one therefore needs to go beyond showing significant correlations to adducing evidence for causal effects of culture. Using panel data that include observations over time may not be informative because, barring major shocks, cultures evolve over very long timespans, ranging from decades to millennia. To assess the causal role of culture on institutions and policy outcomes, scholars in the last decade thus have relied on a different approach that employs instrumental variables, some of them quite imaginative. Briefly, a good instrument should relate to culture in a meaningful way and relate to the dependent factor only through its relation to culture. Luigi Guiso, Paula Sapienza, and Luigi Zingales used historical data on wars and genetic data to gauge the impact of trust on economic exchange.[38] In a joint study with Chanan Goldschmidt and Shalom Schwartz, we

---

[36] See Mark Granovetter, "Economic Action and Social Structure: The Problem of Embeddedness", 91 Am. J. Soc. 481 (1985); Mark Granovetter, "The Impact of Social Structure on Economic Outcomes", 19 J. Econ. Persp. 33 (2005).

[37] For a discussion of networks' structural features, see Amir Barnea, Cesare Fracassi, & Ilan Guedj, "Director Networks", Working Paper (2013); Ronald S. Burt, Martin Kilduff, & Stefano Tasselli, "Social Network Analysis: Foundations and Frontiers on Advantage", 64 Ann. Rev. Psychol. 527 (2013).

[38] Luigi Guiso, Paola Sapienza, & Luigi Zingales, "Does Culture Affect Economic Outcomes?", 20 J. Econ. Persp. 23 (2006).

introduced linguistic variables on grammar of the dominant language to establish an effect of embeddedness/autonomy on the rule of law, corruption, and democratic accountability in nations.[39] Another joint study, with Jordan Siegel and Shalom Schwartz, used past war experience, religion, and societal fractionalization to assess the role of egalitarianism on international investment.[40] Recent studies exploit data on the natural environment such as parasite and pathogen prevalence and on rainfall as instruments for individualism.[41]

3 CULTURE'S CONSEQUENCES FOR CORPORATE GOVERNANCE

3.1 Relevance

So culture matters. But (how) does it matter for corporate governance? (How) does it interact with corporate laws to affect corporate governance? According to Beugelsdijk & Maseland, "many scholars struggle with the concept of culture. It is unclear whether legal origin is seen as culture (it is, just like culture, an exogenous factor) or whether there is a relationship between legal origin and culture."[42]

A key insight here is that culture, as an informal institution, can address the very issues that governance, including corporate governance, calls for regulating. Formal social institutions and formal private arrangements—that is, laws and contracts, respectively— must rely on shared understandings among societal members about persons and property, about interpersonal relations, or about the dynamics of life. I have argued that in a corporate governance setting, cultural orientations regarding these issues would bear on a broad set of questions, including modes of corporate finance, primary approaches to stakeholders, shareholding structures, self-dealing, executive compensation, disclosure, and so forth.[43] The cultural value dimension framework allows for opening the "black box" of culture and forming testable hypotheses about which cultural orientation may be related to a particular corporate governance issue in light of the content meaning of that issue.[44] Moreover, with an appropriate methodology, causal claims about culture's consequences for corporate governance can be made and tested.

---

[39] Amir N. Licht, Chanan Goldschmidt, & Shalom H. Schwartz, "Culture Rules: The Foundations of the Rule of Law and Other Norms of Governance", 35 J. Comp. Econ. 659 (2007).

[40] Siegel et al., *supra* note 29.

[41] See Robbert Maseland, "Parasitical Cultures? The Cultural Origins of Institutions and Development", 18 J. Econ. Growth 109 (2013); Yuriy Gorodnichenko & Gérard Roland, "Culture, Institutions and Democratization", Working Paper (2013); Lewis Davis, "Individual Responsibility and Economic Development: Evidence from Rainfall Data", 69 Kyklos Int'l. Rev. Soc. Sci. 426 (2016).

[42] Beugelsdijk & Maseland, *supra* note 17, at 254.

[43] For a detailed theory, see Amir N. Licht, "The Mother of all Path Dependencies: Toward a Cross-Cultural Theory of Corporate Governance Systems", 26 Del. J. Corp. L. 147 (2001); for a current discussion and review, see Ruth V. Aguilera & Gregory Jackson, "Comparative and International Corporate Governance", 4 Acad. Mgmt. Annals 485 (2010).

[44] Licht, *supra* note 43.

To get a flavor of how culture might impact corporate governance, consider CEO succession—one of the most significant challenges faced by every company, its board, and its shareholders. Early references to culture in this regard tended to be highly impressionistic.[45] Granted, the culture of some countries may engender rather idiosyncratic practices for ensuring the quality of controlling persons. For instance, Vikas Mehrotra et al. report that, in Japan, controlling families may adopt a brilliant executive with an average pedigree with a view to handing him (it's him all right) the family firm.[46] This is a fascinating example that powerfully drives home the point that culture matters for corporate governance, but from this it is hard to generalize a lesson for other countries. Drawing on Hofstede's dimensions, these authors propose in a separate study that the spread of marriage for love helps undermine the family firm as a dominant business institution in many countries by depriving those firms of suitable heirs. This tendency is linked to cultural emphases on power distance, collectivism, and uncertainty avoidance.[47] These authors further find that family firm dominance in the economy interacted with arranged marriage norms and also correlates with lower economic development, suggesting that cultural inertia may also impede convergence to more efficient economic organization.

At the most general level of analysis of the structure of economic systems—sometimes referred to as "varieties of capitalism"[48]—culture has been linked to large-scale variation in such structures. Using the Schwartz dimensions, Frederic Pryor has shown that certain combinations of cultural orientations match the particular economic systems of OECD countries and in fact exert a causal effect on these systems.[49] Wolfgang Breuer and Astrid Salzmann observe that stronger cultural emphases on embeddedness, egalitarianism, and harmony in the Schwartz model correlate with bank-based corporate governance systems, whereas opposite cultural emphases correlate with market-based systems.[50] Their results are robust to legal origin, which has separately been linked to varieties of capitalism.[51] Chuck Kwok and Solomon Tadesse have related the prevalence of bank-based versus

---

[45] See, e.g., Lucian Arye Bebchuk & Mark J. Roe, "A Theory of Path Dependence in Corporate Governance and Ownership", 52 Stan. L. Rev. 127, 169 (1999) ("American culture, for example, resists hierarchy and centralized authority more than, say, French culture. German citizens are proud of their national codetermination. Italian family firm owners may get special utility from a longstanding family-controlled business, while an American family might prefer to cash the company earlier and run the family scion for the U.S. Senate.").

[46] See Vikas Mehrotra et al., "Adoptive Expectations: Rising Sons in Japanese Family Firms", 108 J. Fin. Econ. 840 (2013). The authors are Vikas Mehrotra, Randall Morck, Jungwook Shim, and Yupana Wiwattanakantang.

[47] See Vikas Mehrotra et al., "Must Love Kill the Family Firm? Some Exploratory Evidence", 35 Entrepreneurship Theory & Prac. 1121 (2011).

[48] See Varieties of Capitalism: The Institutional Foundations of Comparative Advantage (Peter A. Hall & David Soskice eds., 2001); see also Curtis J. Milhaupt & Katharina Pistor, Law & Capitalism (2008).

[49] See Frederic L. Pryor, "Culture Rules: A Note on Economic Systems and Values", 36 J. Comp. Econ. 510 (2008).

[50] Wolfgang Breuer & Astrid Salzmann, National Culture and Corporate Governance, in Corporate Governance: Recent Developments and New Trends 369 (Sabri Boubaker et al. eds., 2012).

[51] See, e.g., Rafael La Porta, Florencio Lopez-de-Silanes, & Andrei Shleifer, "The Economic Consequences of Legal Origins", 46 J. Econ. Lit. 285 (2008).

market-based corporate governance systems to cultural emphases on Hofstede's uncertainty avoidance.[52]

3.2 General Relations between Law and Culture

The following sections review the relations between cultural orientations and particular subjects of corporate governance. Prior to that, this section discusses the general relations between culture and law, especially corporate law. As Williamson's model of social institutions explicates, in a standard setting, culture and law may interact. Culture sets informal constraints and provides motivations for developing the law in a culturally compatible fashion. In tandem, societal patterns of compliance with, or deviance from, culturally compatible laws inculcate in societal members the value emphases that these laws reflect.

On a deeper level than formal legal rules there lies the institution of legality—the rule of law or, more roughly, property rights, quality of institutions, or simply institutions. A social norm of legality functions as an interface between the informal and formal institutional level. For any law, including corporate law, to operate as designed there must exist a widely shared social norm of law abidingness and law enforcement. Such a norm of legality means that the legal entitlements of societal members are respected—namely, their personal safety, tangible and intangible property (e.g., shares and other cash-flow rights in firms), and other legal interests (e.g., voting rights). Every legal system by definition calls on people to obey the law, yet countries vary greatly in the degree to which laws are followed. A social norm of legality can ensure that formal laws are followed by drawing its injunctive force from its compatibility with certain cultural values—in particular, values that underscore the legitimacy of personal interests and the moral equality of individuals.[53]

A study with Goldschmidt and Schwartz confirms that cultural emphases primarily on Schwartz's autonomy and on Hofstede's individualism cause countries to have higher levels of legality and lower levels of corruption (which are related).[54] A follow-up study with Amnon Lehavi extends this finding to greater protection of both tangible property and intellectual property in countries.[55] Claudia Williamson and Carrie Kerekes show that when both formal and informal institutional components are included in the analysis, the impact of formal constraints in explaining the security of property is greatly diminished, while informal constraints are highly significant.[56]

Exogenous shocks may take place at either or both levels of institutions. For example, a major war or conquest experience can affect cultural orientations. Such is the case, for

---

[52] Chuck C. Y. Kwok & Solomon Tadesse, "National Culture and Financial Systems", 37 J. Int'l. Bus. Stud. 227 (2006).

[53] See Licht, *supra* note 11.   [54] See Licht, Goldschmidt, & Schwartz, *supra* note 39.

[55] See Amnon Lehavi & Amir N. Licht, "BITs and Pieces of Property", 36 Yale J. Int'l. L. 115 (2011).

[56] See Claudia R. Williamson & Carrie B. Kerekes, "Securing Private Property: Formal versus Informal Institutions", 54 J. L. & Econ. 537 (2011). These authors use measures for culture from the World Values Survey, Schwartz, and Hofstede.

example, with regard to a heritage of state-formation wars during the nineteenth century that promoted an ethos of equality of sacrifice, which today associates positively with egalitarianism.[57] This is also the case with regard to a communist-rule experience, which is negatively linked to egalitarianism.[58] The level of egalitarianism in a country in turn may affect, among other things, legally mandated board representation of non-shareholder constituencies as well as other features that are conceptually compatible with egalitarianism. At the formal institutional level, the most well-known exogenous shock in the social institutions and corporate governance literature is British rule, either colonial or in other modes, which nearly invariably entailed the transplantation of a common law legal system; other colonial powers tended to implement a similar transplantation approach with regard to their home legal system. This heritage has affected a massive set of legal rules, including those on investor rights.[59]

In an exploratory study with Goldschmidt and Schwartz, we observe that countries' affiliation with a common-law origin is associated with lower uncertainty avoidance in Hofstede's model, and with lower harmony in Schwartz's model. Moreover, the scores of legal rules of investor protection constructed by La Porta, Lopez-de-Silanes, Shleifer, and Vishny (LLSV) correlate negatively with these cultural orientations, whereas LLSV's scores of formalism in the court system correlate positively with these orientations.[60] These results are consistent with the view that a history of British rule has left an impact on both the culture and on the general "legal style," with the result that these nations are more receptive to uncertain and open-ended, even entrepreneurial, mechanisms. Another set of analyses shows that classifications of countries according to legal origin and cultural region correlate with one another, in line with Williamson's theory.

In a joint study with Siegel and Schwartz, we document positive correlations between egalitarianism and a set of legal rules that support the weak in the society, especially employees, the sick, and the elderly, thus reflecting a societal stance against abuse of power.[61] Hao Liang and Luc Renneboog show that an index of country-level regulatory framework in relation to sustainability—a facet of corporate social responsibility (CSR)—correlates robustly with countries' legal origin and also with their scores on some of Hofstede's dimensions.[62] These findings together indicate that neither legal nor cultural classifications, when considered in isolation, may sufficiently account for variations in

---

[57] Siegel et al., *supra* note 29.

[58] See Shalom H. Schwartz, Anat Bardi, & Gabriel Bianchi, Value Adaptation to the Imposition and Collapse of Communist Regimes in East-Central Europe, in Political Psychology: Cultural and Cross-Cultural Foundations 217 (Stanley A Renshon & John Duckitt eds., 2000); Jordan I. Siegel, Amir N. Licht, & Shalom H. Schwartz, "Egalitarianism, Cultural Distance, and Foreign Direct Investment: A New Approach", 24 Org. Sci. 1174 (2013).

[59] This literature is too broad to cite here. For a survey see, La Porta et al., *supra* note 51; see also in this volume, chapters 6, 11, and 12.

[60] See Amir N. Licht, Chanan Goldschmidt, & Shalom H. Schwartz, "Culture, Law, and Corporate Governance", 25 Int'l. Rev. L. & Econ. 229 (2005).

[61] Siegel et al., *supra* note 29.

[62] See Hao Liang & Luc Renneboog, "The Foundations of Corporate Social Responsibility", ECGI Working Paper 394 (2013).

countries' legal regimes of corporate governance. Both levels of social institutions should be taken into consideration.[63]

3.2.1 A Note on Legal Transplants

The idea that formal laws and the functioning of the entire legal system may depend on cultural values in turn implicates the transplantation of legal rules—possibly the most prominent means for policy reform, especially in corporate governance. Legal transplantation is explored in detail in other chapters of this volume. Here, it will suffice to make a brief note on the role of culture.

Legal transplantation may occur through different channels. Transplantation may occur involuntarily, as already noted, consequent to colonial occupation. Japan thus received a version of the Illinois business corporation law because the legal team at the headquarters of General Douglas MacArthur, the Supreme Commander of the Allied Powers after World War II, comprised of lawyers from Chicago.[64] Legal transplantation often takes place voluntarily through importation of legal mechanisms by legislators—as Korea did with regard to independent directors and US-like fiduciary duties of board members[65]—or by courts—as Israel did with regard to US-like fiduciary duties of controlling shareholders.[66]

Whatever may be the channel of legal transplantation, the cultural environment of the receiving country plays a significant role in determining the manner and extent to which the transplant integrates with the receiving legal system.[67] People are more likely to comply with the law voluntarily to the extent that a social norm of legality prevails in general and to the extent that the transplant is conceptually compatible with the values that the local law reflects. Young Jeong, in a sober assessment of Korea's corporate governance reform program, thus implicates different facets of Korea's Confucian culture for the limited success with which the US-oriented legal amendments have met.[68] A similar rejection of a legal transplant could take place even when the graft is synthetic rather than harvested from a real

[63] This point thus calls into question the attempt of La Porta et al., *supra* note 51, to disprove an argument that "legal origins [are] merely proxies for cultural variables." Beyond certain shortcomings of their empirical approach, which considers a very limited set of legal rules and cultural orientations, the very hypotheses looks dubious in light of current theory and findings.

[64] See Mark D. West, "The Puzzling Divergence of Corporate Law: Evidence and Explanations from Japan and the United States", 150 U. Pa. L. Rev. 527 (2001).

[65] See *supra* note 6 and accompanying text. The Korean corporate governance reform was not entirely voluntary, however, in that it came in the wake of the 1997 Asian financial crisis which forced Korea to apply for support from international financial institutions. See Hwa-Jin Kim, "Living with the IMF: A New Approach to Corporate Governance and Regulation of Financial Institutions in Korea", 17 Berkeley J. Int'l. L. 61 (1999).

[66] C.A. 817/79, *Kossoy v. Y.L. Feuchtwanger Bank Ltd.*, 38(3) P.D. 253. See Amir N. Licht, "David's Dilemma: A Case Study of Securities Regulation in a Small Open Market", 2 Theoretical Inquiries L. 673 (2001).

[67] I abstract from a related question dealing with the source from which a country may want to import a legal transplant. Cultural proximity would be beneficial here, too. See John Armour et al., "How Do Legal Rules Evolve? Evidence from a Cross-Country Comparison of Shareholder, Creditor, and Worker Protection", 57 Am. J. Comp. L. 579 (2009).

[68] See Young-Cheol David K. Jeong, "Charting Corporate and Financial Governance in Korea in the New Decade", 2 Jindal Global L. Rev. 99 (2011); see also Amir N. Licht, "Legal Plug-Ins: Cultural Distance, Cross-Listing, and Corporate Governance Reform", 22 Berkeley J. Int'l. L. 195 (2004).

legal-system donor. Bernard Black, Reinier Kraakman, and Anna Tarassova thus attributed the colossal failure of a corporate law statute for Russia, which was designed to be more immune to the weaknesses of the court system there, to the country's culture of extreme self-dealing and corruption.[69] One may note that the latter two norms reflect lower autonomy and egalitarianism.

3.3 The Objectives of the Corporation

The debate over the objectives of the business corporation is one of the oldest and probably the most fundamental in corporate law. The proposition that shareholders are the primary beneficiaries of the corporation and hence directors' duties run to them is generally interpreted as calling on corporate fiduciaries to maximize (long-term) shareholder value.[70] The literature often refers to this proposition in shorthand as the "shareholder primacy norm" or the "shareholder wealth maximization norm." In contrast to shareholder primacy there stands an opposite view—the "stakeholder approach"—which calls on corporate fiduciaries to take into account, in addition to shareholders' interest, also the interests of other constituencies, including employees, creditors, customers, and the community.[71]

Legal doctrine regarding the objectives of the corporation varies among jurisdictions. Although common law and civil law jurisdictions often have been characterized as, respectively, shareholder-oriented and stakeholder-oriented,[72] even a cursory analysis challenges such a clear distinction. Thus, the laws of the state of Delaware and of the United Kingdom endorse the shareholder-oriented approach. In Delaware, the ruling in *Gheewalla*[73] underscored shareholder primacy and dispelled any possible ambiguities in the wake of *Credit Lyonnais*.[74] UK law authorizes board members to consider the interests of non-shareholder constituencies but subordinates the latter to a primary objective of promoting "the success of the company for the benefit of its members [shareholders] as a whole."[75] In Canada, however, the Supreme Court's ruling in *BCE*[76] endorsed an approach that balances the interests of different (financial) constituencies. Finally, Indian law is a chimera requiring

---

[69] See Bernard Black, Reinier Kraakman, & Anna Tarassova, "Russian Privatization and Corporate Governance: What Went Wrong?", 52 Stan. L. Rev. 1731 (2000).

[70] See, e.g., Michael P. Dooley, Fundamentals of Corporation Law 97 (1995); D. Gordon Smith, "The Shareholder Primacy Norm", 23 J. Corp. L. 277 (1998).

[71] See Martin Gelter, "Taming or Protecting the Modern Corporation? Shareholder-Stakeholder Debates in a Comparative Light", 7 N.Y.U. J.L. & Bus. 641 (2011); Amir N. Licht, "The Maximands of Corporate Governance: A Theory of Values and Cognitive Style", 29 Del. J. Corp. L. 649 (2004); Michael Bradley et al., "The Purposes and Accountability of the Corporation in Contemporary Society: Corporate Governance at a Crossroads", 62 L. & Contemp. Probs. 9 (1999).

[72] See, e.g., Bradley et al., *supra* note 71; for empirical evidence, see Dan S. Dhaliwal et al., "Nonfinancial Disclosure and Analyst Forecast Accuracy: International Evidence on Corporate Social Responsibility Disclosure", 87 Acct. Rev. 723 (2012).

[73] *N. Am. Catholic Education v. Gheewalla*, 930 A.2d 92 (Del. 2007).

[74] *Credit Lyonnais Bank Nederland, N.V. v. Pathe Communications Corp.*, 1991 WL 277613 (Del. Ch. 1991); see also Lyman Johnson, "Unsettledness in Delaware Corporate Law: Business Judgment Rule, Corporate Purpose", 38 Del. J. Corp. L. 405 (2013).

[75] Section 172 of the Companies Act, 2006 (U.K.).

[76] *BCE Inc. v. 1976 Debentureholders*, 2008 SCC 69, [2008] 3 S.C.R. 560.

directors "to promote the objects of the company for the benefit of its members as a whole, and in the best interests of the company, its employees, the shareholders, the community and for the protection of environment."[77]

In the civil law tradition things are not clearer. German law famously vests the managing board with the responsibility "to manage the corporation as the good of the enterprise and its retinue and the common wealth of folk and realm demand."[78] In China, the 2005 revision of its corporate law requires companies to comply with "social morality" and to "bear social responsibilities."[79] In Sweden, however, the objective of business corporations is to generate profits for shareholders.[80]

The decades-long debate on this subject shows no sign of abating. Meanwhile, recent research provides several insights with regard to the role of values and culture that shed new light on it. First, whatever the law might say on the objectives of the corporation, board members and top executives may adopt strategies that stray from that injunction. A joint study with Renée Adams and Lilach Sagiv finds that in Sweden, a social-democratic economy with a shareholder-oriented company law, board members and CEOs vary systematically in their willingness to endorse strategic actions that benefit shareholders at the expense of other stakeholders or balance the interests of several stakeholders.[81] This individual "shareholderism" stance is linked to directors' personal value profile; the more one endorses entrepreneurial values as guiding principles in one's life, the more one supports shareholder-oriented strategies, and vice versa. Managers apparently draw on their personal values in deciding what is the right thing for the firm, the law notwithstanding.

This finding at the individual level of analysis points to culture at the societal level of analysis as an institution that, in tandem with the law, can exert substantial influence on corporations' strategic behavior in shareholder–stakeholder dilemmas. The cultural orientations that prevails in a country may affect the individual value preferences of managers and thus tilt their strategic decisions in a culturally compatible direction. In addition, and regardless of their personal values, managers may also assess the public expectations of the surrounding social environment, what would be considered publicly legitimate, and so forth, and opt for compatible strategies.[82] Specifically, firms in more egalitarian societies would endorse more stakeholderist strategies, as this cultural orientation expresses a moral equality of all people. Higher harmony may also be related to stakeholderist strategies as it reflects lesser tolerance toward exploitation of the social and natural environment. In the Hofstede model, individualism may relate to shareholderism as the former

---

[77] Section 166(2) of the Companies Act, 2013 (India).

[78] Section 70 of the 1937 Aktiengesetz; see Gelter, *supra* note 71.

[79] Section 5 of the Company Law of the People's Republic of China.

[80] This widely accepted doctrine derives from the Swedish Companies Act, 2005, Ch. 3, § 3, which requires companies with a different objective to state this clearly in the articles of association.

[81] See Renée B. Adams, Amir N. Licht, & Lilach Sagiv, "Shareholders and Stakeholders: How Do Directors Decide", 32 Strategic Mgmt. J. 1331 (2011).

[82] See Licht, *supra* note 43; Ruth V. Aguilera & Gregory Jackson, "The Cross-National Diversity of Corporate Governance: Dimensions and Determinants", 28 Acad. Mgmt. Rev. 447 (2003); Dirk Matten & Jeremy Moon, "'Implicit' and 'Explicit' CSR: A Conceptual Framework for a Comparative Understanding of Corporate Social Responsibility", 33 Acad. Mgmt. Rev. 404 (2008).

connotes selfishness at the expense of others, but this conjecture is qualified by the fact that the opposite orientation, collectivism, focuses on the in-group.

Recent empirical studies provide some support for these hypotheses. A study by Siegel and Barbara Larson finds that subsidiaries of a large multinational company adjust their employment practices to the host countries' egalitarianism levels.[83] In a study with Siegel and Schwartz, we show positive correlations between cultural egalitarianism and national averages of a series of firm-level CSR practices such as paying greater firm surplus to employees, voluntary (i.e., non-legally mandated) nonfinancial (CSR) disclosure, and organizational practices that consider human rights in the process of selecting or terminating suppliers or sourcing partners and which take the general community into consideration more generally.[84] Kurt Desender and Mircea Epure present a more systematic analysis, finding robust relations between egalitarianism and a set of indexes for corporate social performance (CSP).[85] Although highly suggestive, limitations of current data on CSR, among other things, render these findings tentative at this stage.[86]

3.4 Relations with Investors (and Other Stakeholders)

Defined as the institutional framework that regulates the division and exercise of power in the corporation,[87] corporate governance addresses the multiple relations among corporate stakeholders, including shareholders, managers, employees, creditors, and others. This section demonstrates the role that culture may play with regard to key issues in the relations with investors and other stakeholder—namely, earnings management, as a facet of the informational regime that governs public companies, and dividend policy, as a facet of firms' financial relations with its stakeholders.

---

[83] See Jordan I. Siegel & Barbara Z. Larson, "Labor Market Institutions and Global Strategic Adaptation: Evidence from Lincoln Electric", 55 Mgmt. Sci. 1527 (2009).

[84] Siegel et al., *supra* note 29.

[85] Kurt A. Desender & Mircea Epure, "Corporate Governance and Corporate Social Performance", Working Paper (2013); see also Gijs van den Heuvel, Joseph Soeters, & Tobias Gössling, "Global Business, Global Responsibilities: Corporate Social Responsibility Orientations Within a Multinational Bank", 53 Bus. Soc. 378 (2014).

[86] On the role of social networking see David Diaz, Babis Theodoulidis, & Azar Shahgholian, "Social Networking Influence on Environmental and Corporate Performance", Working Paper (2012). Evidence using Hofstede dimensions is somewhat inconclusive. See Ioannis Ioannou & George Serafeim, "What Drives Corporate Social Performance? The Role of Nation-Level Institutions", 34 J. Int'l. Bus. Stud. 834 (2012); Foo Nin Ho, Hui-Ming Deanna Wang, & Scott J. Vitell, "A Global Analysis of Corporate Social Performance: The Effects of Cultural and Geographic Environments", 107 J. Bus. Ethics 423 (2012).

[87] Amir N. Licht, Corporate Governance, in Handbook of Financial Globalization 369, 369 (Gerard Caprio ed., 2013). For similarly spirited definitions, see Jean Tirole, "Corporate Governance", 69 Econometrica 1, 4 (2001) ("[I] define corporate governance as the design of institutions that induce or force management to internalize the welfare of stakeholders."); Luigi Zingales, Corporate Governance, in The New Palgrave Dictionary of Economics (Steven N. Durlauf & Lawrence E. Blume eds., online 2d ed. 2008) ("I define corporate governance as the complex set of constraints that shape the ex post bargaining over the quasi-rents generated by a firm."); Aguilera & Jackson, *supra* note 43 ("Corporate governance may be defined broadly as the study of power and influence over decision making within the corporation.").

3.4.1 Disclosure: Earnings Management

Information asymmetry is pivotal in engendering agency problems. Societies, firms, and individual actors may respond to the challenge posed by agency problems through different measures of disclosure with a view to mitigating these information asymmetries. A disclosure regime regulates the way in which firms communicate with their stakeholders and with market participants more generally. Much of this communication takes place through highly formatted financial statements that are regulated by formal legal rules and accounting standards. Within this formal straitjacket, insiders may still have some wiggle room to massage the financial statements a little bit (short of cooking the books). At the heart of this endeavor lies the financial bottom line—the firm's earnings numbers. Since accounting scholars pioneered the implementation of the cultural value dimension framework, we now have a good deal of research on culture's consequences for various accounting issues,[88] including earnings management.

Earnings management is the practice of exercising judgment in financial reporting to mislead some stakeholders about firm performance or to influence contractual outcomes.[89] Corporate insiders may want to manage earnings numbers in order to be eligible to contingent remuneration, or to meet financial covenants in debt instruments, or to meet analysts' expectations to avoid an embarrassment, and so forth. Earnings can be managed to reduce intertemporal variability in reported earning ("smoothing") or to meet certain targets. In a study of earnings management around the world, Christian Leuz, Dhananjay Nanda, and Peter Wysocki have found a significant negative relation between earnings management and two measures of investor protection through the legal system—namely, legal enforcement (rule of law) and outside investor rights, proxied with LLSV's index.[90] This finding is consistent with the idea that legal systems that better protect investor rights do this also through increasing transparency about "unpleasant" information and reducing insiders' discretion in their communication with the market.

Against this backdrop, Timothy Doupnik has found that Hofstede's uncertainty avoidance correlates positively and individualism correlates negatively with earnings management across a broad cross-section of countries. Culture was found to have greater explanatory power with regard to earnings smoothing and to explain more variation than Leuz et al.'s legal factors.[91] Several subsequent studies corroborate Doupnik's results and also document a negative relation between earnings management and Schwartz's egalitarianism, with some observing that formal legal measures lose significance altogether as predictors for earnings management when culture is entered in the regressions.[92]

---

[88] See Sidney J. Gray, "Towards a Theory of Cultural Influence on the Development of Accounting Systems Internationally", 24 Abacus 1 (1988); Stephen B. Salter & Frederick Niswander, "Cultural Influence on the Development of Accounting Systems Internationally: A Test of Gray's (1988) Theory", 26 J. Int'l. Bus. Stud. 379 (1995).

[89] See Paul M. Healy & James M. Wahlen, "A Review of the Earnings Management Literature and Its Implications for Standard Setting", 13 Acct. Horizons 365 (1999).

[90] See Christian Leuz, Dhananjay Nanda, & Peter D. Wysocki, "Earnings Management and Investor Protection: An International Comparison", 69 J. Fin. Econ. 505 (2003).

[91] See Timothy S. Doupnik, "Influence of Culture on Earnings Management: A Note", 44 Abacus 317 (2008).

[92] See Liming Guan & Hamid Pourjalali, "Effect of Cultural Environmental and Accounting Regulation on Earnings Management: A Multiple Year-Country Analysis", 17 Asia-Pac. J. Acct. &

These findings suggest that societies whose culture emphasizes individual initiative and responsibility to one's actions would channel corporate managers to communicate with stakeholders in a way that does not obfuscate information. Importantly, managers exercise this discretion in reporting above and beyond the call of legal duty. The positive correlation with egalitarianism similarly expresses a shared view that all stakeholders and market participants deserve candor. The findings for uncertainty avoidance suggest that in cultures that perceive uncertainty as threatening, managers may have a stronger inclination to present financial results in a way that conceals actual variability and conveys an image of stability and control. Others in the market tolerate and even expect such behavior as they share the same discomfort with random fluctuations.

When the findings for formal and informal institutions are considered together, the picture that emerges is one of institutional affinities and complementarities, consistent with Williamson's model. Neither law nor culture alone is sufficient for understanding how corporate governance systems function with regard to the informativeness of financial disclosure. Leuz, in another study that uses cultural groupings of countries based on Schwartz dimensions, generalizes this point with regard to investor protection and self-dealing regulation.[93] The upshot is that regulatory regimes that appear similar or even identical, such as IFRS accounting standards or EU directives, may nonetheless exert a differential impact depending on the cultural environment.

3.4.2 Distribution: Dividend Policy

Several theories purport to explain dividend policies.[94] Agency theory holds that dividends may serve to discipline insiders from behaving opportunistically by denying them free funds that could be extracted as private benefits or allow for managerial slack. In this view, discretionary dividend payouts may substitute for legal rights that ensure investor protection. LLSV, however, have documented a positive relation between shareholder rights and dividend payouts around the world.[95] This finding arguably supports an outcome theory of dividends—namely, that minority shareholder rights support pressures to release free cash

---

Econ. 99 (2010); Jeffrey L Callen, Mindy Morel, & Grant Richardson, "Do Culture and Religion Mitigate Earnings Management? Evidence from a Cross-Country Analysis", 8 Int'l. J. Disclosure & Governance 103 (2011); Kurt A. Desender, Christian E. Castro, & Sergio A. Escamilla de Léon, "Earnings Management and Cultural Values", 70 Am. J. Econ. Soc. 639 (2011); Xu Zhang, Xing Liang, & Hongyan Sun, "Individualism–Collectivism, Private Benefits of Control, and Earnings Management: A Cross-Culture Comparison", 114 J. Bus. Ethics 655 (2013). Desender et al. report also for egalitarianism. One study, however, finds the opposite for individualism and uncertainty avoidance—a point that deserves a separate analysis. See Sam Han et al., "A Cross-Country Study on the Effects of National Culture on Earnings Management", 41 J. Int'l. Bus. Stud. 123 (2008).

[93] See Christian Leuz, "Different Approaches to Corporate Reporting Regulation: How Jurisdictions Differ and Why", 40 Acct. Bus. Res. 229 (2010); see also Zhang et al., *supra* note 92; Stephen Salter & Philip A. Lewis, "Shades of Gray: An Empirical Examination of Gray's Model of Culture and Income Measurement Practices Using 20-F Data", 27 Advances Acct. 132 (2011).

[94] See Alon Brav et al., "Payout Policy in the 21st Century", 77 J. Fin. Econ. 483 (2005).

[95] See Rafael La Porta et al., "Agency Problems and Dividend Policies Around the World", 55 J. Fin. 1 (2000).

to shareholders. Dividend payout increases default risk and might limit future investment such that it affects additional stakeholders like creditors and employees.

Jana Fidrmuc and Marcus Jacob have used empirical specifications similar to LLSV's, which they augmented by entering variables for cultural dimensions from Hofstede and Schwartz in addition to the legal environment variables. These tests revealed strong relations between culture and dividend payouts—specifically, positive for individualism and negative for power distance and uncertainty avoidance, and positive for autonomy and egalitarianism (negative for embeddedness and hierarchy). Among the legal factors, only some exhibited significant relations—namely, public enforcement of securities laws and (weakly) an anti-self-dealing index from Djankov et al.'s study.[96]

Several other studies have looked at the relations between culture and dividend payouts, with some obtaining results in line with Fidrmuc and Jacob and others finding differently. Unfortunately, certain studies raise methodological issues that make it difficult to compare their findings, such that the empirical evidence on this subject is in some disarray. Due to scope limitations, I refer to these studies only briefly. The fuller discussion that they deserve is relegated to another occasion.

Dara Khambata and Wei Liu, indeed pioneering this line of inquiry, have reported that a propensity to pay dividends in the Asia-Pacific region associates negatively with uncertainty avoidance and long-term orientation.[97] Sung Bae, Kiyoung Chang, and Eun Kang find that dividend payout in general correlates negatively with uncertainty avoidance, masculinity, and long-term orientation, but the signs flip to significantly positive in a subsample of countries with a high anti-self-dealing legal regime (which is significant but unstable).[98] Liang Shao, Chuck Kwok, and Omrane Guedhami report negative relations with dividend payouts for mastery but, in contrast to other studies, positive relations for embeddedness; shareholder rights, per LLSV's early anti-director rights index, are positively related to dividends only in firm-level tests.[99] Finally, in an interesting paper, Wolfgang Breuer, Oliver Rieger, and Can Soypak introduce behavioral measures intended to capture patience, loss aversion, and ambiguity aversion to explain dividend policies.[100] For robustness checks, these authors enter some dimensions from Hofstede and Schwartz and various legal protection measures, with uneven results.

The decidedly mixed empirical findings on culture, the legal environment, and dividends, combined with the theoretical puzzle that such policies still pose, defy any coherent

[96] Simeon Djankov et al., "The Law and Economics of Self-Dealing", 88 J. Fin. Econ. 430 (2008).

[97] See Dara Khambata & Wei (Wendy) Liu, "Cultural Dimensions, Risk Aversion and Corporate Dividend Policy", 6 J. Asia-Pac. Bus. 31 (2005). Beside its small sample, this study fails to consider other Hofstede dimensions, primarily individualism.

[98] See Sung C. Bae, Kiyoung Chang, & Eun Kang, "Culture, Corporate Governance, and Dividend Policy: International Evidence", 35 J. Fin. Res. 289 (2012). These authors fail to consider individualism/collectivism in light of its very high correlation with long-term orientation. The latter thus might crudely proxy for collectivism.

[99] See Liang Shao, Chuck C.Y. Kwok, & Omrane Guedhami, "National Culture and Dividend Policy", 41 J. Int'l. Bus. Stud. 1391 (2010). These authors use an early release of the Schwartz data and a 21-country sample; they erroneously consider egalitarianism and harmony versus hierarchy and mastery as belonging to a single dimension and report separately for all orientations.

[100] See Wolfgang Breuer, M. Oliver Rieger, & K. Can Soypak, "The Behavioral Foundations of Corporate Dividend Policy: A Cross-Country Analysis", 42 J. Banking & Fin. 247 (2017). Using individual-level and societal-level factors interchangeably, as these authors occasionally do, calls for elaboration.

interpretation of culture's role in this setting. One thing is clear at this stage: When corporate insiders use their discretion to decide on dividend distributions, they comply with implicit injunctions of informal cultural institutions just as much, and perhaps even more strongly, as they respond to formal legal constraints.

3.5 Executive Compensation

Few issues of corporate governance trigger heated debates and (sometimes frenzied) regulatory intervention in the way that executive compensation does. Executive compensation is a complex issue and corporate governance is only one aspect of it.[101] Whether one subscribes to the "managerial power" theory of executive pay or to the "optimal contracting" theory, there is no denying that executive compensation is set by corporate insiders who enjoy discretionary power. This may call for institutional regulation. This section focuses on the role that culture may play in this setting.

In a speech given by the Governor of the Bank of England, Mark Carney, at the World Economic Forum's annual meeting in Davos, stated: "[W]hile regulators . . . can determine the appropriate split of remuneration between fixed and variable elements to limit risks to financial stability, only society, not regulators, can determine whether the absolute and relative levels of compensation are acceptable."[102] Like a good shepherd, Mr. Carney knows his flock. Basing his point on in-depth interviews with UK FTSE100 CEOs, John Hendry observes that these CEOs emphasize values of professional achievement and competitiveness more than the wealth aspects of their pay, which they do not consider as an incentive.[103] Anna Zalewska has found that in British companies, the greater the pay dispersion within the board, the worse firm performance is, in contrast with findings for the US—a result she relates to British boards being less individualistic and hierarchical then their American counterparts.[104]

Separately from asking whether firms pay their top executives for performance, the debate over executive compensation revolves around the question whether managers are paid "too much." As Carney's remarks indicate, societal stances may implicate both the level of pay and, perhaps more acutely, the relative level of executive pay in comparison to some benchmark. Cultural orientations may influence executive pay packages through the channels discussed in this chapter: first, through individual value preferences and beliefs about the "right" pay of the people who are parties to the bargain—namely, the executive herself, the board, the board's compensation committee, and compensation consultants;[105] second,

---

[101] For a survey, see Kevin J. Murphy, Executive Compensation: Where We Are, and How We Got There, in Handbook of the Economics of Finance 211 (George Constantinides, Milton Harris, & René Stulz eds., 2013).

[102] Mark Carney, Speech, Davos CBI British Business Leaders Lunch, Jan. 24, 2014, available at http://www.bankofengland.co.uk/-/media/boe/files/speech/2014/remarks-given-by-mark-carney-at-davos-cbi-british-business-leaders-lunch.pdf.

[103] See John Hendry, "CEO Pay, Motivation and the Meaning of Money", Working Paper (2012).

[104] See Anna Zalewska, "Gentlemen Do Not Talk about Money: Remuneration Dispersion and Firm Performance Relationship on British Boards", 27 J. Empirical Fin. 40 (2013); see also Martin J. Conyon & Kevin J. Murphy, "The Prince and the Pauper? CEO Pay in the United States and the United Kingdom", 110 Econ. J. F640 (2000).

[105] See Adam J. Wowak & Donald C. Hambrick, "A Model of Person-Pay Interaction: How Executives Vary in Their Responses to Compensation Arrangements", 31 Strategic Mgmt. J. 803 (2010); see also

through widely shared beliefs and values about what is acceptable in executive pay, such that straying too far from that consensus would instigate public reaction adverse to the firm;[106] third, indirectly, through culturally consistent legal regulation that affects executive pay.[107] Director networks work to disseminate information (namely, beliefs) about pay practices among connected firms.[108]

There is now substantial evidence that cultural orientations are indeed associated with the structure of executive compensation, in line with the hypothesized mechanisms. Henry Tosi and Thomas Greckhamer have found that total CEO pay, the proportion of variable pay to total compensation, and the ratio of CEO pay to the lowest level employee pay correlate positively with power distance. The first two factors also related positively with individualism.[109] Greckhamer later expanded that analysis, observing more nuanced relations between configurations of cultural dimensions from Hofstede and differences in compensation level and compensation inequality.[110] Consistently with these findings, in a joint study with Siegel and Schwartz, we document negative correlations between egalitarianism and the ratio between CEO wage and average production worker wage.[111] Natasha Burns, Kristina Minnick, and Laura Starks find that CEO tournament pay structure—measured by the gap or ratio between CEO pay and the pay of the next highest-paid executives—associates positively with power distance and with measures of a society's perceived desirability of income inequality and competition from the World Values Survey.[112] Stephen Bryan, Robert Nash, and Ajay Patel examine another prominent feature of executive compensation that focuses on incentivizing executives.[113] These authors observe, while controlling for the legal environment, that the relative use of equity-based compensation associates with individualism (positively) and with uncertainty avoidance (negatively)—namely, with a cultural environment that is compatible with shareholders' interests and entrepreneurship more generally.

Terence R. Mitchell & Amy E. Mickel, "The Meaning of Money: An Individual-Difference Perspective", 24 Acad. Mgmt. Rev. 568 (1999).

[106] See Camelia M. Kuhnen & Alexandra Niessen, "Public Opinion and Executive Compensation", 58 Mgmt. Sci. 1249 (2012); John E. Core, Wayne Guay, & David F. Larcker, "The Power of the Pen and Executive Compensation", 88 J. Fin. Econ. 1 (2008).

[107] See Stephen Bryan, Robert Nash, & Ajay Patel, "How the Legal System Affects the Equity Mix in Executive Compensation", 39 Fin. Mgmt. 393 (2010); Marc van Essen et al., "An Institution-Based View of Executive Compensation: A Multilevel Meta-Analytic Test", 43 J. Int'l. Bus. Stud. 396 (2012).

[108] See Shue, *supra* note 10; see also Trevor Buck & Azura Shahrim, "The Translation of Corporate Governance Changes Across National Cultures: The Case of Germany", 36 J. Int'l. Bus. Stud. 42 (2005).

[109] See Henry L. Tosi & Thomas Greckhamer, "Culture and CEO Compensation", 15 Org. Sci. 657 (2004).

[110] See Thomas Greckhamer, "Cross-Cultural Differences in Compensation Level and Inequality Across Occupations: A Set-Theoretic Analysis", 32 Org. Stud. 85 (2011).

[111] See Siegel et al., *supra* note 29.

[112] See Natasha Burns, Kristina Minnick, & Laura Starks, "CEO Tournaments: A Cross-Country Analysis of Causes, Cultural Influences, and Consequences", 52 J. Fin. Quant. Anal. 519 (2013).

[113] See Stephen Bryan, Robert Nash, & Ajay Patel, "The Effect of Cultural Distance on Contracting Decisions: The Case of Executive Compensation", 33 J. Corp. Fin. 180 (2015).

3.6 The Board of Directors

The board of directors is the epicenter of power relations in the corporation. It is therefore a key component in firms' corporate governance. At first glance, the board is a universal phenomenon. Companies have invariably had boards at least since the East India Company was chartered in 1600. Doctrinally, the board of directors holds the power to manage or direct the management of the company's business. With various secondary differences, this is the law in virtually all common-law jurisdictions as well as in other legal systems.[114] The OECD Principles of Corporate Governance provide a modern rendition of the board's dual mission—namely, to provide strategic advice and monitor the management.[115] Although they lack legal force and may not precisely reflect the corporate laws of all countries, the OECD Principles do reflect a universal consensus on the board's responsibilities.[116]

This image of universality may be misleading, however. When one examines national laws in more detail, numerous differences emerge, especially with regard to the structure of the board (e.g., unitary or two-tiered) and its composition (e.g., worker representation in the board).[117] Recent research indicates that formal legal differences, regardless of whether they are consequential or not, may be just the tip of the iceberg. Both the functioning of the board and its structure may also be shaped by informal, cultural orientations. This section reviews current evidence on these issues.

3.6.1 Operation: Board–CEO Relations

Of the two limbs that constitute the board's dual mission, the responsibility to monitor the management has attracted more scholarly attention than has strategic advice. This special interest in monitoring likely stems from the prominence of agency theory, which underscores the need to monitor corporate insiders lest they utilize their discretionary power opportunistically for their personal benefit. Other theories, however, provide different accounts of the relations between the board of directors and the top management team. These theories adopt perspectives beyond agency, including perspectives based on resource dependence, upper echelons, stewardship, social networks, and institutional.[118] Among the latter, several theories draw on insights from behavioral science and institutional analysis to highlight the role of values, shared beliefs, social norms, and, at bottom, cultural orientations in

---

[114] See Franklin A. Gevurtz, "The Historical and Political Origins of the Corporate Board of Directors", 33 Hofstra L. Rev. 89 (2004); Franklin A. Gevurtz, "The European Origins and the Spread of the Corporate Board of Directors", 33 Stetson L. Rev. 925 (2004).

[115] Organisation for Economic Co-operation and Development, OECD Principles of Corporate Governance 24 (2004) ("VI. The Responsibilities of the Board. The corporate governance framework should ensure the strategic guidance of the company, the effective monitoring of management by the board, and the board's accountability to the company and the shareholders.").

[116] See Amir N. Licht, "State Intervention in Corporate Governance: National Interest and Board Composition", 13 Theoretical Inquiries L. 597 (2012).

[117] See, e.g., Paul L. Davies & Klaus J. Hopt, "Corporate Boards in Europe: Accountability and Convergence", 61 Am. J. Comp. L. 301 (2013).

[118] See Brian K. Boyd, Katalin T. Haynes, & Fabio Zona, "Dimensions of CEO–Board Relations", 48 J. Mgmt. Stud. 1892 (2011).

molding the interactions between the board and the CEO with regard to both monitoring and strategy setting.[119]

Craig Crossland and Donald Hambrick have examined the impact that formal and informal institutions exert on discretion at the top management team, particularly by CEOs.[120] Managerial discretion exists when managers can choose a line of action from a set of viable options. It is a joint product of stakeholder open-mindedness about executive actions and stakeholder inability to block objectionable actions. The scope of discretion thus is affected by what firm stakeholders perceive as possible and acceptable—in other words, on shared beliefs about "what goes with what" or what is "done" or "not done."

Crossland and Hambrick's results indicate two underlying institutional factors ("themes") that are positively linked to managerial discretion. One factor consists of individualism and looseness; the other factor combines informal and formal institutions as well as factual circumstances—namely, uncertainty tolerance (reversed uncertainty avoidance), common law legal origin, employer flexibility, and ownership dispersion. These factors reflect the degree to which a country allows individuals to take unilateral, idiosyncratic actions and the degree to which a country tolerates bold, deviant, and risky actions.[121]

Drawing on these insights, Crossland and Guoli Chen examine the institutional factors that may lead to greater executive accountability in the form of CEO dismissal in the wake of poor financial performance.[122] These authors find that CEOs are more likely to be thus dismissed in countries where managerial discretion is higher, where financial performance measures are more meaningful, for example due to lower earnings management, and also where the legal system has a common-law origin.

These findings weave together several threads that this chapter has already identified. Corporate governance operates differently in different institutional environments in one of its most important tasks. Post-failure CEO dismissal is a particular social norm of accountability that serves to regulate agency problems in firms in a context that is notoriously resilient to formal legal regulation.[123] This norm depends on another social norm regarding managerial discretion, on yet another social norm dealing with earnings management, and on the general style of the legal system. The latter institutions in turn draw on fundamental cultural orientations that promote entrepreneurship as they emphasize individual autonomy and tolerance of uncertainty. Thus, we have here a pyramid of norms in which each stratum interacts with and is conceptually compatible with strata above and below it.[124]

---

[119]   On the link between culture and strategy in connection with the objective of the corporation and CSR, see *supra* text to note 87 et seq.

[120]   See Craig Crossland & Donald C. Hambrick, "Differences in Managerial Discretion across Countries: How National-Level Institutions Affect the Degree to which CEOs Matter", 32 Strategic Mgmt. J. 797 (2011); see also Craig Crossland & Donald C. Hambrick, "How National Systems Differ in their Constraints on Corporate Executives: A Study of CEO Effects in Three Countries", 28 Strat. Mgmt. J. 767 (2007).

[121]   The authors refer to "risk" but conceptually these institutions deal with uncertainty.

[122]   See Craig Crossland & Guoli Chen, "Executive Accountability Around the World: Sources of Cross-National Variation in Firm Performance–CEO Dismissal Sensitivity", 11 Strat. Org. 78 (2013).

[123]   See chapter 37 on private enforcement, and chapter 40 on liability standards.

[124]   See Williamson, *supra* note 20; Licht, *supra* note 11.

3.6.2 Composition: Board Diversity

Until not too long ago, a typical US board was dominated by white, mid-fifties, wealthy male executives who were predominantly Protestant and Republican.[125] From a contemporary comparative perspective, however, boards around the world today exhibit at least some diversity in terms of non-executive (independent) members, gender composition, or employee representation, often due to legal requirements. The composition of boards has attracted special attention, and diversity in board composition is subject to heated debates.[126] Social activists have been calling for even greater gender and ethnic diversity, and policy makers have not been oblivious to these calls, especially in Europe.[127] To paraphrase von Clausevitz on war, legal regulation of board composition has been and remains the continuation of politics by other means.[128] The political skirmishes in Europe over board diversity echo a stream in the corporate governance literature that argues that political forces have stood behind many major corporate governance reforms.[129] Legal reforms in Europe with regard to gender diversity in fact were not confined to boards but have also encompassed political parties.

Culture's role in shaping board composition should be analyzed against this backdrop. Extensive research, both theoretical and empirical, shows that the ways boards fulfill their mission are endogenous. What the board in fact does and how it is structured in a particular firm may be both a cause and an outcome of other factors, including the firm's industry, its stage of development, its financial needs, the individuals in the top management team and on the board itself, and so forth.[130] Informal institutions would be a potentially important part of this setting—again, functioning both as constraints and as motivators ("isomorphic pressures" in the sociological parlance) for molding board composition to accommodate shared values and beliefs.

From a comparative vantage point, cultural orientations thus stand out as factors that may exert a differential effect on board composition in different countries. For example, a cultural emphasis on egalitarianism likely will buttress social norms on gender equality that would facilitate a higher female presence on boards as well as in other institutions—e.g.,

---

[125] James D. Cox, "Changing Perceptions into Reality: Fiduciary Standards to Match the American Directors' Monitoring Function", 1 Bond L. Rev. 218, 218 (1989); Marleen A. O'Connor, "Women Executives in Gladiator Corporate Cultures: The Behavioral Dynamics of Gender Ego, and Power", 65 Md. L. Rev. 465, 468 (2006).

[126] See Deborah L. Rhode & Amanda K. Packel, "Diversity on Corporate Boards: How Much Difference Does Difference Make?", 39 Del. J. Corp. L. 377 (2014).

[127] For EU initiatives, see Deirdre M. Ahern & Blanaid J. Clarke, "Listed Companies' Engagement with Diversity: A Multi-Jurisdictional Study of Annual Report Disclosures", ECGI Law Working Paper 221 (2013).

[128] See Licht, *supra* note 116.

[129] See Mark J. Roe, Political Determinants of Corporate Governance (2003); Peter A. Gourevitch & James Shinn, Political Power and Corporate Control: The New Global Politics of Corporate Governance (2005); see also chapter 3.

[130] See Benjamin E. Hermalin & Michael S. Weisbach, "Endogenously Chosen Boards of Directors and Their Monitoring of the CEO", 88 Am. Econ. Rev. 96 (1998); see also Renée B. Adams et al., "The Role of Boards of Directors in Corporate Governance: A Conceptual Framework and Survey", 48 J. Econ. Lit. 58 (2010); Scott G. Johnson, Karen Schnatterly, & Aaron D. Hill, "Board Composition Beyond Independence: Social Capital, Human Capital, and Demographics", 39 J. Mgmt. 232 (2013).

parliaments. Western Europe indeed provides a good example for such an institutional environment, as it scores particularly high on egalitarianism on average and boasts several interventionist pro-gender-diversity initiatives. Similarly, higher egalitarianism may encourage employee representation in boards as a constituency that is also vulnerable to firm performance, in addition to shareholders. Western Europe again comes to mind.[131] In societies that emphasize entrepreneurship more, which would be reflected in higher individualism, lower uncertainty avoidance, and lower harmony, we would expect board composition to be aligned with (outside) shareholder interests—e.g., by having more independent directors.

Plausible as these hypotheses may seem, relatively little research thus far has addressed the role that culture might play in determining board composition. Jiatao Lee and Richard Harrison find that the percentage of outside directors in boards of multinational firms from 15 countries correlates positively with uncertainty avoidance, individualism, femininity, and power distance.[132] (Except for femininity, similar links were observed for a tendency to consolidate the CEO and Chair positions.) Consistent with the view of boards as endogenous institutions, these findings suggest that the structure of the corporate leadership body also conforms to cultural orientations. These authors did not control for legal requirements, however. That the observed correlations differ from those hypothesized above may suggest that in the sample firms, outside directors do not care solely for outside shareholders but rather for a broader set of stakeholders, who might be less enthusiastic about entrepreneurial strategies.

Johanne Grosvold reports that the percentage of women in the boards of firms from some 50 countries correlates positively with power distance and negatively with uncertainty avoidance, controlling for a set of country- and firm-level factors, though not for legal ones.[133] Grosvold and Stephen Brammer separately examine national average percentages of women on boards across regions classified by culture, legal origin, or other institutions.[134] Although these authors claim that cultural and legal factors appear to play the most significant role in shaping board diversity, their findings do not lend themselves to coherent interpretation.

3.6.3 Structure: Director Networks

In recent years, there has been a flurry of studies on corporate governance and social capital as embodied in social networks. Research thus far has focused on director networks, in which board members also serve as CEOs or as board members in additional companies.[135] It appears that director networks work as advertised, according to social capital theory, to

---

[131] See Aline Conchon, Board-Level Employee Representation Rights in Europe: Facts and Trends, European Trade Union Institute Report (2011); see also, in within-country setting, Pascal Gantenbein & Christophe Volonté, "Is Culture a Determinant of Corporate Governance?", Working Paper (2013).

[132] See Jiatao Lee & J. Richard Harrison, "National Culture and the Composition and Leadership Structure of Boards of Directors", 16 Corp. Governance: Int'l. Rev. 375 (2008).

[133] See Johanne Grosvold, "Where Are All the Women? Institutional Context and the Prevalence of Women on the Corporate Board of Directors", 50 Bus. & Soc. 531 (2011).

[134] See Johanne Grosvold & Stephen Brammer, "National Institutional Systems as Antecedents of Female Board Representation: An Empirical Study", 19 Corp. Governance: Int'l. Rev. 116 (2011).

[135] For a survey see Luc Renneboog & Yang Zhao, The Governance of Director Networks, in The Oxford Handbook of Corporate Governance 200 (Mike Wright et al. eds., 2013); see also Johnson et al., supra note 130.

facilitate information exchange as well as mutual commitment and trust.[136] In some cases this may prove helpful for attaining strategic resources such as information on growth opportunities or outside managerial talent.[137] More extensively connected, and hence more powerful, independent directors are economically and statistically positively correlated with shareholder valuations, possibly because more socially powerful independent directors have better information and more influence.[138]

The upshot may also be detrimental to the interest of the company and of its outside shareholders, however. Several studies have associated more extensive director interlocks with higher CEO pay and with less performance-sensitive CEO pay and tenure, indicating reduced monitoring.[139] Among other things, social acquaintances may engender these adverse effects through compromising the efficacy of formally though not actually independent directors[140] or through propagation of bad practices such as option backdating.[141]

Assessing the relations between culture and board structure in terms of social network configuration begins with the observation that social networks undergird groups. Social networks constitute one's location in the group and one's linkages with other group members. Social networks, however, are merely a structural concept. They are devoid of content meaning, shorn of any normative implications. In the corporate governance context of board structure, individual board members have power that calls for social regulation. They can follow several lines of action that may sustain multiple equilibriums. This is where

---

[136] See, e.g., Christa H. S. Bouwman, "Corporate Governance Propagation through Overlapping Directors", 24 Rev. Fin. Stud. 2358 (2011); Fabio Braggion, "Managers and (Secret) Social Networks: The Influence of the Freemasonry on Firm Performance", 9 J. Eur. Econ. Ass'n. 1053 (2011); Cesare Fracassi, "Corporate Finance Policies and Social Networks", 63 Mgmt. Sci. 2420 (2012); Shue, *supra* note 10.

[137] See, e.g., Luc Renneboog & Yang Zhao, "Us Knows Us in the UK: On Director Networks and CEO Compensation", 17 J. Corp. Fin. 1132 (2011); Joanne Horton, Yuval Millo, & George Serafeim, "Resources or Power? Implications of Social Networks on Compensation and Firm Performance", 39 J. Bus. Fin. & Actg. 399 (2012); David F. Larcker, Eric C. So, & Charles C.Y. Wang, "Boardroom Centrality and Firm Performance", 55 J. Acct. & Econ. 225 (2013); Benjamin Balsmeier, Achim Buchwald, & Stefan Zimmermann, "The Influence of Top Management Corporate Networks on CEO Succession", 7 Rev. Mgmt. Sci. 191 (2013); Thomas C. Omer, Marjorie K. Shelley, & Frances M. Tice, "When Do Well-Connected Directors Affect Firm Value?", 2014 J. Applied Fin. 1 (2014); see also Luc Renneboog & Yang Zhao, "Director Networks and Takeovers", 28 J. Corp. Fin. 218 (2014).

[138] See Kathy Fogel, Liping Ma, & Randall Morck, "Powerful Independent Directors", Working Paper (2014).

[139] See, e.g., Renneboog & Zhao, *supra* note 137; Erik Devos, Andrew Prevost, & John Puthenpurackal, "Are Interlocked Directors Effective Monitors?", 38 Fin. Mgmt. 861 (2009); Rayna Brown et al., What are Friends for? CEO Networks, Pay and Corporate Governance, in Corporate Governance: Recent Developments and New Trends 287 (Sabri Boubaker et al. eds., 2012); Bang Dang Nguyen, "Does the Rolodex Matter? Corporate Elite's Small World and the Effectiveness of Boards of Directors", 58 Mgmt. Sci. 236 (2012); Amir Barnea, Cesare Fracassi, & Ilan Guedj, "Director Networks", Working Paper (2013); Joseph Engelberg, Pengjie Gao, & Christopher A. Parsons, "The Price of a CEO's Rolodex", 26 Rev. Fin. Stud. 79 (2013).

[140] See Byoung-Hyoun Hwang & Seoyoung Kim, "It Pays to Have Friends", 93 J. Fin. Econ. 138 (2009); see also Udi Hoitash, "Should Independent Board Members with Social Ties to Management Disqualify Themselves from Serving on the Board?", 99 J. Bus. Ethics 399 (2011).

[141] See, e.g., John Bizjak, Michael Lemmon, & Ryan Whitby, "Options Backdating and Board Interlocks", 22 Rev. Fin. Stud. 4821 (2009); Cesare Fracassi & Geoffrey Tate, "External Networking and Internal Firm Governance", 67 J. Fin. 153 (2012); Vikramaditya S. Khanna, E. Han Kim, & Yao Lu, "CEO Connectedness and Corporate Frauds", 70 J. Fin. 1203 (2015).

culture comes into play. When one is embedded in a particular cultural environment, one takes for granted "what goes with what" in light of the values and beliefs that one shares with other societal members. Holding a position with a high level of centrality in a network of board members or being located in a structural hole of such a social network thus may entail different implications in different cultures. In sum, social capital is also culturally contingent for board members.

The relations between the individual and the group are the primary issue that every society needs to address. Societal stances on this issue consitute the most fundamental social institution. These stances are captured by their location on Hofstede's individualism/collectivism dimension and in Schwartz's autonomy/embeddedness. As noted, the autonomy/embeddedness and individualism/collectivism dimension overlap conceptually to a degree. Both concern relations between the individual and the collective and both contrast an autonomous with an interdependent view of people. However, the dimensions also differ. For instance, individualism implies self-interested pursuit of personal goals while selfishness is not a characteristic of cultural autonomy. Collectivism more than embeddedness highlights ingroup boundaries as delineating the scope of unquestioning loyalty. The correlation between these dimensions is substantial but far from complete.[142]

Research on culture's consequences for social networks is in its infancy at this stage. Scholars have pointed out the importance of individualism versus collectivism for social network analysis, contrasting Western (usually North American) culture with East Asian (usually Chinese) culture. A related concept is the very elaborate set of relational norms known as guanxi, which traces its roots to Confucian philosophy and calls on individuals to cultivate the right guanxi through extensive, continuing exchanges.[143] For instance, the scope of people that one might trust seems to be substantially narrower in Confucian countries than in Western countries.[144] This is consistent with a collectivist view of ingroup members only as trustworthy, whereas people in individualistic cultures are less likely to hold such a bifurcated view of "most others" for purposes of the "generally speaking question" on trust.[145]

Business organization scholars are beginning to investigate whether the wisdom of social capital in terms of centrality and structural holes (or similar concepts from the current terminological thicket) applies equally in collectivist cultures.[146] The basic idea, as Zhixing Xiao and Anne Tsui put it, is that "[p]eople who stay at the boundary of two ingroups tend to be distrusted by both groups—both ingroups are likely to regard them as outgroup members who do not deserve ingroup treatment . . . Simple and dense networks that represent clear group membership, rather than networks full of structural holes, constitute resources for social actors."[147]

---

[142] See Schwartz 2006, *supra* note 28. There is less conceptual overlap between other dimensions of the two frameworks.

[143] See Chen et al., *supra* note 5.

[144] See Jan Delhey, Kenneth Newton, & Christian Welzel, "How General Is Trust in 'Most People'? Solving the Radius of Trust Problem", 76 Am. Soc. Rev. 785 (2011).

[145] See *supra* text to note 51.

[146] See Johnson et al., *supra* note 130; Sun-Ki Chai & Mooweon Rhee, "Confucian Capitalism and the Paradox of Closure and Structural Holes in East Asian Firms", 6 Mgmt. & Org. Rev. 5 (2009).

[147] Zhixing Xiao & Anne S. Tsui, "When Brokers May Not Work: The Culture Contingency of Social Capital", 52 Admin. Sci. Q. 1, 5 (2007); see also Rong Ma, Yen-Chih Huang, & Oded Shenkar, "Social Networks and Opportunity Recognition: A Cultural Comparison between Taiwan and the United States",

Applying these insights to corporate governance implications of board structure may require careful consideration before extant evidence of the sort mentioned above could be extended to other cultural settings. In doing so, attention should be paid to the dual mission of the board—namely, of strategic advice and of monitoring. The strategy task revolves around board members serving as sources of out-of-firm information and similar resources thanks to external background or linkages. The monitoring task crucially hinges on a certain detachment between directors—especially independent directors—and firm insiders. As the very notion of being "independent" or "external" entails different repercussions in cultures high on collectivism and embeddedness, we should expect such directors to fulfill their tasks differently. Furthermore, since boards are endogenous institutions, we should expect their composition too to reflect the different cultural environment. Outside board members with multiple directorships may not be able to provide valuable information because nobody will supply them with such information, which is reserved for ingroup members. The Japanese family firm practice of adopting adult executives suggests the extent to which societies might go to "familiarize" managers with the firm and its controlling shareholders.[148] On the other hand, such board members might prove to be better monitors if they feel less pressure to socialize within the firm and become part of the ingroup.[149]

The above conjectures are preliminary hypotheses that warrant further theoretical development and empirical testing. In tandem, these cultural differences call for careful assessment of legal measures intended to improve corporate governance by imposing "true and tested" fiduciary duties inspired by common-law sources.[150] A standard common-law duty of loyalty requires any fiduciary, directors included, in the strongest of terms, to act in absolute disinterestedness. Practical issues of implementation aside, such a duty is premised on a view of people as autonomous entities, in line with cultural individualism and autonomy. Such a legal duty may not sit well with a social norm of guanxi in a board whose members maintain extensive relations with other members in the company.

4 CONCLUSION

This chapter has surveyed the literature on culture, law, and corporate governance with a view to establishing the importance of considering both formal (legal) and informal (cultural) institutions in the analysis of corporate governance systems. It is hoped that that goal has been met with some success. In an early paper that called for adopting the cultural value dimension framework for such analyses, I referred to culture as "the mother of all path dependencies."[151] The body of scholarship that has since accumulated seems to support the contention made at that time: "At the risk of stretching the mother metaphor a little bit, it can be argued that culture may indeed be perceived as an old mother. It knows a lot, but some of

32 Strat. Mgmt. J. 1183 (2011); compare Jennifer Merluzzi, "Social Capital in Asia: Investigating Returns to Brokerage in Collectivistic National Cultures", 42 Soc. Sci. Res. 882 (2013).

[148] See *supra* text to note 63.

[149] See Yunsen Chen, Yutao Wang, & Le Lin, "Independent Directors' Board Networks and Controlling Shareholders' Tunneling Behavior", 7 China J. Actg. Res. 101 (2014).

[150] See *supra* text to note 6 et seq.   [151] Licht, *supra* note 43, at 204.

this knowledge might be obsolete today; it is sometimes nagging; it will resist change unless absolutely required. Most importantly, it must not be ignored."

More work can be done toward revealing additional facets of the relations between corporate governance and culture. Institutional environments in Asia (again, think China) and even in Europe differ markedly from those that prevail in English-speaking countries. Understanding these environments will help policy- and lawmakers to develop corporate governance systems more effectively. To achieve this goal we will need to advance our knowledge beyond observing correlations of the sort that was reviewed here toward a more elaborate understanding of the relations between law and culture. Looking to the road ahead, it is fitting to conclude this chapter with a contemporary quotation from Michael Bond, who together with Hofstede and Schwartz, is among the founders of modern cross-cultural research:

> Hypothesizing that this or that Chinese population should be higher (or lower) than mainstream Western norms on this or that construct because this particular Chinese societal context is higher (or lower) than that other comparison context on Hofstede's, House's, Schwartz's, Inglehart's, or Leung and Bond's national-level "cultural" dimension of X will not make the cut—there are simply too many ways to challenge such results, even if confirmed. . . This kind of simplistic, straightforward work informed the earlier cataloguing period of diverse phenomena, which was characterized as the "Aristotelean" era of the cross-cultural discipline. . . That was a time for documenting differences in organizational phenomena across cultural groups, a time for establishing the potential of the cross-cultural enterprise. That agenda was met and, in our opinion, that time has now passed.[152]

---

[152] Michael Harris Bond & Miriam Muethel, "Doing Better Research on Organizational Behaviour in Chinese Cultural Settings: Suggestions from the Notebooks of Two Fellow-Travellers", 8 Mgmt. & Org. Rev. 455, 457–458 (2011).

CHAPTER 7

A BEHAVIORAL PERSPECTIVE ON CORPORATE LAW AND CORPORATE GOVERNANCE

JAAP WINTER

1 INTRODUCTION

LAW and lawyers traditionally have been rather self-occupied. The study of law focuses on the law as a world in and of itself. To understand it, one must understand key legal concepts that have specific meaning within the law, that generate consequences in law, but also how law and rules are made and applied in specific circumstances, and the fundamental, immovable principles as well as the dependent, context-sensitive principles that govern these processes. Unalienable legal notions such as justice and fairness form part of this understanding of law upon which specific rules and decisions are based and which can even limit the application of specific rules. Lawyers, courts, and legal scholars engage in a constant process of ordering these legal concepts, deducing appropriate rules and decisions, seeking consistency and predictability or criticizing the lack thereof, and sometimes pleading or deciding to change course fundamentally because reality has moved on and requires a new approach. In those latter cases one can see a glimpse of the connection between law and reality that the legal process itself often obscures.

In such an inwardly looking legal environment there is little need for lawyers, lawmakers, judges, and legal scholars to have a deep understanding of the reality that is touched by a legal rule or decision. Legal education and legal research as a result also primarily focus on (deepening the) understanding (of) law, legal concepts, and practices from this intrinsic perspective. The economic analysis of law ("Law & Economics") has forced the law to open up to an outside-in perspective. The economic analysis of law questions whether features of the law are economically efficient in terms of maximizing social wealth. Legal rules and case decisions may be consistent, predictable, and even fair, but if they do not facilitate that goods and services end up with those who value them the most, these rules and decisions are not economically efficient and therefore, from an economic perspective, should be changed.

This has forced lawyers to rethink what the objectives of the law actually are and how it can be demonstrated that these objectives are met.

The economic analysis of law has been criticized severely by lawyers ("economic efficiency is not the only or most important end of law," "economic analysis of law requires a set of simplifying assumptions that determine the results of the analysis and therefore cannot be applied to real-life situations," "economic analysis cannot value properly such intrinsically legal notions as fairness and justice," and "economic analysis of law reduces law to an instrument to achieve objectives outside law, destroying the built-in integrity of law").[1] Nonetheless it has become the dominant approach to law, particularly in the field of corporate law and corporate governance.

Much of the economic analysis of corporate law and corporate governance that we have seen is methodically mathematical, seeking to establish significant correlations between data. This may blind us from seeing that economics is basically an attempt to understand human behavior. At its core is the presumption that human beings act as rational economic agents acting in their self-interest. Theories are based on this presumption that have had a profound influence on the understanding of corporate law and corporate governance, the most significant of which is the agency theory. This theory positions managers of a company as agents on behalf of shareholders, who, as residual claimants, are the principals. As rational actors, managers will pursue their own interests, which are not necessarily in line with the interests of the principals, and this perspective has created the dominant approach to corporate law and corporate governance. Agency theory suggests that it is the purpose of corporate law and corporate governance to deal with this "agency problem" in order to ensure that the interests of shareholders as principals are sufficiently protected. The focus has been on the rights shareholders should be able to exercise, on the monitoring of executive directors by non-executive directors and by external auditors, on executive remuneration that seeks to align the interests of executive directors with the interests of shareholders, and on takeover bids as a mechanism to discipline executives. These have also become the dominant themes in the legal analysis of the corporate setting. This, in its turn, has determined to a large extent the extensive regulatory agenda in the field of corporate law and corporate governance of the last decade and a half.

In more recent years the key assumption of the *homo economicus* acting rationally in his self-interest has been challenged by academics from other behavioral fields and also by economists who have taken on the insights from these other fields to develop the study of behavioral economics. Academics from fields such as psychology, neuropsychology, neurology, evolutionary psychology, sociology, and philosophy have started to challenge the assumptions underlying economic as well as legal theorizing.

The field of behavioral studies is enormous and quickly expanding. In this chapter I will not make an attempt to capture all behavioral insights that potentially are relevant for corporate law and corporate governance. I will first set out how the growing body of behavioral knowledge affects the core assumptions of the agency theory, which renders it at best an incomplete approach to corporate law and corporate governance (section 2). I will then address a number of specific areas of corporate law and corporate governance where

---

[1] See, for example, Brian Z. Tamanaha, Law as a Means to an End: Threat to the Rule of Law (2006).

behavioral perspectives are particularly relevant. In section 3, I will address behavioral perspectives relevant to rulemaking in corporate law and corporate governance. These are particularly relevant as after the governance crisis and financial crisis we saw a general tendency to increase (mandatory) rules to enforce responsible human behavior in corporate and financial affairs. The regulatory push completely ignores what rulemaking does to people's sense of responsibility for their behavior. In section 4, I take a closer look at how to understand board performance. The agency theory has triggered an expanding field of financial economics, seeking to correlate elements of boards and their composition as regulated in law to company performance. This is one of the core issues of the current corporate governance debate. However, none of this research can truly explain how boards perform. This would require opening the black box of the board and asks for different, behavioral methods of research.

Section 5 will deal with modern executive remuneration systems, typically in the form of performance-based pay. This seeks to align interests of executives with those of shareholders but is based on flawed mechanical assumptions about human performance.

2 AGENCY THEORY AND ITS DEFECTS

The core idea of agency theory, that managers as agents for shareholders as principals do not necessarily have the interests of shareholders at heart when they take decisions as managers of the company, comes across as sensible. It is a relevant insight for anyone who is interested in relationships within the corporation and it poses relevant regulatory questions on how to deal with the principal–agent conflicts in corporations. In fact, corporate law has dealt with agency problems since its incubation and well before anybody framed the potential conflicts of interests between managers and shareholders, or between controlling shareholder and minority shareholders, as agency problems. Economists have sought to understand and calculate the agency costs triggered by these agency relationships, for example the costs of measuring a manager's performance, the costs of monitoring and bonding activities, the costs of receiving information on the manager's behavior, etc. Elements of corporate law are then judged by their tendency to reduce these agency costs. The more they do, the more efficient in economic terms they are. In order to be able to make those calculations, the theory in an effort to simplify things, takes two crucial starting points: (1) a manager as agent makes rational decisions, and (2) a manager always maximizes his own economic gains.[2] This is where the economic approach, for the sake of being able to build a model that allows for more or less straightforward calculations, takes an absolute turn that does not reflect how people really behave.

From a behavioral perspective criticism can be raised against the agency theory.

---

[2] Michael C. Jensen & William H. Meckling, "Theory of the Firm: Managerial Behavior, Agency Costs and Ownership Structure", 3 J. Fin. Econ. 305 (1976).

2.1 Not that Rational

A vast and expanding body of research suggests that we are not the rational decision makers that agency theory assumes. Our rationality is bounded. Our judgment and thinking, based on information that we are aware of, are limited and biased in systemic, predictable ways.[3] But our awareness is bounded as well, which prevents people from noticing or focusing on useful, observable, and relevant information. Finally, our ethicality is similarly bounded by psychological processes, leading to questionable behavior by individuals who contradict their own preferred ethics.[4]

People rely on a number of simplifying strategies, or heuristics, when making decisions. Heuristics help us to make sense of complex situations in which we need to make decisions. Most of the time we do this intuitively, without any special thought. Kahneman and others have made the distinction between System 1 and System 2 in the mind.[5] System 1 operates automatically and quickly, with little or no effort and no sense of voluntary control. System 2 allocates attention to the effortful mental activities that demand it, including complex computations. In most situations our System 1 thinking is quite sufficient. System 1 thinking, among others, allows us to detect that one object is more distant than another, orient the source of a sudden sound, answer 2 + 2 = ?, and drive a car on an empty road. Errors in our thinking occur frequently in System 1 thinking. These errors are called biases. Numerous cognitive biases have now been identified.[6] Some of the best known, and also relevant to decision making by managers and boards, are the *overconfidence* bias (the tendency to underestimate risks and overestimate own abilities)[7]; the *escalation of commitment* bias (the tendency to increase investment in a decision based on cumulative prior investment despite evidence that the cost of continuing outweighs its expected benefit)[8]; the *availability* bias (the tendency to believe that events in vivid memory have a higher probability of occurring than they actually have)[9]; the *self-serving* bias (the tendency to attribute success to personal factors and failures to external factors)[10]; the *loss-aversion* bias (the tendency to value avoiding losses more than the prospect of gains)[11]; and the *confirmation* bias (the tendency to search

---

[3] Max H. Bazerman & Don A. Moore, Judgment in Managerial Decision Making (7th ed. 2009); Dan Ariely, Predictably Irrational: The Hidden Forces that Shape Our Decisions (2008).

[4] Max H. Bazerman & Ann E. Tenbrunsel, Blind Spots: Why We Fail to Do What's Right and What to Do about It (2011).

[5] Daniel Kahneman, Thinking, Fast and Slow (2011).

[6] See for an overview of biases that may have caused problems for the governance of businesses Alexandre Di Miceli da Silveira, "Corporate Scandals of the 21st Century: Limitations of Mainstream Corporate Governance Literature and the Need for a New Behavioral Approach" (2015), http://ssrn.com/abstract=2181705.

[7] See Catherine M. Schrand & Sarah L.C. Zechman, "Executive Overconfidence and the Slippery Slope to Financial Misreporting" 53 J. Acct. & Econ. 311 (2012) and Kahneman, *supra* note 5, part III.

[8] See Kathryn Kadous & Lisa M. Sedor, "The Efficacy of Third-Party Consultation in Preventing Managerial Escalation of Commitment: The Role of Mental Representations" 21 Contemporary Accounting Research 55 (2004).

[9] See Saulo D. Barbosa & Alain Fayolle, "Where is the Risk? Availability, Anchoring, and Framing Effects on Entrepreneurial Risk Taking" (2007), http://ssrn.com/abstract=1064121 and Kahneman, *supra* note 5, chapter 12.

[10] Bazerman & Tenbrunsel, *supra* note 4, at 73–74.   [11] Kahneman, *supra* note 5, chapter 26.

for and accept as valid or true information that confirms prior held beliefs or preferences).[12] Some of the System 1 biases are so strong that they prevent attentive, effortful System 2 thinking to correct them. Kahneman says: "The best we can do is a compromise: learn to recognize situations in which mistakes are likely and try harder to avoid significant mistakes when the stakes are high. The premise of this book is that it is easier to recognize other people's mistakes than our own."[13]

People are constantly at risk of finding themselves overwhelmed by too much information. To protect themselves against this overload, people consistently engage in information filtering, much of which is carried out unconsciously and automatically. Sometimes this leads to inattentional blindness. A popular example is the clip of the "moonwalking bear" passing through two teams of basketball players that goes unnoticed to the vast majority of viewers.[14] Similarly, people have a tendency not to notice change in their physical environments, as is shown by the "colour-changing card trick."[15] Inattentional and change blindness are likely also to occur in realms outside visual perception.[16] Focalism or the focusing illusion is the tendency of people to overestimate the degree to which their future thoughts will be occupied by an event on which they focus. Or as Kahneman says it: "Nothing in life is as important as you think it is when you are thinking about it."[17]

Our moral judgments are also subject to flaws in our thinking process. People have an innate ability to maintain a belief while acting contrary to it. There is also a tendency to evaluate one's own moral transgressions differently than those of others, applying a self-serving double standard. People tend to focus more on their contribution to a joint effort than on the efforts of others. Organizational practices and language can contribute to ethical fading, framing decisions, for example, as business decisions rather than ethical decisions. Cognitive busy participants in a study were more likely to cheat on a task than less overloaded participants.[18] As long as we cheat by only a little, people also tend to rationalize their behavior so as to benefit from cheating and still maintain a view of themselves as honest people.[19]

It is good to note that not only managers as agents are subject to bounded rationality, bounded perception, and bounded ethicality, but also those who take positions as monitors of managers on the basis of the argument of agency theory, such as non-executive directors and external auditors. The same systemic biases and social pressures may cloud the professional judgment of non-executives.[20]

---

[12] JaeHong Park, Prabhudev Konana, Bin Gu, Alok Kumar & Rajagopal Raghunathan, "Confirmation Bias, Overconfidence, and Investment Performance: Evidence from Stock Message Boards" (2010), http://ssrn.com/abstract=1639470 and Kahneman, *supra* note 5, at 80–81.

[13] Kahneman, *supra* note 5, at 28.

[14] See http://www.youtube.com/watch?v=KB_ITKZm1Ts.

[15] See http://www.youtube.com/watch?v=v3iPrBrGSJM.

[16] Bazerman & Moore, *supra* note 3.   [17] Kahneman, *supra* note 5, at 402.

[18] Bazerman & Tenbrunsel, *supra* note 4.

[19] Dan Ariely, The (Honest) Truth about Dishonesty: How We Lie to Everyone—Especially Ourselves (2012).

[20] Oliver Marnet, Behaviour and Rationality in Corporate Governance (2008); Sven Hoeppner & Christian Kirchner, "Ex-Ante vs. Ex-Post Governance: A Behavioral Perspective" (2014), http://ssrn.com/abstract=2405843. See further section 4.

Cognitive errors may have played a crucial role in governance and financial crises. Ben-David, Harvey, and Graham found that companies with overconfident CFOs apply lower discount rates to value cash flows, use more debt, and are less likely to pay dividends.[21] Schrand and Zechman found that overconfident executives are more likely to initially overstate earnings which start them on the path to growing intentional misstatements or frauds.[22] The availability bias makes us forget after a while that every now and then a big crisis will happen and think that now it is different, which is confirmed by every day and year of good financial performance.[23] The loss aversion bias may have contributed to the collapse of Lehman Brothers. Dick Fuld, CEO of Lehman Brothers, held a capital interest in Lehman Brothers that at one time was valued at $475 million. In the last year leading up to the collapse of Lehman Brothers, Fuld decided to increase the exposure of Lehman Brothers to toxic mortgage-backed securities, at the same time spending hundreds of millions on share buybacks, exposing the company and its shareholders to ever more risks.[24] Kahneman and Tversky found that people are risk-seeking when all the options are bad. If given the option to choose between getting €900 for sure or having a 90% chance of getting €1,000, most people would choose to get €900 for sure. The subjective value of a gain of €900 is more than 90% of the value of a gain of €1,000. But if given the option to choose between losing €900 for sure or having a 90% chance of losing €1,000 most people choose the 90% chance of losing €1,000. The sure loss is very aversive and this drives us to take the risk.[25] *Skin in the game* may be a good thing when all the options are good, but may lead to disaster if the options all become bad.

2.2 Not that Selfish

The assumption that the agent always maximizes his own wealth has also been criticized in behavioral studies. Numerous studies point out that in given situations where a rational self-interested choice would lead to taking a certain decision, the majority of people in fact take the opposite decision. The well-known prisoner's dilemma is a case at hand. Two suspects are put in separate prison cells. Each is told that if neither of them confesses they will both be charged with the crime and be sentenced to one year in jail. Each prisoner is also made an offer: if he decides to confess and to implicate the other, he will go free while the non-confessing partner will be sentenced to 15 years in jail. Finally each of them is told that if they both confess both will be convicted and sentenced to ten years in jail. A rational choice for each of the two prisoners is to defect and get a lower sentence than when not defecting, which is true regardless of whether the other prisoner defects or not. But in reality people often choose to cooperate. This has been demonstrated in hundreds of studies.[26] Similarly,

---

[21] Itzhak Ben-David, Campbell R. Harvey, & John R. Graham, "Managerial Overconfidence and Corporate Policies" (2007) http://www.nber.org/papers/w13711.

[22] Schrand & Zechman, *supra* note 7.

[23] Nassim Taleb, *The Black Swan* 83 (2007).

[24] Lawrence G. McDonald, A Collosal Failure of Common Sense: The Inside Story of the Collapse of Lehman Brothers (2009).

[25] Kahneman, *supra* note 5, at 279–80.

[26] See for example David Sally, "Conversation and Cooperation in Social Dilemmas: A Meta-Analysis of Experiments from 1958 to 1992", 7 Rationality & Society 58 (1995).

in ultimatum games two players need to decide how to divide a sum between the two. The first player makes a proposal to the second player who can either accept or refuse. If the second player rejects, neither receive anything. If the second player accepts, the money is split according to the proposal. If the proposer would be a rational and purely selfish *homo economicus* he would offer the lowest amount possible. If the responder would act as a true *homo economicus* he would accept the lowest amount that can be offered. But in reality the proposer often offers a substantial portion of the stakes, most frequently half. And the responder often rejects the offer when it does not provide him with a substantial portion of the stakes, typically rejecting offers below 30%.[27]

Many of these and other social dilemma games have been played and studied under a wide variety of conditions. They show that people routinely act unselfishly, sometimes sacrificing their own payoffs to increase others' (altruism), sometimes to hurt others (spite).[28] The cooperative behavior of people has been studied at length, by academics from different fields. For example, the volume *Moral Sentiments and Material Interests*, edited by Herbert Gintis and others,[29] provides an overview of research in economics, anthropology, evolutionary and human biology, social psychology, and sociology dealing with the theoretical foundations and policy implications of cooperative behavior. It is clear that forms of reciprocity play a crucial role. Weak reciprocity may occur in the case of repeated interactions between people, when factors such as individual reputation and punishment of norm violators play a role. Under those conditions reciprocity may actually be seen as a form of self-interest. But numerous experiments indicate that people also display strong reciprocity in non-repeated sessions: acting kindly to actions that are perceived to be kind and in a hostile way to actions that are perceived to be hostile, both at the cost of personal gain. Many people exhibit strong reciprocity but not everybody. Most studies indicate that a substantial number, but not the majority, of people behave in a purely selfish way.[30] The results of these experimental studies are also culturally robust in the sense that in no culture is the canonical model of self-regarding behavior supported. The level of behavioral variability across cultures, however, is considerable. Differences between societies in levels of market integration and cooperation in production may explain about half of this behavioral variation.[31] These authors dryly note that the Law & Economics analysis, with its abstraction from reciprocity and other non-self-regarding motives, limits its general relevance.

Many economists have now accepted that the assumption of the rational, personal wealth maximizing *homo economicus* may help economic modeling but has at best only limited relevance for understanding human behavior and developing policy decisions.[32] Jensen and

[27] Martin A. Nowak, Karen M. Page, & Karl Sigmund, "Fairness versus Reason in the Ultimatum Game" 289 Sci. 1773 (2000).

[28] Lynn Stout, Cultivating Conscience: How Good Laws Make Good People (2011).

[29] Moral Sentiments and Material Interests (Herbert Gintis, Samuel Bowles, Robert Boyd, & Ernst Fehr eds., 2005).

[30] Ernst Fehr & Urs Fischbacher, The Economics of Strong Reciprocity, in Moral Sentiments and Material Interests, *supra* note 29, at 151 ff.

[31] Herbert Gintis, Samuel Bowles, Robert Boyd, & Ernst Fehr, Moral Sentiments and Material Interests: Origins, Evidence, and Consequences, in Moral Sentiments and Material Interests, *supra* note 29, at 3 ff.

[32] Eleanore Hickman, "Boardroom Gender Diversity: A Behavioural Economics Analysis", 14 J. Corp. L. Stud. 385 (2014).

Meckling themselves have said that "the economic model is, of course, not very interesting as a model behavior. People do not behave this way. In most cases use of this model reflects economists' desire for simplicity in modeling; the exclusive pursuit of wealth or money income is easier to model than the complexity of actual preferences of individuals".[33]

2.3 Social Context Matters

In yet another aspect, the agency theory is too limited a theory on which to base a full understanding of human interaction in the corporate environment. The agency theory focuses on the pursuit and control of individual agency, not taking into account the social context in which such agency takes place. Individuals operating in that social context form interpretations of the social context, which in turn are socially constructed or constituted. Westphal and others have undertaken extensive research on the social situations in which corporate governance actually takes place, such as social relationships, networks, and institutions that shape individual agency, which becomes contingent on this social context. They note also that an individual's socialization and cumulative personal experiences define what the individual conceives as situationally possible, thus both enabling and constraining the agency of the individual.[34] Westphal, for example, found that increases in a board's social and structural independence from management motivated CEOs to engage in ingratiating behavior toward independent directors, essentially neutralizing the effects of board independence on a variety of corporate policies ranging from the level and form of executive compensation to corporate diversification strategy.[35] Similarly, research has demonstrated that increases of institutional investor ownership prompted CEOs to engage in ingratiatory behavior toward institutional fund managers, which in turn alleviated pressure from institutional owners to adopt a variety of corporate governance reforms.[36] Others claim that the greater the CEO's power over the board, the greater the demographic similarity between the CEO and his/her successor, while board power over the CEO predicted demographic similarity between the CEO's successor and outside directors.[37] Westphal and Bednar found a systemic tendency for outside directors to underestimate the extent to which fellow directors shared their concerns about the firm's corporate strategy when firm performance had been relatively poor.[38] This pluralistic ignorance would be especially severe when the board was relatively diverse. Likewise, more recent scholarship establishes that security analysts systemically underestimated the extent to which fellow analysts shared their reservations about

---

[33] Michael C. Jensen & William H. Meckling, "The Nature of Man", 7 J. Appl. Corp. Fin. 4 (1994).

[34] James D. Westphal & Edward J. Zajac, "A Behavioral Theory of Corporate Governance: Explicating the Mechanisms of Socially Situated and Socially Constituted Agency", 7 Acad. Mgmt. Annals 607 (2013).

[35] James D. Westphal, "Board Games: How CEOs Adapt to Increases in Structural Board Independence from Management", 43 Admin. Sci. Q. 511 (1998).

[36] James D. Westphal & Michael K. Bednar, "The Pacification of Institutional Investors", 53 Admin. Sci. Q. 29 (2008).

[37] Edward J. Zajac & James D. Westphal, "Who Shall Succeed? How CEO/Board Preferences and Power Affect the Choice of New CEOs", 39 Acad. Mgmt. J. 64 (1996).

[38] James D. Westphal & Michael K. Bednar, "Pluralistic Ignorance in Corporate Boards and Firms' Strategic Persistence in Response to Low Firm Performance", 50 Admin. Sci. Q. 262 (2005).

stock repurchase plans, inhibiting them from responding negatively to the adoption of new plans, despite accumulating evidence that repurchase plans are often not implemented.[39] The impact of the gradual acceptance of the agency theory as the dominant theory in corporate governance has also been studied by these researchers. For example, they find that relatively negative appraisals by security analysts in the form of less optimistic earnings forecasts and less positive stock recommendations prompted powerful corporate leaders to symbolically conform to the agency theory prescriptions by increasing the board's formal independence from management without increasing the board's social independence (i.e., appointing directors who lacked formal ties to top managers but who were friends of the CEO).[40] Another study comes to the same result following negative media coverage.[41]

None of these social factors that impact the way executives, non-executives, investors, and analysts interpret the relevant context for their decision making and their actual behavior are taken into account in agency theory based on individual agency of a rational self-regarding agent.

2.4 Groups Matter Too

A specific social context that is key in corporate governance is the context of the group or team within which individuals function. In particular, the board of directors plays a key role in corporate governance and is typically thought of as, and in reality consists of, multiple participants. Also at executive level, although there is a wide variety in size of executive teams and single person (CEO) dominance across countries, to a large extent the executive function is a team effort. Key corporate decisions, therefore, are typically not the result of individual decision making but of group decision making. Agency theory does not shed light on the particularities in decision making by groups.

Cognitive psychologists have long studied the benefits of group decision making versus individual decision making, recognizing that in real life many decisions are taken by groups.[42] In a number of studies, groups appear to be better decision makers than individuals. Groups have advantages in information processing, by having superior memories for information, by having access to more information, which is then exchanged through discussion, and by processing information more thoroughly through discussion. These advantages of groups over individuals may in particular help to overcome the bounded rationality, bounded perception, and bounded ethicality problems that individuals face. On the other hand, the

---

[39] David H. Zhu & James D. Westphal, "Misperceiving the Beliefs of Others: How Pluralistic Ignorance Contributes to the Persistence of Positive Security Analyst Reactions to the Adoption of Stock Repurchase Plans", 22 Org. Sci. 869 (2011).

[40] James D. Westphal & Melissa E. Graebner, "A Matter of Appearances: How Corporate Leaders Manage the Impressions of Financial Analysts about the Conduct of their Boards", 53 Acad. Mgmt. J. 15 (2010).

[41] Michael K. Bednar, "Watchdog or Lapdog? A Behavioral View of the Media as a Corporate Governance Mechanism", 55 Acad. Mgmt. J. 131 (2012).

[42] See for extensive references to research in this field Craig D. Parks & Lawrence J. Sanna, Group Performance and Interaction (1999); Donelson R. Forsyth, Group Dynamics (6th ed. 2013); Stephen M. Bainbridge, "Why a Board? Group Decisionmaking in Corporate Governance", 55 Vand. L. Rev. 1 (2002).

group context creates its own dynamics as a result of which the quality of decision making can deteriorate. Groups typically spend more time on examining information that two or more members have in common than on examining information that only one member brings (*shared information bias*). Groups tend to suffer even more than individuals from the confirmation bias, the tendency to search for and accept as valid or true information that confirms prior held beliefs or preferences. Groups often do not urge restraint but polarize; they amplify either riskier or more cautious strategies. Pluralistic ignorance occurs in groups: members believe their own views or concerns deviate from the rest of the group's views and then seek to conform to what they believe to be the group's views. Within groups, conflicts may arise, which prohibits the group from taking the best decision. Finally groupthink may arise where the group values consensus and unanimity more than reaching the best possible decision. Symptoms of groupthink are overestimation of the capabilities of the group, closed-mindedness, and pressure toward uniformity.

Looking at all the evidence of behavioral studies, undermining the absoluteness of the principal elements of agency theory of rational self-interested wealth maximization, and adding the social and group contexts as additional influences on behavior and decision making, it should be clear that agency theory is indeed an incomplete model for the behavior and decision making of key actors in the corporate setting. Agency theory captures an essential but limited part of the complexity of the behavior of corporate actors that corporate law and corporate governance seek to regulate. The conflict of interest that is central to the agency theory is real in the sense that in every corporate setting the agents' behavior may be determined more by their self-interest than the interest of the corporation or its shareholders. That, however, does not mean to say that this is always the case, and that their behavior will always be to the detriment of corporate well-being. Agency theory cannot explain when, under what circumstances, and why it is more or less likely that the inherent conflict of interests indeed leads to the detrimental behavior of the agent. Nor can it explain when, under what circumstances, and why certain corporate regulatory mechanisms that seek to contain this conflict work well or not so well. It should therefore not be the sole theoretical basis for perceiving governance problems and designing regulatory or non-regulatory solutions to those perceived problems. Agency theory is incomplete and should be supplemented, at least, with insights from behavioral studies.

By unconditionally accepting the agency theory and its principal components, lawyers may make the same mistake economists made when they borrowed from physics to shore up the scientific level of their studies. Economists borrowed from nineteenth-century physics notions such as equilibrium and compared value in economics to energy in physics in order to be able to make mathematical predictions of economic behavior. Physics moved on in the twentieth century, challenging equilibrium thinking with complexity notions and complementing Newtonian action-and-reaction concepts with quantum mechanical perceptions of the world. Mainstream economics did not follow the evolution in physics but kept on bending, stretching, and updating its theories to keep them running, and by doing so became ever further removed from real life. Over the last five decades a number of academics from various academic disciplines, such as Herbert Simon, Daniel Kahneman, Amos Tversky, Richard Thaler, Herbert Gintis, George Akerlof, and Dan Ariely, have studied and amended our understanding of human behavior and decision making, developing the field of behavioral economics. However, in the field of corporate law and corporate governance, much of the behavioral insights developed seem to remain unnoticed, with some exceptions.[43] Instead, the economic approach to corporate law and corporate governance is based on the traditional, outdated model of man as the rational, self-interested actor. It may be that legal scholars are particularly attracted to applying the agency theory to corporate law and corporate governance because law is often and predominantly concerned with preventing things going wrong and seeking redress (punishment, compensation) when they do. This naturally fits with the agency theory, which presumes that agents are out there acting for themselves, to the detriment of principals. Oliver Wendell Holmes in his famous speech "The Path of the Law" put it like this: "If you want to know the law. . . you must look at it as a bad man, who cares only for the material consequences which such knowledge enables him to predict, not as a good one, who finds his reasons for conduct. . . in the vaguer sanctions of conscience."[44] The agency model fits nicely with this bad man presumption. That notion as something that the law particularly is interested in is not the problem in itself. But when corporate law and corporate governance mechanisms are then evaluated or promoted solely on the basis of models applying full rationality and self-interest maximization as assumptions, the analysis becomes flawed. This runs the risk of corporate law and corporate governance regulation that precisely does not strengthen but weakens corporate decision making and responsibility.[45]

3 Rulemaking in Corporate Law and Corporate Governance

The governance crisis of 2001–2003, with a number of high-profile scandals due to governance failures of large listed companies, and the financial crisis of 2007–2009, with financial institutions failing and putting the whole financial system at risk, have led to a surge in regulation in the field of corporate governance, through corporate, securities, and financial regulation. Much of this regulation was promulgated on the basis of the belief that irresponsible behavior in the corporate sector and financial sector had caused these crises and needs to be addressed through regulation in order to prevent another crisis. Much can be said about the forces that push us to respond to every crisis with new regulation seeking to fix the system. A large part can be addressed to our need to have control over our world or at least have the feeling of control. An illusion of control is preferred over a sense of being out of control. Lawmakers feel urged to respond to the outcry of the public, falling victim quickly to the perceived need that "something must be done." Anything that validly presents itself as such a "something," therefore, by some logic of action must be done. There is also a strong, often implicit belief that we can indeed cure things, improve matters, prevent future mistakes through new rules and processes that we put in place. And so every crisis leads to new regulation, piled upon previous regulation that apparently was not enough to prevent

---

[43] See for example Marnet and Hoeppner & Kirchner, *supra* note 20; Donald C. Langevoort, Behavioral Approaches to Corporate Law, in Research Handbook on The Economics of Corporate Law (Claire Hill & Brett McDonnell eds., 2012); Margaret Blair & Lynn A. Stout, "Trust, Trustworthiness, and the Behavioral Foundations of Corporate Law", 149 U. Penn. L. Rev. 1735 (2001).

[44] Oliver Wendell Holmes, Jr., "The Path of the Law", 10 Harv. L. Rev. 457 (1897).

[45] Stout, *supra* note 28.

this crisis from happening. As a result, in many areas of society, whether it be education, academia, health care, legal practice, or the financial-corporate system there is a sense of being overburdened by regulation, of the primary human practice being overshadowed by the regulations that seek to keep those that practice it in the right place, and that actually things are getting worse instead of better as a result.

There are a number of problems with this belief in social engineering through regulation as the solution to problems in our society.

3.1 Regulatory Crowding Out Effect

Rules have a paradoxical effect on people. More and more rules replace the responsibility we feel for our behavior and for the consequences of our behavior to others by the responsibility to comply with the rules. It generates a sense that anything that is not forbidden or covered by the rules is free territory where anything is permissible and where it is not necessary to ponder the consequences to others of one's behavior. In this way, a regulatory intervention of certain aspects of the financial or corporate reality through more mandatory rules shifts these aspects into a different mental category outside the scope of moral reflection. This perverse effect is similar to the crowding out effect of monetary incentives replacing intrinsic motivation for behavior. This effect was established in the well-known case of day care centers that fined parents for coming late to pick up their children, which had the effect of more parents coming late. The social norm, including feelings of guilt, was replaced by a market norm, the fine became a price to pay so parents could decide for themselves whether or not to be late.[46] The crowding out effect of incentives has also been established in economic relations[47] and in relation to legal incentives.[48] We can speak of a regulatory crowding out effect when new rules and procedures seek to address certain specific forms of problematic behavior that were revealed in the crisis but then lead people to believe that anything not covered by the rules must be ethically permissible.[49] A consequence of this effect is that the more rules apply to the practice we engage in, the more we experience a sort of outsourcing of our responsibility to those that make the rules. If our behavior in the not-yet-regulated space is challenged, we respond by saying the lawmaker should have made better or more complete rules. The same applies to more and more regulatory supervision by, for example, security regulators seeking to enforce the rules, which may lead us to believe that if the regulator does not intervene, we no longer have to worry about the consequences of our behavior.[50] The result of the regulatory crowding out effect is that people actually feel less

---

[46] Uri Gneezy & Aldo Rustichini, "A Fine is a Price", 29 J. Leg. Stud. 1 (2000); Ariely, *supra* note 1.

[47] Bruno Frey & Reto Jegen, "Motivation Crowding Theory", 15 J. Econ. Surveys 589 (2001); Ernst Fehr & Simon Gärchter, "Do Incentive Contracts Crowd out Voluntary Cooperation?" USC Center for Law, Economics and Organization, Research Paper no. C01-3 (2002).

[48] Emad H. Atiq, "Why Motives Matter: Reframing the Crowding Out Effect of Legal Incentives", 123 Y.L. J. 1070 (2014).

[49] George Loewenstein, Conflicts of Interest Begin Where Principal–Agent Problems End, in Conflicts of Interest: Challenges and Solutions in Business, Law, Medicine, and Public Policy (Don A. Moore, Daylian M. Cain, George Loewenstein, & Max H. Bazerman eds., 2005).

[50] Kees Cools & Jaap Winter, External and Internal Supervision: How to Make it Work?, in Financial Supervision in the 21st Century (A. Joanne Kellermann, Jakob de Haan, & Femke de Vries eds., 2013).

responsible for (the consequences of) their behavior, while the reason for regulatory intervention in the first place was the lack of responsibility by various actors in the field revealed by the crisis.

3.2 Weakening of our Ability to Make Moral Judgments

A related effect of the increase of rules and procedures, particularly after a crisis, is that more and more rules and procedures reduce our ability to make moral judgments. In an environment where what we should and should not do is described in detail by rules and governed by strict procedures, we run the risk of becoming automatons who mindlessly follow the rules and procedures. In doing so we lose the ability to make moral judgments ourselves about the actions we are about to engage in and their consequences for our own organization, for its clients, customers, shareholders, and others who are affected by these actions. We no longer train our moral muscle, as all we need to know apparently has been described in the applicable rules and procedures. We no longer have to think about the consequences of our actions; what is not filtered out by application of rules and procedures is apparently all right. Thus we lose our practical wisdom.[51] One key element of the notion of practical wisdom that was developed by Aristotle, who referred to this as φρόνησις, is sensitivity to context. In most human practices conflicting demands, interests, principles, circumstances, responsibilities, and views are relevant to deciding what action to take. Sound decision taking requires constant balancing of these demands, interests, principles, circumstances, responsibilities, and views. There is no way that any set of rules can predict in advance how decisions should be taken in each and every context that may occur. This requires discretion to balance each of the relevant factors in order to decide what the right outcome is in the particular context. The thrust to regulate extensively after a crisis reduces this discretion. It imposes certain outcomes from the start, typically with only one of the multiple aims or concerns in mind that may be relevant. The discretion required to balance these multiple and sometimes conflicting aims disappears.[52]

3.3 Another Paradox: We Like the Rules We Say We Hate

Complaints of overregulation abound in many fields of human practice. Our typical response to failures and crises appears to be to try to identify causes and design rules and procedures that seek to ensure that they will not occur again. In the process, we destroy our sense of responsibility, our ability to make moral judgments, and the discretion required to come to balanced decisions. The outcries that the modern regulatory frameworks undermine the professionalism of teachers, academics, doctors, and judges are expressions of these concerns. Yet at the same time, new rules and procedures are designed in all these human practices. Often the request to regulate matters more closely comes from practitioners themselves. I have experienced this once myself in the field of corporate governance. I was

---

[51] Barry Schwartz & Kenneth Sharpe, Practical Wisdom: The Right Way to Do the Right Thing (2010).

[52] Philip Howard, Life Without Lawyers: Restoring Responsibility in America (2009); Schwartz & Sharpe, *supra* note 51.

a member of the Dutch Corporate Governance Committee that drafted the Dutch corporate governance code in 2003. A first draft was published for consultation in the summer of 2003. I discussed the draft with many executives and non-executives. The general response was that the draft presented an excessively regulatory approach to governance and board practices. It contained no less than 113 best practices and that was seen to be way over the top. At one point, however, the executives in particular took a fully opposite view. In the draft code we had provided that the board of management as a matter of best practice should declare in the Annual Report that the internal risk management and control systems operated effectively. We were criticized heavily for not providing any further rules and processes on the basis of which it would be reasonable for a board of management to make such a statement, as a result of which the provision created an unacceptable level of uncertainty. They demanded more detailed rules before they would accept this provision. The Governance Committee did not yield and the provision was included in the final code as best practice provision II.1.4. The provision continued to raise concerns, partly because of the potentially broad scope of the statement. In 2008 it was amended to reflect that the statement relates only to financial reporting risks and that only a reasonable measure of certainty was required that the financial report did not contain mistakes of material substance—current best practice II.1.5.[53]

A core psychological concept may explain what happened here. In psychology a distinction is made between a real object and the object representation in the mind. Real objects can be observed or understood with day vision; we clearly see or understand them. Real objects are for example a car or an iPad, but also relationships such as marriage or team membership. Object representations are the representations we make in our mind of these real objects, the interpretations and the narratives we generate about them. These interpretations and narratives are generated not only on the basis of what we observe and understand but also on the basis of our past experiences, the beliefs we build on them, and the contexts that we believe to be relevant. These interpretations and narratives act as filters, influencing interpretations of future experiences with these real objects. The interpretations and narratives we generate of the objective world are often unconscious; we are not consciously aware of them. It may take deliberate effort and night vision to become aware of these interpretations and narratives.[54] The core insight is that it is not the objective world that influences us and determines our behavior but how we represent and interpret the world.[55]

Rules as real objects seen with day vision can be described as guidelines, orders, or prohibitions relating to our behavior: they tell us what to do and what not to do and sometimes how to do it. At a deeper level of understanding, with night vision, we can expose that rules offer certainty and comfort. To the extent they take out our personal judgments and discretion (rules simply tell us what to do), they also take away our responsibility for getting it right when we exercise our judgment and discretion. Rules reduce our fear of responsibility, of having to explain to our peers, those that rely on us, and the public that we got it

---

[53] See for the 2014 version of the Dutch Corporate Governance Code www.commissiecorporate governance.nl.

[54] The concept of day vision and night vision in the context of the drivers of our behavior has been developed by Erik van de Loo, Roger Lehman, & Howard Book, Night Vision: A Systems-Psychodynamic Approach to Organisations (forthcoming).

[55] Timothy D. Wilson, Redirect: Changing the Stories We Live By (2011).

wrong when we made a judgment. Rules provide safety in a world full of risk. The executives that opposed the in-control best practice provision detected a new responsibility that was imposed on them without the safety of rules and procedures that informed them on what they could rely in making such statements. Clear rules would have reduced their responsibility. This effect may also explain the general and mechanical application of many best practice provisions in corporate governance codes: better to simply (without actually doing anything with the provision beyond formal compliance) apply these provisions, even if they are irritating, than to have to explain why they are not applied and to be challenged on this explanation.[56] We may like freedom of choice and judgment, but when this also creates risky responsibility we often prefer rules to tell us what to do. By allowing the rules to take over, we effectively hand over our responsibility.

A key notion to grasp from a behavioral perspective is that regulatory intervention itself has behavioral effects that may differ entirely from the effects that the intervention seeks to achieve. This behavioral perspective is not an argument against any regulation per se but should caution us, particularly after a crisis, to analyze carefully whether new rules and procedures can truly be expected to work before they are launched or whether any positive effect expected of them is outdone by the weakened sense of responsibility, the weakened ability to make moral judgments, and the eroded discretion that also result from the new rules.

4 Understanding Board Performance

Building on the agency theory, economic and finance research has focused on trying to establish a link between the performance of the firm and aspects of the regulation of boards, in particular requirements of independence, expertise, and diversity.[57] The problem with this research is that it only looks at input variables of board demographics and tries to establish a link between those variables and the outcome variable of firm performance. This assumes a causational relation between board composition and board performance on the one hand and between board performance and firm performance on the other. Both are very difficult to establish. A wealth of research indicates that research into board demographics in relation to firm performance must remain inconclusive if the intermediating process within the board itself is not researched.[58] Agency-based economic and finance research has so far ignored the black box of the board process and interaction as a key factor in board performance. It typically also focuses solely on the perspective of the non-executive gatekeepers as an indicator of board performance and leaves out the primary contribution of the executives who are being monitored. By ignoring the internal board interaction among

---

[56] Jaap Winter, Geen regels maar best practices, in Willems' Wegen: Opstellen aangeboden aan prof. mr. J.H.M. Willems 459 (Van Hassel, Nieuwe Weme eds., 2010).

[57] Jaap Winter & Erik van de Loo, Board on Task: Developing a Comprehensive Understanding of the Performance of Boards, in *Boards and Shareholders in European Listed Companies, Facts, Context and Post-Crisis Reforms* 225 (Massimo Belcredi & Guido Ferrarini eds., 2013).

[58] Daniel P. Forbes & Frances J. Milliken, "Cognition and Corporate Governance: Understanding Boards of Directors as Strategic Decision-Making Groups", 24 Acad. Mgmt. Rev. 489 (1999).

non-executives and between non-executives and executives, this research also ignores the human interaction that is the essence of the board process. The board as a combination of executive and non-executive directors[59] is a social, organizational structure allowing people in different roles to cooperate, debate, and take decisions in order to achieve specific corporate objectives. Both at the level of individual executive and non-executive directors as well as at the level of dynamics of the group as a whole, behavior is driven by factors that cannot be discerned or explained by the agency theory. They can only be investigated and understood by looking into the black box of board interaction, requiring different methodologies, techniques, and concepts. Erik van de Loo and I have developed and described a number of concepts and techniques for this purpose.[60] I summarize them here.

4.1 Board on Task and Board Interaction

In order to appreciate board performance, one has to have an idea of what the board is supposed to be doing. A *board is on task* when it is doing the right things and doing them right. Precisely on this matter corporate law and non-binding corporate governance regulation, even after a good decade of substantial regulation relating to boards, remain surprisingly vague. The notions described in legislation and governance codes typically use very broad terms, not clarifying what they in fact require of executives and non-executives. In the absence of clear guidance from the law, boards need to develop and define their own role with precision.[61] Many organizational theories distinguish two or three basic roles for the board: control, service, and sometimes as a separate role strategy.[62] These theories primarily take the perspective of non-executives to describe the roles of the board. In stewardship theory the role of the board is to facilitate and empower management and the CEO to lead the company, rather than to monitor and control them.[63] This theory takes the role of the executives as the primary role with the board consisting primarily of executive directors. A full understanding of board performance requires addressing both the roles of executives and of non-executives and how these roles relate to one another. We have developed a "matrix of board interaction" to discern with more precision in what fields of interaction executives and non-executives can be expected to interact and what types of involvement can be distinguished. Corporate hygiene (internal risk and control, financial statements), strategy (future

---

[59] In this chapter I make no distinction between one-tier and two-tier boards. In both models the crucial element is the interaction between executives and non-executives. The formal distinction between board models is not the key factor in understanding board performance. The term "board" in this chapter refers to the interaction between executives and non-executives in both one-tier and two-tier models.

[60] Winter & van de Loo, *supra* note 57; Erik van de Loo, Jaap Winter, & Maszuin Kamarudin, Corporate Governance and Boards: System and Behaviour. Developing Board Effectiveness in Malaysia (forthcoming 2015).

[61] The Future of Boards: Meeting the Governance Challenges of the Twenty-First Century (Jay W. Lorsch ed., 2012).

[62] Forbes & Milliken, *supra* note 58; Abigail Levrau & L.A.A. Van den Berghe, "Corporate Governance and Board Effectiveness: Beyond Formalism", 6 IUP J. of Corp. Gov. 58 (2007).

[63] Lex Donaldson & James H. Davis, "Stewardship Theory or Agency Theory: CEO Governance and Shareholder Returns", 16 Austl. J. Mgmt. 49 (1991).

direction of the company, risks, rewards under uncertainty), performance (current performance monitoring, financial and otherwise), people (role of non-executives as employers
toward executives, appointment, dismissal, remuneration), and stakeholders (shareholders,
employees, creditors, others) are areas where non-executives interact with executives. The
involvement of non-executives may vary from ratifying (non-executives blessing the outcome of the analysis of executives, not supposed to say no), probing (challenging the analysis
and outcome, substantively and procedurally), and engaging (contributing beyond probing
and challenging, adding specific knowledge or experience to the analysis), to directing (non-
executives as owners of the process and the content of the decision). These types of involvement, each requiring different behaviors from both non-executives and executives, can be
plotted in a matrix against the fields of interaction. In the field of people, referring to the role
of non-executive directors as employers of executives, codes and regulation typically require
non-executives to take a directive involvement. In other fields the minimum required involvement of non-executives is probing, while in practice non-executives may still be much
more ratifying than probing. In some instances non-executives may have to take a directive role in these fields as well, for example in case of suspicion of financial fraud or when
executives are conflicted, as may be the case in takeover bids. Sometimes non-executives can
engage beyond probing when they have particular expertise or knowledge that may help the
executives. This engaging role typically is for non-executives individually in specific areas
rather than as a group.

The matrix of board interaction does not provide a static description of the fields of interaction and the types of involvement of non-executives. On the contrary, the interaction
is dynamic by nature from field to field, from time to time, and from company to company.

4.2 Organizational Role Analysis

Distinguishing different fields of interaction and different levels of involvement is a first step
to bringing the interaction between executives and non-executives into vision. That in itself,
however, does not explain what boards, non-executives, and executives really do. In practice
we find that board members may still have different expectations, interpretations, views, and
perceptions of what the board, non-executives, and executives do or should be doing. As set
out in section 3.3, these personal narratives to a large extent determine how board members
act in their roles. A valuable framework to deepen our understanding of these board realities
is organizational role analysis (ORA). ORA is a relatively new model, which conceives of the
organization as a system of interrelated tasks, roles, and role-holders.[64] The concept of "role"
comprises the "place" or "area" that is the interface between a person and an organization,
or between personal and social systems.[65] It represents a space impacted on the one hand by
the organization and its definitions (tasks, other roles, system boundaries, resources, etc.)
and on the other by the way this specific person/role holder fills up and shapes this space,
fueled by the specific needs, aspirations, values, attitudes, and perceptions of that person.

---

[64]   Coaching in Depth: The Organizational Role Analysis Approach (John Newton, Susan Long &
Burkard Sievers eds., 2006).

[65]   Burkard Sievers & Ullrich Beumer, Organizational Role Analysis and Consultation: The
Organization as Inner Object, in Coaching in Depth, *supra* note 64, at 65 ff.

From this perspective the "role" is the place where the formal role (as defined by the organization/system) blends with the informal role (the specific way a specific person takes up his or her role). Crucial in all of this is that the role holder assumes what the role requirements are: what is the primary task and how is it to be fulfilled? Individual role holders construct implicit and explicit task ideas. These task ideas will to a large extent determine how an individual will take up his role. Taking up one's role represents a complex and interrelated configuration of interpretations: of the system, of the tasks to be fulfilled, of one's role, of oneself in one's role, and of others in their roles. For a meaningful explanation of the functioning of a system, it is important to map out how the various role holders interpret their own as well as one another's roles in it. These can be referred to as *role ideas*. As a consequence, for any group with a joint task or with interrelated tasks it is essential to become aware of both one's own and of others' role and task ideas. This requires role awareness and role dialogues.[66]

From the matrix of board interaction we can develop role definitions and distinguish role ideas from both the perspective of non-executives and executives. The probing involvement, for example, requires non-executives to receive information from the executives, to review this information critically, to invest time to understand and prepare for a discussion on the basis of the information received and to engage in that discussion in order to truly understand, to distinguish what is known and what is believed, and to grasp what the risks and opportunities are in light of the inevitable uncertainties. If they in fact are not doing so, their efforts do not go beyond a ratifying involvement. Their actual role idea (of being ratifying) does not fit with the role definition (of being probing). Furthermore, a probing role for non-executives requires executives to provide them with all relevant information. But if executives only bury non-executives with all information available without discerning the key elements, the core questions to address and the essential factors to balance, or if they provide information only at a very late stage, they in fact reduce the role of non-executives to merely ratifying. The actual role idea that executives have of the role of non-executives (only being ratifying) again does not fit with the formal role definition (of being probing). Different fields of interaction also require different role definitions and role ideas. For example, in corporate hygiene a certain critical, strict attitude and healthy suspicion of non-executives is required. If a non-executive feels the need to be seen as nice, this will hinder him in being truly probing. At the same time, executives will need to be able to deal with the critical and robust probing attitude of non-executives. If they perceive criticism as a failure or a sign of distrust and develop a practice of delaying or hiding crucial information from non-executives, they frustrate the probing role of non-executives. In the field of strategy, on the other hand, the nature of the interaction is more of a partnering kind, ensuring that best choices are made. Non-executives can improve the thinking process of executives by providing external perspectives and specific expertise. But if executives or non-executives believe that the lack of specific company knowledge on the part of non-executives means that they cannot contribute to the development of strategy in depth, nothing will come of this added value. Again, the role definition requiring a probing involvement is reduced to the role idea of ratifying.

---

[66] Susan Long, John Newton, & Jane Chapman, Role Dialogue: Organizational Role Analysis with Pairs from the Same Organization, in Coaching in Depth, *supra* note 64, at 95 ff.

4.3 Board GPS

In law and in economics the formal system of rights and duties is often taken as a given. A behavioral perspective deepens the scope of the inquiry to what the formal, systemic requirements lead to in the actual behavior of individuals in their roles. The matrix of board interaction seeks to describe the interaction of non-executives and executives in the board at a more granular level, distinguishing fields of interaction and types of involvement. This produces more accurate role definitions. The ORA then provides an approach that helps to identify what role ideas non-executives and executives hold. These internal narratives determine their actual behaviors in their roles as non-executives and executives. In this way the ORA connects the System to the Persons in the board as a Group. If we are to understand board performance in a comprehensive way, we have to apply and combine these three perspectives: Group, Person, and System. This approach, which we call Board GPS, allows us to address behavioral characteristics and factors at personal and group levels, looking into formal and informal leadership in a group, cohesion, conflict resolution, information sharing, reflection, group biases and groupthink,[67] and personal styles, parrhesia,[68] empathy, humility, and biases at personal level.

It is clear that reaching into the black box of a board to uncover the reality of the interaction of non-executives and executives requires different techniques and methodologies. Many empirical techniques such as interviews, questionnaires, and observations from various social and behavioral sciences have not yet been applied to boards that often remain closed environments for external academics to research. However, the corporate governance wave that has rolled on for the last two decades has sharpened the focus on board performance. Many boards are moving beyond formal compliance with rules and best practice standards and seek to enhance their performance by internal and externally facilitated board reviews. Researchers in the Netherlands, some of whom are conducting board reviews themselves, are in the process of connecting academic research into board performance with the practice of board reviews in order to make private information on particular boards available for academic research on an anonymous (both individual board members and companies) basis. Erik van de Loo and I have developed a specific questionnaire, the "Board Reality Questionnaire" (BRQ), in order to collect relevant samples of perceived behavioral and emotional interactions in the board. We use the BRQ when we conduct board reviews. The BRQ asks board members and outsiders who can observe (parts of) the board interaction whether they have observed a series of behaviors and events during the last year. These behaviors and events have been formulated in 150 items, based on the concept of Board GPS and asking about the prevalence of behaviors and events relevant from the perspective of the Group, Person, and System. Participants can indicate whether the behaviors have occurred never, regularly, or consistently, or that they cannot say for the particular behavior or event. The first findings of the BRQ with four boards in 2013 show that non-executives and executives as groups regularly report different and sometimes completely opposing (never versus consistently) scores, and that sometimes the scores also vary strongly within the

---

[67] Forsyth, *supra* note 42.

[68] Michel Foucault, Le courage de la vérité, Le gouvernement de soi et des autres II. Cours au Collège de France (1983–1984) (2009).

groups of non-executives and executives. Where these differences occur this indicates that there is no common perception of behaviors and events. This may cause different narratives and interpretations of the reality of the board to exist or continue, weakening the board's performance. By using the BRQ in board reviews we plan to build up a dataset of observations of board realities. This may help us to uncover in what areas it is more likely that differences of perception and interpretation are to occur, potentially weakening board performance.

5 Executive Remuneration Built to Fail

The agency theory postulates that managers of companies as agents have different interests than shareholders as principals and that managers as rational self-interest maximizers seek to further their interests as much as they can, also when this does not serve the interests of shareholders. One strategy that has been designed and enthusiastically applied to deal with this problem is to align the interests of managers with those of shareholders by various remuneration mechanics. The key element of these is that remuneration should not be fixed but should depend on results achieved that are also in the interest of shareholders. Cash bonuses that depend on profits reported are an example. Stock options that give the right to acquire shares in the company for an exercise price equal to the share price of the day of the grant of the options provide an incentive to enhance company performance that should result in a higher stock price, which makes exercising the stock option profitable. Share grants typically vest depending on the position the company holds in a peer group of companies based on total shareholder return (share price increase plus dividends), usually over a period of three years. Shares held after exercise of stock options or vesting of share grants continue to align the interests of managers with the interests of shareholders.

Earlier criticism by scholars indicated that the design and governance of executive remuneration systems are often poor.[69] Governance regulation, through corporate governance codes and for financial institutions also in EU binding regulation, has attempted to address design and governance problems. But a more fundamental problem remains: modern behavioral research indicates that people cannot handle performance-based variable play, for a number of reasons that I have set extensively elsewhere.[70] I summarize the gist of the arguments.

5.1 Incentives and Behavior

A growing body of research raises serious questions about the effects of monetary incentives. In section 3.1 I mentioned the crowding out effect of monetary incentives.

[69] Lucian Bebchuk & Jesse Fried, Pay Without Performance: The Unfulfilled Promise of Executive Compensation (2004); Michael C. Jensen, Kevin J. Murphy, & Eric Wruck, "Remuneration: Where We've Been, How We Got to Here, What Are the Problems and How to Fix them", ECGI Financial Working Paper series no. 44 (2004), available at http://ssrn.com/abstract=561305.

[70] Jaap Winter, Corporate Governance Going Astray: Executive Remuneration Built to Fail, in Research Handbook on Executive Pay 199 (Randall S. Thomas & Jennifer Hill eds., 2012).

Monetary incentives have the effect that the intrinsic motivation of people and any social reasons they may have to perform a certain task well are displaced by the extrinsic monetary incentive, as a result of which the performance may actually become worse. James offers an alternative explanation, holding that an extrinsic incentive may provide intrinsic satisfaction if the incentive indicates competence, but will not do so if it is perceived as controlling.[71] When the size of the incentive is large it will primarily be perceived as controlling as it rationally compels the agent to attribute its efforts to the incentive rather than his own preferences. This latter effect is also demonstrated when the incentive is withdrawn or substantially reduced, leading the agent to question why he would continue to work hard to reach a certain result. This effect was also demonstrated in the case of day care centers where the number of parents that kept coming late did not decrease.[72] Ariely says: "Once the bloom is off the rose—once a social norm is trumped by a market norm—it will rarely return."[73]

An even more damaging research result is that monetary incentives appear to have a negative effect on performance when a creative, non-mechanical task needs to be executed.[74] Amabile and others have shown consistently that extrinsic rewards stifle creativity.[75] Glucksberg reported that participants who were told they would receive a reward for solving the cognitive complex candle problem faster were actually slower in solving the problem.[76] Other researchers have found that a higher bonus does lead to better results when the job at hand involved only clicking two keys on a keyboard.[77] However, once the task required even rudimentary cognitive skills, the higher incentives led to a negative effect on performance.[78] These results are consistent with the meta-analytical study that Jenkins and co-authors conducted in 1998 on the results of 47 studies known then on the relation between incentive and performance.[79] They found that financial incentives have a significant relationship to the quantity of work delivered, but not with the quality of the work.[80] It is clear that the work of executives is not merely to perform mechanical functions. They constantly need to take decisions in uncertainty, gathering information, weighing pros and cons and risks and rewards. Research indicates that large financial incentives are not helping them to make better decisions, but rather the opposite.

---

[71] Harvey James, "Why Did You Do That? An Economic Examination of the Effect of Extrinsic Compensation on Intrinsic Motivation and Performance", Revision of CORI Working Paper no. 2003-01 (2004), available at http://ssrn.com/abstract=476542.

[72] Gneezy & Rustichini, *supra* note 46.   [73] Ariely, *supra* note 3.

[74] Hoeppner & Kirchner, *supra* note 20.   [75] Teresa M. Amabile, Creativity in Context (1996).

[76] Sam Glucksberg, "The Influence of Strength of Drive on Functional Fixedness and Perceptual Recognition", 63 J. Experimental Psychology 36 (1962).

[77] Dan Ariely, Uri Gneezy, George Loewenstein, & Nina Mazar, "Large Stakes and Big Mistakes", 76 Rev. Econ. Stud. 451 (2009).

[78] Id.

[79] G. Douglas Jenkins, Jr., Atul Mitra, Nina Gupta, & Jason D. Shaw, "Are Financial Incentives Related to Performance? A Meta-Analytic Review of Empirical Research", 83 J. Applied Psychology 777 (1998).

[80] Id.

5.2 Target Setting and Cheating

A key element of variable pay systems is that the targets on the achievement of which the incentives depend are set in advance. The payout is then related to the actual achievement of these targets. Jensen refers to this system as a game that pays people to lie twice. "Tell a manager that he or she will get a bonus when targets are realized and two things are sure to happen. First, managers will attempt to set targets that are easily reachable, and once the targets are set, they will do their best to see that the targets are met even if it damages the company to do so."[81] Performance indicators corrupt immediately when they become targets that need to be met in order to receive a certain award. This was illustrated in the case of Chicago public schools, where a change in how schools were held accountable for student learning led to an increase in cheating by teachers.[82] Target setting in advance for financial incentive purposes was designed on the belief that this would help to base remuneration on objective and measurable factors, thereby limiting the scope for rigging by managers. The opposite is likely to happen. At the same time most managers will maintain that they are honest. The ability to combine cheating with a view of oneself as honest increases when the manager can categorize his actions and find rationalizations that allow him to reinterpret his actions in a self-serving manner.[83]

5.3 (Bad) Luck

The self-serving bias also causes us to systematically overestimate our influence on success and to ignore factors that are often more relevant: timing, circumstances, and pure luck.[84] We tend to create narratives to find meaning in events and we tend to do so in a self-serving way, ignoring that reality is mostly more complex, fuzzy, and messy. As a result we also tend to underestimate our influence on failure and are quick to blame circumstances outside our control. This correlates to an opportunistic shift of perception of what is supposed to be rewarded. When times are good, the creation of value is perceived as the performance that needs to be rewarded, regardless of how much value was actually created by the specific performance of executives. When times are not so good and little or no value has been created, the extraordinary efforts of the executives need to be rewarded. This is confirmed by research indicating that executive pay is most sensitive to industry or market benchmarks when such benchmarks are up, but much less so when they are down. Executives are paid for good luck, but not punished for bad luck.[85] The basis for this self-serving tendency is

---

[81] Michael C. Jensen, "Paying People to Lie: The Truth about the Budgeting Process", 9 Eur. Fin. Mgmt. 379 (2003).

[82] Brian A. Jacob & Steven D. Levitt, "Rotten Apples: An Investigation of the Prevalence and Predictors of Teacher Cheating", 118 Q. J. Econ. 843 (2003).

[83] Nina Mazar, On Amir, & Dan Ariely, "The Dishonesty of Honest People: A Theory of Self-Concept Maintenance", 45 J. Marketing Research 633 (2008).

[84] Taleb, *supra* note 23.

[85] Gerald T. Garvey & Todd T. Milbourn, "Asymmetric Benchmarking in Compensation: Executives are Rewarded for Good Luck but Not Penalized for Bad", 82 J. Fin. Econ. 197 (2006); see also Marianne Bertrand & Sendhil Mullainathan, "Are CEOs Rewarded for Luck? The Ones without Principals Are", 116 Q. J. Econ. 901 (2001).

the motive to affirm self-worth. People react to negative information about themselves by making more self-serving attributions that affirm their worth.[86] When performance targets have not been met, the need to affirm our self-worth creates cognitive dissonance. We will look for other reasons outside our own performance to explain the failure to reach targets.

5.4 Benchmarking for Fairness and Status

Another mechanism that seeks to make the system objective and measurable and less subject to rigging by executives is the process of benchmarking remuneration to remuneration received by executives of companies in a peer group. This benchmarking is an expression of the human reality that we perceive the fairness of our income in relative terms, as compared to what others make for similar or different jobs. Benchmarking of executive pay typically is combined with a policy to reward one's own executives above the median or sometimes in the top quartile of the peer group. If all companies in a peer group apply this policy (and they mostly do), the remuneration of all executives of all peer group companies predictably goes up in a race to be in the top 50% or 25% of remuneration, unrelated to the underlying performance of their companies. A German executive once said at a conference I attended: "I know I am being overpaid, but the benchmark shows I am not being overpaid enough!" The cause of this is probably not the desire to receive more remuneration as such. Benchmarking is also an expression of social status. High remuneration signals high social status among peers. Status is a zero-sum game. If my status moves up by receiving more pay, then the status of others comes down.[87] Research also indicates that the only situation where we may accept a pay cut is when others do so too.[88]

The behavioral research summarized here indicates that substantial executive remuneration through variable pay, target setting in advance, and benchmarking that seeks to solve the agency problem in fact delivers fundamental problems in return which discredit modern executive pay techniques as an effective mechanism to align interests with shareholders.

6 Conclusion

This chapter only addresses a fraction of the behavioral research that could be relevant to aspects of corporate law and corporate governance. It is also only fair to note that much of the behavioral literature cited here does not directly relate to corporate settings but is based on studies of behavior in experimental situations. Some elements of the corporate setting may provide a counter-balance to detrimental behavior that appears to result from these experiments.[89] Nonetheless, the evidence is more than sufficient to merit at least paying careful attention to it in corporate law and corporate governance. This chapter also only touches upon some elements of corporate law and corporate governance, such as

---

[86] Max H. Bazerman & Don A. Moore, Judgment in Managerial Decision Making (7th ed. 2009).
[87] Richard Layard, Happiness: Lessons from a New Science (2d ed. 2011).
[88] Truman Bewley, Why Wages Don't Fall During a Recession (1999).
[89] Langevoort, supra note 43.

rulemaking, board performance, and executive remuneration. Many other areas could be studied from a behavioral perspective. Shareholders play a key role in corporate law and corporate governance. The role of institutional investors in the corporate governance of listed companies has been debated extensively recently, in particular in relation to the question of whether they should be more engaged in the governance of investee companies and what stops them from doing so. The investment model as such seems to be a key driver for the lack of engagement that we see.[90] Behavioral sciences also influence the investment model in all aspects of bounded rationality, bounded perception, and bounded ethicality.[91] In addition, the interaction between executives, non-executives, and (institutional) investors in the governance of the company is often difficult. Each of these three players is under scrutiny to contribute to proper governance relations, but what is to be expected of them in this triangle is in practice often unclear.[92]

Conflicts of interests are a key topic in corporate law and corporate governance. Conflicts may relate to dominating shareholders who may force the company into related party transactions that are detrimental to minority shareholders. Directors may engage in transactions in which they have a personal interest. A typical legal response to conflicts of interest is to require transparency of interest. Research, however, indicates that disclosure may make matters worse. Persons who disclose conflicts may actually feel freer to act selfishly because counterparties have been warned of the risk.[93] Another topic where behavioral insights are crucial is director liability. The personal liability of directors to pay damages has been a cornerstone of corporate law since its inception. In some countries criminal liability plays an additional role. Liability for damages is imposed as a sanction in case of improper managerial behavior through which third parties are compensated. However, beyond compensation the function of sanction is that of deterrence. In corporate law debates this deterrence factor is often assumed to be self-evident. Clearly, whether, to what extent, and under what conditions deterrence through personally liability actually works is a behavioral question beyond mere rational calculation.[94]

Corporate law and corporate governance in the end are all about human behavior in corporate roles. We would learn more about how corporate law and corporate governance function in practice by broadening our perspective from the legal intuitions and

---

[90] Jaap Winter, "Shareholder Engagement and Stewardship: The Realities and Illusions of Institutional Share Ownership", Working Paper (2011), available at http://ssrn.com/abstract=1867564; Mats Isaksson & Serdar Çelik, "Who Cares? Corporate Governance in Today's Equity Markets", OECD Corporate Governance Working Papers no. 8 (2013), http://dx.doi.org/10.1787/5k47zw5kdnmp-en; Serdar Çelik & Mats Isaksson, "Institutional Investors as Owners: Who Are They and What Do They Do?", OECD Corporate Governance Working Papers no. 11 (2013), www.oecd-ilibrary.org/governance/institutional-investors-as-owners_5k3v1dvmfk42-en.

[91] James Montier, Behavioural Investing: A Practitioner's Guide to Applying Behavioural Finance (2007).

[92] Erik van de Loo & Angelien Kemna, Roles, Risks and Complexity: An Exploration of the Triangle Institutional Investors, Executive Boards and Supervisory Boards in the Netherlands, in *Towards a Socioanalysis of Money, Finance and Capitalism* 178 (Susan Long & Burkard Sievers eds., 2012).

[93] Daylian M. Cain, George Loewenstein & Don A. Moore, "The Dirt on Coming Clean: Perverse Effects of Disclosing Conflicts of Interests", 34 J. Leg. Stud. 1 (2005).

[94] See already Alfred F. Conard, "A Behavioral Analysis of Director's Liability for Negligence", 1972 Duke L. J. 895 (1972).

assumptions behind corporate laws and corporate governance regulations, beyond the economic analysis assuming rational self-regarding behavior into other behavioral disciplines that can explain how we truly behave. We both are rational and make cognitive errors, we can be pro-social but also selfish. Regulating corporate law and corporate governance on the assumption of the one-sided notion of rational self-regarding behavior may actually prove counterproductive.[95] Opening up to these insights can help us to improve corporate law and corporate governance regulation.

---

[95] Blair & Stout, *supra* note 43.

CHAPTER 8

....

EMPIRICAL STUDIES OF CORPORATE LAW AND GOVERNANCE

Some Steps Forward and Some Steps Not

....

MICHAEL KLAUSNER[1]

THEORY often does not get us very far in understanding corporate law and governance. Competing plausible theories offer conflicting answers on many questions. For most questions, therefore, we would ideally seek answers based on empirical analysis. But empirical analysis entails its own challenges. Causation is difficult to prove. Reverse causation is often a plausible interpretation of results, as are other endogenous relationships. In addition, unobservable factors are pervasive and the inability to control for them can make results unreliable. Consequently, to address many empirical questions, an exogenous shock would be needed in order to infer causation. But exogenous shocks can be uncooperative in targeting interesting corporate governance questions. Finally, many economists who engage in empirical research on corporate governance lack the knowledge of institutional and legal facts that is needed to carry out empirical analysis of corporate governance questions.

Nonetheless, there are certainly areas of corporate law and governance in which we have learned a lot from empirical analysis. Even where imperfect, if econometric analysis reveals a theoretically reasonable correlation between a corporate governance structure and an outcome variable, and the analysis goes as far as one can go toward controlling for extraneous variables and alternative channels of causation, we can learn from the analysis. Over time, other less-than-perfect analyses may confirm the analysis, or fail to confirm it, so that in the aggregate we have a reasonably good answer to the question we are trying to answer.

On the other hand, a finding of a theoretically *implausible* correlation should not be taken seriously. Regrettably, along with the good empirical work that has been done on corporate governance, there have been too many instances of work by economists who

[1] Nancy and Charles Munger Professor of Business and Professor of Law, Stanford Law School. The author would like to thank Emiliano Catan, John Coates, Allen Ferrell, Ron Gilson, Jeff Gordon, Colleen Honigsberg, and Marcel Kahan for helpful comments on this chapter.

do not understand the underlying institutional and legal arrangements. As a result, their hypotheses and tests have generated implausible results. Regrettably, other economists have followed and entire literatures have developed based on an incorrect understanding of the underlying facts. The literature on takeover defenses and state antitakeover statutes is an example—dating back 30 years and continuing today.[2] The use of governance indices, which I have discussed elsewhere and which I discuss below, is another.[3]

It is obviously not feasible to survey the entire empirical literature on corporate law and governance in one chapter, so I will adopt two somewhat arbitrary constraints. First, I will only discuss the literature on US corporate law and governance.[4] Second, I will address just four areas of the US corporate governance literature—state competition to produce corporate law, independent boards, takeover defenses, and the use of corporate governance indices—to illustrate the good and the bad in empirical work on corporate governance.

Studies of state competition have been the most productive. They have taken our knowledge of the world well beyond where it was when legal academics debated this topic on the basis of theory alone. Studies of board independence are more problematic. Econometric challenges are pervasive, but they are generally acknowledged and while few papers can convincingly claim to have identified causal relationships, some have done so, and the literature as a whole is large and collectively informative. The takeover defense topic is the most problematic area of the empirical corporate governance literature. It is here where economists' lack of knowledge of basic institutional and legal facts has resulted in numerous studies that simply cannot tell us anything because the research design is so out of line with the underlying processes being modeled. The design and use of corporate governance indices are a specific and pervasive instance of economists' lack of knowledge in this area. These indices do not measure corporate governance quality, and have been widely employed with no awareness of what they do or do not measure. The E Index, in fact, is a by-product of an article showing that three quarters of the elements included in the G Index are irrelevant. As I explain in section 4 of this chapter, the same is true of three of the six elements retained in what became the E Index.

1 STATE COMPETITION TO PROVIDE CORPORATE LAW

One of the longest running debates regarding corporate law in the US was the question whether there is a "race to the bottom" or a "race to the top" among the 50 states in the enactment of corporate law.[5] Does the evolution of state corporate law result in improvement or

---

[2] See Emiliano Catan & Marcel Kahan, "The Law and Finance of Antitakeover Statutes", 68 Stan. L. Rev. 629 (2016); John C. Coates IV, "Takeover Defenses in the Shadow of the Pill: A Critique of the Scientific Evidence", 79 Tex. L. Rev. 271 (2000); Michael Klausner, "Fact and Fiction in Corporate Law and Governance", 65 Stan. L. Rev. 1325 (2013).

[3] Klausner, *supra* note 2.

[4] Because of the greater data availability on US firms, a disproportionately large fraction of the empirical corporate governance literature has a US focus in any event.

[5] See Chapter 5: Marcel Kahan, "The State of State Competition for Incorporations."

degradation? Plausible competing theories supported each of these propositions. So, if the question can be answered, it would be with empirical analysis.

When a company in the US goes public, its pre-IPO management and shareholders together choose a state in which to incorporate and in doing so, they choose the corporate law of that state to govern the relationship between its post-IPO managers and shareholders. The incorporation decision is thus a choice of corporate law. Once the company is publicly held, its board decides on an ongoing basis whether to remain incorporated in its initial state of incorporation or to reincorporate in another state. Reincorporation requires the approval of both the board and shareholders. But at the time this debate started, public shareholders were viewed as passive followers of management preferences, and boards were seen as controlled by CEOs.

As of the mid-1970s, the prevailing view was that the states were racing to the "bottom" to convince management to choose them as a state of incorporation—meaning that they were viewed as enacting pro-management, anti-shareholder laws that we would characterize today as suboptimal. States enacted these laws, the theory went, in order to bring fees associated with incorporation into state coffers and income into a state's corporate lawyers' pockets. The content of the laws then perceived to serve managers' parochial interests was primarily protection of management from liability risk—for example, the business judgment rule and rules allowing for a wide scope of indemnification.[6]

The competing view, held by most economics-oriented legal scholars beginning in the late 1970s, accepted the premise that states were racing to attract incorporations, but rejected the view that states did so by enacting suboptimal, pro-management laws. In the view of this more economically oriented group of legal academics, managers would gain by maximizing the value of their firms and thereby increasing the value of their shareholdings and compensation. Therefore pre-IPO managers and investors would initially incorporate their firms in states whose corporate law regimes maximized firm value. Then, after going public, firms' managers would continuously monitor changes in corporate law around the country and reincorporate if a better choice arose.[7] Advocates of this view theorized that state competition, therefore, must be a race to the "top."[8]

A third view, which entered the debate later, raised doubts about the competitiveness of the race. Although this view, also adopted by economically oriented scholars, was framed as a challenge to the theory that the race would reach the top, its logic applied as well to the race-to-the-bottom proposition. This challenge was based on the concept that corporate laws have network externality qualities, as discussed in Chapter 4. One would expect the network externalities present in an entire corporate law regime—court decisions, legal expertise, and investor familiarity—to be even more important than those associated with a particular legal rule or a charter or bylaw term, which was the focus of Chapter 4. If, in fact, state corporate law regimes provide network benefits, then once Delaware led the race one would expect its lead to widen and potentially become so dominant that no state would have a chance of gaining significant market share. If this occurred, why would another state run

---

[6] William L. Cary, "Federalism and Corporate Law: Reflections upon Delaware", 83 Yale L. J. 663, 663–68 (1974).

[7] See Chapter 4: Michael Klausner, "The 'Corporate Contract' Today."

[8] Ralph K. Winter, Jr., "State Law, Shareholder Protection, and the Theory of the Corporation", 6 J. Leg. Stud. 251 (1977).

the race at all? The network externality theory implies that once Delaware acquired a substantial lead, as it had well before the "race" debate started in the 1970s, it would maintain that lead. There would be no point in other states challenging Delaware, and there was no reason to believe that Delaware would reach the "top." The outcome, therefore, would not necessarily be an optimal corporate law regime, as the race-to-the-top theory maintained. This is not to say that Delaware could ignore the care and maintenance of its corporate law; if the law's inherent quality were to fall too far behind that of other states, the network benefits that Delaware provides could be insufficient to attract additional incorporations or to deter exit to other states. There was a possibility that Delaware could be overtaken in the incorporation market. But Delaware would not have to run very fast to keep its leading position, and it would not have to produce an optimal corporate law, independent of the network benefits it provides.[9]

Roberta Romano provided the first major empirical analysis of state competition in the market for corporate law.[10] In this path-breaking article, she found support for the race-to-the-top theory. She found that Delaware was the most common destination among public corporations that changed their state of incorporation. She further found that reincorporation in Delaware was associated with an increase in share price. This result is consistent with Robert Daines's later finding that Delaware firms are valued more highly than firms incorporated elsewhere,[11] a finding that Guhan Subramanian has contested.[12]

Looking at the supply side of the corporate law market, Romano found that state legislatures adopt legal innovations over time in an S-shaped pattern similar to that of firms adopting product innovations in competitive markets. This suggested a competitive market for the states' provision of corporate law. Romano further found that a state's responsiveness to corporate law innovations by other states was correlated with the state's dependence on corporate franchise fee revenues, again supporting the race-to-the-top theory. Delaware, for which franchise fees comprise a higher proportion of state revenues than they do in any other state, was the quickest to imitate other states' legal innovations. Importantly, however, Delaware was not an innovator. It maintained its lead by just keeping up with the competition.

Romano concluded that state competition in corporate law does, in fact, exist. She described Delaware's success as a self-reinforcing "first-mover advantage" stemming from

---

[9] For a more detailed explanation, see Michael Klausner, "Corporations, Corporate Law, and Networks of Contracts", 81 Va. L. Rev. 757, 842–847 (1995) and Lucian Arye Bebchuk & Assaf Hamdani, "Vigorous Race or Leisurely Walk: Reconsidering the Competition over Corporate Charters", 112 Yale L. J. 553 (2002).

[10] Romano tracked the 50 states' adoption of eight innovations in corporate law:

> (1) the explicit elaboration of a standard for director and officer indemnification, (2) the exemption from stockholder vote of mergers involving a specified percentage of the corporation's stock, (3) the elimination of appraisal rights in corporations whose shares trade on a national exchange, (4) antitakeover statutes, (5) the right of shareholders to take action nonunanimously without holding a meeting, and the permission to (6) stagger the board of directors, (7) eliminate cumulative voting, and (8) eliminate preemptive rights.

Roberta Romano, "Law as a Product: Some Pieces of the Incorporation Puzzle", 1 J. L. Econ. & Org. 225, 233 (1985).

[11] Robert Daines, "Does Delaware Law Improve Firm Value?", 62 J. Fin. Econ. 525, 533–38 (2001).

[12] Guhan Subramanian, "The Disappearing Delaware Effect", 20 J. L. Econ & Org. 32 (2004).

a number of sources: the importance of franchise taxes to Delaware's budget; a large body of case law; experienced judges; and the familiarity of lawyers nationwide with Delaware law. These findings, however, are somewhat in tension with one another. If Delaware has these first-mover advantages in promoting shareholder interests, and it already held a commanding share of the incorporation market as of the mid-1980s, how much state competition is there likely to be? Why would a state bother to compete with Delaware? Why would any firm incorporate in a state other than Delaware? Does the Delaware legislature have slack with which to respond to the lobbying efforts of managers and others seeking to promote parochial interests that are not consistent with the maximization of firm value? If other states do not compete vigorously head-to-head with Delaware, will Delaware ever get to the "top"?

A series of articles published between 2002 and 2006 addressed the question whether there really is a race of any sort—to the top or the bottom.[13] One startling finding was that, contrary to the expectations of commentators on both sides of the race debate, there was no nationwide race among the 50 states. Instead, nearly all firms incorporate either in the state in which they are headquartered or in Delaware. Thus, if there is competition among states it would take the form of each state competing with Delaware for the incorporation of firms headquartered in that state. Putting Delaware aside, between 1978 and 2000, the four most successful states at attracting incorporation by out-of-state firms at the IPO stage garnered a total of only 3.5% of firms going public.[14] For firms already public as of 1999, only two states other than Delaware had more than 1% of total out-of-state incorporations. Delaware had 58%.[15] Consequently, there is little out-of-state franchise tax revenue at stake for any state other than Delaware. There may be more potential in-state revenues in large states, but large states are likely to have large budgets in which potential franchise taxes do not make a dent. These findings suggest that states may have no incentive to compete with Delaware.

In an article entitled "The Myth of State Competition in Corporate Law," Marcel Kahan and Ehud Kamar concluded that the amount of franchise tax revenue at stake for any state other than Delaware is too small to matter. Moreover, they found that no state other than Delaware takes significant steps to attract incorporations or to gain significant revenues from incorporation.[16] They based their conclusions on an analysis of states' franchise tax structures, their tax receipts, patterns by which laws are adopted across states, and states' marketing efforts.[17] This paper was not empirical in the sense of compiling statistics and running regressions, but it was deeply empirical in the sense of delving into facts in 50 states in order to determine whether they are participating in any sort of race. Kahan and Kamar's

---

[13] Marcel Kahan, "The Demand for Corporate Law: Statutory Flexibility, Judicial Quality, or Takeover Protection?", 22 J. L. Econ. & Org. 340 (2006); Lucian Arye Bebchuk & Alma Cohen, "Firms' Decisions Where to Incorporate", 46 J. L. & Econ. 383 (2003); Guhan Subramanian, "The Influence of Antitakeover Statutes on Incorporation Choice: Evidence on the "Race" Debate and Antitakeover Overreaching", 150 U. Pa. L. Rev. 1795 (2002); Robert Daines, "The Incorporation Choices of IPO Firms", 77 N.Y.U. L. Rev. 1559 (2002).

[14] Daines, *supra* note 13, at 1573.   [15] Bebchuk & Cohen, *supra* note 13, 389, 391 (at Table 2).

[16] Marcel Kahan & Ehud Kamar, "The Myth of State Competition in Corporate Law", 55 Stan. L. Rev. 679, 748–49 (2002).

[17] Id. at 687–99.

analysis essentially ended the debate. The states are not racing against one another to attract incorporations—neither by trying to appeal to managers' parochial interests nor by trying to appeal to their joint interest with shareholders in maximizing firm value.

As Kahan and Kamar's article was going to press, Nevada was preparing to make a play for incorporation revenue by offering a corporate law that Michal Barzuza has termed "liability-free" for officers and directors. As Barzuza explains and documents, Nevada has targeted a niche of firms whose managers want to be largely free of liability risk in their exercise of fiduciary duty. She and David Smith further find that firms attracted to incorporate in Nevada make good use of the liability-free environment; they are disproportionately more likely than other firms to engage in accounting misstatements.[18] Nevada's market share, however, is in the single digits. Perhaps Nevada will attract more firms seeking liability-lite. We will see. But Nevada's efforts do not challenge the overall story of the race that never was.

Even if there is no race, however, all states have corporate law, and firms still choose between incorporating in Delaware or in their home state. There is still the demand side of the market for corporate law. What factors influence firms' decisions? Are firms choosing between Delaware and their home state based on differences in corporate law or something else?

The choice of Delaware incorporation provides law and legally-related network benefits— a large and continuously growing body of case law, a specialized judiciary that has a steady flow of corporate law cases with which to maintain its skills and knowledge, a large number of lawyers with expertise, and more. But what about firms choosing to incorporate in their headquarters state? Some states keep more in-state incorporations and some states keep fewer. What drives these differences? The fact that the location of a firm's headquarters plays such an overwhelming role in incorporation decisions suggests that differences in state law are not the primary focus of firms' incorporation decisions. As Robert Daines said in a paper on state competition, Oregon retains almost 70% of IPO firms headquartered there, but in 20 years only three out-of-state firms incorporated in Oregon when they went public.[19] If the attraction of Oregon were its corporate laws, then out-of-state firms would presumably see the attraction and incorporate there. There must be other explanations.

In three articles, Daines, Bebchuk and Cohen, and Kahan offer some other empirically based explanations for in-state incorporation, most of which are not based on the content of a state's corporate law. One is that local lawyers who advise firms on their IPOs have their clients incorporate in-state, perhaps in order to retain their business. A second explanation is that in-state firms want to be in a position to influence the corporate law under which they operate. They may believe that if they incorporate at home they will be able to influence their state legislature to enact laws that favor them. This is consistent with Romano's finding, in 1987, that the enactment of state antitakeover statutes was responsive to domestically incorporated firms.[20] Daines finds evidence that firms concerned about future takeovers tend to incorporate in-state and suggests that they may expect to find favor in the state legislature or in the courts when they seek to ward off hostile bidders. Bebchuk and Cohen find that

---

[18] Michal Barzuza & David Smith, "What Happens in Nevada? Self-Selecting into Lax Law", 27 Rev. Fin. Stud. 3593 (2014); Michal Barzuza, "Market Segmentation: The Rise of Nevada as a Liability-Free Jurisdiction", 98 Va. L. Rev. 935 (2012).

[19] Daines, *supra* note 13, at 1576.

[20] Roberta Romano, "The Political Economy of Takeover Statutes", 73 Va. L. Rev. 111 (1987).

large firms headquartered in small states tend to incorporate in-state, from which they infer that such firms expect to have influence over future changes in corporate law. Kahan, on the other hand, finds some support for the proposition that in-state incorporation is influenced by the quality of state law at the time of incorporation. Specifically, he finds that flexibility to opt out of statutory rules tends to attract more in-state incorporations, and the quality of a state's courts does as well.[21]

In sum, empirical work on state incorporation has moved us well beyond the theory-based "race" debate. We have learned that a race among the states may have occurred at one time, but that by the time the debate got started the race was long over and Delaware dominated the market. We have also learned that while Delaware incorporation may be value-enhancing compared to incorporation elsewhere, Delaware's incentive to reach the "top" is weak as a result of its self-perpetuating lead in the market. A reasonable inference from the empirical work is that much of Delaware's value comes from its network benefits, or what Romano had earlier called "first-mover advantages"—its high volume of case law, expert judiciary, expert bar, and familiarity among investors—and that these benefits unique to Delaware render useless efforts by other states to compete. Nonetheless, Romano found that Delaware is not complacent. Its legislature is quick to follow when other states enact a new law to respond to a new situation.

2 INDEPENDENT DIRECTORS

Another battle that raged at a theoretical level in the corporate governance arena was about independent boards. This was not so much a battle among academics but rather a battle between institutional shareholders and advocates for management. Institutional shareholders viewed boards as monitors of management and therefore in need of independence. Management advocates, on the other hand, viewed boards as part of a cohesive management team that could be disrupted by too much independence. One could imagine either role for a board, and hence reasonably view independence as either a virtue or a vice. One could also imagine some boards performing both roles well. Moreover, one could have different views for different companies, depending on the presence of other monitoring mechanisms. Legal academics took positions on one side or another based on a mix of theory, intuition, and ideology.[22]

---

[21] Kahan, *supra* note 13, at 363–64. Bebchuk and Cohen, and Subramanian find that antitakeover statutes are an attraction for in-state incorporation as well. Bebchuk & Cohen, *supra* note 13, at 404–20; Subramanian, *supra* note 13, at 1856, 1852–1853. Kahan, however, attributes this finding to a methodological problem and finds no such association.

[22] Mel Eisenberg has been the champion of the monitoring board. See Melvin Eisenberg, The Structure of the Corporation: A Legal Analysis 140–48 (1976); Melvin Eisenberg, "Legal Models of Management Structure in the Modern Corporation: Officers, Directors, and Accountants", 63 Cal. L. Rev. 375 (1975). Stephen Bainbridge has been an advocate of the board as a more "collegial body using consensus-based decisionmaking." Stephen M. Bainbridge, "A Critique of the NYSE's Director Independence Listing Standards", 30 Sec. Reg. L. J. 370, 384 (2002); Stephen M. Bainbridge, "Independent Directors and the ALI Corporate Governance Project", 61 Geo. Wash. L. Rev. 1034 (1993).

Congress, the SEC, and the stock exchanges settled this debate by fiat in 2002 and 2003. In 2002, Congress enacted the Sarbanes–Oxley Act (SOX), which imposed independence requirements on audit committees, and in 2003, the SEC approved New York Stock Exchange and NASDAQ rules requiring that a majority of public company board members be independent and that all compensation, nominating, and governance committee members be independent.[23] The stock exchange rules specified criteria by which director independence would be determined. They also required independent directors to meet regularly without management present.

At the time these rules were adopted, there was no basis in empirical research to support the proposition that board independence was value-enhancing as a general matter. For that reason, among others, Roberta Romano referred to the SOX-mandated governance requirements as "quack corporate governance."[24]

The lack of evidence was not due to a lack of effort. Many empiricists had tried to measure the impact of independent boards on firm conduct and performance. Empirical analysis of whether independent boards were beneficial to corporations was plagued by inherent methodological problems. Even if an association between independent boards and firm value or performance were found, causation was difficult if not impossible to prove.

Prior to the stock exchange mandates, a firm's choice to have an independent board was an endogenous choice. There are any number of potential causal relationships between board independence and firm performance. CEOs of firms that performed well might have had greater confidence than those at firms that performed poorly, and might therefore have been more likely to give in to institutional shareholder pressure to nominate more independent directors. Or CEOs of firms that performed well may not have wanted to rock the boat by bringing on more independent directors, and shareholders may not have pressured them to do so because performance was good. Conversely, CEOs of firms that performed poorly might have been more likely to add independent directors to their boards, either in response to shareholder pressure or in order to get more strategic advice. Or CEOs of firms that performed poorly may have opposed nomination of independent directors in order to avoid the pressure and risk to their careers that could ensue. The nature and direction of causation were thus ambiguous. Furthermore, additional problems arise as a result of the inability to observe true independence among directors. A director who meets the legal requirements of independence could well have a relationship with a CEO or a personality that makes him or her an unlikely monitor.[25]

---

[23] https://www.sec.gov/rules/sro/34-48745.htm. The stock exchange rules requiring independence do not apply in the case of "controlled" companies in which at least 50% of the voting power is held by the controller. For expositional convenience, I will call a board with a majority of independent directors an "independent board."

[24] Roberta Romano, "The Sarbanes–Oxley Act and the Making of Quack Corporate Governance", 114 Yale L. J. 1521 (2005). On the other hand, even before SOX, the fraction of independent directors on boards, and thus the number of boards with a majority of independent directors, increased substantially. Gordon reports that the median representation of independent directors on boards prior to the time SOX went into effect was 75%. Jeffrey N. Gordon, "The Rise of Independent Directors in the United States, 1950–2005: Of Shareholder Value and Stock Market Prices", 59 Stan. L. Rev. 1465 (2007).

[25] See *In re Oracle Corp. Derivative Litigation* (Oracle), 824 A.2d 917 (Del. Ch. 2003) (contextual analysis of independence in which relationship between two directors and certain board members leads court to conclude the two are not independent).

It is also possible that the benefit of an independent board differs across such factors as industry, firm size, geography, and other less observable factors. The value of an independent board would likely vary as well with the presence of other monitoring mechanisms. Yet another complication is the danger that an independent director, say a CEO from another company, may have conflicts of interest that compromise the contributions he can make to the board. This danger could vary across firms and the fields in which they operate.

In light of these methodological challenges it is not surprising that studies that attempted to uncover a relationship between board independence and firm value or performance failed to yield a clear result. Studies by Bhagat and Black,[26] Hermalin and Weisbach,[27] and Baysinger and Butler[28] all found no correlation. Of course this does not mean there was no relationship. It just means that econometric methods could not be used to reject the null hypothesis that independent boards are unrelated to firm value or performance.

One study, however, used the SOX and stock exchange independence requirements as an exogenous shock in order to analyze the value of board independence for firms that had not voluntarily adopted an independent board before doing so became mandatory. For these firms, the adoption of independent boards was not an endogenous choice; it was imposed on them by the enactment of SOX and the adoption of the related stock exchange rules. This study, by Chhaochharia and Grinstein, found that the board independence mandates had a positive effect on firms that were forced to accept independent boards. Among firms that scored lowest on the authors' measure of board and committee independence prior to SOX and the stock exchange rules, there was a statistically significant and economically substantial increase in abnormal returns when the rules went into effect.[29]

It is difficult to know the extent to which Chhaochharia and Grinstein's results are generalizable to other firms. By the time the stock exchange independence rules went into effect, a large majority of firms already had independent boards. Linck, Netter, and Yang find that as of the end of 2003, when the SEC approved the stock exchange rules, fewer than 10% of boards did not have a majority of independent directors, and those that did not were disproportionately small firms.[30] The firms on which the Chhaochharia and Grinstein study is based, therefore, may well have been systematically atypical, and the reasons behind their

---

[26] Bernard Black & Sanjai Bhagat, "The Non-Correlation Between Board Independence and Long-Term Firm Performance", 27 J. Corp. L. 231 (2002).

[27] Benjamin Hermalin & Michael Weisbach, "The Effect of Board Composition and Direct Incentives on Firm Performance", 20 Fin. Mgmt. 101 (1991).

[28] Barry Baysinger & Henry Butler, "Corporate Governance and the Board of Directors: Performance Effects of Changes in Board Composition", 1 J. L. Econ & Org. 101 (1985).

[29] Vidhi Chhaochharia & Yaniv Grinstein, "Corporate Governance and Firm Value: The Impact of the 2002 Governance Rules", 62 J. Fin. 1789 (2007). Additional studies of the impact of SOX, which do not focus on board independence but rather SOX as a whole, include Haidan Li, Morton P. K. Pincus, & Sonja O. Rego, "Market Reactions to Events Surrounding the Sarbanes–Oxley Act of 2002 and Earnings Management", 51 J. L. & Econ. 111 (2008); Pankaj K. Jain & Zabihollah Rezaee, "The Sarbanes–Oxley Act of 2002 and Capital-Market Behavior: Early Evidence", 23 Contemp. Acct. Res. 629 (2006); Ivy Xiying Zhang, "Economic Consequences of the Sarbanes–Oxley Act of 2002", 44 J. Acct. & Econ. 74 (2007).

[30] James Linck, Jeffry Netter, & Tina Yang, "The Effects and Unintended Consequences of the Sarbanes–Oxley Act on the Supply and Demand for Directors", 22 Rev. Fin. Stud. 3287, 3313 (2009). This figure comes from their Disclosure sample, which includes firms that file with the SEC.

having non-independent boards prior to SOX could explain why the mandatory imposition of independent boards on them had a positive impact.

Other studies looked at the relationship between board independence and performance of specific tasks. These studies produced some evidence that independent boards were slightly better, for example, at firing poorly performing CEOs than were non-independent boards, but the evidence was not strong.[31] Studies also found that, among firms that received tender offers and offers of management buyouts, those with independent boards realized higher returns than those with non-independent boards.[32] Yet another group of studies looked at returns to bidders in tender offers, and found evidence that bidders with independent boards were less likely to overpay in a tender offer.[33] Each of these studies, however, faced the inevitable methodological difficulties affecting those focused on firm value and performance.[34]

In sum, empirical studies of independent boards faced what, for the most part, may be insurmountable empirical challenges. Perhaps future studies can test more precise hypotheses regarding where and when independent boards are valuable. It remains to be seen whether one can observe and collect data that reflect the differences relevant to that sort of refinement. Within the limits of what has been done, however, researchers have generated some useful information—hints that independent boards performed some jobs well.

3 Takeover Defenses

Takeover defenses have been a third topic of intense debate in corporate governance since the 1980s. Institutional shareholders have battled management over the adoption of defenses. Management lobbied state legislatures for, and institutional shareholders lobbied against, the adoption antitakeover statutes. Firms continue to litigate management's use of takeover defenses when bidders mount hostile takeovers. And academics continue to debate the value of takeover defenses in law journals and finance journals.

As is true of other corporate governance debates, theory can only go so far. Empirical research has long shown that target shareholders reap substantial gains from hostile acquisitions.[35] Takeover defenses, therefore, would reduce target shareholder value to the

---

[31] Michael Weisbach, "Outside Directors and CEO Turnover", 20 J. Fin. Econ. 431 (1988).

[32] James Cotter, Anil Shivdasani, & Marc Zenner, "Do Independent Directors Enhance Target Shareholder Wealth During Tender Offers?", 43 J. Fin. Econ. 195 (1997); Chun Lee, Stuart Rosenstein, Nanda Rangan, & Wallace Davidson III, "Board Composition and Shareholder Wealth: The Case of Management Buyouts", 21 Fin. Mgmt. 58 (1992).

[33] John Byrd & Kent Hickman, "Do Outside Directors Monitor Managers?: Evidence From Tender Offer Bids", 32 J. Fin. Econ. 195 (1992); Victor You, Richard Caves, Michael Smith, & James Henry, Mergers and Bidders' Wealth: Managerial and Strategic Factors, in The Economics of Strategic Planning: Essays in Honor of Joel Dean (Lacy Glenn Thomas, III ed. 1986).

[34] For a summary of this literature, see Benjamin E. Hermalin & Michael S. Weisbach, "Boards of Directors as an Endogenously Determined Institution: A Survey of the Economic Literature", 9 Fed. Res. Bank N.Y. Econ. Pol'y Rev. 7 (2003); Sanjai Bhagat & Bernard Black, "The Uncertain Relationship Between Board Composition and Firm Performance", 54 Bus. Law. 921 (1999).

[35] For summaries of early studies that show this, see Gregor Andrade, Mark Mitchell, & Erik Stafford, "New Evidence and Perspectives on Mergers", 15 J. Econ. Persp. 103 (2001); Sanjai Bhagat, Andrei Shleifer, & Robert W. Vishny, "Hostile Takeovers in the 1980s: The Return to Corporate Specialization", Brookings

extent they deter bids or allow management to defeat value-increasing bids. Moreover, if managers feel less pressure from the takeover threat, then all shareholders in the aggregate may be worse off even in the absence of an actual takeover bid. On the other hand, to the extent management uses takeover defenses to reject low bids or to negotiate higher bids, then the presence of the defense could promote shareholder value in firms that receive bids.

Legal academics initially lined up on one side of the debate or the other with only theory to offer, and there were plausible theories on both sides.[36] The question whether takeover defenses tend to be value-enhancing or value-decreasing in the hands of management is therefore an empirical question. It is a question as much about the behavior of target management when using defenses, which of course will vary, as it is a question about the mechanical impact of a takeover defense. From an empirical perspective, when we look at the impact of defenses on firm value, the two are combined—the mechanical potential of a defense and management's use of the defense.

Many economists have tried to analyze the empirical relationship between takeover defenses and firm value. Those efforts began in the 1980s and continue today. But the institutional and legal setting of takeovers and takeover defenses is complex, and few economists have mastered the complexity. As a result, much of the empirical literature in this area is fatally flawed.

In a nutshell, the institutional and legal facts one must understand in order to analyze takeover defenses empirically are the following:

- A poison pill, also known as shareholder rights plans, is a complete bar to a takeover so long as a target board keeps it in place.[37]
- Poison pills were validated by the Delaware Supreme Court in 1985[38] and in most other states by 1990.[39]
- A board can adopt a pill unilaterally at any time, including after a hostile bid has been made.[40] No shareholder approval is required, and the legal treatment of a pill is the same regardless of when it is adopted.

Papers on Econ. Activity, no. 1, 1990, at 1; Gregg A. Jarrell, James A. Brickley, & Jeffry M. Netter, "The Market for Corporate Control: The Empirical Evidence Since 1980", 2 J. Econ. Persp. 49 (1988); and Michael C. Jensen & Richard S. Ruback, "The Market for Corporate Control: The Scientific Evidence", 11 J. Fin. Econ. 5 (1983). Although acquirers' gains are small and sometimes negative, the research summarized in these articles has also shown that total gains to the shareholders of the target and the acquirer are large.

[36] See, e.g., Frank H. Easterbrook & Daniel R. Fischel, "The Proper Role of a Target's Management in Responding to a Tender Offer", 94 Harv. L. Rev. 1161 (1981); Ronald J. Gilson, "A Structural Approach to Corporations: The Case Against Defensive Tactics in Tender Offers", 33 Stan. L. Rev. 819 (1981); Lucian A. Bebchuk, "Comment, The Case for Facilitating Competing Tender Offers", 95 Harv. L. Rev. 1028, 1047 (1982); Martin Lipton, "Takeover Bids in the Target's Boardroom", 35 Bus. Law. 101 (1979).

[37] The detailed mechanics of the pill are unimportant, but the basic mechanism is to massively dilute the shares of a would-be acquirer when the acquirer's shareholding crosses a specified threshold—for example, 20% of outstanding shares. The prospect of dilution stops the acquirer in its tracks until the pill is withdrawn.

[38] *Moran v. Household Int'l., Inc.*, 500 A.2d 1346 (Del. 1985) (upholding the use of a poison pill where no bid is imminent). *Moran* involved the earliest version of the poison pill (a "flip-over" pill), which was quickly replaced by the more powerful "flip-in" pill and pills that had both flip-over and flip-in functionality. But the logic of *Moran* applied to flip-in pills and the court never differentiated between the two in ruling on pills after *Moran*.

[39] *See* Catan & Kahan, *supra* note 2, at 637.

[40] In *Moran*, the court said "The Board has no more discretion in refusing to redeem the Rights than it does in enacting any defensive mechanism." 500 A.2d 1346, 1354 (Del. 1985).

- A board can withdraw a pill unilaterally at any time, and often announces that it will do so if a bid is high enough.
- A board can keep a pill in place indefinitely in response to bid.[41]
- If a bidder cannot convince a target board to withdraw a pill, its only option is to initiate a shareholder vote to replace the board with new directors of its own choosing (who will likely withdraw the pill and allow the takeover to go forward).
- It follows therefore that a takeover defense that could have an impact at the margin, given that all firms have or can have a pill, is one that impedes a shareholder vote to replace a majority of the board of directors with a new board that will withdraw a pill. *This is the key point on which the rest of this discussion hinges.*
- The following defenses can impede that shareholder vote:
  - o A staggered board provided for in a firm's charter can delay the replacement of a target board for up to two years.[42]
  - o A restriction on shareholders' ability to vote in between annual meetings, either by calling a shareholder meeting or voting by written consent in lieu of a meeting, can delay the replacement of a target board for up to one year.[43]
  - o A prohibition on the removal of directors without cause can also delay the replacement of a target board for up to one year.[44]

[41] This rule became clear as a result of *Paramount Communications, Inc. v. Time Inc.*, 571 A.2d 1140 (Del. 1989). For a discussion of the implications, see Jeffrey N. Gordon, "Corporations, Markets, and Courts", 91 Colum. L. Rev. 1931 (1991).

[42] The staggered board could be provided for in a firm's bylaws so long as shareholders cannot, as a practical matter, amend that provision of the bylaws. Since the law requires firms to allow shareholders to amend bylaws unilaterally, this means the staggered board provision in the bylaws would have to be protected from amendment by a supermajority vote requirement in the charter. The combination of the supermajority vote requirement and inside ownership of the firm's shares (which can change over time) could make the staggered board invulnerable to shareholder action.

In addition, for a staggered board to be effective, shareholders must not have the ability to remove a director without cause, and they must not be able to "pack" the board by enlarging it and electing new members that constitute a majority. Under Delaware law, removal without cause is impermissible for a company with a staggered board, unless provided for in a firm's charter. Del. Code Ann. tit. 8, § 141(k)(1). Under other state laws, removal without cause is permissible unless the charter prohibits it. Model Bus. Corp. Act § 8.08. Shareholders will be unable to pack the board if the charter either (a) sets a maximum board size that is low enough in relation to the board's current size to prevent packing, (b) the charter provides that only the board may set the board size, or (c) the charter does not allow shareholders to fill empty board seats. Sometimes the term "effective staggered board" is used to refer to a staggered board that shareholders cannot unilaterally eliminate in any of these ways. One study showed that about 90% of staggered boards are effective. Bebchuk & Cohen, *supra* note 13, at 419. For simplicity in this chapter, I will use the term "staggered board" to refer to an effective staggered board.

[43] Board elections at annual meetings are mandatory, so shareholders can vote to replace their board at their next annual meeting. Voting by written consent and voting at a special meeting are governed either by the terms of a firm's charter or the default rule of the state in which the firm is incorporated. If the law of a state disallows or restricts either means of voting, it can be overridden in a charter provision. The election of new directors in a vote by written consent requires a majority of shares outstanding to be voted in favor, whereas in a vote at a special or annual meeting, only a majority of shares voted is required.

[44] Even if shareholders can call a special meeting or vote by written consent in lieu of a meeting, they must be able to either remove sitting directors or pack the board as explained above in order to elect a majority of the board.

These institutional and legal facts imply certain limitations regarding empirical studies of poison pills, staggered boards, and other defenses—limitations that many studies violate and thus produce results that are uninformative. (I use the term "facts" rather than the more common term, "institutional detail" to make clear that these points are not details and that designing studies inconsistent with these points is not an option.)

3.1 Poison Pill Studies

Between 1986 and 1996, twelve event studies were published on the impact the adoption of a poison pill had on share value.[45] There is an inherent problem with all of these studies—and with *any* effort to measure the impact of a poison pill. A board of directors can adopt a pill unilaterally at any time. If a firm does not have a pill at the moment, it can have one later today. All that must be done is for the firm's board to adopt one. If a firm does not already have a pill, it certainly will adopt one if and when it receives an unwanted bid. Even if the target management is amenable to a sale, it needs a pill in place in order to negotiate a price if there is any chance that a target will "go hostile" in the lingo of M&A lawyers. One study confirmed that among targets of hostile takeover attempts, every target had adopted a pill either before the bid was made or in response to the bid.[46] Consequently, while a poison pill is an effective defense against a hostile takeover, the adoption of a pill is a *nonevent*, and an event study will not measure its impact. Coates explained this point in a critique of the empirical corporate governance literature on takeover defenses as of 2000.[47] As he explained the point, all firms have a "shadow pill" in the sense that all firms can adopt a pill at any time. Consequently, the fact that a pill will be in place whenever it is needed is baked into the price of all shares continuously. As will be evident below, Coates's explanation made little impression on economists writing in this field.

Not surprisingly, the results of pill-adoption event studies ranged from finding no significant abnormal returns to finding statistically significant but economically small returns, both negative and positive.[48] The studies that found a statistically significant negative effect on share prices were those that used the earliest sample period.[49] Robert Comment and William Schwert's study, which was the largest at the time, found statistically significant negative effects only in 1984 (when only nine pills were adopted).[50] As the authors suggested, this may have reflected the market's initial lack of understanding regarding how the pill would work.[51]

More recently, there have been additional studies of poison pills. These have been motivated by studies based on corporate governance indices, discussed in section 4, which include poison pills among their scoring elements. In a broad study of takeover defenses,

[45] See Coates, *supra* note 2, at Appendix A (listing the results of these studies).

[46] See Lucian Arye Bebchuk, John C. Coates IV, & Guhan Subramanian, "The Powerful Antitakeover Force of Staggered Boards: Theory, Evidence, and Policy", 54 Stan. L. Rev. 887, 926–27 (2002).

[47] Coates, *supra* note 2, at 286–91.   [48] Id. at 280–86 (summarizing results of pill studies).

[49] Id. at 284 ("Studies of early pill adoptions show (weak) negative results, whereas the only studies of pill adoptions after 1986 show no statistically significant results for their full samples").

[50] Robert Comment & G. William Schwert, "Poison or Placebo? Evidence on the Deterrence and Wealth Effects of Modern Antitakeover Measures", 39 J. Fin. Econ. 3, 20 tbl. 2, 21 (1995).

[51] Id. at 21.

Cremers and Ferrell found that firms that had adopted poison pills had a lower value than those that did not.[52] For reasons described above, it is doubtful that the direction of causation runs from pill adoption to firm value. Such a relationship would mean the market does not understand that all firms have "shadow pills" despite the fact that the law has been clear on this point for many years. Cremers and Ferrell recognize that the direction of causation could run in the opposite direction, reporting "very modest" support for an inference that firms with low valuation tend to adopt pills.

Emiliano Catan has recently looked more closely at the relationship between poison pills and firm value—cross-sectionally and within-firm over time using quarterly data— in a sample period of 1996 to 2014.[53] In order to separate the adoption of a pill from the announcement of a takeover offer, he focuses only on the adoption of "clear-day" pills— pills adopted when there is no publicly known takeover bid in the offing. Catan finds that firms adopt clear-day pills *after* their value has fallen. Moreover, his firm fixed effects results suggest that this dynamic drives cross-sectional differences in value between firms with and without pills. This empirical finding is consistent with the fact that pill adoption is a non-event and should not affect share value. The inference is further supported by Catan's second finding—that when firms drop their pills, there is no impact on firm value.

One might still ask why firms adopt poison pills on a clear day rather than waiting until a hostile bid is made. The answer is that there is no harm in doing so, and no harm in waiting. Some firms adopt pills on a clear day and some wait. Since all firms will adopt a pill if it is needed, it does not matter when they adopt it. Catan found that after 2004, when ISS threatened to recommend "withhold" votes for members of boards that adopted clear-day pills (or re-adopted them after they expired), clear-day pill adoptions nearly vanished, even though an ISS threat is highly unlikely to result in a board member losing his or her seat, and even though there was no good reason for ISS to make the threat.[54] So even a small threat apparently pushed the balance against adopting pills on a clear day.

3.2 Studies of Staggered Boards

Since a poison pill allows a board to resist a takeover bid indefinitely, if it chooses to do so, a bidder's only response is to give target shareholders an opportunity to remove and replace at least a majority of the target's directors. In a company with dispersed shareholders and dispersed votes, a staggered board is the strongest impediment to doing so.[55] With a staggered board in place, two shareholder elections must occur at two consecutive annual meetings in order to replace a majority of the target's board. This can take two years to occur. It is generally understood that a staggered board is a near bulletproof defense if the target board continues to resist a hostile takeover. In the case of *Air Products and Chemicals, Inc*

---

[52] Martijn Cremers & Allen Ferrell, "Thirty Years of Shareholder Rights and Firm Value", 69 J. Fin. 1167 (2014).

[53] Emiliano Catan, "The Insignificance of Clear-Day Poison Pills" (Sept. 7, 2016), http://ssrn.com/abstract=2836223.

[54] Stephen Choi, Jill Fisch, Marcel Kahan, & Edward Rock, "Does Majority Voting Improve Board Accountability?", 83 U. Chi. L. Rev. 1119 (2016).

[55] Dual-class shares with management holding the multiple-vote shares would be a stronger defense, but this is not common.

v. Airgas, Inc, William Chandler, former Chancellor of the Delaware Court of Chancery stated, "no bidder to my knowledge has ever successfully stuck around for two years and waged two successful proxy contests to gain control of a classified board in order to remove a pill."[56]

Is a staggered board value-decreasing or value-enhancing? Once again, there is theory on both sides. With a staggered board, directors can prevent a takeover from occurring, even if the takeover would be beneficial for shareholders. Since at least 1990, it has been clear that courts will not interfere.[57] A staggered board may therefore deter a would-be acquirer from attempting to take over a target in the first place. Furthermore, with this protection from the takeover threat, a company's board and management may feel less pressure to perform and thus may fail to maximize share value on an ongoing basis. On the other hand, if a board is diligent and loyal, and management is motivated to promote shareholder interests, a staggered board can allow a company to make long-term investments without concern that the market will undervalue those investments and thereby expose the company to a takeover at too low a price. In addition, a staggered board might enhance a target's bargaining power in negotiating a sale with an acquirer. So a staggered board could increase *or* decrease firm value, depending on how a firm's board and management are expected to respond to an acquisition offer. One's view on the question in general depends on one's view of how boards and management tend to respond to hostile bids—and of course boards and managers differ, so the empirical question is about averages.

Despite the fact that economists had been studying takeover defenses since the 1980s, the first empirical study of staggered boards was not published until 2002 (by law professors). This study, by Bebchuk, Coates, and Subramanian, found that staggered boards had a negative impact on shareholder value for a sample of firms that received hostile takeover bids between 1996 and 2000.[58] The authors found that firms with staggered boards were more likely to reject bids and remain independent, and that remaining independent meant lower returns to shareholders as compared with companies that were acquired. They found no evidence of greater bargaining power for targets with staggered boards; when companies with staggered boards were sold, the premiums they commanded were no different from those of firms without staggered boards. The aggregate result of these impacts for firms that received hostile bids meant an average loss of 8% to 10% in share value attributable to a staggered board. In another study, Bebchuk and Cohen directly compared the value of companies with and without staggered boards between the years 1995 and 2002 and confirmed this conclusion, finding that staggered boards were associated with lower Tobin's Q than firms with annually elected boards.[59]

To a large extent, these findings have been confirmed and refined by others. Faleye confirmed that staggered boards are associated with lower firm value and further found that staggered boards are worse at firing poorly performing CEOs than are annually elected

---

[56] *Air Products and Chemicals, Inc. v. Airgas, Inc.*, 16 A.3d 48 (2011).

[57] *Paramount Communications, Inc. v. Time Inc.*, 571 A.2d 1140 (Del. 1989).

[58] Bebchuk, Coates, & Subramanian, *supra* note 46.

[59] Lucian Bebchuk & Alma Cohen, "The Costs of Entrenched Boards", 78 J. Fin. Econ. 409 (2005). Tobin's Q is a measure of firm value. It is defined as the market value of common equity plus the book values of preferred equity and long-term debt divided by the book value of assets.

boards.[60] Masulis, Wang, and Xie found that firms with staggered boards make value-destroying acquisitions more than do firms with annually elected boards.[61]

In general, staggered boards thus seem to reduce firm value—or more precisely, target boards have used them to reduce firm value, on average, and the market has expected them to do so, at least during the sample periods of these studies. As in other areas of corporate governance research, there are methodological challenges. Each of the studies described above considers the possibility that the choice of a staggered board is endogenous—that low value, poorly performing firms may adopt staggered boards to protect management. Each responds to the possibility in reasonable but inevitably imperfect ways. First, they note that shareholders must approve the adoption of staggered boards, and that this is unlikely to happen if a firm is performing poorly. Second, they analyze firms that had had staggered boards at least several years before the years in which value was measured. Another methodological concern is the use of Tobin's Q to measure and compare firm values. Although widely used, this measure is considered by many economists to be an unreliable measure of firm value.[62]

There are, however, recent studies that find a positive relationship between a staggered board and firm value for certain types of firms. Johnson, Karpoff, and Yi analyze staggered boards adopted at the IPO stage and infer that they are used as commitment devices by firms that have important long-term relationships with suppliers or customers.[63] They find that the use of staggered boards by firms that have those relationships enhances value. Cremers, Litov, and Sepe analyze public companies over a 33-year period, from 1978 to 2011, and reach a similar conclusion.[64] They infer that staggered boards are used by firms to maintain commitments to long-term investments and long-term relationships. Emiliano Catan and I, however, have recently taken a closer look at this result and found that it is spurious.[65] Daines, Li, and Wang also find that staggered boards have a positive effect on firm value. They focus on smaller firms, using as a natural experiment a 1990 Massachusetts statute that imposed staggered boards on all companies incorporated in that state.[66] They found that the statute caused an increase in firm value over the next 15 years for small firms and firms with relatively high R&D investment.

---

[60] See Olubunmi Faleye, "Classified Boards, Firm Value, and Managerial Entrenchment", 83 J. Fin. Econ. 501, 522–26 (2007).

[61] See Ronald W. Masulis, Cong Wang, & Fei Xie, "Corporate Governance and Acquirer Returns", 62 J. Fin. 1851, 1853, 1867–69 (2007).

[62] See Phillip Dybvig & Mitch Warachka, "Tobin's q Does Not Measure Firm Performance: Theory, Empirics, and Alternatives" (Mar. 2015), http://ssrn.com/abstract=1562444.

[63] William C. Johnson, Jonathan M. Karpoff, & Sangho Yi, "The Bonding Hypothesis of Takeover Defenses: Evidence from IPO Firms", 117 J. Fin. Econ. 307 (2015).

[64] Martijn Cremers, Lubomir Litov, & Simone Sepe, "Staggered Boards and Long-Term Firm Value, Revisited" 126 J. Fin. Econ. 422 (2017). Data on the years 1978 to 1985 is not relevant to analysis because the antitakeover impact of a staggered board did not begin until the advent of the pill. As explained above, the power of the staggered board lies in the obstacle it poses for an acquirer to have target shareholders replace their board with a board that is willing to disable the firm's pill.

[65] Emiliano Catan & Michael Klausner, "Board Declassification and Firm Value: Have Shareholders and Boards Really Destroyed Billions in Firm Value?" (October 2017), http://ssrn.com/abstract=2994559.

[66] Robert Daines, Shelley Xin Li, & Charles C. Y. Wang, "Can Staggered Boards Improve Value? Evidence from the Massachusetts Natural Experiment" (Mar. 2017), http://ssrn.com/abstract=2836463.

All in all, studies of staggered boards have advanced our understanding beyond the realm of theory. As a matter of mechanics, staggered boards give a board the power to thwart value-increasing takeovers. In the 1990s, the market seems to have believed that boards would exercise that power—hence, the negative correlation between staggered boards and firm value. Evidence from the 2000s that Catan and I analyzed suggests (through a null result) that the market no longer believes boards will use the power that a staggered board provides to thwart the interests of shareholders.

3.3 Studies of Other Takeover Defenses

As explained above, a poison pill is freely available to a board facing a takeover threat, and so long as it is in place it is a complete bar to a takeover. To succeed in acquiring a target, a hostile acquirer must either convince a target board to agree to an acquisition, or it must mount a proxy contest to have target shareholders replace their board with one that will agree to be acquired. The only additional takeover defense that is useful, therefore, is one that impedes the ability of the acquirer to have target shareholders replace their board—with a staggered board being the primary example. Any other defense is, at best, redundant with the pill, and in fact other defenses are less effective than a pill.

Due to a lack of understanding regarding how takeover defenses work, however, many economists have published empirical analyses of other apparent defenses that have no impact on shareholders' ability to replace a board at the margin. Once the pill was held to be legally valid, these defenses could have no additional impact on a firm's exposure to a hostile takeover. Some examples are fair price charter provisions and supermajority vote requirements to approve a merger. These studies began in the late 1980s and continue to be published today. Early studies of takeover defenses were problematic in several ways. Some considered only ineffective defenses; some combined ineffective defenses with staggered boards to create a single takeover-defense or "charter amendment" variable; and some considered staggered boards prior to the advent of the pill, when staggered boards did not provide meaningful takeover protection.[67] Yet others counted up how many defenses a firm had and used that number as a measure of its takeover exposure—more defenses were understood to mean less exposure.[68] None of these approaches makes substantive sense, and therefore the results of these studies are uninformative. More recent articles continue to refer to the conflicting results of the 1980s and 1990s as a puzzle, as opposed to a reflection of methodological errors.[69] The confusion thus continues—most rampantly in the use of

---

[67] See, e.g., Brent W. Ambrose & William L. Megginson, "The Role of Asset Structure, Ownership Structure, and Takeover Defenses in Determining Acquisition Likelihood", 27 J. Fin. & Quant. Anal. 575 (1992); Kenneth A. Borokhovich, Kelly R. Brunarski, & Robert Parrino, "CEO Contracting and Antitakeover Amendments", 52 J. Fin. 1495 (1997); Mark Johnson & Ramesh Rao, "The Impact of Antitakeover Amendments on Corporate Financial Performance", 32 Fin. Rev. 659 (1997).

[68] See, e.g., Borokhovich et al., *supra* note 67; Laura Casares Field & Jonathan M. Karpoff, "Takeover Defenses of IPO Firms", 57 J. Fin. 1857 (2002).

[69] For example, Olubunmi Faleye, in framing his 2007 study of staggered boards, refers to two studies of this sort in the 1980s and 1990s that reached opposite results as raising an unresolved empirical question. Faleye, *supra* note 60, at 502.

corporate governance indices, discussed in section 4, which include multiple takeover defenses that have no impact.

There are, however, two other takeover defenses that *can* have an impact at the margin. The first is a combination of two charter provisions that prevent shareholders from voting to replace a board in between annual shareholder meetings: (a) a prohibition on shareholders calling a special meeting and (b) a prohibition on shareholders acting by written consent in lieu of a meeting.[70] If both these limitations on shareholder voting are present, an acquirer must wait until the target's next annual meeting to mount a proxy contest to replace the target board. The second defense is a charter provision that allows shareholders to replace board members only for cause, which means wrongdoing that goes beyond a difference in judgment regarding whether to allow a takeover to occur. In effect, this provision also requires an acquirer to wait until the next annual meeting to have shareholders replace their board. This delay is not as severe as the delay created by a staggered board, but it could be meaningful. Interestingly, no one has yet studied the actual impact of these restrictions on shareholder voting.

3.4 Studies of State Antitakeover Statutes

Studies of the impact of state antitakeover statutes entail the same types of errors as do studies of firm-level takeover defenses other than staggered boards. Emiliano Catan and Marcel Kahan have recently provided a detailed analysis of this literature, with a focus on the most common and most commonly studied statutes—business combination statutes, fair price statutes, and control share acquisition statutes.[71] As they say, "[c]orporate lawyers and academics generally dismiss these antitakeover statutes as irrelevant."[72] Regarding empirical studies of antitakeover statutes, they state: "The way financial economists approach takeover defenses results in a highly distorted view of takeover protections supplied by state law."[73]

Catan and Kahan's explanation is the same as that provided here with respect to charter-based takeover defenses. Once the poison pill was validated, the only statutory defense that could have an impact would be one that impeded shareholder votes to replace a target board. With the exception of a few states that mandate staggered boards, state antitakeover statutes do not do that, and never did. Therefore, after the advent of the pill and the states' validation of the pill, state antitakeover statutes had no impact on a firm's exposure to hostile takeovers.[74] They were irrelevant. Catan and Kahan explained the point well:

> Business combination, fair price, and control share acquisition statutes apply once a raider has become a major shareholder. . . . But if, as a result of the flip-in pill, a raider never acquires a significant stake, any statute that deals with what a raider can do *once it becomes* a major shareholder becomes moot. Similarly, flip-over pills, which make business combinations once a raider has acquired a large stake prohibitively expensive, render business combination and fair

---

[70] Dual-class stock is another antitakeover defense that can have an impact, but it is rarely present.
[71] Catan & Kahan, *supra* note 2.   [72] Id. at 632.   [73] Id. at 648.
[74] The studies discussed here did not cover state statutes mandating staggered boards nor those that provided for staggered boards as default rules. They covered business combination statutes, fair price statutes, and control share acquisition statutes.

price statutes superfluous [because they do the same thing]. Control share acquisition statutes, moreover, do not even purport to offer meaningful protection against hostile bids that are opposed by the board of the target but are favored (as most "hostile" bids are) by a majority of the target's shareholders.[75]

The Delaware Supreme Court held pills to be valid in 1985. For a few years after that, other state courts split on the validity of the pill, but by 1990, 24 states had validated the pill and none had invalidated it. Those states that validated the pill accounted for the vast majority of firms' states of incorporation.[76] Consequently, even if one assumes that the validity of the pill was still in doubt in the other 26 states, which would be an unrealistic assumption, the window of time and the scope of firms that can be used to study the impact of state antitakeover statutes is very narrow. None of the studies performed to date focuses on state antitakeover statutes within these constraints.

Nonetheless, empirical studies that purport to show impacts of state antitakeover statutes are numerous[77] and continue to be written today.[78] These studies are so flawed as to be utterly uninformative. Catan and Kahan use the term "nonsensical."[79] Catan and Kahan replicated a study by Marianne Bertrand and Sendhil Mullainathan to determine whether the firms they identified as being subject to business combination statutes were also incorporated in states that had validated the poison pill, in which case the business combination statute would have no impact at the margin. They found that this was true of over 50% of the firms whose take-over protection Bertrand and Mullainathan had attributed to business combination statutes.[80] For this reason and others, Catan and Kahan found that Bertrand and Mullainathan's analysis of the impact of business combination statutes was fatally flawed. This mistake was a result of their misunderstanding of how business combination statutes and poison pills work and how they relate to one another.

In sum, the empirical literature on takeover defenses is a mixed bag. Studies of staggered boards have been relatively well conceived and informative. They face inevitable methodological challenges but these studies have moved us beyond intuition, theory, and ideology.

---

[75]   Catan & Kahan, *supra* note 2, at 638–39. Flip-in pills would dilute an acquirer's shareholding in a target once that shareholding reaches a specified threshold. Flip-over pills would dilute an acquirer's interest in the combined company when the acquirer merges with the target, just as a business combination statute would. Today, pills are flip-in.

[76]   Id. at 637, 658.

[77]   Catan and Kahan provide citations to many of these. The following are some examples: Julian Atanassov, "Do Hostile Takeovers Stifle Innovation? Evidence from Antitakeover Legislation and Corporate Patenting", 68 J. Fin. 1097 (2013); Marianne Bertrand & Sendhil Mullainathan, "Enjoying the Quiet Life?: Corporate Governance and Managerial Preferences", 111 J. Pol. Econ. 1043 (2003); Gerald T. Garvey & Gordon Hanka, "Capital Structure and Corporate Control: The Effect of Antitakeover Statutes on Firm Leverage", 54 J. Fin. 519 (1999); Xavier Giroud & Holger M. Mueller, "Does Corporate Governance Matter in Competitive Industries?", 95 J. Fin. Econ. 312 (2010); Kose John & Lubomir Litov, "Managerial Entrenchment and Capital Structure: New Evidence", 7 J. Emp. Leg. Stud. 693 (2010).

[78]   Todd A. Gormley & David A. Matsa, "Playing It Safe? Managerial Preferences, Risk, and Agency Conflicts", 122 J. Fin. Econ. 431 (2016); Jonathan M. Karpoff & Michael D. Wittry, "Institutional and Legal Context in Natural Experiments: The Case of State Antitakeover Laws" (April 2017), http://ssrn.com/abstract=2493913.

[79]   Catan & Kahan, *supra* note 2, at 645.   [80]   Id. at 648–49.

Other studies of takeover defenses have been fundamentally flawed and uninformative. Beginning with early event studies of the poison pill and extending to studies of state antitakeover statutes today, these studies reflect a regrettable (and avoidable) failure on the part of economists to learn the institutional and legal facts of the takeover context. As discussed in section 4, this problem is present as well in the design and use of corporate governance indices.

4 CORPORATE GOVERNANCE INDICES

The use—or, as I will explain, misuse—of corporate governance indices has reached epidemic proportions.[81] The "Governance" or "G" Index created by Gompers, Ishii, and Metrick (GIM),[82] and the "Entrenchment" or "E" Index created by Bebchuk, Cohen, and Ferrell (BCF)[83] are used in hundreds of articles covering a wide range of corporate governance topics.[84] Yet the G and E Indices reflect the same mistakes described above, with some additional mistakes that similarly reflect a failure to understand institutional arrangements and legal rules. For the most part, the elements of the G and E Indices have no impact on entrenchment, or on anything else of importance to corporate governance.

It is doubtful that anyone familiar with the details of corporate charters, bylaws, and state corporate law would have initiated a research program with the hypothesis that the elements contained in the G Index would correlate with firm value or firm performance, let alone the possibility of a causal relationship. The elements of the G Index are a hodgepodge of provisions that range from trivial to important, and from theoretically positive to theoretically negative to theoretically ambiguous in their impact on corporate governance. GIM purposefully did not select the elements of their index based on a substantive judgment regarding their functionality. Instead, as they explained, they took a list of governance provisions that the Investor Responsibility Research Center (IRRC), a nonprofit organization with an interest in corporate governance, tracked for a sample of firms over time, and they combined the provisions that the IRRC tracked into 24 elements that became the G Index. A firm received one point for each IRRC element that it had adopted directly or through operation of state law, and the sum of the firm's points was its G Index score. GIM then performed an econometric analysis that produced surprising results: Firms with low scores (supposedly better governance) had higher value and higher investment returns than firms with high scores (supposedly worse governance). A few years later, BCF analyzed the

---

[81] Lucian Bebchuk's website provides links to 307 studies (including a few of his own) that use the E Index as of January 2018. http://www.law.harvard.edu/faculty/bebchuk/studies.shtml. The G Index was developed before the E Index and presumably has at least as many users. I understand from economist friends that the epidemic quality of these indices' diffusion through the empirical governance literature is due at least in part to a standard referee request: "The authors should control for governance."

[82] Paul Gompers, Joy Ishii, & Andrew Metrick, "Corporate Governance and Equity Prices", 118 Q. J. Econ. 107 (2003).

[83] Lucian Bebchuk, Alma Cohen, & Allen Ferrell, "What Matters in Corporate Governance?", 22 Rev. Fin. Stud. 783 (2009).

[84] See Chapter 9, Allen Ferrell, "The Benefits and Costs of Indices in Empirical Corporate Governance Research."

GIM results and showed that three quarters of the G Index elements were empirically irrelevant to those results. The fact that 18 elements of the G Index were not correlated with firm value or performance was not surprising to those of us familiar with the Index. But the fact that six elements were correlated *was* surprising. As discussed in detail in section 4.2, there is no functional reason why most of those six elements should have any relationship to firm value or investment performance. BCF nonetheless reported correlations and christened these six elements the "E Index." From there, the G and E Indices took on lives of their own and became embedded in the empirical corporate governance literature as a measure of governance quality. None of the economists who have used the indices in this way have questioned their validity, nor have they attempted to understand what the indices mean.

Before explaining why the G and E Indices do not measure management entrenchment or any other aspect of governance quality—a discussion that is necessarily detailed and may challenge the attention span of some readers—I will review the empirical findings regarding the relationship between the G and E Indices and firm value, including recent studies that have begun to look for explanations for the GIM and BCF results. While those of us familiar with the IRRC provisions included in these indices would not have headed down this path at the start, now that we are here, GIM and BCF have presented us with a puzzle: What lies behind the GIM and BCF correlations?

4.1 Empirical Findings Regarding the G and E Indices

As a threshold matter, what did the governance indices intend to measure? GIM describe the G Index as measuring the extent to which a firm has "reduce[d] shareholder rights,"[85] and at another point as measuring "the balance of power between managers and shareholders."[86] Neither of these descriptions is very precise, but in setting the context of their study, they explain: "The rise of the junk bond market in the 1980s [. . .] enable[ed] hostile-takeover offers for even the largest public firms. In response, many firms added takeover defenses and other restrictions of shareholder rights."[87] So it seems GIM thought they were measuring a firm's exposure to hostile takeovers. BCF describe their E Index more precisely as containing elements that "*appear to* provide incumbents *at least nominally* with protection from removal or the consequences of removal"[88]—again, through a hostile takeover or the threat of one. By using the words "appear to" and "at least nominally," BCF hint at the point I make here.

GIM analyzed the correlation of the G Index with firm value and investor returns. Their results were startling and drew the attention of everyone involved in corporate governance research. If an investor had shorted firms in the worst decile of G Index score and held shares in the best decile, he or she would have reaped a return of 8.5% per year from 1990 to 1999. GIM further found that in each sample year firms with bad scores—a lot of supposed protection—had substantially lower value than those with good scores. For example, in 1999, a one-point increase in a firm's G Index score (meaning one more supposedly entrenching element), was associated with an 11.4% lower value, as measured by Tobin's Q. GIM were

---

[85] Gompers et al, *supra* note 82, at 109.   [86] Id. at 144.   [87] See id. at 108.
[88] Bebchuk et al., *supra* note 83, at 788 (emphasis added).

careful not to attribute a causal explanation to these differences. They investigated alternative explanations and concluded that the evidence was insufficient to draw a conclusion regarding causation. One thing they did not do, however, was to analyze the function of the G Index elements—what do these elements actually do? Doing so would have led them to exclude the possibility of a causal relationship with respect to nearly all G Index elements.

BCF took the first step toward looking more closely at the GIM analysis. They found that out of the 24 elements of the G Index, 18 are empirically irrelevant. Six elements, discussed in section 4.2, account for GIM's results. Using those six elements, BCF's long-short strategy would have yielded a 7.4% annual return in equal-weighted portfolios, and a 14.8% return in value-weighted portfolios. Like GIM, BCF also found a strong correlation between the E Index and firm value, measured by Tobin's Q. BCF went a step beyond GIM in analyzing causation by looking at the correlation between E Index scores as of 1990 and firm value between 1998 and 2002, thereby reducing the possibility of reverse causation. They find that the higher a firm's E Index score in 1990 the lower its value between 1998 and 2002 (controlling for value in 1990), from which they suggest a causal relationship between the E Index and firm value.

The literature has gone in two directions with the G and E Indices. A large and growing number of papers blindly add one or both indices to regressions as a measure of good or bad corporate governance. A few, however, have tried to analyze the GIM and BCF results more deeply. The latter path is well worth following. The starting point, as I explain in detail in section 4.2, should be that there can be no causal relationship between the indices and firm value or firm performance—assuming an efficient market and reasonably knowledgeable market participants. The relevant research question, therefore, is: If not causation, what explains the GIM and BCF results? A few papers have shed important light on this question, but the mystery remains unsolved.[89]

A paper that is not directly about the indices but that nonetheless may answer much of the puzzle is Catan's recent paper on poison pills, discussed in section 3.1. He finds that poison pills—an element of both the E and G Indices—tend to be adopted *after* a firm's value declines.[90] This finding is consistent with the nature of poison pills, discussed in section 3.1. A board can adopt a pill unilaterally at any time. If a firm is performing poorly, its board could decide to adopt a pill just in case it attracts a hostile acquirer. It could of course wait until a hostile acquirer appears, but there is no harm (and no benefit) to doing so in advance. Catan's finding and the inherent nature of pills together dispel any notion that a pill causes a drop in firm value.[91] Thus, to the extent poison pills are driving the empirical correlation between the G and E Indices and firm value, the explanation is not that a change in index score causes a change in firm value.

---

[89]   In the interest of brevity, I focus only on papers that try to explain the relationship that GIM and BCF found between index scores and firm value, and not on papers that try to explain the GIM and BCF findings regarding investment returns.

[90]   Catan, *supra* note 53.

[91]   Some economists will argue that firm value may have declined prior to the adoption of the pill because the market anticipated the pill's adoption, and declined in response. Therefore, they would claim, despite the temporal order between pill adoption and decline in firm value, pills do cause a drop in firm value. This story, however, is implausible in light of the nature of pills. Since every firm can and will adopt a pill by the time it is needed, the adoption of a pill is not an event that market participants need

Cremers and Ferrell have provided further refinement of the GIM and BCF results, also focusing on poison pills.[92] Their sample period runs from 1978 to 2006, which allows for more within-firm variation and therefore more power in their firm fixed effects models.[93] In addition, they cluster standard errors at the firm level, which is a methodological advance that has become standard practice since the time BCF published their article. Cremers and Ferrell find that the presence of a poison pill explains much of the negative correlation between the G and E Index and firm value. They show this in both cross-sectional regressions and time series regressions with firm fixed effects. For firms that have adopted poison pills, no other element of the indices has a significant correlation with firm value. Taking this result together with Catan's, the implication is that for firms that adopted a poison pill, the negative relationship that GIM and BCF find between firm value and the G and E Indices is not causal. (Cremers and Ferrell report some evidence of reverse causation as well.)

Cremers and Ferrell, however, also find that for firms that have not (yet) adopted a poison pill, the E Index (minus the pill) is associated with lower firm value—though with statistical significance of only 10%. This warrants further investigation for two reasons. First, since firms that have not adopted a pill can and will do so if they receive a hostile bid, it is not apparent why they should be different with respect to the impact of the G Index elements. Second, in firm fixed effects models Cremers and Ferrell find no statistically significant relationship between firm value and three E Index elements: supermajority vote requirements to amend a charter, to amend bylaws, and to approve a merger. Moreover, they find a *positive* relationship between staggered boards and Q. This leaves only golden parachutes to explain the negative relationship between firm value and the E Index for firms that have not adopted poison pills. More work is needed to untangle these relationships. Nonetheless, Cremers and Ferrell have moved us considerably closer to understanding the GIM and BCF results in a way that is consistent with what we know about how the elements of the E Index work.

Fox, Gilson, and Palia have also weighed in recently with a draft paper that attempts to explain the GIM results for just two years following the Enron scandal in terms of signaling theory.[94] But the signal Fox et al. see in a firm's index score is not costly to low quality firms—precisely because nearly all elements carry no consequence. Therefore, a good index score sends no signal.

4.2   Why the G and E Indices Fail to Measure Entrenchment or Governance Quality

The G Index comprises firm-level provisions and six provisions of state antitakeover statutes, which are combined into 24 elements.[95] A firm is scored based on how many of

---

to anticipate. In fact, to the extent pill adoption could signal an imminent hostile bid, it could trigger an *increase* in share value.

[92] Cremers & Ferrell, *supra* note 52.

[93] The results of relevance to this discussion are from 1985 on, the period following the *Moran v. Household International* case in Delaware, which validated the poison pill and more generally allowed target management to defend against a hostile takeover.

[94] Merritt Fox, Ronald Gilson, & Darius Palia, "Corporate Governance Changes as a Signal: Contextualizing the Performance Link" (November 2016), http://ssrn.com/abstract=2807926.

[95] The G Index includes the following elements:

   • Blank check preferred stock

these elements are present in its charter, bylaws, or the law of the state in which the firm is incorporated. The assumption underlying the index is that the more elements a firm has in its charter, bylaws, or elsewhere, the more it is protected from hostile takeovers.

It is implausible that, as a general matter, a firm with a larger number of G Index elements protects management from hostile takeovers more than a firm with a smaller number of G Index elements. Particular elements of the index provide protection (notably, a staggered board), but the vast majority do not. Moreover, the G Index suffers from the flawed conception that *more* elements matter more—that the accumulation of individually entrenching elements layers on more protection at the margin from hostile takeovers or worse governance in some other sense. As explained in section 3, this is simply not true.

The E Index consists of six G Index elements that BCF found to be the underlying empirical drivers of the GIM results.[96] By omitting 18 G Index elements, which were not only empirically irrelevant to governance but also functionally irrelevant, the E Index is an improvement on the G Index. But the E Index suffers from the same flaws as the G Index on a

- Staggered board
- Shareholders' inability to call a special meeting
- Prohibition on shareholder voting by written consent
- Change in control provision in executive compensation plan
- Golden parachutes
- Indemnification agreements with officers and directors
- Indemnification of officers and directors in bylaws
- Exculpation of outside directors for violations of the duty of care (e.g., under Del. Code Ann. tit. 8, § 102(b)(7))
- Executive severance agreements not contingent on change of control
- Restrictions, such as supermajority vote requirement, on bylaw amendments by shareholders
- Restrictions, such as supermajority vote requirement, on charter amendments by shareholders
- Absence of cumulative voting
- Absence of confidential voting by shareholders
- Supermajority shareholder vote required for mergers
- Unequal voting based on duration of shareholding (not dual-class stock)
- Anti-greenmail charter provision
- Non-shareholder constituency charter provision
- Fair price charter provision or applicable state statute
- Pension parachute
- Poison pill
- Silver parachute
- Anti-greenmail statutory provision applies
- Business combination statute applies
- Non-shareholder constituency statute applies
- Cash-out statute applies
- Fair price statute applies
- Control share acquisition statute applies

[96] The E Index includes the following elements:
- Poison pill
- Staggered board
- Golden parachutes
- Supermajority shareholder vote requirement for bylaw amendments
- Supermajority shareholder vote requirement for charter amendments
- Supermajority shareholder vote requirement for mergers

smaller scale. Five of the six E Index elements are either entirely or nearly irrelevant as measures of entrenchment or governance quality more generally.

So what exactly is wrong with the elements of the G and E Indices? Since the E Index is a subset of the G Index, I will answer this question with respect to the broader G Index and in doing so cover the subset of G Index elements that constitute the E Index. For clarity, in the discussion below, each E Index element will be in **bold** type initially. I will also recap with a summary of why the E Index is fundamentally flawed.

The flaws in the G Index fall into the following categories, each of which is explained further below: (1) Some elements can have no impact on management entrenchment; (2) nearly all other elements can have no impact on entrenchment if a firm has a staggered board; (3) some elements can have an impact on entrenchment only under limited and unusual circumstances; and (4) some elements are either of no relevance to entrenchment or they have an affirmatively beneficial impact on governance. Consequently, neither the G Index nor the E Index is a plausible measure of management entrenchment (or any other governance quality).

4.2.1 Takeover-Related Elements with No Takeover-Related Impact

As explained in section 3, the following elements of the G Index have no impact on a firm's exposure to a hostile takeover:

- **Poison pill in advance of an actual bid**
- Coverage by a business combination statute
- Coverage by a fair price statute or charter provision
- Coverage by a control share acquisition statute
- Coverage by a cash-out statute (which is equivalent to a fair price statute).

The presence of a pill at any point in time before a hostile takeover bid is made is of no consequence, as discussed in section 3. What matters is that when a hostile bid occurs, the target firm has a pill. Once a bid is made, the target board has plenty of time to adopt a pill. All it takes is a board resolution. Therefore at any time prior to the point at which a bid is made, a firm without a pill is no more exposed to a takeover threat than a firm with a pill. As explained above, all firms have a "shadow pill." Consequently, inclusion of a poison pill in the G and E Indices is incorrect.

Once a firm adopts a poison pill, the pill provides complete protection from a hostile takeover so long as it is in place. Consequently, the other provisions listed above have no impact on entrenchment (or anything else). Each provides protection that is not only redundant with that of a pill but less powerful than a pill as well.

Because a pill provides complete protection as long as it is in place, the only governance measures that affect a firm's exposure to a hostile takeover are those that impede a shareholder vote to replace a firm's board with a new board that will disable the pill. None of the elements listed above do that.

The G Index also includes the following provisions:

- A supermajority shareholder vote to amend a charter
- A supermajority shareholder vote to approve a merger

The first of these—a supermajority to amend a charter—is of no consequence with respect to takeover exposure. As a matter of law, a charter amendment requires both board approval and shareholder approval. Since board approval is needed, there is no way for shareholders to amend a charter regardless of whether a majority or supermajority vote is needed. If there is anything in the charter that entrenches management—a staggered board, for example—it will stay there unless the board decides to amend the charter to eliminate it, in which case a shareholder vote of approval is sure to follow with or without a supermajority requirement.[97]

A supermajority vote to approve a merger is also of no consequence and does not belong in the indices. A shareholder vote on a merger can come up in the context of a hostile takeover only after a bidder has succeeded in a tender offer for a majority of the target's shares—that is, a majority of the target's shareholders have already sold their shares to an acquirer. (No shareholder vote is needed for this to happen.) If the acquirer wants to buy the remaining shares, which is typically the case, it must conduct a "back-end merger." This requires a vote of the target shareholders. A majority of the target's votes are already held by the acquirer, and they will obviously be voted in favor of the merger, but if there is a supermajority vote requirement, it is theoretically possible that a large enough minority of shareholders will hold out so that the supermajority threshold (say, 80%) will not be met. But who would hold out? Target insiders, perhaps. But to what end? Their firm is already controlled by the acquirer and they are either out of their jobs or they certainly will be out of jobs if they vote against the merger. Perhaps there is an outside blockholder unrelated to management. But if so, an acquirer will have gotten that blockholder's support in advance. Perhaps a hedge fund could buy up the target's shares after the tender offer in an effort to shake down the acquirer for a higher back-end price. Theoretically, this could happen but it never has. And for a supermajority vote requirement to entrench management, an acquirer must be deterred from the start, which means it must foresee this happening. Not too likely, especially during the period of the GIM and BCF studies.

Neither of these supermajority vote requirements, therefore, belongs in a governance index.

4.2.2 *Treatment of Firms with Staggered Boards*

As explained above, a **staggered board** in conjunction with a pill is a nearly complete defense to a hostile takeover. It imposes a roughly two-year delay on an acquirer seeking to have target shareholders replace their board with a board that will disable the target's pill. For firms with staggered boards, no other takeover defense can have a protective impact at the margin.[98] This means that for all firms with staggered boards, the presence of other elements just runs up the score without adding additional protection from hostile takeovers. On the other hand, it would make no sense to give firms a total score of only 1 for having the strongest takeover mechanism in place and none of the remaining ones that provide no

---

[97] It is possible that the board will want to amend the charter and that a supermajority requirement is so high that the shareholders fail to muster enough votes to carry out the amendment. But this scenario is not a scenario involving management protection.

[98] The exception to this statement is dual-class stock, which is rare.

protection at the margin anyway. This is just one respect in which the premise of tallying up a score for takeover-related elements that are not additive makes no sense.

4.2.3 Takeover-Related Elements with an Impact Only Under Limited Circumstances

Some takeover-related elements of the G Index can have an impact on management entrenchment, but only under limited circumstances. Two of these elements, discussed in section 3, are those that prevent shareholders from voting to replace board members between annual meetings, and thereby delaying an acquirer for up to one year. These elements are (a) a prohibition on shareholders calling a special meeting and (b) a prohibition on their voting by written consent in lieu of a meeting (or, equivalently, a requirement that such votes be unanimous). These provisions are relevant, however, in only two circumstances. First, they are relevant only for firms without staggered boards. The law governing staggered boards requires that directors be elected *at annual meetings only*.[99] Second, each is relevant only if the other is present; one alone is useless.[100] Therefore, one point for either provision alone is not appropriate, nor is assigning two points for both.

Another element that is relevant only under certain circumstances is a **supermajority vote requirement for bylaw amendments**. The analysis here is complicated. As a threshold matter, this provision can be relevant only if the combination of the supermajority threshold and inside share ownership is such that it would be difficult to get a sufficient number of outside shareholder votes to amend a firm's bylaws. For example, if an 80% vote is required to amend a firm's bylaws, and management (or outside shareholder allies) hold over 20% of the firm's shares, then management can effectively veto changes to the bylaws. If management holds 15% it would still be difficult to get enough votes to amend. Since inside ownership changes over time and could change specifically in the context of a takeover-related event, this is not a straightforward item of data.

Assuming that the supermajority threshold is high enough to matter, the next condition that must be met for the supermajority to be relevant to entrenchment is that there is something in the bylaws that entrenches management in the first place, or equivalently, that there is something in the relevant state default rules that is entrenching. In either case, to the extent the supermajority provision prevents the shareholders from amending the bylaws to undo

---

[99] Model Bus. Corp. Act § 8.06 (2007); Del. Code Ann. tit. 8, § 141(d) (2013). As discussed in section 4.2.4, these provisions can be useful for a company with an ineffective staggered board, where shareholders might be able to replace the board immediately by passing a bylaw amendment. It is also possible that, for companies with an effective staggered board, one of these provisions could be used for a bylaw amendment that would facilitate an earlier takeover at the margin. This is what shareholders attempted (unsuccessfully) to do in *Airgas, Inc. v. Air Products & Chemicals, Inc.*, 8 A.3d 1182 (Del. 2010), but especially following *Airgas*, such use of these provisions will not have a substantial impact on entrenchment.

[100] There are relatively minor differences between the two. A vote by written consent requires a majority of outstanding shares, whereas a vote at a special meeting requires only a majority of shares cast. On the other hand, a vote by written consent can be carried out more quickly than a vote at a special meeting. The duration of the delay would depend on when the takeover bid begins in relation to the target's next annual meeting and the extent to which the state law governing the target allows it to delay its annual meeting.

the entrenchment, the offending protective mechanism will remain present. A staggered board is the primary example.[101] Occasionally, bylaws rather than charters provide for a staggered board. If a firm's bylaws provide for a staggered board and that bylaw provision is protected by a supermajority provision, then the supermajority provision is relevant to management entrenchment. But BCF report both that 5% to 7% of firms in their sample have staggered boards provided for in their bylaws[102] and, separately, that 32% to 40% of firms have supermajority provisions applicable to bylaw amendments.[103] Unless these additional super-majority provisions protect an entrenching bylaw provision, they should not be included in the index. Moreover, including this supermajority provision in the index means that a firm with both a staggered board provision in its bylaws and a supermajority requirement for amending its bylaws will receive two points, and a firm with a staggered board provided for in its charter will receive only one point, yet the level of entrenchment is the same.[104]

Even if there is no entrenching provision in a firm's bylaws at a particular time (or an equivalent provision adopted by default from state law), most firms' charters allow their boards to amend bylaws unilaterally—along with shareholders, who always have a unilateral right as well. Consequently, one might ask whether a supermajority vote requirement for shareholder amendments exposes shareholders to such unilateral amendments by boards with no opportunity for shareholders to undo the damage with their own amendment. This scenario is possible but not with respect to seriously entrenching amendments. In Delaware, a board cannot amend bylaws to create a staggered board, and in states that have adopted the Model Business Corporation Act in its original or revised form, a staggered board must be provided for in the charter, not the bylaws.[105] In addition, any other board-imposed amendment must be in line with the board's fiduciary duty to shareholders and consistent with the corporate statute and the firm's charter.[106] Its impact must also be fully disclosed. If an amendment somehow shields management from a hostile takeover, a court will subject it to serious scrutiny. Consequently, a board's opportunity to amend bylaws this way is not substantial. Therefore if there is nothing in the bylaws (or a state default rule) to protect, a super-majority requirement to amend bylaws should not be given credit in an index as entrenching.

Golden parachutes could well be included in section 4.2.1, among the E Index provisions with no impact on entrenchment. Since 1984, golden parachutes are subject to a tax if they are greater than three times an executive's base compensation.[107] Consequently, most golden parachutes are at this level. Golden parachutes alone, therefore, will not impose a high enough cost to deter a hostile bid. It is possible that, when added to other forms of change-of-control payments, such as accelerated options, golden parachutes happen to become an important deterrent to a takeover at the margin for some firms. It is also true that some golden parachutes are larger than the tax-penalty limit. So it is technically possible that a

---

[101] For firms with annually elected boards, then the two provisions that prevent shareholders from voting outside of annual meetings are the other examples.

[102] Bebchuk & Cohen, *supra* note 59, at 419.   [103] Bebchuk et al., *supra* note 83, at 797.

[104] Indeed, the entrenchment of a charter-embedded staggered board is greater because it cannot be undone by a board majority vote. A shareholder vote will always be required, which will add time and uncertainty to a bid.

[105] Del. Code Ann. tit. 8, §141(d); Model Bus. Corp. Act §8.06; Revised Model Bus. Corp. Act §8.06.

[106] *Chesapeake Corp. v. Shore*, 771 A.2d 293 (Del. Ch. 2000).

[107] Internal Revenue Code, §280G.

golden parachute of the right size relative to the gains available to an acquirer could deter an acquirer. But if this were the basis for including golden parachutes in the G or E Index, one would have to include only very large ones—perhaps larger than those that actually exist.

A second potential reason to consider golden parachutes as a negative factor in corporate governance is that they *may* make management indifferent to a takeover at a low price. This seems to be what BCF had in mind. If a golden parachute makes management indifferent to a hostile takeover at a low price and as a result relieves management of pressure to manage the company well, then the golden parachute would be detrimental to shareholders. But will three times base salary have this incentive effect on CEOs and other senior managers? It seems unlikely.

Finally, a golden parachute is generally expected to have a *positive* impact on governance because it will reduce management's resistance to a value-increasing takeover bid. That is, it has an anti-entrenchment impact.[108] It therefore does not belong in an index that supposedly measures negative governance quality.

In sum, golden parachutes can be either a positive or negative influence on corporate governance and firm value—and they may have no influence in either direction. Their impact at the margin depends on other factors. To score a golden parachute as entrenching, especially without considering other factors, is incorrect.

4.2.4 *Elements that are Unrelated to Takeover-Defense and Affirmatively Good for Corporate Governance*

The G Index also contains several elements that are not takeover defenses, that have no bearing on management entrenchment whatsoever, and that are widely understood to be beneficial from a governance standpoint. Three such elements protect board members and managers from litigation and liability risk: (i) director indemnification provided for in bylaws; (ii) director indemnification provided by agreement; and (iii) exculpation of outside directors for monetary liability for violation of the duty of care. All of these protections have exceptions for actions that directors or officers have taken in bad faith.[109] They are not licenses to steal. It is widely agreed that directors and officers should be protected from the expense of shareholder lawsuits, which are often non-meritorious, even if this protection can also extend to individuals who have engaged in misconduct. Indeed, without such protection, it would be difficult to attract outside directors and perhaps even top-level officers to public companies, and those who are attracted would take few risks, regardless of the rewards to shareholders.

4.2.5 *The E Index*

The E Index contains the following elements of the G Index:

- Staggered board
- Supermajority to amend bylaws
- Golden parachute

---

[108] See Marcel Kahan & Edward B. Rock, "How I Learned to Stop Worrying and Love the Pill: Adaptive Responses to Takeover Law", 69 U. Chi. L. Rev. 871 (2002).

[109] See Del. Code Ann. tit. 8, § 145 (allowing companies to indemnify individuals who acted in good faith).

- Supermajority to amend charter
- Supermajority to approve a merger
- Poison pill

Summarizing what has just been explained above, a staggered board is the primary element of the Index with a potential for entrenchment. A supermajority requirement to amend bylaws can, under highly limited circumstances, be entrenching. But treating them as entrenching without taking account of those circumstances is inaccurate. The impact of golden parachutes is even more contingent, and possibly positive. The two other supermajority requirements are not entrenching. And finally, the presence or absence of a poison pill at any point in time is of no consequence and therefore should not be in the index.

So the final tally of E Index elements that can potentially have an impact on entrenchment is three out of six. And of those three, two are highly contingent, and one of those two—golden parachutes—is expected to have positive impact on governance. If researchers want to know whether these three elements have an impact on governance, or if they believe they do ex ante in a particular circumstance, there is no reason to combine them into an index. Each can enter a regression separately and each can be refined to capture situations in which they matter.

While a governance index must simplify complex relationships, the simplification must reflect an understanding of how the elements of the index work. This is not the case with the G Index or the E Index. Their elements do not have any justification in terms of how corporate governance works. These problems, coupled with the fact that researchers mechanically use the indices without understanding them, has resulted in widespread and ongoing confusion in the empirical governance literature.

5 Conclusion

Empirical analysis of corporate governance has taken the field beyond the exchange of theoretical assertions and ideological pronouncements that often characterize legal scholarship, and it has the potential to take us farther. There are methodological barriers that warrant modesty with respect to the interpretation of results and even more so to policy prescriptions. But econometricians will continue to develop methods that reduce those barriers.

A greater problem, though one that can (in theory) be corrected, is the fact that many economists working in this area do not understand the institutional and legal context of their research. This is not only a problem with individual economists who write these articles, it is a problem in the finance and economics research infrastructure. The editors and the referees are no better informed than the authors submitting papers for publication, nor are business school and economics department colleagues who are impressed by publications in top journals.

Catan and Kahan described the situation well: "[J]ust like managers suffer from agency costs that distort behavior, academics (in finance, but also in law—ourselves included) have incentives that can distort behavior. And for empiricists, one of the potential distortions is to embrace variables that can be easily employed in an empirical test and to pay little heed to arguments that the variable has no theoretical validity."[110]

---

[110] Catan & Kahan, *supra* note 2, at 669.

CHAPTER 9

....

THE BENEFITS AND COSTS OF INDICES IN EMPIRICAL CORPORATE GOVERNANCE RESEARCH

....

ALLEN FERRELL

1 INTRODUCTION

....

INTEREST in corporate governance, whether on the part of academics, governmental agencies, shareholder activists, or market commentators, has never been greater. Shleifer and Vishny define corporate governance as "the ways in which suppliers of finance to corporations assure themselves of getting a return on their investment."[1] So defined, few issues could be more fundamental to the operation of the capital markets and the financing of corporations.

Given the diversity of differing, and reasonable, views on which aspects of corporate governance should matter to investors, how they matter and when they matter, the resolution of what constitutes good corporate governance practices is ultimately an empirical question. This chapter will focus on the benefits and costs of the empirical literature's reliance on using corporate governance indices to measure corporate governance in exploring these issues.

2 MEASURING CORPORATE GOVERNANCE

....

2.1 Corporate Governance Indices

Measuring firm characteristics related to firm corporate governance for large numbers of firms over substantial periods of time is one of the most important challenges facing

---

[1] Andrei Shleifer & Robert W. Vishny, "A Survey of Corporate Governance", 52 J. Fin. 737 (1997).

corporate governance research. The issues that must be confronted in such an endeavor include whether there are plausible reasons to believe that whatever firm characteristics are
being measured could reasonably be expected to matter in the first place, adequate breadth
of coverage (both temporally and cross-sectionally), consistency with prior literature, and
standardization. Not all these desirable outcomes are always achievable to researchers at the
same time, such as the potential trade-off between breadth of coverage and one's preferred
measure of corporate governance. As with corporate governance itself, the measurement of
corporate governance will also involve debatable trade-offs.

A common approach in measuring corporate governance is to use corporate governance indices. These indices typically sum the number of a particular set of arrangements
a firm has and assigns the firm a score based on this summation. Indices therefore ignore
weighting particular combinations of arrangements differently from other combinations
in the score assigned to a firm. In so doing, the empirical corporate governance literature
has followed the approach adopted in other areas such as the use of indices in exploring the
effect of country-level legal rules on various outcome measures of interest.[2] It is therefore
not surprising that some of the issues that have arisen with respect to indices measuring the
quality of country-level legal rules have also arisen in the context of measuring firm-specific
governance arrangements.

Of all the indices, the G-Index measure of corporate governance, first introduced in the
seminal paper of Gompers, Ishii, and Metrick,[3] has had the most profound impact on empirical corporate governance research. The G-Index is based on how many of 24 possible corporate governance provisions, each of which purportedly restricts shareholder rights in some
manner, a firm has at a particular point in time. A higher G-Index therefore indicates fewer
shareholder rights. The G-Index provisions include the presence of antitakeover provisions
(such as staggered boards and poison pills), certain types of compensation arrangements
that might arguably help insulate management (such as golden parachutes), and various
types of supra-majority shareholder voting requirements. Some of these provisions can be
found in a corporation's bylaws or corporate charter, some in a firm's contracts with management, and still others are a function of the law of the state the firm is incorporated in.

Building on Gompers, Ishii, and Metrick, another triplet, Bebchuk, Cohen, and Ferrell,
construct another widely used corporate governance index, the E-Index, which consists
of six of the 24 G-Index provisions.[4] They argue that these six provisions in particular can
matter in furthering managerial entrenchment, particularly that of target management
facing a hostile takeover. As with the G-Index, a higher E-Index score is indicative of fewer
shareholder rights. They document that the negative association of the G-Index with firm
value and lower stock returns is accounted for by the E-Index.

To be sure, besides the widely used G- and E-Indices other corporate governance indices
have been proposed in the literature, though they are generally used less frequently. For example, Gillan, Hartzell, and Starks construct a board index intended to capture the strength

---

[2] See, e.g., Rafael LaPorta, Florencio Lopez-de-Silanes, Andrei Shleifer, & Robert W. Vishny, "Law and
Finance", 106 J. Pol. Econ. 1113 (1998).

[3] Paul Gompers, Joy Ishii, & Andrew Metrick, "Corporate Governance and Equity Prices", 118 Q. J.
Econ. 107 (2003).

[4] Lucian A. Bebchuk, Alma Cohen, & Allen Ferrell, "What Matters in Corporate Governance?", 22
Rev. Fin. Stud. 783 (2009).

of board monitoring (based on board size, separation of chair and CEO, separate independent board committees).[5] Brown and Cayler introduced a corporate governance index based on the sum of 51 firm-level provisions.[6] Cremers and Nair utilize an antitakeover index intended to measure a firm's takeover exposure, which consists of summing whether a firm has a staggered board, blank check preferred stock, and restrictions on shareholders' ability to call a special meeting or act through written consent.[7] Coates proposes an index carefully constructed to track the legal impact of various provisions on a firm's takeover exposure.[8] Unlike the typical index approach, his approach considers the interaction of different types of arrangements. In the commercial and advising context, additional corporate governance indices have been used such as the Institutional Shareholder Services' Corporate Governance Quotient Index; the Governance Metrics International's GMI Index; and the Corporate Library's TCL Index, though there are academic concerns regarding these indices' utility.[9]

There are at least three important reasons that can account for the influence of the G- and E-Indices on empirical corporate governance research, at least insofar as the research has focused on the type of provisions tracked by the G- and E-Indices.

First, and perhaps most importantly, these indices are readily calculable from the widely used RiskMetrics database (formerly maintained by the Institutional Responsibility Research Center (IRRC)) covering between 1,400 and 1,800 firms starting in 1990 until 2008 (updated at either two- or three-year intervals). All the firms of the S&P 500 are included as well as a number of others. These firms represent more than 90% of total US stock market capitalization in any given year. As of 2008 and onwards, however, only a subset of the G-Index provisions are covered in the RiskMetrics database rendering it currently impossible to calculate a firm's G- or E-Index scores for more recent years using this database. Given this important and growing gap in the data, and in light of the central role of the G- and E-Indices in empirical corporate governance research, Cremers et al. will be providing this data to researchers for each year starting in 2008 for a large sample of firms while also correcting for some coding issues in the RiskMetrics database.[10] Besides the RiskMetrics database, some of the G-Index provisions are also available from the SharkRepellent database.

Second, readily available indices capturing a range of governance provisions enable researchers to examine the impact of particular corporate governance provisions while accounting for a wider universe of corporate governance provisions. A corporate governance index can readily be broken into its component parts and analyzed in the context of

---

[5] Stuart L. Gillan, Jay C. Hartzell, & Laura T. Starks, "Tradeoffs in Corporate Governance: Evidence From Board Structures and Charter Provisions", 1 Q. J. Fin. 667 (2011).

[6] Lawrence D. Brown & Marcus L. Caylor, "Corporate Governance and Firm Valuation", 25 J. of Accounting and Public Policy 409 (2006).

[7] K.J. Martijn Cremers & Vinay B. Nair, "Governance Mechanisms and Equity Prices", 60 J. Fin. 2859 (2005).

[8] John C. Coates, IV, "An Index of the Contestability of Corporate Control: Studying Variation in Legal Takeover Vulnerability", Working Paper (June 1999).

[9] Robert Daines, Ian D. Gow, & David F. Larcker, "Rating the Ratings: How Good Are Commercial Governance Ratings?", 98 J. Fin. Econ. 439 (2010).

[10] K.J. Martijn Cremers, Allen Ferrell, Paul Gompers, & Andrew Metrick, "Introducing the CFGM Corporate Governance Database: Variable Construction and Comparison to the RiskMetrics and IRRC Governance Databases", Working Paper 2016.

exploring the particular effect of a provision or sub-portion of the index that is of interest. In contrast, much research prior to Gompers, Ishii, and Metrick[11] tended to focus on just one particular provision or a small set of provisions[12] without accounting for the other provisions tracked by these indices.

Third, despite significant skepticism, particularly in the legal academy, concerning the construction of these indices, it is nevertheless the case that an impressive number of academic papers utilizing the G- and E-Indices in a variety of settings, including a number of papers published in top peer-reviewed finance journals, consistently report finding that these indices are associated with various outcome variables of interest, typically some metric of firm performance. For instance, in an interesting paper, Masulis, Wang, and Xie explore the effect of corporate governance, using the G- and E-Indices, on returns experienced by bidders when making an acquisition announcement.[13] They hypothesize that bidders with poor corporate governance will experience greater negative stock returns as these firms are likely to engage in poor acquisitions. Consistent with this hypothesis, they report that "bidder returns decrease by 0.290% (0.435%) per one-standard deviation increase in the [G-Index (E-Index)] . . . "[14] To take another example, Dittmar and Mahrt-Smith investigate whether the market's valuation of a firm's cash holdings depends on the quality of corporate governance.[15] They report that whether one uses the G- or E-Index, the "results show that having less entrenched managers (good governance) substantially and significantly increases the value of a dollar of cash, as evidenced by the positive and significant coefficient on the interaction between governance and cash."[16] As a final example, Giroud and Mueller document that firms with weak corporate governance, using the G- and E-Indices as the measure, have lower labor productivity, make more value-destroying acquisitions, and experience worse operating performance, lower equity returns, and lower firm value when the firm is in a noncompetitive industry.[17] The importance of governance in noncompetitive industries might be the result of firms in these industries facing less pressure from product competition to adopt value-maximizing practices.

While many of these studies focus on the relationship between corporate governance and various metrics for firm performance (typically Tobin's Q), one of the interesting findings from Gompers, Ishii, and Metrick that has generated its own literature is the association between good corporate governance and positive abnormal stock returns.[18] Economically,

[11] Gompers, Ishii, & Metrick, *supra* note 3.

[12] See, e.g., Michael Ryngaert, "The Effect of Poison Pill Securities on Shareholder Wealth", J. Fin. Econ. 377 (1988).

[13] Ronald W. Masulis, Cong Wang, & Fei Xie, "Corporate Governance and Acquirer Returns", 62 J. Fin. 1851 (2007).

[14] Masulis, Wang, & Xie, *supra* note 13, at 1867.

[15] Amy Dittmar & Jan Mahrt-Smith, "Corporate Governance and the Value of Cash Holdings", 83 J. Fin. Econ. 599 (2007).

[16] Dittmar & Mahrt-Smith, *supra* note 15, at 607.

[17] Xavier Giroud & Holger M. Mueller, "Does Corporate Governance Matter in Competitive Industries?", 95 J. Fin. Econ. 312 (2010); X. Giroud and H. Mueller, "Corporate Governance, Product Market Competition, and Equity Prices", 66 J. Fin. 563 (2011).

[18] Martijn Cremers & Allen Ferrell, "Thirty Years of Shareholder Rights and Stock Returns", Working Paper 2013; Lucian A. Bebchuk, Alma Cohen, & Charles C. Y. Wang, "Learning and the Disappearing Association Between Governance and Returns", 108 J. Fin. Econ. 323 (2013); John E. Core, Wayne R. Guay, & Tjomme O. Rusticus, "Does Weak Governance Cause Weak Stock Returns? An Examination of Firm Operating Performance and Investors' Expectations", 61 J. Fin. 655 (2006).

the reported results are striking, with a portfolio that buys (sells) firms with strong (weak) shareholder rights having an annualized abnormal return of 8.7% over 1990–1999. This is deeply puzzling as any impact corporate governance has on stock prices would presumably be a one-time event assuming that the firm does not change its corporate governance, and the market salience of corporate governance does not change over time. In other words, the value of the firm might be lower as a result of poor corporate governance, but this firm value effect should not also generate a different return profile going forward over significant periods of time. Various theories have been proposed for the stock return effect, including the market learning of the importance of good corporate governance over long stretches of time, a lack of robustness, and the relationship between takeover exposure (as reflected in the G- or E-Index) and systematic risk.

Whether all these and similar findings in the literature are due to the direct causal impact of the provisions tracked by the G- and E-Indices (or some subset of these), a correlation of these indices with other more difficult to measure aspects of corporate governance, coding issues, or simply reflect some form of endogeneity inadequately controlled for has been and remains an interesting topic of corporate governance research.

2.2 Measurement Error

While the success of these indices is easy to understand, these indices also have important limitations. I will focus on concerns centered on the construction of the indices in this portion of my discussion.

The theoretical underpinnings of the G-Index, and, in particular, why these 24 provisions in particular might plausibly impact the corporate governance of a firm in a meaningful way, have typically been left at a quite abstract level. For instance, Gompers, Ishii and Metrick themselves argue that the G-Index provisions could create agency costs through "some combination of inefficient investment, reduced operational efficiency, or self-dealing."[19] These types of managerial agency concerns stated at this level of generality, of course, have a long provenance in the literature beginning with Berle and Means,[20] concerns developed by Manne in the corporate control context,[21] and reflected in the vast agency cost literature beginning with Jensen and Meckling.[22] The E-Index has a somewhat more granular justification as it focused on managerial defenses against unwanted changes in corporate control (or at least unwanted by the target's board). In this context, Bebchuk, Cohen, and Ferrell[23] also point out that the presence of some entrenching provisions, such as poison pills, might provide an informational signal to the market as was pointed out by Coates.[24] Managerial

---

[19]   Gompers, Ishii & Metrick, *supra* note 3, at 131.

[20]   Adolf A. Berle & Gardiner Means, The Modern Corporation and Private Property (1932).

[21]   Henry G. Manne, "Mergers and the Market for Corporate Control", 73 J. Pol. Econ. 110 (1965).

[22]   Michael C. Jensen & William H. Meckling, "Theory of the Firm: Managerial Behavior, Agency Costs and Ownership Structure", 3 J. Fin. Econ. 305 (1976). For a survey, see also Lucian A. Bebchuk, "The Case against Board Veto in Corporate Takeovers", 69 U. Chi. L. Rev. 973 (2002).

[23]   Bebchuk, Cohen, & Ferrell, *supra* note 4.

[24]   John C. Coates, IV, "Takeover Defenses in the Shadow of the Pill: A Critique of the Scientific Evidence", 79 Tex. L. Rev. 271 (2000).

entrenchment in the context of a hostile bid has been a prominent concern in the literature since Manne.[25]

The issue that such an abstract justification for an index, whether it be the G-Index or some other corporate governance index, does not lie in the fact that a researcher could reasonably take the opposite view. For example, managerial entrenchment under certain conditions might result in beneficial effects such as empowering managers to negotiate higher acquisition premiums[26] or reducing distortions in incentives to invest in long-term projects.[27] After all, this competing view can also be put to the test using these same indices assuming that it is measuring, even if imperfectly, managerial entrenchment.

Rather, the more powerful critiques have focused on the a priori plausibility of a particular index accurately capturing a firm's corporate governance profile. In short, the claim focuses on whether it is measuring anything at all of importance. For instance, Bebchuk, Cohen, and Ferrell argue that their analysis fails to reveal any basis for viewing 18 of the 24 G-Index provisions as significant.[28] To take an important example, antitakeover statutes (such as business combination statutes) were arguably rendered largely irrelevant once target boards had the ability to block unwanted takeovers with a poison pill so long as the directors remained in office. If directors could ward off an unwanted takeover by this means, the additional incremental protections provided to a target board by an antitakeover statute are rendered superfluous.[29] If correct, this calls into question the numerous corporate governance studies that have focused on the presence of an antitakeover statute important to the corporate governance of firms incorporated in that state.[30] Klausner goes one step further and argues that the only antitakeover provisions that are likely to matter are poison pills and staggered boards (along with dual class shares, which are not one of the 24 G-Index provisions).[31] Romano, Bolton, and Bhagat argue for the superiority of just one corporate governance variable: the dollar value of the median independent director's stockholding.[32]

Indeed, an even further paring back of the firm characteristics that should arguably be included in a measure of corporate governance is possible. As has been clearly recognized since Coates, poison pills can clearly matter a great deal to a firm's corporate governance profile but the extent to which actually having one at any particular point in time should matter is questionable given the unilateral ability of any firm to quickly adopt a poison pill if and when it is desired.[33] In other words, all firms in effect have a "shadow poison pill." Of course, this view is entirely consistent with the fact that a firm's adoption of a pill might well

---

[25] Manne, *supra* note 21.

[26] René M. Stulz, "Managerial Control of Voting Rights: Financing Policies and the Market for Corporate Control", 20 J. Fin. Econ. 25 (1988).

[27] Jeremy C. Stein, "Takeover Threats and Managerial Myopia", 96 J. Pol. Econ. 61 (1988).

[28] Bebchuk, Cohen, & Ferrell, *supra* note 4.

[29] See also Emiliano Catan & Marcel Kahan, "The Law and Finance of Anti-Takeover Statutes", 68 Stan. L. Rev. (forthcoming 2016).

[30] See, e.g., Marianne Bertrand & Sendhil Mullainathan, "Enjoying the Quiet Life? Corporate Governance and Managerial Preferences", 111 J. Pol. Econ. 1043 (2003); Jiaping Qiu & Fan Yu, "The Market for Corporate Control and the Cost of Debt", 93 J. Fin. Econ. 505 (2009).

[31] Michael Klausner, "Fact and Fiction in Corporate Law and Governance", 65 Stan. L. Rev. 1325 (2013).

[32] Sanjai Bhagat, Brian Bolton, & Roberta Romano, "The Promise and Peril of Corporate Governance Indices", 108 Colum. L. Rev. 1803 (2008).

[33] Coates, *supra* note 24.

constitute an important signal to the market concerning the firm's management, such as the management's receptivity to a takeover or private information about the likelihood of the firm facing a takeover bid.

Offsetting these objections to the use of corporate governance indices are two considerations. First, while the indices are undoubtedly noisy measures of corporate governance, they are arguably deployed in a manner reflective of this fact. In Gompers, Ishii, and Metrick itself,[34] for instance, the empirical analysis focuses on the extreme ends of the G-Index distribution (labeled the "democracy" and "dictatorship" firms). That is to say, even with a noisy proxy for corporate governance, firms at either end of the distribution are more likely to have an acceptable noise/signal ratio, thereby at least somewhat mitigating a concern over mismeasurement. Needless to say, whether this is a satisfying response will depend on the extent of one's concerns over mismeasurement (or non-measurement).

Second, the claim that corporate governance has been substantially mismeasured as a result of the literature's reliance on corporate governance indices does not by itself imply that the typical regressions one sees in the literature are necessarily invalid or uninformative. It is worth noting at the outset that in the literature the corporate governance variable, such as an index, is typically (although not inevitably) on the right-hand side of the regressions, i.e. serves as an explanatory variable. On the left-hand side—the dependent variable—there is very often (although not inevitably) some metric related to firm performance, such as Tobin's Q, return on assets, accounting restatements, cost of equity, and excess stock returns. This reflects the simple fact that researchers are usually interested in investigating the potential association of corporate governance, controlling for other variables, to metrics related to firm performance.

In such a regression framework, as is well understood, any measurement error becomes part of the regression error. Assuming the measurement error is correlated with the corporate governance measure being used as an explanatory variable (or, equivalently, is uncorrelated with the "true" unobserved corporate governance), this gives rise to a standard errors-in-variables problem with any ordinary least square regressions that are run using this measure. Specifically, any coefficient from a regression using the corporate governance measure, say the G-Index, will suffer from attenuation bias, meaning the coefficient on the index will be biased toward zero.[35] As a result, if a positive statistically significant coefficient on corporate governance were in fact found, then a researcher could simply note that even despite this bias working against such a finding they were nevertheless able to find one. There is nothing particularly problematic in any of this. Potentially far more troubling is the further fact that if other explanatory variables (of which there might be a significant number) in a regression besides the corporate governance measure are also measured with error, then the bias on the corporate governance coefficient can go either way, i.e. could be biased away from or toward zero. In such a situation, it may be impossible to draw any inferences from the regression, whether or not the coefficients in the regression are statistically significant.

To the extent the critique of corporate governance indices can be translated into an econometric concern over the impact of measurement error (putting aside the argument that the indices in fact do not measure anything), to what extent is such a critique in fact specific to

---

[34] Gompers, Ishii, & Metrick, *supra* note 3.
[35] Jeffrey M. Wooldridge, Econometric Analysis of Cross Section and Panel Data (2002).

the use of any particular corporate governance index? After all, it is the potential measurement error in the non-corporate governance right-hand-side variables, regardless of how corporate governance is measured or whether an aggregate index is used, that can rise to the problematic situation discussed earlier where the bias can be away from or toward zero. But this is an issue that can arise for other measures of corporate governance, even assuming a perfect measure for corporate governance (i.e. no measurement error) could be constructed. Presumably, using an accurate measure of corporate governance, whatever this might consist of, would not remove the measurement error in other standard right-hand side variables.

Consider by way of illustration variables that reflect executive compensation that are often used in the corporate governance literature, such as the value of executive compensation,[36] or the sensitivity of managerial wealth to stock price.[37] To construct these variables, one needs to estimate the value of management's stock options which usually involves approximation, such as using the Black–Scholes pricing theorem.[38] Given these are approximations, these variables will involve measurement error, an issue that would remain even assuming no measurement error in the corporate governance metric. Alternatively, to take another example, variables related to corporate ownership, which are often included on the right-hand side, have known measurement error issues.[39]

3 ENDOGENEITY

Of course, empirical corporate governance research, as is true for empirical corporate finance more generally, must deal with the endogeneity of corporate governance, irrespective of how it is measured.[40] One particular endogeneity concern in the literature has been reserve causation: the possibility that low-valued firms tend to adopt poor corporate governance with any association between corporate governance and firm valuation thereby not being attributable to the causal impact of corporate governance.[41] More generally, researchers are concerned about the potential for omitted variable bias. This arises when a variable is both correlated with a right-hand-side variable (such as corporate governance) and also correlated with the left-hand-side variable (say some metric of firm performance) but is not included in the regression. Obviously the list of potential omitted variables in the context of studying explanatory variables for firm performance is a daunting one.

---

[36] Sudip Datta, Mai Iskandar-Datta, & Kartik Raman, "Executive Compensation and Corporate Acquisition Decisions", 56 J. Fin. 2299 (2001).

[37] See, e.g., John Core & Wayne Guay, "Estimating the Value of Employee Stock Option Portfolios and their Sensitivities to Price and Volatility", 40 J. Acct. Research 613 (2002).

[38] Michael R. Roberts & Toni M. Whited, Endogeneity in Empirical Corporate Finance, in Handbook of the Economics of Finance, Volume 2 (George Constantinides, Milton Harris & René M. Stulz eds., 2012).

[39] Jennifer Dlugosz, Rüdiger Fahlenbrach, Paul Gompers, & Andrew Metrick, "Large Blocks of Stock: Prevalence, Size, and Measurement", 12 J. Corp. Fin. 594 (2006).

[40] See, e.g., Harold Demsetz & Kenneth Lehn, "The Structure of Corporate Ownership: Causes and Consequences", 93 J. Pol. Econ. 1155 (1985).

[41] Kenneth Lehn, Sukesh Patro, & Mengxin Zhao, "Governance Indexes and Valuation: Which Causes Which?", 13 J. Corp. Fin. 907 (2007).

I will first focus on the reverse causation issue before turning to the issue of omitted variable bias writ large.

3.1 Reverse Causation

Cremers and Ferrell comprehensively collected G- and E-Index data for panels of firms for the 1978–1989 period, enabling them to study these indices from 1978 to 2007 after combining their data with the standard Riskmeterics/IRRC data that begins as of 1990.[42] They therefore can directly test the reverse causation hypothesis by examining whether changes in corporate governance (many of these changes occurring in the 1980s) can be attributed to the firm having a low valuation. They find little evidence in support of reverse causation for the G-Index, albeit with an economically modest reverse causation effect with respect to the decision to adopt a poison pill.

On the other hand, with respect to staggered boards, using the same data, Cremers, Litov, and Sepe do report finding reverse causation.[43] The latter finding raises the question as to whether the well-documented association between staggered boards and lower firm valuation is due to reverse causation. It is important to emphasize, however, that this finding, by itself, does not establish that for firms with staggered boards adopted long ago causation does not run from staggered boards to lower firm valuation. For instance, the ability to remain a low-valued firm over time could be a function of having adopted a staggered board. Indeed, this could potentially have been the motivation behind the decision to adopt in the first place. Another related issue is whether the mere fact that low-valued firms adopted staggered boards 20 or 30 years earlier can adequately explain the current association between low-valued firms and staggered boards today without attributing some causal role to staggered boards.

The stability of the corporate governance indices for the 1990s and early 2000s has presented both opportunities and challenges in addressing endogeneity concerns. In exploring the reverse causation issue other papers have exploited the stability of corporate governance during this period. For instance, Bebchuk, Cohen, and Ferrell examine whether a firm's E-Index score as of 1990 has a negative association with firm valuation in the 1998–2002 period.[44] The rationale is that while a firm's 1990 E-Index score is highly correlated with its score in the 1998–2002 period given this stability, a firm's 1990 E-Index score cannot itself be the result of low firm valuation during the 1998–2002 period. To control for the possibility that poor management as of 1990 is responsible for both the existence of entrenching provisions in 1990 and the firm's low valuation in the 1998–2002 period, they further control for firm valuation as of 1990 given that poor management would tend to result in low valuation. They find that the E-Index as of 1990 is negatively associated with firm valuation in the 1998–2002 period. Using similar reasoning, Masulis, Wang, and Xie examine whether for firms that went public prior to 1990 there was a negative association between bidder returns

---

[42] K.J. Martijn Cremers & Allen Ferrell, "Thirty Years of Shareholder Rights and Firm Valuation", 69 J. Fin. 1167 (2014).

[43] K. J. Martijn Cremers, Lubomir P. Litov, & Simone M. Sepe, "Staggered Boards and Firm Value, Revisited", Working Paper (2014).

[44] Bebchuk, Cohen, & Ferrell, *supra* note 4.

and the firm's G- and E-Index scores for bidder acquisitions in the 1990s.[45] They report that the negative association is even stronger for this subsample of firms.[46]

A second issue that has arisen given the stability of corporate governance is when the dependent variable of interest relates to some metric of the firm's future operating performance. Larcker, Richardson, and Tuna point out that given the persistence of corporate governance combined with the documented persistence of firm operating performance, controlling for a firm's current operating performance in a regression could have the result of simply removing the impact of governance that one is attempting to estimate.[47]

While the persistence of corporate governance for much of the period for which researchers have data can be helpful, it has come at the cost of limiting the ability of investigating the impact of within-firm variation in corporate governance through using fixed effects, as there is relatively little within-firm variation to work off. The Gompers, Ishii, and Metrick regressions, for instance, are cross-sectional in nature, i.e. work off differences across firms. This leads directly to the omitted variable concern of the possibility that there are uncontrolled for differences across these firms with the same G-Index scores. Indeed, Cremers and Ferrell document that firms with the same G-Index scores vary widely in terms of their market betas.[48] Firm-fixed effects have the benefit of controlling for any unobserved time-invariant firm-specific characteristics and so, to this extent (but only to this extent), can partially address this concern. With this in mind, Cremers and Ferrell examine within-firm variation in their G- and E-Index scores and document that in fact the G- and E-Indices are negatively related to firm valuation with fixed effects.[49]

It is worth pointing out that the critique that corporate governance has been mismeasured has particular salience in the context of firm-fixed-effects regressions given that potentially useful information from across-firm variation is being discarded. This could increase the noise associated with any mismeasurement of corporate governance. Moreover if the mismeasurement of corporate governance is worse in terms of identifying changes in corporate governance at a firm than comparing corporate governance across firms, then the attenuation bias discussed earlier becomes potentially even more severe.[50]

3.2 Omitted Variables

3.2.1 The Problem

Putting aside the specific concern with reverse causation, omitted variable bias remains an important issue given that firms make a decision to change or not change their corporate governance provisions at every point in time in a sense. This firm decision could be

---

[45] Masulis, Wang, & Xie, *supra* note 13.

[46] On a similar note, see also Dittmar & Mahrt-Smith, *supra* note 15 (using lagged values of the G- and E-Indices using the same reasoning).

[47] David F. Larcker, Scott A. Richardson, & A. Irem Tuna, "Corporate Governance, Accounting Outcomes, and Organizational Performance", 82 The Accounting Review 963 (2007).

[48] Cremers & Ferrell, *supra* note 18.   [49] Cremers & Ferrell, *supra* note 42.

[50] See Todd A. Gormley & David A. Matsa, "Common Errors: How to (and Not to) Control for Unobserved Heterogeneity", 27 Rev. Fin. Stud. 617 (2014); Joshua D. Angrist & Jörn-Steffen Pischke, Mostly Harmless Econometrics: An Empiricist's Companion (2009).

influenced by any number of factors, some of which might be difficult or impossible to observe. Moreover, some of these factors might not be constant over time and therefore would not be removed via a fixed effects regression. This is likely to be particularly true over long stretches of time. Without adequately controlling for all these possible factors, the concern is that any association found between corporate governance and some metric of firm performance is in reality driven by these omitted variables. Unlike measurement error in one variable, if there is omitted variable bias, it is often impossible to know in which direction the bias in any estimated coefficient is, such as the coefficient on corporate governance, without having some information about the omitted variables.

One particular omitted variable bias concern is the quality of management. Coles and Li emphasize the importance in some settings of controlling for managerial fixed effects.[51] Perhaps poor management is more likely to adopt poor corporate governance so as to insulate itself. Some papers, following the approach in Morck, Shleifer, and Vishny,[52] control for this factor using industry-adjusted operating performance as a proxy for the quality of management. While certainly informative, limiting the research question to what is the impact of corporate governance conditional on a given level of managerial quality might be unduly restrictive, as an important effect of poor corporate governance might in fact be poor management and the persistence of poor management. This is the same concern already touched upon in the context of addressing reverse causation by examining within-firm variation in corporate governance.

One standard way to address omitted variable bias (as well mismeasurement of corporate governance and reverse causation) is to find a variable that (i) affects the corporate governance variable but (ii) not the left-hand-side variable except through its effect on corporate governance. While (i) is easily tested, (ii) cannot be directly tested (putting aside over-identification and Hauseman tests for reverse causation that must assume that one (or more) of the instruments is in fact valid). Larcker and Rusticus propose some helpful tests to explore whether an IV (instrumental variables) regression is preferable to a simple OLS (ordinary least squares) regression.[53]

Unfortunately, it is difficult to find plausible instruments in the corporate governance literature. Firm-specific characteristics for these purposes can easily prove problematic. For instance, managerial stock ownership could directly impact firm performance given its effect on managerial incentives (mechanism 1), firm performance could impact decisions concerning managerial stock ownership (mechanism 2), and managerial stock ownership could impact a firm's choices concerning its corporate governance profile, as measured, say by the G- or E-Index, and thereby firm performance (mechanism 3). Mechanisms 1 and 2, which are quite plausible, are problematic from the standpoint of satisfying condition (ii) for instrumental variables.

Moreover, to further compound the difficulty, there are at least two further generic issues. First is the so-called problem of "weak instruments." If the instrument is only weakly

[51] Jeffrey L. Coles & Zhichuan Li, "An Empirical Assessment of Empirical Corporate Finance", Working Paper (2011).

[52] Randall Morck, Andrei Shleifer, & Robert W. Vishny, "Do Managerial Objectives Drive Bad Acquisitions?", 45 J. Fin. 31 (1990).

[53] David F. Larcker & Tjomme O. Rusticus, "On the Use of Instrumental Variables in Accounting Research", 49 J. Acct. & Econ. 186 (2010).

correlated with the endogenous variable, this can lead to biased and therefore unreliable estimates. This can be a particular problem in the corporate governance context given the difficulty of finding suitable instruments in the first place. A weak instrument might be worse than having no instrument at all.[54]

Second, even assuming a valid instrument with sufficient power, one must be careful in generalizing the results to an overall claim. IV estimates will work off the variation in the endogenous variable that is being instrumented that is correlated with the instrument. As a result, one should keep in mind that IV regression results do not necessarily imply that for other sources of variation in the endogenous variable the same results would necessarily hold.

3.2.2 *The Literature and Omitted Variables*

Given all this, the most promising approach in the literature has been to focus on exogenous legal shocks or regulatory discontinuities that alter the impact of corporate governance for some firms. Atanasov and Black have a useful survey on the use of shocks, and in particular legal shocks, as a way of tackling endogeneity concerns.[55]

For instance, Cremers and Ferrell use the Delaware Supreme Court's 1985 decision in *Moran v. Household* which authorized the use of the powerful antitakeover defense of poison pills and indicated judicial acceptance, to some significant extent, of antitakeover defenses more generally.[56] As a result, any harmful effects of antitakeover provisions on firm valuation should be more pronounced after *Household*. Moreover, for firms for which the *Household* decision is irrelevant, there should be no firm valuation effects associated with the decision (the "control group"). Cremers and Ferrell use the G- and E-Indices as their proxy for antitakeover provisions and dual class share firms as their control group. Dual class share companies already had a powerful antitakeover effect that would render superfluous any additional takeover protection approved in *Household*.[57] They find that the G- and E-Indices do have a more powerful negative firm valuation effect post-*Household*. The same finding, however, does not hold for dual class shares.

The paper by Cohen and Wang[58] is particularly interesting in terms of examining legal shocks. They also use Delaware legal decisions as a way of addressing endogeneity but use an event study methodology. They focus on the market's reaction to the Delaware Chancery Court's decision in the *Airgas* decision (which casted significant doubt on the antitakeover effectiveness of some companies' staggered boards) and the Delaware Supreme Court's reversal of that decision (removing this doubt). Specifically, their event study measures market reactions for firms with staggered boards impacted by these decisions (both the Delaware

[54] Larcker & Rusticus, *supra* note 53.

[55] Vladimir Atanasov & Bernard Black, "Shock-Based Causal Inference in Corporate Finance and Accounting Research", Critical Finance Review (forthcoming 2016).

[56] Cremers & Ferrell, *supra* note 42.

[57] Paul A. Gompers, Joy Ishii, & Andrew Metrick, "Extreme Governance: An Analysis of Dual-Class Firms in the United States", 23 Rev. Fin. Stud. 1051 (2010).

[58] Alma Cohen & Charles C. Y. Wang, "How Do Staggered Boards Affect Shareholder Value? Evidence from a Natural Experiment", 110 J. Fin. Econ. 627 (2013).

Chancery Court and the Delaware Supreme Court decisions). Importantly, these decisions were not fully anticipated by the market.

This event study approach is a powerful way of addressing omitted variable bias for three important reasons: (1) firms already incorporated in Delaware were impacted by these decisions whether they liked it or not (i.e. no endogeneous firm decision); (2) the court decisions had substantially differential impact within the universe of companies with staggered boards thereby enabling them to use as a control group firms with staggered boards but unaffected by the *Airgas* decisions; and (3) observing the immediate market reaction to these decisions provides important evidence as to what the market thought (i.e., provides an unbiased, objective ex ante measure of the expected impact of effective staggered boards). Given all this, this approach provides useful insights beyond simply looking at the effects of a firm deciding to adopt or remove a staggered board (within-firm variation) or the cross-sectional effects associated with staggered boards (firms with versus firms without staggered boards) given the omitted variable bias issue that exists even with firm-fixed effects.

There are two potential criticisms of the event study approach to assessing corporate governance provisions. One is the fact that the market might be reacting to an information signal as well as to any direct causal effects of corporate governance. For instance, an event study of a firm's endogenous decision concerning its corporate governance profile might well carry both negative and positive signals relevant to an assessment of firm value. Such a concern, while often present in the context of event study analysis of firm corporate governance decisions, is absent in the context of a legal shock that applies to a number of firms such as in the Cohen and Wang paper.[59] Second, some claim that the market is unable to fully evaluate the effect on managerial incentives of the legal shock.[60] This critique should not be given undue weight, however, without further specific reasons for concluding that the market would somehow be incapable of providing an unbiased estimate of such effects. After all, concerns and market attention over the issue of managerial incentives, and managerial incentives in the context of takeovers, have been actively debated and commented upon for many decades.

4 CORPORATE GOVERNANCE MECHANISMS

In combination with the search for plausible legal shocks or discontinuities, current research has increasingly focused on identifying the exact mechanisms by which corporate governance impacts the performance of the firm. Consider antitakeover defenses. A number of important questions can be asked that go beyond whether there is an association between an index adding up some provisions and some metric of firm performance. Do antitakeover defenses matter to shareholders in terms of reducing the probability of receiving an attractive bid? Do they matter because it removes the disciplinary effect of hostile takeovers thereby resulting in poor operating performance? Or what is the relationship between the importance of takeover exposure and the size and identity of the firm's shareholders? How does the

---

[59] Cohen & Wang, *supra* note 58.   [60] See, e.g., Cremers, Litov, & Sepe, *supra* note 43.

identity of the shareholders interact with and impact corporate governance and the operation of the firm?

For instance, John and Kadyrzhanova investigate the effect of a staggered board (and G-Index scores) on the probability of a takeover when the firm is in an industry experiencing a merger wave.[61] They find that firms without a staggered board are more than three times as likely to receive a takeover bid. Given this, they conclude that the relevance of this aspect of corporate governance is time-varying given the time-varying nature of merger waves. Cremers and Nair focus on the interaction of ownership structure and the types of provisions tracked by the G- and E-Index.[62] They find that public pension fund ownership is important only in the presence of takeover vulnerability and that the market for corporate control is important only in the presence of an active shareholder. Masulis, Wang, and Xie specifically focus on the effect of the G- and E-Index on value-reducing acquisitions.[63] Identifying specific mechanisms, and when those mechanisms might be relevant, is a critical step in moving from broad associations to how corporate governance might actually matter and when.

5 Conclusion

Corporate governance indices will undoubtedly continue to play an important role given their ease of use and their acceptance in the literature. That being said, much recent research has moved beyond measuring associations between these indices and some outcome variable of interest. Increasing importance is being placed on generating testable hypotheses where the causal impact of corporate governance arrangements can be inferred. This tends to align with a research focus on the impact of a particular set of corporate governance arrangements in a specific setting. Event study methodology and legal shocks or regulatory discontinuities will likely play an ever greater role in the future.

---

[61] Kose John & Dalida Kadyrzhanova, "Managerial Entrenchment Waves", Working Paper (2014).
[62] Cremers & Nair, *supra* note 7.   [63] Masulis, Wang, & Xie, *supra* note 13.

CHAPTER 10

....

TAXONOMIES AND LEXIMETRICS

....

MATHIAS M. SIEMS[1]

1 INTRODUCTION

....

THE division of the world into distinct legal families is frequently seen to be one of the cornerstones of comparative law.[2] The corporate law literature also uses taxonomies that divide the world into more or less distinct models, as this chapter will discuss in detail. To set the scene, this introduction will start with an overview of the main rationales for and types of such taxonomies.

One of its main purposes is to understand the complexity of the world. In this respect, "classifying legal systems is similar to reorganizing the books in our library, or the knives in our kitchen."[3] Taxonomies may also help us in describing similarities and differences between countries: to start with, we outline the common features that units of one model share, but subsequently we explain possible complications and overlaps.[4] Taxonomies can also have a more normative dimension. Such a rationale can derive from the taxonomies themselves. For example, it may be shown that mixing models by way of transplanting legal rules from one model to another leads to inconsistent results.[5] There may also be more emotional forms of attachment to a particular model: for example, the belonging to a particular legal family can be a "matter of self-identity" or even an attempt of "insulation" from foreign

....

[1] Professor of Commercial Law, Durham University, and Research Associate, Centre for Business Research, University of Cambridge, UK.

[2] E.g., writing about civil and common law, Ugo Mattei, Comparative Law and Economics 70 (1997) ("most fundamental"); Vernon Valentine Palmer, Mixed Jurisdictions in Elgar Encyclopaedia of Comparative Law 591 (Jan M. Smits ed., 2d ed. 2012) ("basic building blocks").

[3] Jacques Vanderlinden, Religious Laws as Systems of Law—A Comparatist's View, in Religion, Law and Tradition: Comparative Studies in Religious Law 165 (Andrew Huxley ed., 2002).

[4] E.g., for legal families see Ugo Mattei, Teemu Ruskola, & Antonio Gidi, Schlesinger's Comparative Law 260 (7th ed. 2009); William Twining, Globalisation and Legal Theory 152, 178 (2000); Konrad Zweigert & Hein Kötz, An Introduction to Comparative Law 72–73 (3d ed. 1998).

[5] See also section 2.3.

influence.[6] Normative statements can also go further. Some of the research discussed in the following claims that the Anglo-American model of corporate law is more conducive to financial development than that of other legal traditions (i.e., it "works better"). But this is not the only possible relationship to be examined. For example, it may also be analyzed how spatial, institutional, cultural, organizational, and relational proximity are related to each other.[7]

These different rationales are reflected in different types of taxonomies. At a general level, one can distinguish between those based on "ideal" and "real" types.[8] Starting with ideal types may be more typical for the "what works" rationale, whereas research aiming to understand differences may typically focus on real types. However, in practice, these starting points are often less different than they may appear: any ideal types are developed so as to capture actual differences and similarities. Focusing on real types starts with such features but, to avoid the conclusion that all units are unique, it also needs to identify more general "ideal" elements that apply to multiple units.

There is also a link between different rationales and research methods. Research that aims to identify "what works" tends to have a preference for quantitative methods, whereas research aiming to understand differences may prefer qualitative tools. Yet, again, this is not always the case, as quantitative data can also be used for descriptive purposes, and qualitative data too may indicate possible causal relationships. This blurring of different tools can also be seen in the legal scholarship in this field. Since, traditionally, legal scholars did not use quantitative methods, the dominant paradigm was that of understanding similarities and differences in a textual or socio-legal qualitative way. But with the emergence of "leximetrics," the aim for understanding now also includes quantitative data. Economists, by contrast, have long been more willing to use quantitative methods and, since the 1990s, have also frequently included quantitative legal data in their regressions (e.g., in order to determine what stimulates financial development).[9]

A further distinction is between limited taxonomies (i.e., those being concerned with specific topics) and more general ones. Using this distinction as a starting point, section 2 of this chapter outlines common taxonomies in corporate law and governance. In addition, it distinguishes taxonomies which are mainly focused on the law from those which also incorporate non-legal topics (see the overview in Table 10.1). The subsequent Section 3 discusses challenges to these taxonomies. It presents general counter-arguments but also addresses the more specific criticism directed against the quantitative research on legal origins. This is not meant to reject the possibility of quantifying legal differences. Indeed, Section 4 discusses how "leximetric" tools can contribute to the question of whether there are distinct legal families in corporate law. It outlines research conducted at the Centre for Business Research of the University of Cambridge on this topic. In addition, it presents a new leximetric analysis based on investor protection data of the World Bank's Doing Business Report. Section 5 concludes.

---

[6] Mattei et al., *supra* note 4, at 263; Pier Giuseppe Monateri, Methods in Comparative Law: An Intellectual Overview, in Methods of Comparative Law 7 at 9 (Pier Giuseppe Monateri ed., 2012).

[7] Cf. Neil Coe, Philip F. Kelly, & Henry W.C. Yeung, Economic Geography: A Contemporary Introduction 393–94 (2d ed. 2013) (for distinctions in economic geography).

[8] Cf. also Mathias Siems, Comparative Law 87 (2d ed. 2018).   [9] See section 2.3.

Table 10.1 Examples of Taxonomies in Corporate Law and Governance

	Law-focused	Beyond law
Limited classifications	(section 2.1) sources of corporate law types of companies one/two tier board shareholder primacy	(section 2.2) ownership dispersion insider/outsider models shareholder/stakeholder focus
General classifications	(section 2.3) English, French, German, Nordic, socialist legal origins origin/transplant countries	(section 2.4) Anglo-Saxon, Germanic, Latin, and Japanese models of corporate governance regional and cultural models; emerging economies

2 Taxonomies in Corporate Law and Governance

2.1 Limited Classifications: Law-Focused

Some of the limited and law-focused taxonomies differentiate countries according to the relevant sources of corporate law. This often leads to a divide between common and civil law countries similar to the classifications in other areas of law. For example, this distinction may relate to the established view that civil law is based more on statute and common law more on case law.[10] Of course, in corporate law all countries have legislation but it can still be suggested that there are differences: for example, in common law countries the case law on directors' duties tends to be very extensive, with courts often taking account of the case law of other common law jurisdictions. By contrast, the role of case law in the corporate law of civil law countries is more varied; while in bigger jurisdictions such as France and Germany courts have engaged with many questions of corporate law, in smaller jurisdictions statute law is often the sole legal basis.[11]

A more pronounced difference may be that the corporate law of common law countries is said to be less strict than that of civil law countries. A clear version of a strict law can be found in the German law on public companies which states that the entire Companies Act is mandatory unless explicitly stated otherwise.[12] In substance, French and Chinese corporate

---

[10] E.g., Thomas Lundmark, Charting the Divide Between Common and Civil Law (2012); Jan M. Smits, The Making of European Private Law: Towards a Ius Commune Europaeum as a Mixed Legal System 73–94 (2002); Caslav Pejovic, "Civil Law and Common Law: Two Different Paths Leading to the Same Goal", 32 Victoria University of Wellington L. Rev. 817 (2001).

[11] See the comparison of sources of law in eight civil law (and two common law) countries in Mathias Siems & David Cabrelli, Form, Style and Substance in Comparative Company Law, in Comparative Company Law: A Case-Based Approach 364 at 372–74 (Mathias Siems & David Cabrelli eds., 2013).

[12] German Companies Act (Aktiengesetz), § 23(5).

law have a similar tendency toward comprehensive regulation, leaving scarcely any room for contractual freedom.[13] By contrast, in the US, the influential law of Delaware is an example of a "business friendly" law that does not impose many hurdles on companies and their directors. This is often related to the role of regulatory competition in US corporate law,[14] though listed companies also need to comply with the mandatory rules of federal securities law that deal with some topics that in other countries would be seen as rules of corporate law (e.g., proxy voting rules). In the UK, on the one hand, the codified corporate law is more de-tailed and prescriptive than in Delaware, not least due to the influence of EU directives.[15] On the other hand, it can be said that the UK relies less on "hard law" than the US since many topics of corporate governance are addressed in a voluntary code of best practice, which has also inspired such codes in other countries.[16]

This broad difference between common and civil law countries can also be related to "ideal type" taxonomies. The common law model may be said to be similar to contractual theories of corporate law. In particular, this is the case for the view of the company as a "nexus of contracts" as this is seen to imply only default rules of statute law in order to reduce transac-tion costs as well as a belief in the efficient forces of capital markets.[17] The civil law model can be associated with counter-views that refer to the statutorily fixed nature of the company, for instance, that the company is an institution, fiction, or real person, and that the articles too constitute not a simple contract but an objective rule.[18]

Also related to the sources of law is the question of how many forms of business organ-izations countries provide. Common law countries typically start with the view of a uni-tary type of company. Distinctions between closely and publicly held corporations in the US, and between private and public companies in the UK, are therefore seen as two different versions of a single company form. To be sure, there are also some new forms of business organizations, such as limited liability companies and limited liability partnerships, which are addressed in special laws, though often with many references to general corporate law.[19] German law, by contrast, provides two distinct forms of company. The initial form of com-pany, the Aktiengesellschaft, is the equivalent of the public company in other countries. The small company form, the GmbH, was created in 1892 in order to provide smaller and less capital-intensive firms with a more simple legal form that also excludes the personal lia-bility of the shareholders. In the twentieth century, this idea was taken up by a number of

---

[13] See Mathias Siems, Convergence in Shareholder Law 50–52 (2008).

[14] E.g., Roberta Romano, The Genius of American Corporate Law 39–40 (1993).

[15] Cf. Siems, *supra* note 13, at 51.

[16] Ruth V. Aguilera, Michel Goyer, & Luiz Ricardo Kabbach de Castro, Regulation and Comparative Corporate Governance, in The Oxford Handbook of Corporate Governance 23 (Mike Wright, Donald S. Siegel, Kevin Keasey, & Igor Filatotchev eds., 2013); Ruth V. Aguilera & Gregory Jackson, Comparative and International Corporate Governance, 4 Acad. Mgmt. Annals 485, at 511 (2010). See also David Kershaw, Corporate Law and Self-Regulation (this volume).

[17] See, e.g., Brian R. Cheffins, Company Law: Theory, Structure, and Operation 31–46 (1997). For the discussion about "law versus contract" in corporate law see also Reinier Kraakman et al., The Anatomy of Corporate Law: A Comparative and Functional Approach 17–22 (3d ed. 2017).

[18] See, e.g., Nicholas HD Foster, "Company Law Theory in Comparative Perspective: England and France", 48 Am. J. Comp. L. 573 (2000); Siems, *supra* note 13, at 47.

[19] See Mathias Siems, "Regulatory Competition in Partnership Law", 58 Int'l. & Comp. L. Q. 767 (2009) (comparison between the US, the UK, Germany, and France).

other European (and non-European) civil law countries, though not always in two separate companies acts.[20]

Other taxonomies are more closely focused on specific legal rules. In particular, comparing and classifying those rules is useful as far as they have some relevance beyond the particular problem they are aiming to address.[21] For example, a frequent distinction exists between countries with one and two boards. The model with just one board of directors ("one-tier model") was the original one, and this is still the one used in common law countries. When state supervision of companies was reduced in the Germany of the nineteenth century, it was, however, decided that public companies should have two boards: a management board and a supervisory board ("two-tier model"). This German model has spread to some fellow civil law countries, while others, such as France, Italy, and Japan, allow companies to choose between different board models.[22]

Many questions of corporate governance depend on the availability and choice between those two models. This topic is also related to the role of employees in corporate law since some of the two-tier countries require employee representatives on the supervisory board.[23] A similar question, often used for taxonomic purposes, is whether directors primarily have to consider the interests of shareholders or whether they can also consider those of other stakeholders. A typical statement is that in common law countries shareholder interests legally take primacy. The sole or at least primary object of the company is seen as lying in achieving a rise in the share price and high dividends. By contrast, in civil law countries a pluralist, stakeholder approach is often seen as prevailing since it also takes account of the social and financial interests of employees, consumers, and creditors.[24]

2.2 Limited Classifications: Beyond Law

The main focus of this chapter is on legal taxonomies in corporate law. Yet classifications that go beyond legal questions cannot be ignored, not least since legal and non-legal matters often overlap. The following examples aim to illustrate this point.

---

[20] E.g., in France in 1925, in Japan in 1938, and in China in 1993. See Siems, *supra* note 13, at 10.

[21] Thus, this can provide a link to more conceptual taxonomies of legal rules: see, e.g., Michael J. Whincop, "Form, Function and Fiction: A Taxonomy of Corporate Law and the Evolution of Efficient Rules", 24 U.N.S.W. L. J. 85 (2001); John Armour & Michael J. Whincop, "The Proprietary Foundations of Corporate Law", 27 Oxford J. Leg. Stud. 429 (2007) (e.g., on whether a relevant aspect of corporate law is "contractarian" or "proprietary").

[22] On board models see, e.g., Paul L. Davies & Klaus J. Hopt, "Corporate Boards in Europe— Accountability and Convergence", 61 Am. J. Comp. Law 301 (2013); Carsten Jungmann, "The Effectiveness of Corporate Governance in One-Tier and Two-Tier Board Systems", 3 European Company and Financial L. Rev. 426 (2006).

[23] See, e.g., http://www.worker-participation.eu/National-Industrial-Relations/Across-Europe/Board-level-Representation2.

[24] For the discussion see, e.g., Veronique Magnier, Comparative Corporate Governance: Legal Perspectives 15–39 (2017); Martin Gelter, "Taming or Protecting the Modern Corporation? Shareholder-Stakeholder Debates in a Comparative Light", 7 N.Y.U. J. Law & Bus. 641 (2011); Siems, *supra* note 13, at 175–90.

The corporate governance literature often makes a major distinction according to the ownership structure of large public companies: in the UK and the US, dispersed shareholder ownership is relatively common, whereas in other parts of the world ownership is more concentrated as other firms, financial institutions, families, or the state hold major blocks of shares.[25] A frequent point of discussion is whether these factual differences are the result of legal ones, say differences in shareholder protection.[26] Ownership structures can also impact on the way corporate law operates. For example, in companies with concentrated shareholdings it is easier to attain supermajority requirements than in those with dispersed ownership. Thus, it can be suggested that the relatively high majority requirements and the strictness of corporate law in continental Europe compensate for the greater freedom to contract out of statutory corporate law in the UK and the US.[27]

Related to ownership structures is the distinction between "insider" and "outsider" models.[28] As far as companies have concentrated ownership, the dominant shareholders are likely to appoint board members who act on their behalf: e.g., in a family firm, members of that family. Thus, here, the directors are "insiders," in contrast to firms with dispersed shareholder ownership where newly appointed directors tend to be "outsiders" to the company in question. The link to corporate law is that one would expect that in insider systems the main aim is to protect minority against majority shareholders, whereas in outsider systems it is to protect all shareholders against possible misconduct by directors.[29] This corresponds to the distinction that shareholders may be protected by either "voice" or "exit";[30] to some extent this depends on the available legal tools, but the ownership of companies also plays a role, since dispersed owners are more likely than blockholders to be able to be protected by "exit," i.e. by just selling their shares.

Section 2.1 has already raised the discussion of whether directors' duties should be targeted toward shareholders only. Yet, the distinction between shareholder and stakeholder models is not primarily a legal one. For example, Japan is usually seen as a stakeholder country, but this is due to cultural and social factors accounting for the role of stakeholder interests, not provisions of its corporate law.[31] The literature also frequently discusses ideal-type models of the relationship between management, capital, and labor. For example, such ideal-type thinking not only refers to a "stakeholder model" but also to an "organic" or a "social entity" model putting emphasis on the interests of the corporation as a whole.[32]

[25] E.g., The Control of Corporate Europe (Fabrizio Barca & Marco Becht eds., 2001). Cf. also Ronald J. Gilson, "Controlling Shareholders and Corporate Governance: Complicating the Comparative Taxonomy", 119 Harv. L. Rev. 1641 (2006) (discussing different kinds of controlling shareholders as to "complicate the comparative taxonomy").

[26] See section 2.3.   [27] Siems, *supra* note 13, at 53–54.

[28] See, e.g., Ruth V. Aguilera, Kurt A. Desender, & Luiz Ricardo Kabbach de Castro, A Bundle Perspective to Comparative Corporate Governance, in The Sage Handbook of Corporate Governance 380 (T. Clarke ed., 2012); Siems, *supra* note 13, at 174.

[29] For the agency problems in corporate law see, e.g., Kraakman et al., *supra* note 17, at 29–47.

[30] The "voice" and "exit" distinction goes back to Albert O. Hirschman, Exit, Voice and Loyalty (1970).

[31] See Junko Ueda, CSR in Japanese Company Law, 8 European Company Law 113 (2011).

[32] See Stephen Letza, Xiuping Sun, & James Kirkbride, "Shareholding Versus Stakeholding: a critical review of corporate governance", 12 Corporate Governance: An International Review 242 (2004).

2.3 General Classifications: Law-Focused

Going beyond limited classifications, the challenge is that classifying countries means making a decision about some common aspects that matter while disregarding others.[33] With respect to legal taxonomies it may help that comparative lawyers often refer to legal families as relatively coherent "bundles."[34] Thus, it may not be necessary to scrutinize all aspects of the law, but to identify legal rules that are good proxies, at least for a particular area of law.

For corporate law, a group of financial economists has conducted such research, using a quantitative comparative method. The first study by Rafael La Porta et al.[35] was based on a small set of variables for shareholder and creditor protection. The core measurement of shareholder protection was an index on anti-director rights, consisting of six variables: proxy by mail allowed, shares not blocked before the meeting, cumulative voting, oppressed minorities mechanism, preemptive rights to new issues, and the right to call a special shareholder meeting. These topics were coded according to a binary scheme ("1" for yes, and "0" for no), and the corresponding numbers were aggregated for 49 countries. The second study by Simeon Djankov et al.[36] examined the corporate laws of 72 countries. The index of this study was based on a hypothetical case of a self-dealing transaction: specifically, four variables on ex-ante private control, six on ex-post private control, and four variables on public enforcement. The description of the variables specified that some intermediate score (such as 0.5) could also be awarded, and the main analysis was based on aggregates of the three main categories (i.e., ex-ante/ex-post private control; public control).

In both studies, the authors' main aim was to establish whether the strength of shareholder protection matters for financial development. Using variables such as ownership dispersion and stock market capitalization as dependent variables, it was confirmed that legal rules on shareholder protection have a quantifiable effect on financial development. A secondary finding—but of major importance for the current chapter—was that the quality of legal rules varied systematically with the "origin" of a country's legal system, that is, whether it fell into the English "common law" or the French, German, or Scandinavian "civil law" systems. In particular, it was found that countries of English legal origin provided considerably better shareholder protection than those of the other legal origins, in particular French legal origin countries.

Other studies by the La Porta/Djankov et al. group have examined further areas of law.[37] Some of those studies cover most countries of the world and some also include a category of socialist legal origin.[38] Why exactly a particular country belongs to a particular legal origin

---

[33]   See generally Anne Peters & Heiner Schwenke, "Comparative Law Beyond Post-Modernism", 49 Int'l. & Comp. L. Q. 800 at 826 (2000).

[34]   See John Bell, Comparative Law and Legal Theory, in Prescriptive Formality and Normative Rationality in Modem Legal Systems: Festschrift for Robert Summers 19 at 28 (Werner Krawietz, Neil MacCormick, & Georg Henrik von Wright eds., 1995) (on the coherence of legal traditions).

[35]   Rafael La Porta, Florencio Lopez-de-Silanes, Andrei Shleifer, & Robert Vishny, "Law and Finance", 106 Journal of Political Economy 1113 (1998).

[36]   Simeon Djankov, Rafael La Porta, Florencio Lopez-de-Silanes, & Andrei Shleifer, "The Law and Economics of Self-Dealing", 88 J. Fin. 430 (2008).

[37]   For a summary see Rafael La Porta, Florencio Lopez-de-Silanes, & Andrei Shleifer, "The Economic Consequences of Legal Origins", 46 J. Econ. Lit. 285 (2008).

[38]   See La Porta et al., *supra* note 37, at 288–89.

is not explained in detail. Rather, to classify countries, the main consideration is whether, according to a book on foreign law,[39] the main codes of these legal systems are based on a particular foreign model.

Section 3.3 of this chapter discusses the problems with these studies, but at this stage it is useful to refer to a refinement of the legal origin taxonomy by Daniel Berkowitz et al.[40] This latter study re-examined the results of the La Porta et al. study, but also distinguished between origin and transplant countries[41] and then identified whether transplant countries had subsequently transplanted laws from either their original or one of the other origin countries. This classification was used to show that "countries that have developed legal orders internally, adapted the transplanted law, and/or had a population that was already familiar with basic principles of the transplanted law have more effective legality than countries that received foreign law without any similar predispositions."[42] This finding is particularly important for legal reforms in transition economies, which have also been the subject of further quantitative legal studies.[43]

2.4 General Classifications: Beyond Law

The corporate governance literature uses categories that, at least for Western countries, mirror those of common and civil law. On one side, one finds the Anglo-Saxon model. This is seen as pursuing a market-based approach according to which the shareholders' individual interests are to the fore. Moreover, in these countries capital markets are seen as more developed, so that interest in shares is broader and shareholder ownership is often dispersed. Markets more generally are also very competitive with firms often pursuing short-term strategies. In continental Europe, by contrast, what counts more are relations within the company than control through the markets. Management cooperates with the dominant shareholders, and the company's banks and employees also hold a strong position. Accordingly, capital markets are less developed and companies rely more on debt finance and support by the state.[44]

---

[39] Thomas Reynolds & Arturo Flores, Foreign Law: Current Sources of Basic Legislation in Jurisdictions of the World (1989). See also www.foreignlawguide.com.

[40] Daniel Berkowitz, Katharina Pistor, & Jean-Francois Richard, "Economic Development, Legality, and the Transplant Effect", 47 Eur. Econ. Rev. 165 (2003); Daniel Berkowitz, Katharina Pistor, & Jean-Francois Richard, "The Transplant Effect", 51 Am. J. Comp. L. 163 (2003).

[41] As "origin countries" they considered England, France, Germany, the four Scandinavian countries, as well as the US, Austria, and Switzerland (given that "the development of their formal legal order was highly idiosyncratic").

[42] Berkowitz et al., *supra* note 40 (Economic Development), at 165.

[43] For the development of corporate laws in the post-communist countries of Eastern Europe see, e.g., Katharina Pistor, "Patterns of Legal Change: Shareholder and Creditor Rights in Transition Economies", 1 Eur. Bus. Org. L. Rev. 59 (2000); Katharina Pistor, Martin Raiser, & Stanislaw Gelfer, "Law and Finance in Transition Economies", 8 Economics of Transition 325 (2000); Marina Martynova & Luc Renneboog, "Evidence on the International Evolution and Convergence of Corporate Governance Regulations", 17 J. Corp. Fin. 1531 (2011).

[44] Siems, *supra* note 13, at 29. For more details see, e.g., Franklin Allen & Douglas Gale, Comparing Financial Systems (2000); Mark J. Roe, Political Determinants of Corporate Governance: Political Context, Corporate Impact (2006); Marc Goergen, International Corporate Governance 68–77 (2012).

But researchers have also suggested further distinctions. A frequent one is between Anglo-Saxon, Germanic, Latin, and Japanese systems of corporate governance. Here, for example, it is said that the Latin and Japanese models are more network-oriented than the Germanic one, that stock markets are more important in the Germanic and Japanese models than in the Latin one, that the government plays a greater role in the Latin model than in the Germanic and Japanese ones, and that ownership concentration is lower in the Japanese model than in the Germanic and Latin ones.[45]

These categories have also been linked to the research in political science on "varieties of capitalism." The broad distinction is here between liberal and coordinated market economies,[46] but there are also more refined taxonomies that can then be related to topics of corporate governance. For example, it may be said that there are four categories: liberal-market economies that follow a model of shareholder capitalism (e.g., the UK, the US); business-coordinated market economies with employee inclusion that follow a model of stakeholder capitalism (e.g., Germany, Sweden); government-coordinated market economies that follow a model of state-led capitalism (e.g., France, South Korea); and loosely coordinated market economies with strong employee protection that follow a model of family/state capitalism (e.g., Italy, Spain).[47] Moreover, the varieties-of-capitalism literature is helpful in pointing toward "institutional complementarities," thus justifying the notion of general classifications.[48]

Up to now, this subsection has mainly focused on developed countries, in particular from the West. Of course, this is not the full picture. In terms of economic differences, for example, researchers have often examined the specific problems of transition economies and emerging markets in corporate governance,[49] but it is also possible to consider on a global scale how corporate governance and categories of economic policy and wealth[50] are related

---

[45] E.g., James Keenan & Maria Aggestam, "Corporate Governance and Intellectual Capital: Some Conceptualisations", 9 Corporate Governance: An International Review 259 (2001); Jeroen Weimer & Joost Pape, "A Taxonomy of Systems of Corporate Governance", 7 Corporate Governance: An International Review 152 (1999).

[46] Peter A. Hall & David Soskice, An Introduction to Varieties of Capitalism, in Varieties of Capitalism: The Institutional Foundations of Comparative Advantage 1 (Peter A. Hall & David Soskice eds., 2001). See also Katharina Pistor, Legal Ground Rules in Coordinated and Liberal Market Economies, in Corporate Governance in Context: Corporations, States and Markets in Europe, Japan and the US 249 (Klaus Hopt et al. eds., 2005).

[47] Andrew Tylecote & Francesca Visintin, "A New Taxonomy of National Systems of Corporate Governance", 24 Comparative Social Research 71, at 80–81 (2007).

[48] For empirical research see Peter A. Hall & Daniel W. Gingerich, "Varieties of Capitalism and Institutional Complementarities in the Political Economy: An Empirical Analysis", 39 British Journal of Political Science 449 (2009). See also Beth Ahlering & Simon Deakin, "Labour Regulation, Corporate Governance and Legal Origin: A Case of Institutional Complementarity?", 41 Law & Soc'y Rev. 865 (2007) (applying the idea of complementarities to corporate governance and labour regulation).

[49] For the former see, e.g., Bernard Black, Reinier H. Kraakman & Anna Tarassova, "Russian Privatization and Corporate Governance: What Went Wrong?", 52 Stan. L. Rev. 1731 (2000); Pistor et al., supra note 43. For the latter see, e.g., Mariana Pargendler, Corporate Governance in Emerging Markets (this volume).

[50] For such categories see, e.g., Lynge Nielsen, "Classifications of Countries Based on Their Level of Development: How it is Done and How it Could be Done", IMF Working Paper WP/11/31 (2011), at http://www.imf.org/external/pubs/ft/wp/2011/wp1131.pdf; Spyros Economides & Peter Wilson, The Economic Factor in International Relations 115 (2001).

to each other. In terms of geographic scope, Flores et al. discuss how well regional grouping schemes fit international business research models. They also elaborate on various grouping schemes developed in the literature, some solely based on geographic proximity, others including cultural traits and investment patterns.[51]

Cultural and political factors are also of interest for taxonomies in comparative law. The general comparative-law literature sometimes distinguishes between legal systems of professional law, political law, and traditional law—with the latter two categories seen as being more prevalent in non-Western legal systems.[52] Specifically for the relationship between corporate governance and law, the legal-origin view has been criticized for its disregard of culture, arguing, for example, that the role of the law in the corporate governance of East Asian companies cannot be assessed in isolation from its cultural environment.[53] Thus, while some of the "beyond-law" categories support the general legal classifications (see section 2.3), others contest the relevance of Western-based legal origins.

3 Challenging the Value of Taxonomies

3.1 Introduction: Forms of Criticism

The taxonomies discussed in this chapter are relatively diverse. However, it is also possible to present and discuss some common challenges. In particular, classifications are often bound to raise the objection that, on the one hand, they overemphasize differences between categories and, on the other hand, they underemphasize differences within these categories (i.e., in this respect they overemphasize similarities). In the words of Patrick Glenn (writing about legal traditions), it is clear that: "the separation we seek to bring about, for purposes of clarity and recognition, is immediately challenged by information which is inconsistent with the separation we have chosen."[54]

Section 3.2 discusses the problem of overemphasizing differences and similarities. Section 3.3 turns to the more specific problems with the taxonomies that try to quantify legal information about legal origins (i.e., the La Porta/Djankov et al. studies). Overall, this will lead us to doubt the relevance of many of these categories. In addition, Section 4 presents a "bottom-up" leximetric analysis on whether it is possible to identify distinct legal families in corporate law.

---

[51] Ricardo Flores, Ruth V. Aguilera, Arash Mahdian & Paul M. Vaaler, "How Well do Supranational Regional Grouping Schemes Fit International Business Research Models?", 44 J. Int'l. Bus. Stud. 451 (2013).

[52] Ugo Mattei, "Three Patterns of Law: Taxonomy and Change in the World's Legal Systems", 45 Am. J. Comp. L. 5 (1997).

[53] Amir N. Licht, Chanan Goldschmidt, & Shalom H. Schwartz, "Culture, Law, and Corporate Governance", 25 Int'l. Rev. L. & Econ. 229 at 250–51 (2005). See also Amir Licht, Culture and Law in Corporate Governance (in this volume).

[54] H. Patrick Glenn, Legal Traditions of the World 362 (5th ed. 2014).

3.2 Overemphasizing Differences and Similarities

In the general literature on comparative law it is today widely held that the distinction between civil and common law countries is often misleading as it overemphasizes differences.
While some legal scholars doubt whether this distinction can be justified from a historical
perspective, a more frequent view is that we have seen a recent convergence between civil
and common law countries.[55] For example, this can refer to the sources of law: common law
countries are said to have now also reached the "age of statutes,"[56] and it has been said that it
is "fundamentally incorrect" to assume that the civil law judge simply applies a set of complete and self-explanatory rules in a mechanical way.[57]

It can also be objected that there is an overemphasis on the similarities within legal
families. For example, the differences between French and German law are said to be "as
great, or even greater, than those between French and English, or German and English law,"
and England and the US are said to be two legal systems "separated by a common law."[58] The
established categories are also often seen as misleading due to the frequency of mixed forms
of legal systems. This is not only the case for "classical" mixed legal systems such as those
of Scotland and South Africa: for example, treating Italy and Portugal as simply part of the
Romanist-French legal family ignores the German influence on these legal systems. With
respect to Japanese law, treating it as civil law is misleading as it would miss the US influence,
but treating it as common law—or Asian law—would also be misleading as it would miss the
legal transplant of some of the main German codes.[59]

For corporate law in particular there are good reasons to be even more skeptical. Here,
differences tend to be less pronounced than, say, in land and property law. It has even been
said that due to the influence of international trade and legal transplants, a strict division
between legal families never really fitted with commercial and corporate law.[60] More specifically, the development of corporate law has been fairly similar across European countries,
namely, in its beginnings, the establishment of colonial corporations, then the trend to make
the corporate form more widely available, going hand in hand with a codification of corporate law, and subsequently its interpretation and application by courts.[61] It has also been
found that by the end of the nineteenth century the most important features of corporate law
were already relatively uniform across countries.[62]

---

[55] For the first view see Reinhard Zimmermann, "Savigny's Legacy: Legal History, Comparative Law,
and the Emergence of a European Legal Science", 112 Law Q. Rev. 576 (1996). For the second one The
Gradual Convergence: Foreign Ideas, Foreign Influences, and English law on the Eve of the 21st Century
(Sir Basil Markesinis ed., 1994).

[56] Guido Calabresi, A Common Law for the Age of Statutes (1985).

[57] Martin Shapiro, Courts: A Comparative and Political Analysis 126–56 (1981).

[58] For the first quote Reinhard Zimmermann, Roman Law, Contemporary Law, European Law: The
Civilian Tradition Today 113 (2001). For the second one Vivian Grosswald Curran, "Cultural Immersion,
Difference and Categories in US Comparative Law", 46 Am. J. Comp. L. 43 at 55 (1998).

[59] Cf. Zweigert & Kötz, *supra* note 4, at 297–98.

[60] Detlev F. Vagts, Comparative Company Law—The New Wave, in Festschrift für Jean Nicolas Druey
595 at 598–99 (Rainer J. Schweizer, Herbert Burkert & Urs Gasser eds., 2000).

[61] See Siems, *supra* note 13, at 18–19.

[62] Henry Hansmann & Reinier Kraakman, "The End of History for Corporate Law", 88 Geo. L. J. 439
(2001). Similar Aldo Musacchio & John D. Turner, "Does the Law and Finance Hypothesis Pass the Test

In addition, corporate laws have converged to a significant extent. A research monograph by the author of this chapter examined the convergence of the corporate laws of the UK, the US, France, Germany, Japan, and China.[63] Other scholars have also identified various types of convergence in corporate law. Even without formal convergence, there is said to be functional convergence,[64] for example because incompetent directors may be removed but along different statutory paths. There can also be contractual (or institutional) convergence where private arrangements have a similar effect to statute law.[65] An example is the distinction between one- and two-tier board models because committees with wholly independent members in a one-tier system make this system akin to a two-tier structure, and an executive committee with a CEO in a two-tier structure makes it akin to a one-tier structure.

Legal family classifications in corporate law may also overemphasize similarities. The EU has harmonized some aspects of corporate law and many related topics of securities law.[66] This has meant that, for instance, English corporate law has diverged from the corporate law of non-European common law countries such as India and Australia. The partial "Americanization" of some foreign corporate laws has also diluted the legal family classifications. Such US transplants have not led to an "end of history" with just one model of corporate law;[67] rather, lawmakers typically follow a strategy of "cherry picking," with different elements of various legal systems being adopted.[68] As a possible consequence, the group of civil law countries may have diverged in corporate law because some, but not all, of those countries are relatively open toward US influences.[69]

With respect to taxonomies "beyond law," it is also frequently noted that established categories do not fit reality. For example, Ruth Aguilera and Gregory Jackson refer to many studies showing that the distinction between Anglo-Saxon and continental models "only partially account for governance realities in Japan, East Asia, a wide range of European countries, and the new emerging markets."[70] Research by Stephen Letza and colleagues emphasizes the complex, pluralist, and fuzzy nature of corporate governance and recommends that one should stay away from making "permanent, absolute and taken-for-granted" assumptions.[71] For example, this "fuzziness" may challenge the distinction between shareholder and stakeholder models: today, cross-border mergers and investments mean that many larger firms do not simply belong to one of these models but have to accommodate elements of both of them.

---

of History?", 55 Bus. Hist. 524 at 533–34 (2013) (quantitative data on shareholder and creditor protection in 1910, with reference to research by Cheffins and others).

[63] Siems, *supra* note 13.

[64] Ronald J. Gilson, "Globalizing Corporate Governance: Convergence of Form or Function", 49 Am. J. Comp. L. 329, at 337–45 (2001).

[65] Gilson, id., at 346–50 (contractual); David Charny, "The German Corporate Governance System", Colum. Bus. L. Rev. 145, at 165 (1998) (institutional).

[66] See, e.g., Nicola de Luca, European Company Law (2017).

[67] Hansmann & Kraakman, *supra* note 62.   [68] See Siems, *supra* note 13, at 227.

[69] See, e.g., R. Daniel Kelemen & Eric C. Sibbitt, "The Americanization of Japanese Law", 23 U. Pa. J. Int'l. Econ. L. 269 (2002).

[70] Aguilera & Jackson, *supra* note 16, at 486 (with references to 18 studies).

[71] Stephen Letza, James Kirkbride, Xiuping Sun, & Clive Smallman, "Corporate Governance Theorising: Limits, Critics and Alternatives", 50 International Journal of Law and Management 17, at 27 (2008). See also Letza et al., *supra* note 32, at 258.

Thus, as far as such taxonomies are still used in the corporate governance literature, they are often treated as mere "ideal types." For example, in an introductory book on comparative corporate governance it may be useful to outline typical features of, say, the German and the Japanese model of corporate governance, but this is not meant to imply that this is how all actual German and Japanese firms are structured. Thus, talking about such models is more akin to the use of words such as "French fries": the reference to the country in question may have some historical justification but may be of little relevance today.[72]

3.3 Challenging the Quantitative Research on Legal Origins

The La Porta/Djankov et al. studies on "legal origins" have been highly influential,[73] but also highly controversial. Thus, it is worth discussing three main problems of these studies in some detail.

First, these studies assume that the quality of a country's corporate law can be expressed in numbers. The initial La Porta et al. study mainly used a six-variable index on "anti-director rights" coding 49 countries.[74] However, subsequent research has identified many coding errors of the legal rules of various countries.[75] But just correcting these numbers would not be sufficient. Scholars have also raised concerns about the simple aggregation of six variables. Here, one problem is that the same indicator may play a completely different functional role in different countries, or different indicators may play the same role, with their relative importance varying from one context to another.[76] The most severe problem is the selection of variables: not only is the number of variables very limited, it also suffers from a US bias (or, more generally, a common law one) since it does not capture important aspects of the corporate law of other countries. Thus, this index cannot be seen as a meaningful tool to compare the strength of shareholder protection across countries.[77]

The more recent Djankov et al. study on self-dealing[78] may be seen as more advanced:[79] yet, here too, the precise numbers raise various concerns. This study includes

---

[72] France (or Belgium) is said to be the origin country of French fries, yet it is not one of its top exporters (see http://www.todayifoundout.com/index.php/2010/09/the-history-of-french-fries/ and http://www.potatobusiness.com/index.php?view=article&catid=1:latest-news&id=124:us-big-on-french-fries-exports).

[73] Boris Durisin & Fulvio Puzone, Maturation of Corporate Governance Research, 1993–2007: An Assessment, 17 Corporate Governance: An International Review 266 (2009).

[74] La Porta et al., *supra* note 35, and see section 2.3.

[75] E.g., Holger Spamann, "The 'Antidirector Rights Index' Revisited", 23 Rev. Fin. Stud. 468 (2010); Sofie Cools, "The Real Difference in Corporate Law between the United States and Continental Europe: Distribution of Powers", 36 Del. J. Corp. L. 697 (2005).

[76] Ahlering & Deakin, *supra* note 48, at 884–85.

[77] Priya Lele & Mathias Siems, "Shareholder Protection—A Leximetric Approach", 7 J. Corp. Law Stud. 17 at 18–21 (2007). In addition, it should not be seen as indicative for further country differences, e.g., in financial reporting, see Frederick W. Lindahl & Hannu Schadewitz, "Are Legal Families Related to Financial Reporting Quality?", 49 ABACUS 242 (2013).

[78] Djankov et al., *supra* note 36, and see section 2.3.

[79] Cf. Brian R. Cheffins, Steven A. Bank & Harwell Wells, "Law and History by Numbers: Use, But with Care", U. Ill. L. Rev., 1739, at 1751–52 (2014).

more variables and more care has been taken in the coding of the law. It also identifies the principal components of the sub-indices, thus aiming to address the problem of simply aggregating all variables. Yet the coding of some of the sub-indices can be criticized. For example, the sub-index on public enforcement simply asks whether "jail sentences" and "fines" are available, not considering how severe these may be or whether these sanctions are used at all. A potential advantage of the Djankov et al. study could be that it is based on a hypothetical case, thus potentially addressing the home bias of the La Porta et al. study. However, this method too is problematic as it has to assume that the same type of problem exists in all of the legal systems examined. This is unlikely to be the case since social and economic structures differ widely between countries. Thus, in comparative law a strict functional approach is today widely criticized, given that societies differ from each other in their priorities and preferences.[80]

Second, having coded the legal rules, the La Porta/Djankov et al. studies calculate the average scores of the English, French, German, and Scandinavian legal origins. This is based on the belief that the laws of the origin countries spread to all countries of the world through conquest, colonization, and imitation.[81] However, this disregards the ongoing influence of pre-transplant laws, the mixtures and modifications at the moment when copying of foreign law occurs, and the post-transplant period in which the transplanted laws and institutions may be altered or applied differently. For example, the law and finance literature assumes that the transition economies of Eastern Europe are either German or French legal origin countries, whereas in practice they have been influenced by a number of different traditions. Similarly, it is assumed that Japan, South Korea, and China are of German legal origin, whereas a more nuanced analysis would have to take into account the indigenous legal cultures of these legal systems as well as more recent Anglo-Saxon influence. Furthermore, there is a complete disregard of non-Western legal traditions: thus, the legal origin categories also suffer from a Eurocentric bias.[82]

The way these studies use legal origins also shows a conceptual misunderstanding. La Porta/Djankov et al. refer to the mainstream literature on comparative law. However, this overlooks the fact that comparative lawyers emphasize that these categories only have a very modest function. For instance, legal traditions are said to be just "a loose conglomeration of data," and the idea of legal families is said to be "no more than a didactic device" that "merely serve[s] our need to maintain a rough overview."[83] It is therefore doubtful of whether such

---

[80] See discussion in Siems, *supra* note 8, at 37–39.

[81] La Porta et al., *supra* note 37, at 286; Thorsten Beck & Ross Levine, Legal Institutions and Financial Development, in Handbook of New Institutional Economics 251 at 258 (Claude Menard & Mary M. Shirley eds., 2005).

[82] For all these points see Mathias Siems, "Legal Origins: Reconciling Law & Finance and Comparative Law", 52 McGill L. J. 55, at 62–70 (2007).

[83] For these quotes: Glenn, *supra* note 54, at 15–16; Réné David, Major Legal Systems in the World Today: An Introduction to the Comparative Study of Law 21 (3d ed. 1985); Mathias Reimann, "The Progress and Failure of Comparative Law in the Second Half of the Twentieth Century", 50 Am. J. Comp. L. 671, at 677 (2002).

deliberately fuzzy and fluid classifications are reconcilable with quantitative research that relies on well-defined data points.[84]

Third, there are good reasons to doubt the claim that the high quality of shareholder protection in common law countries explains their more developed financial markets.[85] The main problem is whether it can really be said that there is a clear one-way link between law and financial development. It seems more likely that law influences society in multiple ways and with various feedback mechanisms.[86] There has also been research on the evolution of corporate law in the UK and the US showing that financial market developments preceded legal change as the former precipitated the emergence of interest groups prepared to lobby for changes in the law.[87] To capture these dynamics, it would be necessary to use legal data that have a time dimension,[88] as opposed to the mere cross-sectional data of the La Porta/Djankov et al. studies.

Getting these causal relationships right is also crucial for the understanding of legal origins. The La Porta/Djankov et al. research treats these as time-invariant causal variables, i.e. the core of the legal system is seen as immune from economic influence. Yet it does not seem likely that legal systems are locked into particular developmental paths. Thus, here too, it is better to think of a co-evolving, though possibly asynchronic and dynamic interaction between law, politics, and society. This also implies that following the model of another legal origin may not have the desired effect. For example, assuming with La Porta/Djankov et al., that common and civil law countries use distinct legal models, it can be argued that institutions in civil law systems may be well matched to local economic conditions, and that following those of the common law would turn out to be either ineffective or counterproductive.[89]

[84] Nuno Garoupa & Mariana Pargendler, "A Law and Economics Perspective on Legal Families", 7 European J. Leg. Stud. 36 (2014); Siems, *supra* note 82.

[85] In addition, protecting shareholders can have negative side-effects, e.g., on innovation, see Filippo Belloc, "Law, Finance and Innovation: The Dark Side of Shareholder Protection", 37 Cambridge J. Econ. 863 (2013).

[86] Alberto Chong & Cesar Calderon, "Causality and Feedback Between Institutional Measures and Economic Growth", 12 Economics and Politics 69 (2000).

[87] For the UK see Julian Franks, Colin Mayer, & Stefano Rossi, "Ownership: Evolution and Regulation", 22 Rev. Fin. Stud. 4009 (2009); Brian R. Cheffins, Corporate Ownership and Control: British Business Transformed (2008). For the US see Brian R. Cheffins, Steven A. Bank, & Harwell Wells, "Questioning 'Law and Finance': US Stock Market Development, 1930–70", 55 Bus. Hist. 601 (2013); John C. Coffee, "The Rise of Dispersed Ownership: The Roles of Law and the State in the Separation of Ownership and Control", 111 Yale L. J. 1 (2001). See also Musacchio & Turner, *supra* note 62.

[88] For such a study see John Armour, Simon Deakin, Prabirjit Sarkar, Mathias Siems, & Ajit Singh, "Shareholder Protection and Stock Market Development: A Test of the Legal Origins Hypothesis", 6 Journal of Empirical Legal Studies 343 (2009) (finding no statistically significant relationship).

[89] John Armour, Simon Deakin, Viviana Mollica, & Mathias Siems, "Law and Financial Development: What We are Learning from Time-Series Evidence", B.Y.U. L. Rev. 1435, at 1448–53 (2009). See also Simon Deakin, "Legal Origin, Juridical Form and Industrialization in Historical Perspective: The Case of the Employment Contract and the Joint-Stock Company", 7 Socio-Economic Review 35 (2009).

4 LEXIMETRICS: ARE THERE DISTINCT LEGAL FAMILIES?

4.1 Introduction: Calculating Differences without a priori Categories

The general comparative-law literature sometimes complains that the assessment of whether groups of legal systems are similar or different is just too subjective.[90] A likely response is that one should apply quantitative tools to law ("leximetrics")[91] since those may, in principle, be able to provide a more objective assessment.

Quantitative methods have already been mentioned in previous sections of this chapter. But in the studies mentioned, these quantifications of the law were just a side topic of other research questions, such as whether law matters for financial development. Moreover, studies such as those by La Porta/Djankov et al. just calculate the average of certain aggregate values for particular groups of countries.

By contrast, the research discussed in the following starts without such a priori categories in order to find out whether particular countries seem to belong together. This research is based on legal variables related to topics of corporate law, yet, not simply, for example, the aggregate of shareholder protection, since different variables can lead to the same score at the aggregate level. Rather, to highlight the differences between the countries, the differences between each variable in the law of a particular legal system, and the same variable in the law of the other countries have been calculated; subsequently, the absolute values of these differences were added together. Thus, these numbers provide the differences between each pair of countries,[92] which can then be analyzed further with tools of network analysis, for instance.

The following uses this "bottom-up" approach with examples from two comparative datasets on corporate and securities law:[93] section 4.2 outlines research conducted at the

---

[90] Masha Antokolskaia, Harmonisation of Family Law in Europe: A Historical Perspective 27 (2006). See also Mattei, *supra* note 52, at 41 ("absence of quantitative tools to measure analogies and differences among legal systems").

[91] For the terminology see Lele & Siems, *supra* note 77, based on Robert D. Cooter & Tom Ginsburg, Leximetrics: Why the Same Laws are Longer in Some Countries than Others, Research Paper 2003, available at http://ssrn.com/abstract=456520. See also Mathias Siems, "Numerical Comparative Law: Do We Need Statistical Evidence in Law in Order to Reduce Complexity", 13 Cardozo J. Int'l. & Comp. L. 521 (2005) (suggesting the term "numerical comparative law").

[92] Such an approach of pairs (or dyads) is also used in political science and international relations. See, e.g., Thomas Sommerer, Katharina Holzinger & Christoph Knill, The Pair Approach: What Causes Convergence of Environmental Policies?, in Environmental Policy Convergence in Europe 144 (Katharina Holzinger, Christoph Knill, & Bas Arts eds., 2008).

[93] For further examples see Siems & Cabrelli, *supra* note 11 (using this approach to analyze the results of a case-based project dealing with the corporate laws of ten countries); Mathias Siems, "Varieties of Legal Systems: Towards a New Global Taxonomy", 12 Journal of Institutional Economics 579 (2016) (classification of 156 countries, not limited to corporate law).

University of Cambridge, and section 4.3 is based on investor protection variables of the World Bank's Doing Business Report.

4.2 The CBR Research on Differences and Similarities in Corporate Law

Since 2005, researchers at the Centre for Business Research (CBR) of the University of Cambridge have constructed indices for shareholder, creditor, and worker protection. The corresponding datasets are available online, including detailed explanations of the respective legal codings.[94] With respect to shareholder protection, the dataset comprises two indices. The first one has 60 variables, coding the laws of France, Germany, India, the UK, and the US for the years 1970 to 2005. The second one reduces the number of variables to ten, but codes 25 countries, initially for the years 1995 to 2005, and then for the years 1990 to 2013.

Calculating the differences between the five countries of the first CBR index, it was found that legal families have lost some importance.[95] In 1970, French law was still relatively similar to German law but more different from UK, US, and Indian law. But this changed in 2005, since here the data show that the French law on shareholder protection is closer to UK law than it is to German law. Throughout the 35 years covered by this study, the US law of shareholder protection has been very different from the other four countries, including the two common law ones—while Indian law has remained relatively close to UK law.

As a general trend, it was found that the five countries of this first index have converged in shareholder protection law. Likewise, the calculations based on the second CBR index, which covers fewer years but more countries, show convergence of the law. Here too, this trend does not involve an Americanization of corporate law since the US was and has remained relatively different from the other countries. Further trends also show that changes have not occurred along legal family lines.[96]

Another paper[97] focused on the final year of the second dataset with tools of social network analysis (for this technique see section 4.3). The resulting network had some plausible

---

[94] See https://www.cbr.cam.ac.uk/datasets/. For summaries of the research see Mathias Siems & Simon Deakin, "Comparative Law and Finance: Past, Present and Future Research", 166 J. Institutional & Theoretical Econ. 120 (2010); Mathias Siems, The Leximetric Research on Shareholder Protection, in Research Handbook on Shareholder Power 156 (Jennifer Hill & Randall Thomas eds.). See also Zoe Adams & Simon Deakin, Corporate Governance and Employment Relations (in this volume).

[95] For the following see Mathias Siems, "Convergence in Corporate Governance: A Leximetric Approach", 35 J. Corp. L. 729 (2010); John Armour, Simon Deakin, Priya Lele, & Mathias Siems, "How Do Legal Rules Evolve? Evidence From a Cross-Country Comparison of Shareholder, Creditor and Worker Protection", 57 Am. J. Comp. L. 579 at 620–23 (2009); Lele & Siems, *supra* note 77, at 37–43.

[96] Mathias Siems, "Shareholder Protection Around the World ('Leximetric II')", 33 Del. J. Corp. law 111 (2008) (e.g., at 128: "French, Indian, South African, Japanese, and Brazilian law have diverged from UK law while Chinese, Canadian, Czech, Chilean, and Italian law have converged to it"). See also Dionysia Katelouzou and Mathias Siems, "Disappearing Paradigms in Shareholder Protection: Leximetric Evidence for 30 Countries, 1990–2013", 15 J. Corp. Law Stud. 127 (2015).

[97] Mathias Siems, "The Web of Creditor and Shareholder Protection: A Comparative Legal Network Analysis", 27 Ariz. J. Int'l. & Comp. L. 747 (2010).

close ties (e.g., China, Germany, and Latvia; Italy, Brazil, and Spain) whereas others were more counter-intuitive (e.g., Pakistan and the Czech Republic; Spain and India). In addition, this study used more advanced tools to classify the 25 countries of this network. Yet the resulting groups were also not entirely plausible: for example, calculating "factions"[98] led to one faction with three civil law countries (Argentina, Czech Republic, Netherlands), one with Japan, Russia, and three common law countries (US, India, Canada), one with four transition and developing countries (Pakistan, Chile, Mexico, Latvia), one with South Africa and two Western European countries (Germany, France), and one with ten countries from various legal origins and regions (UK, China, Malaysia, Italy, Spain, Brazil, Switzerland, Slovenia, Sweden, Turkey).

Overall, according to the CBR research, differences and similarities between corporate laws are largely unrelated to alleged differences between legal families. A possible response could be that perhaps there is just something wrong with the CBR indices. The following section therefore applies leximetrics to data of the World Bank's Doing Business Report which is associated with the La Porta/Djankov et al. research.[99]

4.3   Applying the Leximetric Method to the DBR Data on Investor Protection

The Doing Business Report (DBR) includes an index on "protecting investors," dealing with three broad topics: disclosure, director liability, and ease of shareholder suits.[100] In total, it has 18 variables.[101] The following analysis is based on the first 14 variables of this index since those address topics of company and securities law (the final four variables are entirely about civil procedure).[102] It was the aim to cover the 25 most populous countries of the world; however, Myanmar had to be excluded as it was not included in the DBR. Thus, Figure 10.1 and Table 10.2, below, cover the remaining 24 most populous countries.

Like the research summarized in the previous section, the analysis of this section is based on the paired country differences of each of the investor protection variables. Figure 10.1 shows the closest country pairs, i.e. the most similar legal systems, in a network figure. It was decided to display the closest 37 of the 276 pairs, with the size of the lines determined

---

[98] The calculation of factions is based on an "algorithm that finds optimal arrangements of actors into factions to maximize similarity to the ideal type" (http://faculty.ucr.edu/~hanneman/nettext/C11_Cliques.html).

[99] See http://www.doingbusiness.org/methodology. The DBR "protecting investor" index makes use of Djankov et al., *supra* note 36 (on self-dealing) and Rafeal La Porta, Florencio Lopez-de-Silanes, & Andrei Shleifer, "What Matters in Securities Laws", 61 J. Fin. 1 (2006) (on securities law). For a similar idea see Michael Graff, "Law and Finance: Common Law and Civil Law Countries Compared—An Empirical Critique", 75 Economica 60 (2008) (applying cluster analysis to the initial study by La Porta et al. 1998).

[100] http://www.doingbusiness.org/data/exploretopics/protecting-investors.

[101] See, e.g., http://www.doingbusiness.org/data/exploreeconomies/china/protecting-investors/ (or any other country).

[102] See also Mathias Siems, Private Enforcement of Directors' Duties: Derivative Actions as a Global Phenomenon, in Collective Actions: Enhancing Access to Justice and Reconciling Multilayer Interests? 93, at 108–09 (Stefan Wrbka, Steven Van Uytsel, & Mathias Siems eds., 2012).

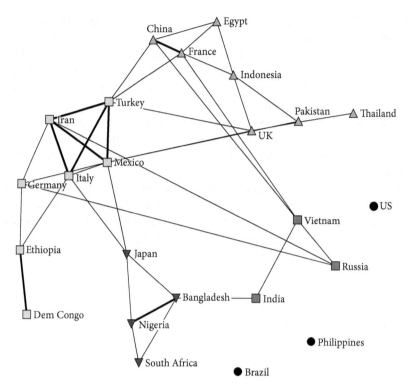

FIGURE 10.1 Network Presentation of Differences in Investor Protection (Basis: DBR 2013).

by the tie strength. The network visualization program (NetDraw) has also shifted the position of countries according to the strength of their relationships, i.e. countries whose shareholder protection is relatively similar are moved closer together. In addition, this program has identified "factions," based on these 37 pairs.[103]

A benevolent reading of Figure 10.1 may identify some similarities between some of the common law countries: a link between Pakistan and the UK, and a clique between Nigeria, Bangladesh, and South Africa. But many of the other similarities are counter-intuitive, for example the clique of Iran, Italy, Turkey, and Mexico, as well as most of the factions.

The network analysis program (UCINET) can also identify "factions" using the entire information of the network, i.e. all 276 valued country-pairs.[104] Table 10.2 presents the results for two to six factions. Again, these categories challenge conventional views. For example, both of the two factions include civil and common law, as well as developed and developing countries. Interpreting the six factions is not easier; for example, it does not seem intuitive what makes, say, India and France, the UK and Turkey, or Germany and Congo (DR) very similar.

---

[103] NetDraw is provided as a supplement to the network analysis program UCINET, available at http://www.analytictech.com/downloaduc6.htm. The precise functions are: Layout > Ordination > Scaling > Iterative Metric MDS (adjust to the nearest Euclidean) and Subgroups > Factions.
[104] See previous note. The precise function is Network > Subgroups > Factions.

Table 10.2 Factions of Investor Protection (Basis: DBR 2013)

Factions	Countries				
6	Philippines	US, Indonesia, Brazil, Pakistan, Egypt	South Africa, Nigeria, Bangladesh, Japan, Mexico, Turkey, UK, Italy	China, India, Russia, Vietnam, Iran, France	Ethiopia, Germany, Congo (DR)	Thailand
5	Philippines	US, Indonesia, Brazil, Pakistan, Egypt	South Africa, Nigeria, Bangladesh, Japan, Mexico, Turkey, UK, Italy	China, India, Russia, Vietnam, Ethiopia, Germany, Iran, Congo (DR), France		Thailand
4	Nigeria, Bangladesh, Philippines	China, India, South Africa, Russia, Japan, Vietnam, Ethiopia, Germany, Iran, Turkey, Congo (DR), France, Italy	US, Indonesia, Brazil, Pakistan, Mexico, Egypt, UK			Thailand
3	Nigeria, Bangladesh, Philippines	China, India, South Africa, Russia, Japan, Vietnam, Ethiopia, Germany, Iran, Turkey, Congo (DR), France, Italy	US, Indonesia, Brazil, Pakistan, Mexico, Egypt, Thailand, UK			
2	India, South Africa, Nigeria, Bangladesh, Russia, Philippines, Vietnam, Germany, Iran, Congo (DR), Italy	China, US, Indonesia, Brazil, Pakistan, Japan, Mexico, Ethiopia, Egypt, Turkey, Thailand, France, UK				

As a result, the DBR data on investor protection confirm the skepticism outlined in the previous sections as regards the relevance of legal families in corporate law. Thus, leximetrics has a destructive potential as it may show that established taxonomies do not stand up to scrutiny. However, it may also be constructive as far as it may illuminate unexpected similarities, and thus motivate the conceptualization of new taxonomies.

5 CONCLUSION

This chapter started with an overview of the different aims that taxonomies can pursue. Given these diverse rationales, it is plausible that there is some variety in the taxonomies used in corporate law and governance. Yet this chapter also explained that some of the classifications have shaped the current debate, notably the "legal origins" research conducted by a group of financial economists.

The idea of "legal origins" is closely related to the discussion in comparative law about "legal families." Categories such as common and civil law—or English, French, German and Scandinavian legal origin—may initially have had a certain plausibility, but at least today there are also good reasons to be skeptical. In particular, leximetric research has shown that, in reality, differences and similarities between legal systems do not fit with these categories. The use of the legal origin categories is therefore highly problematic as far as they take on a life of their own and become mere stereotypes about country characteristics and alleged group differences.

A possible response could be that, in a similar way to some of the corporate governance taxonomies,[105] we may observe a shift from "real" to "ideal" types. Thus, talking, for example, about, "English legal origin" might not necessarily mean that Anglo-Saxon countries tend to have certain commonalities, but would rather describe certain characteristics that any possible group of countries may have in common.

In addition, this chapter suggests that comparative researchers often do not need such a priori categories. As far as a researcher examines a limited group of countries, such as the UK, the US, Germany, and Japan, it is perfectly possible to explain similarities and differences without the use of potentially misleading categories such as English and German legal origin. But even when more countries are examined, the researcher should resist the temptation to classify too early: here, at best, she may try to identify categories with a "bottom-up" approach,[106] being prepared to find the unexpected.

---

[105] Cf. the "French fries" analogy, *supra* note 72.   [106] Such as the factions in section 4.

PART II

SUBSTANTIVE TOPICS

CHAPTER 11

···

EXTERNAL AND INTERNAL ASSET PARTITIONING
Corporations and Their Subsidiaries

···

HENRY HANSMANN AND RICHARD SQUIRE

1 INTRODUCTION

···

ASSET *partitioning* is the use of standard-form legal entities, such as the business corporation, to set boundaries on creditor recovery rights.[1] The corporate form partitions assets in two ways. First, it provides *owner shielding*, meaning that it protects the equityholders' personal assets from the business's creditors. The corporation's particular type of owner shielding is the principle of limited shareholder liability.[2] Second, the corporation provides *entity shielding*, meaning that it protects the business's assets from the equityholders' personal creditors.[3] Entity shielding is not as celebrated as limited liability, but we believe it is the more fundamental type of asset partitioning, because it would be harder to achieve by contract alone, without use of legal enties. By combining entity shielding with owner shielding, the corporation partitions assets from the perspectives of both the business and its owners.[4]

Scholars have identified several economic benefits of corporate asset partitioning. But corporate partitioning also generates costs, and courts have developed equitable remedies

---

[1] Henry Hansmann & Reinier Kraakman, "The Essential Role of Organizational Law", 110 Yale L. J. 387, 390 (2000) (defining asset partitioning).

[2] Henry Hansmann, Reinier Kraakman, & Richard Squire, "Law and the Rise of the Firm", 119 Harv. L. Rev. 1333, 1349–50 (2006) (defining owner shielding).

[3] Id. at 1337 (defining entity shielding). An earlier term for entity shielding is "affirmative asset partitioning." Hansmann & Kraakman, *supra* note 1, at 394. For a discussion of why entity shielding is more difficult to achieve by contract, see id. at 406.

[4] In particular, the corporation provides strong forms of both owner shielding and entity shielding, with the corporation's creditors (normally) unable to collect from the shareholders, and personal creditors unable to assert debt claims against the corporation (although they can seize the shareholders' shares). Weaker forms of both types of asset partitioning can be seen in the general partnership, which merely gives partnership creditors the first claim to the partnership's assets, and each partner's personal creditors the first claim to the partner's personal assets. Id. at 395–96.

that allow unpaid creditors to reach across corporate boundaries to recover. In American law, the most important de-partitioning remedies are veil piercing, enterprise liability, and substantive consolidation, all of which have analogues in the laws of other nations.[5]

Creditors are especially likely to seek a de-partitioning remedy when the debtor is a member of a corporate group, by which we mean a firm organized as a parent entity plus one or more wholly owned subsidiaries. A creditor might ask a court to disregard the boundary separating the parent from its shareholders, which we call an *external* partition. Alternatively, the creditor might seek to cross a boundary that separates one group member from another, which we call an *internal* partition. Several scholars have argued that external partitions provide greater economic benefits than internal partitions and therefore deserve more protection. Most prominently, Frank Easterbrook and Daniel Fischel argued in their 1985 article "Limited Liability and the Corporation" that courts should be more willing to hold a parent entity liable for a subsidiary's debt than to hold a parent's shareholder liable for the parent's debt.[6]

Easterbrook and Fischel's article is deservedly influential. Its analysis of asset partitioning in corporations is, however, incomplete in two important respects. First, it considers only half the story: it analyzes the benefits of owner shielding (that is, limited liability), but not the benefits of entity shielding. Adding entity shielding to the picture reveals several additional benefits of corporate partitioning that de-partitioning remedies could jeopardize. Second, Easterbrook and Fischel did not consider two important characteristics of most corporate groups: their neglect of subsidiary-level accounting and their heavy reliance on intra-group guarantees, which are contractual arrangements in which group members agree to stand behind each other's debts to outside creditors. The presence of these characteristics reveals which potential benefits of corporate partitioning a group's subsidiaries actually provide, and which potential costs they actually generate.

In this chapter, we compare the economic benefits and costs of external and internal corporate partitioning, and we consider our comparison's implications for de-partitioning remedies. Like previous commentators, we argue that the case for enforcing external partitions is stronger than the case for enforcing internal partitions. We add to the previous literature by identifying factors—other than whether a partition is internal or external—that courts should consider when deciding whether to de-partition. We are able to identify these factors because our fuller list of corporate partitioning's costs and benefits makes clearer the relevant trade-offs. For example, we argue that a corporate group's use of intra-group guarantees weighs in favor of disregarding the group's internal partitions. Intra-group guarantees are both evidence of, and contributors to, the agency costs of debt, which de-partitioning remedies can reduce. Because intra-group guarantees are, in essence, de-partitioning by contract, their use in a particular corporate group indicates that the group's subsidiaries serve functions unrelated to asset partitioning's potential economic advantages.

In section 2, we update the standard catalogue of corporate partitioning's costs and benefits to include those identified since Easterbrook and Fischel's article. In section 3, we use this catalogue to analyze the relative economics of external and internal partitioning. In section 4, we identify non-partitioning functions of subsidiaries, which are functions that

---

[5] See *infra* section 5.

[6] Frank H. Easterbrook & Daniel R. Fischel, "Limited Liability and the Corporation", 52 U. Chi. L. Rev. 89, 111 (1985).

de-partitioning remedies do not undermine. Finally, in section 5, we consider whether our cost–benefit analysis predicts how courts actually apply de-partitioning remedies, and we propose general principles for reforming legal doctrine to better reflect the economics of corporate partitioning. In that discussion, we limit our comments to the de-partitioning remedies of veil piercing and enterprise liability, reserving for later work a discussion of substantive consolidation, a remedy that presents unique doctrinal complexities.

2 THE BENEFITS AND COSTS OF CORPORATE PARTITIONING

In this section, we review the main benefits and costs of corporate asset partitioning that scholars have identified. We begin with the benefits that are apparent when owner shielding—meaning, in the business corporation, limited shareholder liability—is considered in isolation. We then expand the list to include three benefits that become evident when the other important aspect of corporate partitioning—entity shielding—is considered. Finally, we describe corporate partitioning's two main costs.

Although our aim is to describe the economics of corporate partitioning generally, in the discussion that follows we focus on the economic consequences of an incorporated firm's external partition. We do so because we believe that the benefits of internal partitioning are a subset of those of external partitioning. Put another way, there is no potential benefit of internal partitioning that is not also a benefit of external partitioning. It thus makes sense to begin by listing external partitioning's benefits; in section 3, we consider whether, and to what extent, each benefit can also arise from the partitions within a corporate group.

We define an *external* partition as the legal barrier dividing a corporation from its ultimate owners: its human and institutional equityholders. And we define an *internal* partition as a legal barrier within a corporate group, by which we mean a parent corporation plus all corporations it wholly owns, directly or indirectly. Under these definitions, if a corporate entity has one or more human shareholders, then the partition separating it from its shareholders is external. Conversely, if a corporation has only one shareholder, and that shareholder is another corporation, then the two entities are members of the same corporate group, and the partition separating them is internal. Finally, if a corporation has multiple corporate shareholders and no human shareholders, then the partition separating it from its shareholders is external unless those shareholders are wholly owned, directly or indirectly, by a common corporate parent.

One more note on terminology before we turn to our catalogue of benefits and costs: The act of incorporating a business firm, and thus introducing an asset partition between it and its owners, can shift value from some creditors to others. For example, if the firm has a high debt–equity ratio, then incorporating it could shift risk from the owners' personal creditors to the firm's creditors. When, however, we speak of corporate partitioning's benefits and costs, we do not mean the offsetting consequences of such a zero-sum transfer. Rather, we define a benefit as a source of economic efficiency: something that increases the sum of social wealth. And we define a cost as a consumption of resources or a deadweight loss— something that reduces social wealth.

We begin our list with the benefits of corporate partitioning that are evident when limited liability is considered in isolation. Because these benefits are well described in prior literature, we merely summarize them here.

2.1 Reduced Need for Equityholders to Monitor Each Other

In the general partnership, partners bear joint-and-several liability for partnership debt, and a partner sued by a partnership creditor can seek contribution from her co-partners.[7] Partners therefore prefer rich co-partners to poor ones, and for this reason might restrict who can become a partner, and also might monitor each other's personal affairs.[8] However, monitoring is expensive, and restricting membership hinders growth and makes partnership shares less liquid. Limited liability eliminates these costs by permitting equityholders to be indifferent to each other's personal fortunes. Pro rata equityholder liability for the firm's debts—a weaker form of owner shielding—provides the same benefit.[9]

2.2 Facilitating Control Transfers

Without limited liability, investors would, by purchasing equity in a firm, make all of their personal wealth available to its creditors. Therefore, transferring ownership from a poor investor to a rich one would confer a windfall on the firm's creditors, at the rich investor's expense. This surcharge on wealthy investors would discourage transfers of control to parties who might be able to run a firm (or monitor its managers) more effectively.[10] Limited liability eliminates the surcharge by making the value of an equity share independent of its owner's wealth. This benefit is distinct from the previous one—reduced need to monitor other shareholders—because it arises even if a firm has, at any particular time, only one owner.

An alternative way to avoid a windfall for a firm's creditors when the firm is sold to a wealthy investor would be to refinance all of the firm's debt, upon the sale's completion, at lower interest rates. Refinancing would, however, entail transaction costs, especially if the old debt agreements contained prepayment penalties. Limited liability makes refinancing unnecessary because it allows ownership to change hands without altering the amount of wealth backing the firm's debts.

2.3 Liquid Shares

Limited liability promotes a liquid market in equity shares, in two ways. First, by making shareholders less concerned about who else owns shares, limited (or pro rata) liability allows

---

[7]   As a pronoun convention, we refer to equityholders as female and creditors as male.
[8]   Paul Halpern, Michael Trebilcock, & Stuart Turnbull, "An Economic Analysis of Limited Liability in Corporation Law", 30 U. Toronto L. J. 117 (1980).
[9]   Henry Hansmann & Reinier Kraakman, "Toward Unlimited Shareholder Liability for Corporate Torts", 100 Yale L. J. 1879 (1991).
[10]   Easterbrook & Fischel, *supra* note 6, at 96.

firms to relax or eliminate restrictions on share transfers. Second, by making a share's value independent of who owns it, limited liability increases the informational value of market prices.[11] An investor can decide whether to buy at the market price without concern that the price results from trading among investors who are poorer than she is.

2.4 Equityholder Diversification

As Henry Manne first observed, limited liability enables shareholders to diversify.[12] In particular, it reduces the volatility of share values by preventing them from dropping below zero. Limited liability therefore makes it easier for investors to reduce the overall riskiness of their portfolios by adding shares of different companies.[13] Moreover, when a firm's shareholders are diversified, its managers can ignore unsystematic risk when deciding how to invest the firm's funds, widening the range of positive-value projects from which they may select.[14]

2.5 Reduced Information Costs for Personal Creditors

Limited liability narrows the factors a prospective creditor must analyze when evaluating a borrower's creditworthiness.[15] The borrower might own shares in a business firm and therefore—without limited liability—be answerable for its debts. The creditor would then have to consider the firm's insolvency risk when analyzing the borrower's credit risk. If, however, the firm is a corporation, then the creditor knows he will not have to compete with its creditors for the borrower's assets. Limited liability thus simplifies lending decisions, which will translate, in a competitive market, into a lower cost of credit.

At first blush, limited liability also seems to reduce information costs for corporate creditors. By denying them access to the shareholders' personal assets, it seems to let corporate creditors ignore those assets when assessing the risk of lending to the corporation. Limited liability is not, however, sufficient to make corporate creditors indifferent to shareholders' personal affairs. Without entity shielding, corporate creditors might be forced to share the corporation's assets with the shareholders' personal creditors. Therefore, corporate creditors will still need to assess the shareholders' personal assets and liabilities when evaluating the corporation's creditworthiness. For this reason, limited liability provides large informational benefits to creditors only when combined with entity shielding—that is, when partitioning is symmetrical rather than asymmetrical.[16]

---

[11] Id.

[12] Henry G. Manne, "Our Two Corporation Systems: Law and Economics", 53 Va. L. Rev. 259 (1967).

[13] Unlike the promotion of efficient control transfers, this benefit of limited liability cannot be achieved by the alternative mechanism of adjusting interest rates to reflect an increase in the amount of personal shareholder wealth backing the firm's debts. If limited liability were suddenly suspended, a downward adjustment of the interest rate on the firm's debt that maintained the expected value of its equity shares would not prevent the increase in the variance of the shares' potential values.

[14] Easterbrook & Fischel, *supra* note 6, at 97.

[15] Richard A. Posner, "The Rights of Creditors of Affiliated Corporations", 43 U. Chi. L. Rev. 499, 507–08 (1976).

[16] Richard Squire, "The Case for Symmetry in Creditors' Rights", 118 Yale L. J. 806, 816 (2009).

There are three other benefits of corporate partitioning that also depend on entity shielding, which are as follows:

2.6 Bankruptcy Simplification

Just as symmetrical partitioning can reduce creditor information costs, it also can simplify bankruptcy proceedings. A public company's bankruptcy would be unmanageable if the bankruptcy court had to take into account not only the company's balance sheet but also each shareholder's personal assets and debts.[17] The symmetrical partition between the company and its owners—blocking creditors in both directions—divides assets and liabilities into legally tractable bundles. It restricts the bankruptcy estate to the assets and liabilities of the company, excluding those of its shareholder. With fewer assets to valuate and proofs of claim to validate, the bankruptcy process can determine the ratio of assets to debts more quickly, permitting faster payouts to unsecured creditors.[18] Faster bankruptcy proceedings are more efficient because they redeploy debtor assets to better uses more quickly and generally have lower administrative costs.[19]

2.7 Protection of Going-Concern Value

An important component of the type of entity shielding provided by the corporation is liquidation protection.[20] Although a shareholder's unpaid personal creditors can seize her shares, they cannot force the corporation to liquidate, a process that in most jurisdictions requires a board resolution followed by shareholder ratification.[21] Liquidation is therefore unlikely unless in the best interests of shareholders generally, such as when the corporation is solvent but its liquidation value exceeds its going-concern value.[22] Without liquidation protection, shareholders could agree to forbid unilateral equity withdrawals, but courts might not enforce such agreements through specific performance, especially against personal creditors who are not parties to the agreements.[23] We see a contrast in the general partnership, whose assets are available for immediate seizure by partners' unpaid personal creditors. For this reason, the traditional rule is that a partner's bankruptcy dissolves the partnership.[24]

Liquidation protection also promotes share transferability. Without liquidation protection, equityholders would wish to prevent sales of equity shares to indebted investors whose creditors could force liquidation of the firm's assets. Conversely, share transferability

---

[17] Id. at 835; Hansmann, Kraakman, & Squire, *supra* note 2, at 1346.

[18] Squire, *supra* note 16, at 835.   [19] Id.

[20] See Hansmann & Kraakman, *supra* note 1, at 403–04 (describing how asset partitioning provides liquidation protection); see also Hansmann, Kraakman, & Squire, *supra* note 2, at 1348.

[21] See, e.g., Del. Gen. Corp. Law § 275.

[22] If a corporation is insolvent, liquidation is contrary to shareholder interests, as the proceeds of the asset sales will go entirely to creditors. Therefore, liquidation protection prevents inefficient dissolution of a firm but not inefficient continuation.

[23] Hansmann, Kraakman, & Squire, *supra* note 2, at 1349.

[24] See, e.g., Unif. P'ship Act § 31(5) (1914).

complements liquidation protection by giving shareholders an alternative way to convert shares to cash.

2.8 Correcting Debt Overhang

Corporate partitioning makes it easier for indebted entrepreneurs to raise funding to start new businesses. Without the option to form a corporation, an indebted entrepreneur might be unable to borrow to fund a prospective business, even if the business has a positive net present value. If the prospective business were to fail, the lender who funded it might have to share its assets with the entrepreneur's prior creditors. Anticipating this, the lender will demand a higher interest rate, which could make the prospective business unprofitable for the entrepreneur. Entity shielding solves this debt-overhang problem.[25] If the entrepreneur commits the new business to a distinct corporate entity that borrows the needed funds, the new lender will have the first claim to the business's assets and therefore will demand less interest, potentially making the undertaking worthwhile for the entrepreneur.[26]

Corporate partitioning also generates two types of cost:

2.9 Higher Agency Costs of Debt

Debt distorts how managers run a business. A firm with debt can take actions that enrich equityholders not by increasing the firm's total value but by shifting risk onto creditors. Termed from the creditors' perspective, such acts of "debtor misconduct" take a variety of forms, including asset shifting, asset substitution, involuntary subordination, debt dilution (for fixed debt), and correlation seeking (for contingent debt). The anticipation of debtor misconduct induces creditors to incur monitoring costs to prevent it and firms to incur bonding costs to reassure creditors that they will not engage in it. If debtor misconduct is undeterred, the value transfers it brings about induce firms to overinvest in risky projects.[27] As defined by Michael Jensen and William Meckling, the direct costs of debtor misconduct,

---

[25] See Elazar Berkovitch & E. Han Kim, "Financial Contracting and Leverage Induced Over- and Under-Investment Incentives", 45 J. Fin. 765, 778 (1990) (showing how project financing—that is, giving creditors who fund a project an exclusive debt claim against it—mitigates the overinvestment problem).

[26] Debt overhang can be a problem even if the indebted entrepreneur plans to finance the new business with her own wealth rather than new debt. Her current creditors, including those who funded her current businesses, will have access to the new business's assets if she is unable to service her prior debt, reducing the new business's expected value to her. Limited liability mitigates this problem if she uses separate corporate entities to house each of her businesses and their associated debt (if any). See Easterbrook & Fischel, *supra* note 6, at 111 (noting that the threat of tort liability would discourage taxicab owners from buying more cabs if they could not incorporate each taxi separately). Strictly speaking, this is not a distinct benefit of limited liability, but rather another way of describing how limited liability makes the value of an equity share independent of its owner's personal wealth. By blocking corporate creditors from seizing shareholder wealth held outside the corporation, limited liability removes a disincentive for the shareholders to increase that wealth.

[27] "Overinvestment" is investment in a project whose expected value to shareholders is positive but whose net present value, considering also its expected impact on creditors, is negative.

plus the monitoring and bonding costs incurred to prevent such misconduct, constitute the "agency costs of debt."[28]

Because every debtor is, at some level of debt, judgment-proof, all debtors face an incentive to engage in misconduct. The incentive increases, however, if business owners can incur debt through corporations to which they have committed only a portion of their wealth. Limited liability shifts business risk from equityholders to creditors, which increases the expected benefit to equityholders of debtor misconduct and thus raises the agency costs of debt.[29]

Incorporating a firm to reduce recoveries for tort creditors can be characterized as a type of debtor misconduct. Whether it actually destroys social wealth depends on the quality of the tort system. If the system is otherwise effective at deterring wealth-destroying torts, then limited shareholder liability leads to underdeterrence. Incorporated firms will overproduce, and they will underinvest in precautions.[30] If, however, the tort system over-deters—perhaps because juries are biased against defendants—then corporate partitioning's judgment-proofing effect could be socially beneficial.[31]

2.10 Accounting Costs

A court cannot enforce an asset partition unless it knows which assets and debts belong on each side. When a corporation fails, the proper division of assets and debts among the corporation, its affiliates, and its shareholders may not be obvious, especially if there is a controlling shareholder. The bankruptcy trustee may have to hire an accountant, whose fees will deplete the estate and thus reduce total creditor recoveries. And creditors might challenge the accountant's conclusions, introducing delay and driving up the estate's legal bills.

Accountants also are hired to confirm or demonstrate compliance with loan covenants and statutory creditor-protection measures such as distribution constraints and fraudulent-transfer law. In this way, accounting costs are monitoring or bonding costs and thus components of the agency costs of debt. Even, however, if a firm scrupulously refrained from debtor misconduct, it probably would still pay accountants to prepare financial statements to reduce information costs for its creditors.

---

[28] Michael C. Jensen & William H. Meckling, "Theory of the Firm: Managerial Behavior, Agency Costs and Ownership Structure", 3 J. Fin. Econ. 305 (1976).

[29] Easterbrook and Fischel argued that limited liability creates value by reducing the need for shareholders to monitor managers. Easterbrook & Fischel, *supra* note 6, at 94. However, it increases creditors' need to monitor, especially by increasing expected returns from debtor misconduct.

[30] See Steven Shavell, "The Judgment Proof Problem", 6 Int'l. Rev. L. & Econ. 45 (1986); Hansmann & Kraakman, *supra* note 9.

[31] Larry E. Ribstein, "The Deregulation of Limited Liability and the Death of Partnership", 70 Wash. U. L.Q. 417, 447 (1992) ("[The] advocacy of unlimited tort liability . . . assumes the efficiency of the tort system."); but see Hansmann & Kraakman, *supra* note 9, at 1918 ("[W]ith unlimited liability, courts would be forced to consider the appropriate scope of enterprise liability more thoughtfully.").

3 INTERNAL PARTITIONING: LEGAL BOUNDARIES WITHIN THE FIRM

We now consider whether, and to what extent, each of corporate partitioning's benefits and costs arises from internal partitioning in particular. The economics of internal partitioning are important, as most publicly traded companies are corporate groups with elaborate subsidiary networks.[32] In 2010, the 100 largest US public companies by revenues had, on average, 245 major subsidiaries.[33] Corporate groups are also the norm in other developed countries: For example, in 2005, large Japanese public companies averaged 108 subsidiaries,[34] and large French firms averaged 68.[35]

In section 2, we identified eight potential benefits of corporate partitioning. In this section, we argue that internal partitioning cannot generate three of these benefits: reduced need to monitor other equityholders, liquid shares, and protection of going-concern value. Four others—reduced creditor information costs, bankruptcy simplification, shareholder diversification, and the correction of debt overhang—are benefits that internal partitioning can provide, but seems rarely to do so in practice. That leaves efficient control transfers as the only common asset-partitioning benefit of subsidiaries. Moreover, subsidiaries seem to provide this benefit only temporarily, until the debts of the acquired entity are paid off or rolled over.

Besides providing fewer economic benefits than external partitioning, internal partitioning also tends to generate higher costs. Accounting costs are higher because subsidiary boundaries often fail to track the firm's real internal divisions. In addition, internal partitions increase the agency costs of debt by facilitating several types of debtor misconduct, including asset shifting, involuntary subordination, and correlation seeking through intra-group guarantees. The implication, which we develop in section 5, is that courts should be less reluctant to disregard the legal partitions within firms than those surrounding them.

We address first the three benefits of corporate partitioning that internal partitioning cannot provide. These are lower inter-shareholder monitoring costs, liquid shares, and protection of going-concern value. External partitioning generates these benefits by preventing conflicts among shareholders who differ in personal wealth and needs for liquidity. These benefits therefore cannot result from internal partitioning, as shareholder conflict cannot

---

[32] In 2010, 95 of the 100 largest US public companies by revenues reported six or more major subsidiaries. Richard Squire, "Strategic Liability in the Corporate Group", 78 U. Chi. L. Rev. 605, 606 n. 1 (2011).

[33] The mean number of subsidiaries for this group was 114. Id.

[34] Akira Mitsumasu, Control and Coordination of Functional Subsidiaries in Japanese Corporate Groups 1 (Aug. 31, 2013) (unpublished DBA thesis, Hitotsubashi University) (on file with Hitotsubashi University Repository), available at https://hermes-ir.lib.hit-u.ac.jp/rs/bitstream/10086/25896/3/ics020201300101.pdf.

[35] See Oren Sussman, "The Economics of the EU's Corporate-Insolvency Law and the Quest for Harmonisation by Market Forces" 29 (University of Oxford, Working Paper No. 2005-FE-16, 2005) (reporting that 92.3 percent of French corporations with more than 5,000 employees had subsidiaries, and that those with subsidiaries averaged 73.9 each), available at http://users.ox.ac.uk/~ofrcinfo/file_links/finecon_papers/2005fe16.pdf.

arise if a corporation—such as a subsidiary in a corporate group—has only one shareholder, or if all its shares are under common control.

There are four other potential benefits of corporate partitioning that internal partitioning could provide in theory but seems rarely to provide in practice. One is bankruptcy simplification. If the members of a bankrupt corporate group operated separately, rarely transacted with each other, and had little overlapping debt, then it might make sense to assign their bankruptcy cases to different judges. Their cases could then proceed in parallel, potentially enabling them to conclude more quickly. In practice, however, we almost never see affiliated debtors assigned to different courts. Instead, when a corporate group fails, its constituent members' cases are administratively consolidated and assigned to a single judge. A collective proceeding makes sense because the affiliated entities often have guaranteed each other's major debts and therefore have common creditors, and because their managers have typically failed to maintain accurate subsidiary-level records, obscuring the proper allocation of assets and debts among them.[36] In such a case, there is no procedural advantage to creating a distinct bankruptcy estate for each constituent entity. On the contrary, the lack of reliable entity-level accounting slows down proceedings and consumes administrative resources. For this reason, enforcing the firm's internal partitions will typically complicate the bankruptcy proceeding rather than simplifying it.

A similar story applies to creditor information costs. Like bankruptcy simplification, lower information costs are a benefit that internal partitioning could, in theory, supply.[37] Just as external partitioning enables a prospective creditor to disregard shareholders' personal affairs when assessing a firm's creditworthiness, so might internal partitions permit a prospective creditor to focus his credit analysis on the particular entity with which he will transact.[38] The cost savings could be considerable if the group's subsidiary boundaries track its real geographical and functional divisions.[39] In practice, however, most firms do not maintain informationally relevant internal partitions. Instead of preparing subsidiary-level financial records and sharing them with creditors, firms neglect entity-level accounts and

---

[36] Squire, *supra* note 32, at 614–16.

[37] Indeed, when Richard Posner first proposed that limited liability could reduce creditor information costs, his focus was the partitions between affiliated corporations. Posner, *supra* note 15, at 509–14.

[38] Id. at 516–17.

[39] Anthony Casey has offered a "selective enforcement" variation on the informational theory of subsidiaries. Anthony J. Casey, "The New Corporate Web: Tailored Entity Partitions and Creditors' Selective Enforcement", 124 Yale L. J. 2680 (2015). He describes a situation in which a single lender makes loans to two (or more) subsidiaries in a corporate group. The loan agreements include cross-default provisions. If one subsidiary defaults, the lender can use information conveyed by the fact of default to decide whether to accelerate the loans to the other subsidiaries. Id. at 2711. The structure thus gives the lender more enforcement options than he would have if the borrowing firm were a single legal entity.

The theory rests on factual assumptions that we find implausible. It presupposes that subsidiaries maintain distinct, accurate financial statements, which—as we discuss—is contrary to the experience of most bankruptcy courts. Without such records, a default by one subsidiary would not convey the information necessary for lenders to make the nuanced enforcement decisions Casey describes. The theory also assumes that a group's managers would allow one subsidiary to default while another is solvent, rather than using profits or assets from the solvent subsidiary to prop up the insolvent one. Yet, managers face strong incentives to prevent any entity in a group from defaulting, precisely because of the widespread use of cross-default provisions, which make a group's debts to multiple creditors immediately payable upon a default on any loan. (Fraudulent transfer law does not deter managers from transferring value within the group to prevent defaults; it merely reverses improper transfers if bankruptcy nonetheless ensues.)

report results only on a consolidated basis.[40] Indeed, bankruptcy courts cite sloppy or indifferent entity-level accounting and tangled internal affairs as their main reasons for applying the de-partitioning remedy of substantive consolidation.[41]

Another practice that undercuts the capacity for subsidiaries to reduce information costs is the widespread use of intra-group guarantees.[42] To see why, suppose that Subsidiaries A and B are members of a corporate group, that Bank One lends to Subsidiary A, and that Subsidiary B guarantees the loan. The guarantee makes the boundary between the subsidiaries irrelevant to Bank One, as both subsidiaries' assets and liabilities will determine the bank's payout if the group becomes bankrupt. In addition, the guarantee widens the exposure of Subsidiary B's creditors beyond Subsidiary B's own operations. They now bear some of Subsidiary A's credit risk: If A defaults, they will have to share Subsidiary B's assets with Bank One.

It is predictable that a corporate group which relies on intra-group guarantees will not bother to prepare accurate entity-level financial reports. The reports would have little value to the group's shareholders, who care only about consolidated results. The reports' only potential audience would be creditors who have extended credit to particular entities within the group. If, however, the creditors have also received intra-group guarantees that tie their

Our perception is that major lenders do not typically make distinct loans to multiple entities in a corporate group. Instead, they lend to the parent, who distributes the proceeds to its subsidiaries, in exchange for which the subsidiaries issue upstream guarantees to the lender. See, e.g., *In re Tousa, Inc.*, 680 F.3d 1298, 1301 (11th Cir. 2012); *In re Owens Corning*, 419 F.3d 195, 201 (3d Cir. 2005). Moreover, Casey lumps together cross-default provisions and intra-group guarantees as "cross-liability provisions," but they have different implications for the possibility of selective enforcement. To forbear enforcing a guarantee from a solvent guarantor when the borrower is insolvent is to forgive a collectible debt, which seems unlikely to be a rational lender strategy.

We believe that intra-group guarantees have a simpler explanation that is more consistent with the observed facts. Lenders seek the guarantees to reduce their information costs and protect themselves against value transfers within the group. And managers issue such guarantees because they reduce the group's cost of debt on the guaranteed loans, partly by reducing the guaranteed creditors' information and monitoring costs, and partly by shifting, through correlation seeking, some of the default risk to the guarantors' general creditors, who are unlikely to charge interest rates that adjust based on whether intra-group guarantees have in fact been issued to other creditors. See Squire, *supra* note 32, at 618, 644.

[40] Squire, *supra* note 32, at 616.

[41] See Christopher W. Frost, "Organizational Form, Misappropriation Risk, and the Substantive Consolidation of Corporate Groups", 44 Hastings L. J. 449, 456 and n. 26 (1993) (collecting cases in which consolidation was ordered because "the assets of the corporate group [could not] be segregated and identified with any particular entity within that group"); Mary Elisabeth Kors, "Altered Egos: Deciphering Substantive Consolidation", 59 U. Pitt. L. Rev. 381, 416 and n. 206 (1998) (citing cases in which consolidation was required due to a lack of accurate subsidiary-level records); William H. Widen, "Corporate Form and Substantive Consolidation", 75 Geo. Wash. L. Rev. 237, 268–69 and n. 100 (2007) (collecting decisions that cite "hopeless entanglement" as grounds for consolidation, and noting that the "entanglement metaphor . . . relates primarily to the failure to maintain business records that properly identify assets with particular corporate names").

[42] This objection to the informational theory of internal asset partitioning was first raised by George Triantis. See George G. Triantis, "Organizations as Internal Capital Markets: The Legal Boundaries of Firms, Collateral and Trusts in Commercial and Charitable Enterprises", 117 Harv. L. Rev. 1102, 1131 (2004) ("[B]anks also typically seek guarantees from affiliates—a pattern that is inconsistent with the specialization economies hypothesis.").

payouts to the performance of the group as a whole, then they too will have little reason to concern themselves with the division of value among entities within the group.[43]

Shareholder diversification is a third economic benefit that internal partitions provide in theory but not often in practice. In a true conglomerate, each subsidiary is a distinct company, making the group akin to an investment portfolio assembled by the parent entity on behalf of its shareholders. Internal partitioning reduces the portfolio's volatility by preventing one company's insolvency from pulling down the others' equity values. However, true conglomerates are rare, as investors have cheaper and more flexible options for diversifying shareholdings, such as mutual funds. Moreover, a group's subsidiaries will effectively diversify risk only if they refrain from lending to each other and from issuing intragroup guarantees, which is unusual. In fact, the typical corporate group is a single business firm organized as a collection of legal entities.

Finally, corporate subsidiaries could serve to correct debt overhang, but, again, firms seem rarely to use them for this purpose. The debt-overhang problem arises when an indebted firm wishes to invest in a new project. If the project is less risky than the firm's existing projects, it will decrease the firm's overall default risk by reducing the variance of the distribution of the firm's potential net asset values. As a result, the project will confer a windfall on the firm's existing creditors at the expense of equityholders. This value transfer could make the new project unprofitable from the shareholders' perspective even if it has a positive net present value. The firm could overcome this problem by organizing itself as a corporate group that houses each investment project, along with the debt used to fund the project, in a separate subsidiary. In reality, however, most corporate groups do not structure themselves this way. Instead, the parent does most of the borrowing and distributes the proceeds to the subsidiaries, which in return issue upstream guarantees. If debt overhang were a problem, this structure would exacerbate it by giving the parent's creditors a claim on the proceeds from any new projects undertaken by the subsidiaries.[44]

The remaining benefit of corporate partitioning identified in section 2 is the facilitation of efficient control transfers. Unlike the others on our list, this benefit is one that corporate subsidiaries do seem to provide with some frequency. However, the benefit is temporary, lasting only until the acquirer pays off or rolls over the target's preexisting debts. Thus, when two firms combine, they typically engage in a "triangular" merger that makes the target firm a subsidiary in the acquirer's corporate group.[45] Maintaining the target as a separate entity denies the target's pre-merger creditors recourse to the acquirer's assets. Such recourse would benefit those creditors at the expense of the acquirer's equityholders,[46] producing a value transfer that would act like a tax on corporate acquisitions, discouraging some wealth-creating combinations.[47] One commonly offered explanation for subsidiaries is a legacy of

---

[43] Squire, *supra* note 32, at 659.

[44] Even without the upstream guarantees, the parent's creditors would be senior to the parent's equityholders in the distribution of proceeds from the subsidiaries.

[45] William T. Allen, Reinier Kraakman, & Guhan Subramanian, Commentaries and Cases on the Law of Business Organization 471 (4th ed. 2012).

[46] The transfer would not occur if the acquirer's and target's insolvency risks were perfectly positively correlated.

[47] To avoid the windfall to the target's creditors, the acquirer could insist on a reduction in the interest rates they are owed, but renegotiating all of the target's debts could require the acquirer to incur significant transaction costs and create holdout problems.

mergers and acquisitions,[48] and we believe that this goal of preventing a windfall for the target firm's preexisting creditors is indeed an important reason that most acquisitions are structured to maintain the target as a distinct entity.

It must be noted, however, that intra-group guarantees undermine this potential benefit of subsidiaries. If a subsidiary results from a merger, and one or more of its creditors subsequently receive downstream or cross-stream guarantees, then those creditors thereby gain access to the acquirer's pre-merger assets, seemingly defeating the purpose of maintaining the target as a distinct legal entity.[49] How then can we reconcile the widespread use of intra-group guarantees with the practice of triangular mergers? One possibility is that acquirers maintain targets as separate entities for some of the non-partitioning reasons for subsidiaries we will discuss in the next part. A second possibility is that the separate subsidiary is meant to prevent a value transfer to the target's creditors at the time of the acquisition, but not later. Thus, as time passes and the subsidiary rolls over its debts, we can expect its lenders to bargain for cross-stream and downstream guarantees that tie their expected payouts to the performance of the group as a whole. These guarantees will reduce those lenders' information costs given the unlikelihood that the group maintains accurate subsidiary-level records. In addition, the guarantees will protect the lenders against value-shifting within the group. Alternatively, the group will replace the subsidiary's debt with new borrowing at the parent level that the subsidiary guarantees. In either case, the subsidiary will cease to serve its positive asset-partitioning function. The group may nonetheless continue to maintain the subsidiary as a separate entity because it serves non-partitioning functions, or because there is no reason to incur the transaction costs of absorbing it into another entity in the group.

In summary, we find that subsidiaries tend to provide only one of corporate partitioning's eight potential benefits with meaningful frequency: the promotion of efficient control transfers. Moreover, they provide this benefit only temporarily, until the newly acquired subsidiary rolls over its debt, at which point intra-group guarantees are issued that pierce the partitions between the subsidiary and the rest of the group.

Turning to the cost side of the ledger, we find that it too is unfavorable to internal partitioning. A subsidiary network facilitates several types of debtor misconduct, including asset shifting, judgment proofing against tort creditors,[50] and involuntary structural subordination. As an example of the last, imagine that HoldCo, the parent entity in a corporate group, takes out a loan from Bank One. Shortly afterward, the group's managers shift all of HoldCo's assets into its wholly owned subsidiary, SubCo. SubCo then uses its increased creditworthiness to borrow at a favorable interest rate from Bank Two. This maneuver harms Bank One by subordinating its claim on HoldCo's assets to Bank Two's claim. It also encourages overinvestment by reducing HoldCo's borrowing costs through an asset transfer

[48] See Posner, *supra* note 15, at 510.

[49] This is not true if the guarantee is upstream, as such a guarantee merely re-prioritizes creditors, and—unlike a cross-stream or downstream guarantee—does not pledge any shareholder wealth that the lender did not have a claim to already. Squire, *supra* note 32, at 638.

[50] See, e.g., Lynn M. LoPucki, "The Death of Liability", 106 Yale L. J. 1, 20 (1996) (arguing that sequestering liability-generating operations in a separate subsidiary prevents tort claimants and other creditors from reaching a firm's most valuable assets).

that, from the perspective of HoldCo's shareholders (as contrasted with its creditors), is costless.[51]

Bank One could insist on a debt covenant forbidding such acts of structural subordination. But monitoring for compliance would be costly, especially because the group could shroud asset shifting in sloppy entity-level accounting.[52] Moreover, the shifting of assets from HoldCo to SubCo would not normally be considered a constructive fraudulent transfer, as a court would probably hold that HoldCo received a reasonable equivalent value through the appreciation in its equity claim in SubCo that the transfer produced.[53]

A more cost-effective way for Bank One to protect itself against involuntary subordination would be to demand an upstream guarantee from SubCo. The guarantee would leave the bank largely indifferent to the division of assets between the two entities.[54] In this way, the widespread use of intra-group guarantees evinces that internal partitioning increases the risk of debtor misconduct. It does not follow, however, that intra-group guarantees produce an overall reduction in the agency costs of debt. Although an intra-group guarantee protects its recipient against asset shifting, it also, though correlation seeking, transfers risk onto the guarantor's preexisting unsecured creditors.[55] Thus, while an upstream guarantee from SubCo would insulate Bank One against asset transfers from HoldCo to SubCo, it simultaneously would take value from SubCo's preexisting general creditors. The value transfer will occur because the probability that the guarantee will be triggered correlates positively with SubCo's insolvency risk,[56] concentrating the guarantee's burden on SubCo's creditors rather than on the group's equityholders. Those creditors will suffer a net reduction in the expected value of their claims even if Bank One pays SubCo a premium equal to Bank One's

[51] Regardless of whether HoldCo or SubCo holds the assets, both entities' creditors must be repaid in full before HoldCo's shareholders can recover. Therefore, the asset shift does not affect the value of the shareholders' residual claims, even though it impairs the claims of HoldCo's creditors.

[52] Discovering the asset shift after the group becomes insolvent and files for bankruptcy is unlikely to be of much help, as Bank One will then be unable to recover the full damages for the breach of the anti-subordination covenant. See Barry E. Adler & Marcel Kahan, "The Technology of Creditor Protection", 161 U. Pa. L. Rev. 1773, 1780 (2013).

[53] Cf. Jack F. Williams, "The Fallacies of Contemporary Fraudulent Transfer Models as Applied to Intercorporate Guaranties: Fraudulent Transfer Law as a Fuzzy System", 15 Cardozo L. Rev. 1403, 1468 (1994) (noting that most judges deem downstream guarantees to be immune from attack as constructive fraudulent transfers, because the guarantees reduce the subsidiaries' cost of credit, which in turn increases the value of the parents' equity stakes).

[54] Phillip I. Blumberg, "Intragroup (Upstream, Cross-Stream, and Downstream) Guaranties under the Uniform Fraudulent Transfer Act", 9 Cardozo L. Rev. 685, 686–87 (1987) (arguing that intra-group guarantees protect lenders from "possible intragroup manipulation of [the borrower's] affairs"); Avery Wiener Katz, "An Economic Analysis of the Guaranty Contract", 66 U. Chi. L. Rev. 47, 73–74 (1999) (noting that a guarantee from a corporate affiliate of the borrower may protect the lender against asset shifting).

[55] Squire, *supra* note 32, at 623–639 (analyzing correlation seeking through intra-group guarantees). In general terms, correlation seeking occurs when a firm sells a contingent claim against itself that has a positive "internal correlation," meaning that the claim's risk of being triggered correlates positively with the firm's insolvency risk. Richard Squire, "Shareholder Opportunism in a World of Risky Debt", 123 Harv. L. Rev. 1151, 1159 (2010). Upon issuance, such a contingent claim reduces expected recoveries for the firm's unsecured creditors. If the firm has priced the contingent claim to capture its full expected value to the claimant, then the consideration the firm receives increases the firm's equity value by a commensurate amount. Id. at 1161.

[56] The risks correlate because a group's entities often make equity and debt investments in each other, and because they typically produce the same goods or services, subjecting them to common supply and demand conditions. Id. It therefore is predictable that, when one entity in a group guarantees the

Table 11.1 Comparison summary: external and internal partitioning

	External Partitioning	Internal Partitioning
Benefits		
Reduced need for inter-equityholder monitoring	Yes	No
Efficient control transfers	Yes	Yes (temporarily)
Liquid shares	*Yes*	No
Shareholder diversification	*Yes*	Rarely
Reduced creditor information costs	Yes	Rarely
Overcoming debt overhang	Yes	Rarely
Liquidation protection	Yes	No
Bankruptcy simplification	Yes	Rarely
Costs		
Agency costs of debt	Moderate	High
Accounting costs	Moderate	High

full expected recovery on the guarantee.[57] Therefore, rather than reducing the total agency costs of debt, intra-group guarantees merely shift the impact of debtor misconduct from creditors who receive guarantees to those who do not.

The enforcement of internal partitions also tends to entail high accounting costs. Whereas an external partition can be enforced if a firm prepares only one consolidated set of financial statements, enforcing internal partitions depends on the firm's preparing separate balance sheets and income statements for each of its constituent entities. In addition, internal partitioning encourages disputes over the company's internal accounting and pricing of intra-group transfers and loans. Such disputes are common in bankruptcy because the debtor's managers will have had little incentive to price internal transfers accurately. The managers' duties are to the group's shareholders, whose claims are unaffected by the pricing of intra-group transfers and loans.[58]

Table 11.1 summarizes our comparison of external and internal partitioning. We have italicized three "yes" entries in the external-partitioning column to indicate benefits that

debt of another, the guarantor will be insolvent when the borrower triggers liability on the guarantee by defaulting on the debt.

[57] It is a straightforward matter to show mathematically that, when the internal correlation is positive, the creditors' expected loss on account of the contingent liability outweighs their expected benefit from the fee. See Squire, *supra* note 32, at 624–28.

[58] The situation would be different if a corporate entity had minority shareholders along with a controlling shareholder and therefore would not be, under the definition we have been using here, a subsidiary within a corporate group. In such a corporation, the minority shareholders care about the pricing of transfers between the corporation and the controller or the controller's affiliates. For a discussion of how minority shareholders can deter opportunism by the controller in this type of corporation, see Triantis, *supra* note 42, at 1125.

external partitioning provides only if a corporation has shareholders who differ in their levels of personal wealth or liquidity requirements. If a corporation has only a single, human shareholder, then its external partition will not provide these benefits, even though it could provide the others in the table.

As Table 11.1 indicates, cost–benefit analysis favors external partitioning. Using a firm's outer boundary to demarcate creditor recovery rights can provide numerous benefits to both creditors and shareholders. By contrast, internal partitioning provides fewer benefits, and its costs are higher, especially if—as is typical—the group neglects subsidiary-level accounting. Such neglect indicates that the group's creditors did not use subsidiary boundaries to economize on credit analysis. It also means that using the internal partitions to delimit creditor recoveries in bankruptcy would require the estate to hire accountants, whose fees would be paid at the expense of the group's general creditors.

4 Non-Partitioning Functions of Subsidiaries

Table 11.1 raises a question. If internal partitioning is costly to enforce and increases the agency costs of debt, and its benefits are either temporary or rare, why do firms have so many subsidiaries? The apparent answer is that subsidiaries serve non-partitioning functions whose benefits outweigh the net costs of internal partitioning, or at least the net costs borne by shareholders. We call these "non-partitioning" functions because, for the most part, de-partitioning remedies such as veil piercing do not compromise them.

One non-partitioning function of a subsidiary is to establish a legal domicile in a particular jurisdiction. For example, a multinational firm might form a corporate entity in a particular country to take advantage of its low tax rate.[59] Similarly, regulated firms such as banks might be required to maintain distinct entities in each state in which they operate. De-partitioning remedies do not interfere with these jurisdictional functions. If a bankrupt company liquidates, disregarding its internal boundaries when calculating creditor payouts will not nullify the tax and regulatory benefits its subsidiaries provided pre-bankruptcy. If the company instead reorganizes, it can maintain its internal entity structure post-bankruptcy even if that structure was not used in bankruptcy to determine payout entitlements.[60]

Another function of subsidiaries is to reduce the transaction costs of spin-offs by preserving transferable bundles of contracts.[61] To see why, suppose that BuyCo acquires TargetCo but wants the option to spin it off cheaply later. During a spin-off, reassigning TargetCo's executory contracts—which might comprise much of TargetCo's real economic value—could be difficult. Most executory contracts contain non-assignment clauses, and

---

[59] William H. Widen, "Report to the American Bankruptcy Institute: Prevalence of Substantive Consolidation in Large Public Company Bankruptcies from 2000 to 2005", 16 Am. Bankr. Inst. L. Rev. 1, 29 (2008).

[60] See *In re Owens Corning*, 419 F.3d 195, 216 (3d Cir. 2005) (noting that, after a deemed consolidation, the firm's subsidiaries can continue to provide their "liability-limiting, tax and regulatory benefits").

[61] Kenneth Ayotte & Henry Hansmann, "Legal Entities as Transferable Bundles of Contracts", 111 Mich. L. Rev. 715, 722 (2013) (introducing the bundled-contracts theory of the corporate form).

non-assignment is the default rule for most employment contracts. These assignment restrictions protect each party to a contract against the risk that the counterparty will transfer its obligations to a third party who will default or otherwise underperform.[62] Most assignment restrictions do not, however, forbid the sale of the entire counter-party to a new owner. Likewise, the common law rule is that the sale of some or all of a corporation's shares does not constitute an assignment of the corporation's contracts. This rule makes economic sense, because a sale of a corporation's shares does not disrupt complementarities among the corporation's contractual positions and its other assets. In other words, changing a firm's ownership is less risky to its counterparties than individual assignments of their contracts would be. Therefore, by preserving TargetCo as a separate subsidiary, BuyCo can later sell it without having to negotiate for waivers from all of its contractual counterparties, which might create holdout problems.

Once again, de-partitioning remedies do not undermine this function of subsidiaries. If a bankrupt company liquidates, its contracts will be cancelled regardless of how creditor payouts are calculated. If it instead reorganizes, any executory contracts (or leases) it chooses to honor will remain with their original entities after the bankruptcy proceeding,[63] preserving the company's contract bundles. Although the subsidiaries might be ignored in the calculation of creditor payouts, including payouts to contractual counterparties whose claims have come due, the subsidiaries can continue to operate as distinct legal persons post-bankruptcy. For this reason, the reorganized company will not be hampered in spinning off any divisions it maintained pre-bankruptcy as separate entities.

5 Legal Implications: Patterns and Presumptions

We now consider our analysis's descriptive and prescriptive implications for creditor remedies that disregard corporate partitions. Descriptively, the distinction between external and internal partitioning corresponds to some, but not all, of the patterns we observe in how courts apply de-partitioning remedies. Prescriptively, our analysis suggests how courts could increase social wealth by bringing doctrine more in line with the economics of corporate partitioning.

The general implications of our analysis are consistent with those of the work of other scholars, beginning with Easterbrook and Fischel. Courts should be less willing to disregard an external partition than an internal one. And they should be especially loath to disregard the external partition of a company with tradable shares, the setting in which shareholders are likely to be most heterogeneous in terms of personal wealth and liquidity needs, and therefore where external partitioning is especially beneficial.

---

[62] Id. at 726.

[63] The Bankruptcy Code empowers trustees to enforce or reject executory contracts selectively and to assign them to third parties, notwithstanding contractual provisions to the contrary. 11 U.S.C. § 365(a),(f). For an argument that selective assignability in bankruptcy may be efficient, see Ayotte & Hansmann, *supra* note 61, at 748.

Turning to more specific implications, our analysis suggests that courts should be more willing to disregard an entity's partition when the entity's managers have failed to keep an accurate record of its assets and liabilities. When such records are absent, asset partitioning does not reduce creditor information costs, correct debt overhang, simplify bankruptcy proceedings, promote share trading, facilitate efficient control transfers, or provide liquidation protection. Therefore, a court can apply a de-partitioning remedy without fear that doing so will undermine these various potential benefits of asset partitioning.

Accurate accounting is also essential for asset partitioning to reduce the agency costs of debt. Legislatures have created creditor-protection measures to reduce those costs. In corporations, the most important measures are fraudulent-transfer law and distribution constraints, both of which rely on accurate recordkeeping. Under fraudulent transfer law, relief is typically available only if a creditor (or bankruptcy trustee acting on creditors' behalf) can show that the debtor did not receive "a reasonably equivalent value" when it transferred an asset or incurred an obligation, and that the debtor was insolvent when the transaction occurred.[64] These are factual showings that require accounting records, including a balance sheet for the time of the transaction. Similarly, distribution constraints presuppose a balance sheet that accurately records the corporation's surplus. Without a balance sheet to cite, creditors cannot prove that a corporation paid dividends out of shareholder capital, which is supposed to remain in the corporation as a cushion against insolvency. Therefore, if managers have failed to keep the accounts necessary for enforcing these boundary-policing measures, courts should be willing to let creditors cross boundaries, especially when equityholders (on whose behalf the managers act) rather than other creditors would bear the consequences.

Our analysis also suggests that courts should be more willing to disregard a corporate partition if the corporation's managers or shareholders have already perforated it by issuing guarantees. A guarantee is voluntary de-partitioning, a waiver of either entity shielding or owner shielding (or both) on behalf of a particular creditor. Therefore, the presence of a guarantee suggests that partitioning's costs outweigh its benefits, at least with respect to the creditor receiving the guarantee.[65] Moreover, if the cost–benefit analysis of enforcing a corporate partition is unfavorable for one creditor, it is likely to be unfavorable for other creditors, even if—perhaps because they are unsophisticated or have small claims—they did not negotiate for guarantees for themselves.[66]

We have already described how intra-group guarantees undercut several potential benefits of internal partitioning. Besides evincing that the recipient creditor did not rely on subsidiary boundaries to economize on information costs, an intra-group guarantee suggests that a subsidiary is no longer serving to facilitate an efficient control transfer or to correct debt overhang. The former is true if a subsidiary's creditor received a cross-stream or downstream guarantee, while the latter is true if the subsidiary itself issued a guarantee. Courts therefore

---

[64] 11 U.S.C. § 548(a).

[65] The guarantee might also indicate that the guarantor has nonadjusting creditors who will not charge a higher interest rate even though the guarantee reduces their expected recoveries.

[66] See Adler & Kahan, *supra* note 52, at 1779 (noting that a firm's creditors often include "small, unsophisticated, or short-term creditors for which negotiating detailed protections may make little sense").

should treat intra-group guarantee as a factor weighing in favor of de-partitioning remedies within corporate groups.

We anticipate an objection. Courts that selectively ignore corporate partitions could disappoint investor expectations and introduce uncertainty into business affairs. We note, however, that this objection does not argue against de-partitioning remedies per se; rather, it argues against applying remedies unpredictably. If courts made clear the circumstances under which they will allow creditors to cross corporate boundaries, expectations and interest rates would adjust accordingly. As discussed below, we believe that de-partitioning criteria can be adopted that promote economic efficiency and that give parties reasonable notice as to when an asset partition will be disregarded.

With these observations in mind, we now address the particular de-partitioning remedies of veil piercing and enterprise liability. Because our expertise is American law, we focus on doctrine developed by American common-law courts. We do, however, offer a few comparative observations about European and Japanese law.

5.1 Veil Piercing

The remedy of veil piercing suspends the rule of limited liability by allowing a corporate creditor to recover from a controlling shareholder. Under American law, the creditor must satisfy both parts of a two-prong test: He must show (1) that the corporation served as the shareholder's mere "alter ego," and (2) that liability for the shareholder is necessary to avoid some injustice.[67] The Japanese Supreme Court has adopted a similar test, permitting recovery from a controlling shareholder if the corporation's legal personality is a "mere formality" that has been "abused."[68] In the United Kingdom, courts occasionally allow a creditor to pierce the veil if the corporation is a "mere façade concealing the true facts."[69]

As these various quoted terms suggest, courts tend to articulate veil-piercing doctrine in vague and conclusory language, making it difficult to evaluate the remedy's economic consequences. If, however, we look at case outcomes, we see that judges—at least in the United States—do often employ the remedy in a manner that protects corporate partitioning's economic benefits and reduces the agency costs of debt. Courts typically consider the first, "alter ego" prong of the veil-piercing test satisfied upon a showing that the corporation failed to follow procedures such as holding board meetings, electing directors, keeping accurate records, and maintaining separate bank accounts.[70] Several of these procedures—especially the last two—bear directly on the agency costs of debt.[71] As noted above, statutory creditor protections such as fraudulent transfer law and distribution constraints presuppose an accurate corporate balance sheet. Therefore, by emphasizing

---

[67] See Kurt A. Strasser, "Piercing the Veil in Corporate Groups", 37 Conn. L. Rev. 637, 640 (2005).

[68] Supreme Court of Japan, Feb. 27, 1969, 23 Saiko Saibansho Minji Hanreishu 511.

[69] Hisaei Ito & Hiroyki Wanabe, "Piercing the Corporate Veil," Comparative Company Law: A Case Based Approach 184 (Mathias Siems & David Cabrelli eds., 2013).

[70] See, e.g., *Van Dorn v. Fut. Chem. & Oil Corp.*, 753 F.2d 565, 570 (7th Cir. 1985).

[71] German courts reportedly also accept the proposition that shareholder liability may be appropriate if shareholder capital and corporate capital were intermingled. Ito & Wanabe, *supra* note 69, at 172.

sound recordkeeping in their alter-ego analyses, courts deter practices that drive up the agency costs of debt.

Regarding the second prong of the American veil-piercing test—the presence of some sort of injustice—studies show that courts are particularly likely to deem it satisfied if the creditor was misled, even if the deception fell short of common-law fraud.[72] We again see an implicit concern with the agency costs of debt, and also with one of the primary benefits of external partitioning: reducing creditor information costs. Creditors are more vulnerable to debtor misconduct and can rely less on the integrity of entity boundaries, if they cannot count on a debtor's attestations about its financial condition and compliance with loan covenants.

In terms of the specific contexts in which courts pierce the veil, the distinctions we have drawn in this chapter predict some, but not all, of the patterns in case outcomes. Thus, courts never pierce the veil to reach the personal assets of public shareholders,[73] which is consistent with our view that corporate partitioning is most beneficial when in the form of an external partition separating a firm from multiple shareholders. On the other hand, there is evidence that, in the context of close corporations, courts are slightly more likely to pierce an external partition (to reach a controlling human shareholder) than an internal partition (to hold a parent liable for the debt of a subsidiary).[74] This observation is unexpected given that, even in a close corporation, external partitioning can provide greater economic benefits. We hypothesize that confounding variables are at work: Courts are perhaps more likely to find that a creditor was misled by a human shareholder than by a corporate entity, or they might consider it more egregious if a firm as a whole, rather than one entity within a corporate group, has failed to respect corporate formalities.

We now consider doctrinal reforms implied by our analysis. We are not the first commentators to notice that the vague terms in which courts articulate veil-piercing doctrine make it difficult for parties and their attorneys to predict when shareholders will be held liable.[75] With respect to the American law of veil piercing, we believe that the first prong in particular could usefully be re-conceptualized and re-articulated. As argued above, the corporate formality that is most important to creditors is the maintenance of accurate entity-level accounts. Other formalities, such as enacting bylaws and holding shareholder meetings, are less relevant. The implication is that courts should ground veil piercing's first prong explicitly, and perhaps exclusively, in accurate accounting, with the dispositive question being

---

[72] See Jonathan Macey & Joshua Mitts, "Finding Order in the Morass: The Three Real Justifications for Piercing the Corporate Veil", 100 Cornell L. Rev. 99, 148 (2014) (finding that courts are significantly more likely to pierce the veil if they find misrepresentation rather than mere undercapitalization); Robert B. Thompson, "Piercing the Corporate Veil: An Empirical Study", 76 Cornell L. Rev. 1036, 1063 (1991) (finding that courts pierced the veil in 94 percent of cases in which they mentioned "misrepresentation" as a factor, making it more important than factors such as undercapitalization (73 percent) and overlapping personnel or business activities (57 percent)).

[73] Peter B. Oh, "Veil-Piercing", 89 Tex. L. Rev. 81, 110 (2010).   [74] Id.

[75] One commentator described the analysis offered in judicial opinions as "jurisprudence by metaphor or epithet. It does not contribute to legal understanding because it is an intellectual construct, divorced from business realities. The metaphors are no more than conclusory terms, affording little understanding of the considerations and policies underlying the court's actions and little help in predicting results in future cases." Phillip Blumberg, The Law of Corporate Groups: Procedural Problems in the Law of Parent and Subsidiary Corporations 8 (1983).

whether the corporation maintained records adequate to support enforcement of standard creditor-protection measures.

Regarding the distinction between external and internal partitioning, we propose that courts employ it to assign evidentiary burdens. When a creditor of a subsidiary seeks the parent's assets, courts should require the defendant to produce annual balance sheets for the subsidiary that are accurate over the span of the plaintiff's loan. Assigning this burden to the defendant makes sense given that internal partitioning has fewer potential benefits than external partitioning and raises a greater debtor-misconduct risk. If the defendant cannot meet the burden, the plaintiff should recover, even if veil-piercing's traditional second prong is not met. Allowing recovery on such facts would reduce the agency costs of debt by penalizing defendants for failing to maintain the records that underpin statutory creditor-protection measures. If, on the other hand, the defendant can produce accurate accounts, courts should presume that the normal creditor-protection measures were effective. The plaintiff should then prevail only upon a clear showing of misrepresentation or deception.

When, by contrast, a plaintiff seeks to pierce a corporation's *external* partition to reach a controlling shareholder's assets, we suggest that the burden lies initially with the plaintiff. Even when shares are not freely tradable, external partitioning often provides benefits that internal partitioning does not, including shareholder diversification, reduced creditor monitoring costs, bankruptcy simplification, and correction of debt overhang. Therefore, when seeking to pierce an external partition, the plaintiff should have to show that the corporation's records are not complete enough to permit enforcement of statutory remedies. In addition, the plaintiff should have to show either that he was deceived or that the partition did not serve external partitioning's main benefits and therefore should be accorded no more respect than a poorly maintained internal partition.

In support of this last type of showing, a plaintiff should be permitted to cite the defendant's grant of a personal guarantee to one of her corporation's creditors. A personal guarantee reduces the degree to which the external partition diversifies the shareholders' equity portfolio, as it puts the shareholder's personal assets—including her investments in other firms—at risk. The guarantee also suggests that the external partition is no longer serving to preserve the benefits of an efficient control transfer. That benefit arises when limited liability prevents an acquired firm's creditors from reaching the acquirer's personal wealth, and yet such access is exactly what a personal guarantee provides. In addition, a personal guarantee suggests that the external partition did not help creditors economize on their information costs, for reasons discussed in section 3. Therefore, if a controlling shareholder has guaranteed any of her corporation's debts, we propose that the inquiry should be the same as in a case involving an internal partition, with the plaintiff prevailing unless there was no deception and the defendant can show that accurate corporate records were maintained.

Why, one might object, should a contractual creditor who has failed to bargain for a personal guarantee enjoy the same remedy—access to the shareholder's personal assets—as the creditor who did? One response is that this objection proves too much: All creditor-protection measures are substitutes for contractual provisions that creditors could, in theory, bargain for (and pay for, through lower interest rates) themselves. If, however, the goal is economic efficiency, then the relevant question is not whether a creditor could have obtained protection contractually but whether a statutory or equitable remedy would more effectively lower the agency costs of debt. Remedies that lower agency costs increase the surplus from credit arrangements, making both lenders and borrowers better off. We note in this regard that the common practice of giving a personal guarantee to a small firm's most important lender—typically a bank—creates perverse incentives, as banks would otherwise charge higher interest rates to firms with greater tort risk. Moreover, bargaining for guarantees entails transaction costs, which is why shareholders almost never give personal guarantees to trade creditors, who have small claims governed by standard-form contracts. To be clear, our argument is not that the issuing of one personal guarantee should invalidate a firm's external boundary for all creditors. Rather, courts should treat the guarantee as evidence that the boundary does not provide most of corporate partitioning's potential economic benefits. The defendant could still prevail by showing that the corporation maintained accurate records and distinct accounts and by rebutting any claim that the plaintiff was deceived.

5.2 Enterprise Liability

Traditional veil piercing is a vertical de-partitioning remedy: It renders shareholders liable for corporate debt. Sometimes, however, the shareholder has committed most of her wealth to other corporations, which may or may not form a corporate group with the original debtor entity. In that situation, American courts sometimes allow the plaintiff to "reverse pierce" and assert claims against these other corporations.[76] To reach their assets, however, the plaintiff must first establish the elements of a piercing claim against the defendant shareholder.

Rather than requiring plaintiffs to take this circuitous route through the shareholder's personal estate, some courts have authorized the alternative de-partitioning remedy of enterprise liability. That remedy allows the creditor of one member of a corporate group to pierce horizontally to reach the assets of other members. The remedy does not, however, open the gates to the shareholder's personal assets: It abrogates internal partitions, not external ones.

The factors that courts consider when deciding whether to impose enterprise liability are much like those that govern the first prong—the alter-ego test—of veil-piercing doctrine. However, while the courts of every US state have endorsed some version of veil piercing, courts in only a handful of states have recognized enterprise liability. Moreover, the list became shorter in 2008 when Texas's highest court repudiated the remedy, holding that mere unity of control or function cannot make one corporation liable for the debt of another.[77] As a result, veil piercing became the only equitable remedy in Texas for abrogating corporate partitioning. Notions of enterprise liability can also be found in British and German company law.[78]

We suspect that enterprise-liability cases are rare in the United States primarily because failed corporate groups typically end up in bankruptcy court, where judges employ a different doctrine—substantive consolidation—to disregard internal partitions.[79] It

---

[76] See, e.g., *Sea-Land Servs., Inc. v. Pepper Source*, 941 F.2d 519 (7th Cir. 1991).

[77] *SSP Partners v. Gladstrong Invest. (USA) Corp.*, 275 S.W. 3d 444 (Texas 2008).

[78] For decisions from the U.K., see *DHN Food Distrib. Ltd. v. Tower Hamlets London Borough Council* [1976] 1 WLR 852; *Littlewoods Mail Order Stores v. Inland Revenue Comm'r* [1969] 1 WLR 1214; *Wallersteiner. Moir* [1974] 1 WLR 991. For a general discussion of de-partitioning remedies in Germany, see Ito & Wanabe, *supra* note 69, at 172.

[79] See, e.g., *In re Owens Corning*, 419 F.3d 195, 211 (3d Cir. 2005).

therefore is unsurprising that the most prominent judicial opinion to endorse enterprise liability in one state (Louisiana) is from a case involving an insurance company,[80] as state regulators rather than federal bankruptcy judges oversee insolvency proceedings involving insurers.[81]

We recognize the need for a doctrine of enterprise liability in collective insolvency proceedings. Our analysis here, however, suggests that courts should more consciously direct the doctrine toward the goals of reducing administrative costs and the agency costs of debt. It follows that courts should be inclined toward imposing enterprise liability when a corporate group has failed to keep accurate entity-level records, especially if the group has also issued intra-group liabilities. Such doctrinal reform would require courts to amend their lists of relevant factors. Currently, American courts do include shoddy internal accounting among the factors weighing in favor of collective liability within the group.[82] But they also consider formalities, such as whether the entities had overlapping directors and officers,[83] that matter little for creditor protection or for the broader question of whether the benefits of enforcing an internal asset partition exceed the costs. Judges also do not weigh the presence of intra-group guarantees in favor of enterprise liability, perhaps because they may be unaware of how such guarantees, via correlation seeking, contribute to the agency costs of debt.

6 CONCLUSION

In this chapter, we have introduced what we believe is a useful distinction between two types of corporate asset partitioning: *external* partitioning versus *internal* partitioning. An external partition is the legal boundary that separates a business corporation from its ultimate, real equityholders: its human and institutional shareholders. Internal partitions are the legal boundaries within a corporate group, meaning a parent entity and its network of wholly owned subsidiaries.

We have argued that distinguishing external partitioning from internal partitioning has both descriptive and prescriptive utility. Descriptively, external partitioning provides more benefits than internal partitioning, and it generates lower costs. External partitioning provides at least eight potential benefits: reduced need for equityholders to monitor each other; liquidation protection; liquid shares; shareholder diversification; reduced creditor information costs; bankruptcy simplification; overcoming debt overhang; and efficient control transfers. Internal partitioning, by contrast, cannot provide the first three benefits on this list, and it rarely provides the next four. Conversely, corporate partitioning's two main costs—accounting costs and the agency costs of debt—tend to be higher when partitioning is internal rather than external.

Prescriptively, our analysis suggests that courts should employ the distinction between external and internal partitioning when applying creditor remedies that disregard corporate partitions, such as veil piercing and enterprise liability. To be sure, to some extent they already do. Studies show that courts are especially unlikely to allow a creditor to pierce a

---

[80] *Green v. Champion Ins. Co.*, 577 So. 2d 249 (La. App. 1 Cir. 1991).
[81] See 11 U.S.C. § 109(b)(2) (barring insurance companies from being debtors in bankruptcy).
[82] See, e.g., *Green v. Champion Ins. Co.*, 577 So.2d at 258.   [83] See, e.g., id. at 257.

public company's external partition, the type of corporate partition with the most favorable cost–benefit analysis. Similarly, courts use the remedy of enterprise liability only to disregard internal partitions, never external ones. The congruence between theory and doctrine is incomplete, however, perhaps because courts often frame de-partitioning doctrine in terms of whether the corporate form has been adequately "respected" rather than whether the economic benefits of partitioning outweigh its costs. We therefore have proposed ways that de-partitioning doctrines could, in light of our analysis, be reformed to increase social wealth.

We are not the first commentators to argue that courts should respect the partition around a firm more than they respect the partitions within it. Thirty years ago, Easterbrook and Fischel argued that courts should be more willing to allow a creditor to pierce the boundary between a corporate subsidiary and the parent than the boundary between the parent and its shareholders. On this point, our conclusions are consistent with theirs. However, the only form of corporate partitioning that Easterbrook and Fischel considered was limited shareholder liability. We have offered a broader analysis that also considers the benefits and costs of entity shielding—the rule that shields a corporation's assets from the shareholders' personal debts. And we have factored into our analysis two important observations about corporate groups: their lack of subsidiary-level financial records and their heavy reliance on intra-group guarantees. For these reasons, we have been able to identify a more complete set of considerations that bear on whether a corporate boundary should be disregarded. For example, we have shown how the presence of intra-group guarantees or personal shareholder guarantees—which are forms of voluntary de-partitioning—evinces that a corporate partition is not providing certain economic benefits, and also that enforcing the partition at the expense of creditors without guarantees is likely to increase the agency costs of debt.

By necessity, our reform suggestions have been broad and summary. We have identified factors we think courts should consider, as well as factors they currently consider but should ignore, when deciding whether to grant a de-partitioning remedy. We have also identified presumptions, based on whether a partition is internal or external, that courts could apply in such cases. A more complete treatment of de-partitioning remedies would consider particular areas of doctrinal conflict, such as the tendency for American bankruptcy courts to apply substantive consolidation more often than appellate courts seem to believe is appropriate.[84] With respect to such issues, we believe that using the economics of asset partitioning generally, and the distinction between internal and external partitioning specifically, to study de-partitioning doctrines is a promising area for future scholarship.

---

[84] See Widen, *supra* note 59, at 28.

CHAPTER 12

···

THE BOARD OF DIRECTORS

···

STEPHEN M. BAINBRIDGE[1]

1 INTRODUCTION

···

WHEN recognizably modern corporations emerged in Anglo-American law in the early nineteenth century, the board of directors was already deeply embedded in their DNA. New York's 1811 Act Relative to Incorporations for Manufacturing Purposes, for example, vested the power to manage the corporation in a board of directors (albeit using the term trustees).[2] Likewise, the United Kingdom's Joint Stock Companies Act of 1844 broadly empowered the board of directors to, inter alia, "conduct and manage the Affairs of the Company."[3] In neither case, moreover, was the statute an innovation. On the contrary, board of directors-like bodies were routine among the modern corporation's antecedents, such as the trading companies created by charters granted by the English crown as far back as the Muscovy Company of 1554.[4]

Similar developments were taking place contemporaneously in Europe. Although many large European businesses of the time remained organized as partnerships, with no governing board, there were emerging entity forms such as the Dutch East India Company that were governed by boards.[5] Interestingly, even though autocratic rule was in its heyday amongst continental governments during much of this period, the antecedents of modern European corporations—like their English counterparts—opted for consensus governance in a board or board-like committee.[6]

---

[1] William D. Warren Distinguished Professor of Law, UCLA School of Law.

[2] Act Relative to Incorporations for Manufacturing Purposes, 1811 N.Y. Laws 151. See Ronald E. Seavoy, The Origins of the American Business Corporation, 1784–1855 65 (1982) ("There could be no more than nine trustees (directors) and they were granted broad powers to manage the business.").

[3] Joint Stock Companies Registration, Incorporation and Regulation Act, 1844, 7 & 8 Vict., c. 110 (Eng.).

[4] Franklin A. Gevurtz, "The Historical and Political Origins of the Corporate Boards of Directors", 33 Hofstra L. Rev. 89, 116 (2004).

[5] Id. at 126–27.

[6] Id. at 167. See generally Franklin A. Gevurtz, "The European Origins and the Spread of the Corporate Board of Directors", 33 Stetson L. Rev. 925 (2004) (arguing that the corporate board of directors is now a worldwide phenomenon but originated in Europe).

Although realworld practice often differs from the statutory ideal, modern corporation statutes still vest ultimate managerial power in neither the corporation's officers (the so-called C-suite) nor its shareholders. Although the differences detail across national boundaries, corporation codes (a.k.a. company laws) establish the board of directors as the key player in the formal decision-making structure. As the influential Delaware code puts it, for example, the corporation's business and affairs "shall be managed by or under the direction of a board of directors."[7]

The formal model of corporate governance thus contemplates a pyramidal hierarchy surmounted neither by a large electorate nor an individual autocrat, but rather by a small collaborative body. This model raises a number of questions: Why are corporate decisions made through the exercise of authority rather than by consensus? Why is corporate authority exercised hierarchically? Put another way, what survival advantage does a large corporation gain by being structured as a bureaucratic hierarchy? Why is the firm's ultimate decision maker a collective rather than an individual? Who, among all the corporation's constituencies, should elect the board?

Section 2 begins the process of answering those questions by looking at the key functions of the board of directors. Although the precise mix of functions varies across national borders, the US unitary board and the German dual board models provide sufficiently useful paradigms that our attention will focus on them. Section 3 turns to the question of why corporations are run by boards of directors rather than, say, by either shareholders or the CEO. It begins by focusing on the separation of ownership and control, discussing how and why the two separated in the corporate form. The focus in this section is mainly on the US experience. Section 3 then turns to developing an economic rationale for vesting control in a group rather than an individual. Section 4 returns to the comparison between the US and German models, exploring the question of which constituencies should be empowered to choose the board of directors. Section 5 discusses the perennial question of whether director independence is to be desired. Finally, while the bulk of this chapter focuses on the theory behind the statutory model, no discussion of the board of directors would be complete without a discussion of how boards so often fail to perform as intended. Section 6 therefore examines how boards fail and the reforms that have been tried to improve their performance.

2 BOARD FUNCTIONS

The roles and functions of the board depend in the first instance on the structure given the board by national (or, in the case of the USA, state) legislation. Although the details vary widely among nations, the US unitary board and the German dual board stand as exemplars of the basic statutory options for board governance. Beyond these statutory requirements, of course, best practice norms and other nonlegal considerations further refine the expected functions of the board.

---

[7] Delaware General Corporation Law § 141(a), Del. Code Ann., tit. 8 § 141(a) (2012) [hereinafter cited as DGCL]. To be sure, many state corporation codes permit shareholders of close corporations to depart from this command by either limiting the powers of the board of directors or even eliminating the board entirely, but the focus herein is on the governance of public corporations.

2.1 The Unitary Board

In the USA's federal system, primary responsibility for creating and regulating corporations is a matter for the states rather than the national government. Among the 50 states, of course, Delaware is far and away the most important. More than half of the corporations listed for trading on the New York Stock Exchange and nearly 60 percent of the Fortune 500 corporations are incorporated in Delaware. Because of the so-called "internal affairs doctrine"—a conflicts of law rule holding that corporate governance matters are controlled by the law of the state of incorporation—Delaware law thus controls the formation and governance of the vast bulk of important public corporations. The most important alternative to Delaware law is the American Bar Association's Model Business Corporation Act (MBCA), which has been adopted in whole by about half the states and in part by many others.

Despite the resulting potential for diversity, there is remarkable uniformity on the basics of board structure. A single board of directors is elected by the shareholders and charged with ultimate decision-making authority within the corporation. Beyond this statutory minimum, there are few housekeeping rules and those are mostly enabling. In most states, for example, there are no rules on board size, term limits, and similar issues.

Instead, the role and functions of the board have been defined mainly by nonlegal norms and expectations. Although the board's functions have therefore varied over time, today they can be sorted into three basic categories. These are management, oversight, and service. Although all three remain important aspects of a board's work, the recent trend has been to elevate the importance of monitoring at the expense of the others.

2.1.1 *Management*

If one looked solely to corporation statutes for guidance, one would assume that the board of directors plays a very active role in the corporation's management. Besides the general allocation of the conduct of the corporation's business and affairs to the board, corporation statutes include many specific mandates that only the board can fulfill. Approval by the board of directors is a statutory prerequisite, for example, to mergers and related transactions such as sales of all or substantially all corporate assets, the issuance of stock, distribution of dividends, and amendments to the articles of incorporation. Approval by the board of directors of related party transactions involving top managers or board members is a statutory option for substantially insulating such transactions from judicial review for fairness. The board typically has non-exclusive power to amend bylaws. And so on.

In fact, of course, the typical modern public corporation is too big for the board to manage on anything resembling a day-to-day basis. As discussed in Part 6.2, moreover, these days most board members are outsiders who have full-time jobs elsewhere and therefore can devote relatively little time to the running of the business for which they act as directors. As early as 1922, the Delaware Chancery Court therefore acknowledged that the directors' principal role was one of supervision and control, with the detailed conduct of the business being a matter that could properly be delegated to subordinate employees.[8]

---

[8] *Cahall v. Lofland*, 114 A. 224, 229 (1921), aff'd, 118 A. 1 (1922).

The formulation of typical modern corporation statutes reflects this shift. MBCA § 8.01(b), for example, provides that the "business and affairs of the corporation" shall be "managed under the direction of" the board.[9] This formulation is intended to make clear that the board's role is to formulate broad policy and oversee the subordinates who actually conduct the business day-to-day. In addition, the statute also provides that corporate powers may be exercised "under the [board's] authority."[10] This formulation allows the board to delegate virtually all management functions to senior corporate officers, who in turn of course will delegate most decisions to subordinate employees.

Even so, modern boards typically retain some managerial functions. Indeed, courts have held that some decisions are so important that the board of directors must make them.[11] In some states, such basic matters as filing a lawsuit[12] or executing a guarantee of another corporation's debts are viewed as extraordinary decisions reserved to the board.[13] In recent years, courts also have imposed substantial managerial responsibilities on the board of directors—especially its independent members—in connection with shareholder derivative litigation, conflict of interest transactions, and mergers and acquisitions.

Best practice also assigns important managerial roles to the board. Broad policy making or, at least, review and approval of major policies, for example, are board prerogatives. Boards are also responsible for hiring the top management team, especially the CEO, and setting their compensation.

2.1.2 Service

A diverse board that includes outsiders can provide a number of services to the top management team. Outsiders can provide access to networks to which insiders do not belong, thereby assisting the firm in gathering resources and obtaining business. Outside directors affiliated with financial institutions, for example, facilitate the firm's access to capital. In addition to simply providing a contact between the firm and the lender, the financial institution's representative can use his board membership to protect the lender's interests by more closely monitoring the firm than would be possible for an outsider. In turn, that reduction of risk should result in the lender accepting a lower return on its loans, thereby reducing the firm's cost of capital.

Another example is the politically connected board member, whose access to legislators and regulators may aid the firm in dealing with the government. Such board members not only assist with obtaining government contracts, but also with clearing red tape and providing the firm with political cover in times of trouble.

---

[9] Model Bus. Corp. Act Ann. § 8.01 [hereinafter cited as MBCA].   [10] Id.

[11] See *Lee v. Jenkins Bros.*, 268 F.2d 357, 365–66 (2d Cir. 1959) (officers have no apparent authority with respect to extraordinary matters, which are reserved to the board).

[12] Compare *Custer Channel Wing Corp. v. Frazer*, 181 F. Supp. 197 (S.D.N.Y. 1959) (president had authority to do so) with *Lloydona Peters Enters. v. Dorius*, 658 P.2d 1209 (Utah 1983) (no authority to do so); *Ney v. Eastern Iowa Tel. Co.*, 144 N.W. 383 (Iowa 1913) (no authority to do so with respect to the corporation's largest shareholder).

[13] Compare *Sperti Products, Inc. v. Container Corp. of Am.*, 481 S.W.2d 43 (Ken. App. 1972) (president had authority) with *First Nat'l Bank v. Cement Products Co.*, 227 N.W. 908 (Iowa 1929) (no authority to do so); *Burlington Indus., Inc. v. Foil*, 202 S.E.2d 591 (N.C. 1974) (president lacked authority, inter alia, because making such guarantees was not part of the corporations' ordinary business).

A core service provided by boards of directors, especially its outside members, is providing advice and counsel to the CEO. By virtue of being outsiders, the board members can offer the CEO alternative points of view. In particular, the board can serve as a source of outside expertise. Complex business decisions require knowledge in such areas as accounting, finance, management, and law. Members who possess expertise themselves or have access to credible external experts play an important role in the board's service function.

2.1.3 Monitoring Managers

Modern public corporations are characterized by a separation of ownership and control, which "produces a condition where the interests of owner and of ultimate manager may, and often do, diverge and where many of the checks which formerly operated to limit the use of power disappear."[14] Economists Michael Jensen and William Meckling later formalized this concern by developing the concept of agency costs,[15] which is now widely recognized as "the fundamental concern of corporate law" and governance.[16]

Agency costs arise because a firm's agents have incentives to shirk. Specifically, the principal reaps part of the value of hard work by the agent, but the agent receives all of the value of shirking. In a classic article, economists Armen Alchian and Harold Demsetz offered the useful example of two workers who jointly lift heavy boxes into a truck.[17] The marginal productivity of each worker is difficult to measure and their joint output cannot be separated easily into individual components, which makes obtaining information about a team member's productivity and appropriately rewarding or punishing it difficult and costly. In the absence of such information, however, the disutility of labor gives each team member an incentive to shirk because the individual's reward is unlikely to be closely related to conscientiousness.

Although agents have strong incentives to shirk once they enter into a contract with the principal, from an ex ante perspective they have strong incentives to agree to contract terms designed to prevent shirking. Bounded rationality and the potential for renegotiation, however, preclude firms and agents from entering into the complete contract necessary to prevent shirking by the latter. Instead, there must be some system of ex post governance by which firms detect and punish shirking. Accordingly, an essential economic function of management is monitoring the various inputs into the team effort: Management meters the marginal productivity of each team member and then takes steps to reduce shirking.

The process just described, of course, raises a new question, namely, who will monitor the monitors? In any organization, one must have some ultimate monitor who has sufficient incentives to ensure optimal productivity without having to be monitored. Otherwise, one ends up with a never-ending series of monitors monitoring lower level

---

[14] Adolf A. Berle & Gardiner C. Means, The Modern Corporation and Private Property 6 (1932).

[15] Michael C. Jensen & William H. Meckling, "Theory of the Firm: Managerial Behavior, Agency Costs and Ownership Structure", 3 J. Fin. Econ. 305 (1976).

[16] Kent Greenfield, "The Place of Workers in Corporate Law", 39 B.C. L. Rev. 283, 295 (1998). For an argument that agency cost theory can be "myopic" with respect to corporate governance regimes outside the "Anglo-Saxon context," see Ruth V. Aguilera, "Corporate Governance and Director Accountability: An Institutional Comparative Perspective", 16 Brit. J. Mgmt. S39, S41 (2005).

[17] Armen A. Alchian & Harold Demsetz, "Production, Information Costs, and Economic Organization", 62 Am. Econ. Rev. 777 (1972).

monitors.[18] Alchian and Demsetz solved this dilemma by consolidating the roles of ultimate monitor and residual claimant.[19] According to Alchian and Demsetz, if the constituent entitled to the firm's residual income is given final monitoring authority, he is encouraged to detect and punish shirking by the firm's other inputs because his reward will vary exactly with his success as a monitor.

Unfortunately, this elegant theory breaks down precisely where it would be most useful. Because of the separation of ownership and control, it simply does not describe the modern publicly held corporation.[20] As the corporation's residual claimants, the shareholders should act as the firm's ultimate monitors. But while the law provides shareholders with some enforcement and electoral rights, these are reserved for fairly extraordinary situations.[21] In general, shareholders of public corporations lack the legal right, the practical ability, and the desire to exercise the kind of control necessary for meaningful monitoring of the corporation's agents.[22] As a result, the legal system evolved various adaptive responses to the ineffectiveness of shareholder monitoring, establishing alternative accountability structures to punish and deter wrongdoing by firm agents, most notably the board of directors.[23]

2.1.4 *Shifting Priorities*

The relative balance between these functions has shifted over time. Survey data and other forms of fieldwork in the 1970s suggested that boards had a mainly advisory role. Survey data from the 1990s, by contrast, showed an emphasis on managerial functions in the sense

[18] See Ronald J. Gilson, "A Structural Approach to Corporations: The Case Against Defensive Tactics in Tender Offers", 33 Stan. L. Rev. 819, 835 (1981) (explaining that "the performance of management must also be monitored, and hiring yet another team of monitors merely recreates the problem one level removed"). As Professor Gilson points out, Dr. Seuss's story of the Hawtch-Hawtcher Bee-Watcher is both an entertaining and highly instructive parable illustrating this point. Id. at 835 n.61.

[19] See Alchian & Demsetz, *supra* note 17, at 783 (arguing that to best incentivize the ultimate monitor, that person should hold a bundle of five rights: "1) to be a residual claimant; 2) to observe input behavior; 3) to be the central party common to all contracts with inputs; 4) to alter the membership of the team; and 5) to sell these rights").

[20] See Thomas S. Ulen, "The Coasean Firm in Law and Economics", 18 J. Corp. L. 301, 312 (1993) ("The modern corporation is, by and large, a publicly-held corporation, and it is not at all clear that the Alchian–Demsetz theory is an apt description of that corporation.").

[21] See generally Michael P. Dooley, Controlling Giant Corporations: The Question of Legitimacy, in Corporate Governance: Past & Future 28, 38 (Henry G. Manne ed., 1982) (discussing "the limited governance role assigned to shareholders.").

[22] Whether the rising tide of shareholder activism requires that the claim made in the text be revised is a question beyond the assigned scope of this chapter. The phenomenon of shareholder activism, however, is one the author has discussed at length elsewhere. See, e.g., Stephen M. Bainbridge, Director Primacy, in Research Handbook on the Economics of Corporate Law 17 (Claire A. Hill & Brett H. McDonnell eds., 2012); Stephen M. Bainbridge, Shareholder Activism in the Obama Era, in Perspectives on Corporate Governance 217 (F. Scott Kieff & Troy A. Paredes eds., 2010); Stephen M. Bainbridge, "Director Primacy and Shareholder Disempowerment", 119 Harv. L. Rev. 1735 (2006); Stephen M. Bainbridge, "The Case for Limited Shareholder Voting Rights", 53 UCLA L. Rev. 601 (2006).

[23] See Oliver E. Williamson, The Economic Institutions of Capitalism: Firms, Markets, Relational Contracting 306 (1985) (arguing that the board of directors "arises endogenously, as a means by which to safeguard the investments" of shareholders).

of broad policy making and setting strategy. By the end of the 1990s, survey data showed that boards were becoming active and independent monitors of the top management team.[24] What drove this shift?

Although the modern understanding of the board's role and function has no single parent, if one were to insist on finding someone to whom to give the bulk of the credit—or blame—the leading candidate would be Professor Melvin Eisenberg. In *The Structure of the Corporation*,[25] "perhaps the most important work on corporate law since Berle and Means's *The Modern Corporation and Private Property*,"[26] Eisenberg argued that boards were essentially passive, with most of their functions captured by senior executives. According to Eisenberg, the board's principal remaining function was selection and supervision of the firm's chief executive. Eisenberg contended, moreover, that most boards failed adequately to perform even that residual task.

As a solution, Eisenberg articulated a corporate governance model that explicitly separated the task of managing large publicly held corporations from that of monitoring those who do the managing. In this monitoring model, directors did not undertake decision making or policy making, which were assigned to senior management. Instead, the board's principal function was to monitor the performance of the company's senior executives. Other functions such as advising the CEO, authorizing major corporate actions, and exercising control over decision making were of minor importance or were merely pro forma.

Eisenberg's model proved highly influential. It informed the role set out for boards of directors in the American Law Institute's *Principles of Corporate Governance: Analysis and Recommendations*.[27] Aspects of his proposals, such as shifting responsibility for interacting with the auditor from management to the audit committee, have long been incorporated into stock exchange listing standards.[28] As early as the late 1970s, guides to corporate governance best practices had widely adopted the monitoring model.[29] Indeed, the monitoring model

---

[24] Renée B. Adams et al., "The Role of Boards of Directors in Corporate Governance: A Conceptual Framework and Survey", 48 J. Econ. Lit. 58, 64–65 (2010).

[25] Melvin Aron Eisenberg, The Structure of the Corporation 139–41 (1976).

[26] Dalia Tsuk Mitchell, "Status Bound: The Twentieth Century Evolution of Directors' Liability", 5 N.Y.U. J. L. & Bus. 63 (2009).

[27] See Evelyn Brody, "The Board of Nonprofit Organizations: Puzzling Through the Gaps Between Law and Practice", 76 Fordham L. Rev. 521, 529–30 (2007) ("The ALI articulated and embraced the independent-board monitoring model, under which an unconflicted board oversees a separate staff that carries out day-to-day operations.").

[28] See generally Stephen M. Bainbridge, The Complete Guide to Sarbanes-Oxley: Understanding How Sarbanes-Oxley Affects Your Business 178–81 (2007) (describing stock exchange listing standards governing audit committees).

[29] See generally Melvin A. Eisenberg, "The Board of Directors and Internal Control", 19 Cardozo L. Rev. 237, 239 (1997) (opining that "the monitoring model of the board has been almost universally accepted"). Several key sources of best practice embraced the model. In 1978, for example, the American Bar Association's Section of Business Law promulgated a Corporate Director's Guidebook that embraced an Eisenberg-like model in which the management and monitoring of management roles were separated, with the latter task being assigned to a board comprised mainly of outside directors. ABA Section of Corporation, "Banking and Business Law, Corporate Director's Guidebook", 33 Bus. Law. 1591, 1619–28 (1978). A formal statement by the Business Roundtable likewise adopted the monitoring model. "Statement of the Business Roundtable: The Role and Composition of the Board of Directors of the Large Publicly Owned Corporation", 33 Bus. Law. 2083 (1978). The absorption of the monitoring model into generally accepted best practice continued throughout the 1990s. See Ira M. Millstein & Paul W. MacAvoy, "The Active Board of Directors and Performance of the Large Publicly Traded Corporation", 98 Colum. L. Rev. 1283, 1288–89 (1998) (reviewing best practice guidelines).

quickly "became conventional wisdom, endorsed by the Chairman of the SEC, the corporate bar, and even the Business Roundtable."[30] By 1997, Eisenberg thus was able to declare that "key structural elements of the monitoring model—including a board that has at least a majority of independent directors, and audit, nominating, and compensation committees—[were] already well-established."[31]

The monitoring model of the board's function received further boosts in the major federal corporate governance laws passed in the wake of the Enron scandal and the subsequent financial crisis of 2007–2008. In the wake of the former and the concurrent bursting of the dot-com bubble, Congress passed the Sarbanes–Oxley Act, much of which was intended to require directors to be more effective monitors of corporate management.[32] The post-financial crisis Dodd–Frank Act likewise "includes significant governance reforms designed to enhance director oversight of compensation and risk."[33]

2.1.5 Critiquing the Monitoring Model

There is an inherent conflict among these roles. Suppose the CEO comes to the board for advice on a proposed project. The board advises the CEO to go forward with the proposal, but the project thereafter fails miserably. The board's role in the original decision inevitably compromises its ability to evaluate and, if necessary, discipline the CEO. The monitoring model seeks to avoid this problem by giving primacy to the board's oversight role.

Yet, in doing so, the monitoring model raises its own set of problems. Do we really want to block boards from playing advisory and service roles? Can we really disentangle those roles from monitoring? Does a focus on monitoring bring its own costs?

2.1.5.1 The Overlap between Monitoring and Management

Eisenberg's somewhat unique theory of corporate law treats it as a species of constitutional law.[34] If we pursue the analogy, his monitoring model can be understood as a separation of powers doctrine. The board and management are individual branches of the corporate government, with clearly delineated duties, which must be kept strictly separate in order to maintain the system of checks and balances on which organizational accountability and thus organizational legitimacy depend.

In practice, however, the line between management and monitoring is fuzzy at best. This is so because while monitoring the performance of senior executives is the board's major function, that task necessarily involves activities best described as managing the corporation.

If the board terminates the CEO due to lagging corporate performance, we might call that a pure example of the monitoring function. If the board terminates the CEO because

---

[30] Jeffrey N. Gordon, "The Rise of Independent Directors in the United States, 1950–2005: Of Shareholder Value and Stock Market Prices", 59 Stan. L. Rev. 1465, 1518 (2007).

[31] Eisenberg, *supra* note 29.

[32] See Renee M. Jones & Michelle Welsh, "Toward a Public Enforcement Model for Directors' Duty of Oversight", 45 Vand. J. Transnat'l L. 343, 346 (2012) ("The monitoring model forms the basis of the Sarbanes-Oxley reforms that sought to strengthen the hand of independent directors vis-à-vis corporate management.").

[33] Id. at 399 n.279.   [34] Eisenberg, *supra* note 25, at 1.

it believes the lagging performance resulted from bad policy decisions by the CEO, that action still fairly could be called monitoring but it also begins to take on managerial aspects. If finding a new CEO whose policy preferences are aligned with those of the board drives the recruitment process, that action takes on an even greater managerial aspect. Providing leadership and guidance to an interim CEO during the interregnum before a new permanent CEO is found also is a common board role, but again is more managerial than oversight in nature.

Not all disciplinary actions rise to the level of termination, of course. In fact, it seems certain that most do not. This is critical because lesser punishments can become almost impossible to distinguish from management. If the board instructs the CEO to change from one policy to another, for example, that order is just as much a management decision as when the CEO instructs a subordinate to do so.

Not only are the two roles almost impossible to untangle, but it also seems clear that performing a management role improves the board's oversight function. On the one hand, the very presence of independent directors who must give their approval to major corporate decisions should go a long way toward encouraging managers to make better and more faithful decisions.

> The mere fact that the top executives know they have to make formal presentations about key issues on a regular basis to an audience that may probe and criticize, and that has the power to remove them, elicits a great deal of valuable behavior. Executives gather facts more carefully and completely, make ideas and judgments more explicit, anticipate and deal with competing considerations, and find modes of articulation that can withstand scrutiny outside the inner circle. The consequence of all these efforts to better "explain and sell" the executive viewpoint may well be to clarify strategic thinking and improve decision-making. . . . Similarly, the fact the top executives know they have to present a proposed major financing, business acquisition, or compensation plan to a board that will ask questions and has power to say "yes" or "no" will tend to limit the range of proposals that the executives dare propose and push them somewhat closer and more reliably toward plans that benefit shareholders. The impact is valuable, even if clearly imperfect.[35]

On the other, managing also makes directors better informed. When the board engages in policy and business strategy decisions, the information the board must gather to make an informed choice inevitably also is relevant to the board's overall evaluation of management's performance.

In the real world, management and monitoring thus are inextricably intertwined. As we have seen, both corporation statutes and case law assign a multitude of managerial functions to the board, with best practice assigning even more. Boards are thus involved in a host of basic corporate decisions, including entering and exiting major lines of business, approving securities offerings or major borrowing, mergers and acquisitions, payment of dividends, risk management, disclosure, auditing, and so on. In many of these cases, of course, the board is reviewing proposals made by management. Because the power to review is the power to decide, the board in these cases is effectively deciding whether the proposal has enough merit to go forward. The board's role in these decisions is thus an executive and

---

[35] Robert C. Clark, Corporate Law 280–81 (1986).

managerial one, rather than one of mere oversight. As a result, even Eisenberg concedes "the board also has important decision-making functions."[36]

2.1.5.2 *Focusing Solely on Monitoring Undermines Other Board Functions*

A slightly different concern arises because the monitoring model contemplates a sort of juridical role for the board, which implies a more formal relationship between the board and management than should or does take place in the real world. Rather than focusing on hiring and firing the CEO, boards typically have a much more richly textured role. Individual directors pass concerns onto the CEO, for example, who in turn bounces ideas off board members. Indeed, even when it comes to discipline, real-world practice likely differs from the formality of the monitoring model. Rather than struggling to overcome the collective action problems that impede firing a CEO, for example, an individual director may try to obtain better performance through a private reprimand. Such seemingly mild sanctions often can be effective without the shaming aspects associated with more formalized disciplinary actions.

2.1.5.3 *Monitoring Can Result in Adversarial Relations*

Finally, requiring boards to focus almost exclusively on monitoring encourages directors to engage in adversarial forms of oversight. Information is the coin of the realm in the world of corporate boards. The more information boards have, the better they are able to carry out their quasi-managerial functions such as advising senior managers, making major policy decisions, and providing networking services. More and higher quality information, of course, also empowers directors to be more effective in their oversight capacity.

The trouble is that the increasing use of independent directors—as explained in section 6.1 below—means that outsiders dominate modern boards. Because these outsiders lack the sort of informal information networks that employment by or routine business dealing with the firm would provide, there is an inherent information asymmetry between modern boards and the top management team. As we will see, outsiders increasingly can rely on external sources of information for some of what they need, but they still remain dependent on management for much key information.

Because information can be used to management's detriment in the board's oversight capacity, however, management has an incentive to use strategically its position as an informational chokepoint. This inherent incentive for managers to withhold information from the board may force the latter to make the difficult decision of whether their firm's unique circumstances counsel weaker oversight and better managerial services by board members or stronger oversight and a less effective managerial role on the board's part. By demanding a strong monitoring role by the outside directors, however, the monitoring model impedes boards from making such tradeoffs. Instead, it pushes the board toward an adversarial relationship with management, which further incentivizes the latter to exercise discretion with respect to the information allowed to reach the board. Obviously, managers will be loath to pass on bad news. Even good news, however, will be massaged, phrased, and packaged, not so as to aid the board in making decisions but to cast management in the best possible light. Ironically, the adversarial relations potentially arising from adherence to the monitoring

---

[36] Eisenberg, *supra* note 31, at 239.

model thus not only make it more difficult for the board to carry out its managerial functions; they also make it harder for the board to serve as an effective monitor.

The aggressive oversight contemplated by the monitoring model may have even more deleterious effects on the management-board relationship than just the perpetuation of information asymmetries. A certain amount of cognitive tension in the board–top management team relationship is beneficial to the extent that it promotes the exercise of critical evaluative judgment by the former. Groups that are too collegial run the risk of submitting to groupthink and various other decision-making errors.[37] If aggressive monitoring fosters an adversarial relation between directors and managers, however, this beneficial form of conflict may transform into more harmful forms. At best, rigid adherence to the monitoring model may transform a collaborative and collegial relationship into one that is cold and distant. At worst, it can promote adversarial relations that result in destructive interpersonal conflict. Adversarial relations between two groups tend to encourage each group to circle the wagons and become defensive vis-à-vis the other. They encourage zero sum gamesmanship rather than collaboration. They divert energies into unproductive areas.

2.1.5.4 *Summary*

In sum, one size does not fit all. The preceding assessment does not deny that the monitoring is a key board function. It does not even deny that monitoring is first among equals. Instead, it simply shows that one size does not fit all.

Firms differ. Every firm has a unique culture, traditions, and competitive environment. A startup with inexperienced entrepreneurs needs an advisory board more than a monitoring one. A company in crisis needs board leadership more than oversight. A well-run, mature corporation staffed by managers with a penchant for hard, faithful work benefits most from a board that provides benevolent oversight and a sympathetic sounding board.

Likewise, different firms have differing arrays of accountability mechanisms. The monitoring board, after all, is not the only mechanism by which management's performance is assessed and rewarded or punished. The capital and product markets within which the firm functions, the internal and external markets for managerial services, the market for corporate control, incentive compensation systems, auditing by outside accountants, are just some of the ways in which management is held accountable for its performance. The importance of the board's monitoring role in a given firm depends in large measure on the extent to which these other forces are allowed to function. For example, managers of a firm with strong takeover defenses are less subject to the constraining influence of the market for corporate control than are those of a firm with no takeover defenses. The former needs a strong monitoring board more than does the latter.

2.1.6 *Unitary Boards Elsewhere*

In addition to the US, the unitary board is the exclusive form or predominant form in a majority of European Union member states.[38] Board functions in EU states following the

---

[37] See generally Stephen M. Bainbridge, "Why a Board? Group Decisionmaking in Corporate Governance", 55 Vand. L. Rev. 1 (2002).

[38] Chris A. Mallin, Corporate Governance 161–62 (3d ed. 2010).

unitary board model tend to be similar to that of boards in the US. The UK's Corporate Governance Code, for example, provides that:

> The board's role is to provide entrepreneurial leadership of the company within a framework of prudent and effective controls which enables risk to be assessed and managed. The board should set the company's strategic aims, ensure that the necessary financial and human resources are in place for the company to meet its objectives and review management performance. The board should set the company's values and standards and ensure that its obligations to its shareholders and others are understood and met.[39]

Although that description seems to contemplate a more managerial role than is the case in US practice, the Code makes clear that the primary role of outside directors is one of monitoring management:

> Non-executive directors should scrutinise the performance of management in meeting agreed goals and objectives and monitor the reporting of performance. They should satisfy themselves on the integrity of financial information and that financial controls and systems of risk management are robust and defensible. They are responsible for determining appropriate levels of remuneration of executive directors and have a prime role in appointing and, where necessary, removing executive directors, and in succession planning.[40]

As is increasingly the case with US boards of directors, moreover, UK boards typically have a number of key committees—such as audit, executive remuneration, and nominating—consisting of non-executive directors.[41] These committees serve to separate the managerial and monitoring functions.

In contrast, Japan also follows a unitary board model, but the functions and composition of Japanese boards differ significantly from the US model. Directors of Japanese corporations typically are insiders, chosen from the ranks of top and middle management.[42] As one might therefore expect, the board's role is less one of monitoring management and more one of achieving consensus on strategic and managerial planning.[43] We have already discussed the advantages and disadvantages of a board focus on monitoring. The advantages and disadvantages of independent-dominated versus insider-dominated boards are discussed *infra* section 5.2.

Many other East Asian economies exhibit high concentrations of corporate control by family groups. In these economies, the controlling shareholder group generally chooses board members.[44]

---

[39] Financial Reporting Council, The UK Corporate Governance Code 8 (2012).   [40] Id. at 10.

[41] Mallin, *supra* note 38, at 168–69.

[42] Takahiro Yasui, Corporate Governance in Japan, in Corporate Governance in Asia: A Comparative Perspective 123, 124 (OECD ed., 2001).

[43] Id.

[44] Il Chong Nam et al., Comparative Corporate Governance Trends in Asia, in Corporate Governance in Asia: A Comparative Perspective 85, 96 (OECD ed., 2001).

2.2 The Dual Board

There are a number of countries whose corporate governance regime departs from the unitary board model, but the best known and most highly developed version is part of the German system known as codetermination. German law in fact has four different statutory models of codetermination, each regulating a different class of corporations.[45] Although some other member states of the European Union also have some form of employee representation, unless otherwise indicated, discussion of codetermination in this section focuses on the 1976 German codetermination statute, which applies to corporations having more than 2,000 employees.

2.2.1 The German Dual Board

Codetermination actually has two principal components: the dual board and works councils. Only the former is of interest for our purposes.[46] The dual board structure consists of a supervisory board that appoints a managing board, with the latter actively operating the firm. Workers are represented only on the former.

The supervisory board concept is difficult to translate into terms familiar to those trained exclusively in US forms of corporate governance. Its statutory mandate is primarily concerned with the appointment and supervision of the managing board.[47] In theory, employees and shareholders are equally represented on the supervisory board. In practice, however, the board is often controlled either by the firm's managers or a dominant shareholder.[48] One of the employee representatives must be from management, and shareholders are entitled to elect the chairman of the board, who has the power to break tie votes.[49] If push comes to shove, which it reportedly rarely does, shareholders thus retain a slight but potentially critical edge.[50]

The powers of the supervisory board are limited. It appoints the members of the corporation's management board and its outsider auditors, calls shareholder meetings, and has the right to inspect the company's books and records. It must approve conflict of interest transactions involving members of the management board, but otherwise has no power to make either operational or strategic decisions.[51]

---

[45] Klaus J. Hopt, "Labor Representation on Corporate Boards: Impacts and Problems for Corporate Governance and Economic Integration in Europe", 14 Int'l. Rev. L. & Econ. 203, 204 (1994).

[46] Works councils are concerned with issues affecting individual plants, rather than the whole firm. In theory at least, works councils have considerable control over shop floor and other issues that affect the personnel of a particular plant. Motohiro Morishima et al., Industrial Democracy in Selected Pacific Rim and European Countries 21–23, presented to the Conference on Industrial Democracy Issues for the 21st Century, Univ. of Illinois, April 12, 1995. Depending on the nature of the issue at hand, the council may be entitled to provision of information, consultation with management, or codetermination. Id. at 21. Their statutory mandate ranges from such minor issues as individual personnel grievances to such major concerns as the introduction of new technology or plant closings. Id. at 21–22. There is empirical data suggesting that works councils have a significantly negative impact on productivity. John L. Cotton, Employee Involvement: Methods for Improving Performance and Work Attitudes 121 (1993).

[47] Hopt, *supra* note 45, at 204.   [48] Id.   [49] Morishima et al., *supra* note 46, at 23.

[50] Id.   [51] See generally Franklin A. Gevurtz, Global Issues in Corporate Law 67–68 (2006).

Although the dual board structure thus formally separates management and monitoring by assigning these functions to two different boards, there are in fact many commonalities between unitary and dual board systems. Just as the unitary board appoints the top management team, the supervisory board appoints the top managers making up the management board. Just as a unitary board supervises and monitors the top management team, the supervisory board oversees the managerial board. Just as the unitary board is ultimately responsible for the accuracy of the corporation's financial disclosures and oversight of internal controls, so is the supervisory board.[52] As a result, it has been suggested that "much of the German dual-board structure can be seen as a mere variation on the basic locus of authority in firms, creating management and supervisory boards where American firms create officers and directors."[53] It is for this reason that much of the discussion below of the economics of boards should apply equally well to the dual board structure as to the unitary board model on which the discussion focuses.

2.2.2 Dual Boards Elsewhere

Dual board structures are most common in continental Europe. Besides Germany, Austria, Denmark, and the Netherlands mandate dual boards. A number of other EU member nations, most notably France, allow companies the option of choosing either a unitary or dual board.[54]

2.2.3 Why a Dual Board?

Given the commonalities between unitary and dual board systems, why did dual boards come into existence and why do they persist? At least in the case of Germany, politics appears to be part—if not the complete—answer. Specifically, the German system of codetermination of which the dual board is a key component reflects a political bargain between labor and capital.[55] This bargain has several dimensions. In an earlier era, when the German economy was capital-poor, codetermination represented a means of encouraging workers to invest in firm-specific human capital despite comparatively low wages. At present, codetermination reflects a political bargain in which employees' pensions are not well funded, but employees have some voice in corporate governance.

Having said that, however, there may be an economic rationale for the dual board. Renée Adams and Daniel Ferreira argue that while the monitoring and service functions of a unitary board appear to "complement each other, board uses any information the CEO provides both to make better recommendations and to implement better decisions."[56] In practice, however, because the CEO is less likely to provide information to actively monitoring boards, "shareholders may optimally elect a less independent or friendlier board that does

---

[52] See generally Mallin, *supra* note 38, at 162–63 (describing commonalities).

[53] Sean J. Griffith, "Governing Systemic Risk: Towards a Governance Structure for Derivatives Clearinghouses", 61 Emory L. J. 1153, 1235 (2012).

[54] Mallin, *supra* note 38, at 213 (listing major EU member nations by board type).

[55] See generally Mark J. Roe, Strong Managers, Weak Owners: The Political Roots of American Corporate Finance 213–15 (1994) (discussing the political origins of codeterminaton).

[56] Renée B. Adams & Daniel Ferreira, "A Theory of Friendly Boards", 62 J. Fin. 217, 218 (2007).

not monitor the CEO too intensively" so as to promote the board's other roles.[57] The dual board structure eliminates the need for boards to make trade-offs between their various roles by limiting the supervisory board's role to monitoring, while managerial and service functions are assigned to the management board.

Yet, this argument does not justify favoring the dual over the unitary board structure. As Adams and Ferreira note, "the role of the audit committee in the sole board systems of the United States and the United Kingdom may be similar to that of supervisory boards."[58] Accordingly, the choice between unitary and dual boards appears to be mainly a function of historical accident, inertia, or political bargaining rather than one of economic advantage.

3 Why a Board?

Ownership and control rights typically go hand in hand. A homeowner may eject trespassers, for example, even using force in appropriate cases. A principal is entitled to control his agent. Each partner is entitled to equal rights in the management of the partnership business.

In the corporation, however, ownership and control are decisively separated. As we have seen, for example, the Delaware General Corporation Law provides that the corporation's "business and affairs . . . shall be managed by or under the direction of the board of directors."[59] In contrast, the firm's nominal owners—the shareholders—exercise virtually no control over either day-to-day operations or long-term policy. Shareholder voting rights are limited to the election of directors and a few relatively rare matters such as approval of charter or bylaw amendments, mergers, sales of substantially all of the corporation's assets, and voluntary dissolution. As a formal matter, moreover, only the election of directors and amending the bylaws do not require board approval before shareholder action is possible. In practice, of course, even the election of directors (absent a proxy contest) is predetermined by virtue of the existing board's power to nominate the next year's board. The shareholders' limited control rights thus are almost entirely reactive rather than proactive.

These direct restrictions on shareholder power are supplemented by a host of other rules that indirectly prevent shareholders from exercising significant influence over corporate decision making. Three sets of statutes are especially noteworthy: (1) disclosure requirements pertaining to large holders; (2) shareholder voting and communication rules; and (3) insider trading and short swing profits rules. These laws affect shareholders in two respects. First, they discourage the formation of large stock blocks. Second, they discourage communication and coordination among shareholders.[60]

Shareholders not only lack significant managerial rights, they also lack most of the other categories of rights associated with control. Shareholders have no right to use or possess corporate property, for example. As one court explained, "even a sole shareholder has no independent right which is violated by trespass upon or conversion of the corporation's

---

[57] Id.   [58] Id. at 235.   [59] DGCL § 141(a).
[60] See generally Stephen M. Bainbridge, "The Politics of Corporate Governance", 18 Harv. J. L. & Pub. Pol'y 671 (1995).

property."[61] Indeed, to the extent that possessory and control rights are the indicia of a property right, the board of directors is a better candidate for identification as the corporation's owner than are the shareholders. As an early New York opinion put it, "the directors in the performance of their duty possess [the corporation's property], and act in every way as if they owned it."[62]

This raises two distinct questions. First, why do we separate ownership and control in the corporate form? Second, why is control ultimately vested in a board of directors rather than, say, the CEO? Taken together, the answers to those questions help us understand the economic logic of the laws mandating that corporations have boards of directors.

3.1 Why Separate Ownership and Control?

3.1.1 An Historical Perspective

According to the widely accepted Berle and Means's account, ownership and control separated as a consequence of the development of large capital-intensive industrial corporations during the late nineteenth century. These firms required investments far larger than a single entrepreneur or family could provide, which could be obtained only by attracting funds from many investors. Because small investors needed diversification, even very wealthy individuals limited the amount they would put at risk in any particular firm, further fragmenting share ownership. The modern separation of ownership and control was the direct result of these forces, or so the story goes.

Professor Walter Werner aptly referred to Berle and Means's account as the "erosion doctrine." According to their version of history, there was a time when the corporation behaved as it was supposed to:

> The shareholders who owned the corporation controlled it. They elected a board of directors to whom they delegated management powers, but they retained residual control, uniting control and ownership. In the nation's early years the states created corporations sparingly and regulated them strictly. The first corporations, run by their proprietors and constrained by law, exercised state-granted privileges to further the public interest. The states then curtailed regulation . . ., and this Eden ended. The corporation expanded into a huge concentrate of resources. Its operation vitally affected society, but it was run by managers who were accountable only to themselves and could blink at obligations to shareholders and society.[63]

The erosion doctrine, however, rested on a false account of the history of corporations. Werner explained that economic separation of ownership and control in fact was a feature of American corporations almost from the beginning of the nation:

> Banks, and the other public-issue corporations of the [antebellum] period, contained the essential elements of big corporations today: a tripartite internal government structure, a share market that dispersed shareholdings and divided ownership and control, and tendencies to

---

[61] *W. Clay Jackson Enters., Inc. v. Greyhound Leasing & Fin. Corp.*, 463 F. Supp. 666, 670 (D.P.R. 1979).
[62] *Manson v. Curtis*, 119 N.E. 559, 562 (N.Y. 1918).
[63] Walter Werner, "Corporation Law in Search of Its Future", 81 Colum. L. Rev. 1611, 1612 (1981).

centralize management in full-time administrators and to diminish participation of outside directors in management.[64]

In contrast to Berle and Means's account, which rests on technological changes during the nineteenth century, this alternative account rests on the early development of secondary trading markets. Such markets existed in New York and Philadelphia by the beginning of the nineteenth century. The resulting liquidity of corporate stock made it an especially attractive investment, which in turn made selling stock to the public an attractive financing mechanism. Stocks were purchased by a diversified and dispersed clientele,[65] including both institutions and individuals. The national taste for speculation also played a part in the early growth of the secondary trading markets and, in turn, to dispersal of stock ownership. As a result of these economic forces, ownership and control separated not at the end of the nineteenth century, but at its beginning.

If this version of history is correct, there never was a time in which unity of control and ownership was a central feature of US corporations. To the contrary, it appears that ownership and control separated at a very early date. In turn, this analysis suggests that the separation of ownership and control may be an essential economic characteristic of such corporations.

3.1.2 A Contractarian Rationale for Separating Ownership and Control

The dominant model of the corporation in legal scholarship is the so-called nexus of contracts theory. "Contract," as used in this context, is not limited to relationships constituting legal contracts. Instead, contractarians use the word contract to refer generally to long-term relationships characterized by asymmetric information, bilateral monopoly, and opportunism. The relationship between shareholders and creditors of a corporation is contractual in this sense, even though there is no single document we could identify as a legally binding contract through which they are in privity.

In a sense, the corporation *is* the nexus of the various contracts among the factors of production comprising the firm. This standard account has a considerable virtue—it emphasizes that the firm is not an entity but rather a set of explicit and implicit contracts establishing rights and obligations among various factors of production. Yet, the standard account fails to capture the more important sense in which the corporation *has* a nexus. Put another way, the standard account understates the role of fiat in corporate governance.

---

[64] Id. at 1637.

[65] A slightly different version of this story is told by Herbert Hovenkamp, who argues that separation of ownership and control is less a function of firm size than of firm complexity. Under this model, neither technological change nor corporate financing was the dispositive factor. Rather, ownership and control separated when, because of a high degree of vertical integration, firms became sufficiently complex to require professional managers. Herbert Hovenkamp, Enterprise and American Law: 1836–1937 357–60 (1991). Notice the close fit between this interpretation and the economic model advanced in this chapter. Under both, the unique attribute of modern public corporations is the hierarchical decision-making structure adopted as an adaptive response to organizational complexity.

3.1.2.1 The Corporation Is a Nexus

Corporate constituents contract not with each other but with the corporation. A bond indenture thus is a contract between the corporation and its creditors,[66] an employment agreement is a contract between the corporation and its workers,[67] and a collective bargaining agreement is a contract between the corporation and the union representing its workers.[68] If the contract is breached on the corporate side, it will be the entity that is sued in most cases rather than the individuals who decided not to perform. If the entity loses, damages typically will be paid out of its assets and earnings rather than out of those individuals' pockets.

One cannot dismiss all of this as mere reification, as some have done. If there were no nexus, employment contracts would cascade—looking rather like a standard hierarchical organization chart—with each employee contracting with his superior. (Debt contracts would be even more complex.) Such a cascade would be costly to assemble, if not impossible.[69] Indeed, most corporate constituents lack any mechanism for communicating with other constituencies of the firm—let alone contract with one another. Instead, each constituency contracts with a central nexus. Accordingly, constituencies must be (and are) linked to the nexus and not each other.

3.1.2.2 The Corporation Has a Nexus

Alchian and Demsetz famously claimed that the firm "has no power of fiat, no authority, no disciplinary action any different in the slightest degree from ordinary market contracting between any two people."[70] Accordingly, they argued, an employer's control over its employees differs not at all from the power of a consumer over the grocer with whom the consumer does business.

If fiat is not an essential attribute of "firm-ishness," the firm would be just a legal fiction describing the space within which the set of contracts are worked out. Power exists within firms, however, and it matters. The corporation has a nexus—and that nexus wields a power of fiat different from that of a consumer over a grocer. Indeed, fiat is the chief characteristic that distinguishes firms from markets. As Ronald Coase explained, firms emerge when it is efficient to substitute entrepreneurial fiat for the price mechanisms of the market.[71] One team member is empowered to constantly and, more important, unilaterally rewrite certain terms of the contract between the firm and its various constituents. By creating a central

---

[66] See, e.g., *Lorenz v. CSX Corp.*, 1 F.3d 1406, 1417 (3d Cir. 1993) ("It is well-established that a corporation does not have a fiduciary relationship with its debt security holders, as with its shareholders. The relationship between a corporation and its debentureholders is contractual in nature."); *Simons v. Cogan*, 549 A.2d 300, 303 (Del. 1988) (holding that "a convertible debenture represents a contractual entitlement to the repayment of a debt").

[67] See, e.g., *Berman v. Physical Med. Assocs.*, 225 F.3d 429, 433 (4th Cir. 2000) (holding that, "as to Berman's claims under the employment agreement and severance benefit agreement, only the corporation owed Berman a contractual duty").

[68] See *John Wiley & Sons, Inc. v. Livingston*, 376 U.S. 543, 546 (1964) (asking "whether the arbitration provisions of the collective bargaining agreement survived the Wiley-Interscience merger, so as to be operative against" successor corporation).

[69] Such a cascade also would be subject to opportunistic disassembly threats in which one or more of the contracting parties seeks to hold up the others.

[70] Alchian & Demsetz, *supra* note 17, at 777.

[71] Ronald Coase, "The Nature of the Firm", 4 Economica (n.s.) 386 (1937).

decision maker—a nexus—with the power of fiat, the firm thus substitutes ex post governance for ex ante contract.

Coordination need not imply fiat, as illustrated by the democratic decision-making processes of many partnerships and other small firms. In the public corporation, however, fiat is essential. All organizations must have some mechanism for aggregating the preferences of the organization's constituencies and converting them into collective decisions. In his important work *The Limits of Organization*,[72] Kenneth Arrow observed that such mechanisms fall out on a spectrum between "consensus" and "authority." A consensus-based decision-making process is one that uses "any reasonable and acceptable means of aggregating [the] individual interests" of the organization's constituents.[73] An authority-based decision-making system is one in which the organization creates a central agency to which all relevant information is transmitted and empowers that agency to make decisions binding the organization as a whole.

The choice between consensus and authority is driven by three considerations: access to information, member interests and preferences, and severity of collective action problems. Consensus-based governance systems work best when each decision maker has comparable access to information and shared interests and their decision-making process is unencumbered by serious collective action issues. In contrast, authority-based decision-making structures tend to arise where there are information asymmetries among potential decision makers, those decision makers have different interests, and the group suffers from significant collective action concerns.

With these criteria being specified, it should be self-evident that efficient corporate governance requires an authority-based decision-making structure. Consider the problems faced by shareholders, who are conventionally assumed to be the corporate constituency with the best claim on control of the decision-making apparatus. At the most basic level, the mechanical difficulties of achieving consensus amongst thousands of decision makers impede shareholders from taking an active role. Put another way, in large corporations, authority-based decision-making structures are desirable because of the potential for division and specialization of labor. Bounded rationality and complexity, as well as the practical costs of losing time when one shifts jobs, make it efficient for corporate constituents to specialize. Directors and managers specialize in the efficient coordination of other specialists. In order to reap the benefits of specialization, all other corporate constituents should prefer to specialize in functions unrelated to decision making, such as risk-bearing (shareholders) or labor (employees), delegating decision making to the board and senior management. This natural division of labor, however, requires that the chosen directors and officers be vested with discretion to make binding decisions. Separating ownership and control by vesting decision-making authority in a centralized nexus distinct from the shareholders and all other constituents is what makes the large public corporation feasible.

Even if one could overcome the seemingly intractable collective action problems plaguing shareholder decision making, the shareholders' widely divergent interests and distinctly different levels of information would still preclude active shareholder participation in corporate decision making. Although neoclassical economics assumes that shareholders

---

[72] Kenneth J. Arrow, The Limits of Organization 63–79 (1974).

[73] Id. at 69. American partnership law is a good example of a consensus-based decision-making structure. Michael P. Dooley, "Two Models of Corporate Governance", 47 Bus. Law. 461, 466–67 (1992).

come to the corporation with wealth maximization as their goal, and most presumably do so, once uncertainty is introduced it would be surprising if shareholder opinions did not differ on which course will maximize share value. More prosaically, shareholder investment time horizons are likely to vary from short-term speculation to long-term buy-and-hold strategies, which in turn is likely to result in disagreements about corporate strategy. Even more prosaically, shareholders in different tax brackets are likely to disagree about such matters as dividend policy, as are shareholders who disagree about the merits of allowing management to invest the firm's free cash flow in new projects.

As to Arrow's information condition, shareholders lack incentives to gather the information necessary to actively participate in decision making. A rational shareholder will expend the effort necessary to make informed decisions only if the expected benefits of doing so outweigh its costs. Given the length and complexity of corporate disclosure documents, the opportunity cost entailed in making informed decisions is both high and apparent. In contrast, the expected benefits of becoming informed are quite low, as most shareholders' holdings are too small to have significant effect on the vote's outcome. Corporate shareholders thus are rationally apathetic. Instead of exercising their voting rights, disgruntled shareholders typically adopt the so-called Wall Street Rule—it's easier to switch than fight—and sell out.[74]

The efficient capital markets hypothesis provides yet another reason for shareholders to eschew active participation in the governance process. If the market is a reliable indicator of performance, as the efficient capital markets hypothesis claims, investors can easily check the performance of companies in which they hold shares and compare their current holdings with alternative investment positions. An occasional glance at the stock market listings in the newspaper is all that is required. Because it is so much easier to switch to a new investment than to fight incumbent managers, a rational shareholder will not even care why a firm's performance is faltering. With the expenditure of much less energy than is needed to read corporate disclosure statements, he will simply sell his holdings in the struggling firm and move on to other investments.[75]

Consequently, it is hardly surprising that the modern public corporation's decision-making structure precisely fits Arrow's model of an authority-based decision-making system. Overcoming the collective action problems that prevent meaningful shareholder involvement would be difficult and costly, of course. Even if one could do so, moreover, shareholders lack both the information and the incentives necessary to make sound decisions on either operational or policy questions.[76] Under these conditions, it is "cheaper and more efficient to transmit all the pieces of information to a central place" and to have

---

[74] Again, the extent to which the growth of shareholder activism challenges this framework is beyond the scope of this chapter, but has been addressed in the works cited *supra* note 22.

[75] Finally, portfolio theory offers yet another justification for separating ownership and control. By virtue of their non-diversified investment in firm-specific human capital, managers bear part of the risk of firm failure. As the firm's residual claimants, however, shareholders also bear a portion of the risk associated with firm failure. Portfolio theory tells us that individual shareholders can minimize that risk through diversification, which managers cannot do with respect to their human capital. Separating ownership and control thus unbundles the risks associated with the firm and allocates each of those risks to the party who can bear it at the lowest cost. We regard this explanation as somewhat problematic, however, due to its managerialist overtones.

[76] Similar analyses apply to other corporate constituents on whose behalf claims to control of the decision-making apparatus might be made, such as employees or creditors.

the central office "make the collective choice and transmit it rather than retransmit all the information on which the decision is based."[77] Accordingly, shareholders will prefer to irrevocably delegate decision-making authority to some smaller group.

3.1.2.3 Locating the Nexus

Under conditions of asset specificity, bounded rationality, and opportunism, the ability to adapt becomes the central problem of organization. Contrary to Alchian and Demsetz's argument, in large public corporations, adaptation is effected by fiat.[78] This is so because, as we have seen, the necessity for a literal nexus—a center of power capable of exercising fiat—within the corporation follows as a matter of course from the asymmetries of information and interests among the corporation's various constituencies.

If the corporation has a nexus, however, where is it located? As we have seen, the Delaware code, like the corporate law of virtually every other state, gives us a clear answer: the corporation's "business and affairs . . . shall be managed by or under the direction of the board of directors."[79] Put simply, the board is the nexus.

Indeed, we can think of the corporation as a vehicle by which the board of directors hires capital by selling equity and debt securities to risk bearers with varying tastes for risk. The board of directors thus can be seen as a sui generis body serving as the nexus for the various contracts making up the corporation and whose powers flow not from shareholders alone but from the complete set of contracts constituting the firm. As an early New York decision put it, the board's powers are "original and undelegated."[80]

3.1.3 Consequences of Separating Ownership and Control

Modern scholars refer to the consequences of separating ownership and control as agency costs,[81] but Berle and Means had identified the basic problem over 40 years before the current terminology was invented: "The separation of ownership from control produces a condition where the interests of owner and of ultimate manager may, and often do, diverge."[82] To ask the question, "Will the board of directors use its control of the corporation to further the selfish interest of the board members rather than the best interests of the corporation's shareholders and other constituencies?," is to answer it. Given human nature, it would be surprising indeed if directors did not sometimes shirk or self-deal. Consequently, much of corporate law is best understood as a mechanism for constraining agency costs.

---

[77] Arrow, *supra* note 72, at 68–69.

[78] Obviously, fiat within firms has limits. Some choices are barred by contract, such as negative pledge covenants in bond indentures. Other choices may be barred by regulation or statute. Still other choices may be unattractive for business reasons, such as those with potentially adverse reputational consequences. Within such bounds, however, adaptation effected through fiat is the distinguishing characteristic of the firm.

[79] DGCL § 141(a). For a summary of comparable state corporation code provisions, see the commentary to MBCA § 8.01.

[80] *Manson v. Curtis*, 119 N.E. 559, 562 (N.Y. 1918).   [81] Jensen & Meckling, *supra* note 15.

[82] Berle & Means, *supra* note 14.

A narrow focus on agency costs, however, can easily distort one's understanding. In the first instance, corporate managers operate within a pervasive web of accountability mechanisms that substitute for monitoring by residual claimants. The capital and product markets, the internal and external employment markets, and the market for corporate control all constrain shirking by firm agents.

In the second, agency costs are the inescapable result of placing ultimate decision-making authority in the hands of someone other than the residual claimant. Because we could substantially reduce agency costs by eliminating discretion, but do not do so, one infers that discretion has substantial virtues. In a complete theory of the firm, neither discretion nor accountability can be ignored because both promote values essential to the survival of business organizations.[83] At the same time, however, the power to hold to account is ultimately the power to decide.[84] Managers cannot be made more accountable without undermining their discretionary authority. Establishing the proper mix of discretion and accountability thus emerges as the central corporate governance question.

Given the significant virtues of discretion, one ought not lightly interfere with management or the board's decision-making authority in the name of accountability. Because the separation of ownership and control mandated by US corporate law has a substantial insulating effect, by constraining shareholders both from reviewing most board decisions and from substituting their judgment for that of the board, that separation has a strong efficiency justification.

3.2 Why a Board? Why Not a CEO?

At the apex of the corporate hierarchy stands not a single individual but a collective—the board of directors. The legal rules governing the board of directors, moreover, put considerable emphasis on the need for collective rather than individual action.[85] A director "has no power of his own to act on the corporation's behalf, but only as one of a body of directors acting as a board,"[86] to cite just one example.

Why this emphasis on collective action? Put another way, why not vest the ultimate power of fiat in an individual autocrat rather than a collegial group?

The commentary to the MBCA's provisions on board meetings provides one answer:

> A well-established principle of corporate common law accepted by implication in the Model Act is that directors may act only at a meeting unless otherwise expressly authorized by statute. The underlying theory is that the consultation and exchange of views is an integral part of the functioning of the board.[87]

---

[83] Dooley, *supra* note 73, at 463–64.   [84] Arrow, *supra* note 72, 78.

[85] At one time, many states in fact required that the board have at least three members, although most have eliminated that requirement. MBCA § 8.03(a) cmt.

[86] Restatement (Second) of Agency § 14 C cmt (1958).

[87] MBCA § 8.20 cmt. An alternative explanation is suggested by Jeffrey Gordon's persuasive demonstration that voting within a corporation is subject to Arrow's impossibility theorem, in the sense that voting on most matters of day-to-day policy would result in cyclical majorities. Although we will rely more heavily on information and incentive-based arguments for the board's authority than does Gordon, he does present a convincing argument that corporate law's authority-based board of directors system is explicable in very large measure as a device for avoiding the cycling problem by restricting

The drafters' argument runs afoul of the old joke that a camel is a horse designed by a committee, yet their "underlying theory" is pervasively reflected in the statutory rules governing corporate boards.[88] The implicit preference for group decision making also finds support in two basic economic principles: bounded rationality and agency costs.[89]

3.2.1 The Board as an Adaptive Response to Bounded Rationality

Vesting decision-making authority in a group rather than a single individual is a high value-added adaptive response to the problem of bounded rationality. Decision making requires the use of scarce resources for four purposes: (1) observation, or the gathering of information; (2) memory, or the storage of information; (3) computation, or the manipulation of information; and (4) communication, or the transmission of information.[90] How do groups minimize these transaction costs vis-à-vis individual decision makers? Multiple

owner voice. Jeffrey N. Gordon, "Shareholder Initiative: A Social Choice and Game Theoretic Approach to Corporate Law", 60 U. Cin. L. Rev. 347 (1991).

[88] Many of these housekeeping rules doubtless seem formalistic or even a little silly, but the requirement that the board act only after meeting as a collective body actually has a sound economic basis. Work by experimental psychologists has found that group decision making, under certain circumstances, can be superior to decision making by individuals. Where evaluation of complex problems requiring the exercise of critical judgment is concerned, the evidence is clear that the performance of a group will be superior to that of the group's average member. This result has been confirmed by experiments requiring performance of a wide variety of tasks. See, e.g., Larry K. Michaelsen et al., "A Realistic Test of Individual versus Group Consensus Decision Making", 74 J. App. Psych. 834 (1989) (test taking in team learning settings); Marjorie E. Shaw, "A Comparison of Individuals and Small Groups in the Rational Solution of Complex Problems", 44 Am. J. Psych. 491 (1932) (puzzle solving); see generally Gayle W. Hill, "Group versus Individual Performance: Are N + 1 Heads Better than One?", 91 Psych. Bull. 517 (1982). For a detailed review of the evidence on group decision making, with applications to corporate law, see Bainbridge, *supra* note 37.

[89] There may also be a behavioral explanation for the board. Research in behavioral economics has identified a number of pervasive cognitive errors that bias decision making. Several of the identified decision-making biases seem especially pertinent to managerial decision making, especially the so-called overconfidence bias. The old joke about the camel being a horse designed by a committee captures the valid empirical observation that individuals are often superior to groups when it comes to matters requiring creativity. Research on brainstorming as a decision-making process, for example, confirms that individuals working alone generate a greater number of ideas than do groups, especially when the assigned task is "fanciful" rather than "realistic." Hill, *supra* note 88, at 527. Individuals often become wedded to their ideas, however, and fail to recognize flaws that others might identify. Peter M. Blau & W. Richard Scott, Formal Organizations 116–21 (1962). In contrast, there is a widely shared view that groups are superior at evaluative tasks. Group decision making presumably checks individual overconfidence by providing critical assessment and alternative viewpoints, which is consistent with the standard account of the board's function. Recall that our taxonomy identified three basic board roles: monitoring, service, and resource gathering. At the core of the board's service role is providing advice and counsel to the senior management team, especially the CEO. At the intersection of the board's service and monitoring roles is the provision of alternative points of view. Put another way, most of what boards do requires the exercise of critical evaluative judgment, but not creativity. Even the board's policy making role entails judgment more than creativity, as the board is usually selecting between a range of options presented by subordinates. The board serves to constrain subordinates who have become wedded to their plans and ideas, rather than developing such plans in the first instance.

[90] Roy Radner, "Bounded Rationality, Indeterminacy, and the Theory of the Firm", 106 Econ. J. 1360, 1363 (1996).

sources of information may make it less costly to gather information, but it seems unlikely that directors qua directors do much to facilitate the observation process. Any such savings, moreover, likely are offset by increased communication costs. By decentralizing both access to information and decision-making power, group decision making requires additional resources and imposes additional delays on the decision-making process.

The relevant advantages of group decision making therefore likely arise with respect to either memory and/or computation. As to the former, groups develop a sort of collective memory that consists not only of the sum of individual memories but also an awareness of who knows what. Consequently, institutional memory is superior when the organization is structured as a set of teams rather than as a mere aggregate of individuals. There is some laboratory evidence, moreover, that the collective memory of groups leads to higher quality output.[91] Group members, for example, seem to specialize in memorizing specific aspects of complex repetitive tasks.

As to the relationship between group decision making and computation-based costs, an actor can economize limited cognitive resources in two ways. First, by adopting institutional governance structures designed to promote more efficient decision making. Second, by invoking shortcuts, i.e., heuristic problem-solving decision-making processes. Here we focus on the former approach, positing that group decision making provides a mechanism for aggregating the inputs of multiple individuals with differing knowledge, interests, and skills. Numerous studies suggest that groups benefit from both the pooling of information and from providing opportunities for one member to correct another's errors.[92] In the corporate context, the board of directors thus may have emerged as an institutional governance mechanism to constrain the deleterious effect of bounded rationality on the organizational decision-making process.

3.2.2 The Board as a Constraint on Agency Costs

Individuals are subject to the temptations to shirk or self-deal. The internal dynamics of group governance, however, constrain self-dealing and shirking by individual team members. In this regard, group decision making has a bi-directional structure. In the vertical dimension, a group may be superior to an individual autocrat as a monitor of subordinates in the corporate hierarchy. In the horizontal dimension, intra-group governance structures help constrain shirking and self-dealing at the apex of the hierarchy.

3.2.2.1 Vertical Monitoring

Suppose an individual autocrat rather than a board of directors capped the corporate hierarchy. Under such circumstances, a bilateral vertical monitoring problem arises. On the one hand, the autocrat must monitor his/her subordinates. On the other hand, someone must monitor the autocrat. In theory, if corporate law vested ultimate decision making authority in individual autocrats, chief executives could be monitored by their subordinates.

---

[91] Susan G. Cohen & Diane E. Bailey, "What Makes Teams Work: Group Effectiveness Research from the Shop Floor to the Executive Suite", 23 J. Mgmt. 239, 259 (1997).

[92] Hill, *supra* note 88, 533.

Economist Eugene Fama contends, for example, that lower level managers monitor more senior managers.[93]

It seems unlikely, however, that such upstream monitoring happens often or in a sufficiently systematic way to provide a meaningful constraint on upper management. In any case, this monitoring mechanism does not take full advantage of specialization. Fama and Jensen elsewhere point out that one response to agency costs is to separate "decision management"—initiating and implementing decisions—from "decision control"—ratifying and monitoring decisions.[94] Such separation is a defining characteristic of the central office typical of M-form corporations. The monitoring mechanisms described herein could be accomplished through a simple pyramidal hierarchy of the sort found in U-form corporations. The M-form corporation adds to this structure a rationalization of decision-making authority in which the central office has certain tasks and the operating units have others, which allows for more effective monitoring through specialization, sharper definition of purpose, and savings in informational costs.[95] In particular, the central office's key decision makers—the board of directors and top management—specialize in decision control. Because low- and mid-level managers specialize in decision management, expecting them to monitor more senior managers thus requires them to perform a task for which they are poorly suited.

A different critique of Fama's hypothesis is suggested by evidence with respect to meeting behavior. In mixed status groups, higher status persons talk more than lower status members. Managers, for example, talk more than subordinates in business meetings.[96] Such disparities result in higher status group members being more inclined to propound initiatives and wielding greater influence over the group's ultimate decision. Consequently, a core board function is providing a set of status equals for top managers.[97] As such, corporate law's insistence on the formal superiority of the board to management begins to make sense. To the extent law shapes social norms, admittedly a contested proposition,[98] corporate law empowers the board to more effectively constrain top management by creating a de jure status relationship favoring the board.

3.2.2.2 *Horizontal Monitoring*

Who watches the watchers? Because all members of the corporate hierarchy—including our hypothetical autocrat—are themselves agents of the firm with incentives to shirk, a mechanism to monitor their productivity and reduce their incentive to shirk must also be created or one ends up with a never-ending series of monitors monitoring lower level monitors. As we have seen, Alchian and Demsetz purported to solve this dilemma by requiring that the

---

[93] See, e.g., Eugene F. Fama, "Agency Problems and the Theory of the Firm", 88 J. Pol. Econ. 288, 293 (1980).

[94] Eugene F. Fama & Michael C. Jensen, "Separation of Ownership and Control", 26 J. L. & Econ. 301, 315 (1983).

[95] Williamson, *supra* note 23, at 320.

[96] Sara Kiesler & Lee Sproull, "Group Decision Making and Communication Technology", 52 Org. Behav. & Human Decision Processes 96, 109–10 (1992).

[97] Robert J. Haft, "The Effect of Insider Trading Rules on the Internal Efficiency of the Large Corporation", 80 Mich. L. Rev. 1051, 1061 (1982) (describing the board as "a peer group—a collegial body of equals, with the chief executive as the *prima inter pares*").

[98] See Stephen M. Bainbridge, "Mandatory Disclosure: A Behavioral Analysis", 68 U. Cin. L. Rev. 1023, 1052–53 (2000) (describing debate).

monitor be given the residual income left after all other workers have been paid, but their otherwise quite useful model has limited relevance to the public corporation.[99]

Consequently, corporate law and governance must provide alternatives to monitoring by the residual claimants. A hierarchy of individuals whose governance structures contemplate only vertical monitoring, such as that hypothesized above, cannot resolve the problem of who watches the watchers. By adding the dimension of horizontal monitoring, however, placing a group at the apex of the hierarchy provides a solution to that problem. Where an individual autocrat would have substantial freedom to shirk or self-deal, the internal dynamics of group governance constrain self-dealing and shirking by individual team members and, perhaps, even by the group as a whole. Within a production team, for example, mutual monitoring and peer pressure provide a coercive backstop for a set of interpersonal relationships founded on trust and other noncontractual social norms. Of particular relevance here are effort and cooperation norms.[100]

While the old adage opines "familiarity breeds contempt," personal proximity to others in fact deeply affects behavior. As people become closer, their behavior tends to improve: "something in us makes it all but impossible to justify our acts as mere self-interest whenever those acts are seen by others as violating a moral principle"; rather, "[w]e want our actions to be seen by others—and by ourselves—as arising out of appropriate motives."[101] Small groups strengthen this instinct in several ways. First, they provide a network of reputational and other social sanctions that shape incentives. Because membership in close-knit groups satisfies the human need for belongingness, the threat of expulsion gives the group a strong sanction by which to enforce compliance with group norms. Because close-knit groups involve a continuing relationship, the threat of punishment in future interactions deters the sort of cheating possible in one-time transactions.[102] Second, because people care about how they are perceived by those close to them, communal life provides a cloud of witnesses whose good opinion we value. We hesitate to disappoint those people and thus strive to comport ourselves in accordance with communal norms. Effort norms will thus tend to discourage board members from simply going through the motions, but instead to devote greater cognitive effort to their tasks. Finally, there is a transaction costs economics explanation for the importance of closeness in trust relationships. Close-knit groups know a lot about one another, which reduces monitoring costs and thus further encourages compliance with group norms. Members of close-knit groups therefore tend to internalize group norms.[103]

---

[99] See *supra* notes 17–23 and accompanying text.

[100] Social norms are relevant to other aspects of decision making besides agency costs. Group norms of reciprocity, for example, facilitate the process of achieving consensus within groups.

[101] James Q. Wilson, "What Is Moral and How Do We Know It?", Commentary, June 1993, at 37, 39. See also Kenneth L. Bettenhausen, "Five Years of Groups Research: What We Have Learned and What Needs to Be Addressed", 17 J. Mgmt. 345, 348 (1991).

[102] See generally Williamson, *supra* note 23, at 48 ("Informal peer group pressures can be mobilized to check malingering . . . . The most casual involves cajoling or ribbing. If this fails, rational appeals to persuade the deviant to conform are employed. The group then resorts to penalties by withdrawing the social benefits that affiliation affords. Finally, overt coercion and ostracism are resorted to.").

[103] The case should not be overstated. Cohesive groups are subject to inherent cognitive biases that limit their effectiveness. A widely cited example is the so-called risky shift phenomenon. There seems to be a polarizing effect in group decision making, so that post-discussion consensus is more extreme

Taken together, these factors suggest that group decision making is a potentially powerful constraint on agency costs. It creates a set of high-powered incentives to comply with both effort and cooperation norms. This analysis thus goes a long way toward explaining the formalistic rules of state corporate law governing board decision making.[104]

4 WHO SHOULD ELECT THE BOARD?

Is it curious that only shareholders get the vote? What about the corporation's other constituencies, such as employees, creditors, customers, suppliers, etc.? Why do they not get a voice in, say, the election of directors? The traditional answer is that shareholders own the corporation. Ownership typically connotes control, of course. Consequently, despite the separation of ownership and control characteristic of public corporations, shareholders' ownership of the corporation might be deemed to vest them with unique control rights. But the nexus of contracts theory of the firm demonstrates that shareholders do not in fact "own" the corporation in any meaningful sense. By throwing the concept of ownership out of the window, the contractarian model eliminates the obvious answer to our starting question—why are only shareholders given voting rights?[105]

than the individual pre-test results. See Norbert L. Kerr, "Group Decision Making at a Multialternative Task: Extremity, Interfaction Distance, Pluralities, and Issue Importance", 52 Org. Behav. and Human Decision Processes 64 (1992). The most significant group bias for our purposes, however, is the "groupthink" phenomenon. Highly cohesive groups with strong civility and cooperation norms value consensus more greatly than they do a realistic appraisal of alternatives. Irving Janis, Victims of Groupthink (1972). In such groups, groupthink is an adaptive response to the stresses generated by challenges to group solidarity. To avoid those stresses, groups may strive for unanimity even at the expense of quality decision making. To the extent groupthink promotes the development of social norms, it facilitates the board's monitoring function. It may also be relevant to other board functions, such as resource acquisition, to the extent that it promotes a sort of esprit de corps. Yet, the downside is an erosion in the quality of decision making. The desire to maintain group cohesion trumps the exercise of critical judgment. Adverse consequences of groupthink thus include not examining alternatives, being selective in gathering information, and failing to be either self-critical or evaluative of others. Studies of meeting behavior, for example, conclude that people tend to prefer options that have obvious popularity. Kiesler & Sproull, *supra* note 96. In the corporate setting, board culture often encourages groupthink. Boards emphasize politeness and courtesy at the expense of oversight. CEOs can foster and channel groupthink through their power to control information flows, reward consensus, and discourage the reelection of troublemakers. The groupthink phenomenon therefore demands close attention with respect to a variety of corporate governance issues, but is most directly relevant to the board composition debate discussed below.

[104] Noting that most corporations—especially outside the USA and UK—have highly concentrated ownership, Morten Bennedsen suggests that a major function of boards is to mediate conflicts between controlling and non-controlling shareholders. Morten Bennedsen, Why Do Firms Have Boards? (March 2002 (copy on file with author)). Of course, this is also an agency cost story, focusing on a different potential set of conflicts.

[105] The extent to which the increasingly important phenomenon of shareholder activism requires us to rethink the issues discussed in this section is beyond the scope of this chapter. As already mentioned *supra* note 22, however, the author has discussed that phenomenon at length elsewhere.

Recall that Arrow identified two basic modes of decision making: consensus and authority. Consensus requires that each member of the organization have identical information and interests so that preferences can be aggregated at low cost. In contrast, authority-based decision-making structures arise where group members have different interests and information.

The analysis that follows proceeds in three steps. First, why do corporations not rely on consensus-based decision making? In answering that question, we begin by imagining an employee-owned firm with many thousands of employee shareholders. (Employees are used solely for purposes of illustration—the analysis would extend to any other corporate constituency.) After demonstrating that Arrow's conditions cannot be satisfied in such a firm, we then turn to the more complex public firm in which employees and shareholders constitute separate constituencies to demonstrate that Arrow's conditions are even less likely to be met in this type of firm. Second, why do corporations not permit multiple constituencies to elect directors? Finally, why are shareholders the favored constituency?

4.1 The Necessity of Authority

4.1.1 Information

Assume an employee-owned corporation with 5,000 employee shareholders. Could such a firm function as a participatory democracy? Not if we hoped that each participant would make informed decisions. As a practical matter, of course, our employee shareholders are not going to have access to the same sorts of information. Assuming at least some employees serve in managerial and supervisory roles, they will tend to have broader perspectives, with more general business information, while line workers will tend to have more specific information about particular aspects of the shop floor.

These information asymmetries will prove intractable. A rational decision maker expends effort to make informed decisions only if the expected benefits of doing so outweigh its costs. In a firm of the sort at bar, gathering information will be very costly. Efficient participatory democracy requires all decision makers to have equal information, which requires that each decision maker have a communication channel to every other decision maker. As the number of decision makers increases, the number of communication channels within the firm increases as the square of the number of decision makers.[106] Bounded rationality makes it doubtful that anyone in a firm of any substantial size could process the vast number of resulting information flows. Even if they were willing to try, moreover, members of such a firm could not credibly bind themselves to reveal information accurately and honestly or to follow prescribed decision-making rules. Under such conditions, Arrow's model predicts that the firm will tend toward authority-based decision making. Accordingly, the

---

[106] Oliver E. Williamson, Markets and Hierarchies: Analysis and Antitrust Implications 46 (1975). In addition to the transaction costs associated with making an informed decision, which by themselves are doubtless preclusive of participatory democracy in the large firm setting, the opportunity cost entailed in making informed decisions is also high and, even more importantly, readily apparent. In contrast, the expected benefits of becoming informed are quite low, as an individual decision maker's vote will not have a significant effect on the vote's outcome. Our employee owners thus will be rationally apathetic.

corporation's employer-owners will prefer to irrevocably delegate decision-making authority to some central agency, such as a board of directors.

Now introduce the complication of separating capital and labor. Nothing about such a change economizes on the decision-making costs outlined above. Instead, as described below, labor and capital can have quite different interests, which increases decision-making costs by introducing the risk of opportunism. In particular, capital and labor may behave strategically by withholding information from one another.

4.1.2 *Interests*

Again, begin by assuming an employee-owned firm with 5,000 employee shareholders. Is it reasonable to expect the similarity of interest required for consensus to function in such a firm? Surely not. In some cases, employees would differ about the best way in which to achieve a common goal. In others, individual employees will be disparately affected by a proposed course of action. Although the problems created by divergent interests within the employee block are not insurmountable, such differences at least raise the cost of using consensus-based decision-making structures in employee-owned firms.

Empirical evidence confirms the existence of such divergent interests within the employee group. Labor-managed firms tend to remain small, carefully screen members, limit the franchise to relatively homogeneous groups, and use agenda controls to prevent cycling and other public choice problems.[107] All of these characteristics are consistent with an attempt to minimize the likelihood and effect of divergent interests.

Now again complicate the analysis by separating capital and labor. Although employee and shareholder interests are often congruent, they can conflict. Consider, for example, the downsizing phenomenon. Corporate restructurings typically result in substantial reductions in force, reduced job security, longer work weeks, more stress, and diminished morale.[108] From the shareholders' perspective, however, the market typically rewards restructurings with substantial stock price increases. The divergence of interest suggested by this example looms large as a bar to the use of consensus in capitalist firms.

4.2 The Inefficiency of Multiple Constituencies

The analysis to this point merely demonstrates that corporate decision making must be made on a representative rather than on a participatory basis. As yet, nothing in the analysis dictates the US model in which only shareholders elect directors. One could plausibly imagine a board of directors on which multiple constituencies are represented. Indeed, imagination is not required, because the supervisory board component of German codetermination provides a realworld example of just such a board. Empirical evidence, however, suggests that codetermination does not lead to efficiency or productivity gains.[109]

---

[107] Greg Dow & Louis Putterman, "Why Capital (Usually) Hires Labor: An Assessment of Proposed Explanations", Brown Univ. Dep't of Econ. Working Paper 96–21 at 63–64 (Sep. 1996).

[108] Michael Useem, Investor Capitalism: How Money Managers Are Changing the Face of Corporate America 164–65 (1996).

[109] See generally Stephen M. Bainbridge, "Participatory Management within a Theory of the Firm", 21 J. Corp. L. 657 (1996) (summarizing studies).

Why not? In Arrow's terminology, the board of directors serves as a consensus-based decision-making body at the top of an authority-based structure. Recall that for consensus to function, however, two conditions must be met: equivalent interests and information. Neither condition can be met when employee representatives are on the board.

The two factors are closely related, of course. Indeed, it is the potential divergence of shareholder and employee interests that ensures employee representatives will be deprived of the information necessary for them to function. Because of the board's position at the apex of the corporate hierarchy, employee representatives are inevitably exposed to a far greater amount of information about the firm than is normally provided to employees. As the European experience with codetermination teaches, this can result in corporate information leaking to the workforce as a whole or even to outsiders. In the Netherlands, for example, the obligation of works council representatives to respect the confidentiality of firm information "has not always been kept, causing serious concerns among management which is required . . . to provide extensive 'sensitive' information to the councils."[110]

Given that providing board level information to employee representatives appears clearly contrary to shareholder interests,[111] we would expect managers loyal to shareholder interests to withhold information from the board of directors in order to deny it to employee representatives, which would seriously undermine the board's ability to carry out its essential corporate governance roles. This prediction is borne out by the German experience with codetermination. German managers sometimes deprive the supervisory board of information, because they do not want the supervisory board's employee members to learn it.[112] Alternatively, the board's real work may be done in committees or de facto rump caucuses from which employee representatives are excluded. As a result, while codetermination raises the costs of decision making, it may not have much effect on substantive decision making.[113]

Although Arrow's equality of information criterion is important, in this context the critical element is the divergence of shareholder and employee interests. The interests of shareholders will inevitably differ as amongst themselves, as do those of employees, but individual constituents of the corporation nevertheless are more likely to share interests with members of the same constituency than with members of another constituency. Allowing board representation for employees thus tends only to compound the problem that gives

[110] Tom R. Ottervanger & Ralph M. Pais, "Employee Participation in Corporate Decision Making: The Dutch Model", 15 Int'l. Law 393, 399 (1981).

[111] One sure result of lost confidentiality will be worker demands for higher wages. This prediction is supported by an empirical study finding that provision of financial and other business information to employees of non-unionized firms had a negative effect on firm profitability, which was attributed to higher wages demanded by the informed employees. Morris M. Kleiner & Marvin L. Bouillon, "Providing Business Information to Production Workers: Correlates of Compensation and Productivity", 41 Indus. & Lab. Rel. Rev. 605, 614–15 (1988). See also Stuart Ogden, "The Limits of Employee Involvement: Profit Sharing and Disclosure of Information", 29 J. Mgmt Stud. 229 (1992) (stating that UK employers are reluctant to provide disclosure of financial information for fear of stimulating workers to make demands respecting pay and working conditions). In a unionized firm, moreover, management will be especially reluctant to inform union members on the board of information that might aid the union in collective bargaining.

[112] Hopt, *supra* note 45, at 206.

[113] Tove H. Hammer et al., "Worker Representation on Boards of Directors: A Study of Competing Roles", 44 Indus. & Lab. Rev. 661, 663 (1991) (Scandinavian experience with codetermination shows it has little substantive effect on corporate decision making).

rise to an authority-based hierarchical decision-making structure by bringing the differing interests of employees and shareholders directly into the boardroom.[114] The resulting conflicts of interest inevitably impede consensus-based decision making within the board. Worker representatives on corporate boards tend to prefer greater labor advocacy than do traditional directors, no doubt in large part because workers evaluate their representatives on the basis of labor advocacy, which also results in role conflicts.[115] The problem with co-determination thus is not only that the conflict of employee and shareholder interests impedes the achievement of consensus, but also that it may result in a substantial increase in agency costs.[116]

[114] The difficulty, of course, is not merely that the interests of employees and shareholders diverge, but also that different classes of employees have divergent interests. As we have seen, this seriously compounds the problem of aggregating constituency preferences.

[115] Cotton, *supra* note 46, at 128 (1993). This conflict is exacerbated in heavily unionized industries, as representatives of a single union might sit on the boards of multiple firms within the industry. In the extreme case, the demise of one firm might redound to the greater good of the greatest number by benefiting union members who work at competing corporations. This creates the potential for perverse incentives on the part of union representatives on the board.

[116] The most obvious problem is the possibility that employee representation will permit management to pursue its own self-interest at the expense of both shareholders and employees by playing worker and shareholder representatives off against each other. Legal and market accountability mechanisms constrain this tendency, but because they are not perfect there remains the possibility that self-interested managers may throw their support behind the side of the board whose interests happen to coincide with those of management in the issue at hand. See William J. Carney, "Does Defining Constituencies Matter?", 59 U. Cin. L. Rev. 385, 420–24 (1990).
This conflict is well-known, of course, but there is a more subtle problem that is often overlooked. Corporate employees have an incentive to shirk so long as their compensation does not perfectly align their incentives with those of the firm's shareholders. In turn, knowing of this phenomenon, the firm's shareholders should expect management to reduce the compensation of the firm's employees by the amount necessary to offset the expected degree of employee shirking. Because ex ante wage adjustments rarely are fully compensatory, due to bounded rationality and the resulting use of incomplete contracts, the firm's shareholders should expect management to monitor the employees and punish ex post those who shirk. Benjamin Klein, "Contracting Costs and Residual Claims: The Separation of Ownership and Control", 26 J. L. & Econ. 367, 368 n.2 (1983). Would it not seem odd that those who are to be monitored should be allowed to choose the monitors? One of the accountability mechanisms that aligns managerial and shareholder interests is monitoring by the board of directors. Allowing employee representation on the board necessarily reduces the likelihood that the board will be an effective monitoring device. Because shareholders "could seek profits by getting highly motivated managers who sweat the labor force," workers have an interest in supporting rules that free management from accountability to shareholders. Roe, *supra* note 55, at 44. Managerial shirking of its monitoring responsibilities thus will often redound to the workers' benefit, which suggests that employee representatives on the board of directors are less likely to insist on disciplining lax managers than are shareholder representatives. If employees are entitled to voting representation on the board of directors, monitoring by the board and its subordinate managers will be less effective, which will cause agency costs to rise.
The validity of this prediction is confirmed by the German experience with codetermination. Conflicts of interest faced by employee representatives on the supervisory board remain a serious but unresolved concern. Employee representation slows the finding of a consensus on the supervisory board and creates a built-in polarization problem. Not surprisingly, it is standard practice for employee and shareholder representatives to have separate pre-meeting caucuses. Hopt, *supra* note 45, at 206–08.

Although it is sometimes asserted that employee representation would benefit the board by promoting "discussion and consideration of alternative perspectives and arguments,"[117] the preceding analysis suggests that any such benefits would come at high cost. In addition, there is reason to doubt whether those benefits are very significant. Workers will be indifferent to most corporate decisions that do not bear directly on working conditions and benefits.[118] All of which tends to suggest that employee representatives add little except increased labor advocacy to the board.

4.3 Why Only Shareholders?

The analysis thus far demonstrates that public corporation decision making must be conducted on a representative rather than a participatory basis. It further demonstrates that only one constituency should be allowed to elect the board of directors. The remaining question is why shareholders are the chosen constituency, rather than employees. Answering that question is the task of this section.

The standard law and economics explanation for vesting voting rights in shareholders is that shareholders are the only corporate constituent with a residual, unfixed, ex post claim on corporate assets and earnings.[119] In contrast, the employees' claim is prior and largely fixed ex ante through agreed-upon compensation schedules. This distinction has two implications of present import. First, as noted above, employee interests are too parochial to justify board representation. In contrast, shareholders have the strongest economic incentive to care about the size of the residual claim, which means that they have the greatest incentive to elect directors committed to maximizing firm profitability.[120] Second, the nature

---

[117] Robert Howse & Michael J. Trebilcock, "Protecting the Employment Bargain", 43 U. Toronto L. J. 751, 769 (1993).

[118] See Michael P. Dooley, European Proposals for Worker Information and Codetermination: An American Comment, in Harmonization of the Laws in the European Communities: Products Liability, Conflict of Laws, and Corporation Law 126, 129 (Peter E. Herzog ed., 1983) (opining: "As to the majority of managerial policies concerning, for example, dividend and investment policies, product development, and the like, the typical employee has as much interest and as much to offer as the typical purchaser of light bulbs").

[119] See, e.g., Frank H. Easterbrook and Daniel R. Fischel, The Economic Structure of Corporate Law 66–72 (1991). An alternative answer based on the model used herein returns to the divergence of interests within constituency groups. Although investors have somewhat different preferences on issues such as dividends and the like, they are generally united by a desire to maximize share value. Board consensus therefore will be more easily achieved if directors are beholden solely to shareholder interests, rather than to the more diverse set of interests represented by employees.

A related but perhaps more telling point is the problem of apportioning the vote. Financial capital is fungible, transferable, and quantifiable. Control rights based on financial capital are thus subject to low-cost allocation and valuation. In contrast, the human capital of workers meets none of these criteria. While one-person/one-vote would be a low-cost solution to the allocation problem, it appears highly inefficient given the unequal distribution of reasoning power and education. If the most competent people and/or those with the most at stake should have the most votes, some more costly allocation device will be necessary.

[120] The superiority of shareholder incentives is a relative matter. Shareholders may have better incentives than other constituencies, but the phenomenon of rational apathy nevertheless limits the extent to which shareholders can be expected to act on those incentives.

of the employees' claim on the firm creates incentives to shirk. Vesting control rights in the employees would increase their incentive to shirk. In turn, the prospect of employee shirking lowers the value of the shareholders' residual claim.

At this point, it is useful to once again invoke the hypothetical bargain methodology. If the corporation's various constituencies could bargain over voting rights, to which constituency would they assign those rights? In light of their status as residual claimants and the adverse effects of employee representation, shareholders doubtless would bargain for control rights, so as to ensure a corporate decision-making system emphasizing monitoring mechanisms designed to prevent shirking by employees, and employees would be willing to concede such rights to shareholders.

Granted, collective action problems preclude the shareholders from exercising mean-ingful day-to-day or even year-to-year control over managerial decisions. Unlike the employees' claim, however, the shareholders' claim on the corporation is freely transfer-able. As such, if management fails to maximize the shareholders' residual claim, an outsider can profit by purchasing a majority of the shares and voting out the incumbent board of directors. Accordingly, vesting the right to vote solely in the hands of the firm's shareholders is what makes possible the market for corporate control and thus helps to minimize shirking. As the residual claimants, shareholders thus would bargain for sole voting con-trol, in order to ensure that the value of their claim is maximized. In turn, because all cor-porate constituents have an ex ante interest in minimizing shirking by managers and other agents, the firm's employees have an incentive to agree to such rules.[121] The employees' lack of control rights thus can be seen as a way in which they bond their promise not to shirk. Their lack of control rights not only precludes them from double dipping but also facilitates disciplining employees who shirk. Accordingly, it is not surprising that the default rules of the standard form contract provided by all corporate statutes vest voting rights solely in the hands of common shareholders.

To be sure, the vote allows shareholders to allocate some risk to prior claimants. If a firm is in financial straits, directors and managers faithful to shareholder interests could pro-tect the value of the shareholders' residual claim by, for example, financial and/or work-force restructurings that eliminate prior claimants—all of which raises the question of why employees do not get the vote to protect themselves against this risk. The answer is twofold. First, as we have seen, multiple constituencies are inefficient. Second, as addressed below, employees have significant protections that do not rely on voting.

Suppose a firm behaves opportunistically toward its employees. What protections do the employees have? Some are protected by job mobility. The value of continued dealings with an employer to an employee whose work involves solely general human capital does not de-pend on the value of the firm because neither the employee nor the firm have an incentive to preserve such employment relationship. If the employee's general human capital suffices for him to do his job at Firm A, it presumably would suffice for him to do a similar job at

---

[121] According to the Coase Theorem, rights will be acquired by those who value them most highly, which creates an incentive to discover and implement transaction cost minimizing governance forms. See Ronald H. Coase, "The Problem of Social Cost", 3 J. L. & Econ. 1 (1960). Although shareholders and employees obviously do not bargain, a basic premise of the law and economics account is that corporate law provides them with a set of default rules reflecting the bargain they would strike if they were able to do so.

Firm B. Such an employee resembles an independent contractor who can shift from firm to firm at low cost to either employee or employer.[122] Mobility thus may be a sufficient defense against opportunistic conduct with respect to such employees, because they can quit and be replaced without productive loss to either employee or employer. Put another way, because there are no appropriable quasi-rents in this category of employment relationships, rent seeking by management is not a concern.

Corporate employees who make firm-specific investments in human capital arguably need greater protection against employer opportunism, but such protections need not include board representation. Indeed, various specialized governance structures have arisen to protect such workers. Among these are severance pay, grievance procedures, promotion ladders, collective bargaining, and the like.[123]

In contrast, shareholders are poorly positioned to develop the kinds of specialized governance structures that protect employee interests. Unlike employees, whose relationship to the firm is subject to periodic renegotiation, shareholders have an indefinite relationship that is rarely renegotiated, if ever. The dispersed nature of stock ownership also makes bilateral negotiation of specialized safeguards difficult. The board of directors thus is an essential governance mechanism for protecting shareholder interests.

If the foregoing analysis is correct, why do we nevertheless sometimes observe employee representation? An explanation consistent with our analysis lies close at hand. In the United States, employee representation on the board is typically found in firms that have undergone concessionary bargaining with unions. Concessionary bargaining, on average, results in increased share values of 8–10 percent.[124] The stock market apparently views union concessions as substantially improving the value of the residual claim, presumably by making firm failure less likely. While the firm's employees also benefit from a reduction in the firm's riskiness, they are likely to demand a quid pro quo for their contribution to shareholder wealth. One consideration given by shareholders (through management) may be greater access to information, sometimes through board representation. Put another way, board of director representation is a way of maximizing access to information and bonding its accuracy. The employee representatives will be able to verify that the original information about the firm's precarious financial situation was accurate. Employee representatives on the board also are well positioned to determine whether the firm's prospects have improved sufficiently to justify an attempt to reverse prior concessions through a new round of bargaining.

---

[122] See generally Oliver Williamson, "Corporate Governance", 93 Yale L. J. 1197 (1984). This is not to say that exit is costless for either employees or firms. All employees are partially locked into their firm. Indeed, it must be so, or monitoring could not prevent shirking because disciplinary efforts would have no teeth. The question is one of relative costs.

[123] As private sector unions have declined, the federal government has intervened to provide through general welfare legislation many of the same protections for which unions might have bargained. The Family & Medical Leave Act grants unpaid leave for medical and other family problems. OSHA mandates safe working conditions. Plant closing laws require notice of layoffs. Civil rights laws protect against discrimination of various sorts. Even such matters as offensive horseplay have come within the purview of federal sexual harassment law.

[124] Brian E. Becker, "Concession Bargaining: The Impact on Shareholders' Equity", 40 Indus. & Lab. Rel. Rev. 268 (1987).

5 SHOULD DIRECTORS BE INDEPENDENT?

As the monitoring model came to dominate thinking about the board's role, the board's composition inevitably came to the fore. A board comprised of insiders is poorly positioned to monitor the CEO. Research on group decision making shows that in mixed status groups, higher status persons talk more than lower status members. Managers, for example, talk more than subordinates in business meetings. Such disparities result in higher status group members being more inclined to propound initiatives and having greater influence over the group's ultimate decision. Group dynamics thus help ensure the CEO's dominance over inside directors. As a practical matter, moreover, the CEO typically serves as the chairman of the board, giving him substantial control over both the selection of new directors and the board's agenda. Not surprisingly, director independence therefore is a longstanding goal of corporate reformers, especially those affiliated with the monitoring model school of thought.

5.1 Mandating Director Independence

5.1.1 Director Independence in USA State Law

State corporation statutes are silent on the issue of board composition. Issues such as board size, director qualifications, and independence are left to private ordering. If state statutory law were all that mattered, firms would thus be free to select the board structure and composition optimal to their unique circumstances.

The state common law of corporations does provide some incentives for corporations to include at least some independent directors on the board. It has long been the case, for example, that approval of related party and other conflicted interest transactions by vote of a majority of the disinterested and independent directors effectively immunizes such transactions from judicial review by invoking the defendant-friendly business judgment rule as the standard of review.[125] In connection with going private transactions initiated by a controlling shareholder, the Delaware Supreme Court called upon boards to create "an independent negotiating committee of its outside directors to deal with [the buyer] at arm's length."[126] Indeed, the Court went on to equate "fairness in this context" to the conduct that might be expected from "a theoretical, wholly independent, board of directors acting upon the matter before them." Similarly, with respect to antitakeover defenses, the Court has held that the validity of such defenses is "materially enhanced . . . where, as here, a majority of the board favoring the proposal consisted of outside independent directors."[127] Taken together with similar decisions in other areas of corporate law, these judicially created safe

---

[125] *Marciano v. Nakash*, 535 A.2d 400, 405 n.3 (Del. 1987) (opining that "approval by fully-informed disinterested directors under section 144(a)(1) . . . permits invocation of the business judgment rule and limits judicial review to issues of gift or waste with the burden of proof upon the party attacking the transaction").

[126] *Weinberger v. UOP, Inc.*, 457 A.2d 701, 709 n.7 (Del. 1983).

[127] *Moran v. Household Int'l., Inc.*, 500 A.2d 1346, 1356 (Del. 1985).

harbors provide substantial incentives for both boards and managers to favor director independence.

Having said that, however, state law typically is far more concerned with director disinterestedness than independence. Consider, for example, the Delaware law on excusal of demand in shareholder derivative litigation. In *Grimes v. Donald*,[128] the Delaware Supreme Court identified three reasons for excusing demand: "(1) a majority of the board has a material financial or familial interest; (2) a majority of the board is incapable of acting independently for some other reason such as domination or control; or (3) the underlying transaction is not the product of a valid exercise of business judgment."[129] As to the first prong, directors are interested if they have a personal financial stake in the challenged transaction or otherwise would be materially affected by the board's actions. Consequently, for example, the Delaware Chancery Court excused demand on director interest grounds where five of nine directors approved a stock appreciation rights plan likely to benefit them.[130]

Although the second prong is framed in terms of independence, it is not concerned with whether a director is generically independent of management. While being employed by the corporation would preclude a director from being deemed independent for all purposes under Sarbanes–Oxley and Dodd–Frank, for example, it does not preclude a finding that the director is independent under state law. This is so, in part, because state law views independence from a transactional perspective rather than one of status. The other critical difference is that state law links independence to self-interest in the underlying transaction. Accordingly, demand is not excused simply because the plaintiff has named a majority of the board as defendants.[131] Indeed, it is not enough even to allege that a majority of the board approved of, acquiesced in, or participated in the challenged transaction.[132] In other words, merely being named as defendants or participants does not render the board incapable, as a matter of law, of objectively evaluating a pre-suit demand and, accordingly, does not excuse such a demand. Instead, demand typically is excused under this prong only if a majority of the board was dominated or controlled by someone with a personal financial stake in the transaction.[133]

State law thus fails to satisfy the more exacting standards of independence pursued by reformers like Ralph Nader or Melvin Eisenberg. Instead, the reformers want independence to be defined by status. In general, any material relationship between the director and the corporation or its top management team would be regarded as disabling the director from being deemed independent as they wished it to be defined.

---

[128] 673 A.2d 1207 (Del. 1996).   [129] Id. at 1216.

[130] *Bergstein v. Texas Int'l. Co.*, 453 A.2d 467, 471 (Del. Ch. 1982).

[131] See *Rales v. Blasband*, 634 A.2d 927, 936 (Del. 1993) (holding that the "mere threat" of personal liability in connection with the litigation is not enough, although a "substantial likelihood" of personal liability in connection therewith will excuse demand).

[132] *Aronson v. Lewis*, 473 A.2d 805, 817 (Del. 1984) ("In Delaware mere directorial approval of a transaction, absent particularized facts supporting a breach of fiduciary duty claim, or otherwise establishing the lack of independence or disinterestedness of a majority of the directors, is insufficient to excuse demand.").

[133] See id. at 814 ("[W]here officers and directors are under an influence which sterilizes their discretion, they cannot be considered proper persons to conduct litigation on behalf of the corporation.").

5.1.2 Director Independence in the Stock Exchange Listing Standards and the Sarbanes–Oxley Act

The Sarbanes–Oxley Act did relatively little to reform boards of directors. Besides some minor tweaking of rules like those governing disclosure of stock transactions by directors and so on, the only substantive changes worked by Sarbanes–Oxley dealt with the audit committee of the board of directors.

Instead, Congress and the SEC left the heavy lifting on board reform to the stock exchanges. All three major exchanges—the NYSE, NASDAQ, and the American Stock Exchange (AMEX)—amended their corporate governance listing requirements to require that a majority of the members of the board of directors of most listed companies must be independent of management. All three also adopted new rules defining independence using very strict, bright-line rules. Finally, all three significantly expanded the duties and powers of independent directors.

The NYSE long required that all listed companies have at least three independent directors.[134] A director was treated as independent unless, inter alia, (1) the director was employed by the corporation or its affiliates in the past three years; (2) the director had an immediate family member who, during the past three years, was employed by the corporation or its affiliates as an executive officer; (3) the director had a direct business relationship with the company; or (4) the director was a partner, controlling shareholder, or executive officer of an organization that had a business relationship with the corporation, unless the corporation's board determined in its business judgment that the relationship did not interfere with the director's exercise of independent judgment.

The NYSE's pre-SOX listing standards also required that listed companies have an audit committee comprised solely of independent directors. The committee had to have at least three members, all of whom must be "financially literate." At least one committee member had to have expertise in accounting or financial management.

As the Enron crisis was peaking, the NYSE appointed a blue ribbon panel of Wall Street Brahmins to evaluate whether the new environment called for changes in the exchange's corporate governance listing standards. The panel reported back with a number of proposed new governance standards, including a mandate that independent directors comprise a majority of any listed corporation's board of directors.[135] The exchange forwarded the proposals to the SEC for approval. At that point, however, the listing standards proposal was caught up in the larger legislative process surrounding Sarbanes–Oxley and final action on the proposal was deferred until that process was completed.

The Sarbanes–Oxley Act expressly addressed the question of board composition only in § 301, which required the SEC to require that the exchanges adopt new rules for audit committees. The specified duties and powers of that committee will be addressed in Chapter 5. Suffice it for present purposes to note that § 301 requires each member of the audit committee to be independent, which was defined therein to mean that the director could not "(i) accept any consulting, advisory, or other compensatory fee from the issuer; or (ii) be an affiliated person of the issuer or any subsidiary thereof."

[134] NYSE, Listed Company Manual § 303.01, http://nysemanual.nyse.com/lcm/.
[135] Report of the NYSE Corporate Accountability and Listing Standards Committee 6 (June 6, 2002).

Section 301's focus on the audit committee is broadly consistent with the general thrust of the Sarbanes–Oxley Act, which as a whole is mainly concerned with accounting and auditing issues. Congress was well aware of the pending exchange rulemaking proposals and presumably was content to leave the details to the SEC and the exchanges so long as the final listing standards met the specified minimum requirements regarding the audit committee. In November 2003, the process concluded when the SEC gave final approval to revised exchange listing standards on director independence.[136]

5.1.2.1 The Majority Independent Board

As approved by the SEC, the NYSE listing standards now require that all listed companies "must have a majority of independent directors."[137] In addition, as we will see below, the NYSE has mandated the use of several board committees consisting of independent directors. Finally, the NYSE's Listed Company Manual provides that: "To empower non-management directors to serve as a more effective check on management, the non-management directors of each listed company must meet at regularly scheduled executive sessions without management."[138] The listed company's Form 10-K must disclose the identity of the independent director who chairs the mandatory executive sessions. Although the rule does not indicate how many times per year the outside directors must meet to satisfy this requirement, emerging best practice suggests that there should be such a meeting held in conjunction with every regularly scheduled meeting of the entire board of directors.

The NASDAQ and AMEX standards are substantially similar. One wrinkle is that NASDAQ expressly states an expectation that executive sessions of the outside directors will be held at least twice a year. Note that all three exchanges exempt controlled companies—those in which a shareholder or group of shareholders acting together control 50 percent or more of the voting power of the company's stock—from the obligation to have a majority independent board.

5.1.2.2 Who Is Independent?

As we saw, Delaware state corporate law asks a very simple question to determine whether a director is independent; to wit, whether "through personal or other relationships the directors are beholden to" management.[139] In contrast, the exchange listing standards use multipart bright line standards to determine whether a director is independent. The NYSE, for example, has five such standards looking at the relationships between the listed company and a director and his immediate family members. A director will not be independent, for example, if that director "is, or has been within the last three years, an employee of the listed company, or an immediate family member is, or has been within the last three years, an executive officer, of the listed company."[140] The NASDAQ and AMEX have substantially similar tests.

The trouble with economic tests is that they fail to capture the myriad of other ways in which individuals can be biased toward others. Many nominally independent directors have full-time jobs as executives at other firms or as partners in business service companies such

---

[136] Exchange Act Rel. No. 48,745 (Nov. 4, 2003).
[137] NYSE Listed Company Manual § 303A.01.   [138] Id., § 303A.03.
[139] *Aronson v. Lewis*, 473 A.2d 805, 815 (Del. 1984).
[140] NYSE Listed Company Manual § 302A.02(b)(i).

as law firms or financial institutions. Directors tend to be white males, educated at top-20 schools, and share a host of other social ties. When their fellow directors get into trouble, the reaction of these nominally independent directors may be one of leniency, motivated by a " 'there but for the grace of God go I' empathy."[141]

The problem is not just one of undue empathy, however. Social ties have a deterrent effect on director behavior that can be just as important, if not more so, than economic relationships. As Delaware Vice Chancellor Leo Strine observes:

> To be direct, corporate directors are generally the sort of people deeply enmeshed in social institutions. Such institutions have norms, expectations that, explicitly and implicitly, influence and channel the behavior of those who participate in their operation. Some things are "just not done," or only at a cost, which might not be so severe as a loss of position, but may involve a loss of standing in the institution. In being appropriately sensitive to this factor, our law also cannot assume—absent some proof of the point—that corporate directors are, as a general matter, persons of unusual social bravery, who operate heedless to the inhibitions that social norms generate for ordinary folk.[142]

Unfortunately, operationalizing this insight proves quite problematic.

The NYSE definition of independence perhaps seeks to address this problem of structural bias by providing that "[n]o director qualifies as 'independent' unless the board of directors affirmatively determines that the director has no material relationship with the listed company."[143] The commentary to that section explains that:

> It is not possible to anticipate, or explicitly to provide for, all circumstances that might signal potential conflicts of interest, or that might bear on the materiality of a director's relationship to a listed company . . . Accordingly, it is best that boards making "independence" determinations broadly consider all relevant facts and circumstances. In particular, when assessing the materiality of a director's relationship with the listed company, the board should consider the issue not merely from the standpoint of the director, but also from that of persons or organizations with which the director has an affiliation. Material relationships can include commercial, industrial, banking, consulting, legal, accounting, charitable and familial relationships, among others.

The commentary thus contemplates an inquiry broad enough to encompass social ties as well as economic relationships ("broadly consider all relevant facts"). Yet, one suspects such inquiries tend to be superficial, at best, and mainly focused on objective factors rather than the sort of soft biases of social ties.

The key problem, of course, is that the board of directors rather than some outside impartial adjudicator is making the independence determination. These directors presumably have at least ties of class, and probably social relations, amongst themselves and with the candidate whose independence is to be determined. The finder of fact is thus structurally biased against making a finding of structural bias. No workable solution to this problem has been forthcoming.

---

[141] *Zapata Corp. v. Maldonado*, 430 A.2d 779, 787 (Del. 1981).
[142] *In re Oracle Corp. Derivative Litig.*, 824 A.2d 917, 938 (Del. Ch. 2003).
[143] NYSE Listed Company Manual § 303A.02(a).

5.1.2.3 Board Committees

The NYSE Listed Company Manual mandates the establishment of three committees of the board of directors: a Nominating and Corporate Governance Committee (§ 303A.04), a Compensation Committee (§ 303A.05), and an Audit Committee (§ 303A.06). All three must be comprised solely of independent directors. As such, they significantly extend the mandate for a board dominated by directors independent of management.

5.1.3 Director Independence Requirements outside the USA

In dual board jurisdictions, director independence is a natural consequence of the board's structure. Top managers are limited to the management board and are excluded from the supervisory board.[144] On the other hand, the employee representatives on the supervisory board are typically not independent of the labor sponsors and the shareholder represent-atives often are beholden to large block holders.[145] Accordingly, the norm of truly inde-pendent board members—beholden to no one—is absent.

In EU states in which the unitary board model dominates, the sole pertinent statutory mandate is the EU Audit Directive, which requires that boards include at least one inde-pendent director with financial expertise.[146] The question of director independence is other-wise left to national best practice codes.

In the UK, for example, the Corporate Governance Code provides that "at least half the board, excluding the chairman, should comprise non-executive directors determined by the board to be independent."[147] The Code recommends that the board consist of "an ap-propriate combination of executive and non-executive directors (and, in particular, inde-pendent non-executive directors) such that no individual or small group of individuals can dominate the board's decision taking."[148] This recommendation presumably is intended to curb any tendency toward Imperial CEOs, as is the Code's provision that the board should select a lead independent director.[149]

In Asia, a number of key economies have adopted statutory requirements that public companies have at least a specified number of independent directors. In Hong Kong, Singapore, India, and the Philippines, for example, UK-like corporate governance codes rec-ommend that companies have independent directors, although none requires a majority of board members be independent. Korea, Thailand, and China all mandate appointment of

---

[144] See Aguilera, *supra* note 16, at S44 ("One of the key goals of this board structure is to ensure the independence of the two boards by making sure that executives are not too powerful.").

[145] Luca Enriques et al., The Basic Governance Structure: The Interests of Shareholders as a Class, in The Anatomy of Corporate Law: A Comparative and Functional Approach 55, 54–74 (Reinier Kraakman et al. eds., 2d ed. 2009).

[146] Id.

[147] Corporate Governance Code, *supra* note 39, at 12. Smaller companies—defined as those "below the FTSE 350 throughout the year immediately prior to the reporting year"—need only have two independent board members to satisfy the Code. Id. at 12 n.6.

[148] Id. at 11.

[149] See id. at 10 ("The board should appoint one of the independent non-executive directors to be the senior independent director to provide a sounding board for the chairman and to serve as an intermediary for the other directors when necessary.").

independent directors.[150] Whether directors in those countries are actually independent of management, however, is a matter of debate.[151] Japan is regarded as the principal outlier in this regard, as neither law nor best practice require director independence to any extent.[152]

5.2 Outsiders on the Board: The Uncertain Case for Director Independence

As we have seen, the board of directors has three basic functions. First, while boards rarely are involved in day-to-day operational decision making, most boards have at least some managerial functions. Second, the board provides networking and other services. Finally, the board monitors and disciplines top management.

Independence is potentially relevant to all three board functions. As to the former two, outside directors provide both their own expertise and interlocks with diverse contact networks. As to the latter, at least according to conventional wisdom, board independence is an important device for constraining agency costs. On close examination, however, neither rationale for board independence justifies the sort of one size fits all mandate adopted by the exchanges at the behest of Congress and the SEC.

5.2.1 *Independence, Interlocks, and Decision Making*

Putting outside directors on the board can create valuable relationships with a variety of potential strategic partners. This is relevant not only to the board's resource gathering function, but also to its monitoring and service functions. Complex business decisions require knowledge in such areas as accounting, finance, management, and law. Providing access to such knowledge can be seen as part of the board's resource gathering function. Outside board members may either possess such specialized knowledge themselves or have access to credible external sources thereof.

Reliance on outside specialists is a rational response to bounded rationality. The expert in a field makes the most of his limited capacity to absorb and master information by limiting the amount of information that must be processed by limiting the breadth of the field in which the expert specializes. As applied to the corporate context, more diverse boards with strong outsider representation likely contain more specialists, and therefore should get greater benefits from specialization.[153]

---

[150] Nam et al., *supra* note 44, at 97.   [151] Id.

[152] Asian Corporate Governance Ass'n, White Paper on Corporate Governance in Japan (2008). For an argument that "board culture in a globalizing world [probably will not] be shifted towards the Anglo-American expectations of independence and accountability," see Aguilera, *supra* note 16, at S43–44.

[153] Conversely, however, note that, because their decisions are publicly observable, board members have a strong incentive to defer to expert opinion. Because even a good decision maker is subject to the proverbial "act of God," the market for reputation evaluates decision makers by looking at both the outcome and the action before forming a judgment. If a bad outcome occurs, but the action was consistent with approved expert opinion, the hit to the decision maker's reputation is reduced. In effect, by deferring to specialists, a decision maker operating under conditions of bounded rationality is buying insurance against a bad outcome. In a collegial, multi-actor setting, the potential for log rolling further encourages deference. A specialist in a given field is far more likely to have strong feelings about the

Having said that, however, a full-time senior employee has other informational advantages over outsiders who devote but a small portion of their time and effort to the firm. At the minimum, the presence of outsiders on the board increases decision-making costs simply because the process takes longer. Outsiders by definition need more information and are likely to take longer to persuade than are insiders.[154] More subtly, and perhaps more importantly, long-term employees make significant investments in firm-specific human capital. Any employee who advances to senior management levels necessarily invests considerable time and effort in learning how to do his job more effectively. Much of this knowledge will be specific to the firm for which he works, such as when other firms do not do comparable work or his firm has a unique corporate culture. In either case, the longer he works for the firm, the more firm-specific his human capital becomes. Such an employee is likely to make better decisions for the firm than an outsider, even assuming equal levels of information relating to the decision at hand. The insider can put the decision in a broader context, seeing the relationships and connections it has to the firm as a whole.

Insider access to information is particularly significant due to the nature of decision making within large corporations. Recall that the corporation is a classic example of an authority-based decision-making structure characterized by the existence of a central agency to which all relevant information is transmitted and which is empowered to make decisions binding on the whole. Unlike many other organizations, the corporation's central agency is not a single autocrat, but rather a multimember body—the board of directors—that usually functions by consensus. Put another way, the board of directors is best understood as a collegial body using consensus-based decision making. Because consensus works best where team members have equal information and comparable interests, insiders may find it easier to reach consensus than would a diverse body of outsiders. Insiders are more likely to have comparable access to information and similar interests than are outsiders. Insiders have many informal contacts within the organization, which both promote team formation and provide them with better access to information. Hence, insofar as efficient decision making is the goal of corporate governance, independence may not be desirable. On the contrary, these factors suggest that an all-insider board might be preferable.

5.2.2 *Independence and Agency Costs*

Corporate law provides a number of accountability mechanisms designed to constrain agency costs. Chief among them is the board of directors, especially the independent directors. To be sure, outsiders have neither the time nor the information necessary to be involved in the minutiae of day-to-day firm management. What outsiders can do, however, is monitor senior managers and replace those whose performance is sub par. Accordingly,

---

outcome of a particular case than a non-expert. By deferring to the specialist, the non-expert may win the specialist's vote in other cases in relation to which the non-expert has a stronger stake. Such log rolling need not be explicit, although it doubtless is at least sometimes, but rather can be a form of the tit-for-tat cooperative game. In board decision making, deference thus invokes a norm of reciprocation that allows the non-expert to count on the specialist's vote on other matters.

[154] Michael P. Dooley & E. Norman Veasey, "The Role of the Board in Derivative Litigation: Delaware Law and the Current ALI Proposals Compared", 44 Bus. Law. 503, 533 (1989).

proponents of the monitoring model have always been among the strongest proponents of director independence.

It is not clear, however, why one would expect independent directors to be an effective constraint on shirking or self-dealing by management. Monitoring the performance of the firm's officers and employees is hard, time-consuming work. Moreover, most outside directors have full-time employment elsewhere, which commands the bulk of their attention and provides the bulk of their pecuniary and psychic income. Independent directors therefore may prefer leisure or working on their primary vocation to monitoring management. As Adam Smith observed three centuries ago,

> The directors of [joint stock] companies, however, being the managers rather of other people's money than of their own, it cannot well be expected, that they should watch over it with the same anxious vigilance with which the partners in a private co-partnery frequently watch over their own. Like the stewards of a rich man, they are apt to consider attention to small matters as not for their master's honour, and very easily give themselves a dispensation from having it. Negligence and profusion, therefore, must always prevail, more or less, in the management of the affairs of such a company.[155]

Other factors impede an independent director from monitoring management, even if he wishes to do so. Although boards meet more often and longer now than they did pre-SOX, board meetings are still few and short relative to the amount of time insiders spend with one another. Moreover, outside directors are generally dependent upon management for information.

Collective action problems also impede the board's ability to effectively monitor and discipline managers. Even though faithful monitoring may be in an individual director's interest, he or she may assume that other directors will do the hard work of identifying sub-par performances, permitting the free rider to shirk. As in any free-riding situation, this will tend to result in suboptimal levels of monitoring. Even in cases of clearly sub-par management performance, moreover, other collective action problems may prevent the board from taking necessary remedial steps. Some director must step forward to begin building a majority in favor of replacing the incumbent managers, which again raises a free-rider problem. Furthermore, if an active director steps forward, he or she must not only overcome the forces of inertia and bias, but also must likely do so in the face of active opposition from the threatened managers who will try to cut off the flow of information to the board, co-opt key board members, and otherwise undermine the disciplinary process. Board members are likely to have developed warm personal relationships with the CEO and other managers, who will in turn have cultivated that type of sentiment. Those relationships make it hard for boards to fire senior managers, especially when personal friendships of long standing are in play. Lastly, some board members will have been responsible for hiring the managers and will need to make the cognitively difficult admission of their error in order to fire the managers.

Finally, the insiders may effectively control nominally independent directors. As we've seen, it has long been common practice for a corporation's outside directors to include lawyers and bankers (of both the investment and commercial varieties) who are currently providing services to the corporation or may wish to provide services in the future.

---

[155] Adam Smith, The Wealth of Nations 700 (1937).

University faculty or administrators, to take another common example, may be beholden to insiders who control corporate donations to their home institutions. None of these outsiders are likely to bite the hand that feeds them.

Even if the independent directors are not actually biased in favor of the insiders, moreover, they often are predisposed to favor the latter. As noted above, outside directors tend to be corporate officers or retirees who share the same views and values as the insiders. Because outside directors are nominated by the incumbent board members and passively elected by the shareholders, structural bias remains one of the key insoluble riddles of corporate governance.

5.2.3 Pre-Crises Empirical Evidence

The logic of the Sarbanes–Oxley Act and the stock exchange board composition rules is that independent directors will be an effective constraint on the agency costs inherent in the corporate separation of ownership and control. As we have just seen, however, theory predicted that independent directors were unlikely to be effective in doing so. Before independent directors can become effective monitors of management, the system must incur costs to remedy the information asymmetry between outsiders and insiders. It also must incur costs to prevent outside board members from shirking. Put another way, hiring agents to watch other agents may compound instead of reducing agency costs.

The empirical evidence on the relationship between board composition and firm performance available when Sarbanes–Oxley was adopted was inconclusive, at best. If independent directors effectively constrain agency costs, one would have expected the evidence to show a correlation between the presence of independent outsiders on the board and firm performance. But it did not.

True, some early studies found positive correlations between independence and performance. Rosenstein and Wyatt, for example, found that shareholder wealth increased when management appointed independent directors.[156] Weisbach studied board decisions to remove a CEO, finding that boards comprised mainly of independent directors were more likely to base the removal decision on poor performance, as well as being more likely to remove an underperforming CEO, than were insider-dominated boards. He also found that CEO removals by outsider-dominated boards added to firm value, while CEO removals by insider-dominated boards did not.[157] Baysinger and Butler found that corporate financial performance tends to increase (up to a point) as the percentage of independent directors increases.[158] Cotter found that boards dominated by outsiders generate higher shareholder gains from tender offers.[159]

---

[156] Stuart Rosenstein & Jeffrey G. Wyatt, "Outside Directors, Board Independence, and Shareholder Wealth", 26 J. Fin. Econ. 175 (1990).

[157] Michael S. Weisbach, "Outside Directors and CEO Turnover", 20 J. Fin. Econ. 431 (1988).

[158] Barry D. Baysinger & Henry N. Butler, "Revolution versus Evolution in Corporation Law: The ALI's Project and the Independent Director", 52 Geo. Wash. L. Rev. 557, 572 (1984).

[159] James F. Cotter et al., "Do Independent Directors Enhance Target Shareholder Wealth During Tender Offers?", 43 J. Fin. Econ. 195 (1997).

Other studies, however, such as that by MacAvoy, found that board composition had no effect on profitability.[160] Klein likewise found little evidence of a general association between firm performance and board composition, but found a positive correlation between the presence of insiders on board finance and investment committees and firm performance.[161] Rosenstein and Wyatt found that the stock market experienced a significantly positive price reaction to announcements that insiders had been appointed to the board when insiders owned more than 5 percent of the firm's stock.[162]

A 1999 meta-analysis of numerous studies in this area concluded that there was no convincing evidence that firms with a majority of independent directors outperform other firms. It further concluded that there was some evidence that a "moderate number" of insiders correlates with higher performance.[163] A 1998 meta-analysis likewise found no evidence that board composition affects financial performance.[164]

A literature review by Wagner et al. further complicated the empirical landscape by effectively splitting the baby.[165] Their meta-analysis of 63 correlations found that, on average, increasing the number of outsiders on the board is positively associated with higher firm performance. On the other hand, increasing the number of insiders on the board had the same effect. In other words, greater board homogeneity was positively associated with higher firm performance, which is not what the Sarbanes–Oxley Act's proponents would have predicted.

There is some evidence that the post-SOX regulatory changes and the new market forces affecting independent directors have had an impact. Robert Felton's review of studies of post-SOX boards of directors found that the average number of companies on whose board a director sits has gone down, presumably because boards and committees meet more often and have to process more information. The amount of time required for board service has especially gone up for members of audit committees, who have a host of new duties. Overall, "the average commitment of a director of a U.S. listed company increased from 13 hours a month in 2001 to 19 hours in 2003 (and then fell to 18 hours in 2004)."[166] Whether this strengthens the case for director independence is questionable, however, because many of the factors discussed in the preceding sections likely would have produced similar increases in effort by insider-dominated boards.

---

[160] Paul MacAvoy et al., ALI Proposals for Increased Control of the Corporation by the Board of Directors, in Statement of the Business Roundtable on the American Law Institute's Proposed "Principles of Corporate Governance and Structure: Restatement and Recommendations" C-1 (Feb. 1983).

[161] April Klein, "Firm Performance and Board Committee Structure", 41 J. L. & Econ. 275 (1998).

[162] Rosenstein & Wyatt, *supra* note 157.

[163] Sanjai Bhagat & Bernard Black, "The Uncertain Relationship between Board Composition and Firm Performance", 54 Bus. Law. 921, 922 (1999).

[164] Dan R. Dalton et al., "Meta-Analytic Reviews of Board Composition, Leadership Structure, and Financial Performance", 19 Strategic Mgmt. J. 269 (1998). A more recent study of Australian firms found that corporate boards "chaired by non-executives and dominated by non-executive directors at the full board and compensation committee levels are no more adept at enforcing CEO pay-for-firm-performance than are executive-dominated boards." Alessandra Capezio et al., "Too Good to Be True: Board Structural Independence as a Moderator of CEO Pay-for-Firm-Performance", 48 J. Mgmt. Stud. 487 (2011).

[165] John A. Wagner et al., "Board Composition and Organizational Performance: Two Studies of Insider/Outsider Effects", 35 J. Mgmt. Stud. 655 (1998).

[166] Robert F. Felton, "A New Era in Corporate Governance", McKinsey Q., Spring 2004, at 28, 60.

Somewhat stronger evidence that the fetish for independence has had at least some beneficial effects is provided by Michael Useem and Andy Zelleke's survey of governance practices. They found that boards of directors increasingly view delegation of authority to management as properly the subject of careful and self-conscious decision making. The surveyed board members acknowledged that they do not run the company on a day-to-day basis, but rather are seeking to provide stronger oversight and supervision. Increasingly, boards are establishing written protocols to allocate decision-making rights between the board and management, although the protocols vary widely, ranging from detailed and comprehensive to skeletal and limited in scope. Useem and Zelleke conclude that executives still set much by the board's decision-making agenda. At the same time, they found that boards have been increasingly asserting their sovereignty in recent years and that an emergent norm requires management to be mindful of what information boards want to hear and what decisions boards believe they should make.[167]

A critical issue, of course, has always been board access to information. Indirect evidence that independent directors now have good access to information is provided by a study by Enrichetta Ravina and Paola Sapienza of independent directors' trading results. The authors found that independent directors earn substantial positive abnormal returns when trading in their corporation's stock. Even more interestingly, the difference between their results and those of the same firm's executive officers is relatively small, although it widens in firms with weaker governance regimes.[168] It seems reasonable to infer from this evidence that outsiders now have good access to material information about firm performance—indeed, that their access to such information is comparable to that of executive officers.[169]

5.3 Does One Size Now Fit All?

The post-SOX regulatory environment rests on the conventional wisdom that board independence is an unalloyed good. As the preceding sections demonstrated, however, the empirical evidence on the merits of board independence is mixed. Accordingly, even though there is some reason to think independent board members are finally becoming properly incentivized and, as a result, more effective, the clearest take-home lesson from the preceding analysis is still that one size does not fit all.

This result should not be surprising. On one side of the equation, firms do not have uniform needs for managerial accountability mechanisms. The need for accountability is determined by the likelihood of shirking, which in turn is determined by management's tastes, which in turn is determined by each firm's unique culture, traditions, and competitive environment. We all know managers whose preferences include a penchant for hard, faithful

---

[167] Michael Useem & Andy Zelleke, "Oversight and Delegation in Corporate Governance: Deciding What the Board Should Decide", 14 Corp. Governance 2 (2006).

[168] Enrichetta Ravina & Paola Sapienza, "What Do Independent Directors Know? Evidence from Their Trading", 23 Rev. Fin. Stud. 962 (2010).

[169] Note that this raises doubts about the extent to which independent directors are relying on stock price-based metrics. If independent directors are performing as well as insiders, it may be assumed that the former—like the latter—have access to material nonpublic information.

work. Firms where that sort of manager dominates the corporate culture have less need for outside accountability mechanisms.

On the other side of the equation, firms have a wide range of accountability mechanisms from which to choose. Independent directors are not the sole mechanism by which management's performance is monitored. Rather, a variety of forces work together to constrain management's incentive to shirk: the capital and product markets within which the firm functions; the internal and external markets for managerial services; the market for corporate control; incentive compensation systems; auditing by outside accountants; and many others. The importance of the independent directors' monitoring role in a given firm depends in large measure on the extent to which these other forces are allowed to function. For example, managers of a firm with strong takeover defenses are less subject to the constraining influence of the market for corporate control than are those of a firm with no takeover defenses. The former needs a strong independent board more than the latter does.

The critical mass of independent directors needed to provide optimal levels of accountability also will vary depending upon the types of outsiders chosen. Strong, active independent directors with little tolerance for negligence or culpable conduct do exist. A board with a few such directors is more likely to act as a faithful monitor than a board that has many nominally independent directors who shirk their monitoring obligations.

The post-SOX standards, however, strap all listed companies into a single model of corporate governance. By establishing a highly restrictive definition of director independence and mandating that such directors dominate both the board and its required committees, the new rules fail to take into account the diversity and variance among firms. The new rules thus satisfy our definition of quack corporate governance. The one size fits all model, they mandate, should be scrapped in favor of allowing each firm to develop the particular mix of monitoring and management that best suits its individual needs. This conclusion becomes even stronger when one considers the adverse albeit unintended consequences of the movement for director independence, as discussed in the next Part.

5.4 A Note on CEO/Chairman Duality

The exchange listing standards require appointment of an independent lead director if the listed company's CEO serves as the chairman of the board of directors. The lead director presumably chairs the executive sessions of the independent board members. Because the lead director's identity and contact information must be disclosed, he also acts as a point person for shareholder relations. The lead director should have a voice in setting the board's agenda, as a check on the CEO/Chairman's control of board meetings. The lead director should serve as a rallying point for the other independent directors in times of crisis, especially those involving CEO termination or succession.

The lead director position was a compromise with those commentators who wanted the exchanges to mandate a non-executive chairman of the board of directors. The proponents of splitting the CEO and board chairman role, however, continued to press the idea and sought to use Dodd–Frank as a vehicle for doing so. In the end, however, Dodd–Frank Section 973 merely directed the SEC to adopt a new rule requiring reporting companies to disclose whether the same person or different persons hold the positions of CEO and Chairman of the Board.[170] In either case, the company must disclose its reasons for doing so.

The legislative history expressly states that the Act "does not endorse or prohibit either method."[171] This is just as well, because neither method has compelling support in the empirical literature. To be sure, an independent chairman of the board is becoming more common:

> Approximately 16 percent of S&P 500 companies now have an independent chair; among S&P Mid and Small Cap companies the figure is higher (23 percent and 27 percent, respectively). In 2008, 95 percent of S&P 500 boards had an independent lead or presiding director, compared with only 36 percent in 2003.[172]

The latter figure represents the impact of exchange listing standards, of course, and thus should not be taken as evidence in favor of a non-executive chairman. The real question is whether the relatively modest number of companies with such an independent chair is due to market failure or reflects optimal board design.

A study by Olubunmi Faleye finds support for the hypothesis that firms actively weigh the costs and benefits of alternative leadership structures in their unique circumstances and concludes that requiring a one size fits all model separating the CEO and chairman positions may be counterproductive.[173] A study by James Brickley, Jeffrey Coles, and Gregg A. Jarrell found little evidence that combining or separating the two titles affected corporate performance.[174] A subsequent study by the same authors found "preliminary support for the hypothesis that the costs of separation are larger than the benefits for most firms."[175]

As John Coates summarizes the field, the evidence is mixed, at best:

> At least 34 separate studies of the differences in the performance of companies with split vs. unified chair/CEO positions have been conducted over the last 20 years, including two "meta-studies." ... The only clear lesson from these studies is that there has been no long-term trend or convergence on a split chair/CEO structure, and that variation in board leadership structure has persisted for decades, even in the UK, where a split chair/CEO structure is the norm.[176]

---

[170] The Wall Street Reform and Consumer Protection Act of 2010 § 953, Pub. L. No. 111–203, 124 Stat. 1376 (2010).

[171] S. Rep. No. 111–176, at 147 (2010).

[172] "Report of the Task Force of the ABA Section of Business Law Corporate Governance Committee on Delineation of Governance Roles and Responsibilities", 65 Bus. Law. 107, 131 (2009).

[173] Olubunmi Faleye, "Does One Hat Fit All? The Case of Corporate Leadership Structure", 11 J. Mgmt. & Governance 239 (2007).

[174] James A. Brickley et al., "Leadership Structure: Separating the CEO and Chairman of the Board", 3 J. Corp. Fin. 189 (1997).

[175] James A. Brickley et al., "Corporate Leadership Structure: On the Separation of the Positions of CEO and Chairman of the Board", Simon School of Business Working Paper FR 95–02 (Aug. 29, 2000), http://ssrn.com/abstract=6124.

[176] John Coates, "Protecting Shareholders and Enhancing Public Confidence through Corporate Governance" (July 30, 2009), http://blogs.law.harvard.edu/corpgov/2009/07/30/protecting-shareholders-and-enhancing-public-confidence-through-corporate-governance/. With respect to the UK, see Aguilera, *supra* note 16, at S47 ("British boards' signature trait is the separation of the CEO and chairman functions.").

Although Coates concludes that splitting the CEO and chairman positions by legislation "may well be a good idea for larger companies," he further concludes that mandating such a split "is not clearly a good idea for all public companies."[177]

Proponents of a mandatory non-executive Chairman of the Board have overstated the benefits of splitting the positions, while understating or even ignoring the costs of doing so. Michael Jensen identified the potential benefits in his 1993 Presidential Address to the American Finance Association, arguing: "The function of the chairman is to run the board meetings and oversee the process of hiring, firing, evaluation, and compensating the CEO. . . . Therefore, for the board to be effective, it is important to separate the CEO and Chairman positions."[178] In fact, however, overseeing the "hiring, firing, evaluation, and compensating the CEO" is the job of the board of directors as a whole, not just the Chairman of the Board.

To be sure, in many corporations, the Chairman of the Board is given unique powers to call special meetings, set the board agenda, and the like.[179] In such companies, a dual CEO-Chairman does wield powers that may impede board oversight of his or her performance. Yet, in such companies, the problem is not that one person holds both posts; the problem is that the independent members of the board of directors have delegated too much power to the Chairman. The solution is to adopt bylaws that allow the independent board members to call special meetings, require them to meet periodically outside the presence of managers, and the like.

Indeed, the influence of an executive chairman may not even be a problem. Brickley, Coles, and Jarrell concluded that the separation and combination of titles is part of the natural succession process. A successful CEO receives a variety of rewards from the company, one of which may be a fancier title. If the power that comes with the combined title came as a reward for sustained high performance, that power may actually redound to the company's benefit.

Turning from the benefit side to the cost side of the equation, even if splitting the posts makes it easier for the board to monitor the CEO, the board now has the new problem of monitoring a powerful non-executive chairman. The board now must expend effort to ensure that such a chairman does not use the position to extract rents from the company and, moreover, that the chairman expends the effort necessary to carry out the post's duties effectively. The board also must ensure that a dysfunctional rivalry does not arise between the chairman and the CEO, both of whom presumably will be ambitious and highly capable individuals. In other words, if the problem is "who watches the watchers?," splitting the two posts simply creates a second watcher who also must be watched.

In addition, a non-executive chairman inevitably will be less well informed than a CEO. Such a chairman therefore will be less able to lead the board in performing its advisory and networking roles. Likewise, such a chairman will be less effective in leading the board

---

[177] Coates, *supra* note 177.

[178] Michael C. Jensen, "Presidential Address: The Modern Industrial Revolution, Exit, and the Failure of Internal Control Systems", 48 J. Fin. 831, 866 (1993).

[179] James Verdonik and Kirby Happer, Role of the Chairman of the Board 2 (explaining that "one of the duties of the Chairman is to call meetings of the Board of Directors and the shareholders . . . . Chairmen often set the agenda for Board meetings"), www.academia.edu/14812228/Role-of-the-chairman-verdonik-happer.

in monitoring top managers below the CEO, because the chairman will not know those managers as intimately as the CEO.

6 How and Why Boards Fail

Boards of directors have long had bad press. In the eighteenth century, Adam Smith famously complained that one could not expect that the directors of a joint stock company, "being the managers rather of other people's money than of their own, . . . should watch over it with the same anxious vigilance with which the partners in a private copartnery frequently watch over their own."[180] Almost two centuries later, William O. Douglas complained that there were too many boards whose members did "not direct"[181] and dismissed directors as "business colonels of the honorary type—honorary colonels who are ornamental in parade but fairly useless in battle."[182]

More recently, the SEC in 2009 complained that the financial crisis had "led many to raise serious concerns about the accountability and responsiveness of some companies and boards of directors."[183] In the same time frame, prominent Canadian corporate governance commentator Stephen Jarislowsky argued that corporate "boards 'have enormous responsibility for'" the financial crisis of 2007–2008.[184]

Despite this long history of complaints about board performance, there seems little doubt that the rise of the monitoring model has been accompanied by important improvements in board behavior. In 1995, only one in eight CEOs was fired or resigned under board pressure; by 2006, almost a third of CEOs were terminated involuntarily.[185] Over the last several decades, the average CEO tenure has decreased, which also has been attributed to more active board oversight.[186] In sum, boards of directors, "which once served largely as rubber stamps for powerful CEOs, have become more independent, more powerful, and under more pressure to dump leaders who perform poorly."[187]

In addition to the evidence from CEO terminations, other studies confirm a general improvement in board performance. Studies of post-SOX boards of directors find that average board size has increased, presumably because companies are adding more independent directors rather than replacing incumbent insiders.[188] Conversely, the average number of

---

[180]   Adam Smith, An Inquiry into the Nature and Causes of the Wealth of Nations 264–65 (Edwin Cannan ed., 1976) (1776).

[181]   William O. Douglas, "Directors Who Do Not Direct", 47 Harv. L. Rev. 1305 (1934).

[182]   William O. Douglas, Democracy and Finance 46 (1940).

[183]   Facilitating Shareholder Director Nominations, Exchange Act Rel. No. 60,089 (June 10, 2009).

[184]   Janet McFarland, Jarislowsky Blames Financial Mess on Lax Governance Rules, Globe & Mail (Toronto), Oct. 24, 2008, at B12.

[185]   Chuck Lucier et al., "The Era of the Inclusive Leader", Strategy & Bus., Summer 2007, at 3.

[186]   Denis B.K. Lyons, "CEO Casualties: A Battlefront Report", Directors & Boards, Summer 1999, at 43.

[187]   Lauren Etter, Why Corporate Boardrooms Are in Turmoil, Wall St. J., Sept. 16, 2006, at A7.

[188]   Houman B. Shadab, "Innovation and Corporate Governance: The Impact of Sarbanes-Oxley", 10 U. Pa. J. Bus. & Emp. L. 955, 997 (2008) ("To become SOX compliant, companies tended to add independent directors rather than replace insiders, which is reflected in public company board size increasing on average by 8.4 percent from 2001 to 2004 (which reversed the prior 12-year trend in decreasing board size).").

companies on whose boards a director sits has gone down, presumably because boards and committees meet more often and have to process more information.[189]

Michael Useem and Andy Zelleke's survey of governance practices provides additional evidence for improved board performance.[190] They found that boards of directors increasingly view delegation of authority to management as properly the subject of careful and self-conscious decision making.[191] The surveyed board members acknowledged that they do not run the company on a day-to-day basis, but rather are seeking to provide stronger oversight and supervision.[192] Increasingly, boards are establishing written protocols to allocate decision-making rights between the board and management, although the protocols vary widely, ranging from detailed and comprehensive to skeletal and limited in scope.[193] Useem and Zelleke conclude that executives still set much of the board's decision-making agenda.[194] At the same time, they found that boards are increasingly asserting their sovereignty in recent years and that a norm is emerging among managers that, at the very least, they must be mindful of what information boards want to hear and what decisions directors believe the board should make.[195]

6.1 Room for Improvement

While many modern boards demonstrably outperform their predecessors, it would be Pollyannaish to deny that there is still much room for improvement. The financial crisis of 2007–2008, for example, revealed widespread board failures in areas such as enterprise risk management. According to a 2002 survey of corporate directors, 43 percent said that their boards had either an ineffective risk management process or no process for identifying and managing risk at all.[196] According to the same survey, 36 percent of directors felt they had an incomplete understanding of the risks faced by their companies.[197]

A 2008 Towers Perrin survey of CFOs suggests that risk management remained underdeveloped when the financial crisis hit. Seventy-two percent of the respondents, for example, "expressed concern about their own companies' risk management practices and ability to meet strategic plans."[198] Instructively, 42 percent "foresaw more energized involvement by boards of directors in risk management policies, processes and systems,"[199] which implies that

---

[189] James S. Linck et al., "The Effects and Unintended Consequences of the Sarbanes–Oxley Act on the Supply and Demand for Directors", 22 Rev. Fin. Stud. 3287 (2009) (finding that the average number of directorships held by a director in a large firm decreased after SOX).

[190] Useem & Zelleke, *supra* note 168.

[191] Id. at 2.   [192] Id.   [193] Id.   [194] Id. at 11.   [195] Id.

[196] Carolyn Kay Brancato & Christian A. Plath, Corporate Governance Handbook 2005 75 (2005). This finding is supported by a 2003 study, in which 45 percent of respondent directors said their firms had no risk management plan. Susan Schmidt Bies, "Director and Officer Responsibility: A Plan for Action", 8 Fordham J. Corp. & Fin. L. 81, 86 (2003).

[197] Brancato & Plath, *supra* note 197, at 75.

[198] Towers Perrin, "Financial Crisis Intensifies Interest in Risk Management Among CFOs" (Sept. 2008), http://www.soa.org/library/essays/rm-essay-2008-shimpi.pdf.

[199] Id.

pre-crisis boards were inadequately engaged with risk management. This inference finds support in a 2006 observation that risk management was still "a work in progress at many boards."[200]

Respondents to the Towers Perrin survey pointed to these failures as a root cause of the financial crisis. Sixty two percent of respondents blamed "poor or lax risk management at financial institutions as a major contributor to the current financial mess."[201] Instructively, surveyed CFOs were more likely to point to risk management failures by boards as a reason for the financial crisis than either the complexity of financial instruments or speculation (55 percent and 57 percent, respectively).[202]

Still another widely asserted criticism is that boards have failed to rein in allegedly run-away executive compensation. In an influential critique, for example, Lucian Bebchuk and Jesse Fried argued that "directors have been influenced by management, sympathetic to executives, insufficiently motivated to bargain over compensation, or simply ineffectual in overseeing compensation."[203] As a result, they claim, executive pay has greatly exceeded the levels that would prevail if directors loyal to shareholder interests actually bargained with managers at arm's-length.[204] Many other commentators have leveled similar criticisms at boards.[205]

6.2 Why Boards Fail

The reasons boards continue to struggle include the outsider status of most directors, in-adequate time, misspent time, inadequate information, improper skill sets, and insufficient incentives. Ironically, while many of these concerns are longstanding, they have almost all been compounded by recent reforms, especially those focusing on increasing director independence.

As a result of the repeated reforms increasing the number of independent directors, boards today are dominated by part-timers, the vast majority of whom have full-time employment elsewhere, which commands the bulk of their attention and provides the bulk of their pecuniary and psychic income.[206] This has had a number of unintended adverse consequences.

---

[200] Michel Crouhy et al., The Essentials of Risk Management 85 (2006).

[201] Towers Perrin, *supra* note 199.   [202] Id.

[203] Lucian Bebchuk & Jesse Fried, Pay without Performance: The Unfulfilled Promise of Executive Compensation 5 (2004).

[204] See id. at 2 (arguing "the pay-setting process in publicly traded companies has strayed far from the arm's-length model" because "managerial power has played a key role in shaping managers' pay arrangements").

[205] Michael B. Dorff, "Confident Uncertainty, Excessive Compensation & the Obama Plan", 85 Ind. L. J. 491, 493 n.7 (2010) (citing authorities).

[206] See Colin B. Carter & Jay W. Lorsch, Back to the Drawing Board: Designing Corporate Boards for a Complex World 22 (2004) (observing that "most directors today . . . are *very* part-time"; emphasis in original).

6.2.1 Time Constraints

Historically, moreover, directors did not spend much time together working as a group.[207] Board meetings were few and short. According to one survey, for example, during the 1980s directors in large manufacturing companies averaged a total of 14 board and committee meetings per year, with the average board meeting lasting only three hours.[208]

To be sure, as we have seen, the legislative and regulatory fallout from the financial crises of the last decade resulted in directors devoting greater time to board service. Yet, independent directors by their very nature remain part-timers, which has very real costs:

> Independent directors are part time participants in a corporation's affairs. By definition they are outsiders. However intelligent, hardworking or strong minded they may be they do not have the time or the mandate to challenge management's judgments except as to a discrete number of issues. If they spend all of their time trying to audit the auditors and assure that executive compensation is reasonable, they will have no time for focusing on important business and strategy matters.[209]

It appears, moreover, that much of the time directors do spend directing is misspent. Given that time is a scarce resource—especially for the sort of successful individuals likely to be tapped for board memberships—this is a potentially serious problem with contemporary board governance.

Much of the additional time appears to be devoted to oversight activities, which is hardly surprising given that both the Sarbanes–Oxley and Dodd–Frank Acts reinforced the monitoring model's influence.[210] If so, the additional time and effort being expended by directors may have important costs. The rise of the monitoring model long has threatened to generate unproductive adversarial conflict between boards and management. A certain amount of cognitive tension in the board–top management team relationship is beneficial to the extent that it promotes the exercise of critical evaluative judgment by the former.[211] Groups that are too collegial run the risk of submitting to groupthink and various other decision-making errors.[212] If aggressive monitoring fosters an adversarial relation between directors and managers, however, this beneficial form of conflict may transform into more harmful forms. At best, rigid adherence to the monitoring model may transform a collaborative and collegial relationship into one that is cold and distant.[213] At worst, it can promote

---

[207] See id. (noting that "part-time directors don't spend much time together").

[208] The Conference Board, Membership and Organization of Corporate Boards 25 (1990).

[209] Roberta S. Karmel, "Realizing the Dream of William O. Douglas—The Securities and Exchange Commission Takes Charge of Corporate Governance", 30 Del. J. Corp. L. 79, 132 (2005).

[210] See Bainbridge, *supra* note 109, at 59–60 (discussing how Sarbanes–Oxley and Dodd–Frank codified the monitoring model).

[211] See Daniel P. Forbes & Frances J. Milliken, "Cognition and Corporate Governance: Understanding Boards of Directors as Strategic Decision Making Groups", 24 Acad. Mgmt. Rev. 489, 497 (1999) ("Cognitive conflict can help to prevent the emergence of groupthink in cohesive groups by fostering an environment characterized by a task-oriented focus and a tolerance of multiple viewpoints and opinions.").

[212] See *supra* note 103.

[213] See Carter & Lorsch, *supra* note 207, at 19 (discussing ways in which increasing power of the board may disrupt its relations with management).

adversarial relations that result in destructive interpersonal conflict.[214] As noted above, adversarial relations promote conflict rather than collaboration and divert energies into unproductive areas.[215] Unfortunately, as Peter Wallison observes, the "congressional imprimatur" Sarbanes–Oxley put on the monitoring model has compounded the problem by encouraging "an adversarial relationship between managements and boards that will, over time, impair corporate risk-taking and thus economic growth."[216]

Even if a firm's board and management maintain an appropriately balanced relationship, the additional time and effort elicited by the Sarbanes–Oxley Act may not be directed productively. Boards today "are more focused on compliance with standards and regulations than they are on obtaining a competitive advantage."[217] This leaves boards with less time to devote to their traditional functions, including management oversight.

6.2.2 Compounding the Board's Inherent Information Disadvantage

At the minimum, the presence of outsiders on the board increases decision-making costs simply because the process takes longer. Part-time outsiders by definition need more information and are likely to take longer to persuade than are full-time insiders.[218] In addition to having greater access to formal intra-firm information flows by virtue of being full-timers, insiders have lots of informal contacts within the firm, which provide even better access to information than are available to outsiders whose interactions with firm employees is limited.[219] More subtly, and perhaps more importantly, long-term employees make significant investments in firm-specific human capital.[220] Any employee who advances to senior management levels necessarily invests considerable time and effort in learning how to do his job more effectively. Much of this knowledge will be specific to the firm for which he works, such as when other firms do not do comparable work or his firm has a unique corporate culture.[221] An employee who has made significant investments in firm-specific human capital is likely to make better decisions for the firm than an outsider, even assuming equal levels of information relating to the decision at hand. The insider can put the decision in a broader context, seeing the relationships and connections it has to the firm as whole.

---

[214] See id. at 52 (discussing how tension between the board and management can cause "the board's ability to perform effectively" to suffer).

[215] Cf. Bainbridge, *supra* note 109, at 49 ("Relational teams . . . respond to external monitoring efforts by 'circling the wagons' around the intended subject of sanctions.").

[216] Peter J. Wallison, Capital Punishment, Wall St. J., Nov. 4–5, 2006, at A7.   [217] Id.

[218] Dooley & Veasey, *supra* note 155, at 533. Board dysfunctionality can be the result of having too little or too much information. On some boards, directors are deprived of information. Ralph D. Ward, Saving the Corporate Board: Why Boards Fail and How to Fix Them 1 (2003). At other corporations, however, "indigestible overload of information" is dumped on directors. Id.

[219] See Ward, *supra* note 219, at 123 (asserting that "outside board members are amazingly out of touch with the corporation for which they bear ultimate legal responsibility").

[220] See Stephen M. Bainbridge, "Interpreting Nonshareholder Constituency Statutes", 19 Pepp. L. Rev. 971, 1006–07 (1992) (discussing ways employees develop firm-specific human capital).

[221] See Raghuram G. Rajan & Luigi Zingales, "Power in a Theory of the Firm", 113 Q.J. Econ. 387, 392 (1998) (discussing how managers invest in firm-specific human capital).

6.2.3 Compounding the Generalist Problem

In contrast to insiders, independent directors have little incentive to invest in firm-specific human capital. As noted, they typically have full-time jobs elsewhere and often serve on multiple boards simultaneously. As a result, they tend to be generalists with little firm-specific knowledge, skills, or expertise.[222] Modern boards thus tend to be "composed of individuals who are not qualified to assess the strategic viability of the corporations they direct."[223]

> Corporate casualties in the most recent crisis represent instances of board members lacking expertise. In years past, some of Merrill Lynch's board members were leaders of prestigious colleges and universities. However, nothing would indicate that these individuals had meaningful accounting or financial expertise. Their backgrounds and lack of corresponding expertise raise concerns as to their ability to effectively monitor an investment bank such as Merrill. Similarly, Citigroup has been criticized for a board that had a dearth of independent directors with a financial background. Critics have attributed the independent board members' lack of financial skill as a major contributing factor to the company's problems.[224]

Unfortunately, the rules mandating director independence virtually ensure that this problem will remain insoluble. The standards defining what constitutes independence effectively rule out "just about anybody who has firsthand knowledge of the company and its industry."[225] While independent directors can develop such knowledge over time, doing so can be a very lengthy process.[226] Many independent directors thus never develop more than a "rudimentary understanding of their companies' workings."[227]

While at least some long-serving directors may develop a reasonable knowledge of the company's inner workings, long service can give rise to close friendships between nominally independent directors and the managers with whom they serve.[228] This can compromise the director's ability to take strong action when management falters. In some cases, but not all, long-serving directors "may find it difficult to be truly independent in deciding what's in the shareholders' best interests."[229]

6.2.4 Compounding the Improper Incentives of Independent Directors

The most basic way of incentivizing people to do a good job is to pay them for doing so.[230] Oddly, however, it long was against the law for corporations to compensate directors at all.[231] Because boards at that time consisted mainly of people associated with the firm, such as founding entrepreneurs, insiders, or representatives of major shareholders, their stake in the

---

[222] See Carter & Lorsch, *supra* note 207, at 53 ("Directors are the archetypal generalists in a world that values and needs specialization.").

[223] Nicola Faith Sharpe, "Rethinking Board Function in the Wake of the 2008 Financial Crisis", 5 J. Bus. & Tech. L. 99, 109 (2010).

[224] Id. (footnotes omitted).   [225] Carter & Lorsch, *supra* note 207, at 45.   [226] Id.

[227] Id. at 45.

[228] See id. at 49 (discussing relationship between service length and interpersonal relations).

[229] Id.

[230] For an application outside the common practice, see M. Todd Henderson & Fredrick Tung, "Pay for Regulator Performance", 85 S. Cal. L. Rev. 1003 (2012).

[231] See Charles M. Elson, "Director Compensation and the Management-Captured Board—The History of a Symptom and a Cure", 50 S.M.U. L. Rev. 127, 135–48 (1996).

company provided alternative incentives for good performance.[232] As independent directors with no such stake in the company became more common, however, legislatures and courts recognized that compensation now was a necessary incentive and changed the law to allow it.[233] By the mid-1970s, almost all public corporations paid their directors, and the amount of director compensation grew rapidly in the following years.[234]

Unfortunately, the combination of growing cash compensation and management's control of the board nomination process acted "to align the interests of the outside directors with current management rather than with the shareholders. . . . Directors whose remuneration is unrelated to corporate performance have little personal incentive to challenge their management benefactors."[235] In response, Charles Elson proposed a radical change in the form of director compensation:

> To ensure that directors will examine executive initiatives in the best interest of the business, the outside directors must become substantial shareholders. To facilitate this, directors' fees should be paid primarily in company stock that is restricted as to resale during their term in office. No other form of compensation, which serves to compromise their independence from management, should be permitted. The goal is to create within each director a personally based motivation to actively monitor management in the best interest of corporate productivity and to counteract the oversight-inhibiting environment that management appointment and cash-based/benefit-laden fees create.[236]

In 1996, a NACD blue ribbon panel adopted many of Elson's ideas, recommending the use of stock-based compensation and further opining that directors should personally invest an amount in company stock sufficiently large so as to decouple the director's financial interests from those of management.[237] The core idea rapidly caught on, although few firms went so far as to eliminate all cash compensation and benefits. According to a 2007 report by the Conference Board, 90 percent of surveyed companies made some form of stock-based compensation to directors, with 38 percent paying all or part of the basic retainer in stock.[238]

In theory, this change in board compensation practices should align director incentives with the interests of shareholders. If directors have skin in the game, their interests will be more closely aligned with those of the shareholders. The problem is that the practice of paying directors in stock occurred simultaneously with a dramatic increase in the use of

---

[232] *First Nat'l Bank of Allen v. Daugherty*, 250 P. 796, 797 (Okla. 1926) ("Corporate offices are usually filled by those chiefly interested in the welfare of such institutions by reason of interest in stock or other advantages and such interests are presumed to be the motive for executing duties of office without compensation.").

[233] See Elson, *supra* note 232, at 144–46 (discussing evolution of state corporation codes and case law toward allowing director compensation).

[234] See id. at 147 ("By 1975, virtually all public companies compensated their directors and, among manufacturing companies, the median annual compensation, including fees and retainers, had grown to $6000, with the largest companies paying a median of $13,000.").

[235] Id. at 162–64.   [236] Id. at 165.

[237] National Association of Corporate Directors, Report of the NACD Blue Ribbon Commission on Director Professionalism (1996).

[238] The Conference Board, Directors' Compensation and Board Practices in 2006 6–8 (2007).

stock options to pay management.[239] There's some evidence that stock-based compensation is associated with an increase in managerial manipulation of financial results.[240]

The incentives of directors with substantial stock holdings or in-the-money options are more closely aligned with managers than those of shareholders.[241] As a result, if managers inflate the company's stock prices by manipulating financial data or otherwise cooking the books, "directors may go along because they also stand to benefit."[242] There is thus an inherent tension between the competing goals of ensuring director independence and incentivizing them to perform at a high quality level. The more stock a director owns, the less independent the director becomes.[243]

6.2.5 *The Lost Benefits of Insider Representation*

Oliver Williamson suggests that one of the board's functions is to "safeguard the contractual relation between the firm and its management."[244] Insider board representation may be necessary to carry out that function. Many adverse firm outcomes are beyond management's control. If the board is limited to monitoring management, and especially if it is limited to objective measures of performance, however, the board may be unable to differentiate between acts of god, bad luck, ineptitude, and self-dealing. As a result, risk-averse managers may demand a higher return to compensate them for the risk that the board will be unable to make such distinctions. Alternatively, managers may reduce the extent of their investments in firm-specific human capital, so as to minimize non-diversifiable employment risk. Insider representation on the board may avoid those problems by providing better information and insight into the causes of adverse outcomes.

Insider representation on the board also will encourage learned trust between insiders and outsiders. Insider representation on the board thus provides the board with a credible source of information necessary to accurate subjective assessment of managerial performance. In addition, however, it also serves as a bond between the firm and the top management team. Insider directors presumably will look out for their own interests and those of their fellow managers. Board representation thus offers some protection against dismissal for adverse outcomes outside management's control.

---

[239] See Charles M. Yablon, "Bonus Questions—Executive Compensation in the Era of Pay for Performance", 75 Notre Dame L. Rev. 271, 272 (1999) (observing that there has been a "substantial increase in the use of stock options, performance-based bonuses and other forms of pay for performance" since the early 1990s).

[240] Jap Efendi et al., "Why Do Corporate Managers Misstate Financial Statements? The Role of Option Compensation and Other Factors", 85 J. Fin. Econ. 667, 667 (2007) (observing that "the likelihood of a misstated financial statement increases greatly when the CEO has very sizable holdings of in-the-money stock options"); Jesse M. Fried, "Hands-Off Options", 61 Vand. L. Rev. 453, 456 (2008) (citing evidence that "managers ... often inflate the short-term stock price before selling to boost their trading profits").

[241] Carter & Lorsch, *supra* note 207, at 48 (noting the conflict of interest faced by managers and directors "loaded up with stock and options").

[242] Id.

[243] See id. (noting link between increasing stock ownership and loss of "some aspects" of the director's independence).

[244] Williamson, *supra* note 23, at 298.

Such considerations likely explain the finding by Klein of a positive correlation between the presence of insiders on board committees and firm performance.[245] They also help explain the finding by Wagner et al. that increasing the number of insiders on the board is positively correlated with firm performance.[246]

6.3   Boards-R-Us: A New Direction for Reform

As the preceding discussion confirms, the myriad of reforms of the last decade have for the most part simply compounded the problems that lead to board failure. Accordingly, Todd Henderson and this author recently proposed a new direction for board reforms.[247]

Bainbridge and Henderson propose permitting independent firms (e.g., partnerships, corporations, etc.) to provide board services. They call these businesses "board service providers" (BSPs). The idea would be for a corporation, such as Microsoft or ExxonMobil, to hire another entity, call it Boards-R-Us, to provide director services, instead of the group of unrelated individuals it currently hires to provide these services.

Companies provide almost all the goods and services in our economy, including such professional services as accounting or law, because they offer some well-known advantages compared with sole proprietorships. For instance, providing director services as a group would allow directors to decrease individual risk in ways that are more efficient than third-party insurance. It would also allow directors to deploy experts as needed to address particular problems as they arise, just as consultancies and law firms do.

Board members currently have to get expertise from outsiders hired typically by the CEO, which creates conflict-of-interest problems. (Conflict problems arising from BSPs could be handled through rules limiting cross-selling of services, just as Sarbanes–Oxley did for accounting and consultancy services.) Allowing these experts to be under the same roof would reduce this problem, as well as transaction costs. Finally, service firms have reputations that exceed those of individual members, meaning the potential for slack or opportunism is reduced. When an individual acts alone, only one reputation is at stake, but when a firm acts, it is effectively betting the reputation of the firm each time.

Hiring a BSP to provide board services instead of a loose group of sole proprietorships will increase board accountability, both from markets and judicial supervision. For instance, BSPs traded in public markets will be disciplined to provide quality services at competitive prices, and courts may be more willing to enforce fiduciary duties against companies than against individuals.

There currently is no market for directors. They find their way onto boards largely through personal connections, often with the CEO, or the opaque headhunter process, and because

---

[245]   See Klein, *supra* note 162.

[246]   See Wagner et al., *supra* note 166.

[247]   Stephen M. Bainbridge & M. Todd Henderson, "Boards-R-Us: Reconceptualizing Corporate Boards", 66 Stan. L. Rev. 1051 (2014). The summary in this section is borrowed with permission from M. Todd Henderson & Stephen M. Bainbridge, Rethinking Corporate Boards: Why Companies Need "Board Service Providers," Bloomberg Businessweek (Aug. 22, 2013), http://www.businessweek.com/articles/2013-08-22/rethinking-corporate-boards-why-companies-need-board-service-providers.

votes are private and decisions are made collectively, the accountability to shareholders is greatly diminished. Although it is possible for any individual to run for a board seat on any company, the publicity and voting costs are prohibitive. A BSP with a national reputation and the ability to provide all director functions would be able to reduce the cost of winning board seats. For instance, BSPs can use their brand and economies of scale to lower the costs of communicating with and persuading shareholders to hire them.

Bainbridge and Henderson do not argue that all public companies should hire BSPs to provide their board services. Companies should merely have the choice to use BSPs—and to understand their potential benefits—just as they do for all other services they require.

CHAPTER 13

EXECUTIVE REMUNERATION

GUIDO FERRARINI AND MARIA CRISTINA UNGUREANU

1 INTRODUCTION

EXECUTIVE pay lies at the heart of current discussion on corporate governance reform. Increased disclosure, monitoring by the media, and institutional investor activism often suggest that the levels and structures of executive remuneration are divorced from corporate performance, and represent a sharp conflict of interest between management and shareholder interests. Moreover, "excessive" compensation at banks and other financial institutions is widely believed to have contributed to the financial crisis by incentivizing managers to take excessive risks. In the present chapter we consider executive remuneration from a transatlantic perspective, looking at corporate practices, regulation, and investor behavior both in Europe and the US. The remainder of this introductory section introduces the main problems of executive pay from the perspective of agency costs theory, banking theory, and corporate social responsibility. In section 2, we analyze the main policy issues concerning executive pay, such as design problems, remuneration governance, disclosure of pay policies and amounts, and prudential regulation of pay structure at banks. In section 3 we examine the regulation of pay governance and disclosure, focusing on EU law, comparative law, and international practice. In section 4 we analyze the regulation of pay structure at financial institutions (banks in particular) focusing on the international principles and standards, on the Dodd–Frank Act, and CRD IV. Section 5 concludes.

1.1 Agency Costs

The principal–agent model has generated two competing views of executive pay.[1] Under the first view, executive pay remedies the agency costs generated by the misalignment of management and shareholder interests in the dispersed ownership company. Shareholders

---

[1] Guido Ferrarini & Niamh Moloney, "Executive Remuneration in the EU: The Context for Reform", 21 Oxford Rev. Econ. Pol'y 304 (2005).

in dispersed ownership systems have only a fractional interest in firm profits, are not fully incentivized to discipline, and have limited opportunities to monitor management.[2] Management's unobserved actions, particularly where personal costly decisions (e.g., laying off employees) and private beneficial activities (e.g., consuming perquisites) are involved, can reduce shareholder wealth and give rise to agency costs. Whether, and the extent to which, a manager will fully pursue the shareholders' agenda depends on how she is incentivized. Agency theory suggests that the performance-based pay contract, which links pay to shareholder wealth via performance indicators such as share prices or accounting-based targets, is a powerful way of attracting, retaining, and motivating managers to pursue the shareholders' agenda.[3] In the dispersed ownership context, this approach has dominated the pay debate and pay practices since the early 1990s and still enjoys considerable support as making management more sensitive to shareholders' interests.[4]

According to a second view, executive pay can also be regarded as an agency cost in itself in that it provides a powerful and opaque device for self-dealing by conflicted managers.[5] In practice, pay is not set by shareholders; instead, it is set on their behalf by the board of directors, which is expected to align shareholder and managerial incentives.[6] Nonetheless, a conflicted board may use the pay-setting process to influence pay and extract rents in the form of pay in excess of that would be optimal for shareholders, given weaknesses in the design of pay contracts and in their supporting governance structures.[7] In other words, executive pay raises an additional agency problem: How can the effectiveness of the executive pay contract as a remedy for manager/shareholder agency costs be protected from conflicts between the board, as pay-setter, and the shareholders?[8] The equity-based incentive contract may, as post-Enron scholarship argues, deepen conflicts of interest between shareholders and managers by generating perverse management incentives to manipulate financial disclosure, particularly earnings, and distort share prices, which can lead to catastrophic

---

[2] Michael Jensen & William Meckling, "Theory of the Firm: Managerial Behavior, Agency Costs and Ownership Structure", 3 J. Fin. Econ. 305 (1976).

[3] Michael Jensen & Kevin Murphy, "Performance Pay and Top-Management Incentives", 98 Journal of Political Economy 225 (1990); Michael Jensen & Kevin Murphy, "Remuneration: Where We've Been, How We Got to Here, What Are the Problems, and How to Fix Them", 44 ECGI Finance Working Paper (2004), available at: www.ecgi.org; Martin J. Conyon & Dennis Leech, "Top Pay, Company Performance and Corporate Governance", 56 Oxford Bulletin of Economics and Statistics 229 (1994); Brian J. Hall & Jeffrey Liebman, "Are CEOs Really Paid Like Bureaucrats?", 113 Q.J. Econ. 653 (1998).

[4] Bengt Holmstrom & Steven N. Kaplan, "The State of U.S. Corporate Governance: What's Right and What's Wrong?", 15 J. Appl. Corp. Fin. 8 (2003); Rajesh K. Aggarwal & Andrew A. Samwick, "Executive Compensation, Strategic Competition, and Relative Performance Evaluation: Theory and Evidence", 54 J. Fin. 1999 (1999); Conyon & Leech (1994).

[5] Lucian Arye Bebchuk, Jesse M. Fried, & David I. Walker, "Managerial Power and Rent Extraction in the Design of Executive Compensation", 69 U. Chi. L. Rev. 751 (2002); Jennifer Hill & Charles M. Yablon, "Corporate Governance and Executive Remuneration: Rediscovering Managerial Positional Conflict", 25 U.N.S.W. Law Journal 294 (2002); Lucian Bebchuk & Jesse Fried, Pay without Performance: The Unfulfilled Promise of Executive Compensation (2004).

[6] Jensen & Murphy (2004).   [7] Bebchuk et al. (2002); Bebchuk & Fried (2004).

[8] Jensen & Murphy (2004); Jeffrey N. Gordon, "Executive Compensation: If There's a Problem, What's the Remedy? The Case for 'Compensation Disclosure and Analysis'", 30 J. Corp. L. 675 (2005); Jensen & Murphy (1990); Michael C. Jensen & Kevin J. Murphy, "CEO Incentives—It's Not How Much You Pay, but How", 3 J. Appl. Corp. Fin. 64 (2010).

corporate failures. The consequences of such a cycle of ever higher share prices, and their impact on pay, have been examined as "the agency costs of overvalued equity."[9]

The relationship between agency problems and the executive pay incentive contract takes on an additional complexity in continental European firms, characterized by concentrated shareholdings and long-term shareholder commitment.[10] Here, incentives and conflicts change, as concentration of control (possibly intensified by cross shareholdings, pyramidal ownership structures, proxy voting by financial institutions connected to the company, and voting pacts) recasts the agency problem which executive pay is designed to resolve. The agency costs which trouble the dispersed ownership company are reduced, as block-holding shareholders have both incentives and resources to monitor managers effectively. As a result, there is less need for an incentive contract to control the conflict between management and shareholder interests that is remedied by executive pay. There is also less probability of the agency problem which derives from executive pay arising. However, other concerns may emerge with regards to concentrated shareholdings regarding also executive pay.

1.2 Financial Stability

The traditional agency approach does not fully explain the problems of bankers' pay and their possible impact on financial stability. No doubt, a widespread post-crisis view holds that the failure of banks both in Europe and the US may have been at least partially caused by flawed remuneration structures, including short-term incentives that may have led bank managers to take risks which in the long run appeared to be excessive. Nonetheless, empirical research has shown that banks that failed in the crisis somehow complied with best practices as to corporate governance and executive remuneration.[11] A paper by Rüdiger Fahlenbrach and René Stulz analyzes a sample of 98 large banks across the world and finds "no evidence that banks with a better alignment of CEOs' interests with those of their shareholders had higher returns during the crisis."[12] The authors rather identify "some evidence that banks led by CEOs whose interests were better aligned with those of their shareholders had worse stock returns and a worse return on equity." According to their study, CEOs had substantial wealth invested in their banks, with the median CEO portfolio including stocks and options in the relevant bank worth more than eight times the value of the CEO's total compensation in 2006. Similar equity holdings should have led CEOs to focus on the long term, avoiding too much risk and excessive leverage for their banks. Instead, the study shows that a bank's stock return performance in 2007–2008 was negatively related to the dollar value of its CEO's

---

[9] Jensen & Murphy (2004).

[10] Guido Ferrarini & Niamh Moloney, "Executive Remuneration and Corporate Governance in the EU: Convergence, Divergence, and Reform Perspectives", 1 Eur. Company & Fin. L. Rev. 251 (2004). The relevant arguments are developed and shown also empirically in Roberto Barontini, Stefano Bozzi & Guido Ferrarini, "Executive Remuneration Standards and the 'Conformity Gap' at Controlled Corporations", 21 Journal of Management and Governance 573 (2017).

[11] Andrea Beltratti & René Stulz, "The Credit Crisis around the Globe: Why Did Some Banks Perform Better?", 105 J. Fin. Econ. 1 (2012); Renée Adams, "Governance and the Financial Crisis", ECGI Finance Working Paper No. 248 (2009), available at www.ssrn.com.

[12] Rüdiger Fahlenbrach & René M. Stulz, "Bank CEO Incentives and the Credit Crisis", 99 J. Fin. Econ. 11 (2011).

holdings of shares in 2006, and that a bank's return on equity in 2008 was negatively related to its CEO's holdings in shares in 2006.

However, another stream of literature highlights possible agency costs in banks caused by inadequate remuneration structures. A paper by Lucian Bebchuk, Alma Cohen, and Holger Spamann on executive compensation at Bear Stearns and Lehman Brothers focuses on the link between substantial short-term incentives and excessive risk taking.[13] The authors argue that the large losses on shares that the top financiers suffered when their firms melted down do not offer a full picture of their payoffs, which should include what the same executives cashed out in the 2000–2008 period and what they owned initially. In the observed timeframe, the relevant executives received large amounts of cash bonus compensation and "regularly took large amounts of money off the table by unloading shares and options." Indeed, performance-based compensation paid to top executives at Bear Stearns and Lehman Brothers substantially exceeded the value of their holdings at the beginning of the period. Bebchuk et al. argue that this provides a basis for concern about the incentives of the two banks' executives. Rather than producing a "tight alignment" of their interests with long-term shareholder value, the design of performance-based compensation provided executives of the relevant firms with substantial opportunities "to take large amounts of compensation based on short-term gains off the table and retain it even after the drastic reversal of the two companies' fortunes."

In order to get the full picture, the remuneration of other bank employees (such as traders) should also be taken into account, particularly that of high earners who contribute to risk taking by the firm.[14] Even though precise empirical data are lacking, it is well known that many of these employees were paid short-term incentives before the crisis in amounts much greater than that of their fixed salaries. As explained by Diamond and Rajan (2009):

> Given the competition for talent, traders have to be paid generously based on performance. But many of the compensation schemes paid for short-term risk-adjusted performance. This gave traders an incentive to take risks that were not recognized by the system, so they could generate income that appeared to stem from their superior abilities, even though it was in fact only a market-risk premium.[15]

No doubt, assuming that CEOs and other top managers were awarded the right incentive schemes—i.e., not only short-term, but also long-term incentives—the fact that other employees had mainly short-term incentives should not be a source of great concern, provided that sound risk management systems were in place and an effective oversight was exercised on risk takers by their superiors. However, as widely acknowledged in the aftermath of the crisis, this was not always the case at large banks, where risk management systems were often deficient, and CEOs and top managers frequently did not have proper controls over the financial operations. Moreover, the problems were exacerbated by the huge

---

[13] Lucian Bebchuk, Alma Cohen, & Holger Spamann, "The Wages of Failure: Executive Compensation at Bear Stearns and Lehman 2000–2008", 27 Yale J. Reg. 257 (2010).

[14] Ing-Haw Cheng, Harrison Hong, & Jose A. Scheinkman, "Yesterday's Heroes: Compensation and Creative Risk-Taking", ECGI Finance Working Paper No. 285 (2010), available at www.ssrn.com.

[15] Douglas W. Diamond & Raghuram G. Rajan, "The Credit Crisis: Conjectures about Causes and Remedies", 99 Am. Econ. Rev. 606 (2009).

amounts promised by banks to their employees. As colorfully described by Professor Alan Blinder, traders and other employees were often offered:

> the following sort of go-for-broke incentives when they place financial bets: Heads, you become richer than Croesus; tails, you get no bonus, receive instead about four times the national average salary, and may (or may not) have to look for another job . . . Faced with such skewed incentives, they place lots of big bets. If heads come up, they acquire dynastic wealth. If tails come up, OPM [other people money] absorbs almost all losses.[16]

1.3 Social Issues

The criticism of excessive pay also concerns non-financial firms and, across sectors, portrays a social perspective. Indeed, populist and political resentment against income disparity is on the rise, particularly in the present context of economic uncertainty, leading to a lack of confidence in the integrity and fairness of large corporations. The US was the first to officially address the social implications of high executive pay.[17] In September 2013 the SEC proposed new rules on disclosure by public companies of the ratio of CEO pay to median employee pay, as required under Section 953(b) of the Dodd–Frank Act.[18] This approach has been the subject of intense debate and has garnered significant media attention.[19] Its supporters, including pension funds and other socially-minded investors, argue that the ratio represents material information for investors and that looking at the overall compensation framework of a single company can help rein in excessive executive pay.[20] In contrast, business organizations, major law firms, and other market constituencies argue that the pay ratio would provide little or no insight for investors, who are rather interested in the correlation between CEO pay and the company's financial performance, also in comparison with pay practices at other public companies.[21]

The reported ratio is expected to be very high, even for CEOs whose compensation is relatively modest. Whilst the US is attempting to deter excessive executive pay by holding boards

---

[16] Alan S. Blinder, After the Music Stopped: The Financial Crisis, the Response, and the Work Ahead (2014).

[17] Kevin J. Murphy, The Politics of Pay: A Legislative History of Executive Compensation, in Research Handbook on Executive Pay 11 (Randall S. Thomas and Jennifer G. Hill eds., 2012).

[18] Section 953(b) of Dodd–Frank directs the SEC to amend its executive compensation disclosure rules to require public companies to disclose (1) the median of the annual total compensation of all employees, other than the CEO; (2) the annual total compensation of the CEO; and (3) the ratio of the median employee annual total compensation to the CEO annual total compensation. The Dodd–Frank Wall Street Reform and Consumer Protection Act, Pub. L. No. 111–203 (2010).

[19] AFL-CIO, Dodd–Frank, section 953(b): Why CEO-to-Worker Pay Ratios Matter for Investors (2013), available at www.aflcio.org.

[20] For example, the Council of Institutional Investors recommends that compensation committees consider the "goals for distribution of awards throughout the company" and "the relationship of executive pay to the pay of other employees" as factors in developing their executive pay philosophy. Council of Institutional Investors, Corporate Governance Policies (2010), available at http://www.cii.org/CouncilCorporateGovernancePolicies/.

[21] For an analysis of the debate including critics, Gary Shorter, "The 'Pay Ratio Provision' in the Dodd–Frank Act: Legislation to Repeal It in the 113th Congress" (October 2013), available at https://www.fas.org/sgp/crs/misc/R43262.pdf.

accountable both to shareholders and society through mandated disclosure, some European countries target similar goals through different measures.[22] For example, France uses taxation as a means to rebalance pay differences between corporate executives (and high earners in general) and other employees, through a 75 percent "super tax" payable by employers on compensation over €1m.[23] In Germany, changes to the Corporate Governance Code were effected requiring supervisory boards (1) to set maximum payout levels on the total and individual pay of executive board members and (2) to consider the relationship between executive board members' remuneration and that of staff generally.[24] In Switzerland, following a public referendum against excessive salaries in March 2013 (the "fat cat initiative"), the voters' majority called for new constitutional rules to control executive pay and improve the corporate governance of listed companies.[25] As the referendum's outcome was not directly enforceable, the Federal Council adopted an interim ordinance,[26] which intends to improve the corporate governance of Swiss listed companies and empowers shareholders to express a binding vote on executive compensation. The new ordinance is particularly striking as it includes penal provisions for breaches of its rules and for executives being granted or accepting excessive compensation.

2 POLICY ISSUES

2.1 Design Problems

Performance pay may suffer from a number of inherent design defects which damage the performance link at the heart of the incentive contract's effectiveness as an interest-alignment device, and which provoke conflicts between management and shareholders or, potentially, between management/controlling shareholders and minority shareholders (according to the particular shareholder/management profile in blockholding companies). These defects heighten the need for an effective governance and disclosure matrix for pay setting if the alignment process is to work. We highlight three main design challenges: proxies for firm performance, stock options, and long-term pay.[27]

---

[22] Tower Watson, Executive Remuneration—Europe. Corporate Governance Developments (2014), available at: www.towerwatson.com.

[23] French General Tax Code, Article 750, Public Finances General Directorate, Tax Policy Directorate, Minister of Economy, Finance and Industry, available at http://www.impots.gouv.fr/portal/deploiement/p1/fichedescriptive_1006/fichedescriptive_1006.pdf.

[24] German Corporate Governance Code, 2013, available at www.corporate-governance-code.de.

[25] Text of initiative (in German) Eidgenössische Volksinitiative "gegen die Abzockerei," available at http://www.admin.ch/ch/d/pore/vi/vis348t.html. Brief in English available at http://www.lexology.com/library/detail.aspx?g=d97687f6-db1d-430e-b157-3c3432b5ed1a.

[26] Ordinance against Excessive Compensation with respect to Listed Stock Corporations. (OaEC, 2014). See information on http://www.lexology.com/library/.

[27] Ferrarini & Moloney (2005); Guido Ferrarini, Niamh Moloney, & Maria-Cristina Ungureanu, "Executive Remuneration in Crisis: A Critical Assessment of Reforms in Europe", 10 J. Corp. L. Stud. 73 (2010).

2.1.1 Proxies for Firm Performance

Share price is ordinarily the best available proxy for shareholder wealth and reflects overall corporate performance more effectively than business-line linked, target-specific bonuses. But the danger arises when generating incentives to inflate earnings and manage disclosure to generate short-term share-price increases. Equity-based compensation also risks over-compensation of executives who preside over a period of market growth and under-compensation of those caught in a period of overall poor market performance. It is, however, difficult to construct a better alternative for shareholder wealth, given that it does reflect the market's perception of the company's current and future cash flows, and so its perceptions of management performance and investment opportunities.[28] The risk of management inflating the share price, however, demands that the governance matrix, which monitors management and supports pay setting, whether it be independent directors, institutional investors, or controlling shareholders, is robust and establishes risk-adjustment mechanisms in the remuneration policy.

2.1.2 Share Options

Share options pose a second major design problem. They can create potentially powerful incentives by linking pay to shareholder returns expressed via the share price. They can incentivize executives to take efficient but personally stressful decisions and promote greater efforts to increase the global value of the company and the share price.[29] They have an attractively asymmetrical pay structure in that they reward success but do not appear to penalize failure: Executives are not likely to equate the failure to make a gain with an actual loss. Options can also act as a powerful inducement to attract talent and can incentivize executives to stay. At the same time, share options also display a number of inherent inefficiencies and possible risks,[30] such as the following:

1   Relative performance. Fixed price options, where vesting is independent of performance, can deliver very large gains for executives whenever the market is rising, even if the company is under-performing its competitors.[31] This problem can be avoided by linking the option's exercise price to a market or peer-group index such that executives are rewarded only when they outperform the competition, or linking exercise to the achievement of performance conditions.

---

[28] Kevin J. Murphy, "Corporate Performance and Managerial Remuneration: An Empirical Analysis", 7 J. Acct. & Econ. 11 (1985); Jensen & Murphy (1990).

[29] Jeffrey N. Gordon, "What Enron Means for the Management and Control of the Modern Business Corporation: Some Initial Reflections", 69 U. Chi. L. Rev. 1233 (2002).

[30] Bebchuk et al. (2002).

[31] Alfred Rappaport, "New Thinking on How to Link Executive Pay with Performance", 77 Harv. Bus. Rev. 91 (1999); Menachem Brenner, Rangarajan K. Sundaram, & David Yermack, "Altering the Terms of Executive Stock Options", 57 J. Fin. Econ. 103 (2000); Don M. Chance, Raman Kumar, & Rebecca B. Todd, "The 'Repricing' of Executive Stock Options", 57 J. Fin. Econ. 65 (2000); Angela B. Morgan & Annette B. Poulsen, "Linking Pay to Performance—Compensation Proposals in the S&P 500", 62 J. Fin. Econ. 489 (2001); Keith W. Chauvin & Catherine Shenoy, "Stock Price Decreases Prior to Executive Stock Option Grants", 7 J. Corp. Fin. 53 (2001).

2 Repricing. The capacity for share options to be re-priced when the share price falls on poor corporate performance (rather than on sector-wide movements) further weakens the incentive justification and damages the alignment mechanism.[32] This was a common practice in the US prior to changes in accounting regulations.[33]

3 Impact on dividend policy. If share options appropriately align shareholder and management incentives, management should be incentivized to allocate cash flow to shareholders in the form of dividends. Share options can distort this alignment as the value of options drops with dividend payment, incentivizing management to reduce dividends.[34]

4 Dilution. Share options carry the risk of dilution and, therefore, of a reduction in earnings per share and entrenchment of management voting power.[35] Dilution also raises difficulties in blockholding companies, where controllers may see their dominant position weakened.

Option grants can, however, be structured to avoid incentive alignment weaknesses. The share option problem then becomes one of how to ensure good supporting governance in, and disclosure of, pay setting, rather than a difficulty with the option as a tool of executive pay per se. Design problems are in the hands of the board, as pay setter, and its allied monitoring structures. If the board strategy is aligned with shareholder interests, structure problems can be mitigated. Although the connection between bad governance and suboptimal pay structures is not entirely clear,[36] the link between optimal shareholder interest alignment and good governance drives regulatory responses to remuneration.

2.1.3 Long-Term Pay

One of the concerns in the discussion regarding executive pay design has been that it is insufficiently focused on the long term, leading to reckless, short-term decision-making by executives and to financial bubbles.[37] However, combating short-termism appears to be high on the post-crisis agenda, as shown by the Kay Review in the UK, suggesting that "companies should structure directors' remuneration to relate incentives to sustainable long-term business performance. Long-term performance incentives should be provided

---

[32] Brenner et al. (2000); Chance et al. (2000).

[33] Mary Ellen Carter & Luann J. Lynch, "An Examination of Executive Stock Option Repricing", 61 J. Fin. Econ. 207 (2001).

[34] Richard A. Lambert, William N. Lanen, & David F. Larcker, "Executive Stock Options Plans and Corporate Dividend Policy", 24 J. Fin. Quant. Anal. 409 (1989); Scott J. Weisbenner, "Corporate Share Repurchases in the 1990: What Role Do Stock Options Play?", FEDS Working Paper No. 2000-29 (2000), available at www.ssrn.com; Markus C. Arnold & Robert M. Gillenkirch, "Stock Options as Incentive Contracts and Dividend Policy", University of Frankfurt Finance & Accounting Working Paper Series (2002), available at www.ssrn.com.

[35] Morgan & Poulsen (2001); Chauvin & Shenoy (2001).

[36] Brenner et al. (2000); Marianne Bertrand & Sendhil Mullainathan, "Agents with and without Principals", 90 Am. Econ. Rev. 203 (2000); Carter & Lynch, 2001.

[37] David I. Walker, "The Challenge of Improving the Long-Term Focus of Executive Pay" 51 Boston College Law Review 435 (2010); Bebchuk & Fried (2004).

only in the form of company shares to be held at least until after the executive has retired from the business."[38] In addition, corporate governance scholars suggest that executives should be encouraged to focus on the long term by holding a large fraction of their equity after it vests. Bhagat and Romano, in particular, recommend that incentive compensation should consist only of restricted stock and restricted stock options—restricted in the sense that the executive cannot sell the shares or exercise the options for two to four years after his or her last day in office. They contend that such an incentive compensation package will focus management's attention on the long-run and discourage investment in high-risk, value-destroying projects.[39] Bebchuk and Fried also focus on equity-based compensation as a way for tying incentives to long-term results.[40] They particularly analyze the optimal design of limitations on unwinding, arguing that an executive receiving an equity-based grant should not be free to unwind the received equity incentives for a specified period of time after vesting, after which she should be permitted to unwind the equity only gradually. Moreover, they advocate that firms adopt arrangements designed to ensure that executives cannot easily evade both the prescriptions that require executives to hold equity for the long term and those that prevent gaming.

2.2 Governance Mechanisms

The effectiveness of the incentive contract largely depends on the management of agency problems between the board and shareholders and on adequate monitoring by, inter alia, independent directors and, ultimately, shareholders.

2.2.1 Boards

A board may become passive or captured by management, and hence poorly incentivized to bargain for optimal incentive pay in shareholder interests. The addition of independent directors to the board (or board remuneration committee) may provide a solution and is a dominant theme of regulatory responses to remuneration, albeit adjusted, in blockholding systems, to reflect the influence of controlling shareholders.[41] Independent, well-resourced, informed, and competent directors should be able to withstand any overbearing influence of senior management and be more likely to judge performance in the shareholders' interests and with respect to the company's performance.[42]

---

[38] The Kay Review of UK Equity Markets and Long-Term Decision Making (July 2012), available at www.gov.uk; European Commission, Communication on long term financing of the European economy, available at http://www.ec.europa.eu (March 2014)

[39] Sanjai Bhagat & Roberta Romano, "Reforming Executive Compensation: Focusing and Committing to the Long-Term", 26 Yale J. Reg. 359 (2009).

[40] Lucian A. Bebchuk & Jesse M. Fried, "Paying for Long-Term Performance", 158 U. Pa. L. Rev. 1915 (2010).

[41] Guido Ferrarini & Marilena Filippelli, "Independent Directors and Controlling Shareholders around the World", ECGI Working Paper No. 258 (2014) available at www.ssrn.com.

[42] Reinier Kraakmann, Disclosure and Corporate Governance: An Overview Essay, in Reforming Company and Takeover Law in Europe (Guido Ferrarini et al. eds., 2004).

There are, however, certain impediments to optimizing the presence of independent directors. Independent directors in given circumstances may be reluctant to disturb the status quo, or may be incentivized to set pay in a manner beneficial to them where they are serving executive directors. They may lack expertise on pay or have insufficient time to become expert. Disclosure flows to independent directors on corporate performance may be unreliable. Reputational factors, which may result in an independent director who is regarded as "tough on pay" being blacklisted from other boards may arise. The empirical evidence on the effectiveness of independent directors is equivocal.[43] It has also been suggested that independent directors have not always controlled executive pay but rather presided over its explosion.[44]

One way out of this impasse is to impose rigorous controls on the independence of nominally independent directors, which can only be achieved to a limited degree in blockholding systems. Composed primarily of independent directors and exercising pay-setting functions delegated from the board, the remuneration committee can act as an objective control on the pay-setting process. However, the remuneration committee may be particularly ineffectual in blockholding companies playing, in effect, a fictional role as pay is set by the controlling shareholders directly, although it has a potentially important role in minority shareholder protection.

While external remuneration consultants provide expertise in the complex area of pay design and improve disclosure flows to the remuneration committee, they are also vulnerable to capture by the board and may exacerbate problems by acting as a camouflage mechanism to legitimize suboptimal pay decisions, unless selected by and accountable to the remuneration committee.[45]

2.2.2 *Shareholders*

The effectiveness of back-stop shareholder monitoring of the incentive contract and the pay-setting process lies at the core of the pay-setting problem in the dispersed-ownership context. As effective monitors, whether via direct shareholder voice mechanisms, such as votes on pay, or via indirect lobbying, shareholders suffer from the collective action problem and from lack of information. Collective action problems are exacerbated in the case of executive pay as shareholders are unlikely to see substantial individual gains from a potential reduction in executive pay, and may suffer if management incentives are damaged. An examination of the optimality of pay decisions requires careful case-by-case analysis of disclosure which, even where it is made available, can be difficult for shareholders. Institutional investors are, albeit controversially, often regarded as potentially strong corporate monitors. The extent to which institutional investors can bear on the pay process is, however, doubtful.[46]

---

[43] Roberta Romano, "The Sarbanes-Oxley Act and the Making of Quack Corporate Governance", 114 Yale L. J. 1521 (2005).

[44] Sanjai Bhagat & Bernard Black, "The Non-Correlation between Board Independence and Long-Term Firm Performance", 27 J. Corp. L. 231 (2002).

[45] Bebchuk et al. (2002); Jensen & Murphy (2004).

[46] Brian R. Cheffins & Randall S. Thomas, "Should Shareholders Have a Greater Say over Executive Pay? Learning from the US Experience", 1 J. Corp. L. Stud. 277 (2001); Jeffrey Gordon, "'Say on Pay': Cautionary Notes on the U.K. Experience and the Case for Shareholder Opt-In", 46 Harvard J. Legislation 323 (2009).

The collective action problem arises and is aggravated by the need for institutions to have diversified holdings,[47] which dilutes the ability of institutional investors to focus on company-specific issues. Institutions may not communicate effectively as a group and so fail to influence the board. Agency problems can also arise within an institutional investor, where, for example, an investor's corporate governance team faces pressure from other internal groups which provide services to a company's management.[48] Institutional investors may also be prone to short-termism and ill-equipped to undertake successful long-term monitoring of executive pay strategies. However, there is some US evidence that large shareholders (5 percent and over) can act as an effective governance mechanism with respect to remuneration.[49] Law, and particularly mandatory disclosure, appears to matter in this context, as the changes to UK company law in 2002 requiring a shareholder vote on the Director's Remuneration Report, appeared to galvanize institutional investors into action, as we argue below.

However, a significant development in the last few years has been the rise of shareholder engagement. This mainly depends on the re-concentration of ownership in the hands of institutional investors and on the willingness of many of these to behave as active investors.[50] While there are also other issues to debate (such as corporate social responsibility), remuneration stands out in particular as a topic on which investors have significant interest.[51] Generally, companies engage with shareholders on executive compensation well ahead of the annual general meeting. While initially engagement occurred primarily in cases in which a "no" recommendation had been issued by proxy advisors on a company's pay policy or other negative feedback had come from significant shareholders, it is accepted today that dialogue with shareholders should take place in all circumstances.[52] Indeed, not only pay practices but also corporate performance drive proxy advisors' recommendations and voting by institutional investors.[53] Therefore, a negative recommendation or vote could be issued simply on the basis of a perceived disconnect between between pay and corporate performance or shareholder return, regardless of how carefully remuneration structures comply with best practices.

---

[47]   Klaus Hopt, "Modern Company and Capital Market Problems. Improving European Corporate Governance after Enron", ECGI Working Paper No. 5 (2002), available at www.ecgi.org.

[48]   Roberta Romano, "Less Is More: Making Institutional Investor Activism a Valuable Mechanism of Corporate Governance", 18 Yale J. Reg. 174 (2001).

[49]   Bertrand & Mullainathan (2001).

[50]   Ronald J. Gilson & Jeffrey N. Gordon, "The Agency Costs of Agency Capitalism: Activist Investors and the Revaluation of Governance Rights", 113 Colum. L. Rev. 863 (2013); Brian R. Cheffins, "The Corporate Governance Movement, Banks and the Financial Crisis", ECGI Law Working Paper No. 232 (2014) available at: www.ecgi.org.

[51]   European Commission, Summary of the informal discussions concerning the initiative on shareholders engagement (March 2013), available at http://ec.europa.eu.

[52]   European Commission (2003).

[53]   ISS (International Shareholder Services), 2011 U.S. Post Season Report (2011), available at www.iss.com; ISS (International Shareholder Services) 2012 Proxy Season Review. World Markets (2013), available at www.iss.com.

2.3 Disclosure

Disclosure may provide the least costly way to manage the range of potential agency costs by ensuring that shareholders have sufficient information on remuneration as well as on any potential conflicts in the remuneration-setting process. It is also a more limited form of intervention in governance, which would allow flexibility and increase transparency in remuneration-setting in dispersed and blockholding ownership companies.[54] Disclosure requirements prompt the board to justify pay choices and the pay-setting process, and can also enhance the accountability and visibility of the remuneration committee. They can also sharpen shareholder monitoring, particularly by inducing institutional shareholders to play a more active role. Disclosure of pay lowers the cost of monitoring by raising the reputation of institutional investor monitors by signalling or publicizing the results of their active approach and generating greater deterrence effects. It also facilitates communication between institutional investors and with company management.

While disclosure is traditionally associated with minimal regulatory intervention, there are costs involved. The benefits of potentially greater shareholder activism must be weighed against popular and political reaction to enhanced disclosure of executive pay. With enhanced disclosure, pay questions are played out in the media, influenced by labour, captured by private interests (such as those of political activists and union personnel), and politically infused. Remuneration committees may be vulnerable to responding to political and workforce pressures and adopting suboptimal remuneration structures which are not sufficiently sensitive to performance.[55] Disclosure which focuses on headline pay levels invites popular hostility and does not assist shareholders in assessing remuneration structures, and the pay-setting process is destabilizing.[56] By contrast, disclosure which makes it easier to assess the pay-performance relation/incentive structure and the effectiveness of governance can remedy some of the structural and process weaknesses of executive remuneration. Among other possible drawbacks of excessive disclosure, there is the risk that disclosure may result in an increase in pay due to a ratcheting effect.

2.4 Mandatory Pay Structure

In a previous paper we argued that the case for regulating the structure of bankers' pay appears to be rather weak.[57] First, it is far from proven that pay structures generally contributed to excessive risk taking before the recent crisis. According to some of the studies cited above, corporate governance and compensation structures of CEOs at banks that failed were not necessarily flawed. Second, even assuming that compensation structures were flawed—in particular, those of traders and other middle-managers taking excessive risks for banks—the need for their regulation would not be automatically established. In fact, excessive risk taking could be curbed directly through prudential regulation of banking activities, rather than by modelling the incentives of bank employees, also given that regulators

---

[54] Ferrarini et al. (2009).   [55] Romano (2001).   [56] Murphy (1995).
[57] Guido Ferrarini & Maria Cristina Ungureanu, "Economics, Politics, and the International Principles for Sound Compensation Practices: An Analysis of Executive Pay at European Banks", 62 Vand. L. Rev. 429 (2011).

may not be professionally qualified for designing pay structure.[58] Thirdly, mandating pay structures hampers the flexibility of compensation arrangements, which need tailoring to individual firms and managers, also in light of the latter's portfolios of their own bank securities. Moreover, in this context, bank boards may lose one of their key governance functions, finding it more difficult to align executives' incentives to corporate strategy and risk profile. This may also create problems in keeping and attracting managerial talent, particularly from countries that adopt a more liberal stance or from firms that are not subject to regulatory constraints (such as hedge funds or private equities).

Nonetheless, competent authorities should supervise bankers' compensation from the perspective of bank safety and soundness. Rather than designing compensation structures ex ante, which is a matter for institutions and their boards, they should analyze the impact of actual remuneration structures on risk taking and conduct their surveillance activities accordingly, for instance by imposing higher capital requirements to institutions adopting "aggressive" or inappropriate remuneration mechanisms. Moreover, supervisors should check bank compliance with compensation governance requirements and with the disclosure requirements concerning remuneration policies. Rather than interfering with pay structures, this type of regulation aims to ensure that organizational structures and procedures are in place for the setting of pay in compliance with safety and soundness requirements.

3 Regulating Pay Governance and Disclosure

3.1 EU Law

Disclosure, shareholder voice, and the independent director all appear in the EU's strategy for executive pay. The EU's initial approach, set out in the 2004 and 2005 Recommendations, was based on pay governance.[59] A number of directives adopted under the Financial Services Action Plan also form part of the EU's pay matrix by improving disclosure, both generally and with respect to pay, and by addressing insider dealing risks.[60]

3.1.1 The 2004–2005 Recommendations

To achieve its objectives, the Commission employed a non-binding Recommendation, avoiding a "one-size-fits-all" solution at the firm and Member State levels. The 2004 Recommendation was the EU's first attempt to address best practice with respect to pay governance. It uses disclosure and shareholder voice mechanisms to support efficient pay and recommends: disclosure of company pay policy, either in a distinct remuneration report or in the annual report; detailed disclosure concerning individual directors' pay; a

---

[58] Blinder (2013).   [59] Ferrarini et al. (2010).

[60] Niamh Moloney, The EU and Executive Pay: Managing Harmonization Risks, in Research Handbook on Executive Pay 466 (Randall S. Thomas and Jennifer G. Hill eds., 2012).

shareholders' vote on company pay policy, which can be either binding or advisory; and a priori approval of share-based schemes. The Recommendation does not engage with pay design, although support for performance-based pay is implicit across the Recommendation.

The role of the board in pay setting is addressed by the parallel 2005 Recommendation on the role of non-executive directors, which highlights remuneration as an area in which the "potential for conflict of interest is particularly high" and recommends that boards should have an "appropriate balance" of executive and non-executive directors such that no individual or group of individuals can dominate decision-making and there is a "sufficient" number of "independent" non-executive directors; board committees should be created for issues particularly vulnerable to conflict of interest (including remuneration); and the remuneration committee (its functions are delineated in some detail) should be composed exclusively of non-executive or supervisory directors, a majority of whom should be independent. The Recommendation also provides guidelines on the notion of "independence."

Member States were free to adopt the Recommendations (implementation was not mandatory) either through legislation or, as has been the dominant method, through soft law, typically based on the local Corporate Governance Code and, for many Member States though not all, on the related "comply or explain" principle.[61] Poor compliance need not necessarily follow from soft law implementation; companies that voluntarily adopt more rigorous corporate governance structures can be rewarded by a positive effect on firm value.[62]

3.1.2 The 2009 Recommendation

Executive pay in non-financial firms was pulled into the Commission's wider financial crisis reform agenda with the adoption of a 2009 Recommendation on Directors' Remuneration, which had to be implemented by the Member States by the end of 2009. Through it the Commission moved closer to the problematic, but politically appealing, design sphere. Noting that remuneration structures have become increasingly complex, too focused on the short term and leading, in some cases, to "excessive" remuneration not justified by performance,[63] the Commission adopted a series of voluntary principles concerning the structure of remuneration. The 2009 Recommendation focuses in particular on the pay/performance link, on long-term sustainability and on restricting "excessive" variable pay.

---

[61] European Commission, Report on the Application by the Member States of the EU of the Commission Recommendation on the Role of Non-Executive or Supervisory Directors of Listed Companies and on the Committees of the (Supervisory) Board (COM SEC(2007) 1021) (2007).

[62] Manuel Ammann, David Oesch, & Markus M. Schmid, "Corporate Governance and Firm Value: International Evidence", 18 Journal of Empirical Finance 36 (2011); Reena Aggarwal & Rohan Williamson, Did New Regulations Target the Relevant Corporate Governance Attributes?, Georgetown University Research Paper (2006), available at www.ssrn.com; Valentina Bruno & Stijn Claessens, "Corporate Governance and Regulation: Can There Be Too Much of a Good Thing?", 19 J. Fin. Intermediation 461 (2010); Vidhi Chhaochharia & Luc Laeven, "Corporate Governance Norms and Practices", 18 J. Fin. Intermediation 405 (2009).

[63] European Commission, Communication from the Commission accompanying Commission Recommendation complementing Recommendations 2004/913/EC and 2005/162/EC as regards the regime for the remuneration of directors of listed companies and Commission Recommendation on remuneration policies in the financial services sector {C(2009) 3159} {C(2009) 3177} (April, 2009).

The Recommendation addresses remuneration policy disclosure, suggesting that the remuneration policy be clear and easily understandable, that an explanation be provided concerning how performance criteria relate to firms' long-term interests and with respect to whether those criteria were fulfilled, and that "sufficient information" be provided concerning termination payments, vesting, and other restrictions, and concerning the peer groups on which the remuneration policy is based. The Recommendation touches upon the remuneration committee, buttressing its independence and suggesting that one member have knowledge and experience concerning remuneration. The Recommendation also considers design issues, suggesting that performance criteria promote long-term sustainability and include relevant non-financial criteria, that variable pay be withheld when performance criteria are not met, and that arrangements be made to claw back variable pay awarded on the basis of data which proves to be misstated. Moreover, termination payments should not exceed a fixed amount and, in general, not be higher than two years of non-variable pay.

However, the Recommendation goes further and appears imbued with a concern to reduce pay levels. The suggestion that undefined "limits" should be placed on variable pay is particularly troubling, given the benefits of incentive alignment, and represents an undue incursion into corporate autonomy.[64] The Recommendation similarly suggests that remuneration committees should ensure that executive director remuneration is "proportionate" to that of other executive directors and other staff members. While efforts have been made by some Member States to address proportionality concerns, this is not widespread and there is little evidence that intervention in support of "reasonable" pay works.[65]

The Recommendation's suggestions with respect to the deferral of pay are similarly intrusive. It suggests: that the "major part" of variable pay should be deferred for a "minimum period" of time; that restrictions on share-based pay and that the vesting of shares and the exercise of share options be subject to predetermined and measurable performance criteria; that shares should not vest for at least three years after their award and that share options or similar rights should not be exercisable for three years. The Commission has also suggested that a certain number of shares be retained by directors until the end of their mandate. Performance share plans, particularly linked with director shareholding periods, have proved to be a very useful mechanism for aligning director interests more effectively with long-term performance and are already a feature of several European Codes.[66]

3.1.3 Recent Proposals

In 2014 the European Commission proposed a revision of the Shareholder Rights Directive (SRD), including measures to improve the corporate governance of listed companies in an effort to increase the transparency and long-term sustainability of these companies. The new

---

[64]   Richard A. Posner, "Are American CEOs Overpaid, and, if So, What if Anything Can be Done about It?", 58 Duke L. J. 1013 (2009).

[65]   Randall Thomas, International Executive Pay: Current Practices and Future Trends, in International Executive Pay: Current Practices and Future Trends (Randall Thomas ed., 2009).

[66]   The UK Corporate Governance Code, Financial Reporting Council (2014), Italian Corporate Governance Code, Italian Corporate Governance Committee (2011), French Corporate Governance Code of Listed Corporations, AFEP-MEDEF (2013).

Directive, which was adopted in 2017, aims to encourage shareholders to engage more with the companies they invest in and to take a longer-term perspective on their investments.[67]

The amended SRD strengthens shareholder rights to exercise proper control over management, including a binding "say on pay." This comes as a reaction to the insufficient link between management pay and performance, which has determined harmful short-term tendencies. In addition, the new directive enhances transparency on remuneration policy and the actual remuneration of individual directors, and improves shareholder oversight of directors' remuneration. Each listed company in the EU will be required to put its remuneration policy to a binding shareholder vote at the general meeting. However, Member States may provide for the vote on remuneration policy to be advisory. Shareholders will also vote on a company's remuneration report, which describes how the remuneration policy has been applied in the last year, but their vote would be advisory only. Where the shareholders vote against the remuneration report, boards will need to explain in their next remuneration report how the vote of the shareholders has been taken in account.

Companies will have to provide a clear, understandable remuneration policy, in line with the business strategy, long-term interests, and sustainability of the firm. The policy will set clear criteria and explanations for the award of fixed and variable remuneration; explain how the pay and employment conditions of employees of the company were taken into account when establishing the remuneration policy; indicate the main terms of the contracts of directors and the decision-making process leading to their determination. The remuneration report also will need to be clear and understandable, including information on the total remuneration split out by component; the relative proportion of fixed and variable remuneration; how the total remuneration complies with the adopted remuneration policy; and how the performance criteria were applied. Once the shareholders have approved the remuneration policy, a company will not be permitted to pay remuneration to directors other than in accordance with that policy.

The Directive does not regulate the level of remuneration and leaves decisions on this to companies and their shareholders. The transparency and voting requirements are similar to those already in place for UK quoted companies. However, there are no detailed requirements for disclosure. Other Commission proposals also have an impact on the approach to remuneration policies by the companies. Notably, the Recommendation on the quality of corporate governance reporting ("comply or explain" principle) provides guidance to listed companies, investors, and other interested parties so as to improve the overall quality of corporate governance statements.[68]

3.2 Comparative Regulation

The EU regulatory framework based on non-binding recommendations proved unsuccessful in embedding good practices with respect to remuneration governance across

---

[67] Directive (EU) 2017/828 of the European Parliament and of the Council of 17 May 2017 amending Directive 2007/36/EC as regards the encouragement of long-term shareholder engagement.

[68] Commission Recommendation of 9 April 2014 on the quality of corporate governance reporting ('comply or explain') (2014/208/EU), OJ L 109/43.

Europe's largest companies.[69] Significant differences continued to persist across Member States' regulatory regimes and in pay governance practices.[70] Institutional investors were not persuasive in demanding better practices either, which may reflect the difficulties they faced in assessing industry-wide practices given generally poor disclosure.

3.2.1 From Soft to Mandatory Regulation

Either anticipating or following the Commission's proposals, Belgium, Portugal, Spain, Italy, and the UK were the first jurisdictions to consider moving remuneration governance and disclosure into law. Belgium adopted a law aimed primarily at reinforcing boards in listed companies,[71] which lifted a number of the national Corporate Governance Code provisions to the legislative level. As a result, the creation of a remuneration committee became mandatory and the publication of a corporate governance statement including a remuneration report was required. The Portuguese market regulator issued a 2010 Regulation on Corporate Governance, which provides for mandatory description of the remuneration policy and disclosure of individual director remuneration.[72] The regulation also requires firms to report on the composition of the remuneration committee and the fact that at least one of its members has knowledge and experience in remuneration policy issues. In Spain, the Law on Sustainable Economy, in effect since March 2011, delegated the Ministry of Economy and Finance and the market supervisor (CNMV) to determine the structure and content of companies' remuneration report.[73] The CNMV issued a regulation requiring disclosure of remuneration in a standard annual report format.[74] Similarly, in 2011 in Italy the Securities Commission (CONSOB) adopted new rules on transparency of remuneration,[75] requiring uniform and detailed disclosure of compensation practices and setting standards characteristics to be included in the remuneration report. The regulation also makes provisions for shareholder vote on both the previous year's policy and the proposed future policy.

The UK has traditionally had the most extensive set of governance requirements in force with respect to executive compensation in Europe. Listed companies have been required to prepare a Directors' Remuneration Report since 2002 and submit it to the advisory

---

[69] Commission, Report on the application by Member States of the EU of the Commission Recommendation on directors' remuneration (2007) (SEC(2007) 1022); Commission, Report on the application by the Member States of the EU of the Commission Recommendation on the role of non-executive or supervisory directors of listed companies and on the committees of the (supervisory) board (2007) (COM SEC(2007) 1021).

[70] Ferrarini et al. (2009, 2010); Roberto Barontini et al., Directors' Remuneration before and after the Crisis: Measuring the Impact of Reforms in Europe, in Boards and Shareholders in European Listed Companies: Facts, Context and Post-Crisis Reforms 251 (Massimo Belcredi and Guido Ferrarini eds., 2013).

[71] Law on the reinforcement of corporate governance in listed companies (2010).

[72] CMVM Regulation No. 1/2010 Corporate Governance (2010).

[73] Law No. 2/2011 of 4 March 2011 on Sustainable Economy (last amended by Law No. 2/2012 of June 29, 2012).

[74] New section 61ter, Securities Market Law ("Ley del Mercado de Valores"), CNMV (1989).

[75] Art. 84-quarter, Consob. Regulation 11971/1999 implementing Italian Legislative Decree No. 58 of 24 February 1998, concerning the discipline of issuers.

vote of shareholders.[76] Despite similar regulatory measures, during the recent crisis, UK companies—banks in particular—raised serious concerns for what many observers considered as "excessive executive pay."[77] This led the government in 2011 and 2012 to announce a reform directed to curb executive pay through greater remuneration transparency, more shareholder powers, and more diverse board and remuneration committees.[78]

3.2.2 Say on Pay

Pressure over dealing with "inappropriate" executive compensation, be it understood as either "excessive" or misaligned with shareholder value, has led to initiatives giving investors greater influence over executive pay through a vote on companies' remuneration policies and packages, i.e., through the "say-on-pay" process.

In the US, votes on pay are mandatory under the 2010 Dodd–Frank Wall Street Reform and Consumer Protection Act, but the voting result is not binding. Most European jurisdictions, in their governance codes, introduced an advisory vote on the remuneration policy and a binding vote on equity-based incentive schemes. Few regulators went further, introducing binding votes on pay policy, in the hope that such votes would determine corporations to be more conservative with respect to the total amount paid to their executives and that this would be more driven by corporate performance. The Netherlands, Sweden, and Norway, however, had already required binding say on pay before the crisis.[79]

Post-crisis reforms not only regard the nature of the vote (binding or advisory), but also the possible shift of voting requirements from best practice principles to legislation. Spain and Italy were among the first countries to introduce a similar rule in their corporate laws, while France has extensively debated the issue at government level.[80] For a long time, in the UK the shareholder advisory vote on executive compensation has been non-binding on companies and their boards. Since spring 2012, however, the government moved toward a binding regime through a range of proposals, including: an annual binding vote on future remuneration policy; an annual advisory vote on how the company's pay policy was implemented in the previous year; and a binding vote on "exit payments" of more than one year's salary.

The effects of say on pay started to be felt soon after the launch of these reforms. The case of UK companies failing to receive majority support for their pay policies in 2011 could be considered representative for the history of "say on pay."[81] In the US, by comparison, the

---

[76] The Directors' Remuneration Report Regulations (2002). Schedule 7A of the Companies Act 1985, re-enacted in Regulation 11 and Schedule 8 of the Large and Medium-Sized Companies and Groups (Accounts and Reports) Regulations 2008, available at www.legislation.gov.uk.

[77] Ferrarini & Ungureanu (2010).

[78] The Large and Medium-sized Companies and Groups (Accounts and Reports) (Amendment) Regulations 2013. Department of Business, Innovation & Skills (2013).

[79] David Larcker, Allan L. McCall, & Gaizka Ormazabal, "Outsourcing Shareholder Voting to Proxy Advisory Firms", 58 J. L. & Econ. 173 (2015); Yonca Ertimur, Fabrizio Ferri, & David Oesch, "Shareholder Votes and Proxy Advisors: Evidence from Say on Pay", 51 J. Accounting Research 951 (2013).

[80] Consultation sur la remuneration des dirigeants d'enterprise (2012), available at www.tresor. economie.gouv.fr.

[81] For example, at the AGM of Barclays, over 25 percent of shareowners voted against the company's pay plan at a very tumultuous meeting; Barclays Stung by Shareholder Pay Revolt, April 27, 2012, BBC

impact of the recent reform introducing say on pay may be seen as modest. Amongst the Russell 3000 companies with say-on-pay votes occurring between September 2011 and June 2012, 2.4 percent failed to achieve shareholder support levels of 50 percent or higher. These results point to a slight rise in say-on-pay failure rates compared to 2011, when 1.6 percent of Russell 3000 companies failed over the same timeframe.[82]

No doubt, "say-on-pay" has increased the power of proxy advisory firms, especially the two largest, Institutional Shareholder Services (ISS) and Glass Lewis and Co. Similar to rating agencies prior to the financial crisis, these firms have implicitly been granted by regulators significant power as to the shaping of corporate governance policies in US public companies and their influence has spread over to Europe and Asia as well.[83] Research has consistently shown a strong correlation between recommendations of proxy advisors and proxy voting by institutional shareholders.[84] The influence of these firms is enhanced by the fact that investors may find it less costly to pay a fee for the advisory firms' reports and rely on their recommendations especially in highly technical, if not arcane, matters like incentives structure for top executives and the link between incentives and corporate performance. However, large institutional investors such as Fidelity, Vanguard, BlackRock, and T. Rowe Price still assign analysts to study executive compensation at their portfolio companies, develop internal policies, and make voting determinations.

Studies show that, historically, a negative recommendation from ISS will, on average, influence between 13.6 percent and 20.6 percent of votes cast on management-sponsored proposals.[85] Companies that receive a negative recommendation from ISS almost always fail their say-on-pay vote, whereas no company that receives a positive ISS recommendation fails its say-on-pay vote. The policies that advisory firms prefer also influence decisions by the non-executive directors of public companies. However, there is evidence that such influence may not be for the better in terms of shareholder value enhancement. For example, research found that, when public companies implement certain principles defined by proxy advisers as "best practices" (in this case with regard to stock option exchange programs), gains in shareholder value are on average 50 percent to 100 percent less than at other firms.[86] Conflicts of interest

News, available at www.bbc.co.uk/news/business. Shareholder discontent over pay also contributed to the exit of insurer Aviva's CEO, who resigned five days after 54 percent of shareowners voted against pay at the company's annual meeting; Aviva Rocked by Shareholder Rebellion over Executive Pay, Guardian, May 3, 2012, available at www.guardian.co.uk/business. Over 40 percent of WPP investors voted "no" on pay, prompting the company's compensation committee chair to reach out to investors prior to the upcoming AGM to defend a 30 percent pay raise for the company's CEO; WPP Shareholders Vote against £6.8m Pay Packet for Sir Martin Sorrell, Guardian, June 13, 2012, available at www.guardian.co.uk/media.

[82] Institutional Shareholder Services (2011, 2012).

[83] Ertimur et al. 2013; Massimo Belcredi et al., "Say-on-Pay in a Context of Concentrated Ownership. Evidence from Italy", CONSOB Working Papers No. 76 (2014), available at www.ssrn.com.

[84] Larcker et al. (2013); Ertimur et al. (2013).

[85] Jennifer E. Bethel & Stuart L. Gillan, The Impact of Institutional and Regulatory Environment on Shareholder Voting, 31 Financial Management 29 (2002); Jie Cai, Jacqueline L. Garner, & Ralph A. Walkling, "Electing Directors", 64 J. Fin. 2389 (2009); David F. Larcker, Allan L. McCall, & Brian Tayan, The Influence of Proxy Advisory Firm Voting Recommendations on Say-on-Pay Votes and Executive Compensation Decisions, The Conference Board: Trusted Insights for Business Worldwide (2012), available at http://www.gsb.stanford.edu.

[86] Larcker et al. (2013).

of proxy advisory firms have also become an issue, so that regulators from Europe and the US have proposed to regulate these firms; and the policy debate continues.[87]

As a result of the ambiguous benefits of proxy advisors and of increased shareholder activism, several investors have reduced their reliance on advisors' recommendations. In 2013 Blackrock (the world's largest asset manager) announced that they were no longer following ISS recommendations and released their comprehensive voting policies for each main jurisdiction.[88] These policies sometimes go against practices which, in a given jurisdiction, are generally accepted, such as performance based remuneration for non-executive directors in German companies; poor disclosure of remuneration policies in Greek companies; excessive severance payments in Italian companies. They also emphasize the importance of aligning the performance metrics of variable pay to the execution of strategy at UK companies, where long-term compensation plans are known to be rather complex.

Several investors and representative associations have put forward principles with regard to remuneration, setting out their own views on the role of shareholders and directors in relation to remuneration and the manner in which remuneration should be determined and structured. For example, the National Association of Pension Funds (NAPF) in the UK updated its remuneration guidelines and published a "Remuneration Principles" document. The Guidelines track the Principles of the UK Corporate Governance Code, and give guidance on how each principle should be applied and what investors might look for in particular, followed by a voting recommendation. The revisions of the NAPF's remuneration guidelines include a new list of practices that are likely to cause investor concern and may even trigger a vote against Directors' Remuneration Reports and/or new share plans.[89] Investors often act in concert when addressing governance issues of investee companies, with the aim of building a meaningful voice, as in the case of the GC100 and Investor Group (Group formed by GC100 representing FTSE100 companies and the Corporate Governance Forum, a network of leading institutional investors) who issued their own Directors' Remuneration Reporting Guidance.[90] The guidelines substantially change the requirements for the contents of the directors' remuneration report and include some significant new disclosures, expecting companies not to adopt a "boilerplate" approach and be innovative in order to meet their specific needs.

Other large investors—including Fidelity, Legal & General, and Vanguard—went as far as sending alerts to the CEOs of large companies, communicating changes in their voting policy on remuneration and conditioning a positive vote on specific provisions, which largely go beyond the current regulatory and governance requirements, and trying to ensure a better alignment between executive compensation and the longer-term performance of the company. In 2013 Fidelity sent a letter to Europe's 350 largest companies requiring them (and anticipating otherwise a negative vote) to lengthen the required term of the LTIP by

---

[87] For EU see ESMA, An Overview of the Proxy Advisory Industry. Considerations on Possible Policy Options (March 2012), available at http://www.esma.europa.eu/. For US see SEC, Opening Statement at the Proxy Advisory Services Roundtable (December 2013), available at www.sec.org.

[88] BlackRock, Proxy voting guidelines for European, Middle Eastern and African securities (2014), available at www.blackrock.com.

[89] NAPF Coporate Governance Policy and Voting Guidelines (2013), available at http://www.napf.co.uk.

[90] GC100/Investors group, Directors' Remuneration Reporting Guidance (2013), available at: http://uk.practicallaw.com/groups/uk-gc100-investor-group.

distinguishing between "vesting periods" and "holding periods" of the incentive, requiring a holding period of minimum five years and a minimum three-year vesting period. Legal & General sent a letter to FTSE 250 companies calling them to provide certain enhancements in their remuneration disclosure, warning them in regard to unclear explanations on the performance measures behind incentive schemes; making significant "golden hello" payments; providing matching schemes to new recruits; not considering the experience of the individual when recruiting external candidates. L&G specifically anticipates voting against remuneration in companies that do not provide sufficient information on performance measures, unless full explanation on the lack of transparency is provided. In anticipation of the 2014 proxy season, Vanguard sent letters to approximately US 350 companies to proactively engage with them on governance issues. The letters are tailored to the individual companies and identify governance practices at the companies that Vanguard believes are not in line with what the asset manager views as best practices.

Clearly, we have entered into a new chapter of executive pay governance and the ways in which companies respond to shareholder engagement have evolved significantly: "[T]he process has become less defensive and more proactive."[91]

3.3 Some Empirical Data

In this section, we summarize the outcomes of our previous paper on firms' remuneration practices before and after the crisis, with particular emphasis on the governance process and the quality of disclosure.[92] Our original paper compared the data collected for the years 2007 and 2010, thus providing evidence on the evolution of pay practices in response to the recent financial crisis and to the remuneration reforms adopted by European policy makers.

3.3.1 Statistics on Governance

Following the 2005 Recommendation, most EU corporate governance codes endorsed the setting up of a remuneration committee with a majority of independent directors. Only the German Corporate Governance Code did not specifically recommend the formation of a remuneration committee. Moreover, the 2009 German Act on the Appropriateness of Management Board Remuneration marked a departure from European corporate law and practice by requiring that the full supervisory board decide on individual management board pay (including salary and incentive-based pay).[93] Reflecting this regulatory framework, our analysis found a widespread recourse to the remuneration committee, both before and after the crises, in all countries except Germany, where only about half of the companies in our sample established this committee, with a slight increase in 2010. Again with the exception of German firms, the independence requirement (i.e., the committee should only include non-executive members, with a majority of independent directors) was fulfilled by

---

[91] Michael Segal, "Compensation Season 2014: Shareholder Engagement" (2013), available at http://blogs.law.harvard.edu/corpgov/2013/12/20/compensation-season-2014-shareholder-engagement/#!.

[92] Barontini et al. (2013).

[93] Act on the Appropriateness of Management Board Remuneration (Gesetz zur Angemessenheit der Vorstandsvergütung, 'VorstAG') (2009).

most of the companies having a remuneration committee (about 80 percent of the sample, with a small increase from 2007). However, several compensation committees still did not fulfil the composition criteria established by either best practice or regulation.

Requirements concerning the presence and role of compensation consultants in continental European countries are weak compared to the UK.[94] In the UK, the Directors' Remuneration Report Regulations of 2002 require that firms disclose consultant information. Although the Commission supports the presence and independence of remuneration consultants in its 2004 and 2009 Recommendations, strong disclosure requirements are not found in continental Europe, where the relevant provisions are rather patchy. Our analysis showed that all UK companies used a third-party consultant to advise them on compensation levels and design since before the crisis. Furthermore, all UK firms in our sample make a statement regarding their independence, i.e., non-engagement in other consulting services for the management. In the other jurisdictions, the presence of an external consultant is usually not disclosed. Similar disclosure gaps bar an accurate review of the remuneration governance process.

3.3.2 Statistics on Disclosure

Current disclosure criteria require remuneration statements to be clear and easily understandable, to provide detail on the alignment between pay and performance, and to be transparent about the individual directors' compensation packages. However, significant differences existed amongst national jurisdictions as to pay disclosure before the financial crisis. In our paper, we found that disclosure of remuneration generally improved post-crisis in all jurisdictions, even though the levels of compliance vary greatly across countries. We showed that compliance with the remuneration statement requirement was quite strong across jurisdictions before the crisis and improved post-crisis at the few non-compliant firms. All of the remaining variables for the remuneration policy showed a significant increase in compliance for the whole sample, with the exception of performance criteria for bonuses.

As to individual disclosure, increased compliance (even though not statistically significant) was observed for the two variables capturing disclosure of the annual compensation components for executive and non-executive directors. On average, disclosure of individual share schemes is lower, although some countries (in particular the UK, Italy, and France) show significant improvements. However, the jurisdictions where remuneration disclosure and governance standards were lower prior to the crisis (Greece and Portugal in particular) did not show substantial improvements post-crisis.

These findings show that the firms' approach to compliance is strongly dependent on their home country's approach to regulation and governance culture. Firms generally tend to reflect the way in which EU regulations are implemented at the national level—either through mandatory legislative requirements or best practice guidelines—and the level of detail in the formulation of the relevant standards.

[94] Conyon (2011).

4 REGULATING PAY STRUCTURE

4.1 Long-Term Remuneration

Investor initiatives and political developments continue to exert pressure over executive compensation, especially on the design and structure of long-term incentives.[95] The public debate and regulatory initiatives have resulted in heightened scrutiny of executive pay by the shareholders and shareholder advisory groups, particularly focusing on the relationship between executive pay and firm performance. A related theme for investors is that a greater portion of incentive pay should relate to long-term performance, as it is widely believed that anything less than three-year performance periods would carry the risk of significant compensation being paid for performance that is not truly sustainable.[96]

The combination of these forces has accelerated the adoption of performance-linked long-term incentive programs. A decade ago, plain-vanilla stock options filledup the compensation packages of executives, while terms such as restricted stock, full-value awards, or performance shares were almost unheard of.[97] Research has shown that a majority of individuals view stock options as a "gift."[98] As a result, they significantly discount the value of stock options and view them as something that is a "nice to have" rather than an essential element of their compensation plan. Today, plain-vanilla options are on the decline, while restricted stock and performance shares are a regular part of the long-term incentive lexicon, especially in public companies.[99] In a pay-for-performance world, equity compensation is increasingly becoming a reward for achievement of success. The problem with paying for upside potential is not only reflected in cash bonuses but also in short-term gains through stock options.[100] Initial values mean far less than what is finally delivered (or not) to the employee. Performance criteria add another layer of complexity to a compensation program, but performance may also add the secret ingredient of direct alignment that allows for a compelling discussion between the company and its stakeholders on current and potential value.

The key condition to any reward is making sure that the linkage between achievement and payout is reasonable and comprehensible. Investors pay more attention to changes in

---

[95] Barontini et al. (2013); Massimo Belcredi & Guido Ferrarini, Corporate Boards, Incentive Pay and Shareholder Activism in Europe: Main Issues and Policy Perspectives, in Boards and Shareholders in European Listed Companies: Facts, Context and Post-Crisis Reforms 1 (Massimo Belcredi and Guido Ferrarini eds., 2013); Steven N. Kaplan, "CEO Pay and Corporate Governance in the U.S.: Perceptions, Facts, and Challenges", 25 J. Appl. Corp. Fin. 8; Murphy (2013).

[96] Association of British Insurers (ABI), Principles for Executive Remuneration (2013), available at https://www.ivis.co.uk/guidelines; Ertimur et al. (2013).

[97] Hamid Mehran & Joseph Tracy, "The Effect of Employee Stock Options on the Evolution of Compensation in the 1990s", 7 Economic Policy Review 17 (2001).

[98] Peter Cappelli & Martin Conyon, "Stock Option Exercise and Gift Exchange Relationships: Evidence for a Large U.S. Company", NBER Working Paper No. 16814 (2011), available at http://www.nber.org/papers/w16814.

[99] David I. Walker, "Evolving Executive Equity Compensation and the Limits of Optimal Contracting", 64 Vand. L. Rev. 611 (2011).

[100] Patrick Bolton, José Scheinkman, & Wei Xiong, "Executive Compensation and Short-Termist Behaviour in Speculative Markets", 73 Rev. Econ. Stud. 577 (2006).

the proportion of shares issued and shares conveyed to employees; they scrutinize time-based stock plans (i.e., restricted stock, time-vested stock) and performance share plans with a lower than three-year performance period.[101] They value stock ownership and retention requirements, which are considered to reinforce executives' "shareholder mindset." Similar concerns have led to legal changes and governance codes reviews in major markets over the last few years, either requiring or recommending deferral of annual incentives and/or longer vesting periods for long-term incentives for senior executives in all listed companies (not just financial services). As we move into the era of "say-on-pay," performance hurdles are also being added to these awards.[102]

As a result, companies are working to balance their compensation philosophy and executive pay programs have come under closer scrutiny. Equity compensation has become more volatile and complex during the past two decades, requiring more planning, expertise, and pragmatism.[103] The growing focus on aligning pay with long-term performance has driven many companies to grant performance-vested long-term incentives,[104] apply not lower than three-year performance measurement periods, align plans with two or more performance measures, make executive directors maintain a substantial ownership interest for the duration of their employment, and establish stock ownership plans for directors. Several companies are moving away from full vesting and toward pro-rata vesting of equity, toward more disciplined target setting and greater consideration of strategic, non-financial performance measures in annual and long-term incentives.[105]

4.2 FSB Principles

Compensation structures at banks are considered by the FSB principles along lines that reflect, to a large extent, general best practices already adopted before the crisis.[106] However, pre-crisis practices mainly emphasized the alignment of managers' incentives with shareholder wealth maximization. The principles break new grounds by requiring financial institutions to align compensation with prudent risk taking. Accordingly, compensation should be adjusted for all types of risk, including those considered difficult to measure, such as liquidity risk, reputation risk, and capital cost. Compensation outcomes should be symmetric with risk outcomes. Deferment of compensation, traditionally used as a retention mechanism (on the basis that a "bad leaver" would generally lose unpaid deferrals), should

---

[101] David Yermack, "Shareholder Voting and Corporate Governance", 2 Annual Review of Financial Economics 103 (2010); ISS (International Shareholder Services), 2011 U.S. Post Season Report (2011), available at www.iss.com; ISS (International Shareholder Services) 2012 Proxy Season Review. World Markets (2013), available at www.iss.com.

[102] Barontini et al. (2013).

[103] Walker (2010); Jeffrey N. Gordon, "Executive Compensation and Corporate Governance in Financial Firms: The Case for Convertible Equity-Based Pay", Columbia Law and Economics Working Paper No. 373 (2010); available at: www.ssrn.com.

[104] Clearbridge, The ClearBridge 100 Report (2013), available at http://www.clearbridgecomp.com.

[105] Equilar, Equity Trends Report (2013) available at www.equilar.com; GMI Ratings, 2013 CEO Pay Survey (2013) available at www3.gmiratings.com; BlackRock, Time to Rethink Executive Incentive Programs (2012), available at www2.blackrock.com.

[106] Ferrarini & Ungureanu (2011).

make compensation payout schedules sensitive to the time horizon of risks. In particular, a substantial portion of variable compensation (i.e., 40–60 percent) should be payable under deferral arrangements over a period of not less than three years, provided that this period is correctly aligned with the nature of the business, its risks, and the activities of the employee in question. Furthermore, a substantial portion (i.e., more than 50 percent) of variable compensation should be awarded in shares or share-linked instruments, as long as the same create incentives aligned with long-term value creation and the time horizons of risk. In any event, awards in shares or share-linked instruments should be subject to an appropriate retention policy.

The principles also tackle concerns relative to bonuses, which famously emerged during the recent crisis. They require "malus" and "clawback" mechanisms, which enable boards to reduce or reclaim bonuses paid on the basis of results that are unrepresentative of the company's performance over the long term or later prove to have been misstated. They consider "guaranteed" bonuses (i.e., contracts guaranteeing variable pay for several years) as conflicting with sound risk management and the pay-for-performance principle. Severance packages need to be related to performance achieved over time and designed in a way that does not reward failure.

The FSB principles represent a political compromise between the various interests at stake in the area of compensation, incorporating traditional criteria and adapting them to new circumstances by focusing on long-term incentives, in order to counter the role allegedly played in the crisis by short-term incentives; tracking already existing practices, but extending the same to a greater number of bank employees; and widening the powers of supervisors by explicitly making pay at financial institutions subject to prudential supervision. Similar to other international financial standards, the principles remain at a sufficient level of generality and allow for flexibility in implementation; in several instances, financial institutions are permitted to depart from a given principle or standard, if application of the same would lead to unsound consequences.

4.3 Dodd–Frank

The FSB principles were implemented along different models.[107] Some jurisdictions follow a primarily supervisory approach to implementation, involving principles and guidance and the associated supervisory reviews. In other jurisdictions the model includes a mix of regulation and supervisory oversight, with new regulations often supported by supervisory guidance that illustrates how the rules can be met. The US initially followed the supervisory model of implementation. However, with the enactment of the Dodd–Frank Wall Street Reform and Consumer Protection Act on July 21, 2010,[108] a mixed model of implementation was adopted. The Act includes two sets of provisions on executive compensation. On the one side, there are those applicable to all listed companies,[109] touching upon issues like say on

---

[107] Financial Stability Board, Thematic Review on Compensation: Peer Review Report (2010), available at www.financialstabilityboard.org.

[108] The Dodd–Frank Wall Street Reform and Consumer Protection Act ("The Act"), Pub. L. No. 111-203, enacted July 21, 2010.

[109] Provisions contained in Title IX of the Act: sections 951, 952, 953, 954, 955 of the Act.

pay; independence of compensation committees; enhanced proxy disclosure; "clawbacks" of incentive compensation; and disclosure of employee and director hedging. On the other, Section 956 of the Act (headed "Enhanced Compensation Structure Reporting") requires Federal regulators of financial institutions to issue new rules in two areas.[110] First, they must jointly prescribe regulations or guidelines requiring each covered financial institution to disclose to the appropriate federal regulator the structure of all incentive-based compensation arrangements in a manner sufficient to determine whether the same provide an executive officer, employee, director, or principal shareholder of the covered financial institution with excessive compensation or could lead to material loss to the covered institution. Second, they must prescribe regulations or guidelines that prohibit any type of incentive-based payment arrangements that encourage inappropriate risks by covered financial institutions by providing an executive officer, employee, director, or principal shareholder with excessive compensation or that could lead to material financial loss to the covered financial institution.

In February 2011 the federal agencies jointly exercised their mandate by approving a proposal on incentive-based compensation arrangements for "covered financial institutions."[111] These are institutions under the supervision of the respective federal regulator, with total consolidated assets of $1 billion or more.[112] The Rule supplements existing rules and guidance adopted by the relevant agencies regarding compensation, including the Interagency Guidance on Sound Incentive Compensation Policies referred to above.

The use of "standards" rather than "rules" analytically defining the compensation structure not only reflects the international Principles, but also the federal regulators' willingness to avoid a "one-size-fits-all" approach and keep the needed flexibility in compensation arrangements. Under the proposed standards of "reasonable" (as opposed to "excessive") compensation, "balanced" arrangements, and "appropriate" risk taking, the institutions concerned have to tailor their remuneration policies to their businesses and risks, assuming responsibility for the relevant arrangements through good corporate governance and internal control mechanisms. At the same time, the regulators will be in a condition to influence the supervised institutions' compensation practices through general guidance and individual inspections. To this effect, the proposed Rule also requires the covered financial institutions to submit an annual report to regulators describing the structure of incentive-based compensation arrangements.

Specific rules apply to "larger covered financial institutions,"[113] such as bank holding companies with consolidated assets of more than $50 billion. In addition to mandating wider disclosure to the Federal regulators, the proposed Rule requires similar institutions to defer at least 50 percent of the incentive-based compensation payments to executive officers over

---

[110] The FED, the OCC, the OTS, the FDIC, the NCUA, the SEC, and the FHFA are mandated by section 956 of the Act to jointly prescribe regulations or guidelines with respect to incentive-based compensation practices at covered financial institutions.

[111] The FDIC issued Notice of Proposed Rulemaking on incentive-based compensation arrangements (February, 2011), available at http://www.fdic.gov/news/news/press/2011/pr11027.html. In similar lines with the FDIC proposal, the SEC issued Rules on Incentive-based Compensation for Large Broker-Dealers and Investment Advisors (2011); available at http://www.sec.gov/news/press/2011/2011-57.htm.

[112] Explanatory definitions S. III, § 3, section 956 of the Act.

[113] For the federal banking agencies and the SEC, the term "larger covered financial institution" refers to those covered financial institutions with total consolidated assets of $50 billion or more. Section 956, the Act.

a period of a minimum three years, with the release of the deferred amount to occur no faster than on a pro-rata basis.[114] A "malus" mechanism also applies, in that the deferred amount should be adjusted for actual losses incurred by the institution or other measures of performance during the deferral period. Moreover, if the covered financial institution has consolidated assets of $50 billion or more, the board of directors (or a board committee) shall identify those covered persons (other than executive officers) who individually have the ability to expose the institution to possible "substantial" losses. These covered persons may include, for example, traders with large position limits and other individuals who have the authority to place at risk a substantial part of the capital of the covered financial institution. The board of directors (or a board committee) must approve the incentive-based compensation arrangements for covered persons after determining that the same effectively balance the financial rewards and the range and time horizon of risks associated with the covered person's activities.

4.4 CRD IV

The European regulation in this area was deeply overhauled by CRD IV. The new regime applies on a consolidated basis, i.e., to "institutions at group, parent company and subsidiary levels, including those established in offshore financial centres" (Article 92(1)). The ratio for an EU-wide scope of application is "to protect and foster financial stability within the Union and to address any possible avoidance of the requirements laid down in this Directive" (67th considerandum). The new regime applies to different categories of staff including senior management, risk takers, staff engaged in control functions, and any employee receiving total remuneration that takes them into the same remuneration bracket as senior management and risk takers, whose professional activities have a material impact on their risk profile (Article 92(2)). In this regard, the Commission has recently adopted a delegated Regulation including regulatory technical standards on the identification of risk takers.[115]

Article 92(2) requires inter alia that the remuneration policy should be consistent with sound and effective risk management and should not encourage risk taking in excess of the tolerated risk level of the institution. Moreover, the remuneration policy should be in line with the business strategy, objectives, values, and long-term interests of the institution, and incorporate measures to avoid conflicts of interest.

Article 94, para. 1 provides several requirements for the variable elements of remuneration. Some of them are rather generic, such as the one requiring performance pay to be based on a combination of the assessment of the performance of the individual and of the business unit concerned and of the overall results of the institution. In addition, performance should be assessed in a multi-year framework in order to ensure that the assessment process is based on longer-term performance and that the actual payment of performance-based components of remuneration is spread over a period which takes account of the underlying

---

[114] S. III, § 5, section 956 of the Act.

[115] Commission Delegated Regulation of 4.3.2014 supplementing Directive 2013/36/EU of the European Parliament and of the Council with regard to regulatory technical standards with respect to qualitative and appropriate quantitative criteria to identify categories of staff whose professional activities have a material impact on an institution's risk profile, available at http://ec.europa.eu/.

business cycle of the credit institution and its business risks. Moreover, the total variable remuneration should not limit the ability of the institution to strengthen its capital base. Furthermore, the fixed and variable components of total remuneration should be appropriately balanced and the fixed component should represent a sufficiently high proportion of the total remuneration to allow the operation of a fully flexible policy on variable remuneration components, including the possibility to pay no variable remuneration component.

Other requirements in Article 94, para. 1 are more specific, particularly regarding the "bonus cap" that the European Parliament asked to include in CRD IV. Under Article 94(1)(g), the variable component should not exceed 100 percent of the fixed component of the total remuneration for each individual. However, Member States may set a lower maximum percentage (as Belgium and the Netherlands did, by setting 50 percent and 20 percent respectively). Moreover, Member States may allow shareholders of the institution concerned to approve a higher maximum level of the ratio between fixed and variable remuneration provided the overall level of the variable component shall not exceed 200 percent of the fixed component of the total remuneration for each individual. Member States may also set a lower percentage. In any case, approval of a higher percentage should occur through a special procedure that is described in detail by Article 94(1)(g)(ii).

The official justification for this bonus cap is to avoid excessive risk taking (65th considerandum). However, the provision has generated some debate, particularly on whether the bonus cap is suitable to prevent excessive risk taking by bank managers and traders. As stated by Kevin Murphy, several arguments show that neither the objective to reduce excessive risk taking nor the one to reduce perceived excesses in the level of banking remuneration will be achieved by capping variable remuneration.[116]

First, the bonus cap may lead to an increase in the level of fixed remuneration, making banks more vulnerable to business cycles and therefore increasing the risk of bank failure. Anecdotal evidence already shows that fixed pay at large European banks is on the rise[117]. Secondly, the traditional bonus system at investment banks, which is characterised by below-market salaries and high bonus opportunities, provides strong incentives to avoid "bad" risks and to take "good" ones. On the contrary, the new system—which will be characterized by above-market salaries and "capped" bonuses—provides incentives to take "bad" risks and avoid "good" ones. In fact, if bad risks materialize, the bank manager will not suffer, for her remuneration is to a large extent fixed. But, if the bank shuns good risks and the relevant profits, the responsible manager will not be worse off given that his bonus is capped. Indeed, the bonus cap reduces incentives to create value, which is the main purpose of variable pay. Third, executive remuneration is largely set by the markets, so that a bonus cap could also have unintended consequences on the firms' ability to hire people of adequate standing in the international market for managers. In the end, remuneration "will reflect a less-talented workforce as the top producers leave for better-paying opportunities in financial firms not subject to the pay restrictions." In other words, the cap "will not lead to lower levels of overall remuneration after adjusting for ability and the risk of the remuneration package."[118] Furthermore, the cap on variable pay may reduce the competitiveness of the EU

---

[116] Murphy (2013).

[117] Steve Slater, London Banks Are Responding to Bonus Caps with Higher Salaries, Reuters (Nov. 28, 2013), available at www.reuters.com; Nicholas Comfort, Bloomberg News, "Deutsche Bank Seeks Shareholders' Permission to Ease Bonus Cap." (April 10, 2014).

[118] Id.

banking sector relative to non-EU banks and other nonbank financial intermediaries which are not subject to similar restrictions. Fourth, the mandatory cap also reflects a "one-size-fits-all" approach, which is clearly too rigid for different types of credit institutions that are presented with different levels of risk exposure, so that an incentive structure which is appropriate for one firm is not necessarily suited to another. Moreover, the EU bonus-cap applies to all credit institutions, without regard to their size and therefore to systemic risk considerations.

5 Conclusions

In this chapter, we have analyzed the current trends in the regulation and practice of executive remuneration. No doubt, the role of regulation is on the rise, particularly after the recent financial crisis, and the standards as to pay governance and structures are spreading from the financial sector to the non-financial one. As a consequence, today's remuneration practices are shaped not only by the need to reduce managerial agency costs at listed companies through appropriate incentives, but also by the hard and soft laws tackling corporate governance and remuneration structures. While the governance prescriptions (such as those on remuneration committees and say on pay) are intended to reduce the agency costs relative to incentive pay, the regulation of pay structures has an impact on incentives and the quantum of remuneration. Moreover, this type of regulation also responds to social issues and political pressures, thus reflecting concerns about inequality in the distribution of wealth and incentives to undertake "excessive" risks in the financial sector.

We then examined the main policy questions concerning incentive pay, including the optimal design of stock options, their impact on dividends and dilution, and the importance of long-term pay. Amongst the governance mechanisms, we have considered both the role of boards and independent directors, and that of shareholders under say on pay rules, taking into account the rise of shareholder engagement in listed companies across the Atlantic. As to the structure of pay, we have highlighted the special problems of banks and the main policy issues concerning regulation of pay at financial institutions.

We have subsequently analyzed regulatory developments in Europe in the last ten years and most recent proposals by the Commission, comparing the same with developments at Member State level and in the US. In particular, we have highlighted the impact of say on pay rules on shareholder activism, expanding on the role of proxy advisors and the behaviour of the largest institutional investors, who have shown an autonomous and active stance on executive remuneration issues at large listed companies. We lastly focused on the regulation of pay structures, showing that long-term incentives are clearly favored for both financial and non-financial companies by either regulators or institutional investors. However, financial institutions are the main target of post-crisis reforms, first at the international level through soft-law initiatives like the FSB principles and standards, and second at US and EU levels, where the FSB principles have been implemented along partially diverging routes. CRD IV, in particular, has marked a new trend in the regulation of bankers' pay, by imposing a bonus cap that we have criticized from an economic perspective and which clearly goes beyond what is required by the international principles.

....

CHAPTER 14

INSTITUTIONAL INVESTORS IN CORPORATE GOVERNANCE

....

EDWARD B. ROCK[1]

1 INTRODUCTION

....

Effective and sustainable shareholder engagement is one of the cornerstones of the corporate governance model of listed companies, which depends on checks and balances between the different organs and different stakeholders. Greater involvement of shareholders in corporate governance is one of the levers that can help improve the financial and non-financial performance of companies, including as regards environmental, social, and governance factors, in particular...

Institutional investors and asset managers are often important shareholders of listed companies in the European Union and can therefore play an important role in the corporate governance of those companies, but also more generally with regard to their strategy and long-term performance. However, the experience of the last years has shown that institutional investors and asset managers often do not engage with companies in which they hold shares and evidence shows that capital markets often exert pressure on companies to perform in the short term, which may jeopardise the long-term financial and non-financial performance of companies and may, among other negative consequences, lead to a suboptimal level of investments, for example in research and development, to the detriment of the long-term performance of both the companies and the investors.[2]

LIKE poets and revolutionaries, corporate law scholars and policy makers dream. If only we could find the silver bullet, the wonder drug, we could solve the manager-shareholder

[1] Martin Lipton Professor of Law, NYU School of Law. Many thanks to Glenn Booraem, Georg Ringe, and to participants in the Columbia Law School authors' workshop for helpful comments and suggestions. This chapter was completed in 2015 and updated in 2017 to take into account the EU's May 2017 enactment of the Amendments to the Shareholder Rights Directive.
[2] Directive (EU) 2017/828 of the European Parliament and of the Council of 17 May 2017 amending Directive 2007/36/EC as regards the encouragement of long-term shareholder engagement, paras. 14–15. The goal of increasing shareholder engagement is implemented in Article 3g (Engagement Policy) through a "comply or explain" strategy.

agency cost problem that is the focus of much of corporate law. For a while in the 1980s, some thought that the hostile tender offer was that magic potion. Then, beginning in the late 1980s, attention shifted to institutional investors, where it has stayed, on and off, ever since. Noting that shares of publicly held corporations are largely held by institutions, and that shareholding among institutions is concentrated, some have viewed institutional investors as having the potential to act as the responsible owners that corporate law seems to presume: shareholders that, by virtue of their holdings, will have the skills and incentives to keep an eye on managers and check departures from maximizing firm value, to prevent "short termism," and to do whatever else one wants responsible owners to do.

As with other utopian dreams, reality has proved to be less exciting and less transformative. In this chapter, I try to synthesize what we have learned about institutional investors in corporate governance over the last 30 years or so.

2 Who and What are "Institutional Investors"?

Robert Clark provides a basic framework for understanding how institutional investors fit within the historical evolution of finance.[3] The first stage, characteristic of the nineteenth century, was the age of the promoter-investor-manager, exemplified by Rockefeller or Carnegie. The second stage, characteristic of the first part of the twentieth century, was the age of the professional business manager who took on the management of the corporation, while leaving the financial claims to the owners of shares. This stage was exemplified by managerial giants such as Alfred Sloan who led the way in creating the modern, publicly held business corporation. The third stage, characteristic of the late twentieth century, was the age of the portfolio manager in which the selection of the financial claims (stock, bonds, etc.) was professionalized, while leaving the beneficial ownership to the capital supplier. This age of financial intermediaries is the age of the institutional investors, with great stock pickers like Peter Lynch as representative heroes.

In this age of intermediated finance, the investment function—where to invest money that is being saved—is separated from the savings decision and given to professionals, the "money managers." By professionalizing the investment function, which had been bundled with the savings decision, the third stage parallels the professionalization of the management function that characterized the second stage of capitalism. The most prominent "traditional" intermediaries are public and private pension funds, mutual funds, insurance companies, and endowments (collectively referred to as "institutional investors"). More recently, as will become apparent later, activist hedge funds have emerged as a distinct category of specialized professional investors.

Clark's description, and the above taxonomy, is most applicable to economies with corporations with dispersed public ownership, most prominently the US and the UK. In

---

[3] Robert Charles Clark, "The Four Stages of Capitalism: Reflections on Investment Management Treaties", 94 Harv. L. Rev. 561 (1981).

economies dominated by publicly held firms with concentrated ownership, such as the countries of continental Europe, this description is less accurate but the trend lines point in the same direction. In this chapter, I primarily focus on the US experience, with secondary attention to drawing lessons for the UK and continental Europe.[4]

As is now widely recognized, institutional ownership of equities has been transformed over the last 60 years. In 1950, institutions held $8.7 billion in equities (6.1% of total); in 1980, institutions held $436.2 billion in equity (18% of total); in 2009, they held $10.239 trillion (40.4% of total).[5] In this growth, mutual funds have been especially prominent, going from owning $70 billion in 1980 to $7.2 trillion in 2009.[6]

The effect of this growth has been to concentrate ownership of publicly held firms in institutional hands. Between 1987 and 2009, the institutional ownership in the top 1000 US corporations grew from 46.6% to 73%.[7] In 2009, the 25 largest corporations by market value had an average institutional ownership of over 60%.[8]

The concentration of ownership within these firms is impressive as well. Table 14.1, drawn from data in the 2010 Conference Board report, shows institutional ownership in the 25 largest corporations, and the ownership of the top five, ten, 20, and 25 institutions in each. As this table makes clear, both the level and the concentration of institutional ownership in even the largest companies is high.

Two factors seem to have driven the trends over time: regulation and market forces. The extraordinary growth of institutional investors in the US owes much to the 1974 enactment of ERISA which mandated that pension commitments be fully funded by segregated pools of assets.[9] This led to the creation of independent corporate pension funds to fund "defined benefit" plans (in which employees' pensions were a certain percentage of final salary). It also eventually pushed corporations to shift to "defined contribution" plans in which the employer and employee each contribute to a tax-advantaged retirement account (almost invariably managed by a mutual fund) to support the employee after retirement. From an employer's perspective, the great virtue of a "defined contribution" plan is that it is fully funded from the beginning and all investment risk falls on the employee. From an employee's perspective, the benefit of a defined contribution plan is complete portability, a significant advantage for a mobile workforce.

---

[4] There is a large literature. For an insightful recent contribution, see Ronald J. Gilson & Jeffrey N. Gordon, "The Agency Costs of Agency Capitalism: Activist Investors and the Revaluation of Governance Rights", 113 Colum. L. Rev. 863 (2013). Earlier contributions include: Bernard S. Black, "Shareholder Passivity Reexamined", 89 Mich. L. Rev. 520 (1990); John C. Coffee, Jr., "Liquidity versus Control: The Institutional Investor as Corporate Monitor", 91 Colum. L. Rev. 1277 (1991); Edward B. Rock, "The Logic and (Uncertain) Significance of Institutional Shareholder Activism", 79 Geo. L. J. 445 (1991); Bernard S. Black, "Agents Watching Agents: The Promise of Institutional Investor Voice", 39 UCLA L. Rev. 811 (1992); Mark J. Roe, "A Political Theory of American Corporate Finance", 91 Colum. L. Rev. 10 (1991); Mark Roe, Strong Managers, Weak Owners: The Political Roots of American Corporate Finance (1994).

[5] Matteo Tonello & Stephan Rahim Rabimov, The 2010 Institutional Investment Report: Trends in Asset Allocation and Portfolio Composition (Nov. 11, 2010) (Conference Board Research Report), No. R-1468-10-RR, 2010 at p. 22 tbl.10, available at SSRN: http://ssrn.com/abstract=1707512.

[6] Conference Board Research Report, *supra* note 5, at 8, Chart 2a.

[7] Conference Board Research Report, *supra* note 5, at 27, Tbl. 13, Chart 14.

[8] Conference Board Research Report, *supra* note 5, at 29, Tbl. 16.

[9] For an overview of these developments, see Gilson & Gordon, *supra* note 4 at 878–84.

Table 14.1 Institutional Ownership concentration in the 25 largest US Corporations (by market value; as of 03/26/2010)

Company	Market value ($millions)	% of total shares outstanding held by institutions	% held by top 5 institutions	% held by top 10 institutions	% held by top 20 institutions	% held by top 25 institutions
Exxon Mobil Corp	$314,153.50	48.20%	13.40%	17.40%	22.80%	25%
Microsoft	260,131.90	63.7	17.1	23.5	29.5	31.9
Apple Inc.	209,379.00	70.8	18.5	26.2	34.5	37
Wal-Mart Stores, Inc.	208,662.50	35.9	8.6	12	15.7	17.2
Berkshire Hathaway Inc.	200,900.50	25	10.4	14.8	18.3	19.2
General Electric Co.	195,740.50	49.4	12.7	17	22.8	24.8
Procter & Gamble Co.	184,993.50	58	16.5	20.6	26.7	29.1
Bank of America Corp.	179,572.90	54.9	14.9	20.3	26.8	28.9
Google, Inc.	179,104.10	79.6	21.5	32.2	41.4	44.1
JPMorgan Chase & Co.	178,865.00	73.3	17.9	25.6	33	35.8
Johnson & Johnson	177,169.10	63.9	14.9	20.1	27.3	29.6
IBM Corp.	167,909.10	61.3	15.3	20.9	28.1	30.6
Wells Fargo & Co.	161,742.30	75.2	21.7	32.9	41.5	44.3
AT&T Inc.	154,870.40	55.1	16.9	23	29.1	31.4
Cisco Systems, Inc.	151,500.30	73.4	17.5	24.1	31.3	33.8
Chevron Corp.	149,481.70	62.2	17.2	22.3	29.1	31.7
Pfizer Inc.	138,285.20	69.7	16.9	22.9	30.5	33.2
Oracle Inc.	128,940.40	60.8	17.9	25.3	32.5	34.7
Coca-Cola Enterprises Inc.	125,975.00	63.5	23.6	32.5	38.4	40.4
Hewlett-Packard Co.	125,274.90	77.4	19	27.6	36.3	39.4
Citigroup Inc.	123,088.90	37.8	13.4	17.9	22.1	23.5
Intel Corp.	122,853.80	63.2	15.3	20.6	27.6	30
Merck & Co., Inc.	116,606.30	73.4	21.6	33.3	41.3	43.8
PepsiCo, Inc.	110,052.60	66.2	15.1	21.6	29	31.6
Philip Morris International Inc.	97,215.10	71.7	22.7	30	37.7	40.4
Goldman Sachs Group	91,077.10	54.9	18.8	27.4	36.4	39.2

At the same time, the growth of institutional investors has made them remarkably efficient managers of capital. Vanguard's 500 Index fund allows investors to invest in a basket of securities that tracks the S & P 500 stock index for as low as five basis points (i.e., 0.05% per year).[10] This extraordinarily low price reflects, among other things, massive economies of scale.

When all these factors are brought together, the critical fact that must ground any analysis of corporate governance is the "de-retailization" of the capital markets.[11] Any sensible discussion must begin from the fact that between 60% and 70% of the shares of medium and large public corporations are held by institutional investors, and that even in the largest corporations, a significant percentage of the shares are held by a handful of investors.

3 The Governance of Money Managers

The governance of money managers themselves is quite varied. There are four or five different models, as illustrated by some of the leading firms. First, there are for-profit asset managers, some of which are publicly held (e.g., BlackRock and State Street are both NYSE companies), while others are privately held (e.g., Fidelity Management & Research Company, which acts as the investment advisor to Fidelity's family of mutual funds).[12] Included in this group are (for-profit) insurance companies and savings institutions.

Second, there are "mutual" and nonprofit management companies. For example, Vanguard's management company is owned by the Vanguard funds, and thus indirectly by Vanguard participants,[13] while CREF, the College Retirement Equity Fund, is a nonprofit corporation whose trustees are directly elected by participants, with votes weighted by dollar amount in an account.[14]

Third, there are public-employee pension funds in which the governing managers or boards are appointed by politicians or directly elected by voters. At CalPERS, the board includes six elected members, three appointed members, and four ex officio state officials.[15] The NYCERS board "consists of eleven members: the Mayor's Representative, the City Comptroller, the Public Advocate, the heads of the three unions with the largest number of participating employees, and the five Borough Presidents."[16] By contrast, the NY State & Local Retirement System is headed by the elected NY State Comptroller.[17]

---

[10] See, e.g., https://investor.vanguard.com/mutual-funds/vanguard-mutual-funds-list?assetclass=stk.
[11] Brian G. Cartwright, Gen. Counsel, SEC, Speech by SEC Staff: The Future of Securities Regulation (Oct. 24, 2007) (transcript available at http://sec.gov/news/speech/2007/spch102407bgc.htm). https://www.sec.gov/news/speech/2007/spch102407bgc.htm (checked 5/18/2015).
[12] http://investing.businessweek.com/research/stocks/private/snapshot.asp?privcapId=6480833.
[13] https://about.vanguard.com/what-sets-vanguard-apart/why-ownership-matters/.
[14] See, e.g., CREF 2012 Proxy Statement at p. 2, available at http://www1.tiaa-cref.org/ucm/groups/content/@ap_ucm_p_tcp/documents/document/tiaa04031044.pdf.
[15] http://www.calpers.ca.gov/index.jsp?bc=/about/board/home.xml.
[16] http://www.nycers.org/%28S%28onotmx555bn5qxfzwp0blu55%29%29/about/Board.aspx.
[17] https://www.osc.state.ny.us/retire/about_us/index.php.

Finally, there are the union-related funds that have been prominent governance activists. With respect to shareholder proposals, which require minimal investments, the AFL-CIO has filed proposals using its $28 million "Reserve Fund."[18] The joint union-employer pension funds (known as "Taft-Hartley Plans" after the key regulation) collectively hold approximately $400 billion in assets (of which $100 billion is in common stock), but have not been active, largely because discretion is delegated to outside money managers in order to avoid the risk of liability under ERISA.

Governance structure affects activism in predictable ways. The union funds pursue a labor agenda. The public pension funds respond to political pressure.[19] For-profit money managers such as BlackRock rarely engage in aggressive activism, although increasingly they engage with companies and support dissident shareholders.[20]

4 The Organization of Share Voting by Institutional Investors

With the thousands of public companies held by institutional investors, each with an annual meeting and a variety of matters to vote on, voting shares is a huge task. Major institutional investors establish dedicated proxy voting departments that are responsible for developing voting guidelines and voting proxies.

To get a sense of how proxy voting is organized at major institutional investors, and what sort of people are involved, consider Exxon Mobil's three largest shareholders: BlackRock, State Street, and Vanguard, each of which owns more than 3% of the company.[21] At BlackRock, for example, there is a "Corporate Governance and Responsible Investment" (CGRI) team that acts as a central clearinghouse across its various portfolios.[22] The CGRI team has 20 professionals working out of six offices around the world,[23] has responsibility for voting proxies, and has developed general Proxy Voting Guidelines.[24] Since 2009, the group has been headed by Michelle Edkins, who has made a career of corporate governance analysis, previously as managing director at Governance for Owners and, earlier, as Corporate

---

[18] Marcel Kahan & Edward Rock, "The Insignificance of Proxy Access", 97 Va. L. Rev. 1347, 1377–79 (2011).

[19] Roberta Romano, "Public Pension Fund Activism in Corporate Governance Reconsidered", 93 Colum. L. Rev. 795 (1993).

[20] Barry Burr, "Money Managers Increasing Activism on Governance—But Quietly, Pensions & Investments", Mar. 19, 2012, available at http://www.pionline.com/article/20120319/PRINT/303199980/money-managers-increasing-activism-on-governance-8212-but-quietly; David Benoit & Liz Hoffman, BlackRock's Fink Sounds the Alert, Wall St. J. Mar. 25, 2014, available at https://www.wsj.com/articles/blackrocks-fink-sounds-the-alert-1395787125.

[21] Tonello & Rabimov, *supra* note 5, at 30.

[22] Blackrock, "2013 Corporate Governance & Responsible Investment Report: Taking the Long View", available at http://www.fossilfuelsreview.ed.ac.uk/resources/Evidence%20-%20Investment%2C%20Financial%2C%20Behavioural/BlackRock%20-%20Responsible%20Investment%20Report.pdf.

[23] Id. at 8.

[24] BlackRock, Proxy Voting Guidelines for U.S. Securities (2018), available at http://www.blackrock.com/corporate/en-us/literature/fact-sheet/blk-responsible-investment-guidelines-us.pdf.

Governance Director at Hermes in London.[25] Daniel Oh, VP for the Americas on the CGRI team, was previously part of the corporate governance team at State Street, and still earlier was a corporate governance advisor at ISS.[26]

At State Street, the:

> Corporate Governance Team is responsible for implementing the Proxy Voting and Engagement Guidelines (the "Guidelines"), case-by-case voting items, issuer engagement activities, and research and analysis of governance-related issues. The implementation of the Guidelines is overseen by the SSgA Global Proxy Review Committee ("SSgA PRC"), a committee of investment, compliance and legal professionals, who provide guidance on proxy issues as described in greater detail below. Oversight of the proxy voting process is ultimately the responsibility of the SSgA Investment Committee.[27]

Rakhi Kumar leads the group as the head of Corporate Governance.[28] A Yale MBA, she spent time earlier in her career at Proxy Governance Inc.

At Vanguard, proxy voting is delegated to the "Proxy Voting Group," which, in turn, is overseen by the "Proxy Oversight Committee" made up of senior officers and reporting to the board.[29] The Proxy Voting Group applies the general proxy voting guidelines to specific instances, and is responsible for:

> (1) managing proxy voting vendors; (2) reconciling share positions; (3) analyzing proxy proposals using factors described in the guidelines; (4) determining and addressing potential or actual conflicts of interest that may be presented by a particular proxy; and (5) voting proxies. The Proxy Voting Group also prepares periodic and special reports to the Board and any proposed amendments to the procedures and guidelines.[30]

The Proxy Voting Group is led by Glen Booraem, who joined Vanguard in 1989 and has spent his entire career in fund accounting and administration roles.[31] In addition to leading

---

[25] Michelle Edkins, LinkedIn, at https://www.linkedin.com/profile/view?id=144306472&authType=OUT_OF_NETWORK&authToken=qvNy&locale=en_US&trk=tyah2&trkInfo=tarId%3A1405698584327%2Ctas%3Amichelle%20edki%2Cidx%3A1-1-1.

[26] Daniel Oh, LinkedIn, at https://www.linkedin.com/profile/view?id=97148005&authType=NAME_SEARCH&authToken=ach1&locale=en_US&srchid=13939147214057022287008&srchindex=1&srchtotal=1&trk=vsrp_people_res_photo&trkInfo=VSRPsearchId%3A13939147214057022287008%2CVSRPtargetId%3A97148005%2CVSRPcmpt%3Aprimary.

[27] State Street Global Advisors, Proxy Voting and Engagement Principles at 3 (Mar. 2014), available at https://www.ssga.com/investment-topics/environmental-social-governance/2017/Proxy-Voting-and-Engagement-Guidelines-EU-20170320.pdf.

[28] Rakhi Kumar, LinkedIn, at https://www.linkedin.com/profile/view?id=17196181&authType=NAME_SEARCH&authToken=snkV&locale=en_US&trk=tyah2&trkInfo=tarId%3A1406212829801%2Ctas%3Arakhi%20kuma%2Cidx%3A1-1-1.

[29] Vanguard's Proxy Voting Guidelines, https://about.vanguard.com/vanguard-proxy-voting/voting-guidelines.

[30] Id. at 7.

[31] Glenn Booraem, Passive Investors, Not Passive Owners, available at https://personal.vanguard.com/us/insights/article/proxy-commentary-042013.

Vanguard's corporate governance program, he is also responsible for fund accounting, administration, and compliance services.[32]

Other major institutional investors organize the proxy voting/corporate governance functions the same way. At Fidelity, Mark Lundvall is the Vice President of Investment Proxy Research, having earlier worked on corporate governance and compliance at Vanguard.[33] Gwen Le Berre, Director of Proxy & Governance at Charles Schwab, is responsible for the development of Schwab's corporate governance policies and oversees the implementation of its proxy voting guidelines.[34] She came to Schwab from BlackRock's Corporate Governance and Responsible Investment group, with similar functions at Barclays.[35] Not surprisingly, some corporate governance professionals have spent time at a proxy advisory firm such as ISS, Proxy Governance Inc., or IRRC.[36] Public pension funds, such as CalPERS and CalSTRS, approach corporate governance and proxy voting in the same way.[37]

Given the number of companies in the portfolio, and the legal pressures to vote shares, the role inevitably includes a compliance function. Simply voting the shares, without even considering *how* to vote them, is an enormous task. In addition, especially in recent years and especially at the largest institutional investors, these groups have become increasingly active in corporate governance. From an incentive perspective, however, these activities are not treated as an investment function: unlike with portfolio managers, the compensation of governance professionals is not typically linked to the performance of the portfolios.

Proxy voting groups at institutional investors invariably subscribe to the major proxy advisory firms ISS and Glass Lewis. From what one can tell from the outside, there is a significant difference in the use made of the information and recommendations of those services.[38] At institutions with large in-house proxy voting groups, ISS and Glass Lewis are mainly

---

[32] https://www.conference-board.org/bio/index.cfm?bioid=2944; see also, Glen Booraem, Controller at Vanguard, C-SUITE Daily, June 25, 2014, available at http://www.csuiteinsight.com/2014/06/interview-with-glenn-booraem/.

[33] Mark Lundvall, LinkedIn, at https://www.linkedin.com/profile/view?id=3710006&authType=NAME_SEARCH&authToken=iAYS&locale=en_US&trk=tyah2&trkInfo=tarId%3A1406213028343%2Ctas%3Amark%20lundvall%2Cidx%3A1-1-1.

[34] Id.

[35] Gwen Le Berre, LinkedIn, at https://www.linkedin.com/profile/view?id=24044566&authType=NAME_SEARCH&authToken=qYOc&locale=en_US&trk=tyah2&trkInfo=tarId%3A1406213047175%2Ctas%3Agwen%20le%20berre%2Cidx%3A1-1-1.

[36] Daniel Oh (VP, Americas, Corporate Governance and Responsible Investment, BlackRock), LinkedIn profile *supra* note 27; Edward Gehl (Director of Proxy Research at Fidelity), LinkedIn, at https://www.linkedin.com/profile/view?id=7248772&authType=NAME_SEARCH&authToken=OtzO&locale=en_US&srchid=1393914721405702495939&srchindex=1&srchtotal=5&trk=vsrp_people_res_photo&trkInfo=VSRPsearchId%3A1393914721405702495939%2CVSRPtargetId%3A7248772%2CVSRPcmpt%3Aprimary.

[37] CalPERS global proxy voting policy, available at https://www.calpers.ca.gov/eip-docs/investments/policies/shareowner/proxy-voting-policy/global-proxy-voting.pdf; CalSTRS Names Head of Corporate Governance, http://www.calstrs.com/news-release/calstrs-names-head-corporate-governance (Sept. 4, 2008).

[38] Stephen Choi, Jill Fisch, & Marcel Kahan, "Who Calls the Shots? How Mutual Funds Vote on Director Elections", 3 Harv. Bus. L. Rev. 35, 55–63 (2013).

useful as information aggregators.[39] Smaller institutions seem to rely more heavily on the proxy advisory firms' recommendations.[40]

On high-value, high-profile issues such as contested mergers, proxy voting groups consult with the managers of the portfolios that hold the relevant shares. Otherwise, portfolio managers are typically less involved. Indeed, some report that portfolio managers sometimes oppose governance activism for fear that it may make it more difficult to arrange meetings with management.

5 THE PROMISE OF INSTITUTIONAL SHAREHOLDER ACTIVISM

The 2017 amendments to the EU's Shareholder Rights Directive, quoted above, accurately express the conventional view that "effective and sustainable shareholder engagement is one of the cornerstones of the corporate governance model of listed companies, which depends on checks and balances between the different organs and different stakeholders."[41] The frustration, going back at least as far as Berle and Means (1932), is that shareholders in public corporations with dispersed ownership do not perform that function. Much corporate law scholarship and policy making has focused on how to remedy or adapt to this failing.[42] The move towards ensuring that the board of directors is dominated by independent directors can best be understood as one type of solution to the lack of shareholder engagement: Because shareholders themselves do not monitor managers, we need a new player in the boardroom to play that role for the benefit of passive shareholders. Likewise, for some, hostile

[39] See, e.g., Vanguard's Proxy Voting Guidelines at 1; State Street's 2014 Global Proxy Voting and Engagement Principles at 3 ("SSgA retains Institutional Shareholder Services Inc. ('ISS'), a firm with expertise in proxy voting and corporate governance. SSgA utilizes ISS's services in three ways: (1) as SSgA's proxy voting agent (providing SSgA with vote execution and administration services); (2) for applying the Guidelines; and (3) as providers of research and analysis (relating to general corporate governance issues and specific proxy items.").

[40] Choi, Fisch, & Kahan, *supra* note 39, 316–28.

[41] Directive (EU) 2017/828 of the European Parliament and of the Council of 17 May 2017 amending Directive 2007/36/EC as regards the encouragement of long-term shareholder engagement, paras. 14–15. These sections trace back to the EU's 2011 The EU Corporate Governance Framework, COM(2011)164 final (2011) at 3, available at http://ec.europa.eu/internal_market/company/docs/modern/com2011-164_en.pdf. See, also, Michel Barnier, http://ec.europa.eu/commission_2010-2014/barnier/docs/speeches/20101025/speech_en.pdf: "Last but not least, shareholders must play their role fully. Too often, shareholders are only interested in the highest possible dividends. That is understandable but it fuels short-termism. We have spoken for years about shareholders rights. It is time to also talk about shareholders' obligations. All these measures put together will make a difference and lead to better corporate governance in companies, to more responsibility and more accountability. We still need to debate how we put these measures in place—but I am clear we will not be able to rely only on voluntary codes."

At the time, Barnier was European Commissioner for Internal Market and Services and a Vice President of the European Commission.

[42] See, generally, John Armour, Henry Hansmann, & Reinier Kraakman, Agency Problems and Legal Strategies, in The Anatomy of Corporate Law: A Comparative and Functional Approach (2d ed., R. Kraakman et al. eds., 2009).

tender offers can provide a lever of managerial accountability that passive shareholders do not supply.

In the late 1980s, with the decline of the hostile tender offer, attention shifted to the rise of institutional investors as a potential solution to the separation of ownership and control. Institutional investors combined large stakes with professional management, at a time when the increased concentration of shareholdings reduced the costs of collective action. Perhaps, optimists thought, institutional investors would emerge from their historic lassitude that was summarized by the phrase "Wall Street Walk": Shareholders dissatisfied with management would (or should) sell their shares rather than engage in corporate governance activism. With the increased institutional holdings, perhaps institutional investors would emerge to provide the missing lever of corporate governance, to hold the management to account for its performance.

6 How Best to Explain Institutional Investor Passivity? Two Competing Hypotheses

Given the traditional passivity of institutional investors, policy makers needed to understand why they had played so minor a role in corporate governance. Two explanations were offered: excessive regulation and inadequate incentives.

6.1 The "Excessive Regulation" Hypothesis

In the late 1980s, Mark Roe and Bernard Black separately catalogued the dizzying array of regulatory barriers to activism found in state corporate law, federal securities law, federal regulation of investment companies (mutual funds), state insurance company regulation, and pension regulation.[43] Moreover, as Roe demonstrated, many of these barriers were erected as part of a political decision to *prevent* institutional investors from playing an active role in corporate governance.

Together, these analyses implicitly proposed "excessive regulation" as the explanation for why institutional investors, despite their size and expertise, were not more active in corporate governance. If only these largely unnecessary regulations were reduced or eliminated, they seemed to suggest, we could expect institutions to take a more prominent role.

---

[43] Roe, A Political Theory, *supra* note 4; Roe, Strong Managers, Weak Owners, *supra* note 4; Black, Shareholder Passivity Reexamined, *supra* note 4; Black, Agents Watching Agents: The Promise of Institutional Investor Voice, *supra* note 4.

6.2 The Inadequate Incentives Hypothesis

During this same period, other scholars argued that the source of institutional investor passivity was to be found in their lack of or misaligned incentives.[44] Institutional investors are intermediaries, competing against each other for investors' funds. Many of the largest institutions offer low-cost diversification, by tracking stock indices or the equivalent.

This industry structure has a variety of implications, almost all of which point away from serious engagement with corporate governance. First, the market for money managers is highly competitive, with money flowing to funds offering higher returns. To the extent that competing funds track indices, superior returns can *only* come from lowering costs, leaving little money for activism. Outside of the hedge fund sector, discussed below, even "active managers" will typically only depart slightly from an indexing strategy.[45]

Second, the costs of activism are borne by the activist while the benefits are enjoyed by all the shareholders, potentially leading to both "rational apathy" (when the private costs exceed the private benefits) and the "free rider problem" (when shareholders refuse to incur costs, hoping to benefit from other shareholders' activism). As shareholding becomes more concentrated, and the costs of coordination among shareholders drops, both of which have occurred in the last 20 years, shareholders can capture more of the gains, allowing them to move beyond rational apathy.

Third, institutional investors' revenue model is typically a percentage of assets under management. In such a system, the dominant incentive is to increase fund or fund complex size. This can be done via a variety of avenues, including both marketing and performance. There is thus a link with fund performance, but it will be indirect.

Fourth, money managers may have perverse incentives with regard to activism: To the extent that funds depart from an index, but still compete with managers of similar funds, a fund's *relative* performance improves when "underweighted" companies in their portfolio perform *badly*.[46] If Fund A has 4% of X Corp and 2% of Y Corp, and competes with Fund B, with 4% of X Corp and 4% of Y Corp, the worse that Y Corp performs, the better Fund A's relative performance vis-à-vis Fund B. Indeed, to the extent that relative performance is determinative, Fund A would have a financial incentive to vote against a merger that would benefit Y Corp or elect incompetent directors.

Fifth, consistent with the old "Wall Street Rule," noted above, portfolio managers still believe that involvement in everyday corporate governance is a tough way to make money and would prefer to devote their efforts to selecting better investments. Moreover, corporate governance activism can make it difficult for portfolio managers to gain access to the management of portfolio companies, making their jobs more difficult.

---

[44] Rock, *supra* note 4; Coffee, *supra* note 4; Jill E. Fisch, "Relationship Investing: Will It Happen? Will It Work?", 55 Ohio St. L. J. 1009 (1994).

[45] How to Spot a Closet Index Fund, Bloomberg Businessweek, Sept. 6, 2004, available at http://www.businessweek.com/stories/2004-09-05/how-to-spot-a-closet-index-fund; Chris Flood, UK Regulator Urged to Tackle "Index Clones", Sept. 24, 2013, available at http://www.ft.com/cms/s/0/d05e39e0-2467-11e3-8905-00144feab7de.html#axzz3FmBfEgzt.

[46] Simon C. Y. Wong, How Conflicts of Interest Thwart Institutional Investor Stewardship, Butterworths Journal of International Banking and Financial Law (Sept. 2011), available at: http://ssrn.com/abstract=1925485.

Finally, asset managers face a variety of conflicts of interests. It is difficult to compete for corporate pension business while criticizing the company. When the asset manager is part of a larger group including an investment bank, the bankers may pressure asset managers not to antagonize current or prospective clients by, for example, voting against the CEO's pay.[47]

6.3 A Natural Experiment: Partial Deregulation of Institutional Investors

In the years since 1990, concentration of ownership has continued to increase and many of the regulations that Black and Roe identified have been relaxed. Thus, the 1992 reform of the proxy rules allows institutions to talk with other institutions about the performance of the management without fear of liability for improper solicitation of proxies.[48] Regulation Fair Disclosure, effective in 2000, prevents corporate managers from punishing active investors by providing selective disclosure of important information only to friendly portfolio managers, thereby protecting active shareholders from at least one form of retribution.[49]

Yet institutional investors have not emerged as shareholders' champion. While not conclusive, the evidence strongly suggests that the primary explanation for institutional investor passivity is inadequate incentives, rather than excessive regulation.

7 CAN WE FIX THE INCENTIVE PROBLEMS?

7.1 The European Commission's 2017 Amendments to the Shareholder Rights Directive

The European Commission, as reflected in the 2011 Green Paper, has been frustrated by the same shareholder passivity that has frustrated US observers.[50] In its proposal to amend the Shareholder Rights Directive,[51] it observed that:

> The financial crisis has revealed that shareholders in many cases supported managers' excessive short-term risk taking. Moreover, there is clear evidence that the current level of

---

[47] Id.

[48] United States, Securities and Exchange Commission, Regulation of Communication among Shareholders, 1992, Securities Exchange Act of 1934 Release No. 31,326, 57 Fed. Reg. 48,276, Oct. 16.

[49] Securities and Exchange Commission, Final Rule: Selective Disclosure and Insider Trading, 17 CFR Parts 240, 243, and 249, Release Nos. 33–7881, 34–43154, IC-24599, File No. S7-31-99, RIN 3235-AH82, available at adopting release available at http://www.sec.gov/rules/final/33-7881.htm.

[50] The EU efforts follow earlier efforts in the UK to develop a "Stewardship Code" to "enhance the quality of engagement between asset managers and companies to help improve long-term risk-adjusted returns to shareholders." Financial Reporting Website, https://www.frc.org.uk/Our-Work/Codes-Standards/Corporate-governance/UK-Stewardship-Code.aspx (copy of Stewardship Code, first published in July 2010 and subsequently revised in September 2012 is available on the FRC website). The Stewardship Code seems to have only had a modest impact on UK corporate governance. Iris H.-Y. Chiu, "Reviving Shareholder Stewardship: Critically Examining the Impact of Corporate Transparency Reforms in the UK", 38 Del. J. Corp. L. 983 (2014).

[51] Proposal for a Directive of the European Parliament and of the Council amending Directive 2007/36/EC as regards the encouragement of long-term shareholder engagement and Directive 2013/34/EU as

"monitoring" of investee companies and engagement by institutional investors and asset managers is sub-optimal. Institutional investors and their asset managers do not sufficiently focus on the real (long-term) performance of companies, but often on share-price movements and the structure of capital market indexes, which leads to suboptimal return for the end beneficiaries of institutional investors and puts short-term pressure on companies.

Short-termism appears to be rooted in a misalignment of interests between asset owners and asset managers. Even though large asset owners tend to have long-term interests as their liabilities are long-term, for the selection and evaluation of asset managers they often rely on benchmarks, such as market indexes. Moreover, the performance of the asset manager is often evaluated on a quarterly basis. As a result many asset managers' main concern has become their short-term performance relative to a benchmark or to other asset managers. Short-term incentives turn focus and resources away from making investments based on the fundamentals (strategy, performance and governance) and longer-term perspectives, from evaluating the real value and longer-term value creative capacity of companies and increasing the value of the equity investments through shareholder engagement.[52]

In its 2017 Amendments to the Shareholder Rights Directive, in an effort to address this lack of engagement, the EU adopted a variety of measures, including the requirement that institutional investors and asset managers develop and disclose (on a "comply or explain basis") a policy on shareholder engagement: "Institutional investors and asset managers shall develop and publicly disclose an engagement policy that describes how they integrate shareholder engagement in their investment strategy. The policy shall describe how they monitor investee companies on relevant matters, including strategy, financial and non-financial performance and risk, capital structure, social and environmental impact and corporate governance, conduct dialogues with investee companies, exercise voting rights and other rights attached to shares, cooperate with other shareholders, communicate with relevant stakeholders of the investee companies and manage actual and potential conflicts of interests in relation to their engagement."[53] In addition, institutional investors are expected to disclose the results of their policies, how they vote in general meetings, and an explanation for how they vote.[54] The Amendments also seek to encourage institutional investors to incentivize asset managers to manage for the medium- to long-term performance of assets.[55]

Are these attempts to encourage or force institutional investors to play a more significant and productive role in corporate governance likely to succeed? In this regard, it is worth reviewing the US experience with a very similar set of reforms.

7.2 The 1988–2013 Mutual Fund "Experiment": Imposing Obligations on Mutual Funds

In 1988, the Department of Labor issued the legendary "Avon Letter" which declared that proxy voting rights are plan assets subject to the same fiduciary standards as other plan

---

regards certain elements of the corporate governance statement, COM(2014) 213 final, available at http://eur-lex.europa.eu/legal-content/EN/TXT/?uri=COM:2014:213:FIN (Apr. 9, 2014).

[52] Id. at 4.   [53] 2017 Amendments to Shareholder Rights Directive, Art. 3g(1)(a).

[54] Id. at Art. 3g(1)(b).   [55] Id. at Art. 3h.

assets.[56] In subsequent letters, the DOL amplified on this responsibility.[57] Since then, the SEC has repeatedly made clear that, under the Investment Company Act and Investment Advisors Act, the voting of proxies is a matter of money managers' fiduciary duties.

The SEC raised the stakes in 2003 when it promulgated two related releases that together imposed an obligation to disclose proxy voting policies and proxy votes on registered investment management companies (the managers of mutual funds) and investment advisors (the individuals who work for the managers of mutual funds).[58] In promulgating these new rules, the SEC focused on (1) mutual funds' large holdings; (2) advisors' and investment management companies' fiduciary obligations to their investors to vote proxies responsibly and in the interests of the investors; (3) mutual funds' historic passivity; and (4) the potential for conflicts of interest between mutual funds duties to their investors and their commercial interests. One can almost feel the SEC's frustration that, despite 15 years of emphasizing money managers' fiduciary responsibility to vote proxies, nothing much had changed.

The SEC justified imposing new obligations on mutual funds on two grounds: (1) investors' "fundamental right" to information on how mutual funds vote and (2) the ways in which transparency will allow investors to hold mutual funds accountable for how they vote, thereby controlling conflicts of interest and inducing more responsible "stewardship":

> Proxy voting decisions by funds can play an important role in maximizing the value of the funds' investments, thereby having an enormous impact on the financial livelihood of millions of Americans. Further, shedding light on mutual fund proxy voting could illuminate potential conflicts of interest and discourage voting that is inconsistent with fund shareholders' best interests. Finally, requiring greater transparency of proxy voting by funds may encourage funds to become more engaged in corporate governance of issuers held in their portfolios, which may benefit all investors and not just fund shareholders.[59]

Further, the SEC seemed to expect that disclosure of mutual fund proxy voting would lead investors to choose funds based on how active they are in corporate governance:

> A number of commenters, including an overwhelming number of individual investors, strongly supported the Commission's proposal to require a fund to disclose its complete proxy voting record. Many of these commenters stated that this disclosure would improve

---

[56] Letter from Alan D. Lebowitz, Deputy Assistant Secretary, Department of Labor, to Helmuth Fandl, Chairman of the Retirement Board, Avon Products Inc. (Feb. 23, 1988) (reprinted at 15 Pens. Rptr. (BNA) 391).

[57] For a useful summary of the evolution of the Department of Labor's views, beginning in 1988, see Clifton Perry, "Gathering Strength: The Reinforcement of Fiduciary Responsibility for Proxy Voting", Pension Consultants White Paper (Oct. 2004), available at http://www.pension-consultants.com/cimages/file_85.pdf; James McRitchie, Fiduciary Duty to Announce Votes (Part 2): Historical Background, at http://corpgov.net/2014/05/fiduciary-duty-announce-votes-part-2-historical-background/#more-19148.

[58] Proxy Voting by Investment Advisers, Investment Advisers Act Release No. IA—2106, 68 FR 6585 (Feb. 7, 2003); Disclosure of Proxy Voting Policies and Proxy Voting Records by Registered Management Investment Companies, Release Nos. 33-8188, 34-47304, IC-25922, 2003 SEC Lexis 3143 (2003).

[59] IC-25922 at *18.

shareholders' ability to monitor funds' voting decisions on their behalf and that it would allow investors to make more informed decisions when choosing among funds . . .

After careful consideration of these comments, we continue to believe that requiring funds to disclose their complete proxy voting records will benefit investors by improving transparency and enabling fund shareholders to monitor their funds' involvement in the governance activities of portfolio companies.[60]

In addition, the SEC expected that "more conscientious" mutual fund voting would lead to increases in firm value:

A third significant benefit of the amendments comes from providing stronger incentives to fund managers to vote their proxies conscientiously. The amendments could increase the incentives for fund managers to vote their proxies carefully, and thereby improve corporate performance and enhance shareholder value. The improved corporate performance that could result from better decisionmaking in corporate governance matters may benefit fund investors. In addition, other equity holders may benefit from the improvement to corporate governance that results from more conscientious proxy voting by fund managers. We note that assets held in equity funds account for approximately 18% of the $11 trillion market capitalization of all publicly traded US corporations, and therefore funds exercise a considerable amount of influence in proxy votes affecting the value of these corporations.[61]

Further, the release provided guidance on what sort of proxy voting policies mutual funds should have:

We do expect, however, that funds' disclosure of their policies and procedures will include general policies and procedures, as well as policies with respect to voting on specific types of issues. The following are examples of general policies and procedures that some funds include

---

[60] Id. at *28–*29. See, also, the SEC's benefit cost analysis:

The amendments to the registration statement and reporting forms that we are adopting will benefit fund investors, by providing them with access to information about how funds vote their proxies.

First, the amendments will provide better information to investors who wish to determine:

- to which fund managers they should allocate their capital, and
- whether their existing fund managers are adequately maximizing the value of their shares.

The investment adviser to a mutual fund is a fiduciary that owes the fund a duty of "utmost good faith, and full and fair disclosure." This fiduciary duty extends to all functions undertaken on the fund's behalf, including the voting of proxies relating to the fund's portfolio securities. An investment adviser voting proxies on behalf of a fund, therefore, must do so in a manner consistent with the best interests of the fund and its shareholders. The increased transparency resulting from proxy voting disclosure may increase investors' confidence that their fund managers are voting proxies in accordance with their fiduciary duties. Without disclosure about how the fund votes proxies, fund shareholders cannot evaluate this aspect of their managers' performance. To the extent that investors choose among funds based on their proxy voting policies and records, in addition to other factors such as expenses, performance, and investment policies, investors will be better able to select funds that suit their preferences. Further, insofar as investors may over-emphasize certain of these factors, e.g., past performance, in selecting funds, it may be beneficial to provide additional information to use in selecting funds. On a related point, we anticipate that over time, commercial third-party information providers will offer services that will enable investors to better analyze proxy voting by funds. These developments will further facilitate the benefits to fund investors from proxy vote disclosure (Id. at *72–74; footnotes omitted).

[61] Id. at *75–*76 (footnote omitted).

in their proxy voting policies and procedures and with respect to which disclosure would be appropriate:
- The extent to which the fund delegates its proxy voting decisions to its investment adviser or another third party, or relies on the recommendations of a third party;
- Policies and procedures relating to matters that may affect substantially the rights or privileges of the holders of securities to be voted; and
- Policies regarding the extent to which the fund will support or give weight to the views of management of a portfolio company.

The following are examples of specific types of issues that are covered by some funds' proxy voting policies and procedures and with respect to which disclosure would be appropriate:

- Corporate governance matters, including changes in the state of incorporation, mergers and other corporate restructurings, and anti-takeover provisions such as staggered boards, poison pills, and supermajority provisions;
- Changes to capital structure, including increases and decreases of capital and preferred stock issuance;
- Stock option plans and other management compensation issues; and
- Social and corporate responsibility issues.[62]

Finally, the SEC gave advice on how funds might handle conflicts of interest:

> Advisers today use various means of ensuring that proxy votes are voted in their clients' best interest and not affected by the advisers' conflicts of interest. An adviser that votes securities based on a pre-determined voting policy could demonstrate that its vote was not a product of a conflict of interest if the application of the policy to the matter presented to shareholders involved little discretion on the part of the adviser. Similarly, an adviser could demonstrate that the vote was not a product of a conflict of interest if it voted client securities, in accordance with a pre-determined policy, based upon the recommendations of an independent third party. An adviser could also suggest that the client engage another party to determine how the proxies should be voted, which would relieve the adviser of the responsibility to vote the proxies.[63]

7.3 The Effects of the SEC Release

Mutual funds complied with the requirements of the release. They now have proxy voting guidelines[64] and disclose their proxy voting.[65] Not surprisingly, funds have adopted voting guidelines that rather closely follow the SEC guidelines for what such guidelines should look like. Thus, guidelines typically take positions on general governance matters like classified boards, independent directors, anti-takeover provisions, and compensation.

Note how the SEC's release shaped the *substance* of mutual funds' engagement. By describing "best practices" for proxy voting guidelines, the SEC effectively mandated a

---

[62] Id. at *23–*24.

[63] Proxy Voting by Investment Advisers, IA-2106, 68 FR 6585 at *6588 (footnotes omitted).

[64] See, e.g., Vanguard's at https://about.vanguard.com/vanguard-proxy-voting/voting-guidelines/ and Fidelity's at http://personal.fidelity.com/myfidelity/InsideFidelity/InvestExpertise/governance.shtml#fulltext.

[65] How Our Funds Voted, Vanguard, https://about.vanguard.com/vanguard-proxy-voting/how-our-funds-voted/. The report for Vanguard's Index 500 fund (which tracks the S & P 500 index and thus has approximately 500 companies in it) runs to 256 pages.

particular "guidelines" approach to shareholder engagement, and rejected the perfectly re-spectable view that governance is endogenous to firms. It would take an unusually assertive and brave mutual fund to announce the following (entirely fictional) approach:

> We believe that there are no general principles or best practices in corporate governance. Rather, we believe that optimal governance depends on firm specific factors and that market pressures, even in the absence of regulation, drive most firms to adopt optimal governance arrangements. In addition, we believe that most shareholder voting is irrelevant to firm value, a distraction to corporate management, and does not contribute (and can interfere with) maximizing the financial performance of your fund. Therefore, we will routinely vote with management unless we become aware of a specific problem at a particular company. In those cases, we will decide how to vote on a case by case basis, taking into account all factors and discussing issues with management and other shareholders.

I am not aware of any funds that have announced this approach, even though such an approach, many believe, would be optimal for investors in widely diversified funds.

The SEC, in emphasizing money managers' fiduciary duties, and the extent to which conflicts of interest may breach those duties, created a compliance challenge. By then indicating reliance on guidelines or a predetermined policy of voting based on "the recommendations of an independent third party," the SEC gave a boost to "guideline based voting" (noted above), as well as to the proxy advisory industry. A subscription to ISS and Glass Lewis can be viewed as a kind of "ERISA insurance."[66]

So the SEC achieved its immediate goal, namely the routine disclosure of proxy voting policies and proxy votes. But has this disclosure led investors to choose funds based on those policies or votes? And has this new disclosure mandate increased firm value?

I have not found any evidence that investors seeking to maximize returns pay *any* attention to either the policies or the votes. In particular, I cannot find any evidence that investors *choose* funds based on how the fund voted its proxies. There is, however, evidence that labor and environmental groups use the voting reports to determine whether mutual funds comply with the groups' guidelines, and to criticize those that do not.[67]

Further evidence of compliance with the SEC requirements, and of the transformation of proxy voting into a "compliance function," is the creation of "proxy voting groups" at large mutual fund complexes, described above, staffed with people whose compensation does not depend on the performance of the companies or funds for which they vote proxies. The very existence of these groups indicates portfolio managers' *lack* of interest in voting routine proxies (although they clearly do weigh in on major decisions like mergers). Given that portfolio managers select investments and are judged based on the performance of the investments they select, this itself is strong evidence that an individual fund's routine proxy voting does not have any measurable effect on performance. The lack of incentive compensation for proxy voting groups eliminates any straightforward "pay for performance" penalty for votes that reduce firm value. Although mutual funds reliably support "performance

[66]   Leo E. Strine, Jr., "Toward Common Sense and Common Ground? Reflections on the Shared Interests of Managers and Labor in a More Rational System of Corporate Governance", 33 J. Corp. L. 1, 16 (2007).
[67]   See e.g. AFL CIO's annual report: http://corpgov.net/2013/02/afl-cio-key-votes-survey-results-for-2012/; also have pdf on file. See, also, http://proxydemocracy.org/.

compensation" for portfolio companies because of the incentive effects, proxy voting groups are not, themselves, compensated in this way.

With ten years of experience with the SEC's mutual fund release, we can begin to measure the effect of these mandates on firm value. The preliminary results are not encouraging. In an important paper, Larcker, McCall, and Ormazabal (2015) use the Dodd–Frank mandated "say on pay" votes to study the impact of proxy advisory firms on shareholder voting and firm value.[68] Their key findings are:

> proxy advisory firm recommendations have a substantive impact on say-on-pay voting outcomes, a substantial number of firms change their compensation programs in the time period before formal shareholder votes in a manner consistent with the features known to be favored by proxy advisory firms in an effort to avoid negative voting recommendations, and the stock market reaction to these compensation program changes is statistically negative.[69]

The first two findings support the conventional wisdom. Consistent with other research, the recommendations by ISS and Glass-Lewis have a significant effect on how mutual funds vote. The second finding confirms that, when proxy advisory recommendations matter, portfolio firms will tailor their conduct to comply and thereby avoid a negative recommendation.

The most important, and intriguing, finding is the third; namely, that complying with ISS guidelines to avoid a negative recommendation is correlated with a *decline* in firm value. Larcker et al. interpret this result as suggesting that "outsourcing voting to proxy advisory firms appears to have the unintended economic consequence that boards of directors are induced to make choices that decrease shareholder value."[70] An alternative explanation for the results is that firms identify themselves as out of compliance with proxy advisory firm recommendations by disclosing these changes, and that "lack of compliance" is evidence that firms are badly governed, leading to a fall in stock price. If, however, this were the explanation, then one would predict that *future* performance of these firms would decline; Larcker et al., however, show that this is not the case. As interesting and suggestive as these results are, more research is clearly needed to determine whether and to what extent proxy advisory firms' recommendations are value increasing or decreasing.

What can we learn from the last 25 years during which the US has experimented with using fiduciary duties and disclosure to induce mutual funds, an important subset of institutional investors, to be more active in corporate governance? The most immediate lessons are discouraging. While regulation clearly changes behavior—it led mutual funds to adopt proxy voting guidelines, to disclose their proxy voting, and to subscribe to proxy advisory services—it failed to achieve its core goal, namely, transforming mutual funds into shareholders' champions that assume a role in corporate governance commensurate with their shareholdings. Indeed, in an example of the law of unintended consequences, the effects of the effort may well be negative on the core measure of firm value. Not surprisingly, the fundamental incentive structure outlined above—in which institutional investors, as intermediaries, have minimal incentives to become active in corporate governance—seems to undermine even the best-intended regulatory intervention. It is very difficult to force anyone to be free.

---

[68] David F. Larcker, Allan L. McCall, & Gaizka Ormazabal, "Outsourcing Shareholder Voting to Proxy Advisory Firms", 58 J. L. & Econ. 173 (2015).
[69] Id. at 173.   [70] Id.

There is little reason to believe that the European Commission's reforms will fare any better. Now that the amendments to the Shareholder Rights Directive have been adopted, one can predict that institutional investors and asset managers will reliably comply (rather than explain why they did not), will dutifully create and disclose policies for engagement, and will disclose their votes at general meetings. Likewise, one can predict that institutional investors will turn to proxy advisors for assistance. Finally, one suspects that this greater engagement will not increase firm or portfolio value.

8 The New Reality: Institutional Investors and Activist Hedge Funds

But these negative assessments may be too quick. Although traditional institutional investors have not emerged as active "stewards," there has been a more modest, although still important, change in institutional investor behavior: Institutional investors are engaging with management in a much more active way than ever before; and, rather than always supporting management, institutional investors are now willing to support hedge funds and other corporate governance activists when they are convinced that doing so will increase firm value.[71] As one hedge fund manager explains, "The brute force of ownership is not required anymore because the big institutional players listen to both sides and are willing to back the activist fund if they believe in them . . . You can win with persuasion and ideas."[72]

Hedge fund activists include some familiar names from the 1980s like Carl Icahn and Nelson Peltz, as well as newer players like Bill Ackman, Daniel Loeb, and Jana Partners. Although exact figures are hard to come by, Icahn is said to have $20 billion available,[73] while Ackman has around $12 billion.[74] Overall, corporate activist hedge funds are estimated to have a total of around $100 billion.[75] While these are very large sums, they are small relative to the amounts managed by the largest institutional investors. As of 2017, the largest included: BlackRock ($5.1 trillion), State Street ($2.5 trillion), Vanguard ($4 trillion), and

---

[71] Marcel Kahan & Edward B. Rock, "Hedge Funds in Corporate Governance and Corporate Control", 155 U. Pa. L. Rev. 1021, 1045 (2007); David Gelles & Michael J. De La Merced, New Alliances in Battle for Corporate Control, N.Y. Times, Mar. 18, 2014 at B1, available http://dealbook.nytimes.com/2014/03/18/new-alliances-in-battle-for-corporate-control/?_php=true&_type=blogs&ref=business&_r=0.

[72] Alexandra Stevenson, No Barbarians at the Gate; Instead, a Force for Change, N.Y. Times, Jan. 6, 2014, available at http://dealbook.nytimes.com/2014/01/06/no-barbarians-at-the-gate-instead-a-force-for-change/, quoting Gregory Taxin, president of $1.5 billion hedge fund Clinton Group and a co-founder of Glass Lewis & Company, a leading proxy advisor.

[73] Having returned outside investors' money in 2011, Icahn relies on his own considerable resources: Forbes estimates his net worth at $20 billion. Steven Bertoni, Carl Icahn Unleashed: Wall Street's Richest Man Is on the Attack – Just Ask Michael Dell, Forbes (Apr. 15, 2013), http://www.forbes.com/sites/stevenbertoni/2013/03/27/carl-icahn-unleashed-wall-streets-richest-man-is-on-the-attack-just-ask-michael-dell/

[74] Rob Copeland, Ackman's Pershing Square L.P. Fund Rose 3.8% Last Month, Wall St. J., http://blogs.wsj.com/moneybeat/2014/02/04/ackmans-pershing-square-l-p-fund-rose-3-8-last-month/?link=mtkw.

[75] Stevenson, *supra* note 73. See also Beth Jinks and Laura Marcinek, Bankers Pitching Avoidance Advice as Activists Amass Record Cash, Bloomberg (Jan. 6, 2014), http://www.bloomberg.com/news/

Fidelity ($2.1 trillion). They are also small relative to the market capitalization of the largest companies. As of September 29, 2017, the median market cap for the S & P 500 was $20 billion; the smallest market cap was $2.7 billion; the largest $796 billion.[76]

Hedge funds, in contrast to traditional institutional investors, engage with particular companies over firm-specific issues. Their activities can usefully be divided into corporate governance activism (e.g., pressuring management over business issues such as asking management to spin off a division, nominating a "short slate" of directors, and pushing for changes in corporate financing such as buying back stock or paying a dividend), and corporate control activism (e.g., blocking acquirers from completing a merger, blocking targets from agreeing to a merger, pushing the board to sell the company, and even making bids for the company).

The biggest difference between hedge funds and traditional institutional investors is hedge funds' business model. For traditional institutions, activism, when it occurs, is a response to unexpected and undesired problems that emerge in portfolio companies. Once problems arise, institutional investors must decide whether to sell the position (the "Wall Street Walk"), to intervene to improve it, or to do nothing. As we saw above, institutional investors' incentives to intervene are very weak.

By contrast, for activist hedge funds, activism is ex ante and strategic.[77] Activists first identify a problematic company, then decide whether intervention can improve matters. If activists conclude that an intervention is warranted, they buy a stake in order to intervene. When combined with high-powered performance-based incentives (typically between 1% and 2% of money under management plus between 15% and 20% of gains), hedge funds, unlike traditional institutions, have strong financial incentives to get involved. When an engagement is effective, the gains to the hedge fund can be huge. Moreover, activist hedge funds typically do not have the same conflicts of interest as institutional investors, as they do not sell money management services to portfolio companies.

The links between activist hedge funds and traditional institutional investors are critical to understanding hedge funds' influence and institutional investors' contemporary roles in corporate governance. First, because activist hedge funds do not have sufficiently large positions to prevail in medium or large cap companies, they must convince the other shareholders—mainly the traditional institutional investors—to support them. Hedge funds play an important "catalyst" role in facilitating shareholder action.

Second, the border between the "investor" side and the "issuer" side has become increasingly permeable, with increasing mobility of corporate governance professionals between the investor and issuer "sides" of the table. Stephen Brown, Director of Corporate Governance at TIAA-CREF, became the CEO of the Society of Corporate Secretaries and Governance

---

2014-01-06/bankers-pitching-avoidance-advice-as-activists-amass-record-cash.html (estimating $89 billion in activist hedge funds as of the 2013 third quarter compared to $66 billion at the end of 2012).

[76]   S & P Dow Jones Indices, S & P 500 fact sheet, available at http://us.spindices.com/indices/equity/sp-500.

[77]   Kahan & Rock, *supra* note 72, at 1069.

Professionals and then joined KPMG's "board leadership" group.[78] Bess Joffe, by contrast, left Goldman Sachs to become Managing Director of Corporate Governance at TIAA-CREF.[79] Linda Scott, managing director at Governance for Owners and, before that, Director of Corporate Governance at TIAA-CREF, is now SVP and Associate Corporate Secretary at JPMorgan Chase.[80] Abe Friedman, founder and managing partner of CamberView Partners, a boutique advisory firm that advises issuers, came from BlackRock. Chris Young, after six years as Director of M & A and Proxy Fight Research at ISS, is now managing director and head of contested situations at Credit Suisse where he advises issuers.[81] And, of course, John Wilcox, after a long career at the leading proxy solicitor Georgeson, became SVP and head of corporate governance at TIAA-CREF, and is now chairman of Morrow Sodali, which works with issuers in developing institutional investor relationships.[82]

Third, and critically, a significant (but undisclosed) amount of activist hedge fund capital is raised from traditional institutions. According to the 2010 Conference Board report, hedge fund and other alternative investment assets have grown from under $2 billion in 1990 to around $1.5 trillion in 2009.[83] This growth has been fueled by institutional investment. As of 2009, the largest 200 defined benefit plans had invested around $70 billion in hedge funds alone.[84]

Institutional investor investment in activist hedge funds potentially align interests in a variety of interesting ways. First, it insulates institutional investors from criticism by those opposed to the activists' agenda, and avoids antagonizing portfolio companies and incurring the wrath of portfolio managers. Second, encouraging activism through hedge funds allows for much higher-powered financial incentives than would be politically acceptable within institutional investors. Third, the arrangement allows for a division of labor, with the hedge funds developing expertise in pressuring management. Having induced activism through investments in hedge funds, institutional investors quite reasonably may choose to take a more passive reactive role. Fourth, the investments partially align the financial interests of the institutional investor and the hedge fund. Finally, major institutional investors only invest in hedge funds after significant due diligence. The process associated with institutional investors' *investment* in hedge funds provides some assurance to the general investing public of the activists' bona fides. Institutional investors are now far more willing to consider proposals for change made by the activist hedge funds than they used to be.

At the same time, hedge funds' high-powered financial incentives create grounds for concern. Hedge funds exist to make money, and will likely attempt to do so, whether or not it benefits shareholders as a group. Thus, for example, hedge funds have sought to acquire companies and, of course, sought to do so at the lowest possible cost. Hedge funds have also

---

[78] Stephen Brown, LinkedIn, at https://www.linkedin.com/in/stephenlbrown/.

[79] Bess Joffe, LinkedIn, at https://www.linkedin.com/in/bessjoffe/.

[80] Linda Scott, LinkedIn, at https://www.linkedin.com/in/linda-scott-36239737/.

[81] Christopher Young, LinkedIn, at https://www.linkedin.com/in/christopher-young-jd-cfa-7043154/.

[82] John C. Wilcox, LinkedIn, at https://www.linkedin.com/in/john-c-wilcox-a861b216/.

[83] Conference Board report at Chart 20 (p. 49).

[84] Conference Board Research Report, *supra* note 5, at p. 52, Tbl. 20 (this category includes all hedge funds and is thus far broader than the subset of hedge funds that engage in corporate governance activism; at the same time, defined benefit plans are a small subset of institutional investors).

used tactics such as "empty voting" that serve the hedge funds' interest at the expense of the other shareholders.[85]

The potential constraints induced by the need to form a coalition can be usefully illustrated by the Air Products/Air Gas battle.[86] In 2012, Air Products, an industrial gas producer, launched a hostile bid for Air Gas, a supplier of gas delivered in canisters. Air Gas, which had a staggered board and a poison pill, resisted Air Products's above market bid on the grounds that it undervalued the company. Eventually, Air Products launched a proxy fight to elect a short slate of directors. Air Products nominated three independent directors who were committed to taking a "second look." After prevailing in a hard-fought contest, with support of ISS, hedge funds, and traditional institutions, the newly elected directors, with separate counsel and investment banking advice, surprised many by concluding that the Air Products' offer, though a premium above market value, substantially undervalued Air Gas, and became the most vociferous proponents of resisting the Air Products offer. Air Products ultimately refused to raise its offer, and the bid failed. Air Gas's stock price has remained above the offer price and, in fact, has increased nearly 50%. The newly elected outside directors seem to have been right.

From a corporate governance perspective, one of the most interesting features of the battle was that Air Products did, in fact, identify and elect genuinely independent directors and not a slate committed to selling the company.[87] The best explanation one heard for this "unusual" tactic is that the institutions and the hedge funds that held Air Gas shares were genuinely unsure of the value of Air Gas, and would not have supported a more partisan slate.

The world has changed when F. William McNabb, III, chairman and CEO of Vanguard, publicly salutes certain interventions by activist hedge funds:

> The nature of activist investing has changed significantly since the 1980s. Today, we're seeing a greater trend toward constructive activists rather than destructive activists. Activists are not inherently good or bad. They often raise legitimate questions.
>
> And when they raise legitimate questions and tie their business cases to long-term shareholder value—that gets our attention. There have been a number of cases where a board wasn't asking the right questions and eventually lost touch with how the company was being run, and how it was being perceived by investors. I'll share two instances where Vanguard has sided with activist campaigns in recent years.
>
> - **Canadian Pacific Railway:** In 2012, activist Bill Ackman went in and identified some vulnerabilities in Canadian Pacific Railway. We agreed—as did many other large investors— that the company had been poorly run and governed. Ackman brought in an experienced CEO and a number of directors they thought could make a difference. It's been an activist success story—by and large.
> - **Commonwealth REIT:** Another example of us supporting an activist: Earlier this year, Corvex and Related Companies waged a successful campaign to replace the

---

[85] See, e.g., Henry T. C. Hu & Bernard Black, "The New Vote Buying: Empty Voting and Hidden (Morphable) Ownership", 79 S. Cal. L. Rev. 811 (2006).

[86] For a full description, see *Air Prods. & Chems., Inc. v. Airgas, Inc.*, 16 A.3d 48 (Del. Ch. 2011).

[87] As Chancellor Chandler pointed out, Air Products could have nominated a slate with strong priors in favor of selling, e.g., a slate of "three . . . Bebchuks." Id. at 123 n. 487.

entire board of Commonwealth REIT. This was a company with a track record of poor performance and poor governance, and they were ultimately held accountable. Commonwealth was using a third-party management firm, RMR, that was run by family members of Commonwealth leadership. RMR extracted value from the public company. They didn't operate it well, but they were paid well nonetheless. We supported wiping the slate clean. In the case of Commonwealth, we were the largest shareholder. We were important to Corvex's case, but at the end of the day, I don't think they needed us. 81% of Commonwealth shareholders voted to remove the company's board.[88]

The constraining effects of coalition building have some interesting implications. We should be more worried about cases in which hedge funds can act on their own than when a coalition with other shareholders is required. Thus, for example, the squeeze-out threshold in the EU for completing a takeover under the Takeover Directive (95% in Belgium, Germany, France, Italy, and the Netherlands; 90% in Spain, Sweden, and the UK)[89] is an invitation to hedge funds to acquire a blocking position. Especially at the 95% level, it would seem close to "hedge fund malpractice" not to buy a blocking position, especially in private equity deals in which the sponsor's financing requires owning 100%. Some worry that similar hold-out problems can be created by "majority of the minority" provisions, whether in a controlling shareholder context or a management-sponsored LBO. This suggests that such provisions should be used sparingly. It also raises the possibility that the doctrinal effect of such provisions should be revisited.[90]

9 Conclusion

The preceding discussion suggests that, try as we might, we are unlikely to transform institutional investors into "stewards" of portfolio companies. The emergence of activist hedge funds raises an even more fundamental question that applies equally to institutional investors: Do we, as a society, actually *want* shareholders to act like owners? Highly incentivized, focused actors can be and often are socially disruptive. In the US during the 1980s, the disruption accompanying hostile tender offers resulted in anti-takeover

---

[88] F. William McNabb III, "Getting to Know You: Sharing Practical Governance Viewpoints, John Weinberg Center for Corporate Governance", Oct. 30, 2014, available at http://www.lerner.udel.edu/sites/default/files/WCCG/PDFs/events/Transcript%20_UDel%20Corp%20Governance%2010%2030%20 2014_%20FINAL%20for%20UD%20website.pdf.

[89] Commission Staff Working Document, Report on the Implementation of the Directive on Takeover Bids, SEC (2007) 268 (Brussels, 21.02.2007), available at http://ec.europa.eu/internal_market/company/docs/takeoverbids/2007-02-report_en.pdf.

[90] But see Edward Rock, "MOM Approval in a World of Active Shareholders" (Working Paper 2017). Relatedly, bond covenants that were arguably optimal in an era of passive bondholders and under-enforcement may result in suboptimal selective over-enforcement as hedge funds overcome bondholders' classic collective action problems and exploit poorly drafted covenants, without having to convince institutional holders to join with them. Marcel Kahan & Edward Rock, "Hedge Fund Activism in the Enforcement of Bondholder Rights", 103 Nw. U. L. Rev. 281 (2009).

legislation, as well as judicial decisions that limited shareholders' ability to proceed unilaterally.[91] Mark Roe's political history of US corporate finance provides numerous examples of regulatory pacification of active or potentially active shareholders.[92] Whenever hedge funds have emerged as activists, they have produced a backlash as their single-minded, incentive-driven focus—whether on shareholder value maximization or blocking a transaction or exploiting ambiguities in bond contracts—has made people nervous. The rise of hedge funds in Europe has led to calls to constrain them.[93]

When one reads the EU's 2017 Amendments to the Shareholder Rights Directive, and the discussions leading up to it, one gets the distinct impression that shareholders who act too much like shareholders, with single-minded focus on maximizing shareholder value today, are *not* what is sought. Too often, it seems, with a focus on maximizing profits, they push for unpleasant things like closing plants, moving work to China, firing employees, or putting competitors out of business. Rather, the EU seems to be searching for a very different sort of shareholder, a shareholder more like a rich uncle who, while demanding, is ultimately focused on doing what is best for the family as a whole, one who "can be encouraged to take an interest in sustainable returns and longer term performance" even at the cost of lower returns. The US experience makes clear that traditional institutions and hedge funds are not this sort of investor and it is unlikely that regulation can transform them into this sort of "patient capital."

---

[91] For a discussion of how a self-regulating market economy stresses social relationships in a way that inevitably produces public regulatory countermeasures in a democracy, see Jeffrey N. Gordon, "Corporations, Markets, and Courts", 91 Colum. L. Rev. 1931, 1971–82 (1991) (using Karl Polanyi's The Great Transformation as a lens through which to understand the Delaware Supreme Court's restriction of hostile takeovers in *Paramount v. Time*).

[92] Roe, Strong Managers, Weak Owners, *supra* note 4.

[93] Alexandros Seretakis, "Taming the Locusts? Embattled Hedge Funds in the E.U.", 10 N.Y.U. J. L. & Bus. 115 (2013). For a more extensive treatment of the effects on hedge fund activism of the Shareholder Rights Directive, see Alessio M. Pacces, "Hedge Fund Activism and the Revision of the Shareholder Rights Directive" (July 5, 2017). European Corporate Governance Institute (ECGI) Law Working Paper No. 353/2017. Available at SSRN: https://ssrn.com/abstract=2953992 or http://dx.doi.org/10.2139/ssrn.2953992.

CHAPTER 15

··

SHAREHOLDER ACTIVISM
A Renaissance

··

WOLF-GEORG RINGE[1]

1 INTRODUCTION

WHEN considering shareholder activism, the likes of Chris Hohn, Carl Icahn, Bill Ackman, Nelson Peltz, T. Boone Pickens, CalPERS, and Atticus are commonly at the forefront of people's minds. As minority shareholders they commonly use their equity stakes in targeted corporations to sway management, arguably towards short-term value enhancement.[2] This can occur via proxy battles or voting contests, negotiations behind closed doors with management boards, publicity, litigation, and so forth. In recent years, activist investors seem to have honed their tactics.[3] However, in relation to a concept that not only encompasses various strategies for intervention but also applies to a multitude of minority shareholder profiles, care must be taken not to overgeneralize.[4]

Shareholder activism has become an important and integral part of our corporate governance reality. This chapter takes stock of the phenomenon of shareholder activism and evaluates its importance for the shape of today's debate on shareholders and shareholder empowerment. My main focus will be on the evolution of activist shareholder structures in the UK, the US, and continental Europe as well as historical developments, the guises and traits

[1] Professor of Law, Director of the Institute of Law & Economics, University of Hamburg; Visiting Professor, University of Oxford. Many thanks to Simon Deakin, Zohar Goshen, Amir Licht, Ed Rock, and Paul Davies for comments on an earlier draft of this chapter.
[2] Bill George & Jay Lorsch, How to Outsmart Activist Investors, Harv. Bus. Rev., May 2014.
[3] Dan McCrum & David Gelles, Stirrers and Shakers, Fin. Times, Aug. 22, 2012, at 7; Economist, Anything You Can Do, Icahn Do Better, Feb. 15, 2014, at 51.
[4] Brian R. Cheffins & John Armour, "The Past, Present, and Future of Shareholder Activism by Hedge Funds", 37 J. Corp. L. 51, 54–55 (2011); Gavin Davies & Tom Platts, "Shareholder Activism in Practice", 23 J. Int'l. Bank. & Fin. L. 100 (2008).

of shareholder activism, regulatory constraints, and finally the perspectives for shareholder activism following the financial crisis that plagued the global economy from 2007 to 2011.[5]

My main arguments are as follows: first, the seemingly straightforward term "shareholder activism" may cover a range of different activities, and may be exercised by a broad variety of activist investor types. Second, the importance and the effect of shareholder activism will very much depend on the prevailing shareholder structure under which it operates; and the economic benefits that we attach to shareholder activism may likewise vary depending on the environment in which it occurs. Third, I document that shareholder activism has seen something of a renaissance lately, with hedge fund activism becoming more refined, and also popular following the 2007–2009 global financial crisis.

I proceed as follows. Section 2 explores the concept of shareholder activism and emphasizes the importance of the shareholder structure under which it operates. Section 3 then looks back in time and seeks to explain the historical developments of shareholder activism, mostly in the US, UK, and continental Europe. This allows us to discuss the various methods of activist shareholders in section 4 and the corresponding regulatory constraints (section 5). Finally, section 6 demonstrates that activist shareholders suffered badly during the global financial crisis, but that more recent years seem to suggest that they are experiencing a "comeback." Section 7 concludes.

2 SHAREHOLDER ACTIVISM IN CONTEXT

A share in a company may afford the owning shareholder a range of rights and liabilities under the prevailing jurisdiction, but it is the way in which these rights are utilized in conjuncture with investment strategies of profit maximization that define shareholder activism.[6] In parallel, the legal protection given to a share as an asset not only plays a crucial role in stimulating economic activity in equity markets but also enables the modern syndicate to prosper.[7]

In its most general form, shareholder activism means nothing more than an active, engaging shareholder who does not simply consider the investment made as purely financial, but as strategic. The most obvious way in which shareholders may voice their demands is to exercise the voting rights associated with share ownership. One of the main problems of shareholder voting is that small shareholders generally have weak incentives to exercise their voting rights. This is the well-known phenomenon of "rational apathy" of (dispersed) shareholders.[8] The relationship between vote and benefit is usually so unfavorable for

---

[5] See Larry Elliott, Global Financial Crisis: Five Key Stages 2007–2011, Guardian, Aug. 7, 2011, available at <http://www.guardian.co.UK/business/2011/aug/07/global-financial-crisis-key-stages> (last visited Oct. 31, 2017).

[6] As opined by Lord Millet in *Her Majesty's Commissioners of Inland Revenue v. Laird Group Plc* [2003] UKHL 54 para 35.

[7] Iris Chiu, The Foundations and Anatomy of Shareholder Activism 110 (2010).

[8] Kenneth J. Arrow, The Limits of Organization (1974). See Mark J. Roe, "A Political Theory of American Corporate Finance", 91 Colum. L. Rev. 10 (1991); Bernard S. Black, "Shareholder Passivity Reexamined", 89 Mich. L. Rev. 520 (1990); Eddy Wymeersch, Shareholder(s) matter(s), in Unternehmen, Markt und Verantwortung – Festschrift für Klaus J. Hopt zum 70. Geburtstag am 24. August 2010, 1565, 1571 (2010).

retail investors that the rational investor will not seriously engage in the business strategy in order to make an informed decision or to vote. Activist shareholders, by contrast, overcome this passivity—for various reasons—and actively monitor the company's strategy and management's decisions. Activism comes in many different shapes. During the 1980s, it appeared in the form of corporate raiders dictating company policies, or as leveraged buyout funds taking public companies private in order to change corporate policy. More recently, some pension funds have exerted pressure on management in publicly listed companies, often in the form of behind-the-scene negotiations. The latest activist trend can be seen in hedge funds which have discovered corporate activism as their business model. In any case, it is important to bear in mind that each shareholder activist will pursue their own style of trading and methods for engaging with management boards, within the relevant legal and regulatory environments.[9] Without doubt these varying facets accord a degree of complexity to the meaning of shareholder activism.

In general terms, early forms of shareholder activism encompassed all forms by which shareholders engaged with targeted corporations on matters of company policy. This broad meaning was subsequently broken down into formal and informal activism.[10] Shareholder activism of a formal nature takes place in the public domain, for example at annual general meetings. Gillan and Starks consider there to be three residual categories to formal shareholder activism: namely, "transacting" shareholders, whereby shareholders voice their views on the performance of the targeted corporation by purchasing or selling shares; "activist blockholders" who focus on influencing decision making by gaining a minority control in the targeted corporation and voicing their views; and finally shareholders who seek to implement their changes by gaining control of the company, availing themselves of a (hostile) takeover.[11] Informal shareholder activism, in contrast, occurs in private, behind closed doors, and away from the prying eyes of the public. It therefore rarely attracts any media attention, rendering it near impossible to prove unless one has access to an activist's private database.[12] Although the above goes some way in defining the generalist traits of shareholder activists, the evolution of shareholder structures, regulatory regimes, and stock markets in the UK, US, and continental Europe has played a crucial role in influencing activist engagements. Shareholder activism in other parts of the world has been less pertinent, and is beyond the scope of this chapter.[13]

---

[9] Stuart L. Gillan & Laura T. Starks, "The Evolution of Shareholder Activism in the United States", 19 J. Appl. Corp. Fin. 55 (2007) [hereinafter Gillan & Starks, Evolution of Shareholder Activism].

[10] Lauren Talner, The Origins of Shareholder Activism (Investor Responsibility, 1983), quoted in R. Franklin Balotti, Jesse A. Finkelstein & Gregory P. Williams, Meetings Of Stockholders (Aspen, 1996), at para 5.4; Henry Schäfer & Christian Hertrich, Shareholder Activism in Germany: Theoretical Considerations and Empirical Evidence (2011), at 5.

[11] Stuart L. Gillan & Laura T. Starks, "A Survey of Shareholder Activism: Motivation and Empirical Evidence", 2 Contemp. Fin. Dig. 10 (1998).

[12] See, e.g., Willard T. Carleton, James M. Nelson, & Michael S. Weisbach, "The Influence of Institutions on Corporate Governance Through Private Negotiations: Evidence from TIAA-CREF", 53 J. Fin. 1335 (1998); Marco Becht, Julian Franks, Colin Mayer, & Stefano Rossi, "Returns to Shareholder Activism: Evidence from a Clinical Study of the Hermes U.K. Focus Fund", 22 Rev. Fin. Stud. 3093 (2009).

[13] For shareholder activism in Japan, see, e.g., John Buchanan, Dominic Heesang Chai, & Simon Deakin, "Agency Theory in Practice: A Qualitative Study of Hedge Fund Activism in Japan", 22 Corp. Governance 296 (2014); and, more generally, John Buchanan, Dominic Heesang Chai, & Simon Deakin,

2.1 Shareholder Activism: UK/US

Despite diversified shareholder structures being present in both the UK and US they have evolved into their current forms for differing reasons. The diversified shareholder structure seen in the UK has to a greater extent been developed by responding and adapting to the regulatory changes that have taken place over the past century and the globalization of stock markets.[14] Whilst the shareholder structures of corporations were historically comprised of "local" regional owners, the diversification of stock ownership in the UK only really commenced from the offset of the 1990s as UK insurance companies and pension funds began to emerge on stock markets. In parallel, foreign investors materialized as equity investment strategies became globalized due to the growing internationalization of corporate activities.[15] Akin to the UK, the shareholder structures of large US listed corporations are also dispersed in nature, but arguably for different reasons. To start with, dispersed ownership arrived in the United States much earlier: scholars disagree on the precise background, but, most commonly, the early twentieth century is named as the decisive period, though the developments that paved the way for equity dispersion had begun in the last quarter of the nineteenth century.[16] According to Mark Roe, an important feature was legislation enacted in 1940, which, by restricting the power of large financial conglomerates, inadvertently constrained the control of large blockholders in American corporations.[17] By restraining the operations of large blockholders it became possible to not only protect minority shareholders but to facilitate the diversification of US corporate shareholder structures. Influential in the diversification of both UK and US corporate shareholder structures was the mergers-and-acquisitions wave in the first half of the twentieth century. Equity exchanges during mergers and acquisitions furthermore dispersed the ownership of stock in both the UK and the US as the shareholdings of existing investors became diluted.[18]

In such a shareholder environment, activist shareholders are seen as those amongst the vast, anonymous shareholder body who actually take an interest in the company's affairs and in monitoring the management, contrary to what an ordinary shareholder would do. Activist shareholders are largely associated with a positive contribution to the business of the company, since they invest time and resources to make informed decisions and to engage in corporate strategy. Mostly, the realization of their plans will depend on the support of larger

Hedge Fund Activism in Japan: The Limits of Shareholder Primacy (2012). For evidence, see Yasushi Hamao, Kenji Kutsuna, & Pedro P. Matos, "U.S.-Style Investor Activism in Japan: The First Ten Years", Working Paper 2011, available at http://ssrn.com/abstract=1785281.

[14] Brian R. Cheffins, Corporate Ownership and Control: British Businesses Transformed (2008).

[15] The Kay Review of UK Equity Markets and Long-Term Decision Making, Final Report (URN 12/917, July 2012), at 10 [hereinafter Kay Review].

[16] See John C. Coffee, Dispersed Ownership: The Theories, the Evidence, and the Enduring Tension between "Lumpers" and "Splitters," in The Oxford Handbook of Capitalism (Dennis C. Mueller ed., 2012) 463, 474.

[17] Mark J. Roe, Strong Managers, Weak Owners: The Political Roots of American Corporate Finance (1994) at 102 ff. See 15 USC. §§ 80a-1 to 80a-64 (Investment Company Act of 1940) and §§ 80b-1 to 80b-21 (Investment Advisers Act of 1940).

[18] Julian Franks, Colin Mayer, & Stefano Rossi, "Ownership: Evolution and Regulation", 22 Rev. Fin. Stud. 4009 (2009).

institutional investors.[19] Recent evidence supports the view that this is indeed happening increasingly. A concrete example is Jana Partners, an activist hedge fund, teaming up with the Ontario Teachers' Pension Plan to bring about change at McGraw-Hill, the education and data company.[20] In this case, activist shareholders act as governance intermediaries, actively monitoring company performance and then presenting to companies and institutional investors concrete visions for business strategy. In this scenario, activists can serve to reduce the market's undervaluation of voting rights to the advantage of all shareholders.[21]

2.2 Shareholder Activism: Continental Europe

In contrast, the shareholder structures of continental European corporations (and many other countries of the world) have historically been dominated by blockholders and arguably continue to be so despite an increase in foreign investors. As recently as 2001 it was reported that the shareholder structures of more than 50% of European corporations consisted of a single majority blockholder.[22] This contrasted greatly with the shareholder structures of UK and US corporations as they were comprised of less than 3% of blockholders.[23] Today prominent families and large financial institutions remain the majority shareholders of corporations in continental Europe.[24] For example, it has been reported that a family blockholder is present on circa 66% of all listed companies in Italy whilst circa 10% of the Borsa Italiana is controlled by a sole Italian family.[25] This phenomenon is not only seen in Italy as other countries in continental Europe and beyond are experiencing a similar degree of domination by blockholders in national corporations and stock markets. Take Sweden as an illustration: about 50% of the market capitalization on the Stockholm Stock Exchange is controlled by a single Swedish family—the Wallenbergs—due to their shareholdings in listed companies.[26] A small number of very wealthy families are commonly able to exert a high degree of control over corporations in several continental European countries via pyramids, dual class shares, cross shareholdings, and differential voting shares.[27] For example, a

---

[19]   Ronald J. Gilson & Jeffrey N. Gordon, "The Agency Costs of Agency Capitalism: Activist Investors and the Revaluation of Governance Rights", 113 Colum. L. Rev. 863 (2013). See this concept in more detail *infra* section 6.3.

[20]   McCrum & Gelles, *supra* note 3.   [21]   Gilson & Gordon, *supra* note 19.

[22]   Marco Becht & Colin Mayer, Introduction, in The Control of Corporate Europe (Fabrizio Barca & Marco Becht eds., 2001).

[23]   Franks, Mayer, & Rossi, *supra* note 18.   [24]   Kay Review, *supra* note 15, paras 2.29 and 8.16.

[25]   Julian Franks, Colin Mayer, Paolo Volpin, & Hannes F. Wagner, "The Life Cycle of Family Ownership: International Evidence", 25 Rev. Fin. Stud. 1675 (2012); European Commission, Impact Assessment on the Proportionality between Capital and Control in Listed Companies (SEC(2007) 1705, Dec. 12, 2007), available at http://ec.europa.eu/internal_market/company/docs/shareholders/impact_ assessment_122007.pdf (last visited Oct. 31, 2017), at para. 19.

[26]   John A. Doukas, Martin Holmén, & Nickolaos G. Travlos, "Diversification, Ownership and Control of Swedish Corporations", 8 Eur. Fin. Mgmt. 281, 285 (2002).

[27]   Randall Morck, Daniel Wolfenzon, & Bernard Yeung, "Corporate Governance, Economic Entrenchment, and Growth", 43 J. Econ. Lit. 655, 688 ff. (2005). For the legal framework in Europe, see ISS, Shearman & Sterling LLP & ECGI, Report on the Proportionality Principle in the European Union, available at http://ec.europa.eu/internal_market/company/docs/shareholders/study/final_report_en.pdf (last visited Oct. 31, 2017); Shearman & Sterling LLP, Proportionality between Ownership and Control in EU Listed Companies: Comparative Legal Study (May 2007).

pyramidal structure can enable a family to gain control of a corporation via a small outlay that enables them to establish a chain of ownership relations.[28] As an illustration, if a family directly owns 50% of a corporation, which itself has a 50% stake in another corporation the family will indirectly gain a 25% controlling interest in the latter corporation form their initial outlay.[29] In the alternative, the industrial success experienced in Germany was attributed in part to a system of cross-shareholdings and interlocking directorates between banks, insurance companies, and institutional firms. This web of mutual participations appears to be eroding in recent years.[30] Historically, however, these cross-shareholdings were credited for having protected German companies from hostile takeovers due to the stability of ownership and continuity that they provided.[31] After the end of World War II, only one out of three relevant public takeovers had succeeded until the trend was broken by the Mannesmann–Vodafone takeover in 1999/2000.[32]

It has been argued that this concentration of block ownership of corporations in many countries outside of the US and the UK is directly attributable to a country's corporate governance regime; namely, the notion that a lack of minority shareholder protection leads to a concentration of ownership structures.[33] With a lack of regulatory protection shareholders are often forced to protect their investments by directly exercising control via the ownership of large blocks of shares.[34] In summary, it could be argued that the degree of minority shareholder protection given by the prevailing regulatory systems played an instrumental role in the evolution of shareholder structures of corporations in the UK and US vis-à-vis those in continental Europe and beyond.[35] The causality aspect of this account is, however, not certain.

In such a business environment of concentrated ownership, shareholder activism necessarily has an entirely different role and meaning than in a dispersed, US/UK style system. One aspect is that other stakeholders carry out the monitoring duties in such countries—typically blockholders, families, or banks (depending on the country). In a stable and solid corporate environment, the symbiotic relationship between company and controller can continue for a long time. Activists are then smaller shareholders who rebel against the controlling shareholder and attempt to bring about change, usually acting or purporting to act on behalf of all other shareholders.[36] This differs from the UK/US context, where activists

---

[28] Heitor V. Almeida & Daniel Wolfenzon, "A Theory of Pyramidal Ownership and Family Business Groups", 61 J. Fin. 2637, 2657 ff. (2006).

[29] Id. at 2638.

[30] Wolf-Georg Ringe, "Changing Law and Ownership Patterns in Germany: Corporate Governance and the Erosion of Deutschland AG", 63 Am. J. Comp. L. 493 (2015).

[31] Alberto Onetti & Alessia Pisoni, "Ownership and Control in Germany: Do Cross-Shareholdings Reflect Bank Control on Large Companies?", 6 Corp. Ownership & Control 54, 57 (2009). The German AG (Aktiengesellschaft) is a "public" corporation that is not necessarily (but can be) listed on a stock market.

[32] Id.

[33] Rafael La Porta, Florencio Lopez-de-Silanes, Andrei Shleifer, & Robert W. Vishny, "Legal Determinants of External Finance", 52 J. Fin. 1131, 1149 ff. (1997); Rafael La Porta, Florencio Lopez-de-Silanes, Andrei Shleifer & Robert W. Vishny, "Law and Finance", 106 J. Polit. Econ. 1113, 1151 (1998).

[34] Franks, Mayer & Rossi, *supra* note 18.   [35] Id.

[36] European Corporate Governance Network, Preliminary Report—The Separation of Ownership and Control: A Survey of 7 European Countries (1997), Volume 1, p. 13. See also Matteo Erede, "Governing Corporations with Concentrated Ownership Structure: An Empirical Analysis of Hedge Fund Activism in Italy and Germany, and Its Evolution", 10 Eur. Company & Fin. L. Rev. 328, 346 ff. (2013). In the perspective taken in this chapter, the controller's active monitoring of the company itself is not a form

typically understand themselves as advocates of shareholders generally, and the opponent would be the corporate management.

Where a dominant or even controlling shareholder is present, the strategies and tactics pursued by activist shareholders need to be fundamentally different from their US/UK counterparts, and their situation is probably more difficult. They might nevertheless be successful, as the French example shows.[37] In other countries like Brazil they are also gaining ground.[38] In this context of corporate governance conflict between dominant blockholders and minority shareholders, institutional investors are considered to usefully exploit shareholder activism techniques in order to build an opposition and a counterbalance to controlling shareholders. They thereby strengthen and support the voice and the position of minority shareholders.[39]

To illustrate, consider the example of the merger between VW and Porsche, which was proposed in 2009. Both companies were dominated by family and state ownership, and Porsche already owned 53% of VW at the time. Minority shareholder Norges Bank Investment Management was the only investor to voice early concerns, stating that the proposed transactions were "unacceptable" as they "leave the impression of being designed to suit the needs of the Porsche controlling families."[40] They also accused VW chairman and Porsche co-owner Ferdinand Piëch of being exposed to heavy conflicts of interest and of violating principles of good corporate governance.[41] Even though the merger was eventually consummated, the example illustrates that "activism" in this context does not simply mean shareholder engagement—rather, it may be understood as a rebellion of minority shareholders against an unrestrained reign by the controllers.

It is important to understand the fundamental differences between types of shareholder activism depending on the shareholder structure and environment. Critics may argue against this distinction, claiming that "shareholder activism" in all situations has a similar structure: the common element is always an initiative against the "controller"—whether the controller is the board (as in the US/UK context) or a dominant shareholder (as in Europe), or both. This perspective overlooks, however, that activism in a controlling shareholder world differs on a number of fundamental points. It is, first of all, more difficult to push

---

of shareholder activism. For a different understanding in the German context, see Peter Hommelhoff, Aktionärs-Aktivismus im dualistischen System?—ein Zuruf im EU Corporate Governance-Diskurs, in Liber amicorum für Martin Winter 255 (Michael Hoffmann-Becking, Uwe Hüffer & Jochem Reichert eds., 2011).

[37] Carine Girard & Stephen Gates, "The Professionalization of Shareholder Activism in France", 3(4) Directors Notes 1 (2011).

[38] Marta Viegas & Oduvaldo Lara Júnior, "Activism Gains Ground in Brazil", Int'l. Fin. L. Rev., Sept. 2014, available at http://www.iflr.com/Article/3383533/IFLR-magazine/Activism-gains-ground-in-Brazil.html.

[39] José M. Garrido & Angel Rojo, Institutional Investors and Corporate Governance: Solution or Problem?, in Capital Markets and Company Law 427, 437, 447 (Klaus J. Hopt & Eddy Wymeersch eds., 2004); in a similar vein, see Jaap W. Winter, Cross-border Voting in Europe, in Capital Markets and Company Law 387, 388 f (Klaus J. Hopt & Eddy Wymeersch eds., 2003).

[40] Vibeke Laroi & Chris Reiter, Norway Oil Fund Asks VW to Call Off Porsche Takeover, Reuters, Oct. 8, 2009, available at http://www.bloomberg.com/apps/news?pid=newsarchive&sid=aCAhhoxuxEQQ.

[41] Christoph Ruhkamp, Norwegens Ölfonds attackiert VW-Aufsichtsratschef Piëch, Frankfurter Allgemeine Zeitung, Oct. 8, 2009, at 15.

through activist initiatives for minority shareholders in a controlled firm, since the "controller" normally has the voting power to sanction the incriminated act or behavior. Second, the minority activist will usually find it more difficult to argue their case, and to show that their own ideas will benefit all shareholders, not just the majority.

2.3 Jurisdictional Influences on Shareholder Activism

By investing in the stock of a corporation, a shareholder risks losing potential returns on their investment should the targeted corporation underperform. Thus, shareholders generally have an interest in ensuring that the economic performance of the company within which they own a share is sustained or, alternatively, improved.[42] Shareholder activists will often engage in a proactive manner with their targeted companies in order to ensure that strategies are adopted that will generate abnormal returns on their investments.[43] However, the extent to which a shareholder activist can exert influence on their targeted corporation is often constrained by the prevailing laws, regulations, and realities of the country within which they are operating. This naturally adds to the complexity of comparing shareholder activism between nations. For example, it has been argued that the right to vote is often one of the most effective modes of activism for shareholders. However with fluctuating threshold requirements at general meetings, the scope for activism by voice is often inherently facilitated or hindered when acting in one nation or another. For example, whilst the UK's typical voting block lies at circa 10%, this is almost double that required in the US. Continental European countries, on the other hand, require considerably higher thresholds: in France circa 20%, and in Germany up to 57% in certain cases.[44]

The combination of a low voting threshold, recourse to proxy voting by a dispersed shareholder structure, and certain regulatory requirements has unquestionably facilitated shareholder activism in the US and enabled the emergence of adversarial voting against the boards of targeted corporations in comparison to the preference for informal activism in the UK.[45] In relation to continental Europe it becomes evident that voting patterns of shareholder activists fluctuate greatly from one nation to another. This is predominately due to the governing laws and regulations of European nations. It appears that shareholder activism is more adversarial in nature in nations that offer minority shareholder protection against managerial and controlling shareholder influences.[46] This is the case in France, Greece, Belgium, and Sweden, where the voting patterns of activists are decidedly confrontational in nature.[47] In contrast, shareholder activists in Italy and Germany often opt for more subdued activist strategies.[48] This is particularly so in Germany where shareholder activists have limited room for maneuver due to the historical existence of cross-shareholdings and

---

[42] Paolo Santella, Enrico Baffi, Carlo Drago, & Dino Lattuca, "Legal Obstacles to Institutional Investor Activism in the EU and in the US", 23 Eur. Bus. L. Rev. 257 (2012).

[43] Id.   [44] Schäfer & Hertrich, *supra* note 10, at 12.

[45] Santella et al., *supra* note 42.   [46] Id.   [47] Id.

[48] Massimo Belcredi & Luca Enriques, Institutional Investor Activism in a Context of Concentrated Ownership and High Private Benefits of Control: The Case of Italy, in Research Handbook on Shareholder Power 383 (Jennifer G. Hill & Randall S. Thomas eds., 2015); Massimo Belcredi, Stefano Bozzi,

the presence of employee representatives on supervisory boards irrespective of the trend towards a market-orientated system.[49] With ownership patterns in Germany shifting, however, hedge-fund activism may find new investment opportunities in Germany too.[50]

In summary, it can be argued that the voting patterns of shareholder activists in continental Europe are influenced by national laws and regulations, shareholder structures, and the existence of control enhancing mechanisms (CEMs).[51] In contrast, whilst the UK's legal and cultural environment supposedly fosters shareholder activism there is relatively little evidence of actual shareholder activism. This could in part be due to the fact that the vast majority of shareholder influence is exerted behind closed doors in the UK.[52] Informal talks between institutional investors and management are common, supported by a low removal threshold of corporate directors.[53] The US market, however, remains at the forefront of activist engagement and has experienced the greatest volume of successful shareholder activism to date.

3 HISTORICAL DEVELOPMENT OF SHAREHOLDER ACTIVISM

A close nexus between stock-market trading and corporate ownership was originally established during the Gilded Age and the takeover wave of the 1980s in the US.[54] In considering the historical development of shareholder activism, it is beneficial to take into consideration the impact that regulation and ownership structures had on the development of shareholder activism, in addition to the evolution of shareholder activism from its origins in the US stock market to subsequent developments seen elsewhere.

& Carmine di Noia, Board Elections and Shareholder Activism: The Italian Experiment, in Boards and Shareholders in European Listed Companies 365 (Massimo Belcredi & Guido Ferrarini eds., 2013); Erede, *supra* note 36.

[49] Santella et al., *supra* note 42; Onetti & Pisoni, *supra* note 31, at 73. For recent evidence of shareholder activism in Germany, see Ann-Kristin Achleitner, André Betzer, & Jasmin Gider, "Do Corporate Governance Motives Drive Hedge Fund and Private Equity Fund Activities?", 16 Eur. Fin. Mgmt. 805 (2010); Christian Thamm & Dirk Schiereck, "Shareholder Activism in Deutschland—Eine Bestandsaufnahme", 1 Corporate Fin. 17 (2014); Wolfgang Bessler, Wolfgang Drobetz, & Julian Holler, "The Returns to Hedge Fund Activism in Germany", 21 Eur. Fin. Mgmt. 106 (2015).

[50] Bessler, Drobetz, & Holler, *supra* note 49, at 108, 143.

[51] Santella et al., *supra* note 42. CEMs are typically shareholder agreements, cross-shareholdings, multiple voting rights, pyramid structures, etc.

[52] Becht et al., *supra* note 12.

[53] Companies Act 2006, s 168 states that directors can be removed at any time, without cause, by a simple 50% majority.

[54] Allen D. Boyer, "Activist Shareholders, Corporate Directors, and Institutional Investment: Some Lessons from the Robber Barons", 50 Wash. & Lee L. Rev. 977, 978 (1993). The Gilded Age spans from circa the end of the Civil War to the beginning of World War I and was marked by a lack of government regulation of the economy and rapid industrialization. The Merger Wave of the 1980s in contrast was fueled predominantly by junk bonds and driven by corporate raiders.

3.1 Impact of Regulation on the Development of Shareholder Activism

The enactment of regulation by lawmakers and market conditions have often had a twofold impact on shareholder activism; namely either acting as a deterrent, by, for example, erecting obstacles with the purpose of hindering investors from gaining majority holdings in companies, or alternatively facilitating shareholder activism, by for example deregulating fixed commission rates and thus increasing the incentives for fund managers to maximize returns for investors. If one takes the US as an illustration, it becomes evident that regulations have often been enacted in response to developments on the stock market.[55] For example, the Buttonwood Agreement of 1792[56] was a response to a market crash at the time and the virtual cessation of credit, trading, and liquidity. The agreement itself set minimum stockbroking commissions and was in force until the 1970s upon which commission rates became fully negotiable as fixed commission rates were abolished completely.[57] It has been argued that a combination of the deregulation and the technological advances at the time, such as the arrival of the personal computer, facilitated the ease in which stocks were traded on the stock market for the first time.[58]

The enactment of the Glass–Steagall Act in 1933[59] was furthermore a response to market events and in this particular case a direct response to the 1929 stock market crash, a nation-wide commercial bank failure, and the Great Depression. The Act itself led to a clear demarcation between the activities of investment and commercial banking as it was considered that the overzealous investment strategies of commercial banks were directly responsible for the 1929 stock market crash. In particular, it has been argued that the Glass–Steagall Act contributed towards a rapid decline in shareholder activism.[60] However, subsequent legislation such as codification of shareholder entitlement by the Securities and Exchange Commission (SEC) in 1942 yet again facilitated shareholder activism. This instance marked the advent of the first shareholder proposal rule.[61] The rule enabled shareholders to submit proposals for vote at (annual) general meetings and facilitated the predominant means by which shareholders could actively participate in postwar company life. The rationale behind the rule, as stated by Commissioner O'Brian in 1943, was to reincarnate the widely attended meetings that were characteristic of the times when companies were geographically limited and locally owned.[62] The rule arguably paved the way for shareholder engagement and

---

[55] Gilson & Gordon, *supra* note 19.

[56] The Buttonwood Agreement in essence led to the investment community on Wall Street and the creation of the New York Stock Exchange.

[57] Cheffins & Armour, *supra* note 4, at 72.   [58] Id. at 71–72.

[59] The Glass–Steagall Act, also known as the Banking Act of 1933, inter alia created the Federal Deposit Insurance Corporation (FDIC) and imposed conditions on the banks that received its protection.

[60] Santella et al., *supra* note 42, at 258.

[61] For (sparse) data on shareholder activism between 1900 and 1950, see John H. Armour & Brian R. Cheffins, Origins of "Offensive" Shareholder Activism in the United States, in Origins of Shareholder Advocacy 253 (Jonathan G.S. Koppell ed., 2011).

[62] Bevis Longstreth, SEC Commissioner, in a speech entitled The S.E.C. and Shareholder Proposals: Simplification in Regulation (Dec. 11, 1981), at 3, available at http://www.sec.gov/news/speech/1981/121181longstreth.pdf.

activism, which is illustrated by the fact that a mere 50 proposals were recorded annually in the 1940s whilst an average of 220 proposals were recorded by 1969, and circa 650 proposals were recorded annually by 1979.[63]

The abolition of the Glass–Steagall Act in 1999 and subsequent deregulations played a prolific role in fuelling competition in the American financial landscape and arguably triggered an increase in the exploitation of investment banking opportunities by, inter alia, engaging in risk-averse investment strategies during mergers and acquisitions.[64] However, the Bull Market of the late 1980s and early 1990s saw a downturn in shareholder activism as investors took a step back and relied on the gadflies to uphold shareholder rights.[65] Nevertheless, subsequent financial disasters, such as those seen at Enron and Tyco, in addition to the credit bubble of the mid-2000s, presented the ideal platform for a re-emergence of shareholder activism as hedge funds took center stage.[66] With an availability of cheap debt, market conditions were ripe for activists to lobby their targeted corporations for the distribution of cash to shareholders or for the sale of the corporation itself.[67] Paradoxically, the financial crisis that plagued the recent global economy from 2007 to 2011 marked the most recent downturn in shareholder activism.

3.2 Impact of Ownership Structures on the Development of Shareholder Activism

As mentioned above, the shareholder structures of most corporations in the UK and the US are widely dispersed, whilst those of continental European corporations are dominated mostly by blockholders. If one takes the UK as an illustration, it becomes apparent that a dispersed ownership structure and an emergence of shareholder activism were in essence driven by policy. In contrast, when considering Germany and the structure of the "Germany Inc." it becomes evident that the domination of blockholders on the shareholder structures of corporations fuelled shareholder activism as minority shareholders rebelled against their controlling influence.

In the first instance, as opined by Brian Cheffins, the dispersion of ownership in England only emerged after World War II as families began to unwind their controlling stakes in companies to benefit, inter alia, from tax incentives that favored diversification and the managerial revolution.[68] Furthermore, it was the legal reforms that were enshrined in the Companies Act of 1948[69] that gave minority shareholders a voice for the first time in the

---

[63] Id.

[64] Michael Galanis, "Vicious Spirals in Corporate Governance: Mandatory Rules for Systemic (Re) Balancing?", 31 Oxf. J. Leg. Stud. 327 (2011).

[65] James Surowiecki, To the Barricades, The New Yorker, June 9, 2003, available at http://www.newyorker.com/magazine/2003/06/09/to-the-barricades (last visited Oct. 31, 2017).

[66] John Armour & Brian Cheffins, "The Rise and Fall (?) of Shareholder Activism by Hedge Funds", 14(3) J. Alternative Inv. 17, 20 (2012).

[67] Cheffins & Armour, supra note 4, at 91–92.

[68] Cheffins, supra note 14, at, chs. 2–4.

[69] The Companies Act of 1948 regulated company law in England.

UK. However, despite being relatively groundbreaking in nature as they represented the first statutory remedy for shareholders in England, they proved relatively inadequate in reality.[70] Lord Hoffman shed further light on the matter by stating that it was not until 1980 that Parliament gave the unfairly treated minority shareholder the power to "slay the dragon" by passing into law the "unfair prejudice" remedy, which is now found in section 994 of the Companies Act 2006.[71] Thus, despite reforms occurring in 1948 it was only in 1980 that minority shareholders finally gained a voice in the UK stock market. For various reasons, however, they did not take up the legal instruments that were available to them. The "unfair prejudice" remedy ultimately only really applies to small, quasi-partnership companies, and is unsuitable for large public companies.[72] The other minority shareholder activism tool, the derivative claim, suffered a setback in the famous case of *Prudential Assurance v. Newman Industries Ltd*, the only reported case where a UK institutional investor brought a derivative suit against directors of a portfolio company.[73] Despite the recent codification and extension of this remedy in the 2006 Act,[74] it has not gained great prominence for activist investors to date.

So in sum, although shareholder rights became enforceable by law, many investors, and especially institutional investors, were cautious about engaging in activism. This was also due to fears of either being found guilty of market abuse because of potentially being privy to insider information or being considered to be acting in concert within the definition of the City Code on Takeovers and Mergers.[75] As such, activism per se did not really materialize in full until the UK's 2008 banking crisis led to a call on institutional investors to take a more proactive approach in the enforcement of corporate governance. Consequently, shareholder activists began to gain a reputation for overcoming apathy and actively engaging in the strategies of their targeted corporations.

In the second instance, the ownership structure of the "Germany AG," which was characterized by a concentration of ownership due to extensive cross-shareholding networks, and long-term relational financial ties between banks, insurance companies, and

---

[70] Lord Hoffman as cited in the foreword to the first edition to Robin Hollington, Shareholders' Rights (now 8th edition, 2016). Section 459(1) Companies Act 1985 (now section 994 Companies Act 2006) enables a shareholder to apply to the court by petition for an order on the ground that the company's affairs were being or had been conducted in a manner which was unfairly prejudicial to the interests of some members of the company.

[71] Lord Hoffman as cited in the foreword to Hollington. See *supra* note 70.

[72] Academic studies show that there are only six unfair prejudice petitions involving publicly traded companies that resulted in a judicial decision between 1998 and 2006, three of which involved allegations of misfeasance by the company's directors. See John Armour, Enforcement Strategies in UK Company Law: A Roadmap and Empirical Assessment, in Rationality in Company Law: Essays in Honour of D.D. Prentice 71 (John Armour & Jennifer Payne eds., 2009).

[73] *Prudential Assurance Co. Ltd v. Newman Industries Ltd* [1982] Ch 204. See on this Brian R. Cheffins & Bernard S. Black, "Outside Director Liability Across Countries", 84 Tex. L. Rev. 1385, 1407 (2006); Armour, *supra* note 72, at 115; also Geof P. Stapledon, Institutional Shareholders and Corporate Governance 132 (1996).

[74] The derivative claim is now restated in ss. 260 ff. Companies Act 2006.

[75] Chiu, *supra* note 7, at 29. The aim of the City Code on Takeovers and Mergers is to ensure fair and equal treatment of all shareholders during takeovers and furthermore provide a framework for the manner in which takeovers are to be conducted.

institutional firms, guaranteed not only ownership stability and continuity but also acted as a shield against hostile takeovers.[76] With blockholders dominating the shareholder community and, to a degree, the supervisory board, minority shareholders were left with no other option but to engage in activism in order to maximize the returns on their investments. In any case, the abolishment of the capital gains tax on the sale of cross-shareholdings in early 2002 marked a pivotal change in Germany's former low-liquidity insider market.[77] The removal of capital gains tax on the sale of cross-shareholdings opened the floodgates to foreign investors who had previously only held circa 18% of German stocks.[78] As foreign investors arrived on the German market so too did shareholder activists. This pivotal change undermined the ownership networks that had shielded German corporations from takeovers for decades. Out of the three relevant public takeovers that had taken place after the end of World War II only one was a success until Vodafone's acquisition of Mannesmann.[79]

In summary, it becomes evident that regulatory changes have not only been influential on the extent of shareholder activism but that developments in global markets and ownership structures have played an equally influential role on the commonality of shareholder activism.

3.3 Origins and Evolution of Shareholder Activists

As mentioned above, a close nexus between corporate ownership and stock-market trading was first established during the Gilded Age and the takeover wave of the 1980s in the US. The Gilded Age and the 1980s became synonymous with corporate raiders buying shares to gain control of their targeted corporations. However, the primary goal of gaining control of their targeted corporations was not in pursuit of making returns from the corporation's operational profits but to raise the firm's listed value to maximize the returns as shares were subsequently sold at peak prices.[80] Buying or selling businesses, or threatening to do so, became more lucrative than actually running a company, and consequently led to the takeover wave of the 1980s.

---

[76] John W. Cioffi, "Corporate Governance Reform, Regulatory Politics, and the Foundations of Finance Capitalism in the United States and Germany", 7 German L. J. 533, 540 (2006); Onetti & Pisoni, *supra* note 31, at 72; Ringe, *supra* note 30.

[77] Nigel Holloway, The End of Germany AG, Forbes, June 11, 2001, available at http://www.forbes.com/global/2001/0611/024.html (last visited Oct. 31, 2017). See in more detail Ringe, *supra* note 30.

[78] Holloway, *supra* note 77.

[79] Onetti & Pisoni, *supra* note 31, at 57. There were two unsuccessful takeover attempts: in 1989 Veba's attempt to take over Feldmühle Nobel and in 1990/1991 Pirelli's attempt to take over Continental AG. One successful takeover attempt was Krupp's 1992 takeover of Hoesch AG which ended in ThyssenKrupp being formed.

[80] Boyer, *supra* note 54, at 978.

3.3.1 *Corporate Raiders and the Takeover Wave of the 1980s*

The takeover wave of the 1980s was characterized by daring takeover bids that were engineered by corporate raiders on the basis of aggressive and innovative financial techniques.[81] An activist cohort subsequently established itself in the US which specifically targeted underperforming corporations in the hope of improving operational performance before exiting. Amongst others, the operating performance of a targeted corporation was often improved by initiating changes to the firm's strategy. The cohort included renowned raiders such as Carl Icahn, the Bass Brothers, and Coniston Partners. However, despite their apparent success, it remains undisputed that the purchase of these shareholdings was financed predominately out of debt with limited equity which generated short-term gains and left no company safe from a hostile bid.[82] In consequence of their aggressive strategies, opposition to corporate raiders soon mounted, not only on the part of the targeted corporations themselves via the implementation of defense strategies but also on the part of the government, which took action to protect the interests of targeted corporations. Although takeover defense strategies became plentiful the most successful was colloquially known as the "poison pill" defense. The "poison pill" defense was developed by Martin Lipton, a New York attorney, in order to help El Paso Co. fend off a hostile takeover bid.[83] The "poison pill" as a takeover defense strategy can either come in the form of a flip-in or flip-over but fundamentally consists of a strategy whereby the target corporation attempts to reduce the value of or dilute its stock in order to ward off a hostile bid.[84]

The 1980s also marked the re-emergence of institutional shareholder activism as pension funds, mutual funds, insurance companies, and managed trust funds submitted proposals and forced management boards to reform, inter alia, executive remuneration packages and defense strategies against threats of takeover.[85] These strategies were dramatic in nature and a far cry from previous engagements which had consisted of the strategy of "voting with their feet."

3.3.2 *Institutional Investors*

The rapid growth of institutional investors in the 1980s was primarily in response to an increased proportion of household savings being invested directly in equity and corporate bonds via private-funded pension schemes and life-insurance policies as the longevity of the aging population increased.[86] Larger portfolios meant that many institutional investors

---

[81] Cheffins & Armour, *supra* note 4, at 75–76.

[82] Michael R. Patrone, "An International Comparison of Corporate Leeway to Ward Off Predators", 25 Butterworths J. Int'l. Banking & Fin. L. 355, 355 (2010).

[83] Id.

[84] A flip-in poison pill is the more frequently used out of the two and enables existing shareholders to purchase further stock at a discount when the poison pill is activated by a hostile bidder. This has the effect of diluting the would-be acquirer's stock in the target and thus deters a hostile acquisition. In contrast, a flip-over enables shareholders to purchase the acquirer's shares at a discounted price but only after the merger has taken place. In the last 15 years the poison pill has only been triggered intentionally twice. Id.

[85] Santella et al., *supra* note 42.   [86] Id.

could no longer dispose of large blocks of stock on the market at any one time and were thus forced to alter their strategies from one centered on exit to one that advocated activist engagement in pursuit of profit maximization.[87] Additionally, the disposal of large stocks on the market at any one time was no longer an option as it risked triggering sharp falls in stock valuation, a market crash, and a probable reduction in the value of portfolios.[88]

Although the rapid growth and subsequent increase in institutional investor portfolios forced investment strategies to be altered, the rise of institutional shareholder activism in the UK was predominantly driven by policy. Policy makers in the UK were the driving force in advocating that institutional shareholders engage in activism in response to wider corporate governance concerns and the social good.[89] The policy-led drive for activism in the UK was more in keeping with a shareholder's responsibility and accountability to the market at large as opposed to promoting investment strategies tailored towards profit maximization. Scholars such as Christoph van der Elst further argue that this policy-led drive for activism in pursuit of greater corporate governance was also widespread in continental Europe and was subsequently embodied in regulations and corporate governance codes.[90] It is argued that institutional investors are best placed to enforce corporate governance as, unlike individual investors, they are operating within a professional capacity and thus have the necessary expertise to manage the investment funds within their portfolios.[91] Irrespective of the origins in the surge of activist engagements, it should be noted that institutional investors are often constrained in their ability to partake in shareholder activism due to their own conflicts of interests.

Conflicts of interests usually derive from the business relationships between the target corporation and the institutional investor, which often compels the latter to concur with management even if this were to conflict with their fiduciary duties.[92] As an illustration, a US mutual fund that is associated with a financial institution may err on the side of caution when engaging in shareholder activism so as not to jeopardize the business relationships between present or future clients of their parent company.[93] In other words, it has been argued that conflicts of interests arise between banks and insurance companies due to their day-to-day business dealings with corporate management, between private pension funds and their governing corporate managers, and with public pension funds due to external political influences.[94]

In summary, the extent to which institutional investors engage in shareholder activism, and thus utilize the power granted to them by laws and regulations, is constrained by the

---

[87] Jason M. Loring & C. Keith Taylor, "Shareholder Activism: Directorial Responses to Investors' Attempts to Change the Corporate Governance Landscape", 41 Wake Forest L. Rev. 321, 324 (2006).

[88] Id.   [89] Chiu, *supra* note 7, at 18.

[90] Christoph van der Elst, "Revisiting Shareholder Activism at AGMs: Voting Determinants of Large and Small Shareholders", ECGI Finance Working Paper No. 311/2011, available at http://ssrn.com/abstract=1886865, at 12.

[91] Id.

[92] Santella et al., *supra* note 42; Iman Anabtawi & Lynn Stout, "Fiduciary Duties for Activist Shareholders", 60 Stan. L. Rev. 1255, 1285 ff. (2008).

[93] Marcel Kahan & Edward B. Rock, "Hedge Funds in Corporate Governance and Corporate Control", 155 U. Pa. L. Rev. 1021, 1054 ff. (2007).

[94] Bernard S. Black, "Agents Watching Agents: The Promise of Institutional Investor Voice", 39 UCLA L. Rev. 811, 826 ff. (1992).

eventual occurrence of conflicts of interests.[95] Nevertheless, despite the affect a potential conflict of interest may have on the degree of activist engagement, institutional investors still represent one of the largest forms of shareholders in the US, having increased their shareholdings in US equities from a mere 10% in 1953 to over 70% in 2006.[96] In comparison, the size of institutional shareholdings in European corporations tends to fluctuate from circa 80% in the UK to 20% in Italy, with Germany and France experiencing shareholdings of up to 30% and 60% respectively.[97]

3.3.3 Hedge Funds

Nearly two decades after corporate raiders dominated stock markets, hedge funds began to re-emerge, filling the gap that had been left by institutional investors due to their concerns over conflicts of interests and regulatory constraints.[98] Despite re-emerging in the 1990s it was only in the twenty-first century that hedge funds took center stage as shareholder activists.[99] Their ability to take the stock market by storm with over $1 trillion under management, a cutting-edge investment strategy which centered on corporate activism, and a cut-throat "do what it takes" mentality were arguably in part a result of their organizational structure and the subsequent lack of regulation governing their operations.[100]

By comparing hedge funds with institutional investors it is possible to shed some light on their unique business structure that has enabled them to pursue a strategy of corporate activism away from the prying eyes of the public and policy makers. Although hedge funds are commonly managed from the US or the UK, they are typically incorporated in offshore jurisdictions and are thus subjected to a minimal degree of public oversight and regulation.[101] An intrinsic lack of regulation and public oversight has enabled hedge funds to increase their market power whilst diversifying their risks by benefiting, inter alia, from derivatives and high levels of leverage.[102] Furthermore, unlike institutional investors, hedge funds are not constrained by potential and/or actual conflicts of interests in pursuing their investment strategies. This is predominately due to the fact that they avoid investing in large entities where wider interests can often conflict with a duty towards their investors.[103] By

---

[95] Assaf Hamdani & Yishay Yafeh, "Institutional Investors as Minority Shareholders", 17 Rev. Fin. 691 (2013).

[96] Gillan & Starks, Evolution of Shareholder Activism, *supra* note 9, at 57.

[97] Santella et al., *supra* note 42.

[98] On hedge fund activism generally, see Eveline Hellebuyck, Activist Hedge Funds and Legal Strategy Devices, in Legal Strategies: How Corporations Use Law to Improve Performance 277 (Antoine Masson & Mary Shariff eds., 2009); Sean Geraghty & Harriet Smith, Shareholder Activism as a Strategy for Hedge Funds, in Hedge Funds and the Law ch. 8 (Peter Astleford & Dick Frase eds., 2010).

[99] Cheffins & Armour, *supra* note 4, at 80; Eddy Wymeersch, "Shareholders in Action: Towards a New Company Paradigm?", 4 Eur. Company L. 50, 53 ff. (2007).

[100] Stephen Taub, "Proxy Warriors, Institutional Investor" (Jan. 16, 2003), available at http://www.institutionalinvestor.com/Article/1035728/Proxy-Warriors.html (last visited Oct. 31, 2017).

[101] European Parliament, The Economic Consequences of Large Shareholder Activism, Study No. IP/A/ECON/IC/2009-004, EP Policy Department Economic and Scientific Policy (2009), at 23 [hereinafter European Parliament, Economic Consequences].

[102] Id.

[103] European Parliament, Hedge Funds: Transparency and Conflict of Interest, Study No. IP/A/ECON/IC/2007-24, EP Policy Department Economic and Scientific Policy (2007), at 26.

rather opting to invest in corporations that enable them to make trading-induced profits with a quick turnaround, hedge funds do not run the risk of being confronted with potential conflicts of interest.[104] Targeted corporations are subsequently undervalued, presenting the ideal opportunity for profit maximization via shareholder activism.

Their often aggressive tactics in the pursuit of profit maximization in the short term can be attributed to the performance-based compensation schemes for hedge fund managers which contrast greatly with the fixed compensation fees earned by institutional investors.[105] This compensation scheme typically comprises of an annual fixed fee that ranges from 1–2% of portfolio assets in addition to a performance-based fee ranging from 15–25% of the profits earned annually.[106] This arguably aligns the interests of fund managers and investors in generating maximum returns on investments. Thus, shareholder activism is purely an element of a hedge fund's investment strategy as opposed to the concurrent enforcement of corporate governance that is pursued by many other institutional investors today.[107]

As such, markets fully anticipate that the engagement by a hedge fund in a targeted corporation will undoubtedly lead to an improvement in the target's operational performance.[108] It is therefore common to witness steep increases in stock prices as hedge funds make their initial stock purchase in the target. New empirical data from the US and Europe illustrate that hedge fund engagement mostly involves advantages for other shareholders. According to these studies, the initial investment decision by an activist hedge fund is usually related to a substantial increase in their returns.[109] These increased returns are apparently a consequence of real improvements and reliable profits, and not a mere redistribution to the detriment of debtholders and other stakeholders.[110] Further, the holding periods of hedge funds are much longer than previously anticipated.[111]

These positive effects for the shareholders of a company in which a hedge fund invests need to be distinguished from the question of whether a hedge fund brings profit for its own

---

[104] Id.

[105] Mark Mietzner, Denis Schweizer, & Marcel Tyrell, "Intra-Industry Effects of Shareholder Activism in Germany: Is There a Difference between Hedge Fund and Private Equity Investments?", 63 Schmalenbach Bus. Rev. 151, 156 (2011).

[106] William N. Goetzmann, Jonathan E. Ingersoll, Jr., & Stephen A. Ross, "High-Water Marks and Hedge Fund Management Contracts", 58 J. Fin. 1685 (2003).

[107] Kahan & Rock, supra note 93, at 1028. See also Andreas Engert, "Transnational Hedge Fund Regulation", 11 Eur. Bus. Org. L. Rev. 329 (2010).

[108] See the overview provided by Steven M. Davidoff, A Standard Criticism of Activist Investors that No Longer Holds Up, N.Y. Times, July 10, 2013, at B5.

[109] Alon Brav, Wei Jiang, Frank Partnoy, & Randall S. Thomas, "Hedge Fund Activism, Corporate Governance, and Firm Performance", 63 J. Fin. 1729 (2008) [hereinafter Brav et al., Hedge Fund Activism]; April Klein & Emanuel Zur, "Entrepreneurial Shareholder Activism: Hedge Funds and Other Private Investors", 64 J. Fin. 187 (2009); Becht et al., supra note 12; Lucian Bebchuk, Alon Brav & Wei Jiang, "The Long-Term Effects of Hedge Fund Activism", 115 Colum. L. Rev. 1085 (2015). See also Marco Becht, Julian Franks, & Jeremy Grant, "Hedge Fund Activism in Europe", ECGI Finance Working Paper 283/2010 [hereinafter Becht et al., Hedge Fund Activism in Europe]; Marco Becht, Julian Franks, Jeremy Grant, & Hannes Wagner, "The Returns to Hedge Fund Activism: An International Study", ECGI Finance Working Paper 402/2014 [hereinafter Becht et al., Returns to Hedge Fund Activism].

[110] Brav et al., Hedge Fund Activism, supra note 109.

[111] Bidisha Chakrabarty, Pamela C. Moulton, & Charles Trzcinka, "Institutional Holding Periods", Working Paper 2013, available at http://ssrn.com/abstract=2217588.

investors.[112] However, empirical evidence from 2007 indicated that hedge funds make absolute returns from circa 5–7% on the initial share price after commencing activism in the US, whilst further empirical evidence from 2008 indicated that hedge funds make absolute returns of circa 12% for the duration of a two-to-three-year period following activist engagement.[113] Of interest here is that these empirical studies did not have access to the private databases of their sample and relied solely on publically available information in reaching their conclusions.[114] By contrast, another empirical study from 2008 was conducted with full access to the sample hedge fund's private database, including the fund's trades and asset values, and concluded that a dependence on public information alone would have omitted approximately 12 out of a total of 30 engagement cases.[115] This is a clear illustration of the intrinsic lack of publicly available information on activist engagements by hedge funds and the secretive manner in which they protect their engagements. However, having been accountable for up to half of the daily activity on the New York Stock Exchange (NYSE) and the London Stock Exchange (LSE) in 2005 alone, it is likely that they will remain an important and controversial feature in stock markets for some time to come.[116]

Regulatory strategies following the financial crisis target hedge funds in particular.[117] It is notable, however, that none of these new regulatory instruments target the implications of hedge fund activity for the functioning of traditional corporate governance mechanisms. It is clear that hedge funds' sophistication in exploiting the traditional categories and tools of corporate governance poses significant challenges for regulators and lawmakers.[118] For example, the European AIFM Directive and the US Dodd–Frank Act limit themselves to certain rules on the supervision of hedge fund managers, and do not pursue an activities-based approach.[119]

3.3.4 *Private Equity Funds*

The twenty-first century also marked the emergence of private equity funds which have frequently been compared with hedge funds due to their innate similarities. Nevertheless, despite their concurrent reputations for activist engagement and similar remuneration structures for fund managers, they arguably deploy different investment strategies. As opposed to the short-term investment strategies of hedge funds, private equity funds will typically focus on long-term investments which are innate to closed-end funds. Investments

---

[112] A body of scholarship is skeptical on this question; see in particular Simon Lack, The Hedge Fund Mirage: The Illusion of Big Money and Why It's Too Good to Be True (John Wiley & Sons ed., 2012).

[113] Chiu, *supra* note 7, at 75.

[114] For some evidence on non-US hedge fund activism see Dionysia Katelouzou, "Myths and Realities of Hedge Fund Activism: Some Empirical Evidence", 7 Va. L. & Bus. Rev. 459 (2013).

[115] Becht et al., *supra* note 12.

[116] Financial Services Authority, Hedge Funds: A Discussion of Risk and Regulatory Engagement, Discussion Paper DP 05/4, June 2005, at 14.

[117] See *infra*, section 6.4.

[118] On this, Wolf-Georg Ringe, "Hedge Funds and Risk-Decoupling: The Empty Voting Problem in the European Union", 36 Seattle U. L. Rev. 1027, 1033 (2013).

[119] See House of Commons, Treasury Committee, Banking Crisis: International Dimensions (HC 615, 2009), p. Ev 90f. There are just a few such abstract provisions, in particular on risk and liquidity management, see Arts. 12 ff. of the AIFM Directive. More on both pieces of regulation below section 6.4.

of a closed-end fund in targeted corporations will usually last five years, at which point in time the fund will exit passing the proceeds to their investors.[120] Adopting a long-term investment strategy with a corporation arguably implies that a private equity fund will be inclined to adopt a "hands-on approach" with the board as they are of the opinion that this method is the most effective in generating value before the firm is either sold or rejoins the market.[121] This contrasts greatly with the strategies deployed by hedge funds as they typically avoid majority or sole ownership, preferring to reap rewards as minority shareholders.[122] With a long-term outlook, it is more common for private equity funds to actively engage in the strategy and management of their targets; an engagement policy which is argued to be pivotal in generating shareholder wealth and enabling a fund to exit with profit.[123] A study conducted by Acharya and co-authors revealed that private equity funds play an active role in the strategy of the targeted firm, with 89% of interviewees citing value creation and 56% of interviewees citing exit as their principal priorities.[124]

4 Methods of Shareholder Activism

From the offset of the 1980s shareholder activists have been playing the market instead of carefully protecting the value of their holdings.[125] By operating under a common set of assumptions, namely public information and commercial consensus, investors are able to strike bargains by purchasing undervalued shares which they subsequently sell at abnormal prices after having improved the operational performance of their targeted corporation.[126]

It was traditionally viewed that shareholders turned to activism when they were dissatisfied with the management or the operational performance of the targeted corporation by commonly opting to vote with their feet by exit. However, the modern-day approach witnesses the purchase of shares in the hope of generating short-term gains via activist engagement.[127]

But what techniques do activists use? Empirical evidence in the US suggests that activism (in particular by hedge funds) encompasses a wide range of activities, from the subtle pressure on the incumbents through letters, other communications, and meetings to the requisition of a shareholder meeting, possibly involving the drama of a management change, or the commencement of litigation or a takeover bid from the activist.[128] Practitioners report

---

[120] European Parliament, Economic Consequences, *supra* note 101, at 25.

[121] Cheffins & Armour, *supra* note 4, at 59.   [122] Id.

[123] Chiu, *supra* note 7, at 98 ff.

[124] Viral V. Acharya, Oliver F. Gottschalg, Moritz Hahn, & Conor Kehoe, "Corporate Governance and Value Creation: Evidence from Private Equity", 26 Rev. Fin. Stud. 368 (2013).

[125] Boyer, *supra* note 54, at 978.

[126] Id, at 990.

[127] On the distinction between various forms of shareholder activism, see *supra* section 2.

[128] William W. Bratton, "Hedge Funds and Governance Targets", 95 Geo. L. J. 1375 (2007); Brav et al., Hedge Fund Activism, *supra* note 109.

an even more diverse set of tactics.[129] Recognizing that activism involves an evolutionary decision-making behavior, researchers have provided empirical evidence on activism in the US by modelling activism as involving four distinct phases: demand negotiations, board representation, threat of proxy fight, and proxy contest.[130]

4.1 "Voting with the Feet"

"Voting with the feet" or the "Wall Street Rule" is a traditional form of shareholder activism whereby activists opt to sell their stock rather than partaking in often costly and futile efforts of reform in pursuit of increasing the value of their investments.[131] It is worth bearing in mind that this passive approach to activism used to be rooted in the respect of traditional values as opined by Brian Cheffins. Cheffins argues that this traditional method of activism was nestled in the Chandelerian exhortation which first and foremost respects the managerial revolution and thus leads to the unquestionable acceptance of managerial power on the boards of companies.[132] However, in today's economy this method of exit can be both complex and costly for an activist. An increase in the size of shareholdings, especially in relation to those held by institutional investors, has rendered this form of activism more hazardous due to the risks posed by disposing of large volumes of stock on the equity markets at any one time. The risks can be threefold in nature, triggering a sharp fall in the valuation of the stock, a stock market crash, or a reduction in the overall value of the investor's portfolio.[133] However, institutional investors aside, it can be argued that modern-day activists generally acquire small quantities of stock in a targeted corporation to minimize their risk exposure and remain anonymous to management boards by not exceeding the thresholds that trigger disclosure obligations.[134]

4.2 Purchase of Stock

The present trend to purchase small quantities of stock enables shareholder activists to seek not only the most opportune moment for action but also support from other activist investors before striking with an element of surprise to gain the upper hand in communications with the targeted corporation. This strategy often improves the success rate of their

---

[129]   Martin Lipton, Dealing with Activist Hedge Funds, Harvard Law School Forum on Corporate Governance and Financial Regulation, Nov. 6, 2014, http://blogs.law.harvard.edu/corpgov/2014/11/06/dealing-with-activist-hedge-funds-3.

[130]   Nickolay Gantchev, "The Costs of Shareholder Activism: Evidence from a Sequential Decision Model", 107 J. Fin. Econ. 610 (2013).

[131]   Jayne W. Barnard, "Shareholder Access to the Proxy Revisited", 40 Cath. U. L. Rev. 37, 45 (1990).

[132]   Alfred D. Chandler, The Visible Hand: The Managerial Revolution in American Business (1977); Alfred D. Chandler, Scale and Scope: The Dynamics of Industrial Capitalism (1990).

[133]   Loring & Taylor, *supra* note 87, at 324.

[134]   According to recent research, the median stake of activist hedge funds at the beginnings of an activist campaign is only 6.3%. See Alon Brav, Wei Jiang & Hyunseob Kim, "Hedge Fund Activism: A Review", 4 Foundations & Trends in Fin. 185 (2009).

interventions as, on the one hand, targeted corporations are by default left with a limited time period within which to prepare defense strategies. On the other hand, the shareholder activist can carefully select support from fellow activist investors whilst mitigating the likelihood of freeriding. A case in point was Knight Vinke's target of HSBC in 2007. Knight Vinke was able to target HSBC with a shareholding of less than 1% via the use of informal methods of activism. In the first instance, Knight Vinke wrote to HSBC in 2007 asking the board for, inter alia, an independent non-executive Chairman and an in-depth review of its strategy and management structure. These demands were reiterated in 2008 in a letter signed by not only Knight Vinke but also six of the world's largest institutional investors that had by then amassed shareholdings in HSBC. HSBC responded publically to the second letter stating that the majority of demands had already been met and took further steps to, inter alia, replace almost a third of the non-executive board members whilst selling part of their non-core banking network. This was arguably a success for an activist with a minority holding that deployed informal methods of activism, but it is worth bearing in mind that little evidence is commonly available on private negotiations between shareholders and companies as and when they actually occur.[135] An exception to this is the clinical study[136] of the Hermes UK Focus Fund where the authors were granted access to the fund's private databases and were able to ascertain that focused engagements with the support of other institutional investors, on private meetings and letters, etc., generated substantial returns on investments and especially so when changes to the structure of the board and the target's strategy were demanded.[137] Had the authors relied on public information alone they would have been unaware of at least 12 out of the 30 reported engagement cases.[138] A further study,[139] which compared positive abnormal returns between public and private interventions, concluded that private interventions generated higher returns than those conducted in the public domain but were also more expensive to run.[140] Accordingly, "voice" and participation at annual general meetings are often a popular strategy for activist engagement.

4.3 "Voice"

"Voice" is arguably one of the most common methods of shareholder activism and as such has often been cited as a distinguishing feature of shareholder activism. Shareholder activists are commonly referred to as investors who via voice aim to alter the status quo of a targeted corporation without altering the manner in which the firm is controlled.[141] The activist method of "voice" itself encompasses a broad spectrum of activities including shareholder proposals, proxy contests, influencing the strategy of targeted corporations, and voting at shareholder

---

[135] Van der Elst, *supra* note 90, at 4.   [136] Becht et al., *supra* note 12.
[137] Van der Elst, *supra* note 90.   [138] Becht et al., *supra* note 12.
[139] Becht et al., Hedge Fund Activism in Europe, *supra* note 109.
[140] Gantchev, *supra* note 130.
[141] Gillan & Starks, Survey of Shareholder Activism, *supra* note 11.

meetings. A shareholder activist will attempt to persuade the management board of their targeted corporation to pursue certain strategies via the private communication of information in the hope that this will enable returns on investments to be maximized.[142] However, the effectiveness of the use of "voice" as a method of shareholder activism is dependent on the degree of publicity used and the credibility of the actual message.[143] For example, Apple recently bowed to renewed pressure from CalPERS for shareholders to have a greater say on the election of directors.[144] It is interesting to note that in pursuit of a drive to hold management boards to account for their actions CalPERS has convinced a total of 77 large US corporations to implement majority voting in the last two years alone, and is currently targeting a total of 17 corporations that are holding out.[145] This clearly highlights the effectiveness of a credible and public message in instigating desired changes in a targeted corporation. However, it is also worth bearing in mind that the legal environment within which a shareholder activist operates can also play a pivotal role in facilitating or restraining their recourse to "voice." This is particularly so in relation to their ability to vote on certain matters at the general meeting.

The participation of shareholder activists at annual and other general meetings is historically low in Europe and highly dependent on regulatory constraints pertaining, inter alia, to conflicts of interest, national and cross-border proxy voting, and the separation of ownership.[146] In contrast, the US has always experienced a considerably higher degree of participation despite the existence of legal barriers. For example, although shareholder engagement at general meetings was facilitated in the UK under the Companies Act of 2006, investors continued to refrain from intervening in the management of large corporations as they believed that it was neither their role nor their duty to do so.[147] It was only following the call on investors to take a more active role in enforcing corporate governance after the 2008 banking crisis that shareholders began to actively engage with management in the UK. In contrast, the legal environment in the US established numerous barriers for shareholder activists that sought to actively influence the management board of targeted corporations by "voice."[148] For example, despite the fact that the former proxy regulation Rule 14a-8 enabled a selection of shareholder proposals, it neither allowed director nominations nor objections to be made against management's proposals—arguably impeding the influence of shareholder activists.[149] Nevertheless, despite the presence of these former barriers, activist engagements still became an inherent part of corporate governance in the US.[150] This is illustrated by the fact that attendance at annual general meetings reached 87% in 2006 and 79% in 2010, considerably higher than that seen in Germany, or the UK for that matter (respectively 60% and 68% in 2010).[151] Many have argued that the rationale behind the higher turnout at shareholder meetings in the US in comparison with that experienced

---

[142] Doron Levit, "Soft Shareholder Activism", Working Paper, Finance Department University of Pennsylvania (2012), available at http://ssrn.com/abstract=1969475, at 3.

[143] Id.

[144] Dan McCrum, Apple Yields to Governance Reform Call, Fin. Times, Feb. 23, 2012.

[145] Id.   [146] Santella et al., *supra* note 42.

[147] The Companies Act 2006 currently regulates company law in the UK.

[148] Gillan & Starks, Survey of Shareholder Activism, *supra* note 11.

[149] Id.   [150] Id.   [151] Santella et al., *supra* note 42.

in Europe hinges on the widespread recourse to proxy voting by the dispersed shareholder base in the US.[152]

4.4 Litigation

Litigation is often considered to be the last resort for a shareholder activist due to its unpredictable nature and the fact that it rarely leads to immediate results. Not only does its use hinge on the substantive laws and regulations of the jurisdiction within which a shareholder activist is operating, but a shareholder activist will also have recourse to different forms of litigation dependent on where they are operating. For example, litigation can include the pursuit of damages against the directors of targeted corporations, injunctive relief for the enforcement of inquiry requests, the contestation of resolutions passed at general meetings, or derivative actions whereby the shareholder activist brings an action on behalf of the targeted corporation in order to uphold the firm's rights if the directors cannot or will not enforce them.[153] As an illustration, in contesting resolutions made at general meetings, actions are often brought in the name of the actual shareholder in Germany, whereas shareholder activists have typically used legal loopholes to sue in France.[154] Nevertheless, although shareholders have the ability to bring a civil action on behalf of the company against a director (or against a third party) in the UK, shareholders rarely do so and the courts have the ultimate right to refuse the claim in any case. For example, the abandoned Equitable Life litigation is illustrative of the hurdles that are faced in reality when seeking legal redress for acts that amount to a director's legal breach of their duties in the UK.[155] Despite the varying use of litigation in Europe, full proxy fights and threats to litigate are commonly used by shareholder activists in the US. This is particularly true of hedge funds operating in the US, as they commonly have the financial means to pursue the matter to the end should they wish to do so. In light of this, corporations in the US will more often than not concede to the demands of hedge funds before class actions and less common derivative actions are even made.[156]

In summary, it is clear that shareholder activists engage in various methods of activism in pursuit of realizing their ultimate goal of profit maximization. However, the prevailing regulatory regimes can often facilitate or hinder their activist strategies. It is common for targeted corporations opting to ignore activist demands to receive negative press. These firms are often relegated on governance ratings whilst their directors diminish their chances for re-election.[157]

---

[152] Id.

[153] Eric Engle, "What You Don't Know Can Hurt You: Human Rights, Shareholder Activism and SEC Reporting Requirements", 57 Syracuse L. Rev. 63 (2006).

[154] Van der Elst, *supra* note 90, at 7: in Germany "approximately 12 per cent of general meeting resolutions are contested every year"; Carine Girard, "Comparative Study of Successful French and Anglo-Saxon Shareholder Activism", Working Paper 2009, at 28.

[155] Chiu, *supra* note 7, at 23.   [156] Id, at 88.

[157] Luc Renneboog & Peter G. Szilagyi, "Shareholder Activism through the Proxy Process", ECGI Finance Working Paper No. 275/2010, available at http://ssrn.com/abstract_id=1460578, at 5.

5 REGULATORY CONSTRAINTS

The announcement by BNP Paribas in August 2007 that it would cease the activities of three hedge funds specializing in US mortgage debt and the subsequent bankruptcy of Lehman Brothers in September 2008 not only marked the commencement of the most farreaching crisis to hit the global economy since the Great Depression but also saw calls for greater regulation and government intervention.[158]

However, it has been argued that no single entity can collate all the requisite information in order to draft rules that would be adequately binding for all.[159] If one takes the UK as an illustrative example, it becomes evident that it is a combination of both legal obligations which are derived from, amongst others, the Companies Act 2006,[160] the Criminal Justice Act 1993,[161] the Financial Service and Markets Act 2000,[162] and industry benchmarks for best practices which are embodied in the UK Corporate Governance Code[163] and the Stewardship Code,[164] that govern the activities of investors today. As the current most prominent regulatory constraints on shareholder activism concern proxy access, acting in concert, and insider dealing, these will form the focus of this section of the chapter.

5.1 Proxy Access

Shareholder activism through the proxy process has always been subject to considerable debate amongst regulators and academics. On the one hand, it is argued that proxy access is an inherent right of shareholders and places them in a better position to monitor the performance of corporations and corporate governance. On the other hand, it is argued that by giving shareholders greater access to the boards of corporations they will pursue changes for personal benefit at the cost of the firm's long-term future. Additionally, the laws and regulations that govern proxy access by shareholders vary considerably from one nation to another often constraining their use by activists.

Although the majority of European jurisdictions recognize the benefits of affording minority shareholders rights to protect their interests, the laws and regulations governing proxy access remain stringent when compared to those that are currently in place in the US.[165] For example, in the UK, under the Companies Act 2006, shareholders may submit proposals

---

[158] Elliott, *supra* note 5.

[159] Friedrich A. Hayek, "The Use of Knowledge in Society", 35 Am. Econ. Rev. 519, 530 (1945).

[160] The Companies Act 2006 governs company law in the UK.

[161] The Criminal Justice Act 1993 governs, inter alia, insider dealing in the UK.

[162] The Financial Services and Markets Act 2000 regulates financial services and markets in the UK.

[163] The UK Corporate Governance Code details good corporate governance principles for predominantly those corporations that are listed on the London Stock Exchange.

[164] The Stewardship Code is fundamentally a set of guidelines for institutional investors operating on UK equity markets.

[165] Peter Cziraki, Luc Renneboog, & Peter G. Szilagyi, "Shareholder Activism Through Proxy Proposals: The European Perspective", 16 Eur. Fin. Mgmt. 738 (2010).

for vote at general meetings provided they own at least 5% of the corporation's issued stock, whilst ownership of 5% of the corporation's stock also enables shareholders to requisition an extraordinary shareholder meeting and propose their own nominees to the board.[166] The situation is similar in Germany where the German Stock Corporation Act[167] decrees that new agenda items and extraordinary meetings can be demanded by shareholders that own at least 5% of the corporation's voting capital.[168] Therefore, it would appear that shareholders in the UK and Germany, amongst other European nations, are in a strong position to engage in activism if they are of the opinion that the boards of their targeted corporations are not addressing their concerns in an adequate manner.[169] Nevertheless, the logistics of national and cross-border proxy voting and the ability to meet quorum requirements have often acted as a barrier to the use of the proxy process by activists in Europe. According to Manifest, with the increased dispersion of ownership in Europe and an unduly cumbersome system of proxy voting due to the need for cross-border chains of intermediaries, the ability to vote and satisfy quorum requirements became both time-consuming and prone to errors.[170] The July 2007 Shareholder Rights Directive was designed to remove these hurdles to the proxy process for shareholders by facilitating the exercise of basic shareholders' rights and enabling national and cross-border proxy voting.[171] The Directive, in essence, provides shareholders with the tools needed to not only monitor management boards but also to facilitate their involvement in the corporation's activities via, inter alia, advanced access to information ahead of general meetings.[172]

By comparison, the current situation in the US is arguably more conducive to the submission of proxy proposals by shareholders at general or annual general meetings. However, this has not always been the case as significant barriers used to exist for shareholders seeking proxy access, for example, to monitor the performance of the board of a company in the US. In particular, as mentioned, the former proxy regulation Rule 14a-8 on the submission of proxy proposals by shareholders excluded areas of fundamental importance such as the ability to make director nominations.[173] The recent economic crisis and subsequent calls for

---

[166] See Companies Act 2006, s. 303.

[167] Amongst others, the German Stock Corporate Act (Aktiengesetz) determines the powers of the corporate bodies of a German public company (Aktiengesellschaft). The corporate bodies of a German public company are the Management Board and the Supervisory Board.

[168] In fact, these thresholds have been harmonized by the European Shareholders Rights Directive: Directive 2007/36/EC of the European Parliament and of the Council of 11 July 2007 on the Exercise of Certain Rights of Shareholders in Listed Companies, [2007] OJ L184/17.

[169] Peter Baldwin, John Phillips, Lizanne Thomas, & Jennifer Lewis, "Anything You Can Do . . . How the Dodd-Frank Act Might Influence Further Reform of UK Corporate Governance", 26 Butterworths J. Int'l. Banking & Fin. L. 153, 154 (2011).

[170] Santella et al., *supra* note 42, at 267, with reference to Manifest, Cross-Border Voting in Europe: A Manifest Investigation into the Practical Problems of Informed Voting across EU Borders (May 2007).

[171] Santella et al., *supra* note 42. See also *supra* note 167.

[172] Marco Scalera, "Investor Engagement in Europe in the Wake of the Shareholder Rights Directive Implementation", available at http://www.conference-board.org/retrievefile.cfm?filename=DN-006-10.pdf&type=subsite (last visited Oct. 31, 2017), at 2.

[173] Gillan & Starks, Survey of Shareholder Activism *supra* note 11.

greater accountability of corporate boards by, for example, the Dodd–Frank Act[174] led to the SEC's proposal of rules that would enable shareholders with access to the proxy statements of companies to nominate directors. The proposals were subsequently enacted under Rule 14a-11 permitting shareholders, satisfying certain requirements, to include director nominees on the proxy materials of a corporation that are distributed to shareholders.[175] Further amendments were also made to Rule 14a-8(i)(8) in narrowing the types of shareholder proposals that could be excluded under the "election exclusion." The rationale behind the amendments lay in the need to empower shareholders to hold boards to account for their actions by, inter alia, facilitating communication between shareholders in the proxy process and improving corporate suffrage.[176]

A study on shareholder activism through the proxy process found that proxy proposals were generally targeted at underperforming corporations and/or those with a poor governance structure.[177] Specifically, the authors ascertained that it was more likely for proposals to be submitted against corporations that have ineffective and entrenched CEOs and management that lacks the incentive to act in the best interests of the firm.[178] This conclusion was supported by the fact that out of their sample the majority of proposals made were in relation to takeovers, the removal of the management board, and poison pills.[179] However, it is worth noting that the sample period ranged from 1996 to 2005 and thus occurred during the time when greater regulatory constraints existed on proxy access.

5.2 Acting in Concert

Cooperation between shareholders is not uncommon if one considers that a shareholder activist will usually hold a minority shareholding and will thus commonly hold insufficient stock to realize their goals.[180] However, a greater degree of strategic care is currently required not to fall foul of the laws and regulations that govern acting in concert, which could in certain jurisdictions even risk triggering a mandatory bid for the targeted corporation.

In Europe, the Directive on Takeover Bids defines acting in concert as cooperating under the guise of an agreement with the offeror or the offeree corporation to either acquire control of the offeree corporation or hinder the bid that has been made.[181] Under the rules of the Directive, those found to be acting in concert are required to make a mandatory offer to the

---

[174] Dodd–Frank Wall Street Reform and Consumer Protection Act, Pub. L. No. 111-203, §971, 124 Stat. 1376 (2010) ("Dodd–Frank Act") is a US federal statute that was passed following the 2007–2009 financial crisis with the aim of making the US financial system more transparent and accountable ultimately protecting taxpayers' money.

[175] A part of Rule 14a-11 has however been declared unlawful, see *Business Roundtable and Chamber of Commerce v. US Securities and Exchange Commission*, D.C. Cir., No. 10-1305, July 22, 2011.

[176] Securities and Exchange Commission, Facilitating Shareholder Director Nominations, available at http://www.sec.gov/rules/final/2010/33-9136.pdf (last visited Oct. 31, 2017), p. 1.

[177] Renneboog & Szilagyi, *supra* note 157.   [178] Id. at 3.

[179] Id. at 9, 10.

[180] Empirical material at Rafel Crespi & Luc Renneboog, "Is (Institutional) Shareholder Activism New? Evidence from UK Shareholder Coalitions in the Pre-Cadbury Era", 18 Corp. Governance: An Int'l. Rev. 274 (2010). See further, Ian MacNeil, "Activism and Collaboration Among Shareholders in UK Listed Companies", 5 Cap. Markets L. J. 419 (2010).

[181] Articles 2(1)(d) and 5 of Directive 2004/25/EC.

other shareholders of the targeted corporation if together they surpass a "control" threshold, usually fixed at about 30% of the voting rights.[182] The same concept of acting in concert is also relevant for the block disclosure rules under the EU Transparency Directive.[183] Depending on the context and depending on the jurisdiction, the precise definition of "acting in concert" has been implemented in different ways.[184] The resulting legal uncertainty has prompted the European Securities and Markets Authority (ESMA), on the request of the European Commission, to publish a White List of "innocent" activities.[185] The concept of "acting in concert" and its divergent interpretations may chill shareholder activism, a development which policy makers may or may not welcome.[186]

The situation is slightly more complex in the US where there are numerous barriers to prevent acting in concert.[187] For example, section 13(d) of the Exchange Act[188] requires a shareholder or group owning more than 5% of a listed company's shares to file a "Schedule 13D" publicly. A "Schedule 13D" discloses all parties involved in addition to their intended aims in relation to the targeted corporation. However, it was recently clarified that shareholders are able to communicate, plan, and even act together to effect policy changes without disclosing their affiliation under section 13(d) of the Exchange Act.[189] It is only on the grounds of acquiring, holding, voting, or disposing of their shareholdings that they must disclose their group arrangement in a Schedule 13D filing.[190]

The above clearly outlines the complexity of acting in concert and the restricting effect it can have on activist engagement. It should, however, be noted that the fundamental aim behind the laws and regulations on acting in concert is to protect the interests of minority shareholders by granting them the right to exit on fair terms when the controlling shareholders change.[191]

5.3 Market Abuse and Insider Dealing

Many of the activities that activists are pursuing touch on the limits of legally permissible market behavior. For example, in circumstances in which the activist shareholder has engaged in previous communication with the target company's board, it is possible that inside

---

[182] For Germany, see for example § 35(2) and § 29(2) Wertpapiererwerbs- und Übernahmegesetz [WpÜG] (German Takeover Law).

[183] Article 10 of Directive 2004/109/EC.

[184] Leading to proposals for greater harmonization in the EU. See European Securities Markets Expert Group, Preliminary Views on the Definition of Acting in Concert between the Transparency Directive and the Takeover Bids Directive, Nov. 2008.

[185] European Securities and Markets Authority (ESMA), Information on Shareholder Cooperation and Acting in Concert Under the Takeover Bids Directive, ESMA/2013/1642 (Nov. 12, 2013).

[186] On the topic generally, see Martin Winner, "Active Shareholders and European Takeover Regulation", 11 Eur. Company & Fin. L. Rev. 364 (2014).

[187] Santella et al., *supra* note 42.

[188] Securities Exchange Act of 1934 governs the trading of stocks, bonds, and debentures in the US.

[189] Clarification given in Second Circuit's July 2011 Opinion: *CSX Corp. v. The Children's Investment Fund Management*.

[190] Id.

[191] Santella et al., *supra* note 42.

information has been divulged, which would restrict the shareholder from being able to deal in the company's shares. Moreover, in some instances it is possible that the actual strategy being pursued by the activist shareholder is itself inside information, thus requiring disclosure to the market as a whole.

Insider dealing not only risks undermining the shareholder voting process but also has negative repercussions on timing paramount for the proper functioning of the stock markets.[192] By trading on inside information, investors are selling and buying at the most opportune moment in time but are breaching their fiduciary duty or other relationship of trust and confidence whilst they are in possession of stock information that is not publicly available. These actions ultimately undermine confidence in the integrity and fairness of stock markets.[193]

In establishing the cause of the 1929 financial crash, US Congress ascertained that widespread insider dealing had played a pivotal role and so enacted the Securities Exchange Act of 1934 with the principle aim of deterring unfair transactions.[194] With an increase in corporate takeovers and coincidental abuses of cash tender offers, the Williams Act of 1968 was passed to make full and fair disclosure a mandatory requirement. This legislation ultimately enabled the SEC to fine and prosecute offenders like the corporate raider Ivan Boesky. Ivan Boesky was fined $100 million in 1986 for having launched takeover bids on the basis of information that was obtained illegally. By acting on inside information, Ivan Boesky was able to purchase stock in his targeted corporations before his takeover bid went public.[195] This enabled him to reap rewards as the stock's value subsequently rose. The proactive approach taken to tackle insider dealing in the US was not mirrored by legislators in the UK, as it was only in 1980 that insider dealing became a criminal offence there.

In the UK, dealing on insider information was considered legitimate and widespread until the late 1950s when it began to be considered an unethical practice. Nevertheless, the practice was as widespread as ever in the 1960s and 1970s and was even being depicted as the crime of being something in the City by the Financial Editor of The Sunday Times in 1973.[196] It was only in 1980 that insider trading became a criminal offence in the UK and is currently enforceable under the Criminal Justice Act 1993.[197] However, as cases are rarely prosecuted

---

[192] Laurie B. Smilan, David A. Becker, & Dane A. Holbrook, Wolf Pack Attacks and Williams Act Protections: What Every Company Should Know about Shareholder Activist Hedge Funds, in Securities Litigation & Enforcement Institute 235 (Bruce D. Angiolillo ed., 2006) Boyer, *supra* note 54, at 1033.

[193] Securities and Exchange Commission, Insider Trading, available at http://www.sec.gov/answers/insider.htm (last visited Oct. 31, 2017).

[194] William R. McLucas, John H. Walsh, & Lisa L. Fountain, "Settlement of Insider Trading Cases with the SEC", 48 Bus. Law. 79 (1992).

[195] Stephen Chapman, Drawing the Wrong Lesson from the Ivan Boesky Affair, Chicago Tribune, Dec. 5, 1986, available at http://articles.chicagotribune.com/1986-12-05/news/8604010030_1_takeovers-ivan-boesky-affair-insider (last visited Oct. 31, 2017).

[196] Margaret Cole, Insider Dealing in the City, speech by Margaret Cole, then Director of Enforcement, Financial Services Authority, at the London School of Economics, Mar. 17, 2007, available at http://www.fsa.gov.uk/library/communication/speeches/2007/0317_mc.shtml (last visited Oct. 31, 2017).

[197] Criminal Justice Act 1993 governs all criminal law in the UK.

under this Act, the Financial Service and Markets Act 2000[198] subsequently came into force, giving the FSA wide-ranging powers to prosecute offenders for insider dealing.[199] Insider dealing has been subject to European regulation since the 2003 Market Abuse Directive.[200]

With the identities of shareholder activists constantly evolving, hedge funds have recently become a focal point for regulators in many jurisdictions as the inherent nature of their operations often makes them vulnerable to involvement in market abuse, advertently or inadvertently.[201] As pointed out by a former Chairman of the SEC, William H. Donaldson, hedge funds present a unique challenge as the vast majority are not registered with the SEC, which limits the SEC's ability to detect matters such as fraud before stock markets or investors are affected.[202] Inherently, this would arguably also be applicable to other regulators and governing bodies due to the tendency for hedge funds to register offshore in order to benefit from lighter regulatory oversight and weaker control environments.[203] However, as market dynamics and investor strategies continue to evolve, regulators and governing bodies have to constantly respond and adapt in order to maintain the fairness and integrity of the equity markets.

6 SHAREHOLDER ACTIVISM DURING THE FINANCIAL CRISIS AND IN THE FUTURE

Allen Boyer argues that the market has never altered the role of a shareholder activist but has always defined that role.[204] It is therefore tenable that the abundance of world trade agreements since the 1960s facilitated the liberalization of worldwide capital flows and contributed to the denationalization of the corporate and financial landscape.[205] The free flow of financial capital within and across national borders not only altered the power dynamics between governments, shareholders, and corporations but also facilitated the realization of abnormal returns on investments by shareholder activists. This was particularly the case for hedge funds that were able to reap returns by deploying activist strategies. Nevertheless, as the market facilitated the realization of activist strategies it also restricted their reach as illustrated by the recent financial crisis and the initial demise of private equity

---

[198] Financial Service and Markets Act 2000 established the former Financial Services Authority (FSA), which regulated insurance, investment corporations and banking.

[199] Cole, *supra* note 196.

[200] Directive 2003/6/EC of the European Parliament and of the Council of 28 January 2003 on insider dealing and market manipulation (market abuse) [2003] OJ L96/16; now replaced by Regulation (EU) No 596/2014 of the European Parliament and of the Council of 16 April 2014 on market abuse (market abuse regulation) [2014] OJ L173/1.

[201] Financial Services Authority, *supra* note 116, at 54.

[202] William H. Donaldson, Testimony Concerning the Long and Short of Hedge Funds: Effects of Strategies for Managing Market Risk, US Securities and Exchange Commission, available at http://www.sec.gov/news/testimony/052203tswhd.htm (last visited Oct. 31, 2017).

[203] Financial Services Authority, *supra* note 54, at 14.

[204] Boyer, *supra* note 54, at 998.   [205] Galanis, *supra* note 64, at 358.

and hedge fund activity. In short, research has documented that activist hedge funds are thus heavily pro-cyclical.[206]

6.1 Initial Demise of Private Equity and Hedge Funds

During the financial crisis, the outlook for activists, in particular hedge funds and private equity firms, was bleak. A reduction in available liquidity, private companies seeking a quick exit from their private equity shareholders, and potential targets shying away from listing on the main markets due to costs and regulatory obligations seemed to create the advent of a "buyer's strike" or the end of the locust era.[207] Faced with higher startup costs and an increasingly competitive market, private equity and hedge funds were perceived to be finding it ever more difficult to amass sufficient returns to remain profitable.[208] Some scholars even heralded the near "eclipse" of private equity.[209]

However, it is now evident that that shareholder activism has not just survived but dramatically prospered over the past years since the crisis. During crisis times, falling profits and dividends will force management boards to be more responsive to demands for disposals by shareholders.[210] For example, Chris Hohn, the founder of The Children's Investment Fund Management (TCI), gained notoriety in 2005 after having succeeded in removing Rolf Breuer and Werner Seifert from the board of Deutsche Börse and in stopping attempts to acquire control of the London Stock Exchange.[211] Following heavy losses of 43% in 2008, and the departure of various founding partners, little was heard of the fund on the market. However, recent filings with the SEC indicate that activity is once again well under way: as per the quarterly 13-F reports The Children's Investment Fund Management (UK) LLP increased its portfolio of US shares to levels equal to those seen at the fund's peak in 2008.[212] More recently, TCI seems to have fully regained its pre-crisis strength.[213] Additionally, recent figures on the hedge fund industry indicate that activist hedge funds alone now have a total of $66 billion under management after recent years have seen strong capital inflows and record

---

[206] Mike Burkart & Amil Dasgupta, Activist Funds, Leverage, and Procyclicality, SRC Discussion Paper No 40, July 2015, available at http://eprints.lse.ac.uk/65095/1/LEQSPaper16.pdf.

[207] The Kay Review of UK Equity Markets and Long-Term Decision Making, February Interim Report (2012), at 26. For evidence on the decline of shareholder activism during the financial crisis, see Becht et al., Returns to Hedge Fund Activism, *supra* note 109.

[208] Financial Services Authority, *supra* note 116, at 34.

[209] Brian R. Cheffins & John Armour, "The Eclipse of Private Equity", 33 Del. J. Corp. L. 1 (2008).

[210] Long Live Activism, Fin. Times, Nov. 4, 2008, at 8.

[211] Ivar Simensen, Activist Investors Seek Success in Germany, Fin. Times, Dec. 7, 2007, 11; William Hutchings, Where are They Now? Chris Hohn, Fin. News, July 9, 2010, available at http://www.efinancialnews.com/story/2010-07-09/fn100-where-are-they-now-chris-hohn (last visited Oct. 31, 2017).

[212] Hutchings, *supra* note 211.

[213] Louise Armitstead, TCI Has Record Year—But this Time Charity Won't Benefit, Telegraph, Jan. 7, 2014, available at http://www.telegraph.co.uk/finance/newsbysector/banksandfinance/10556696/TCI-has-record-year-but-this-time-charity-wont-benefit.html (last visited Oct. 31, 2017).

profits in 2013.[214] As a note of caution, however, the future success of shareholder activism looks likely to be constrained with new regulations coming into force over the next few years and a growing concern over the implementation of short-term investment strategies.

6.2 Activism post the Financial Crisis

The 2008/2009 global financial crisis has intensified the debate about the role that investors play or should play in corporate governance. To some, increasing shareholder influence and facilitating shareholder intervention when necessary is part of the essential reforms; activism in particular is often hailed as the solution for effectively monitoring management. To others, activism by shareholders who potentially have short-term interests is part of the problem, not a solution. Lawmakers are still undecided to what extent (and when) shareholder activism can improve firm value and performance or to what extent (and when) shareholder activism can produce distortions that make matters worse. Research by financial economists that seeks further light on these questions will provide valuable input to the questions with which decision makers are struggling.

In any case, following the struggle of hedge funds and private equity funds during the crisis, the ensuing recession and more recent years have undoubtedly played a role in the rise of more targeted and more focused shareholder activism.[215] For many investors, voting their shares has become a legitimate method to express dissatisfaction with the performance of a specific board member. In addition, the weak stock market performance since 2007 has increased the clout of activist investors, and low interest rates have given hedge funds record investment volumes. At the same time, the slight economic recovery since 2009 has given companies time to reduce debt and to build cash piles which make them interesting targets for activists.[216] This may help explain why shareholder activists in recent times have also begun targeting larger and blue-chip companies such as Apple, Procter & Gamble, and Sony, generating a profound echo in the corporate world and in the media.[217] It is said that activism has outpaced any other hedge fund strategy performance over the past years.[218]

Advances in technology have surely helped foster this development. The rise of the Internet, along with greater disclosure obligations, has made it easier to access information about target companies, board members, and financial data.[219] It has further encouraged

---

[214] Stephen Foley, Activist Hedge Funds Increase Corporate Bond Risk, says Moody's, Fin. Times, Mar. 10, 2014.

[215] McCrum & Gelles, *supra* note 3 at 7; Economist, *supra* note 3, at 51; Joseph Cyriac, Ruth De Backer, & Justin Sanders, Preparing for Bigger, Bolder Shareholder Activists, Insights & Publications, Mar. 2014, available at http://www.mckinsey.com/insights/corporate_finance/preparing_for_bigger_bolder_shareholder_activists.

[216] Paul Parker, head of global corporate finance and M&A at Barclays Capital, is cited as saying "The percussive theme song is unmistakable; use it or lose it. Excess capital must be used or returned to shareholders." See McCrum & Gelles, *supra* note 3.

[217] Stephen F. Arcano & Richard J. Grossman, Activist Shareholders in the US: A Changing Landscape, Skadden, Arps, Slate, Meagher & Flom LLP Insight, June 17, 2013, available at http://www.skadden.com/insights/activist-shareholders-us-changing-landscape-0 (last visited Oct. 31, 2017).

[218] Stephen Foley, Activist Investors' Success Owes Much to Wider Bull Run, Fin. Times, Mar. 2, 2015.

[219] Justin Fox, Ackman, Icahn and their Pals Are Keepers, BloombergView, Jan. 12, 2015.

greater shareholder collaboration. Shareholder activism can therefore be said to have become more targeted in character.[220]

6.3 The "Teaming Up" Strategy

Finally, the techniques of shareholder activism seem to have changed. Along with new technological advantages come broader alliances that activists are seeking to build with traditionally passive institutional investors. In most cases, the realization of activists' plans (in particular in large target companies) will depend on the support they get from larger institutional investors.[221] As a consequence, hedge funds may seek to form coalitions with these institutions, sometimes even before they invest. Scholars such as Ronald Gilson and Jeffrey Gordon have argued that the ultimate solution to shareholder passivity may be a new breed of activist shareholder—those who do not bring about change themselves, due to the small stakes they hold, but who can pressure for change by teaming up with normally rather passive institutions such as pension funds and mutual funds.[222] According to this view, such activist investors, in particular hedge funds, fill a vacuum that is created by the increased remoteness of investment and shareholder apathy.[223]

Practitioners confirm this trend. According to reports from the law practice, activists are now receiving greater support from traditional institutional investors, including those that might not themselves agitate for change.[224] This development goes hand in hand with the feeling that supporting activists has largely lost the stigma that it used to have among traditional investors, which once may have viewed activists as a disruptive influence acting contrary to the long-term interests of the company.[225] One recent example of this phenomenon actually happening is Jana Partners, an activist hedge fund, teaming up with the Ontario Teachers' Pension Plan to bring about change at McGraw-Hill, the education and data company.[226] Another example is the 2014 alliance between activist fund Legion Partners Asset Management LLC and pension fund California State Teachers' Retirement System (CalSTRS) to press retailer Perry Ellis International Inc. into considering strategic

---

[220] Dunstan Prial, Shareholder Activism More Focused, Targeted, Fox Business, May 25, 2012, available at http://www.foxbusiness.com/industries/2012/05/25/shareholder-activism-more-focused-targeted/ (last visited Oct. 31, 2017).

[221] Stephen Foley, Activist Hedge Fund Managers Get Board Welcome, Fin. Times, Dec. 23, 2013 ("Activists also have the ear of the traditional large fund management groups, which are themselves pressing management to be more responsive to shareholder concerns.").

[222] Gilson & Gordon, *supra* note 19. See also Marcel Kahan & Edward Rock, "Embattled CEOs", 88 Tex. L. Rev. 987 (2010).

[223] Gilson & Gordon, *supra* note 19, at 896 ff.

[224] Svea Herbst-Bayliss, Activist Investors Get More Respect amid Strong Returns, Reuters, Nov. 17, 2013, available at http://www.reuters.com/article/2013/11/18/us-investment-summit-activism-idUSBRE9AH02K20131118 (last visited Oct. 31, 2017); Charles Nathan, Debunking Myths about Activist Investors, Harvard Law School Forum on Corporate Governance and Financial Regulation, Mar. 15, 2013, available at https://blogs.law.harvard.edu/corpgov/2013/03/15/debunking-myths-about-activist-investors/ (last visited Oct. 31, 2017); David Bernstein, Do Investors Want to Vote?, IFLR.com, Dec. 9, 2014, available at http://www.iflr.com/Article/3400945/Do-investors-want-to-vote.html (last visited Oct. 31, 2017); Arcano & Grossman, *supra* note 217.

[225] Arcano & Grossman, *supra* note 217.   [226] McCrum & Gelles, *supra* note 3.

alternatives.[227] CalPERS, the largest pension fund in the US, is also reported to be toying with the idea.[228] A recent report by business consultancy FTI found that 76% of the institutional investors they interviewed in December 2014 were backing shareholder activism by supporting the actions of traditional activists as well as using their own tactics.[229]

Related strategies for activists include the possibility of convincing proxy advisors such as ISS to support their campaigns[230] or to team up with other activists, building a "wolf pack."[231] According to some, institutional shareholders are even reportedly encouraging activists to agitate at underperforming companies in their portfolio.[232]

Apart from these few sketchy examples, the "teaming up" phenomenon seems to be developing into a broader market trend, and a positive one, since the support by conventional investors serves as an additional check on the validity and long-term viability of the activists' plans.[233] Activists are viewed as suitable governance intermediaries, actively monitoring company performance and then presenting to companies and institutional investors concrete visions for business strategy. The pension fund's support gives them additional credibility, both in relation to the target company and to the wider market, and may discredit the common complaint about activists' short-term perspectives.[234] The collaboration between a passive investment fund and an activist investor can thus be understood as a win-win scenario in three ways: It bolsters the position of the activist, giving them more influence and credibility. At the same time, activist influence is welcome support for large institutional investors who do not need to invest their own resources in detecting strategic investment possibilities. Finally, such joint initiatives may serve as a "screening" process to give other investors, or the wider, market an indication of which activist projects are legitimate for the shareholder body as a whole, since the support by the traditional investor promises an increased likelihood of long-term orientation and value creation. Taking all of these points together, the teaming-up strategy holds great promise—and activists can effectively serve to reduce the market's undervaluation of voting rights to the advantage of all shareholders.[235] It should be noted that the "teaming-up" concept needs to be seen within the respective regulatory framework, and existing legal barriers—for example, as discussed, on "acting in concert"—should be reconsidered in the light of these positive market trends.[236]

---

[227] Ronald Orol, Teaming Up with CalSTRS Helps Activist Funds Get Their Way, TheDeal.com, Aug. 4, 2014, available at http://www.thedeal.com/content/consumer-retail/teaming-up-with-calstrs-helps-activist-funds-get-their-way.php (last visited Oct. 31, 2017).

[228] Id.

[229] FTI Consulting, 2015 Shareholder Activist Landscape: An Institutional Investor Perspective, available at http://www.fticonsulting.com/global2/critical-thinking/reports/shareholder-activism-2015.aspx.

[230] See, e.g., the initiative by Hermes campaigning against the proposed chairman at Infineon, the German semiconductor manufacturer. Hermes succeeded in convincing both Glass Lewis and RiskMetrics to support them. See Richard Milne & Daniel Schäfer, Activists Draw Blood in Fight for Infineon, Fin. Times, Jan. 28, 2010.

[231] Alon Brav, Amil Dasgupta & Richmond Mathews, "Wolf Pack Activism", Working Paper, Nov. 2014, available at http://ssrn.com/abstract=2529230.

[232] Arcano & Grossman, *supra* note 217.

[233] See for further detail David Gelles & Michael J. de la Merced, New Alliances in Battle for Corporate Control, N.Y. Times, Mar. 19, 2014, at 1.

[234] Orol, *supra* note 227.   [235] Gilson & Gordon, *supra* note 19.

[236] On acting in concert see *infra* section 5.2.

Modern hedge fund activism can thus be said to be an improved, more sophisticated version of its predecessors. The "teaming-up" concept has a double advantage: hedge funds cannot do it alone; they must convince fellow shareholders that their ideas are beneficial for the entirety of the shareholders, including the typically long-term oriented pension funds. But this step additionally amounts to a de facto "vetting process," whereby checks and balances are created: if and insofar as activists need to convince other funds that their strategic plans are beneficial for the company as such (and do not create idiosyncratic benefits for the hedge fund), this process mitigates the potential extraction of short-term private benefits and ensures that activism is channeled into mutually beneficial activities.

6.4 New Regulatory Constraints

It is apparent that the width and depth of the recent financial crisis has reignited the regulatory debate on shareholder activism, when previously many seemed content to leave control to the mechanisms of the market as a whole.[237] The new regulatory reforms that look set to constrain the activities of hedge funds in particular over the coming years are the US Dodd–Frank Act of 2010 and the European Directive on Alternative Investment Fund Managers.[238]

6.4.1 US Dodd–Frank Act of 2010

The Dodd–Frank Act is the main US regulatory response to the global financial crisis. It arguably represents one of the most significant changes to the US financial regulatory system since the Great Depression.[239] The fundamental aim of the Act is to prevent another financial crisis by reining in the activities of Wall Street and abolishing the bailout of institutions that are argued to be too large to fail. The principal changes that will affect the scope of shareholder activism are those that are related directly to hedge funds, the SEC, and the strengthening of shareholder rights.

As part of the "shadow banking system," hedge funds have traditionally been largely exempt from the scope of regulators. This exemption from regulatory oversight has enabled hedge funds to operate freely, transferring vast volumes of capital and risk on equity markets in the pursuit of maximizing their investments. This operational freedom has often risked the stability of financial markets or damaged trade execution and settlement processes.[240]

---

[237] Galanis, *supra* note 64, at 361 ff. See also Engert, *supra* note 107.

[238] Long Titles: Restoring American Financial Stability Act of 2010 and Directive 2011/61/EU of the European Parliament and of the Council of 8 June 2011 on Alternative Investment Fund Managers and Amending Directives 2003/41/EC and 2009/65/EC and Regulations (EC) No 1060/2009 and (EU) No. 1095/2010.

[239] John G. Finley, How Financial Reforms Will Impact Private Equity Hedge Funds, Harvard Law School Forum on Corporate Governance and Financial Regulation, June 8, 2010, available at http://blogs.law.harvard.edu/corpgov/2010/06/08/how-financial-reforms-will-impact-private-equity-hedge-funds (last visited Oct. 31, 2017).

[240] Financial Services Authority, *supra* note 116, at 18.

Thus, Title IV of the Act (or the "Private Fund Investment Advisers Registration Act" of 2010) requires hedge funds managing over $100 million to register as investment advisors with the SEC and disclose the requisite financial data required for monitoring risk and protecting investors.[241] It is hoped, on the one hand, that the disclosure of financial information will mark an end to the "shadow" financial system within which hedge funds previously operated. On the other, it is hoped that the requirement to register with the SEC will enable the assessment of systemic risk and thus help maintain the stability of the financial market.

In parallel, by strengthening a shareholder's ability to influence matters such as executive pay and the enforcement of greater accountability, it is hoped that the current system supporting the realization of short-term gains will be reversed.[242] This should in theory give board members the incentive to minimize taking risks with excess leverage which inherently had a detrimental effect on the long-term performance of their firms and negatively affected the stability of the economy as a whole.[243] Whether the Act does indeed transform the stability of the US economy remains to be seen, as it does not appear to have the same farreaching consequences as the Glass–Steagall Act did.

6.4.2 European Directive on Alternative Investment Fund Managers

The European Directive on Alternative Investment Fund Managers (the "AIFM Directive"), which came into force on July 21, 2011, has the aim of rectifying the regulatory gaps and inconsistencies that previously governed the operations of collective investment undertakings over the value of €100 million, such as hedge funds and private equity funds.[244]

The Directive not only applies to the worldwide activities of alternative investment fund managers based in the European Union but also the activities conducted inside the EU by alternative investment fund managers that are based in third countries. By stipulating that an alternative investment fund manager will need to obtain prior authorization from national authorities in order to operate, the Directive is creating a "passport system" under which alternative investment fund managers will have the authority to market alternative investment funds in the EU.[245] Once a "passport" has been obtained, the alternative investment fund manager will need to satisfy additional requirements, namely the preparation of an annual report which is to be made available to investors, the disclosure of specific information such as a description of their investment strategy, and reporting to regulatory authorities on a regular basis on matters such as liquidity, risk management arrangements,

---

[241] Senate Committee on Banking, Housing, and Urban Affairs, Chairman Chris Dodd (D-CT), Summary: Restoring American Financial Stability—Create a Sound Economic Foundation to Grow Jobs, Protect Consumers, Rein in Wall Street, End Too Big to Fail, Prevent Another Financial Crisis, available at http://banking.senate.gov/public/_files/FinancialReformSummaryAsFiled.pdf (last visited Oct. 31, 2017), at 7.

[242] Id. at 9.   [243] Id.

[244] The AIFM Directive had to be implemented into local law of Member States by July 22, 2013.

[245] Eilís Ferran, "After the Crisis: The Regulation of Hedge Funds and Private Equity in the EU", 12 Eur. Bus. Org. L. Rev. 379, 399ff (2011); Dan Awrey, "The Limits of EU Hedge Fund Regulation", 5 L. & Fin. Markets Rev. 119 (2011).

and leverage. Furthermore, the Directive will also exert a degree of influence on the pay and bonus schemes of an alternative investment fund's personnel by, for example, stipulating that 40% of bonuses must be deferred for at least three to five years with the potential for earlier recovery should relevant investments perform badly.

Despite its purported aim, the Directive has come under heavy criticism since the first draft was published in April 2009. Many have urged that the Directive is not a proportionate response to the 2007–2009 financial crisis, having targeted hedge funds despite major reports, such as the de Larosière Report[246] and the Turner Review,[247] concluding that hedge funds did not play a significant role in the crisis.[248] Furthermore, it appears that the Directive in part goes against the advice set out in the G20's 2009 Global Plan for Recovery and Reform. The G20's Global Plan not only advocated a supervisory and regulatory framework that was more globally in sync but also encouraged regulators and supervisors to reduce the capacity for regulatory arbitrage and resist protectionism in pursuit of promoting global trade and investment.[249] As such, it will be a matter of time for the full effectiveness of the Directive to be determined.

6.4.3 Assessment

Despite these concerns, it is submitted that regulatory efforts overall have been relatively modest, and for good reason.

Both the AIFM Directive and the Dodd–Frank Act limit themselves to certain rules on the supervision of hedge fund managers, and do not pursue an activities-based approach that would address specific corporate governance methods used by activists.[250] Given that potential pathologies of corporate governance—such as empty voting, for example—can be pursued by any investor (and not just hedge funds), it would appears pointless to regulate such behavior on an individual, hedge fund basis. Insofar as these tactics pose governance problems, these problems are best dealt with by general corporate law.

Broader hedge fund market regulation can be meaningful, instead, in addressing market concerns such as market stability and integrity, that is, a more macroprudential-oriented approach. In this context, the newly introduced regulatory framework can contribute to a smooth functioning of the market and strengthen market oversight powers for regulators.

---

[246] High Level Group on Financial Supervision in the EU, chaired by Jacques de Larosière, Report, Feb. 25, 2009, available at http://ec.europa.eu/internal_market/finances/docs/de_larosiere_report_en.pdf.

[247] The Turner Review: A Regulatory Response to the Global Banking Crisis, Mar. 2009, available at http://www.fsa.gov.uk/pubs/other/turner_review.pdf.

[248] Louise Armitstead, European Commission Unveils Tough Hedge Fund Directive, Telegraph, Apr. 29, 2009.

[249] G20 Global Plan For Recovery And Reform, Apr. 2, 2009, available at http://www.cfr.org/financial-crises/g20-global-plan-recovery-reform-april-2009/p19017 (last visited Oct. 31, 2017), at paras. 13, 14.

[250] On this, Ringe, *supra* note 118, at 1033; House of Commons, Treasury Committee, Banking Crisis: International Dimensions (HC 615, 2009), p. Ev 90f. There are just a few such abstract provisions, in particular on risk and liquidity management. See Arts. 12 ff. of the AIFM Directive.

6.5 Short Termism

The rationale behind equity markets is twofold: namely, that investors can reap the benefits generated from linking their savings to business profits and that the operational performance of corporations can be improved by the efficient allocation of capital.[251] The efficiency of the market, in other words the smooth functioning of a market whereby investors have recourse to liquidity and transparency, is thus dependent on long-term strategies that do not take into consideration day-to-day stock fluctuations.[252] The reality of the equity markets, however, could not be further from this definition as the regulatory framework has a tendency to support liquidity and trading activity over a period of long-term ownership.[253] It is argued that this short termism could not only be having a detrimental effect on market efficiency but could also be jeopardizing the long-term growth and success of corporations.[254]

Arguably, it is shareholder engagement, and thus shareholder activism, which has encouraged corporations to focus on short-term financial gains at the cost of a corporation's growth and development in order to generate abnormal returns on investments.[255] If one takes hedge funds as an illustration, it becomes evident that long-term investment strategies would risk excessive leverage and exposure to fluctuations in a sector or the market as a whole. The hedge fund manager is therefore pursuing short-term strategies to satisfy the demands of investors who at times of uncertainty, as is presently the case, have a preference for immediate cash flows and dividends as opposed to growth over the long term.[256] Private equity funds have also been criticized despite typically engaging in longer-term strategies. It has been argued that the boards of corporations owned by private equity funds are under increasing pressure to refrain from investing in the business for its long-term future and instead ensure that earnings are increased so that a speedy refinancing or early exit can be achieved by the private equity manager.[257] Boards of takeover targets are also often forced to concede to shareholder activism, as was the case in the takeover of Cadbury by Kraft. Sir Roger Carr, who was the Chairman of Cadbury at the time of the takeover, is quoted as having stated that the board did not feel it an option to reject a high bid even if they were of the opinion that it was not in the corporation's long-term interests.[258]

This chapter does not purport to seriously address these complaints, let alone the question of whether short-term perspective is really detrimental to value creation.[259] It suffices to point out that the "teaming-up" strategy discussed above may serve as an effective check on too much alleged short termism.[260] In summary, it has become evident from the above that market conditions have been the driving force in defining the role of shareholder activists. Accordingly, whether shareholder activists will opt to engage in long-term investment strategies for the benefit of a corporation as a whole not only depends on the demands of

---

[251] Short-Changed: The British Stockmarket is Not Fit for Purpose, Economist, Mar. 3, 2012.

[252] Kay Review, Interim Report, *supra* note 207, at 7.

[253] Short-Changed, *supra* note 251.

[254] Department for Business, Innovation & Skills, A Long-Term Focus for Corporate Britain: A Call For Evidence, Oct. 2010, at 8.

[255] Kay Review, Interim Report, *supra* note 207, at 8.

[256] Geordie Clarke, Never Mind Short-Term Fads, Take the Longer View, Fin. Times, Mar. 3, 2012, at 9.

[257] Kay Review, Interim Report, *supra* note 207, at 35.   [258] Id. at 13.

[259] See for further analysis, chapter 16 by Mark Roe.   [260] See *infra* section 6.3.

their investors but also on market conditions and the knock-on effects of the new regulatory constraints that are currently coming into force in the US and the EU.

7 CONCLUSION

This chapter paints a largely positive picture of activist investors' engagement in corporate governance. Exploring the historical roots and the methods of shareholder activists, I argue that shareholder structure is an important variable to determine the shape and the importance of activist engagement. In all environments, however, the key question to address is how to constrain self-serving activist behavior while harnessing its positive effects. Regulation has only a modest share in this context. The recent trend of forming coalitions between activists and conventional institutional investors may however be seen as a promising strategy that serves as a screening test on legitimate agendas while giving activists more credibility.

Shareholder activists have rebounded strongly after the financial crisis. Even though policy makers seized the opportunity of introducing more regulation to contain hedge funds, for example, in both the US and the EU, regulation is and should play a modest role in this field. A market supervision approach, monitoring systemic concerns, coupled with individual steps to address specific corporate governance problems appears to be the right way forward.

In sum, there's life in the old dog yet. Whilst some predicted the end of hedge funds and private equity a few years ago, they have emerged from the financial crisis stronger than ever. Having honed their tactics and enhanced their credibility, they are here to stay—constantly updating their strategies.

CHAPTER 16

....

CORPORATE SHORT-TERMISM

In the Boardroom and in the Courtroom

....

MARK J. ROE

1 INTRODUCTION

....

THE belief that short-term stock market trading undermines corporate decision making at the top has long been part of the corporate governance discourse and policy making, and in recent years has picked up articulate judicial adherents. One of the most vivid and effective classic attacks on financial market short-termism came as the takeover wars of the 1980s opened up, via Martin Lipton's well-known justification to further empower managers to defeat hostile takeovers: "It would not be unfair," he wrote, "to pose the policy issue as: Whether the long-term interests of the nation's corporate system and economy should be jeopardized in order to benefit speculators interested . . . only in a quick profit . . . ?"[1] Over the years the chairs of the Securities and Exchange Commission, Congress,[2] business analysts,[3] and the business media have regularly excoriated trading markets as perniciously shortening corporate time horizons, justifying corporate law rules that insulate boards from markets. And more recently, leading Delaware corporate law judges have indicated in off-the-bench analyses that the short-termist issue is something they take seriously as people with deep experience in corporate lawmaking and policy. This all leads us to the question posed here: Should short-termism weigh heavily, or at all, in corporate lawmaking today?

Management's attention to quarterly earnings is well known, inducing dubious, perhaps misleadingly illegal, shifts in sales and profits.[4] The question I pose here, though, is whether

---

[1] Martin Lipton, "Takeover Bids in the Target's Boardroom", 35 Bus. Law. 101, 104 (1979).

[2] E.g., Examining Short-Termism in Financial Markets: Hearing Before Senate Subcomm. on Econ. Policy of the Comm. on Banking, Hous. & Urban Affairs, 111th Cong. 2 (2010), available at http://www.gpo.gov/fdsys/pkg/CHRG-111shrg61654/pdf/CHRG-111shrg61654.pdf.

[3] Robert H. Hayes & William J. Abernathy, Managing Our Way to Economic Decline, Harv. Bus. Rev., July–Aug. 2007, at 67; Edmund S. Phelps, "Short-termism Is Undermining America", 27 New Persp. Q. 17 (2010).

[4] E.g., John Graham, Campbell R. Harvey, & Shiva Rajgopal, "Value Destruction and Financial Reporting Decisions", 62 Fin. Analysts J. 27, 31, 36–37 (2006) [hereinafter Graham et al., Value Destruction]; Alfred Rappaport, "The Economics of Short-Term Performance Obsession", 61 Fin. Analysts J. 65, 65–66 (2005).

such earnings management systemically degrades real investment and real economic activity, and, most pointedly, whether the policy tools available to courts making corporate law are appropriate for remedying the purported problem.

The short-termist argument is afflicted with five substantial debilities. First, one must evaluate the American economy from a system-wide perspective. The American economy is replete with venture capital markets, private equity markets, and many privately held firms. As long as venture capital markets, private equity markets, privately held firms, and similar conduits mitigate or reverse enough of any short-term tendencies in the public securities market, then the purported problem is not a systemic economic issue. We would have no corporate law reason to reorient the system to pick up one type of slack.

Second, the evidence that the stock market is, net, short-termist is inconclusive. There is indeed much evidence supporting the conclusion that it undervalues long-term value. But there is also much evidence that stock market sectors often overvalue the long term, most obviously in the intermittent bubbles in technology and other new industries. The lofty price-earnings multiples long accorded Amazon, Apple, and Google are suggestive of a market that appreciates the long term; the dot.com bubble of a decade ago suggests that the markets can over-value the long term. Hence, we cannot focus solely on evidence of short-termism in our evaluation, but must evaluate excessive long-termism as well. Intermittent over-valuation in the stock market is not a virtue, but its frequent occurrence tells us that the market is not uniformly short term. This over–under problem is what one would expect from an imperfect institution: sometimes it overshoots, sometimes it undershoots, and sometimes it is on target.

Third, mechanisms inside the corporation may well be important sources of short-term distortions and these internal distortions can be, and would be, exacerbated by insulating boards further from external financial markets. The CEO is still the most important decision maker inside the firm, and human psychology suggests that CEOs will typically want good results to occur on their watch, and prefer that poor results be pushed into the future, beyond their tenure. With average overall tenure for CEOs now at seven years, the typical CEO can expect about three more years at the top. Moreover, senior managers not yet at the top but with an eye on their future job prospects in the labor market want strong results before the next headhunter calls them. There is considerable evidence consistent with managerial distortions being a major source of short-term focus. Boards and managers may well have leeway in setting the horizon for compensation and that horizon may be shorter than it needs to be: the time duration for executive pay packages appears to be shorter than the duration of institutional investor holdings.

Fourth, courts are not well equipped to evaluate this kind of economic policy and should leave this task to other regulatory institutions that have better remedies available than courts do. Some, like the Federal Reserve and the US Treasury, are better positioned than courts to assess the extent, location, and capacity for lawmaking to ameliorate the purported problem. For reasons similar to those that underpin the business judgment rule, courts should be as reluctant to make economic policy decisions as they are to second-guess unconflicted board business decisions.

Fifth, the widely held view that short-term trading has increased dramatically in recent decades is unquestioned but may well misinterpret the data. The duration for holdings of the country's major stockholders, such as mutual funds at Fidelity and Vanguard, and major pension funds, has not shortened. Rather, a high-velocity trading fringe is moving stock rapidly through their computer systems. But these new high-velocity trading patterns do not affect the major stockholding institutions and, hence, should not yet affect corporate law thinking.

Each of these five problems with the short-termist view for corporate lawmaking is largely independent of the other four. Each could alone justify the view that courts and corporate lawmakers should not allow short-termism to join the considerations that go into the law-making balance. It is at least possible that the arguments proxy for a view that stakeholders should be better attended to, or that managers should have more autonomy generally. Regardless, the five together make the standard corporate governance case based on the view of excessive short-termism untenable.

2 THE INFLUENCE OF
THE SHORT-TERMIST ARGUMENT

In this section, I recount the persistent influence of the short-termist argument on corporate law policy thinking, particularly its implication that managers should be isolated from financial markets so that they may be free to pursue longer-term horizons. Of course, the long term is not to be preferred, just for its own sake, if it yields poorer returns and wastes resources. The short-termist view is rather that financial mechanisms induce corporate directors and managers to favor immediate but lower-value results over more profitable long-term results.

2.1 Takeovers in the Boardroom

Rapid trading in stock markets, with a diminishing breed of long-term holders, is thought to be the primary culprit in inducing too strong a focus on short-term results inside the corporation. Quarterly results trump long-term investment, particularly long-term technological development.[5] These pernicious effects of securities markets are then emphasized by those seeking to influence policy-making that would insulate managers and boards from markets. Thus, Martin Lipton, the corporate world's most prominent and persistent promoter of board autonomy over the decades, offered short-termism as a primary reason why hostile takeovers needed to be stopped. "It would not be unfair," he wrote in the well-known Business Lawyer article quoted above, "to pose the policy issue as: Whether the long-term interests of the nation's corporate system and economy should be jeopardized in order to

---

[5] See John R. Graham, Campbell R. Harvey, & Shiva Rajgopal, "The Economic Implications of Corporate Financial Reporting", 40 J. Acct. & Econ. 3, 5 (2005) [hereinafter Graham et al., Economic Implications] (78% of CFOs state in a survey that they would sacrifice some real value for smoother reported earnings); Kevin J. Laverty, "Economic 'Short-Termism': The Debate, the Unresolved Issues, and the Implications for Management Practice and Research", 21 Acad. Mgmt. Rev. 825, 831 (1996); James M. Poterba & Lawrence H. Summers, "A CEO Survey of U.S. Companies' Time Horizons and Hurdle Rates", MIT Sloan Mgmt. Rev., Fall 1995, at 43, available at http://sloanreview.mit.edu/article/a-ceo-survey-of-us-companies-time-horizons-and-hurdle-rates/.

benefit speculators interested . . . only in a quick profit . . .?"[6] Shareholder-induced corporate short-termism, he argued, threatened the overall health of the economy.[7] And he indicated that it still does: the first key issue facing boards in 2013 was that money managers "are wildly skewed to short-term results."[8]

And those views on shareholder short-termism, as reasons for managerial and board-room autonomy, were rebroadcast in the 1980s, the 1990s, and the last decade,[9] justifying board insulation from leveraged buyout pressures, from hedge fund activism, and from capital markets generally. The view justifies board autonomy from more market influence via five-year board terms. Overall, it is perhaps corporate law's longest-running modern re-frain: financial short-termism demands that managers and boards be further insulated from financial markets, with enhanced autonomy to resist market pressure for performance, for fear that the pressure will over-emphasize short-term results.

The issue has persisted in media and corporate discourse. Arthur Levitt and William Donaldson, chairs of the Securities and Exchange Commission, saw the securities markets' propensity to induce corporate short-termism as a problem needing public attention.[10] Prominent executives and corporate analysts have pushed forward parallel points.[11] Media attention to short-termism has further delegitimized the securities markets' influence on corporate decision making.

2.2 Current Views from the Delaware Judiciary

Today, the state corporate judiciary decides corporate election rules, the ease of insurgent proxy contests, and the rules governing the occasional takeover offers. Influential thinkers and decision makers in the Delaware corporate lawmaking structure have come to see the short-termist argument as important and as one that should influence corporate law election rules and electoral frequency. None has articulated this broad view in judicial decisions, but they have offered the power of the short-termist view in off-the-bench writings, with the ju-dicial attention to short-term horizons narrower and more transactional.[12] The thesis here is that although the subject is ripe for out-of-court consideration, it is not one that should

---

[6] Lipton, *supra* note 1, at 104.   [7] Id.

[8] Martin Lipton et al., Some Thoughts for Boards of Directors in 2013 (Dec. 31, 2012), available at https://corpgov.law.harvard.edu/2012/12/31/some-thoughts-for-boards-of-directors-in-2013/.

[9] For full citations, see Mark J. Roe, "Corporate Short-Termism—In the Boardroom and in the Courtroom", 68 Bus. Law. 977, 981–83 nn.9–11 (2013) [hereinafter Roe, Corporate Short-Termism].

[10] Arthur Levitt, Chairman, SEC, Speech at the Center of Law and Business, New York University: Renewing the Covenant with Investors (May 10, 2000), available at http://www.sec.gov/news/speech/spch370.html.

[11] Michael E. Porter, "Capital Disadvantage: America's Failing Capital Investment System", 70 Harv. Bus. Rev., Sept.–Oct. 1992, at 65; Robert Monks, Corporate "Catch-22", Wall St. J., Jan. 5, 1988, at 25; John G. Smale, What About Shareowner's Responsibility, Wall St. J., Oct. 16, 1987, at 28.

[12] See the discussion of *Airgas*, *infra* notes 42–47 and accompanying text.

influence on-the-bench thinking for election rules, proxy rules, and the rules governing takeovers.

Thus, Justice Jacobs of the Delaware Supreme Court seeks means by which Delaware's corporate law can bolster long-term investment capital,[13] justifying three-year board terms.[14] Leo Strine, as vice-chancellor of the Delaware Court of Chancery, viewed the short-termism problem as a "substantial policy dilemma."[15] "It is jejune," he said, "to demand that CEOs and boards manage for the long term when the stockholders who can replace them buy and sell based on short-term stock price movements, rather than the long-term prospects of firms."[16] And vice chancellor Laster recently argued that time horizon differences between blockholders and other shareholders could create serious conflicts of interest inside the boardroom.[17]

With important judges thinking in their extra-judicial analytics that short-termism is a problem and wondering whether corporate law could help combat the problem, we must consider whether the issue should affect corporate lawmaking more directly. I conclude here that it should not.[18]

[13] Jack B. Jacobs, "'Patient Capital': Can Delaware Corporate Law Help Revive It?", 68 Wash. & Lee L. Rev. 1645, 1661–63 (2011).

[14] William T. Allen, Jack B. Jacobs & Leo E. Strine, Jr., "The Great Takeover Debate: A Meditation on Bridging the Conceptual Divide", 69 U. Chi. L. Rev. 1067, 1096, 1100 (2002); Jacobs, *supra* note 13, at 1660 (reiterating that boards need more insulation from shareholder elections—to plan for the long term—via multi-year election terms).

[15] Leo E. Strine, Jr., "One Fundamental Corporate Governance Question We Face: Can Corporations Be Managed for the Long Term Unless Their Powerful Electorates Also Act and Think Long Term?", 66 Bus. Law. 1, 1–2 (2010) (hereinafter Strine, Fundamental Question) (Strine is now Delaware's chief justice; the article was written while he was a vice chancellor). "Many activist investors hold their stock for a very short period of time and may have the potential to reap profits based on short-term trading strategies that arbitrage corporate policies . . . . [T]here is a danger that activist stockholders will make proposals motivated by interests other than maximizing the long-term, sustainable profitability of the corporation." Id. at 8.

[16] Id. at 17.

[17] J. Travis Laster & John M. Zeberkiewicz, "The Rights and Duties of Blockholder Directors", 70 Bus. Law. 33, 50 (2015) ("[T]he blockholder director's duties to the corporation require that the director manage for the long term, while the blockholder director's duties to the investor require that the director manage for an exit"). See also *In re Trados Inc. S'holder Litig.*, 73 A.3d 17 (Del. Ch. 2013); Jack Bodner, Leonard Chazen, & Donald Ross, "Vice Chancellor Laster and the Long-Term Rule" (Mar. 11, 2015), http://corpgov.law.harvard.edu/2015/03/11/vice-chancellor-laster-and-the-long-term-rule/. As we see below in sections 4 and 5, the vice chancellor's conclusions here, like the other Delaware conclusions, do not comport with the overall evidence, which does not point to detrimental short-termism as on average afflicting blockholders and investors.

[18] The short-termism issue is not just American, but international. John Kay, The Kay Review of UK Equity Markets and Long-Term Decision Making: Final Report (July 2012), available at https://www.gov.uk/government/uploads/system/uploads/attachment_data/file/253454/bis-12-917-kay-review-of-equity-markets-final-report.pdf; OECD, Financial Market Trends: Long-Term Investment and Growth (2011).

3 The Short-Termist View

3.1 The Argument

The core short-termist concept is that because securities traders hold their stock for such a short duration, they look for strong corporate results only during the period they hold the corporation's stock so that they can sell profitably.[19] Many institutional investors, such as mutual funds, are afflicted with this short horizon because they seek to show strong short-run results so that they can attract new investors to their funds.[20] Pension fund managers seek good short-term results so that they can renew their management contracts and obtain new ones,[21] while hedge fund managers are often compensated on immediate results.[22] And because they cannot evaluate complex, long-term, technologically sophisticated information well, they rely on simple signals to evaluate the value of the corporate stock in their portfolio. Quarterly earnings results accordingly loom larger than they would otherwise because of their relative simplicity.[23]

For the trading argument to have traction, these stock market trading structures need a transmission mechanism into the corporation to affect corporate time horizons. That is, even if the short-term traders furiously moved a company's stock every nanosecond, managers could still be fully free to decide on corporate investments and time horizons, as the furious traders would typically pay no attention to the firm's horizons and would be incapable of intervening in corporate-governance decision making even if they paid attention. So more is needed—a transmission mechanism from the market to the boardroom.

In an earlier era, the transmission mechanism from short-term holding to corporate action was thought to be the hostile takeover. In the current era it would be shareholder activism and executive compensation, with boards more willing to fire CEOs if short-term financial results are poor, partly because directors fear for their own jobs or reputations. If senior management is compensated based on stock market returns, then management will tend to replicate the time horizons of the market. The end result would then be that boards and senior managers would forgo long-term value maximization for short-term results, all toward the end of pleasing the stock market.

By breaking the transmission mechanism (via longer election periods for directors or via greater managerial and board autonomy from the market), corporate leaders have sought to foster sensible long-term corporate behavior. Is this action wise?

---

[19] Rappaport, *supra* note 4, at 66 ("Today, the average holding period in professionally managed funds is less than a year and annual portfolio turnover is greater than 100%.").

[20] See Aspen Institute, Business & Society Program, Overcoming Short-termism: A Call for a More Responsible Approach to Investment and Business Management, Sept. 9, 2009, at 2, available at http://www.aspeninstitute.org/sites/default/files/content/docs/pubs/overcome_short_state0909_0.pdf.

[21] See id.; Jenny Anderson, Pension Funds Still Waiting for Big Payoff from Private Equity, N.Y. Times, Apr. 10, 2010, at B1.

[22] See Carl Ackermann, Richard McEnally, & David Ravenscraft, "The Performance of Hedge Funds: Risk, Return, and Incentives", 54 J. Fin. 833, 834 (1999).

[23] For sophisticated academic modeling of the phenomena, see Jeremy Stein, "Efficient Capital Markets, Inefficient Firms: A Model of Myopic Corporate Behavior", 104 Q. J. Econ. 655 (1989).

3.2 The Evidence in Favor

There is indeed hard evidence supporting the short-termist argument. Matched samples of privately held and publicly held firms show that the privately held firms invest more in their firm's operations than the publicly held half of the sample.[24] Matched samples of firms that went public and similar firms that did not show key personnel leaving the public firm shortly after the offering, which suggests an inability of the relevant firm to manage and create for the long term.[25] Corporate managers attuned to short-term thinking (as evidenced by their persistent reference to the short term in their communications with investors) had a short-term investor base with higher turnover than average. (Whether the first fact is caused by the second is not shown, but the possibility that causation runs from shareholder horizons to managerial orientation cannot be dismissed.[26]) Private equity funds with shorter time horizons invest in firms at a later development stage than those with a longer horizon.[27]

In addition, there is evidence that markets underestimate long-term corporate cash flows.[28] And there is evidence that mispriced public firms invest in line with the time horizons of their major investors.[29] Earnings management and earnings manipulation are regularly evidenced.[30] Initial public offers often use dual class stock, with insiders obtaining higher voting rights that insulate them from stock market pressure. More generally, corporate managers regularly bemoan the pressure from shareholders to produce strong quarterly results[31] and report in a prominent study that they would give up shareholder value to report better earnings.[32]

Thus we have the basic corporate argument for pernicious stock market short-termism and the evidence in its favor.

---

[24] John Asker, Joan Farre-Mensa, & Alexander Ljungqvist, "Corporate Investment and Stock Market Listing: A Puzzle?", 28 Rev. Fin. Stud. 342 (2015). Cf. Alex Edmans, "Short-Term Termination Without Deterring Long-Term Investment: A Theory of Debt and Buyouts", 102 J. Fin. Econ. 81 (2011) (blockholders incentivized to ascertain reasons for any poor short-term performance).

[25] Shai Bernstein, Does Going Public Affect Innovation? (Oct. 14, 2012) (unpublished manuscript) (available at www.ssrn.com/abstract=2061441).

[26] François Brochet, Maria Loumioti, & George Serafeim, "Speaking of the Short-Term: Disclosure Horizon and Managerial Myopia", 3 Rev. Acct. Stud. 1122 (2015).

[27] Jean-Noel Barrot, Investor Horizon and the Life Cycle of Innovative Firms: Evidence from Venture Capital (Dec. 2012) (unpublished manuscript) (available at www.ssrn.com/abstract=2024601).

[28] Angela Black & Patricia Fraser, "Stock Market Short-Termism—An International Perspective", 12 J. Multinational Fin. Mgmt. 135 (2002).

[29] François Derrien, Ambrus Keckés, & David Thesmar, "Investor Horizons and Corporate Policies", 48 J. Fin. Quant. Anal. 1755 (2013).

[30] Brian J. Bushee, "The Influence of Institutional Investors on Myopic Investment Behavior", 73 Acct. Rev. 305 (1998); Daniel A. Cohen et al., "Real and Accrual-Based Earnings Management in the Pre- and Post-Sarbanes Oxley Periods", 83 Acct. Rev. 757 (2008); Sugata Roychowdhury, "Earnings Management Through Real Activities Manipulation", 42 J. Acct. & Econ. 335 (2006).

[31] Graham et al., Economic Implications, *supra* note 5; Claire L. Marston & Barrie M. Craven, "A Survey of Corporate Perceptions of Short-Termism Among Analysts and Fund Managers", 4 Eur. J. Fin. 233 (1998).

[32] Graham et al., Value Destruction, *supra* note 4, at 31.

4 Difficulties with the Basic Argument: Concept

But the short-termist argument faces counter-arguments that largely neutralize the idea that fears of short-termism should bear weight in corporate lawmaking. One class of counter-arguments is primarily theoretical, the other primarily factual. As far as I can tell, several of these theoretical arguments that I present here are new to the discourse.[33]

4.1 Market Correctives

If short-term stock market pressures are inducing firms to give up value over the long run, then firms and markets would have incentives to develop institutions and mechanisms to facilitate that long-run profitability. Those that do will over the long run make more money. For example, if short-term trading reduced firms' time horizons perniciously, then some investors could profit by trading for the long term, by placing longer-term bets, and by developing credible mechanisms so that they will hold onto profitable long-term ventures. Such efforts may be incomplete in inducing the system to improve,[34] but the market system would have incentives to push in that direction. If small stockholders find it not to be worthwhile to evaluate long-term, complex information, then the market has incentives to produce mechanisms that facilitate larger block holdings for longer time periods. Persistent rules and politics stymieing such efforts are plausible, particularly in the United States, which has had a long history until recently of cutting finance down and keeping blockholders small, intermittent, and ineffective; I previously analyzed these rules as likely to hinder blockholder efforts to overcome the information transmission breakdowns.[35] But market incentives to counterbalance have arisen, even if restrained and insufficient.

Private equity could correct some short-termism. If the public markets are inducing a publicly held firm to be excessively short-term oriented, then private equity holders, often with time horizons of years, sometimes stretching toward a decade, could buy the company, take it off the public market, and reorient its business model toward the longer term. If a firm produced poor profits because it overly focused on quarterly results, the marketplace incentives would be to move the firm into private equity's hands, where the horizons are longer. For transactional examples that were widely reported in the business press, one can

---

[33] See Roe, Corporate Short-Termism, *supra* note 9.

[34] Andrei Shleifer & Robert W. Vishny, "The Limits of Arbitrage", 52 J. Fin. 35 (1997).

[35] See Mark J. Roe, Strong Managers, Weak Owners: The Political Roots of American Corporate Finance 19–49 (1994) [hereinafter Roe, Strong Managers, Weak Owners].

look to the private equity investments in Dollar General, a mass-market retailer, and Seagate Technologies.[36]

Aggregate data is consistent with private equity providing a longer-term alternative to public markets, when that alternative is useful. Firms that private equity takes private have increased patenting efforts in the target firms' core areas of strength.[37] An older study finds increased spending on research after firms are taken private.[38] These suggest a shorter-than-optimal public market; but they also point to an existing cure to the problem. And other studies find that higher inside block ownership is associated with more long-term investment.[39] A recent study shows that hedge fund ownership is associated with "better quality, higher impact innovations" than those in firms lacking hedge fund ownership.[40] Shareholder value holds up over the long term after activist hedge fund intervention.[41]

More generally, product market competition can partially correct short-term financial markets. For some excessive short-termism, the firm will find itself behind the curve technologically or otherwise at a later date. When it finds itself lagging, it will have the incentive to catch up.

4.2 Trade-Offs

If stock markets are indeed excessively inducing corporate short-termism, and if board and managerial isolation from financial markets is a partial solution, then unintended costs need to be accounted for in any cost–benefit analysis of a policy of insulating boards and managers from stock market influence, as there are obvious costs that come from further insulating them. If managers drift away from efficient, competitive behavior, financial markets can sting them into returning to a better corporate strategy. If boards and managers can freely dismiss market signals as the misguided views of short-term traders, if corporate policy makers bless that view, and if their blessing of that view leads to further isolation of boards and managers from markets, then the corrective could (1) go too far and (2) facilitate

---

[36] Josh Lerner, Morten Sorensen, & Per Strömberg, "Private Equity and Long-Run Investment: The Case of Innovation", 66 J. Fin. 445, 455–56 (2011).

[37] See discussion of the Dollar General and Seagate Technologies buyouts in Roe, Corporate Short-Termism, *supra* note 9, at 987–89.

[38] Frank R. Lichtenberg & Donald Siegel, "The Effects of Leveraged Buyouts on Productivity and Related Aspects of Firm Behavior", 27 J. Fin. Econ. 165 (1990).

[39] Jennifer Francis & Abbie Smith, "Agency Costs and Innovation: Some Empirical Evidence", 19 J. Acct. & Econ. 383 (1995) (management and block ownership associated with more indicators of innovation); James Mahoney, Chamu Sundaramurthy, & Joseph Mahoney, "The Effects of Corporate Antitakeover Provisions on Long-Term Investment: Empirical Evidence", 18 Managerial & Decision Econ. 349 (1997).

[40] Ying Wang & Jing Zhao, Hedge Funds and Corporate Innovations, 44 Fin. Mgmt. 353 (2015).

[41] Shane Goodwin, "Myopic Investor Debunked: The Long-Term Efficacy of Shareholder Advocacy in the Boardroom" (SSRN working paper, June 2014), available at www.ssrn.com/abstract=2450214; Lucian Bebchuk, Alon P. Brav, & Wei Jiang, "The Long-Term Effects of Hedge Fund Activism", 115 Colum. L. Rev. 1085 (2015); Lucian A. Bebchuk, "The Myth that Insulating Boards Serves Long-Term Value", 113 Colum. L. Rev. 1637 (2013).

managerial drift. These managerial agency costs are well known. The point here is that there is a trade-off of costs and benefits, even if the market turned out to be, net, short-term oriented.

4.3 Short-Termism in the Courtroom: Limits to Judicial Correctives

Is the courtroom an appropriate venue to consider short-termism? Proponents of board autonomy may well wish that short-termism be part of the judicial decision-making mix and could hope that, if the short-termist view proved to be persuasive in the courtroom, it would affect the atmospherics of corporate judicial decision making. Litigants have pressed that view on the Delaware Chancery Court.[42] However, although astute judges have sympathized with the short-termist view in off-the-bench analyses, the record does not indicate that the short-termist view is yet regularly being explicitly weighed in the corporate lawmaking. Still, with the off-the-bench statements common and clear, one has to assess whether off-the-bench thinking affects judicial courtroom perspectives that are not fully articulated.

Consider the recent *Airgas* takeover opinion, which was a major decision. It does display courtroom viability for the short-termism argument—rejected at first in the opinion and then seen to be relevant in the decisional mix.

The target firm defendants asserted in *Airgas* that the target's short-term stockholder base justified strong defensive antitakeover measures. Said Chancellor Chandler:

> Defendants' argument . . . [is] based on the particular composition of Airgas's stockholders (namely, its large "short-term" base). In essence, Airgas's argument is that "the substantial ownership of Airgas stock by these short-term, deal-driven investors poses a threat to the company and its shareholders."[43]

And

> [The defendants assert that the board should have more defensive room because of a] risk . . . that a majority of Airgas's [excessively short-term focused] stockholders . . . will tender into Air Products' offer despite its inadequate price tag, leaving the [longer-term] minority "coerced" into taking $70 as well.[44]

The Chancellor rejected this short-termist argument, at first: "The defendants do not appear to have come to grips with the fact that the [short-term] arbs bought their shares from long-term stockholders who viewed the increased market price generated by Air Products' offer as a good time to sell."[45]

The Chancellor's strong rejection of the time horizons argument, however, did not persist to the opinion's conclusion. He ultimately ruled for the defendants and, with time horizons in mind, he turned the defendants' assertion into a question: Were enough stockholders "so 'focused on the short-term' that they would 'take a smaller harvest in the swelter of

---

[42] See *Air Prods. & Chems., Inc. v. Airgas, Inc.*, 16 A.3d 48, 108–09 (Del. Ch. 2011).
[43] Id. at 108.   [44] Id. at 109.   [45] Id. at 108–09 (footnotes omitted).

August over a larger one in Indian Summer?'" he asked, quoting the defendants.[46] Yes, he concluded: Both sides' experts testified that the short-term arbitrageurs would tender "regardless of whether the price is inadequate," even if it failed to reflect the company's long-term value.[47] The rhetoric of short-termism was in play in *Airgas*, in the context of a takeover.

Courts are not the right institution to do this kind of economic policy making. Consider that the judicial deference embedded in the business judgment rule is based largely on the presumption that judges are poorly positioned to make, or to second-guess, board-room business decisions. The corporate judiciary ought to be even more reluctant to assess whether the corporate economy is too short term, too long term, or just right. Even a state legislature, with its parochial funding concerns, is ill-placed to make such judgments be-yond firms operating primarily within the state's own borders. To allow short-termism issues into the courtroom is to facilitate a type of business and economic engineering that the best business judges rightly decline to do in more compelling situations, such as that of a single mistaken business decision for a firm.[48]

Other institutions and other policy makers are better suited to assess how well the economy is handling time horizons. Moreover, other policy avenues beyond corporate law-making, such as tax policy or policy on ownership structure, are better suited to handle any short-termism, if policy makers conclude that stunted horizons are real and pernicious.

On ownership structure and short-termism, a long-standing view has seen impediments to large blockholding as inducing more short-termism than is optimal, particularly because some information travels badly from inside the firm to diffuse public markets. Blockholders, I have previously argued, could better handle complex, technological, and subtle informa-tion than diffuse stock markets. They could signal to public stock markets the blockholder's view that a managerial long-term decision was good for shareholder value.[49] Says the global managerial director of McKinsey & Company in discussing the problems of short-termism, "[t]he most effective ownership structure tends to combine some exposure in the public markets (for the discipline and capital access that exposure helps provide) with a significant, committed, long-term owner."[50]

---

[46] Id. at 111.   [47] Id. at 111–12.

[48] Even favored corporate structural solutions, like giving long-term shareholders greater voice in the corporation, see Colin Mayer, Firm Commitment (2013); Julia Werdigier, A Call for Corporations to Focus on the Long Term, N.Y. Times Dealbook, May 14, 2012, available at http://dealbook.nytimes.com/2012/05/14/group-calls-on-companies-to-focus-on-long-term-goals/, can readily backfire. Jesse M. Fried, "The Uneasy Case for Favoring Long-Term Shareholders", 124 Yale L.J. 1554 (2015).

[49] For blockholder suppression as increasing the short-term problem, see Roe, Strong Managers, Weak Owners, *supra* note 35, at 240–47. For the concept that diffusion erodes complex information flow, see Stein, *supra* note 23. For evidence associating blockholders with more long-term innovation, see Julian Atanassov, "Do Hostile Takeovers Stifle Innovation? Evidence from Antitakeover Legislation and Corporate Patenting", 68 J. Fin. 1097 (2013). For the idea that even blockholders who trade can encourage long-term investments by processing information more effectively than small shareholders, see Alex Edmans, "Blockholder Trading, Market Efficiency, and Managerial Myopia", 64 J. Fin. 2481 (2009).

[50] Dominic Barton, Capitalism for the Long Term, Harv. Bus. Rev., Mar. 2011, at 85, 90.

4.4 Regulatory Correctives

Consider, moreover, that the other remedy that has often been prominently touted over the years has been a Tobin tax on rapid trading. When policy thinkers such as Joseph Stiglitz, Lawrence Summers, or the blue-ribbon Aspen Institute have considered short-term stock markets a problem, they have turned to a Tobin tax as the appropriate mechanism to reduce short-termism, not to using corporate law to increase board and managerial insulation.[51]

Thus, three of the most prominent policy measures to reduce unwarranted short-termism have been a Tobin tax on securities trading, a sliding-scale capital gains tax tied to the length of the holding period, and facilitating more and larger blockholders. The corporate judiciary and state legislatures constructing corporate law cannot implement most such measures, and cannot well assess whether such measures would be the best means to mitigate any securities market short-termism.

5 Difficulties with the Basic Short-Termist Argument: Facts

The short-termist theory faces offsetting facts, which make it unwise to place much weight on the theory for corporate policy making. First, even if the stock market is excessively short-run focused and even if there are transmission mechanisms that bring excessively short-term financial markets' time horizons into corporate decision making, policy makers need to see the American economic system as a whole, where there are counter-measures. Second, there is considerable evidence of stock market long-termism. Third, substantial, albeit unheralded, sources of excessive short-termism come from inside the corporation. The average duration for executive compensation appears to be shorter than the average duration of institutional-investor stock-market holdings, for example. Fourth, the purported shortening of investor holding periods during recent decades may be exaggerated. Fifth, the new short-termism, if it exists, may be an appropriate reaction to changes in the economic environment: more rapid technological change, increased globalization, and government short-term policies. If the facts of the firm's basic business surroundings are changing more quickly than ever, the firm's business horizons should indeed change and become shorter.

I take each of these in turn.

5.1 The Economic System

Alternatives to public ownership can be structured to plan for the long term: venture capital markets and private equity markets; privately held firms; and government financing of

---

[51] See Aspen Inst., *supra* note 20; Joseph E. Stiglitz, "Using Tax Policy to Curb Short-Term Trading", 3 J. Fin. Services Research 101, 109 (1989); Lawrence H. Summers & Victoria P. Summers, "When Financial Markets Work too Well: A Cautious Case for a Securities Transactions Tax", 3 J. Fin. Services Research 261, 272 (1989).

long-term research, to name the basics.[52] If these alternative economic institutions provide much of the long-term orientation that securities markets purportedly do not, and if securities markets provide substantial other benefits—in diversification, liquidity, and aggregation of capital from disparate investors—then the system's complementarity may make the short-termism problem a problem for one firm or another, but not a problem for the American economy overall.

True, these sectors may not be big enough. Or they may not be long-term enough—venture capital and private equity often have horizons of five to ten years. Perhaps that is not long enough. Privately held firms may weaken as their founders age. Governments make mistakes. The point is not that these institutions are fail-safe but that they are offsets, and often substantial offsets.

5.2 Stock Market Long-Termism

The substantial evidence of financial market long-termism tends to be ignored in this debate, although public firms are often overinvesting compared to their private counterparts.[53] Financial economists return results that are inconsistent with institutional investors causing corporate short-termism. "Indeed," say two prominent researchers, "we document a positive relation between industry-adjusted expenditures for [property, plant, and equipment] and R&D and the fraction of shares owned by institutional investors."[54] After analyzing "corporate expenditures for property, plant and equipment (PP&E) and research and development (R&D) for over 2500 US firms," they conclude that "[w]e find no support for the contention that institutional investors cause corporate managers to behave myopically."[55] In industries dependent on outside capital, public firms "generate patents of higher quantity, quality, and novelty compared to their private counterparts."[56] And again, "[c]ontrary to the view that institutional ownership induces a short-term focus in managers, we find that their presence boosts innovation."[57] Particularly when managers are less entrenched, the authors find, institutions induce the firm to innovate more effectively.

---

[52] On government research funding, see Mariana Mazzucato, The Entrepreneurial State: Debunking Public vs. Private Sector Myths (2013).

[53] Sreedhar T. Bharath, Amy K. Dittmar, & Jagadeesh Sivadasan, Does Capital Market Myopia Affect Plant Productivity? Evidence from Going Private Transactions (Dec. 2010) (unpublished manuscript) (available at www.ssrn.com/abstract=1735508). Overinvestment would map to a long-standing critique of managerial incentives in public firms, evidencing not pernicious short-termism but empire-building, excessive continuance in dying industries, and excessive long-termism.

[54] Sunil Wahal & John J. McConnell, "Do Institutional Investors Exacerbate Managerial Myopia?", 6 J. Corp. Fin. 307, 307 (2000).

[55] Id.

[56] Viral V. Acharya & Zhaoxia Xu, Financial Dependence and Innovation: The Case of Public Versus Private Firms, 124 J. Fin. Econ. 223 (2017). For industries that do not depend on outside capital, the private firms do no better than the public ones.

[57] Philippe Aghion, John Van Reenen, & Luigi Zingales, "Innovation and Institutional Ownership", 103 Am. Econ. Rev. 277, 302 (2013).

Companies whose managers' compensation is tied to volatile stock prices overinvest in R&D, compared to companies whose managers' compensation is not so closely linked.[58] The bulk of the studies show institutional ownership to be associated with higher R&D intensity;[59] firms that become more insulated from financial markets reduce long-term R&D investments.[60] Takeover protection has been one of the most prominent policy prescriptions induced by those who see stock-market-induced short-termism as a serious problem. If the prescription were on average correct, then isolating boards and management from takeovers would lead to higher R&D and other results. But, although two studies are consistent with this view,[61] as many or more studies do not find such increases following takeover protection.[62] The most recent extensive studies on the issue find that patents and innovation

[58] Carl Hsin-Han Shen & Hao Zhang, "CEO Risk Incentives and Firm Performance Following R&D Increases", 37 J. Banking & Fin. 1176 (2013). The influence of the stock market here may well be pernicious, by inducing managers to overinvest in less-than-profitable R&D, so as to falsely signal good corporate prospects. But the point is that the stock market is not facilitating R&D cuts—the usual short-termist bête noir—but inducing greater R&D, contrary to the short-termist prediction.

[59] Gary S. Hansen & Charles W. Hill, "Are Institutional Investors Myopic? A Time-Series Study of Four Technology-Driven Industries", 12 Strategic Mgmt. J. 1 (1991). To the same effect: Yixing Tong & Feida Zhang, "Does the Capital Market Punish Managerial Myopia?" (SSRN working paper, Feb. 2014), available at http://researchrepository.murdoch.edu.au/id/eprint/22202/; Barry D. Baysinger, Rita D. Kosnick, & Thomas A. Turk, "Effects of Board and Ownership Structure on Corporate R&D Strategy", 34 Acad. Mgmt. J. 205, 205–14 (1991); Li Eng & Margaret Shackell, "The Implications of Long-Term Performance Plans and Institutional Ownership for Firms' Research and Development (R&D) Investments", 16 J. Acct., Audit. & Fin. 117 (2001); Jennifer Francis & Abbie Smith, "Agency Costs and Innovation: Some Empirical Evidence", 19 J. Acct. & Econ. 383 (1995); Peggy M. Lee & Hugh M. O'Neill, "Ownership Structures and R&D Investments of U.S. and Japanese Firms: Agency and Stewardship Perspectives", 46 Acad. Mgmt. J. 212, 212–25 (2003).

[60] "[Our] results contradict the managerial myopia hypothesis: firms significantly decrease R&D intensity relative to industry R&D intensity following an antitakeover amendment." Lisa K. Meulbroek, Mark L. Mitchell, J. Harold Mulherin, Jeffry M. Netter, & Annette B. Poulsen, "Shark Repellents and Managerial Myopia: An Empirical Test", 98 J. Pol. Econ. 1108, 1115 (1990). A noticeable part of the finance literature on short-termism depends on the firm sensitivity to state-based takeover rules and charter terms. There is good reason to find this literature even more indeterminate than the text argues, as using state antitakeover legislation as a variable is questionable. Emiliano M. Catan & Marcel Kahan, "The Law and Finance of Anti-Takeover Statutes", 68 Stan. L. Rev. 629 (2016). It's questionable because since the early 1990s, all American firms have a "shadow poison pill," in that they, even if there is no antitakeover legislation and even if the firm has not put antitakeover tactics in place in advance, ward off most takeovers by putting in a poison pill at the last minute. John C. Coates, "Takeover Defenses in the Shadow of the Pill: A Critique of the Scientific Evidence", 79 Tex. L. Rev. 271 (2000).

[61] William N. Pugh, Daniel E. Page, & John S. Jahera, Jr., "Antitakeover Charter Amendments: Effects on Corporate Decisions", 15 J. Fin. Res. 57 (1992); Ali R. Malekzadeh, Victoria B. McWilliams, & Nilanjan Sen, "Antitakeover Amendments, Ownership Structure, and Managerial Decisions: Effects on R&D Expenditure" (Working Paper, St. Cloud State University, 2005), available at https://pdfs.semanticscholar. org/5aa2/cd98fef4387a5e7535204f8a89342002b19b.pdf?_ga=2.5073331.1844801519.1520300575-1062556537.1520300575. Cf. Andrei Shleifer & Lawrence H. Summers, Breach of Trust in Hostile Takeovers, in Corporate Takeovers: Causes and Consequences 33 (Alan J. Auerbach ed., 1988) (lower managerial incentives to invest in innovation, managerial effort, and firm-wide human capital when shareholders have strong takeover power).

[62] Ravi Jain & Sonia Wasan, "Adoption of Antitakeover Legislation and R&D Expenditure", 6 Inv. Mgmt. & Fin. Innovations 63 (2009); Mark S. Johnson & Ramesh P. Rao, "The Impact of Antitakeover Amendments on Corporate Financial Performance", 32 Fin. Rev. 659 (1997); Paul Mallette,

decrease "for firms incorporated in states that pass antitakeover laws relative to firms incorporated in states that do not."[63]

Consider the regular, but intermittent high valuations accorded to one sector or another of the financial market. At the very beginning of the twenty-first century, there was a boom, many now say bubble, in internet stocks.[64] New companies arose, went public, and were accorded high—sometimes astronomical—valuations.[65] These high valuations can be, and should be, interpreted as stock market long-termism. The market was valuing firms with no immediate earnings as very good investment prospects. Indeed, analysts concluded that many high-tech, dot.com firms would have needed to grow at unprecedented rates for the high prices of the late 1990s to be accurately predicting long-term prices.[66] Stock market beneficiaries of the concomitant rising equity prices invested more in capital—i.e., more in the long term—than they otherwise would have.[67] The "run-up in equity prices allowed for new projects to be undertaken by these [high-priced] firms—projects that otherwise would likely be underfunded."[68]

Nor were the dot.com bubble and its concomitant market overvaluation unique. Railroads, automobiles, the telephone, and plastics have at various times been overvalued.[69] Of course, these bubbles and their manifestation of excessive long-termism are not testimonials to our having an efficacious stock market. They are themselves problems. The point is not that markets are therefore efficient, or even that they are good. The point of overvaluation is that it fits better with a market that is giving excessive weight to the long term. It is not short-term.[70]

More prosaically, analysts sympathetic to the short-termist viewpoint should focus on the planning horizons for firms that must focus on returns over decades. Oil production companies, for example, invest in oil fields that will produce for multiple decades, often over a good fraction of a century.[71] These firms are disproportionately public firms with scattered,

"Antitakeover Charter Amendments: Impact on Determinants of Future Competitive Position", 17 J. Mgmt. 769 (1991).

[63] Atanassov, *supra* note 49; Mahoney, Sundaramurthy, & Mahoney, *supra* note 39, at 349 ("This paper's empirical results indicate that the average effect of antitakeover provisions on subsequent long-term investment is negative."); Meulbroek et al., *supra* note 60. Again, weaknesses afflict studies using antitakeover provisions in this way, which is common in finance. See *supra* note 61.

[64] John M. Griffin, Jeffrey H. Harris, Tao Shu, & Selim Topaloglu, "Who Drove and Burst the Tech Bubble?", 66 J. Fin. 1251, 1284 (2001).

[65] See Robert J. Hendershott, "Net Value: Wealth Creation (and Destruction) During the Internet Boom", 10 J. Corp. Fin. 281, 282 (2004); Alexander Ljungqvist & William J. Wilhelm, Jr., "IPO Pricing in the Dot-Com Bubble", 58 J. Fin. 723, 723 (2003).

[66] Eli Ofek & Matthew Richardson, "Dot.com Mania: The Rise and Fall of Internet Stock Prices", 58 J. Fin. 1113 (2003); Eli Ofek & Matthew Richardson, "The Valuation and Market Rationality of Internet Stock Prices", 18 Oxford Rev. Econ. Pol'y 265 (2002). But cf. Lubos Pastor & Petro Veronesi, "Was There a Nasdaq Bubble in the Late 1990s?", 81 J. Fin. Econ. 61 (2006).

[67] Murillo Campello & John R. Graham, "Do Stock Prices Influence Corporate Decisions? Evidence from the Technology Bubble", 107 J. Fin. Econ. 89 (2013); Michael Jensen, "Agency Costs of Overvalued Equity", 34 Fin. Mgmt. 5 (2005).

[68] Campello & Graham, *supra* note 67.   [69] Jensen, *supra* note 67, at 6 n.5.

[70] The end-of-bubble psychology might be interpreted as short-termist, when the investor expects the bubble to burst shortly. Long-term lofty price–earnings ratios for Amazon and other companies cannot be so easily reinterpreted.

[71] Brian Hicks & Chris Nelder, Profit from the Peak: The End of Oil and the Greatest Investment Event of the Century 23 (2008).

trading stockholders. At the same time, the bond market has historically had little problem in making long-term financing commitments to much of the American economy.[72]

5.3 Short-Termism Inside the Corporation

Short-termism can arise inside the corporation and can do so in ways that would be exacerbated by insulating boards further from markets.

The first intuition is simple: The CEO is still the most influential corporate decision maker in most large public firms. It is basic human nature that the CEO will want good results to come to fruition during his or her tenure. With the average CEO's tenure at about seven years,[73] many CEOs could well think that there are only a few years left to their time as CEO. They have personal reasons to emphasize projects that will have good results during those few years, as a matter of personal pride.[74] Older CEOs put their firms on a low-risk path when their firms become more insulated from shareholder influence (while younger CEOs do the opposite).[75] Older CEOs reduce research and development as well as their firm's overall riskiness by diversifying more.[76] While some of these CEOs may worry that they will be replaced by powerful shareholders, an equally logical hypothesis is that they favor short-term results because they want results to be good before they retire. A "one standard deviation increase in CEO age decreases [a measure of R&D intensity] by almost 20%."[77]

---

[72] Cláudia Custódio, Miguel A. Ferreira, & Luís Laureano, "Why Are US Firms Using More Short-Term Debt?", 108 J. Fin. Econ. 182, 182, 211 (2013). They find that debt markets have become less willing to finance long-term operations than previously. They link the shortening debt maturity largely to the increasing number of new, smaller, riskier firms accessing the bond market. This suggests an issue that is not one for corporate law courts but is one that arises from the changing nature of the economy.

[73] Steven N. Kaplan & Bernadette A. Minton, "How Has CEO Turnover Changed?", 12 Int'l. Rev. Fin. 57, 58 (2012) (seven years in the 1992 to 2007 period; six from 2000 to 2007).

[74] Id. at 67. The problem is more complex and causation need not be one way. Financial markets could press firms to produce results, which in turn could press boards to fire CEOs more frequently, which in turn could press CEOs to emphasize immediate firm performance. But the fact that older CEOs seem more susceptible to under-investment suggests that some of the cause emanates from the CEO, in that older CEOs are more likely to expect their current position to be their last.

[75] Jon A. Garfinkel, Jaewoo Kim, & Kyeong Hun Lee, The Interactive Influence of External and Internal Governance on Risk Taking and Outcomes: The Importance of CEO Career Concerns (Aug. 2013) (unpublished manuscript) (available at http://ssrn.com/abstract=2171005).

[76] Matthew A. Serfling, "CEO Age and the Riskiness of Corporate Policies", 25 J. Corp. Fin. 251 (2014).

[77] Jaideep Chowdhury, Managerial Myopia: A New Look 6 (Jan. 24, 2012) (unpublished manuscript) (available at http://ssrn.com/abstract=1991429) ("[F]aced with [a] one unit increase in growth opportunities[,] there is a 35.29% drop in the increase in investments when there is [a] one standard deviation increase in CEO age. My results point[] to significant deviations from optimal investments as CEO[s age].". For theory consistent with the idea that younger CEOs will invest more than older ones, see Canice Prendergast & Lars Stole, "Impetuous Youngsters and Jaded Old-Timers: Acquiring a Reputation for Learning", 104 J. Pol. Econ. 1105, 1126 (1996); Xiaoyang Li, Angie Low, & Anil Makhija, "Career Concerns and the Busy Life of the Young CEO", 47 J. Corp. Fin. 88 (2017). For theory that younger CEOs will invest less, see Bengt Holmström, "Managerial Incentive Problems: A Dynamic Perspective", 66 Rev. Econ. Stud. 169, 179 (1999); David S. Scharfstein & Jeremy C. Stein, "Herd Behavior and Investment", 80 Am. Econ. Rev. 465, 476 (1990).

Several empirical studies show entrenched, older CEOs investing less than younger ones.[78] These results suggest that enhancing CEO autonomy from financial markets will lead to more short-termism, not less. One study, for example, finds that CEOs increase their firms' research and development spending during their first year as CEO, and reduce it in their final years as CEO.[79] Managers not at the top of the firm but who are mobile want to show good short-term results to managerial labor markets.[80] This is short-termism, and potentially pernicious short-termism, but it originates in managerial labor markets, not stock markets. And internal organizational metrics can overemphasize immediate results.[81] Lastly here, overconfident managers, who abound at the top, suggest several authors, "are likely to delay recognition of losses . . . , [perceiving] poorly performing negative NPV projects . . . as positive NPV projects."[82]

Overall, there is considerable evidence that the internal organizational structure of the large firm is a source of significant short-term impulses. More prosaically, boards and executives do have capacity to design longer-term compensation contracts to mitigate market features they see as deleteriously short-term, if they wish to.[83]

A commonly cited short-termist mechanism is that corporate managers are unable to communicate complex or technological information to a diffusely held market of nonexperts. But if this is a primary problem, a significant improvement could come from rules that facilitated blockholders in the large American corporation instead of impeding these blocks from forming, persisting, and participating in corporate governance. Such blockholders would have incentives to process the more complex information that distant, smaller stockholders cannot readily process and understand.[84] That the core cure that is promoted is often to insulate boards from stockholders, by according boards greater autonomy, and not to facilitate more blockholding[85] or lengthen the duration of executive

---

[78] Yakov Amihud & Baruch Lev, "Risk Reduction as a Managerial Motive for Conglomerate Mergers", 12 Bell J. Econ. 605, 609 (1981); Marianne Bertrand & Sendhil Mullainathan, "Enjoying the Quiet Life? Corporate Governance and Managerial Preferences", 111 J. Pol. Econ. 1043, 1072 (2003); Paul A. Gompers, Joy L. Ishii, & Andrew Metrick, "Corporate Governance and Equity Prices", 118 Q.J. Econ. 107, 133 (2003); Li, Low & Makhija, *supra* note 77; Andrei Shleifer & Robert W. Vishny, "Management Entrenchment: The Case of Manager-Specific Investments", 25 J. Fin. Econ. 123, 125 (1989).

[79] Patricia Dechow & Richard Sloan, "Executive Incentives and the Horizon Problem: An Empirical Investigation", 14 J. Acct. & Econ. 51, 52 (1991).

[80] Tim S. Campbell & Anthony M. Marino, "Myopic Investment Decisions and Competitive Labor Markets", 35 Int'l. Econ. Rev. 855, 858 (1994); Bengt Holmström & Joan Ricart i Costa, "Managerial Incentives and Capital Management", 101 Q. J. Econ. 835, 841 (1986); M.P. Naryanan, "Managerial Incentives for Short-Term Results", 40 J. Fin. 1469, 1470 (1985); Richard P. Rumelt, Theory, Strategy and Entrepreneurship, in The Competitive Challenge 137 (David J. Teece ed., 1987).

[81] Laverty, *supra* note 5, at 831–32, 840–47; Kevin J. Laverty, "Managerial Myopia or Systemic Short-Termism? The Importance of Managerial Systems in Valuing the Long Term", 42 Mgmt. Decision 949 (2004).

[82] Anwer S. Ahmed & Scott Duellman, "Managerial Overconfidence and Accounting Conservatism", 51 J. Acct. Res. 1, 2 (2013).

[83] Cf. Brian D. Cadman, Tjomme O. Rusticus, & Jayanthi Sunder, Stock Option Grant Vesting Terms: Economic and Financial Reporting Determinants, 18 Rev. Acct. Stud. 1159 ("Vesting schedules are longer in growth firms where lengthening the executive's investment horizon is more important and . . . firms with more powerful CEOs and weaker governance grant options with shorter vesting periods.").

[84] This is the view I offered in Roe, Strong Managers, Weak Owners, *supra* note 35, at 240–47.

[85] See Lipton, *supra* note 1.

compensation, makes it plausible that for some adherents the excessive short-termist theory is proxying for a more general managerialist view of what makes the corporation run well.

5.4 Interpretive Error?

It is a widely held view that the holding duration of equity has dramatically shortened in recent decades. Trading volume is up and traders' average holding periods are down. Those developments make even the limited shareholder attention span of the 1970s flicker as shareholders buy and sell, in this view. Program traders can move much stock through the system in microseconds.

For example, Delaware's judicial leader, Leo Strine, when chief of the chancery court, where the country's major corporate litigation usually transpires, bemoans stock churning and the rapid turnover of a typical public company's stockholder base.[86] Short-termism and stock turnover are being taken as serious corporate issues by important corporate policy makers.

As we have seen, however, churning would not in itself be dispositive for a short-termist view for corporate lawmaking, if (1) short-term trading did not much affect corporate decision making because, say, no transmission mechanism brought those trading horizons into the firm's decision-making process, (2) there were sufficient market correctives if it did affect corporate decision making, or (3) the costs of correction were too high. The prior three sections discuss these three possibilities. This section discusses a fourth reason for continued reticence in corporate lawmaking here—that interpreting the market turnover data as showing a shortening duration for America's core stockholders may well be erroneous. Its duration may not even be shortening.

Consider this possibility: Starting in 1985, 100 shareholders each hold 100 shares of the XYZ Corporation for three years. They sell their shares, after holding onto them for three years, to other investors, who in turn hold their shares for three years and then resell them. The average, median holding duration for each 100-share shareholder is three years.

Thereafter, by 2013, 10 of those 100 shareholders become active traders. These active traders sell their shares every four months to a new set of shareholders. For this group we have 10 holders every four months, 30 holders every year, and 90 holders every three years. For 90 holders, the average duration of ownership is four months. For another 90 holders, the average duration is still three years. One might be tempted then to say that for the entire stock of 180 holders of XYZ stock during the past year, the average duration for holding was only 20 months, while in the good old days it was 36 months. Holding duration has nearly halved.

These statements would be accurate counts, but the question is whether they are the best way to interpret the changing holding duration for policy-making purposes. For 90% of the shareholder mass, their turnover period and their holding duration are just as they always have been. For 90% of the shareholders, nothing has changed and their holding period has not shortened.

---

[86] Strine, Fundamental Question, *supra* note 15, at 10, 11, 17. Strine is now chief justice of the state's supreme court.

This analytical problem is hardly unique to short-termism. When a distribution is skewed and not symmetrical, the average—the mean—can fail to describe properly the population and its change over time.

Emerging evidence suggests that this interpretive consideration is in play for the duration of stock ownership in the United States. For example, two of America's primary shareholders—Fidelity and Vanguard—have holding durations that have not budged since 1985.[87] The overall holding duration for mutual funds and pension funds—America's core stockholder class—increased during the quarter century from 1985 to 2010.[88] These institutional investor holding durations seem to exceed the managers' time-to-realization—the duration—for executive pay.[89]

The authors of the stock holding duration study report that they investigated "institutional investors' holding durations since 1985 and find that holding durations have been stable and, if anything, slightly lengthened over time." In 1985, the average duration for stock holding in the United States was 1.2 years; in 2010 it had increased to 1.5 years.[90] This data erodes the typical short-termist factual foundation on directionality.

True, even if this reinterpretation of the data trends comes to be seen as accurate, the short-termist view can persist, but it would have to be recast. The typical holding duration has not shortened, short-termists would concede, but they could contend that it is still too short-term now, just as it was too short before. So, as a policy matter, shareholders must be neutered from corporate governance influence. And, even if shareholders' typical holding duration is somewhat less short-term today than in the 1980s, they might argue, their corporate strength and influence have changed. Proponents of the short-termist view would argue that shareholders have become more powerful—staggered boards are largely gone, many firms have majority voting, SEC rules favor shareholder voice, and hedge funds allow some shareholders influence that disaggregated holdings do not. Others would argue the contrary—that the central governance event of the past quarter century was the hostile takeover's demise, with offsetting shareholder gains in strength being pale, weak substitutes for the lost takeover.[91]

---

[87] Martijn Cremers, Ankur Pareek, & Zacharias Sautner, Stock Duration and Misvaluation, at 11 (Feb. 14, 2013) (unpublished manuscript) ("While [s]tock [d]uration lengthened [from 1985 to 2010], share turnover has substantially increased from 72% per year . . . to 276% per year.").

[88] Id. at 44. From less than a year for pension funds to over two years, and from just over a year for mutual funds to just under 1.5 years.

[89] Compare Radhakrishnan Gopalan, Todd Milbourn, Fenghua Song, & Anjan V. Thakar, "Duration of Executive Compensation", 69 J. Fin. 2777, 2793–95 (2014) ("[T]he average total compensation for an executive in our sample is $2,214,425, which comprises $447,365 of salary, $143,252 of bonus, $908,969 of stock options, and $711,228 of restricted stock . . . . The average executive pay duration in our sample is 1.218 years. Thus, executive pay vests on average about one year after it is granted.") With Cremers et al., *supra* note 87 (duration of stock holding increased somewhat from 1985 to 2010).

[90] Id. at 3. The study, however, would not pick up intra-quarterly trading, as it tracks the persistence of holdings, quarter to quarter (as the holding data is available only for end-of-quarter reports). Round-trip trading inside a quarter would not diminish the measured duration number.

[91] One might logically critique the text's distinction if the program traders were the marginal corporate governance players, so that shareholders had become more powerful and the program traders were the new powers in corporate governance. But this is not so. Program traders do not participate in governance. Short-term theorists might counter that executive compensation is tied to stock price and short-term traders set the stock's price. But, if this is so, then the short-term problems lie inside the firm, as compensation could be tied to other measures or to longer-term stock price averages.

People could disagree here on the overall direction of shareholder power, but the point is that this disagreement is a very different argument from one that says that shareholders have been becoming more short-term over the past quarter century and that corporate America needs a remedy for the shortening of that duration. The most recent data analysis suggests the contrary.

5.5 More Powerful Core Causes? Speeding Technology, Increasing Globalization, and Unstable Government Policy

Whether or not stock markets are moving faster, the world is moving faster in the twenty-first century than it moved in the twentieth. Technological change is faster, the Internet is destroying old distribution systems, computers change how business is done, and modern telecommunications make global markets local. International trade more quickly hits local businesses that were once isolated from world markets. Government policies—whether it is the American fiscal cliff or the European potential for an imploding euro—make it hard for businesses to plan for the long term.

Keep in mind again that conventional long-term production requiring massive investment does happen in large public firms: shale oil and gas are being produced for the long term,[92] as are oil and gas from conventional fields that must be developed with infrastructure investment requiring 30- or 40-year horizons. These investments do not support the idea that the stock market cannot handle the very long term.

But other investments do not have the same long-term luxury. Consider the speed of technological change. Earlier we noted that financial markets have not deterred major technological firms from their tasks. Amazon, Apple, and Google come to mind as public companies with a focus on innovation and the long term.

> Amazon's CEO is aggressive on the issue. In 1997, the year Amazon.com went public, its chief executive, Jeff Bezos, issued a manifesto: "It's all about the long term," he said. He warned shareholders "we may make decisions and weigh tradeoffs differently than some companies" and urged them to make sure that a long-term approach "is consistent with your investment policy." Amazon's management and employees "are working to build something important, something that matters to our customers, something that we can tell our grandchildren about," he added.[93]

There is also a reverse side to the disruption wrought by rapid technological change, such as that which Amazon has pursued. Critics might look at bricks-and-mortar bookstores that fail to expand, invest, and discover new means to market their business. If the companies are public, critics might blame public markets for that unwillingness to invest. But the underlying problem may well be simpler, in that technological changes are eroding the viability of such firms' business models.

---

[92] World Energy Council, 2010 Survey of Energy Resources 92 (2010), available at http://www.worldenergy.org/wp-content/uploads/2012/09/ser_2010_report_1.pdf.

[93] James B. Stewart, Amazon Says Long Term and Means It, N.Y. Times, Dec. 17, 2011, at B1. Cf. Amar Bhide, Efficient Markets, Deficient Governance, Harv. Bus. Rev., Nov.–Dec. 1994, at 128, 135.

Finally here, consider the reported corporate reaction to the risks emanating from uncertainty about government policy and from the deepening inability of Washington to effectively address economic issues.[94] "At Vanguard, [the large mutual fund complex,] we estimate that policy uncertainty has created a $261 billion drag on the U.S. economy."[95] To observers looking at ownership structure, stock market trading of these firms' equity may seem to be the root cause of the drop-off in investment spending—a basic indicator of a preference for the short term over the long term. But identification of misshapen markets rather than policy as the more fundamental cause may be mistaken here.

Consider former Federal Reserve Chair Ben Bernanke's PhD thesis:

> When Ben S. Bernanke wrote his doctoral thesis in 1979, he could have been channeling the quandary that C.E.O.'s face today. "Uncertainty about the long-run environment which is potentially resolvable over time thus exerts a depressing effect on current levels of investment," he wrote at the Massachusetts Institute of Technology. "Uncertainty provides an incentive to defer such investments in order to wait for new information."[96]

The corporation may indeed now need to plan more for the short run than for the long run. But this explanation for the shortened planning horizon lies more in the nature of shortening technological life cycles, globalization, and changing government policy than in the financial markets external to, or the structures internal to, the large public firm.

6 THE SHORT-TERMIST ARGUMENT AS PROXY

The short-termist argument is closely associated with two views of corporate governance and may proxy for, or be used to bolster, these views. These views, though, must stand on their own. They get no extra weight and no extra persuasive power by using the short-termist argument.

6.1 As Proxy for the Need for Managerial Insulation

Shareholders, it has been said, are best served by managers with enormous discretion and autonomy. It is asserted that shareholders will not be well informed generally, will disagree with one another on corporate strategy, and will disrupt boardroom decision making if given too much authority to affect corporate decision making directly.[97]

The short-termist view may proxy here for the managerialist view, in that managerialists see shareholders as afflicted by a wide range of debilities, and see boards as needing to be

---

[94] Scott R. Baker, Nicholas Bloom, & Steven J. Davis, Measuring Economic Policy Uncertainty 1–2 (Jan. 1, 2013) (unpublished manuscript), available at http://ssrn.com/abstract= 2198490.

[95] Bill McNabb, Uncertainty Is the Enemy of Recovery, Wall St. J., Apr. 29, 2013, at A17.

[96] Andrew Ross Sorkin, "Shareholder Democracy" Can Mask Abuses, N.Y. Times DealBook, Feb. 25, 2013, available at http://nyti.ms/15Lvwoh.

[97] Stephen M. Bainbridge, "Director Primacy: The Means and Ends of Corporate Governance", 97 Nw. U. L. Rev. 547 (2003).

separated from shareholders' influence in order to coherently lead the corporation and keep it competitive.

Here I make no claim on the appropriateness of this view, positively or negatively. I do assert, however, that this view gains no added persuasive power from the short-termist argument, which is insufficiently strong, empirically and theoretically, to affect corporate rulemaking. Perhaps boards need to be left largely unaffected by shareholders, but the short-termism argument is not one of the reasons for it. The board insulation view must stand or fall on its own, without reference to short-termism. But one way to see the short-termist argument is that managerialists can offer it to policy makers as "cover" from public criticism. Short-termism justifies protecting managers; it resonates with public and popular prejudices on the functioning of financial markets. Even better for the managers if legislative and judicial decision makers with authority over the structure of power in the corporation believe short-termism to be pernicious and needing correction.

6.2 As Proxy for the Need to Attend to Stakeholders

Similarly, the view is widely but not universally held that short-term-oriented shareholders induce firms to be less attentive to the firm's other stakeholders, to government regulation, and to societal values generally. The firm that is excessively solicitous of short-term shareholders will in this view treat labor badly, will sell defective products, will take excessive risks with public funds in the financial sector, and will degrade the environment, all in ways that make our society worse off.[98] Shareholder voice degrades each of these stakeholders in the corporation, many think. Short-termism is the catch-all term to embody these negatives.

But this is an incorrect use of the short-termist view. We ought not to conflate corporate bad behavior with short-termism. Bad behavior could be long-term or short-term.[99]

Many perceive these negatives as serious faults of the large public corporation, warranting public policy attention. I do not evaluate this view here. But the purported tendency of shareholders to shorten the corporate time horizon must not figure into the balance. The stakeholder view, like the managerialist view, must stand or fall on its own.

7 Conclusion: No More than Watchful Waiting

We have here evaluated the long-standing short-termist argument in corporate law, using modern thinking and data on markets and the economy, and have found it wanting. It

---

[98] Cf. Christophe Moussu & Steve Ohana, Are Leveraged Firms Focused on the Short-Run? Evidence from Health and Safety Programs in U.S. Firms (Dec. 12, 2012) (unpublished manuscript) (available at http://ssrn.com/abstract=2188303).

[99] Cf. Fried, *supra* note 48, at 20 (long-term shareholders' interests are not necessarily more aligned with stakeholders than short-term shareholders).

should be given no weight in corporate lawmaking. The short-termist argument suffers from five substantial weaknesses.

First, policy makers must evaluate the American economy from a system-wide perspective. System-wide, the American economy is replete with venture capital markets, private equity markets, and many privately held firms, all of which are capable of the longer-term planning that the public firm is thought in some circles to be capable of. As long as venture capital markets, private equity markets, and other conduits mitigate or reverse enough of any short-term tendencies in the public securities market, then the purported problem is less systemic. While these institutions are themselves imperfect, they must still be considered when evaluating whether stock market short-termism, if it is excessive, is a system-wide problem.

Second, the evidence that financial markets are excessively short-term is widely believed but not proven, and there is much evidence pointing in the other direction. We have seen bubbles and overvalued companies with little more than a business plan, strongly suggestive that financial markets can be excessively long-term. Markets undershoot and overshoot, as one should expect. We see technology companies and prosaic natural resources companies making major long-term investments that far exceed stock market holding periods and CEO job tenure.

Third, mechanisms inside the corporation may well be important sources of short-term distortions and these internal distortions can be, and would be, exacerbated by further insulation of boards from external financial markets. It seems obvious (but underexamined) that CEOs will prefer that good results occur on their watch, and that poor results be pushed off into the future, beyond their tenure. There is considerable evidence consistent with this likelihood that a major source of short-term focus originates inside the corporation and not outside in financial markets. Senior managers with an eye on a new position want good results and they want them soon.

It is not impossible that the short-termist view captures a rhetorical high ground in the case for board autonomy by contrasting the positive connotation of patient long-term capital against short-term frenzy. But it is at least possible that some of the phenomenon is better captured by contrasting dynamic firms that change and adapt quickly, i.e., in the short run and sometimes due to shareholder pressure, with lackluster, encrusted organizations that do not move as nimbly.

Fourth, if proponents of the short-termist view are seeking to influence courts and state legislatures that make corporate law, their view should be rejected. Courts are poor places to make this kind of basic economic policy. They may even find it difficult to assess accurately whether the economy is too short term, too long term, or just right. If such considerations are to make their way into economic policy, these should be national policies, coordinated with tax policy, and perhaps implemented via the tax code, securities laws, and the rules that influence the size of stockholdings, not via parochial corporate law.

Fifth, the widely held view that short-term trading has increased dramatically in recent decades is unquestioned but should be examined, as that view may misinterpret the data. The best recent evidence indicates that the duration for holdings of the country's major stockholders, such as mutual funds at Fidelity and Vanguard, and major pension funds, has not shortened. Instead, a high-velocity trading fringe is moving stock rapidly through their computer systems. Their holdings, when averaged into market-wide data, make the duration appear to be shortening across the entire financial market. But these new trading patterns do not affect the major stockholding institutions and, hence, should not affect corporate law thinking.

Any one of these features should induce substantial caution among corporate law policy makers before using the short-termist view to buttress law that would further insulate managers from markets. It is at least possible that the arguments proxy for a view that stakeholders should be better attended to, or that managers should have more autonomy generally. Regardless, in combination, they tell us that corporate law courts and corporate lawmaking legislators should view the short-termist argument for further board and CEO insulation as one that should be accorded no weight today.

ACKNOWLEDGMENTS

Thanks for comments and discussions go to Martin Bengtzen, Martin Fridson, Jesse Fried, William Organek, Federico Raffaele, Edward Rock, David Sorkin, Dmitry Stepanov, Leo Strine, and Norman Veasey. A prior, extended form of this piece can be found at 68 Bus. Law. 977 (2013).

CHAPTER 17

··

MAJORITY CONTROL AND MINORITY PROTECTION

··

ZOHAR GOSHEN AND ASSAF HAMDANI

1 INTRODUCTION

··

MINORITY protection is a central issue for legal systems that regulate firms with a controlling shareholder. Concentrated ownership is the predominant ownership structure of public companies around the world, and even in the United States and the United Kingdom, where dispersed ownership is the norm, firms with concentrated ownership make up a substantial portion of publicly held companies. In this organizational structure, a person or entity—the controlling shareholder—holds an effective majority of the firm's voting and equity rights.[1]

Despite the costs of illiquidity and suboptimal diversification associated with being a controlling shareholder, concentrated ownership remains prevalent throughout the world. Several theories attempt to make sense of this apparent anomaly. These theories identify justifications for the presence of controlling shareholders and offer explanations for cross-jurisdictional differences in the prevalence of the concentrated ownership structures.

The prevailing view posits that controllers are drawn to what corporate lawyers and economists call "private benefits of control."[2] These benefits can be both pecuniary, where controlling shareholders may be able to engage in self-dealing transactions or tunnel funds, and nonpecuniary, such as enhanced social status and ego.[3]

---

[1] Our definition of concentrated ownership structure sets it apart from dual class firms and pyramidal structures. In the United States, Delaware courts have declined to quantify the precise percentage of stock necessary to constitute an "effective majority," choosing instead to engage in a factual inquiry of the exercise of actual control in each case. See, e.g., *Kahn v. Lynch Comm'ns Systems*, 638 A.2d 1110 (Del. 1994).

[2] See Lucian A. Bebchuk, "A Rent Protection Theory of Corporate Ownership and Control", Nat'l Bureau of Econ. Research, Working Paper No. 7203 (1999), at http://papers.ssrn.com/sol3/papers.cfm?abstract_id=168990; Simeon Djankov, Rafael La Porta, Florencia Lopez-de-Silanas, & Andre Shleifer, "The Law and Economics of Self-Dealing", 88 J. Fin. Econ. 430 (2008).

[3] Another perspective takes a more positive view of concentrated ownership, emphasizing the governance role of controlling owners. This view argues that an investor's significant equity stake in a firm leads to more effective monitoring of management, and considers the private benefits associated with controlling ownership to be a reward or compensation for this monitoring. See, Ronald J. Gilson,

In this chapter, we provide a brief summary of our new explanation of the value of corporate control for controllers–entrepreneurs and the prevalence of concentrated ownership.[4] We then use our new framework to offer a blueprint for the corporate law regime governing firms with controlling shareholders. In our view, holding a control block allows the entrepreneur–controlling shareholder to pursue her business idea (i.e., any concept that she genuinely believes could produce an above-market rate of return) under conditions of asymmetric information and differences of opinion in the manner she sees fit, even against minority investors' objections. We call the subjective value entrepreneurs attach to their business idea or vision the entrepreneur's *idiosyncratic vision*.

Both our novel explanation and the existing ones for the prevalence of controlling ownership have a foundation in reality, and indeed, both may be at play in a single firm. While pecuniary and nonpecuniary private benefits of control may be a strong motive for many controlling shareholders, the pursuit of their idiosyncratic vision notwithstanding investors' objection may motivate others to hold a control block. Moreover, our theory can explain the prevalence of concentrated ownership even in countries with strong investor protection and offers important implications for corporate law governing firms with controlling shareholders.

Corporate control matters in our framework because business ideas take time to implement. The successful implementation of a business idea requires many decisions, ranging from day-to-day management issues to major strategic choices. Perhaps the most important decision is whether to continue a project notwithstanding some setbacks. Due to either asymmetric information or differences of opinion between entrepreneurs and investors, there may be substantial disagreements over whether the project should be continued and in what fashion. The entrepreneur will therefore want to retain control over a wide range of management decisions to successfully pursue her vision. In short, control enables controlling shareholders to capture the value that they attach to the execution of *their* vision.[5]

Henry Ford's story is the best illustration of the importance of control for entrepreneurs-controlling shareholders in pursuing their idiosyncratic vision. Ford did not invent the automobile, nor did he own any valuable intellectual property in the technology. Therefore, he had to compete with hundreds of other entrepreneurs who were attempting to create a "horseless carriage." Ford had a unique vision regarding car production, however. In the first firm that Ford founded, the Detroit Automobile Company, investors retaining control resulted in tensions over the automobile production timeline. While Ford's investors demanded that cars be immediately produced and sold, Ford insisted on perfecting the design prior to production. This difference of opinion led to delays, frustration on both sides, and the eventual shutdown of the firm by its investors.[6] Ford's second attempt, the Henry

---

"Controlling Shareholders and Corporate Governance: Complicating the Comparative Taxonomy", 119 Harv. L. Rev. 1641, 1663–64 (2006).

[4] Our theory is fully developed elsewhere. See, Zohar Goshen and Assaf Hamdani, "Corporate Control and Idiosyncratic Vision", 125 Yale L. J. 560 (2016).

[5] It is important not to confuse business vision with nonpecuniary benefits of control. Non-pecuniary benefits of control refer to the value (e.g., personal satisfaction, pride, fame, political power) that only the entrepreneur derives from the execution of her business idea. In contrast, the pursuit of business vision—if properly harnessed—will equally benefit all shareholders in the corporation.

[6] M. Todd Henderson, The Story of Dodge v. Ford Motor Company: Everything Old is New Again, in Corporate Law Stories 40 (Mark Ramseyer ed., 2009).

Ford Company, was also controlled by investors. Again, after designing a car, Ford resisted the investors' pressure and did not move swiftly into production. Eventually, his obstinacy led to the investors replacing Ford with Henry Leland, changing the company name to the Cadillac Automobile Company and producing the car designed by Ford with great success.[7] Finally, on his third attempt—the Ford Motor Company—Ford insisted on retaining control. This time, with no outside investor interference, Ford transformed his ideas of car design and production (i.e., his idiosyncratic vision) into one of the greatest corporate success stories of all time.[8]

While Henry Ford's story demonstrates the perils of asymmetric beliefs and investor control from the entrepreneur's perspective, asymmetric information also introduces the risk of agency costs for investors. Entrepreneurs are not always right. For Henry Ford's investors, it was difficult to know whether Ford was pursuing a viable vision or simply wasting valuable money and time on an unattainable project. More importantly, entrepreneurs might behave opportunistically. An entrepreneur may continue a failing project out of personal interest, or, in the type of concentrated ownership structure discussed in this chapter, exploit her dominant position to consume private benefits at the expense of minority shareholders. She can, for example, pursue pecuniary benefits by entering into self-dealing transactions,[9] engaging in tunneling,[10] or employing family members. In addition, she can also capture nonpecuniary benefits such as boosting her ego and social or political status through her influence on corporate decisions.[11] These risks, called agency costs, arise when the interests of agents and their principals are not perfectly aligned.

Protecting investors against agency costs is in an unavoidable conflict with allowing entrepreneurs to pursue their idiosyncratic vision. The more freedom an entrepreneur has to pursue her business vision, the more exposed the investors are to agency costs, and vice versa. Entrepreneurs and investors allocate control and cash-flow rights to resolve the inevitable trade-off between agency costs and idiosyncratic vision. In a firm with concentrated ownership, the entrepreneur must hold a substantial fraction of cash-flow rights to secure the ability to pursue her vision. This allows the controller to pursue her vision while reducing (due to the controller's considerable share of cash-flow rights) minority shareholders' exposure to management agency costs. The controlling shareholder is willing to bear the costs of holding a large block of shares in exchange for gaining incontestable control, which enables her, through the pursuit of her idiosyncratic vision, to generate an appropriate return on her investment and effort while simultaneously generating pro-rata benefits for investors.

---

[7] Id. at 45.   [8] Id. at 47.

[9] See Djankov et al., *supra* note 2. Based on their study of 72 countries, the authors suggest that regulation of self-dealing transactions is best done by disclosure and ratification by disinterested shareholders. The analysis of the relative efficiency of rules regulating self-dealing was developed several years earlier. See Zohar Goshen, "The Efficiency of Controlling Corporate Self-Dealing: Theory Meets Reality", 91 Cal. L. Rev. 393 (2003) [hereinafter Goshen, Controlling Self-Dealing] (introducing and applying the property rule/liability rule analysis to minority-shareholders' protection) [hereinafter Goshen, Controlling Self-Dealing].

[10] See, e.g., Bernard Black et al., "Law and Tunneling", 37 J. Corp. L. 1 (2011); Simon Johnson et al., "Tunneling", 90 Am. Econ. Rev. 22 (2000).

[11] See, e.g., Harold Demsetz & Kenneth Lehn, "The Structure of Corporate Ownership: Causes and Consequences", 93 J. Pol. Econ. 1155 (1985).

But, although controlling shareholders hold control primarily in order to *increase the size of the pie* (via the pursuit of vision), there is a risk that they might attempt to dictate the *pie's distribution* (via the consumption of private benefits). Minimizing this risk, i.e., the risk of control-agency cost, is at the center of minority protection.

On the policy level, our theory of the value of control for entrepreneurs offers important lessons for the regulation of firms with controlling shareholders. The existing corporate law literature associating control with consumption of private benefits solely focuses on minority protection from agency costs. However, within our framework of the concentrated ownership structure, controlling shareholders' right to pursue their idiosyncratic vision also plays, and should play, a critical role in corporate law. Specifically, any legal regime governing firms with controlling shareholders encounters an inevitable trade-off between the goals of protecting minorities and allowing controllers to pursue their idiosyncratic vision. Corporate law must balance these conflicting goals instead of pushing for only one of them. Our analysis in the remainder of this chapter focuses mostly on Delaware, the jurisdiction with the most developed corporate case law and jurisprudence.

2 THE TRADE-OFF BETWEEN MINORITY PROTECTION AND CONTROLLER RIGHTS

As delineated above, corporate law should recognize the controller's right to pursue her vision while simultaneously protecting investors from expropriation through self-dealing and other methods of value diversion. Finding the appropriate doctrinal balance is challenging because of the inevitable conflict between minority protection and controller rights, especially since distinguishing between legitimate corporate decisions that enhance business vision and those that lead to unequal distributions can be difficult. The same asymmetric information and diverging beliefs that make the contracting process between investors and entrepreneurs challenging makes the enforcement of the rules against self-dealing challenging as well. Minority-protecting measures may lead to costly errors, and efforts to police the prohibition on non-pro-rata distributions may require legal or governance measures that would undermine the controller's management rights.

To illustrate the interplay between minority protection and controller rights, assume that the entrepreneur owns 60% of a firm. The entrepreneur genuinely believes that a specific component produced only by one particular company is necessary for the development of a new product. It so happens, however, that the company producing the component is 100% owned by the entrepreneur. Accordingly, the entrepreneur wishes for her 60%-owned firm to buy the components from her wholly owned company. If the entrepreneur were the sole owner of both firms, she could simply buy the component under whatever terms she desired. But, with investors owning 40% of the firm's shares, there is an understandable suspicion that the entrepreneur is abusing this transaction to divert value from minority shareholders to her wholly owned corporation, and ultimately, to herself.

This illustration underscores the at-times opaque line between unfair self-dealing and business decisions that are necessary for implementing the controller's vision to the benefit of the controlling and minority shareholders alike. Protecting the minority against inappropriate value diversion requires some constraints on the entrepreneur's ability to exercise control. These constraints can take the form of ex post review by courts with regards to the fairness of the transaction, or an ex ante requirement to secure approval by a majority of the minority shareholders.[12] Thus, the need to provide the minority with protection against agency costs will necessarily require curtailing some of the controller's freedom to pursue her idiosyncratic vision that she would have otherwise enjoyed as a single owner.[13]

One might argue that constraining self-dealing need not interfere with the controller's ability to pursue her vision. After all, the argument goes, if the controller does not intend to expropriate the minority, why would she care about the extra supervision? If the transaction is on arm's length terms, the court will find it to be fair ex post,[14] or minority shareholders will grant their approval ex ante. This argument would be correct in an ideal world without transaction costs. In the real world, however, plaintiffs sometimes bring suits without merit[15] and courts make mistakes.[16] Likewise, under a rule that requires a majority-of-minority vote, minority shareholders might strategically attempt to hold out or simply err in evaluating the proposed transactions.[17] This conclusion also applies to other prophylactic measures required for creating an effective minority-protection regime.[18] Accordingly, protecting minority shareholders against agency costs inevitably interferes with the controller's right to pursue her business vision.

The trade-off between minority protection and controller rights has obvious implications for the design of corporate law. It requires lawmakers and courts to seek an optimal balance between minority protection and controlling shareholder freedom to make managerial decisions. More practically, the nature of minority protection should depend on enforcement considerations. Enforcing a given protection may be too costly not only because of the direct compliance costs incurred by corporations or courts but also due to the unavoidable cost of interfering with the entrepreneur's pursuit of her idiosyncratic vision.

---

[12] Goshen, Controlling Self-Dealing, *supra* note 9.

[13] The single owner standard is useful not only as a benchmark for the protection of investors, but also as a benchmark for the controller's right to secure business vision. See, e.g., Lucian A. Bebchuk, "The Sole Owner Standard for Takeover Policy", 17 J. Leg. Stud. 197 (1988).

[14] For a case in which the court concluded that a controlling shareholder had a strong idiosyncratic vision (without using this term, of course), and therefore approved a series of long-term self-dealing transactions as fair, see *Cookies Food Products, Inc. v. Lakes Warehouse Distributing, Inc.*, 430 N.W. 2d 447 (Sup. Iowa 1988).

[15] Janet Cooper Alexander, "Do the Merits Matter? A Study of Settlements in Securities Class Actions", 43 Stan. L. Rev. 497 (1991); Roberta Romano, "The Shareholder Suit: Litigation Without Foundation?", 7 J. L. Econ. & Org. 55 (1991).

[16] See Goshen, Controlling Self-Dealing, *supra* note 9 (explaining the inefficiencies associated with a fairness test).

[17] See id. (reviewing opportunism and inefficiencies associated with majority-of-minority voting).

[18] Modern corporate governance relies on a variety of gatekeepers and enforcement measures to constrain agency costs. These include, for example, financial reporting and other disclosure duties, requiring outside auditors and setting standards for their work, and requirements for outside independent directors. These measures could interfere with the controller's ability to manage the firm in a way that limits her ability to capture the full value of her idiosyncratic vision.

3 CONTROLLER RIGHTS

Analysis of the controlling shareholder's side of the corporate contract focuses on the scope of the controller's rights vis-à-vis the scope of minority protection. The division of cash-flow rights and control rights is a zero-sum game between entrepreneurs (controlling shareholders) and investors (minority shareholders), such that any freedom granted to the controller to pursue her vision will increase minority exposure to agency costs, and vice versa.

3.1 Property Rule Protection: Preserving Control

To preserve the entrepreneur's incontestable control and the ability to pursue her idiosyncratic vision, her right to make management decisions should be afforded property rule protection.[19] In this context, property rule protection means that the market (i.e., minority shareholders) or courts cannot unilaterally take control rights away from the controller in exchange for an objectively determined compensation. Instead, the controller can prevent a non-consensual change of control from ever taking place at all.[20]

Property rule protection of controller rights has clear implications analogous to standard private property protections. For example, controllers cannot be forced to sell their control block even when doing so would clearly benefit the corporation or its minority shareholders.[21] Furthermore, the controller is generally free to exit her investment by selling her control block whenever she wants and for whatever price she sees fit.[22]

Property rule protection for controlling shareholder management rights extends further to a broad range of corporate actions. Controllers can lose control not only when they sell their shares, but also when the company takes action—such as issuing shares—that dilutes

---

[19] See generally Guido Calabresi & A. Douglas Melamed, "Property Rules, Liability Rules, and Inalienability: One View of the Cathedral", 85 Harv. L. Rev. 1089 (1972).

[20] The need for property rule protection arises from the fundamental justification for allocating control and management rights to the entrepreneur. The controller–entrepreneur is the one who has the unique vision or subjective assessment concerning the project's value (idiosyncratic vision). Any objectively determined compensation for a non-consensual taking will rarely be fair to the entrepreneur. The extensive academic literature on property and liability rules suggests that a property rule protection is appropriate when business vision is present. See Henry E. Smith, "Property and Property Rules", 79 N.Y.U. L. Rev. 1719, 1722–31, 1755–56 (2004).

[21] See Bershad v. Curtiss-Wright, 535 A.2d 840 (Del. 1987). But see generally Jens Dammann, "Corporate Ostracism: Freezing Out Controlling Shareholders", 33 J. Corp. L. 681, 694 (2007) (explaining an innovative proposal for a regime under which minority investors could force the controller out).

[22] Some limits are imposed, however, on the identity of the buyer. See Harris v. Carter, 582 A.2d 222 (Del. Ch. 1990) (prohibiting sale of control to a known looter and imposing limited duties of investigation on controlling shareholders). In Hollinger, Delaware's Chancery Court allowed the board to use a poison pill to prevent a controlling shareholder from selling his control block. We believe, however, that this holding applies only when the sale of the block is in clear violation of the controller's fiduciary duties. See Hollinger Int'l., Inc., v. Black, 844 A.2d 1022, 1085–86 (Del. Ch. 2004) (allowing the board to deploy a poison pill when sale of control was the culmination of an improper course of conduct by the controller and in violation of his contractual obligations).

their holdings. Companies with controlling shareholders cannot take actions that would cause the controller to lose her control, even when doing so would benefit the corporation or minority investors.

Consider the following hypothetical. A bank must increase its capital to meet new capital adequacy requirements. The bank has two options: issuing new shares or selling one of its subsidiaries. The bank's controlling shareholder, who owns 51% of the shares, has her own liquidity problems that prevent her from buying additional shares of the bank. Issuing new shares would therefore dilute the controller and may cause her to lose her controlling position. How should the board decide between the two options? At first glance, directors' fiduciary duties seem to require them to choose the option that best serves the company's interests while disregarding the controller's interest in preserving control. Under Delaware case law, however, the board might be prohibited from taking steps that would make the controller lose corporate control "in the absence of a threatened serious breach of fiduciary duty by the controlling stockholder."[23] Therefore, the board may decide to sell a subsidiary merely because issuing new shares would force the controller to lose control.[24]

This outcome runs against the traditional notions of shareholder value maximization because it allows value-reducing actions in light of a need to protect the controller's rights. Yet a regime under which minority shareholders, the board, or courts could compel the controller to lose control—whether by a forced sale, dilution, or any other action—is inconsistent with the need to provide controllers with a property rule protection for their right to make managerial decisions and pursue their business vision. It is important to note that this outcome is not justified by the need to provide controllers with private benefits to reward them for their willingness to monitor management. Instead, it is based on the parties' mutual consent ex ante on an arrangement that would enable entrepreneurs to pursue their idiosyncratic vision to the benefit of both minority investors and the entrepreneur.

3.2 Management Rights: Business Judgment Rule and Board Composition

Application of the business judgment rule strengthens the controlling shareholder's control over management decisions in pursuit of her idiosyncratic vision. The business judgment rule embodies the principle that courts should generally refrain from interfering with business decisions made by controllers or their representatives. The entrepreneur–controller

---

[23] See *Mendel v. Carroll*, 651 A.2d 297, 306 (Del. Ch. 1994). For an analysis of this decision and its implications, see John C. Coffee, Jr., "Transfers of Control and the Quest for Efficiency: Can Delaware Law Encourage Efficient Transactions While Chilling Inefficient Ones?", 21 Del. J. Corp. L. 359, 390–96 (1996).

[24] Note that this treatment of the controller differs from that of minority shareholders (or investors at widely held firms). We normally allow management to use rights offerings even when that might coerce investors into a choice between dilution and increasing their investment. For evidence that a controller's need to preserve control affects firm decisions concerning capital structure, see, e.g., Thomas Schmid, "Control Considerations, Creditor Monitoring, and the Capital Structure of Family Firms", 37 J. Banking & Fin. 257 (2013) (finding evidence consistent with the hypothesis that family firms in Germany use firms' capital structure to optimize control over the firm).

is willing to make a significant equity investment in exchange for the right to pursue her business vision. The allocation of control particularly matters in light of the asymmetric information and differences of opinion between the entrepreneur and the investors/market. Some of the greatest breakthroughs in business ideas were "crazy" before they became "visionary." These ideas would have never come to pass in the absence of control. What then should be the nature of protection of idiosyncratic vision?

Application of the business judgment rule recognizes the controlling entrepreneur's right to exercise control over any issue that could affect the firm's value. Controlling shareholders should be free to set the firm's direction and make all management decisions. This includes the right to assume a managerial role (if the controller is an individual) as well as the right to appoint and fire managers. This has two implications for corporate law doctrine and policy. First, courts should generally refrain from interfering with business decisions that controllers or their representatives make—in other words, follow the business judgment rule.[25] The controller–entrepreneur retains control because of her expectation that asymmetric information or differences of opinion would induce investors to make decisions that would destroy her vision. The existence of asymmetric information and differences of opinion, moreover, should give courts pause before they attempt to intervene in business decisions. Like investors, courts may make decisions or take actions that, from the entrepreneur's perspective, would destroy her vision.

The business judgment rule is often justified on the grounds that judicial review of non-conflicted transactions is unnecessary in a concentrated ownership environment where the controlling shareholder's significant equity stake provides sufficient incentive to maximize value for all investors.[26] The need to allow the entrepreneur–controller to pursue her idiosyncratic vision, however, provides another explanation for the business judgment rule. The entrepreneur should have the freedom to implement her business plan even when investors and courts believe that such a plan is not value-enhancing.

Moreover, controllers' management rights have significant implications for corporate governance reforms designed to enhance board independence at firms with controlling shareholders. Traditionally, the controllers' voting power enables them to appoint any candidate they wish to the board. Recent corporate governance reforms, however, constrain the controllers' power to appoint directors. Listing requirements, for example, require boards or board committees to maintain a certain percentage of directors who are independent, not only from the company, but also from the controller.[27] Some legal systems go even further and empower minority shareholders to influence board composition by, for example, appointing their own representatives to the board.[28]

---

[25] For the rationale underlying the business judgment rule, see *In re Walt Disney Co. Derivative Litig.*, 907 A.2d 693, 698 (Del. Ch. 2005) ("[R]edress for [directors'] failures . . . must come . . . through the actions of shareholders . . . and not from this Court."); *Aronson v. Lewis*, 473 A.2d 805 (Del. 1984) ("[D]irectors are better equipped than the courts to make business judgments.").

[26] See Lucian A. Bebchuk & Assaf Hamdani, "The Elusive Quest for Global Governance Standards", 157 U. Pa. L. Rev. 1263, 1281 (2009) (advocating for varying governance standards between companies with and without a controlling shareholder, and explaining that controlling shareholders provide the beneficial means and incentive to monitor management).

[27] See the stock exchange rules Nasdaq Rule 4350(c)(1) and Section 303(a) of the NYSE's Listing Company Manual.

[28] See, e.g., Bernard Black & Reinier Kraakman, "A Self-Enforcing Model of Corporate Law", 109 Harv. L. Rev. 1911, 1947–49 (1996) (describing virtues of cumulative voting as mechanism for minority

These measures may be necessary to enforce the rule against self-dealing.[29] Board reforms aim to make the board more effective in monitoring those with power—the CEO or the controlling shareholder. However, asymmetric information and differences of opinion could prevent the controller–entrepreneur from credibly communicating her beliefs regarding her business vision not only to investors but also to skeptical independent board members. Thus, the need to balance controller rights and minority protection should also shape board reforms at firms with controlling shareholders. Since the presence of minority representatives, or even just fully independent board members, could interfere with the controller's ability to manage, the controller should at least have the power to appoint a majority of the board (which in turn should have the power to appoint the CEO and other managers). Presently, this necessity to balance those conflicting goals in firms with concentrated ownership is reflected in exceptions to the NASDAQ and NYSE listing rules for controlled companies.[30]

3.3 Right to Sell Control for a Premium

Whether controlling shareholders can sell their shares for a premium is one of the most important and controversial questions for firms with controlling shareholders.[31] Delaware recognizes the right of controlling shareholders to sell at a premium, subject to the restriction on selling control to a looter (the "market rule").[32] As explained above, the controller's right to sell at any time is the essence of her property right. But what about the right to sell for a premium not shared by minority shareholders?

The right to sell for a premium that is not shared by minority shareholders seems to contradict the idea of pro-rata value distribution. Nevertheless, the property rule protection counsels in favor of allowing controllers to sell their stake at a premium without sharing it

representation); Carrado Malberti & Emiliano Sironi, "The Mandatory Representation of Minority Shareholders on the Board of Directors of Italian Listed Corporations: An Empirical Analysis", Bocconi Legal Studies Research Paper No. 18, available at http://ssrn.com/abstract=965398 (reviewing minority representation reforms in Italy).

[29] See Bernard Black & Woochan Kim, "The Effect of Board Structure on Firm Value: A Multiple Identification Strategies Approach Using Korean Data", 104 J. Fin. Econ. 203 (2012) (reporting evidence that reforms enhancing director independence positively affected Korean firms); Jay Dahya, Orlin Dimitrov, & John J. McConnell, "Does Board Independence Matter in Companies with Controlling Shareholders?", 21 J. Appl. Corp. Fin. 67 (2009) (finding corporate value is consistently higher in controlled firms with independent directors).

[30] Indeed, under NASDAQ Rule 4350(c)(5) a controlled company is exempt from the requirement of Rule 4350(c) of the NASDAQ Marketplace Rule requiring a majority of independent directors on the board. A similar exemption exists under Section 303A of the NYSE's Listed Company Manual.

[31] The common-law norm to sell control for a premium is explained clearly in *Zeitlin v. Hanson Holdings, Inc.*, 397 N.E.2d 387, 388–89 (N.Y. 1979) ("It has long been settled law that, absent looting of corporate assets, conversion of a corporate opportunity, fraud or other acts of bad faith, a controlling stockholder is free to sell, and a purchaser is free to buy, that controlling interest at a premium price."). But see William D. Andrews, "The Stockholder's Right to Equal Opportunity in the Sale of Shares", 78 Harv. L. Rev 505 (1965) (arguing for a sharing of control premium with minority shareholders).

[32] See *Abraham v. Emerson Radio Corp.*, 901 A.2d 751, 758 (Del. Ch. 2006); *Harris v. Carter*, 582 A.2d 222, 234 (Del. Ch. 1990).

with the minority shareholders. A key premise underlying the objection to controllers' right to sell for a premium is that a control premium serves as a proxy for private benefits and thus for minority expropriation. Under this view, imposing constraints on controllers' ability to sell for a premium would decrease the risk of inefficient sales motivated by the prospect of consuming private benefits at the expense of minority shareholders.[33]

As demonstrated above, however, a control premium is not necessarily a proxy for private benefits of control or the magnitude of minority expropriation. Instead, it could also reflect the value of the entrepreneur's idiosyncratic vision from either the buyer's or the seller's perspective. A seller who believes that she could earn above-market return on her shares would insist on a premium for selling her stake even if, had she stayed in control, she would have shared the profits from her realized idiosyncratic vision on a pro-rata basis with minority shareholders. In this sense, the seller is only taking a premium that is reflecting her pro-rata share of what she expects to receive. Consequently, a buyer that believes she could make an even greater above-market return on the new investment would be willing to pay such a premium. Thus, under our framework, the new controller's willingness to pay a premium for buying control does not suggest that she intends to exploit minority investors.[34]

However, corporate law in many jurisdictions appears to not subscribe to this rationale, instead imposing the so-called equal-opportunity rule that requires the buyer of more than a certain percentage of a firm's shares (usually around 30%) to make a tender offer that would take the shareholder to at least 50% share ownership.[35] To be sure, the equal-opportunity rule could protect the minority against a sale to a looter. (After all, we do not rule out the possibility that a control premium can reflect private benefits of control.) Moreover, it does not prevent the controller from selling her shares for a premium. Rather, it requires the buyer to offer the same premium to all shareholders. Yet, forcing the buyer to pay a premium to all shareholders raises the acquisition's total costs, thereby effectively barring a range of control-motivated transactions in which the buyer's expected increase in corporate value is insufficient to justify paying the premium demanded by the current controller to all shareholders. Thus, to the extent that a control premium is a proxy for business vision instead of private benefits, the costs imposed by the equal opportunity rule—in terms of discouraging efficient transactions—are expected to be higher.[36]

---

[33] See Lucian A. Bebchuk, "Efficient and Inefficient Sales of Corporate Control", 109 Q. J. Econ. 957 (1994).

[34] At the same time, our framework could lend support to the equal-opportunity rule. After all, investors in our framework allow the controller to preserve control in order to enable the controller to pursue idiosyncratic vision that would then be shared with investors. When the controller exits the joint investment she takes her pro-rata part of her business vision from the buyer, leaving minority shareholders to wait until the new buyer realizes his idiosyncratic vision. The claim could thus be that the seller must first perform her contractual commitment to the minority (pay the promised share of idiosyncratic vision) before she can ask the minority to enter a new contract with the buyer.

[35] See, e.g., U.K. City Code on Takeovers and Mergers, Rule 36 (stating a purchaser crossing 30% triggers a mandatory offer for over 50% of the company); EU Takeover Directive (Directive 2004/25/EC [adoption: codecision COD/2002/0240]) (mandating that "Member States must ensure that [a controller] is required to make a bid as a means of protecting the minority shareholders of that company. Such a bid must be addressed at the earliest opportunity to all the holders of those securities for all their holdings at the equitable price").

[36] See Bebchuk, *supra* note 33.

4 MINORITY RIGHTS

An analysis of the minority shareholder's side of the corporate contract focuses on the threats facing minority shareholders in corporate structures with a controlling shareholder and the type of protection that should be provided to enforce minority rights.

4.1 Type of Protection

Just as the protection of controllers' rights can exist as a property or a liability rule, minority shareholders can receive either property or liability rule protection against the possible exploitation by a controlling shareholder.[37] Under a liability rule, the controller can engage in self-dealing transactions without minority shareholders' consent, subject to her duty to pay an objectively fair price. This pecuniary commitment is supervised by courts. On the other hand, under a property rule, the controller cannot engage in self-dealing without securing the minority's consent, typically by a majority-of-the-minority vote.

Indeed, legal regimes could also leave protection against the controlling owner's self-dealings up to the unconstrained forces of the market, allowing for individualized solutions.[38] Shareholders would consider the risk of possible self-dealing as a threat to their investments when deciding on share ownership, leading the market to offer protections that mitigate this risk and assuage investor fears. However, markets are not perfectly efficient, and information costs undermine the efficacy of market-based solutions to the point of relatively diminishing standards.[39] Therefore, property- and liability-based protections are more efficient than a non-interventionist approach.

The need to balance controller and minority rights dictates the desirable form of minority protection. A property rule provides the minority with consent-based protection that is vulnerable to holdouts and other problems that can prevent the controller from getting minority approval even for a value-enhancing transaction, risking interference with the controller's management right. In contrast, a liability rule provides the minority with fair-compensation-based protection. This form of protection is vulnerable to judicial error, but it is less likely to interfere with the controller's management rights.[40]

Given the nature of these tradeoffs, a liability rule theoretically strikes the optimal balance between protecting the minority against agency costs and preserving idiosyncratic vision.[41]

---

[37] See Goshen, Controlling Self-Dealing, *supra* note 9, at 408.

[38] Id. at 404. See also, Frank H. Easterbrook & Daniel R. Fischel, "Corporate Control Transactions", 91 Yale L. J. 698 (1982) (arguing that legal rules should imitate what parties would bargain for in absence of negotiating costs).

[39] See Goshen, Controlling Self-Dealing, *supra* note 9, at 405.

[40] To be sure, as Delaware's case law demonstrates, majority-of-the-minority votes may play an important role in scrutinizing self-dealing transactions even under a liability rule. Yet it authorizes courts to approve self-dealing transactions notwithstanding the minority objection, thereby reducing the risk of errors resulting from hold-outs or differences of opinion between the controller and investors.

[41] Note that specialized courts would not only enhance minority protection, but also reduce the risk of excessive interference with controlling shareholders' rights. Specialized courts are less likely to err. This in turn would decrease the cost—in terms of undermining controller rights—of rules designed

However, the actual effect of protections based on property or liability rules depends on the judicial system, market efficiency, and institutional investors of a given jurisdiction.[42]

In the presence of transaction costs, which include negotiation and adjudication costs, the choice between a liability rule and a property rule depends on which rule encourages and facilitates efficient transactions and discourages inefficient ones. In other words, a rule that facilitates the pursuit of idiosyncratic vision and the curtailment of agency cost should be implemented. A property rule, requiring approval by a majority of the minority of shareholders, involves high negotiation costs. These costs stem from dissemination of information and administration of the voting process, including the risk of strategic voting and hold-outs during the vote. On the other hand, although a liability rule does not rely on negotiations and thus does not entail high negotiation costs, negotiations do take place in the "shadow of the law."

Adjudication costs are relatively low in the presence of a property rule, where the courts need to only determine the procedural integrity of the shareholder approval process. Under a liability rule, the courts are called upon to examine the merits of a deal and opine as to its overall "fairness," which can require significant financial modeling by economic experts and has to rely upon a judicial system competent enough to navigate such complex cases. Costs of erroneous rulings are another type of adjudication cost. In the context of valuation, it is often the case that no "objective" market-based value exists, so the court must rely on a compilation of subjective assessments. In addition to increasing direct adjudication costs, this also increases the risks of mistakes, leading to high indirect adjudication costs as well.

Therefore, where negotiation costs are high due to a lack of sophisticated investors, and only a minimal level of judicial efficacy exists, the balance of negotiation and adjudication costs may weigh in favor of a liability rule. The opposite holds true where adjudication costs caused by judicial inefficiency outweigh negotiation costs. In some circumstances, negotiation and adjudication costs will point to the same direction, where either both will be high or both will be low. When both types of costs are high, a property rule is desirable because the risk of minority exploitation is sufficiently high that the private sector is better suited to respond. It is more likely that markets will react and improve minority protection than it is that governments will overcome path-dependency and improve courts' efficacy. Conversely, when both types of costs are low, a liability rule is desirable because the risks to investors are likely lower and liability protection provides greater ability to contract for alternative protections. An assessment of the relative weights of these two categorical transaction costs can indicate which rule is appropriate in a given context.

As demonstrated, there is no single efficient mechanism for the protection of the minority from corporate self-dealing. Rather, the choice between a property rule requiring majority-of-the-minority approval before every conflicted transaction and a liability rule allowing controller discretion subject to the court's objective evaluation of a transaction's fairness depends on the unique characteristics of each jurisdiction and how those characteristics impact the balance of the transaction costs. Ultimately, the rule that achieves the lowest

---

to protect minority shareholders. See, e.g., Luca Enriques, Off the Books, But on the Record: Evidence from Italy on the Relevance of Judges to the Quality of Corporate Law, in Global Markets and Domestic Institutions: Corporate Law in a New Era of Cross Border Deals (Curtis Milhaupt ed., 2003).

[42] See generally Goshen, Controlling Self-Dealing, *supra* note 9.

transaction costs, thereby encouraging efficient transactions and discouraging inefficient ones, should be chosen.

4.2 Pro-Rata Share: Identifying Self-Dealing

The principal form of minority protection is the strong regulation prohibiting non-pro-rata distributions of a firm's assets. Minority shareholders' main concern is that the entrepreneur–controller will engage in self-dealing, tunneling, or other methods of capturing more than her pro-rata share of cash-flow rights. Therefore, in exchange for the controller's freedom to pursue her idiosyncratic vision by executing her business idea as she sees fit, the controller commits to share proportionally with the minority any cash flows that the project will produce. If she seeks any preference over the minority, she should negotiate with the minority investors and obtain their approval—either before entering the joint investment or before obtaining the preference. Otherwise, any non-pro-rata distribution will be subject to strict judicial scrutiny.[43]

A legal regime governing companies with controlling shareholders thus should accomplish two important tasks: first, create a workable distinction between neutral business decisions and self-dealing; and second, implement adequate mechanisms to govern self-dealing transactions. The distinction between self-dealing and other transactions has considerable judicial consequences. Under Delaware law, for example, this distinction determines whether a lawsuit challenging a transaction will be carefully reviewed under the plaintiff-friendly entire fairness standard or quickly dismissed under the defendant-friendly business judgment rule.[44] However, drawing the line between cases that deserve close scrutiny and those that do not is often difficult. Only rarely are cases straightforward; for example, when the controller sells her privately owned asset to the publicly traded firm that she controls, this would most likely constitute self-dealing. In many cases, however, it is unclear whether the mere fact that the controller's interests with respect to certain corporate actions are not fully aligned with those of the minority justifies close scrutiny.[45]

In considering the difficulty of characterizing a transaction as conflicted or non-conflicted, the *dividend distribution* question underlying the *Sinclair* case is instructive.[46] Should courts protect the minority against the risk that a controlling shareholder will use a pro-rata dividend distribution to advance her own interests? The *Sinclair* court answered this question with a clear answer: "No." Rather, it held that pro-rata dividend distributions do not amount to self-dealing and should thus be reviewed only under the business judgment rule.[47] Is this the most desirable outcome?

---

[43] *Weinberger v. UOP, Inc.*, 457 A.2d 701 (Del. 1983) (discussing elimination of minority shareholders via merger between corporation and its majority owner); *Jones v. H. F. Ahmanson & Co.*, 460 P.2d 464, 469 (Cal. 1969).

[44] See generally Steven M. Haas, "Towards a Controlling Shareholder Safe Harbor", 90 Va. L. Rev. 2245 (2004).

[45] See Dammann, *supra* note 21 (noting that the Delaware test makes it difficult for plaintiffs to establish self-dealing because "while it may be possible to show that the course of action taken by the corporation benefited the controlling shareholder, it is extremely difficult to prove that this advantage came at the expense of other shareholders").

[46] See *Sinclair Oil Corp. v. Levien*, 280 A.2d 717 (Del. 1971).   [47] Id.

For purposes of our discussion, assume that a pro-rata distribution could be used to sat-isfy the controller's own liquidity needs while denying the corporation highly profitable growth opportunities. In other words, assume that a pro-rata dividend distribution could be harmful to minority shareholders. Nevertheless, a legal rule that would aspire to supervise the controller and prevent such "abusive" distributions would be too costly.

Any rule that tries to scrutinize pro-rata dividend distributions would necessarily in-terfere with the controller's management rights and her ability to pursue her idiosyncratic vision. First, control over the firm's capital structure—the amount of capital that is required and how to finance the firm's operations—might be an integral part of implementing an entrepreneur's vision.[48] External intervention would therefore significantly interfere with the controllers' ability to make management decisions concerning their vision. Second, distinguishing "legitimate" dividend distributions from illegitimate ones is prone to errors because of asymmetric information and differences of opinion.[49] A court required to im-plement this distinction will have to assess the decision to pay dividends in light of its alter-native, i.e., a decision to retain the dividend amount and invest it in potential projects. But, how will the court determine that the business opportunity abandoned by the corporation in order to facilitate the dividend distribution was indeed a good business opportunity? Will the court assume responsibility for the investment forced upon the controlling owner when it rules that the dividend is illegal? Lastly, even if courts were to accurately deter-mine that a certain dividend is illegal, effective enforcement would itself require excessive intervention.

A disgruntled controller prohibited from paying a dividend may decide, for example, to avoid investments and instead deposit the dividend amount in the firm's bank account in order to distribute the same amount in the near future. Clearly, courts would not take away the controller's rights to make management decisions by forcing the controller to put the money to other, more profitable uses. In other words, effectively enforcing the

---

[48] In a world with no transaction costs the firm's capital structure (i.e., its debt to equity ratio) can be determined using any combination of dividends, leverage, and share issuance, with the same effect on corporate value. Similarly, buying a risky investment with no leverage is the same as buying a solid investment with leverage. See Merton Miller, "The Modigliani-Miller Propositions after Thirty Years", 2 J. Econ. Persp. 99 (1988) (discussing Modigliani and Miller's theorems about the irrelevance of capital structure and dividend policy for corporate value). But, in a world with transaction costs, vision as to a business idea is no different than vision as to capital structure. A controlling shareholder decision to issue new shares and invest in a project should be treated in the same manner as her decision to avoid a project and distribute the money.

[49] Any investment offers a combination of risk and expected returns that are calculated based on estimates of future events or consequences. An investment with an expected return that equals the market pricing of a similar risk offers a zero net present value (NPV). In efficient markets all investments are zero NPV, but to make our point it is sufficient to assume that most of them are. If the expected return on the investment is lower (higher) than the market pricing of the risk that it carries, then it offers a negative (positive) NPV and should be avoided (is a bargain). A controller decision to forego an investment in order to distribute dividends will harm minority shareholders only if the avoided investment was positive NPV (negative NPV should be avoided, and zero NPV leaves shareholders with many alternatives for reinvesting the dividend). Deciding about an investment's NPV would require courts to decide whether the investment is good or bad. Courts cannot make such a decision. Indeed, avoiding such decisions is a major justification for the business judgment rule.

non-distribution of dividends would ultimately require courts to abandon the business judgment rule.

Our discussion of *Sinclair* thus shows that the omnipresent tension between controller management rights and minority protection should shape the legal distinction between self-dealing and other transactions. The interests of controlling shareholders, to be sure, are not always fully aligned with those of minority investors. Yet not every conflict of interest justifies legal intervention to protect the minority.

4.3 Mid-Stream Changes

The preceding analysis provides support for Delaware's approach to self-dealing transactions. In this section, however, we explain that the same approach fails to protect minority shareholders against unilateral mid-stream changes to the firm's governance. Controlling shareholders can enjoy more than their pro-rata share of cash-flow rights by using their control to change the firm's governance arrangements mid-stream either directly—through changes in the charter or bylaws—or indirectly through a business combination, such as a merger. These changes could be inconsistent with the initial contract between the entrepreneur and investors.[50]

Consider, for example, the link between control and cash-flow rights. Under the one-share-one-vote rule, the controller's willingness to make a significant equity investment in order to secure his controlling position alleviates management agency costs and asymmetric information concerns. Once he raises funds from investors, however, the controller might be tempted to unravel this arrangement and find ways to preserve incontestable control without having to incur the costs associated with holding a large equity block.[51] A necessary element in any minority-protection scheme is, therefore, a protection against the unilateral, mid-stream changes to the firm's governance arrangement.

Indeed, on several occasions, minority shareholders did attempt to challenge such changes in Delaware courts, but without success. Courts refused to review these changes under the entire fairness standard, holding that the disparate *economic* impact of such changes on the controller did not amount to self-dealing as long as the *legal* effect was equal.[52]

This legal approach assumes that absent a clear restriction in the charter the controller has the right to change the allocation of control rights, thereby exposing the minority shareholders to agency costs. This approach may stem from the fact that Delaware courts use a single test for two distinct tasks—identifying self-dealing transactions and coping with mid-stream changes. However, mid-stream governance changes by controlling shareholders require a separate legal framework that first identifies cases of mid-stream changes, and second, makes a decision on the nature of protection that minority shareholders should enjoy.

---

[50] Jeffrey N. Gordon, "The Mandatory Structure of Corporate Law", 89 Colum. L. Rev. 1549 (1989) (explaining risk of opportunistic charter amendment).

[51] See, e.g., Black et al., *supra* note 10.

[52] See *Williams v. Geier*, 671 A.2d 1368, 1378 (Del. 1996) ("[T]here was on this record . . . no non-pro-rata or disproportionate benefit which accrued to the Family Group on the face of the Recapitalization, although the dynamics of how the Plan would work in practice had the effect of strengthening the Family Group's control."); see also *eBay Domestic Holdings v. Newmark*, 16 A.3d 1 (Del. Ch. 2010).

5 "Difficult Cases"

In this section, we consider two examples of transactions that have occupied courts and scholars alike and are not easily classified as dealing with either minority protection or controller rights. We first address freezeout transactions. Transactions of this type raise an inevitable and difficult tension between minority protection and controller rights. Second, we consider Delaware's indeterminate approach concerning transactions in which both the controller and the minority sell, for equal consideration, 100% of the firm to a third party. In these cases, the need for minority protection is substantially weaker than in a freezeout transaction. At the same time, however, subjecting these transactions to closer scrutiny is unlikely to interfere with the controller's right to secure her business vision.

5.1 Freezeout Transactions

In a freezeout transaction, the controlling shareholder of a publicly traded company buys out minority shareholders in order to take the company private. Although freezeouts have been subject to extensive analysis by legal scholars,[53] courts continue to struggle with the proper approach to regulating these transactions.[54]

Let us start with controller rights. Reviewing freezeout transactions through the lens of the inevitable conflict between minority protection and controller rights calls for providing controllers with an option to discontinue their partnership with the minority by taking the firm private. Buying out the minority may be required when keeping the firm public interferes with the realization of idiosyncratic vision,[55] or when a minority-protection regime proves too costly. Additionally, bolstering minority protection increases the likelihood that minority-protection measures will interfere with the controller's freedom to pursue her vision, thereby creating an increased need to make it possible for controllers to take the corporation private.[56] Furthermore, there is an obvious difficulty in forcing an

---

[53] See, e.g., Lucian A. Bebchuk & Marcel Kahan, Adverse Selection and Gains to Controllers on Corporate Freezeouts, in Concentrated Corporate Ownership 247 (Randall Morck ed., 2000); Ronald J. Gilson & Jeffery N. Gordon, "Doctrines and Markets: Controlling Controlling Shareholders", 152 U. Pa. L. Rev. 785, 785 (2003); Zohar Goshen & Zvi Wiener, "The Value of the Freezeout Option, Berkeley Program in Law & Economics", Working Paper Series (Mar. 1, 2000); Guhan Subramaman, "Fixing Freezeouts", 115 Yale L. J. 2 (2005).

[54] See, e.g., In re CNX Gas Corp., 4 A.3d 397 (Del. Ch. 2010) (developing the unified standard for reviewing controlling shareholder freezeout transactions). See also In re MFW Shareholders Litigation, 67 A.3d 496 (Del. Ch. 2013) (holding that freezeout mergers could be subject to the business judgment rule if the controller allows the firm to adopt certain procedural safeguards).

[55] For example, an entrepreneur may believe it is no longer possible to implement her vision while complying with the extensive disclosure duties imposed on public companies. In this case, the only way for the entrepreneur–controller to implement her plan and capture the value she attaches to the project is by taking the firm private. See Harry DeAngelo, Linda DeAngelo, & Edward M. Rice, "Going Private: Minority Freezeouts and Shareholder Wealth", 27 J. L. & Econ. 367 (1984) (finding the source of efficiency to be the elimination of the costs attendant to the regulation of public ownership).

[56] Assume a liability rule protection against self-dealing under which courts make errors in 20% of the cases: in half of them they approve unfair transactions and in the other half they block fair transactions.

entrepreneur to "work" for others—minority investors—for as long as the investors wish or demand.[57] As a matter of legal doctrine, the need to provide the controller with an option to buy out the minority explains why Delaware courts have abandoned the requirement that freezeout transactions satisfy a business purpose test.[58]

For minority shareholders, however, freezeout transactions present a substantial risk of expropriation on a large scale. Controlling shareholders might opportunistically use the option to buy out the minority at unfair prices while taking advantage of their superior access to information concerning the firm's true value.[59] The risk of expropriation calls for effective measures to protect minority shareholders in freezeout transactions.

However, a property rule protection—requiring a freezeout transaction to be conditional on a majority-of-the-minority vote—might undermine the controller's ability to take the firm private in order to preserve her idiosyncratic vision.[60] Providing minority shareholders with the power to veto a freezeout may inhibit the goal of preserving the controller's idiosyncratic vision in two respects. First, asymmetric information or strategic voting considerations might lead minority shareholders to vote against going-private proposals that are fair to the minority, thereby preventing the controller from an exit that could be vital for securing her business vision. Second, forcing the controller to keep the firm public has the same practical consequence as preventing dividend distribution. The court would have to interfere with management decisions, normally protected by the business judgment rule, to make sure the controller continues to work efficiently for the minority. Therefore, despite the high risk of expropriation, protection for minority shareholders in freezeout transactions should tilt toward a liability rule protection.[61]

A narrow reading of the Delaware Chancery Court's decisions in *CNX Gas* is consistent with favoring liability rule protection for minority shareholders in the context of a freezeout. It is possible to read the decision as requiring controlling shareholders to allow the board to use a poison pill to prevent a freezeout.[62] However, in a subsequent decision, the court

When the court approves an unfair transaction, the direct damage is the given transfer of wealth from the minority to the controller (i.e., zero sum transfer), while the indirect damage of under-deterrence is limited due to the small percentage of such mistakes. However, when the court erroneously blocks a fair transaction the damage is not limited to over-deterrence and zero sum transfer, as it also includes the frustration of business vision. The last damage might in some cases be too high to tolerate. Thus, due to the potential incidence of such cases the legal system should contain a safety valve when minority shareholder protections are involved—the ability to take the company private.

[57] See Uniform Partnership Act (1997) § 601 (explaining partnership is at will).

[58] See *Weinberger v. UOP, Inc.*, 457 A.2d 701 (Del. 1983) (explaining that allowing controllers to buy out the minority only if they present convincing business reasons for taking the firm private would overly burden controllers, especially given the role played by asymmetric information). See also *Jones v. H. F. Ahmanson & Co.*, 460 P.2d 464, 469 (Cal. 1969).

[59] See *Coggins v. New England Patriots Football Club, Inc.*, 492 N.E.2d 1112 (Mass. 1986) (reviewing controller opportunism to the detriment of minority shareholders under the old "business purpose" test).

[60] See also Benjamin E. Hermalin & Alan Schwartz, "Buyouts in Large Companies", 25 J. Leg. Stud. 351 (1996) (calling for protecting the minority with a liability rule to provide the controller with optimal incentives to encourage her entrepreneurial effort).

[61] To be sure, a legal regime could adopt of variety of measures to protect the minority, such as approval by special committees of the board and shifting the burden of proof to controllers. Yet, some form of an exit option should be left open even when the minority objects.

[62] See *In re CNX Gas Corp.*, 4 A.3d 397, 415 (Del. Ch. 2010) ("[A] controller making a tender offer does not have an inalienable right to usurp or restrict the authority of the subsidiary board of directors.

seems to suggest that a poison pill is required only if the controller wishes to avoid judicial review of the transaction under the entire fairness standard.[63] In other words, the court allowed controllers to choose between a liability rule (judicial review) and a property rule (majority-of-the-minority vote and board veto). Allowing controllers to choose the legal regime that would apply to their going-private transaction seems consistent with the pursuit of idiosyncratic vision.[64] However, a regime that would compel controllers to subject their going-private transaction to a board's deployment of a poison pill would unnecessarily delay the freezeout by forcing the controller to replace the directors before merging.

5.2 Sale to Third Party

The last example we consider is a transaction in which a third party, unrelated to the controller, buys all the company's shares from both the controller and the minority shareholders. In a transaction of this type, the controller—with a majority of the votes—can effectively force the minority to sell their shares (an implied drag-along option). Delaware courts have reviewed such transactions under different levels of scrutiny, depending on whether the controller and the minority received equal consideration. A sale to a third party raises genuine minority protection concerns when the consideration for the controller differs from that payable to the minority. Cases of this type create a conflict between the controller and the minority over the allocation of the sale proceeds. The controller might abuse her control over the target by bargaining with the third party buyer for a transaction that would benefit the controller at the expense of the minority. Not surprisingly, courts have subjected these transactions to the searching entire fairness test.[65]

In contrast, when a third party buyer offers equal consideration to all shareholders, minority shareholders should not need any protection. After all, with the largest equity stake and no apparent conflict, the controller could be relied on to work diligently to achieve the best feasible bargain. Yet Delaware case law on this issue is in remarkable disarray. While some decisions hold that these transactions do not require close scrutiny,[66] others have allowed minority shareholders to proceed with claims that the controller's need for

A subsidiary board, acting directly or through a special committee, can deploy a rights plan legitimately against a controller's tender offer . . . to provide the subsidiary with time to respond, negotiate, and develop alternatives.").

[63] See id.

[64] For this reason, we also support the recent decision in *In re MFW S'holders Litig.*, 67 A.3d 496 (Del. Ch. 2013) (holding that a freezeout merger could be subject to the business judgment standard of review if the controller both (i) allowed a special committee of independent directors to veto the transaction; and (ii) conditioned the transaction on a majority-of-minority shareholder vote).

[65] See *In re John Q. Hammons Hotels Inc. S'holder Litig.*, Civil Action No. 758-CC, 2009 WL 3165613 (Del. Ch. 2009) (requiring procedural protections in order to apply the business judgment rule); *Ryan v. Tad's Enters., Inc.*, 709 A.2d 682, 689 & n.9 (Del. Ch. 1996), aff'd, 693 A.2d 1082 (Del. 1997) (applying entire fairness when the controlling stockholder received a benefit that was not shared with the minority shareholders in an asset sale).

[66] See *Trenwick Am. Litig. Trust v. Ernst & Young, L.L.P.*, 906 A.2d 168, 202 n.95 (Del. Ch. 2006) ("[T]ransactions where the minority receive the same consideration as the majority, particularly a majority entitled to sell its own position for a premium, had long been thought to fall within the ambit of non-conflict transactions subject to business judgment rule protection.").

cash—liquidity—created a conflict of interest that justified the court's review of the transaction.[67] Delaware courts' willingness to treat the controller's liquidity needs as creating a conflict that justifies judicial review is especially puzzling given their reluctance to treat the controller's liquidity needs as justifying judicial review in other contexts, such as pro-rata dividends.[68] Despite this seemingly inconsistent approach, the answer to the courts' treatment may lie, not in the nature of the conflict, but rather in the absence of business vision concerns.

To begin, the controller can sell her block at a premium, thereby taking her share of the idiosyncratic vision, while enabling the minority to stay and share in the expected profits arising from the buyer's idiosyncratic vision. Alternatively, the controller can freeze the minority out to pursue her idiosyncratic vision in a wholly owned corporation, subject only to minority shareholders' right to receive an appraisal and entire fairness protection.[69] However, in contrast to these situations, the right to drag-along the minority does not protect the controller's idiosyncratic vision: The controller sells the corporation and ends her pursuit of the vision. Why, then, does the controller receive the right to force the minority to sell their shares along with her?

The answer is to allow the *buyer* to pursue her business vision in a wholly owned corporation. Instead of buying just the control block and then freezing out the minority subject to appraisal rights and entire fairness review, the buyer is willing to pay an equal premium to the minority to avoid the costs of a freezeout (i.e., time, effort, uncertainty, and litigation). In this scenario, the controlling seller who forces the minority to sell together with her assumes the role of an auctioneer. However, the controller has substantial holdings that normally induce her to maximize sale price. Thus, unlike the board of directors of a widely held firm that assumes the role of an auctioneer subject to both duty of loyalty and a heightened duty of care (i.e., *Revlon* duties),[70] the controller is only subject to the duty of loyalty.

Of course, the controller can avoid the role of an auctioneer by selling only her block. Obviously, she will simply do just that unless selling with the minority will result in a higher price. Put differently, the seller needs the minority to sell with her not because doing so will allow her to get the right price for her business vision, but because it will allow her to extract a higher share of the *buyer's* idiosyncratic vision. Accordingly, a controller cannot, for example, decide to take a cash offer over a higher valued bid while dragging along the minority to satisfy her liquidity needs, as this would be a breach of her duties as an auctioneer.

---

[67] See *McMullin v. Beran*, 765 A.2d 910 (Del. 2000) (stating duty-of-loyalty claim could be filed against the parent for negotiating an all-cash transaction to satisfy a liquidity need); *N.J. Carpenters Pension Fund v. Infogroup, Inc.*, 2011 WL 4825888, at *4, *9–10 (Del. Ch. 2011) (denying motion to dismiss when the director, who was also a large stockholder, was in desperate need of liquidity to satisfy personal judgments, repay loans, and fund a new venture). See also *In re Synthes, Inc. S'holder Litig.*, 2012 WL 3594293, at *10 (Del. Ch. 2012) (NO. CIV.A. 6452) ("[I]t may be that there are very narrow circumstances in which a controlling stockholder's immediate need for liquidity could constitute a disabling conflict of interest irrespective of pro rata treatment.").

[68] See *Sinclair Oil Corp. v. Levien*, 280 A.2d 717 (Del. 1971) (explaining pro-rata dividend payments are subject to business judgment rule, even if paid for clear benefit of controlling shareholder/parent).

[69] See, e.g., Del. Gen. Corp. L. § 262 (providing for appraisal rights); *Kahn v. Lynch Commc'ns Sys., Inc.*, 638 A.2d 1110, 1115 (Del. 1994) (entire fairness).

[70] *Revlon, Inc. v. MacAndrews & Forbes Holdings, Inc.*, 506 A.2d 173 (Del. 1986).

Our framework thus calls for a different treatment of controllers' liquidity needs across transactions. A regime that imposes stricter scrutiny on dividend distributions would inevitably interfere with the controllers' management rights and might undermine their ability to preserve their idiosyncratic vision. These concerns cease to apply when the controller decides to sell the whole corporation to a third party. By putting her management rights up for sale, and also forcing the minority to sell, the controller signals that she is no longer concerned with the firm's implementing *her* idiosyncratic vision. Moreover, a sale to the highest bidder also means that asymmetric information is no longer an issue. In other words, employing judicial review is less likely to be costly here. Thus, even a relatively small risk of a conflict of interest may call for judicial scrutiny.

6 SUMMARY

In publicly held companies with concentrated ownership, minority protection is a central concern of firm regulation. The presence of a controlling shareholder who owns only a fraction (albeit a majority) of cash-flow rights leads to potential agency costs for minority shareholders. In our framework, however, the need to protect minority shareholders from these inevitable agency costs must be balanced against preserving controlling shareholders' ability to pursue their idiosyncratic vision. This tension determines the type of protection that should apply to both the controllers' rights to make management decisions and the minority's rights to receive a pro-rata share of the firm's cash flows.

The value of control lies at least partially in the freedom for an entrepreneur to pursue her idiosyncratic vision associated with her business idea. This pursuit commonly takes place under the conditions of asymmetric information and differences of opinions. Consequently, this chapter discussed the need for property rule protection of the controlling owner's right to control. Property rule protection guarantees that minority shareholders or courts cannot unilaterally take control rights away from the controller, even for objectively fair compensation. The deferential business judgment rule further strengthens the controlling shareholder's ability to manage the company in pursuit of her idiosyncratic vision. Property rule protection extends to a broad range of corporate actions by the board, such as preserving the controlling shareholder's control even when it is not value-maximizing and protecting the ability of controllers to sell their control block for a premium.

On the other hand, the form of minority protection is also an important question for any legal regime. Minority protection can take two primary forms. Liability rule protection guarantees the minority shareholders that they will receive objective compensation for any unfair self-dealing by a controlling owner after an ex post entire fairness review by the courts. Property rule protection requires a majority-of-the-minority vote ex ante before any self-dealing transaction can be consummated in the first place, essentially guaranteeing the minority the subjective value of their consent. Transaction costs inform which rule should be utilized. Differences in the relative size of negotiation and adjudication costs based on the efficacy of judicial systems, efficiency of markets, and presence of institutional investors suggest a liability rule in some jurisdictions and a property rule in others.

Minority protection is characterized fundamentally by the principle of equal, or pro-rata, distribution. Under this imperative, controlling shareholders have agreed to allow minority shareholders to share equally the proceeds arising from the controller's freedom to pursue her idiosyncratic vision. However, the application of this principle can be difficult in reality because of the frequently unclear division between conflicted and non-conflicted transactions. Finally, certain kinds of transactions, such as freezeouts and sales of 100% of a controlled company to a third party, present unique problems in achieving an optimal balance between securing the controller's ability to pursue her business vision and protecting the minority shareholders against agency costs and exploitation.

CHAPTER 18

....

DEBT AND CORPORATE GOVERNANCE

....

CHARLES K. WHITEHEAD[1]

1 INTRODUCTION

....

WITHIN the traditional framing,[2] lenders rely on loan covenants and monitoring to minimize agency costs, restrain borrower misbehavior, and manage credit risk.[3] A borrower's commitment to making principal and interest payments may also reduce the agency costs of free cash flow.[4] Debt, however, can be a clunky governance device.[5] Financial contracts are incomplete and covenants are imprecise—reflecting, among other things, the difficulty of predicting a borrower's future actions and circumstances when first agreeing on a

---

[1] Myron C. Taylor Alumni Professor of Business Law, Cornell Law School, and Professor and Director, Law, Technology & Entrepreneurship Program, Cornell Tech. Portions of this chapter are derived from Charles K. Whitehead, "The Evolution of Debt: Covenants, the Credit Market, and Corporate Governance", 34 J. Corp. L. 641 (2009) [hereinafter Whitehead, Evolution of Debt]. I appreciate the valuable research assistance provided by Eric DiMuzio and Shandy Pinkowski.

[2] I mark the traditional framing as the agency–cost model published in Michael C. Jensen & William H. Meckling, "Theory of the Firm: Managerial Behavior, Agency Costs and Ownership Structure", 3 J. Fin. Econ. 305, 308–10 (1976).

[3] See id. at 337–38. Empirical work suggests that public debt covenants, which are typically less restrictive than bank covenants, see Greg Nini et al., "Creditor Control Rights and Firm Investment Policy", 92 J. Fin. Econ. 400, 401 (2009), also reduce agency costs. See, e.g., Matthew T. Billett et al., "Growth Opportunities and the Choice of Leverage, Debt Maturity, and Covenants", 62 J. Fin. 697, 729 (2007).

[4] See Michael C. Jensen, "Agency Costs of Free Cash Flow, Corporate Finance, and Takeovers", 76 Am. Econ. Rev. 323, 324 (1986) (noting that debt contracts bind managers, while promises to pay dividends do not); see also René M. Stulz, "Managerial Discretion and Optimal Financing Policies", 26 J. Fin. Econ. 3, 4 (1990) (suggesting that debt, which reduces investment in all states, addresses the agency costs of overinvestment).

[5] References to "governance" and "corporate governance" in this chapter are to mechanisms to reduce or deter agency costs arising from management incentives or actions that impede the maximization of firm value.

loan's terms.[6] If the terms are too flexible, the borrower may pursue projects that benefit its shareholders, potentially at the lender's expense.[7] If the terms are too strict, the borrower may forgo projects that are valuable to the firm and, potentially, its creditors.[8] Over time, as new information arises, lenders can renegotiate the loan's terms—including modifying outdated covenants and waiving events of default—but only to the extent the original agreement was broad enough in the first place to capture the borrower's future actions or circumstances.[9]

As Oliver Williamson has described, the way a firm is governed is closely related to how it raises capital.[10] A corollary to Williamson's insight is that change in the capital markets can also result in change in corporate governance.[11] This chapter traces debt's evolving role as a corporate governance device (sometimes referred to as "debt governance") in light of developments in the private credit market. It starts by reviewing debt as it was traditionally structured—illiquid and largely reliant on covenants and monitoring, with contract providing creditors a long-term say in how borrowers were managed. The chapter then explains how the relationship between creditors and borrowers has evolved over time as traditionally private instruments have become more liquid. Today, lenders can manage credit risk through purchases and sales of loans and other credit risk,[12] potentially lowering capital costs,[13] but

---

[6] See George G. Triantis & Ronald J. Daniels, "The Role of Debt in Interactive Corporate Governance", 83 Cal. L. Rev. 1073, 1093–94 (1995) ("[C]ovenants are imperfect predictors of when bank exit or intervention is optimal . . . ."); see also Jensen & Meckling, *supra* note 2, at 338 (anticipating that the costs of writing exhaustive covenants would be "non-trivial").

[7] See, e.g., Jensen & Meckling, *supra* note 2, at 335 ("[I]f the owner has the opportunity to first issue debt, then to decide which investments to take, . . . he can transfer wealth from the (naïve) bondholders to himself as equity holder."); see also George Triantis, "Exploring the Limits of Contract Design in Debt Financing", 161 U. Pa. L. Rev. 2041, 2043 (2013) [hereinafter Triantis, Limits of Contract Design] (citing studies that indicate that lenders price covenants).

[8] See, e.g., Jensen & Meckling, *supra* note 2, at 338 ("[C]ovenants occasionally limit management's ability to take optimal actions on certain issues.").

[9] A classic example of activities that fall outside an agreement's terms is Marriott's 1992 spin-off of Marriott International (containing Marriott's most profitable operations) to its shareholders, causing a substantial decline in the value of Marriott's bonds. The spin-off was not prohibited by the bond indenture's terms. See F. John Stark, III et al., "'Marriott Risk': A New Model Covenant to Restrict Transfers of Wealth from Bondholders to Stockholders", 1994 Colum. Bus. L. Rev. 503, 516–19 (1994). Lenders, accordingly, have an incentive to over-regulate a firm's risk taking in an effort to protect their own investments. See Kose John et al., "Corporate Governance and Risk Taking", 63 J. Fin. 1679, 1681 (2008) (finding that corporate risk taking positively correlates with shareholder protection and that growth correlates with risk taking); see also George G. Triantis, "Financial Contract Design in the World of Venture Capital", 68 U. Chi. L. Rev. 305, 315 (2001) (noting that renegotiation "lies at the heart" of banks' relational lending).

[10] See Oliver E. Williamson, "Corporate Finance and Corporate Governance", 43 J. Fin. 567, 579–81 (1988).

[11] See Whitehead, Evolution of Debt, *supra* note 1, at 643–46.

[12] See id. at 656–57.

[13] There is substantial literature on why firms choose to fund with varying amounts of debt, beginning with the Modigliani–Miller claim that, absent frictions, capital structure is irrelevant to firm value. See, e.g., Franco Modigliani & Merton H. Miller, "The Cost of Capital, Corporation Finance and the Theory of Investment", 48 Am. Econ. Rev. 261, 268–69 (1958). Scholarship regarding tax and other real-world frictions demonstrate that firm value may be enhanced through a capital structure that includes both debt and equity. See Franco Modigliani & Merton H. Miller, "Corporate Income Taxes and the Cost of Capital: A Correction", 53 Am. Econ. Rev. 433, 442–43 (1963). But see Merton H. Miller, "Debt and Taxes",

also weakening their incentives to monitor and enforce covenant protections.[14] Loans and lending relationships have evolved in response to those changes, providing new means for debt to influence corporate governance.[15] In particular, actions affecting a borrower's credit quality are more likely to be reflected in the price at which its loans and other credit instruments trade in the secondary market.[16] Those changes can affect the borrower's cost of capital, providing managers with a real-time incentive to minimize risky behavior—an emerging discipline that may complement the traditional protections provided by covenants and monitoring.[17]

2 DEBT'S TRADITIONAL ROLE

Most public company debt is private, and most private loans are made or arranged by commercial banks (although increasingly they involve nonbank lenders).[18] Even among public firms, which typically have access to larger pools of capital,[19] roughly 80% maintain private credit arrangements.[20]

Loans are illiquid within the traditional framing of the firm. The difficulty in trading loans reinforced the lenders' (often banks') reliance on monitoring and covenants in order to manage a borrower's credit risk.[21] Portfolio theory suggested there were less costly means for lenders to do so,[22] but they required a liquid market for the purchase and sale of credit, which

32 J. Fin. 261, 267 (1977) (suggesting that the inclusion of income taxes at the personal level nullifies the advantages of debt). I do not address that scholarship in this chapter, except to the extent it relates to our principal focus on debt governance.

[14] See Whitehead, Evolution of Debt, *supra* note 1, at 646–47. New credit instruments have been blamed for the 2008 financial crisis, calling into question the viability of a corporate governance mechanism that relies, in part, on an increasingly liquid credit market. From the perspective of debt governance there are important differences between those instruments—primarily tied to subprime mortgages—and unsecured corporate debt. By their nature, subprime mortgage instruments rely principally on collateral to manage credit risk. Unsecured loans, however, are much more dependent on covenants and monitoring, without offsetting protection. See id. at 647–48.

[15] See id. at 663–67.   [16] See id. at 668.

[17] See *infra* notes 110–115 and accompanying text; see also Triantis, Limits of Contract Design, *supra* note 7, at 2043 ("To the extent that debt investors price agency costs, a firm can lower its cost of capital by reducing the inefficiencies of debtor-creditor conflict.").

[18] See Joshua D. Rauh & Amir Sufi, "Capital Structure and Debt Structure", 23 Rev. Fin. Stud. 4242, 4250 (2010). Many firms use public and private sources of debt capital, including bank debt, program debt (such as commercial paper), and public bonds. See id. Investment-grade firms rely predominantly on senior unsecured debt and equity, while lower-credit firms rely on a combination of secured bank debt, senior unsecured debt, subordinated bonds, convertible securities, and equity. See id. at 4244.

[19] See id. at 4243–44 (noting that firms with lower credit quality do not have access to certain debt markets).

[20] See Nini et al., *supra* note 3, at 401 (citation omitted).

[21] See Douglas W. Diamond, "Financial Intermediation and Delegated Monitoring", 51 Rev. Econ. Stud. 393, 410 (1984).

[22] Markowitz first demonstrated the benefits of portfolio diversification in the early 1950s, for which he won the Nobel Prize in Economics in 1990. See generally Harry Markowitz, "Portfolio Selection", 7 J. Fin. 77 (1952).

did not exist at the time.[23] Diversification's benefits, therefore, applied principally to public common stock, with lenders instead relying on contractual protections to manage loan-related risks. As described below, other characteristics affecting debt governance included borrower reputation,[24] the reduction in free cash flow,[25] and loan maturity.[26] Together, they provided creditors with tools to oversee a borrower's business and operations.

2.1 Low-Cost Monitoring

Within the standard construct of the firm, lenders rely on long-term relationships in order to monitor borrowers and their credit quality.[27] Banks can access quasi-public information about borrowers in the ordinary course of business—for example, through deposit taking and providing financial advice.[28] Doing so permits banks to monitor borrowers in more detail and at lower cost than other creditors.[29] It also allows banks to detect and deter managerial slack at an early stage, minimizing potential losses and providing shareholders and other investors with a credible signal of the borrower's performance.[30] The resulting benefits can be tangible—the borrower's capital costs may decline as other investors, including shareholders, freeride on the enhanced oversight provided by self-interested bank monitors.[31] That reliance, however, can increase a bank's bargaining power over the borrower. The bank's presumptive knowledge of a borrower's credit quality can create a hold-up problem if the bank demands a greater return as a condition to making (or rolling over) a loan. In response, the borrower may look to diversify its funding sources, relying on other lenders in order to dilute the bank's ability to appropriate rents.[32] Weighing against those benefits, however, is the

[23] See *infra* notes 75–76 and accompanying text.

[24] See *infra* notes 52–55 and accompanying text.

[25] See *infra* notes 56–69 and accompanying text.

[26] See *infra* notes 70–73 and accompanying text.

[27] See Scott L. Lummer & John J. McConnell, "Further Evidence on the Bank Lending Process and the Capital-Market Response to Bank Loan Agreements", 25 J. Fin. Econ. 99, 113 (1989) ("Over time, the bank becomes privy to information not available to outside claimholders, and, based on this information, periodically revises the terms of the credit agreement.").

[28] See, e.g., Fischer Black, "Bank Funds Management in an Efficient Market", 2 J. Fin. Econ. 323, 326, 329 (1975).

[29] See, e.g., Eugene F. Fama, "What's Different About Banks?", 15 J. Monetary Econ. 29, 35–37 (1985).

[30] See Triantis & Daniels, *supra* note 6, at 1077–78; see also Clifford W. Smith, Jr. & Jerold B. Warner, "On Financial Contracting: An Analysis of Bond Covenants", 7 J. Fin. Econ. 117, 122, 124 (1979) (describing, and noting support for, bond covenants as a necessary means to align shareholders and bondholders).

[31] See Joel Houston & Christopher James, "Bank Information Monopolies and the Mix of Private and Public Debt Claims", 51 J. Fin. 1863, 1888 (1996) ("Overall, our results are consistent with the widely held view that banks create durable transaction-specific information as part of an ongoing relationship.").

[32] See Raghuram Rajan, "Insiders and Outsiders: The Choice between Informed and Arm's-Length Debt", 47 J. Fin. 1367, 1392 (1992). Of course, the bank-borrower relationship can change after a loan is made. As J. Paul Getty is said to have observed, "If you owe the bank $100, that's your problem. If you owe the bank $100 million, that's the bank's problem." See Simon Johnson & James Kwak, 13 Bankers: The Wall Street Takeover and the Next Financial Meltdown 184 (2011). A later, unexpected downturn in the borrower's affairs may force the bank to make additional loans or forestall a default rather than risk a write-down of the value of its original investment. See Arnoud W.A. Boot, "Relationship Banking: What Do We Know?", 9 J. Fin. Intermediation 7, 16 (2000). New financial instruments, however, may permit

likelihood that less-informed creditors will seek stricter covenants in order to more closely control a borrower's actions in light of the higher cost of monitoring.[33]

2.2 Covenants

In a perfect world, creditors would be as familiar as a borrower's managers with projects that require new financing. In the real world, with costly monitoring,[34] lenders have only limited information, which potentially allows managers to invest in less profitable projects that may benefit them personally or favor one class of investors over another.[35]

In order to attract new lending at low cost, managers must credibly commit to behave in a manner consistent with the creditors' interests. That commitment is particularly important to debt holders, since shareholders (who benefit from directors' fiduciary duties, and who may exercise voting control over the board[36]) are interested in increasing the firm's risk-taking once debt is in place. Doing so may enhance shareholder returns without raising the limit on their losses. Lenders typically do not share (or share less) in any incremental returns.

Covenants provide one solution by contractually limiting how managers operate the borrower's business. By protecting lenders, tighter covenants can improve the firm's borrowing capacity, decrease costs, and increase share price through the debt capital available to fund new projects and the positive signal provided by new lending.[37] Covenants also act as early warning "trip wires,"[38] when breached, that enable lenders to reassess a borrower's credit quality and mitigate loss by renegotiating a loan's terms.[39]

Covenants, however, are imperfect predictors of management behavior. Lenders may not be able to anticipate a borrower's future actions or circumstances at the time the loan is made.[40] Consequently, covenant violations are not uncommon, but they typically do

a lender to transfer all or a portion of a borrower's credit risk to others, raising the lender's relative bargaining power and enabling it to more effectively enforce its covenant protections. See *infra* note 103 and accompanying text.

[33] See Raghuram Rajan & Andrew Winton, "Covenants and Collateral as Incentives to Monitor", 50 J. Fin. 1113, 1114 (1995) (noting that banks often need incentives to perform monitoring, which may hinge on covenants triggered by "information that is not costlessly available to the public"); Joanna M. Shepherd et al., "What Else Matters for Corporate Governance?: The Case of Bank Monitoring", 88 B.U. L. Rev. 991, 1007–08 (2008) (summarizing the monitoring advantages of banks).

[34] See Kenneth J. Arrow, Pareto Efficiency with Costly Transfers, in Studies in Economic Theory and Practice 73, 74 (Nina Assorodobraj-Kula et al. eds., 1981) (noting that transaction costs are ubiquitous).

[35] See Yakov Amihud et al., "A New Governance Structure for Corporate Bonds", 51 Stan. L. Rev. 447, 453–54 (1999); Jensen & Meckling, *supra* note 2, at 335 (describing how a manager can theoretically reallocate wealth to himself and the shareholders); Smith & Warner, *supra* note 30, at 118–19 (summarizing major sources of conflict between bondholders and shareholders).

[36] No state affirmatively grants debt holders the right to vote, although a few state codes make it optional. See, e.g., Cal. Corp. Code § 204(a)(7) (West 2014); Del. Code Ann. tit. 8, § 221 (West 2014).

[37] See Fama, *supra* note 29, at 37.   [38] See Triantis & Daniels, *supra* note 6, at 1093.

[39] See Ilia D. Dichev & Douglas J. Skinner, "Large-Sample Evidence on the Debt Covenant Hypothesis", 40 J. Acct. Research 1091, 1097 (2002) (citations omitted) (discussing how violations are treated in practice across firms in different financial condition); Daniel R. Fischel, "The Economics of Lender Liability", 99 Yale L. J. 131, 138–40 (1989) (summarizing the considerations bearing upon lender opportunism).

[40] See Jensen & Meckling, *supra* note 2, at 338.

not result in lenders accelerating repayment of the loan or taking control of the borrower.[41] Instead, the violations are often waived by the lenders, but can be costly to a borrower because renegotiations may prompt closer scrutiny of the borrower's credit quality
and tighter covenant restrictions in both the renegotiated and future loans.[42] Managers,
therefore, have a strong incentive to ensure the firm complies with the loan's original
terms.[43]

A loan's terms may also adjust in response to changes in a borrower's circumstances.[44]
A pricing grid is one example. Normally, a decline in cash flow would cause the borrower, in
light of its riskier position, to be better off under the loan's original terms than if it entered
into a new loan, creating a strong incentive for it to avoid renegotiation. A pricing grid can
adjust the amount of interest that is payable based on changes in a borrower's riskiness, as
measured by its financial ratios or credit rating. By increasing interest payments, the pricing
grid shifts the relative bargaining power to the lender, which can restructure the loan to reflect the borrower's new circumstances. Conversely, improved performance can cause a drop
in the interest the borrower must pay, reflecting its better credit quality.[45] Together, the grid
establishes minimum performance standards for the borrower and rewards actions that
minimize risk to the lender.[46]

A creditor can also use covenants to limit a borrower's use of funds that are available
to repay its loan.[47] The effect of the limit is likely to depend on the borrower's characteristics. A start-up firm with high growth opportunities, for example, is likely to benefit if
management's hands are relatively untied, permitting them to allocate capital to the most
profitable projects. Such a firm, however, often has fewer tangible assets against which
a loan can be made. The lender may then rely on shorter maturities[48] or more costly loan
restrictions in order to manage its exposure to the borrower.[49] A slower-growing firm, by
contrast, faces the possibility of managers making unprofitable investments. In that case,
covenants restricting overinvestment or a borrower's ability to incur debt may benefit the
lender. Explicitly limiting capital expenditures, particularly after a decline in the firm's
credit quality, is likely to enhance operating performance and cause a rise in stock price.[50]
Although there is a risk that some covenants will limit profitable activity, that cost can be

---

[41] See Dichev & Skinner, *supra* note 39, at 1122.

[42] See Frederick Tung, "Leverage in the Board Room: The Unsung Influence of Private Lenders in
Corporate Governance", 57 UCLA L. Rev. 115, 141–44 (2009).

[43] See Nini et al., *supra* note 3, at 410; see also Michael R. Roberts & Amir Sufi, "Control Rights
and Capital Structure: An Empirical Investigation", 64 J. Fin. 1657, 1666 (2009) ("[C]reditors use their
acceleration right to extract amendment fees, reduce unused credit availability, increase interest rates,
increase reporting requirements, increase collateral requirements, and restrict corporate investment."
(citations omitted)); Smith & Warner, *supra* note 30, at 151–52 (predicting that private debt initially
contains stricter restrictions because it is easier for them to be renegotiated).

[44] Examples of loan agreement contingencies appear in Michael R. Roberts & Amir Sufi,
"Renegotiation of Financial Contracts: Evidence from Private Credit Agreements", 93 J. Fin. Econ. 159,
165 (2009), and Tung, *supra* note 42, at 147–50.

[45] See Roberts & Sufi, *supra* note 44, at 165.   [46] See Tung, *supra* note 42, at 148–49.

[47] See Sudheer Chava & Michael R. Roberts, "How Does Financing Impact Investment? The Role of
Debt Covenants", 63 J. Fin. 2085, 2088 (2008).

[48] For a discussion of the use of maturity to manage risk, see *infra* notes 70–73 and accompanying text.

[49] See Billett et al., *supra* note 3, at 721–22.   [50] See Nini et al., *supra* note 3, at 415–17.

offset by the ability, among a small group of lenders, to inexpensively renegotiate covenants that become too restrictive.[51]

2.3 Reputation

A borrower's reputation can affect the covenant types that lenders demand and, in turn, the means by which lenders oversee corporate governance.[52] A firm that repeatedly accesses the credit market has an economic interest in developing a reputation as a "good" borrower, acting in a manner consistent with lender expectations. Lenders may begin to relax their reliance on covenants and monitoring for borrowers with established reputations.[53] Nevertheless, as Michael Jensen and William Meckling famously noted, even "sainthood" cannot drive agency costs to zero.[54] Lenders and borrowers have short-term memories, so the incentives that make reputation valuable in the near-term can shift with changes in the marketplace. Actions that prompt a poor reputation may be forgotten over time.[55]

2.4 Free Cash Flow

Debt can help curb excessive management spending, in large part through contractual provisions, like loan covenants, that require the debtor to make specified payments (principal and interest), meet minimum financial criteria, report periodically, and operate within bounds specified by the creditors.[56] Loans, therefore, can reduce the

---

[51] See Patrick Bolton & David S. Scharfstein, "Optimal Debt Structure and the Number of Creditors", 104 J. Pol. Econ. 1, 19–20 (1996) (noting that ease of negotiation varies by the number of creditors); Stewart C. Myers, "Determinants of Corporate Borrowing", 5 J. Fin. Econ. 147, 158 (1977) (characterizing value-maximizing debt contracts as "extremely difficult to write"); Smith & Warner, *supra* note 30, at 151–52 (predicting that private lenders start with more restrictive covenants and modify the terms going forward).

[52] Credit ratings historically have provided an important assessment of market reputation, see Claire A. Hill, "Regulating the Rating Agencies", 82 Wash. U. L. Q. 43, 74 (2004) (suggesting that markets believe that the agencies are independent); Frank Partnoy, "The Siskel and Ebert of Financial Markets?: Two Thumbs Down for the Credit Rating Agencies", 77 Wash. U. L. Q. 619, 622–23 & n.13 (1999), even though recent findings regarding conflicts of interest, inadequate staffing, and a failure to follow their own guidelines have drawn the rating agencies' credibility into question. See, e.g., Div. of Trading & Markets, U.S. Sec. & Exch. Comm'n, Report to Congress on Assigned Credit Ratings 12–13 (2012); Gretchen Morgenson, Debt Watchdogs: Tamed or Caught Napping?, N.Y. Times, Dec. 7, 2008, at 1.

[53] See Douglas W. Diamond, "Monitoring and Reputation: The Choice between Bank Loans and Directly Placed Debt", 99 J. Pol. Econ. 689, 690 (1991) ("Reputation effects eliminate the need for monitoring when the value of future profits lost because of information revealed by defaulting on debt is large."); Amir Sufi, "Information Asymmetry and Financing Arrangements: Evidence from Syndicated Loans", 62 J. Fin. 629, 630 (2007) (noting that reputation reduces information asymmetry).

[54] Jensen & Meckling, *supra* note 2, at 351.

[55] See William W. Bratton, Jr., "Corporate Debt Relationships: Legal Theory in a Time of Restructuring", 1989 Duke L.J. 92, 141–42 (1989).

[56] See Williamson, *supra* note 10, at 572. A description of standard loan covenants appears in Tung, *supra* note 42, at 144–50.

agency costs of free cash flow, making less cash available to be spent at the managers' discretion.[57]

The board typically has discretion to suspend dividend payments, but suspending interest payments usually is a breach of the firm's debt obligations. Thus, debt financing increases the risk of bankruptcy, and greater leverage increases a firm's risk of incurring the real costs of financial distress—the actual costs of bankruptcy, as well as a rise in risk premiums demanded by customers, suppliers, and employees.[58] In order to reduce those risks, managers are motivated to maximize profitability, including by reducing business expenses, working harder, and investing more carefully.[59] Incurring greater debt may signal a manager's confidence in the company's future by requiring a commitment to making profitable investments (in order to pay amounts owing under the indebtedness) and a willingness to be monitored by outsiders.[60] Furthermore, greater leverage permits superior managers to signal their quality, separating them from managers who potentially suffer a greater risk of bankruptcy.[61] Managers have a direct, personal stake in avoiding bankruptcy, since directors and officers of bankrupt firms tend to do poorly in the labor market.[62]

On balance, entrenched managers[63] are more likely to prefer lower levels of borrowing in order to reduce monitoring and minimize the limitations imposed by

---

[57] See, e.g., Jensen, *supra* note 4, at 324; Stulz, *supra* note 4, at 4.

[58] See Milton Harris & Artur Raviv, "Corporate Control Contests and Capital Structure", 20 J. Fin. Econ. 55, 58 (1988). Greater leverage can also be used to deter a hostile takeover, perhaps incurred to finance a defensive self-tender offer that increases management's percentage of voting control, with entrenched managers weighing the benefits of continued control against the potential cost and disciplining effect of greater indebtedness. See René M. Stulz, "Managerial Control of Voting Rights: Financing Policies and the Market for Corporate Control", 20 J. Fin. Econ. 25, 26–27 (1988).

[59] See Sanford J. Grossman & Oliver D. Hart, Corporate Financial Structure and Managerial Incentives, in The Economics of Information and Uncertainty 107, 108–09 (John J. McCall ed., 1982); see also Milton Harris & Artur Raviv, "Capital Structure and the Informational Role of Debt", 45 J. Fin. 321, 323 (1990) ("The optimal amount of debt is determined by trading off the value of information and opportunities for disciplining management against the probability of incurring investigation costs."); Michael C. Jensen, Active Investors, LBOs, and the Privatization of Bankruptcy, Statement Before the H. Ways and Means Comm., reprinted in 2 J. Appl. Corp. Fin. 35, 41–42 (1989) (showing that higher levels of debt-to-value incentivize resolving insolvency without liquidation); Jeffrey Zwiebel, "Dynamic Capital Structure under Managerial Entrenchment", 86 Am. Econ. Rev. 1197, 1198–99 (1996) ("[T]hrough bankruptcy, debt enables the future retention of managers to depend on current as well as anticipated future investments.").

[60] See Diamond, *supra* note 53, at 713–14; Hayne E. Leland & David H. Pyle, "Informational Asymmetries, Financial Structure, and Financial Intermediation", 32 J. Fin. 371, 372 (1977).

[61] See, e.g., Grossman & Hart, *supra* note 59, at 109–10 (considering the issuance of debt "as being an example of . . . bonding behavior") (emphasis omitted). The resulting rise in the borrower's stock price can further enhance a manager's job security. See Philip G. Berger et al., "Managerial Entrenchment and Capital Structure Decisions", 52 J. Fin. 1411, 1413 (1997) ("[O]ur findings also seem consistent with a conjecture that most firms have less leverage in their capital structure than is optimal, and that managers who sense threats to their security increase leverage permanently as a value enhancing action.").

[62] See, e.g., Stuart C. Gilson, "Management Turnover and Financial Distress", 25 J. Fin. Econ. 241, 242 (1989) (noting that a majority of financially distressed firms saw management turnover and that none of the departing managers "hold a senior-management position at another exchange-listed firm during the next three years").

[63] In this chapter, a manager is considered entrenched when it is difficult for the shareholders to remove her and, consequently, she is able to use the firm to further her own interests rather than those of

creditors.[64] Less debt reduces the risk of financial distress and, in turn, the risk to managers of losing the private perks of their position.[65] Nevertheless, in some cases, entrenched managers may incur higher levels of indebtedness. A manager whose interests are aligned with the shareholders (e.g., where compensation is tied to the firm's stock price) may prefer riskier policy choices that are more likely to benefit shareholders at the creditors' expense.[66] Entrenched managers may be less risky—more willing to adopt conservative investment policies[67]—and, therefore, lenders may be more willing to provide those managers with lower-cost financing.[68] In that case, a greater reliance on debt may reflect weaker corporate governance rather than signal an improvement in managerial performance.[69]

2.5 Maturity

Loan maturities can also affect corporate governance. Debt with a short-term maturity motivates managers to invest in profitable projects or risk the loss of future, near-term financing. Before rolling over an existing loan or extending a new one, lenders must be convinced of management's ability to operate the firm profitably; any doubts may be reflected in increased capital costs.[70] Likewise, if funding is short term, successful management can be

the shareholders. See Michael S. Weisbach, "Outside Directors and CEO Turnover", 20 J. Fin. Econ. 431, 435 (1988).

[64] See Sudip Datta et al., "Managerial Stock Ownership and the Maturity Structure of Corporate Debt", 60 J. Fin. 2333, 2342 (2005) (finding that entrenched managers seek debt with longer maturities to insulate themselves from monitoring).

[65] See Gerald T. Garvey & Gordon Hanka, "Capital Structure and Corporate Control: The Effect of Antitakeover Statutes on Firm Leverage", 54 J. Fin. 519, 521 (1999) (finding that managers protected by takeover statutes reduce leverage, which suggests debt may be a takeover defense); Leonard L. Lundstrum, "Entrenched Management, Capital Structure Changes and Firm Value", 33 J. Econ. & Fin. 161, 172 (2009) ("We conclude that the positive relationship between ownership and the change in leverage is confined to the 'entrenchment' range of managerial share ownership.").

[66] See Jeffrey L. Coles et al., "Managerial Incentives and Risk-Taking", 79 J. Fin. Econ. 431, 432 (2006). Perhaps the best-known case law illustration of the tension between shareholders and creditors is found in footnote 55 of the Delaware Chancery Court's decision in *Credit Lyonnais Bank Nederland, N.V. v. Pathe Communications Corp.*, 1991 WL 277613 (1991). There, Chancellor Allen posed a hypothetical where a firm's sole asset was a judgment ($51 million) against a solvent debtor. The case was on appeal, with the firm receiving offers to settle for an amount that would satisfy both shareholders and debt holders. Diversified shareholders, nevertheless, would be likely to reject the settlement offers and appeal, since the additional upside if the firm won would be theirs, whereas the downside of losing would be borne by both shareholders and debt holders.

[67] See John et al., *supra* note 9, at 1680.

[68] See Kose John & Lubomir Litov, "Managerial Entrenchment and Capital Structure: New Evidence", 7 J. Empirical Legal Stud. 693, 694–95 (2010) ("[F]irms with entrenched managers . . . rely more on debt to meet their external financing needs.").

[69] See id.

[70] See Nini et al., *supra* note 3, at 401; see also René Stulz, Does Financial Structure Matter for Economic Growth? A Corporate Finance Perspective, in Financial Structure and Economic Growth: A Cross-Country Comparison of Banks, Markets, and Development 143, 151, 160 (Asli Demirgüç-Kunt & Ross Levine eds., 2001).

reflected in a lower cost of refinancing, resulting in a decline in the firm's capital costs that benefits shareholders as well as creditors.[71]

Longer-term debt postpones a borrower's need for refinancing. The longer maturity may reflect less need for creditor oversight, or it may reflect concerns over the borrower's near-term capacity to repay the loan.[72] Repayment, however, depends on the borrower's future earnings, so longer maturities may also help motivate managers to pursue longer-term, value-additive projects.[73]

3 Private Credit Market Liquidity

Within the traditional framing of the firm, a bank's familiarity with a borrower made it less costly for it to extend loans than a more arm's-length creditor.[74] That same advantage also made it more difficult for the bank to resell loans to less knowledgeable purchasers, a classic "lemons problem" that impeded the creation of a liquid credit market.[75] The lending business, however, began to transform in the 1970s and 1980s, driven by increasing competition (both for depositors and borrowers), innovation in the marketplace, and changes in financial regulation.[76] Developments in technology also eroded the banks' informational advantage over nonbanks, making it easier for new market participants to assess a borrower's

[71] See Myers, *supra* note 51, at 1559 ("Borrowing short … offer[s a] setting for continuous and gradual renegotiation."); see also Michael J. Barclay & Clifford W. Smith, Jr., "The Maturity Structure of Corporate Debt", 50 J. Fin. 609, 612 (1995) (noting that short-term debt increases a lender's power and can encourage the exercise of growth options).

[72] See Mark J. Flannery, "Asymmetric Information and Risk Debt Maturity Choice", 41 J. Fin. 19, 20 (1986) (noting that insiders in quality firms perceive long-term premiums generated by uncertainty as excessive, while insiders in lower-quality firms prefer longer-term debt).

[73] See Oliver Hart & John Moore, "Debt and Seniority: An Analysis of the Role of Hard Claims in Constraining Management", 85 Am. Econ. Rev. 567, 568 (1995).

[74] See *supra* notes 27–29 and accompanying text.

[75] See Diamond, *supra* note 21, at 409 (noting that if bankers can observe each other's information and actions, they face no group moral hazard problem). For the classic description of the effects of informational asymmetries on markets, see George A. Akerlof, "The Market for 'Lemons': Quality Uncertainty and the Market Mechanism", 84 Q. J. Econ. 488 (1970); see also Darrell Duffie, "Innovations in Credit Risk Transfer: Implications for Financial Stability" 7 (Bank for Int'l. Settlements, Working Paper No. 255, 2008) (describing Akerlof's insight in the context of loan sales).

[76] See Gary B. Gorton & George G. Pennacchi, "Banks and Loan Sales: Marketing Nonmarketable Assets", 35 J. Monetary Econ. 389, 392–93 (1995). For example, the banks' greater regulatory capital requirements prompted an increase in loan securitizations and syndications as banks moved assets from their balance sheets in order to reduce their capital requirements. See Charles K. Whitehead, "What's Your Sign?—International Norms, Signals, and Compliance", 27 Mich. J. Int'l. L. 695, 723 n.146, 724 (2006) (describing regulatory changes and their impact); Arthur E. Wilmarth, Jr., "The Transformation of the U.S. Financial Services Industry, 1975–2000: Competition, Consolidation, and Increased Risks", 2002 U. Ill. L. Rev. 215, 230–31 (situating banks within broader market developments); Patricia Jackson et al., "Basel Committee on Banking Supervision, Capital Requirements and Bank Behaviour: The Impact of the Basel Accord" 6 (Basle Committee on Banking Supervision, Working Paper No. 1, 1999) (suggesting how banks could manipulate balance sheets to meet requirements).

credit quality.[77] Banks, as a result, began to reassess corporate lending and loan trading, with many adopting new strategies to minimize costs.[78]

Among the new approaches, banks began to diversify their exposure to credit risk, which required a liquid market to buy and sell loans and other credit instruments. New technologies could measure risk and diversification across loan portfolios, enabling banks to decide which assets to buy and sell, and at what price, in order to optimize a portfolio's return-to-risk relationship.[79] The costs traditionally associated with loan resales were offset by the real benefits of managing credit risk, among them more profitable loan portfolios.[80] The lending business evolved as banks originated loans for sale to others and bought and sold credit risk in order to better manage their exposure.[81] A portion of the gains could be

[77] See Gerald F. Davis & Mark S. Mizruchi, "The Money Center Cannot Hold: Commercial Banks in the U.S. System of Corporate Governance", 44 Admin. Sci. Q. 215, 221–22 (1999) (describing the decline in senior corporate managers as bank directors as reflecting a shift by banks away from the traditional lending business).

[78] See Franklin Allen & Douglas Gale, "Financial Markets, Intermediaries, and Intertemporal Smoothing", 105 J. Pol. Econ. 523, 538–41 (1997) (discussing the negative impact of competition on an inter-temporally smoothed economy); Franklin Allen & Anthony M. Santomero, "What do Financial Intermediaries do?", 25 J. Banking & Fin. 271, 278 (2001) (describing securitization in mortgage and other markets); Allen N. Berger et al., The Transformation of the U.S. Banking Industry: What a Long, Strange Trip It's Been, 1995 Brookings Papers on Econ. Activity 55, 60 (1995) ("[T]hese rules may have given some banks incentives to reorganize their on-balance sheet portfolios or to shift into off-balance sheet activities."). For example, from the mid-1970s, the asset-backed securities market was fueled by the drive toward lower-cost financing. See Lowell L. Bryan, Breaking Up the Bank: Rethinking an Industry Under Siege 76, 82–83 (1988). Banks reportedly moved subprime mortgage assets off their balance sheets due to the greater capital requirements to which they were subject on the banks' balance sheets compared to securities firms. See Charles W. Calomiris, "The Subprime Turmoil: What's Old, What's New, and What's Next" 47–48 (Oct. 2, 2008), available at https://www.imf.org/external/np/res/seminars/2008/arc/pdf/cwc.pdf. Assets that were traditionally held by banks moved to a "shadow" banking system comprised of structured investment vehicles and other financing conduits set up to minimize the effect of regulatory capital requirements. See, e.g., Floyd Norris, No Way to Make a Loan, N.Y. Times, Oct. 19, 2007, at C1; Timothy F. Geithner, President and Chief Executive Officer, Fed. Reserve Bank of N.Y., Remarks at the Economic Club of New York: Reducing Systemic Risk in a Dynamic Financial System (June 9, 2008), available at http://www.newyorkfed.org/newsevents/speeches/2008/tfg080609.html. As former Citigroup Chairman and CEO, Charles Prince, told Rep. Barney Frank, off-balance sheet financing was necessary because on-balance sheet financing "would have put Citigroup at a disadvantage with Wall Street investment banks that were more loosely regulated and were allowed to take far greater risks." Nelson D. Schwartz & Julie Creswell, What Created This Monster? N.Y. Times, Mar. 23, 2008, at BU1. Those vehicles raised funds primarily by selling short-term commercial paper and medium-term notes to money market funds and other investors. The proceeds of those sales were then used to purchase longer-term mortgage loans (or, in some cases, mortgage-backed securities). See Gretchen Morgenson, Debts Coming Due At Just the Wrong Time, N.Y. Times, June, 14, 2009, at B1. Assets owned by the conduits were used to make payments on the outstanding securities, as well as provide collateral in the event of default. See Markus K. Brunnermeier, "Deciphering the Liquidity and Credit Crunch 2007–2008", 23 J. Econ. Perspect. 77, 79–80 (2009).

[79] See Whitehead, Evolution of Debt, *supra* note 1, at 664–65.

[80] See A. Sinan Cebenoyan & Philip E. Strahan, "Risk Management, Capital Structure and Lending at Banks", 28 J. Banking & Fin. 19, 36 (2004) ("[C]ontrolling for activities, the buy-and-sell banks are safer than otherwise similar banks."); see generally Katerina Simons, "Why Do Banks Syndicate Loans?", New England Econ. Rev., Jan.–Feb. 1993, at 45, 46 (contrasting syndications and loan sales).

[81] See Charles W. Calomiris, U.S. Bank Deregulation in Historical Perspective 335 (2000); John B. Caouette et al., Managing Credit Risk: The Next Great Financial Challenge 93 (1998); see also

passed on to borrowers, potentially enhancing a bank's competitiveness and lowering the borrowers' real cost of capital.[82]

The result was greater liquidity in the private credit market, in part through loan syndication, collateralized loan obligations (CLOs), and credit default swaps (CDS). Within loan syndications, one or more "lead banks" (or "arrangers") negotiates the terms of a loan and invites other lenders to participate at origination. Interests in a loan, whether or not syndicated, can also be sold in the secondary market, which riskier borrowers and nonbank investors tend to dominate.[83] Through CLOs, a portfolio of loans can be sold to a special purpose vehicle that, in turn, issues multiple tranches of CLO securities in order to fund the purchase. Converting loan assets to securities, and then transferring interests through the capital markets, enhances their liquidity.[84] Finally, credit derivatives enable lenders to transfer credit risk to other investors. Using CDS,[85] for example, a lender can sell all or a portion of a borrower's credit risk without transferring the loan itself. In effect, CDS permit lenders to outsource credit risk to CDS investors who can assume (and manage) a borrower's credit risk without funding the working capital component of the loan.[86] Doing so enables

Patrick Bolton & Xavier Freixas, "Equity, Bonds, and Bank Debt: Capital Structure and Financial Market Equilibrium Under Asymmetric Information", 108 J. Pol. Econ. 324, 326–37 (2000) (noting that securitization allows banks to provide flexible financing to firms with large public debt).

[82]   See A. Burak Güner, "Loan Sales and the Cost of Corporate Borrowing", 19 Rev. Fin. Stud. 687, 689–90 (2006) (noting that borrowers extract concessions for permission to engage in sales); see also Joseph P. Hughes & Loretta J. Mester, "Bank Capitalization and Cost: Evidence of Scale Economies in Risk Management and Signaling", 80 Rev. Econ. & Stat. 314, 315 (1998) (noting that diversification reduces the marginal cost of risk, which provides an incentive to incur more risk); Duffie, *supra* note 75, at 7–8 (discussing other forms of credit risk transfer).

[83]   A description of the syndicated loan market, and how it differs from secondary trading, can be found in Sufi, *supra* note 53, at 634.

[84]   See Tamar Frankel, "Securitization: The Conflict Between Personal and Market Law (Contract and Property)", 18 Ann. Rev. Banking L. 197, 218 (1999).

[85]   A CDS permits a counterparty to a swap contract to buy or sell all or a portion of the credit risk tied to a credit instrument, such as a loan or bond. See, e.g., Morton Glantz, Managing Bank Risk: An Introduction to Broad-Base Credit Engineering 531 (2003). The CDS customer pays the "writer" of the swap a periodic fee in exchange for a contingent payment in the event of a credit default. See id. at 540; see also Blythe Masters & Kelly Bryson, Credit Derivatives and Loan Portfolio Management, in Handbook of Credit Derivatives 47–48 (Jack Clark Francis et al. eds., 1999) (noting that credit events often also include "bankruptcy, cross acceleration, restructuring, repudiation" and, if measurable, significant price decreases "in a specified reference obligation issued or guaranteed by the reference entity"). If a credit event occurs, typically involving default by the borrower, the CDS writer typically pays the counterparty an amount sufficient to make it whole, see Glantz, *supra*, at 540; accord Masters & Bryson, *supra*, at 48, or purchases the referenced loan or bond at par, see Masters & Bryson, *supra*, at 49. Although there are important differences, a CDS in substance is economically similar to a term insurance policy written against the credit downgrade of the referenced borrower. See, e.g., Adam B. Ashcraft & João A.C. Santos, "Has the CDS Market Lowered the Cost of Corporate Debt?", 56 J. Monetary Econ. 514, 515 n.5 (2007) (noting that CDS, unlike insurance, do not require trading in the underlying asset).

[86]   See Charles K. Whitehead, "Reframing Financial Regulation", 90 B. U. L. Rev. 1, 4 n.9 (2010). A description of different credit derivatives appears in Glantz, *supra* note 85, at 538–42, and Masters & Bryson, *supra* note 85, at 47–55.

lenders to manage credit exposure more efficiently, providing value-maximizing managers with an incentive to continue to grow the private credit market.[87]

Balanced against liquidity's benefits is the risk that by "decoupling" economic and control rights—for example, through CLOs or CDS—a lender may have less interest in monitoring the borrower or acting for those who own economic interests in the loan. Purchasers of credit risk may be better able to manage that risk through diversification, but they may also be less able to oversee borrowers as effectively as the originator, resulting in increased agency costs and an overall decline in corporate governance.[88]

Those costs are similar to agency costs that arise in the public market, but with a critical difference: Unlike firms that issue public bonds, information regarding private borrowers is often less accessible.[89] Some portion of the cost is offset by the creditors' ability to buy and sell credit risk more efficiently.[90] Nevertheless, investors may demand higher returns to compensate for the greater risk—a result that is unlikely to be sustained if there are less-costly means to mitigate the agency costs. Designing resale arrangements to address the problems of limited information can reduce the lemons problem, increasing a bank's ability to transfer loans at lower cost and enhancing profitability.[91] Market participants, therefore, have looked to change how loans are structured and, by extension, they have shaped new forms of debt governance.[92] As discussed below, a key to that change has been the response of the private credit market to shifts in the source of capital, as providers have moved from bank lenders (within the traditional framing) to bank and nonbank investors in an increasingly liquid credit market.

---

[87]   See Ronald J. Gilson & Charles K. Whitehead, "Deconstructing Equity: Public Ownership, Agency Costs, and Complete Capital Markets", 108 Colum. L. Rev. 231, 247–51 (2008) (noting better risk management decreases cash-flow volatility and risks of real financial distress in ways that cannot be duplicated by shareholders); see also Robert C. Merton & Zvi Bodie, "The Design of Financial Systems: Towards a Synthesis of Function and Structure", 3 J. Inv. Mgmt. 1, 14–15 (2005) (suggesting that markets will turn financial products into commodities once incentive problems are resolved); Robert C. Merton, "Financial Innovation and Economic Performance", 4 J. Appl. Corp. Fin. 12, 19 (1992) (predicting specifically tailored risk management products). For an investigation of growth in the market, see Beverly Hirtle, "Credit Derivatives and Bank Credit Supply", 18 J. Fin. Intermediation 125, 126 (2009) (reporting mixed results).

[88]   See Frank Partnoy & David A. Skeel, Jr., "The Promise and Perils of Credit Derivatives", 75 U. Cin. L. Rev. 1019, 1030–34 (2007).

[89]   Much of the new credit market has been concentrated among large banks. See, e.g., Bernadette A. Minton et al., "How Much Do Banks Use Credit Derivatives to Hedge Loans?", 35 J. Fin. Serv. Res. 1, 2–3 (2009); Wilmarth, *supra* note 76, at 334–35. Part of the reason may be the informational asymmetry that historically has given banks a competitive edge over nonbank lenders. See Viral V. Acharya & Timothy C. Johnson, "Insider Trading in Credit Derivatives", 84 J. Fin. Econ. 110, 111 (2007). Trading among a small group of informed investors, however, can still result in the public release of a substantial amount of private information through competitive pricing. Others can rely on that information to make their own investment decisions, resulting in an overall increase in market size. See Craig W. Holden & Avanidhar Subrahmanyam, "Long-Lived Private Information and Imperfect Competition", 47 J. Fin. 247, 248, 255 (1992).

[90]   See Ashcraft & Santos, *supra* note 85, at 515 (finding a small reduction in public bond and bank loan spreads after CDS start to trade); see also Black, *supra* note 28, at 331 (discussing the relationship among interest rates, loan term severity, and firm value).

[91]   See George G. Pennacchi, "Loan Sales and the Cost of Bank Capital", 43 J. Fin. 375, 376 (1988).

[92]   See id. at 387–88.

3.1 Syndication

A loan is more likely to be syndicated as information about the borrower becomes more accessible (e.g., through reliance on a credit rating or based on public information).[93] For less well known borrowers, the number of lenders may be capped and resales restricted in order to encourage direct monitoring and renegotiation if a covenant is breached.[94] Participants in the original syndicate are more likely than later purchasers to have long-term relationships with the borrower, enabling them to monitor the borrower at lower cost and facilitating coordination.[95] Thus, a lead bank's traditional governance role in overseeing a borrower may be replaced by the collective oversight of the syndicate's members.

As a condition of sale, a purchaser can also require the lead bank to continue to hold a portion of the loan until it matures.[96] By retaining economic risk, the bank can credibly commit to continued monitoring and, as necessary, enforcing a loan's covenants.[97] A lender can also commit to monitoring if, as is often the case, other relationships with the borrower continue to motivate oversight. Those relationships, however, may be of questionable value

---

[93] See Steven A. Dennis & Donald J. Mullineaux, "Syndicated Loans", 9 J. Fin. Intermediation 404, 407 (2000).

[94] See Sang Whi Lee & Donald J. Mullineaux, "Monitoring, Financial Distress, and the Structure of Commercial Lending Syndicates", 33 Fin. Mgmt. 107, 120 (2004) (noting the existence of more concentrated syndicates in secured loans, which are known to involve greater credit risk, to encourage monitoring and negotiation); see also Rebecca S. Demsetz, Bank Loan Sales: A New Look at the Motivations for Secondary Market Activity 8 (Federal Reserve Bank of New York Staff Report No. 69, 1999), available at http://www.ny.frb.org/research/staff_reports/sr69.pdf ("A strong credit quality reputation may improve access to the secondary market, particularly as a loan seller.").

[95] See Sufi, *supra* note 53, at 631–32; see also Joseph G. Haubrich, "Financial Intermediation: Delegated Monitoring and Long-Term Relationships", 13 J. Banking & Fin. 9, 10, 17 (1989).

[96] That condition is now mandatory for most securitizations, even though not a legal requirement for loan syndication. Section 941 of the Dodd–Frank Act added new Section 15G to the U.S. Securities Exchange Act of 1934 (Exchange Act), which generally requires securitizers to retain at least five percent of the credit risk of any asset included in a securitization. See Dodd–Frank Wall Street Reform and Consumer Protection Act, Pub. L. No. 111-203, § 15G, 124 Stat. 1376, 1891–1896 (2010) (codified at 15 U.S.C. § 78o-11 (2012)). The requirement generally does not apply to asset-backed securities comprised of "qualified residential mortgage[s]" (no credit risk retention required) or that otherwise meet underwriting standards established by regulation (less than five percent credit risk retention required). See 15 U.S.C. § 78o-11(c)(1)(B). Securitizers are prohibited from directly or indirectly hedging or transferring the credit risk they are required to retain, unless permitted by regulation. See 15 U.S.C. § 78o-11(c)(1)(A). Final rules implementing the section 941 requirements subsequently were adopted in a flurry of regulatory actions intended to require securitizers to maintain some risk exposure to securitized loans and other assets. See Department of the Treasury, Federal Reserve System, Federal Deposit Insurance Corporation, Federal Housing Finance Agency, Securities and Exchange Commission, and Department of Housing and Urban Development, Credit Risk Retention (Oct. 22, 2014), available at http://www.federalreserve.gov/aboutthefed/boardmeetings/bcreg20141022a1.pdf.

[97] See Gorton & Pennacchi, *supra* note 76, at 394; see also Diamond, *supra* note 21, at 394 (noting that, as the number of lenders increases, there are either large expenditures for monitoring or a free-rider problem since no security holder has a significant stake in doing so); Pennacchi, *supra* note 91, at 383, 387 (modeling diminishing returns as the portion of a loan that is sold increases).

to the extent they result in a conflict between the economic interests of syndicate members and the originating lender.[98]

3.2 Changes in Covenants

Covenant levels may drop if creditors are unable at low cost to monitor a borrower's compliance with its obligations or to renegotiate the terms following breach. Public bonds typically contain less restrictive covenants than loans,[99] in part due to the public availability of information, the higher cost to directly monitor and enforce compliance, and a decline in the ability (or, for higher-quality borrowers, the need) to mitigate credit risk through contract.[100] For private borrowers, covenants levels may increase as one means to offset the greater monitoring costs that arise with more opaque firms.[101] Thus, non-syndicated loans structured for resale (typically leveraged, risky loans to nonbank, institutional investors) may contain higher covenant levels tied to observable public information. In addition, by tightening covenants, lenders can more quickly discover changes in a borrower's financial position. And by tying covenants to observable data, purchasers can mitigate the increased cost of direct monitoring.[102]

Transferring credit risk may also enable a creditor to enforce its covenant protections more effectively. The decline in exposure can enhance the lender's relative bargaining power, enabling it to more easily refuse to renegotiate a loan unless the terms are attractive. In the extreme, a creditor who transferred its economic risk may have less incentive to renegotiate or restructure a loan altogether, potentially reducing the value of the borrower's outstanding debt or even pushing the borrower into bankruptcy.[103] Consequently, growing liquidity has

---

[98] See Henry T. C. Hu & Bernard Black, "Debt, Equity, and Hybrid Decoupling: Governance and Systemic Risk Implications", 14 Eur. Fin. Mgmt. 663, 681–82 (2008).

[99] See, e.g., Amihud et al., *supra* note 35, at 462; Rauh & Sufi, *supra* note 18, at 4254 ("Bank debt is generally viewed as the least information sensitive, as banks write covenants into loan agreements.").

[100] See Christopher James, "Some Evidence on the Uniqueness of Bank Loans", 19 J. Fin. Econ. 217, 231–32 (1987) ("The announced ability to borrow may be good news for small firms . . . but not much news at all for large firms . . . that have other ways of disseminating information."); Smith & Warner, *supra* note 30, at 150–51 (discussing difficulty of enforcing trust indentures); Triantis & Daniels, *supra* note 6, at 1089 (suggesting that, for firms with both types of debt, bank debt is the least costly); see also Mark Carey et al., The Economics of the Private Placement Market 3 (Board of Governors of the Federal Reserve System, Staff Study No. 166, 1993), available at http://www.federalreserve.gov/pubs/staffstudies/1990-99/ss166.pdf (discussing the difference between a firm's observable credit risk and information problems).

[101] Higher covenant levels also may reflect bank incentives to transfer lower-quality assets to third parties—with the result that covenants may be lower for those borrowers most in need of closer monitoring. See Duffie, *supra* note 75, at 7.

[102] See Steven Drucker & Manju Puri, "On Loan Sales, Loan Contracting, and Lending Relationships", 22 Rev. Fin. Stud. 2835, 2837 (2009).

[103] See Hu & Black, *supra* note 98, at 682 ("Even a creditor with zero, rather than negative, economic ownership may want to push a company into bankruptcy."); see also Patrick Bolton & Martin Oehmke, "Credit Default Swaps and the Empty Creditor Problem", 24 Rev. Fin. Stud. 2617, 2618 (2011) (suggesting that CDS empower creditors to extract more in negotiation, but conceding that they may not negotiate even if it would be efficient).

prompted the rise of specialist investors (sometimes referred to as "vultures") who look to influence a firm's management through its debt covenants. Loans purchased by those investors are often distressed, with the discount in purchase price (and potential for substantial return) offsetting the greater cost of monitoring.[104] Investors use the borrower's breach of its covenants to force a change in policies or a change in control. This provides another pair of eyes over distressed borrowers, where the potential for management opportunism can be greatest.[105]

3.3 Reputation

Reputation can also mitigate agency costs, although as noted earlier,[106] its influence may not be significant or long lasting. A reputable borrower is more likely to be able to obtain loans with fewer restrictions than a borrower with a less well known or reputable credit history. The potential benefits can incentivize a borrower to act in a manner consistent with its lenders' interests.[107] For example, prior to the 2008 financial crisis, private equity sponsors saw a substantial rise in "covenant-lite" (or "cov-lite") loans, which, as the name suggests, have fewer covenants (typically, fewer maintenance covenants) than most commercial loans. Competition among bankers for new business is likely to have contributed to the climb. Reputation may have also played a role. The private equity market is comprised of a limited group of participants that interact frequently, suggesting that a reputation as a "good" borrower may have had substantial and positive economic consequences.[108]

Bank reputation can also be important.[109] The manner in which a bank structures a loan or monitors a borrower may not be apparent to investors at the time the loan is sold. The purchaser, instead, must rely on the lender's reputation based on prior sales. Structuring a bad loan or failing to monitor a borrower can hurt that reputation. Consequently, so long as loan sales are a significant part of its business, concerns over reputation may induce an originating bank to continue to monitor a borrower, even after its credit risk has been transferred.[110]

---

[104] See Edith S. Hotchkiss & Robert M. Mooradian, "Vulture Investors and the Market for Control of Distressed Firms", 43 J. Fin. Econ. 401, 402 (1997).

[105] See Michelle M. Harner, "Trends in Distressed Debt Investing: An Empirical Study of Investors' Objectives", 16 Am. Bankr. Inst. L. Rev. 69, 82–87 (2008).

[106] See *supra* notes 54–55 and accompanying text.

[107] See *supra* notes 52–55 and accompanying text.

[108] See Whitehead, Evolution of Debt, *supra* note 1, at 662. Market participants also attributed a portion of the decline in covenant levels to the increased ability to hedge risk in the credit market and the weakening incentives of banks to screen and monitor borrowers. See id.

[109] See Dennis & Mullineaux, *supra* note 93, at 407 (noting reputable lenders are more likely to syndicate); see also Drucker & Puri, *supra* note 102, at 2856–58 ("[M]ore restrictive covenants increase the likelihood of sale when lead lenders are ranked low.").

[110] See Lee & Mullineaux, *supra* note 94, at 121 ("[R]eputable banks may experience more free riding within the syndicate, representing an implicit cost of establishing and maintaining a reputation."); see also Dianna Preece & Donald J. Mullineaux, "Monitoring, Loan Renegotiability, and Firm Value: The Role of Lending Syndicates", 20 J. Banking & Fin. 577, 580 (1996) (noting banks must initially evaluate a loan and engage in monitoring the lead lender).

4 Debt's Evolution

Lending has changed in response to greater liquidity in the private credit market. Syndicate structure, covenant levels, and reputation are all means to reduce the resulting agency costs and balance the potential decline in debt governance.

A further change has resulted from greater liquidity in the credit market itself. For public debt, secondary trading prices inform managers of how the market assesses a borrower's credit quality.[111] Likewise, as the private credit market becomes more liquid, one would expect actions that affect a firm's credit quality increasingly to be reflected in changes in the price at which a firm's loans and other credit instruments trade. Those changes may affect a borrower's cost of capital, providing a discipline through the feedback furnished by market participants that complements the traditional protections provided by contract.[112]

Loan agreements already include features, like pricing grids,[113] that adjust the real cost of capital based on pre-agreed changes in a borrower's financial condition or credit rating. Going forward, lenders can also rely on the secondary pricing of credit instruments in order to assess a firm's credit quality and, if necessary, determine the cost of hedging their credit exposure. A borrower's actions that change the price at which its existing loans or other credit instruments trade can influence the price and non-price terms on which lenders are prepared to make subsequent loans. Since most loan pricing is tied to default risk, actions that increase credit risk will result in a corresponding increase in a borrower's cost of capital.[114]

As a result, growth in secondary trading may begin to overtake the role of covenants and monitoring in corporate governance. Covenants can be over- or under-inclusive, reflecting the difficulty of anticipating future events and drafting terms that properly reflect them. By contrast, since firms access the credit market on a regular basis,[115] changes in credit pricing that directly affect a firm's cost of capital may provide a more efficient and timely alternative.[116] More costly debt can affect a firm shortly after a change in its credit risk, either through a higher interest rate on an existing loan or the greater cost of a new loan. That cost, in turn, may lower the firm's share price and, like public equity, discipline managers by affecting compensation, retention decisions based on share price performance, and the possibility of a hostile takeover.

To be clear, covenants and monitoring are likely to continue to play an important role in corporate governance, but some portion of the traditional reliance may be offset by the feedback provided by an increasingly liquid credit market. The trick, as the markets become

---

[111] See Amihud et al., *supra* note 35, at 460.

[112] See Lars Norden & Wolf Wagner, "Credit Derivatives and Loan Pricing", 32 J. Banking & Fin. 2560, 2563–64 (2008); Whitehead, Evolution of Debt, *supra* note 1, at 645–46.

[113] See *supra* notes 44–46 and accompanying text.

[114] See Francis A. Longstaff et al., "Corporate Yield Spreads: Default Risk or Liquidity? New Evidence from the Credit Default Swap Market", 60 J. Fin. 2213, 2214–15 (2005).

[115] See Triantis & Daniels, *supra* note 6, at 1083–84.

[116] As Judge Easterbrook has noted, "Additional ways to price or trade financial instruments ought to strengthen the capital market as a disciplinary force. What makes the capital market more efficient not only makes governance less important—in what field does it retain a comparative advantage?—but also makes governance better." Frank H. Easterbrook, "Derivative Securities and Corporate Governance", 69 U. Chi. L. Rev. 733, 737–38 (2002).

more complete, will be to balance that new discipline against the traditional role played by covenants and monitoring.

5 Conclusion

Traditional debt governance is premised on debt's relative illiquidity. Banks with access to private information were able to extend loans at lower cost than other lenders, but looked to covenants and monitoring as a principal means to manage credit risk. The last four decades have witnessed the transformation of the traditional bank–borrower relationship, resulting in growth in the private credit market. Over time, with greater liquidity, changes in a firm's credit quality may increasingly be reflected in the pricing of its credit instruments. This may create a more efficient "real-time" alternative that supplements a lender's traditional reliance on covenants and monitoring. In short, as noted at the outset of this chapter, changes in the capital markets have affected capital structure, and changes in how a firm raises capital have also affected corporate governance.[117]

Those changes prompt a question: To what extent should new financial regulation—beyond its focus on market integrity, customer protection, and systemic risk—take into account its effect on corporate governance? Consider, for example, the new federal regulation of credit derivatives. In a frictionless world, a firm's equity and debt prices should move in tandem when new information is discovered.[118] In practice, CDS often have reacted first to new credit information—with prices moving ahead of changes in equity and debt,[119] as well as preceding the public announcement of a negative change in a firm's credit rating.[120] A change in CDS pricing, therefore, often mirrored an increase or decrease in a firm's credit quality before a change in its debt or equity price. The result was more timely (and potentially more accurate) feedback on changes in a firm's riskiness,[121] particularly in light of recent

---

[117] See *supra* notes 10–11 and accompanying text.

[118] A loan, in that world, is economically equivalent to the lender owning a riskless claim on the borrower and also issuing a put option on the borrower to the borrower's shareholders. If the value of the borrower's assets falls below the face value of the loan, then the borrower defaults—with the shareholders, in effect, exercising their right to "put" the firm to the lender in satisfaction of its claims. The implication is that there is a correlation between the value of a firm's debt (including credit derivatives tied to that debt) and equity, so that market prices should adjust at the same time and to the same information. See Robert C. Merton, "On the Pricing of Corporate Debt: The Risk Structure of Interest Rates", 29 J. Fin. 449, 455–60 (1974).

[119] See Roberto Blanco et al., "An Empirical Analysis of the Dynamic Relation between Investment-Grade Bonds and Credit Default Swaps", 60 J. Fin. 2255, 2256, 2268–71 (2005) (noting in 25 of 27 cases that the CDS market contributed to price discovery in credit spreads); Lars Norden & Martin Weber, "Informational Efficiency of Credit Default Swap and Stock Markets: The Impact of Credit Rating Announcements", 28 J. Banking & Fin. 2813, 2830 (2004) (leading stock market); Jorge A. Chan-Lau & Yoon Sook Kim, "Equity Prices, Credit Default Swaps, and Bond Spreads in Emerging Markets" 19 (Int'l. Monetary Fund, Working Paper No. 04/27, 2004) (noting CDS dominates one-day discovery horizons).

[120] See John Hull et al., "The Relationship between Credit Default Swap Spreads, Bond Yields, and Credit Rating Announcements", 28 J. Banking & Fin. 2789, 2802–03 (2004).

[121] See Glantz, *supra* note 85, at 537.

concern over LIBOR and the credit-rating process.[122] That feedback, in turn, affected new credit extended to the firm, providing the borrower with a real-time incentive to manage its risky projects and activities.[123]

Part of the difference in responsiveness reflected the special access of banks that traded CDS to quasi-public information about borrowers.[124] With the passage of the Dodd–Frank Act, however, CDS have become subject to the federal securities laws. As a result, trading in CDS based on material non-public information is prohibited, and those instruments are likely to become less informative.[125] Prohibiting insider trading in CDS may not be a bad outcome. But to what extent should the impact of CDS on corporate governance be part of the analysis around the new regulation? Should that effect, and the weakening of a debt governance tool, inform part of the policy makers' deliberations? These questions mirror the evolving nature of debt and debt governance described in this chapter. They also suggest a need to take a more expansive view of the effect of new financial regulation on how corporations are governed.

[122] See, e.g., Office of Credit Ratings, Sec. & Exch. Comm'n, Credit Rating Agency Independence Study 46–47 (2013) (discussing the proportion of rating agency revenue from "ancillary services"); Libor Scandal, Fin. Times, http://www.ft.com/intl/indepth/libor-scandal (last visited Oct. 29, 2014).

[123] See, e.g., Pierre Paulden & Caroline Hyde, Citigroup, Credit Suisse Link Loans to Swaps in Shift, Bloomberg (Oct. 29, 2008), http://www.bloomberg.com/apps/news?pid=newsarchive&sid=a9lKCX0P4 6hg (reporting that Citigroup and Credit Suisse were among banks tying corporate loan rates to CDS).

[124] See Acharya & Johnson, *supra* note 89, at 116 (noting significant information flow from the CDS market to the equity market where there are a large numbers of insiders or gains to hedging are substantial); Minton et al., *supra* note 89 (describing concentration of CDS in large banks).

[125] A "security-based swap" is a "security" subject to the Exchange Act. See 15 U.S.C. § 78c(a)(10) (2012). Included within the definition of "security-based swap" are swaps that are based on a single security or loan or on the occurrence, nonoccurrence, or extent of the occurrence of an event relating to an issuer or issuers of securities. See 15 U.S.C. § 78c(a)(68) (2012). Extending the definition of security to security-based swaps subjects trading in those instruments to section 10(b) of, and Rule 10b-5 under, the Exchange Act, which prohibits the purchase or sale of a security when in possession of material, non-public information. See 17 C.F.R. § 240.10b5-1(a) (2013).

CHAPTER 19

·····································

ACCOUNTING AND
FINANCIAL REPORTING
Global Aspirations, Local Realities

·····································

LAWRENCE A. CUNNINGHAM[1]

1 INTRODUCTION

"You manage what you measure," the late Louis Lowenstein noted when explaining the importance of accounting in corporate governance, and the insight remains durable. Highlighting the functions of corporate accounting and financial reporting worldwide, this chapter explores how aspirations for a universal system are often disappointed by local realities that explain persistent diversity. Section II provides context and background by summarizing the history and progress of contemporary efforts to move accounting from its diverse local roots to a unified global stage. Section III identifies the varying functions of accounting and reporting laws around the world and reflects on how related forces contribute to persistent divergence in financial reporting.

Despite a gloomy assessment of the prospects for achieving a universal system of accounting, a more profound and happier truth should be stressed at the outset. The goal of international accounting is instrumental in promoting cross-border economic exchange, not an artistic aspiration for pure uniformity of financial reporting. Although pure accounting harmony appears to be an impossible dream, its pursuit has helped to facilitate the expansion of global capitalism, a substantial accomplishment. There is work ahead to promote prosperous convergence, but progress is significant in absolute terms and probably in relation to what might be attained by continued investment in international standards.

---

[1] Henry St. George Tucker III Research Professor of Law, George Washington University. This chapter is adapted and updated from my previous work, especially Lawrence A. Cunningham, "The SEC's Global Accounting Vision: A Realistic Appraisal of a Quixotic Quest", 87 N.C. L. Rev. 1 (2008).

2 Accounting Contributes to Globalization

Through the late twentieth century, accounting systems in most countries developed within the traditions of each country and varied considerably across them. But, as globalization took hold in the century's final decades, an appetite for a universal system emerged. After numerous fits and starts, beginning from 1973, international standards ripened in the twenty-first century into a comprehensive system achieving international recognition. But the struggle continues.

2.1 Struggle

The quest for international accounting standards is motivated by increased cross-border capital flows manifested in worldwide stock market listings, foreign ownership of domestic securities, and an expansion of transnational business combinations. Unsurprisingly, differences in national accounting standards and their application interfered with expanding these desirable activities. Accountants produced different reports of income and equity for identical underlying transactions, a phenomenon famously illustrated the German auto-maker Daimler-Benz's traditional German accounting results differed radically from the US accounting standards it applied when it first listed in the United States.[2]

Internationalization of accounting standards has historically centered in London. There, in 1973, a group of accountants began a process of articulating global standards.[3] The organization, originally called the International Accounting Standards Committee (IASC), was formed by agreement among professional accountancy organizations in Australia, Canada, France, Germany, Ireland, Japan, Mexico, the Netherlands, the United Kingdom, and the United States.[4] By 1983, IASC included all professional accountancy bodies that were also members of the International Federation of Accountants.[5]

Between 1973 and 1987, IASC issued twenty-six accounting standards (and by 2000 had issued a total of forty-one standards).[6] However, IASC lacked an effective governance structure and the political clout to attract adherents.[7] Its standards were too vague and contained numerous optional approaches to reporting identical transactions. The products were usefully adopted by developing countries that lacked accounting standards.[8] But IASC's founding countries largely ignored the standards, preferring to use their own.

---

[2] See David Waller, "Daimler-Benz Gears Up for a Drive on the Freeway", Fin. Times, Apr. 29, 1993, at 18; Breeden Announces Daimler-Benz Will File to Trade Stock in US Markets, 25 SEC Reg. & L. Rep. (BNA) 477 (Apr. 2, 1993).

[3] See Gary John Previts & Barbara Dubis Merino, A History of Accountancy in the United States: The Cultural Significance of Accounting 361 (rev. ed. 1998).

[4] See David R. Herwitz & Matthew J. Barrett, Accounting for Lawyers 174 (4th ed. 2006).

[5] Id. at 174–75.

[6] See Acceptance from Foreign Private Issuers of Financial Statements Prepared in Accordance with International Financial Reporting Standards Without Reconciliation to US GAAP, 72 Fed. Reg. 37,962, 37,964 n.23 (proposed July 2, 2007) (codified at 17 C.F.R. §249.220f).

[7] See Herwitz & Barrett, *supra* note 4, at 175–76.   [8] See id. at 175.

Efforts to strengthen IASC were redoubled in 1988 with backing from the International Organization of Securities Commissions (IOSCO).[9] IASC began to review its standards, omit optional treatments, enhance disclosure, and "specify in greater detail how each standard was to be interpreted."[10] The result was a formal 1995 agreement between IASC and IOSCO on a joint program to develop standards comprehensively.[11] This project led IOSCO, in 2000, to endorse IASC revisions while letting national regulators add requirements such as disclosure, specificity, and reconciliation.[12]

During the 1990s, the US Securities and Exchange Commission (the SEC) emphasized that, to achieve requisite stature, IASC needed to develop a comprehensive, high-quality, generally accepted basis of accounting.[13] It would be characterized by transparency, comparability, and full disclosure and would be susceptible to rigorous interpretation and enforcement. On process, the SEC prescribed modeling IASC's governance structure after that of the US accounting standard-setting body, the Financial Accounting Standards Board (FASB).

The SEC was able to exert this power over IASC because of how, along with US GAAP, it had consolidated a position as the gold standard in financial reporting. Beginning in 1983, non-US companies interested in accessing US capital markets were required to use US GAAP, at least by reconciling their home-country statements to it.[14] Adding to its influence, some multinational enterprises adopted US GAAP completely, including Daimler-Benz, which switched from German GAAP to US GAAP in 1993 to gain its US listing.[15]

US GAAP's leadership paralleled US leadership in capital markets, which New York had dominated throughout the second half of the twentieth century. Traditionally, the United Kingdom was a strong competitor in capital market advancement, where London long rivaled New York. In the early 1990s, after the collapse of the Soviet Union and the end of the Cold War, world trade expanded and capital flows began to move more freely and rapidly across more national borders.

The existence of multiple, alternative accounting systems can increase the costs of cross-border deals. Multinational enterprises based in various countries moved from domestic accounting regimes toward internationally useful and recognized systems. Most often, this meant a shift from national accounting systems to US GAAP, although interest grew in the standards that IASC offered. The appetite for a universal accounting system increased during the late 1990s and early 2000s as market integration accelerated.

Signaling belief in the possibility of moving from country-specific accounting standards to an international approach, the SEC issued a concept release in 2000 outlining essential elements of international standards.[16] The SEC did not pursue this concept, however, as

---

[9] Id.   [10] Id.

[11] See A.A. Sommer, Jr., "IOSCO: Its Mission and Achievement", 17 Nw. J. Int'l. L. & Bus. 15, 24–25 (1997).

[12] See Herwitz & Barrett, *supra* note 4, at 175.

[13] International Accounting Standards, Securities Act Release No. 33-7801, Exchange Act Release No. 34-42430, 65 Fed. Reg. 8,896, 8,897 (Feb. 23, 2000) (codified at 17 C.F.R. pts. 230 & 240).

[14] See Adoption of Foreign Issuer Integrated Disclosure System, Securities Act Release No. 33-6437, 47 Fed. Reg. 54,764, 54,764 (Dec. 6, 1982).

[15] See Waller, *supra* note 2.

[16] International Accounting Standards, Securities Act Release No. 33-7801, Exchange Act Release No. 34-42430, 65 Fed. Reg. 8,896, 8,897 (Feb. 23, 2000) (codified at 17 C.F.R. pts. 230 & 240) (stating that the desired attributes of international standards are effective, independent, and high quality standards

accounting scandals at Enron and other companies diverted its attention. Instead, it entered a period of domestic regulatory activity that produced and implemented the Sarbanes–Oxley Act of 2002.

Meanwhile, the IASC, boasting more than one hundred professional accountancy bodies by 2000, revised its governance along the lines that the SEC had recommended.[17] It modeled itself closely after FASB, renamed itself the International Accounting Standards Board (IASB), and renamed its standards as International Financial Reporting Standards (IFRS). IASB propounded new and revised international accounting provisions that were destined to set a new gold standard in financial reporting.

IASB also began a vigorous marketing campaign with numerous countries and blocs to gain recognition.[18] This led the European Union to pass legislation in 2002 requiring all EU-listed companies to use IFRS beginning in 2005 (subject to the European Union's endorsement of each new standard as it was produced).[19] Additionally, IASB's campaign led scores of other countries, from Australia to Singapore, to embrace its standards (subject, in most cases, to the same endorsement mechanism).[20] Others, including Japan and the United States, agreed with IASB to work to converge national standards and IFRS.[21]

During this period, coordination accelerated between the United States and European Union. In 2004, the SEC and the Committee of European Securities Regulators (CESR)[22] agreed to increase collaboration on accounting convergence, including a commitment to concentrate on the consistent application, interpretation, and enforcement of IFRS.[23] Within one year, the SEC unveiled a "roadmap" to convergence (including ending the US reconciliation requirement for non-US issuers by 2009 or sooner),[24] and CESR declared that US GAAP was substantially equivalent to the European Union's IFRS.[25] In both Europe and the US, as elsewhere, IFRS required making significant cultural adjustments from historical traditions.[26]

accompanied by capable firms with quality controls and backstopped by regulatory oversight conducting the auditing).

[17] See Strategic Working Party, International Accounting Standards Committee, Recommendations on Shaping IASC for the Future (1999).

[18] See David Tweedie, "Setting a Global Standard: The Case for Accounting Convergence", 25 Nw. J. Int'l L. & Bus. 589, 592–93 (2005) (showing the reflections of IASB's principal leader).

[19] Eur. Parl. Doc. PE 308.463, available at http://www.europarl.europa.eu/meetdocs/committees/juri/20020225/461067EN.pdf.

[20] See Donald T. Nicolaisen, "A Securities Regulator Looks at Convergence", 25 Nw. J. Int'l. L. & Bus. 661, 664–65 (2005).

[21] See Press Release, International Accounting Standards Board, IASB and Accounting Standards Board of Japan Agree to Next Steps in Launching Joint Project for Convergence (Jan. 21, 2005), available at http://www.iasb.org/news; Financial Accounting Standards Board & International Accounting Standards Board, Memorandum of Understanding, "The Norwalk Agreement" (Oct. 28, 2002), available at http://www.fasb.org/resources/ccurl/443/883/memorandum.pdf.

[22] CESR has now been replaced by the European Securities and Markets Authority (ESMA).

[23] See Press Release, SEC, SEC-CESR Set Out the Shape of Future Collaboration (June 4, 2004), available at http://www.sec.gov/news/press/2004-75.htm.

[24] See Roadmap for the Potential Use of Financial Statements Prepared in Accordance with International Financial Reporting Standards by US Issuers, 73 Fed. Reg. 70,816 (proposed Nov. 21, 2008) (to be codified at 17 C.F.R. pts. 210, 229, 240, 244, & 249).

[25] See Nicolaisen, *supra* note 20, at 673–74.

[26] Martin Gelter & Zehra G. Kavame, Whose Trojan Horse? "The Dynamics of Resistance Against IFRS", 36 U. Pa. J. Int'l. L. 89 (2014).

In 2006, the SEC and CESR reaffirmed and deepened their earlier commitment in a formal work plan to intensify joint investment in IFRS.[27] Meeting the roadmap commitment, the SEC ended the reconciliation requirement in 2007 and broached letting US issuers choose to adopt IFRS instead of US GAAP.[28] In 2008, however, the financial crisis sidetracked the SEC, much as the Enron-period scandals had earlier, this time under the weight of the Dodd–Frank Act of 2010. In 2012, the SEC staff issued its final report on the work plan. It might have endorsed IFRS and recommended that the Commission do so, but it did neither, putting its fate in the United States in limbo.

2.2 Standstill

IASB's impressive showing was reinforced by enthusiasm for the notion that IFRS largely took the form of principles as opposed to rules. This enthusiasm was a stunning turn-about since IASC standards set from 1973 to 1987 and into the late 1990s were criticized and did not catch on because they were too loose.[29] Earlier objections to IASC's relatively vague standards were based on the requirement that an accounting system must provide definiteness.

Specifically, an accounting system must enable preparing financial statements that meet basic criteria that are recognized worldwide for reliability and usefulness. Such a system is reliable when it is capable of transparently capturing, aggregating, and summarizing vast quantities of transactions with varying qualities, which is possible only if standards are sufficiently comprehensive to address most transaction types and categories.

To be useful, an accounting system must facilitate comparability across enterprises. Thus, one risk of principles that are too generic is that the role of subjective judgment diminishes the comparability of resulting statements. Yet that risk of excessive generality was offset by several forces, which together made a global turnabout from criticizing to applauding IASC's standards, which came to be called "principles-based."

Foremost among these forces, in the earlier period, there was less pressure for countries supporting IASC to adopt its standards. For example, countries like Australia, Britain, Germany, and France had respected systems; therefore, IASC standards were generally only taken up by less developed countries that lacked accounting traditions, such as countries in Eastern Europe and former members of the Soviet Union. The pressure equation changed as the value of international standards increased to developed countries amid post-Cold War globalization.

Moreover, to command acceptance among far-flung participants, from the European Union to the United States and scores of other countries, it is helpful for accounting standards to be written at a relatively high level of generality. If too detailed or overly tailored

---

[27] Press Release, SEC, SEC and CESR Launch Work Plan Focused on Financial Reporting (Aug. 2, 2006), available at http://www.sec.gov/news/press/2006/2006-130.htm.

[28] See, "SEC Concept Release on Allowing US Issuers To Prepare Financial Statements in Accordance with International Financial Reporting Standards," Securities Act Release No. 8831, Exchange Act Release No. 56,217, Investment Company Act Release No. 27,924, 72 Fed. Reg. 45,600, 45,607 (Aug. 7, 2007) [hereinafter SEC Concept Release on Domestic IFRS].

[29] See Herwitz & Barrett, *supra* note 4, at 175.

to specific attributes of particular nations, the standards appeal only to those nations and not to others.

In addition, literal and functional translation costs are proportional to the relative generality or specificity of the original text. Because of language differences, it is necessary to translate the standards from their original language, English, into other languages. More general language is easier to translate into other languages and easier for readers of the translated texts to comprehend.

Finally, the relative generality of IFRS was more appealing in the early 2000s than before because of events in the United States that reverberated worldwide. It was tempting to attribute the Enron debacle to how US GAAP were highly detailed and dense with rules. Enron's managers—and managers at other companies in the heady period—appeared to manipulate US GAAP's rules by designing transactions that could opaquely avoid triggering adverse accounting results and enable reporting beneficial ones.[30] Critics of US GAAP, and foes of using rules in regulation generally, offered such examples as evidence that rules are costly and that it is better to regulate and design accounting systems using principles.[31]

The force of globalization and related harmonization efforts led to substantial but incomplete convergence in accounting standards worldwide. IFRS has many followers. Its standard-setters have worked closely with FASB to evolve US GAAP in harmony. However, there are still significant differences in the content of IFRS versus US GAAP on many topics.[32] Centrally promulgated IFRS are often adopted in a slightly different form by given countries or companies, which prepare statements to comply with country-specific variations.[33] Related auditing opinions tend to attest to the country-specific versions of IFRS rather than to the IASB version.[34] There is also a wide variety of applications of given IFRS standards.[35] Variety extends to the form of presentation,[36]

---

[30] See William W. Bratton, "Enron, Sarbanes–Oxley and Accounting: Rules Versus Principles Versus Rents", 48 Vill. L. Rev. 1023, 1030 (2003).

[31] The complaints overstated the case. See William C. Powers, Jr. et al., Report of Investigation by the Special Investigative Committee of the Board of Directors of Enron Corp. 3–4 (2002).

[32] See International Accounting Standards: Hearing Before the Subcomm. on Securities, Insurance, and Investment of the S. Comm. on Banking, Housing and Urban Affairs, 110th Cong., at D1413 (Oct. 24, 2007) (testimony of Jack Ciesielski, President, R&G Associates); Elaine Henry, Steve W.J. Lin, & Ya-Wen Yang, "The European-U.S. 'GAAP Gap': IFRS to U.S. GAAP Form 20-F Reconciliations", 23 Acct. Horizons 121 (2009) (revealing a widening of the gap compared to previous findings from 1999).

[33] See SEC, Staff Observations, *infra* note 35 ("We found that the vast majority of companies asserted compliance with a jurisdictional version of IFRS and that most also asserted compliance with IFRS as published by the International Accounting Standards Board, commonly referred to as the IASB.").

[34] Id. ("In the vast majority of the companies we reviewed, the company's auditor opined on the company's compliance with the jurisdictional version of IFRS that the company used, but did not opine on the company's compliance with IFRS as published by the IASB.").

[35] See SEC, "Staff Observations in the Review of IFRS Financial Statements" (July 2, 2007), http://www.sec.gov/divisions/corpfin/ifrs_staffobservations.htm [hereinafter Staff Observations]; see also SEC, Staff Comments on Annual Reports Containing Financial Statements Prepared for the First Time on the Basis of International Financial Reporting Standards (2007), http://www.sec.gov/divisions/corpfin/ifrs_reviews.htm.

[36] See SEC, Staff Observations, *supra* note 35. (finding that companies based in the same jurisdiction and industries sometimes used different formats for their income statements).

bottom-line income statement figures,[37] cash flow statements,[38] and a variety of transactional matters.

Despite powerful forces of globalization, then, the project of establishing a single-set of high-quality accounting standards has proven to be monumentally elusive. Some of the reasons may be found in the local character of traditional accounting, which produces significant counter-pressures, as discussed next.

3 ACCOUNTING STILL REMAINS A LOCAL LANGUAGE

The following discussion uses familiar classifications from legal scholarship to highlight aspects of accounting that are affected by national variation. Underlying cultural and legal features shape the development of accounting standards. Those features explain the variability of traditional accounting standards from nation to nation, as well as the continuing differences between IFRS and US GAAP. The pressure of these features, which tend to be sticky, also explains sustained variation in the application of uniform international accounting standards.[39]

3.1 Legal Origins

National accounting systems are connected to local legal traditions. A broad contrast among legal traditions distinguishes common law and civil law.[40] Accounting standards in common law countries, such as the United States and United Kingdom, traditionally obtained authority through general acceptance by the profession;[41] accounting systems in civil law countries, including most continental European countries (the Netherlands is the major exception), obtain legitimacy by enactment as law.[42] Japanese accounting exhibited a blending of these traditions.[43]

These origins play out in different views on how to apply identical accounting requirements. A salient manifestation of how legal origins influence the application of identical accounting requirements concerns the principle that financial statements should present a true and fair view of the business and financial condition of an enterprise.

---

[37] Id. (discussing the wide variations in calculations made in each system).

[38] See SEC, SEC Concept Release on Domestic IFRS, *supra* note 28, at 45,606 n.40.

[39] See SEC, SEC Concept Release on Domestic IFRS, *supra* note 28, at 45,608 ("[I]t is likely that not everyone will apply accounting standards consistently or appropriately.").

[40] See Edward L. Glaeser & Andrei Shleifer, "Legal Origins", 117 Q. J. Econ. 1193, 1193–97 (2002); Rafael La Porta, Florencio Lopez-de-Silanes, & Andrei Shleifer, "The Economic Consequences of Legal Origins", 46 J. Econ. Lit. 285, 285–87 (2007).

[41] This is also true for Dutch accounting, despite a civil law tradition, and due in part to its use of a specialized commercial and company law court. See Miller, European Accounting Guide 700 (David Alexander & Simon Archer eds., 3d ed. 1998).

[42] Id. at 1–2.   [43] Id. at 1,149.

This edict, perhaps the most famously flexible and contingent notion in all of accounting, can mean different things in different cultures and contexts. For example, in England, "fair" denotes that reports are within a range of fidelity to business records and economic reality; "true" negates its opposite—false.[44] But, until the United Kingdom joined the European Union, the concept of "true and fair" was alien to non-Dutch Europe; the European Union's 1978 Fourth Directive introduced the requirement.[45]

The Italian translation of "true and fair" is "true and correct" (*rappresentare in modo veritiero e corretto*),[46] which is then equated with Italian civil law requiring "straightforwardness and truth" (*evidenza a verita*). [47] Many translations replace the compound phrase with a single word. In Greece, this is the equivalent of "real"; in Belgium, France, Luxembourg, the Netherlands, and Spain, it is the equivalent of "faithful."[48] In the United States, the concept is embedded in the requirement that financial statements "fairly present" an enterprise's financial condition and results of operations.[49]

Substantive disagreements exist concerning the relationship between the principle and other accounting standards. Conflicts arise when applying the standards could impair the objective. There are at least three alternative approaches to resolving such a conflict.[50] In the United Kingdom, an override is called for so that the true and fair view is privileged and conflicting standards are subordinated; in Europe, overriding the written rules is repugnant, despite the "true and fair" view concept; and in the United States, overrides have generally not been used because litigation risks induce people to comply with rules.[51]

These legal origins explain some of the observed and persistent divergence among companies purporting to use IFRS.[52] Across the European Union, differences are

---

[44] Alternatively, "true" is defined as complying with the letter of rules and "fair" as complying with the spirit of rules. Tom K. Cowan, "Are Truth and Fairness Generally Acceptable?", 40 Acct. Rev. 788, 788–94 (1965).

[45] See Lawrence A. Cunningham, "Semiotics, Hermeneutics, and Cash: An Essay on the True and Fair View", 28 N.C. J. Int'l. & Com. Reg. 893, 902–13 (2003).

[46] In earlier legislation, Italy translated the phrase as "faithful picture" (*quadro fedele*). See Miller, European Accounting Guide, *supra* note 41, at 581.

[47] Id. at 583 (citing Civil Code, Article 2217, section 2). Italian accounting also requires true and correct presentation with clarity and precision (*chiarezza e precisione*). Id. (citing Civil Code, Article 2423, section 2).

[48] See Christopher Nobes, "The True and Fair View Requirement: Impact on and of the Fourth Directive", 24 Acct. & Bus. Res. 35, 42 (1993). Similar translation differences exist across Europe, such as right-looking (Denmark), according to facts (the Netherlands), and true and appropriate (Portugal). Id.

[49] See Cunningham, *supra* note 45, at 902–13.   [50] Id. at 902–13.

[51] Id. at 908–09. See generally Jonathan Rickford, "Legal Approaches to Restricting Distributions to Shareholders: Balance Sheet Tests and Solvency Tests", 7 Eur. Bus. Org. L. Rev. 135, 147 (2006); David Alexander & Eva Eberhartinger, "The True and Fair View in the European Union", 18 Eur. Acct. Rev. 571 (2009); David Alexander & Eva Jermakowicz, "A True and Fair View of the Principles/Rules Debate", 42 Abacus 132, 139 (2006); Lisa Evans & Christopher Nobes, "Some Mysteries Relating to the Prudence Principle in the Fourth Directive and in German and British Law", 5 Eur. Acct. Rev. 361, 363–65 (1996). The override approach was enacted as formal French law though its meaning remains uncertain C. Com. (France) art. L 123–14 al. 3. See Christian De Lauzainghein, Jean-Louis Navarro, & Dominique Nechelis, Droit Comptable 361 (3d ed. 2004) ("même vingt ans après son introduction dans notre droit la notion demeure souvent bien floue") (Google translation: "even twenty years after its introduction into our law, the concept often remains very fuzzy").

[52] The evidence summarized above attributed variation among IFRS users to different legal origins.

significantly influenced by the legal origin of the firm's home country (i.e., common law or civil law traditions).[53] It appears unlikely that any international standard will be capable of reconciling these disagreements. After all, local cultural influences will retain a role in how any principle is applied.

3.2 Securities Regulation

Legal traditions continue to influence the shape of securities regulation in different countries. Securities regulation, in turn, influences accounting standards. The most forceful examples of these relationships appear in the contexts of investor protection and enforcement intensity.[54] In the United States, investor protection is among the chief purposes of securities regulation, and accounting principles are designed to bolster investor protection.[55] In many other countries, interests of constituencies other than investors matter, and investor protection is one among several competing goals of securities regulation.[56]

Enforcement intensity refers to the relative strength of legal institutions equipped to police adherence to securities regulations, including accounting provisions.[57] The United States employs an intense enforcement apparatus, one that includes the SEC, private litigation, and various other state and federal authorities.[58] Few countries match this level of enforcement intensity, and many exhibit a weak enforcement program.

These differences pose implications for a range of accounting issues. A general example concerns the preferred form that standards assume, ranging from detailed rules to vague principles. Indeed, it is possible to understand the relative rules-density of US GAAP as a product of an intensive enforcement environment.[59] Thus, litigation threats may lead preparers and auditors to value clarity in accounting standards, leading to extensive provision of detailed guidance.[60] Unlike US companies, European and Asian companies and constituents may be able to accept relatively more generic accounting standards, in part because of the comparatively lower level of private and public enforcement of securities laws through regulation, prosecution, and litigation.

Predicting the effects of cultural variance on the future of IFRS is not easy. It is conceivable that relative enforcement intensity and the value of investor protection can converge worldwide. That would mean making legal changes to US regulations in order to reduce the role of liability risk and litigation threats on preparers and auditors. These changes would curtail

---

[53] See Donna L. Street, "International Convergence of Accounting Standards: What Investors Need to Know" (Oct. 2, 2007) at 9, available at http://www.sec.gov/comments/s7-20-07/s72007-24.pdf. see also D. Jetuah, Citigroup Lays out IFRS-US GAAP Gulf, Accountancy Age, Aug. 30, 2007 (reporting on similar results from Citigroup survey).

[54] See John C. Coffee, Jr., "Law and the Market: The Impact of Enforcement", 156 U. Pa. L. Rev. 229, 230–34 (2007); see also Howell E. Jackson, "Variation in the Intensity of Financial Regulation: Preliminary Evidence and Potential Implications", 24 Yale J. Reg. 253, 279–85 (2007).

[55] See Thomas Lee Hazen, The Law of Securities Regulation 9–10 (5th ed. 2005).

[56] Id. at 17–19.   [57] See Jackson, *supra* note 54, at 278–79.   [58] Id. at 279.

[59] See George J. Benston, "Public (US) Compared to Private (UK) Regulation of Corporate Financial Disclosure", 51 Acct. Rev. 483, 484–85 (1976); Stephen A. Zeff, "A Perspective on the US Public/Private-Sector Approach to the Regulation of Financial Reporting", 9 Acct. Horizons 52, 66 (1995).

[60] See Cunningham, *supra* note 45, at 1473 nn.266–68.

demand for detail or increase those levels in other nations. Both prospects entail momentous changes with uncertain prospects and payoffs. Even substantial reductions in the scope of legal liability for accounting violations are unlikely to eliminate litigation as a dispute resolution mechanism in the United States.[61] Intensifying enforcement activity in other countries is possible but is by no means certain or desirable.

3.3 Corporate Governance

Corporate governance, referring to the combination of corporate purpose and organizational arrangements designed to achieve it, varies worldwide. Broadly defined, corporate purposes range from a shareholder profit maximization philosophy to a pluralistic conception of corporate constituencies that includes shareholders, creditors, employees, suppliers, communities, and the state.[62] Organizational arrangements reflect these purposes through devices such as the design, composition, and duties of boards of directors.

Boards may have one or two tiers, members may be elected by shareholders only or by other groups, and duties may range from maximizing profits to assuring the corporation's long-term sustainability. Accounting in systems characterized by shareholder profit maximization may naturally emphasize the measurement of profit from period to period, whereas more pluralistic systems may emphasize net worth and consistent levels of profit over time.

In addition, the role of employees, at both the senior executive levels and the broader level of laborers, can have significant effects on accounting philosophy. Labor plays an active role in corporate governance in many countries, a role rarely held in the United States.[63] For example, employees are formally represented on boards of directors in Germany.[64]

For senior executives, the most pronounced global difference concerns levels and forms of compensation. US corporations pay executives considerably greater compensation than elsewhere, often by staggering multiples and often in the form of stock options and other compensation that is contingent on varying measures of corporate performance.[65] Thus, setting the benchmarks of corporate performance and calculating compensation levels play a more important role in accounting systems such as those in the United States than in some other systems. However, such benchmarks assume less or no importance where executive compensation packages are more modest.

---

[61] An additional explanation for the relatively greater use of principles in IFRS is simply its relative youth. Repeated application of even the vaguest standard reduces that vagueness. A maturing IFRS can be expected to metamorphose from principles to rules. There are also reasons to challenge as overstated the conventional view that IFRS are "principles-based" and US GAAP is "rules-based." See Lawrence A. Cunningham, "A Prescription to Retire the Rhetoric of 'Principles-Based Systems' in Corporate Law, Securities Regulation, and Accounting", 60 Vand. L. Rev. 1411 (2007).

[62] In Germany, to give a well-known example, short-term profits are subordinated to long-term financial survival. See Wolfgang Ballwieser, Germany: Individual Accounts, in 2 Transnational Accounting 1241 (Dieter Ordelheide & KPMG eds., 2d ed. 2001).

[63] See Brett H. McDonnell, "The Curious Incident of the Workers in the Boardroom", 29 Hofstra L. Rev. 503, 513 (2000) (book review).

[64] Id. at 515.

[65] See Charles M. Yablon, "Bonus Questions—Executive Compensation in the Era of Pay for Performance", 75 Notre Dame L. Rev. 271, 279–81 (1999).

In the most general terms, the varying corporate purposes and organizational designs around the world reflect varying forms of capitalism.[66] National accounting tradition- ally reflects competing conceptions of capitalism. Although these and other distinctive traditions are converging, enduring diversity in views on capitalism are likely to continue to exert influence at national levels, posing challenges to the formulation, acceptance, applica- tion, and enforcement of international standards.[67]

3.4 Corporate Finance

Even within corporate governance systems that exhibit family resemblance, there may be differences in corporate finance that lead to sharply different conceptions of accounting's purpose and audience. Corporate finance refers to the sources of capital employed to fund a business organization and the entity's resulting capital structure. The chief categories of cap- ital are equity and debt securities. The combination, identity, and role that the two forms of investment play influence the audience for whom accounting is designed.[68]

Needs and interests of debt and equity investors differ. For equity investors, accounting standards and statements should be useful to form judgments concerning business value.[69] Standards quality is evaluated in terms of the relationship between reported accounting figures and resulting stock market prices or returns. On the other hand, for debt investors, accounting standards should make contract negotiation more efficient. Standards quality is evaluated in terms of whether they translate into financial statements that are useful for establishing covenants and other contractual provisions that regulate the rights and duties of lenders and borrowers.

Corporate finance characteristics also influence the relative importance of transparency that accounting can provide. Anglo-American finance is oriented toward equity and open capital markets, often attracting dispersed and uninvolved equity owners, making trans- parency in financial reporting vital.[70] Traditionally, Euro-Japanese finance relies on banks, which exercise considerable power within corporations.[71] This reduces the importance of reporting transparency for external users.

The relative needs of equity or debt investors also bear on how accounting standards and statements address uncertainty. The traditional US approach to uncertainty is conservatism, meaning asymmetric recognition of losses compared to gains.[72] However, investors and

[66] See David Levi-Faur, "The Global Diffusion of Regulatory Capitalism", 598 Annals Am. Acad. Pol. & Soc. Sci. 12 (2005).

[67] See Corporate Governance Regimes: Convergence and Diversity (Joseph A. McCahery et al. eds., 2002).

[68] The list of potential audiences for accounting information can be extended beyond debt and equity investors to include regulators, vendors, tax authorities, management, and potential merger partners.

[69] See Ray Ball, Ashok Robin, & Gil Sadka, Is Accounting Conservatism Due to Debt or Share Markets? A Test of "Contracting" versus "Value Relevance" Theories of Accounting, Working Paper 1 (Oct. 26, 2005).

[70] See Lawrence A. Cunningham, "Commonalities and Prescriptions in the Vertical Dimension of Global Corporate Governance", 84 Cornell L. Rev. 1133, 1136–39 (1999).

[71] Id. at 1142.

[72] See Sudipta Basu, "The Conservatism Principle and the Asymmetric Timeliness of Earnings", 24 J. Acct. & Econ. 3, 7–8 (1997).

other constituencies may have different demands for relative conservatism. In general, debt demands greater conservatism than equity.[73] Managers compensated heavily using stock options or other devices based on reported accounting results will demand a different level of conservatism than managers not so compensated. Managerial demand for conservatism relative to that demanded of equity or debt investors will differ accordingly.

Corporate finance also can influence the relative weight assigned to the income statement or balance sheet. This sometimes follows from the traditional forms of capital structure that prevail. To the extent that debt capital dominates, the balance sheet assumes greater importance to provide a basis for estimating solvency; where equity capital dominates, the income statement warrants a more central role in evaluating business performance. It is also possible for the relationship between financial and tax reporting (and the role of the state) to influence the relative importance of, and the relationship between, the income statement and the balance sheet. Accounting for inventory illustrates both points.

It is conceptually defensible to assume that goods in inventory are sold either in the direct order that they are produced (first-in-first-out, or FIFO) or in reverse order of production (last-in-first-out, or LIFO). In a period of rising prices, FIFO is more faithful to economic reality in the balance sheet, because it lists the inventory assets at more current values; conversely, LIFO is more faithful to economic reality in the income statement, because it records the costs of goods sold at more current costs. US GAAP permits choosing between these measurements, allowing enterprises to determine whether balance sheet or income statement fidelity is more important; IFRS requires using FIFO, suggesting balance sheet primacy.

Concerning taxation, the US Internal Revenue Code, requires conformity between inventory accounting for financial and tax reporting purposes.[74] Specifically, a company must use LIFO for both or FIFO for both. The rationale is simple. In a period of rising prices, FIFO results in reporting higher income compared to LIFO. Thus, managers may prefer FIFO for financial accounting to show investors higher income but prefer LIFO for tax accounting to pay lower taxes. The Internal Revenue Code's conformity requirement reflects how US culture generally considers tax and financial accounting separate subjects with generally different standards, whereas in many countries the two subjects are substantially co-extensive.[75]

A broader point about the cultural contingency of giving greater weight to the income statement or balance sheet is the question of which emphasis is more susceptible to manipulation (sometimes referred to as "tunneling").[76] In countries with dispersed equity ownership, such as the United States, controlling persons have greater incentives to manipulate the income statement, as their payoffs are a function of earnings per share.[77] In countries with

---

[73] See William W. Bratton, "Shareholder Value and Auditor Independence", 53 Duke L. J. 439, 477 (2003).

[74] Internal Revenue Code § 446(a); see *Thor Power Tool Co. v. Comm'r*, 439 U.S. 522 (1979).

[75] E.g., A. Frydlander & D. Pham, "Relationship Between Accounting and Taxation in France", 5 Eur. Acct. Rev. Supplement 845, 845–46 (1996); Dieter Pfaff & Thomas Schröer, "The Relationship Between Financial and Tax Accounting in Germany", 5 Eur. Acct. Rev. Supplement 963, 967–69 (1996).

[76] See John C. Coffee, Jr., "A Theory of Corporate Scandals: Why the United States and Europe Differ", 7 Stud. Int'l. Fin. Econ. & Tech. L. 3, 15 (2005); Simon Johnson et al., "Tunneling", 90 Am. Econ. Rev. (Papers & Proc.) 22 (2000).

[77] See John C. Coffee, Jr., Gatekeepers: The Professions and Corporate Governance 81, 88–91 (2006).

concentrated ownership, such as in Europe and Japan, the incentives are to manipulate the balance sheet, as controlling person payoffs come from allocating corporate assets to themselves rather than serving as stewards for other claimants.

It is not obvious whether IFRS provisions are designed to influence managerial propensity to manipulate the income statement or the balance sheet. It is likewise uncertain whether accounting standards could eliminate those propensities by proper design. Still, the cultural differences that lead to these alternative incentives matter in assessing universal accounting standards, both in production and application. Currently, it is more important for investors in US companies to constrain discretion over the income statement and for investors in European companies to constrain discretion over the balance sheet.[78]

Time horizons, referring to the distinction between the long-term and short-term, can be of great significance in conceiving appropriate accounting standards. Consider the case of traditional German accounting, which permitted and sometimes required the recognition of revenue or expense through hidden reserves across multiple time periods.[79] Although relevant in some countries, these have little to do with recognition concepts in US or UK accounting, which reflect more immediate time periods.

The use of hidden reserves, also followed in other European countries, including Austria, Denmark, Finland, and Switzerland, and to lesser degrees in Spain, would constitute earnings management in the United States and United Kingdom and would be a violation of both accounting standards and securities laws.[80] Even if these principles were abandoned for enterprises using IFRS, traditional knowledge and associated sensibilities would likely play a part in applications. The effect of this is that preparers in different countries could, in good faith, apply identical standards in different ways.

3.5 The Market

The relative role of markets in corporate activity covered by accounting reports can influence the character of accounting standards and the attitudes of those applying them. An example appears in the fundamental accounting issue of measuring assets. In general, there are two choices: measuring assets based on observed transactions (known as historical cost accounting) and measuring assets based on prevailing market conditions (known as fair value accounting).

National accounting systems take differing stances on whether to prefer historical cost or fair value accounting in general and in specific circumstances. Many are dual-attribute models, in which some items are measured using historical cost and others are measured using fair value. The choice is determined according to trade-offs between accounting's goal of relevance and that of reliability.

---

[78] But, if all use the same set of standards, it may be impossible to make these distinctions. On the other hand, a single set of global accounting standards may make the kinds of tunneling activities in which managers or insiders are engaged more transparent. See Vladimir Atanasov, Bernard Black, & Conrad S. Ciccotello, "Unbundling and Measuring Tunneling", 2014 U. Ill. L. Rev. 1697 (2014).

[79] See Enno W. Ercklentz, Jr., 2 Modern German Corporation Law 442–45 (1979).

[80] See id.; Donald E. Kieso et al., Intermediate Accounting 826 (10th ed. 2001).

The appeal of historical cost accounting is that measurements arise from observed transactions, such as the purchase price of an asset, which leads to reliable figures. Judgments are required to allocate that cost over the asset's life. As time passes, the historical cost figure becomes less relevant in the context of prevailing conditions.

The virtue of fair value accounting is that measurements are based on prevailing conditions, such as market prices of an asset, which leads to relevant figures.[81] But, cost allocations may require adjustment; a limitation occurs when exact market prices are inaccessible (either because the asset does not trade on a market, the asset trades infrequently, or the asset has few substitutes), making it less reliable than historical cost figures.

US GAAP traditionally preferred historical cost accounting, subject to a "lower of cost or market principle" that used market values when these were lower.[82] A US trend toward favoring fair value accounting began in the late twentieth century.[83] For its part, IFRS favors fair value accounting, in part as a product of the projects designed to converge IFRS and US GAAP.[84] Other national accounting systems vary in their relative preference for historical cost and fair value accounting. Thus, any choice IFRS makes will entail cultural adjustment in some countries.

Further, a putative advantage of fair value accounting is its use of markets as a basis for asset measurement. Yet a limitation arises if markets are imperfect or unavailable to measure particular assets. When that occurs, preparers and auditors must estimate fair value using judgments based on hypothetical valuation modeling tools.

This activity raises a broad question of how much deference these actors should receive when making such judgments compared to how much power investors and other users of financial statements should have to challenge those judgments. The national significance of this question will vary according to local investor demographics, including the mix of debt and equity in a capital structure and the degree of ownership concentration or dispersion.

3.6 The State

The role of the state varies across nations, even within capitalist societies. In comparative terms, the social democrat traditions prevalent in many continental European nations demand a state role consciously committed to protecting its citizens, including in the context of economic policy. The European practice of designating some corporations as "national champions" illustrates this sensibility as does assigning a special status to some constituent groups, such as labor unions. In contrast, US sensibilities, certainly among conservatives and even among many centrists and liberals, evince a more individualistic proclivity that

---

[81] See Lawrence A. Cunningham, "Finance Theory and Accounting Fraud: Fantastic Futures versus Conservative Histories", 53 Buff. L. Rev. 789, 792–93 (2005).

[82] Id.

[83] See Stanley Siegel, "The Coming Revolution in Accounting: The Emergence of Fair Value as the Fundamental Principle of GAAP", 42 Wayne L. Rev. 1839 (1996).

[84] A prominent international accounting standard reflecting this appetite is IAS No. 39, Financial Instruments: Recognition and Measurement. See IASC Foundation, "IAS 39 Financial Instruments: Recognition and Measurement" (2005) (describing the steps by which IAS No. 39 affects the IFRS' plan).

reduces the role of the state in economic life (and other spheres). Thus, there are no or few national corporate champions in the United States, and constituents vie for shifting political and economic power.

The consequence of these sensibilities is illustrated by differences between traditional French accounting compared to US (and UK) accounting. French accounting is heavily linked to, and co-extensive with, state fiscal policies,[85] while in the United States, tax accounting and financial accounting are distinct. Also, the US/UK income statement is designed to present information in forms useful to decision making by equity owners, whereas traditional French income statements were organized according to a statutory scheme that reflected an orientation toward the French state.[86] Similarly, US/UK balance sheets conceptualize assets in economic terms, while traditional French accounting conceives of them in a "patrimonial sense" of interests in tangible property.[87]

The state's role also bears on relative accounting conservatism. States may prefer a level of conservatism designed to generate desired tax revenue from corporations subject to tax within their jurisdiction. The exact appetite various states have for relative accounting conservatism may depend on population demographics, the manner of raising fiscal revenue, and the influence of economic theories on national policy, such as views on what supply-side effects have on production and total tax revenue. Whatever a state's appetite is, it may differ from those of the state's constituents and from those prevalent in other countries.

A state's net appetite for relative accounting conservatism may also be influenced by the demands of corporations and their constituents domiciled within the country. In countries that tend to identify national champions among their corporate elite, a national solicitude toward their interests is likely to interact with fiscal policy making. The net appetite also likely will be influenced by the historical relationship between financial and tax accounting. In the United States, because these accounting systems have been distinct, financial accounting can generally be evaluated independently of fiscal policy. For countries in which financial and tax accounting are co-extensive, the state's interest will continue to influence desired choices within financial accounting.[88]

The state interest manifests in many matters of international affairs. Even when political blocs endorse IFRS, it does not mean that all member countries follow suit or companies within them do. Some members of the European Union, for example, are notorious for ignoring EU directives, especially the Czech Republic, Greece, Italy, Luxembourg, and Portugal.[89] Many members, including such diverse countries as Cyprus, Germany, Hungary, and Spain, have altered IFRS to reflect local needs.[90] Beyond the European Union, IFRS

---

[85] See Cunningham, *supra* note 45, at 919–22.

[86] See Jacques Richard, France: Group Accounts, in 2 Transnational Accounting 1137 (Dieter Ordelheide & KPMG eds., 2d ed. 2001).

[87] Id.

[88] See Eva Eberhartinger & Margret Klostermann, "What If IFRS Were a Tax Base? New Empirical Evidence from an Austrian Perspective" (SSRN, Working Paper No. 1080512, 2008), available at www.ssrn.com/abstract_id=1080512; Wolfgang Schön, "The Odd Couple: A Common Future for Financial and Tax Accounting?", 58 Tax L. Rev. 111 (2005).

[89] See Tobias Buck, Italy Under Fire for Worst Record on EU Market Laws, Fin. Times, July 19, 2005, at 9.

[90] See David Henry, "A Better Way to Keep the Books?", Bus. Wk., Sept. 15, 2008, at 35.

endorsers include such assorted countries as Armenia, Iraq, and Kuwait.[91] Considering this diversity, it may be naïve to believe that accounting standards will be enforced uniformly in all these places.

It may be highly unlikely for countries to do so when national interest warrants non-compliance. An example is the experience of Japan in the late 1990s. When accounting rules required Japanese banks to record big losses on large loans in the 1990s, Japan's government intervened against doing so to avert a national financial crisis.[92] For another, after IASB adopted rules for financial instruments, the French government lobbied the European Union to obtain an exception to reduce volatility in reports of French banks.[93] Steps like these will continue and, depending on frequency, could stealthily destroy global uniformity.

4 CONCLUSION

Pressure of global capitalism has induced the drive toward universal accounting standards, and it can be difficult for any centralized authority to control that journey. It may be possible to bridge diversity using a universal set of accounting standards that concentrates on points of congruence while appreciating the consequences of difference. After all, in-choate but real convergence has occurred in important aspects of modern culture. These aspects include melding of legal traditions, coalescing around some forms of capitalism, and expanding global coordination and governance in many spheres of human activity. Yet diversity endures in many of those spheres, including those that affect accounting, especially law, economics, politics, and language.

Other cultural phenomena have proven more or less susceptible to such transcendence. Consider the metric system—a standardized, uniform method of measurement. This innovation was important to expanding international trade. It was begun by France in the late eighteenth century and was gradually adopted by all countries except the United States and two smaller ones.[94] Even in the United States, however, people are familiar with the metric system, and its use is widespread in everything from consumer goods to industrial production.

Although accounting is more complex and involves more than just measurement, measurement is an important aspect of accounting. Accounting's more complex attributes explain the hackneyed adage that accounting is the language of business.

Thousands of languages exist in the world, and hundreds are in use in the United States alone. Still, English has emerged as a widely spoken, nearly universal language, at least among active participants in international matters. On the other hand, conscious efforts to create a universal language have failed. The infamous example is Esperanto. This was a

---

[91] For a detailed list of countries requiring or permitting IFRS, see IAS Plus, Use of IFRS by Jurisdiction, available at http://www.iasplus.com/en/resources/ifrs-topics/use-of-ifrs.

[92] See Charles K. Whitehead, "What's Your Sign? International Norms, Signals, and Compliance", 27 Mich. J. Int'l. L. 695, 728 (2006).

[93] See Floyd Norris, Europe Closer to Accepting Uniform Accounting Rules, N.Y. Times, May 10, 2012, at B1.

[94] See MetricConversion.us, The Metric System, http://www.metricconversion.us/system.htm.

high-quality language, grammatically sound and coherent, with a sizable vocabulary capable of extensive expression. Yet it never caught on and is not widely used anywhere.

Today's accounting is more like the metric system than Esperanto. It is widely recognized if not universally embraced or uniformly implemented and has contributed substantially to the proliferation of global capitalism and related prosperity. That is quite an achievement, though the quest for a truly uniform system of accounting is elusive. It was shrewd or lucky that proponents set their sights on the bold vision of universal accounting, as such an outsized target equipped participants and followers to achieve the more realistic and practical objective.

In the nineteenth century, Max Weber explained how capital accounting was a precondition to the flourishing of capitalism.[95] The spread of reliable systems of accounting contributed to the flourishing of capitalism even though those systems were imperfect, incomplete, and incompatible across countries. Today, a global financial reporting system may be seen as a pre-condition to globalization, and one that has already substantially been achieved despite inherent imperfections and persistent shortfalls from pure comparability.[96] IFRS has helped to draw more countries into capitalist traditions. Its limits may simply reflect the different forms of capitalism and the different conceptions of corporate purpose and constituencies in the world.

The initial inspiration for international standards was to promote global capitalism, to facilitate cross-border capital flows, deals, and listings, an instrumental value, rather than the intrinsic beauty or Platonic value of an elegant universal ideal system. It has succeeded to a very large degree. We can accept both that the pure idea of universal accounting is a dream and that the practical efforts people took in its name have been valuable.

[95]   Max Weber, Economy and Society 85–86 (Guenther Roth & Claus Wittich eds., Ephraim Fischoff trans., Bedminster Press 1968) (exploring how the development of capital accounting was a precondition to the flourishing of capitalism during the eighteenth and nineteenth centuries).

[96]   See Bernard S. Black, "The Legal and Institutional Preconditions for Strong Securities Markets", 48 UCLA L. Rev. 781 (2001).

CHAPTER 20

....

RELATED PARTY TRANSACTIONS

....

LUCA ENRIQUES[1]

1 INTRODUCTION

....

THIS chapter covers transactions between a corporation and a "related party," a term of art that usually comprises counterparties who, thanks to their influence over corporate decision makers, may secure better terms for themselves than they would get following arm's-length bargaining.

First of all, it highlights the reasons why related party transactions ("RPTs") are so common around the world (section 2). Next, it better identifies the phenomenon as a specific class of potentially value-diverting behavior by dominant shareholders and managers, i.e., as an instrument for tunneling,[2] and asks why many jurisdictions provide for specific regulations on RPTs in addition to general rules or standards against controllers' abuse (section 3). Then, it describes the legal tools that policy makers and legal scholars commonly or increasingly consider as useful to tackle tunneling via RPTs:[3] prohibitions, procedural safeguards, mandatory disclosure, external independent advice, and ex post standard-based judicial review (section 4). Because of the focus on RPTs, this section does not include non-transaction-based, structural measures to prevent tunneling and dominant shareholders'

[1] University of Oxford and ECGI. I wish to thank András Hanák, Merritt Fox, Zohar Goshen, Michael Klausner, Georg Ringe, Chuck Whitehead, and especially Amir Licht and Alessio Pacces, for their comments on an earlier draft. Fianna Jurdant and Nadia Zainuddin provided useful information on Asian reforms focusing on related party transactions. Usual disclaimers apply. Throughout this chapter, by "companies" or "corporations" I mean listed companies unless it is otherwise clear from context.
[2] See Simon Johnson et al., "Tunneling", 90 Am. Econ. Rev. 22, 22 (2000) (defining "tunneling" as "the transfer of resources out of a company to its controlling shareholder"). The term tunneling is used, as here, to refer both to dominant shareholders and managers extraction of wealth by Vladimir A. Atanasov, Bernard S. Black & Conrad S. Ciccotello, "Unbundling and Measuring Tunneling", 2014 U. Ill. L. Rev. 101, 101.
[3] Although the main focus throughout the chapter is on RPTs, mention will also be made, when relevant to our purposes, to rules with a broader or narrower scope than those on RPTs strictly defined.

abuse, like limits on deviations from one-share-one-vote,[4] board composition requirements, or measures affecting the company's ownership (including the mandatory bid rule or oppression remedies); such tools' operation is not, whether by design or necessarily, dependent on abuse involving RPTs.

Finally, this chapter concludes that no regulation of RPTs (or tunneling) can succeed in preventing (minority) shareholder expropriation in the absence of sophisticated enforcement actors, i.e., experienced courts and/or active, committed securities regulators, operating in a social context that rejects tunneling as a business practice (section 5).

2 WELCOME TO TUNNELLAND

You are the founder and sole owner of a flourishing incorporated firm in Tunnelland, a notoriously business-unfriendly country: its punitive and inefficient tax system imposes unbearable tax rates, but leaves tax collection in the hands of unsophisticated, or selectively sophisticated (corrupt), tax officials.[5] Its politicians are strongly inclined to grabbing value from businesses by seizing corporate assets or allocating them to third parties, whether via legitimate enforcement of existing business-unfriendly laws or by exercising "raw power."[6] In addition, Tunnelland's courts are slow, unpredictable, and corrupt. Finally, its bankruptcy law is pro-creditors and liquidation-oriented and its banking system prone to liquidity crises: in the event of a credit crunch, firms face the risk of a value-destroying bankruptcy procedure due to illiquidity problems that are beyond firm owners' control.

If you are successful, you will soon experience how difficult it is, given the weakness of the institutional framework, to have satisfactory long-term, complex contractual relationships with business partners. You will then find it convenient to expand into adjacent industries, such as the production of materials or the supply of services you need for your initial business[7]: by governing these supply relationships by fiat within your firm, you will reduce the transactions costs thereof.

In such a setting, a constant worry of yours will be how to minimize the risk of government expropriation and of value destruction due to creditor rights enforcement. How much wealth should you leave within your corporation? The easy answer is: as little as is strictly

---

[4] Most notably, that is the route taken by Israel in the last twenty years, which has culminated in a ban on pyramids. See, e.g., Federico Cenzi Venezze, "The Costs of Control-Enhancing Mechanisms: How Regulatory Dualism Can Create Value in the Privatization of State-Owned Firms in Europe", 15 Eur. Bus. Org. L. Rev. 499, 513–14 (2014). For empirical evidence that in Korea a higher degree of separation between ownership and control correlates with greater RPTs activity see Minjung Kang, Ho-Young Lee, Myung-Gun Lee, & Jong Chool Park, "The Association between Related-Party Transactions and Control-Ownership Wedge: Evidence from Korea", 29 Pacific-Basin Fin. J. 272 (2014).

[5] One may think of 1990s Russia as vividly described by Bernard Black, Reinier Kraakman, & Anna Tarassova, "Russian Privatization and Corporate Governance: What Went Wrong?", 52 Stan. L. Rev. 1731, 1758–59 (2000).

[6] See Curtis Milhaupt, "Property Rights in Firms", 84 Va. L. Rev. 1145, 1153 (1998).

[7] See, e.g., Randall Morck, "Finance and Governance in Developing Economies", 3 Annual Review of Financial Economics 375 (2011) (describing LG's expansion from the original cosmetic cream business to very loosely related businesses like plastics, insurance, and oil refinery).

sufficient to keep the firm viable. How will you transfer wealth that is not strictly neces-sary for the corporation's viability into safer pockets? Again, there is an easy answer: in the way that makes it hardest for creditors, including the state as tax collector, and enforcement agents (public prosecutors, securities regulators, and courts) to detect and prove that you have transferred value out of the firm for nothing. The best way to do that is via transactions with yourself and/or entities you control. You will have made sure that there are plenty of these entities: in fact, your legal and tax advisors will have easily persuaded you to grant formal ownership rights over as many of the company's assets as possible to "third" parties connected to yourself, such as wholly owned companies, possibly even better if operating from a foreign jurisdiction. By doing so, you will have reduced the risk that those assets end up in the hands of tax authorities and/or creditors if things go wrong.

Your advisors will have more generally recommended that you structure your whole business as a web of connected, but formally separate, entities, each involved in a different production phase, typically with a holding company in charge of financing operations, one or more operating companies producing the goods or providing the services (the core firm(s)), and other satellite companies in charge of supplying the core firm(s) with components and other goods or services, like real estate or distribution. Once such a corporate group is in place,[8] RPTs will become routine and, correspondingly, it will be harder to find them suspicious, especially if businesses structured as corporate groups are a common organizational form within the economy. If RPT terms are such that the oper-ating corporation receives less than it gives away, you can routinely transfer wealth from its coffers to your (affiliates') pockets.

Unfortunately, there are still countries around the world displaying at least some of the business-unfriendly features of Tunnelland.[9] In such countries, tunneling via RPTs is, in a way, a physiological, and possibly even social welfare enhancing, reaction to badly functioning institutions. It may be the case that, in their absence, the cost of running a business would be even higher for entrepreneurs, fewer firms would exist and those coun-tries would be even less prosperous.[10]

An even higher number of countries have proved as business-unfriendly as Tunnelland until fairly recently.[11] There, tunneling via RPTs, or possibly RPTs without tunneling, may still be common because of path dependence, i.e., because in the past the institutional envir-onment made it convenient for businessmen to adopt business structures (practices) that may now be costly (for tax reasons or for the rents the dominant shareholders still extract through them) to disentangle (abandon).[12]

Of course, the point here is not to justify business practices that are almost universally viewed as harmful to investors and financial markets. Rather, as anticipated, it is to illustrate why RPTs are so common in many countries around the globe. The fictitious example of Tunnelland also shows what the minimal quality of property rights institutions must be in

---

[8] See Klaus J. Hopt, Groups of Companies, chapter 23 in this volume.

[9] One may think of Russia or Venezuela.

[10] Yet, it goes without saying that one cannot expect capital markets to develop so long as "defensive" tunneling is pervasive. See *infra* notes 13 and 23–27 and accompanying text.

[11] One may think of Italy or South Korea.

[12] See generally Lucian A. Bebchuk & Mark J. Roe, "A Theory of Path Dependence in Corporate Ownership and Governance", 55 Stan. L. Rev. 127 (1999).

any given system for RPTs to be rather a key issue for reform-minded policy makers aiming to boost domestic capital markets than a "second-worst" solution to a dysfunctional institutional environment. Finally, the example highlights how, in bad institutional environments, RPTs may be frequent also in closely held corporations with no distinction between controlling and non-controlling shareholders. Once corporations plan for a listing and try to raise outside capital, the controlling shareholders' private costs (including the tax implications) of disentangling complex organizational structures and the related web of RPTs may be higher than the increase in the IPO price they may secure by doing so. That is especially the case if credibly committing not to engage in tunneling is costly or even impossible, for example because the legal regime is too lax to serve as a credible commitment device.

Eventually, in countries with better functioning institutions, RPTs are not just the remnants of darker ages. Whenever an agency relationship exists, as is the case between shareholders as a class and creditors, between controlling and minority shareholders, and between managers and shareholders in dispersed ownership companies, the party with de facto residual rights of control over corporate assets, i.e., the agents, will appropriate as much value as they can expect to get away with, after factoring in the probability of detection and punishment.[13] RPTs are, again, an effective technology to appropriate value, because of the same attractive features highlighted above: first, they are easier to disguise as legitimate business transactions; second, thus disguised, they are not taxed as corporate distributions.[14]

At the same time, no one denies that RPTs exist that create value for all parties involved.[15] That may more easily be the case in closely held companies incurring higher transaction

---

[13] Scholars tend to associate RPT-based tunneling more with dominant shareholders than with managers, who are said to appropriate private benefits via excessive compensation (see Lucian A. Bebchuk & Assaf Hamdani, "The Elusive Quest for Global Governance Standards", 157 U. Pa. L. Rev. 1263, 1304–05 (2009)). However, there is no reason why, other things being equal, managers should prefer excessive compensation to RPTs as a tunneling technique. As a matter of fact, in jurisdictions where tunneling is widespread and unchecked for by legal and non-legal institutions, not only do manager-controlled companies often enter into RPTs (see, e.g., Merritt B. Fox & Michael A. Heller, What Is Good Corporate Governance?, in Corporate Governance Lessons from Transition Economy Reforms 3, 18 (Merritt B. Fox & Michael Heller eds., 2006)), but it is also the case that such companies soon become shareholder-controlled, whether because managers themselves succeed in securing a controlling ownership stake (usually via "equity tunneling:" see Atanasov et al., Unbundling, *supra* note 2, at 110–111) or because someone else acquires control in their stead. Control is simply too valuable to remain "up for grabs" for long. See Lucian A. Bebchuk, "A Rent-Protection Theory of Corporate Ownership and Control" (1999), National Bureau of Economic Research Working Paper No. w7203, available at http://www.nber.org/papers/w7203. Hence, even in such jurisdictions we observe no managerial tunneling in equilibrium: dominant shareholders themselves will keep managers on a tight leash. It is where institutions effectively address tunneling that one can observe dispersed ownership in equilibrium and, possibly, excessive managerial compensation. This form of tunneling is more common than others in such an environment, because it is hard to detect: executive pay is inevitable and determining what is reasonable compensation highly subjective.

[14] Of course, the same is usually true of excessive compensation. See note 13. Hwang and Kim report that in Korea RPTs are also used to transfer wealth to heirs so as to avoid estate and gift taxes. See Sunwoo Hwang & Woochan Kim, "When Heirs Become Major Shareholders. Evidence on Pyramiding Financed by Related-Party Sales", 41 J. Corp. Fin. 23 (2016).

[15] RPTs may even be entered into at favorable terms for the corporation and correspondingly unfavorable ones for the related party, whenever the latter has an interest in supporting the former (so-called propping), if only to keep extracting private benefits of control from it in the future. See Atanasov et al., Unbundling, *supra* note 2, at 108.

costs when dealing with unconnected market participants, due to higher information costs on both sides.[16] But listed companies may enter into entirely fair RPTs as well.

For instance, a company's labs may start developing a new product, but the finance department may later find that it is impossible to bring it to market, e.g. due to financial constraints and the need to concentrate R&D investment in other, more promising areas. The dominant shareholder may be in the best position to buy the project from the company and have a company wholly owned by himself work on it. Selling to a third party may be worse as an alternative, if the project is better developed with the dominant shareholder's unique entrepreneurial input and/or if it is hard for any third party to understand the project's chances of success: any offer from such third party will discount the higher perceived risk of failure. If the dominant shareholder buys the project for more than its net present value to the company, then the transaction is both fair and efficient.

This stylized example also shows how difficult it will be for third parties, be they minority shareholders, financial analysts, the company's audit firm, enforcement agents, or the public at large, to understand whether a RPT is in the best interests of the company: to do so, they would not only need to gauge what the right value of the project to the company would be if it realized it internally, but also assess whether it would be possible to find a third party willing to offer a price higher than the sum of (1) the price offered by the controlling shareholder and (2) the transaction costs that finding another buyer and negotiating with him would involve.

More debatable is whether even RPTs harmful to the company and/or its minority shareholders, and tunneling more broadly, may be efficiency-justified as the quid pro quo for the "public" (or shared) benefits minority shareholders enjoy as a consequence of the monitoring/entrepreneurial effort undertaken by dominant shareholders.[17] Note that there is no reason why minority shareholders themselves should a priori dislike a system thus designed. Provided ways are found for the dominant shareholder to pre-commit to a given level of private benefits extraction, minority shareholders may in fact understand the virtues of a regime that maximizes the sum of their (direct and indirect) losses from private benefits of control and of their gains from public benefits of control. In other words, they may be ready to tolerate private benefits extraction, so long as the contribution to the company's value by the dominant shareholder compensates for that.

---

[16] See, e.g., Luca Enriques et al., Related Party Transactions, in Reinier Kraakman et al., The Anatomy of Corporate Law 145, 146 (3d ed. 2017). Savings in transaction costs may be such that a below-market rate or price for a given RPT may be justified (i.e., involve no harm to the corporation). See, e.g., David Kershaw, Company Law in Context 478 (2d ed. 2012).

[17] For this proposition see María Gutiérrez Urtiaga & Maria I. Sáez Lacave, "A Carrot and Stick Approach to Discipline Self-Dealing by Controlling Shareholders" 7, ECGI—Law Working Paper No. 138 (2010), available at http://ssrn.com/abstract=1549403; Ronald J. Gilson & Alan Schwartz, "Constraints on Private Benefits of Control: Ex Ante Control Mechanisms Versus Ex Post Transaction Review", 169 J. Institutional & Theoretical Econ. 160, 162 (2013). Both models crucially rely on the verifiability of tunneling levels whether by markets via disclosure (Gutiérrez Urtiaga and Sáez Lacave) or courts (Gilson and Schwartz). See also Jens Dammann, "Corporate Ostracism: Freezing Out Controlling Shareholders", 33 J. Corp. L. 681, 705–25 (2008) (a system allowing for unfair related party transactions coupled with a structural ex post remedy may be more efficient for some companies than a transaction-based approach to tunneling control). But see contra Alessio M. Pacces, Rethinking Corporate Governance 96–97, 151–52 (2012): "[s]tealing is always inefficient ex ante."

The problem with this idea is, again, that private benefits extraction is hard to verify by a third party like a court or even an arbitrator. Even a comprehensive system of mandatory disclosure may be insufficient for the purpose: no disclosure regime can be expected to succeed in forcing dominant shareholders to confess how much they are stealing from their controlled company.[18]

No legal regime explicitly subscribes to the "quid pro quo" view of private benefits extraction.[19] But laxity in regulation and enforcement of anti-tunneling provisions has traditionally been common around the world.[20] That is tantamount to an implicit legalization of pecuniary private benefits extraction;[21] it also provides a strong incentive for parties to devise contractual or, better, non-legal (and especially reputation-based) constraints on tunneling. A credible device to commit to moderate tunneling is family ownership itself: so long as the dominant family member has descendants who may be at the company's helm some day, he can be expected to stop short of subtracting so much value as to make the company no longer profitable in the long run.[22]

Finally, tunneling not only raises distributional concerns in the relationship between insiders (managers or controlling shareholders) and (minority) shareholders,[23] but has an intuitively negative effect on capital markets as a whole and their dynamic efficiency. First, pervasive tunneling may have chilling effects on the IPO market: if a prospective listed company is unable to signal its controllers' intention not to engage in tunneling and/or to credibly commit to higher standards, it may desert the IPO market, leaving it to tunneling-prone issuers.[24] Second, a high level of tunneling (actually, of private benefits of control more generally) may lead to distortions in the market for corporate control (the highest-value user may be unable to buy control from the incumbent controlling shareholder, if the former is unable to extract as high private benefits)[25] and in ownership structures more generally (no one will relinquish control to the market if the private benefits of control to be extracted are high).[26] Finally, tunneling may well lead to distortion in managerial and strategic

---

[18] Cf. Alessio M. Pacces, "Controlling the Corporate Controller's Misbehaviour", 11 J. Corp. L. Stud. 177, 193 (2011) (highlighting the unattainable conditions for ex post mandatory disclosure to work effectively in this area).

[19] What comes closest to that are rules allowing for individual unfair transactions to go through in the context of corporate groups. See *infra* note 107 and accompanying text.

[20] See, e.g., Sang Y. Kang, "'Generous Thieves': The Puzzle of Controlling Shareholder Arrangements in Bad-Law Jurisdictions", 21 Stan. J.L. Bus. & Fin. 57, 85–95 (2015).

[21] See Gutiérrez Urtiaga & Sáez Lacave, *supra* note 17, at 14; Gilson & Schwartz, *supra* note 17, at 162.

[22] See Kang, *supra* note 20.

[23] The ability of relatively efficient markets to discount tunneling risk makes distributional concerns less troublesome anyway: a company's share price should reflect information about known (uncompensated for) past tunneling and expectations about (uncompensated for) tunneling yet to come (or to detect). Thus, shareholders buy shares at a price that discounts the predictable harm resulting from tunneling. They may miscalculate the amount of undetected and future tunneling, but that is no different from miscalculating future earnings. Incidentally, the tunneling discount makes tunneling more socially acceptable even when detected: minority shareholders deserve no particular sympathy if the price they paid compensated them ex ante for taking that risk. But see *infra* notes 24–27 and accompanying text for the various inefficiencies arising from tunneling.

[24] See, e.g., Fox & Heller, *supra* note 13, at 19.

[25] See, e.g., Lucian A. Bebchuk, "Efficient and Inefficient Sales of Corporate Control", 109 Q.J. Econ. 957 (1994).

[26] See, e.g., Bebchuk & Roe, *supra* note 12. See also *supra* note 13.

choices within individual companies, as controlling shareholders will choose transactions and strategies allowing them to extract more value via tunneling than those that maximize overall firm value.[27]

3 Related Party Transactions versus Tunneling versus Conflicted Transactions

Because RPTs are a usual suspect as a vehicle for tunneling, a number of jurisdictions provide for specific provisions addressing RPTs as such. For instance, accounting standards, including the US GAAP and the International Financial Reporting Standards (IFRS), provide for disclosures on (material) related party (relationships and) transactions.[28] Similarly, the UK has since long provided for procedural safeguards and immediate disclosure of larger RPTs.[29] Italy has followed the UK example in 2010.[30] Under the influence of international economic organizations such as the OECD and the World Bank,[31] many Asian countries,[32] including India,[33] have recently broadened the scope of RPT rules and tightened their content.

If RPTs do not necessarily involve tunneling and tunneling itself can be the outcome of behavior not involving RPTs, why do those jurisdictions single out RPTs for specific regulation

---

[27] See, e.g., Lucian A. Bebchuk, Reinier Kraakman & George Triantis, Stock Pyramids, Cross-Ownership, and Dual Class Equity: The Mechanisms and Agency Costs of Separating Control from Cash-Flow Rights, in Concentrated Corporate Ownership 295, 301–03 (Randall K. Morck ed., 2000).

[28] See Research and Dev. Arrangements, Statement of Fin. Accounting Standards No. 57 (Fin. Accounting Standards Bd. 1982); International Accounting Standards Board, International Accounting Standard No. 24 (EC Staff Consolidated version of 20 July 2010, available at http://ec.europa.eu/internal_market/accounting/docs/consolidated/ias24_en.pdf). No mention of materiality is made in the International Accounting Standard 24. However, it is an overarching principle of IFRS that disclosure is only to be made when it is material. See International Accounting Standards Board, International Accounting Standard No. 1, para. 31 (EC Staff Consolidated version of 18 Feb. 2011, available at http://ec.europa.eu/internal_market/accounting/docs/consolidated/ias1_en.pdf): "An entity need not provide a specific disclosure required by an IFRS if the information is not material."

[29] See Paul L. Davies & Sarah Worthington, Gower & Davies Principles of Modern Company Law 689–90 (9th ed. 2012). Note, however, that the UK's definition of RPT is different from the IAS 24's. Similar rules are also in place in Hong Kong since the 1980s.

[30] See Regulations Containing Provisions Relating to Transactions with Related Parties (adopted by CONSOB with Resolution no. 17221 of 12 March 2010, later amended by Resolution no. 17389 of 23 June 2010, available at http://www.consob.it/mainen/documenti/english/laws/reg17221e.htm).

[31] The World Bank's Doing Business Report has been instrumental in focusing lawmakers' minds on improving RPTs laws by ranking countries, inter alia, according to how strictly (according to a methodology derived from Simeon Djankov, Rafael La Porta, Florencio Lopez-de-Silanes & Andrei Shleifer, "The Law and Economics of Self-Dealing", 88 J. Fin. Econ. 430 (2008)) they regulate them. See International Finance Corporation, Doing Business 2017 66 (14th ed. 2016), available at http://www.doingbusiness.org.

[32] See, e.g., OECD, Guide on Fighting Abusive Related Transactions in Asia 25–31 (2009).

[33] See, e.g., Ernst & Young, India Inc.—Companies Act 2013. An overview 42–43 (2013), available at www.ey.com/Publication/vwLUAssets/India_Inc_Companies_Act_2013/$FILE/India_Inc_Companies_Act_2013.pdf.

rather than dealing, more broadly, with conflict-of-interest transactions or, even better, any kind of tunneling?

To answer this question, let us first identify RPTs by reference to their accounting definition, taking the one in the International Financial Reporting Standards as an example. According to International Accounting Standard 24,[34] "[a] related party transaction is a transfer of resources, services or obligations between a [corporation] and a related party, regardless of whether a price is charged."[35] Who qualifies as a related party is, in turn, defined very analytically in the same Standard so as to include all entities and persons, such as directors and controlling shareholders, that may presumptively have a significant influence on a corporation's decision on whether to enter into a transaction and under what terms, together with their (again broadly and analytically identified) affiliates.[36]

A key component of the RPT definition is in the preposition "between:" technically, no RPT exists if the transaction does not have the corporation (or an affiliate of its) on one side and a related party on the other. Hence, various transactions with tunneling potential entered into directly between the controller and shareholders do not qualify as RPTs because the company is not a party to the transaction. Such is, for example, the case of: (1) "internal tender offers," by which a controlling shareholder aims to take the company private via a bid for all of the shares he does not already own; (2) sales of the controlling block at a premium incorporating the present value of future private benefits; and (3) share purchases other than from the company itself on the basis of inside information.[37]

Other tunneling transactions do not qualify as RPTs because the counterparty to the corporation is not a related party, although the dominant shareholder may indirectly gain from the transaction to the detriment of (some of the) minority shareholders.[38] Such may be the case when a side deal exists between the controller and the company's counterparty. For example, the latter pays a kickback to the former in exchange for an above-market discount from the controlled entity: these transactions would clearly qualify as conflict-of-interest transactions, but they are not between the company and a related party.

No RPT is entered into in the following case either: suppose a company is controlled by a parent also active in the same business. For antitrust or regulatory reasons, the latter has to divest part of its business. Instead of selling its own assets, it may force the subsidiary to sell its own and even to select a buyer that will not challenge the parent's dominant position in the market, when possibly another competitor would have done so and paid more for the assets (assuming the subsidiary will no longer be active in that market after the sale, selling

---

[34] International Financial Reporting Standards were previously known as International Accounting Standards. Confusingly, standards adopted prior to renaming, like the one dealing with related party transactions, have kept their previous name of International Accounting Standards (IAS) followed by the relevant number.

[35] See International Accounting Standard 24, *supra* note 28.

[36] Id. at 2–4 (using 857 words to define related parties).

[37] See Vladimir Atanasov, Bernard S. Black & Conrad S. Ciccotello, "Law and Tunneling", 37 J. Corp. L. 1, 16 (share sales on the basis of inside information are at the expense of prospective shareholders. Id. at 23).

[38] To be sure, under the UK Listing Authority Listing Rules for Premium listed companies RPTs are defined more broadly to include also transactions (other than in the ordinary course of business) "between a listed company and any person the purpose and effect of which is to benefit a related party" (UK Listing Authority Listing Rules, LR 11.1.5.R(3)).

to an aggressive competitor would have harmed the parent's profitability, but not necessarily the subsidiary's).

Another example may be that of a secondary offering at a discount over the market price, but the price of which is still inflated because of negative information that has not yet been disclosed or because of false or misleading statements that keep market prices artificially high. If (some of the) minority shareholders subscribe to the newly issued shares and the controller does not, the former, together with any other new shareholder, will lose and the controller will correspondingly gain (to be sure, together with other non-subscribing shareholders).[39]

Transactions by which minority shareholders are forced to sell their shares to the company or the controlling shareholder, when executed outside the framework of a merger with a related party (as can be the case in Europe following a takeover bid,[40] where they are known as squeeze-outs) are also transactions in which the interest of the controller is clear, equity tunneling may take place, but no transaction between the company and a related party would occur.

Finally, according to its accounting notion, a RPT involves a transfer of resources. When value is transferred between the company and the related party that does not qualify as a resource, no RPT is involved. Such is for example the case where the controller appropriates a mere business idea (or a corporate opportunity).[41]

Of course, the fact that RPTs are subject to specific rules not applying to other tunneling techniques, and vice versa, can be fully justified. There might be tunneling transactions falling under a category of transactions normally displaying no potential for abuse, which yet happen to transfer value to the related party due to some idiosyncratic features of theirs. As an example, consider the case of an undercapitalized two-layer pyramidal group which operates at both layers in an industry (e.g., banking) where capital ratios are required at a consolidated level. Suppose that the higher-layer company is undercapitalized while the lower-layer company is well capitalized. The dominant shareholder at the top of the group will have an interest in raising new capital at the lower level of the pyramid, so as to minimize his burden in the recapitalization. That may, however, come at the expense of the lower-layer

---

[39] See Jesse M. Fried, "The Uneasy Case for Favoring Long-Term Shareholders", 124 Yale L. J. 1554, 1604–06 (2015). For empirical evidence from Chile on this form of tunneling see Borja Larrain & Francisco Urzúa, "I. Controlling Shareholders and Market Timing in Share Issuance", 109 J. Fin. Econ. 661 (2013).

[40] See, e.g., Edward Rock et al., Fundamental Changes, in Kraakman et al., *supra* note 16, at 171, 190–91.

[41] The point is tricky, however, because there is no doubt that a RPT is entered into if the controller indeed pays a price for the business idea. In the absence of a formal deal, there is a transfer of value between the company and the controller, but what is transferred would arguably not qualify as a "resource," because there is no evidence thereof in the company's books. This makes sense from an accounting perspective, because in the absence of a resource (i.e., asset), there can be no entry for the tacit transaction in the company's accounts. It makes much less sense if RPTs are the subject of procedural rules or other mandatory disclosure rules. This example shows how the automatic transplant of accounting concepts into regimes aimed to substantially or procedurally regulate behavior may be problematic. Examples of regulations transplanting the accounting definitions of RPTs to define the scope of procedural safeguards include Italy's CONSOB Regulation on RPTs (*supra* note 30) and the European Union's new regulatory framework for RPTs (see Directive (EU) 2017/828 of the European Parliament and of the Council of 17 May 2017 amending Directive 2007/36/EC as regards the encouragement of long-term shareholder engagement, O.J. L132, May 20, 2017, 1, and more precisely Art. 1(4) thereof, which inserts a new Article 9c in Directive 2007/36/EC).

company's profitability. Yet applying the special rules on RPTs to all new share issues to prevent idiosyncratic tunneling transactions such as the one just described may lead to burdensome, over-inclusive regulation: other things being equal, in such a case ex post judicial review would sound like a better solution.

At the same time, when the law treats differently two tunneling techniques allowing a controller to reach exactly the same expropriation outcome, the controller may engage in "tunneling arbitrage" and choose the more loosely regulated technique.[42] For instance, should a legal system provide that the procedural safeguards for RPTs have to be followed in the case of parent-subsidiary mergers, while much looser rules apply to tender offers initiated by the dominant shareholder and followed by a squeeze-out (again executed other than via a merger), the latter will be the preferred avenue to freeze out minorities.[43]

So why do reform efforts in various jurisdictions in recent years focus on RPTs as opposed to, for example, the broader (and, in many jurisdictions, more traditional) category of conflict-of-interest transactions?[44] One plausible explanation (in addition to the more prosaic one that the international policy debate is framed in terms of RPTs and domestic policy makers are just receptive of that language) is that rules applying to RPTs are more easily complied with and enforced than rules on conflicts of interest. Intuitively, the question of whether a "conflict of interest" exists in a given transaction is much more subjective and uncertain than the question of whether someone is a related party (although there is room for discretion in that respect as well). More precisely, it would be harder for companies as well as for regulators to set up, respectively, an effective compliance program or supervisory policies for conflict of interest transactions than for RPTs, especially if the special procedure has to apply (and enforcement powers are to be used) as soon as negotiations of an RPT start. Detecting a RPT is easier than deciding on a case-by-case basis whether on a given issue a director or a dominant shareholder may have a direct or indirect interest (in some jurisdictions: that conflicts with that of the corporation). In the case of the former, a "map" of related parties is relatively easy to draw and update, of course with the collaboration of "direct" related parties such as directors and dominant shareholders. Identifying "interests," especially indirect ones, equally implies the collaboration of directors and dominant shareholders, but, first, their discretion will be wider because of the subjective call

[42] See Atanasov et al., Law and Tunneling, *supra* note 37, at 40.

[43] This was the case in Delaware with reference to parent-subsidiary mergers, on the one hand, and tender offers launched by an already dominant shareholder, on the other: courts treated internal tender offers more leniently than mergers, until they recognized that the two transaction forms are functionally equivalent. See, e.g., Suneela Jain et al., "Examining Data Points in Minority Buy-Outs: A Practitioners' Report", 36 Del. J. Corp. L. 939, 941–48 (2011). Legal scholars' criticism of Delaware's bifurcated approach to such pairs of transactions was instrumental to the Court's acknowledgment of their functional equivalence. See especially Ronald J. Gilson & Jeffrey N. Gordon, "Controlling Controlling Shareholders", 152 U. Pa. L. Rev. 785 (2003); Guhan Subramanian, "Fixing Freezeouts", 115 Yale L. J. 2 (2005). The role legal academics had in such evolution in Delaware case law illustrates how sophisticated, functionally minded legal scholars may sometimes be as important as sophisticated courts in ensuring that the law in action works effectively to protect minority shareholders.

[44] Conflict-of-interest (or self-interested) transactions are a traditional focus of corporate law rules in many jurisdictions and are still the target of anti-tunneling provisions in some of them. Such is the case in France (special rules for transactions in which either directors or controlling shareholders have a direct or indirect interest: Code de Commerce (C. Com.) Art. L225-38) and in Belgium (for transactions in which directors have a conflicting interest: Code des Sociétés Art. 523).

that is needed to decide whether an interest has arisen with regard to a specific transaction (and whether it may conflict with the corporation's interest); second, the identification exercise would have to be undertaken for each and any individual transaction, which makes a properly formalized procedure or supervisory policy necessarily over-inclusive, and therefore burdensome. For the company, it would in fact imply asking directors and dominant shareholders to self-scrutinize each corporate transaction as opposed to providing an updated list of their affiliated persons and entities. True, this issue is less serious when the applicable rules provide for no special safeguards already to be complied with ahead of a formal resolution, for example, by the board. And yet, even when legal rules only pertain to the final stages of a transaction (e.g., requiring the additional approval by the shareholder meeting and detailed disclosure over the transaction), the risk remains higher of failing to apply the relevant rules to a conflicted transaction than to a RPT.

4 Legal Tools Against Tunneling via RPTs

Turning to the question of how legal systems can prevent RPTs from being used for tunneling purposes, the key issue is how to minimize that risk (i.e., to have rules that are effective enough to give rise to few "false negatives") without stifling value-creating transactions (i.e., avoiding "false positives" as much as possible) and more generally without imposing higher costs.[45] Because a number of context-specific factors and variables will determine what the best solution is for any given jurisdiction,[46] no attempt is made here to rank the legal tools described below, let alone recommend any of them as suitable. Rather, the conditions for them to be effective and their limits will be sketched out in very general terms.

4.1 Prohibitions

The seemingly most draconian way to address tunneling via RPTs is a simple prohibition of RPTs as such. Straightforward as it may seem, that strategy has two main drawbacks: it would also rule out value-creating RPTs that insiders may otherwise have entered into on fair terms for the corporation and, more importantly, it "may not [even] accomplish much":[47] unless an equally well enforced prohibition on any form of tunneling is in place,[48] insiders would just avoid RPTs as an expropriation technique and use functionally equivalent substitutes. In other words, a prohibition on RPTs is only effective if the enforcement system can tackle tunneling more broadly. That requires enforcement actors to use open-ended standards to respond to insiders' ingenuity in devising seemingly legitimate

---

[45] See, e.g., Pacces, *supra* note 18, at 191.

[46] See Zohar Goshen, "The Efficiency of Controlling Corporate Self-Dealing: Theory Meets Reality", 91 Cal. L. Rev. 393, 414–25 (2003).

[47] Enriques et al., *supra* note 16, at 146.

[48] See Troy A. Paredes, "A Systems Approach to Corporate Governance Reform: Why Importing US Corporate Law Isn't the Answer", 45 Wm. & Mary L. Rev. 1055, 1149–51 (2003).

value-diverting transactions. However, if an enforcement system is so sophisticated as to be capable of dealing with tunneling in all its forms, then there is no reason for using such a raw technique as a per se prohibition to prevent corporate theft. Conversely, and for the same reasons, a prohibition on RPTs would ineffectively tackle tunneling exactly where, on its face, it would be most justified to protect minority shareholders, i.e., in countries with bad enforcement institutions.

One may counter that a prohibition will be better than nothing and that, however little, it will raise the costs of tunneling, making it less profitable. Yet it remains true that if enforcement institutions are bad enough, the costs of evading the prohibition on RPTs will still be low: for instance, a counterparty will be related to the corporation if it is in turn controlled by a related party. Assessing whether a *control* relationship exists inevitably leaves much room for discretion and for clever lawyers' tricks to disguise it.

True, it might be the case that in countries which have neither excessively bad nor particularly good enforcement institutions, a RPT prohibition may indeed lower the amount of tunneling in the economy. But even there, prohibitions may be self-defeating in the long-term: because individual RPTs can be entirely fair for the company, and sometimes even necessary (as in crisis situations in which outsiders may be unwilling to do business with the company), value-creating transactions may be entered into in violation of the prohibition. As it happens, one of the parties to the RPT may ex post find it convenient to renege on it. It may then opportunistically use the prohibition to free itself from its obligations. In those cases, the pressure for judges to come up with doctrines or interpretations eroding the automatism of RPT prohibitions will be strong. With time, prohibitions "in action" may end up looking ever more similar to ex post standards.[49]

Prohibitions selectively targeting a specific category of RPTs, i.e., loans to related parties such as directors and executives, have traditionally been more common in Europe[50] and gained traction in the US and China in the first half of the 2000s. In the US, Congress banned loans to officers and directors[51] after WorldCom and other corporate scandals highlighted both the magnitude of the phenomenon and how loans could be used to circumvent executive compensation disclosure rules or delay compliance therewith.[52] In the wake of widespread abuse, China banned debt guarantees to shareholders from companies and their affiliates.[53]

---

[49] This may be part of the explanation for how, back in the nineteenth century, an ex post fairness review of RPTs prevailed on a (seeming) prohibition thereon in the United States. For an in-depth analysis of the relevant case law and for the doctrinal basis for such an outcome in Delaware, New Jersey, and New York, see David Kershaw, "The Path of Corporate Fiduciary Law", 8 N.Y.U. J. L. & Bus. 395, 444–83 (2012).

[50] See Luca Enriques, "The Law on Company Directors' Self-Dealing: A Comparative Analysis", 2 Int'l. & Comp. Corp. L. J. 297, 303–07 (2000).

[51] 15 U.S.C. 78m (k).

[52] See Lucian Bebchuk & Jesse Fried, Pay Without Performance: The Unfulfilled Promise of Executive Compensation 115–17 (2004).

[53] See, e.g., Henk Berkman, Rebel A. Cole, & Lawrence J. Fu, "Expropriation Through Loan Guarantees to Related Parties: Evidence from China", 33 J. Bank. Fin. 141, 144 (2009).

4.2 Procedural Safeguards

Most jurisdictions provide for rules on how to enter into RPTs. Procedural rules may apply to RPTs as such (as is the case in India and Italy), to a broader set of transactions that include some or all RPTs (as is the case in France, where procedural rules apply to all transactions in which a director has a direct or indirect interest[54]), or to a subset of RPTs (as is the case in Germany, with its very narrow rules applying to transactions in which the director is the counterparty or acts in the counterparty's name[55]). Often jurisdictions provide for different procedural rules depending on whether the related party is a director or a controlling shareholder (e.g., Belgium). Sometimes, quantitative thresholds or qualitative features are used to define the scope of procedural rules (e.g., in the UK and Italy).

In general, procedural rules can be defined as more or less strict, depending on how effectively insulated corporate decision makers are from the dominant insiders and on the extent to which they put such "independent" decision makers in control over the negotiating process. Relatedly, a crucial element for rules' effectiveness is decision makers' access to relevant information and their ability to process it as disinterested executives would.

The focus here is on two of the main procedural safeguards that at least some jurisdictions currently deploy: approval by a majority of independent shareholders and approval by disinterested/independent directors.

4.2.1 MOM Approval

A popular idea in academia as well as among policy makers is that the most effective procedural safeguard against tunneling is a veto power over RPTs for a majority of the shareholders other than the related party itself (a majority of the minority, or MOM, in companies with a dominant shareholder).[56] An increasing number of countries (including the UK, Israel, and all major East Asian countries, with the notable exceptions of Japan and South Korea[57]) provide for such a requirement with respect to larger, non-routine transactions.

A MOM requirement does ensure that only fair RPTs are entered into, provided at least four conditions are met:

(a) Minority shareholders have a real opportunity to cast their vote.
(b) Voting shareholders do so sincerely, for example being truly unrelated themselves to the related party and having been paid no bribe to vote in favor.

---

[54] Code de Commerce (C. Com.) Art. L225-38. For the UK, see *supra* note 38.

[55] AktG § 112. BGB § 181. A recent trend, especially in scholarship, toward extending the scope of § 112 has not gone very far yet. See Mathias Habersack, § 112, 2 Münchener Kommentar zum AktG 1371, Rn. 10 & 16 (Wulf Goette, Mathias Habersack & Susanne Kalss eds., 4th ed. 2014), available at Beck-online (§ 112 does not extend to shadow management board members, but does extend to family members of the board member in very specific circumstances).

[56] See Assaf Hamdani & Yishai Yafeh, "Institutional Investors As Minority Shareholders", 17 Rev. Fin. 691, 692 (2013) ("Financial economists, legal scholars, the Organisation for Economic Co-Operation and Development, and others have urged lawmakers to subject certain self-dealing transactions to a vote by 'disinterested' shareholders").

[57] See Asian Roundtable on Corporate Governance, Reform Priorities in Asia. Taking Corporate Governance to a Higher Level 66 (2011).

(c) The MOM approval is the outcome of a well-informed decision-making process, following full disclosure of all material information about the RPT.

(d) Shareholder voting takes place at a moment in time when vetoing the RPT is still a viable choice for the corporation.

Condition (a) would seem to always apply and hence not be even worth mentioning. However, the Russian experience in the 1990s reminds us that where enforcement institutions are dysfunctional enough, even MOM clauses are deprived of their "self-enforcing" appeal.[58] A famous account of asset stripping after privatization in Russia includes an anecdote of how Mikhail Khodorkovski, then the dominant shareholder at Yukos, managed to obtain the legally required shareholder vote for a number of tunneling transactions involving its subsidiaries:

> Yukos owned only 51% of the shares in the subsidiaries, and needed 75% of the votes of the shareholders who participated in a shareholder meeting to authorize the share issuance (plus a majority of the votes of noninterested shareholders). Khodorkovski's solution was bold, if not exactly legal: The day before the subsidiaries' shareholder meetings, Yukos arranged for a compliant judge to declare that the minority shareholders were acting in concert, in violation of the Antimonopoly Law. The judge disqualified everyone but Yukos and its affiliated shareholders from voting. When minority shareholders arrived at the meetings, they were greeted by armed guards; most were barred from voting or attending on the basis of this court order. Yukos' shares were voted and were counted as noninterested; the proposals all passed.[59]

That was also a case in which condition (b) (sincere voting) was not met. In the absence of broad-scope rules on who is disqualified from voting, MOM approval may just pay lip service to minority shareholder protection. In countries where families often control listed companies, like Hong Kong, excluding the related party but counting votes from "relatives, such as cousins, nephews, and uncles, as well as friends and other members of the board of directors"[60] may easily lead to routine general meeting approval of RPTs.[61]

Less blatant cases of conflicted voting are those where shareholders are (controlled by) current or potential providers of financial services to the company (and/or its dominant shareholder):[62] in countries with smaller capital markets and a small presence of international institutional investors and/or independent asset managers, shareholders of that kind may well ensure that RPTs are routinely passed.[63]

---

[58] See Bernard Black & Reinier Kraakman, "A Self-Enforcing Model of Corporate Law", 109 Harv. L. Rev. 1911, 1959–60 (1996).

[59] Black et al., Privatization, *supra* note 5, at 1771.

[60] See Yan-Leung Cheung, P. Raghavendra Rau, & Aris Stouraitis, "Tunneling, Propping, and Expropriation: Evidence from Connected Party Transactions in Hong Kong", 82 J. Fin. Econ. 343, 350 (2006).

[61] Id.

[62] The Delaware case *Hewlett v. Hewlett Packard Co.*, 2002 Del. Ch. LEXIS 35, while not dealing with a tunneling transaction, aptly shows how difficult it is for a plaintiff to prove that an institutional investor's vote may have been tainted by conflict of interest.

[63] For Israeli evidence of that see Hamdani & Yafeh, *supra* note 56, at 706–08, 711–13 (analyzing Israeli companies' shareholder votes on RPTs in 2006). The most blatant example of "friendly" institutional investor voting on a RPT comes from South Korea: in August 2017, Samsung's CEO, Lee Jae-yong, was convicted for making payments to foundations close to South Korea's president in exchange for state pension funds' favorable vote in a merger between two Samsung affiliates that cemented the CEO's

Condition (c) presupposes rules ensuring that full disclosure is made of information shareholders need in order to make an informed decision about the transaction.[64] In addition, it presupposes that shareholders are able to make good decisions on individual business transactions as opposed to decisions on how to invest.[65]

To be sure, a disinterested, albeit less well-informed, decision maker may generally be preferable to one with the relevant knowledge but a clear conflict of interest: that MOM approval may also lead to false negatives does not mean that shareholders would be better off without it.

Finally, disinterested shareholders may well approve a RPT which appears not to be the best deal for the company, when the alternative unconnected transaction would now be less convenient to the company after taking prospective transaction costs into account. Suppose the shareholder meeting is convened to approve the sale of an asset to a related party for a (fair) price of $100. Once the proposed transaction is disclosed, an unrelated party credibly declares that it would buy the same asset for $102, subject to due diligence etc. If the company has to spend more than $2 in transaction costs to negotiate with the unrelated party, disinterested shareholders will vote for the RPT even if, by now, they are aware that the company would have gained more by searching for another buyer on the market.[66]

Of course, a MOM requirement also makes it more likely that a fair RPT (i.e., a transaction in the best interests of the company) will not be entered into. That may be the case when:

1   Shareholders are ill-informed about the real value to their corporation of the asset to be bought (sold), thinking it is worth less (more) than the related party offers.
2   One or more shareholders have the power to hold out and no agreement is (or may be) reached on the side payment that they request to vote in favor of the transaction.[67]
3   The marginal transaction costs of obtaining MOM approval, including the longer time and the publicity needed to finalize it, are such as to make the transaction no longer worth entering into or practicable.

control over the *chaebol*. See Bryan Harris, Samsung Heir Sentenced 5 Years in Jail, Fin. Times, August 25, 2017, available at https://www.ft.com/content/63f25122-892d-11e7-bf50-e1c239b45787.

[64] For a more general analysis of why shareholder voting outcomes may deviate from efficient ones see Michael C. Schouten, "The Mechanisms of Voting Efficiency", 2010 Colum. Bus. L. Rev. 763, 780–808.

[65] See Rock et al., *supra* note 40, at 174.

[66] Assuming that the transaction costs of dealing with the related party were half those of dealing with an outsider (say, $1.5 versus $3), the company would originally have been better off selling to the outsider for 102. Note, incidentally, that the stylized example in the text is unlikely. Similarly, a scenario in which the company starts negotiations both with an outsider and a related party will be infrequent. Even assuming that the negotiation process itself can be shaped in such a way as to rule out favoritism and hence persuade the outsider to compete with the related party, the outsider should know that the related party will have better information about the value of the asset than the outsider, so that either the related party will outbid the oustider or the outsider will have paid too much for the asset. Ex ante, this is likely to discourage the outsider from starting negotiations. (I am grateful to Luigi Zingales for this insight.)

[67] Compare Edward B. Rock, Institutional Investors in Corporate Governance, chapter 14 in this volume (reporting that some worry about extensive use of MOM approval in the presence of hedge fund activism).

The transaction cost issue is the reason why jurisdictions that provide for MOM approval (e.g., the UK, Hong Kong, Singapore) do so only for RPTs above a given size, typically when their value is above 5% of the company's market capitalization. France is an exception, because the exemption is only for routine self-interested transactions (i.e., those the company itself assesses to be entered into in the ordinary course of business and at market conditions). However, MOM approval in France is only ex post, at the annual meeting, and denial of approval of a properly board-approved transaction has very little practical impact, if any.[68]

4.2.2 Disinterested or Independent Directors' Approval

Jurisdictions may require involvement of independent directors in the approval process, as is the case in Belgium (for intra-group transactions specifically[69]) and Italy,[70] or make it strongly advisable, as under Delaware case law with regard to some transactions with controlling shareholders.[71] Within or across jurisdictions, however, approval merely by disinterested directors is sometimes sufficient: such is the case in Belgium and Delaware for transactions with directors and in France generally for transactions in which a director or a substantial shareholder have an interest.

For independent directors (and a fortiori for merely disinterested ones) to play an effective role in the protection of minority shareholders, the key issue is of course how truly independently from controllers one can expect them to act. In part, that will depend on how "independence" is defined and, primarily, on whether being nominated by the controlling shareholder precludes that qualification. Even when a director is nominated and appointed with the involvement of minority shareholders (like in Israel, Italy, and Spain[72]) substantial independence is not guaranteed, as that is mainly a function of an individual's assertiveness, ability not to succumb to boardroom biases,[73] and reputational and career concerns.[74]

Even assuming that an independent director has such personal qualities and concerns, a handicap she still faces is her inferior knowledge of a company's business.[75] The presence of what are to her unknown unknowns may well allow insiders opportunistically to filter the pieces of information based upon which her decision will be made.

---

[68] See, e.g., Enriques, The Law, *supra* note 50, at 327–328.   [69] Code des Sociétés Art. 524.

[70] CONSOB Regulation on Related Party Transactions, *supra* note 30, Art. 7 & 8.

[71] In Delaware, approval of freezeout transactions by a special committee of independent directors reverses the burden of proof that the transaction is entirely fair upon the plaintiff. See, e.g., Claire Hill & Brett McDonnell, "Sanitizing Interested Transactions", 36 Del. J. Corp. L. 903, 922–23 (2011).

[72] See María Gutierrez & Maribel Sáez, "Deconstructing Independent Directors", 13 J. Corp. L. Stud. 63, 86 (2013). In Israel, "[e]ach public company has to appoint at least two outside directors, who must be independent from both the controlling shareholder and the management and whose candidacy must be approved not only by a majority of shareholders but also by a third of minority shareholders." Hamdani & Yafeh, *supra* note 56, at 698. Cumulative voting, which allows for minority shareholder representation in the board, is mandatory in Argentina, the Philippines, Russia, and Poland. See Tatiana Nenova, "A Corporate Governance Agenda for Developing Countries", 217 Contaduría y Administración 181, 201 (2005).

[73] Andrew Keay, "The Authorizing of Directors' Conflicts of Interest: Getting a Balance?", 12 J. Corp. L. Stud. 129, 143–46 (2012).

[74] Cf. Luca Enriques et al., The Basic Governance Structure: Minority Shareholders and Non-Shareholder Constituencies, in Kraakman et al., *supra* note 16, 79, 85.

[75] Keay, *supra* note 73, at 152.

Independent director involvement may also vary in intensity. The weakest involvement requirement is for independent directors to give non-binding advice on RPTs, like in Belgium and, limited to smaller transactions, in Italy. Such a requirement does not prevent the dominant shareholder, or at least non-independent directors, from being part of the internal decision-making process. Yet, provided that the negative advice is to be disclosed and private enforcement tools are available to shareholders, non-binding negative advice can serve shareholder interests by giving them a persuasive piece of circumstantial evidence of tunneling before the court. Further, the market may use it as a signal of the dominant shareholder's inclination for tunneling, although that will be of little consequence if control is incontestable and the company has no prospect of raising more equity. Finally, especially when the negative advice is to become public, boards will tend not to deviate from the independent directors' advice.[76]

Involvement is stronger with a requirement that the transaction be approved not only by the board as a whole but also by a majority of the independent directors. Here, it makes a difference whether their decision is made in the same room and at the same time as the board's decision, and whether interested directors, and especially the CEO or the dominant shareholder, are present.

Still stronger is an independent directors' binding advice, in which case they do have a veto power over the RPT. Whether that power is effective (will be exercised as often as necessary to protect shareholders' interests) depends not only on the directors' substantial independence and on whether they have full access to information, but also on whether they can be assisted by experts (lawyers, investment bankers, etc.) of their own choice at the company's expense (like in Italy[77]), and on how late in the negotiation process they are involved: the later they are to express themselves on the RPT, the more likely that a number of alternatives will no longer be practically available, so that the RPT may have become the only viable way ahead for the corporation and favorable advice a forgone conclusion.

The strongest form of involvement is finally the "independent negotiating committee" (or "special committee") Delaware courts have since long nudged boards into using when a parent–subsidiary merger or an MBO is on the agenda:[78] the board delegates a small number of independent directors to conduct negotiations on the transaction and to decide upon it, usually having freedom to search for alternative counterparties. Because of their total control over the process, special committees have various advantages over shareholder MOM approval: their involvement is more timely, their (access to) information better, no serious holdout risk exists,[79] and the procedural costs should be lower. The crucial point is always whether one can expect independent directors to make decisions in the best interests of the company rather than in the related party's.[80]

---

[76] That is the case at least in Belgium. See Koen Geens, Corporate Boards in Belgium, in Corporate Boards in Law and Practice 120, 142 (Paul Davies & Klaus Hopt eds., 2013).

[77] See CONSOB Regulation on Related Party Transactions, *supra* note 30, Art. 7–8 (for larger transactions, independent directors may hire advisors of their choice at the company's expense).

[78] See, e.g., Edward B. Rock, "Saints and Sinners: How Does Delaware Corporate Law Work?", 44 UCLA L. Rev. 1009, 1026 (1997) ("language in Weinberger led to the near universal use of 'special committees' of independent directors in MBOs." See *Weinberger v. UOP, Inc.*, 457 A.2d 701, 709 (Del. 1983)).

[79] Unless they may be held liable for damages in case of a negligent decision, in which case, other things being equal, they may have a preference for vetoing the transaction.

[80] For a negative assessment see Gutierrez & Sáez, Deconstructing, *supra* note 72, at 81.

4.2.3 Independent Directors and MOM Approval?

All in all, neither MOM approval nor the independent directors' role ensures that tunneling via RPTs will not occur. To lower that risk, a jurisdiction may think of combining the two procedural safeguards discussed above. There are obvious synergies between the two: as (then) Vice-Chancellor Strine put it, the independent directors' role "is important because the directors have the capability to act as effective and active bargaining agents, which disaggregated stockholders do not."[81] They may thus screen RPTs and ensure that their terms are better for the shareholders: the risk that shareholders approve unfair transactions because it is too late for alternative solutions to be considered[82] should go down considerably. But, again in Chancellor Strine's words, "because bargaining agents are not always effective or faithful, [MOM approval] is critical, because it gives the minority stockholders the opportunity to reject their agents' work."[83] Ex ante, it will prompt independent directors to negotiate harder.[84]

Net of the higher direct transaction costs, compared to MOM approval alone, the combination of independent directors and MOM approval may also lower the risk that value-creating transactions will not be entered into. In fact, approval by well-reputed independent directors may act as a credible signal of a transaction's fairness to minority shareholders. These, in turn, may be more inclined to vote for the proposed RPT rather than siding with opportunistic activist investors who, by holding out, may aim to extract value from the company.

No main jurisdiction has so far addressed RPTs by combining independent directors and MOM approval. The one which has come closest is Delaware: for endgame transactions such as MBOs and freeze-outs, its courts have held that combining both a special committee and MOM approval grants a company and its dominant shareholder the protection of the business judgment rule, and therefore virtually insulates the transaction from judicial review.[85]

4.3 Disclosure

One of the core functions of mandatory disclosure has traditionally been to cast light on self-interested transactions.[86] Mandatory disclosure is still today a widely used technique to

---

[81] *In re Cox Communications, Inc. S'holders Litig.*, 879 A.2d 604, 606 (Del. Ch. 2005).

[82] See *supra* note 66 and accompanying text.

[83] *In re Cox Communications, Inc.*, *supra* note 81, at 606.

[84] Richard Booth, "Majority-of-the-Minority Voting and Fairness in Freezeout Mergers", 59 Vill. L. Rev. Tolle Lege 87, 93 (2014).

[85] *In re MFW S'holders Litig.*, 67 A.3d 496 (Del. Ch. 2013). Because a special committee is sufficient to reverse the burden of proof that the transaction is entirely fair, which also means some degree of insulation from judicial review, it is unclear how worthy it is for a company (and its controlling shareholder) to go through the hassle of MOM approval and the ensuing risk of activist investor holdouts. See Viktor Lewkow et al., Going Private Transactions—MFW's Bumpy Road to Business Judgment Review, Cleary Gottlieb Mergers & Acquisitions and Corporate Governance Report 7, 7–8 (May 2014).

[86] See Paul G. Mahoney, "Mandatory Disclosure as a Solution to Agency Problems", 62 U. Chi. L. Rev. 1047, 1066–73 (1995).

address RPTs. In isolation, mandatory disclosure may be insufficient to prevent tunneling, which is well documented even via transactions that are publicly disclosed.[87] Its importance is more in supporting internal decision makers' independence (they will act more assertively if they know the RPT under consideration will be subject to public scrutiny) and in facilitating private and public enforcement against tunneling.

Financial reporting standards nowadays require disclosure (and therefore the audit)[88] of information relating to material RPTs almost everywhere.[89] In addition to accounting standards' requirement for periodic information about RPTs, the US SEC requires companies to annually disclose RPTs above $120,000 so long as the related party has a material interest in the transaction.[90] In Europe, as elsewhere, companies going public have to provide detailed information of material transactions with related parties in their prospectuses.[91]

All of these rules and standards rely on a company's necessarily discretionary assessment of whether a transaction (or a related party's interest) is material for disclosure purposes. Especially if that assessment is not itself made by independent directors, embarrassing RPTs may well remain hidden from the public's view.[92] And even independent directors may not always be in the best position to make that call: if they approve the transaction themselves, given a choice on whether their judgment should be subject to public scrutiny, they will naturally tend to favor opacity.

Some jurisdictions also provide for ad hoc, immediate disclosure of larger RPTs, whether as a step in the process leading to MOM approval (UK) or as an independent requirement once the transaction has been entered into (Italy; the UK for "smaller transactions"). In the former case, because disclosure is made well in advance of the shareholder meeting where MOM approval is scheduled, there is the additional advantage that attention from the media, financial analysts, and activist investors may pressure the company into obtaining better terms for (minority) shareholders or even into abandoning the transaction altogether.[93]

Even when ex post, ad hoc disclosure has an additional advantage over periodic disclosure in IFRS-compiled financial statements: while in the former case details about the individual

---

[87] For empirical evidence relating to China between 1996 and 2006 see Guohua Jiang et al., "Tunneling Through Intercorporate Loans: The China Experience", 98 J. Fin. Econ. 1 (2010); Yan-Leung Cheung et al., "Buy High, Sell Low: How Listed Firms Price Asset Transfers in Related Party Transactions", 33 J. Bank. & Fin. 914 (2009).

[88] Reliability and completeness of RPT-related information in financial statements is usually supported by auditors' review thereof. See, e.g., Kershaw, *supra* note 16, at 507.

[89] For the US and the EU, see *supra* note 28.

[90] Securities and Exchange Commission, Regulation S-K, Item 404.

[91] For the EU, see Commission Regulation (EC) No 809/2004, April 29, 2004, implementing Directive 2003/71/EC of the European Parliament and of the Council as regards information contained in prospectuses as well as the format, incorporation by reference and publication of such prospectuses and dissemination of advertisements, as amended, Annex 1, No. 19 (O.J. L149, April 30, 2004, 3, 31).

[92] Cf. Geeyoung Min, "The SEC and the Courts' Cooperative Policing of Related Party Transactions", 2014 Colum. Bus. L. Rev. 663, 698.

[93] For the same reason, disclosure as an independent requirement would be more effective if it were to be made before the transaction is finalized. Notice, however, that even with disclosure to the market prior to MOM approval, renegotiation is highly unlikely if, like in the UK, the applicable rules allow for the transaction to be finalized before it, with the only proviso that it must be approved by shareholders.

transaction are normally to be provided, according to International Financial Reporting Standards, RPTs "of a similar nature may be disclosed in aggregate except when separate disclosure is necessary for an understanding of the effects of related party transactions on the financial statements of the entity."[94] The wording, again, grants a company (its audit firm) discretion in the choice of whether to aggregate RPTs (in objecting to that choice).

Finally, given the discretion in disclosing RPTs, rules requiring public disclosure as to who is in the position to engage in RPTs with the corporation can also help detect tunneling. Ownership disclosure rules allow the market to have updated information about who has or may have an influence over the company's management.[95]

4.4 Third Party Advice and Fairness Opinions

To tackle the issue of insufficient (independent director and/or) shareholder information, some jurisdictions require that companies make an independent financial advisor's opinion available to shareholders,[96] whether in anticipation of their vote on the transaction or as a supplement to information on the transaction itself. Voluntary use of independent third parties as advisors in the negotiation process, be they lawyers or investment banks, is also common practice.[97] Such advice usually includes (when it is not confined to) a fairness opinion, which the law may then require to disclose.[98]

Because fairness valuations imply a high degree of discretion,[99] the value of the independent experts' fairness opinions ultimately rests upon the experts' reputation. Their effectiveness as a tool to protect investors is thus as doubtful as that of gatekeepers more generally,[100] the main concern being, as usual, that outside experts, even when chosen by

[94] IAS 24, *supra* 28, at 6 (§24). David Buchuk et al., "The Internal Capital Markets of Business Groups: Evidence from Intra-Group Loans", 112 J. Fin. Econ. 190, 208–10 (2014) (connecting evidence of absence of tunneling via related lending transactions in Chile to reforms providing for disclosure of all such loans individually in the financial statements).

[95] See, e.g., Luca Enriques, Matteo Gargantini & Valerio Novembre, "Mandatory and Contract-based Shareholding Disclosure", 15 Uniform L. Rev. 713, 720 & 735 (2010) (describing ownership disclosure as "mainly a tool for ensuring better corporate governance by guaranteeing that the market knows who has an influence over management").

[96] Such is for example the case in Belgium (for intra-group transactions: Code des Sociétés Art. 524(2)) and Singapore (see Rule 921, Singapore Exchange Mainboard Rules).

[97] Also nudged by statutes and/or case law providing that directors may reasonably rely on experts' reports. See, e.g., Del. Code Ann. tit. 8, § 141(e). For Germany see Holger Fleischer, "Directors' Liability and Financial Crisis: The German Perspective", 88 Il Diritto Fallimentare e delle Società Commerciali 454, 463–64 (2013) (describing the case law outlining the conditions under which directors can rely on independent experts' opinions).

[98] That is the case in Italy: see CONSOB Regulation on Related Party Transactions, *supra* note 30, Art. 5(5) (if a fairness opinion is released, it has to be disclosed).

[99] See, e.g., Steven M. Davidoff, "Fairness Opinions", 55 Am. U. L. Rev. 1557, 1573–80 (2005).

[100] See generally John C. Coffee Jr., Gatekeepers. The Professions and Corporate Governance 2-10 (2006) (defining gatekeepers as agents acting as "reputational intermediary[ies] to assure investors as to the quality of the 'signal' sent by the corporate issuer," including investment bankers providing fairness opinions in parent-subsidiary mergers among gatekeepers, and outlining reasons for the failure of gatekeepers in the early 2000s).

independent directors, may be less independent than they look, as they usually stand to gain much more from other advisory and investment banking roles than from providing fairness opinions.[101]

In addition, as a piece of information instrumental to shareholder voting on the transaction, the fairness assessment per se is not particularly informative.[102] What can be helpful is information the fairness opinion is based upon, like management's projections of future cash flows, and the assumptions and methods the advisor has used.[103] Delaware is the only main jurisdiction that has developed a wide body of case law on the scope of required disclosure on fairness opinions,[104] while Italy's CONSOB Regulation on RPTs requires information about fairness opinion contents roughly equivalent to Delaware case law.[105] Other countries appear to be less detailed in their requirement for fairness opinion disclosure.

4.5 Ex Post Standard-Based Review

Jurisdictions often rely also on ex post judicial enforcement of one form or another of a "don't tunnel" standard to tackle RPTs. Generally, what the various manifestations of ex post standard-based review have in common is that courts look into the merits of a RPT to find out whether its terms were "fair" to the corporation, i.e., whether it suffered any prejudice (broadly or strictly identified) therefrom.[106]

Different standards of review may apply to different RPTs within the same jurisdiction. Notably, corporate law in many countries, including France and Italy, provide for more lenient standards when RPTs also qualify as intra-group transactions.[107]

---

[101] See, e.g., Davidoff, *supra* note 99, at 1586–88; Wai Yee Wan, "Independent Financial Advisers' Opinions for Public Takeovers and Related Party Transactions in Singapore", 30 Corp. & Sec. L. J. 32, 33 (2012).

[102] See *In re Pure Res., Inc., S'holders Litig.*, 808 A.2d 421, 449 (Del. Ch. 2002) ("the disclosure of the banker's 'fairness opinion' alone and without more, provides stockholders with nothing other than a conclusion, qualified by a gauze of protective language designed to insulate the banker from liability").

[103] See Blake Rohrbacher & Mark Zeberkiewitz, "Fair Summary: Delaware's Framework for Disclosing Fairness Opinions", 63 Bus. Law. 881, 891, & 900–05 (2008).

[104] For surveys of such case law see id., passim; id., "Fair Summary II: An Update on Delaware's Disclosure Regime Regarding Fairness Opinions", 66 Bus. Law. 943, passim (2011) (focusing especially on cases dealing with investment bankers' conflicts of interest).

[105] See CONSOB Regulation, *supra* note 30, Annex 4.

[106] Matters are more complicated in the US, where ex post review looks not only into a transaction's substantial fairness, but also its procedural fairness. See, e.g., Melvin A. Eisenberg, "The Divergence of Standards of Conduct and Standards of Review in Corporate Law", 62 Fordham L. Rev. 437, 451–57 (1993).

[107] See Hopt, *supra* note 8. The justification for a looser approach on such transactions is that these are routine, repeat transactions, the individual review of which by courts would be practically incompatible with the very group business form; in addition, no matter whether the individual transaction is fair to the individual group entity, synergies arising from repeated intra-group RPTs or lower transaction costs may make both the parent and its subsidiaries better off in the longer run. Cf. Dammann, *supra* note 17, at 706–09 (albeit with no explicit reference to group law).

Ex post standard review can be an alternative to the legal safeguards analyzed so far, in which case a jurisdiction comes closest to a pure liability rule on RPTs.[108] The country which is closest to a pure liability rule model among the main ones is Germany: leaving aside a very specific provision on purchases from some related parties in the two years following the company's formation[109] and non-binding corporate governance code recommendations enacted in 2015,[110] its procedural rules only apply to RPTs in which the director is formally on both sides of the transaction.[111] Ex post enforcement relies on the prohibition of concealed distributions,[112] on directors' duty of loyalty, and on the very broad domain of the criminal provision on breach of trust (Untreue).[113]

In form, Delaware is similar to Germany, because no remedy can be successfully obtained if the RPT is judged to have been entered into on fair terms. However, as a matter of practice if not of substance, Delaware case law nudges corporations into subjecting RPTs to procedural safeguards: the more rigorously these safeguards are complied with, in form as well as in substance, the less the judges will be inclined to rule for the plaintiffs by finding that its terms themselves are substantially unfair.

When ex post standard-based review goes together with procedural (ex ante) safeguards, the two legal tools can interact in at least three ways. First, ex post review may strengthen (minority) shareholder protection by working as an additional safeguard to procedural ones. That is the case if a remedy (such as damages and/or nullification) is available if the transaction is judged to be unfair, proof of compliance with ex ante safeguards having no bearing on the outcome of the case. Examples of standard-based remedies that help police tunneling via RPTs are often found in criminal, bankruptcy, and tax law. In France prosecution for abuse of corporate assets (abus de biens sociaux) complements procedural safeguards relying on shareholder meeting ratification of RPTs, while in Italy criminal penalties for tunneling are only relevant, for practical purposes, in the event of bankruptcy, on a count of "fraudulent bankruptcy."[114] In bankruptcy, actions to recover assets for the benefit of creditors, such as the actio pauliana, can also be used to tackle tunneling.[115] Ex post review is finally the technique tax laws use to deal with RPTs aimed to minimize a company's tax burden (so-called transfer pricing).[116]

---

[108] See Goshen, *supra* note 46, at 408.   [109]   AktG § 52.

[110] See § 4.3 & 5.5, German Corporate Governance Code as amended in 2015 (available at http://www.dcgk.de/en/code.html).

[111] See *supra* note 55 and accompanying text.

[112] See, e.g., Wolfgang Schön, Transfer Pricing–Business Incentives, International Taxation and Corporate Law, in Fundamentals of International Transfer Pricing in Law and Economics 47, 58 (Wolfgang Schön & Kai A. Konrad eds., 2012) (clarifying that, however, "these rules only bite when asset diversion either leads to insolvency of the company or when the assets of the company do not fully cover the subscribed capital").

[113] See Pierre-Henri Conac, Luca Enriques, & Martin Gelter, "Constraining Dominant Shareholders' Self-Dealing: The Legal Framework in France, Germany, and Italy", 4 Eur. Comp. & Fin. L. Rev. 491, 500, 520–21 (2007).

[114] Id. at 518–20, 523.

[115] See, e.g., Irit Mevorach, "Transaction Avoidance in Bankruptcy of Corporate Groups", 11 Eur. Comp. Fin. L. Rev. 235, 242 (2011).

[116] See, e.g., Wolfgang Schön, Transfer Pricing, the Arm's Length Standard and European Union Law, in Allocating Taxing Powers within the European Union 73, 73–74 (Isabelle Richelle, Wolfgang Schön, & Edoardo Traversa eds., 2013). According to some, an effective and sophisticated tax system may itself contribute to preventing tunneling. See Mihir A. Desai et al., "Theft and Taxes", 84 J. Fin. Econ. 591 (2007). But see Atanasov et al., Law and Tunneling, *supra* note 37, at 12, for a negative assessment of tax law as an anti-tunneling device (in the US, but with arguments of more general import).

The opposite occurs when a remedy for violations of ex ante safeguards is only available if the transaction is also judged to be unfair, in which case ex post standard-based review effectively weakens ex ante safeguards.[117] Even MOM approval, on its face a property rule (i.e., a rule that requires consent of the relevant party, in our case—minority—shareholders), proves to be very much akin to a liability rule if defendants may prove that a RPT that has not been MOM-approved is still valid because it has caused no damage to the corporation.[118]

Finally, procedural safeguards may trump ex post standard-based review: such is the case when compliance with ex ante safeguards immunizes the transaction, i.e., prevents judges from declaring a transaction void or even from finding for the plaintiff in a liability suit despite evidence that the transaction is, in fact, harmful to the corporation.[119]

5 THE CHALLENGES OF ENACTING EFFECTIVE AND ENDURING REFORMS

Reform-minded policy makers aiming to improve domestic capital markets' attractiveness have recently singled out RPTs among tunneling techniques and designed special prophylactic rules, relying mainly on procedural and disclosure requirements.

For such reforms to be effective in the long run two elements are crucial: first, the law in action has to follow through on the reformed law on the books; second, the new legal environment must be either supported by relevant market players or in tune with social perceptions about tunneling.

Good enforcement institutions are key because, first, in this area there is no such thing as an effective bright line rule,[120] and even self-enforcing provisions prove illusory.[121] Second, substantial fairness is intuitively hard to evaluate, as the convenience of a transaction to a corporation is known only, at most, to corporate insiders.[122] Third, even procedural rules will require difficult judgment calls on the part of enforcers (be they prosecutors, lawyers, judges, or supervisory authorities officials). Such rules may indeed better screen tunneling (as they do introduce a filter). But when, for whatever reason, the filter does not work, ex post enforcement will often be not much easier than when substantial fairness review is required. Enforcers will have to resolve questions such as whether a control relationship exists (a key component of the notion of related party), disclosure has been complete, pivotal votes were

---

[117] For instance, in France RPTs that have not been approved by the board are void only if they harm the corporation. See Code de Commerce (C. Com.) Art. L225-42.

[118] See Goshen, *supra* note 46, at 409.

[119] For practical purposes, such is the case in Delaware in the event of approval by disinterested directors of a transaction in which a director has an interest, because in that case the business judgment rule applies. See, e.g., Enriques, *supra* note 50, at 322–23. See also *supra* note 85 and accompanying text (for the similar consequences of special committee and MOM approval of freezeout transactions).

[120] See *supra* notes 47–48 and accompanying text.

[121] See *supra* text preceding note 59 (while the Yukos case is extreme, we have shown throughout this chapter that there is generally ample room for manoeuvring to avoid the application of RPT rules).

[122] See *supra* text following note 16.

sincere, and/or independence (disinterestedness) was just formal (ostensible) or substantial (real) as well. Most of the times, none of these questions will have a straightforward answer.

Only by seeing more and more cases can enforcers develop the "smell"[123] that is needed to discern bad RPTs from good. This is why the ease by which private and public enforcement actors can start a case and collect evidence is not only key to assessing a jurisdiction's anti-tunneling regime,[124] but also relevant to predicting how likely it is that the law in action will evolve in the right direction.

The problem is that even reform-minded policy makers will hesitate to unleash incompetent judges by easing shareholder access to justice. Unpredictability of outcomes and outright wrong decisions, no matter whether in favor of plaintiff shareholders or defendant insiders, may well harm an equity market's reputation no less than the absence of avenues for judicial redress.

That may explain why in countries with traditionally weak enforcement institutions (think, for example, of Italy or Brazil) it is often securities regulators who have taken the lead in enforcing anti-tunneling rules. Not only can securities regulators hire experienced professionals from the market, but, given their investor protection mission, they may also perform their enforcement tasks zealously.

But even fervent enforcement by a committed securities regulator, backed, as it may, by law reforms tightening RPT rules, can reveal itself to be no more than a flash in the pan in countries where either no social norm against tunneling exists (i.e., where "don't engage in tunneling" is not a specification of the prohibition on theft)[125] or market players do not themselves effectively demand high compliance rates and strict enforcement.

Unless social norms evolve in unison with the new stricter rules and thus make tunneling socially unacceptable,[126] the social perception may soon become one of overzealous bureaucrats harassing successful entrepreneurs/employers for the benefit of anonymous and often foreign investors, at which point it will be easy for the powerful business elite to obtain laxer enforcement and/or a "reparation law."[127]

---

[123] Cf. Charles M. Yablon, "On the Allocation of Burdens of Proof in Corporate Law: An Essay on Fairness and Fuzzy Sets", 13 Cardozo L. Rev. 497, 502 n.16 (1991) (reporting how Delaware practitioners used to refer to fairness review as the "smell test[:] . . . if the terms of the underlying transaction stink badly enough, the courts will find a way to abrogate any procedural protections supplied by the business judgment rule").

[124] Goshen, *supra* note 46, at 409.

[125] Cf. Sviatoslav Moskalev & Seung C. Park, "South Korean Chaebols and Value-Based Management", 92 J. Bus. Ethics 49, 57–59 (2010) (discussing the reasons why "the South Korean public has [long] tolerated the unethical practice of tunneling"); Luca Enriques, "Do Corporate Law Judges Matter? Some Evidence from Milan", 3 Eur. Bus. Org. L. Rev. 765, 781–82 (2002) (suggesting that in the past tunneling by dominant shareholders was socially accepted in Italy).

[126] On the relationship between corporate governance and social norms see generally Amir N. Licht, Culture and Law in Corporate Governance, chapter 6 in this volume.

[127] In 1995 Belgian lawmakers enacted a "loi de réparation" to replace a 1991 law requiring a shareholder vote for all transactions in which a majority of directors had an interest, following large companies' and financial media's accusation that the 1991 law was making it impossible to manage corporate groups. See Lucien Simont, "Conflits d'Intérêt: Les Implications des Nouveaux Articles 60 et 60bis", 1996 Revue pratique des sociétés 369, 372.

Social norms can switch to anti-tunneling mode in two ways. The easier one is when "obey the law" is a social norm itself: anti-tunneling rules will almost automatically convert into social norms. Unfortunately, the "obey the law" norm is far from universal.[128]

When no such norm exists, a "tunneling shock" will be necessary[129] (and perhaps not even sufficient). Think of spectacular instances of tunneling at an individual company (e.g. at Italy's Parmalat) or across the market (e.g. in Russia or the Czech Republic after privatization or in East Asian countries in the run-up to the 1990s East Asian crisis) affecting one or more large firms' viability and therefore harming wider constituencies than investors, such as employees, suppliers, and entire communities. When that happens, a backlash may ensue and tolerance for tunneling may fall. That will be fertile ground for effective corporate governance reforms, so long as, of course, intolerance for tunneling stabilizes as well, i.e., it is not just an ephemeral outbreak of moralism with no roots in deeply felt social convictions about loyalty bonds.[130]

Finally, there might be situations in which market players themselves may not only pressure politicians to enact stricter anti-tunneling provisions, but also keep the pressure high on enforcement agents and the government, so that there are no second thoughts. Large international institutional investors and independent financial media are the best candidates for that job, while global law firms and leading issuers may set the right tone at the top of the legal and business elites.[131] But that kind of dynamics is rarely observed: independent institutional investors may have too little at stake in an individual jurisdiction's equity market to keep the pressure high. Further, in many jurisdictions independent financial media, when they exist, find it hard to retain their independence for long.

6 Summary

This chapter has given an overview of related party transaction regulation from a comparative perspective. It has first shown how RPTs are a common phenomenon in many jurisdictions, whether as a political risk management tool in countries with bad quality institutions, as a more elegant way than outright theft to misappropriate corporate value by dominant shareholders, or as a tool to create synergies or better allocate resources between connected businesses. Next, it clarified the distinction between tunneling and RPTs and showed why it can make sense to have specific rules on the latter. Subsequently, it analyzed

---

[128] See Amir. N. Licht, "Social Norms and the Law: Why Peoples Obey the Law", 4 Rev. L. & Econ. 715, 736–42 (2008).

[129] Leaving aside even more serious shocks, like wars (of state formation), which are arguably the most effective drivers of cultural change. See, e.g., Jordan I. Siegel, Amir N. Licht & Shalom H. Schwartz, "Egalitarianism and International Investment", 102 J. Fin. Econ 621, 625 (2011).

[130] Cf. William L. Cary, "Federalism and Corporate Law: Reflections upon Delaware", 83 Yale L. J. 663, 671 (1974) ("the Ambassador from a South American country . . . came to seek [my] advice because he wanted to encourage the investment of outside capital into private firms in his country . . . I asked first, 'Are your stock exchange facilities adequate?' And he replied, 'No, that really isn't the question . . . . The trouble with management in my country is that their only loyalty is to their relatives' ").

[131] See generally Curtis J. Milhaupt & Katharina Pistor, Law and Capitalism 203–04 (2008).

some of the most common legal tools to regulate RPTs: prohibitions, procedural safeguards (independent director and majority-of-the-minority approval), disclosure, external independent advice, and ex post standard-based review. As a conclusion, it sketched out the conditions for anti-tunneling law reforms to be effective.

CHAPTER 21

....

CONTROL SHIFTS VIA SHARE ACQUISITION CONTRACTS WITH SHAREHOLDERS (TAKEOVERS)

....

PAUL DAVIES[1]

1 INTRODUCTION

....

THIS chapter analyzes the regulatory issues which arise when a person, typically a company (the "acquirer"), makes an offer to one or more shareholders of a "target" company to acquire their shares in sufficient quantities to give it control of the target. The mechanism discussed in this chapter is a technique for shifting control of a company which is capable of embracing a wide variety of types of control shift. Through the share acquisition, control may move from an existing controlling shareholder (or controlling shareholder group) to the acquirer or, in a dispersed shareholding structure, from the management of the target company to the acquirer (which itself may be management or shareholder controlled). The shareholders of the target company may exit entirely from their interest in the target (as in a cash bid) or they may replace that interest with an interest in the combined entity (as where the acquirer offers its own equity as consideration in the offer). In the latter case it is even possible that the shareholders of the target will end up with the dominant economic interest in the combined group, where the target has a larger market capitalization than the acquirer (sometimes referred to as a "reverse takeover"). For this reason the US term for the subject matter of this chapter—"tender offer"—is perhaps more appropriate than the UK term—"takeover bid" or "takeover offer." The former term focuses on the mechanism—the invitation to offer shares to the acquirer—whilst the latter hints at a substantive outcome.[2] Insofar as the share acquisition process can be used to effect a "merger of equals" (the shareholders of the acquirer and

[1] Senior Research Fellow, Harris Manchester College and Allen & Overy Professor of Corporate Law Emeritus, Oxford University, and ECGI.
[2] The UK term also suggests that, in contractual terminology, the acquirer's communication to the shareholders is an offer to contract rather than an invitation to treat, which may or may not be the case.

target having a roughly equal economic interest in the combined entity), the characterization of this as a "takeover" is somewhat misleading. Nevertheless, we will use the term "takeover" as a shorthand way of referring to a shift in control through an offer to acquire shares directly from the target shareholders, on the grounds that, in global usage, this term seems to have the edge.[3]

Section 2 seeks to identify the "corporate law" issues involved in the regulation of takeovers; section 3 considers how those issues could be resolved in the light of an overarching criterion of increasing the productive efficiency of companies. Section 4 analyzes the choices actually made in four jurisdictions: UK, US, Germany, and Japan.

2 CONTROL SHIFTS VIA SHARE ACQUISITIONS AND CORPORATE TRANSACTIONS

The legal technique at the heart of the takeover could hardly be simpler or more familiar. Typically, shareholders may contract to sell their shares, on or off-market, at any time to someone who is willing to purchase them for a consideration which the seller finds acceptable.[4] In most cases the share sale has no implications for control of the company. But the legal technique does not alter if acquisition is intended to shift control. If control is acquired from a single shareholder all that is necessary is one contract for the sale of shares. Where control is acquired from multiple non-controlling shareholders, mechanisms for coordinating the offers and acceptances need to be put in place, but at root there is simply a set of conditional contracts between acquirer and shareholders. It might thus be thought that the law of contract provides all the regulation that is necessary.

However, takeover regulation around the world recognizes three principal areas where contract may need to be supplemented by takeover-specific rules. In each case, the underlying question is whether the control-shift by share acquisition should be regulated simply as a series of parallel contracts (implying little or perhaps no supplementation of the contractual rules) or whether it should be regulated by analogy with a corporate transaction (i.e., a decision binding on the company taken by the shareholders in general meeting or a board decision), which might imply a substantial supplementation of the contractual rules. As we shall see, the salience of each of the three potential areas of regulation depends to a significant extent on whether the shareholding structure of the target company is concentrated or dispersed.

In this chapter the acquirer's communication to the target shareholders will be referred to as an "offer" even if contractually it is the target shareholders who offer their shares for purchase by the acquirer.

[3] The term takeover is often used in a wider sense, i.e. whenever the shareholders of one company end up with a dominant interest in the combined entity, even if the combination is brought about, not by an offer to acquire shares (a "takeover" in my terminology), but via a statutory merger procedure.

[4] In close companies there may be restrictions imposed via the company's internal rules on the free transfer of shares, but such restrictions are rare for public companies and generally prohibited by stock exchange rules if the shares are publicly traded.

2.1 Coordination Costs of Target Shareholders

With multiple shareholders in the target company, coordination among those shareholders may be costly and thus found only at a low level. Contract law has some techniques for generating coordination. For example, the acquirer may make its commitment to buy any shares offered to it conditional upon receiving offers to sell covering in total a certain proportion of the voting rights in the target (e.g., 50%, 75%, or even 90%),[5] so that the acquirer either obtains control or no shares are transferred. However, a widely recognized problem, which takeover-specific laws seek to address, is the ability of the acquirer to exploit target shareholders' coordination problems so as to enable it to acquire the target at a price which, overall, does not reflect its true value. A classic example was the "Saturday night special," i.e., an offer, open only for a short period, to acquire shares at an attractive price, which offer would be shut off once the acquirer had obtained de facto control (say around one-third of the voting rights) of the company. Non-accepting shareholders would later receive offers for their shares at a much lower price (if they received an offer at all), reflecting the absence now of a control-shift premium and, perhaps, the market's adverse assessment of the acquirer's plans for the company. The impact of the scheme is to incentivize shareholders to be quick to tender all their shares into the offer, even though collectively they would likely be better off not accepting the offer but negotiating a uniform price with the acquirer as if they were a single shareholder.

Where all or a controlling block of shares are held by one or a coherent group of shareholders, the target shareholders' coordination costs are substantially reduced, perhaps even eliminated. Nevertheless, provisions addressing target shareholders' coordination problems are widely found in takeover regimes around the world, even in jurisdictions characterized by controlling shareholders. This is probably because even those jurisdictions contain (or may contain in the near future) some companies with dispersed shareholdings and because the arguments for permitting acquirers to exploit target shareholders' coordination problems seem weak. Exploitation is likely to result in inefficient transfers of control as companies are transferred at less than their fundamental value, perhaps to acquirers who intend to 'loot' the target. Acquirers may thus be motivated by the goal of acquiring assets cheaply, not by the goal of operating the acquired company more efficiently. Wealth is transferred from existing shareholders to the acquirer, but no societal benefit occurs in the shape, for example, of increased operating efficiencies. Addressing target shareholders' coordination problems is thus a method of maximizing the number of efficient control shifts by eliminating competition from one set of inefficient acquirers (or acquirers no more efficient than the existing controllers).[6]

The analogy with a corporate decision (e.g., a decision by the shareholders in general meeting to remove the members of the board or to instruct the board to adopt a new strategy, to which a takeover is often the functional equivalent) suggests various ways of addressing these coordination problems. Procedurally, takeover rules might seek to impose minimum

---

[5] These percentages may be expressed as percentages of the total voting rights in the company (thus including voting rights held by the acquirer before the offer is launched) or as percentages of the voting rights offered for.

[6] See generally L.A. Bebchuk, "Toward Undistorted Choice and Equal Treatment in Corporate Takeovers", 98 Harv. L. Rev. 1695 (1985).

periods during which the offer must remain open (so that target shareholders have the opportunity to analyze it properly) and require that information should be disclosed about the offer by both acquirer and target (to the same end). Substantively, the corporate decision analogy suggests that all accepting shareholders should receive the same price (i.e., they should all be "voting" on the same proposition). Thus, purchases from shareholders who sell in the market to the acquirer at a higher price or from shareholders who accept the offer late in the process after the acquirer has raised the level of its offer should cause the price available to all shareholders to be revised upwards. The provisions mentioned in this paragraph are widely found in takeover rules around the world.

It may even be that the corporate decision analogy is taken to the point of making a majority acceptance of the offer binding on all the target shareholders. This means the acquirer is entitled to squeeze out non-accepting shareholders at the offer price. Often squeeze out is available only at a very high level of acquirer post-bid shareholding (e.g., 90% of the voting rights),[7] but some jurisdictions are more open to squeeze out at lower levels of post-bid share ownership.[8] Where squeeze out is available, it can be said to address the target shareholders' coordination problems from the acquirer's perspective. A shareholder may refuse an offer from an efficient acquirer even when it is pitched above the pre-bid market price because she calculates that she will be even better off if the bidder acquires control but she remains in the company. If enough shareholders take this view, insufficient shareholders will accept the offer for control to pass. The bidder may have to offer nearly the whole of its expected gains from the transaction to the target shareholders to persuade them to accept its offer—but this will substantially reduce the incentives for potential acquirers to put offers on the table.[9] One way to break out of this vicious circle may by to provide acquirers with rights to squeeze out non-accepting minorities at the same price as was accepted by the majority, so that the option of staying in and benefiting from the acquirer's control is taken off the table.

2.2 Centralized Management

Control of the company or its assets can be shifted to another in many ways other than through an acquisition of the company's shares directly from their existing holders. A company many engage in a statutory merger which, provided the jurisdiction's merger procedure permits cash to be used as merger consideration, can be used to replicate almost exactly the

---

[7] Typically a freestanding squeeze out right, tied to the takeover is made available, as in the European Union (Directive 2004/25/EC, Art. 15 - hereinafter "Takeover Directive"). In jurisdictions without comprehensive takeover codes, the merger rules may be adapted to this end. For example, Delaware dispenses with the need for target shareholder approval of the merger if the acquiring company already holds 90% of each outstanding class of stock (Delaware General Corporation Law (DGCL) § 253).

[8] The UK Listing Rules (5.2.11A) permit de-listing of the target (normally a potent threat in the light of the loss of liquidity) following a takeover bid by a previously non-controlling acquirer provided the acquirer ends up with at least 75% of the voting rights of the class to be de-listed and the de-listing proposal was part of the offer. Similarly DGCL § 251(h) dispenses with the need for target shareholder approval (see previous note) if the normally required level of approval has been acquired in a tender offer – but this relaxation is not available after a hostile takeover.

[9] Sandford Grossman & Oliver Hart, "Takeover Bids, the Free Rider Problem and the Theory of the Corporation", 11 Bell J. Econ. 42 (1980).

result of a cash or share (or combined) takeover offer.[10] Or the company may simply sell the assets it owns rather than the acquirer buying the shares in the company holding the assets in question. Or a company may issue or repurchase shares with a consequent impact on control of the company. All these transactions, however, involve a corporate decision, often more than one. In particular, in all the above transactions the incumbent management of the target company has, de jure or de facto, a veto over the transaction. This veto right may arise because only the board may initiate the transaction (as with a statutory merger in many jurisdictions) or because, even where the decision could be initiated by the shareholders alone, the coordination problems of dispersed shareholders make it difficult for them to secure the necessary level of shareholder agreement. Of course, shareholder consent may be required for these transactions as well (jurisdictions tend to vary quite considerably on this matter),[11] but the crucial point is that, one way or another, the consent of the target board is at least a precondition of the transaction.

The contrast with the takeover is stark, since that transaction is formally between acquirer and target shareholders. The incumbent management appears to be sidelined. However, the formal position is highly misleading. Management is in fact in a strong position to protect itself by self-help: its powers of centralized management will often permit it to take action which renders a takeover offer unattractive to the acquirer, so that management may be in a good position to derail a bid it does not favor. For example, it may issue new shares to a friendly investor or conditionally dispose of the assets the acquirer is keen to obtain. Thus, in relation to target management, the core issue for takeover regulation is whether the standard powers routinely conferred upon the boards of public companies should be constrained during takeover offers precisely in order to allow shareholders to contract freely with the acquirer. Should takeover rules ensure that the transaction is in fact, as well as formally, one subject solely to the joint decision of the acquirer and target shareholders? More colloquially, should the rules facilitate "hostile" bids[12] (i.e., offers to which the incumbent management objects) or only "friendly" bids (i.e., those supported by incumbent management)?

There is a linkage between the first and second areas of potential takeover regulation. Management, if allowed to insert itself into the takeover process, might operate so as to protect dispersed shareholders against bidder exploitation. Management might act as the single counter-party, on behalf of all shareholders, with whom the acquirer has to deal. There is a potential trade-off here, but the trade-off is more apparent than real if effective and low-cost protection against bidder opportunism can be provided directly and without relying on target management.

It will be apparent that the centralized management point, like the coordination problems of target shareholders, is highly sensitive to the shareholder structure of the target company.

---

[10] Indeed, where the acquisition is supported by target management, the question of whether transfer of control takes place via a takeover or a statutory merger procedure becomes a second-order question, which revolves around questions such as, which is more tax efficient, which is more likely to give the acquirer the level of control it seeks, which offers the fewest opportunities for a competing acquirer to emerge? See J. Payne, The Use of Schemes of Arrangement to Effect Takeovers: A Comparative Analysis, Oxford Legal Studies Research Paper No. 51/2014.

[11] Reinier Kraakman et al., Anatomy of Corporate Law ch. 7 (3rd ed. 2017).

[12] "Hostile," that is, to the incumbent management, not to the target shareholders. See note 15 on the difficulty of classifying bids as "friendly" or "hostile."

Where there is a single or cohesive group of shareholders with a controlling block in the target, the debate about centralized management is largely irrelevant. The board of such a company are highly unlikely to exercise their powers to block an offer the controlling shareholder is minded to accept, since they will owe their positions on the board to election by the controlling shareholder.[13] On the other hand, the controlling shareholder is less reliant on the governance benefits of a takeover than are dispersed shareholders. The controller can make use at low cost of the standard corporate law governance mechanisms (most obviously, dismissal of the board) to remove underperforming management, without relying on an acquirer to do this job. Equally, if the controlling shareholder concludes it is in her interest to merge the company with another, she is well placed to hire an investment bank to seek out a company which might want to bid for her company.[14]

From this it is sometimes concluded that this second area of takeover regulation is important only for dispersed shareholding companies (or jurisdictions). However, this is not the case. Assume the controller (or controlling group) does not have de jure control of the company (more than 50% of the votes) but only de facto control (e.g., 20–30% of the votes)— the remainder of the votes being dispersed. Absent a takeover offer, a de facto controller relies on the apathy or lack of coordination among the majority shareholders to sustain her control of the company in the general meeting. A takeover offer, however, may generate very different decision dynamics from those in play at a general meeting. At a meeting the de facto controller's position ultimately turns on the dispersed shareholders' assessment that the certain costs of trying to coordinate with the other non-controlling shareholders so as to outvote the de facto controller outweigh the uncertain gains from taking control and implementing a new business strategy for the company. A takeover offer, by contrast, quantifies the benefits of the new strategy (in the shape of the offer consideration) and removes the need for the shareholders to coordinate amongst themselves as against incumbent management in order to produce a control shift. Thus, there can be no guarantee for the de facto controller that the acceptance patterns in relation to the takeover offer will reflect the voting patterns at a general meeting; in fact, an attractive offer is likely to secure acceptance from the majority, especially if the de facto controller had been extracting private benefits of control. Consequently, the rules on the involvement of management in the bid process may be crucial for the de facto controller who, through the management she has appointed, may wish to take action aimed at derailing the bid.

A challenge to the de facto control of the company may be even more plausible if that control is held, not by a single shareholder, but by a coordinated group of large shareholders. The acquirer may be able to detach one of those shareholders from the group and thus increase its chances of success with the offer—assuming that that shareholder is not effectively bound by contract with the other group members not to defect. By extension, a takeover offer could be used to make even de jure control contestable where that control is held by a group of shareholders, one or more of whom can be induced to defect from the controlling group.

Contrary to what is sometimes argued, it follows that restrictions on the use of the powers of centralized management during a takeover may operate, not only to make

---

[13] This will be true even of "independent" directors.
[14] A substantial number of takeovers are initiated by the target company.

managerial control contestable in a wholly dispersed shareholding environment, but also to make de facto control and even de jure control by a group of shareholders contestable. Whether to inhibit the use of the powers of centralized management becomes a salient issue, not only for dispersed shareholding jurisdictions, such as the US and the UK, but also for jurisdictions where block-holding is more common. Thus, Professor Culpepper concludes, on the basis of a cross-country examination of patterns of shareholdings and hostile bids,[15] that "some [shareholding] concentration is not inconsistent with an active market for corporate control."[16] He points particularly at Australia and Canada as countries with a higher percentage of hostile bids as a proportion of overall deal activity than the US and the UK despite moderately high levels of shareholder concentration. One might also point to France as a country with shareholder concentration around the Canadian/Australian level where (see section 3.2.1) the regulatory constraints on management intervention in takeover offers have recently been almost completely relaxed for fear of unwelcome foreign takeover offers succeeding. Unless irrational, this legislative reaction suggests that hostile bids are feasible in that country, at least for a significant proportion of domestic companies.[17]

Of course, the self-interest of the incumbent management may not lie in blocking a bid but in promoting it to the shareholders, for example, in a management buy-out or a private equity buy-out where the acquirer intends to keep on the incumbent management and give them a higher economic stake in the business than was available to them when the target was in public ownership. Incumbent management cannot force the shareholders to accept a bid they regard as suboptimal, but they may recommend them to do so, a recommendation which may carry considerable weight with the shareholders given management's access to "soft" inside information. The standard remedies against bias in this context are disclosure of potential conflicts of interest and, possibly, third-party opinions on the fairness of the proposed transaction, to be disclosed along with recommendation.

---

[15] The available commercial data on hostile bids is notoriously difficult to interpret in relation to the issues discussed in this chapter. Typically, a bid is classified as hostile only if it remained opposed by management throughout the offer period. Along one dimension this approach can be supported: a bid that is initially opposed but later accepted by management may indicate management negotiating with the bidder on behalf of shareholders rather than management acting in a self-interested way. But a bid that is always "friendly" (or becomes so) may simply reflect a regulatory structure that makes managerial opposition fruitless, so that the hostile bid data underestimate the impact of the takeover rules. With some exaggeration, one might say that, where regulation outlaws defensive measures by management, hostile bids will not show up because management will not oppose the acquirer on grounds of futility, whilst, where regulation permits defensive measures, hostile bids will not show up because acquirers will not launch them!

[16] Pepper C. Culpepper, Quiet Politics and Business Power 34–35 (2011).

[17] The argument in this paragraph is not that hostile bids will inevitably emerge at some particular level of dispersal of shareholding. Clearly, existing controlling shareholders or the state may block the development of takeover regulation that facilitates hostile bids. The argument is rather that the question of how takeover regulation is structured becomes a salient question long before a high level of dispersal is achieved. For an analysis of the factors that might affect the evolution of takeover laws in developing countries see John Armour, Jack B. Jacobs, & Curtis J. Milhaupt, "The Evolution of Hostile Takeover Regimes in Developed and Emerging Markets: An Analytical Framework", 52 Harv. Int'l. L. J. 219, Part IV (2011).

2.3 Agency Costs of Non-Controlling Shareholders

We have just seen that debates about shareholders' coordination costs and the exercise of management powers arise most strongly in dispersed shareholding contexts. By contrast, non-controlling agency costs arise, as the term implies, where there is a controlling shareholder. Assuming the controlling shareholder(s) have enough voting shares to pass control to the acquirer, the deal will occur whether the non-controlling shareholders are in favor of it or not, provided that the controlling shareholder is in favor.[18] No powers of centralized management will be deployed to block the deal and the controlling shareholders who negotiated the deal will not be subject to significant coordination costs. The central questions for the non-controlling shareholders are: (1) are they entitled to receive an offer at all where control is transferred from an existing controller to a new one (i.e., do they receive an exit right) and (2) if so, is the offer to be on the same terms as those offered to the controllers?

Standard contract law does not require the acquirer to make an offer to all the holders of the shares carrying voting rights in the company. If a deal with one or some shareholders gives the acquirer control, it may choose not to offer for the remainder of the shares. Nor does standard contract law require the same price to be offered to all those who own the same good. By contrast, an analogous corporate transaction (e.g., sale of corporate assets) would see the consideration received by the company and the rules on distributions would normally follow an equality principle, i.e., all shareholders participate in the distribution pro rata to their economic interest in the company.[19] If this analogy were followed, non-controlling shareholders would have the right to exit the company on the same terms as had been made available to the controlling shareholder, i.e., the premium attaching to the controlling shares would be shared among all the target shareholders.

3 THE GOALS OF TAKEOVER REGULATION

The previous section has shown the tension between the purely contractual mechanism of the takeover offer and the different rules that would apply if an equivalent transaction were effected through the corporation. The position of the target shareholders as a group, of incumbent management and of non-controlling shareholders would be regulated in a significantly different way according to the regulatory model chosen. The purpose of using the device of the analogous corporate transaction was to illuminate the central choices that need to be made in takeover regulation. The purpose was not to argue that the corporate analogy should trump the contractual analysis, either wholly or partly, or vice versa. Except in relation to target shareholders' coordination costs, where the corporate analogy has gained traction with rulemakers for the reasons pointed out above, the debate between the

---

[18] The non-controlling shareholders may have some leverage if the acquirer needs to obtain a very high level of acceptances, for example, in order to squeeze out the non-accepting shareholders to obtain 100% control of the company. This is a common objective of private equity bidders.

[19] However, the sale would not normally require the consent of the minority shareholders (except possibly in a related party transaction). By analogy, takeover regulation does not contemplate making the control shift conditional on the consent of the non-controlling shareholders.

contractarians and the corporatists has not resulted in a clear victory for either side. Nor is it the case that in relation to centralized management and non-controlling shareholders' agency costs that jurisdictions have ended up in the same mode on both questions. The UK, for example, is contractarian in relation to centralized management (target board excluded from exercising its powers to frustrate an offer) but corporatist in relation to non-controlling shareholders (exit opportunity on the same terms as the controlling shareholder). Delaware is similarly eclectic, but the other way around: allowing the incumbent management to "just say no" but more respectful of the principle that a controlling shareholder should be able to sell her shares without sharing the control premium with other shareholders.

In order to make choices between the contractarian and the corporate approaches some higher level of theory is required. In line with modern corporate law scholarship, one might say that the goal of takeover regulation should be to maximize the number of efficient shifts of control and to minimize the number of inefficient shifts. A rule which produces the best combination of these two objectives is thus to be preferred. Also in line with that scholarship, an efficient shift of control can be said to be one that reduces the costs of production through the corporate form. Reducing production costs is the general societal interest which company law serves.[20]

Operationalizing this general principle through detailed takeover rules is, however, far from straightforward. A starting point might be to test the efficiency of takeover rules by reference to their impact on the share price of target and acquiring companies. If the joint value of target and acquirer companies is maximized, the above principle might be said to be satisfied. In fact, the empirical evidence, mainly from the US, has long shown that the value of the target company is enhanced by a takeover (comparing the pre-bid price with the level at which the deal is consummated),[21] whilst the evidence on the post-bid value of the acquirer has been mixed. More recent research suggests that the gains to the acquirer have been underestimated in the past.[22] Even on the more pessimistic assessment of the gains, the joint wealth of the acquirer and target shareholders is maximized.[23]

3.1 Efficiency Arguments for Takeovers

As Romano pointed out some time ago,[24] takeovers may operate to increase the value of the companies involved for their shareholders for reasons which are linked to reduced costs of production but also for reasons which are not. In the former case, increased shareholder value correlates with society's interest in takeovers; in the latter case, it does not. Let us look at the efficiency arguments first.

[20] Anatomy, *supra* note 11, ch 1.5.
[21] M. Jensen & R. Ruback, "The Market for Corporate Control: the Scientific Evidence", 11 J. Fin. Econ. 5 (1983)—gains of about 30% at the time of the announcement of the takeover.
[22] B. Espen Eckbo, "Takeovers and Economic Efficiency", 6 Annual Review of Financial Economics 51 (2014).
[23] A point of importance to shareholders who have holdings in both acquirer and target, a position many institutional shareholders will find themselves in. However, the more pessimistic evidence does raise the question of why acquirers launch takeovers, a question we address below.
[24] Roberta Romano, "A Guide to Takeovers: Theory, Evidence and Regulation", 9 Yale J. Reg. 119 (1992).

The principal arguments in favor of takeovers from an efficiency perspective relate to the reduction of agency costs (for dispersed shareholders)[25] and synergy gains. The threat of a takeover can operate as a powerful incentive to management to promote the interests of the shareholders and one that operates at low cost for the shareholders. The takeover threat will be there at all times, it is argued, and not just when an offer is imminent. This is an argument in favor of preserving the contractual stance of the law in relation to takeovers, for a management which can derail a bid aimed at displacing it will feel less exposed to takeover threat than one which cannot. Ensuring that an acquirer can effectively appeal over the heads of the incumbent management to the shareholders (in a "hostile" bid) maximizes the disciplinary impact of the takeover. However, the intensity of the takeover threat is not a function simply of the rules regulating it (notably rules restraining the exercise of powers of management during the takeover process), but also of the incentives for bidders to launch takeovers. There is some evidence that very poorly performing companies are not attractive targets[26] and clear evidence that takeover activity is highly correlated with the business cycle.[27] So the disciplinary threat of the takeover may not operate perfectly, but it does not look as if it can be written off completely.

The synergy gains from a takeover flow from the economies of scale or scope which result from redrawing the boundaries of the firm. Management's reasons for opposing a disciplinary takeover are clear (the purpose of the takeover is to remove the incumbent management team). They are likely as well to oppose a takeover driven by synergies, since in that situation too they risk being replaced by the bidder's team or being demoted from running their own show to being subordinate to a higher level of management.[28] However, managerial opposition to a synergistic bid is not inevitable: an MBO is defined by its retention of the incumbent management team whilst we noted above that a private equity acquirer might wish to keep on the existing team and in fact offer them financial incentives which compensate for their newly subordinate position, or the CEO and other senior managers of the target may have the opportunity to move into equivalent positions in the combined group. Nevertheless, in the absence of such options, the self-interest of the incumbent management is likely to prejudice them against the acquisition.

In consequence, whether the bid rules permit incumbent management to exercise their powers so as to derail a bid of which they disapprove becomes an important question—perhaps the central question in takeover regulation. Preserving the contractual nature of the takeover offer permits a potential acquirer to appeal, via a "hostile" takeover, over the heads of the incumbent management, when it is conflicted, to the shareholders of the target. This policy also permits the shareholders of the target to vote on a business plan for the company

---

[25] As we noted in section 2, concentrated shareholders are well placed to change underperforming management through the exercise of their governance rights.

[26] Julian Franks & Colin Mayer, "Hostile Takeovers and the Correction of Managerial Failure", 40 J. Fin. Econ. 163 (1996), but cf. Randall Morck, Andrei Shleifer, & Robert Vishny, Characteristics of Targets of Hostile and Friendly Takeovers, in Corporate Takeovers: Causes and Consequences (A. Auerbach ed., 1988).

[27] Eckbo, *supra* note 22, § 2.1.

[28] Franks & Mayer (*supra* note 26) found that 90% of the directors of the targets they studied were no longer with the company two years after the acquisition. (In interpreting this statistic it should be remembered that a UK board (at least then) would typically have a higher percentage of executives on it, at least half, than a US board. So top managers departed, not just independent directors.)

that represents an alternative to the plan being pursued by incumbent management, but without the target shareholders having to incur the cost of developing or implementing that alternative. In somewhat the same way as activist shareholders, seeking a change of management policy without a change of control, the takeover can operate as a method of putting alternative investment propositions before the shareholders in a manner that neatly sidesteps their coordination costs.[29]

As we noted in section 2, the hostile takeover is a mechanism of potential benefit not only to shareholders in dispersed shareholding companies, but also to non-controlling shareholders where the company has a de facto controller or even where the company has a de jure controlling group, provided the solidarity of the group is open to question. The threat of the takeover may make the controlling group more respectful of the interests of the non-controlling shareholders. However, one may wonder why controlling shareholders would not accept a synergy-driven offer from an acquirer since the target shareholders' gains from such an acquisition would go predominantly to its controlling shareholders and the controlling shareholders would be well-placed to negotiate effectively with the potential acquirer. If the controlling shareholders would typically accept an efficient offer, regulating the exercise of managerial powers in relation to a synergistic bid in order to facilitate an acquisition would be a much less important question for controlled companies.

The controller's behavior is likely to be conditioned on whether her controlling position gives her access to benefits which are not available to the non-controlling shareholders ("private benefits of control"—pbc). Where this is not the case, the financial incentives of the controller are aligned with the incentives of the non-controllers and there is little reason to fear that the controller will use her influence over the management of the company to block an efficient bid. Where pbc are being extracted, this argument cannot be relied on. If the pbc are financial (i.e., the controller is diverting more than her pro-rata share of the firm's revenues to herself), the controller may calculate that her currently enhanced share of the smaller pie is worth more to her than her pro-rata share of the bigger pie resulting from the control shift. Where the pbc are non-financial (e.g., the prestige and social recognition flowing from controlling an important company), the controller may attach a very high price to that benefit—a sort of controller's "consumer surplus." In either case, the controller will be disposed to block the takeover offer.[30]

There are two legal strategies which could be deployed to induce takeovers in this situation, both involving insistence on the contractarian model. One would be to sideline management in the acquisition process, so that the controller cannot deploy her influence over

---

[29] On activist investors see Ronald Gilson & Jeffrey Gordon, "The Agency Costs of Agency Capitalism: Activist Investors and the Revaluation of Governance Rights", 113 Colum. L. Rev. 863 (2013) and Mike Burkart & Samuel Lee, "Signaling to Dispersed Shareholders and Corporate Control", 82 Rev. Econ. Stud. 922 (2015). In a cash bid the target shareholders are being offered the discounted present cash value of the alternative strategy (or some proportion of that value); in a share-exchange offer there is the opportunity to benefit from the implementation of that strategy.

[30] Where the pbc arise out of actual management of the company, the controller may be unwilling to relinquish that managerial role, even if she is making a poor job of it. Consequently, the availability of a hostile takeover may be an important disciplinary tool in such cases. However, as performance declines, the controller will suffer financially, and this is likely to generate a change of mind on the value of a management renewal, especially if there is a controlling group (e.g., a family) only some of whom are involved in the management of the company.

management to block the bid. This might be effective where the control is de facto or is held de jure by an unstable group of shareholders. Alternatively, the controller could be permitted to sell her shares at the price which reflects her pbc. This strategy might induce control shifts even in the case of secure de jure control. In order to make the acquisition of the target financially viable from the bidder's point of view, the acquirer would need to be left free not to offer the same level of consideration to the non-controlling shareholders and perhaps even not to offer to acquire their shares at all. The mandatory bid rule (MBR—required of European Union (EU) states by the Takeover Directive),[31] would become suspect in this analysis, for that rule requires a person acquiring de facto control to offer an exit right to all the other shareholders at an "equitable" price, defined as a price at least equal to the highest price paid over the previous six to twelve months in the acquisition of the controlling shares. In most cases, therefore, under the MBR the acquirer will not be able to engage in price discrimination.[32] The tendency of the MBR is thus to inhibit transfers of control by controllers who extract pbc. Where the acquirer intends to earn a return on the investment involved in the takeover by increasing the operating efficiency of the target, then the societal interest in control shifts is harmed. Where, on the other hand, the bid is motivated by a plan to extract even higher pbc than currently, the inhibition is to be welcomed from a societal point of view, as we see below.

3.2 Inefficient Takeovers

Takeovers may be inefficient for three main reasons. First, the joint wealth of target and acquirer shareholders may be increased but for reasons which are unrelated to any increase in the productive efficiency of the target. Second, the joint value of the two companies may not be expected to increase, but the acquirer's management nevertheless have an incentive to launch the takeover and the target's shareholders an incentive to accept it. Third, those responsible for making the takeover decision may aim to bring about only efficient transfers of control and to block inefficient ones, but their decision making is poor so that they achieve their aim with only a low level of accuracy.

3.2.1 Wealth Transfers

In the first case, the gains to acquirer and target shareholders are achieved, not by increased operating efficiencies in the target, but by a wealth transfer from some other group to

---

[31] Art. 5. The definition of control is left to the Member States. Most have adopted a "bright-line" rule, i.e. a fixed percentage of the voting rights and fixed that percentage around 30%. This is arguably too high to catch all cases of de facto control: L. Enriques & M. Gatti, "Creeping Acquisitions in Europe: Enabling Companies to be Better Safe than Sorry", 15 J. Corp. L. Stud. 55 (2015).

[32] If the bidder is able to acquire a block of shares just below the threshold which triggers the mandatory bid and to do so in secret (perhaps through equity swaps), it might then wait out the reference period (6 to 12 months) before making a public offer at significantly below the highest price paid for the block. Or it might make a "low ball" offer, enough to get it over the threshold, but not much more. Going over the threshold in a voluntary offer does not trigger a mandatory bid. See Klaus J. Hopt, "European Takeover Reform of 2012/2013 – Time to Re-Examine the Mandatory Bid", 15 Eur. Bus. Org. L. Rev. 143 at 3.2.3.

those shareholders.[33] Since there are no gains to productive efficiency, the societal case for facilitating the takeover disappears. In fact, the prospect of redistribution may have an adverse effect on the target's current productive efficiency, so that there may be efficiency gains from blocking such takeovers.

The range of candidates which has been put forward as likely to suffer adverse redistribution is wide: target employees, target creditors, consumers of the target's products, taxpayers of the jurisdiction in which the target is located, even citizens generally in the target's jurisdiction. In principle, most of these inefficient transfers can be addressed by rules separate from those which deal with the three areas identified above. All jurisdictions have some rules which constrain the bidder from initiating an offer for certain categories of target, either at all or without the consent of some governmental agency. All countries have put in place controls over the acquisition of targets which are particularly important for the polity in question, for example, defense contractors, banks, crucial infrastructure suppliers. Sometimes, these controls are overtly discriminatory against foreign acquirers; and sometimes the claims of the target to "public interest" protection seem rather weak. Sometimes the rules apply to wide swathes of the domestic economy, sometimes to only narrow sectors. Whenever these rules apply, the acquirer ends up dealing with the state before it can talk effectively to the shareholders of the target.

In these cases regulation of the takeover process is driven by, often ill-articulated, notions of national security or of sovereignty. So the implementation of these policy concerns via rules separate from the formal takeover rules seems sensible. Nevertheless, there is a tendency for states to buttress these separate rules when configuring their takeover laws. Thus, in 2014 the French legislature made a number of important changes to the French takeover laws, including the removal of a "no frustration" rule which had previously applied to the management of target companies, in large part because of what was seen as a threat of takeovers from foreign acquirers who would reduce jobs and investment in France.[34] Improving target management's freedom to "just say no" was seen as a way of reducing foreign takeovers which, it was claimed, would leave French citizens less well off.

Tax-driven takeovers are a more obvious form of wealth transfer, i.e., from taxpayers to the shareholders of the acquiring and target companies, which may be accompanied by no improvements in productive efficiency. However, the legislature is in a good position to combat through the tax code control shifts driven by tax consideration. Tax law can set the incentives for takeovers, for example, through rules relating the deductibility of interest on loans taken out to finance takeover or rules on the availability of target tax losses to acquiring companies or which discourage companies from altering their tax domicile through a takeover in order to achieve a lower tax burden.[35] Using takeover rules to this end appears unnecessary.

---

[33] We leave on one side the situation where the gains are partly from operating efficiencies and partly from a wealth transfer.

[34] A. Pietrancosta, "The Latest Reform of French Takeover Law: The 'Florange Act' of March 29, 2014", 42 Revue Trimestrielle de Droit Financier 3 (2014).

[35] The incentive for US companies to do "tax inversion" deals by acquiring foreign targets was reduced in 2014 through rulemaking by the US Treasury: AstraZeneca Aims to Ward Off Pfizer by Highlighting "Tax Inversion Risks," Fin. Times, Nov. 6, 2014.

The consumer interest in competitive markets is normally addressed through competition (antitrust) law separate from takeover regulation. Within a contractual model of takeover regulation the shareholders of the target might well accept a competition-reducing offer, because the acquirer would be able to finance an attractive offer for the target's shares on the back of its expected monopoly or oligopoly rents. In a corporatist model, the self-interest of the managers in blocking a control shift might be better aligned with the interests of consumers, but this cannot be relied on, for example, where the management of the target are offered attractive positions with the acquirer. Separate competition regulation also seems sensible since anti-competitive moves can result from transactions other than control shifts via share acquisitions, for example, through the acquisition of assets from a competitor which is seeking to exit that particular line of business. From a competition standpoint these transactions should be treated equally.

Specific takeover regulation might be thought to have a bigger role to play in protecting corporate constituents (i.e., creditors and employees) against wealth-transfers via takeover bids. Creditors in fact feature rarely in takeover regulation, even though a control shift which lowers the credit-rating of the target (e.g., where its assets are used as security for loans taken out to fund the acquisition) reduces the value of the loan to the lender. Probably, this is because financial creditors are thought well positioned to protect themselves through contract, for example, a change of control clause in the initial loan contract that permits the lender to recall the loan when a control shift occurs. The lender can then decide whether to recall the loan or seek to renegotiate the terms of the loan under the threat of recall (or, of course, do neither of these things).[36]

3.2.2 *Wealth Transfers and Employees*

Employees, by contrast, do receive explicit recognition in at least some takeover codes. In the EU the Takeover Directive requires the provision of information to employees or their representatives and gives some opportunity for the employee representatives to make their views on the proposed acquisition known.[37] Some national laws go further: the French reforms referred to above extend the information right into a consultation right and make the receipt of the works council's opinion[38] a precondition (usually) for the distribution to the shareholders of the target board's opinion on the offer, which is itself a mandatory step in the bid process.[39] This requirement has some potential for slowing down the acquisition

[36] William Bratton, "Bond Covenants and Creditor Protection: Economics and Law, Theory and Practice, Substance and Process", 7 Eur. Bus. Org. L. Rev. 39, at § 3.3 (2006).

[37] Takeover Directive, Arts. 6.1, 8.2 and 8.5.

[38] Some sort of works council is now mandatory in the EU in all but the smallest enterprises or establishments where the employees wish to establish one. See Directive 2002/14/EC. The composition of the works council varies from country to country, but essentially it is a body representative of all the employees in the workplace whose powers are defined by statute. It thus contrasts with firm-level collective bargaining where, formally at least, only union members are represented in the bargaining and the scope of the bargaining is more influenced by agreement between employer and union. The powers of the works council also vary: they are noticeably strong in Germany and the Netherlands, but weak in, for example, the UK, where the firm-level representation space has been occupied by trade unions. France is an intermediate case where union and works-council-based systems to some degree compete at workplace level.

[39] Pietrancosta, *supra* note 34, 45–46.

process and for giving target management more time to set up defenses against the bid or to seek an alternative acquirer whom the incumbent management regards more favorably. The French reforms also require the acquirer post-bid to report to the works council at intervals over the following two years on its implementation of any commitments made to the employees in the bid process. The UK Takeover Code now also contains a somewhat similar post-bid requirement, introduced as a result of the decision by a foreign bidder to reverse its commitment not to close a particular plant after it had acquired control of the target.[40] Such rules are likely somewhat to constrain acquirer opportunism in relation to statements made about employment matters in the acquisition process.

The obvious objection to such rules in takeover codes is that a takeover is only one of a number of corporate events which might have an adverse impact on the employees. A transfer of assets or simple competition in the product market might produce similar management decisions adverse to the interests of the employees. Therefore, employee protections, it could be argued, should be general, if they are deployed at all, and, in particular, are difficult to justify if confined to takeovers. In fact, the EU does have information and consultation requirements in these additional areas,[41] so that the objection is not so much to the substantive scope of the EU rules as to the legislative technique of generating multiple, but not identical, information and consultation requirements rather than a single overarching regime.

The utility of information and consultation rights is open to question, even from the point of view of the employees themselves. It is not clear why target shareholders should be influenced by the adverse impact of the offer on the employees, at least in a cash offer. It is possible that the information disclosed could be used to bolster the possibilities available to employee organizations outside the offer process itself, for example, to deploy more effectively industrial or political resources against the offer.[42] And, as indicated, within the offer process consultation rights may have a limited hold-up value for the employees.

From our point of view, the more salient question is how the objective of avoiding wealth transfers from the employees impacts on the configuration of takeover rules in the core areas identified above. A strategy, often advocated, is to allow target management freedom to take defensive measures, thus relying on the self-interest of management in blocking bids to act as a proxy for the protection of employee interests. A weak version of this strategy can be found in US "constituency statutes" which permit or require target boards to take into

---

[40] The Takeover Code (UK), rule 19.1, n.3. The acquirer is committed to statements of intention made during a bid for 12 months post-bid or for the period mentioned in the statement "unless there has been a material change of circumstances." Enforcement is by the Panel, though it is unclear what steps it might be prepared to take. Rule 24.2 requires the acquirer to state what implications, if any, the acquisition has for employment or the employees' pension scheme. The commitment rules arose out of the acquisition of Cadbury plc. by Kraft Inc., in the course of which the bidder unwisely committed itself to keeping open a plant the incumbent management had decided to close, only to discover upon acquisition that the previous management had good reasons for its decision.

[41] See for asset transfers Directive 2001/23/EC; for dismissals on economic grounds generally Directive 98/59/EC; and for changes proposed by incumbent management which are likely to lead to "substantial changes in work organisation or in contractual relations" Directive 2002/14/EC.

[42] For example, if the government is responsive to the interests of organized labor and has the formal power to make life difficult for the acquirer—perhaps because the proposed acquisition is by a foreign company in a sensitive part of the economy—the employees' views may weigh heavily with the acquirer when deciding whether to bid and how to formulate its plans for the target.

account non-shareholder interests when formulating their response to the offer. The utility of such statutes depends, for employees, on how closely aligned the incentives of managers and employees are in fact and, for society, on how closely those interests are aligned with societal interests. In the absence of alignment, such statutes could operate so as to increase the discretion of management by diluting their accountability to the shareholders without any clear gain to the employees or to society.[43]

A stronger version of this strategy would be to institutionalize employee voice within the acquisition process, perhaps via employee representation at board level or via a strong role for the works council[44] in the acquisition process. It is important to be clear what the societal interest in such employee voice mechanisms might be. The mere fact that takeovers are often associated with job loss as the acquirer implements its plans post-acquisition seems a poor basis for giving employees a voice in the control-shift decision itself (as opposed to laws which seek to mitigate the adverse impact of the subsequent restructuring on the employees). The societal interest in takeovers, it is suggested in this chapter, lies in their potential to increase the productive efficiency of companies. Short-term losses to employees are not decisive evidence of an inefficient transfer of control.[45] Such losses are not even inconsistent with the view that, in the longer term, employees gain from higher productive efficiency (e.g., because the company will fail completely in the medium term if it does not adapt to competitive pressures or because, again in the medium term, the target company will end up employing more workers than at the time of its acquisition).

For the employee voice argument to be convincing it needs to be shown that takeovers (or a certain class of takeovers) are routinely driven by wealth transfers from employees even where the prior arrangements with the employees are productively efficient (and, ideally, that there are no or only limited offsetting efficiency gains from takeovers in such cases). An early statement of such a theory was provided by Shleifer and Summers[46] on the basis of firm-specific human capital investment by employees in return for implicit[47] promises by management to exercise their discretion (especially in relation to the maintenance of employment) in a way that favors employee interests. Although this theory was described in the US context as "clever but not convincing,"[48] the subsequent development of the "varieties of capitalism" literature[49] suggests that in "coordinated market" economies the story of transfer of wealth from employees in a takeover is a plausible one. In a "liberal market" economy, such as the US, coordination of the inputs necessary for production occurs, both within and outside firms, mainly across markets, i.e., principally by explicit contract. In coordinated market economies, such as Germany and Japan, there is strategic coordination of those contributing to the productive process through institutions operating to some extent

---

[43] A litigation challenge to the directors' decision will be more difficult to mount if the statute requires the directors to consider the interests of multiple groups but leaves the balance to be struck to the incumbent board than if their obligation is to consider the interests of only a single group.

[44] See *supra* note 38.

[45] For example, where the former management had allowed parts of the business to become overmanned or had failed to address the lack of competitiveness of that business.

[46] A. Shleifer and L. Summers, Breach of Trust in Hostile Takeovers in Corporate Takeovers: Causes and Consequences 33 (A. Auerbach ed., 1988).

[47] That is, not observable by third parties, including courts.

[48] Romano, *supra* note 24, 15–19.

[49] The seminal work was Varieties of Capitalism (P. Hall and D. Soskice eds., 2001).

independently of markets. Although the coordinated market analysis has implications for a wide range of policies and institutions in society, in terms of labor contracting and takeovers it follows quite closely the Shleifer and Summers argument. For example, a somewhat idealized picture of Germany, a prototypical coordinated economy, is one in which adversarial, distributional issues are handled largely outside the firm—through multi-employer collective bargaining—leaving scope for firm level labor representation bodies, notably works councils, to develop informal arrangements over efficient working practices and skill acquisition in exchange for greater security of employment and greater promotion opportunities. Board-level representation in Germany functions as a way of verifying that the management of the company has stuck to its promises, i.e., it functions as a governance substitute for the unavailable direct enforcement of implicit contracts.[50]

In this analysis, the takeover appears as a threat to the informal arrangements put in place by incumbent management. The new management team might renege on the informal commitments made by the previous management team in pursuit of short-term shareholder gain. The risk of this outcome would reduce generally the credibility of management promises made as part of cooperative deals and so thus reduce also the ex ante incentives for employees to enter into such deals. Of course, the new management team might be as committed as the previous team to the high-level coordination of corporate strategy and human resources policy. The acquirer might be expecting to gain from the takeover through productive efficiencies in an entirely different area of corporate strategy than the terms and conditions, explicit and implicit, upon which the workers are employed. These arguments point in the direction, not of prohibiting takeovers, but of creating a space for strong employee voice in the selection of offers which will proceed and those which will be blocked. In Germany this is achieved by permitting the management board to exercise its powers of centralized management to discourage takeovers, provided the management's action is approved, post-bid, by the supervisory board, upon which the employees are represented, perhaps to the extent of half the seats.[51]

I am not aware of direct evidence about the capacity of codetermined boards to distinguish between efficient and inefficient takeover offers in coordinated market economies, as compared to boards with no employee representation. However, there is evidence that coordinated market economies and liberal market economies are equally good at generating economic growth,[52] and that the reduced costs of labor contracting under the German system are considerable and may outweigh the additional costs in that system of contracting for equity capital.[53]

Finally, it should be noted that the mechanism for giving employees voice in takeover decisions in Germany is not one developed ad hoc for the takeover situation. Board representation is an integral part of the corporate governance system of that country and operates

[50] Paul Davies, Efficiency Arguments for the Collective Representation of Workers, in The Autonomy of Labour Law ch 15, § 5 (A. Bogg, C. Costello, A. Davies & J. Prassl eds., 2015)—also available at http://ssrn.com/abstract=2498221.

[51] In Germany, half the seats on the supervisory board in companies with 2,000 plus employees are allocated to worker representatives and one-third in companies below this number (except in the coal and iron and steel industries where specially strong arrangements apply).

[52] P.A. Hall and D.W. Gingerich, "Varieties of Capitalism and Institutional Complementarities in the Political Economy: An Empirical Analysis", 39 British Journal of Political Science 449 (2009).

[53] Paul Davies, supra note 50.

in relation to all aspects of corporate strategy setting. The same is true of other European countries which use board-level representation or works council input to provide employee voice in takeovers. Employee voice is not just a device for preventing wealth transfers from employees to shareholders in takeovers but an integral part of the arrangements which, at least in association with certain productive technologies, generate and reinforce the company's productive efficiency.

3.2.3 Inefficient Transfers of Control Involving Wealth Transfers between or within Acquirer and Target Shareholders

In all the above cases the transfer of control is inefficient because there may be little or no increase in productive efficiency, but the joint wealth of the shareholders of the acquirer and target is increased because of a transfer of wealth to them from non-shareholder groups. In these cases, it is likely that control shifts will occur if the decision is left wholly to the target shareholders. In this section we consider cases where the joint wealth of the shareholders of the acquirer and the target shareholders is not increased, but, nevertheless, the acquisition occurs because there is a wealth transfer between acquirer and target shareholders or within those groups. Since these transfers are also financed by a redistribution of wealth rather than by an increase in wealth resulting from greater operational efficiency, there is no public policy reason to facilitate such acquisitions.

3.2.3.1 Acquirer Empire Building

First, there will be a transfer of wealth from bidder to target shareholders where the bidder offers a premium price to the shareholders of the target company but has no realistic prospect of obtaining synergies from the control shift or better management performance in the target to recoup the money spent on paying the target shareholders above the pre-bid, undisturbed price of their shares. In effect, there is a wealth shift from bidder shareholders to target shareholders.[54] Such acquisitions may occur because the management of the bidder is more incentivized to increase the size of the acquirer than its profitability, perhaps because their pay packets are tied more to the size than to the profitability of the enterprise or because they obtain significant reputational rewards from running bigger companies or because the bankruptcy risk of the company is reduced if its operations are diversified. Such behavior is perhaps particularly likely where the bidder has a large free cash flow and so can easily finance an acquisition, and the management prefers to engage in such action rather than return the surplus to the acquirer's shareholders.[55]

Acquirer management behavior of this type tends not to be covered in takeover-specific rules, probably because expansion of the enterprise can take many forms other than a takeover offer. Consequently, this problem is usually addressed through the general corporate governance rules applying to the acquirer. Where shareholding in the acquirer is concentrated, management aggrandisement is unlikely, but it may be replaced by acts of controlling shareholder aggrandisement, which general corporate governance rules may find difficult

---

[54] This is clear if the acquisition is wholly for cash; but even where it is wholly for shares, the target shareholders gain a disproportionately large share of the combined enterprise.

[55] Michael Jensen, "A Free Cash Flow Theory of Takeovers", 76 Am. Econ. Rev. 323 (1986).

to control.[56] Where shareholding is dispersed, sophisticated institutional shareholders may have been able to lobby for rules that require acquirer management explicitly to obtain shareholder consent for large transactions.[57] Alternatively, the applicable governance rules may make it feasible for shareholders to respond effectively to a drop in the price of the acquirer's shares on the announcement of an inefficient offer by the acquirer, for example, by credibly threatening the removal of the management if they proceed without informal shareholder approval.

A variation of this problem is where the offer is initially wealth enhancing, but the offer is amended in the course of the takeover process so as to involve overpayment for the target's shares. This is a particular risk where competitive bidding occurs and is sometimes referred to as the "winner's curse," i.e., bidder management gets carried away with enthusiasm for winning the auction without noticing that the price offered is destroying the financial foundation of the acquisition. However, the winner's curse is not to be explained entirely by the dysfunctional psychology of auctions. The initial bidder will have incurred substantial sunk costs in identifying the target and launching the offer. Those costs are likely to be thrown away if a competitor succeeds, as will be clear to the shareholders. Whether the costs of the acquisition are recoverable within a reasonable time-frame, by contrast, may not become clear until sometime in the future, so that management may think it will have an easier time with its shareholders if it pursues the course of winning the auction. Much depends on the ability of the market to identify overpayment at the time of the offer (and then mark down the price of the acquirer's shares) and on the intensity of the accountability of acquirer management to shareholders under the general corporate governance rules.

However, some rules specific to takeovers (or to mergers and acquisitions more generally) may help to moderate the winner's curse. "Break fees," i.e., payments by the target company to the initial offeror if the deal is ultimately completed with an alternative offeror, may, if substantial, recompense the initial bidder for its search and launch costs, and thus reduce the incentive to participate over-actively in an auction. On the other hand, such arrangements tend to reduce the incidence of competitive bidding (because the target is worth less in the hands of a subsequent bidder, to the extent of the break fee) but equally to increase the probability of the bid being completed. Because the break fee is part of an agreement between target management and acquirer, break fee agreements tend to be strictly controlled in systems which place the bid decision in the hands of the target shareholders, because they reduce shareholder choice, but approached more favorably in systems which allow target management a substantial role in the acceptance decision.[58]

---

[56] Here approval by the shareholders as a class is not likely to be effective and "majority of the minority" approval is difficult to justify since there will normally be a plausible commercial explanation for the acquisition.

[57] As in the UK. See Financial Conduct Authority, Listing Rules, § 10. This requirement was one of the factors that led to the failure of Barclays plc. to put forward a takeover proposal for Lehman Brothers over the weekend of September 12–15, 2008: the size of the financial guarantees of Lehman Brothers' obligations, which the US authorities insisted Barclays should provide, made shareholder approval necessary. See Financial Services Authority, Statement, 20 January 2010 (available at fsa.gov.uk/pubs/other/lehman.pdf).

[58] See J.C. Coates, IV, "M&A Break Fees: U.S. Litigation vs. U.K. Regulation", in Regulation versus Litigation ch 9 (Daniel P. Kessler ed., 2011). The UK Rules are now tighter than when this article was written, since break fees (previously limited to 1% of the deal value) are now entirely prohibited except in limited cases; for example, with a competing bidder where the initial offer was not recommended

An alternative technique to reduce the incentive to pursue an auction to the bitter end, which has less impact on the incidence of auctions, is to facilitate pre-bid acquisition of shares of the target by the bidder. These can then be sold into the winning bidder's offer at a substantial profit, if it loses out in the auction.[59] Insider dealing rules tend to facilitate such precautionary action by not requiring a prospective bidder to reveal its intentions prior to dealing in the market.[60] On the other hand, disclosure requirements for "large" shareholdings put a cap on the size of the stake a potential acquirer can build up before the market becomes aware of its existence and the price of the target's shares increases. Sometimes the disclosure rules are supplemented by rules enabling companies to take the initiative to demand information of a suspected investor about its stake in the company, if any.[61]

More generally, competitive bidding raises the price paid to target shareholders, conditional on a bid being made, but the extent to which the prospect of an auction discourages the launching of bids in the first place and the impact of reduced bidding activity on shareholder wealth is unclear.[62]

3.2.3.2 Controlling and Non-Controlling Shareholders

A second form of wealth transfer may occur where there is a controlling shareholder in the target company. In this case, there may be a transfer of wealth from the non-controlling shareholders in the target to the controlling shareholder and the shareholders of the acquirer. The controller may agree to sell her stake to the acquirer who intends to extract pbc—or to extract a higher level of pbc than the existing controller. Since such an acquisition will depress the price of the non-controlling shares, a wealth transfer occurs. In egregious cases of post-acquisition behavior by the acquirer ("looting"), liability may be imposed on the selling controlling shareholder to share her control premium with the non-controlling shareholders, thus incentivizing the selling controller to do some investigation of the acquirer's intentions.[63] More generally, the mandatory bid rule, imposing an obligation

(Takeover Code UK, rule 21.2). Coates found that bids in the UK were twice as likely to face a competitor than bids in the US, which also affected completion rates, because, in both countries, bids without competition were completed in 90% of instances but, with competition, in only 60% of instances (§ III.B).

[59] "Toe-hold" bidding is associated with lower winning premiums and a higher probability of winning: S. Betton and B. Eckbo, "Toeholds, Bid Jumps, and Expected Payoff in Takeovers", 13 Rev. Fin. Stud. 841 (2000).

[60] The latest version of the EU rules on insider trading is, however, ambiguous on this matter. See Art. 9.4 of Regulation (EU) No 596/2014. This contains an exemption for inside information obtained in the course of a public takeover where that information is used to effect the acquisition but it is also stated that "This paragraph shall not apply to stake-building."

[61] The UK has a low disclosure threshold (3% of the voting rights in the company), disclosure within two trading days (not including the day of acquisition), with economic interests under equity swaps counting toward the threshold: Financial Conduct Authority, Disclosure and Transparency Rules § 5. In addition, there is a company-initiated interrogation scheme (Companies Act 2006, Part 22), which can lead to the disenfranchisement of shares whose beneficial ownership is not disclosed to the company.

[62] What is clear is that the UK regulation opts for maximizing shareholder wealth conditional on a bid rather than maximizing the number of bids. The ban on break fees, strict disclosure rules, the presence of a mandatory bid rule and the associated restriction on partial bids, other strict equal treatment rules, and the minimum time periods for bids to be open are all conducive to the emergence of a competing bid.

[63] This is the approach to the problem favored by US law, which in general applies a "market rule" to sales of control, i.e. the seller is entitled to whatever she can get for the controlling shares, but not in the

on the buyer of the controlling block, may help to reduce the incidence of wealth-shifting transfers of control. Assume that the potential acquirer intends to gain from the transaction by extracting greater pbc than the seller currently extracts and to run the company less efficiently than the current controller. If this acquisition succeeds and the non-controlling shareholders remain in the company, they will be much worse off, because the post-bid share price of the company will reflect both the higher pbc of the new controller and the less efficient operation of the company. However, in order to secure the current controller's acceptance of the offer, the potential acquirer will have to pay the existing controller a price which at least reflects that controller's pbc as well as the pre-bid market price of the shares. Given that the acquirer will run the company less efficiently, so that its overall value is less post the acquisition than before it, the transaction will not occur if the price the existing controller will demand has to be extended to all the shareholders. Without that extension, the acquisition will likely go ahead provided the pbc of the new controller plus the post-bid market price of the acquired shares exceed the existing controller's reservation price. Unlike in the situation discussed in section 2, where the MBR potentially blocked efficient sales of control, here it operates to block (or reduce the likelihood of) inefficient sales of control.[64]

3.2.4 Inefficient Sales of Control Resulting from Intended Efficient Control Shifts

In this section we consider cases where the parties to the acquisition intend to produce an efficient control shift but they end up with an inefficient result. Operating efficiencies rather than wealth shifts motivate the acquisition, but the result is not efficient. There are two reasons why this may occur. First, the market value of acquirer and bidder companies may fail to reflect their fundamental value. Consequently, efficient companies may be undervalued and become takeover targets whilst overvalued acquiring companies may be in a position to make offers (especially share offers) which do not reflect their true value. Second, whether a particular acquisition pays off is determined only after the acquisition (ex post), whilst those deciding whether to make the acquisition have to decide ex ante, normally in the absence of full information about the target. If acquirers are not good at distinguishing takeovers likely to be efficient from those likely to be inefficient, then an inefficient

---

case of looting and analogous situations (R.C. Clark, Corporate Law 478–498 (1986).) Neither federal law nor most US states have an MBR, but in Delaware an acquirer who wishes to move, by means of a merger, to 100% ownership after obtaining a controlling stake in the target will find that fiduciary duty law applies particularly strongly to ensure that the non-controlling shareholders receive a fair price. See *Kahn v. M & F Worldwide Corp* (88 A.3d 635 (Del. 2014)).

[64] Assume there are 100 shares outstanding, of which existing controller holds half, and the company pre-bid is worth 110, of which the controller extracts 10 by way of pbc, so that the shares are each worth 1. Existing controller's reservation price for the control block is 60 (50 +10). New controller proposes to extract pbc of 40 and to run the company so that its overall value falls to 90. Post-bid shares will be worth 0.5 each. New controller can afford to pay 60 for control block (i.e., 1.2 per share) because that block will be worth 65 to it (25 + 40). To pay that price for all the shares, however, means paying 120 for a company worth 90. L. Bebchuk, "Efficient and Inefficient Sales of Corporate Control", 109 Q. J. Econ. 957 (1994); E.-P. Schuster, "The Mandatory Bid Rule: Efficient, After All?", 76 Mod. L. Rev. 529 (2013), arguing that MBR is an efficient rule because it places bidders competing to acquire a controlling stake in a company in the same position.

takeover may result in a high number of cases even if all those involved are trying to avoid this result.

The first argument obviously raises very fundamental questions about the utility of stock prices, which affects not just takeover regulation, but the whole question of the appropriate level of accountability of management to shareholders. The most common argument that markets misprice companies is that securities markets take a short-term approach to company valuation. Investments that pay off in the short term are more highly valued by investors than investments that pay off in the long term, whilst there is no reason to equate the societal interest in corporate development with short-term payoffs. This is a long-standing debate,[65] which is still not close to being resolved. It is clearly a debate of relevance mainly to dispersed shareholding companies, since controlling shareholders are necessarily there for the long term. It is plausible that a market populated by "speculators," i.e., those interested only in short-term gains, would operate so as inappropriately as to discount long-term increases in share value. However, in both the US and the UK, the major dispersed shareholding jurisdictions, the biggest section of the market is held by institutional shareholders—pension funds, insurance companies, mutual funds—which do not have short-term goals. Often their holdings reflect an underlying drive to provide income in old age. So it is a puzzle why investors with a long-term investment horizon should be thought to be driven by the acquisition of short-term gains.

There are possible explanations for the puzzle, arising out of the relations between the institutional shareholders and their asset managers or the way in which asset owners are regulated. These explanations suggest that the market valuation of shares is not inevitably short termist. Indeed, the current fashion for investor "engagement" in the UK and the EU is premised upon the notion that the long-term interests of institutional shareholders and managers in the development of companies would be aligned, if only they could concentrate on them.[66] The implications of this debate for takeover regulation are clear: for those who think the market misvalues companies, especially targets, giving target management a veto over takeover offers is the preferred strategy, because of management's greater information about the company,[67] whilst those who think the market does not misprice are anxious to take advantage of the hostile takeover to reduce shareholders' managerial agency problems.[68]

---

[65] For an early discussion see Paul Marsh, Short-Termism on Trial (1990); for early skepticism see Robert Shiller, Fashions, Fads and Bubbles in Financial Markets, in Knights, Raiders and Targets ch. 3 (J. Coffee, L. Lowenstein, & S. Rose-Ackerman eds., 1988); for a discussion of market prices in the financial crisis and their implications for corporate governance, see E. Fox, M. Fox, & R. Gilson, "Economic Crisis and Share Price Unpredictability: Reasons and Implications", ECGI Working Paper in Law, 243/2014; and for the status of the Efficient Capital Market Hypothesis after the crisis, see R. Kraakman and R. Gilson, "Market Efficiency after the Financial Crisis: It's Still a Matter of Information Costs", 100 Va. L. Rev. 313 (2014). The empirical evidence does not support the view that acquirers routinely failed to engage in innovation or R&D expenditures: Eckbo, *supra* note 22, § 3.

[66] The Kay Review of UK Equity Markets and Long-Term Decision Making, Final Report (2012, URN 12/917), stressing the absence of trust; along the same lines Colin Mayer, Firm Commitment (2013).

[67] M. Lipton, "Takeover Bids in the Target's Boardroom", 35 Bus. L. 101 (1979–1980) and "Twenty-Five Years After 'Takeover Bids in the Target's Boardroom': Old Battles, New Attacks and the Continuing War", 60 Bus. L. 1369 (2005). Lipton, famously, invented the "poison pill" discussed below in § 3.

[68] L. Bebchuk, "The Myth that Insulating Boards Serves Long-Term Value", 113 Colum. L. Rev. 1637 (2013).

The second suggested way in which misvaluation occurs builds on information asymmetry. The bidder lacks full information about the target and so may be prone not to bid when an acquisition would be efficient or to bid when it would not. One potential legal strategy would be to require potential targets to make information available to potential bidders, but, given the opportunistic behavior by competitors which this might engender, the decision whether to provide a "data room" is invariably left to target management, not something required of them. This creates an incentive for bidders proposing particularly risky acquisitions—for example, a highly leveraged acquisition by a private equity company—to proceed only via a friendly takeover, which includes some access to the target's books before an offer is made.[69] If the proposed acquisition is on a share-exchange basis, then the risks of an inefficient transfer of control fall in part on target shareholders as well. It is unlikely that dispersed target shareholders are better placed than the bidder to evaluate the offer, and so this may be an argument in favor of a role for target management in deciding whether the acquisition goes ahead, but only where the information the target management holds cannot credibly be communicated to target shareholders.

4 SOME NATIONAL SYSTEMS

Having identified the crucial areas for takeover regulation (section 2) and the (conflicting) policy objectives which determine how these areas could be regulated (section 3) we now turn in section 4 to analysis of choices made by selected jurisdictions. We will examine the UK, the US (focusing on Delaware for state law), Germany, and Japan, focusing, for want of space, mainly on the second principal issue in takeover regulation, i.e., the role of target management and the hostile bid. In each case it is important to view takeover regulation in the context of the corporate governance system of the jurisdiction as a whole. Placing takeover regulation in context will help us to see (1) whether different formal systems are functionally equivalent[70] and (2) whether even functionally different systems are equally efficient because of complementarities.[71]

4.1 The United Kingdom

We start with the UK, because it is in many ways a straightforward system. The principal, but not exclusive, body of rules, is the Takeover Code, which now has a statutory basis.[72]

---

[69] With the risk for the target that no offer may in fact emerge, leading the market to downgrade the former target's share price, on the assumption that the potential bidder discovered some adverse facts the market does not yet know.

[70] R. Gilson, "Globalizing Corporate Governance: Convergence of Form or Function", 49 Am. J. Comp. Law 329 (2001).

[71] That is, the notion that a feature of a country's corporate governance system is more efficient because of its coexistence with another feature of that system than it would be on its own. Indeed, on its own that feature might be a second-best choice, but its functioning together with the other feature makes it first best.

[72] Under Part 28 of the Companies Act 2006. The Takeover Code is still made and enforced by practitioner-panels operating in real time (www.thetakeoverpanel.org.uk).

Its central feature is the allocation of the decision on the bid wholly to the shareholders of the target company. Once the board has reason to believe that an offer might be imminent, it needs the consent of the shareholders in general meeting to take any action "which may result in any offer or bona fide possible offer being frustrated or in shareholders being denied the opportunity to decide on its merits."[73] This is a strong effects-based rule which reverses the normal allocation of powers between board and management during the bid. Management good faith is not a defense if the action frustrates the bid. The rule extends to the initiation of litigation to defend the company's interests. Prior shareholder approval before the bid emerges is not enough to satisfy the rule. In short, hostile bids are facilitated. In addition, by imposing minimum periods during which the offer must be open, the Code encourages the emergence of competing offers. The competitor has an equal information right with the initial (and perhaps preferred) bidder[74] and break fees and other arrangements designed to reduce shareholder choice are normally not allowed.[75]

Having side-lined target management, the UK Code is unable to rely on that source to protect target shareholders and so needs to address directly the issue of coercive offers. The Code contains a wide range of rules requiring disclosure of information (by the management of both target and acquirer), laying down timetables with minimum offer periods, and requiring equal treatment of those who accept early with those who accept late in the offer period or outside the offer, even before it was launched, including a mandatory bid rule.[76] Particularly important is Rule 31.4. This provides that, even after the acquirer has received the level of acceptances which it requires, the offer must remain open to non-accepting shareholders for a further 14 days. Target shareholders who regard the offer as inadequate and so do not want to accept it but are even less enamored of becoming minority shareholders in a company controlled by the acquirer can thus order their preferences by (1) not initially accepting the offer and (2) changing their minds when it becomes clear that a majority of fellow shareholders have accepted it.[77]

Finally, the UK Code contains a mandatory bid rule, though it was not initially part of the Code. In a dispersed shareholder setting, the MBR does not function so as to block (or discourage) sales of control by existing controlling shareholders, whether those sales are efficient or inefficient. Its function appears to be to control bidder coercion as against the shareholders as a class.[78] Without it, the acquirer could carry out a market raid at a high price, but not offer for the shares of those who did not respond to the market raid. If this is its function, it is not clear that the trigger is set at the right level: in a dispersed context, a holding of less than 30% may well be enough to give the holder de facto control of the company.[79]

Overall, the UK Code is target shareholder friendly, in a way that maximizes shareholder wealth conditional on a bid being made, rather than by maximizing the number of offers. An acquirer who is not in a position to offer for all the shares in the target company at the highest

---

[73] Rule 21.   [74] Rule 20.2.   [75] Rule 21.2. See *supra* note 58.

[76] P. Davies, The Nature of Equality in European Takeover Regulation, in Takeovers in English and German Law ch. 2 (J. Payne ed., 2002).

[77] See Bebchuk, *supra* note 6.

[78] On similar grounds partial bids are not normally permitted (rule 36) and offers which result in the acquirer holding less than 50% of the voting rights are ineffective, i.e. bidder does not acquire the shares assented to the offer (rule 10).

[79] Enriques & Gatti, *supra* note 31.

price paid for any of them is likely to find the UK rules discouraging. Furthermore, the UK rules, whilst sidelining management in relation to defensive measures, nevertheless permit target management to negotiate on behalf of target shareholders. Partly through the force of their recommendations to shareholders and partly by permitting or denying the acquirer access to the target's books, the management of UK target companies can play an active role in the takeover process even though subject to the "no frustration" rule. Thus, bid premiums in the UK and the US, which allows target management a significant role in the takeover decision, are not significantly different.[80]

There is a convincing political economy cum method-of-rulemaking story to explain the orientation of the UK Code. The adoption of the Code in 1968, after a series of fiercely contested takeovers when target management freely exercised their powers in attempts to block bids, occurred at a time when pension funds and insurance companies had acquired commanding share of the UK public market. The institutions' interest in investee companies was primarily financial, unlike that of the controlling families whom they were replacing, and so they had an interest in promoting rules likely to generate high-premium takeovers. As important, the UK government decided not to legislate on takeover rules but to leave that matter to a self-regulatory exercise by a group of financial interests coordinated by the Bank of England.[81] This gave institutional shareholders more influence over the setting of the rules than management or other groups, such as employees, who might have been more effective in a standard legislative process.[82] The "no frustration" rule was adopted from the beginning and has retained its place despite its adverse impact on non-shareholder interests in a number of cases.[83] The choice of rules which maximize target shareholder wealth conditional upon a bid being made (rather than to maximize the number of offers) is probably explicable by the desire of the institutions' representative bodies (which did the negotiating) to avoid a situation where one institution did better out of an acquisition than the others.

The role of the institutions is also crucial in explaining one other mystery about UK takeover rules. If the Code is so strong at ruling out post-bid takeover defenses, why does this not push management into adopting pre-bid shareholder defenses, such as non-voting or weighted voting shares or voting cap arrangements, all of which general UK corporate law permits and which the Code does not control because the defenses are put in place before a bid is imminent? If companies take this step, the ban on post-bid defensive measures becomes an irritation rather than a real block on effective defenses.[84] Such arrangements might be put in place at the point at which the company goes public, thus giving investors the option of buying on this basis or not buying at all. Offers of this type are common in New York; rare in London. The answer seems to be the strong opposition of UK institutions to departures from "one share, one vote." The opposition of the UK institutions to non-voting

---

[80] Coates, *supra* note 58 at Table 1: the mean was about 30% in both countries.

[81] Although it is no longer the case that the Panel is a self-regulatory body (see above) its rules and working practices still strongly reflect this origin.

[82] See J. Armour & D. Skeel, "Who Writes the Rules for Hostile Takeovers, and Why? The Peculiar Divergence of US and UK Takeover Regulation", 95 Geo. L. J. 1727 (2007).

[83] Most recently in the takeover of Cadbury plc. by Kraft Foods Inc. in 2010. The Panel engaged in a preemptive review of the Code, which, however, left the "no frustration" rule intact. See Panel Consultation Paper 2010/2.

[84] On these grounds Arlen and Talley argue against a no frustration rule: "Unregulable Defenses and the Perils of Shareholder Choice", 152 U. Pa. L. Rev. 577 (2003).

shares is legendary and of long standing. The position is not that they discount the price of shares which do not carry equal voting rights, but that they will not buy them at all.[85] Coordination amongst the UK institutions thus extends beyond lobbying for rules they favor to establishing market practice.[86]

Finally, the shareholder friendly approach of the Code fits in well with the general orientation of UK corporate law, which retains its classical, nineteenth-century position of giving shareholders strong governance rights over management.[87] Shareholders by ordinary majority vote at any time may remove all or any of the directors from office without cause and 5% of the shareholders may convene a meeting, whether the board agrees or not, to put such a resolution before the shareholders. As the prehistory of the Code showed, however, the governance rights were not enough to dissuade management from the use of their powers to block bids.[88] Managers may have reasoned that the opportunity to argue things out later with the shareholders was more attractive than certain execution now in the hands of the acquirer. In any event, the "no frustration" rule shifts the burden of action from shareholders (to remove managers who blocked bids) to management (wishing to take defensive action) and moves the decision from the future (when passions may have cooled) to the present (when a bid is on the table).

However, David Kershaw has argued that the "no frustration" rule adds nothing to what the English common law fiduciary duties of directors would have required—other than, one might suggest, a much more effective enforcement mechanism via the Takeover Panel.[89] This is a very difficult argument to assess, since there was only one English case applying the fiduciary "proper purposes" rule to defensive measures by target management before common law decision making was overtaken by the Panel. This was the first-instance decision in *Hogg v. Cramphorn*,[90] which did indeed decide that the defensive tactics adopted in response to a non-coercive bid without shareholder approval constituted a breach of that rule. How the courts would have further developed the proper purposes doctrine in the takeover context is a highly speculative question, especially as the counterfactual could take more than one form. In the complete absence of a takeover code it seems likely that the English courts would have been forced, as with the courts in Delaware and Japan, to use fiduciary duty law to distinguish between "legitimate" and "illegitimate" offers, rather than to impose a blanket ban on defensive action, as the UK Code does, for that would have left target shareholders unprotected against bidder opportunism. As we shall see below, however, the

---

[85] See Paul L. Davies, "Shareholder Power in the United Kingdom", in Research Handbook on Shareholder Power 355 (Randall Thomas and Jennifer Hill eds., 2015). An interesting question for the future is whether foreign institutions, now the dominant players in the market, will take a similar line.

[86] Of course, management has greater freedom pre-bid to take commercially plausible action which makes the company a less attractive target, e.g. entering into a joint-venture arrangement, because an effects-based pre-bid rule would constrain centralized management too tightly, even from the shareholders' point of view. As a matter of law pre-bid defensive measures are controlled by fiduciary duties, where the test is whether the "dominant" purpose of the directors is to entrench themselves or to promote the company's commercial interests. But such action is also scrutinized by institutional shareholders, albeit not by reference to the bright-line standard which is applied to non-voting shares.

[87] Davies, *supra* note 85.   [88] This is recounted in Armour and Skeel, *supra* note 82, § II.B.

[89] David Kershaw, "The Illusion of Importance: Reconsidering the UK's Takeover Defence Prohibition", 56 Int'l. & Comp. L. Q. 267 (2007).

[90] [1967] Ch 254.

courts in those two jurisdictions draw the line between legitimacy and illegitimacy in rather different ways, so there would have been a range of choices for the English courts to make when fashioning a full set of takeover rules on the back of fiduciary duties law. In any event, a simple "no frustration" rules is unlikely to have resulted. If the counterfactual is the Takeover Code and Panel, as they stand, except for the absence of a "no frustration" rule, the English courts would have had to puzzle out whether the omission of that rule from an otherwise target-shareholder friendly set of rules represented a deliberate decision to permit defensive measures or whether a "no frustration" rule was implicit in the Code's structure. In either case, there is good reason to think that the institutional shareholders had more success in shaping the rules of the Code than they would have had in influencing court decisions, where lobbying is not an accepted part of judicial decision making.[91]

The Takeover Code's "no frustration" rule thus adds materially to the power of target shareholders in takeovers, albeit by way of extension of characteristics already present in the UK corporate governance system rather than by way of a novel addition.

4.2 The United States

The US takeover rules are an almost complete contrast with those in the UK, but the practical results of their operation seem not to be as different as the contrast at the level of the formal rules would suggest. Let us look first at the formal rules.

The Williams Act 1968[92] contains provisions which inhibit the acquirer to a significant extent from taking advantage of the coordination problems of dispersed shareholders—though the Act stops short of a mandatory bid rule. The other two major areas of takeover regulation (defensive measures, minority protection against controlling shareholders) have been left to state law. State legislation, which has been partial rather than comprehensive, has generally favored defensive measures, sometimes through constituency statutes[93] and sometimes through more robust measures.[94] However, these legislative provisions have been superseded in fact by a remarkable piece of private ordering (the shareholder rights plan—hereafter the "plan"—or "poison pill") which has provided target management with a high level of input into the takeover decision.[95] Where the plan has been accepted by the courts, as it has in Delaware and most other states, it has become the primary mechanism for forcing acquirers to deal with the management of the target company rather than appeal over their heads to the target shareholders in a hostile bid.

---

[91] On the differences between courts and other forms of rulemaking from a "lobbying" point of view, see Armour & Skeel, *supra* note 82.

[92] Amending the Securities Exchange Act 1934, §§ 13 and 14. 1968 was also the year in which the first version of the UK Takeover Code was adopted.

[93] Above § 2.B.ii.

[94] Some of the more extreme statutes were struck down as unconstitutional on the grounds that the Williams Act had preempted the area in which the states sought to legislate. However, state regulation outside the area of proxy solicitation was upheld. For more detail see J. Seligman, T. Paredes, & L. Loss, Fundamentals of Securities Regulation 868–81 (6th ed. 2014).

[95] E. Catan & M. Kahan, "The Law and Finance of Anti-Takeover Statutes", 68 Stan. L. Rev. 629 (2016) pointing out the insignificance of other defensive devices and the relevance of this fact for empirical research.

The plan, in its dominant "flip in" version,[96] provides for the issue of warrants to subscribe for shares at an attractively low price when an investor acquires a proportion of the company's voting rights which is set out in the plan (e.g., 15%). The warrants are made available to all shareholders except the one who has crossed the threshold. Where the acquirer obtains the shares by purchases in the market or by private treaty with a large shareholder, the impact of the plan, if triggered, is to dilute the acquirer's holding (in both voting and financial terms) below the threshold and to do so whenever the threshold is crossed. The acquirer might seek to avoid this "show stopper" by making an offer for shares conditional upon a high percentage of the target shareholders accepting the offer, so that the dilution will apply only to the small percentage of non-accepting shares.[97] However, if the plan is triggered also by an offer for more than a certain percentage of the voting shares, the target shareholders will have every incentive to exercise their rights and then assent them to the offer, thus destroying the financial basis of the acquirer's offer of so much per share.[98] In either case, proceeding is too risky a business for the acquirer. No acquirer is known to have launched and succeeded in a bid in the face of a plan. Instead, it needs to get the rights removed, which the plan will provide can be done by the directors of the target company at low or no cost to the company, thus forcing the acquirer to deal with target management as well as target shareholders.

The second crucial feature of the shareholder rights plan is the ease with which it can be adopted. Under Delaware law[99] the adoption of a plan is within the powers of the board, so that no shareholder consent is required.[100] Not only is the decision within the unilateral control of the board, but it can be taken speedily, since only a board resolution is needed.[101]

---

[96] Early versions of the pill gave target shareholders rights to shares in the acquiring company ("flip over") but doubts about the effectiveness of such plans led to their replacement by "flip-in" plans: W. Allen, R. Kraakman, & G. Subramanian, Commentaries and Cases on the Law of Business Organization § 12.3 (4th ed. 2012).

[97] The plan might be tailored so as to produce the required level of dilution even at a high threshold level.

[98] In this case the exclusion of the acquirer from the warrants is probably unnecessary. The increase in the number of shares bid for is in itself enough to destroy the acquirer's offer, even if the acquirer's pre-bid holding is also pro-rata increased. Formulating the plan in this way, as is done in the French version of the plan (Commercial Code (France) Art. L233–32, as amended by Loi n° 2014–384 of 29 March 2014) avoids the legal risk arising from unequal treatment of shareholders, which is a substantial one in some European jurisdictions. Under the French version, the warrants may be issued by the board of the target when a bid is launched; if this happens, the acquirer is permitted to withdraw its offer; and the board can then withdraw the warrants. P. Davies, E. Schuster, & E. van de Walle de Ghelcke, The Takeover Directive as a Protectionist Tool? in Company Law and Economic Protectionism—New Challenges to Economic Integration 105 (Ulf Bernitz and Wolf-Georg Ringe eds., 2010) § V(b). However, it should be noted that pre-bid shareholder approval is needed to confer this power on the board, and the French poison pill leaves the target unprotected from an actual acquisition of de facto control through the market or private treaty.

[99] As interpreted in *Moran v. Household International Inc* 500 A 2d 1346 (1985).

[100] By contrast, in the EU the issuance of shares, including warrants granting entitlements to subscribe for shares, requires shareholder approval, though that approval can be given in advance (for periods up to five years) (Directive 2012/30/EU, originally enacted in 1977).

[101] Hence, given the disclosure rules relating to shareholdings, it matters little to the ability of the board to defend against a bid whether it actually has a plan in place or not (M. Klausner, "Fact and Fiction in Corporate Law and Governance", 65 Stan. L. Rev. 1325 (2013)).

However, the effectiveness of this piece of private ordering depends crucially on the courts' view of its relationship to the fiduciary duties of directors. The Delaware courts easily accepted that for the directors, by adopting a plan, to put themselves in a position where they could decide whether or not to block an offer, if one were made, was not a breach of fiduciary duty.[102] So the question became whether failure to redeem a plan in the face of a particular offer, so as to permit the bid to proceed, was a breach of fiduciary duty. This decision of the board has always been subject to court review. It was relatively easy for the courts to conclude that it was legitimate for the board to stymie a bid which was structurally coercive of target shareholders, because the shareholders' decision in that situation could not be regarded as a reliable expression of their wishes.[103] Absent coercion, the analogy with the UK approach would indicate that the pill should routinely be redeemed. The Delaware courts never adopted this approach. In fact, as time went on, although the standard of court review was always formally more exacting than a business judgment rule,[104] the courts became increasingly deferential to the board's views.[105] The board could refuse to redeem if this were necessary to protect their existing business strategy (even though productive efficiencies might indicate a change of strategy)[106] and, more recently, if the board thought the offer "substantively" coercive (apparently meaning that the shareholders might take a lower view of the company's value than the directors thought appropriate).[107] The only serious qualification to the courts' deference to management was the duty imposed on the board to seek out the highest bidder for the company if the board had in fact decided to sell the company.[108]

As might be expected, the very different UK and US rules produced different experiences in relation to hostile bids. In both jurisdictions hostile bids are uncommon, but they are more common and more likely to succeed in the UK than in the US. Armour and Skeel report that "in the United Kingdom, 0.85% of takeovers announced during the period 1990–2005 were hostile, compared with 0.57% in the United States. Of these hostile bids, 43% were successful in the United Kingdom, as opposed to just 24% in the United States."[109] More striking, however, is their assessment that "in the United States, the overall level of takeover activity, adjusted for the size of the economy, actually seems slightly higher than in the United Kingdom, even during the 1990s."[110] This is surprising because, if the thesis about

---

[102]   See note 99—an issue which would clearly be debatable under the English or Japanese improper purposes doctrine, since the plan's only purpose is to give the target board that power.

[103]   *Unocal Corp v. Mesa Petroleum Co* 493 A 2d 946 (1985).

[104]   It was whether the board had reasonable grounds for believing that the acquisition presented a threat to the corporation's interests and whether the board's response was proportionate in relation to the threat. See previous note.

[105]   R. Gilson, "Unocal Fifteen Years Later (and What We Can Do About it)", 26 Del. J. Corp. L. 491 (2001).

[106]   *Paramount Communications Inc v. Time Inc* 571 A 2d 1140 (1989). But the board must have an objective which plausibly promotes shareholder value: *eBay Domestic Holdings Inc v. Newmark* 16 A 3d 1 (2010)—defense of "corporate culture" by itself not enough.

[107]   *Air Products and Chemicals Inc v. Airgas Inc*, 16 A.3d 48 (2011).

[108]   *Revlon Inc v. MacAndrews and Forbes Holdings Inc* 506 A 2d 173 (1986). On the significance of *Revlon*, see L. Johnson & R. Ricca, "The Dwindling of Revlon", 71 Wash. & Lee L. Rev. 167 (2013).

[109]   *Supra* note 82, 1739.

[110]   *Supra* note 82, 1741. Coates, *supra* note 58, § III.C found that the UK bid rate was only 80% of the US rate (after controlling for the relative size of the economies). See also S. Rossi & P. Volpin, "Cross-Country Determinants of Mergers and Acquisitions", 74 J. Fin. Econ. 277 (2004).

managerial hostility to disciplinary and synergistic control shifts is correct, one would expect target management to use the power given to them by the plan to reduce substantially the incidence of takeovers.[111]

There are two broad categories of explanation of this fact. The first is that the plan simply diverted acquirers into another method of obtaining control, i.e., a proxy fight to replace the directors with the acquirer's nominees, who would repeal the plan. Given that under Delaware law directors can normally be removed by shareholders only at the annual meeting through a failure to re-elect (not at any time, as in the UK), even this change of procedure would seem to imply some significant costs for the acquirer.[112] For most of the recent period, however, even this opportunity has not been available, because boards were "classified" or "staggered" (only one-third of the board retiring each year), so that a proxy victory in two successive general meetings would be necessary to pass control. The combination of the plan and the staggered board made this alternative route impassable.[113]

The alternative explanation is that the corporate governance system in the US adapted to this grant of power by the plan to target boards by developing mechanisms to influence the way in which directors exercise the power. "Just say no" may be an accurate description of the formal power held by target directors under the plan, but "just say no" did not become an accurate description of how target directors behaved. Two developments in US corporate governance, occurring at the same time as the plan became widespread, but not necessarily because of the prevalence of the plan, altered the incentives of target management directors in a direction more friendly to the interests of target shareholders. One development, high-powered share-based remuneration schemes for executive directors and top managers, re-channeled the self-interest of executives in the direction of accepting bids which were wealth-enhancing for target shareholders. Such schemes might provide handsome recompense for an executive who lost his job in a control shift, especially if the normal vesting period requirements were waived on the takeover, and generate an incentive for that executive to negotiate the best price for the target shares which could be obtained. At the same time the arrival of the independent non-executive director as the dominant type of board member (at least in numerical terms) generated pressure in the same direction, since the incentives of the non-executives were to be seen to do a good job for target shareholders in order to enhance their reputation and increase the likelihood of higher-status non-executive positions in the future. The combined effect of these two developments was to change "just say no" into "just say yes, if it is a good price."[114]

---

[111] Of course, it could be that the US takeover rate would be even higher but for the plan.

[112] See *supra* note 94, at 812 for the advantages of the takeover as against a proxy fight, even in the absence of a staggered board. Indeed, the takeover emerged initially as a response to the costs of a proxy fight.

[113] L. Bebchuk, J. Coates, & G. Subramanian, "The Powerful Antitakeover Force of Staggered Boards: Theory, Evidence, and Policy", 54 Stan. L. Rev. 887 (2002). Classification of the board under § 141(d) DGCL rests on either such a provision being in the company's initial certificate of incorporation or by-laws or be adopted by shareholder vote through a subsequent by-law amendment. Today, however, staggered boards are less common than they were and their impact on corporate performance is much disputed.

[114] M. Kahan & E. Rock, "How I Learned to Stop Worrying and Love the Pill: Adaptive Responses to Takeover Law", 69 U. Chi. L. Rev. 879 (2002). At the same time staggered boards were becoming less prevalent, as institutional shareholder power grew, so that staggered boards became more difficult

Does this mean that the UK and the US have ended up in the same place (at least in relation to Delaware corporations)? There is one potentially important difference. If the management of the Delaware target company genuinely believe[115] that the value of the company in their hands is greater than its value in the hands of the acquirer and they can convince another set of corporate insiders (the independent directors) that this is the case, but it is difficult for them to convey that argument credibly to outsiders (target shareholders), then they have a greater possibility of keeping the target independent in the US than in the UK. Under a "shareholders decide" rule, target management runs the risk of being misunderstood by the investors or, what is usually the same thing, the market. Since the most plausible version of the efficient capital market hypothesis (the semi-strong version) accepts that sometimes there is information available to insiders which is not available to the market and a more skeptical view might be that there are periods when the market suffers from failures to value companies accurately,[116] the Delaware arrangement might be thought to have advantages.[117]

Another potential advantage of the Delaware arrangement is that it relies heavily on private ordering, i.e., decisions taken at company level rather than by legislatures or other general rulemakers. The plan, the staggered board and the incentive remuneration system are all examples of private ordering; only the independent director requirements result from regulation. Enriques, Gilson, and Pacces[118] have argued that, in general, firm-level decision making on the role of management in the takeover is to be preferred. Whether protection of the existing strategy of the company or exposing target board management to the risk of removal if they perform badly will better promote the wealth of target shareholders depends heavily upon the circumstances of each company and, within a company, may vary from time to time.[119] A mandatory exclusion, as under the UK Code, prevents shareholders from committing themselves not to assent to a takeover offer for a period of time, as the newly fashionable policy of engagement might be thought to require from time to time.[120] However, the Delaware arrangements do not fully measure up to the default model proposed by these authors. They propose that the default should be that shareholders decide, both because on average shareholder decision making is more likely to be wealth-enhancing than

to obtain or to maintain (M. Kahan & E. Rock, "Embattled CEOs", 88 Tex. L. Rev. 987 (2009–2010)). Consequently, the defensive power of the plan became less, though by no means negligible.

[115] If they do not, the financial gains from the control shift are likely to mean that they do not persist in their opposition.

[116] Fox, Fox, & Gilson, *supra* note 65.

[117] Of course, to the extent that US institutional shareholders become able and willing to exercise their general governance rights, for example to remove staggered boards or directors of whom they disapprove, incumbent management may become less incentivized to back its own judgment against a potential acquirer. Kahan & Rock, *supra* note 114 (Embattled CEOs).

[118] L. Enriques, R.J. Gilson, & A.M. Pacces, "The Case for an Unbiased Takeover Law (with an Application to the European Union)", 4 Harv. Bus. L. Rev. 85 (2014). They make the same argument in relation to the MBR.

[119] There is some evidence from the US that takeover defenses among companies going public are common in firms that have substantial contractual commitments to business partners—customers, suppliers, or strategic partners (W. Johnson et al., "The Bonding Hypothesis of Takeover Defenses: Evidence from IPO Firms", 117 J. Fin. Econ. 307 (2015). But see the comments of Klausner, *supra* note 101, at 1325.

[120] M. Kahan & E. Rock, "Corporate Constitutionalism: Antitakeover Charter Provisions as Pre-Commitment", 152 U. Pa. L. Rev. 473 (2003).

board decision making, and because a shareholder default means that it can be altered only with shareholders' consent. It is the management's burden to persuade the shareholders to alter the default rather than the other way around. This is likely to be the better arrangement because the burden of persuasion is more easily discharged by management than dispersed shareholders.[121] On this view, the shareholder rights plan places the burden of action the wrong way around.

4.3 Germany

The formal rules in Germany look very much like the US ones where there is a plan in place, except that the rules result from legislation rather than private ordering. Under the relevant statute, the management board may take defensive measures provided the supervisory board approves, subject to their fiduciary duties and their obtaining shareholder approval where the measure is one which, if taken outside a takeover bid, would require shareholder approval.[122] Scrutiny by reference to directors' duties is likely to be light, as in Delaware, but in this case for the reason that German company law does not equate corporate value with shareholder value. The board is free, even obliged, routinely to consider a range of "stakeholder" interests, so that the fact that the directors' decision does not and is not intended to maximize shareholder wealth does not of itself render that decision suspect.

More constraining are likely to be the rules on shareholder consent, which are in general imposed more widely in European corporate systems than in Delaware.[123] These are likely to make the adoption of a German rights plan difficult without shareholder consent, but that may do no more than push the German management in the direction of other defensive measures, such as the conditional sale of assets whose acquisition is important to the acquirer.[124] Furthermore, the German system has not developed the two adaptive devices

---

[121] The EU Takeover Directive requires Member States which do not make a "no-frustration" rule mandatory to permit companies incorporated in their jurisdiction to opt into that rule, by shareholder supermajority vote (as needed to alter the company's articles). No company is known ever to have opted in. European Commission, External Study on the application of the Directive on Takeover Bids, 190 (available at http://ec.europa.eu/internal_market/company/docs/takeoverbids/study/study_en.pdf).

[122] Wertpapiererwerbs- und Übernahmegesetz (WpÜG), § 33(1). Germany has a mandatory two-tier board system (except for European Companies incorporated in Germany). Management is normally in the hands of the management board; the supervisory board may not be allocated management powers but can make certain management board decisions subject to its approval; and shareholders have only limited decision-making rights. However, in the case of defensive measures, shareholder approval, which can be given in advance for periods of up to 18 months, can replace supervisory board approval, but apparently is rarely sought, perhaps because a 75% majority of the shareholders is required and minority shareholders are likely to be less accepting of defenses than the supervisory board.

[123] See *supra* note 11.

[124] Carsten Gerner-Beuerle, David Kershaw, & Matteo Solinas, "Is The Board Neutrality Rule Trivial? Amnesia About Corporate Law In European Takeover Regulation", 22 Eur. Bus. Org. Rev. 559 (2011) come close to the view that other provisions of German law will always require shareholder consent for defensive actions, so that the WpÜG provisions are irrelevant. Two responses: general corporate law usually requires shareholder consent in advance (up to five years in advance often being permitted) rather than post bid, as under the "no frustration" rule. It is thus not possible to equate voting outcomes in general meetings in advance with outcomes in takeover offers. See § I.B above. Second, in relation to asset sales the authors have to rely on what might be argued to be an overextended interpretation

which have proved important in Delaware. High-powered share-based remuneration systems have not taken hold in Germany and, after the financial crisis, legislative reforms have pushed in the opposite direction.[125] "Golden parachutes" are far from excluded but the equity interest of German management board members in their company is likely to be substantially less than in a comparable Delaware company. In addition, German rulemakers have been lukewarm about requirements for independent directors on supervisory boards, probably because of the presence of employee representatives on the supervisory boards of large companies.[126] The German corporate governance code goes no further than to state that "The Supervisory Board shall include what it considers an adequate number of independent members."[127] So there may be few independent directors pushing for consideration of the acquirer's case, whilst the employee representatives on the supervisory are likely to tilt the board against takeovers, at least where adverse short-term consequences for the employees are likely to follow.

It is thus reasonable to conclude that German management boards are not under the same incentives as directors of Delaware companies to use their defensive powers in the interests of target shareholders.[128] However, traditionally this has been an unimportant question in

---

of the *Holzmüller* doctrine for the proposition that crown jewel sales would require shareholder approval. *Holzmüller* ((1982) BGHZ 83, 122) was a surprising decision of the Federal High Court (Bundesgerichtshof) which increased the decision-making powers of the shareholders beyond the apparently closed list of matters on which shareholders can decide, as laid down in § 119 of the German Companies Act (AktG). The extension was to large-asset transactions which impacted adversely on the exercise of shareholder rights. This decision has been reined in significantly by the subsequent *Gelatine* decision ((2004) Doc. No. II ZR 154/02). Both *Holzmüller* and *Gelatine* concerned intra-group restructurings, not takeovers. It is suggested that it is unlikely that the German courts would use *Holzmüller* to impose the contractual model of defensive measures on German companies when the legislative history of the WpÜG shows the legislature had wished to adopt the corporate model. For English translations of these decisions see A. Cahn and D. Donald, Comparative Company Law 695–721 (2010).

[125] § 87(1) of the AktG provides: "The supervisory board shall, in determining the aggregate remuneration of any member of the management board (salary, profit participation, reimbursement of expenses, insurance premiums, commissions, incentive-based compensation promises such as subscription rights and additional benefits of any kind), ensure that such aggregate remuneration bears a reasonable relationship to the duties and performance of such member as well as the condition of the company and that it does not exceed standard remuneration without any particular reasons. The remuneration system of listed companies shall be aimed at the company's sustainable development. The calculation basis of variable remuneration components should therefore be several years long; in case of extraordinary developments, the supervisory board shall agree on a possibility of remuneration limitation." The German Corporate Governance Code (4.2.3), enforceable on a "comply or explain" basis adds: "Benefit commitments made in connection with the early termination of a Management Board member's activity due to a change of control shall not exceed 150% of the severance cap." That cap is set at two years' total compensation.

[126] P. Davies and K. Hopt, "Corporate Boards in Europe-Accountability and Convergence", 61 Am. J. Comp. L. 301, § II.B (2013). If half the seats are taken by employee representatives and half the shareholder seats were allocated to independent directors (who must not have links to important shareholders), large shareholders might feel that they could not rely on the board to protect their interests.

[127] German Corporate Governance Code, § 5.4.2 (available at http://www.dcgk.de/en/home.html).

[128] J. Gordon, "An American Perspective on Anti-Takeover Laws in the EU: A German Example", in Reforming Company Law in Europe (G. Ferrarini, K.J. Hopt, J. Winter, & E. Wymeersch eds., 2004).

Germany, given the shareholding structure of German companies. In the past that structure has been highly concentrated. In the 1990s the average size of the largest shareholding in a German public company was 57%.[129] The historically very small number of hostile takeovers in Germany needs no other explanation: a hostile bid is pointless if management is likely to have been pursuing the policies preferred by the controlling shareholder and if the management are not likely to be willing to take defensive steps which the controlling shareholder opposes.

A precondition for the issue of defensive measures to move center-stage in Germany is some deconcentration of the shareholding structure of German companies. Mannesman, unusually, had such a structure, which facilitated its takeover by the UK company Vodafone in 2000. This event alerted the German government and management and employee interest groups to the salience of the issue. It led the German government to oppose, successfully, the adoption of a mandatory "no frustration" rule at EU level and to enact the domestic legislation putting into the hands of the supervisory board the approval of defensive measures. Ringe has provided recent evidence of a more general de-concentration of shareholdings in German companies.[130] Issues relating to the scope of management board freedom to block hostile bids, to their incentives to do so, and to the incentives of the supervisory board to sanction such measures are thus likely to become more important in the future.

However, it would be wrong to read in a straight line from deconcentration to the acceptance of a higher level of hostile takeovers. Employee representatives on the board might still play an important role in discouraging takeovers. More importantly, if it is the case that the German system of coordination lowers the cost of labor contracting more than it raises the cost of equity finance,[131] it would not be in the societal interest routinely to promote hostile bids, even if shareholders were willing to accept the offers made.

4.4 Japan

In relation to takeovers Japan has many similarities to Germany, that is, the issue of the hostile takeover (and thus of defensive measures) has not been a live one until recently, because other elements of the corporate governance system had made takeovers unfeasible and perhaps unnecessary. However, changes in the surrounding governance environment appear to have gone further than in Germany and to have opened up a lively debate about the appropriate role for takeovers in general, and hostile bids in particular. That debate, in which courts, government, and the Tokyo stock exchange have all participated, has not produced a clear resolution of the issues and the rules, still inchoate, chart an uncertain course between the contractual and corporate models. Japan, like Germany, can be viewed as a coordinated market economy, so that the question of whether facilitating hostile bids would increase the productive efficiency of Japanese companies raises a wide range of difficult questions.

---

[129] M. Becht & C. Mayer, Introduction, in The Control of Corporate Europe Table 1.1 (F. Barca and M. Becht eds., 2001).

[130] Wolf-Georg Ringe, "Changing Law and Ownership Patterns in Germany: Corporate Governance and the Erosion of Deutschland AG", 63 Am. J. Comp. L. 493 (2015).

[131] See the discussion above at § 2.2.2.

Although the US occupying power after the Second World War sought to impose a highly deconcentrated shareholding structure in place of the family control which had prevailed pre-war, what resulted by the mid-1960s was not retail ownership of large Japanese companies but ownership by other corporations, insurance companies, and banks, in an elaborate pattern of cross-holdings with a "main bank" at the center. This made hostile takeovers difficult or even impossible to mount so long as the system of cross-holdings remained solid—though it is doubtful whether takeover protection was the primary driver of this development.[132] In fact, not only takeovers but external governance mechanisms in general were weak at this time. What developed instead was a system of internal governance, dominated by the interests of the employees. For core employees as a whole this development was symbolized by the emergence of lifetime employment contracts. For management, the system rewarded long and loyal service in an additional way. Top management was invariably appointed from the managers who had worked their way up through the company, and the chances of moving from a management position in one company to another in mid-career were limited. The board was an executive, not a monitoring, board. Having reached the top, the leading executives secured the loyalty of subordinate management by maximizing their opportunities for promotion within the company. This system has been called the "company community."[133]

The incentives generated by this arrangement were to increase steadily the size of Japanese public companies, but not necessarily their profitability. During the good times, which lasted until the 1990s, this tension was not normally apparent, for the success of Japanese public companies in global markets normally provided a satisfactory return to external investors, despite their limited governance powers. In those cases where there were idiosyncratic failings which internal management did not address, the main bank would intervene as a matter of last resort. From the 1990s onwards, three factors put this setup under pressure. The Japanese economy ground to a halt in the "lost decade"; given the opportunities provided by globalization Japanese banks became less willing to tie up capital in patient cross-holdings when that capital could be more profitably used in support of investment banking; and with the removal of restrictions on capital flows, foreign investors appeared on the Tokyo market in substantial quantities and with different expectations of external governance rights.[134]

Given these changes, attempts to revive and expand external governance mechanisms appeared in practice and moved center-stage in policy discussions. As for hostile takeovers, in the absence of a Japanese Takeover Code and Panel, disputes were handled by the ordinary courts on the basis of general corporate law, notably a "proper purpose" doctrine not dissimilar to the UK concept. As befits a coordinated market economy, however, an important role was also played by government guidelines, issue by the Ministry of Economy, Trade and Industry (METI), to which the courts paid attention, whilst the Tokyo Stock Exchange

---

[132] J. Franks, C. Mayer, & H. Miyajima, "The Ownership of Japanese Corporations in the 20th Century", 27 Rev. Fin. Stud. 2580 (2014) explain this development by reference to the need to finance Japanese industry during the crisis period of the 1950s and early 1960s in the absence of institutions which effectively protected the interests of retail investors.

[133] Zenichi Shishido "Reform in Japanese Corporate Law and Corporate Governance: Current Changes in Historical Perspective", 49 Am. J. Comp. Law 653 (2001).

[134] For a brief account see Armour, Jacobs, & Milhaupt, *supra* note 17, § II.C.1

sought to hold a balance between investors and issuers. As suggested, these only partially co-ordinated developments have not (yet) crystallized into a coherent set of rules.

The leading court decisions are consistent with a contractual approach. In the Livedoor case[135] the High Court disallowed defensive measures the shareholders had not approved, applying the proper purposes standard.[136] In Bulldog Sauce[137] the Supreme Court allowed discriminatory defensive measures which had been approved by the shareholders.[138] However, it would be wrong to interpret the Japanese rules as a simple "shareholders de-cide" approach. The METI guidelines of 2005 suggested that the maintenance of "corporate value" is the appropriate object of takeover defenses and "corporate value" is a concept not to be equated with shareholder value—although those guidelines suggested that the "rea-sonable will" of the shareholders was also an important element. The court decisions rec-ognize that the proper purposes doctrine allows defensive measures without shareholder approval against "abusive" takeovers (undefined). The Supreme Court in Bulldog Sauce seemed to attach less importance to shareholder approval of the measures than to its char-acterization of the takeover as abusive, apparently on the grounds that the bidder, a US ac-tivist hedge fund, had no clear plans for increasing the target's corporate value. To underline this point the study group, whose report had lain behind the METI guidelines, issued an-other report in 2008 pointing out that shareholder approval was not the sole criterion for legitimacy (whilst also saying that defensive measures should not be used to entrench in-cumbent management).[139] The TSE has played a moderating role, largely in the interests of investors. Whilst the METI guidelines state that rights plans are potentially legitimate, they also suggest that these should not normally discriminate among shareholders of the same class and should be subject to removal by shareholder vote. The TSE, however, used its power over listing conditions to encourage the adoption instead of what is in effect a board proced-ure for assessing the implications for corporate value of an acquirer of, for example, 20% of the voting rights, on the basis of which assessment rights might be issued.[140]

How these competing perspectives will be resolved will depend, it is suggested, on the more general evolution of corporate governance in Japan. The recent developments noted above indicate a greater role for external governance in Japan than in the latter part of the twentieth century. However, the role of the hostile takeover in that context is far from ob-vious. The hostile takeover carries potentially high costs in terms of undermining the in-ternal governance system which constitutes a major "path dependency" in that country. In other words, policy makers would have to be convinced, before they introduced a strong

---

[135] Tokyo High Court, Order, 23 March 2005; 1899 Hanrei Jiho 56.

[136] It was in principle unlawful to issue share options in order to dilute the position of a potential bidder and entrench current directors in office.

[137] Supreme Court, Aug. 7, 2007.

[138] In this case the defensive measures involved the compulsory squeezeout of the bidder at a very attractive price and so was a sort of "reverse greenmail." The shareholders' support for this rather extraordinary measure was probably a reflection of the fact that their interest in the company was not primarily financial.

[139] Corporate Value Study Group's Report on Takeover Defenses, 1968, available at http://www.dir.co.jp/english/souken/research/report/macro/mlothers/08072201mlothers.pdf.

[140] For more detail on the developments outlined in the paragraph see Curtis J. Milhaupt, Takeover Law and Managerial Incentives in the United States and Japan, in Enterprise Law: Contracts, Markets and Laws in the US and Japan ch. 9 (Z. Shushido ed., 2014).

system of external governance, that the switching costs from a predominantly internal to predominantly external form of governance would be less than the benefits to be obtained. They would also need to overcome the likely opposition from incumbents who would lose out from the switch (essentially the management of public companies). Thoughtful analysis by Japanese scholars tends toward the view that greater engagement (Japanese-style) between newly significant institutional shareholders and corporate management is the most likely development. In that context, hostile takeovers might come to play only a modest role.[141]

5 Conclusions

From the 1960s onwards takeovers have served up to interested spectators a never-ending, if somewhat episodic, spectacle combining drama and technical innovation of the highest order by clever lawyers and bankers, at least in the United States and United Kingdom. Consequently, there has been a tendency to analyze takeovers as an isolated phenomenon, which the contractual structure of the takeover offer somewhat encourages. However, the complex policy issues underlying the setting of the detailed rules on takeovers can be resolved only in the context of an analysis of the central features of the broader corporate governance arrangements in a particular jurisdiction. One obviously relevant feature is the level of shareholder concentration in a particular jurisdiction or company, though, as we noted in section 2.2, this does not mean that takeovers are relevant only in jurisdictions with highly dispersed patterns of shareholding.

More important, and more difficult to handle, is the relationship between takeover regulation and features of the governance system which are less easy to quantify. One can look at this relationship relatively narrowly, that is, as concerning only the interaction of the board/top management and the shareholders. It is trite to remark that in all jurisdictions board rules set both board authority and board accountability and that jurisdictions vary in the balance which is struck between these two desirable characteristics. Takeovers are a potentially powerful tool for encouraging accountability and so their facilitation sits more naturally in jurisdictions where accountability is highly regarded and the standard governance mechanisms for providing accountability may not function at low cost. The UK, with its dispersed shareholdings, is the exemplar here. In jurisdictions where the balance between authority and accountability has been struck traditionally more in favor of authority, some skepticism about the complete exclusion of management from the takeover decision is likely to be found, as in Delaware law. Delaware law also shows, however, the ability of the market (albeit at some cost) to "contract around" the initial allocation of decision-making power to

---

[141] Zenichi Shishido & Takaaki Eguchi, The Future of Japanese Corporate Governance: Internal Governance and the Development of Japanese-Style External Governance through Engagement in Research Handbook on Shareholder Power (Randall Thomas & Jennifer Hill eds., 2015). Some support for this view can be gained from the failure of activist hedge funds to establish a significant role in Japan. See John Buchanan, Dominic Heesang Chai and Simon Deakin, Hedge Fund Activism in Japan: The Limits of Shareholder Primacy (2012).

the board by adapting other features of the governance system (in this case, remuneration and board composition practices) so as to shape management's exercise of that power.

More broadly, takeovers can be looked at in the context of the governance system for providers of other inputs into the company, especially the employees. Systems that use mechanisms of corporate governance to regulate the process whereby a company contracts for labor as well as for equity capital are likely to find the unfettered takeover disruptive of those arrangements. This may lead, as in Germany, to an attempt to insert management firmly into the decision-making process on the takeover or, as in Japan, to uncertainty as to how takeovers should be regulated.

Finally, analysis should not be static. In all systems some movement toward alternative approaches is usually within contemplation, awaiting only the right set of events to trigger change. Japan shows this dynamic most openly. However, share deconcentration in Germany, the emphasis on engagement by shareholders in the UK, and the growing power of institutional shareholders in the US may have an impact on takeover regulation in those countries in the future. It is not inconceivable that UK institutions might want to be able to opt out of the "no frustration" rule in order to "engage" with shareholders, that US institutions might become powerful enough to block the routine adoption of plans, or that German institutions might want greater input into takeover defenses. Even with the growth of "activist" hedge funds,[142] which have stolen some of the governance thunder of hostile takeovers, takeover regulation looks likely to continue to be in a state of "becoming" rather than of having "arrived" at some final destination point.

---

[142] *Supra* note 29.

CHAPTER 22

··

MERGERS, ACQUISITIONS, AND RESTRUCTURING
Types, Regulation, and Patterns of Practice

··

JOHN C. COATES JR.[1]

1 INTRODUCTION

··

THE core goal of corporate law and governance is to improve outcomes for participants in businesses organized as corporations, and for society, relative to what could be achieved through contract, property, and other less "regulatory" bodies of law. One way that corporate law and governance achieves that goal is to regulate significant transactions—particularly mergers, acquisitions, and restructuring, with an eye toward the two core values served by fiduciary duty doctrines: to ensure care and loyalty on the part of corporate decision makers. This chapter considers ways in which M&A—which will be the chapter's shorthand for the general class of significant corporate transactions, including restructuring—is specially regulated, both within the formal body of corporate law and as that law interacts with other bodies of law, particularly securities (including listing standards), antitrust, industry-specific regulation, and regulations of cross-border transactions.

The chapter proceeds as follows. First, the concepts of "M&A" and "restructuring" are defined, and they are distinguished from other corporate transactions or activities. Second, major types of M&A transactions are briefly reviewed, using recent examples to illustrate the choices M&A participants have for effecting an M&A transaction. Third, the core goals of regulation are sketched[2]:

[1] John F. Cogan Professor of Law and Economics, Harvard Law School. Copyright John C. Coates Jr.; all rights reserved. Thanks for research assistance to Jason Wasser. For disclosure of financial interests potentially relevant to this chapter, see http://www.law.harvard.edu/faculty/COI/2013_Coates_John. html.

[2] The emphasis here is on how corporate law and governance go beyond background contract, tort, and property law in the M&A context. Important practical regularities in how those bodies of law are deployed in M&A—for example, contract clauses allocating risk, managing disputes, or redressing fraud—are neglected in this chapter, even though they are as important as the topics covered here. For more on those topics, see John C. Coates IV, "Managing Disputes Through Contract: Evidence from

1. To clarify authority and control over M&A by corporate decision makers;
2. To reduce transaction costs and overcome collective action problems;
3. To constrain and improve outcomes of conflict-of-interest transactions;
4. To protect dispersed owners of public companies;
5. To deter or mitigate looting, asset-stripping and excessive M&A-related leverage; and
6. To cope with the side effects of other regulations.

In addition to these corporate law or governance related goals, M&A transactions face special treatment under other bodies of law (antitrust, industry-based regulation, regulation of foreign ownership of business, and tax) that sometimes interact with corporate law and governance, and the goals of these laws as applied to M&A are also briefly reviewed. Fourth, the modes of regulation are summarized, dividing laws or regulations into those that constrain M&A transactions and those that facilitate them. Fifth and finally, empirical research is summarized to present the different types of transactions that are actually chosen and (where available) what effects the laws that apply to them have in the world's two largest M&A markets (the US and the UK) and (as a contrasting example, and more selectively, given data limitations) in a developing nation (India), which now accounts for ~4% of global M&A. Throughout, the chapter notes similarities and differences of the choices and modes of regulation across transaction types and countries.

The chapter concludes with more general observations about what these variations in types and modes imply. Some differences, for example, seem to reflect longstanding differences in deep structural features of the markets (such as ownership structure). But other differences seem to reflect the way that (as in chaotic systems) seemingly small differences in starting conditions can ramify and persist in the face of otherwise generally similar conditions and strong market pressures. Minor variations in similar laws with similar goals in similar legal systems, in other words, can have real effects on the amount and nature of economic activity.

2 TERMINOLOGY AND SCOPE: WHAT ARE M&A AND RESTRUCTURING TRANSACTIONS?

The concepts "mergers and acquisitions" (M&A) and "restructuring" are primarily used as business terms, not as legal terms of art. They are not sharply defined, instead referring to fuzzy sets of similar transactions. As commonly understood by practitioners and used in this chapter, the core of M&A is a deliberate transfer of control and ownership of a business

M&A", 2 Harv. Bus. Rev. 301 (2012); "Evidence-based M&A: Less Can Be More When Allocating Risk in Deal Contracts", 27 J. Int'l., Banking, Fin. & L. 708 (2012); and Contracting to Lie: A Discussion of Abry Partners v. F & W Acquisition (Del.Ch. 2006), Legalworks 22nd Annual Mergers & Acquisitions Institute (May 17, 2006), available at http://bit.ly/Ut7dum. Also not addressed are insolvency and bankruptcy laws, which often have important effects on restructuring transactions, and M&A conducted by insolvent companies.

organized in one or more corporations.[3] "Restructuring" is a deliberate, significant and unusual alteration in the organization and operations of a business, commonly in times of financial or operational distress, typically accompanied by changes in ownership or finance, as when a company merges two divisions, or sells off a business unit.

M&A and restructuring commonly occur together, and can bleed into one another, as well as other, unusual but less dramatic business decisions: bulk sales of inventory, organic growth through advertising campaigns, office closures, layoffs, and so on. M&A differs from those events, and from restructuring, in that M&A typically refers to the transfer of control of a business as an entirety, even if the buyer may consequently choose to restructure the target or itself. Restructuring differs from ordinary business events in that it is more significant, disruptive of prior operations and strategy, and not part of ongoing or routine business activity. M&A and restructuring are commonly accompanied by changes or transactions in capital (borrowing, buybacks, stock sales, etc.), either as part of the transactions or in parallel, but differ in that they change fundamental business operations and not purely finance.

M&A and restructuring are the most important transactions an incorporated business can undertake, rivaled only by initial organization or liquidation. The combination of change on multiple dimensions with deliberation and importance gives these transactions their characteristic drama and complexity. Their importance and complexity also makes them challenging for corporate law and governance.

Characteristically, M&A transactions involve a purchaser or buyer and a seller. The business being transferred is commonly called the "target," which may be separately incorporated, or may consist of an operating unit or division—a collection of assets, employees, relationships, etc.—owned along with other businesses by a single entity. In some M&A transactions, however, there is no clear purchaser or seller—two companies combine their assets in what is commonly called a merger of equals.[4]

3 What Are the Major Types of M&A Transactions?

M&A transactions fall into a variety of types. A standard typology focuses on the legal nature of the transaction, dividing M&A into asset purchases, stock purchases, and mergers (or schemes of arrangement). The most primitive M&A transaction consists simply of the purchase of all of the assets used in (and so control over) a business. Where the target sells all of its assets, it typically then liquidates or otherwise distributes the price paid to its owners. (Something must also be done about the target's liabilities, of course; the buyer may assume them, or they may be paid in the target's liquidation, or they may be maintained in force if the target retains the price paid for its assets, or some combination.) In May 2007, for example,

---

[3] Throughout, the chapter refers to "corporations" as a stand-in for the various types of corporate entities, including partnerships.

[4] Julie Wulf, "Do CEOs in Mergers Trade Power for Premium? Evidence from 'Mergers of Equals'", 20 J. L. Econ. & Org. 60–101 (2004) (analyzing such transactions).

iStar Financial purchased Freemont Investment's commercial real estate mortgage lending business, and the parties structured their deal as a purchase of assets for $1.9 billion in cash, with liabilities of the target divided between the buyer and seller.[5]

Where target assets are extensive, complex, or hard to specify, or their transfer is subject to regulatory requirements, or contract consents—think of the purchase of the individual assets of a company such as Barclays or Citigroup—asset purchases can be cumbersome, time-consuming, and lengthy. The corporate form creates a simple, and often vastly simpler, alternative: a buyer can purchase all of the stock (and thus control) of the corporation that owns a business, rather than its assets. AT&T's attempted acquisition of T-Mobile from Deutsche Telekom in 2011 was structured as a stock purchase.[6]

In India, stock purchases represent the dominant type of M&A transaction, followed by asset purchases, because ownership is typically concentrated in the hands of a single or small number of related shareholders, even when a target company is listed. In the five-year period ending 2008, for example, the average stake transferred in a domestic Indian M&A deal was only 53%, and in cross-border deals, involving a foreign bidder, only 16% of deals involved a 100% acquisition—a feature of the Indian M&A market partly explained by India's extensive regulation of foreign ownership of Indian companies, discussed more below. Examples of partial in-bound acquisitions include Vodafone's acquisition of 67% of Hutchison and Vedanta's acquisition of 59% of Cairn India.

When a target corporation has more than a small number of shareholders and the goal of the buyer is to obtain 100% ownership, stock purchases begin to increase transaction costs, making a simpler method of purchasing ownership more attractive. In the US, this is accomplished through the use of statutorily authorized mergers. Other statutory mechanisms exist in the US—consolidations, mandatory share exchanges, etc.—but mergers are the most straightforward and by operation of law result in the transfer of assets of one corporation to another, without the need to specify or purchase individual assets, and through which all owners have their stock converted into an agreed-upon form of "currency" or deal consideration (cash, stock of the buyer, etc.).

Commonly, it is desirable for purchasers to create new subsidiary corporations to carry out an acquisition. If done by merger, the resulting "triangle" of companies (parent/buyer, acquisition subsidiary, and target company) is described as having engaged in a "triangular" merger (target into subsidiary being called "forward" and the reverse being called "reverse"). AT&T's May 2014 agreement to buy DirecTV is structured as a forward triangular merger[7]; Comcast's February 2014 agreement to buy Time Warner Cable is structured as a reverse triangular merger.[8]

In the UK and India, a similar result can be obtained through what is termed a scheme of arrangement. Vodafone's April 2012 offer for Cable & Wireless was effected as a scheme of arrangement[9]; an example from India is the combination of Centurion Bank with HDFC Bank in 2008.[10] More commonly in the UK (and to a lesser extent in the US), a purchaser can achieve a similar result by making a public bid (or tender offer) for the target's stock—that is, to use the tools of mass communication to offer to buy stock of multiple shares

---

[5] http://1.usa.gov/1roU57G.   [6] http://1.usa.gov/1oShgDg.

[7] http://1.usa.gov/1nApnqH.   [8] http://1.usa.gov/1mQipKJ.   [9] http://bit.ly/1o67v3o.

[10] http://1.usa.gov/1ixfh2o.

simultaneously, at a set price with a specified currency. This enables the stock purchase to occur more cheaply than could be done through individual shareholder-by-shareholder purchases. Kraft's January 2010 acquisition for Cadbury was structured as a bid.[11]

In a bid or tender offer, some shareholders may not tender, either because they (sincerely or strategically) choose to "hold out" for a higher price, or because they may not be aware of the offer (despite the bidder's best efforts at publicity) or even that they own the relevant stock (suppose the shareholder has a diversified portfolio and is traveling or busy and has failed to delegate authority over her stock dealings to a responsible agent). In that case, some statutorily authorized transaction—a freezeout or squeezeout, as they are often called—amounting economically to the equivalent of a call option on the stock may be necessary to convey 100% ownership of the target (and its businesses). The transaction thus consists of two formal steps—bid plus squeezeout—that produce the same result as a reverse triangular merger or scheme of arrangement.[12] Another step that might precede or fall between those steps is an initial stock purchase by the buyer from the target, or from selling shareholders of the target. Freezeouts also sometimes occur outside the context of an arm's-length acquisition, as when a controlling shareholder or parent company freezes out a minority stake in a controlled public subsidiary, generally pursuant to a single-step merger.[13] The freezeout of public investors in Levi-Strauss in 1996 by the Haas family is an example.[14]

In addition to these basic types of M&A transactions, there are other types, less common but not uncommon. In a spin-off, ownership interests in one business are distributed to shareholders of a company that retains other businesses, resulting in a transfer of effective control to a newly constituted board and management of the "spinco," and transfer of ownership to the shareholders of the spinning corporation—followed typically by a divergence over time in the ownership of the two companies. Alternatively, a company can place one business in a corporation and sell its stock to the public for cash. Or these can be combined, with an initial carve-out followed by a spin-off. More complexity is possible and not uncommon. A new company can be created, along with two subsidiaries, and each of two separate companies can merge with each subsidiary (a top-hat or double dummy structure).[15] It is possible to combine three separate businesses at once in a new single enterprise, through a combination of the above simple legal types, or to transfer control and ownership of one company followed immediately by a further resale, spin-off, or carve-out (or both) of one of that company's businesses.

---

[11] http://bit.ly/1klM36a.

[12] Id. ("Kraft Foods is today commencing the procedure under Chapter 3 of Part 28 of the 2006 Act to acquire compulsorily all of the outstanding Cadbury Shares . . . which it does not already hold or has not already acquired contracted to acquire or in respect of which it has not already received valid acceptances"); http://1.usa.gov/1nwPtYF (Amgen tender offer document dated September 3, 2013 describing agreement with target Onyx Pharmaceuticals, Inc. pursuant to which Amgen would acquire 50% of Onyx's shares in the tender offer, followed by a freezeout merger to acquire the remaining shares).

[13] E.g., http://1.usa.gov/1pjcRfi (Form 8-K filed by PepsiCo. announcing freezeout mergers between it and two controlled public subsidiaries) (last visited June 9, 2014).

[14] http://1.usa.gov/SkxYiM (SEC filing describing Levi-Strauss transaction).

[15] In the acquisition of NYSE Euronext by IntercontinentalExchange in 2013, such a structure was provided for as an alternative to the initial structure, to be used if certain conditions were not met. http://1.usa.gov/1pESZjA.

Larger businesses are not typically organized as single companies, but as holding companies with multiple subsidiaries in multiple layers. (Morgan Stanley has ~2,800 subsidiaries, for example, and is not the most complex financial institution in the world.[16]) As a result, it is common for the buyer in an M&A transaction to want—after the initial "main" transaction—to move pieces of the target's business (often in multiple subsidiaries) into multiple subsidiaries of the purchaser, so as to achieve economies, avoid or reduce the costs of regulation, or for other reasons. As a result, the overall M&A transaction may take many steps. In Bank of America's acquisition of Countrywide, it used an initial forward triangular merger, followed by at least three sets of major stock or asset purchases at the subsidiary level, taking place over more than a year.[17]

M&A transactions also use a variety of types of currencies or forms of consideration. Cash is common, as is stock of the buyer. Buyers can also "pay" the target's owners with their own debt, i.e., promise to pay cash later—something commonly referred to as "seller financing," or by exchanging assets for assets, or by assuming debt of the target or the seller. Forms of currency can be mixed, as in a one-step fixed blend (e.g., 50% cash, 50% stock), or by using all cash in one step, followed by all stock in a second step, or by offering target shareholders a choice, perhaps constrained by specified limits.[18] If non-cash is used and the transaction involves delay between the moment the parties agree upon a price and the completion of the transaction, the value of the non-cash currency can fluctuate or can be fixed by contract. Deal currency is a separate choice from the legal form of the transaction—so asset purchases can be for cash or stock, as can stock purchases, mergers, and bids.

A final way to break down M&A transactions by type is by the nature of the parties or financing for the deal. Targets and buyers alike can have a single or small set of shareholders—private companies—or dispersed owners with stock listed on an exchange—public companies.[19] Buyers can have existing businesses—strategic buyers— or may be newly formed solely to carry out the transaction, typically raising the price of the deal by issuing equity to a sponsor (such as a private equity fund) and debt to banks or investors in the leveraged loan market, sometimes combined with sales of bonds or preferred stock—financial buyers. Acquisitions by financial buyers are commonly called "buyouts," and where newly issued debt is used to generate the currency used in the deal, the buyouts are called leveraged buyouts or LBOs. Where the seller is also a private equity fund, the deal is commonly referred to as a secondary buyout; where the seller is a company with other businesses, a buyout of one its divisions or subsidiaries is commonly referred to as a divisional buyout.

---

[16] Dafna Avraham, Patricia Selvaggi, & James Vickery, "A Structural View of U.S. Bank Holding Companies" FRBNY Economic Policy Review 65 (2012).

[17] *MBIA Ins. Corp. v. Countrywide Home Loans, Inc., et al.*, 936 N.Y.S.2d 513 (N.Y. Sup. Ct. 2012). Readers should be aware that the author was a testifying witness on behalf of MBIA in the MBIA case.

[18] E.g. http://1.usa.gov/1pjcRfi (PepsiCo. freezeout merger agreements offering controlled public subsidiary shareholders choice of stock or cash subject to aggregate limits); see Wachtell, Lipton, Rosen, & Katz, "Takeover Law and Practice", 1–156, 77–81 (Mar. 2014), available at http://bit.ly/1u4P8wY (discussing mixed consideration alternatives).

[19] For general discussion of the many ways in which M&A varies across ownership of target companies, see John C. Coates, The Powerful and Pervasive Effects of Ownership on M&A, Olin Center Discussion Paper No. 669 (June 2010), available at papers.ssrn.com/sol3/papers.cfm?abstractid=1544500.

A final observation about deal types: many economically identical (or highly similar) M&A transactions can be accomplished through more than one combination of legal components. One-step mergers are similar to tender offers followed by freezeouts. A cash bid can achieve much the same effect as a stock-for-stock merger coupled with a buyback of shares. A leveraged buyout is similar to a buyout funded with cash on hand, followed by new borrowings to replace the cash. A purchase of all assets plus target liquidation can produce economically equivalent results as a merger. And so on. This fact can make it hard to regulate M&A transaction effectively through simple, clear rules. Coupled with differences in legal treatment of different forms of M&A transaction, the economic similarity of different transaction forms can also make it hard for conventional doctrinal analysis to rationalize fully, or even to identify adequately the goals served by, every feature of M&A law and regulation.

4 What Roles Exist for Regulation of M&A Transactions?

Let us turn to the goals of regulation of M&A transactions. Within the traditional scope of corporate law, three major regulatory goals pertaining to M&A exist: (1) to enhance and clarify authority and control over a corporation as applied to M&A, setting baseline entitlements to participate in related decision making; (2) to facilitate M&A by overcoming collective action problems and transaction costs; (3) to constrain and improve the outcomes associated with conflicts of interest; and (4) to deter or mitigate looting, asset-stripping, and excessive M&A-related leverage. If the owners of a party are dispersed, an additional goal of M&A law is (5) to protect those owners, a goal that sometimes overlaps or extends into the domain of securities regulation and listing standards. As discussed below, a major "mode" or method of regulation of M&A is to impose approval and disclosure requirements—and where owners are dispersed, these requirements have important side effects on M&A process and outcomes, so that another goal of M&A regulatory design is (6) to cope with those side effects. Finally, other bodies of law apply specially to M&A, and while not within the scope of corporate law and governance as generally understood today, those bodies of law interact with corporate law and governance sufficiently that they must be taken into account as well.

The material in this section is not meant to present a comprehensive list of all possible justifications for regulation of M&A, nor is it meant to justify regulation overall or in any given instance. Rather, the justifications that are commonly offered for (or common rationalizations of) major types of actual regulation (discussed more below) are presented, with only passing reference to costs or unintended consequences of regulation. This choice of presentation reflects not a naïve embrace of the nirvana fallacy. Many efforts to regulate M&A fail for the reason already noted above (i.e., that M&A can sometimes be structured in many different ways, sometimes so as to successfully evade a given law or regulation), and all regulatory efforts impose at least some costs. Instead, the material simply reflects standard arguments for entrenched modes of regulation, which all those who are interested in M&A contend with, whether in designing deals, complying with law, or proposing reforms to M&A regulation.

4.1 Enhancing and Clarifying Authority, Control, and Baseline Entitlements

An important function of corporate law is to establish "default" or baseline entitlements to control over a corporation. Even if no one set of entitlements is best in all settings, a clear baseline economizes on contracting costs. Because M&A transactions are so fundamental and significant, and have potentially dramatic effects on the value of a company (and therefore on common stock), it is natural to set a baseline right for common shareholders to participate in the decision whether to engage in an M&A transaction. This is particularly likely when an M&A transaction involves either (1) a sale or liquidation of a company (as when all of a target's assets are purchased for cash) or (2) an acquisition in which the buyer issues a significant amount of equity. (If an M&A transaction is structured as a stock purchase, a role for shareholders emerges from contract and property; but if the transaction is structured in other ways, or if statutes provide overrides (as in a merger or squeezeout), it does not.)

However, because M&A is not a clearly defined category—as discussed above—and bleeds into routine transactions, it is hard to map shareholder participation onto all M&A transactions, without sweeping in many transactions for which shareholder governance would not be efficient as a baseline. (Shareholders can obtain or broaden such governance rights by contract, such as a voting or shareholders agreement.) Dividing M&A into subsets where shareholder governance is usefully required and where it is not, then, is one role for corporate law.

In addition, M&A creates opportunities and incentives for corporate decision makers (boards, officers, employees) to conflict with one another (and with shareholders) over whether, when, and how to engage in such transactions, and for some to pursue transactions without actual authority. Even if each agent or decision maker is free of a personal conflict of interest, the dramatic nature of a change in control and ownership, or of a significant and abnormal shock to normal operations, may lead agents to deviate from normal corporate practices. For example, one officer may in good faith pursue a transaction and agree to negotiate exclusively with one potential counterparty, only to have other officers, or the board, disagree with this method of pursuing a transaction and try to stop the deal. An M&A transaction can involve contracts that commit a company to take on operations (perhaps at a subsidiary of a target) that are not subject to adequate controls, and can thus undermine the control authorized corporate decision makers customarily have over a company or its assets.

Corporate law clarifies who decides, and how, and who will have control and responsibility over the combined company after the deal. Because of M&A's significance, and because corporate actors and third parties alike often have a greater need to rely on the fact of appropriate authorization in an M&A context, corporate law typically imposes explicit or implicit requirements on M&A that differ from those applicable to more ordinary business decisions. For example, when does a corporate officer need to notify or obtain explicit authority from the board to sell a business, or enter into a contract to buy one, or sell a potentially controlling block of stock?[20] If shareholder approval is required, what vote is required, and through what mechanism? If not, are disclosures to shareholders required, and if so,

---

[20] *Jennings v. Pittsburgh Mercantile Co.*, 202 A.2d 51 (Pa. 1964) (officer did not have apparent authority to enter into a sale/leaseback transaction of all of company's real estate); *Grimes v. Alteon, Inc.*, 804 A.2d 256 (Del. 2002) (chief executive officer did not have authority to bind the company to a promise to sell 10% of any new stock to an existing shareholder, without board authorization).

when? These aspects of M&A-related laws can be understood as (efficiently) communicating to all concerned a clear set of default procedures for authorization of M&A transactions.

4.2 To Facilitate M&A by Overcoming Collective Action Problems and Transaction Costs

A second goal of M&A law is to facilitate M&A transactions. As noted above, asset purchases can generate extensive transaction costs under background conditions of property and contract law, which can prevent the transfer of control and ownership of business and so reduce social welfare. If a large bank had to obtain consent from each borrower to transfer each of its loans to a buyer, the costs might overwhelm the benefits from the sale, even if the buyer could efficiently combine the target's operations with its own. The structure of corporate law—which permits control and ownership of a collection of assets to be transferred via purchase of stock—facilitates M&A. However, even stock purchases can generate non-trivial transaction costs if ownership is dispersed. While technology (mass communication) has overcome some of these costs, collective action problems may impede M&A under certain circumstances. If an M&A transaction requires individual consents from dispersed shareholders, each shareholder may have an economic incentive to hold out in an attempt to remain an equity owner of a business whose value will be enhanced by the bidder after the transaction; if each shareholder has that incentive, then none may sell, preventing value-increasing transactions from occurring.[21] Law can overcome those incentives by providing mechanisms to force target shareholders to accept a proposed M&A transaction under specified circumstances, as in a merger, scheme of arrangement, or squeezeout.

4.3 To Constrain Conflicts of Interest

A more controversial set of legal constraints on M&A is designed to constrain or improve the outcomes of conflicts of interest that arise in the M&A context. Such conflicts can take a variety of forms, some obvious, some less so. In a management buyout or MBO, officer-fiduciaries of the target participate as owners of the buyer, and so face a clear conflict.[22] In a freezeout of minority investors by a controlling shareholder or parent company, again, the conflict is clear.[23] A controlling shareholder may cause two controlled subsidiaries to merge, or one to acquire the other, and if one of the subsidiaries is wholly owned while the other is not, the transaction's terms may be designed to favor the wholly owned over the partly owned subsidiary.[24] Absent legal protections, management or the control shareholder would

---

[21] Michael Bradley, "Interfirm Tender Offers and the Market for Corporate Control", 53 J. Bus. 345–76 (1980); Sanford J. Grossman and Oliver D. Hart, "Takeover Bids, the Free-Rider Problem, and the Theory of the Corporation", 11 Bell J. Econ. 42–64 (1980).

[22] E.g., *Mills Acquisition Co. v. MacMillan, Inc.*, 559 A.2d 1261 (Del. 1989).

[23] E.g., *In re Cox Communications Inc. Shareholders Litigation*, 879 A.2d 604 (Del. Ch. 2005); *Kahn v. M&F Worldwide Corp.*, 88 A.3d 635 (Del. 2014).

[24] E.g., *In re Southern Peru Copper Corp. Shareholder Derivative Litigation*, 52 A.3d 761 (Del. Ch. 2011).

be tempted to offer an unfairly low price; investors, anticipating this, would refuse to invest, or would impose a severe discount on the value they would place on the shares. Since investors would not know in advance when such a conflict transaction might occur, the cost of capital would be higher for all firms. In a hypothetical bargain designed to maximize the joint gain to both the conflicted party and investors, the parties would agree to some degree of legal protection, and corporate law can economize on bargaining costs by imposing such protections as a default.[25]

Other conflicts are less direct but clear and significant. Fiduciaries may propose a spin-off in which they are given the right to buy a controlling stake.[26] A fiduciary may sell a public company to an arm's-length buyer but simultaneously engage in negotiations to buy back part of the public company from the buyer.[27] A control shareholder who also serves as a fiduciary may divert an opportunity to sell the company as a whole by offering to sell a control block in lieu of the whole-company transaction.[28]

Still other conflicts are real but may not be as stark. Fiduciaries may favor one bidder over another, not in return for an explicit quid pro quo (e.g., in the form of a payment) but to curry goodwill in the hope of obtaining post-deal employment, or perhaps out of malice toward a bidder or gratitude for some past favor. Fiduciaries may prefer one set of transaction-related agents (investment bankers, lawyers, lenders) for the same kinds of reasons. Those agents may have incentives distorted if they own equity in a party with interests opposed to their client.[29] Fiduciaries may seek to sell their company "too early" or "too cheaply" to trigger "golden parachutes" or vesting under option plans or retirement plans, or in return for benefits from the buyer.[30] Fiduciaries of a target may have business or social ties to a buyer.[31]

Conflicts can exist at the shareholder level (between control and minority shareholders), between shareholders and the board, among board members, between the board and officers, and between officers and the company. The range of potential conflicts created by an M&A transaction is enormous—and the opportunity to hide payoffs or benefits from the transactions is generally larger than is true in the ordinary course of corporate decision

---

[25] John C. Coates IV, "'Fair Value' as a Default Rule of Corporate Law: Minority Discounts in Conflict Transactions", 147 U. Penn. L. Rev. 1251 (1999).

[26] E.g., *Robert M. Bass Group, Inc. v. Edward P. Evans, et al.*, 552 A.2d 1227 (Del. Ch. 1988).

[27] E.g., Steven Bertoni, Carl Icahn Attacks Ebay, Marc Andreessen, & Scott Cook, Shareholder Letter, Forbes (Jan. 24, 2014), http://onforb.es/1dBt8FD; see also *In re El Paso Corp. Shareholder Litigation*, 41 A.3d 432 (Del. Ch. 2012).

[28] E.g., *Thorpe v. CERBCO, Inc.*, 676 A.2d 436 (Del. 1996).

[29] E.g., *In re El Paso Corp. Shareholder Litigation*, 41 A.3d 432 (Del. Ch. 2012); see also John C. Coates, Clayton Rose, & David Lane, El Paso's Sale to Kinder Morgan, HLS 13–08 (July 25, 2012), available at casestudies.law.harvard.edu/el-pasos-sale-to-kinder-morgan.

[30] E.g., *Smith v. Van Gorkom*, 488 A.2d 858 (Del. 2012); John C. Coates, Clayton Rose, & David Lane, Barclays Capital and the Sale of Del Monte Foods, HLS 13–07 (July 27, 2012), available at casestudies.law.harvard.edu/barclays-capital-and-the-sale-of-del-monte-foods/.

[31] E.g., *Cinerama, Inc. v. Technicolor, Inc.*, 663 A.2d 1156 (Del. 1995) (holding merger satisfied fairness standard where majority of board of directors was disinterested and two directors who were interested disclosed); see also *Orman v. Cullman*, 794 A.2d 5 (Del. Ch. 2002) (independent directors not found "beholden" conflicted fiduciary simply because of longstanding business relations or co-service as directors).

making. In all of these circumstances, corporate law and governance may be able to improve on outcomes for shareholders by constraining the process or nature of the transaction.

4.4 To Protect Dispersed Owners

Corporate law (and closely related securities regulations) can also protect the interests of dispersed owners in the M&A context. Where an M&A transaction requires shareholder approval or consent, law can usefully specify what information and process needs to be followed to obtain that approval (particularly how long shareholders must be given to consider whether to approve). The information required and process to be followed may differ if the shareholders are dispersed, and so likely to be less informed, to be able to protect their own interests, or to act quickly than a small number of owners. Because bids can be structured to have a coercive effect on dispersed shareholders—the reverse of the collective action problem discussed above—dispersed shareholders may need protection even when they are informed, active, and sophisticated.[32] Even where a transaction does not require (as a baseline entitlement) shareholder approval, dispersed shareholders may still need information to decide whether they should use other legal rights (e.g., through normal voting rights to elect directors, or the right to sue in response to conflicts of interest). Without specific approval rights, moreover, shareholders may suffer the effects of M&A before they can mobilize to protect their interests with normal voting rights or other governance mechanisms. This risk seems more acute for bidders, whose value may be destroyed by poorly conceived acquisitions, than for targets, which generally attract bids at prices over market prices.

4.5 To Deter or Mitigate Looting, Asset-Stripping, and Excessive M&A-Related Leverage

Particular risks toward which M&A law may be directed include the risk of looting, asset-stripping, or excessive leverage from debt-financed M&A. Looting here means theft or clear violation of fiduciary duties or other legal obligations (arising under contract, tort, property, or other bodies of law) resulting in a transfer of value from a company to a person in control of the company. Looting harms not just shareholders, but also creditors, employees, and others who depend on the continued functioning of the business. Looting is by definition already made illegal by non-M&A law. But because M&A results in a change of control, it can increase the risk of looting, and M&A-related duties may enhance the effectiveness of such laws, such as the imposition of a duty of care on decision makers who are selling not to sell to a person with a reputation as a looter.

A similar potential result of M&A is asset stripping. Asset stripping is the transfer out of a business (often via M&A) of value (as in a transaction at an unfair price), or of revenue or earnings-generating assets of a company. Even if those transfers are at a fair price, they may insure that certain creditors will not be paid, while others (and perhaps shareholders,

---

[32] E.g., Lucian Bebchuk, "The Case Against Board Veto in Corporate Takeovers", 69 U. Chi. L. Rev. 973 (2002).

too) obtain value from the transaction or the company, in violation of normal payment priorities.[33] The result is that the company is left insolvent (immediately or over time, as contingent liabilities are realized), and with non-operating assets that are incapable of generating growth or future revenues or earnings. Asset stripping includes conduct that verges on or in fact may constitute fraud in contexts where complexities associated with valuation and proof of intent[34] may make fraud claims grounded in tort or other doctrines difficult or impossible. Asset stripping can also result in what would (in an insolvency or bankruptcy proceeding) be treated as preferential payments, and sometimes also involves transactions implicating conflicts of interest (where for example insiders or control persons are the recipients or beneficiaries of the transfers).

Where a target has only one shareholder after an M&A transaction, as when a private company is the buyer, the result of asset stripping is to harm creditors. Where a target continues to have dispersed owners after control has passed, it may also harm shareholders. Where value is itself taken, the harm of asset stripping is clear. Where revenue or earnings-generating potential is taken (but value is not clearly reduced), the harm is not direct, but flows from the reduction (or, in the limit, elimination) of the possibility that a target business nearing insolvency may recover, by virtue of having an uncertain future expected value reduced to a certain or near-certain insolvency or by virtue of having residual assets distributed in a non-pro rata fashion (the anticipation of which can reduce the value of all firms potentially subject to this technique).

As with looting, other laws of general application—rules about dividends (actual or constructive), fraudulent conveyance, theft, fiduciary duties, fraud, or preferential payments— may constrain asset stripping. However, it is a common risk for corporate claimants in the M&A context, and can be amplified by M&A, due to the transfer of control and the ability of an M&A participant to camouflage asset stripping with the pretext of ordinary post-deal consolidation or restructuring. The difficulties of proof and enforcement may justify tighter legal constraints in the M&A context, absent which M&A may be induced by the possibility of successful asset stripping.

A final if less extreme example—and therefore one that generates more public policy debate over whether it should be regulated—is the incurrence of excessive debt as a result of an M&A transaction. Even if assets are not removed, M&A that is funded by new debt, or for which debt is part of the deal currency, the target (or bidder) may be left with more debt than it can repay. This is most likely to be true if the surviving company already had significant debt in place prior to the M&A transaction, such that the related creditors were not (at the time of the transaction) able to price the risk of insolvency arising from the increased debt.

Contract creditors can (in theory[35]) demand covenants to prevent, or a price that reflects, the risk of M&A-related increases in debt, as well as asset stripping. Tort creditors cannot do

---

[33] Cf., e.g., *MBIA Ins. Corp. supra* note 17 (refusing to grant motion for summary judgment on a claim alleging de facto merger under New York law based on same transaction, also finding no meaningful conflict between Delaware and New York law on question) with *MBIA Insurance Corp. v. Countrywide Financial Corp.*, N.Y. Supr. Ct. (Apr. 29, 2013); *In re Countrywide Financial Corp. Securities Litigation*, 588 F.Supp.2d 1132 (C.D. Cal. 2008) (granting motion for summary judgment against claim alleging de facto merger under Delaware law).

[34] PLSRA § 21D(b)(2); FRCP Rule 9(b).

[35] David Musto & Jillian Popadak, "The Pricing of Bond Covenants", Working Paper (2014) document that change-of-control covenants re-emerged in the buyout wave of the 2000s, but only after it was too late to protect lenders or other creditors affected by those buyouts.

so, however, nor (due to transaction costs) can employees, many kinds of contract counterparties (e.g., with warranty claims), or other third parties that may be affected by a resulting
insolvency. Laws aimed at preventing sudden and excessive M&A-related increases in debt
may protect these parties. Even contract creditors (such as banks) may lack appropriate
incentives to prevent excessive risk, due to moral hazard or internal agency problems, and
tax laws may induce levels of debt that are excessive relative to what would otherwise be socially optimal. Transaction costs may also be reduced if law sets baseline restrictions on excessive debt for the benefit of contract creditors (who then do not need to contract for those
restrictions). Regulatory strategies aimed primarily to prevent systemic risk or tax-induced
speculative excess may include restrictions on debt-financed M&A.

4.6 To Cope with the Effects of Other Regulations

All of the laws justified by the foregoing rules are likely to produce unintended and sometimes pernicious consequences, given the difficulties of enforcement and achieving precise, targeted goals through general laws. For example, a rule facilitating M&A by allowing
shareholders to be forced to accept transaction via statutory merger or squeezeout mechanism may make inefficient transactions easier for a conflicted fiduciary to pursue.
Disclosure obligations may chill bids. Constraints on conflicts of interest may make efficient
transactions less likely. Shareholder approval requirements may create opportunities for
third parties to compete for a target during the shareholder approval period. Private actors
may attempt to respond to these consequences in ways that either undermine the purpose
of the laws or create additional problems. For example, private contract can mitigate the risk
of post-announcement bid competition (e.g., through break fees), which thereby undermine the shareholder approval or consent requirement that creates the risk of competition.
Fiduciary obligations to obtain the best reasonably available price may lead targets to insist
upon "no-shop" or "go-shop" clauses in M&A contracts.[36]

Another, second-order role for corporate law, then, is to mitigate unintended
consequences and private responses to first-order corporate laws. Specialized courts, regulatory agencies, or other means to address evasions and enforce laws governing M&A can
be understood in this way, as can a variety of laws and regulations focused on the process of
approving an M&A transaction as well as a variety of exemptions from otherwise applicable
M&A-related requirements. First-order structural laws are (almost by definition) important, so much so that they are taken for granted by practitioners. For instance, it would not
occur to most M&A lawyers (or judges, for that matter) to ask whether shareholders should
have any role in approving the liquidation of their investment in an M&A transaction. The
nuances of second-order laws that mitigate the effects of first-order laws, by contrast, can
be of first-order practical importance, as they are more likely to be modified by lawmakers
(such as judges) and be affected by choices of transaction participants and their lawyers.

---

[36] Guhan Subramanian, "Go-Shops vs. No-Shops in Private Equity Deals: Evidence and Implications",
63 Bus. Law. 739 (2008); *In re The Topps Co. 12 Shareholders Litig.*, 926 A.2d 58 (Del. Ch. 2007) (permitting
a board to undertake a post-signing 'go shop' period rather than a full auction process).

4.7 Antitrust, Industry Regulation, Foreign Ownership, and Tax

Finally, M&A implicates a variety of third party or social interests. M&A is a fast way to achieve monopoly power, and is typically regulated separately under general antitrust laws to prevent or remediate such power.[37] Industry-based regulations (e.g., banking, airlines, telecommunications, utilities) are often aimed at preserving or stabilizing firms that produce public goods (systems of payment, communication, transportation, or energy production) that are vital to society and the economy. One means to prevent private interference with those systems often includes rules specifying who may obtain control over companies in those industries, and M&A is often regulated specially in those industries.[38] Foreign ownership of domestic business can raise political concerns that range from the cross-culturally intuitive to the less so—e.g., in the defense, yogurt, or tea industries—and so cross-border M&A is often regulated specially.[39] M&A can be a way for owners to liquidate or realize cash from profits built up in a business, and in most income tax regimes, tax is typically

[37] E.g., Hart-Scott-Rodino Antitrust Improvements Act of 1976 § 5 (prohibiting mergers and acquisitions that constitute "unfair . . . competition"); Clayton Act of 1914 § 7 (prohibiting the acquisition of stock or assets where "the effect of such acquisition may be substantially to lessen competition, or to tend to create monopoly"); Federal Trade Commission Act of 1914 § 5 (declaring "unfair methods of competition in or affecting commerce, and unfair or deceptive acts or practices in or affecting commerce . . . unlawful").

[38] See, e.g., Bank Holding Company Act of 1956 § 1972; Airline Deregulation Act of 1978; William Gillespie and Oliver M. Richard, Economics Analysis Group, U.S. Dept. of Justice, Antitrust Immunity and International Airline Alliances ("Recent decisions by the U.S. Department of Transportation . . . to grant immunity from the U.S. antitrust laws to large groups of airlines in alliances relating to international air transportation represent a significant development."), available at http://1.usa.gov/1lo9QXT; Telecommunications Act of 1996; Federal Power Act of 1920.

[39] For the US, see the Defense Production Act of 1950 § 721, as amended by the Foreign Investment and National Security Act of 2007 (known as the Exon-Florio Amendment) and implemented by Executive Order 11858 and regulations at 31 C.F.R. Part 800, authorizes the Committee on Foreign Investment in the United States (CFIUS) to inspect M&A deals that may produce foreign control of a U.S. entity. Roughly 100 deals require filings under Exon-Florio in the US per year, and only a small number go through a second-stage review, and an even smaller number have been blocked. For one of the few, see Sara Forden, Obama Bars Chinese-Owned Company from Building Wind-Farm, Businessweek.com (Sep. 28, 2012), http://bloom.bg/1knObKB. For yogurt in France, see France Flouts the Pepsi Challenge, Telegraph (July 24, 2005) (French Labour Minister, among other officials, pledged to do "all we can" to defeat PepsiCo bid for Danone.), available at http://bit.ly/1knOoNT. For tea in China, see US Government Accountability Office, Foreign Investment: Laws and Policies Regulating Foreign Investment in 10 Countries, GAO-08320 (Feb. 2008) at 44 (noting that tea production is protected industry in China). Foreign acquisitions in the UK are not governed by a single legislative framework, the UK is generally perceived as open to foreign investment, and the EU's "single market" rules have encouraged openness generally in Europe. The UK government nonetheless has authority block deals that affect the national interest, water companies, or media companies, if they are against the "public interest," as well as in "important" manufacturing concerns, and there have been six interventions since 2003 on national security grounds, and one on "public interest" grounds. As common in the EU, the UK owns a "golden share" blocking a transfer of control over key companies, such as Rolls-Royce (due to its nuclear business) and BAE systems (defense). Id. at 99–100. Although India has liberalized significantly in the past 20 years, India remains stricter than the US or the UK in regulating foreign M&A of domestic businesses across more industries. Id. at 65–72.

linked to such realizations, and more generally, tax systems are often linked to transactions, including M&A.[40]

While M&A-related laws emerging from antitrust, industry regulation, foreign ownership, and tax are not formally part of corporate law, and a detailed review is beyond the scope of this chapter (and book), they have important implications for the ways corporate law regulates M&A. Such laws can create incentives for certain kinds of M&A transactions versus others; or impose delays or notice requirements that collaterally inform the public or relevant corporate decision makers or potential competing bidders; or constrain how ownership and control can be allocated after a transaction. For those reasons, M&A practitioners tend to be highly aware of these related bodies of law, and corporate law is sometimes modified in response to their effects.

5   WHAT MODES EXIST FOR REGULATION OF M&A TRANSACTIONS?

In this section, the analysis moves from potential purposes for law to actual law. The material is organized around mode of regulation, with some serving multiple purposes. The presentation is not meant to be exhaustive, but illustrative, with examples from the US, the UK, and India.

5.1   Facilitating M&A

5.1.1   Collective Action: Mergers and Schemes of Arrangement

One purpose of M&A law is to facilitate M&A. One way the law does this is to assist decision makers in overcoming collective action problems. One method of doing this is to permit an M&A transaction to be "forced" upon shareholders, even without their consent, provided certain procedural conditions are satisfied. One example—our first mode of M&A regulation—is the statutory merger, which effectively allows a share of common stock to be converted into some other thing (or even, in the limit, nothing[41]), in connection with the

---

[40] See Internal Revenue Code § 368 for conditions for tax-free treatment. In general terms, US law requires recognition of capital gain, and taxes it, upon the occurrence of many M&A deals, unless they qualify for "tax-free" (really, tax-deferred) treatment, and even then, imposes a tax on any consideration other than stock received in the transaction. In the UK, cash consideration will typically trigger tax, but tax may be deferred even upon the receipt of qualifying notes or debt from the buyer (as well as stock); stock transfer taxes may arise in bids structured as stock purchases, however. Laurence Levy, Jeremy Kutner and Simon J. Little, Public Mergers and Acquisitions in the UK (England and Wales): Overview, Practical Law (May 1, 2013), available at http://us.practicallaw.com/8-502-2187#a688792.

[41] See Odyssey Partners, L.P. v. Fleming Companies, Inc., 735 A.2d 386 (Del. Ch. 1999) (finding that the net asset value of company was zero or less, as a partial basis for holding that conflict of interest transaction involving majority shareholder and creditor of company was not entirely unfair); see also S. Muoio & Co. LLC v. Hallmark Entertainment, 2011 WL 863007 (Del. Ch. Mar. 9, 2011); In re Vision Hardware Group, Inc., 669 A.2d 671 (Del. Ch. 1995), aff'd sub nom Young v. Vision Hardware Group, Inc., 676 A.2d 909 (Del. 1996); In re Hanover Direct, Inc. Shareholders Litigation, 2010 WL 3959399 (Del. Ch. Sep. 24, 2010).

legal combination of the issuing corporation with some other corporation, provided the statutorily specified steps for a merger are completed. Every US state provides for a merger,[42] and compulsory share exchanges, with much the same result, are also permitted by statute in a majority of US states.[43] Typically, a statute requires one corporation to be designated as the "surviving" or "continuing" corporation, which by operation of law succeeds to all assets and liabilities of the two combining companies. That choice is generally independent of whether one or both combining companies' shareholders continue as shareholders.

As noted above, one company that is formally "combining" in a US merger may be a newly created shell corporation, wholly owned by a true party-in-interest (e.g., a parent/buyer), solely for the purpose of merging with another (e.g., a target). In such a triangular relationship, the statutory requirements of the merger apply to the shell and the target, the formally combining entities, rather than to the parent/buyer and the target, as might occur in a less formalistic legal treatment. The "currency" used in a merger—i.e., whatever the combining corporations' stock is to be converted into—need not even be owned as property by one of the combining companies, so long as the parties to the related agreement and plan of merger include a company that does own that currency. Another result of this combination of formalism and flexibility is that in the US the merger can also be used in post or extra-M&A reorganizations, for example to shuffle the hierarchy of related corporations, or to effect a recapitalization or reorganization, or to interpose a new holding company or intermediate holding company between an operating company and its shareholders or parent and company.

In the UK, the primary example is the scheme of arrangement,[44] which provides for mergers as well as a broader array of restructuring or combination transactions. Schemes of arrangement have their origin in stand-alone recapitalizations or reorganizations by financially distressed companies,[45] and are not limited to arrangements in which two or more companies be combined. But they can be, and UK law now expressly contemplates them to be used to coordinate shareholders in the approval of M&A transactions, effectively imposing the results on dissenting (or inattentive) shareholders.[46] In both jurisdictions, then, a statutory device originally aimed at different original goals (combinations, recapitalizations) has been repurposed to the other goal, and both goals are now commonly pursued together and separately through that device.

India, too, permits schemes of arrangement, but they play a less important role than in the UK, because among Indian companies dispersed control is rare, even in listed companies with dispersed ownership.[47] A related point is that corporate governance generally is less

---

[42] E.g., DGCL § 251.   [43] E.g., NYBCL § 913.

[44] UK Companies Act 2006, Parts 26–28.

[45] John Tribe, "Companies Act Schemes of Arrangement and Rescue: The Lost Cousin of Restructuring Practice", 7 J. Int'l. Banking & Fin. L. 386 (2009).

[46] Jennifer Payne, "Schemes of Arrangement, Takeovers and Minority Shareholder Protection", 11 J. Corp. L. Stud. 67 (2011).

[47] Shaun J. Mathew, "Hostile Takeovers in India: New Prospects, Challenges, and Regulatory Opportunities", 3 Colum. Bus. L. Rev. 800, 833 (2007) (noting that as of 12/31/06 average ownership percentage of BSE 500 companies was 49.55%); Vikramaditya S. Khanna and Shaun J. Mathew, "The Role of Independent Directors in Controlled Firms in India: Preliminary Interview Evidence", 22 Nat'l L. Sch. of India Rev. 35 (2010), at 53 (majority of independent directors surveyed understood their role to be primarily advisors to control shareholders, known as "promoters" in India).

protective of minority investors in India (although it has been improving in that regard[48]), with the result that control shareholders may find it more useful to preserve minority investment even after an M&A transaction than in the US or the UK, where it is difficult for control shareholders to exploit their control positions at the expense of minority investors.

5.1.2 Call Rights: Squeezeouts

A second way that law can facilitate M&A is to provide corporate decision makers with "calls" on stock. That is, provided a designated process is followed, a corporation can force its shareholders (typically less than a majority) to accept cash in lieu of their shares. By allowing controllers to "squeeze out" minority shareholders in this way, the law creates a means by which a bidder can obtain 100% ownership following a control acquisition, while avoiding the freeriding problem noted above. In the US, squeezeouts are typically achieved via merger—either under a special statutory provision designed for this purpose,[49] or under the more general-purpose merger statute described above;[50] occasionally, they are achieved via reverse stock split, in which a corporation via charter amendment converts all shares into a smaller fraction (e.g., three for one) and provides cash in lieu of fractional shares.[51] In the UK, squeezeouts are achieved pursuant to a provision of the Takeover Code, now embodied in the Companies Act 2006, which expressly permits a more straightforward conversion of minority shares into cash ("compulsory acquisitions") following a bid (and also provides shareholders equivalent "put" rights, to force such a conversion).

5.2 Constraining M&A

5.2.1 Notice and Disclosure

The least restrictive mode of regulation that is designed to constrain M&A requires special notices and disclosure. Advance notice to a board of directors of the parties is typically required for agents to have authority to engage in significant transactions, although norms vary on how far in advance, how frequently, and in how much detail a board should be informed prior to formal board authorization. In conflict-of-interest transactions, at least, the safest practice would include advance notice at the earliest point that a conflicted fiduciary becomes aware of a transaction that has a material chance of occurring.[52] It may be tempting

---

[48] B.S. Black and V.S. Khanna, "Corporate Governance Reforms Increase Firms' Market Values", Working Paper (Oct. 2007), available at http://ssrn.com/abstract_id=914440.

[49] See DGCL §§ 251(g) and 253.   [50] See DGCL § 251(c).

[51] E.g., see Maryland Code of Pub. Gen. L. § 2-309; see also *Milton Applebaum v. Avaya, Inc.*, 805 A.2d 209 (Del. Ch. 2002) (holding proposed stock split complies with Delaware statute).

[52] An interesting and undeveloped question may arise if the target is or may become insolvent before or as a result of the transaction, in which case even a sole shareholder may face a conflict in pursuing or designing a transaction, in which case notice to creditors may become an effective requirement as a result of duties owed by that shareholder (or a board) of the insolvent company. E.g., *In re Central Illinois Energy Co-op*, 2012 WL 3638027 (Bank. C.D. Ill. 2012); *North American Catholic Educational Programming Foundation, Inc. v. Gheewalla*, 930 A.2d 92 (Del. 2007) (directors owe duties to corporation and shareholders, but creditors may protect interest through derivative action when corporation is in "zone of insolvency"); *Prod. Res. Gp., L.L.C. v. NCT Gp., Inc.*, 863 A.2d 772, 776 (Del. Ch. 2004) (same).

for officers facing a conflict to treat notice to a single board member, such as a chairman or lead director, as the equivalent, but individual directors do not on their own have (as a default matter) authority to act on behalf of a corporation, and if the chairman or lead director chooses to not pass the information on to the full board, the conflicted officer may find the transaction in legal jeopardy.[53]

Bidders or targets are sometimes also required to give advance notice to be given to shareholders, although how and when this is accomplished varies with jurisdiction and transaction structure.[54] In the US, a company's board may bind it to a merger agreement without advance notice to shareholders, but the agreement must thereafter be noticed to and approved by shareholders,[55] and for public companies, entry into any "material" agreement (including an M&A agreement) requires disclosure within four business days.[56] In the UK, listed companies must give notice to shareholders "as soon as possible" after terms are agreed for large transaction, defined to include those involving more than 5% of gross assets, profits, consideration, or gross capital.[57]

Bids or tender offers for stock of public companies can only be completed if target shareholders are given advance notice and time to consider the offer.[58] If a buyer is using non-cash-deal currency and the target is held by more than a small number of investors, US law will treat an M&A transaction as if it were a securities offering to the target shareholders and require extensive disclosures in advance of any shareholder commitment to the deal.[59]

Heightened disclosure requirements apply to a major class of conflict-of-interest transactions—those in which insiders ("affiliates") or controlling shareholders buy out the public shareholders and cause the target to "go private."[60] Advance notice is also typically

---

[53] E.g., *Southeastern Pennsylvania Transportation Authority v. Rubin et al.*, 2011 WL 1709105 (Apr. 29, 2011).

[54] If a shareholder approval is required, discussed below, advance notice of the meeting will be required both under state corporate law and under stock exchange rules. E.g., DGCL 213 (setting of record date for meeting) and 222 (notice of meetings); NYSE Rules § 4; Amex Rules Part 7; NASDAQ Rule 5620.

[55] DCGL 251.

[56] SEC Form 8-K. "Material" for this purpose is not defined in a specific way, but would clearly include any merger agreement for a target, and the instructions to the SEC's form indicates that material agreements include those for property, plant, and equipment if the consideration is 15% or more of a company's fixed assets. Filings are also required for any material amendment or termination of a material agreement, for the completion of the acquisition or sale of significant assets (equal to 10% or more of the company's assets), for private sales of more than 1% of the company's equity securities, for material changes in rights of security holders, for changes of control, and for changes to the company's charter or bylaws. In addition, SEC Regulation S-X requires pro forma and audited target financial statements to be filed on the bidder's Form 8-K if the target's assets or income exceed 20% of the bidder's assets or income.

[57] UK Listing Authority Listing Rule 10.4. If the transaction exceeds 25% of those measures, shareholder approval must also be obtained, as discussed below.

[58] In the US, see Securities and Exchange Act § 14(d)-(f); SEC Regulations 14D and 14E; Schedule T-O (form used for tender offers); in the UK, see Takeover Code, Rule 24.

[59] SEC Rule 145; Securities Act of 1933 and Form S-4 (form used for M&A-related offerings).

[60] SEC Rule 13e-3. SEC Form 8-K also requires disclosure of contracts with directors or officers, subject to specific exceptions, and SEC Regulation 14A Item 404 separately requires disclosure of specified "related party" transactions involving more than $60,000 or 5% of consolidated gross revenues in the issuer's next proxy statement, including any deal-related proxy statement, such as will be required to obtain any required shareholder approval.

required to be given to antitrust regulators for any significant transaction.[61] Transactions that are premised on the expectation of layoffs may trigger advance notice requirements benefiting employees.[62]

5.2.2 *Special Approvals*

M&A transactions are typically subject to approvals of parties. In the US, these requirements mainly arise on the target side, and effectively arise on the buyer's side only when stock is being used as deal currency. Where common stock is used as deal currency and more than 20% of the buyer's pre-deal outstanding shares are to be issued, US stock exchange rules require shareholder approval from the buyer.[63] In deals involving stock as deal currency in the UK, preemptive rights provide existing buyer shareholders with some ability to protect their interests, not by voting on the deal, but by investing on the same economic terms as are being offered to target shareholders.[64] In addition, in the UK, listed companies must obtain shareholder approval for any "substantial acquisition," that is, one involving a target with more than 25% of a bidder's gross assets, profits, gross capital, or market capitalization.[65] No equivalent general requirement for bidder shareholder approval exists in the US.

Where the structure is a purchase of shares, property and contract law effectively require approval of target shareholders, subject to the deal-facilitating laws summarized above. Where the structure is a purchase of assets, the law augments rules of basic corporate governance by requiring special board and shareholder approvals for the target. But because most businesses conduct asset purchases in the ordinary course of business, the dividing line between those that do and those that do not require special votes is either arbitrary or

---

[61] In the US, the Hart-Scott-Rodino Antitrust Improvements Act of 1976, as amended (15 U.S.C. § 18a), and related rules require both buyer and target to file, and a buyer to obtain clearance, prior to the acquisition of more than ~$70 million in value of equity securities (the amount is adjusted annually in line with growth in the economy). Mergers and most acquisitions of assets constituting a business also require such filings. In Europe, including the UK, a similar mandatory notification and clearance requirement exists under Regulation (EC) 139/2004 ("Merger Regulation") for deals involving parties with global revenues over €5 billion and EU-wide revenues over €250 million, or if global revenues are over €2.5 billion, EU-wide revenues exceed €100 million for two or more parties, combined turnover in each of three EU-member states exceeds €100 million, and turnover in each of those member state by at least two of the parties exceeds €25 million. In addition, a deal involving a UK company may also entail a formally voluntary but practically desirable filing and clearance from the newly created Competition and Markets Authority if UK revenues are over £70 million or the deal will create or enhance a 25% share of the supply of goods or services in the UK.

[62] In the US, e.g., Workers Adjustment and Retraining Notification (WARN) Act, 12 USC §§ 2101–2109.

[63] NYSE Rule 312.03(c); see also Amex Rule 712; NASDAQ Rule 5635. Here, unlike US state corporate law, the stock exchange rules are less formalistic, and are triggered for the parent/buyer issuing the stock, even if the parent/buyer is not a formal party to the merger, and even if the issuance is achieved in a series of steps.

[64] UK Companies Act 2006, sections 561–577.

[65] UK Listing Authority, Listing Rule 10.1. For an empirical analysis suggesting that this requirement improves outcomes for bidders in the UK, see Marco Becht, Andrea Polo, & Stefano Rossi, "Does Mandatory Shareholder Voting Prevent Bad Acquisitions?", 29 Rev. Fin. Stud. 3035 (2016).

uncertain. In Delaware, the trigger for shareholder approval is the sale of "substantially all" a target's assets, with all of the vagueness such a standard implies.[66]

In the US, the law imposes special approval requirements for mergers. In Delaware, for example, mergers must generally be approved by both combining companies' boards of directors and shareholders, in each case by majority vote.[67] As noted above, triangular mergers effectively eliminate these requirements for bidders, but not for targets.[68] In the UK, schemes of arrangement are subject to even higher requirements, by both 75% in value and 50% of the number of each class of "members" (i.e., shareholders), and by a court, following receipt of an independent valuation report.[69] (However, court approval appears to be a pure formality in the UK, if shareholder approval and a reputable expert report are obtained.[70]) In the US, a few states also offer a court-approved transaction path; California's is occasionally used because it can reduce the regulatory burdens of federal securities regulation due to an exemption for court-approved stock issues.[71] Requiring shareholder approval by the remaining minority of target shareholders following a bid would only exacerbate the collective action problem described above. Hence, no such approval is required in the case of post-bid squeezeouts, or else the law permits the controlling shareholder to effectively force through the merger over the objections of a minority shareholder.

Where M&A transactions involve a conflict of interest, they are typically governed by special approval requirements, either formally or through judicial incentives. In the UK, the Companies Act requires shareholder ("member" in UK parlance) approval of "substantial property transactions" involving directors and connected persons, which would cover deals structured as asset purchases.[72] In Delaware, management buyouts structured as a merger are not formally subject to any different statutory requirements than any other M&A transaction, but because they present conflicts of interest, they face heightened judicial scrutiny unless subject to approval by a special committee of independent directors,[73] and failure to obtain such an approval will itself be a negative factor in the court's assessment. One might think that court incentives of this sort might not have a strong effect for public companies, because dispersed shareholders would not use them, due to collective action problems, but the derivative lawsuit mechanism in the US enables any shareholder to sue on behalf of all,

---

[66] *Hollinger Int'l., Inc. v. Black*, 844 A.2d 1022 (Del. Ch. 2004), aff'd 872 A.2d 559 (Del. 2005).

[67] This is generally true even if the merger is essentially immaterial for the buyer. The formal requirement of board approval applies, for example, if the cash to be issued to target shareholders is a tiny amount relative to the buyer/parent's assets. Where a triangular structure is used, the approvals under US state corporate law are generally applied formalistically to the combining companies, and not to the parent/buyer. Hence, the approvals for the shell corporation involved are pro forma, since subsidiary directors are typically officers, and an officer can also approve the merger on behalf of the parent company as sole shareholder of the subsidiary. A board's approval is only required at one point in time, and does not need to continue throughout the M&A process: under DGCL § 146, a merger may proceed to stockholder vote even if a board has changed its recommendation on how to vote.

[68] See Ehud Kamar, "Does Shareholder Voting on Acquisitions Matter?", 64 Am. L. & Econ. Rev. 64 (2006).

[69] UK Companies Act 2006, sections 904–918.   [70] Payne, *supra* note 46.

[71] Cal. Corp. Code § 25142; Securities Act of 1933 § 3(a)(9).

[72] UK Companies Act 2006, section 190.

[73] *Barkan v. Amsted Indus., Inc.*, 567 A.2d 1279 (Del. 1989); see M&F Global, *supra* note 23.

and nearly all large transactions—particularly those involving conflicts of interest—generate such lawsuits.[74]

In addition to board and shareholder approvals, M&A transactions are often subject to other approvals. Regulators (antitrust, industry-focused, or national security-focused) must approve (or be given an opportunity to object to) significant M&A transactions, subject to court review. Contracts (e.g., bond indentures, loan agreements) may also require third-party consents, typically in circumstances where a change of control could reasonably be expected to increase or change the risks or value of the deal participants' performance. Such consents may effectively be "bought out" by M&A participants, however, either through explicit redemption or prepayment rights, or through renegotiation of contract terms. Similarly, preferred stock holders typically have approval rights unless the buyer effectively "rolls over" the preferred and preserves its dividend and other rights and powers. If a buyer uses a triangular deal structure, typically the preferred stock will be "rolled over" at the subsidiary level, which may be undesirable for the buyer, in which case the buyer may create incentives for preferred holders to exchange their stock for buyer (parent) company equivalents.[75]

Where a class of preferred (or special class of common stock) has separate approval rights, an M&A deal can be "held hostage" by holders of that class, who may seek more value to flow to them to induce them to permit the transaction to be completed. This risk is most acute if the stock is neither common nor participating preferred (and so would not normally share directly in the benefits of the deal to the combining companies, other than through risk reduction), and if the class is either held by a small number of investors, or may be purchased on the market (as when the preferred is listed on an exchange), in which case hedge funds or other active investors may buy up the stock precisely to hold out against the deal.

5.2.3 Augmented Fiduciary Duties and Other Legal Obligations

As with all corporate decisions, M&A transactions must be approved by corporate decision makers who are subject to fiduciary duties of care and loyalty, but in the US, M&A transactions are generally subject to heightened judicial (as well as public) scrutiny, whether or not pursuant to formally distinct doctrinal treatment.[76] It is no accident that the few instances in which US courts have held directors personally liable for breaching their duty of care have been in the context of M&A transactions.[77] Conventional wisdom among US

---

[74] Robert M. Daines & Olga Koumrian, "Recent Developments in Shareholder Litigation Involving Mergers and Acquisitions" (Cornerstone Research, Mar. 2012), available at http://bit.ly/1yads5t; Steven M. Davidoff, Corporate Takeover? In 2013, a Lawsuit Almost Always Followed, N.Y. Times (DealBook) (Jan. 12, 2014), available at http://nyti.ms/1lt6lkg.

[75] See, e.g., *Kirschner Brothers Oil, Inc. v. Natomas Co.*, 185 Cal. App. 3d 784 (1986).

[76] Directors and officers of UK companies are also subject to fiduciary duties, see generally Gower and Davies, Principles of Modern Company Law (9th ed. Paul Davies & Sarah Worthington eds., 2012), but it is significantly more difficult for dispersed shareholders to bring lawsuits to enforce such duties in the UK in a cost-effective manner, so these duties are less constraining and less significant to M&A practice than in the US. See generally John C. Coates et al., "Program on the Legal Profession: The Legal Profession of the United Kingdom", available at http://bit.ly/1pJoLdo (contrasting US and UK legal systems, including availability of contingent fees, attorneys' fees, discovery, and representative actions).

[77] *Supra* note 28; see Bernard Black, Brian Cheffins, & Michael Klausner, "Outside Director Liability", 58 Stan. L. Rev. 1055 (2006).

practitioners that the sale of a company should include at least two board meetings, at least one of which is lengthy; that a publicly held target company's board should obtain a fairness opinion from an investment bank in order to become reasonably informed about the relative value of the deal; that approval should be preceded by advance notice, review of deal documents or summaries, comparison of options, and preferably some process designed to insure that the deal represents the best reasonably obtainable value. Fairness opinions so obtained are themselves subject to judicial review for the adequacy of the underlying analyses, under both state law and federal securities law.[78]

All of this remains true despite the fact that the Delaware legislature subsequently enabled and most corporations have elected to immunize ("exculpate") directors from liability for breaches of care, even in the M&A context, and the leading Delaware court has disclaimed any per se rule requiring any particular "blueprint" for a sale.[79] US securities law reinforces this heightened duty of care when a deal involves stock currency and the target is publicly held. In such deals, the buyer is effectively issuing stock to the public (through the deal), with the result that its directors and officers have potential anti-fraud liability if they do not conduct (or have conducted for them) adequate "due diligence" to see that the prospectus delivered in advance of closing is accurate, materially complete, and complies with technical regulatory requirements.[80]

The content of fiduciary duties may also be shifted in subtle ways depending on the nature of a transaction. For example, in Delaware, a company selling itself for cash faces slightly different and effectively more stringent judicial review than one that accepts a merger with all stock as the deal currency, even if the buyer is a much larger company, and in such situations, the target board may not openly prefer one bidder on the ground that its bid will benefit any "constituency" other than shareholders.[81]

In the UK, the Takeover Code (and now the Companies Act) forbids target directors from taking actions that tend to "frustrate" any bidder, essentially requiring them to be neutral between bidders—even if the target directors believe (for example) that one bidder is a stronger business partner than another. UK rules also effectively require target boards to remain "neutral" between different bidders. In the US, if a transaction involves contract provisions designed to deter competition that may arise after a bid emerges, those provisions (and possibly the entire deal) will also be subject to heightened judicial scrutiny, and while favoritism among bidders is not formally precluded, it is discouraged as a result of this review.[82]

---

[78] For US state law, see, e.g., *In re Toys "R" Us, Inc. Shareholder Litigation*, 877 A.2d 975 (Del. Ch. 2005); *In re Rural Metro Corp. Stockholders Litigation*, 88 A.3d 54 (2013); for US federal securities law, see *Herskowitz v. Nutri/System, Inc.*, 857 F.2d 179 (3d Cir. 1988), cert denied, 489 U.S. 1054, 109 S.Ct. 1315, 103 L.Ed.2d 584 (1989) (investment bank could be held liable under federal securities laws where the investment bank permitted its fairness opinion to be included in proxy solicitation materials, but without a genuine belief or reasonable basis for concluding that the economic assumptions upon which the fairness opinion was based were accurate).

[79] See DGCL § 102(b)(7); Edward P. Welch & Robert S. Saunders, "Freedom and its Limits in the Delaware General Corporation Law", 33 Del. J. Corp. L. 845 (2008); *Barkan, supra* note 73.

[80] Securities Act of 1933 § 11; *Escott v. BarChris Construction Corp.*, 283 F. Supp. 643 (1968).

[81] *Revlon, Inc. v. MacAndrews & Forbes Holdings, Inc.*, 506 A.2d 173 (Del. 1986); *Barkan, supra* note 73.

[82] Id.; *Unocal Corp. v. Mesa Petroleum Co.*, 493 A.2d 946 (Del. 1985).

The strongest judicial review in the US is reserved for conflict-of-interest transactions—a sufficiently stringent type of review to deserve separate attention (discussed in the next section). In addition, one type of conflict transaction—insider trading—in the US is subject to extra regulation in the context of tender offers.[83]

5.3 Fairness Review, Appraisals, and Minimum Payment Requirements

M&A is sometimes subject to special "fairness" approval requirements, designed to insure that the transaction is "fair" to a designated set of beneficiaries—typically, shareholders (or non-controlling shareholders in the case of transactions in which controlling shareholders participate directly)—or, alternatively, that those beneficiaries receive fair compensation for any change in ownership or rights caused by the transaction. "Fairness" is as vague as it sounds, and is typically evaluated on a case-by-case basis, with a view toward whether target shareholders are being treated equally, whether the transaction provides them with value equivalent to the value of their shares prior to the transaction, and whether controlling fiduciaries are benefiting at their expense.

In the US, Delaware law requires that for any conflict of interest transaction, fiduciaries must affirmatively show that the deal is "entirely fair," that is, at a fair price and the result of a fair process. All deal terms and elements of the process leading to the deal are subject to heightened ex post scrutiny, unless the deal meets stringent ex ante conditions.[84] If a court finds that the deal is not "entirely fair," the result is that the fiduciaries are found to have violated their duties, with possible reputational implications.[85] The remedies available are not limited to compensation, but may exceed the compensatory value, potentially including the equivalent of punitive damages (although not typically so characterized).[86]

In addition, in the US, appraisal rights may be an alternative form of fairness review available, but only for specified M&A transactions.[87] Appraisal rights permit any common shareholder to seek a judicial determination of the "fair value" of their shares, measured as

---

[83] SEC Rule 14e-3.

[84] Those conditions effectively and non-waivably precommit the target to a process that includes not only independent approval by a board, but also approval by disinterested shareholders. See *M&F, supra* note 23.

[85] E.g., *Valeant Pharmaceuticals Int'l. v. Jerney*, 921 A.2d 732 (De. Ch. Dec. 1, 2006) (decision by directors to pay large cash bonuses to themselves and officers in connection with proposed transaction was found to fail entire fairness review).

[86] *Weinberger v. UOP, Inc.*, 457 A.2d 701 (Del. 1983) (lower court awarded arbitrary $1 per share after freezeout merger found to fail entire fairness test but merger price found to be above fair price for shares); Valeant, *supra* note 85 (president required to disgorge entire bonus and reimburse company for half of fees advanced by company for joint defense of president and CEO).

[87] On one aspect of the complex relationship between the "fair price" component of the entire fairness standard of review in Delaware with the "fair value" standard in appraisal settings, see, e.g., *In re Orchard Enterprises, Inc. Stockholder Litigation* 88 A.3d 1 (Del. Ch. Feb. 28, 2014) (fair price is a point estimate, fair value a range, so while fair value might exceed a merger price by more than 200%, that does not compel a finding of unfairness, although it is "certainly evidence of financial unfairness"). See also cases cited in note 41 *supra* (cases in which fair value or fair price is found to "approach" or be zero, or less, due to insolvency).

if the transaction had not occurred (hence, excluding deal synergies), based on the value of the target firm as a whole, divided pro rata among common shareholders. Triggering transactions include cash mergers, mergers that rely upon short-form "squeezeout" procedures that avoid a shareholder vote, and stock-for-stock mergers involving private buyers or targets.[88] In Delaware (and indeed, in many US states), appraisal rights are not available in connection with asset or stock purchases, even if they have the same economic effects as a merger.[89]

UK law regulates conflicts of interest differently, depending on whether the transaction is a bid or a scheme. For bids, elements of the Takeover Code create incentives for bidders to never obtain controlling but less than full ownership interests. For example, bidders are required to launch a "mandatory" acquisition bid at a regulated price once they acquire more than 30% of the target's stock or if they acquire more shares after having acquired 30% but less than 50%, preventing creeping control bids and certain stock purchases raising a conflict of interest; bidders must obtain acceptances from at least 50% in the bid; and are required to conduct "squeezeouts" once they obtain 90% ownership, and are constrained to pay a price that is at least equal to the highest price paid for shares (and no less than the price paid in their control bid).[90] Together, these rules prevent or substantively regulate with bright-line rules some of the types of M&A transactions that commonly involve conflicts of interest in the US. For transactions structured as schemes of arrangement in the UK, court approval is required, following receipt of a report from an independent "expert" finding that the share exchange ratio in the scheme is reasonable.[91]

In India, squeezeouts are pursued through schemes of arrangement, and historically have been subject to little real judicial oversight or other regulation.[92] The new Companies Act 2013 introduced one new protection similar to those required by UK law on schemes and induced by US fiduciary duty law—fairness opinions from independent investment banks on the value paid. It remains to be seen if the new statute will achieve minority shareholder protection absent broader judicial reforms to enhance the speed and efficacy of enforcement.[93]

5.4 Regulation of Deal Terms, Deal Process, and Deal-Related Debt

Both the US and the UK impose further restrictions on the substance and process for M&A transactions. Tender offers in the US and bids in the UK must offer all target shareholders

---

[88] DGCL § 262; Coates, "Fair Value," *supra* note 25.

[89] *Hariton v. Arco Elecs., Inc.*, 188 A.2d 123, 125 (Del. 1963).

[90] Takeover Code Rule 9 (mandatory offer upon reaching 30% or acquiring more shares after having reached 30%, limited to cash or cash substitute, and at no less a price than the highest price paid during the 12 months prior to the offer); Companies Act §§ 979 (squeezeouts at 90%).

[91] Companies Act, Part 27, Chapter 2, section 909.

[92] Umakanth Varottil, "Corporate Governance in M&A Transactions", 24 National Law School of India Review 50 (2013).

[93] Umakanth Varottil, "The Protection of Minority Investors and the Compensation of their Losses: A Case Study of India", Working Paper 2014/0001 (Feb. 2014), available at http://law.nus.edu.sg/wps/ ("The Indian court system is plagued by delays, costs, and other inefficiencies . . . [n]early 32 million cases are pending before different levels within the Indian judiciary").

the same consideration. Mergers in the US and schemes in the UK, by contrast, need not, although equal treatment is a strong norm generally followed, except where the point of the transaction is to provide ongoing ownership to a buyer or controller and cash to minority shareholders. Stock purchases, by contrast, do not necessarily benefit all target shareholders, and can be sequenced over time in such a way as to benefit some target shareholders differently (subject, in the UK, to the mandatory bid rule described above, and, in the US, to fiduciary duty constraints on self-dealing). Asset purchases in some formal sense treat all shareholders equally, in that the consideration for the transaction flows to the corporation, which they own collectively; however, the control shareholders and/or board of a company selling assets need not then distribute that consideration to shareholders, and may thereafter use it in ways that may not benefit all shareholders equally.

Both the US and the UK impose limits on pre-bid solicitations of support for M&A transactions involving public targets. In the US, SEC proxy rules effectively limit bidders from obtaining support agreements from more than ten shareholders of a public target without going public (and filing documents with the SEC) for the deal,[94] while in the UK, the Takeover Code forbids bidders from obtaining pre-bid agreements from more than six target shareholders.

Restrictions on the use of debt to finance M&A vary significantly across countries. In India, banks are not permitted to finance share acquisitions, including whole-company deals. However, this requirement is imposed on banks, rather than on deals, creating an imbalance between foreign acquirers (who can finance bids from foreign banks) and domestic acquirers (who are generally dependent on local banks for finance).[95] The Indian Finance Ministry is considering relaxing these restrictions. Even if they are relaxed, however, India's laws further ban "financial assistance,"[96] making debt-financed buyouts of private targets difficult, and those of public targets even more so.

Like India, and consistent with the EU's bank-protective Second Company Law Directive,[97] the UK generally forbids companies from providing "unlawful financial assistance" to a bidder to facilitate a bid or other stock purchase involving a public target,[98] although this prohibition was essentially eliminated for private targets in 2008. In addition, and perhaps more importantly, the UK requires that bids be fully financed before they are launched, with cash on hand or fully committed agreements from lenders, subject to "very limited" conditions.[99]

---

[94] SEC Rule 14a-2. Section 13(d) of the Securities and Exchange Act forces disclosure if the stock owned by supporting shareholders aggregates more than 5%.

[95] Umakanth Varottil, "Financing Domestic M&A" (June 2, 2014), available at http://bit.ly/1nGGnbJ.

[96] India Companies Act 2013, section 67.

[97] 77/91/EEC (13 December 1976), as modified in 2012/30/EU (25 October 2012).

[98] Companies Act, §§ 677–683. Assistance that is provided "out of distributable profits" is permitted in certain limited transactions, such as for employee compensation schemes. Unlawful financial assistance is a crime in the UK. Id., section 680. Schemes of arrangement involving creditors are exempted, id., section 681, but not those involving only shareholders, as in mergers via scheme, id. Separately, companies must be careful not to make illegal "disguised distributions" in the form of debt-financed M&A. See *Trevor v. Whitworth* (1887) 12 App Cas 409.

[99] Takeover Code, Rule 2.7; Slaughter and May, When Will a Commitment Letter Constitute a Firm Commitment?, Financing Briefing (July 2008).

The US M&A market does not have a similar "certain funds" or similar requirement relating to bids and offers. Nor does the US forbid "financial assistance." Indeed, it was something sufficiently common in the 1980s to have earned a catchphrase: "junk-bond boot-strap bust-up two-tier takeover."[100] US tax law was modified in the 1980s to limit interest deductions for debt that trades at a discount at original issuance, curtailing the tax subsidy of more extremely leveraged financing structures,[101] and US bank supervisors have imposed modest constraints on the ability of banks to take on excessive risks in the "leveraged loan" market that funds the largest buyouts.[102]

Instead, the US leans on target fiduciary duties and court-developed M&A-specific successor liability doctrines to reinforce contract and general creditor-protection laws such as fraudulent conveyance statutes.[103] Because target fiduciaries are not strictly required to remain neutral as between bidders, they have more flexibility than in the UK to prefer a bidder based on financing certainty, and they are at risk if they sell to a looter.[104] More generally, even when a buyer seeks to limit the liabilities it takes on—for example, by purchasing assets or employing a subsidiary to carry out the deal—it may find that many special types of liabilities are imposed on the buyer/parent by virtue of control of the target's business.[105] In addition, depending on deal structure, post-deal consolidation choices, and the relevant jurisdiction's law, a buyer or its subsidiaries may become subject to all of a target business's

---

[100] Martin Lipton, "Takeover Bids in the Target's Boardroom", 35 Bus. Law. 101 (1979).

[101] See generally Internal Revenue Service, Guide to Original Issue Discount (OID) Instruments, Publication 1212 (Dec. 2013), available at http://www.irs.gov/pub/irs-pdf/p1212.pdf.

[102] E.g., Office of the Comptroller of the Currency, Federal Reserve System, and Federal Deposit Insurance Corporation, Interagency Guidelines on Leveraged Lending, 78 Fed. Reg. 17,766 (Mar. 22, 2103) (setting forth tightened principles for agency-supervised banks to engage in leveraged lending, including lending for buyouts; stating that "Generally, a leverage level after planned asset sales (that is, the amount of debt that must be serviced from operating cash flow) in excess of 6X Total Debt/EBITDA raises concerns for most industries . . . ").

[103] See J. H. Ginsberg, M. Burgess, D.R. Czerwonka, & Z.R. Caldwell, Am. Bankr. Inst. L. Rev. (2011) (describing fraudulent conveyance law, noting uncertainties in how that law is applied to buyouts, and recommending more rule-like revisions, such as specifying probability at which cash-flow insolvency becomes "reasonably foreseeable").

[104] E.g., *Michael R. Harris v. Donald J. Carter, et al.*, 582 A.2d 222 (Del. Ch. 1990).

[105] E.g., in the US: Comprehensive Environmental Response, Compensation and Liability Act (CERCLA), 42 U.S.C. § 9607 et seq. (environmental liability based on control of real property, not formal ownership or control at time environmental harm created); National Labor Relations Act, 29 U.S.C. § 158(a)(5) (collective bargaining contracts and duty to bargain based on bargaining unit, not on formal corporate structure); the Civil Rights Act of 1964, 42 U.S.C.A. § 2000d (liability for unlawful discrimination may run to successor); Financial Institutions Reform, Recovery, and Enforcement Act of 1989 (FIRREA), 12 U.S.C. § 1821(k), and Federal Deposit Insurance Corporation Improvement Act of 1991 (FDICIA), Pub. L. No. 102–242, 105 Stat. 2236 (codified in scattered sections of 12 U.S.C.) (liability for bank fraud may run to successor, not limited to formal corporate party engaged in fraud); see generally Mark J. Roe, "Mergers, Acquisitions, and Tort: A Comment on the Problem of Successor Corporation Liability", 70 Va. L. Rev. 1559 (1984) (discussing successor liability in tort); John H. Matheson, "Successor Liability", 96 Minn. L. Rev. 371 (2011) (discussing state and federal common law successor liability doctrines); Michael Carter, "Successor Liability Under CERCLA: It's Time to Fully Embrace State Law", 156 U. Pa. L. Rev. 767 (2008) (successor liability under CERCLA).

liabilities under common law doctrines variously labeled "agency," "de facto merger," or "successor liability."[106] While such doctrines do little more than fraudulent conveyance statutes to constrain total leverage resulting from a given deal, they do constrain the temptation to use M&A or restructuring to shift or amplify risks to creditors, or to extract value in violation of conventional priorities among claimants.

5.5 Bans or Structural Limits

Finally, many laws effectively ban or impose structural limits on M&A. At the request of a creditor, a court in the US may be willing to enjoin transactions that would cause a company to become insolvent, particularly if they involve transfers of value to shareholders or a subset of creditors. Banking laws in the US forbid acquisitions by banks of nonbank, or vice versa,[107] while in the UK the separation of banking and commerce is preserved through the discretion of bank supervisors to refuse permission for nonbanking entities to enter banking on prudential ("safety and soundness") grounds. M&A transactions that would create monopolies or monopoly power are banned, unless (as is typical) a buyer is prepared to divest parts of the target's business to reduce competitive concerns. Defense contractors, airlines, and telecommunications companies are typically forbidden from being acquired by foreign or foreign-controlled buyers, and restrictions on foreign ownership typically extend to more industries in developing nations.[108]

---

[106] See cases in *supra* note 33; see also *Magnolia's at Bethany, LLC v. Artesian Consulting Engineers, Inc.*, 2011 Del. Super. LEXIS 435 (Del. Super. Sep. 19, 2011) (Delaware Superior Court articulating de facto merger doctrine as requiring transfer of all assets from one corporation to another, payment made in stock issued by transferee to shareholders of transferor, and agreement by transferee to assume all debts and liabilities of transferor); *Xperex Corp. et al. v. Viasystems Technologies Corp.*, C.A. No. 20582-NC (July 22, 2004) (Delaware Chancery Court articulating broadly framed "de facto merger" doctrine to prevent "sham transactions to achieve mischief" or "to seek to shelter assets from creditors"); *Ramirez v. Amsted Industries, Inc.*, 431 A.2d 811 (Supr. Ct. N.J. 1981) (New Jersey court articulating "flexible" de facto merger test based on multiple factors, including continuity of ownership, cessation of target business, continuity of management, and assumption of liabilities ordinarily needed to operate business); *Kaminksi v. Western MacArthur Co.*, 175 Cal. App. 3d 445 (Ct. App. Cal. 1985) (California court articulating broadly framed "substantial continuity" doctrine imposing tort liability on continued product lines and businesses, regardless of corporate form); *U.S. v. Generations Healthcare, LLC*, 2012 U.S. Dist. LEXIS 116431 (U.S.D.Ct. N.D. Ill. Aug. 14, 2012) (US District Court articulating successor liability doctrine for purposes of False Claims Act as part of US federal common law); *Fitzgerald v. Fahnestock & Co., Inc.*, 286 A.D.2d 573, 574 (N.Y. App. Div. 2001) (New York case stating factors for finding of de facto merger).

[107] Bank Holding Company Act of 1956 § 1972; see also Investment Company Act of 1940 §6 and Internal Revenue Code §§ 851-852 (together effectively limiting the ability of mutual funds to invest in control stakes of portfolio companies); in Europe, see also the "UCITS" directives, 2001/107/EC (the "Management Directive") and 2001/108/EC (the "Product Directive") (1/21/02) 85/611/EEC (12/20/85) and 2009/65/EC, which ban collective investment schemes from purchasing more than 5% of the securities of any issuer.

[108] See *supra* note 38.

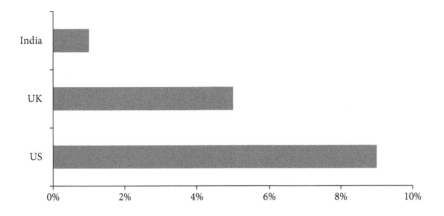

FIGURE 22.1 Deal Volume/GDP in US, UK, and India, 2013.

6 What Types of M&A Transactions Actually Take Place, and What Effects Does Law Have?

What effects do the foregoing laws have on the patterns of deal making in the US, the UK, and India? Although complete data necessary to answer such a question are not available, public data does provide a basis for some general observations about such patterns.

First, as illustrated in Figure 22.1, the overall US legal environment is highly conducive to M&A. US M&A levels are the highest in the world. This is true both in dollars and in numbers of deals, absolutely and (as depicted in the figure) relative to the size of the relevant economies, for both public and private targets, and across a range of industries. UK law is also highly facilitating, with robust M&A markets, albeit modestly less so for public targets than in the US. In part this is due to the rigidity of some UK laws that benefit target shareholders conditional on a bid, but also have modest inhibitory effects on bidders considering whether to initiate a bid.[109] The UK's ban on financial assistance also likely has a constraining effect on buyouts, although buyout volumes in the UK and elsewhere in Europe suggest that the UK's ban on financial assistance has had only limited effect, in part because its focus on debt incurred for transactional purposes does not extend to debt incurred near in time but not as part of a stock purchase.[110] Deals in India have increased in significance, both absolutely and relative to the Indian economy, but remain well below levels in the US and the UK.

Second, deal structures are highly dependent on the ownership structures and sizes of the companies involved. In the US, as illustrated by Figure 22.2, deal structures take on a

---

[109] See John C. Coates, M&A Break Fees: U.S. Litigation versus U.K. Regulation, in Regulation versus Litigation: Perspectives from Economics and Law (Daniel Kessler ed., 2011).

[110] L. Enriques, "EC Company Law Directives and Regulations: How Trivial Are They?", 7 U. Pa. J. Int'l. Econ. L. 1 (2006); Eilis Ferran, "Regulation of Private Equity-Backed Buyout Activity in Europe", ECGI Law Working Paper No. 84/2007 (May 2007).

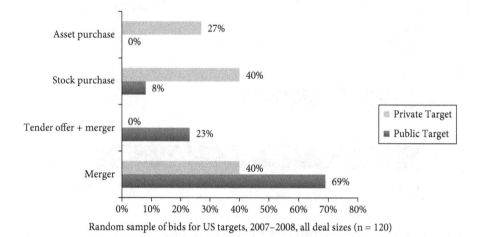

Random sample of bids for US targets, 2007–2008, all deal sizes (n = 120)

FIGURE 22.2 US Target Deal Structures by Ownership of Target.

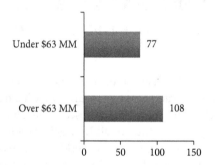

FIGURE 22.3 Mean Deal Duration in Days, by Deal Size in the US.

completely different distribution for public and private targets. In the UK, deals for larger public targets are more likely to use a scheme of arrangement than smaller deals, which are more likely to rely on bids.[111] In India, M&A transactions are almost completely structured as asset and stock purchases, owing to the concentrated controlling ownership structures, even among India's largest public companies.[112]

Third, deal regulation has a clear impact on the way deals proceed. For example, as illustrated in Figure 22.3, deals take substantially longer to complete if they are large enough to trigger antitrust review in the US than if they do not.[113] Similarly, as illustrated in Figure 22.4, deals are substantially more likely to be withdrawn once announced, if they involved

---

[111] Levy et al. *supra* note 40. One advantage of schemes is they can be structured so as to not trigger the small but non-trivial stamp tax liability imposed in the UK (but not in the US), only transfers of stock via bids. See Payne, *supra* note 46.

[112] For an overview of M&A in India, see Kosturi Ghosh, Ipsita Chowdhury, & Vallishree Chandra, "Public Mergers and Acquisitions in India: Overview", available at http://us.practicallaw.com/3-503-1108?q=India.

[113] The trigger for review under the Hart-Scott-Rodino Act in the years of the sample (2007–2008) was ~$63 million. Coates, *supra* note 17. These bids are from the same sample used to create Figure 22.2.

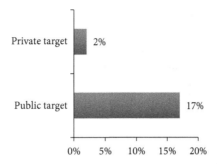

FIGURE 22.4 Withdrawn Bids by Target Ownership in the US.

a public target in the US.[114] Some effects show up across jurisdictions too: acquisitions of US public targets (most of which are mergers that involve at least some non-cash consideration, and so require registration of securities with the SEC) typically take 60 to 90 days from announcement to complete; those of UK public targets take 25 to 30 days from announcement; and those of Indian public targets either occur simultaneously with the announcement (where they are structured as sales of control blocks owned directly or indirectly by one individual or family controlling shareholder to another) or take four to six months (where they are structured as asset purchases or, less commonly, bids for public company shares), or up to a year in the rare scheme of arrangement.[115] Bid withdrawal rates are far higher in India for private target deals than in either the US or the UK, and while some of the differences may be attributable to non-legal factors, the legal process for M&A is likely to be a partial cause as well.

A fourth empirical finding is also clear: M&A transactions generally generate significant gains to target shareholders who sell, regardless of jurisdiction. Premiums over pre-deal market prices for public targets average between ~25% and ~50%, depending on time period and sample, in each of the US, UK, and India.[116] (In India, however, those gains may not be shared with minority shareholders in the typical deal structure, in which a control block is sold without a corresponding acquisition of other shares.) Comparisons of observed premiums across jurisdictions are difficult, in aggregate, due to differences in ownership, finance, and the economics motivating deals, so it is less clear whether law has an important influence on the relative benefits of M&A to target shareholders.

Data on and studies of topics of more general social, political, and economic interest—such as whether M&A transactions are good for bidders or society as a whole—are far more problematic. Part of the difficulty is that M&A is endogenous to a large number of forces, beyond corporate law, or even the law of M&A generally: finance, macroeconomic activity, monetary policy, politics, tax, culture, etc. Controlling for such factors is necessary to draw reliable inferences about the effects of law, but doing so is difficult if not impossible, given limits on the degree or frequency of variation in or observability of such factors.[117] As a

---

[114] Id.

[115] See, e.g., http://www.sec.gov/Archives/edgar/data/1144967/000119312508203048/dex41.htm.

[116] For the US, see Richard Bruner, Applied Mergers and Acquisitions (2004), chapter 3, exhibit 3.3 (summarizing studies, all finding positive returns to target shareholders).

[117] Pavel G. Savor and Qi Lu, "Do Stock Mergers Create Value for Acquirers", 64 J. Fin. 1061 (2009).

result, it remains a topic of some dispute even in the largest M&A jurisdiction whether M&A is, on balance, good for bidders.[118]

Similarly, the effects of M&A generally on non-shareholder constituencies, such as employees or creditors, are disputed. M&A generates substantial transaction costs, which might be viewed as wasteful rents (from a social perspective) if the net result of M&A to both bidder and target shareholders from a typical deal is zero or nearly so. In the US, the tax shield from higher leverage incurred through debt-financed M&A may also represent a form of rent seeking, but it is unclear why managers would not incur similar levels of tax-reducing debt without M&A (other than, perhaps, as a form of agency cost, in which taxpayers may be benefiting at shareholder expense). Employees are commonly laid off following mergers, particularly among general managers, as the buyer can achieve economies in management (e.g., no need for two highly paid general counsels), but the most highly paid employees often receive side payments in the form of vested options or stock, or golden parachutes, and many find employment quickly. Some M&A transactions lead to more widespread layoffs, but it is hard to test whether such layoffs would have occurred anyway, as when M&A is a channel for globalization, or whether the firms involved are able to create new jobs at a faster pace than they would have done without M&A. Labor unions used to oppose hostile takeovers, but union pension plans now commonly embrace corporate governance strategies that tend to increase M&A. Few M&A transactions generate antitrust concern sufficient to attract more than minimal review by US antitrust agencies. Banks and other lenders are sufficiently unconcerned about the effects of M&A on risk or debt levels that they commonly omit event-risk covenants that would provide protection in the M&A context. Larger creditors may be protected by other means, while smaller creditors are "non-adjusting," in the sense that the benefits of seeking contract protections may be outweighed by the transaction costs of doing so, making non-action by larger creditors of uncertain significance for estimating the effects of (leveraged or leverage-increasing) M&A on creditors generally.

7 CONCLUSION: WHAT DO THE VARIATIONS IN TYPES AND MODES IMPLY ABOUT LAW GENERALLY?

What general conclusions can we draw from this survey? At a very high level, corporate and securities law across jurisdictions treats M&A transactions differently from other, less

---

[118] Id. For a study of the combined effect of M&A in the 1990s on bidders and targets, and on operational performance following mergers, see Gregor Andrade, Mark Mitchell and Erik Stafford, "New Evidence and Perspectives on Mergers", 15 J. Econ. Persp. 103 (2001). The largest, relatively recent studies suggest M&A transactions involving private US targets is good, on average, for owners of public company bidders, if only modestly so, while bids for public targets are often if not always bad. E.g., Jie Cai, Moon H. Song and Ralph A. Walkling, "Anticipation, Acquisitions and Bidder Returns: Industry Shocks and the Transfer of Information across Rivals", 24 Rev. Fin. Stud. 2241 (2011); Jeffry Netter, Mike Stegemoller and M. Babjide Wintoki, "Implications of Data Screens on Merger and Acquisitions Analysis: A Large Sample Study of Mergers and Acquisitions from 1992 to 2009", 24 Rev. Fin. Stud. 2315 (2011).

dramatic and more routine types of transaction. Against a background of other laws that shape and structure the M&A process (tax, antitrust, etc.), corporate and securities law simultaneously facilitate M&A, by reducing collective action costs and the risk of strategic hold-up, but also impose tighter disclosure, process, and substantive constraints on M&A transactions. As a general rule, constraints are tighter for deals involving public companies, where dispersed owners are in need of more information and are less capable of protecting their own interests without additional protections, and are tightest for transactions in public companies that represent conflicts of interest (or would do so if permitted).

A second take-away from the survey is that different countries regulate M&A differently, and exhibit different patterns in M&A forms. These differences reflect at least in large part longstanding differences in structural features of the markets, particularly ownership structure, which itself may be at least in part a function of corporate law and governance. In the US, ownership dispersion led to the use of the collective-action cost-economizing merger; in the UK, greater institutional political power achieved shareholder-protective takeover regulation that has been extended largely, if incompletely, to schemes; and in India, schemes are used much less frequently, relative to simpler negotiated stock purchases, in part because the latter do not trigger a number of legal requirements imposed on the former, but also because they are unnecessary given the frequency of control blocks even among large listed companies, and because bidders often appear content to acquire control, rather than 100% ownership, as is typical in the US and the UK.

But other cross-country variations also seem to reflect the way that (as in chaotic systems) seemingly small differences in starting conditions can ramify and persist in the face of similar legal, historical, and economic conditions (common law, English language and heritage, republican democracies, long coastlands, dependence on trade, and for the past 20 years, at least, a relatively unmixed commitment to regulated capitalism) and strong market pressures to produce an efficient method to allocate resources rapidly through M&A. In the UK, courts play a background role in M&A, even when formally required to approve a scheme. Contested litigation is rare, and bright-line rules set (at least initially) by stock exchanges (which in turn are dominated by institutional investors) screen out whole classes of transactions that might harm the interests of shareholders, while other laws that protect creditors (e.g., against "financial assistance") derive from the bank-centered governance politics of the early European Community. In the US, by contrast, the watchword is flexibility, but also litigation. Courts are central, even without a formal role in approving any given deal, and lawsuits are so commonplace as to transform the (Delaware) courts into a quasi-regulatory agency creating "regulation" as much as resolving disputes, driving deal-related disclosure decisions as much as the rival regulatory body (the SEC) with formal authority over disclosure. In India (with admittedly a very different history and more recent path to its current international position and economic and legal structure), litigation is common, but unavailing, given the delays in the court system; the regulatory body overseeing the stock exchanges has achieved the most discipline over corporate controllers in the M&A context, but M&A regulation is multifarious and frequently overshadowed in a given deal by the complex and often informal body of regulations of ownership of business itself. These differences in the details of how M&A is regulated are far greater than an outside observer might expect. Minor variations in similar laws with similar goals in similar legal systems, in other words, can have real effects on the amount and nature of economic activity.

A third and final bottom line of the survey is that some constraining aspects of M&A law can sometimes be evaded, and are. This stems from the fact that the corporate form—by interposing a legal entity between owners and businesses—makes it possible for economically equivalent transactions to be accomplished with a variety of transactional forms—asset purchases, as with non-corporate actors, but also stock purchases (including bids and tender offers) and mergers, schemes and squeezeouts. Because M&A law does not apply equally to all methods of pursuing a given transaction, opportunities arise for M&A to be structured to reduce the effect of or avoid some of these laws. Hence, we see the move from bids to schemes in the UK, illustrating both the incentive to avoid unnecessary (stamp) taxes, but also the greater flexibility of the scheme. Similarly, in the US, we see the emergence of the tender offer as a mechanism for hostile takeovers in the 1980s, followed by its use in negotiated acquisitions (followed by squeezeout mergers), to reduce the time needed to obtain control, while ensuring 100% ownership. Moreover, shifts in deal patterns respond to legal changes, and are themselves of economic consequence. Ironically, these patterns of avoidance are evidence that the law does in fact sometimes bind. If M&A laws were trivial or its constraints inconsequential, such patterns would not appear.

CHAPTER 23

....

GROUPS OF COMPANIES
A Comparative Study of the Economics, Law, and Regulation of Corporate Groups

....

KLAUS J. HOPT[1]

1 GROUPS OF COMPANIES: PHENOMENON, AGENCY PROBLEMS, AND REGULATION

1.1 The phenomenon of the groups of companies

GROUPS of companies rather than single independent companies are the modern reality of the corporation, and most of them are multinational groups. As an example, take the Pirelli group in Italy, which is not one of the very biggest. It has over 100 companies in more than 30 countries, 16 of them in the European Union, with over 30,000 employees and an annual turnover of almost six billion euros.[2] Modern business can be organized in different ways: the integrated firm working only with its own labor force is rare. More common is distribution by commercial agents or appointed dealers. As the firm becomes bigger, it sets up branches and, especially in trade that crosses over borders, it establishes separate companies as subsidiaries of the firm and forms multinational groups. The groups differ greatly as to structure, organization, and ownership. In the US, groups with 100%-owned subsidiaries are common. In continental Europe, the parents usually own less—very often much less—of the subsidiaries, just enough to maintain control. Some groups have holding structures—for example, the large US banks—and Swiss banks are

---

[1] The original version of this article of 2015 has been published in ssrn, ECGI and the online version of this handbook. In the meantime there have been new developments with much new material. The present version is an update to the end of 2017.

[2] Francesco Chiappetta & Umberto Tombari, "Perspectives on Group Corporate Governance and European Company Law", 9 Eur. Company & Fin. L. Rev. (ECFR) 261, 265 (2012).

beginning to follow.[3] In Europe—for example, in Germany and Italy—pyramids[4] are common, i.e., hierarchical groups with various layers of subsidiaries and subsidiaries of subsidiaries forming very complicated group nets. Groups are run very differently: some are tightly steered by the parent from the top, while others are loosely combined with largely autonomous profit centers and sometimes with fierce group-internal competition.[5] If groups cooperate, they sometimes choose to jointly hold certain subsidiaries. Special—often cultural—problems arise if, as in rare cases, multinational groups have two parents from different countries. Accordingly, the economic concepts of the group differ.[6]

Groups also have different legal forms. This depends on the various corporate forms available in different jurisdictions and sometimes on an international level, such as the Societas Europaea (SE) in the European Union. Legal group regulation, if any, depends on these legal forms,[7] which means that there are stock corporation groups,[8] limited liability company groups, SE groups such as the German Allianz insurance giant,[9] and also groups with commercial partnerships such as parents or subsidiaries. The choice of the form is most often tax-driven.[10] In law, the concept of the group depends on the legal concept of control by the parent. There are different legal concepts of control according to the purpose of the regulation. For accounting purposes, but in some countries also under general corporate law, formal control by at least 51% of the shareholdings is the legal test. For antitrust and in countries with a special group law as in Germany, substantive control concepts are used, taking into consideration that economic control may be possible with much less than 50%

[3] Jeffrey N. Gordon & Wolf-Georg Ringe, "Bank Resolution in the European Banking Union: A Transatlantic Perspective on What it Would Take", http://ssrn.com/abstract=2361347, August 2014, 45.

[4] Marcello Bianchi, Magda Bianco, & Luca Enriques, Pyramidal Groups and the Separation Between Ownership and Control in Italy, in The Control of Corporate Europe 154–87 (Fabrizio Barca & Marco Becht eds., Oxford 2001); Marcello Bianchi et al., "Regulation and Self-Regulation of Related Party Transactions in Italy: An Empirical Analysis", CONSOB Working Paper 75 (2014); Heitor V. Almeida & Daniel Wolfenzon, "A Theory of Pyramidal Ownership and Family Business Groups", 61 J. Fin. 2367 (2006); Joseph P.H. Fan, T. J. Wong, & Tianyu Zhang, "Institutions and Organizational Structure: The Case of State-Owned Corporate Pyramids", 29 J. L. Econ. & Org. 1217 (2013); High Level Group of Company Law Experts, A Modern Regulatory Framework for Company Law in Europe, Report for the European Commission (November 2002), ch. V: Groups and Pyramids, 94–100.

[5] John H. Dunning, Multinational Enterprises in the 1970's: An Economist's Overview of Trends, Theories and Policies, in European Merger Control 3–23 (Klaus J. Hopt ed., Berlin, New York 1982).

[6] Christian Kirchner, "Ökonomische Überlegungen zum Konzernrecht", Zeitschrift für Unternehmens- und Gesellschaftsrecht (ZGR) 214–34 (1985).

[7] Forum Europaeum Corporate Group Law, "Corporate Group Law for Europe", 1 Eur. Bus. Org. L. Rev. (EBOR) 165, at 185–87 (2000); John Kluver, "European and Australian Proposals for Corporate Group Law: A Comparative Analysis", 1 EBOR 287, 292–293 at 292–93 (2000).

[8] Aktienkonzern in Germany.

[9] Peter Hemeling, chief legal counsel of the German insurance giant Allianz, on the choice of the SE for the parent: Die Societas Europaea (SE) in der praktischen Anwendung, lecture (Bonn, Zentrum für Europäisches Wirtschaftsrecht 2008).

[10] Wolfgang Schön, "Perspektiven der Konzernbesteuerung", 171 Zeitschrift für das gesamte Handelsrecht und Wirtschaftsrecht (ZHR) 409–45 (2007).

depending on the shareholder structure, shareholder presence, and voting behavior in the general assembly, and other economic facts.

The objectives of group regulation under corporate law are usually twofold: the main objective is the protection of the minority shareholders and the creditors of the subsidiaries in the group. Under this objective, group regulation follows a bottom-up model. A second objective that appears frequently in many countries—including European countries as well as Australia,[11] for example—concerns the corporate law provisions aimed at assisting business and the economy by recognizing corporate groups as organizational forms and by facilitating group management. Here the regulatory perspective is rather top-down. In countries with strong protectionism and in most emerging countries, the emphasis is more on the organizational side.[12] This chapter concentrates on group regulation with the first objective, i.e., on agency problems in corporate groups and their regulation. Special problems arise for multinational groups, an old phenomenon that was already well known in the nineteenth century,[13] for groups with the state or state enterprises as parent,[14] for financial groups as evidenced by the financial crisis, and for listed groups, i.e., groups in which the parent or a subsidiary or even both are listed. These problems cannot be dealt with here in more detail.

1.2 Empirical Data on Groups and their Use for Regulation

Empirical data on groups are available, but they are usually collected for specific purposes. More recently there has been growing research on corporate ownership with a view toward corporate governance law and codes.[15] Ownership differs considerably between the various countries: dispersed ownership in the US[16] and in the UK[17] as prototypes;[18] and controlling family enterprises and groups of companies as the general rule in continental European

---

[11] For Europe Christoph Teichmann, "Europäisches Konzernrecht: Vom Schutzrecht zum Enabling Law", Die Aktiengesellschaft 2013, 184. For Australia see Kluver, *supra* note 7, at 290–91.

[12] For Spain see José M. Embid Irujo, "Trends and Realities in the Law of Corporate Groups", 6 EBOR 65, 79–81 (2005).

[13] Dual-headed structure, Peter Böckli, Schweizer Aktienrecht (4th ed. Zurich 2009), § 11 comments 149–153 with references; on the difficulties of bi-national groups, many of which failed for nonfinancial reasons, Wilhelm F. Bayer, "Horizontal Groups and Joint Ventures in Europe: Concepts and Reality", in Groups of Companies in European Laws 3–17 (Klaus J. Hopt ed., Berlin, New York 1982).

[14] Prototypes are the trading companies of the seventeenth century, such as the Dutch East India Company, the South Sea Company, or the Mississippi Company. Cf. Paul Frentrop, A History of Corporate Governance 1602–2002 49–114 (Amsterdam, Deminor 2003).

[15] Ronald J. Gilson, From Corporate Law to Corporate Governance, chapter 1 in this volume. An extensive collection of the corporate governance codes of many countries is available at the European Corporate Governance Institute (ECGI), Brussels.

[16] Marco Becht, Beneficial Ownership in the United States, in Barca & Becht, *supra* note 4, at 285–99. But this is just the general rule, exceptions are becoming more frequent, in particular in the field of new technology and for start-up companies.

[17] Marc Goergen & Luc Renneboog, Strong Managers and Passive Institutional Investors in the UK, in Barca & Becht, *supra* note 4, at 259–84.

[18] This is just a prevailing pattern. In continental European countries, groups with dispersed shareholders are on the advance: for example, the German Stock Exchange in Germany and most of the German DAX 30 corporations.

states, but also often found in Far Eastern countries and in emerging economies.[19] Empirical data on multinational enterprises and groups of companies are collected by international organizations such as the OECD, UN, G20, Basel, and others.[20] Data on groups are also collected by studies on economic concentration and are used for antitrust and merger control regulation in many industrialized countries, including Germany, the European Union, and the US.[21]

Of particular relevance when studying the regulation of corporate groups are data on conduct and transactions in groups. Usually they are not collected systematically but are set out by regulatory agencies, in case studies, by national and international court cases, and by reports from practice.[22] Much of the existing group law is not codified law but is case law by courts, such as the German limited liability group law, and sometimes by supervisory agencies, such as the former Belgian Banking Commission.[23] The extensive legal contributions of academia in many countries with group law do not usually add much in the way of empirical data.

1.3   Agency Problems: The Controlling Shareholder and Minority Shareholders, Creditors, and Other Stakeholders

It is generally understood that there are three main agency problems to be dealt with in corporate law: conflicts between managers and shareholders, conflicts among shareholders and here essentially between the controlling shareholder and the minority shareholders, and conflicts between the shareholders as a group and other stakeholders, in particular the creditors of the company and its workforce.[24] Sometimes the concept of stakeholders is

---

[19]   Unternehmensgruppen in Mittel- und Osteuropäischen Ländern (Klaus J. Hopt, C. Jessel-Holst & Katharina Pistor eds., Tübingen 2003); Haftungsrisiken für die Konzernmutter, in Mittel- und Osteuropa (Martin Winner ed., Baden-Baden 2013) for Middle and Eastern European countries; Klaus J. Hopt & Katharina Pistor, "Company Groups in Transition Economies: A Case for Regulatory Intervention?", 2 EBOR 1, 4–9 (2001).

[20]   See for example OECD Guidelines for Multinational Enterprises of 1976, updated 2011.

[21]   Cf. German Monopolies Commission, biannual reports on economic concentration; on concentration in Germany, see Volker Emmerich & Mathias Habersack, Konzernrecht (10th ed. Munich 2013) § 1 III comments 19–28; for France see Paul Le Cannu & Bruno Dondero, Droit des sociétés (6e éd. Paris 2015) nos 1525 et seq.

[22]   Chiappetta & Tombari, *supra* note 2, at 265–68 with experience from the Pirelli Group; Vladimir Atanasov, Bernard Black, & Conrad S. Ciccotello, "Law and Tunneling", 37 J. Corp L. 1 (2011) at 25 et seq. with tunneling cases from the US; Bianchi et al. 2014, *supra* note 4, for Italian regulation and self-regulation of related party transactions; on binational groups Bayer, *supra* note 13.

[23]   For a list of landmark cases on German group law, see Klaus J. Hopt, Legal Elements and Policy Decisions in Regulating Groups of Companies, in Groups of Companies 81 (Clive M. Schmitthoff & Frank Wooldridge eds., London 1991); for the former Belgium Banking Commission, Pierre van Ommeslaghe, Les groupes de sociétés et l'expérience du droit belge, in Groups of Companies in European Laws 59 (Klaus J. Hopt ed., Berlin, New York 1982).

[24]   Reinier Kraakman et al., The Anatomy of Corporate Law 35 (3d ed. Oxford 2017), cited as Anatomy, at 25 et seq. More recently protecting external constituencies is getting increased attention, id. at 92–100, also in the European Union under the corporate social responsibility movement and the reporting requirements on non-financial information.

conceived more broadly, encompassing consumers; municipalities, regions, and countries interested in keeping groups and group members within their area; the state as a tax authority; and even non-personal public goods such as the environment, fundamental rights, and others.

The classic agency conflict concerns the managers as agents of the shareholders. This conflict exists if the shareholders are dispersed as is common in the US, the UK, and some other countries.[25] Much corporate law in the various countries deals with this conflict.[26] For controlling shareholders and for the parent in a group of companies, this agency conflict is hardly relevant because the controlling shareholder will ultimately prevail against the management, not only in the parent company but also in the subsidiaries, either by superior influence on the board or by voting power in the general assembly. It is true that under special circumstances—for example, in multinational groups—control may not be exercised so easily, especially if labor sides with the management of the subsidiary, or if state agencies in the country of the subsidiary pursue country-specific interests. But this is the exception.[27] As to groups of companies, the two most discussed principal–agent conflicts concern the minority shareholders and the creditors (as well as the employees).

1.3.1 *Minority Shareholders versus the Controlling Shareholder*

This agency problem occurs most frequently in continental European countries where family companies and groups of companies are common.[28] The controlling shareholder may abuse that control position in various ways, such as self-dealing and similar related party transactions, thereby reaping private benefits of control.[29] The corporate laws of most countries cope with this problem of controlling shareholder opportunism by various strategies and mechanisms of minority protection.[30]

As we shall see, many jurisdictions deal with this agency problem without distinguishing whether these conflicts arise in the independent corporation or in a group of companies. Yet in groups of companies, this agency problem has several particular features.[31] First and most conspicuous is the fact that the controlling shareholder in the subsidiary may not just act opportunistically in his own private interest; he may act responsibly in the interest not

---

[25] See *supra* 1.2.

[26] Anatomy, *supra* note 24, at 49–77; cf. the survey on group law in Germany, France, UK, USA, the European Union and Switzerland in Peter Böckli, *supra* note 13, § 11; Eddy Wymeersch, *Groups of Companies in the EEC, A Survey Report to the European Commission on the Law Relating to Corporate Groups in Various Member States* (Berlin, New York 1993).

[27] A special case includes the groups that are controlled by two or more shareholders at parity, so-called parity groups (Gleichordnungskonzerne). There the problem is the sharing of the control, not the agency conflict with the management of the subsidiary.

[28] *Supra* 1.2.

[29] For an international comparison of private benefits of control, see Alexander Dyck & Luigi Zingales, "Private Benefits of Control: An International Comparison", 59 J. Fin. 537 (2004); Anatomy, *supra* note 24, at 79–108, in particular 103–08, 164–65; for a more positive evaluation of private benefits of control, see Alessio M. Pacces, Rethinking Corporate Governance, The Law and Economics of Control Powers (London, New York 2012).

[30] Anatomy, *supra* note 24, at 79–108, 87–88, as to creditor protection 121–23.

[31] Cf. Emmerich & Habersack, *supra* note 21, § 1 III 3 and in more detail for German group law *infra* 2.2.

only of the parent, but of the group as a whole and/or other subsidiaries. While the controlling shareholder of an independent corporation has an individual interest in the well-being of "his" corporation which somewhat reduces the risk of opportunism at the expense of the minority shareholders, this is not necessarily the case if he has important stakes in other companies as a parent of the group or as a controlling shareholder of the parent. In this case, what may be disadvantageous for him in the one company may at the same time be beneficial for the other companies. This is what makes the agency conflict in the group generally more complex and acute than in the controlled independent company.

Second, steering a group of companies implies making difficult business judgment decisions that may be appropriate or even necessary for the group though they are disadvantageous or even harmful for the subsidiary. This implies a much more difficult balancing of interest between the subsidiary and the parent (and other subsidiaries) than between the minority and the majority in an independent corporation. Examples are easy to find: in most groups, there is a central cash management where the moneys of the subsidiaries are pooled. It is very common that the parent takes contributions from the subsidiaries for the group that may or may not be economically and/or legally justified from the perspective of the subsidiary, for example for services rendered within the group or more generally for the alleged benefits of belonging to the group. The parent or another group member may be in financial difficulties and need the help of the subsidiary. The parent may need to make a decision about where in the group layoffs or cut-downs should be effectuated or, more positively, which of the subsidiaries in the group should be attributed the opportunity to develop a promising new product or where, usually for tax reasons, a new subsidiary should be brought up that may take away business from the others. In a sense, the latter cases present a horizontal agency problem, not just a vertical one as in the independent corporation. This is not to say that such balancing cannot be done in jurisdictions without separate provisions for groups, but it is considered by some jurisdictions the reason for treating the agency problem in groups of companies separately and differently.

Third, the agency problem is exacerbated if the controlling shareholder in the group holds only a block of shares that is enough for control instead of 100%.[32] As seen before, depending on how control is defined, this may be just a 51% block, or even considerably less in corporations in many continental European countries in which the attendance rate of the common shareholders at the general assembly is low. In Germany, for example, this is sometimes under 30%. With the mandatory bid provision for takeovers in many European countries, 30% is usually considered control for the purposes of acquiring control in the sense of the takeover acts.[33] This line of exercising control with relatively smaller stakes is prolonged in a number of continental European countries by pyramiding,[34] i.e., exercising control over a subsidiary by another subsidiary and so on. The actual economic stake of the controlling shareholder at the top of the pyramid may thus become very small, with the consequence that his risk in the lowest part of the pyramid may be minimal. The temptation to take hidden private profits somewhere in the group increases correspondingly.

---

[32]   Luca Enriques & Paolo Volpin, "Corporate Governance Reforms in Continental Europe", 21 J. Econ. Perspect. 117, 122–25 (2007).

[33]   Klaus J. Hopt, "European Takeover Reform of 2012/2013—Time to Re-Examine the Mandatory Bid", 15 EBOR 143, 173–76 (2014).

[34]   See *supra* note 4.

Fourth, in a group of companies, the agency conflict may not just be one that concerns the minority shareholders in the subsidiary. The minority shareholders in the parent corporation may also be affected. This is the case if the management of the parent, in agreement with the controlling shareholder, takes the business decision to invest heavily in a risky subsidiary without shareholder consent in the general assembly of the parent corporation. The famous German Holzmüller case is a good example of this.[35]

1.3.2 Creditors versus the Controlling Shareholder

The other main agency problem concerns the creditors. As for the minority shareholder agency problem, this conflict is well known in general corporate law for the independent company, and a number of jurisdictions do not have separate rules for this problem in group situations.[36] But again creditors of groups may be more exposed to controlling shareholder opportunism than creditors of independent companies.[37]

The above-mentioned special features of the conflict also apply here: a smaller incentive of the controlling shareholder to act in the sole interest of the subsidiary because of his stakes in other companies, difficult financial and investment decisions in steering the whole group, exacerbated risk in pyramidal groups, and agency problems not only for the creditors of the subsidiary but also of the creditors of the parent.

Furthermore, quite apart from the precarious situation of involuntary creditors, it is usually more difficult for a creditor of a subsidiary to evaluate the risk he runs than for a creditor of an independent company. The situation is just more opaque, and the divisions between the assets of group members are more blurred. This is true whether or not the creditor knows that the debtor company is a group member. Disclosure under the various national and international transparency provisions is relatively well established as far as the parent corporation is concerned, in particular because of group accounting,[38] but transparency is much less developed as far as the subsidiaries are concerned. As a consequence, the general creditor risk—ex ante: misrepresentation of value; ex post: intra-group transactions, asset dilution, asset distribution, and debt dilution[39]—is generally higher in groups of companies than in independent companies.

1.3.3 Labor and Other Stakeholders versus the Controlling Shareholder

Similar problems arise for employees and other stakeholders, whether these problems are considered to be agency conflicts[40] or not. The decision of whether employees are hired or fired may not just depend on the business situation of the subsidiary but may follow the interest of the group. Restructuring in groups of companies, in particular in multinational

---

[35] German Bundesgerichtshof, Decisions BGHZ 83, 122 (1982), *Holzmüller* case; but see also the BGHZ 159, 30 (2004), *Gelatine* case.

[36] Anatomy, *supra* note 24, at 109–43: Transactions with Creditors.

[37] Anatomy, *supra* note 24, at 121–23; Marianne Bertrand, Paras Mehta, & Sendhil Mullainathan, "Ferreting Out Tunneling: An Application on Indian Business Groups", 117 Q. J. Econ. 121 (2002) with experience from India. See also *infra* note 105.

[38] See *infra* 3.2.   [39] Anatomy, *supra* note 24, at 111–16.

[40] For employees in this sense, Anatomy, *supra* note 24, at 105–07.

groups, belongs to the most controversial issues for labor. For example, in the case of a take-over threat against an independent company, labor will often seek a coalition with the management and the controlling shareholder against the minority shareholders; in other cases, however, the controlling shareholder in the group may take decisions in labor issues in the interest of the whole group. In a number of countries the employees may have a say in the co-determined board of the independent company, but this does not help if the decision is finally made at the top of the group, unless there is a special group codetermination there as well. Germany has such a group codetermination system, but only German labor has its representatives sitting on the board of the parent.[40a]

Many countries deal with this labor agency problem in groups with specific labor group provisions. In some countries there is even a full-fledged labor group law, either codified or developed by case law. This whole area of group-specific provisions in employment law, industrial relations, and labor codetermination is highly complicated and controversial and cannot be treated here.[41]

Similar group problems arise in other areas of the law, including competition law, tax, and environment. These areas will be briefly mentioned later when we look at the different regulatory models for dealing with groups, but they cannot be treated in more detail here.

2 Groups of Companies: Regulatory Models, Legal Strategies, and Mechanisms

2.1 Regulation by General Corporate and/or Civil Law

Many countries deal with the agency problems we have described by law, either general law or group law. As we shall see, most of this law is mandatory,[42] such as disclosure and group accounting as a reaction to opaqueness, the principles of related party transactions and tunneling, basic standards for directors and controlling shareholders in groups when making decisions that affect minority shareholders, creditor protection provisions, and insolvency law. When we deal with these strategies and mechanisms, we shall look at their function, whether the provisions are mandatory, and what room is left for self-protection or for enabling law, in particular for creditor protection.[43] But it should be mentioned here that certain countries can do without rules for groups of companies, or at least with very

---

[40a] As to the conformity of the German labor co-determination regime with European Law see the judgment of the European Court of Justice, 18 July 2017, C-566/15, ECLI:EU:C: 2017:562 (*Konrad Erzberger ./. TUI AG*), with critical comments by Mathias Habersack, "Germany first?", NZG 2017, 1021, and the controversial discussion before and after the judgment.

[41] See Simon F. Deakin, Employment Law and Industrial Relations, in chapter 39 in this volume. See also *infra* note 81.

[42] Klaus J. Hopt, "Directors' Duties and Shareholders' Rights in the European Union: Mandatory and/or Default Rules?", 61 Rivista delle Società 13–32 (2016). As to mandatory corporate law in the context of disclosure, see Anatomy, *supra* note 24, at 247–48.

[43] *Infra* 5.1.

few of them. This is the case in Sweden, for example, where there seems to be no felt need to deal with group agency problems in more detail. This is astonishing because in Sweden the shareholding structure is characterized by strong owners and weak minorities. The pertinent studies suggest that the reason may be that the country is small and social control is effective.[44] Furthermore, creditor protection in general—and more specifically in groups of companies—may be irrelevant or much less relevant for large voluntary creditors who can choose with whom they contract and can bargain for secured credit. Yet this is not the case for involuntary creditors, and even small and medium voluntary creditors may not really have the choice to protect themselves.

If countries choose to address the group agency problems more specifically, they can follow three regulatory models: first, they can choose between regulation by general corporate and/or civil law (section 2.1) and regulation by special corporate group law (section 2.2). These two models can and usually will be combined with group regulation by areas of law (section 2.3). The prototype of the first regulatory model is the UK.[45] There corporate group law as such (apart from group accounting, for example) is non-existent. The general civil and corporate law provisions for dealing with agency problems of minority shareholders and creditors are used for independent companies as well as for groups of companies. Many other countries follow the same route. As for the corporate law in these countries dealing with group problems, there are considerable differences between the various forms of corporations—for example, stock corporations—particularly if they are listed, limited liability companies, commercial partnerships, and in Europe the European company (SE).

In all these countries, the legitimacy of forming groups—i.e., creating different legal entities within the group and thereby partitioning assets[46] among the creditors of these entities—is principally uncontested, though in US academia there are pleas for unlimited shareholder liability for corporate tort creditors.[47] In the UK, the separate legal personality doctrine following the Salomon case[48] has been firmly upheld by the courts for groups as well.[49] But as we shall see, there are various civil or corporate law concepts that may catch group situations. One example is the concept of the shadow director who exercises de facto control in the company. The parent may qualify as such a shadow director—for example, in the context of wrongful trading under section 214 of the Insolvency Act 1986—though instructions given as directors of the parent are not a sufficient basis for this.[50] Another example is piercing the corporate veil.[51] Still, it has been said that "[i]t is clear that British law

---

[44] Jonas Agnblad, Erik Berglöf, Peter Högfeldt, & Helena Svancar, Ownership and Control in Sweden: Strong Owners, Weak Minorities, and Social Control, in Barca & Becht, *supra* note 4, at 228–58.

[45] Paul L. Davies & Sarah Worthington, Gower & Davies' Principles of Modern Company Law paras 9-21 to 9-23, on group accounts 21-9 to 21-12 (10th ed. London 2016); Paul L. Davies, Introduction to Company Law 95 (2d ed. Oxford 2010); Janet Dine, The Governance of Corporate Groups (Cambridge 2000); D.D. Prentice, Groups of Companies: The English Experience, in Hopt, *supra* note 23, at 99–130.

[46] As to the concept and the economic advantages of asset partitioning, see Anatomy, *supra* note 24, at 9, 110.

[47] Henry Hansmann & Reinier Kraakman, "Toward Unlimited Shareholder Liability for Corporate Torts", 100 Yale L. J. 1879 (1991).

[48] *Salomon v. A. Salomon & Co. Ltd.*, (1897) Appeal Cases 22.

[49] Davies, *supra* note 45, at 96.

[50] *Re Hydrodan (Corby) Ltd* (1994) 2 BCLC 180; *Re Paycheck Services 3 Ltd* (2009) 2 BCLC 309, CA; both referred to by Davies 2010, *supra* note 45, at 97; see *infra* 6.1.

[51] See *infra* 6.3.

is at one end of the spectrum as far as the regulation of liability within groups is concerned." There, the group problems are "solved by a combination of creditor self-help, general company law strategies as section 214, or the unfair prejudice remedy[52] and targeted statutory interventions, such as the requirement for group accounts."[53]

2.2 Regulation by Special Corporate Group Law

Many other jurisdictions have chosen to deal with group agency conflicts by more or less extensive special corporate group law. The prototype for this second regulatory model is Germany, with its separate, extensively codified law of corporate groups. A number of other countries have basically followed the German example, specifically Brazil, Portugal, Hungary, the Czech Republic, Slovenia and Croatia.[54] The German group law has been described elsewhere in more detail,[55] so it suffices here to summarize its key elements. First, it is important to see that in Germany, group law is codified only for stock corporations (Aktien-Konzernrecht).[56] Group law for limited liability companies (GmbH) and for commercial partnerships exists and is extensive, but it is pure case law, which is rather different from codified corporate group law.[57] Second, German codified group law distinguishes between contractual groups and de facto groups. Contractual groups are formed by contract between the parent and the subsidiary, but de facto groups are formed by unilateral declaration.[58] In a contractual group, the parent is allowed to steer the group in the sole group's interest, but the parent has to pay for this legal privilege by being obliged to make good the losses of the subsidiary and by adequate compensation for the minority shareholders of the subsidiary. The legislator's thought was that the freedom to steer the group would be such an attractive incentive for the parent that in most cases it would enter such a group contract. Yet this hope turned out to be vain. Corporate reality in Germany is different: contractual

---

[52] Davies, *supra* note 45, at 232–38.   [53] Davies, *supra* note 45, at 99 and 100.

[54] On group law in Germany, Portugal, Slovenia, Hungary, and Italy, Christoph Teichmann, "Konzernrecht und Niederlassungsfreiheit—Zugleich Rezension der Entscheidung EuGH, Rs. 186/12 (Impacto Azul)", ZGR 2014, 45, 49–62; id., *supra* note 11, at 191–95. See also European Model Company Act (EMCA) 2017, available at < https://ssrn.com/abstract=2929348>, General Comments in Chapter 15 on Groups of Companies, there also Albania and Turkey are mentioned.

[55] Tobias H. Tröger, "Corporate Groups, A German's European Perspective", in German and Nordic Perspectives on Company Law and Capital Markets Law (Holger Fleischer, Jesper Lau Hansen & Wolf-Georg Ringe eds., Tübingen 2015), 157–99; Emmerich & Habersack, *supra* note 21. An old but still useful description of German Aktienkonzernrecht in English is by Herbert Wiedemann, "The German Experience with the Law of Affiliated Enterprises", in Hopt, *supra* note 23, at 21–43.

[56] The German Aktien-Konzernrecht is regulated in the Stock Corporation Act third book on affiliated enterprises (Arts. 291–328) together with general definitions (Arts. 15–19). There are also general corporate group disclosure duties (Arts. 20–22), but they have lost their relevance because of more far-reaching capital market disclosure rules under European law. The authoritative commentary on German Konzernrecht is Volker Emmerich & Mathias Habersack, Aktien- und GmbH-Konzernrecht (8th ed. Munich 2016).

[57] Emmerich & Habersack, *supra* note 21, parts 4, 5, and 6; see list of landmark cases in Hopt in Schmitthoff & Wolodridge, *supra* note 23, at 84 n.15.

[58] Stock Corporation Act, Arts. 18, 302, 309.

groups are rare (and due to diminished tax benefits they are becoming even rarer)[59] and, apart from the few above-mentioned countries, the concept of corporate groups has not been attractive abroad. In the de facto group—i.e., control by the parent without such a group contract—the parent must fully compensate any subsidiary at the end of the year for all acts and transactions caused by the parent that are contrary to the subsidiary's own interest.[60] This rule is complemented by a mandatory group report of the directors of the parent, by group audit, examination by the supervisory board of the parent, and by the right of each shareholder of the parent to have an investigation at the order of the court. Yet the efficacy of these mechanisms is an open question.[61] Furthermore, new case law has established the liability of the shareholders for threatening the solvency of the corporation in closely held firms.[62]

Italy introduced a special codified group law in 2004. The core is made up of Articles 2497–2497-septies of the Italian Civil Code on the activity of "direction and co-ordination of companies" exercised by holding companies.[63] Apart from various rights and duties of directors and group members, and protective measures such as disclosure, the main achievement of this reform was to provide for a liability of the holding company and its directors toward the subsidiary's shareholders and creditors if the legal requirements are met. As we shall see, this liability can be avoided if compensatory damages are paid. The existence of a group need not be proven by the shareholders or creditors, but is presumed. In addition, the rules on conflict of interest have been tightened: they govern the (independent) corporation as well as groups of companies. Under certain circumstances, the minority shareholders also have a right of withdrawal.

A third group of countries includes France, with its Rozenblum doctrine[64] and the crime of abuse of corporate assets,[65] and Belgium, with group provisions for publicly listed companies belonging to a group.[66] The Rozenblum doctrine has been developed as case law by criminal courts and is characterized by a more flexible balancing of interests of the parent and the subsidiary. This may be more functional than the German solution, but the

---

[59] Emmerich & Habersack, *supra* note 21, § 11 comment 6: rare for stock corporations, more frequent for limited liability companies (GmbH).

[60] Stock Corporate Act, Arts. 18, 311. See in more detail *infra* 6.2.

[61] Cf. Jochen Vetter in Aktiengesetz Kommentar § 311 comments 8 and 9 (2d ed. Karsten Schmidt & Marcus Lutter eds., Cologne 2010), but with the remark that German practice has learned to live with the law.

[62] So-called Existenzvernichtungshaftung, i.e., responsibility for "annihilating the existence of an enterprise." Johanna Kroh, Der existenzvernichtende Eingriff (Tübingen 2013).

[63] Paola Fasciani, "Groups of Companies: The Italian Approach", 4 ECFR 195, 202–31 (2007); Umberto Tombari, Diritto dei gruppi di Imprese (Milan 2010).

[64] Cass. crim., 4 February 1985 (*Rozenblum*), Dalloz 1985, 478, Revue des Sociétés 1985, 648; later on Cass. crim., 23 April 1991, Revue des Sociétés 1991, 785; Cass. crim., 9 December 1991, Revue des Sociétés 1992, 358, all three decisions with comment by Bouloc; see the case law report by Marie-Emma Boursier, "Le Fait Justificatif de Groupe dans L'Abus de Biens Sociaux: Entre Efficacité et Clandestinité", Revue des sociétés 2005, 273. See *infra* 5.3.

[65] See *infra* 4.3.3.

[66] Yves De Cordt & Patricia Colard, Groups of companies governance in Belgium, in Festschrift für Klaus J. Hopt zum 70. Geburtstag vol. 2, 3043 at 3047–50 (Stefan Grundmann et al. eds., Tübingen, New York 2010); van Ommeslaghe, *supra* note 23; Xavier Dieux, "Le groupe de sociétés: phénomène ou institution? Illustration dans un droit frontalier", Revue Trimestrielle de Droit Financier/Corporate Finance and Capital Markets Law Review 2017, 35.

subsidiary is better protected by German group law.[67] Other European countries, such as Spain[68] and Sweden,[69] as well as Japan[70] have no comprehensive group law, but various legal provisions for groups.

The situation in the European Union is still in its developmental stage. The Forum Europaeum Corporate Group Law,[71] the High Level Group of Company Law Experts,[72] the Reflection Group[73], the Forum Europaeum on Company Groups (FECG)[73a], The Informal Company Law Expert Group (ICLEG)[73b], the European Company Law Experts (ECLE)[73c] and the European Model Company Act 2017[73d] have all advocated European harmonization by core group rules, more or less in line with the French Rozenblum doctrine. In its Company Law Action Plan of 2012, the European Commission had announced its intention to proceed in this direction,[74] but then the difficult discussion on the Shareholder Rights Amendment Directive[74a] and the Brexit process required more attention. In any case a full-fledged European group law is not in sight and cannot be recommended too.[74b]

---

[67] Cf. Anatomy, *supra* note 24, at 133.   [68] Embid Irujo, *supra* note 12.

[69] Knut Rohde, Groups of Companies in Scandinavian Company Law, in Hopt, *supra* note 23, at 142–52; but see also *supra* section 2.1 for social control.

[70] Eiji Takahashi, "Die Zukunft des japanischen Konzernrechts – Die Reform des Aktienrechts von 2014", AG 2014, 493; id., "Recht und Wirklichkeit der verbundenen Unternehmen in Japan", in German and Asian Perspectives on Company Law 335 (Holger Fleischer, Hideki Kanda, Kon Sik Kim & Peter O. Mülbert eds., 2016). Formerly id., "Japanese Corporate Groups under the New Legislation", 3 ECFR 287–309 (2006).

[71] Forum Europaeum Corporate Group Law, *supra* note 7, at 197–207.

[72] High Level Group of Company Law Experts, *supra* note 4, ch. 5.1–4, at 94–100.

[73] Reflection Group, Report on the Future of EU Company Law (for the European Commission), Brussels, 5 April 2011, ch. 4, 59–75, 79–80.

[73a] Forum Europaeum on Company Groups, "Proposal to Facilitate the Management of Cross-Border Company Groups in Europe", ECFR 2015, 299, in German language also in ZGR 2015, 507. See also Corporate Governance im grenzüberschreitenden Konzern (Peter Hommelhoff, Marcus Lutter & Christoph Teichmann eds., Berlin 2017).

[73b] The Informal Company Law Expert Group (ICLEG), Report on the recognition of the interest of the group, October 2016.

[73c] European Company Law Experts (ECLE), "A Proposal for the Reform of Group Law in Europe", 18 EBOR 1–49 (2017).

[73d] European Model Company Act, *supra* note 54, Section 15.16. Cf. ECFR Symposium in Vienna 2015 on this Model Act, ECFR 2016, 198–374.

[74] European Commission, Action Plan: European Company Law and Corporate Governance—A Modern Legal Framework for More Engaged Shareholders and Sustainable Companies, 12 December 2012, COM(2012) 740 final; Peter Hommelhoff, "Ein Neustart im europäischen Konzernrecht", Kölner Schriften zum Wirtschaftsrecht (KSzW) 02.2014 I 63; Taskforce on European Company Groups (Peter Hommelhoff et al.), Proposal to facilitate the management of cross-border company groups in Europe, draft of November 20, 2014; Tröger, *supra* note 55, at 17–41; Klaus J. Hopt, "Europäisches Gesellschaftsrecht im Lichte des Aktionsplans der Europäischen Kommission vom Dezember 2012", ZGR 2013, 165–215. The Proposal for a Ninth Directive had not been successful, see the comprehensive survey on groups of companies in the EU by Stefan Grundmann, European Company Law—Organization, Finance and Capital Markets § 31 (2d ed. Cambridge 2012). As to the proposal for related party transactions more specifically see *infra* section 4.2 with note 117.

[74a] See *infra* note 117a.

[74b] ECLE, *supra* note 73c, at 41 et seq.; cf. also Peter O. Mülbert, "Auf dem Weg zu einem europäischen Konzernrecht", 179 ZHR 645 (2015); Holger Fleischer, "Europäisches Konzernrecht: Eine akteurzentrierte Annäherung", ZGR 2017, 1; Jessica Schmidt, "Europäisches Konzernrecht", Der Konzern 2017, 1; Marc

2.3 Regulation by Areas of Law

In comparative law, the two above-mentioned regulatory models of dealing with group agency conflicts are usually contrasted with each other. But this is misleading. In those countries that apparently do not have group law, this is also true only as far as corporate group law is concerned. In the UK, group accounting existed well before it was made mandatory by EU regulation.[75] But group law provisions and very often quite extensive group law legislation exists in many countries, though in fields other than corporate law. The list is long and includes group law in accounting and auditing,[76] conflict of law,[77] securities regulation,[78] banking and other financial institutes,[79] insolvency,[80] labor,[81] competition law,[82] product

Amstutz, Globale Unternehmensgruppen, Geschichte und Zukunft des europäischen Konzernrechts (Tübingen, 2017).

[75] Davies, *supra* note 45, at 96.

[76] Grundmann, *supra* note 74, § 16 (Seventh Directive). As to the IFRS special regime for publicly traded groups see id., *supra* note 74, § 18. Audit of consolidated accounts is standard all through Europe. See also *infra* section 4.1.

[77] Moritz Renner, "Kollisionsrecht und Konzernwirklichkeit in der transnationalen Unternehmensgruppe", ZGR 2014, 452–86.

[78] Konzernrecht und Kapitalmarktrecht (Peter Hommelhoff, Klaus J. Hopt & Marcus Lutter, eds., Munich et al. 2001), with general report and country reports; Klaus J. Hopt, "Konzernrecht: Die europäische Perspektive", 171 ZHR 199, 231–32, 233–35 (2007); High Level Group of Company Law Experts, *supra* note 4, ch. 5.4, at 99–100: no separate listing of subsidiaries in the parent is listed.

[79] "Basel Committee on Banking Supervision (Bank for International Settlements), Joint Forum, Principles for the supervision of financial conglomerates", September 2012; id., "Corporate governance principles for banks", July 2015; Jens-Hinrich Binder, "Interne Corporate Governance im Bankkonzern", in Handbuch Corporate Governance von Banken 686 (Klaus J. Hopt & Gottfried Wohlmannstetter, eds., Munich 2011); Tobias Tröger, "Konzernverantwortung in der aufsichtsunterworfenen Finanzbranche", 177 ZHR 475 (2013); id., "Organizational Choices of Banks and the Effective Supervision of Transnational Financial Institutions", 48 Tex. Int'l. L. J. 177 (2013); Peter O. Mülbert & Alexander Wilhelm, "Risikomanagement und Compliance im Finanzmarktrecht – Entwicklungen der aufsichtsrechtlichen Anforderungen", 178 ZHR 502, 530–34 (2014); Guido Ferrarini, "Understanding the Role of Corporate Governance in Financial Institutions: A Research Agenda", ECGI Law Working Paper No, 347/2017, March 2017; Klaus J. Hopt, "Corporate Governance of Banks and Other Financial Institutions after the Financial Crisis", 13 J. Corp. L. Stud. 219–53 (2013); id., "Corporate Governance von Finanzinstituten", ZGR 2017, 438–59. For the European Solvency II directive and the supervision of insurance companies see Meinrad Dreher & Christoph Ballmeier, "Solvency II und Gruppenaufsicht", ZGR 2014, 753.

[80] Horst Eidenmüller & Tilmann Frobenius, "Ein Regulierungskonzept zur Bewältigung von Gruppeninsolvenzen: Verfahrenskonsolidierung im Kontext nationaler und internationaler Reformvorhaben, Zeitschrift für Wirtschaftsrecht (ZIP)", suppl. to issue 22, 1–20 (2013); Heribert Hirte, "Towards a Framework for the Regulation of Corporate Groups' Insolvencies", 5 ECFR 213–36 (2008); Michele Reumers, "Cooperation between Liquidators and Courts in Insolvency Proceedings of Related Companies under the Proposed Revised EIR (European Insolvency Regulation)", 10 ECFR 554 (2013) pleading for cooperation in multinational insolvencies; as to veil piercing in insolvency in New Zealand see Davies, *supra* note 43, at 100. The revised European Insolvency Regulation of 20 May 2015 contains also provisions on group insolvency, Art. 56 et seq., further harmonization of European insolvency law is under way.

[81] Cf. Paul L. Davies, "Labour Law and Multinational Groups of Companies", in Hopt, *supra* note 23, at 208; the fundamental monography by Christine Windbichler, Arbeitsrecht im Konzern (Munich 1989).

[82] Strict parent liability according to the European Court of Justice, 8 May 2013, Case 508/11 P (ENI), Europäische Zeitschrift für Wirtschaftsrecht (EuZW) 2013, 544 with note Nehl; European Court

liability,[83] and other public law such as tax,[84] environment, and others. Apart from some observations on group law accounting, these area-specific group laws cannot be treated in this chapter,[85] since their objective is not the solution of group agency conflicts[86] but depends on the specific—and highly diverse—regulatory goals in each of these areas.

2.4 Legal Strategies and Mechanisms

In the following sections, selected legal strategies and mechanisms for dealing with group agency conflicts will be analyzed, including disclosure and accounting (section 3), related party transactions (section 4), standards for the directors and for the controlling shareholder (section 5), transactions with creditors (section 6), and control transactions (section 7). This is done with an emphasis on those jurisdictions that follow the second model, i.e., regulation by special corporate group law. For countries that follow the first model, examples alone are juxtaposed with what is done under the second model, since doing otherwise would necessarily be a repetition of general corporate law dealing with agency problems, as reported in the other chapters of the book, in particular under Part II: Substantive Topics.

3 Disclosure and Accounting

3.1 General Disclosure under Corporate Group Law

Disclosure and accounting are the most commonly used instruments for protecting minority shareholders and creditors in independent companies as well as in groups of companies.[86a] Today much of this disclosure in Europe is harmonized.[87] There is a long discussion about

---

of Justice, 26 September 2013, Neue Zeitschrift für Gesellschaftsrecht (NZG) 2014, 65 and further judgments; Thomas Weck, "Das gesellschaftsrechtliche Trennungsprinzip – Verabschiedung einer Illusion im Kartellrecht", NZG 2016, 1374; Meinrad Dreher, "Groups of Undertakings and Competition—Regulatory Approaches in Europe", 2 EBOR 187–221 (2001); Christian Kersting, "Wettbewerbsrechtliche Haftung im Konzern", Der Konzern 445 (2011).

[83] Brigitte Haar, "Piercing the Corporate Veil and Shareholders' Product and Environmental Liability" in American Law as Remedies for Capital Market Failures—New Developments and Implications for European and German Law after "Centros", 1 EBOR 317–352 (2000) mainly for the USA.

[84] Schön, *supra* note 10, at 409; Hopt, *supra* note 78, at 206.

[85] But see the chapters in this volume, part V on adjacent areas: chapter 38 on insolvency law; chapter 39 on employment and industrial regulation; chapter 40 on capital markets/securities law; chapter 41 on financial regulation and chapter 43 on tax law.

[86] Unless the concept of agency conflict is very broadly understood as encompassing more remote stakeholders and even non-personal public goods such as environment, fundamental rights, and others; *supra* 1.3.

[86a] Christian Leuz, Peter W. Wysocki, "The Economics of Disclosure and Financial Reporting Regulation: Evidence and Suggestions for Future Research", 54(2) J. Acct. Research 525 (2016).

[87] Konstantinos Sergakis, La Transparence des Sociétés Cotées en Droit Européen (2013).

why disclosure rules should be mandatory as they are in all core jurisdictions. The arguments for mandatory disclosure are both theoretical and empirical.[88] Without mandatory disclosure, there is an underproduction of information. Bad news is preferably suppressed. Voluntary disclosure of bad news may harm the company, in particular if other companies hide such news. Standardized mandatory disclosure helps the investors and the market to evaluate disclosure. Empirical evidence seems to support these arguments for publicly traded firms.[89] Group-specific disclosure[90] relates to the fact of control, to the relationship and transactions between the parent and the subsidiaries, and to the formation of the group at the stage of mere block building. The European Transparency Directive requires notification on changes in voting rights from 5% up at several thresholds.[91] In general, disclosure is much stricter in the US and the UK, while it is more lenient in continental Europe and Japan.[92]

An interesting example of limited disclosure is the German group dependency report for de facto groups.[93] This mandatory report by the management board of the subsidiary contains the details on the relationship between the corporation and the parent and other affiliated companies. It must be audited by the auditor of the company and by the supervisory board of the subsidiary. It is neither published nor available to the shareholders because it contains all the details of the internal life of the group. But the individual shareholders may ask the court for a special investigation if the auditors have refused to provide the audit certificate or have qualified it. In legal academia there has been a call for mandatory disclosure of the group dependency report to the shareholders; however, the legislators fear that this would be counterproductive because in practice the dependency report would become much less meaningful.

3.2 Group Accounting

As mentioned before, a special area of group law is group accounting. Consolidated accounts, though with many differences as to the reach and content, must be provided under various national and international group accounting provisions, including GAAP in the US and International Accounting Standards (IAS) and, as of 2001, International Financial Reporting Standards (IFRS) in many other countries. The European Union has decided to basically follow IFRS standards for group accounting, but has reserved the right not to follow any specific standard. While IFRS standards apply for consolidated accounts, the accounting

---

[88] Anatomy, *supra* note 24, at 247–54; Hanno Merkt, "Creditor Protection Through Mandatory Disclosure", 7 EBOR 95–122 (2006).

[89] For references for and against, see Anatomy, *supra* note 24, at 246–48.

[90] For the various group disclosure rules in Italy, see Fasciani, *supra* note 63. For Switzerland cf. Peter Weber, Heinz Zimmermann, & Beate Brändli, "The Price Effects of Disclosure of Significant Holdings in Listed Companies: The Case of Groups Acting in Concert", 3 Schweizerische Zeitschrift für Wirtschaftsrecht (SZW) 198 (2012).

[91] Rüdiger Veil, Transparency of Major Shareholdings and Financial Instruments, in European Capital Markets Law 310–47 (Rüdiger Veil ed., Oxford, Portland 2013). But see also the critical evaluation of this kind of disclosure by Lucian A. Bebchuk & Robert J. Jackson, "The Law and Economics of Blockholder Disclosure", 2 Harv. Bus. L. Rev. 39 (2012).

[92] Anatomy, *supra* note 24, at 147–251.

[93] Stock Corporation Act, Art. 312; cf. Emmerich & Habersack, *supra* note 21, § 26.

standards regarding annual financial accounts, i.e., those for the members of a group, differ greatly between the Member States.[94] While in the UK the issuer has an option to also prepare the annual financial accounts following IFRS standards, in France, Germany, Spain, and Sweden the annual financial accounts must be prepared in accordance with national accounting law. As far as listed companies are concerned there is a fair amount of convergence in Europe, but not for closely held groups.[95] There is work on more harmonization between US GAAP and IFRS, but progress is still slow.

3.3 Special Investigation with Group Dimension and the Role of Auditors and Independent Experts

Disclosure on groups of companies may be mandatory, but its effectiveness depends on enforcement, and enforcement differs greatly among the jurisdictions. As mentioned before with regard to the German dependency report, this is a task for the auditors as gatekeepers,[96] for special investigation procedures, and, on capital markets, for the stock exchanges and the various capital markets' supervisory agencies. Group auditing is a special area of group law. In Europe it is harmonized to a considerable degree.[97] In France there is good experience with the expert de gestion and the special reports by the commissaire aux comptes.[98] In Australia the Australian Capital Markets Authority has broad investigatory powers and even the right to start civil proceedings.[99]

The special investigation procedure is a very promising mechanism since the shareholders may ask the court to appoint special experts to investigate suspected transactions and possible abuses in independent companies as well as in groups of companies. In the Netherlands this has been said to be a "most effective mechanism," and Switzerland has also had good experiences with it. Meanwhile in Germany, where the Stock Corporation Act has different rules for special investigation in the (independent) company and in groups of companies, the experience with the latter is less impressive, a fact that may be due to difficult valuation problems (valuation rules are not harmonized in the European Union) and lawsuits that last many years. The Forum Europaeum Corporate Group Law and the High Level Group of Company Experts have recommended that Europe provide for a harmonized mechanism of special investigation.[100]

---

[94] On IFRS there is a vast literature. On financial accounting information in Europe, see Hendrik Brinckmann, Periodic Disclosure, in Veil, *supra* note 91, § 18 comments 30–34. The Forum Europaeum Corporate Group Law, *supra* note 7, at 191–96 and the High Level Group of Company Law Experts 2002, *supra* note 4, at 95–96 pleaded for better information on the single group members, in particular the subsidiaries.

[95] Hopt, *supra* note 78, at 208–09, 213–16.

[96] On gatekeepers, see Anatomy, *supra* note 24, at 42–43, 122–23.   [97] *Supra* section 2.3.

[98] Le Cannu & Dondero, *supra* note 21, nos 948 et seq., 1329 et seq. (expert de gestion), nos 508 et seq. (commisaires aux comptes); Maurice Cozian, Alain Viandier & Florence Deboissy, Droit des sociétés nos 1153 et seq. (30th ed. Paris 2017).

[99] Kluver, *supra* note 7, at 298 et seq.

[100] Forum Europaeum Corporate Group Law, *supra* note 7, at 207–17; Christine Windbichler, "'Corporate Group Law for Europe': Comments on the Forum Europaeum's Principles and Proposals for a European Corporate Group Law", 1 EBOR 265, 273 (2000); High Level Group of Company Law Experts, *supra* note 4, ch. 3.4, at 57–59; Klaus J. Hopt, "Comparative Corporate Governance: The State

4 RELATED PARTY TRANSACTIONS

4.1 Related Party Transactions and Specific Disclosure

Disclosure and accounting—rendered effective by the help of auditors and independent experts if needed—makes agency conflicts transparent. While this may lead to appropriate behavior of the agents or self-protective measures by the principals, these beneficial effects cannot be taken for granted, for the agents' temptation to skim off private benefits may be too great. This is also true for controlling shareholders and parents in groups of companies as agents of minority shareholders and creditors. Strong temptations arise for them in conflicted transactions, in particular in related party transactions (section 4) and control transactions (section 7). Conflicted transactions are part of the more general problem of conflicts of interest in corporate law that cannot be dealt with here in more detail.[101] Related party transactions are regulated extensively by corporate law for directors and officers,[102] but if they involve controlling shareholders they present special problems.[103] This is even more true for groups of companies. There such transactions between members of the group are far less visible and, since they are part of the normal group-internal business relations, it is hard—if not impossible—for minority shareholders of a subsidiary to judge whether they are made at arm's length or whether and to what extent private benefits have been extracted.[104] Related transactions can take very different forms and may include straightforward self-dealing as well as cash flow tunneling, asset tunneling, and equity tunneling.[105] Accordingly,

---

of the Art and International Regulation", 59 Am. J. Comp. L. 1 at 57–58 (2011). Cf. also ECLE, *supra* note 73c, at 45. European Model Company Act contains a provision on special investigation, Sections 15.12, 15.14.

[101] See Klaus J. Hopt, Trusteeship and Conflicts of Interest in Corporate, Banking, and Agency Law: Toward Common Legal Principles for Intermediaries in the Modern Service-Oriented Society, in Reforming Company and Takeover Law in Europe 51–88 (Guido Ferrarini, Klaus J. Hopt, Jaap Winter, & Eddy Wymeersch eds., 2004); id., "Conflict of Interest, Secrecy and Insider Information of Directors, A Comparative Analysis", 10 ECFR 167–93 (2013). Cf. the recent book on conflict of interest by Christoph Kumpan, *Der Interessenkonflikt im deutschen Privatrecht* (Tübingen 2014).

[102] Hopt, *supra* note 101, at 167.

[103] See Anatomy, *supra* note 24, ch. 6 on related party transactions and specifically for controlling shareholders 149; Luca Enriques, "Related Party Transactions: Policy Options and Real-World Challenges (With a Critique of the European Commission Proposal)", ECGI Law Working Paper No. 267/2014 (2014); Holger Fleischer, "Related Party Transactions bei börsennotierten Gesellschaften: Deutsches Aktien(konzern)recht und Europäische Reformvorschläge", 69 Betriebs-Berater 2691–700 (2014).

[104] OECD, Related Party Transactions and Minority Shareholder Rights (Paris 2012); J.H. Farrar & S. Watson, "Self-Dealing, Fair Dealing and Related Party Transactions: History, Policy and Reform", 11 J. Corp. L. Stud. 495 (2011).

[105] Atanasov, Black, & Ciccotello 2011, *supra* note 22; Simeon Djankov, Rafeal La Porta, Florencio Lopez-de-Silanes, & Andrei Shleifer, "The Law and Economics of Self-Dealing", 88 J. Fin. Econ. 430 (2008); Simon Johnson, Rafael La Porta, Florencio Lopez-de-Silanes, & Andrei Shleifer, "Tunneling", 90 Am. Econ. Rev., Papers and Proceedings 22 (2000); Jeremy Grant, Tom Kirchmaier, & Jodie A. Kirshner, "Financial Tunnelling and the Mandatory Bid Rule", 10 EBOR 233 (2009); Klaus J. Hopt, Self-Dealing and Use of Corporate Opportunities and Information: Regulating Directors' Conflict of Interest, in *Corporate Governance and Directors' Liabilities* 285 (Klaus J. Hopt & Gunther Teubner eds., Berlin, New York 1985).

the reactions by legislators and courts are manifold. A recent empirical study suggests that for listed companies, disclosure combined with consent of disinterested shareholders may be the best solution.[106] Special mandatory disclosure rules for related party transactions exist in many places, such as the US, the European Union, Germany and other continental European states, as well as Japan.[107] An empirical analysis of regulation and self-regulation of related party transactions has come up with interesting data for Italy.[108] Many of these disclosure rules are not found in the corporate law of these countries but are rather part of the securities laws, prominently in the US and in the European Union (the European Transparency Directive of 2004 as revised in 2013), or are national and international accounting rules, such as annual disclosure following US GAAP and IAS/IFRS. In most of these disclosure rules, one can find specific provisions for block holders, generally starting at 5%, and transactions with controlling shareholders. The test is usually that all material related party transactions that have not been concluded at arm's length—i.e., not under normal market conditions— should be disclosed. Many of these rules make distinctions according to the size and legal form of the firm. For non-listed firms, the requirements, if any, are much more lenient, while for listed companies, stricter disclosure rules for related party transactions may exist under the listing requirements of the stock exchanges than under the law. The dependency report under German group law has already been mentioned.[109] This report is not publicly available but is audited and given to the board of the subsidiary in order to protect the confidentiality of group-internal transactions. At the end, if one does not just look at corporate law, a considerable amount of convergence between the US, Europe, and Japan can be observed as far as disclosure of related party transactions is concerned.[110] This is particularly true for related party transactions in listed companies for both directors and controlling shareholders.

4.2 Procedural Regulation of Related Party Transactions

Disclosure helps against related party transactions, but it is not sufficient. In most jurisdictions it is supplemented by mandatory rules. While these rules originally were substantive, it became clear that fixing ceilings or the outright prohibition of certain related party transactions is too inflexible an approach and may sometimes run against the interest of the shareholders. This is also true in groups of companies where transactions between the members of the group may be economically beneficial. While a number of substantive rules are kept—for example, in tax law under the arm's length standard—more modern regulation is procedural. Usually there are consent requirements: either ex ante or sometimes ex post; by the whole board or by independent directors; in important cases by the

---

[106] Djankov et al., *supra* note 105, 2008; for an enumeration of legal strategies and remedies see Pierre-Henri Conac, Luca Enriques, & Martin Gelter, "Constraining Dominant Shareholders' Self-Dealing: The Legal Framework in France, Germany, and Italy", 4 ECFR 491–528 (2007); Andrew Keay, "The Authorising of Directors' Conflicts of Interest: Getting a Balance?", 12 J. Corp. L. Stud. 129 (2012). As to the practical difficulties see Alessandro Pomelli, Related-Party Transactions and the Intricacies of Ex Post Judicial Review: The Parmalat/Lactalis Case, ECFR 2016, 73.

[107] Anatomy, *supra* note 24, at 148–52, 277–89.   [108] Bianchi et al. 2014, *supra* note 4.

[109] *Supra* section 3.1.   [110] Anatomy, *supra* note 24, 150–52.

shareholders; and sometimes by the supervisory agency.[111] An example of a conflict of interest procedure occurs under Belgian law where a board committee of three independent directors is in charge of carrying out an assessment of the decision or transaction.[112] In groups of companies, these consent requirements may not work fully because the board of the subsidiary is most often dependent on the parent, and consent resolutions by the general assembly are of little use if the parent is in control. Then the consent of independent directors or a decision of only the minority shareholders as in Australia[113] may help.[114] An interesting experiment is found in Italy where the minority needs to be represented on the board by a minority representative. This seems to be more effective than independent directors.[115]

The European Commission considered introducing a rule for related party transactions that would have required the consent of the general assembly for transactions upon a threshold of 5% of the assets of the company.[115a] Similarly, transactions that have had a relevant impact on the profit or turnover of the corporation would have been subjected to such a consent requirement. A similar rule exists under the Listing Rules of the FSA in the UK.[116] Yet the reactions in the Member States, in particular in Germany, were highly critical because the shareholder constituency, shareholder behavior in the general meetings, and the rules governing shareholder rights and voting differ greatly among the Member States. On the other side the case for moving forward on a European level has been made convincingly several times, for example by the Forum Europaeum on Company Groups.[117] In general, the experience with shareholder approval of major transactions and the uncertainties under the German *Holzmüller* case suggested a careful balancing of the benefits and disadvantages of such a rule. In any case, such an initiative on the part of the European Commission would

---

[111]   Keay, *supra* note 104; OECD, *supra* note 104, at 35 et seq.: a long comparative list on shareholder approval requirements for related party transactions (excluding salaries). For Belgium it should be remembered that originally much of the Belgian group regulation was autonomously developed by the Belgian Securities Commission (Commission bancaire, as it was called at that time), Van Ommeslaghe, *supra* note 23, at 59, 79–91.

[112]   De Cordt & Colard, *supra* note 66, at 3046–53.

[113]   Kluver, *supra* note 7, at 295–297 on specific authorization procedure by minority shareholders; Barbara Mescher & Brett Bondfield, "Corporate Groups and the Duty of Directors to Act in Their Company's Best Interests", 8 Journal of Applied Research in Accounting and Finance 2–12 (2013).

[114]   For details, see Anatomy, *supra* note 24, at 85–86.

[115]   Bianchi et al. (2014), *supra* note 4, at 24, 25. See also Corrado Malberti & Emiliano Sironi, "The Mandatory Representation of Minority Shareholders on the Board of Directors of Italian Listed Corporations: An Empirical Analysis" (2007), available at http://www.sssn.com/abstract=965398.

[115a]   On this draft directive see Klaus J. Hopt, "Corporate Governance in Europe, A Critical Review of the European Commission's Initiatives on Corporate Law and Corporate Governance", NYU J. L. & Bus. 12 (2015) 139-213.

[116]   Paras 11.1.7 and 11.1.11 of the Listing Rules, of Financial Conduct Authority (FCA) as of January 2015 www.fsa.gov.uk/pubs/other/listing_rules.pdf (5% up).

[117]   Forum Europaeum on Company Groups, *supra* note 73a; cf. already the proposal of the Forum Europaeum Corporate Group Law, *supra* note 7. As to other reactions see Tim Drygala, Europäisches Konzernrecht: Gruppeninteresse und Related Party Transactions, Die Aktiengesellschaft 198, 208–10 (2013); see also the contributions by Enriques and Fleischer, *supra* note 103. For Germany see Jochen Vetter, "Regelungsbedarf für Related Party Transactions?", 179 ZHR 273 (2015). For Italy see Bianchi et al. 2014, *supra* note 3.

have needed to take better into consideration the group problem—for example, by pro-viding for a minority shareholder vote or otherwise neutralizing the decisive influence of the parent. In the end, the final version of the shareholder rights amendment directive of May 17, 2017 provides a more modest version.[117a] The compromise is a more lenient defi-nition of related party transactions that is up to the Member State to concretize as well as a Member State option that allows to choose between the approval of the general assembly and the approval by the administrative or supervisory board, in the latter case the director or the shareholder concerned being excluded from the vote or at least from having a de-termining role in the approval process. This leaves German Konzernrecht more or less un-touched. While with the directive of 2017 some harmonization as to group law in European law has been reached, there is more to be done on the European level and in particular on the Member State level.[117b]

Similar to the case as for mandatory disclosure,[118] the auditors also have a role in related party transactions. The special investigation procedure by independent experts described above may help to expose hidden abuses. Other gatekeepers such as evaluation experts can help. Under the Belgian procedure, the board committee of three independent directors can ask for the assistance of one or more independent experts who are to provide technical advice.[119]

5 Standards for the Directors and for the Controlling Shareholder

5.1 Standards for the Directors and the Controlling Shareholders in Independent Corporations and in Groups of Companies

Regulating related party transactions may practically cover a large part of the agency conflicts of directors and controlling shareholders in independent companies as well as in groups. But opportunism is not just a temptation for specific transactions; there are many other situations and business decisions that may be conflicted, such as acquisition, alloca-tion, and distribution decisions made in the group that have different impacts for the var-ious group member companies. It is therefore important to set the right standard for the directors if an agency conflict arises. The usual standard for the director when dealing with

---

[117a] Directive (EU) 2017/828 of the European Parliament and of the Council of 17 May 2017 amending Directive 2007/36/EC as regards the encouragement of long-term shareholder engagement, OJEU 20.5.2017 L 132/1, Art. 9c: Transparency and approval of related party transactions. Cf. Andreas Tarde, "Die verschleierte Konzernrichtlinie", ZGR 2017, 360; Rüdiger Veil, "Transaktionen mit Related Parties im deutschen Aktien- und Konzernrecht", NZG 2017, 521.

[117b] ECLE, *supra* note 73c, at 44 et seq.   [118] *Supra* section 3.3.

[119] De Cordt & Colard, *supra* note 66, at 3052.

such conflicts is the duty of loyalty.[120] This duty is a fairness concept that is most open and flexible and will only be concretized ex post and over time by the courts. Traditionally, the duty of loyalty is very strict in the US, the UK, and other Commonwealth countries. One of the reasons for this is the fact that this duty of company directors has its origins in the strict fiduciary position of the trustee under old English trust law. Due to the particularities of US American procedural law, a considerable amount of case law has emerged. The situation in continental Europe is very different because the duty of care has traditionally played a greater role than the duty of loyalty. Only more recently has the latter become important while the former has lost some of its significance due to the import of the business judgment rule into continental Europe.[120a] Many differences still exist, however, as to the reach, the burden of proof, the litigation, and the cultural perception of certain kinds of business behavior that may or may not be acceptable socially. In some countries, these agency conflicts are not only dealt with by corporate law, but also and sometimes very much so by criminal law. For example, in France, self-dealing is a criminal abus des biens sociaux[121] and apparently the most frequently applied criminal rule of company law.[122] In the aftermath of the financial crisis, criminal prosecution of directors is also on the advance in countries such as Germany, Austria, and Ireland.[122a]

In groups of companies it is more difficult to find the right standard for the directors since there the conflicts are not only within the company—i.e., between the director and the shareholders—but also beyond the company between the different member companies of the group and possibly their shareholders. In fact, the group-specific duties and liabilities of directors are manifold, including limits to granting loans to directors in the group,[123] prohibition on competition in the group, and limits to passing on information to other group members.

Standards for the controlling shareholders have been developed more slowly, unless, as in exceptional cases, they can be considered shadow directors.[124] They differ considerably under the national corporate laws, and the differences are striking as far as enforcement and litigation are concerned.[125] While in the US the standard is entire fairness or utmost good faith and loyalty, the standards are more lenient in continental European countries and in Japan, a fact that is due to the different shareholder structure and the economic and political influence of controlling shareholders and groups. In France there is the relatively vague concept of abuse of majority power.[126] Under German stock corporation law the use of the influence of a person over the corporation to the detriment of the corporation or its shareholders

---

[120] For comparative details, see Anatomy, *supra* note 24, at 161–65; Hopt, *supra* note 101, with examples and case law, 175 et seq.: fraud, loans and credit to directors, self-dealing, competition with the company, corporate opportunities, wrongful profiting from positions, remuneration, and ongoing duty of loyalty.

[120a] Klaus J. Hopt, Die business judgment rule, Ein sicherer Hafen für unternehmerische Entscheidungen in Deutschland und der Schweiz, in Festschrift für Peter Nobel 217–34 (Bern 2015).

[121] Art. L. 241-3, L. 242-6 Code de commerce, Conac, Enriques, & Gelter, *supra* note 104, at 518–19.

[122] Cozian et al., *supra* note 98, nos. 910 et seq., 2036.

[122a] Klaus J. Hopt, Responsibility of Banks and Their Directors, Including Liability and Enforcement, in Functional or dysfunctional – the law as a cure? Risk and liability in the financial markets 159 (Lars Gorton, Jan Kleinemann & Hans Wibom eds., Stockholm, Juridiska fakulteten 2014).

[123] Hopt, *supra* note 78, at 236.

[124] This concept is more important for creditor protection and therefore dealt with *infra* section 6.2.

[125] Anatomy, *supra* note 24, at 162–65.   [126] Cozian et al., *supra* note 98, nos. 910, 935.

is forbidden.[127] This is not specifically addressed to controlling shareholders, but it is most important for those. Apart from this provision, it took a very long time for the courts to accept that there are duties of loyalty not only between the controlling shareholder and the company, but also of the controlling shareholder to his minority shareholders.[128]

5.2 Specific Standards for Balancing the Interests of Member Companies in Groups

For groups of companies, the standards used by the various jurisdictions for evaluating the transactions and business relations in groups of companies differ greatly. In many countries there are rules that try to uphold the interest of the group members against the parent and compensate in one way or another the subsidiaries for damages suffered by intragroup transactions. In Germany, France, and Italy, an evaluation of the overall operation of an individual subsidiary and its individual transactions with the controlling company must be made.[129] In this context it has been mentioned that a rule that focuses on the individual transactions may be inefficient since in some cases it disfavors the controlling shareholder by free-riding minority shareholders while in other cases it lets the controller reap excessive private benefits.[130] German group law is the most stringent as it does not allow for weighing up the disadvantages or advantages the subsidiary derives from being a member of the group. The disadvantages are measured from the viewpoint of an independent corporation only. Italian group law is more flexible because it allows the consideration of compensatory advantages for the subsidiary.[131] Spain has been advised to follow the Italian example.[132] The French Rozenblum doctrine[133] allows an even more flexible balancing of the interests of the parent and the subsidiary. The criminal courts that developed this rule allow the subsidiary to also take into consideration the interest of the group, not only its own advantages

---

[127] Art. 117 of the German Stock Corporation Act.

[128] *Linotype* case, German Bundesgerichtshof, Decisions BGHZ 103, 184 (1988) concerning an abusive dissolution of a limited liability company by the majority shareholder. There is later case and abundant legal literature on fiduciary duties of shareholders towards each other, Uwe Hüffer & Jens Koch, Aktiengesetz (12th ed. Munich 2016) § 53a comments 20–25, as to corporate groups comments 24–25.

[129] Anatomy, *supra* note 24, at 163–64.

[130] Jens Dammann, "Corporate Ostracism: Freezing Out Controlling Shareholders", 33 J. Corp. L. 683–744 (2008), summing up at 744.

[131] Art. 2497 para 1 Codice civile (since the reform of 2004): vantaggi compensativi; Vincenzo Cariello, "The 'Compensation' of Damages with Advantages Deriving from Management and Coordination Activity (Direzione e Coordinamento) of the Parent Company (article 2497, paragraph 1, Italian Civil Code)", 3 ECFR 330 (2006); Embid Irujo, *supra* note 12, at 85; Fasciani, *supra* note 63, at 219 et seq.; for group corporate governance, Chiappetta & Tombari, *supra* note 2, at 268–71 with the Pirelli experience.

[132] Embid Irujo, *supra* note 12, at 85–87, proposal to follow the Italian example; Mónica Fuentes, "Corporate Groups and Creditors Protection: An Approach from a Spanish Company Law Perspective", 4 ECFR 529 (2007); see also Pablo Girgado, "Legislative Situation of Corporate Groups in Spanish Law", 3 ECFR 363, 368–69 (2006).

[133] *Supra* section 2.2.

from belonging to the group.[134] The requirements for doing so are threefold: the stable structure of the group, a coherent group policy by the parent, and an equitable distribution of benefits and costs among the group members. For Europe the Forum Europaeum Corporate Group Law, the High Level Group of Company Law Experts, the Reflection Group, and the European Model Companies Act have recommended following and further developing the French Rozenblum doctrine by legally acknowledging the group management.[135] The European Commission has responded to this recommendation, and, according to its Action Plan of 2012, will come up with such an initiative.[136] But it is expected that the form of this initiative will be a mere recommendation or at the most a directive rather than a regulation that is directly applicable in the Member States, and its content will be more on the side of the group than that of the minority shareholders. In the end, it may be concluded that, while there is some convergence on the standards for directors, controlling shareholders, and the parents in groups of companies despite different ownership regimes,[137] this convergence is and will be considerably less than has been observed for disclosure, and we shall see that for creditor protection there is even less convergence.

6 Transactions with Creditors

6.1 Creditor Self-Help and Guarantees by the Parent

The principle is unequivocal: no claims of creditors beyond the debtor corporation. This principle of separate legal personality that is most tightly upheld in the UK under the Salomon doctrine[138] also stands firm for groups of companies and is mandatory.[139] However, there is room for self-help on the part of the creditors and for voluntary action by the debtor parent. As was said before, large voluntary creditors of a group member will usually look after themselves and either refrain from dealing or bargaining to secure their credit by collateral. By monitoring the debtor in their own interest, it is sometimes said that these large creditors also protect the interests of the smaller, unsecured, or involuntary creditors. Yet this

---

[134] Cozian et al., *supra* note 98, at 2037 et seq.; Le Cannu & Dondero, *supra* note 21, at 1582; Maggy Pariente, "The Evolution of the Concept of 'Corporate Group' in France", 4 ECFR 317, 321–30 (2007): group interest; Boursier, *supra* note 64.

[135] Forum Europaeum Corporate Group Law, *supra* note 7, at 197–207; Hopt, *supra* note 78, at 222 et seq.; High Level Group of Company Law Experts, *supra* note 4, ch. 5.5, at 96–98; Reflection Group 2011, *supra* note 73; Pierre-Henri Conac, "Director's Duties in Groups of Companies—Legalizing the Interest of the Group at the European Level", 10 ECFR 194–226 (2013). See now also the European Model Companies Act, *supra* note 54, Section 15.16.

[136] EU Commission, Action Plan 2012, *supra* note 74; for reactions in Germany, see Hopt, *supra* note 74, at 165–215; Teichmann, *supra* note 11; Drygala, *supra* note 117.

[137] On path dependency and convergence for the regulation of conflict of interest and the duty of loyalty see Hopt, *supra* note 101, at 16–171. For a discussion of the limited relevance of ownership regimes for related party transactions and pertinent standards of directors and controlling shareholders, see Anatomy, *supra* note 24, at 166–69.

[138] *Supra* section 2.1.

[139] *Supra* section 3.1. On creditor protection see The Law and Economics of Creditor Protection (Horst Eidenmüller & Wolfgang Schön eds., The Hague 2008).

is true only in specific situations, in particular when the debtor gets into financial difficulties; even then, however, if a creditor is secured, he can sit back without risking his credit.

On the other hand, the parent corporation may have commercial reasons for loosening the asset partition within the group. Corporate guarantees given by the parent for their subsidiaries are a prime example. Such guarantees (letter of comfort, Patronatserklärungen, lettre de patronage)[140] differ considerably as to their form and binding force. They may be given to a particular creditor of the group member company or can be part of a general declaration to the market, sometimes in the annual report as in the case of the Deutsche Bank. Hard and soft forms should be distinguished carefully: in the former case, the parent stands up as a second debtor or as a guarantor of the debt;[141] in the latter, this is a more or less meaningful letter of intent depending on its wording and the circumstances in which it is issued. So the letter of comfort may be treated as a mere statement of present fact, not a promise about future conduct.[142] In France, a distinction is made between the obligation de moyens and the obligation de résultat, with only the latter giving the creditor a full guarantee of repayment.[143] In the bond market, such guarantees are frequent, but again with highly different reach and content.[144] In a way, the German contractual groups can also be mentioned in this context, since by entering such a group contract, the parent voluntarily accepts liability to the creditors of the subsidiary in return for liberty to steer the group in the group interest.[145] But in the end, as practice shows and theory confirms, self-help is not a full substitute for creditor protection by mandatory law.[146]

6.2 Standards for the Directors and the Controlling Shareholders

In the stage before outright insolvency, mandatory law protects group creditors mainly through the standards and liability of the directors and controlling shareholders. General creditor protection by disclosure rules was described above. Legal capital requirements, controversial as they are, and protection by limitations on asset distributions to shareholders are

---

[140] T.W. Cashel, "Groups of Companies—Some US Aspects", in Schmitthoff & Wooldridge, *supra* note 23, 20, at 38–40 with English and American case law. As to German case law see Klaus J. Hopt in Handelsgesetzbuch (Commercial Law Commentary) § 349 comments 22 et seq. (38th ed. Adolf Baumbach & Klaus J. Hopt eds., Munich 2018).

[141] Examples: German Bundesgerichtshof, Neue Juristische Wochenschrift (NJW) 144, 3443 (2010); Court of Appeals of Düsseldorf, Wertpapier-Mitteilungen (WM) 601 (2011).

[142] *Kleinwort Benson Ltd. v. Malaysia Mining Corp. Bhd* (1989) 1 All ER 785, CA, also referred to by Davies 2010, *supra* note 45, 96 note 73.

[143] See the French cases discussed by Pariente, *supra* note 134, at 341–43.

[144] *Re Polly Peck International plc (in administration)* (1996) 2 All ER 433, also referred to by Davies 2010, *supra* note 45, 95 note 73; William W. Bratton, "Bond Covenants and Creditor Protection: Economics and Law, Theory and Practice, Substance and Process", 7 EBOR 39 (2006). These guarantees must be distinguished from subordination agreements among creditors; cf. Gower & Davies, *supra* note 45, para 31-10. See more generally Mark K. Oulds in Schuldverschreibungsrecht (Klaus J. Hopt & Christoph Seibt eds., Cologne 2017), Ch. 3 at 3.34 et seq.

[145] Hopt in Schmitthoff & Wooldridge, *supra* note 23, at 104–05; *supra* section 2.2.

[146] Peter O. Mülbert, "A Synthetic View of Different Concepts of Creditor Protection, or: A High-Level Framework for Corporate Creditor Protection", 7 EBOR 357, 375–77 (2006).

not treated here.[147] In normal times, these standards of conduct protect both shareholders and creditors. Actions of the management with the consent of the parent that are harmful to minority shareholders are usually also harmful to the creditors of the subsidiary.

Yet when the corporation gets into financial difficulties, in particular if insolvency is foreseeable, the standards change and the duties of the management become stricter. In principle, this is true for most jurisdictions. Prototypes are the wrongful trading of directors in the UK, the French responsabilité pour insuffisance d'actif, the Belgian action en comblement du passif, and the German liability of the management of the limited liability company for negligent payments after the company has become insolvent or illiquid.[148] While these concepts of creditor protection differ considerably as to their reach, standards, entitled claimants,[149] and doctrinal nature, in the present context it suffices to state that they are functionally similar. It is true that most of these mechanisms come into play only when the company is actually insolvent, not before, and the receiver brings the claim against the director or controlling shareholder. But the liability is rooted in the wrongful conduct of the directors before, namely in the vicinity of insolvency, and the standard is not only fraud but negligence. The difficulty for the courts in applying this standard is on the one hand not to discourage directors from taking risks that may reasonably be expected to save the company, but on the other side not to allow them to engage in risky speculations at the expense of the creditors if the company has no prospects to go on (gambling for resurrection). The liability imposed on the directors is special insofar as it is not just a normal tort liability with the requirement of causation of the specific damage, but the judge may order the director to make a partial or full contribution to the assets of the insolvent company.

The group aspect of these mechanisms consists in holding liable the controlling parent as de facto director or shadow director. This functional extension of the notion of director is used by many jurisdictions, including the US, the UK, France, Germany, Italy, the Netherlands, Spain, and Switzerland.[150] These jurisdictions vary in the requirements for this liability of the controlling shareholder. Some are very reticent to do so. The prototype is the UK. There a company is not regarded as a shadow director by reason only that the

---

[147] Id. at 383–94.

[148] For a comparison of the situation in the UK, France, and Belgium, see Forum Europaeum Corporate Group Law, *supra* note 7, at 245–257; Hopt, *supra* note 78, at 225 et seq.; for a comparison of UK and German law, see Felix Steffek, *Gläubigerschutz in der Kapitalgesellschaft* (Tübingen 2011); for the UK see Paul Davies, "Directors' Creditor-Regarding Duties in Respect of Trading Decisions Taken in the Vicinity of Insolvency", 7 EBOR 301 (2006); on wrongful trading under UK law, see Gower & Davies, *supra* note 45, para 9-6 and Davies 2010, *supra* note 45, at 86–90; for France Cozian et al., *supra* note 98, at 422 et seq., 2057 et seq., with extensive case law, 413. Cf. European Model Companies Act 2017, *supra* note 54, Section 10.04 on Wrongful Trading.

[149] The German liability is directly to the damages creditors. Wrongful trading results in a full liability toward the company.

[150] Gower & Davies, *supra* note 45, para 9-7 on section 214 Insolvency Act. For Italy see Alexandra Mohn, *Die Gesellschaftsgruppe im italienischen Recht* (Berlin 2012); for Italy and Spain see Fuentes, *supra* note 132, at 541–44; for Switzerland see Karl Hofstetter & Renate Lang, "Konzern(mutter)haftung", in Entwicklungen im Gesellschaftsrecht VIII 231 (Peter V. Kunz, Oliver Arter, & Florian S. Jörg eds., Bern 2013); for the Netherlands Kroh, *supra* note 62, at 333 et seq. See also the German concept of Existenzvernichtungshaftung mentioned *supra* section 2.2 note 62. In Germany the concept of the shadow director is less important for catching the parent than in other countries because of the existence of a full-fledged separate group law.

directors of the subsidiary are accustomed to act on the instructions of the parent.[151] This led commentators to state: "So, this is not 'group law' by the back door."[152] But functionally it is, though in a very limited and carefully balanced way. Case law in some other jurisdictions seems less restrictive. The French courts treat controlling shareholders and parents as dirigeant de fait if they continuously mix themselves into the management and control of the company or subsidiary.[153]

A different instrument for holding parent companies liable well before insolvency should still be mentioned. In Switzerland, the parent may be held liable for the debts of the subsidiary if it creates the factual appearance of an economic unity of the group.[154] This concept is based on the reliance of the creditors and on the responsibility of the parent for this reliance. This instrument has gained some sympathy in Germany, Austria, and France, but the case law is rare and the majority of legal academia is not convinced.[155]

6.3 Indemnification, Veil-Piercing, Subordination, and Substantive Consolidation

Four other mechanisms of creditor protection against controlling shareholders and group parents should be mentioned, two used before and independent of insolvency law—namely indemnification and veil-piercing—and two others that are typical insolvency law mechanisms—subordination and substantive consolidation.

A very farreaching, group-specific means of creditor protection is indemnification. It is a mechanism codified in the German Stock Corporation Act for protecting the creditors of the subsidiary in a de facto group of companies, and it characterizes the regulatory model of special group law regulation described above. As mentioned there,[156] the parent must fully compensate any subsidiary at the end of the year for all acts and transactions caused by the parent that are contrary to the subsidiary's own interest. This is a much more dangerous mechanism than merely mixing into the management and control of the subsidiary as the aforementioned condition for treating the parent as a de facto director. Instructions to the subsidiary are not necessary, mere recommendations or advice may qualify for the requirement of causation, and the recommendations need not be addressed to the directors of the subsidiary but may consist in resolutions taken by the general assembly and in acts of the representatives of the parent in the board of the subsidiary.[157] The relevant criterion is the disadvantage for the subsidiary under an arm's length standard for fully independent

---

[151] As to the different wording of this in the Company Act 2006 and the Insolvency Act 1986, see Gower & Davies, *supra* note 45, para 9-7.

[152] Paul Davies & Jonathan Rickford, "An Introduction to the New UK Companies Act: Part I, Part II", 5 ECFR 48 and 239 (2008) at 64 note 70.

[153] See the cases reported by Cozian et al., *supra* note 98, nos 356 et seq., 2058.

[154] Konzernvertrauenshaftung, see Hofstetter & Lang, *supra* note 150; Böckli, *supra* note 13, § 11 comments 475–79; Peter Nobel, Das Obligationenrecht, Das Aktienrecht: Systematische Darstellung, in Berner Kommentar (Zürich 2017), § 4 N 392 et seq.; Benedict Burg & Hans Caspar von der Crone, "Vertrauenshaftung im Konzern", SZW 417 (2010).

[155] Pariente, *supra* note 134, at 333.   [156] *Supra* section 2.2.

[157] Emmerich & Habersack, *supra* note 21, § 25 passim, in particular comments 2–4.

companies. In practice even all kinds of group contributions (Konzernumlagen) to the parent or to other subsidiaries for which there are no equivalent individual benefits for the subsidiary are considered to be disadvantages.[158]

Veil-piercing or lifting the corporate veil is another mechanism that is used in many jurisdictions, both outside insolvency and in insolvency. It means that the veil created by the limited liability of the legal person is pierced, and the two entities or persons are treated as only one for the purposes of liability. This is obviously a very crude instrument that runs against the very economic and legal reasons for asset partitioning. It is therefore generally used with caution. At one end of the spectrum is the UK where the courts seem to be very reluctant to use this instrument and treat it as definitely more demanding than the concept of the shadow director.[159] In *Adams v. Cape Industries*, an asbestos case, the court upheld the limited liability of the parent against the asbestos victims of products distributed by one of its subsidiaries.[160] The observation of a UK expert is telling: "(L)ifting the veil as a means of achieving group liability is a non-starter even in relation to what may be considered the most deserving case, namely the tort victims of a subsidiary company."[161] German courts also lift the corporate veil only rarely and under very tight requirements.[162] On the other end of the spectrum seems to be the US, where the courts use this mechanism more frequently.[163] To be sure, we are dealing here with the corporate law mechanism of lifting the veil. When it comes to competition law, for example, there is much more willingness on the side of the antitrust authorities and the courts to hold the parent responsible for antitrust violations of its subsidiary.[164] As mentioned above, group legislation and regulation for specific areas is special since it has very different regulatory objectives. For competition law, this may amount to a liability of the parent without real negligent behavior if a subsidiary commits an antitrust violation, a rather controversial result.

The two mechanisms that are common to insolvency law in many countries are subordination and substantive consolidation. Subordination is known in many countries including Austria, Germany, Italy, Spain, the US, and New Zealand, but not in the UK.[165] In

---

[158] Id. § 25 comment 26 with case law.

[159] Davies, *supra* note 45, at 98; Gower & Davies, *supra* note 45, ch. 8 on limited liability and lifting the veil, 8–17: small role in British company law.

[160] *Adams v. Cape Industries* (1990) Ch 433, CA, briefly resumed by Davies 2010, *supra* note 45, at 97–99.

[161] Eilis Ferran, Company Law and Corporate Finance 31 et seq. (London 1999). But see Charles Mitchell, "Lifting the Corporate Veil in the English Courts: An Empirical Study", 3 Company, Financial and Insolvency L. Rev. 15 (1999): veil-piercing in the UK is quite frequent despite the different rhetoric of English judges; Davies (2010), *supra* note 45, at 97 mentions that the courts have become more restrictive.

[162] "Durchgriff," Markus Roth in Baumbach & Hopt, *supra* note 140, annex § 177 a comment 51b-f; Hüffer & Koch, *supra* note 128, § 1 comments 15 et seq.

[163] Robert B. Thompson, "Piercing the Corporate Veil: An Empirical Study", 86 Cornell L. Rev. 1036 (1991); David Millon, "Piercing the Corporate Veil, Financial Responsibility, and the Limits of Limited Liability", 56 Emory L. J. 1309 (2007); Steven Presser, Piercing the Corporate Veil (2013); Jonathan Macey & Joshua Mitts, "Finding Order in the Morass: The Three Real Justifications for Piercing the Corporate Veil" 100 Cornell L. Rev. 99 (2014); Peter S. Spiro, "Clarifying the Rules for Piercing of the Corporate Veil", 26 J. Corp. L. 479 (2001), available at http://ssrn.com/abstract=2363647, 2013; cf. also Haar, *supra* note 83. But Stephen Bainbridge, "Abolishing Veil Piercing", 26 J. Corp. L. 479 (2001).

[164] See *supra* note 82.

[165] Martin Gelter & Juerg Roth, "Subordination of Shareholder Loans from a Legal and Economic Perspective", 5 Journal for Institutional Comparisons 40 (2007); for the US see Irit Mevorach,

subordination, the controlling shareholder's or parent's debt claims are subordinated to the claims of all other creditors. This does not fully amount to what is now called a voluntary debt equity swap,[166] since the subordinated claims still rank before all equity that is held by the parent and other shareholders. The requirements for subordination as an insolvency mechanism differ considerably, reaching from inequitable behavior[167] to automatic subordination of shareholder credits given to the company under German insolvency law.

The insolvency regime can go further and allow the insolvency courts to consolidate the insolvency proceedings of several group members.[168] Consolidation can be merely procedural, in which case the companies belonging to the group are treated as a single unit under one bankruptcy proceeding. Consolidation can also be substantive, when the assets and/ or debts of the different group members are pooled together. Procedural consolidation is possible, for example, under the New Zealand Companies Act 1993, and substantive consolidation is provided for under US insolvency law.[169] Under French and Belgian insolvency law, intermingling of assets (action en confusion de patrimoine) may lead to extending the insolvency of one company to another.[170] But this mechanism should be used with caution and is applied only when there is a real intermingling of the assets of the two corporations, and usually a fault on the side of the parent is necessary.[171] The normal legal and commercial relationship between parent and subsidiary is not sufficient. Usually the insolvencies of multinational groups present particular difficulties. These difficulties are due not only to the different applicable laws and competent receivers and insolvency authorities, but also to the open or, in most cases, hidden opportunism of the latter in favor of their own national companies and creditors. Efforts to agree on international consolidation have been going on for a long time, but up to now only some steps in the direction of procedural consolidation have been made.

In the end, it may be concluded that creditor protection, in particular in corporate groups, is considered by many jurisdictions to be an agency conflict that needs to be regulated. But the strategies and mechanisms used for doing so are equivalent in function only on very basic terms. Fundamental differences remain in policy and even more so in legal doctrine. While we have observed a certain trend toward convergence for minority protection in the independent company and groups of companies by disclosure and, though less so, by standards, we would hardly dare to confirm this for creditor protection as well.

"Appropriate Treatment of Corporate Groups in Insolvency: A Universal Rule", 8 EBOR 179 (2007) and David A. Skeel & Georg Krause-Vilmar, "Recharacterization and the Nonhindrance of Creditors", 7 EBOR 259 (2006); for New Zealand, Davies 2010, *supra* note 45, at 99–100; for Germany Mülbert, *supra* note 146, at 394–99; Anatomy, *supra* note 24, at 131–32.

[166] But cf. Anatomy, *supra* note 24, at 131 note 158.

[167] See the Deep Rock doctrine in the US (*Taylor v. Standard Gas and Electronic Corporation*, 306 U.S. 307 (1939)), Anatomy, *supra* note 24, 132; Skeel & Krause-Vilmar, *supra* note 165, at 263–64.

[168] Mevorach, *supra* note 165, at 187–93.

[169] Mevorach, *supra* note 165, with further references.

[170] For France, see Art. L. 621-2 al. 2 code de commerce; Pariente, *supra* note 134, at 333–40 (2007); Cozian et al., *supra* note 98, at 1522, 2054 et seq.; Kroh, *supra* note 62, at 274 et seq. For Belgium see Van Ommeslaghe, *supra* note 23, 59 at 92 et seq.

[171] Pariente, *supra* note 134, at 331–33. It is mentioned that this mechanism may also be used outside of the insolvency, but in principle it is an insolvency law mechanism; Cozian et al., *supra* note 98, at 2054: exceptional.

7 CONTROL TRANSACTIONS

The second large category of conflicted transactions in corporate law besides related party transactions are control transactions, i.e., transactions by which the control over the corporation is transferred to another person or enterprise, usually by a public takeover.[172] The two typical agency problems in takeovers are between the directors and the shareholders of the target, on the one hand, and between the majority and the minority shareholders of the target as to the premium and a possible exit, on the other.[173] In the first conflict, there are the fundamentally different positions of the UK and many continental European states that have the anti-frustration rule, and the US and other continental European states that give the directors full liberty to decide whether to refuse or to accept the bid.[174] As to the second conflict, a similar divide exists concerning the mandatory bid and the sharing rule for the minority shareholders.[175] In takeovers the situations and problems are different when the shareholders are diverse on the side of the target or there is a controlling shareholder.[176]

Takeover regulation was developed first and primarily in the US and the UK where there is no—or no consistent—group law. In countries such as Germany, with an extensive, codified group law, takeover regulation appeared only very late. This is no coincidence since group law deals with some of the agency problems of minority shareholders at a later stage, namely when the group exists and the minority needs protection. Takeover regulation, in particular by the mandatory bid, comes in at a much earlier stage and allows the exit of the minority shareholders at the same price as those shareholders who accept the bid. The mandatory bid is a protective mechanism at the stage when a new controlling bidder might come in. The mandatory bid has therefore been considered functionally to be a group law provision, offering protection by exit before the (new) group is formed.[177] This is true even in cases of mere transfer of control by the takeover from the former controlling shareholder in the target to the new controlling shareholder whose bid has succeeded. The shareholders do not know in advance how the new controlling shareholder will use his control power and therefore might prefer an early exit at a fair price.[178] The exit after the takeover has been successful, either by squeeze-out or sell-out, can be allowed by takeover law and/or general corporate law. It is always the exit of a minority from a company with a controlling shareholder. This exit exists in independent companies as well as in groups of companies. As to squeeze-out

---

[172] Fundamental changes may also imply a change of control, but under nearly all corporate laws, shareholder consent in the general assembly is necessary, and special provisions for creditor protection exist. Cf. Anatomy, *supra* note 24, ch. 7, 171–203.

[173] Bidder agency problems between directors and controlling shareholders on the one hand and minority shareholders on the other are dealt with by general corporate law, not specifically by takeover law. See Anatomy, *supra* note 24, at 208.

[174] Anatomy, *supra* note 24, at 212–15, 215–21; Klaus J. Hopt, "Takeover Defenses in Europe: A Comparative, Theoretical and Policy Analysis", 20 Colum. J. Eur. L. 249 (2014).

[175] Anatomy, *supra* note 24, at 227–30.

[176] Anatomy, *supra* note 24, at 209–10, and 211–31: no controlling shareholder; 229, 231–36: acquisition from an existing controlling shareholder.

[177] Klaus J. Hopt, Europäisches Übernahmerecht 36–38 (Tübingen 2013); Hopt, *supra* note 33, at 15 EBOR 143, 169–71 (2014). As to the exit strategy, see Anatomy, *supra* note 24, at 88, 227–30.

[178] Anatomy, *supra* note 24, at 233.

and sell-out regulation[179] the dangers for the minority may be greater in groups.[180] As to convergence, the findings are mixed. On the one hand, takeover regulation has spread from the US and the UK all over continental Europe and well beyond into Japan and other countries. But as to dealing with agency conflicts, the policies remain fundamentally different as the cleavage between the countries with and without the anti-frustration rule and with and without the mandatory bid shows.

8 Conclusion

1. The phenomenon of the groups of companies is very common in modern corporate reality. The empirical data on groups of companies are heterogeneous because they are collected for very different regulatory and other objectives.

2. Two main agency problems arise in groups of companies: between the controlling shareholder and the minority shareholders and between the shareholders viz. the controlling shareholder and the creditors. The conflict between labor and other stakeholders and the controlling shareholder is dealt with by labor law, industrial relations, and other fields of law.

3. There are three main regulatory models for dealing with groups of companies: regulation by general corporate and/or civil law (prototype: the UK); regulation by special group law (prototype: Germany); and regulation by areas of the law such as banking, competition, and tax law (to be found in many countries, either combined with the first or the second model).

4. The main strategy for dealing with groups of companies is disclosure and group accounting. It is effectuated by special investigation with a group dimension and by the help of auditors and independent experts. A fair amount of international convergence, at least for listed companies, can be observed.

5. Related-party transactions are a main area of concern for corporate and group law provisions. Specific disclosure is usually combined with consent requirements and other procedural regulation of related-party transactions.

6. In addition, appropriate standards for directors and controlling shareholders for dealing with agency conflicts in groups of companies have been developed in many countries. The duty of loyalty is an open standard to be concretized ex post by the courts. There is some convergence, but many differences remain, in particular as far as specific standards for balancing the interests of member companies in groups are concerned. The strict, codified German group law standard stands against more flexible standards in Italy, France, and other countries.

7. Protection of creditors can be achieved to a certain degree by self-help and guarantees by the parent. But mandatory protection is still considered necessary. There are various national standards for the directors and controlling shareholder in the independent

---

[179] See the comprehensive comparative study by Christoph van der Elst & Lientje van den Steen, "Balancing the Interests of Minority and Majority Shareholders: A Comparative Analysis of Squeeze-out and Sell-out Rights", 4 ECFR 391 (2009).

[180] For the same reasons as discussed in section 1.3.

company as well as in groups of companies. These standards become stricter if insolvency is approaching. The concept of the shadow director plays an important role in extending liability to the controlling shareholder and the parent.

8. There are various other mechanisms for creditor protection in the independent company and in the group of companies. Some of them, such as indemnification and veil-piercing, are used when the corporation is still doing well and is operating as a going concern. Others are mechanisms of insolvency law, such as subordination and substantive consolidation. Creditor protection is still very path-dependent, and convergence is much less advanced.

9. A second group of conflicted transactions besides related party transactions comprise control transactions, in particular public takeovers. Takeover law was first developed in the US and the UK and from there has moved into other countries. Takeover law grew up separately from group law and only arrived in countries with group law such as Germany at a very late stage. The mandatory bid can be understood functionally as a group protection measure that allows the shareholders of the target to opt for an early exit at a fair price (group entry control or Konzerneingangskontrolle). There is some convergence, in particular in Europe, but fundamental differences remain as to the anti-frustration rule and the mandatory bid.

CHAPTER 24

....

CORPORATE SOCIAL RESPONSIBILITY AND CORPORATE GOVERNANCE

....

CYNTHIA A. WILLIAMS

1 INTRODUCTION

....

CORPORATE social responsibility is a topic that has been given increased attention in the last two decades in practice and in theory, both in management and law. Defined in an influential 1970s article as "the firm's considerations of, and response to, issues beyond the ... economic, technical, and legal requirements of the firm to accomplish social benefits along with the traditional economic gains which the firm seeks,"[1] the European Commission more simply defined it in 2011 as "the responsibility of enterprises for their impacts on society."[2] As the Commission stated in adopting that definition, "[e]nterprises should have in place a process to integrate social, environmental, ethical, human rights and consumer concerns into their business operations and core strategy in close collaboration with their stakeholders."[3] Thus, the emphasis has shifted from philanthropy and attention to corporate action "beyond law" to an inquiry into how a company conducts its business. Indicative of this shift, many academics and practitioners in management now refer to the topic as corporate responsibility, not corporate social responsibility, as will this author.[4]

What is some evidence of a developing norm of corporate responsibility? Few global companies today fail to highlight their social initiatives and performance on their websites,

---

[1] Keith Davis, "The Case for and against Business Assumption of Social Responsibilities", 16 Am. Mgmt. J. 312, 312 (1973).
[2] European Commission, A Renewed European Union Strategy 2011–14 for Corporate Social Responsibility, COM(2011) 681, 3.1.
[3] See id.
[4] See Céline Gainet, "Exploring the Impact of legal Systems and Financial Structures on CR", 95 J. Bus. Ethics 195, 197 (2010) (discussing shift in nomenclature from "corporate social responsibility" to "corporate responsibility," for, among other reasons, encompassing the concept of both social and environmental responsibilities in a single term).

while over 90% of the Global 250 companies voluntarily disclose more environmental, so-cial, and governance (ESG) information than required by law.[5] Voluntary, transnational standards of best social and environmental practices are proliferating in virtually every industry, many with associated certification schemes and requirements for third-party at-testation or auditing.[6] These voluntary initiatives are increasingly being supplemented by domestic and multilateral government actions to encourage, or in some cases require, companies to pay closer attention to the social and environmental consequences of their actions and to disclose more information about those consequences.[7]

Investors have also become more attentive in recent years to environmental and social risks in portfolio companies, and therefore more concerned with corporate responsibility. Global assets under management with sustainability screens have risen 61% since 2012, to US$21.4 trillion at the start of 2014.[8] Institutions managing US$45 trillion of invested capital have committed to the UN Environment Program's Principles for Responsible Investment (PRI), which require investors to incorporate ESG issues into investment practices across their asset classes.[9] As of 2015, over US$92 trillion of the world's invested capital backs the Carbon Disclosure Project (CDP)'s work with 2,000 companies around the world to gather data on those companies' greenhouse gas emissions.[10] These data are then provided to Bloomberg for incorporation with other ESG data that Bloomberg has been selling (since 2009) to investors around the world.[11] Indeed, corporate responsibility itself has become an industry, one a critical NGO noted has rendered London "awash with PR consultants, social auditors, firms providing verification or 'assurance' for companies' social and environmental reports, and bespoke investment analysts all vying for business."[12]

While these trends indicate that corporate responsibility has achieved some place within mainstream corporate and investor activities, that place is deeply contested, in both theory and practice. Everything from the history of corporate responsibility, its importance, its effects, and its legitimacy is subject to challenge, depending on the underlying corporate governance system of the country in question, how countries arrange their social welfare provision, the relationship of the state to the market, and even the theory of the nature of the corporation one holds. In important respects corporate responsibility is both too strong and too weak: too strong an assertion of a social role for the corporation and its directors to coexist comfortably with the view of the purely economic role of the corporation within shareholder-focused corporate governance systems, and yet too weak for academics taking

---

[5] See KPMG, "The KPMG Survey of CR Reporting" 2013, available at http://www.kpmg.com/Global/en/IssuesAndInsights/ArticlesPublications/corporate-responsibility/Documents/corporate-responsibility-reporting-survey-2013-exec-summary.pdf.

[6] See Margaret M. Blair, Cynthia A. Williams, & Li-Wen Lin, "The New Role for Assurance Services in Global Commerce", 33 J. Corp. L. 325 (2008).

[7] See Parts II, B, 2 and III, *infra*.

[8] Global Sustainable Investment Alliance, "The Global Sustainable Investment Review" 2014, available at http://www.sustainabilityHQ.com.

[9] United Nations Environment Program Principles for Responsible Investment, available at http://www.unpri.org/about-pri.

[10] Carbon Disclosure Project, Catalyzing Business and Government Action, available at http://www.cdp.net/en-US/Pages/About-Us.aspx.

[11] See Table 24.3, *infra*, for a summary of the environmental and social data that Bloomberg now sells to its broker and dealer clients.

[12] Christian Aid, Behind the Mask: The Real Face of Corporate Social Responsibility 8 (2004).

a stakeholder view of the corporation who are concerned with global problems they view companies as having helped to create, including climate change, environmental degradation, exploitative labor conditions, and worsening economic inequality.

This chapter will proceed as follows. Section 2 will describe voluntary corporate responsibility initiatives, followed in section 3 by some of the more significant legal developments on the topic. Section 4 will discuss empirical evidence about the financial and social effects of corporate responsibility, including interactions with corporate governance structures. Section 5 will evaluate these corporate responsibility trends, and Section 6 will conclude.

2 VOLUNTARY CORPORATE RESPONSIBILITY INITIATIVES

2.1 Corporate Responsibility Reporting

The clearest demonstration of the evolution of corporate responsibility from academic theory to mainstream business practice is in the trends with respect to corporate reporting of ESG information.[13] While some jurisdictions are starting to require ESG reporting (as described below), much of this reporting is still voluntary. It can thus be interpreted as an indication of companies' perceptions of the social expectations of business, even as companies seek to manage those expectations through their corporate responsibility reporting.[14]

The most comprehensive source of data on ESG reporting is that done by KPMG in the Netherlands. KPMG published its first ESG report in 1993, and its most recent in 2013. In 1993, 12% of the top 100 companies in the OECD countries (ex. Japan) published an environmental or social report.[15] By 2013, 76% of the top 100 companies in the Americas published a separate corporate responsibility report, as did 73% of top 100 companies in Europe and 71% in Asia.[16] Of the largest 250 companies globally, reporting rates are 93%.[17] The Global Reporting Initiative (GRI)'s voluntary, multi-stakeholder framework for ESG reporting has emerged as the clear global benchmark: 78% of reporting companies worldwide and 82% of

---

[13] For an excellent overview of the evolution of corporate responsibility as an academic theory in the management literature, see Archie V. Carroll, "Corporate Social Responsibility: Evolution of a Definitional Construct", 38 Bus. & Soc'ty 268 (1999).

[14] See Sara B. Feldner & Kati T. Berg, "How Corporations Manage Industry and Consumer Expectations via the CR Report", 8(3) Public Relations J. (2014), available at http://www.prsa.org/prjournal; Ronen Shamir, "The De-Radicalization of Corporate Social Responsibility", 30 Critical Sociology 669, 675 (2004).

[15] See Ans Kolk, "A Decade of Sustainability Reporting: Developments and Significance", 3 Int'l. J. Environment & Sustainable Devel. 51, 52 Figure 1 (2004). KPMG has changed the format of the report since its original 1993 report on corporate responsibility reporting, so direct comparisons are not possible between the Global 250 in 1993 and the Global 250 in 2013.

[16] KPMG, "The KPMG Survey of CR Reporting" 2013, at 10, available at http://www.kpmg.com/Global/en/IssuesAndInsights/ArticlesPublications/corporate-responsibility/Documents/corporate-responsibility-reporting-survey-2013-exec-summary.pdf (last visited March 5, 2015).

[17] See id.

the Global 250 use GRI as the basis for their corporate responsibility reporting.[18] Of particular note, slightly over half (59%) of the Global 250 now have their reports "assured," most often (two-thirds of the time) by the specialist bureaus of the major accountancy firms.[19]

In addition to the quantity of corporate responsibility reporting, KPMG also evaluates the quality of reporting. Here, European companies generally do substantially better than those in Asia or the Americas (average quality scores of 71 out of 100 in Europe versus 54 for companies in the Americas and 50 in Asia Pacific).[20] Within the Global 250, companies are starting to see more opportunities than risks from social and environmental factors, such as for the development of new products and services. Eighty-seven percent of the Global 250 identify climate change, material resource scarcity, and trends in energy and fuel as "megatrends" that will affect their business.[21] Ultimately, KPMG concludes that "[m]any companies no longer see corporate responsibility as a moral issue, but as core business risks and opportunities."[22] This conclusion is consistent with the views of prominent management academics Michael Porter and Mark Kramer,[23] and Abagail McWilliams and Donald Siegel,[24] who (among others) have argued for companies to use corporate responsibility initiatives as part of their business strategies to promote competitive advantage.

2.2 Substantive Corporate Responsibility Initiatives

2.2.1 *Private Initiatives*

The focus on expanded ESG disclosure has occurred concomitantly with the proliferation of transnational, voluntary standards for what constitutes responsible corporate action. Thus, over the past two decades such standards have been developed by states; public/private partnerships; multi-stakeholder negotiation processes; industries and companies; institutional investors; functional groups such as accountancy firms and social assurance consulting groups (many of which did not exist more than ten years ago); NGOs; and non-financial ratings agencies.[25] Standards have been developed in just about every industry, from apparel[26] to

---

[18]   See id at 11. The Global Reporting Initiative is now in its fourth iteration. It has been developed by, and is used by, thousands of companies, governments, and non-profit entities around the world to report on the economic, environmental, social and governance effects of entities' actions. See Global Reporting Initiative, available at http://www.globalreporting.org.

[19]   See KPMG 2013 Report, *supra* note 16, at 11.   [20]   See id. at 14.   [21]   See id. at 14–15.

[22]   See id. at 15.

[23]   See Michael E. Porter and Mark R. Kramer, "Strategy and Society: The Link Between Competitive Advantage and Corporate Social Responsibility", Harv. Bus. Rev. 78 (Dec. 2006).

[24]   See Abagail McWilliams & Donald S. Siegel, "Creating and Capturing Value: Strategic Corporate Social Responsibility, Resource-Based Theory, and Sustainable Competitive Advantage", 37 J. of Mangmt. 1480 (2011).

[25]   See Benedict Kingsbury, Nico Krisch, & Richard B. Stewart, "The Emergence of Global Administrative Law", 68 L. & Contemp. Probs. 15 (2005). The implications of these standards for theories of corporate governance, regulation, and economic development are profound, some of which the author has explored in prior work. See Cynthia A. Williams & John M. Conley, "An Emerging Third Way? The Erosion of the Anglo-American Shareholder Value Construct", 38 Corn. Int'l. J. J. 493 (2005).

[26]   See, e.g., The Fair Labor Associations, http://www.FLA.org, or the Workers' Rights Consortium, http://www.workersrights.org. For a discussion of these and other standards for the global supply chain

chemicals,[27] extractives such as oil, gas and minerals[28] to conflict-free diamonds[29]; sustainable fisheries[30] and forestry;[31] project finance;[32] and fair-trade goods such as coffee, tea, cocoa, and cotton,[33] to name just a few examples. Thousands of individual companies have adopted voluntary codes of conduct establishing standards for responsible behavior, and some companies then engage third-party certifiers to ensure that their suppliers and subsidiaries are meeting those standards.[34] Multi-sector codes have also been developed with standards that are designed to apply across industries. Of particular note here is Social Accountability 8000 (SA 8000), which is based on the International Labor Organization (ILO)'s Fundamental Principles and Rights at Work,[35] but adds a commitment to a living wage, and a commitment to compliance with UN international human rights protections.[36] SA 8000 also includes a requirement for independent monitoring of code compliance prior to certification that specific productive facilities meet the SA 8000 standards. Another multi-sector example is the Ethical Trading Institute (ETI), which is a London-based tripartite labor, industry, and NGO organization working to incorporate ILO protections into supply chains for products bound for the Western markets.[37] ETI works in a deliberative

in the apparel industry, see Dara O'Rourke, "Outsourcing Regulation: Analyzing Non-Governmental Systems of Labor Standards and Monitoring", 31 Pol'y Stud. J. 1 (2003).

[27] See Responsible Care, http://www.canadianchemistry.ca/responsible_care/index.php/en/responsible-care-history; Jean M. Belanger, "Responsible Care in Canada: The Evolution of an Ethic and a Commitment", 27 Chem. Int'l. 2 (March–April) 2005. The standards developed for responsible industrial chemicals production are in place in over 60 countries, as of 2015, and now include greenhouse gas reporting and assurance.

[28] See the Voluntary Principles on Security and Human Rights, available at http://www.voluntaryprinciples.org.

[29] See the Kimberly Process, http://www.kimberleyprocess.com.

[30] See, e.g., the Marine Stewardship Council certification process, http://www.msc.org.

[31] See Forest Stewardship Council: Principles and Criteria for Forest Stewardship, available at http://www.fsc.org. Competition between the forest standards promulgated by business versus those promulgated by NGOs has been extensively studied by leading students of regulation and political theory. See Benjamin Cashore, Graeme Auld, & Deanna Newsom, Governing through Markets: Forest Certification and the Emergence of Non-State Authority (2004); Errol Meidinger, "The Administrative Law of Global Private-Public Regulation: the Case of Forestry", 17 Eur. J. of Int'l. Law 47, 51 (2006).

[32] See The Equator Principles, http://www.equator-principles.com. See also John M. Conley & Cynthia A. Williams, "Global Banks as Global Sustainability Regulators: The Equator Principles", 33:4 J. L. & Policy Rev. 542 (2011).

[33] See http://www.fairtrade.net/standards/our-standards.html for an overview of the fair trade requirements and current standards.

[34] See Blair, Williams, & Lin, *supra* note 6. The University of Minnesota Law School, under the leadership of international human rights scholar Prof. David Weissbrodt, has an extensive collection of human rights materials online, including copies of hundreds of firms' codes of conduct. See https://www1.umn.edu/humanrts/business/codes.html.

[35] The International Labour Organization's 1998 Declaration on Fundamental Principles and Rights at Work focuses on four core rights: freedom of association and rights to collective bargaining, freedom from forced labor or prison labor, freedom from child labor exploitation and non-discrimination. See International Labour Organization, available at http://www.ilo.org/declaration/lang--en/index.htm.

[36] See Social Accountability 8000, available at http://www.sa-intl.org.

[37] See Ethical Trading Initiative, available at http://www.ethicaltrade.org.

fashion, using monitoring, evaluation, and ongoing learning to both improve standards for the 9.8 million people incorporated into the 70 companies' supply chains (as of 2015), but also to teach workers their rights and how to advocate for them independently.[38]

2.2.2 *Multilateral Initiatives*

A number of significant multilateral instruments have also been developed or recently strengthened by organizations comprised of government representatives. While these instruments do not establish binding treaty obligations, they do articulate governments' expectations of responsible corporate action. Four are of particular note: the OECD's Guidelines for Multinational Enterprises; the ISO 26,000 Corporate Responsibility standards; the UN's Global Compact; and the UN's more recent "Protect, Respect and Remedy" framework articulating states' and companies' human rights responsibilities.

The OECD's Guidelines, initially promulgated in 1976 and most recently amended in 2011, encourage companies to promote sustainable development, and include standards based on ILO and UN treaty obligations, including standards of transparency, labor protection, international human rights protection, responsible supply chain management, environmental protection, anti-bribery standards, and fair tax contributions (added in 2011 and unique among international corporate responsibility standards).[39] A number of aspects of the OECD approach are of particular importance. First, the standards are developed through tripartite participation of governments (through the OECD itself), business (the Business and Industry Advisory Committee to the OECD), and labor (the Trade Union Advisory Committee to the OECD). This approach is typical of the "social partners" view of economic life in Europe. Second, the OECD is starting to develop sector-specific guidance for responsible business conduct in a number of areas: agricultural supply chains, financial sector due diligence, textile and garment supply chains, extractive sector stakeholder engagement, and mineral supply chains. Third, the OECD countries, which include most of the developed economies (excepting Brazil, Russia, India, and China), all commit to establish National Contact Points (NCPs) to whom challenges may be brought where individuals feel their OECD rights have been violated. Labor, in particular, has been proactive in using these NCPs to address violations, and by so doing a record of global labor rights and responsibilities is slowly being developed.[40]

The International Standards Organization (ISO), which has developed thousands of technical standards since its establishment after World War II, developed the ISO 26000 standard for corporate responsibility in 2010, after five years of consultation among standards bodies.[41] Unlike most of its standards, against which certification can occur, ISO

---

[38] See Ethical Trading Initiative, available at http://www.ethicaltrade.org/news-and-events/press-resources/eti-key-achievements.

[39] See Guidelines for Multinational Enterprises, available at http://www.oecd.org/corporate.mne.

[40] See John Evans, Organizing Workers Globally: The Need for Public Policy to Regulate Investment, in The Embedded Firm: Corporate Governance, Labor, and Finance Capitalism, 343–53 (Cynthia A. Williams and Peer Zumbansen eds., 2011).

[41] See "ISO 26,000-Social Responsibility", available at http://www.iso.org/iso/home/standards/iso26000.htm.

26000 is not a standard to provide guidance for certification. It does, however, provide a useful definition of corporate responsibility:

> CSR is the responsibility of an organization for the impacts of its decisions and activities on society and the environment, through transparent and ethical behavior that contributes to sustainable development, including health and the welfare of society, takes into account the expectations of stakeholders, is in compliance with applicable laws and with international norms of behavior, and is integrated throughout the organization and practiced in its relationships.[42]

ISO 26000 is important as evidence of the developing global norm of corporate responsibility: developed with representation from 90 countries and 40 international or regional organizations, it was drafted with input from consumers, governments, industry, labor, NGOs and "service, support, research, academics and others,"[43] and so can credibly claim to represent a global consensus about companies' social responsibilities. To read the specific standards one must buy them (somewhat ironic where one responsibility principle is transparency, but an apparently successful business model), but an outline of the topics is available. ISO 26000 defines general principles of accountability, transparency, ethical behavior, respect for stakeholder interests, for rule of law, for international norms and human rights as the field of corporate responsibility; and core subjects include governance, human rights, labor practices, the environment, fair operating practices, consumer issues, and community involvement.[44]

The United Nations began its work on corporate responsibility in 2000 under Secretary General Kofi Annan with the Global Compact, a policy initiative in which businesses commit to respect ten principles that cover four areas of concern (international human rights, labor protection, environmental protection, and anti-corruption).[45] By 2015, 12,000 businesses, academic institutions, and NGOs in 140 countries had signed onto the Global Compact. Governance efforts are underway to make corporate commitments to the Global Compact framework meaningful, including requirements for participants to communicate annually on their progress regarding the four areas of concern. Still, by 2008 close to 15% of companies had been de-listed from the Global Compact for failing to report on their progress, and the Global Compact continues to be criticized for its lack of specificity.[46]

Among multilateral frameworks, the UN's Guiding Principles on Business and Human Rights, adopted by the UN Human Rights Council in 2011, seems to have the greatest potential to develop into a baseline global legal framework for companies' social responsibilities. (The OECD Principles only apply to companies in or from adhering countries.) The UN Guiding Principles set out the core spheres of obligation for states and companies with respect to human rights: states have the duty to *protect* their citizens from violations by third

---

[42] See id.   [43] See id.

[44] See Guidance on ISO 26,0000, available at https://www.iso.org/obp/ui/ #iso:std:iso:26000:ed-1:v1:en:sec:A.

[45] See UN Global Compact Annual Review 2010, available at http://www.unglobalcompact.org/docs/ news_events/8.1/UNGC_Annual_Review_2010.pdf.

[46] See Jette Steen Knudsen, "Which Companies Benefit Most from UN Global Compact Membership?", available at http://www.EuropeanBusinessReview.com/?p=3167 (citing statistics, and asserting that the Global Compact is primarily useful for large companies to fill a governance void as they operate in less developed countries).

parties, including companies, by promulgating laws and regulations; companies have the responsibility to act with due diligence to *respect* citizens' human rights; and both states and companies have the duty to provide access to *remedies* for victims. Developed after the failure in 2004 of the UN Human Right's Commission's Draft Norms on the Responsibilities of Transnational Corporations and Other Business Enterprises with Regard to Human Rights, which "business vehemently opposed,"[47] the Protect, Respect, and Remedy framework was developed in a six-year process led by Prof. John Ruggie of Harvard University. The international human rights obligations applicable to companies through the Guiding Principles include those in the Universal Declaration of Human Rights, the International Covenants on Civil and Political Rights and on Economic, Social and Cultural Rights, and the Core Conventions of the ILO.[48] The state duty to protect human rights is now being incorporated into many European and other countries by the establishment of National Action Plans to disseminate and implement the Guiding Principles.[49] At the same time, an NGO called the Business and Human Rights Resource Centre, supported by the UK and German governments, has launched a ranking of companies' human rights records in response to the Guiding Principles.[50] The combination of global standards supported by and being implemented by a broad array of governments, a standards-development process that was inclusive, transparent and well-balanced between companies, labor, and NGOs, and a dedicated NGO collecting data and publicizing it, gives the UN Guiding Principles the potential to become the de facto global corporate responsibility standard.

3 SIGNIFICANT LEGAL REQUIREMENTS

For the most part, corporate responsibility standards are voluntary, with the exception of new legislation in India, which has required companies to establish a corporate responsibility committee of the board and contribute 2% of net profits to corporate responsibility initiatives as of 2014,[51] building upon strong cultural foundations for the social obligations of successful companies (and people) in India.[52] That said, many of the topics that corporate

---

[47] See "UN Guiding Principles", available at http://www.reports-and-materials.org/sites/default/files/reports-and-materials/Ruggie-protect-respect-remedy-framework.pdf.

[48] See id.

[49] See Guidelines for the UN Guiding Principles, available at http://www.ohchr.org/EN/Issues/Business/Pages/NationalActionPlans.aspx.

[50] See Phil Bloomer, Human Rights and Big Business: New Ranking Aims to Drive Race to the top, Guardian, Jan. 14, 2015.

[51] See Price Waterhouse Coopers, Handbook on Corporate Social Responsibility in India, available at http://www.pwc.in/assets/pdfs/publications/2013/handbook-on-corporate-social-responsibility-in-india.pdf.

[52] See Peter Cappelli, Harbir Singh, Jitendra Singh, & Micael Useem, "The India Way: Lessons for the US", 24 Acad. Mgmt. Perspectives 6 (2010) (arguing that business managers in India eschew explicit concern with shareholder value, but invest in employee training, employee empowerment, and a social mission, leading to strong growth and successful companies). The Tata Steel Company is one example, among many, of companies with extensive community social responsibility and employee welfare and training initiatives going back over a century. See http://www.tatasteel.com/corporate/heritage/a-century-of-trust.asp.

responsibility addresses are subject to domestic regulation, such as labor rights, environmental protection, consumer protection, anti-discrimination, or anti-bribery. And these regulatory standards have implications for the degree to which voluntary corporate responsibility initiatives are necessary to fill important gaps, either in a domestic or transnational context. As has been argued by Dirk Matten and Jeremy Moon, in countries with stakeholder corporate governance systems and more expansive social welfare arrangements, corporate responsibility is "implicit" in doing business according to law, so companies do not need to be as "explicit" about taking on social responsibilities, as do leading companies in more shareholder-oriented countries.[53] As will be discussed below, recent empirical evidence suggests that these underlying regulatory standards effectively shape the sustainability culture within countries, and have both an effect on how companies handle corporate responsibility issues and an effect on the sustainability outcomes at the country level.[54] To the extent that governments have regulated corporate responsibility per se, however, such regulation is focused on disclosure.

By 2015, many European countries or their stock exchanges, and the EU itself, require some environmental or social disclosure, to varying degrees of specificity.[55] The EU's requirement is a directive that entered into force on 6 December 2014; member states will need to transpose it into national legislation within two years.[56] It will require approximately 6,000 large companies and "public interest organizations," such as banks and insurance companies, to "prepare a non-financial statement containing information relating to at least environmental matters, social and employee-related matters, respect for human rights, anti-corruption and bribery matters."[57] This requirement builds upon EU accounting rules (the EU Accounts Modernization Directive) that have, since 2003, required companies to report on environmental and labor issues "to the extent necessary" to provide investors with an accurate view of the company's financial position and the risks to that position.[58]

In addition to the new EU non-financial disclosure requirements, the Nordic countries have been leaders in requiring corporate reporting that is more comprehensive than the reporting required by the EU's 2003 Accounts Modernization Directive. Since 2008, public companies in Sweden must make a sustainability report consistent with GRI.[59] Since

---

[53] See Dirk Matten & Jeremy Moon, " 'Implicit' and 'Explicit' CSR: A Conceptual Framework for a Comparative Understanding of Corporate Social Responsibility", 33:2 Acad. Mgmt. Rev. 404 (2008).

[54] See Part IV, D, *infra.*

[55] See Beate Sjåfjell & Linn Anker Sørensen, Directors' Duties and Corporate Social Responsibility (CSR), in Boards of Directors in European Companies: Reshaping and Harmonising their Organisation and Duties 153 (Hanne Birkmose, Mette Neville, & Karsten Engsig Sørensen eds., 2013).

[56] See Directive 2014/95/EU of the European Parliament and of the Council of 22 October 2014, amending Directive 2013/34/EU as regards disclosure of non-financial and diversity information by certain large undertakings and groups, Official Journal of the European Union L330/1-330/9.

[57] See id. at ¶ 6.

[58] See Sjåfjell & Sørensen, *supra* note 55. For further discussion of the 2003 Accounts Modernization Directive, see Cynthia A. Williams & John M. Conley, "Triumph or Tragedy? The Curious Path of Corporate Disclosure Reform in the UK", 31:2 William & Mary Env. L.J. 317 (2007).

[59] See Jan Bertil Anderson and Frida Segenmark, "Sustainable Companies: Barriers and Possibilities in Swedish Company Law", Univ. of Oslo Res. Paper No. 2013-09 (April 11, 2013), available at http://www.ssrn.com/abstract=2248584.

January 2009, approximately 1,100 large companies in Denmark, as well as institutional investors and loan providers, have been required to publish an annual corporate responsibility report, following a 2008 government Action Plan on Corporate Responsibility.[60] Companies may use their annual reporting to the UN Global Compact as the framework for their public disclosure, and institutional investors may report on their incorporation of the Principles of Responsible Investment (PRI) developed by the UN Environment Program.[61] And as of 1 July 2013, Norwegian companies must report on labor issues, gender equality, anti-discrimination and environmental issues, including reporting on what they are doing to incorporate these issues and human rights concerns into management practices.[62]

These examples are indicative of a global trend toward required corporate responsibility reporting. According to a 2015 report by the Initiative for Responsible Investment of the Hauser Institute for Civil Society at the Kennedy School, Harvard University, 23 countries have enacted legislation within the last 15 years to require public companies to issue reports including environmental and/or social information.[63] These countries include Argentina, China, Denmark, the EU, Ecuador, Finland, France, Germany, Greece, Hungary, India, Indonesia, Ireland (specific to state-supported financial institutions after the 2008 financial crisis), Italy, Japan, Malasia, the Netherlands, Norway, South Africa, Spain, Sweden, Taiwan, and the UK.[64] Of these countries, France is particularly noteworthy, having been a leader by requiring publicly listed companies to report data on 40 labor and social criteria since 2002, followed by requirements in 2009 for companies with more than 500 employees in high-emitting sectors to publish their greenhouse-gas (GHG) emissions.[65]

In addition to these reporting initiatives, seven stock exchanges require social and/or environmental disclosure as part of their listing requirements: Australia's ASX, Brazil's Bovespa, India's Securities and Exchange Board, the Bursa Malasia, Oslo's Børs, the Johannesburg Stock Exchange, and the London Stock Exchange.[66] Moreover, seven countries have enacted policies following those of the UK and Sweden, which since 2000 have required pension funds to disclose the extent to which the fund incorporates social and environmental information into their investment decisions.[67] These countries include Australia, Belgium, Canada, France, Germany, Italy, and Japan.[68]

---

[60] See Karin Buhmann, "Company Law as an Agent for Migration of CR-Related International Law into Company Self-Regulation? The Case of the CR Reporting Requirement", 8:2–3 Eur. Company L. 65, 68 (2011).

[61] See id. For more information on the PRI, see United Nations Environment Program Principles for Responsible Investment, available at http://www.unpri.org/about-pri/.

[62] See Sjåfjell & Sørensen, *supra* note 55, at 26–27.

[63] See "Initiative for Responsible Investment, Corporate Social Responsibility Disclosure Efforts by National Governments and Stock Exchanges" (March 12, 2015), available at http://hausercenter.org/iri/wp-content/uploads/2011/08/CR-3-12-15.pdf.

[64] See id.   [65] See id., citing the New Economic Regulations Act in France, 2002.

[66] See id.

[67] For a discussion of this requirement in the UK, and other early social and environmental disclosure requirements, see Williams & Conley, *supra* note 25 (arguing that differences in the "shareholder wealth maximizing" norm between the UK and US were substantial enough to cast doubt on the idea of an "Anglo-American corporate governance" system).

[68] See Initiative for Responsible Investment report, *supra* note 63.

Notably missing from any of these lists of comprehensive ESG disclosure is the United States, which does have specific disclosure requirements in certain regulatory contexts but no general ESG disclosure framework. Since 1986, the Environmental Protection Agency has required facility-by-facility disclosure concerning the release into the environment and/or management through recycling of over 650 chemicals through the Toxic Release Inventory.[69] The US Securities and Exchange Commission (SEC) requires substantial corporate governance disclosure from its publicly listed companies, as do most countries. Nevertheless, generalized requirements for environmental or social disclosure tend to be narrower than those described above.

Current SEC regulations require disclosure of environmental litigation against any government agency where a penalty of $100,000 is sought,[70] and the SEC has issued guidance for listed companies regarding the extent to which they should disclose climate risks to their future profitability, either from physical changes associated with climate change, or from regulatory initiatives designed to mitigate climate risk.[71]

Four relevant disclosure requirements (with rulemaking directives to the SEC) were enacted as part of the Dodd–Frank Wall Street Reform and Consumer Protection Act of 2010, each targeting an aspect of a company's social record: the ratio of the CEO's total pay to the median employee pay[72]; mine safety disclosure[73]; "conflict minerals" disclosure where tin, tantalum, tungsten, or gold from the Democratic Republic of the Congo or neighboring countries were incorporated into listed companies' products[74]; and "publish what you pay"

---

[69] See Toxic Release Inventory, available at http://www2.epa.gov/toxics-release-inventory-tri-program/learn-about-toxics-release-inventory.

[70] See Reg. S-K, Instructions to Item 103, No. 5(C), 17 C.F.R. § 229.103 (2015). For a discussion of this requirement, as well as an analysis of the statutory authority of the SEC to require much more extensive social and environmental disclosure, see Cynthia A. Williams, "The Securities and Exchange Commission and Corporate Social Transparency", 112 Harv. L. Rev. 1197 (1999).

[71] See "Commission Guidance Regarding Disclosure Related to Climate Change", Rel. 33-9106, 34-61469 (Feb. 8, 2010), available at https://www.sec.gov/rules/interp/2010/33-9106.pdf.

[72] See Dodd–Frank Wall Street Reform and Consumer Protection Act of 2010 ("Dodd–Frank"), § 953(b)(2). The SEC's proposed rule to implement this provision was published on September 18, 2013 on a three to two divided vote, and the final rule promulgated close to two years later, on August 5, 2015. Pay Ratio Disclosure Proposed Rule, Rel. No. 33-9452; 34-70443 (Sept. 18, 2013), available at https://www.sec.gov/rules/proposed/2013/33-9452.pdf; Pay Ratio Disclosure Final Rule, Rel. No. 33-9877; 34-75610 (Aug. 5, 2015), available at http://www.sec.gov/rules/final/2015/33-9877.pdf. The pay ratio rule does not go into effect until January 1, 2017, so it will be some time before the effect of the rule can be judged.

[73] See Dodd–Frank Wall Street Reform and Consumer Protection Act of 2010 ("Dodd–Frank"), § 1503. The Securities and Exchange Commission has implemented this requirement as Item 104 of Regulation S-K, 17 C.F.R. § 229.104. This section was added to Dodd–Frank after an explosion in April, 2010, at the Upper Big Branch Mine in West Virginia, killed 29 miners. It soon became clear that Massey Energy, the owner of the mine, had a practice of ignoring the Federal Mine Safety and Health Act of 1977, having received over 1,300 notifications of violations about that particular mine in the years leading up to the explosion. Democracy Now, Massey Energy Mine Cited for 1,300+ Safety Violations in Years Leading up the Deadly Explosion, April 7, 2010, available at http://www.demoCRacynow.org/2010/4/7/massey_energy_mine_cited_for_1.

[74] See Dodd–Frank, § 1502, enacted as 15 USC. § 13(p).

transparency disclosure for extractive company payments to host countries.[75] These latter two disclosure provisions have been challenged in litigation by the National Association of Manufacturers (challenging conflict mineral disclosure), and the American Petroleum Institute (challenging publish what you pay), joined in both instances by the US Chamber of Commerce.

The SEC's implementing rule on conflict mineral disclosure, requiring listed companies to engage in a due diligence process to determine if their supplies of the named minerals were from mines supporting armed rebels or the Congolese army, was generally upheld by the District Court[76] and Court of Appeals for the District of Columbia Circuit, with one exception identified by the Court of Appeals.[77] That exception held that required language in reports to the SEC and on a company's website that minerals "have not been found to be DRC conflict free" where a company's due diligence could not exclude the possibility of conflict minerals in their supply chains violated companies' First Amendment rights.[78] That aspect of the Court of Appeals' decision was further reviewed and subsequently upheld by the Court of Appeals,[79] but the rest of the rule has gone into effect, requiring companies to evaluate whether their supplies are conflict free and to report on their due diligence procedures, without using the offending required language.

The 2012 "publish what you pay" rule promulgated by the SEC in response to Dodd–Frank was vacated by the District Court for the District of Columbia Circuit for failing to include any exemptions for public disclosure where host countries prohibit it (such as Angola, Cameroon, China, and Qatar), and for interpreting Dodd–Frank to require public disclosure rather than considering disclosure only to the SEC.[80] As of August, 2015, the SEC had not reissued the rule.

Generally, however, there is a clear trend toward an increasing number of environmental and social disclosure requirements around the world. A report by KPMG, UNEP, GRI, and the Unit for Corporate Governance in Africa which identified individual reporting initiatives in 45 countries found 180 such initiatives in 2013, three times the number they had found in 2006.[81] Such reporting initiatives included ESG/sustainability disclosure frameworks, such as GRI; requirements or recommendations for disclosure of individual

[75] See Dodd–Frank, § 1504, enacted as 15 USC. § 13(q).

[76] *National Association of Manufacturers, Inc. v. SEC*, 956 F.Supp.2d 43 (D.D.C. 2013).

[77] See *National Association of Manufacturers, Inc. ("NAM") v. SEC*, 748 F.3d 359 (D.C. Cir. 2014).

[78] See *NAM*, 748 F.3d at 372–373.

[79] Soon after the Court of Appeals decision in *NAM v. SEC*, the Court of Appeals for the District of Columbia Circuit, en banc, decided another disclosure case, rejecting a claim by companies that required country-of-origin disclosure for meat products violated their First Amendment rights, and using a lower level of constitutional scrutiny ("rational basis") than had been applied in the *NAM* litigation challenging the conflict minerals disclosure. See *American Meat Institute v. US Department of Agriculture*, 730 F.3d 18 (D.C. Cir. 2014) (en banc). After *American Meat Institute* the SEC obtained further review of the conflict minerals disclosure, seeking to persuade the court to uphold its entire rule using the rational basis process of analysis. The *NAM* court's original decision finding a First Amendment violation was upheld at *National Assn. of Manufacturers v SEC*, No. 13-5252 (D.C. Cir. Aug. 18, 2015) (on petitions for panel rehearing).

[80] See *American Petroleum Institute v. SEC*, No. 12-1398 (D.D.C. July 2, 2013).

[81] See KPMG, "UNEP, Global Reporting Initiative and Unit for Corporate Governance in Africa, Carrots and Sticks: sustainability reporting policies worldwide" 8 (2013), available at https://www.globalreporting.org/resourcelibrary/carrots-and-sticks.pdf.

topics (e.g., GHGs) or addressed to specific industries (e.g., mining); or were standards regarding sustainability assurance. Of these 180 reporting initiatives, 72% were mandatory, compared to 58% mandatory in 2006.

4 EMPIRICAL FINDINGS

The trends described above of increasing voluntary corporate ESG disclosure, increasing numbers of voluntary corporate responsibility standards and multilateral frameworks, and increasing numbers of jurisdictions imposing standards for required ESG disclosure suggest that corporate responsibility is becoming important in the institutional and normative frameworks shaping companies' actions. Notwithstanding these trends, the concept of corporate responsibility remains contested from a number of perspectives. In the following sections, some empirical evidence about these trends in relation to institutions of corporate governance will be discussed, followed by a number of critical perspectives.

Two caveats, however, with regard to this discussion of the interaction of corporate responsibility and corporate governance. The topic of corporate responsibility has been given increasing academic attention in the past decades, as the table prepared by Timothy Devinney, University Professor of International Business at the University of Leeds, indicates (see Table 24.1). Table 24.1 shows the number of published articles on corporate responsibility within various fields, based on a database Devinney constructed.

The following discussion aims to bring forward a number of the more evocative empirical research findings about corporate governance influences on corporate responsibility, particularly those with implications for the future of this field. It clearly does not purport to be a comprehensive review of this burgeoning literature. Second, the empirical literature on corporate responsibility is equivocal in many respects, as will be discussed below. This is arguably not very different from the equivocal results of corporate governance research generally, as Ruth Aguilera, Kurt Desender, Michael Bednar, and Jun Ho Lee have shown in an argument for better understanding the effects of external corporate

Table 24.1 Number of Academic Articles on Corporate Responsibility

Area	< 1990	1991–1995	1996–2000	2001–2005	2006–2010
Environmental Sciences	2	0	2	13	61
Economics	19	6	9	46	174
Management	189	149	217	604	1460
Sociology	14	4	10	105	295
Psychology	3	0	2	6	17
Law	23	3	11	50	153

Source: Timothy M. Devinney's Database of Articles on Corporate Responsibility.*

* It should be noted that some significant number of articles in psychology, particularly industrial and organizational psychology, are published in management journals.

governance (law, the market for corporate control, external auditors, stakeholder activism, ratings agencies, and the media) on internal corporate governance and financial results.[82] As with corporate governance, equivocal empirical results here simply suggest there is more work to be done.

4.1 Corporate Responsibility and Financial Performance

One of the perennial debates in this field is whether corporate responsibility initiatives lead to better firm-level financial performance, the "business case" for corporate responsibility.[83] There are a number of aspects to this debate, but two primary issues are: first, whether corporate responsibility initiatives pay off, or whether instead they are a waste of money and evidence of unaddressed agency costs; and second, if financial performance is found to be better in firms with robust responsibility initiatives, which way does causation go? Do better-performing firms invest in corporate responsibility because they have higher slack resources, or do the investments come first and the better financial results follow?

The research addressing both of these issues has led to a welter of conflicting results, which is likely due to three primary factors. First, the breadth of issues encompassed within "corporate responsibility" means different studies are very often looking at different things, while using the same generic labels, as Judith Walls, Pascual Berrone, and Philip Phan have argued in narrowing their own scope of quantitative analysis, as discussed below.[84] Moreover, there are different mechanisms by which corporate responsibility initiatives may contribute to a company's results, as discussed by Archie Carroll and Kareem Shabama in arguing for a broader concept of "the business case" for corporate responsibility.[85] These differing mechanisms, including "business benefits of (1) reducing costs and risks; (2) strengthening legitimacy and reputation; (3) building competitive advantage; and (4) creating win-win situations through synergistic value creation,"[86] would affect results depending on the type of corporate responsibility issue and initiative being examined, the size of the firm, the industry, and the social and legal context.[87]

Second, there are mediating variables that until recently were not being carefully disaggregated. A widely cited study by Abagail McWilliams and Donald Siegel from 2000 that discusses the equivocal financial results in studies of corporate responsibility is based on this point, showing that R&D intensity and advertising intensity of industries explain any significant financial out-performance from corporate responsibility, while recognizing close

---

[82]   See Ruth V. Aguilera, Kurt Desender, Michael K. Bednar, & Jun Ho Lee, "Connecting the Dots: Bringing External Corporate Governance into the Corporate Governance Puzzle", Acad. Mgmt. Annals 2015.

[83]   See Archie B. Carroll & Kareem M. Shabama, "The Business Case for Corporate Social Responsibility: A Review of Concepts, Research and Practice", Int'l. J. of Mgmt. Revs. 85 (2010).

[84]   See Judith A. Walls, Pascual Berrone, & Philip H. Phan, "Corporate Governance and Environmental Performance: Is there Really a Link?", 33 Strat. Mgmt. J. 885, 886 (2012) for further discussion of this point.

[85]   See Carroll & Shabama, *supra* note 83, at 92.   [86]   Id. at 95.   [87]   See id.

correlations between corporate responsibility and R&D and advertising.[88] As studies have become more sophisticated in identifying the mediating variables, the results are starting to be more consistent in showing positive financial results from corporate responsibility.

Third, until recently the data were not very good. Early studies had only a firm's own disclosure to "measure" a firm's social or environmental performance, and some of that disclosure was undoubtedly exaggerated. Today there are multiple databases collating much better quantitative and qualitative sources of information about firms' actual social and environmental performance—such as the data Bloomberg sells to its clients. The misspecification issues are well-known and being addressed by targeted studies. As a consequence, certain results are emerging that substantiate the early (2003) meta-analytic result of Marc Orlitzky, Frank Schmidt, and Sara Rynes that corporate responsibility investments can pay off.[89] A number of examples follow.

In a paper showing superior corporate responsibility performance from companies in countries with a Scandinavian legal origin, and then German and French legal origins, and the superiority of all three in comparison to the common law countries (results discussed in more detail in section 4.4 below), Hao Liang and Luc Renneboog show that better corporate responsibility performance also increases firm value, as measured by Tobin's Q.[90] This finding is consistent with the results of Bob Eccles, Ioannis Ioannou, and George Serafeim, who demonstrate based on 18 years' worth of observations of 90 matched pairs of high-sustainability versus low-sustainability companies that companies with a strategic focus on ESG issues show financial outperformance, and stock market and accounting value premiums.[91] As Eccles, Ioannou, and Serafeim recognize, these are long-term strategies and not consistent with short-term market pressures or results. One can hypothesize that in the United States, where short-term activist shareholders are becoming increasingly powerful, corporate responsibility initiatives will be under pressure. More recent work by Serafeim and colleagues Mozaffar Khan and Aaron Yoon shows that management attention to material sustainability risks yields financial outperformance of 3–8%, evaluated within industries using specific concepts of industry-relevant materiality being developed in the United States by the Sustainability Accounting Standards Board (SASB).[92]

If some corporate responsibility initiatives lead to better financial performance, in some industries and legal contexts, a follow-on question is why. Here a number of very

---

[88] See Abagail McWilliams and Donald L. Siegel, "Corporate Social Responsibility and Financial Performance: Correlation or Misspecification?", 21 Strat. Mgmt. J. 603 (2000).

[89] This study is a widely cited (over 3,300 citations to 2015) meta-analysis of 52 prior studies, and it shows better financial performance of firms with better environmental and social records, although the magnitudes of the financial correlations, while statistically significant, are modest. See Marc Orlitzky, Frank L. Schmidt, & Sara L. Rynes, "Corporate Social and Financial Performance: A Meta-Analysis", 24 Org. Stud. 403 (2003).

[90] See Hao Liang and Luc Renneboog, "Law and Finance: The Foundations of Corporate Social Responsibility", Tilburg University Center for Economic Research, European Corporate Governance Institute (ECGI) Finance Working Paper No. 394/2013 (Jan. 2014), available at http://papers.ssrn.com/sol3/papers.cfm?abstract_id=2360633.

[91] See Robert G. Eccles, Ioannis Ioannou, & George Serafeim, "The Impact of Corporate Sustainability on Organizational Processes and Performance", 60:11 Mgmt. Sci. 2835 (2014).

[92] See Mozaffar Khan, George Serafeim, & Aaron Yoon, "Corporate Sustainability: First Evidence on Materiality", Harvard Business School Working Paper 15-073 (March 2015), available at http://papers.ssrn.com/sol3/papers.cfm?abstract_id=2575912.

recent empirical studies show that important mediating variables are innovation and trust. Companies with a longer-term management focus[93] or a stakeholder orientation[94] promote innovation within the firm and higher levels of trust of the firm among various external stakeholders. In one study, Caroline Flammer and Aleksandra Kacperczk used a "natural experiment" to demarcate a shareholder from a stakeholder orientation of a firm, which was the enactment in various states of the United States of "other constituency" statutes.[95] In the law literature, these statutes, which give directors the statutory discretion to consider constituents other than shareholders in making decisions, particularly decisions to resist takeovers, have generally been interpreted to be relatively unimportant, and underutilized, albeit with the potential to create ambiguity regarding directors' duties.[96] What Flammer and Kacperczk found, however, based on regressions on 159,558 firm-year observations, is that measures of innovation—the number of patents issued and the number of citations to those patents— increased significantly (went up between 6.4% and 6.8%) in companies in states that enacted an "other constituency" statute.[97] They interpret these results to show that the protections of other constituency statutes allow for greater experimentation within the firm, which results in both more "flops" and more "hits" on which the firm can get a patent.[98] In another study, Flammer and Pratima Bansal found an increase in firm value after the firms adopted longer-term management compensation plans, and also found improved operating performance on each of three metrics (return on assets, net profit margin, and sales growth).[99] In year one after the firm adopted the longer-term plan, operating performance declined, which Flammer and Bansal suggest shows that "increased long-term orientation may take some time to materialize into higher profits."[100] Flammer and Bansal's results were mediated by increases in innovation after firms adopted a longer-term orientation, as measured by increasing investment in R&D; and increases in social capital investments and performance (legitimacy, reputation, and trust).[101]

Empirical results from Jordi Surroca, Josep Tribó, and Sandra Waddock support the theory that intangibles like innovation are a necessary mediating variable that explains the relationship between corporate responsibility and better financial performance.[102] Their study shows that corporate responsibility strategies and operating procedures positively influence intangibles of innovation, human capital improvements, reputation, and corporate culture,

---

[93] See Caroline Flammer & Pratima Bansal, "Does Long-Term Orientation Create Value? Evidence from a Regression Discontinuity" (2014) available at http://papers.ssrn.com/sol3/papers.cfm?abstract_id=2511507 (showing that firms that adopted longer-term executive compensation plans showed an increase in firm value and operating performance after the adoption of those plans).

[94] See Caroline Flammer & Aleksandra Kacperczk, "The Impact of Stakeholder Orientation on Innovation: Evidence from a Natural Experiment", available at http://papers.ssrn.com/sol3/papers.cfm?abstract_id=2353076.

[95] See id.

[96] See American Bar Association, "Other Constituency Statutes: Potential for Confusion", 45:4 Bus. Law. 2253 (1990).

[97] See id. at 23–24.   [98] See id.   [99] See Flammer & Bansal, *supra* note 93, at 4.

[100] Id.

[101] See id. Social performance is measured using the Kinder, Lydenberg, Domini (KLD) index of social performance. KLD is a socially-responsible investment fund which has collected an extensive database of quantitative and qualitative data since 1991, which data it uses to construct its investment portfolios. KLD's data is widely used in empirical studies of CSR.

[102] See Jordi Surroca, Josep A. Tribó, & Sandra Waddock, "Corporate Responsibility and Financial Performance: The Role of Intangible Resources", 31 Strat. Mgmt. J. 463 (2010).

and that these intangibles are significantly related to corporate financial performance.[103] If the effects on intangibles are statistically "pulled out," then corporate responsibility performance does not show significant effects on corporate financial performance.[104] These mediating influences are stronger in growth industries versus mature industries, and causality is shown in both directions in both growth and mature industries: better financial performance supports some of the same intangibles and leads to better corporate responsibility performance, and vice versa.[105] Taken together, Surroca et al. conclude that it is the necessity of understanding the mediating variables that explains many of the mixed results of previous investigations of the business case, and explains some of the modesty of the Orlitzky et al. results in their 2003 meta-analysis.[106]

A comprehensive review in 2014 of empirical studies of the financial results of corporate responsibility by Gordon Clark, Andreas Feiner, and Michael Viehs found that 90% of studies show that sound sustainability standards lower firms' cost of capital; 80% of studies show that the stock price performance of companies is positively influenced by good sustainability practices; and 88% of studies show that better E, S, or G practices result in better operational performance.[107] While the answers are thus becoming clearer on the empirical questions related to the business case, it is not fully settled under what conditions corporate responsibility leads to better firm performance when it does, or the direction of causality.[108] As Devinney put the question in 2009: What are the corporate responsibility competencies that can be linked to which specific performance outcomes, and through which operational and managerial competencies?[109]

4.2 Board Composition and Committees

One structural feature that would seem to indicate a seriousness of purpose about corporate responsibility, or at least the potential for a connection between a governance mechanism and corporate social performance, would be a board committee dedicated to the topic. Yet the empirical evidence is mixed on this point. Judith Walls, Pascual Berrone, and Philip Phan made the methodological observation that there are different aspects to a company's social performance, and so the mixed results from empirical studies could be a function of failing to untangle competing parameters.[110] Moreover, the strategic use of disclosure to manage stakeholder relationships may obfuscate performance: the worst environmental performers

---

[103] See id. at 480.   [104] See id. at 482.   [105] See id.   [106] See id.

[107] See Gordon L. Clark, Andreas Feiner, & Michael Viehs, "From the Stockholder to the Stakeholder: How Sustainability Can Drive Financial Outperformance" (2015), available at http://papers.ssrn.com/sol3/papers.cfm?abstract_id=2508281. This report is an excellent resource because it analyzes the empirical literature on the financial effects of sustainability initiatives by type of initiative (E, S, or G) and by various financial measures of interest (cost of debt capital; cost of equity capital; operating performance; and effect on stock prices). The study also separately identifies scientifically sound meta-studies and literature reviews.

[108] See Timothy M. Devinney, "Is the Socially Responsible Corporation a Myth? The Good, the Bad and the Ugly of Corporate Social Responsibility", Acad. Mgmt. Persp. 44 (May 2009).

[109] See id. at 52–53.

[110] See Walls, Berrone, & Phan, *supra* note 84.

might use the most environmental disclosure to manage public relationships, for instance, while the worst social performers (community, labor, and supply chain management) might use the least social disclosure.[111] Since disclosure was used as the evidence for corporate social performance in many previous studies, such patterns would produce conflicting—and inaccurate—results. Thus, Walls et al. only evaluated environmental performance (not environmental disclosure) as a function of various aspects of governance (size of a company, board structure, ownership, executive power, and executive compensation).[112]

The authors found two noteworthy effects regarding the board. First, the existence of a specialized environmental board committee was related to both better and worse environmental performance, suggesting that board committees could be established either to promote better environmental performance or as a reaction to environmental problems.[113] Second, more independent, larger, and less diverse boards were associated with worse environmental outcomes, possibly because of a lack of in-depth knowledge of environmental risks to the company.[114] Moreover, an important interaction Walls et al. describe is between a strong CEO (having both the role of CEO and Chairman of the Board) and an insider board: companies with this configuration have better environmental outcomes than do companies with a split CEO/Chair and more independent board.[115] As Walls et al. state "This interesting finding suggests that powerful CEOs may be important for environmental outcomes, and that the vision of such CEOs can be fostered by boards consisting of supportive inside directors."[116] The same general pattern was demonstrated by Surroca and Tribó, who found that increased independence of the board, split CEO and Chair, and the presence of independent committees reduced corporate social performance. Surroca and Tribó interpreted these results to suggest that corporate responsibility is a strategy for management entrenchment and thus indicative of agency concerns.[117] That is, by establishing stronger ties with internal and external constituents, particularly employees and community elites, the top management team insulates themselves from the accountability mechanisms of an independent board and Chair.[118]

That a dedicated corporate responsibility committee on the board cannot be taken as an unambiguous signal of support for the topic is suggested in Table 24.2, which lists the top 25 companies in the world, by market capitalization, and some features of their corporate governance and responsibility arrangements.

From this table we can see both corporate responsibility leaders with dedicated committees (Johnson & Johnson; Novartis), as well as those companies in industries that have been subject to pointed social criticism (JPMorgan Chase, criticized for its role in the financial crisis; Coca-Cola for its role in water depletion in India and contributing to obesity generally through its products). Notable as well is that of the top 25 companies in the

---

[111] Indeed Mallin et al. found suggestions of this kind of strategic use of disclosure, while not exactly that pattern. See Christine A. Mallin, Giovanna Michelon, & Davide Raggi, "Monitoring Intensity and Stakeholders' Orientation: How Does Governance Affect Social and Environmental Disclosure?", 114(1) J. of Bus. Ethics 29 (2013).

[112] See Walls et al, *supra* note 84, at 886. Walls et al. used environmental performance data that has been collected by KLD.

[113] See id.   [114] See id. at 902.   [115] See id.   [116] See id. at 902.

[117] See Jordi Surroca & Josep A.Tribó, "Managerial Entrenchment and Corporate Social Performance", 35 (5-6) J. of Bus. Fin. & Acctng., 748 (2008).

[118] See id. at 770.

Table 24.2 Board Structures for Corporate Responsibility, Global Top 25 Firms

Company Name	SIC Code	Sector	Exchange	Ticker	Country	Market Cap ($US billion)	Is CSR / Sustainability a separate board committee?
Apple Inc	3571	Electronic Computers	NMS	AAPL	USA	752.21$	No
Exxon Mobil Corp.	2911	Petroleum refining	NYS	XOM	USA	369.26$	No
Berkshire Hathaway Inc.	6331	Fire, marine, and casualty insurance	NYS	BRK B	USA	362.56$	No
Microsoft Corporation	7372	Prepackaged software	NMS	MSFT	USA	359.77$	No
Johnson & Johnson	2834	Pharmaceutical preparations	NYS	JNJ	USA	287.34$	Yes
Wells Fargo & Co.	6021	National commercial banks	NYS	WFC	USA	286.70$	Yes
Novartis AG Basel	2834	Pharmaceutical preparations	NYS	NVS	Switzerland	278.23$	Yes
China Mobile Limited	4812	Radiotelephone communications	NYS	CHL	Hong Kong	276.48$	No
Wal-Mart Stores, Inc.	5331	Variety stores	NYS	WMT	USA	270.68$	No
General Electric Co	3699	Electrical machinery, equipment, & supplies, not elsewhere classified	NYS	GE	USA	263.15$	No
Nestle S.A.	2024	Ice cream and frozen desserts	NBB	NSRG Y	Switzerland	252.02$	No
Roche Holding Ltd.	2834	Pharmaceutical Preparations	NBB	RHHB Y	Switzerland	239.01$	Yes
Toyota Motor Corp	3711	Motor vehicles and passenger car	NYS	TM	Japan	231.14$	Yes
Procter & Gamble Co.	2841	Soap and other detergents, except specialty cleaners	NYS	PG	USA	230.91$	Yes
JPMorgan Chase & Co	6021	National commercial banks	NYS	JPM	USA	230.39$	Yes
Facebook, Inc.	7371	Computer programming services	NMS	FB	USA	223.39$	No
Pfizer Inc	2834	Pharmaceutical preparations	NYS	PFE	USA	213.07$	No
Alibaba Group Holding Ltd	5961	Catalog and mail-order houses	NYS	BABA	Cayman Isl.	208.99$	No

2	3	3a	5	4.a	4.b		9
Within mandate of another committee? If so, which?	CSR / Sustainability on website as separate category?	CSR / Sustainability	GRI report?	Which level?	Independently "assured" / third-party certified / audited?	3rd Party Firm	NASDAQ OMX CRD Global Sustainability Index
Not listed	Yes	Sustainability	Other	G3—Level C	N/A	N/A	
Public Issues & Contributions	Yes	Both	Both—GRI & IPEICA/API/OGP	G3—Level A	+	Lloyd's Register Quality Assurance, Inc.	
Not listed	No	N/A	No	N/A	N/A	N/A	
Regulatory & Public Policy	Yes	CSR	Yes	G4	N/A	Not disclosed	
Science, Technology & Sustainability	Yes	CSR	Yes	G4—Core	Assured	Not disclosed	
Corporate Responsibility	Yes	CSR	Yes	G3—Level B	N/A	Not disclosed	
Governance, Nomination & Corporate Responsibilities	Yes	CSR	Yes	G4	N/A	Not disclosed	
Not listed	Yes	Sustainability	No	N/A	N/A	N/A	
Compensation, Nominating & Governance	Yes	CSR	Yes	G3—Level B	N/A	Not disclosed	
Governance & Public Affairs	Yes	Sustainability	Yes	G3—Level A	N/A	N/A	
Not listed	Yes	CSR	Yes	G4	N/A	Not disclosed	
Corporate Governance & Sustainability	Yes	Sustainability	Yes	G4—Level A	+	Not disclosed	
CSR Committee	Yes	Sustainability	ISO 26000	N/A	Reviewed	Deloitte	
Governance & Public Responsibility	Yes	Sustainability	Yes	G3—Level A	N/A	Not disclosed	
Public Responsibility	Yes	CSR	Yes	G3—Level B	N/A	Not disclosed	
Not listed	Yes	Sustainability	No	N/A	N/A	N/A	
Corporate Governance	Yes	CSR	Yes	G3—Level B	N/A	Not disclosed	
Not listed	Yes	Sustainability	No	N/A	N/A	N/A	

(continued)

Table 24.2 Continued

Company Name	SIC Code	Sector	Exchange	Ticker	Country	Market Cap ($US billion)	1 Is CSR / Sustainability a separate board committee?
Verizon Communications Inc	4813	Telephone communications, except radiotelephone	NYS	VZ	USA	201.62$	No
Chevron Corporation	2911	Petroleum refining	NYS	CVX	USA	198.83$	No
Oracle Corp.	7372	Prepackaged software	NYS	ORCL	USA	193.35$	No
Coca-Cola Co (The)	2086	Bottled and canned soft drinks & carbonated waters	NYS	KO	USA	188.60$	Yes
Disney (Walt) Co. (The)	7812	Motion picture and video tape production	NYS	DIS	USA	179.95$	No
AT&T Inc	4813	Telephone communications, except radiotelephone	NYS	0.00	USA	179.66$	Yes
Amazon.com Inc.	5961	Catalog and mail-order houses	NMS	AMZN	USA	179.23$	No
					Total	**6,656.54$**	Yes
							No
							N/A
							Yes %
							36.0%

Source: Credit for the Table is due to Taras Koulik, JD/MBA 2015, Osgoode Hall Law School, York University.

2	3	3a	5	4.a	4.b		9
Within mandate of another committee? If so, which?	CSR / Sustainability on website as separate category?	CSR / Sustainability	GRI report?	Which level?	Independently "assured" / third-party certified / audited?	3rd Party Firm	NASDAQ OMX CRD Global Sustainability Index
Corporate Governance & Policy	Yes	CSR	No	N/A	N/A	Not disclosed	
Public Policy	Yes	CSR	Other—IPIECA/API/OGP	N/A	N/A	N/A	Removed
Not listed	Yes	Both	Yes	G3—Level B	N/A	Not disclosed	
Public Issues & Diversity Review	Yes	Sustainability	Yes	G4—Level A	+	Ernst & Young	
Not listed	Yes	CSR	Yes	G3—Level B	N/A		
Public Policy & Corp. Reputation	Yes	Both	Yes	G3—Level C	+	Deloitte	
Not listed	Yes	Sustainability	No	N/A	N/A	N/A	
	Yes	CSR	Yes	G1—Level A	+		
	No	Sustainability	No	G1—Level B	N/A		
	N/A	Both	N/A	G1—Level C	Reviewed		
		N/A	Other—IPIECA/API/OGP	G2—Level A	Assured		
Not Listed %			Both—GRI & IPEICA/API/OGP	G2—Level B			
36.0%			ISO 26000	G2—Level C			
				G3—Level A			
				G3—Level B			
				G3—Level C			
				G4—Core			
				G4			
				G4			
				N/A			

world, by market capitalization, 19 of which are from the United States, only one, Berkshire Hathaway, does not have a portion of its website dedicated to corporate responsibility or sustainability issues. Berkshire Hathaway may not need such a page, given that its CEO, Warren Buffett, is known for a clear commitment to simple guiding principles, such as this one prominently featured on the company's website:

> Given the variety and complexity of ethical questions that may arise in the Company's course of business, this Code of Business Conduct and Ethics serves only as a rough guide.
> Confronted with ethically ambiguous situations, the Covered Parties should remember the Company's commitment to the highest ethical standards and seek advice from supervisors, managers or other appropriate personnel to ensure that all actions they take on behalf of the Company honor this commitment. When in doubt, remember Warren Buffett's rule of thumb:
> " . . . I want employees to ask themselves whether they are willing to have any contemplated act appear the next day on the front page of their local paper—to be read by their spouses, children and friends–with the reporting done by an informed and critical reporter."[119]

But that even Alibaba, a Chinese Internet sales company incorporated in the Cayman Islands which is being investigated for extensive sales of counterfeit products online,[120] would include a "sustainability" page on its website suggests at least two things: global companies feel pressure from social actors to be seen to embrace positive social and environmental values; and companies' disclosure cannot be understood as an unambiguous signal of actual corporate responsibility.

4.3 Patterns of Shareholder Ownership

As noted in the introduction to this chapter, there is evidence that some types of institutional shareholders are paying more attention to ESG issues, and that this is one source of pressure on companies also to pay more attention.[121] Trillions of dollars of invested capital supporting initiatives such as the UN Environment Program's Principles of Responsible Investment or backing the Carbon Disclosure Project's efforts to get better data on company's management of GHG emissions send a signal to companies that at least some investors care about these topics. Of potentially greater significance, since 2009, Bloomberg has included 79 environmental and social data points in the information it sells to brokers and dealers throughout the world, as indicated in Table 24.3.

---

[119] See Berkshire Hathaway, Inc. Code of Business Conduct and Ethics, available at http://www. berkshirehathaway.com/govern/ethics.pdf. Unlike every other top company's website, Berkshire Hathaway's also has no pictures.

[120] See Scott Cendrowski, "Nothing to See Here says Alibaba's Ma—and Customers Seem to Agree", available at http://www.fortune.com/2015/02/03/nothing-to-see-here-says-alibabas-ma-and-customers-seem-to-agree (quoting one "obsessive" Chinese customer that "of course" there are counterfeit goods being sold on Alibaba's Chinese website, but that there is a difference between "a fake Coach purse and tainted baby food").

[121] See Ruth V. Aguilera, Deborah E. Rupp, Cynthia A. Williams, & Joyti Ganapathi, "Putting the 'S' Back in Corporate Social Responsibility: A Multi-Level Theory of Corporate Social Responsibility", 32:3 Acad. Mgmt. Rev. 836 (2007) (discussing various motives for employees, managers, shareholders, customers, NGOs, and countries to pressure companies to adopt corporate responsibility initiatives, and theorizing about interactions among those entities and motives, and effects on the firm).

Table 24.3 Bloomberg Social and Environmental Metrics Chart

Number	Name	Description
Social Metrics		
1	Social Disclosure Score	Proprietary Bloomberg score based on the extent of a company's social disclosure as part of Environmental, Social and Governance (ESG) Data.
2	Number of Employees—CSR	This is the total number of company employees at the end of the reporting period disclosed in the company's Corporate Responsibility reports.
3	Employee Turnover %	Number of employees that left the company within the past year expressed as a percentage of the average total number of employees.
4	% Employees Unionized	Number of employees that belong to labour unions as a percentage of the total number of employees.
5	% Women in Workforce	Number of women employed at the company expressed as a percentage of the total number of company employees.
6	% Women in Management	Percentage of women employed in management positions at the company.
7	% Minorities in Workforce	Number of minorities employed at the company expressed as percentage of the total number of employees.
8	Lost Time Incident Rate	Total number of incidents resulting in lost time from work, per 200,000 hours worked or per 100 full time equivalent employees, assuming employees work 40 hours per week and 50 weeks per year.
9	Total Recordable Incident Rate	Total number of recordable incidents, per 200,000 hours worked or per 100 full time equivalent employees, assuming employees work 40 hours per week and 50 weeks per year.
10	Fatalities—Employees	Number of employees who have died on a company site or on a company facility or as a result of a company's operations.
11	Fatalities—Total	Total number of employees and contractors who have died on a company site, at a company facility, or as a result of a company's operations.
12	Social Supply Chain Management	Indicates whether the company has implemented any initiatives to reduce the social risks in its supply chain. Social risks might include poor working conditions, the use of child or forced labour, lack of a living, fair or minimum wage, etc.
13	Sustain Sup Guidelines Encomp ESG Area Pub Disclsd	Indicates whether a supplier's guidelines, which encompass all Environmental, Social, and Governance (ESG) areas, are publically disclosed.
14	Community Spending	Amount of money spent by the company on community-building activities in millions.

(continued)

Table 24.3 Continued

Number	Name	Description
15	Total hours spent by Firm—Employee Training	Hours the company spent on employee training during the reporting period as reported by the company.
16	Health and Safety Policy	Indicates whether the company has recognized its health and safety risks and responsibilities and is making any effort to improve the management of employee health and/or employee safety.
17	Fair Remuneration Policy	Indicates if the company has demonstrated a group-wide commitment to ensure payment of a fair (could be defined as minimum, living, or some other criteria) wage to all group employees, even in those countries that do not legally require a minimum wage.
18	Training Policy	Indicates whether the company has implemented any initiatives to train new and existing employees on career development, education, or skills.
19	Employee—CSR training	Discloses whether the company conducts training courses for employees on Corporate Social Responsibility (CSR).
20	Equal Opportunity Policy	Indicates whether the company has made a proactive commitment to ensure non-discrimination against any type of demographic group.
21	Human Rights Policy	Indicates whether the company has implemented any initiatives to ensure the protection of the rights of all people it works with.
22	Policy Against Child Labour	Indicates whether the company has implemented any initiatives to ensure the prevention of child labour in all parts of its business.
23	Business Ethics Policy	Indicates whether the company has established ethical guidelines and/or a compliance policy for its non-management/executive employees in the conduct of company business.
24	Anti-Bribery Ethics Policy	Indicates whether the company has policies in place to prevent bribery of its employees, executives, and directors by others, and/or prevention of involvement in any corrupt business practices limiting open competition by deception, including but not limited to: cartels, collusion, fraud, embezzlement, nepotism, price fixing, and preferred patronage.
25	Whistle Blower Protection	Indicates whether the company has systems and policies in place for the reporting of internal ethical compliance complaints without retaliation or retribution, including but not limited to access to confidential third-party ethics hotlines or systems for confidential written complaints.
26	UN Global Compact Signatory	Indicates whether the company is a signatory of the United Nations Global Compact.

Table 24.3 Continued

Number	Name	Description
Environmental Metrics		
1	Environmental Disclosure Score	Proprietary Bloomberg score based on the extent of a company's environmental disclosure as part of Environmental, Social, and Governance (ESG) data.
2	Direct CO_2 Emissions	Direct Carbon Dioxide (CO_2) Emissions of the company, in thousands of metric tons.
3	Methane Emissions	Total amount of methane emitted by the company, in thousands of metric tons.
4	Direct Nitrous Oxide (N_2O) Emissions	Direct nitrous oxide (N_2O) emissions of the company, in thousands of metric tons.
5	Direct Methane Emission in CO_2 Equivalent	Direct methane (CH_4) emissions of the company, in thousands of metric tons of carbon dioxide equivalent (CO_2e).
6	Direct Nitrous Oxide Emissions in CO_2 Equivalent	Direct nitrous oxide (N_2O) emissions of the company, in thousands of metric tons of carbon dioxide equivalent (CO_2e).
7	GHG Scope 1	Scope 1/Direct Greenhouse Gas (GHG) emissions of the company, in thousands of metric tons.
8	GHG Scope 2	Scope 2/Indirect Greenhouse Gas (GHG) Emissions of the company in thousands of metric tons.
9	Total GHG Emissions	Total Greenhouse Gas (GHG) emissions of the company, in thousands of metric tons.
10	Nitrogen Oxide Emissions	Total amount of nitrogen oxide (NO_x) emitted by the company, in thousands of metric tons.
11	Sulfur Dioxide Emissions	Total amount of sulfur dioxide (SO_2) emitted by the company, in thousands of metric tons.
12	VOC Emissions	Total amount of volatile organic compounds (VOCs) emitted by the company, in thousands of metric tons.
13	Carbon Monoxide Emissions	Total amount of carbon monoxide (CO) emitted by the company, thousands of metric tons.
14	ODS Emissions	Total amount of ozone-depleting substances (ODSs) emitted by the company, in thousands of metric tons.
15	Particulate Emissions	Total amount of particulates emitted by the company, in thousands of metric tons.
16	Total Energy Consumption	Total Energy Consumption figure in thousands of megawatt hours (MWh).
17	Electricity Used	Total Amount of Electricity used by the company, in thousands of megawatt hours (MWh).

(continued)

Table 24.3 Continued

Number	Name	Description
18	Total Water Use	Total amount of water used to support a company's operational processes, in thousands of cubic meters.
19	Total Water Withdrawal	Amount of water diverted for use by the organization from all sources, but not limited to surface, ground, saltwater, municipal, in thousands of cubic meters.
20	Surface Water Withdrawals	Amount of water diverted for use by the organization from all surface freshwater sources, including but not limited to lakes, rivers and streams, in thousands of cubic meters.
21	Groundwater Withdrawals	Amount of water withdrawn by the organization from underground reservoirs, in thousands of cubic meters.
22	Municipal Water Use	Amount of water diverted for use by the organization from municipal water treatment facilities, in thousands of cubic meters.
23	Total Water Recycled	Amount of process water and cooling water used by the company's operations that was derived from internal recycling/reuse processes, in thousands of cubic meters.
24	Water Recycled	Percentage of water usage from recycled sources.
25	Water Use	Amount of water used for company processes that is not immediately returned to the environment in the same uncontaminated state, in thousands of cubic meters.
26	Discharges to Water	Amount of discharges to water that influence the biophysical or chemical quality of the water.
27	Total Waste	Total amount of waste the company discards, both hazardous and non-hazardous, in thousands of metric tons.
28	Hazardous Waste	Amount of hazardous waste the company discards, in thousands of metric tons.
29	Waste Recycled	Total amount of waste the company recycles, in thousands of metric tons.
30	Waste sent to Landfills	Amount of company waste sent to landfills, in thousands of metric tons.
31	Number Spills	Actual number of spills of hazardous materials by the company in the period.
32	Number of Environmental Fines	Number of environment fines paid by the company in the period.
33	Environmental Fines	Total amount of environmental fines paid by the company in the period, in millions.
34	Environmental Accounting Cost	Cost of environmental conservation and other environmental initiatives undertaken during the normal course of business as defined by company.
35	Investments in Operational Sustainability	Amount of money spent by the company, in millions, on operational environmental and social compliance and other internal environmental and social initiatives, as defined by the company.
36	Energy Efficiency Policy	Indicates whether the company has implemented any initiatives to make its use of energy more efficient.

Table 24.3 Continued

Number	Name	Description
37	Emissions Reduction Initiatives	Indicates whether the company has implemented any initiatives to reduce its environmental emissions to air.
38	Environmental Supply Chain Management	Indicates whether the company has implemented any initiatives to reduce the environmental footprint of its supply chain.
39	Green Building Policy	Indicates whether the company has taken any steps toward using environmental technologies and/or environmental principles in the design and construction of its buildings.
40	Waste Reduction Policy	Indicates whether the company has implemented any initiatives to reduce the waste generated during the course of its operations.
41	Water Policy	Indicates whether the organization has undertaken any initiatives to reduce the quantity of water used or to improve the efficiency of its processes, and whether the company is considering the potential stress to its areas of operation.
42	Sustainable Packaging	Indicates whether the company has taken any steps to make its packaging more environmentally friendly.
43	Environmental Quality Management	Indicates whether the company has introduced any kind of environmental quality management and/or environmental management system to help reduce the environmental footprint of operations.
44	Climate Change Opportunities Discussed	Indicates whether the Management Discussion and Analysis (MD&A) and its equivalent section of the company's annual report discuss business opportunities related to climate change.
45	Risks of Climate Change Discussed	Indicates whether the Management Discussion and Analysis (MD&A) and its equivalent section of the company's annual report discuss business risks related to climate change.
46	Climate Change Policy	Indicates whether the company has outlined its intention to help reduce global emissions of the Greenhouse Gases that cause climate change through its ongoing operations and/or the use of its products and services.
47	New Products— Climate Change	Indicates whether the company has developed and/or launched products during the current period only which address future impacts of climate change and/or which mitigate customers' contributions to climate change by reducing Greenhouse Gas (GHG) emissions.
48	Biodiversity Policy	Indicates whether the company has implemented any initiatives to ensure the protection of biodiversity.
49	Verification Policy	Indicates whether the company's environmental policies were subject to an independent assessment for the reporting period.

Source: Bloomberg Reports, March, 2015. Credit due to Patrick Egit, Osgoode Hall Law School J.D. 2014 and LL.M. 2015.

Following the logic of Robert Daines, Ian Gow, and David Larcker, presumably Bloomberg would not be collecting, analyzing, and selling this information if there were not a market for it.[122] Bloomberg has only sold these data since 2009, which gives further evidence of corporate responsibility as an emerging trend.

Richard Johnson and Daniel Greening have shown that the type of investors in a company has a significant effect on a company's environmental and social performance.[123] Firms with higher percentages of long-term, pension fund investors had significantly better performance on social issues and environmental issues than firms with lower percentages, although the effect on social issues was modest.[124] Donald Neubaum and Shaker Zahra replicated these results in 2006, finding that large (1% holdings) pension fund investors had a significant and positive effect on companies' social and environmental performance, particularly where funds coordinated their activism. Mutual fund and investment bank holdings had a significant and negative effect on corporate social performance, but only when these funds engaged in activism, not when they were simply passive investors.[125] These findings have implications for corporate responsibility going forward, as short-term shareholder activists become more visible, at least in the US.[126] Moreover, these findings have broader social welfare implications given the emerging research discussed above that shows a long-term management perspective fuels innovation.[127]

4.4 Corporate Responsibility, Legal Origins, and Corporate Governance Systems

Consistent with what one might predict, empirical evidence shows that both country-level sustainability ratings and company-level corporate responsibility ratings are higher in countries with a stakeholder-oriented corporate governance system than in countries with a shareholder-oriented corporate governance system. One quantitative study using MSCI (Morgan Stanley Capital, International) Intangible Value Assessment data, supplemented with specific social and environmental data from MSCI's Risk Metrics, found that:

> among different legal origins, the English common law—widely believed to be mostly share-
> holder oriented—fosters CSR the least; within the civil law countries, firms of countries with

---

[122] See Robert M. Daines, Ian D. Gow, & David F. Larcker, "Rating the Ratings: How Good are Corporate Governance Ratings?", 98 J. Fin. Econ. 439 (2010) (while finding the quality of corporate governance ratings to be suspect given little correlation among the ratings from different providers, the fact that these ratings agencies have a commercially viable business shows that investors value the information).

[123] See Richard A. Johnson & Daniel W. Greening, "The Effects of Corporate Governance and Institutional Investor Types on Corporate Social Performance", 42:5 Acad. Mgmt. J. 564 (1999) (using KLD data).

[124] See id.

[125] See Donald O. Neubaum & Shaker A. Zahra, "Institutional Ownership and Corporate Social Performance: the Moderating Effects of Investment Horizon, Activism, and Coordination", 32:1 J. Mgmt. 108 (2006) (using KLD data).

[126] See William W. Bratton & Michael L. Wachter, "Shareholders and Social Welfare", 36 Seattle L. Rev. 489 (2013) (discussing shareholder activists and the corporate policies they promote).

[127] See text accompanying notes 93–105, *supra*.

German legal origin outperform their French counterparts in terms of ecological and environmental policy, but the French legal origin firms outperform German legal origin companies in social issues and labor relations. Companies under the Scandinavian legal origin score highest on CSR (and all its subfields).[128]

The authors of this study, Hao Liang and Luc Renneboog, also find from the analysis of country-level sustainability ratings and financial development that countries with higher financial development (which tend to be those with shareholder-oriented corporate governance systems) have lower country-level sustainability ratings, including lower environmental responsibility ratings, and lower social responsibility and solidarity ratings.[129] While the law and finance literature has emphasized the greater financialization of countries with a common-law legal origin,[130] Liang and Renneboog's results suggest that financialization per se does not occupy the field of important social welfare outcomes.

A similar pattern for the importance of legal origins was found in another empirical study using a different data source (Innovest), but examining only differences between the Scandinavian legal system, the "civil and German" legal system, and the common law system (Great Britain and Ireland) within the EU.[131] In that study Céline Gainet again found that Scandinavian countries outperformed those based on civil and German law with regard to environmental performance, and that both outperformed countries in the EU with a common law origin.[132] Gainet found the pattern with respect to social performance to be mixed (Scandinavian countries outperformed both civil and common law in one year, but the common law countries in Europe, Great Britain, and Ireland outperformed the civil law countries in two years.) These mixed results may have been due to the short time frame (2004 to 2007) over which the social performance of the companies was being examined, given data availability, or they demonstrate convergence in labor protections at the EU level, as Gainet suggests.[133]

---

[128] See Hao Liang & Luc Renneboog, "The Foundations of Corporate Social Responsibility, Tilberg Law and Economics Center Discussion Paper No. 2013-023", available at http://ssrn.com/abstract=2371103. Robert M. Daines, Ian D. Gow, & David F. Larcker, Rating the Ratings: How Good are Corporate Governance Ratings? The MSCI Intangible Value Assessment (IVA) developed a series of 29 ESG scores from 1999 to 2011 using multiple sources of quantitative and qualitative data for the top 1,500 companies in the MSCI World Index, the top 25 companies in its emerging markets index, and the top 275 companies by market capitalization for the FTSE 100 and FTSE 250 and the ASX 200. Liang and Renneboog note that the governance factors within these 29 ESG scores account for less than 2% of the weight of the composite ESG score for a company, while the weight of the labor relations, industry-specific risks in relation to carbon emissions, and environmental opportunity factors add up to 80%. Id. at 8. Liang and Renneboog supplemented the MSCI IVA data with Risk Metrics data on environmental and social factors.

[129] See id. at 23.

[130] See Rafael la Porta, Florencio Lopez-de-Silanes & Andrei Shleifer, "The Economic Consequences of Legal Origins", 46 J. Econ. Lit. 285 (2008).

[131] See Gainet, *supra* note 4, at 212. Innovest uses quantitative and qualitative data evaluating 40 aspects of company action using 20 sources, attempting to capture actual company performance. Social metrics include governance of social issues, human capital measures, stakeholder capital measures, product and services evaluation, and relationships within emerging markets. For environmental measures, Innovest examines total EVA (economic value added) versus waste, and also five aspects of environmental risk and opportunities: historical liabilities, operating risk, sustainability and eco-efficiency risk, material risk, and strategic profit opportunities. Id. at 202.

[132] See id.   [133] See id. at 213.

These studies give evidence of an important vector by which law structures the corporate social relationship, the legal origins vector, which shapes, among other things, a country's views on the proper role of the state in the economy. Where, as in the common law system, the state's role in the economy is understood to be more limited in addressing economic inequality or promoting and protecting labor or environmental interests than among Scandinavian countries or those based on civil law legal families, there is more pressure for voluntary corporate responsibility initiatives to address these issues, as Matten and Moon have argued.[134] The above evidence suggests those voluntary initiatives are less effective in promoting social and environmental social welfare than are the types of laws and institutional arrangements found in the Scandinavian and civil law legal contexts.

5 IMPLICATIONS AND ANALYSIS

Whether attention to corporate responsibility does lead to financial outperformance in some cases, and what those cases are, does not settle the "case of corporate responsibility," for there is a much deeper disagreement with which this chapter concludes. That is the perennial, one might say religious,[135] debate over the purpose of the firm. Is it "simply" to produce products and services that create economic rents to be distributed to rights' holders according to pre-existing contractual, statutory, and (possibly) normative obligations? (Given that close to 70% of new companies ultimately fail, that task cannot be taken as too simple.)[136] Or does the firm also have a social obligation to minimize harm to people and the natural environment in its pursuits of profits, or even a positive duty to promote social welfare beyond its creation of economic rents? In corporate governance and law, this debate tracks the competition between a shareholder versus stakeholder view of directors' and officers' fiduciary obligations. The literature on each side of this debate is so extensive that the following will simply sketch out aspects of the various positions that have direct implications for differing views regarding corporate responsibility, and then give some indications of why it might be possible, and important, to narrow the gap between these seemingly irreconcilable positions.

5.1 Shareholder Primacy

Milton Friedman's articulation of firms' responsibilities is the iconic expression of a predominantly economic perspective on the nature of the firm:

> There is one and only one social responsibility of business—to use its resources and engage in activities designed to increase profits so long as it stays within the rules of the game, which is to say, engages in open and free competition without deception or fraud.[137]

---

[134] See id. at 49.   [135] See id. at 44.
[136] See Startup Failure Rate by Industry, available at http://www.statisticbrain.com/startup-failure-by-industry.
[137] See Milton Friedman, The Social Responsibility of Business is to Increase its Profits, N.Y. Times Magazine 6 (Sept. 13, 1970).

This statement was part of a *New York Times* article in which Friedman contributed to a vigorous debate that was then ongoing within the business community. Some academics and members of the business community in the US had begun to argue that companies had responsibilities to respond to civil rights and anti-war unrest, as well as strategic interests in providing an attractive alternative to collectivist social movements like Marxism, socialism, and organized labor, by paying greater attention to making a positive social contribution.[138] Friedman and others taking his view responded that the social contribution firms make from running a profitable business, employing people, paying taxes, and distributing some part of net profits to shareholders *is* the business firm's positive social contribution. A concern that later writers in this vein articulated is that trying to create additional social benefits beyond those that flow from honest profit-making within the confines of law will dilute management's focus, undermine economic performance, and thereby ultimately undermine social welfare.[139]

A number of arguments for a narrow view of managers' and directors' obligations devolve from shareholders' special position in the firm. One theoretical perspective, the contractarian view of the corporation as articulated by Steve Bainbridge (among others), asserts that an implicit term of the contract between shareholders and the firm is that the directors and managers will act in the shareholders' best interests, understood as maximizing their wealth.[140] A pragmatic perspective suggests that given the broad discretion directors and top managers have to run the firm, and given that in shareholder-oriented corporate governance systems only shareholders have direct rights to vote or to sue,[141] it is

[138] See id. (e.g., note Friedman's statement that "[t]he businessmen believe that they are defending free enterprise when they declaim that business is not concerned 'merely' with profit but also with promoting desirable 'social' ends; . . . In fact they are—or would be if they or anyone else took them seriously— preaching pure and unadulterated socialism. Businessmen who talk this way are unwitting puppets of the intellectual forces that have been undermining the basis of a free society these past decades."). See Davis, *supra* note 1, for a delineation of the perspectives in that historical debate.

[139] See Henry Hansmann & Reinier Kraakman, "The End of History for Corporate Law", 89 Geo. L. J. 439, 442–43 (2001) (writing that "[t]he point is simply that now, as a consequence of both logic and experience, there is convergence on a consensus that the best means to this end—the pursuit of aggregate social welfare—is to make corporate managers strongly accountable to shareholder interests and (at least in direct terms) only to those interests.").

[140] See Stephen M. Bainbridge, "Director Primacy: The Means and Ends of Corporate Governance", 97 Nw. U. L. Rev. 547 (2003). There are other theoretical arguments for shareholder primacy, such as those based on a concept of shareholders as principals and managers and directors as agents in an agency relationship. For a critical summary of this view see Bratton & Wachter, *supra* note 126.

[141] While Canada is often included as a country having a shareholder-oriented corporate governance system, that is no longer correct. Canada permits non-shareholder constituents to bring derivative actions (sue) by statute, and the Supreme Court of Canada has twice articulated a stakeholder perspective on the firm and directors' obligations. See *Peoples Department Stores Inc. (Trustee of) v. Wise*, 2004 SCC 68, [2004] 3 S.C.R. 461 (stating at [42] that "[w]e accept as an accurate statement of law that in determining whether they are acting with a view to the best interests of the corporation it may be legitimate, given all the circumstances of a given case, for the board of directors to consider, inter alia, the interests of shareholders, employees, suppliers, creditors, consumers, governments and the environment"); *BCE Inc. v. 1976 Debentureholders*, 2008 SCC 69, [2008] 3 S.C.R 560 (stating at [82] that "the question is whether, in all the circumstances, the directors acted in the best interests of the corporation, having regard to all relevant considerations, including, but not confined to, the need to treat affected stakeholders in a fair manner, commensurate with the corporation's duties as a responsible corporate citizen.").

not surprising that firms and their managers will act in shareholders' interests in order to avoid being sued, voted out of office, or thrown out of office in a hostile takeover, as recently argued by Leo Strine, Jr., the Chief Justice of the Delaware Supreme Court.[142] In another recent article, CJ Strine argues that acting in shareholders' interests is not only pragmatic but legally required, and so corporate responsibility could be a breach of fiduciary duty.[143] This argument will be discussed in more detail below.

From the shareholder-oriented perspective, corporate responsibility is too much responsibility to impose on directors. Advancing social policy goals is the job of government, not business.[144] In contrast, directors are elected by the shareholders to run the firm in the shareholders' interests. Balancing other constituents' interests by making "tradeoffs between the welfare of shareholders and that of non-shareholder constituencies"[145] is problematic because it is inconsistent with the proper exercise of directors' power to advance shareholders' interests, and because it risks undermining accountability by allowing directors to act in their own self-interest while claiming to act in other constituents' interests.[146]

Given this perspective, the importance of the business case is obvious. If corporate responsibility initiatives do not make money for the firm, they fail. While many other business strategies can also fail, such as mergers and acquisitions, where half to two-thirds do not make money for the acquiring firm and resulting entity,[147] mergers and acquisitions at least aim to make money for the firm, and so their legitimacy as a business strategy is not in doubt. Corporate responsibility initiatives do not have that legitimacy of motivation, from the critics' perspective (although "strategic corporate responsibility" is intended to be profitable,[148] and many responsibility initiatives are profitable, as discussed above).[149] As a result, in this view, corporate responsibility is too strong a concept: it risks economic underperformance, it usurps government's policy roles, and it is beyond the boundaries of directors' and managers' legitimate exercise of power by seeking to advance non-shareholder interests.

---

[142] See Leo E. Strine, Jr., "Making it Easier for Directors to 'Do the Right Thing'?", 4 Harv. Bus. L. Rev. 235 (2014), available at http://papers.ssrn.com/sol3/papers.cfm?abstract_id=2539098.

[143] See Leo E. Strine, Jr., "The Dangers of Denial: The Need for a Clear-Eyed Understanding of the Power and Accountability Structure Established by the Delaware General Corporation Law, ('Dangers of Denial')", University of Pennsylvania Law School Institute for Law and Economics Research Paper no. 15-08, available at http://ssrn.com/abstract=2576389.

[144] See, e.g., David L. Engel, "An Approach to Corporate Social Responsibility", 32 Stan. L. Rev. 1 (1979) (directors are not well suited to balance competing social policy interests, which is the job of legislators); Daniel R. Fischel, "The Corporate Governance Movement", 35 Vand. L. Rev. 1259 (1982) (redress for those concerned about a lack of corporate social accountability is through the political process, not through disrupting the "voluntary arrangements that private parties have entered into in forming corporations").

[145] Stephen M. Bainbridge, "Corporate Social Responsibility in the Night-Watchman State", 115 Colum. L. Rev. Sidebar 39, 49 (2015) (briefly summarizing his prior work discussing this concern).

[146] See id.

[147] See Robert F. Bruner, Deals From Hell: M&A Lessons that Rise above the Ashes Ch.1 (2005).

[148] See Porter and Kramer, *supra* note 23, and McWilliams & Siegel, *supra* note 24, for examples of strategic corporate responsibility.

[149] See text accompanying notes 84–108, *supra*.

5.2 Stakeholder theory

In contrast, to many academic critics of corporate responsibility, it is still too weak a concept. There are a number of strands to this thinking, as with the shareholder perspective. One is stakeholder theory, which is the major theoretical competitor to shareholder primacy. Stakeholder theory is generally attributed to Ed Freeman,[150] although he attributes the idea to "a very old tradition that sees business as an integral part of society rather than an institution separate and purely economic in nature."[151] From the perspective of stakeholder theory, economic value is created by voluntary relationships among many parties who cooperate to create successful businesses. It is an ethical theory about the values of management in relationships with those parties, and also a management theory about how to create and manage successful companies. As Freeman states, "[c]apitalism works because entrepreneurs and managers put together and sustain deals or relationships among customers, suppliers, employees, financiers, and communities."[152] This theory does not deny that shareholders are important stakeholders in the firm, but does reject the view that shareholders' interests are the only interests that managers and directors should consider in managing a successful firm.[153]

From a stakeholder perspective, successful companies incorporate and rely upon multiple social and natural inputs, such as an educated workforce, the physical infrastructure for the production, transportation, and distribution of goods, an effective legal system, and natural capital inputs of water, air, commodities, and so forth. Since some significant portion of the inputs of corporate success, including financial inputs, have been contributed by parties other than shareholders, those parties also have interests to be considered in determining the responsibilities of managers and directors and in distributing the outputs of corporate action. Some, perhaps many, of those interests will be protected by contractual or regulatory arrangements, but others cannot be specified ex ante, and so must depend on corporate participants to fairly balance multiple parties' legitimate claims ex post, as in Margaret Blair and Lynn Stout's team production theory of corporate law.[154]

To some stakeholder theorists, corporate responsibility is too modest, given its emphasis on disclosure and voluntarism. Some serious, even extreme, human rights problems persist despite two decades of corporate responsibility initiatives and expanded ESG disclosure. Andy Crane has shown that "modern slavery" (traditional slavery, bonded labor, human trafficking, and forced labor) is endemic in some industries (agriculture, mining, extraction, construction, brickmaking, carpet weaving, domestic work, and sex work); global estimates range from 12 million to 30 million people enslaved throughout the world.[155] The limits of corporate responsibility can be seen in the problem of slavery in the West African cocoa

---

[150] See R. Edward Freeman, "The Politics of Stakeholder Theory", 4 Bus. Ethics Q. 409 (1994).

[151] R. Edward Freeman & Jeanne Liedtka, "Stakeholder Capitalism and the Value Chain", 15 Eur. Mgmt. J. 286, 286 (1997). Freeman and Liedtka attribute stakeholder theory to other writers in management in the 1960s, including Eric Rhenman, Igor Ansoff, and Russell Ackoff.

[152] Id. at 287.   [153] Id.

[154] Margaret M. Blair & Lynn A. Stout, "A Team Production Theory of Corporate Law", 85 Va. L. Rev. 248 (2003).

[155] Andrew Crane, "Modern Slavery as a Management Practice: Exploring the Conditions and Capabilities for Human Exploitation", 38 Acad. Mgmt. Rev. 49 (2013) (citing the ILO and academic studies).

industry, for instance. That problem was widely publicized by NGOs, putting pressure on multinational companies to sign the Harkin/Engel Cocoa Protocol in 2001, which specifically directed the industry to self-regulate.[156] According to Crane, that Protocol has led to "pilot programs" to determine the most effective ways to eliminate the slavery, and "a mooted, but much delayed, program for monitoring and enforcement."[157] In other words, 14 years later the problem has not been solved by industry initiatives. Tragic evidence of the insufficiency of long-established voluntary company codes of conduct and industry responsibility initiatives continues to accumulate. The Rana Plaza collapse in Bangladesh in 2013, which killed 1,134 people producing clothes for 29 global clothing companies,[158] or Barrick Gold's settlement of claims in 2015 that its security personnel had raped 137 women in Papua New Guinea over a period of decades show some limits to the reach of the voluntary approach.

Moreover, the "business case" may never be strong enough to overcome the economic disincentives to invest in higher labor costs or expensive pollution abatement without a supportive regulatory framework that creates a level playing field for competition. Many of the business drivers of corporate responsibility depend on consumers being willing to pay more for goods produced in a socially responsible fashion; employees being selective about where they will work, choosing only the most responsible employers; and investors generally investing and disinvesting based on social parameters.[159] Jan Wouters and Leen Chanet bring both a moral and a pragmatic argument to show the limits of each aspect of this business case.[160] As a matter of morality, they argue that the business case is a means to the end of responsible business conduct, not an end in itself, and should be evaluated as such: "[I]f respect for human rights is fundamental to our society, whether or not ensuring such respect would bring economic advantages is irrelevant; achieving it remains our final goal."[161] From a pragmatic perspective, neither the ethical consumer movement nor socially responsible investor pressure are strong enough to make a demonstrable contribution to the business case without a supportive regulatory environment, such as by requiring fair trade labeling of products at the point of purchase, or requiring consistent, comparable ESG disclosure by public companies.[162] Olivier DeSchutter also argues for the importance of a supportive regulatory framework.[163] Using an environmental example, he states:

> for a government, the most direct solution to [advance] environmentally responsible conduct is simply to let the price of energy go up [via high taxes], to collect high fees for waste disposal (calculated according to volume) and to oblige companies to internalize the costs of the pollution they create. There would simply be no ground on which to build the business case for CSR, if we bracket these public interventions away.[164]

---

[156] See id. at 58.   [157] Id.

[158] See Clean Clothes Campaign, Compensation is Long Overdue, available at http://www.cleanclothes.org/ranaplaza.

[159] See Aguilera et al., *supra* note 121, for discussions of each of these factors as drivers for companies adopting corporate responsibility initiatives.

[160] See Jan Wouters and Leen Chanet, "Corporate Human Rights Responsibility: A European Perspective", 6 Nw. J. Int'l. H. Rts. 262 (2008).

[161] Id. at 267.   [162] See id. at 267–70.

[163] See Olivier DeSchutter, "Corporate Social Responsibility European Style", 14 Eur. L. J. 203 (2008).

[164] Id. at 221.

Whether the voluntary "business case" is stronger than these assessments suggest may depend on the reputational benefits and risks of corporate responsibility or irresponsibility, and the role of the media in amplifying those benefits or risks. Estimates indicate that 70% to 80% of a company's market value today is based on "intangibles" such as brand reputation, intellectual capital and goodwill.[165] High-profile tragedies such as the Rana Plaza collapse or the Deepwater Horizon explosion cause industry-wide reputational harm and societal (and investor) pressures for redress.[166] As BP found out after the Deepwater Horizon explosion, a gap between a company's reputation and the company's actual performance creates the potential for "reputational risk," which may amplify the effects of media coverage of responsibility issues.[167] Apple is an interesting counter-example here, however. While its reputation may have suffered somewhat from a series of critical media coverage in 2010 concerning the harsh conditions under which Apple products are produced in China,[168] that negative media coverage has not dented Apple's position as the world's largest company by market capitalization.[169] This disconnect between media coverage of a social responsibility issue and consumer reactions was encapsulated brilliantly in the title of an article that empirically studied the limits of the business case, at least insofar as it depended on ethical consumption: "Sweatshop Labor is Wrong Unless the Shoes are Cute."[170]

Another criticism builds on assertions about the strategic use of the business case as an argument for voluntary corporate responsibility rather than regulatory intervention. From this perspective corporate responsibility is a business strategy employed specifically to resist regulation, thus undermining the ability of society to cause companies to limit and then internalize negative externalities. Ronen Shamir has argued that companies have "constructed" the field of corporate responsibility through teaching in business schools, through lobbying, and through litigation, as "an essentially voluntary and non-enforceable domain" in order to "resist the legalization of their social duties."[171] He has also argued that "through a set of social events, workshops, and public ceremonies," businesses "shape notions such as 'social responsibility' and 'social change' in ways that are amenable to business and employers' concerns," thus "preventing the use of law as a means for bringing

[165] See Robet G. Eccles, Scott C. Newquist, & Roland Schatz, "Reputation and its Risks", Harv. Bus. Rev. (Feb. 2007), available at https://hbr.org/2007/02/reputation-and-its-risks.

[166] See Clark, Feiner & Viehs, *supra* note 107, at 14, indicating that after the Deepwater Horizon tragedy BP stock lost 50% of its value, and the oil majors generally lost 18.5%. Five years later, BP's share price is still underperforming its peer group by about 37%. See id.

[167] See Eccles et al., *supra* note 165, discussing how BP's "Beyond Petroleum" public relations campaign and widely reported research projects on solar power led to greater disillusion among consumers after the Deepwater Horizon explosion.

[168] See Richard Bilton, "Apple Failing to Protect Chinese Factory Workers", BBC Panorama (Dec. 18, 2014), describing a BBC Documentary airing in December, 2014, in which a number of BBC reporters got jobs in a Foxconn factory working on Apple products, and reported on conditions of their work and lives there.

[169] See Table 24.2, *supra*, showing Apple's market capitalization at $752 billion as of March, 2014, twice as large as the next largest company, Exxon Mobil ($369 billion).

[170] See Neeru Paharia, Kathleen Vohs, & Rohit Deshpandé, "Sweatshop Labor is Wrong Unless the Shoes are Cute: Cognition Can Both Help and Hurt Moral Motivated Reasoning", 121 Org. Behav. & Human Decision Processes 81 (2013).

[171] See Ronen Shamir, "Between Self-Regulation and the Alien Tort Claims Act: On the Contested Concept of Corporate Social Responsibility", 38 Law & Soc'y Rev. 635 (2004).

greater social responsibility."[172] His interpretation is supported by an historical analysis by Rami Kaplan, in which Kaplan argues that "corporate responsibility was devised [in the 1950's] by the corporate capitalist elite, broadly defined, as an instrument for pre-empting governmental intervention."[173]

Thus, from both the stakeholder and the sociological perspective, corporate responsibility is too weak, and yet too strong. It is an insufficient constraint on how companies do business in a world of accelerating pressures on natural capital and ill-distributed opportunities for human flourishing. At the same time, however, it is effectively undermining the conditions for putting more substantive regulation in place.

5.3 Evaluating the Arguments

By 2015, the argument that corporate responsibility requires companies and the board to take on an essentially political role for which they are ill-suited rings hollow, given the extensive involvement of American companies in law-making, lobbying, litigation to narrow regulation, and constitutionally protected electoral politics.[174] But two arguments for shareholder primacy that are advanced in the US law literature remain important to address: the idea that balancing multiple stakeholders' interests will undermine accountability and allow directors and managers too much discretion to act in their own self-interest; and the argument that it is legally required for boards and managers to act in the interests of shareholders, and shareholders only, such that corporate responsibility initiatives could be a breach of fiduciary duty. This author will address the second argument first, because if shareholder primacy is required by law, that ends the discussion, at least in the United States.

Two points that are relevant to both issues are given insufficient attention in the law literature, however, and so will be highlighted in advance. First, the data do not support the view that corporate responsibility initiatives inevitably cause financial losses; in fact, on the contrary. In an overwhelming majority of cases there is no trade-off between a company's financial health and actions that arise from a broad concept of social obligation, as the studies evaluated by Clark, Feiner, and Viehs show.[175] The management literature is much more sophisticated on this point than is the law literature. Second, many of the arguments in the law literature against corporate responsibility ignore what large companies are saying they are doing, around the world. As set out above, 93 per cent of the world's largest companies discuss their environmental and social initiatives, many in great detail, and many including substantiated, audited data about the effects of those initiatives.[176] Unless one considers *everything* that a

---

[172] Shamir, *supra* note 14, at 676.

[173] See Rami Kaplan, "Who Has Been Regulating Whom, Business or Society? The Mid-20th-Century Institutionalization of 'Corporate Responsibility'," Socio-Economic Rev. 1 (2014).

[174] See Cynthia A. Williams and John M. Conley, "Trends in the Social [Ir]responsibility of American Multinational Corporations: Increased Power, Diminished Accountability", 25 Fordham Envir. L. Rev. 46 (2013) (discussing these trends, and including discussions of *Citizens United v. Federal Election Comm'n.*, 558 US 310 (2010), which expanded corporations' and unions' First Amendment rights regarding electoral participation, and *Royal Dutch Shell v. Kiobel*, 133 S. Ct. 1659 (2013), which narrowed the potential Alien Torts Claims Act accountability of multinational corporations).

[175] See text accompanying notes 84–108, *supra*. See also Clark, Feiner, & Viehs, *supra* note 107.

[176] See text accompanying notes 5–6, *supra*.

company says about its social responsibilities to be unsubstantiated public relations, then it should be incumbent upon judges and law professors who write about these matters to consider these facts in their analyses.

5.3.1 Shareholder versus Stakeholder Theory

The proper understanding of the implications of corporate boards' legal obligations for issues of corporate responsibility has become a matter of vigorous debate again in the United States, inspired by Prof. Lynn Stout's short, sharply critical book, written for a popular audience, entitled *The Shareholder Value Myth: How Putting Shareholders First Harms Investors, Corporations and the Public.*[177] That book has inspired multiple, equally critical reactions by respected scholars,[178] including a number from CJ Strine.[179] CJ Strine recognizes that "directors are generally empowered to manage the corporation in a way that is not dictated by what will best maximize the corporation's current stock price,"[180] but argues that "advocates for corporate social responsibility" make a more fundamental claim, and "pretend that directors do not have to make stockholder welfare the sole end of corporate governance within the limits of their legal discretion."[181] He rejects the argument of "these well-meaning commentators" that "the business judgment rule is cloaking a system of law giving directors the ability to act for any reason they deem appropriate."[182] Evaluating the arguments in this debate can provide the context for a number of observations regarding shareholder primacy, stakeholder theory, and corporate responsibility.

First, it is inaccurate to argue that shareholders have no special place in corporate law in Delaware and in the United States generally. They clearly do. Shareholders are the only group entitled to vote for the board and to approve important corporate transactions, although creditors can also exert control rights through their contracts; shareholders are the only group with rights to bring suit derivatively on behalf of a solvent corporation[183]; and the board's fiduciary duties run "to the corporation and its shareholders."[184] These legal rights matter and should not be treated as unimportant, as Prof. Stout's arguments can sometimes seem to do.

As just stated, the Delaware Supreme Court has in a number of cases articulated the fiduciary duties of directors as advancing the interests of "the corporation and its

---

[177] Lynn Stout, The Shareholder Value Myth: How Putting Shareholders First Harms Investors, Corporations, and the Public (2010). Professor Stout has been a prolific critic of shareholder primacy in the law literature from economic and legal perspectives, but it is her short popular book that seems to have inspired this iteration of the corporate responsibility debate. See, e.g. Lynn A. Stout, "The Toxic Side Effects of Shareholder Primacy", 161 U. Penn. L. Rev. 2003 (2013); Blair & Stout, *supra* note 154 (the team production theory of boards' responsibilities).

[178] See, e.g, Jonathan Macey, "Sublime Myths: An Essay in Honor of the Shareholder Value Myth and the Tooth Fairy", 91 Tex. L. Rev. 911 (2013) (critically reviewing The Shareholder Value Myth).

[179] See Strine, *supra* notes 142 and 143.   [180] Strine, Dangers of Denial, *supra* note 143, at 4.

[181] Id. at 3.   [182] Id. at 7.

[183] If a corporation is insolvent, creditors "have standing to maintain derivative claims against directors on behalf of the corporation for breaches of fiduciary duties." *North American Catholic Educ. Prog. Foundation, Inc. v. Gheewalla*, 930 A.2d 92, 101 (Del. 2007).

[184] See *Unocal Corp. v. Mesa Petroleum Co.*, 493 A.2d 946 (Del. 1985) (board's obligation is to act in "the best interests of the corporation and its shareholders"); *Paramount Communications v. Time*, 571 A.2d 1140 (Del. 1989) (same).

shareholders." When these interests conflict, the Court has upheld board actions that frustrate shareholders' short-term financial interests in favor of the board's well-considered views about the company's longer-term strategies and prospects (as CJ Strine recognizes but does not discuss in any detail).[185] In *Paramount Communications v. Time*, the Delaware Supreme Court upheld the directors' power to reject the shareholders' views and take defensive measures against a well-above-market tender offer.[186] While it might be argued that this simply reflects the authority structure of Delaware corporate law, since it is the directors and not the shareholders who have the statutory power to manage the company,[187] the Time board's actions were demonstrably not shareholder wealth maximizing. If fiduciary principles required shareholder wealth maximizing in general, the directors' actions in *Paramount v. Time* would not have been upheld.

There is one circumstance where shareholders' wealth must be maximized, and that is where the shareholders are being cashed out, as in *Revlon, Inc. v. MacAndrews & Forbes Holdings, Inc.*[188] In that circumstance, "the duty of the board . . . change[s] from the preservation [of the company] as a corporate entity to the maximization of the company's value at a sale for the stockholders' benefit."[189] *Revlon* duties have also been found where the control structure of a company is being changed, such as where a publicly held company with dispersed shareholders is being pursued by a company with a controlling shareholder, and will become a controlled company if the transaction goes forward. *Paramount v. QVC* was such a case.[190] But these are the only circumstances where the board's obligation is to maximize share value, according to the Delaware Supreme Court. Moreover, shareholder pressure cannot put a company into *Revlon* mode: that determination is reserved to the board.[191]

A former Chief Justice of the Delaware Supreme Court, Norman Veasey, has interpreted these precedents as follows:

> [I]t is important to keep in mind the precise content of this "best interests" [of the corporate entity] concept—that is, to whom this duty is owed and when. Naturally, one often thinks that directors owe this duty to both the corporation and the stockholders. That formulation is harmless in most instances because of the confluence of interests, in that what is good for the corporate entity is usually derivatively good for the stockholders. There are times, of course, when the focus is directly on the interests of stockholders [citing *Revlon and Paramount*

---

[185] See id. at 4 (stating that "To the extent that these commentators argue that directors are generally empowered to manage the corporation in a way that is not dictated by what will best maximize the corporation's current stock price, they are correct," citing *Paramount Communications, Inc. v. Time*, 571 A.2d 1140, 1154 (Del. 1989) and *Air Products and Chemicals, Inc. v. Airgas, Inc.*, 16 A.3d 48, 112 (Del. Ch. 2011)).

[186] *Paramount Communications, Inc. v. Time*, 571 A.2d 1140, 1154 (Del. 1989).

[187] As Bob Joffe, the Cravath lawyer who represented Time in the oral argument before the Delaware Supreme Court, put the point, "Your Honor, Delaware law does not require that every important corporate decision be put to a shareholder plebiscite or referendum."

[188] 506 A.2d 173 (Del. 1986).   [189] Id. at 182.

[190] 637 A.2d 34 (Del. 1994) (holding that *Revlon* duties are triggered by a change in control or a break-up of the company).

[191] Chancellor Chandler made this point in discussing the evolution of the Paramount standard in *Air Products and Chemicals, Inc. v. Airgas, Inc.*, 16 A.3d 48, 102 (Del. Ch. 2011).

Comms. v. QVC]. But, in general, the directors owe fiduciary duties to the corporation, not to the stockholders.[192]

Moreover, as Prof. Stout and others emphasize, the protection of the business judgment rule allows directors to make decisions that are in the longer-term interests of the corporation, such as investing in research and development, building new plants, or paying employees well, notwithstanding some shareholders who would rather have the company's money spent on them.[193] As a practical matter, there is going to be no liability for a board that frustrates some shareholders' short-term interests and decides to pay its employees more than the minimum wage, or reduces the prices its products could be sold for so that more employees can buy the product—Walmart did the former in 2015,[194] and the Ford Motor Company did the latter in 1915, a decision that was upheld by the Michigan Supreme Court in *Dodge v. Ford*.[195] This argument about the business judgment rule frustrates CJ Strine

[192] E. Norman Veasey & Christine T. DiGuglielmo, "What Happened in Delaware Corporate Law and Governance from 1992–2004? A Retrospective on Some Key Developments", 153 U. Penn. L. Rev. 1399, 1431 (2005).

[193] See Stout, *supra* note 177, at 2, 24–46. Other scholars have made this argument about the power of the business judgment rule as well. See, e.g., Lynne Dallas, "The New Managerialism and Diversity on Corporate Boards of Directors", 76 Tul. L. Rev. 1363 (2002); Einer Elhauge, "Sacrificing Corporate Profits in the Public Interest", 80 N.Y.U. L. Rev. 733, 770–772 (2005).

[194] See Doug McMillon, "CEO Walmart, In Letter to Associates Walmart CEO Doug McMillon Announces Higher Pay", Feb. 19, 2015, available at http://blog.walmart.com/in-letter-to-associates-walmart-ceo-doug-mcmillon-announces-higher-pay. In the letter, McMillon states that "today, we're announcing a series of important changes that demonstrate our commitment to you, our associates" because the CEO concluded that "it's clear to me that one of our highest priorities must be to invest more in our people this year." There is no discussion of this decision being anything other than employee-focused. CJ Strine might consider this a "confession case," and by his logic, "if a fiduciary admits that he is treating an interest other than stockholder wealth as an end in itself, rather than an instrument to stockholder wealth, he is committing breach of fiduciary duty." Strine, Dangers of Denial, *supra* note 143, at 20. It is unlikely that the shareholders of Walmart would prevail in a suit based on that theory, though, given the business judgment rule, and given the likely positive effects of a decision like this one on employees' "citizenship behavior," which presumably translates into positive financial outcomes. See Russell Cropanzano, Deborah Rupp, Carolyn Mohler, & Marshall Schminke, "Three Roads to Organizational Justice", in 20 Research Personnel and Human Resources Mgmt. 1–113 (2001) (discussing three decades of literature in organizational psychology showing that employees who perceive that they are being treated fairly are more productive, more engaged in the company, have lower absentee rates, and stay longer in the job).

[195] *In Dodge v. Ford*, 204 Mich. 459, 170 N.W. 668 (1919), the Michigan Supreme Court stated that "there should be no confusion (of which there is evidence) of the duties which Mr. Ford conceives that he and the stockholders owe to the general public and the duties which in law he and his co-directors owe to protesting, minority stockholders. A business corporation is organized and carried on primarily for the profit of the stockholders." 170 N.W. at 683. This is the oft-quoted language from this opinion. It is, however, dicta. What is often not discussed is that the Michigan Supreme Court refused to enjoin the Ford Motor Company's plans to increase production and reduce the cost of its cars, in part so that more of its employees could buy the cars. The Dodge Brothers had argued that Henry Ford wanted to expand production and cut costs "not for the good of the company but to give more employment" and to allow more people to buy the cars. Id. at 678. Because of the business judgment rule, the Court refused to find that Henry Ford's plan was legally impermissible, and so it did not enjoin the company's actions, as had been requested, stating that "[t]he judges are not business experts." Id. at 684. It did order a higher dividend to be paid because it found that the company could expand production, cut the costs of cars, and engage in some of its plans for vertical integration and still have substantial assets available from

and Prof. Bainbridge, among others, but Prof. Stout (and others) are correct that this is how the law operates.[196] CJ Strine is undoubtedly correct that there could be problems if a board makes a social or environmental decision that has no conceivable long-term benefit to the company and thus the shareholders, but in today's world it is hard to imagine what such a decision would be, given social expectations that companies will act as responsible citizens and the reputational implications of frustrating those expectations. It is much more likely that a managerialist decision would create problems, such as a company giving a retiring CEO an apartment in New York, maid service, and fresh flowers for life, which raises duty of loyalty concerns not implicated by corporate responsibility.[197]

Thus, the law—at least as decided by the Delaware Supreme Court—does not yet require shareholder wealth maximizing as the standard of conduct in order for boards to meet their fiduciary obligations, except in the circumstances described as being in "*Revlon* mode." Consistent with CJ Veasey's view, we can conclude that shareholders are important beneficiaries of fiduciary obligations in Delaware, of course, but only so long as their interests and the corporation's long-term interests are in harmony. Corporate responsibility initiatives are one type of strategy to promote the corporation's long-term financial well-being, as the empirical evidence shows, and thus there is no fiduciary breach.

However, even if it is lawful, is a multi-stakeholder focus going to mask officers' and directors' self-interest—and thereby undermine accountability—as has been argued?[198] On both the question of self-interest and that of accountability the prioritizing of shareholders' interests as it has been instantiated in the US over the last three decades has itself masked self-interest and created new agency problems. Regarding self-interest, as Lynne Dallas argued over a decade ago, "[a] 'new' managerialism has arisen that consists of short-term decision making and window dressing to impress the stock market at the expense of improving underlying corporation value."[199] In particular, the shift to stock option compensation "provides unique opportunities for managerial self-dealing."[200] By 2015, the tight coupling of managers and markets has allowed managerial rent extraction in the US to an historically unprecedented degree.[201]

which to pay dividends. Thus, the opinion can support either CJ Stine or Prof. Stout's views. That is, there is great latitude for company directors to act to promote the welfare of their employees, the communities in which they operate, their customers and suppliers, or even the environment (Stout's view), but only so long as there is a plausible justification for how that advances the company's long-term financial well-being (Strine's view).

[196] See Strine, Dangers of Denial, *supra* note 143, at fn. 72, discussing Bainbridge's view that this latitude is an "unintended consequence" of the business judgment rule.

[197] GE's Jack Welch was forced to give up $2.5 million per year in retirement benefits of exactly this kind—use of an $11 million company apartment in NY for life, maid service, weekly fresh flowers and wine delivery, dry cleaning—when the benefits were disclosed by his second wife in a contested divorce proceeding. See Matt Murray, Rachel Emma Silverman, & Carol Hymowitz, GE's Jack Welch Meets Match in Divorce Court, Wall St. J. (Nov. 27, 2002), available at http://www.wsj.com/articles/SB1038347809827912908.

[198] See, e.g., Bainbridge, *supra* note 145.   [199] Dallas, *supra* note 193, at 1363.

[200] Id. at 1377.

[201] Both Chrystia Freeland and Thomas Piketty provide statistics on this point, and both identify executive compensation systems in the US as contributing significantly to rapidly increasing economic inequality in the US. Chrystia Freeland, Plutocrats: The Rise of the New Global Super-Rich and the Fall of Everyone Else 211–222 (2012); Thomas Piketty, Capital in the Twenty-First Century 294–303; 330–335; 505–515 (2014).

With respect to accountability, we are back to the question of accountability to whom or what, and here the Delaware precedents provide a clear answer: accountability must be to the corporation and its shareholders, taking a long-term perspective on corporate well-being. Yet today's concern is that shareholders are putting short-term pressure on companies in ways that are unproductive for the future success of the corporate enterprise.[202] Activist investors exert a significant part of this pressure, and an empirical debate is raging over their economic influence.[203] In terms of their influence on corporate decisions, Bill Bratton and Michael Wachter show that activist investors seek one of four things: that more money be given back to shareholders, in the form of share buybacks or special dividends; that the company sell itself or its premium assets; that the company increase leverage; or that the company cut costs.[204] Some of the actions to cut costs might be productive, such as finding ways to save energy or use fewer physical inputs. Others destroy longer-term value, such as putting off needed maintenance of plant and equipment, delaying marketing campaigns, cutting back on research and development,[205] or even engaging in financial reporting fraud or value-destroying mergers and acquisitions, a concern identified by none other than Michael Jensen.[206]

In 2014, S&P 500 companies spent 95% of their earnings on share buybacks and dividends, and they look set to spend over 100% in 2015.[207] This level of share buybacks is so high that Larry Fink, head of the world's largest asset manager, Blackrock, has written to all of the CEOs in the S&P 500, expressing concerns that corporate leaders are meeting activists' short-term pressures while "underinvesting in innovation, skilled workforces or essential capital expenditures necessary to sustain long-term growth."[208] One can argue that giving money back to shareholders is exactly what companies should be doing if they have no positive net present value investments to make. It is bizarre to think that American companies, with their incredible confidence, creativity, and organizational capacity, cannot find better, more productive uses of all of their earnings than giving them back to shareholders (with the not incidental benefit of keeping stock prices high and fueling a stock market rally),[209]

---

[202] See Jesse M. Fried, "The Uneasy Case for Favoring Long Term Shareholders", 124 Yale L. J. 1554 (2015) (arguing that companies that repurchase or sell large volumes of their own shares can manipulate the stock prices, which undermines (in the case of repurchases) putting corporate money to more productive use).

[203] See John C. Coffee, Jr. & Darius Palia, "The Impact of Hedge Fund Activism: Evidence and Implications", Columbia University Law and Economics Working Paper No. 489, available at. http:// papers.ssrn.com/sol3/papers.cfm?abstract_id=2496518 (finding evidence on most important questions regarding hedge fund activism ambiguous).

[204] See William B. Bratton & Michael Wachter, *supra* note 126, at 508, 513. See generally William B. Bratton & Michael Wachter, "The Case Against Shareholder Empowerment", 158 U. Penn. L. Rev. 653 (2010).

[205] See J.R. Graham, C.R. Harvey & S. Rajgopal, "The Economic Implications of Corporate Financial Reporting", 40:1 J. Acct. & Econ. (Dec. 2005).

[206] See Michael Jensen, "The Agency Costs of Overvalued Equity", 34:1 Fin. Mgmt. 5–19 (2005).

[207] See Edward Luce, "US Share Buybacks Loot the Future", Fin. Times (April 26, 2015), available at http://www.ft.com/intl/cms/s/0/1aaac576-e9bb-11e4-a687-00144feab7de.html#axzz3ZJldjIW1.

[208] Id. quoting Larry Fink.

[209] See Lu Wang & Callie Bost, "S&P Companies Spend Almost All Profits on Buybacks", Bloomberg (Oct. 6, 2014) (stating that "buybacks have helped fuel one of the strongest rallies of the past 50 years as stocks with the most repurchases gained more than 300 percent since March 2009").

particularly in light of the enormous technical challenges facing the world from climate change, which scientists tell us requires a rapid transition to a low-carbon economy. A more productive system would encourage managers and directors to manage their companies well and fairly for the longer term, which will benefit tomorrow's shareholders in addition to today's, but which will also give management greater latitude to pursue the positive implications of fair employment policies, high-quality research and product development, good relationships with suppliers, and careful approaches to natural capital. In stylized form, that is what we see in stakeholder economies such as Scandinavia, the Netherlands, France, Germany, or Austria, albeit under pressure, and that is what three-quarters of senior executives globally say they would want to see for their companies.[210]

5.3.2 *Corporate Responsibility Reconciliation*

This chapter will conclude by trying to reconcile competing views of corporate responsibility as simultaneously too strong and too weak, assuming differing views of managers' and directors' obligations from shareholder and stakeholder perspectives, but rejecting the view that corporate responsibility is somehow inconsistent with boards' fiduciary duties even in a shareholder system. Even Friedman believed that business has an obligation to conform "to the basic rules of the society, both those embodied in law and those embodied in ethical custom."[211] Economic theory recognizes negative externalities as one type of market failure justifying regulation. Each of the shareholder partisans quoted above thought that policies to address serious social problems should be developed through laws passed by democratic political processes, not by decisions of private companies' boards of directors.[212] Looking at the self-regulatory initiatives that businesses have participated in can be used as a framework to determine which issues are broadly seen to demand regulatory solutions. At least in theory, the need for more hard law regulating social responsibility issues should be a point of agreement between those who consider corporate responsibility too strong when devolved to corporate boards for decision, and those who consider it too weak because it is voluntary and predominantly process based by emphasizing disclosure.

As both DeShutter and Wouters and Chanet argue, there is a range of regulatory approaches that can be used to produce a facilitative framework that permits voluntary initiatives to be more effective. In today's world, creative regulatory and voluntary approaches to the negative externalities of human rights abuses, labor exploitation, climate change, and declining natural resources (including, most critically, water) are both hypothesized and in place in some parts of the world, but in need of serious scaling up to meet the full scope of global challenges. These approaches can be canvassed for best practices and further learning.

---

[210] See Jonathan Bailey & Jonathan Godsall, Short-Termism: Insights from Business Leaders, McKinsey & Company and CPPIB (Canadian Pension Plan Investment Board), Dec. 26, 2013 (findings from a global survey of 1,038 C-suite executives or board members, indicating that 79 percent felt pressure to deliver financial results in 2 years or less, even though 73 percent thought a reasonable strategic planning horizon should be at least 3 years). McKinsey and CPPIB are co-founders of Focusing Capital on the Long Term, which is described as "a collaborative initiative that is developing practical tools and approaches to help institutional investors and corporate directors enhance long-term value creation." See www.FCLT.org.

[211] See Friedman, *supra* note 137, at 6.

[212] See, e.g., Friedman, *supra* note 137; Fischel and Engel, *supra* note 144.

Moreover, the accounting industry has developed and is continuing to develop approaches to integrated financial and non-financial reporting, and true-value accounting to incorporate the cost of negative externalities.[213] Implementing intellectually justified integrated reporting and accounting systems could go a long way toward providing the information and prices necessary to support capital and products markets that actually work the way market theories suggest they should work, including fully internalizing in the prices of products the social costs of producing and using those products. Beyond such strategies, the voluntary initiatives that companies have adopted to date in just about every industry provide important information about what companies consider feasible. They also provide sources of empirical data about the effects of voluntary initiatives as a way to evaluate what more is needed to address particular social and environmental issues in each industry. If additional substantive regulation is needed to advance sustainability goals, Scandinavian legal and corporate governance approaches may be the most logical place to start to find models that work, at least as a good first approximation.

6 Conclusion

In conclusion, this author will offer the following anecdote. At a conference in Berlin on corporate responsibility four years ago, funded by the German government and held with some fair degree of pomp and circumstance in the German Parliament Offices Building, Dirk Matten, a leading management academic, described the importance of corporate responsibility using the following analogy. Having been told once by Jeremy Moon that of all the things that do not cure a cold, whiskey is the nicest, Matten said that his thinking on corporate responsibility is similar: that of all the things that won't cure contemporary capitalism, corporate responsibility is the nicest. At the least, in his view, it doesn't make the problems worse.

This chapter concludes by agreeing with Matten's assessment, with one important caveat. Corporate responsibility initiatives have likely improved the conditions of employment for at least hundreds of thousands of people around the world who would otherwise be subject to the mandates of unrestrained globalization. It certainly brings more attention to the environmental problems and opportunities of many productive processes and industries, and has thus motivated companies to develop innovative products and solutions to address those problems. It gives latitude to people who want to be change agents within organizations, and promotes deeper thinking among people and teams in organizations about the effects of the investments, products, services, and relationships they are developing. As the empirical evidence is starting to show, it can even be a smart business strategy.

Corporate responsibility does not fundamentally change underlying power relationships between companies and citizens, however, since companies are volunteering to act to address social and environmental problems—or not. It might dissuade governments from

---

[213] See, for instance, KPMG International, "A New Vision of Value: Connecting Corporate and Societal Value Creation" (2014), available at http://www.kpmg.com/global/en/issuesandinsights/articlespublications/press-releases/pages/corporate-societal-value-creation.aspx; Integrated Reporting <IR>, http://www.theiirc.org/.

regulating, however, and in that sense is making problems worse. It leaves gaping holes, such as its failure to establish "no go" zones. We will no doubt see "responsible tar sands mining" before the decade is out, which would be an intellectually bankrupt concept and a tragic development for the stability of the climate. As economic development proceeds apace throughout the world, improving millions of people's standard of living, there are still *billions* of people living on the equivalent of $2 a day or less. While those billions of people may surely benefit from greater access to productive enterprise, the underlying normative and material conditions of that access matter greatly. So to the extent that we actually want to solve any of the underlying global problems of modern capitalism, stronger medicines than the pleasant whiskey of corporate responsibility are required.

CHAPTER 25

....

COMPARATIVE CORPORATE GOVERNANCE IN CLOSELY HELD CORPORATIONS

....

HOLGER FLEISCHER

1 INTRODUCTION

....

THE modern corporate governance movement in Europe and the world has, over the last two decades, dealt predominantly with listed, or at least publicly held companies. This focus becomes particularly clear when looking at three key texts in the UK, US, and German debate: (1) The British Cadbury Report released in 1992 with its widely recognized basic definition of corporate governance[1] recommended the introduction of a Code of Best Practice, aiming first and foremost at the boards of listed companies.[2] (2) The Principles of Corporate Governance, put out by the American Law Institute in 1994, target publicly held corporations in their key parts that deal with company structure.[3] (3) The German

---

[1] Report of the Committee on the Financial Aspects of Corporate Governance (Gee 1992) marg. n°. 2.5: "Corporate Governance is the system by which companies are directed and controlled"; from a British perspective, Mark Cardale, A Practical Guide to Corporate Governance (5th ed. 2014) marg. n°. 1-001: "The Cadbury definition is the one accepted for the principal purposes of this book since it is the definition which has most successfully stood the test of time and is most widely adopted"; from a comparative perspective, Klaus J. Hopt, "Comparative Corporate Governance: The State of the Art and International Regulation", 59 Am. J. Comp. L. 1, 6–7 (2011): "For the purposes of this comparative study, the broad definition of the Cadbury Commission of 1992, written at the beginning of the modern corporate governance movement, is best suited: corporate governance is 'the system by which companies are directed and controlled.'"

[2] Report, *supra* note 1, marg. n°. 3.1: "The Code of Best Practice is directed to the boards of directors of all listed companies registered in the UK, but we would encourage as many other companies as possible to aim at meeting its requirements."

[3] American Law Institute, Principles of Corporate Governance (American Law Institute Publishers 1994) Introductory Note to Parts III and III-A (Structure of the Company): "1. Scope. Parts III and IIIa are directed largely to publicly held corporations."

Corporate Governance Code published in 2002, according to its preamble, primarily addresses listed companies.[4]

In contrast, corporate governance issues in close corporations have been neglected for far too long.[5] This is due to a number of factors: (1) The legal reform debate regarding improved company management and monitoring, has been sparked by scandals in listed companies; for example, the spectacular breakdown of Polly Peck, BCCI, and Barings in the UK,[6] and German companies such as Philipp Holzmann, Metallgesellschaft, or Bremer Vulkan finding themselves on the brink of insolvency or beyond[7]. (2) Publicly held companies as a group are far more homogeneous than their privately held counterparts, which may take widely diverging forms, ranging from large third- or fourth-generation family-owned companies to medium-sized closely held companies and incorporated sole traders.[8] (3) Companies listed on the stock exchange are better illuminated than close corporations. The wide-reaching disclosure requirements of accounting and capital markets law along with constant monitoring by analysts and the economic press produce an incessant flow of empirical information that the legislator and academia can use to formulate well-founded recommendations. In contrast, the data on close corporations is far less available, and therefore far less certain.[9]

It is only in recent times that researchers have begun to explore the corporate governance issues of closely held corporations more thoroughly.[10] It is at this point that this

---

[4] German Corporate Governance Code, Preamble: "Primarily, the Code addresses listed corporations and corporations with capital market access pursuant to section 161(1) sentence 2 of the Stock Corporation Act. It is recommended that companies not focussed on the capital market also respect the Code" [official translation].

[5] From a British perspective, Institute of Directors, "Corporate Governance Guidance and Principles for Unlisted Companies in the UK" (2010) 6: "The corporate governance needs of unlisted companies have, to date, been relatively neglected by governance experts as well as by policy-makers"; from a German perspective Marc-Philippe Weller, "Corporate Governance in geschlossenen Gesellschaften: Status quo und Anforderungen", 41 Zeitschrift für Unternehmens- und Gesellschaftsrecht 386, 387–8 (2012).

[6] For more detail, see Cardale, *supra* note 1, marg. n°. 1–014.

[7] For more detail, see Holger Fleischer, Von "bubble laws" und "quack regulation"—Zur Kritik kriseninduzierter Reformgesetze im Aktien- und Kapitalmarktrecht, in Festschrift Priester 75, 80 et seq. (Peter Hommelhoff ed., 2007).

[8] On the enormous range of close corporation forms in German business practice, see Holger Fleischer, MünchKommGmbHG § 1 marg. n°. 17 et seq. (2d ed. 2015); from a UK perspective Company Law Review Steering Group, Modern Company Law for a Competitive Economy, The Strategic Framework, February 1999, marg. n°. 5.2.20: "First, the character of small companies is very diverse."

[9] See Fleischer, *supra* note 8, Introduction, marg. n°. 198: "The availability of data for close corporations is precarious, as would be expected, given that the Federal Bureau of Statistics last carried out a survey in 1990" (translation); from an economic perspective, Venky Nagar, Kathy Petroni, & Daniel Wolfenzon, "Governance Problems in Closely Held Corporations", 46 J. Fin. Quant. Anal. 943, 944 (2011): "A key difficulty in studying governance problems between controlling and minority shareholders in closely held corporations is the lack of data."

[10] Looking internationally, Gregor Bachmann, Horst Eidenmüller, Andreas Engert, Holger Fleischer, & Wolfgang Schön, Regulating the Closed Corporation (De Gruyter 2014); Corporate Governance of Non-Listed Companies (Joseph A. McCahery & Erik P. M. Vermeulen eds., 2008); Company Law and SMEs (Mette Neville & Karsten Engsig Sørensen eds., 2010); early contributions from the US include Henry G. Manne, "Our Two Corporation Systems: Law and Economics", 53 Va. L. Rev. 259 (1967); Frank H. Easterbrook & Daniel R. Fischel, "Close Corporations and Agency Costs", 38 Stan. L. Rev. 271 (1986).

chapter begins, by firstly identifying the fundamental governance problems in closely held corporations (2) and going on to explain their governance framework consisting of company law, model articles, articles of association and shareholder agreements, with specialized codes playing only a subordinate role (3). This is followed by an analysis of the internal governance of closely held corporations (4), the design of share transfer restrictions (5), and provisions for shareholder exit and exclusion (6). This analysis is completed by a detailed examination of the governance of shareholder conflicts (7).

2 Fundamental Governance Problems in Closely Held Corporations

Closely held corporations are not merely mini-public companies. They differ in a striking way from the typical *Berle Means* textbook corporation with its atomistic shareholder structure around which the international corporate governance debate has raged unabated for the last 30 years.[11] It is therefore worth starting this discussion with an exploration of these differences, as they provide the key for understanding the specific governance problems faced by closely held corporations.

2.1 Typical Characteristics of Closely Held Corporations

Small details aside, closely held corporations are characterized by a handful of traits that distinguish them from a typical publicly owned company.[12]

2.1.1 *Shareholder Involvement in Management*

A key feature of a closely held corporation is shareholder participation in the management, direction, and operation of the business. Shareholders regularly play a double role as director or employee in the company, and their remuneration is often the main source of income and return on investment. As a result, the usual separation of ownership and control typical for publicly owned corporations is often foreign to closely held corporations.[13] Rather, shared ownership goes hand in hand with control over company resources. It is also not rare for shareholders to invest all or a large proportion of their wealth into the corporation,

---

[11] See Adolf Augustus Berle & Gardiner C. Means, The Modern Corporation and Private Property (932); most recently in detail, Gerald F. Davis, "Twilight of the Berle and Means Corporation", 34 Seattle U. L. Rev. 1121 (2012).

[12] For the following, see Holger Fleischer, "Internationale Trends und Reformen im Recht der geschlossenen Kapitalgesellschaft", Neue Zeitschrift für Gesellschaftsrecht (NZG) 1081, 1082 f. (2014); from a U.S. perspective *Donahue v. Rodd Electrotype Co.*, 328 N.E.2d 505, 511 (Mass. 1975).

[13] For the fundamental differences from an economic perspective, Eugene F. Fama & Michael C. Jensen, "Separation of Ownership and Control", 26 J. L. & Econ. 301, 303 (1983): "We call these organizations open corporations to distinguish them from closed corporations that are generally smaller and have residual claims that are largely restricted to internal decision agents."

meaning that, unlike their counterparts in publicly traded companies, they do not have a broadly diversified investment portfolio. On the other side of the ledger, the collective action problem that regularly drives publicly held shareholders into rational apathy seldom features, as the individual shareholders have a much higher stake in the game.

2.1.2 Smaller Number of Shareholders

Typically, a closely held corporation has a small number of shareholders, often family members or friends bound by close bonds of trust. The smaller number of shareholders makes coordination of their interests easier, and contract negotiations cheaper, than could be achieved with a greater number of shareholders, and which would be practically impossible in a publicly traded corporation. Usually, the small number of shareholders corresponds with a smaller company—many closely held corporations are modest companies with a local customer base. There are however exceptions, so that company size itself is not the sole determining factor.

2.1.3 Share Transfer Restrictions

Another key characteristic of the publicly listed company, the ability to freely trade shares, is limited in the closely held corporation context. Depending on national law, the relevant provisions may be contained in legislation, the articles of association, or a shareholder agreement—enabling shareholders to control the composition of the shareholder group while maintaining and improving social capital within their organization.[14]

2.1.4 No Ready Market for Shares

Finally, there is no ready (secondary) market for the shares of closely held corporations—preventing dissatisfied shareholders from simply following the "Wall Street Rule" to sell their investment, as shareholders in public corporations often do. These same limitations often render conflicts regarding the payment of dividends more pointed, as minority shareholders are unable to balance out an unequal distribution with "homemade dividends," i.e. divesting themselves of their shares.[15] Even when there are no legal limitations on the selling of shares, minority shareholders have greater difficulty in finding a buyer, particularly as a reliable valuation for their holding is often lacking.[16]

---

[14] For more on family owned corporations, Jean-Luc Arregle, Michael A. Hitt, David G. Sirmon, & Philippe Very, "The Development of Organizational Social Capital: Attributes of Family Firms", 44 Journal of Management Studies 73 (2007); generally on closely held corporations, Frauke Wedemann, Gesellschafterkonflikte in geschlossenen Kapitalgesellschaften 89 et seq. (2013).

[15] Daniel R. Fischel, "The Law and Economics of Dividend Policy", 67 Va. L. Rev. 699 (1981); Merton H. Miller & Franco Modigliani, "Dividend Policy, Growth, and the Valuation of Shares", 34 J. Bus. 411 (1961); from a comparative perspective, Holger Fleischer & Jennifer Trinks, "Minderheitenschutz bei der Gewinnthesaurierung in der GmbH", NZG 289 (2015).

[16] On the problems of valuation, see Holger Fleischer, Unternehmensbewertung im Personengesellschafts- und GmbH-Recht, in Rechtshandbuch Unternehmensbewertung § 22 marg. n°. 4 et seqq. (Holger Fleischer & Rainer Hüttemann eds., 2015); Shannon P. Pratt, Valuing a Business. The Analysis and Appraisal of Closely Held Companies (5th ed. 2008).

2.1.5 *Broad Spectrum of Shareholders and Applications*

All this needs to be qualified with the statement that the closely held corporation, as the "legal work horse"[17] of the corporate world, is suited to a wide range of applications. It is the legal form of choice for inexperienced company founders and for highly professional market actors alike, providing the legal structure for a heterogeneous group of uses that includes startups, strategic joint ventures between big corporate players, and investment vehicles for private equity investors. This range of uses has implications for the legislator tasked with creating a functioning, yet flexible framework for closely held corporations that adequately reflects their regulatory meeds.

2.2 Typical Governance Issues and Conflicts in Closely Held Corporations

In light of the above, it hardly merits saying that the governance mechanisms for publicly traded companies cannot simply be transferred to closely held corporations.[18] The issues are fundamentally different from the outset: in a publicly listed corporation with a broad shareholder base, *vertical* governance problems predominate; the key challenge for the legislator and shareholders is to preserve the alignment of managerial and shareholder interests by means of institutional arrangements. In contrast, closely held corporations are far more troubled by *horizontal* governance issues,[19] requiring statutory or contractual mechanisms to resolve conflicts between majority and minority shareholders.

The typical governance issues in closely held corporations seem to extend across international boundaries, with remarkable similarities existing between the German GmbH, the English private company, the French SARL, or the US close corporation.[20] The task for the legislator across the board is to provide a functional framework that meets the needs of closely held corporations as well as possible, thereby helping to reduce transaction costs during the foundation phase.[21] Overall, allowing for share transfer restrictions is indispensable for the stability of the company, but it is equally important to provide carefully crafted exit and exclusion rights that preserve the ability of the company to continue operation. The biggest challenge, however, lies in the governance of shareholder conflicts. The goal here

---

[17] Arthur Meier-Hayoz & Peter Forstmoser, Schweizerisches Gesellschaftsrecht § 18 marg. n°. 9 (11th ed. 2012) (translation).

[18] On this, see Frank H. Easterbrook & Daniel R. Fischel, "Close Corporations and Agency Costs", 38 Stan. L. Rev. 271, 277 (1986): "Closely and publicly held corporations tend to have different types of governance mechanisms because of their different economic structure."

[19] Generally on the difference between vertical and horizontal governance issues, Mark J. Roe, The Institutions of Corporate Governance, in Handbook for New Institutional Economics 371, 372 (Claude Menard & Mary M. Shierley eds., 2005).

[20] For more on this and on the emergence of new types and subtypes of private limited liability companies, Fleischer, *supra* note 12, at 1088 et seqq., with further references.

[21] In the same vein, Frank H. Easterbrook & Daniel R. Fischel, The Economic Structure of Corporate Law 237 (1991): "Development of special close corporation statutes reflects the utility of a set of presumptive rules tailored to closely held corporations."

is predominantly to restrict the ability of majority shareholders to unfairly profit from the company,[22] while also providing sufficient mechanisms to prevent ex post opportunism by minority shareholders, and to resolve deadlocks.

3 GOVERNANCE FRAMEWORK FOR CLOSELY HELD CORPORATIONS

The governance framework for closely held corporations is made up of various regulatory elements that are partially corporate and partially contractual in nature, and which vary in their ability to bind the parties.[23]

3.1 Legislation

Legal persons are a creature of the national legislator, without whom they would not exist.[24] Therefore, legislation is the first, and essential layer of the governance regime for closely held corporations. Conceptually however, individual jurisdictions address this question in different ways, referred to in the British company law discussion as either stand-alone or integration models.[25]

3.1.1 Stand-Alone Models

Many countries have independent codes for their private limited liability companies. The historical prototype is the German GmbH Act of 1892, representing Germany's most successful legal export, which found a footing prior to World War I in Portugal in 1901 and Austria in 1906, before being taken up in France in 1925, Turkey in 1926, Belgium in 1935, and Switzerland in 1936. It found equal favour outside of Europe, in Brazil in 1919, Korea in 1931, Argentina in 1932, and Mexico in 1934. Today, versions of the GmbH can be found in over

---

[22] Similarly, from an economic perspective, Nagar, Petroni & Wolfenzon, *supra* note 9, at 943: "The main governance problem in close corporations is the majority shareholders' expropriation of minority shareholders."

[23] With some variance, see also McCahery & Vermeulen, *supra* note 10, at 5 et seqq., the "three pillars of the governance framework" differentiating between: "company law," "contract," and "optional guidelines."

[24] See also from a European perspective, ECJ [1988] ECR 5483 marg. n°. 19—Daily Mail, according to which a company "beyond the national jurisdiction that regulates its founding and existence, does not exist"; similarly from a U.S. perspective, Justice John Marshall, "Trustees of Dartmouth College v. Woordward" (1819) 17 U.S. 518, 636, according to whom a company is an "artificial being, existing solely in contemplation of state law."

[25] See Company Law Review Steering Group, *supra* note 8, marg. n°. 5.2.23: "A wide variety of approaches is possible and various models have been proposed and adopted in other jurisdictions; some have been found wanting, here and abroad. We have broken this down into two broad kinds of approach, which we shall call the 'free standing' and the 'integrated' approach."

100 countries across the world.[26] Many jurisdictions that have taken on the GmbH concept have sought to improve upon the German model, or to give it a slightly different form. This applies particularly to Romanic jurisdictions which place a greater emphasis on the "personal" (*intuitus personae*) elements of the GmbH.[27]

3.1.2 Integrated Approaches

The situation in Anglo-Saxon jurisdictions, with their traditional uniform company model is quite different.[28] In the United Kingdom where the Companies Act 1862 required a minimum of seven founding shareholders to establish a limited liability company,[29] hardly anyone envisioned small, closely held corporations: "First, they were all public"[30]. It is only during the last thirty years of the nineteenth century that the number of smaller companies began to increase significantly,[31] with it, the amount of available practice-based literature.[32] This development was further advanced by the groundbreaking 1892 decision *Salomom v. Salomon*, in which the House of Lords confirmed that while the act required seven founding shareholders, it did not require they be independent, thus condoning what in effect was a "one-man company."[33] The regulatory requirements were tightened up in the Companies Act 1900 in response to numerous fraudulent companies, which had the unfortunate side-effect of making company foundation less attractive for small and medium-sized companies. After serious protests, Parliament appointed a reform commission which did not base their final report on the German GmbH, but rather put forward its own proposals.[34] These recommendations saw the Companies Act 1907 differentiate between public and private companies for the first time, with relaxed regulations for the latter. According to the legal definition in s. 37(1), a company was considered a private company when its articles of

---

[26] For an international picture, Marcus Lutter, Limited Liability Companies and Private Companies, in International Encyclopaedia of Comparative Law, Vol. XIII/1 (Alfred Conard & Detlev Vagts eds., 2006).

[27] From a French perspective, see Maurice Cozian, Alain Viandier, & Florence Deboissy, Droit des sociétés marg. n°. 1079 (27th ed. 2014).

[28] See Stephen Mayson, Derek French, & Christopher Ryan, Company Law 58 (30th ed. 2013): "British company law traditionally regards private and public companies as two variants of the same basic form of legal organisation, unlike legal systems in Continental Europe which tend to treat them as different forms of organisations."

[29] Ron Harris, "The Private Origins of the Private Company: Britain 1862-1907", 33 Oxford J. Leg. Stud. 339, 343 (2013): "The 1862 Act, like those of 1844, 1855 and 1856, did not distinguish between companies based on the number of incorporators and shareholders, on capital, or on transferability of shares."

[30] According to a sub-title in Harris, *supra* note 29, at 342.

[31] Compare the numbers in Harris, *supra* note 29, at 343 et seqq.

[32] Foundational Francis B. Palmer, Private Companies; Or How to Convert your Business into a Private Company, and the Benefit of So Doing (Nabu Press 1877).

[33] *Salomon v. Salomon* [1897] AC 22 (HL); commenting on this decision Paul L. Davies & Sarah Worthington, Gower & Davies' Principles of Modern Company Law marg. n°. 2–3: (9th ed. 2012): "Not only did it finally establish the legality of the 'one person' company (long before EC law required this) and showed that incorporation was as readily available to the small private partnership and sole trader as to the large public company."

[34] See Report of the Company Law Amendment Committee, Parliamentary Papers, 1906, Vol. XLIV, Cmnd 3052, 17 et seqq.

association[35] provided for restrictions on share transfer, limited the number of shareholders to a maximum of 50, and forbade the public offer of company shares or bonds. In the intervening period, the United Kingdom has remained true to its uniform company model; isolated calls for the introduction of specific reforms for small companies[36] have not met with much response.[37] The matter arose most recently in the preparation for the Companies Act 2006, where a freestanding approach was once again rejected for fears of complications in transforming from a private to a public company.[38] Despite this, the reform did take the needs of small and medium-sized corporations into consideration under the slogan "Think Small First"[39] and introduced model rules for private companies.[40]

It took even longer for the required adjustments to be made in the United States, where the close corporation was regarded as the "orphan of corporate law"[41] until well into the twentieth century. The legislation of most of the states in the US were designed for large public corporations, and did not suit small companies with their distinct needs.[42] These were normally accommodated in practice by specific shareholder agreements, which contained voting agreements, restrictions on the transfer of shares or pre-emption rights that were progressively acknowledged with some reservations by the courts. This approach resulted in the gradual development of a common law of close corporations,[43] closely tended by the lawyers of the day.[44] The first specific legislative step was taken in 1948 in New York, followed by a comprehensive regulation in North Carolina in 1955. Today, many states have their own close corporation statutes, albeit with considerable variations.[45] They mostly consist of a separate chapter in the local corporation legislation, which comes into play when the shareholders vote it into their articles of association. General opinion is mixed with regard

[35] Emphasizing this, Timothy W. Guinnane, Ron Harris, Naomi R. Lamoreaux, & Jean-Laurent Rosenthal, *Ownership and Control in the Entrepreneurial Firm: An International History of Private Limited Companies*, Yale University Economic Growth Center Discussion Paper No. 959 (2007), available at http://ssrn.com/abstract=1071007, 28: "Whereas in Germany a company became private by organizing under a different law from a corporation, in Britain a company became private by including in its articles of association the above provisions."

[36] See also A New Form of Incorporation for Small Firms: a Consultative Document (H.M.S.O. 1981), Cmnd 8171.

[37] For more on this, DTI, Company Law Review: the Law Applicable to Private Companies (1994); for a summary, Mayson, French, & Ryan, *supra* note 28, at 27 et seq.

[38] See Company Law Review Steering Group, *supra* note 8, marg. n°. 5.2.27 et seq.

[39] Company Law Review Steering Group, Final Report, July 2011, marg. n°. 1.53 et seqq.

[40] More under III 2.

[41] Abram Chayes, "Madame Wagner and the Close Corporation", 73 Harv. L. Rev. 1532 (1959).

[42] See the conclusion at the time of Robert Kramer, "Foreword", 8 Law & Contemp. Probs. 433, 434 (1953): "One of the most striking facts about the close corporation is the extent to which it is the creation of business men and their counsel rather than of the courts or the legislatures. Most corporate legislation is admittedly drafted for the publicly owned company, at least in this country. Unlike Great Britain and Continental Europe, we have made little attempt in our corporate statutes to provide for the problems and the needs of the close corporation."

[43] For a detailed analysis, Harwell Wells, "The Rise of the Close Corporation and the Making of Corporation Law", Berkeley Bus. L.J. 263, 297 et seqq. (2008).

[44] See for example, William L. Cary, "How Illinois Corporations May Enjoy Partnership Advantage: Planning for the Closely Held Firm", 48 Nw. U. L. Rev. 427 (1953).

[45] Detailed analysis in Dennis S. Karjala, "An Analysis of Close Corporation Legislation in the United States", 21 Ariz. St. L.J. 663 (1989).

to the advantages and disadvantages of this regulatory method.[46] Legal practice shies away from the uncertainties of special regulations that have yet to be subject to intense judicial scrutiny, or is reluctant to make use of them for other reasons.[47]

In continental Europe, the single legislative model has won new supporters in the Nordic states: Denmark, Finland, and Sweden now regulate publicly owned and closed corporations under one legislative instrument, although Norway is continuing with its dual approach.[48]

3.2 Model Articles

The term 'model articles' refers to articles of association provided by the legislator which business founders are free to adopt in whole or in part as an alternative to developing their own customized articles. Of these, the most prominent example is the UK Model Articles for Private Companies, issued by the Secretary of State pursuant to sec. 19(1) of the Companies Act 2006.[49] Some US states have adopted a similar approach in their close corporation statutes.[50] In continental Europe, by contrast, this regulatory technique did not gain a strong footing until the advent of fast-track incorporation procedures, with online registration processes like those in Spain, Italy, Greece, and Poland requiring the adoption of immutable model articles or sample protocols.[51] Germany took a step towards model articles with the reforms of 2008, stipulating the use of a sample protocol for the simplified, more cost-effective incorporation procedure contained in §2 para. 1a sentence 2 GmbHG. France also introduced a *modèle des statuts types* for single member private liability companies (EURL) in 2009.[52] While the use of model articles does permit a more rapid incorporation procedure with lower costs, for companies with multiple shareholders these advantages are often obtained at a price: the enforced waiver of customized agreements, for example on voting rights or dividend clauses.[53] The question as to whether the benefit of increasing the speed

---

[46] For example, William S. Hochstetler & Mark D. Svejda, "Statutory Needs of Close Corporations—An Empirical Study: Special Close Corporation Legislation or Flexible General Corporation Law", 10 J. Corp. L. 849 (1985).

[47] For more on this, see Brian R. Cheffins, "U.S. Close Corporation Legislation: A Model Canada Should Not Follow", 35 McGill L. J. 160, 179 et seqq. (1989).

[48] See Jan Andersson, The Making of Company Law in Scandinavia and Europe—Experimentation and Innovation versus Harmonization, in German and Nordic Perspectives on Company Law and Capital Markets Law 27, 33 (Holger Fleischer, Jesper Lau Hansen, & W. Georg Ringe eds., 2015); Mette Neville, The Regulation of Close Corporations in Danish Company Law in an International Regulatory Context, in Private Company Law Reform in Europe: The Race for Flexibility (A. Jorge Viera González & Christoph Teichmann eds., 2015).

[49] For an in-depth analysis, Mayson, French, & Ryan, *supra* note 28, at 75 et seq.

[50] See Hochstetler & Svejda, *supra* note 46, at 865 et seqq.

[51] For a short overview, Frederik Karsten, "Kann man eine GmbH auf einem Bierdeckel gründen?" GmbH-Rundschau (GmbhR) 958 (2007); for more detail, Michal Romanowski & Bartosz Makowicz, "Polnisches GmbH-Recht: Das neue beschleunigte Gründungsverfahren 'S24' " GmbHR 736 (2012).

[52] Further detail in Philippe Merle, Sociétés commerciales marg. n°. 236 (18th ed. 2015); from a comparative perspective Markus Peifer, "Gründung und Führung einer Einpersonen-S.A.R.L. französischen Rechts", GmbHR 1145 (2009).

[53] Criticizing this from a Spanish perspective, Mercedes Sánchez Ruiz, Las sociedades familiares como paradigma de las sociedades de capital cerradas, in Régimen jurídico de la empresa familiar 43, 49 (Mercedes Sánchez Ruiz ed., 2010): "endemic standardisation of articles of association" (translation).

of incorporation outweighs limiting the potential to tailor the articles of association to a business's specific needs is, as yet, still open to international investigation and debate.[54]

For regular incorporation procedures, however, model articles are still the exception. The Dutch legislator rejected their introduction, citing concerns about flexibility,[55] although the Dutch Association of Notaries quickly stepped into the breach to offer sample protocols. Other countries refer potential company founders to professional expertise—New Zealand, for example, has discontinued its practice of offering professionally drafted model articles via the Companies Office website, instead advising business founders to deal directly with a private service provider.[56] On the supranational level, the European Commission recently revived the idea of a uniform template for articles of association in its SUP proposal,[57] after previous attempts at model articles for the European Private Company turned out to be unsuccessful.[58]

3.3 Articles of Association

Across the globe, it is not the statutes, but rather the articles of association that include the most important governance regulations for closely held corporations.[59] This is usually due to the broad scope that legislation allows for shareholders to determine the internal affairs of the company.

3.3.1 Primacy of Private Ordering

Wide-ranging party autonomy for shareholders has been a hallmark of the German GmbH Act since its entry into force in 1892.[60] The economic advantages are clear: shareholders can

[54] More detail on the simplification of creating articles of association, Frauke Wedemann, Gesellschafterkonflikte in geschlossenen Kapitalgesellschaften 370 et seqq (2013).

[55] See Christoph Van der Elst & Erik P. M. Vermeulen, The Dutch Private Company—Successfully Relaunched?, in La simplification du droit des sociétés dans les États membres de l'union européenne 165, 176 (Yves De Cordt and Édouard-Jean Navez eds., 2015).

[56] See New Zealand Companies Office, Note: "Historically you could purchase draft constitutions online from third party authors via the Companies Office. This option has been discontinued. Now you must deal with the constitution authors directly"; retrievable under http://www.business. govt.nz/companies/learn-about/starting-a-acompany/how-to-apply/constitution-optional/ third-party-constitutions.

[57] See European Commission, Proposal for a Directive of the European Parliament and of the Council on single-member private limited liability companies, COM(2014) 21 final, Article 11: "uniform template of articles of association."

[58] See Hartmut Wicke, Model Articles for the Societas Privata Europaea, in The European Private Company—Societas Privata Europaea (SPE) 183 (Heribert Hirte & Christoph Teichmann, 2013).

[59] For Germany, see the Draft Bill for a Close Corporation Act including Legislative Reasoning and Annexes, 1891, 96: "First and foremost, the content of the articles of association is determinative." (translation); Fleischer, supra note 1 Introduction, marg. n°. 21: "the primary source for the internal organization of a GmbH."

[60] See Draft Bill, supra note 59, at 25, according to which there is no reason to create binding norms due to the lack of "greater public" participation, and that members of a GmbH are in a position to protect their own interests.

establish custom made organizational structures with membership rights according to their own special needs. In the absence of any negative externalities, such agreements improve efficiency by increasing the common benefit of the company founders.[61] However, much of this liberal spirit was lost in the twentieth century, particularly in jurisdictions like Italy or the Netherlands, who based their close corporation legislation (too) closely on that for stock corporations.[62] It is only in recent times that there has been an almost universal return to private ordering in the law of closely held corporations. In France, for example, the *liberté contractuelle* resurfaced 20 years ago with the introduction of the *société par actions simplifiée* (SAS).[63] The Delaware Limited Liability Act has sought to allow the greatest possible effect for private ordering since 2004,[64] while the Court of Chancery takes an even stronger line, offering the members of LLCs "the maximum amount of contract, private ordering and flexibility."[65] The English Department of Business, Industry and Skills put forward almost identical wording in the consultation paper for the Companies Act reform of 2006.[66] Japan formally included the principle of private ordering in its corporations legislation of 2005, giving shareholders a broad contractual scope for establishing the articles of association in closely held corporations.[67]

3.3.2 *Scope of Private Ordering*

The freedom to determine the internal operations of a company is an important expression of private ordering. One key feature of this "libertà di autorganizzazione"[68] is the organizational freedom with respect to internal governance rules and decision-making procedures, namely the ability to choose between different management structures and the ability to drop

---

[61] See also Lucian A. Bebchuk, "Limiting Contractual Freedom in Corporate Law: The Desirable Constraints on Charter Amendments", 102 Harv. L. Rev. 1820, 1826 (1989): "Economic theory suggests that, under the assumed conditions, parties left free to design their contractual arrangements will adopt efficient terms—terms that will maximize the size of the contractual pie available for division among the parties"; similarly, Melvin Aron Eisenberg, "The Structure of Corporation Law", 89 Colum. L. Rev. 1461, 1463 (1989): "The reasons for the bargain principle usually apply to bargains among the shareholders in a closely held corporation concerning the corporation's structural and distributional rules."

[62] See for Italy, Giuseppe Zanarone, Della società a responsabilitá limitata, vol. 1 (2010), 121 with note 232: "small stock corporation without stocks" (translation); for the Netherlands, Maarten J Kroeze, "Flexibility and Function of Private Company Statutes", 8 Eur. Bus. Org. L. Rev. 121, 122 (2007): "The private company statute was, and still is, an almost 100 per cent copy of the public company statute."

[63] See Merle, *supra* note 52, marg. no. 591–1: "The great novelty of this SAS is to give absolute priority to the shareholders' contractual freedom which expresses itself in the articles of association"; most recently, Paul Le Cannu, La SAS: un cadre legal minimale, Rev. soc. 2014, 543.

[64] § 18-1101(b) Del. LLC Act.

[65] *In re Grupo Dos Chiles, LLC,* 2006 Del. Ch. LEXIS 45, *5–6.

[66] See Department of Trade and Industry, Modern Company Law for a Competitive Economy, 1998, marg. no. 5.2: "maximum amount of freedom and flexibility to those organising and directing the enterprise."

[67] See Zenichi Shishido, "Does Law Matter to Financial Capitalism? The Case of Japanese Entrepreneurs", 37 Fordham Int'l. L.J. 1087, 1098 (2014): "In the corporate law reform of 2005, the principle of freedom of contract was formally acknowledged and established. Now, at least in closely held corporations [. . .] Japanese shareholders can plan their inter-relationships as freely as their counterparts in the United States."

[68] Reform Commission Mirone, Scheda di sintesi, February 2000, Art. 3 sub 3.

individual organizational elements. In addition, an informal process for gathering information as well as simplified decision-making processes are now often possible, representing an "intramural informality in close corporations."[69] To take an example from the UK company law reform: a private company is not required to appoint a company secretary, and may choose not to convene an annual general meeting; in addition, resolutions can be made in writing via circulated email.[70] This newly won freedom also presents itself in the liberalization of corporate shares. The Dutch close corporation law, for example, now allows shares without voting rights, shares with multiple voting rights or staggered voting rights, as well as shares with no dividend rights.[71] A shareholder cannot, however, completely waive all rights, and shares that provide neither voting rights nor dividend rights are not permitted under the law.[72]

3.3.3 *Limitation to Private Ordering*

Potential limitations to private ordering were recently discussed as part of the question of whether the duty of loyalty or other functionally similar remedies[73] have a mandatory or default character.[74] The US LLC forms the pointy end of the liberalization scale, with §18-1101(c) Del. The LLC Act permits the complete exclusion of fiduciary duties, naturally with the condition that the implied contractual covenant of good faith and fair dealing remain intact.[75] In contrast, according to the leading interpretation, the recently introduced Article 803 (3) OR only permits a specific and ad hoc exemption from the duty of loyalty for Swiss close corporation shareholders, but no general exemption.[76]

3.4 Shareholder Agreements

In addition to the articles of association, shareholder agreements[77] (*pactes d'actionnaires*[78], *Gesellschaftervereinbarungen*[79]) may contain further provisions for the internal affairs of

---

[69] According to the sub-heading in Elvin R. Latty, "The Close Corporation and the New North Carolina Business Corporation Act", 34 N.C. L. Rev. 432, 456 (1956).

[70] Department of Trade and Industry, Companies Act 2006. A summary of what it means for private companies.

[71] For more detail, van der Elst & Vermeulen, *supra* note 55, at 165, 180 et seqq.

[72] Art. 2:190 NBW.

[73] For the UK remedy of unfair prejudice and its derogations, see recently Rita Cheung, "Shareholders' agreements: shareholders' contractual freedom in company law" J.B.L. (2012) 504.

[74] See Bachmann et al., *supra* note 10, at 50 et seq.; for more detail, Klaus Ulrich Schmolke, Grenzen der Selbstbindung im Privatrecht 667 et seqq (2014).

[75] For more detail, Darren Guttenberg, "Waiving Farewell Without Saying Goodbye: The Waiver of Fiduciary Duties in Limited Liability Companies in Delaware, and the Call For Mandatory Disclosure", 86 S. Cal. L. Rev. 869 (2013) and relevant footnotes.

[76] See Marc Amstutz & Fernand Chappuis, in Basler Kommentar, OR Art. 803 marg. n°. 11 (4th ed. 2012).

[77] Monographically, Graham Muth & Sean Fitzgerald, Shareholders' agreements (6th ed. 2012).

[78] Monographically, Jean-Jacques Daigre & Monique Sentilles-Dupont, Pactes d'actionnaires (1995).

[79] For a collection of country reports, Gesellschaftsrechtliche Nebenabreden (Simon Laimer, Christoph Perathoner, & Susanne Bärlin eds., 2013).

closely held corporations. These agreements enjoy extensive use all over the world, as they assist shareholders more clearly to regulate their relationships with each other. The most common agreements cover voting rights, transfer restrictions, and exit rights, as well as the composition or remuneration of management or supervisory boards. Conceptually, they are separate contractual agreements between all or some of the shareholders that operate *alongside* the articles of association, as the Italian term *patti parasociali* and the Spanish term *pactos parasociales* suggest.[80] As a classical contract, it can only bind its immediate parties; in contrast to the articles of association, it can only be altered with the consent of all parties. In most jurisdictions, the existence and the content of shareholder agreements remain hidden from the curious gaze of outsiders. Noteworthy exceptions are the UK, and some of the former Commonwealth states such as Malaysia, where a copy of all shareholder agreements must be lodged with the Companies Commission.[81] Some continental European jurisdictions, for example France, Italy, and Portugal, require the disclosure of shareholder agreements only in listed companies.[82]

Usually, statutory law says little, if anything at all about shareholder agreements. There are, however, individual codifications which generally alert shareholders to the permissibility of these agreements or even directly address some specific types. Article 17(1) of the Portuguese Commercial Company Act (*Código das Sociedades Comerciais*, CSC), for example, renders legally binding all shareholder agreements entered into by all or some partners. Similarly, Article 17(b) of the UK Companies Act 2006 provides that all shareholder agreements are regarded as part of the company's constitution.[83] Other jurisdictions are more selective, for instance, §7.32 US Revised Model Business Corporation Act (RMBCA) lists, and thus authorizes, only specific types of shareholder agreements. Some other jurisdictions single out voting agreements as the most important contractual device, as in Article 281 Belgian Companies Act (*Code des Sociétés*, C. soc.), where the exercise of voting rights may be the subject of an agreement between shareholders.

The overall trend around the world today is generally to respect and enforce shareholder agreements between company members. The courts have moved on from the open hostility displayed most prominently in a famous line of cases handed down by the New York Court of Appeals ("the Big Four").[84] Russia, one of the few jurisdictions under which shareholder agreements had remained unenforceable, amended its Limited Liability Companies Act to allow them in 2009.[85] Today, most jurisdictions grant shareholders significant latitude to enter into shareholder agreements. The best illustration comes from voting agreements, once viewed as incompatible with statutory corporate governance, they are nowadays recognized as lawful and enforceable, provided they observe certain limits. One typical limitation is spelled out in Article 17(3) Portuguese Commercial Company Act, which declares null and void any voting agreement that obliges a shareholder always to follow the instructions or

---

[80] Monographically, Davide Proverbio, I patti parasociali (2010).

[81] See sec. 30 UK Companies Act 2006.   [82] See for Italy Art. 122(1) Testo Unico.

[83] For more detail, Alexander Schall in Alexander Schall, Companies Act sec. 17 marg. n°. 2 and sec. 29 marg. n°. 5 et seqq (Beck 2014).

[84] See Jeffry D. Bauman, Alan R. Palmiter, & Frank Partnoy, Corporations, Law and Policy (6th ed. 2007) 354.

[85] Further detail, Karina L. Pulec, "Legal Restraints on the Use of Shareholders' Agreements for Structuring Foreign Investment Deals in Russia", 45 Cornell Int'l. L.J. 487 (2012).

approve proposals put forward by the company or one of its bodies or to exercise voting rights in return for special benefits. Article 281 Belgian Companies Act contains a similar list, with the proviso that these agreements must have an expiry date and always be justified in terms of shareholder interests.

Breaches of shareholder agreements are almost universally subject to liability sanctions. However, these are unlikely to be an appropriate remedy due to the difficulties in proving the damages incurred. As a result, practitioners across the board recommend liquidated damages clauses as an indirect enforcement mechanism. Moreover, many jurisdictions allow for specific performance and injunctions, as seen in §7.31(b) RMBCA, which expressly stipulates that a voting agreement is subject to specific performance. However, a number of jurisdictions, including Argentina and Japan, still reject this approach.

From a doctrinal perspective, the most difficult issue is whether shareholder resolutions that deviate from a shareholder agreement can be set aside by a shareholder rescission suit. This question has been vexing German corporate law scholarship for three decades: two Federal Court of Justice cases from the 1980s stated that a breach of an omnilateral shareholder agreement may be subject to a motion to set aside a shareholder resolution.[86] In contrast, many scholars hold with the "separation theory," arguing that articles of association and shareholder agreements should be kept strictly apart.[87] Internationally, this second view holds sway in many jurisdictions including Argentina, Belgium, Portugal, and Switzerland. The Danish Companies Act (*lov om aktie- og anpartselskaber*, SEL) has authoritatively decided the issue, stipulating in Article 82 that shareholder agreements are neither binding on the limited liability company nor with regard to resolutions passed at general meetings. There are, however, many countries that show scholarly support for a legal "spillover" from the contractual to the corporate hemisphere.

3.5 Corporate Governance Guidelines

In contrast to listed companies, corporate governance guidelines do not yet play a significant role for closely held corporations. This is easily explained, as the corporate governance debate originated from the need to protect *external* investors. In addition, the principal-agent problems both company types face are considerably different: the corporate governance principles for listed companies cannot therefore simply be transposed to non-listed companies, let alone closely held corporations. That being said, there are some initial cautious attempts being made to develop a tailored corporate governance framework for unlisted companies. The Belgian *Buysse* Corporate Governance Code is one pioneering example, providing special rules for family enterprises in addition to recommendations for all non-listed companies.[88] Other recommendations, such as the Finnish Central Chamber

---

[86] BGH NJW 1983, 1910; NJW 1987, 1890.

[87] For more detail, Jan Lieder, Schuldrechtliche Nebenabreden im deutschen Gesellschaftsrecht, in Aktuelle Entwicklungen im deutschen, österreichischen und schweizerischen Gesellschafts- und Kapitalmarktrecht 2012 231, 244 et seqq. (Holger Fleischer, Susanne Kalss, & Hans-Ueli Vogt eds., 2013).

[88] Code Buysse I, Corporate Governance Recommendations à l'attention des entreprises non cotées en bourse, 2005; Code Buysse II, Corporate Governance Recommendations à l'attention des entreprises non cotées en bourse, 2009.

of Commerce initiative "Improving corporate governance of unlisted companies"[89] and the British "Corporate Governance Guidance and Principles for Unlisted Companies,"[90] have a somewhat different focus, concentrating on larger unlisted or small and mid-size listed companies. It remains to be seen whether it is helpful or even feasible to draw up a voluntary corporate governance code for closely held corporations. The Colombian Framework of Good Corporate Governance for Small and Medium-Sized Enterprises provides one potential way forward, by serving as a model of reference for businesses attempting to craft their own corporate governance guidelines.[91]

4 INTERNAL GOVERNANCE OF THE COMPANY

The pivotal issue for internal corporate governance in closely held corporations is the interaction between corporate bodies or organs.

4.1 Corporate Organs

Around the globe, almost all general statutory schemes consist of two decision-making organs: the shareholders' meeting and the board of directors. In most jurisdictions the latter is also mandatory,[92] although the company's capacity to act does not, at least theoretically, require a board of directors, as general agency concepts could be used.[93] In France, directors were long viewed by the legislation as agents (*mandataires*) of the company.[94] One exception to the mandatory requirement for a board of directors comes from Delaware. According to §351 DGCL, appropriate provisions in the articles may permit a close corporation to be managed by its shareholders. The most recent British corporate law reform did not follow this bold move, however, confining itself instead to introducing a less formal decision-making process for private companies to better accommodate shareholder-directors.[95]

Occasionally, co-determination may call for a mandatory supervisory board—although this usually only applies to larger companies. For the German GmbH, for example, the threshold is 500 employees. Additionally, EU company law requires medium-sized and

---

[89] Finland Central Chamber of Commerce, Improving Corporate Governance of Unlisted Companies, January 2006.

[90] Institute of Directors, *supra* note 5.

[91] Guía Colombiana de Gobierno Corporativo para Sociedades cerradas y de Familia, September 2009.

[92] For Germany, see § 6 (1) GmbHG: "The company must have one or more managing directors" (translation).

[93] Discussing this point, Bachmann et al., *supra* note 10, at 85 et seq.; Amitai Aviram, "Officers' Fiduciary Duties and the Nature of Corporate Organs", 2013 U. Ill. L. Rev. 763 (2013).

[94] See Dominique Vidal, Droit des sociétés 204 et seq., 517 et seq. (7th ed. 2010).

[95] Paul L. Davies & Jonathan Rickford, "An Introduction to the New UK Companies Act: Part II", 5 Eur. Company & Fin. L. Rev. 239, 261 (2008): "This mechanism is available to all private companies, but it is expected to be attractive especially to those with a high degree of overlap between membership and management."

large corporations to engage an auditor, but opinions are divided as to whether this auditor qualifies as a corporate organ. Many jurisdictions also permit the creation of additional corporate organs, for example, advisory boards or committees. Shareholders are free to determine the name, function, and competences of these additional organs, as long as the exclusive responsibilities of the general shareholders' meeting and the board of directors remain intact.

4.2 Allocation of Powers between Shareholders and Directors

4.2.1 Omnipotence versus Parity Theory

Casting an eye across the globe reveals two basic models for allocating powers between shareholders and directors, snappily captured in the Swiss doctrine as the omnipotence theory and the parity theory.[96] The first is one of shareholder supremacy in which the board of directors is subordinated to the shareholders' meeting. This hierarchical structure has been included in §37(1) German GmbH law since its first enactment in 1892, allowing shareholders to pass a resolution issuing binding instructions for directors, even for the day to day running of the business. Portugal, Spain, and Japan also provide a similar organizational framework.[97] The Netherlands, where previously shareholders in a *besloten vennootschap* were only permitted to issue general instructions, has recently moved in the same direction with their closed corporation reform of 2012. Pursuant to Article 239(4) NBW, the articles of association may now provide that the board of directors has to behave according to the (specific) instructions of another body of the corporation.[98] In Italy, shareholders who represent at least one-third of the issued share capital of a *società a responsabilità limitata* can force a decision of the shareholders meeting in accordance with Article 2479 Abs. C.c.

The alternative approach, based on the principle of parity, is used in Switzerland. Although Article 804(1) OR nominates the shareholders' meeting as the supreme governing body of the company, Article 810(1) OR has put some checks and balances in place, by stating that directors have an inalienable duty of "overall management" ("Oberleitung").[99] British law follows a similar concept, albeit as a default rule, by vesting the board of directors with the management of the company (model Art. 3).[100] As a consequence, it is the directors, and they alone, who may exercise these powers.[101] The only way in which the shareholders can

---

[96] See Rolf Watter & Katja Roth Pellanda, in Basler Kommentar, OR II Art. 810 marg. n°. 1 (4th ed. 2012); most recently with respect to stock corporation law Daniel M. Häusermann, "Wider das Paritätsprinzip", Schweizerische Zeitschrift für Wirtschaftsrecht (SZW) 255 (2014).

[97] See for Portugal, Art. 259 CSC; for Spain Art. 160 LSC.

[98] See van der Elst & Vermeulen, *supra* note 55, at 165, 181; from a comparative perspective Sven Hirschfeld, Die niederländische "bv" nach dem Gesetz zur Vereinfachung und Flexibilisierung des bv-rechts (flex-bv), Recht der Internationalen Wirtschaft 134 et seq. (2013).

[99] See Watter & Roth Pellanda, *supra* note 96, Art. 810 marg. n°. 5 et seqq.

[100] See Mayson, French & Ryan, *supra* note 28, at 466 et seq.

[101] See *Automatic Self Cleansing Filter Syndicate Co v. Cuninghame* [1906] 2 Ch 34; also *John Shaw & Sons (Salford) Ltd v. Shaw* [1935] 2 KB 113, 114: "If the powers of management are vested in the directors, they and they alone can exercise these powers. The only way in which the general body of the shareholders can control the exercise of the powers vested by the articles in the directors is by altering their articles, or, if opportunity arises under the articles, by refusing to re-elect the directors of whose

control the exercise of these powers is by passing a special shareholder resolution (model Art. 4) requiring a majority of not less than 75%.[102] However, the ability of shareholders to remove directors at any time by ordinary resolution under s. 168 CA 2006, induces the directors to regularly follow the business strategy preferred by the majority shareholder. Australia[103] and the USA[104] have a similar division of power as the statutory or common law default—leading to the development of shareholders' agreements that give minority holders a voice in the control and management of the corporation.

4.2.2 *Default and Mandatory Competences of the Shareholder Meeting*

Reflecting the high degree of organizational freedom granted by many jurisdictions,[105] the competences of the shareholder meeting are mostly default powers.[106] This enables shareholders to modify the distribution of powers between the corporate organs as they think fit. Mandatory involvement of shareholders is usually limited to those decisions that impact on their legal or contractual rights. These include alterations to the articles of association, an increase or re-duction of share capital and structural changes such as mergers, divisions, conversions, or decisions to wind up the company voluntarily.[107] An example can be found in Article 27(1) of the Commission's Draft SPE Regulation.[108]

4.2.3 *Mandatory Competences of the Board*

In most continental European jurisdictions, the mandatory competences of the board are fairly limited. Under German law, for example, they include the board's power to repre-sent the company in relation to third parties and the specific-conduct duties in the interests of creditors such as the duties to keep the books of the company, to prepare the annual accounts, to communicate with the Commercial Register and to initiate insolvency proceed-ings if necessary.[109] Similarly, under UK law, the mandatory functions of directors relate to

---

actions they disapproved. They cannot themselves usurp the powers which by the articles are vested in the directors anymore than the directors can usurp the powers vested by the articles in the general body of the shareholders."

[102] See Brenda Hannigan, Company Law marg. n°. 8–7 (3d ed. 2012).

[103] See Art. 198A Corporations Act; R. P. Austin & I. M. Ramsey, Ford's Principles of Corporation Law marg. n°. 7.120 (15th ed. 2012).

[104] See §141(a) DGCL; John Coffee, "Bylaw Battlefield: Can Institutions Change the Outcome of Corporate Control Contests", 51 U. Miami L. Rev. 605, 608 (1997): "Common law decisions have long recognized that a shareholder resolution, passed at a shareholders' meeting, directing the board to take a specified action was ineffective."

[105] See above, 2.5.2.   [106] See Bachmann et al., *supra* note 10, at 92 et seqq.

[107] See Bachmann et al., *supra* note 10, at 94 et seq.; for the UK Davies & Worthington, *supra* note 33, marg. n°.

[108] See Édouard Jean Navez, The Internal Organization of the European Private Company: Freedom of Contract under National Constraints?, in The European Private Company—Societas Privata Europaea (SPE) 147, 160 et seqq. (Heribert Hirte and Christoph Teichmann eds., 2013).

[109] See Wolfgang Zöllner and Ulrich Noack, in Baumbach/Hueck, GmbH-Gesetz § 37 marg. n°. 18 (20th ed. 2013).

the production of the annual accounts and reports and the regular administration of the company, in particular its communications with Companies House.[110]

5 Share Transfer Restrictions

Closely held corporations are built on mutual trust and loyalty between their founders. This close-knit setting lends importance to the matter of "who" a shareholder is—success, or the lack of it, is often contingent on shareholders sharing goals and values. Conversely, a lack of personal bonds or latent conflicts between shareholders may endanger the organizational capital of a close corporation. Against this backdrop, there is a legitimate interest in restricting share transfers to keep out strangers and undesirable co-shareholders.[111] These transfer restrictions constitute one of the core characteristics of a close corporation.[112] However, they vary greatly in type and operation across jurisdictions, making them an attractive subject for comparative company law research.[113]

5.1 Default Rules

An initial question in this field is whether the national legislator should set the free transfer of shares as the default rule, or whether some restrictions should apply. A comparative glance across a range of jurisdictions reveals a somewhat mixed bag of results. One has to consider, however, that some codifications apply only to close corporations under stand-alone legislation, while others do not differentiate between publicly and closely held corporations.[114]

The majority of jurisdictions begin from the perspective that shares are freely transferable, while allowing for transfer restrictions in the articles or in shareholder agreements. This group includes most US states, Germany, Italy, Denmark, Sweden, Finland, Japan, Argentina, and Australia with statutory and contractual transfer restrictions being equally common in these countries. In contrast, other countries have opted for the opposite default rule, requiring the company's consent for share transfers. This is the case for example in Norway and Switzerland, where share transfers require the consent of the shareholder meeting. Similarly, the model rules for private companies in the UK and Ireland require

---

[110]   See Davies & Worthington, *supra* note 33, marg. n°. 14–21.

[111]   For further details, see Lars-Göran Sund and Per-Olof Bjuggren, "Family-Owned, Limited Close Corporations and Protection of Ownership", 23 Eur. J. L & Econ. 273, 274 (2007); Lars-Göran Sund, Jan Andersson, & Kajsa Haag, "Share Transfer Restrictions and Family Business: The Minority Saherholderperspective", 26 Eur. Bus. L. Rev. 437 (2015).

[112]   See above, 2.1.3.

[113]   See the national reports in Die Übertragung von GmbH-Geschäftsanteilen in 14 europäischen Rechtsordnungen (Susanne Kalss ed., 2003); see also Lars-Göran Sund, Jan Andersson, & Edward Humphreys, "A European Company and Share Transfer Restrictions" 23 Eur. Bus. L. Rev. 483, 490 et seqq. (2012); Wedemann, *supra* note 14, 103 et seqq.

[114]   See also Sund, Andersson, & Humphreys, *supra* note 113 , at 490: "[I]n countries with only one general law for all limited companies, such as in Sweden and Finland, fewer restrictions are acceptable."

director approval.[115] Still other jurisdictions, including Belgium, France, Portugal, and Spain have taken a middle course, a statutory consent requirement, with generous exceptions for share transfers between spouses, direct relatives (ascendant or descendent), or fellow shareholders.[116] The basic idea here is that these potential shareholders are not strangers to the company, and that a smooth intergenerational succession is in the best interests of the company. The Netherlands provides a fourth variation, stating that, unless the articles of association provide otherwise, a shareholder looking to dispose of shares must first offer them proportionally to the other shareholders.[117] As a final option, the legislator may require shareholders of close corporations to provide for transfer restrictions in the articles of association without any further specification. This is the approach taken in the European Commission's original Draft Proposal for a European Private Company[118] and in the Malaysian Companies Act.[119]

The existence of valid statutory or contractual transfer restrictions raises the question of what mechanisms are available to protect shareholders "locked in" to the company. Some countries provide statutory relief, such as Switzerland which provides a right to resign from the company with good cause in Article 786(3) OR where the articles of association prohibit exit or the shareholder meeting refuses to consent. A similar withdrawal right has been put in place in Italy under Article 2469(2) C.c. for close corporation shareholders. In cases of valid transfer prohibitions, Portugal grants a statutory withdrawal right after 10 years of shareholding under Article 229(1) CSC. According to the new Dutch law, a shareholder may freely sell shares if they have been offered but not been bought by co-shareholders or other candidates within a three-month period.[120] In Japan, a company which does not ratify a share transfer must instead nominate a designated purchaser, with both the buyer and the seller authorized to ask the court to set the purchase price.

5.2 Types of Share Transfer Restrictions and their Legal Limits

Restrictions on share transferability come in different shapes and forms. Despite their great variety, one can discern a certain standardization around the world. The most common take the form of inalienability clauses, consent clauses, pre-emptive rights, and buy-sell agreements. Occasionally, the national legislator itself will provide a list of potential clauses to enable shareholders to make an informed decision. One nice illustration comes from the statutory regime of the French simplified stock corporation (SAS) that explicitly mentions inalienability and consent clauses.[121] Sweden has provided a similar "à la carte" approach in the Swedish Companies Act since 2006, discarding its former restrictive regulation as it was no longer in line with international standards.[122] The new regulation describes and explains

---

[115] For the UK, see model article 26(1).
[116] For France, see for example Art. L. 223–213 and Art. L. 223–216. C. com.
[117] See Art. 2:192a NBW.
[118] See Art. 8 (1) in conjunction with Annex I, Chapter III, points 6 to 10.
[119] See s. 15(1) Companies Act 1965.   [120] See Art. 2:195 NBW.
[121] Art. L. 227-13 and Art. L. 227-14 C. com.
[122] For further details, see Jan Andersson, Redemption of Shareholders, in Shareholder Conflicts 161, 164 et seqq. (Paul Krüger Andersen, Nis Jul Clausen, & Rolf Skog eds., 2006).

the function of consent clauses, rights of first refusal, and post-sale purchase right clauses in great detail. The Swiss law on private limited liability companies provides a third example, detailing the various permissible forms of transfer restriction agreement as an exhaustive list in Article 786(2) No. 1-5 OR.[123]

Statutory mention of such clauses is helpful for legal practitioners, as it implicitly confirms their legality. A good illustration comes to us from Article L. 227-13 French C. com., which stipulates that the articles of association of an SAS may specify the inalienability of shares for up to ten years. In other jurisdictions, the validity of such clauses is less clear. US courts usually apply a reasonableness test to transfer restrictions, which would likely find indefinite inalienability clauses invalid, based on the venerable property law rule against unreasonable restraints on alienation.[124] According to Article 2:195 Dutch NBW, the articles of association may exclude transferability of shares for a specific period of time—based on legislative history, a fixed period of five years would not be contrary to the principles of reasonableness and fairness. Still other jurisdictions, such as Germany and Switzerland, consider inalienability clauses to be valid, but still protect the interests of locked-in shareholders with a mandatory right of withdrawal for good cause in the GmbH legislation.[125] Guidance is given for other common share transfer restrictions in § 202(c) DGCL which specifically identifies five permissible categories: first-options agreements, first refusal agreements, consent agreements, buy-sell agreements, and provisions prohibiting transfer to designated classes of persons.[126] Should the court find that a clause is not valid in a specific case, §349 DGCL dictates that the corporation still has the option, for a period of 30 days after the judgment setting aside the restriction becomes final, to acquire the shares at a fair value determined by the Court of Chancery.

5.3 Judicial Review of Consent Clauses

As we have seen, consent clauses in the articles or in legislation are often used to control the composition of the shareholder base. Where the responsible company organ—shareholder meeting or board of directors—refuses to grant its consent, the question comes down to whether, and to what extent, the courts will scrutinize this refusal. English courts are generally very hesitant in this regard, only stepping in to apply a subjective standard when the directors have unduly exercised their voting rights: "It is trite law that the court will not interfere with the exercise by directors of a discretion not to register a transfer if their decision was one which a reasonable board of directors could bona fide believe to be in the interests of the company."[127] The same is true for Ireland, where the shareholder looking to dispose of

---

[123] Matthias Oertle and Shelby R. du Pasquier, in Basler Kommentar, OR II Art. 786 marg. n°. 5 (4th ed. 2012).

[124] Individual cases listed in James D. Cox and Thomas Lee Hazen, The Law of Corporations § 14:10, 36 et seq. (3d ed. 2010); see also § 6.27(c)(3) RMBCA.

[125] For Germany, see Jochem Reichert and Marc-Philippe Weller, in Münchener Kommentar zum GmbH-Gesetz § 15 marg. n°. 393 (2d ed. Holger Fleischer & Wulf Goette eds., 2015); for Switzerland, see Art. 787 (3) OR.

[126] For further details on all of these, see Robert A. Ragazzo & Frances S. Fendler, Closely Held Business Organizations 396 et seqq. (2d ed. 2012).

[127] *Tett v. Phoenix Property and Investment Co Ltd* [1985] 1 BCC 99327, 99344.

their shares must prove bad faith on the part of the directors, and for Australia, where a refusal to grant consent is only unlawful when it amounts to fraud on the minority.[128] At least in theory, US courts offer slightly more protection, holding that consent to transfer may not be unreasonably or arbitrarily withheld.[129] However, as has been correctly observed in legal scholarship, reasonableness and arbitrariness are often in the eye of the beholder.[130] Under German law, there is considerable disagreement on the appropriate test: some authors grant the decision-making body an absolute discretion, others call for a proportionate and reasonable exercise of judgment, while still others demand good reason for the refusal to grant consent.[131]

5.4 Legal Assessment of Drag-Along and Tag-Along Clauses

Joint venture and private equity agreements in the guise of a closely held corporation often contain drag-along and tag-along clauses.[132] The former permit a shareholder to demand fellow shareholders offer their shares to a third party at the same price and the same conditions. The latter protects minority shareholders from being left behind when the majority shareholder decides to sell, enabling them to offer their shares for sale on the same terms as the majority shareholder.

Despite their widespread use, the enforceability of drag-along and tag-along rights has received little attention in legal scholarship, and relevant case law is also thin on the ground. A comparative analysis, while providing some valuable indications, does not yield any clear-cut answers. Authors in common law jurisdictions like Australia, Ireland, Malaysia, the UK, and the USA usually point out that there is no prohibition against these clauses and that, in principle, they are enforceable.[133] Recent UK legislation has even formally recognized them in the Growth and Infrastructure Act 2013 with respect to "employee shareholders."[134] Civil law countries in Europe seem to be more cautious; Japanese scholars have expressed doubts as to whether these clauses could be inserted into the articles of association rather than being restricted to shareholder agreements. In general, tag-along rights are subject to less criticism than drag-along rights.[135]

---

[128] For Australia, see Austin & Ramsay, *supra* note 103, marg. n°. 21.370.

[129] See, for example, *Rafe v. Hindin*, 288 N.Y.S.2d 662, 665 (App. Div.).

[130] Ragazzo & Fendler, *supra* note 126, at 399.

[131] On this, Reichert & Weller, *supra* note 125, § 15 GmbHG marg. n°. 408 et seqq.

[132] For further details on their form and commercial background, see Holger Fleischer & Stephan Schneider, "Tag along und Drag along-Klauseln in geschlossenen Kapitalgesellschaften", Der Betrieb 961 (2012); Isabel Sáez Lacave & Nuria Bermejo Gutiérrez, "Specific Investments, Opportunism and Corporate Contracts: A Theory of Tag-along and Drag-along Clauses", 11 Eur. Bus. Org. L. Rev. 423 (2010).

[133] See for example, Corporation Law Committee of the Association of the Bar of the City of New York, The Enforceability and Effectiveness of Typical Shareholders Agreement Provisions, Bus. Law. 1153, 1174 et seq. (2010).

[134] See the newly added s. 205A(1)(5)(j) Employment Rights Act 1996: "state whether the employee shares are subject to drag-along rights or tag-along rights and, if they are, explain the effect of the shares being so subject."

[135] On judicial review of drag along clauses as a means of preventing abuse under German law, Fleischer & Schneider, *supra* note 132, at 967.

In so far as drag-along rights are concerned, US case law seems to suggest that they are enforceable where they serve a reasonable corporate purpose.[136] One UK case from 2005 expressed some reservation in a particular case where the compulsory transfer restriction was only later included in the articles of association by means of an amendment.[137] An Italian court ruling from Milan upheld a drag-along clause under the condition that it ensure a fair price for the minority shareholders.[138] According to Article 2:192 Dutch NBW, the articles of association may specify situations when the shareholder is obliged to transfer shares—thus seeming to accommodate drag-along rights, although in the preparatory documents, the reform legislator cautioned against imposing duties on minority shareholders that were too far-reaching and unreasonable.[139]

6 SHAREHOLDER WITHDRAWAL AND EXPULSION

6.1 Withdrawal Rights

It is a common refrain in company law that a shareholder cannot unilaterally withdraw his investment from the company, effectively locking in the capital contribution. This "lock-in" feature presents a stark contrast to partnership law, where the default position allows all individual partners to disassociate from the firm.[140] Locked-in capital has been identified in legal scholarship as a crucial factor in the rise of the large public corporation in the nineteenth century, as it enabled managers to pursue long-term corporate goals irrespective of shareholders' personally motivated liquidity demands.[141] The inability of shareholders to unilaterally trigger dissolution is equally important in closely held corporations, as it ensures the stability of newly established business and prevents opportunistic shareholders from holding the company to ransom by threatening to leave or dissolve the firm.[142] This, in turn, is a precondition for the willingness of shareholders to provide specific investments.

There is, however, a considerable downside to capital lock-in in a close corporation.[143] Unlike shareholders in the public corporation, minority shareholders in a close corporation

---

[136] *Minnesota Invco of RSA #7, Inc. v. Midwest Wireless Holdings LLC*, 903 A.2d 786 (Del. Ch. 2006).

[137] *Constable v. Executive Connections Ltd* 2 BCLC (2005) 638, 652; also, Brenda Hannigan, "Altering the Articles to Allow for Compulsory Transfer: Dragging Minority Shareholders to a Reluctant Exit" J. Bus. L. 471 (2007).

[138] Tribunale Milano, April 1, 2008, Giur. comm. 2009, II, 1029.

[139] See Kamerstukken II 2008/09, 31 058, No. 6, 13; also, Erik Vorst, "Aandeelhoudersovereenkomst of statuten: balanceren voor de praktijkjurist", Weekblad voor privaatrecht, notariaat en registratie 447, 456 (2013).

[140] From a US perspective, §§ 601, 602 Revised Uniform Partnership Act; John A. C. Hetherington and Michael P. Dooley, "Illiquidity and Exploitation: A Proposed Statutory Solution to the remaining Close Corporation Problem", 63 Va. L. Rev. 1 (1977).

[141] See Margret M. Blair, "Locking in Capital: What Corporate Law Achieved for Business Organisations in the Nineteenth Century", 51 UCLA L. Rev. 387 (2003).

[142] See Edward B. Rock & Michael L. Wachter, "Waiting for the Omelet to Set: Match-Specific Assets and Minority Oppression in the Close Corporation", 24 J. Corp. L. 913, 919, 922 (1999): "beneficial lock-in."

[143] Id. at 923: "But the very provisions that protect against opportunistic exit create the problem of opportunistic lock-in."

are unable to follow the "Wall Street rule" and sell their shares on the open market. The illiquidity of their investment leaves them vulnerable to oppression by the majority shareholder, and without an effective exit route in cases of fundamental changes to the corporate structure. In the face of this, national legislators and courts have to make a policy choice whether and to what extent minority shareholders should be granted protection in the form of exit rights. Although almost every jurisdiction has chosen to do so, the individual approaches vary widely, both with respect to the preferred instrument, and their substantive requirements.

6.1.1 Categories of Exit Rights

Exit rights for minority shareholders come in different shapes and forms. Categorizing them is a difficult task, as some find their legal basis in company law, others in insolvency law, and still others in contract law. There are, however, two distinctions that may provide a workable systemization.[144] The first may be linked to the specific technique employed to provide an exit route: the legislator may empower the court to declare the dissolution of the company under certain conditions (winding-up remedy), or grant minority shareholders a statutory right to be bought out by the majority shareholder (buyout remedy or withdrawal right). These two remedies are not mutually exclusive. The second distinction concerns the substantive reasons for allowing a minority shareholder to exit: whether it be to provide relief from oppression or abuse by the majority shareholder (oppression remedy) or in the face of fundamental changes in the structure of the company initiated by the majority shareholder, even where these changes are not necessarily detrimental to the minority shareholder (appraisal rights).

6.1.2 Oppression Remedies

A majority shareholder can take unfair advantage of his position in a myriad of ways, which will be analysed separately.[145] The question here is whether these maneuvers give rise to a statutory remedy—which in most jurisdictions is a resounding yes. The equitable remedies available under English law are perhaps the best known internationally. Ever since the introduction of the Companies Act in 1862, company law has made provision for a winding up on just and equitable grounds.[146] Currently this provision is contained in s. 122(1)(g) Insolvency Act 1986 (IA 1986). The leading authority, *Ebrahimi v. Westbourne Galleries Ltd*, concerned the removal of a director in a "quasi-partnership" company made up of three members. Although the articles of association provided expressly for the removal of a director by ordinary resolution, the House of Lords decided that it was inequitable for the majority to exercise their power as they did, and ordered the company be wound up on just and equitable grounds.[147] Today, the classic winding-up remedy has taken a backseat to the

---

[144] See also the categorization by Paul Pieter de Vries, Exit Rights of Minority Shareholders in a Private Limited Company 7 et seq. (2010): "Exit rights can be divided into the following four categories: (a) winding-up remedies; (b) oppression remedies; (c) appraisal rights; and (d) exit rights at will."

[145] See below, 7.1.   [146] Mayson, French & Ryan, *supra* note 28, at 583 et seqq.

[147] *Ebrahimi v. Westbourne Galleries Ltd* [1972] 2 WLR 1289.

unfair prejudice regime set out in s. 994 CA 2006. This may see the court order the majority shareholder, or the company itself, to purchase the shares of a minority shareholder to remedy demonstrated unfair and prejudicial treatment.[148] Similar oppression remedies have also evolved in the US, where many corporation law statutes now expressly empower the courts to dissolve a company on application from a minority shareholder where the directors of that company are guilty of fraud, gross mismanagement, or the oppression of minority shareholders.[149] Instead of an involuntary dissolution, courts can, and in practice most commonly do, order a buyout of the aggrieved party's shares.[150]

Among the European civil law jurisdictions, the Scandinavian jurisdictions have historically been more restrictive with regard to exit rights for minority shareholders.[151] Compulsory dissolution under Danish and Finnish law is confined to cases of serious abuse of majority powers. A court-ordered redemption of shares by the majority shareholder requires the minority to demonstrate either a breach of the Companies Act or the articles of association, or a deliberate abuse of power that is likely to continue. Only the Norwegian Private Limited Companies Act offers broader protection, providing aggrieved shareholders with a right to withdraw from the company not only in cases of abuse of power, but also in cases of serious and permanent conflicts of interest regarding the running of the company, unless the redemption procedure would seriously harm the activities of the company, or would otherwise be unreasonable.[152]

The Dutch approach is also worth mentioning, with its detailed rules for resolving shareholder disputes, known locally as *geschillenregeling*.[153] The basic rule is contained in Article 2:243 NBW, which states that a shareholder, whose rights or interests are harmed by the conduct of one or more co-shareholders in such a way that continued membership can no longer be reasonably expected, may file a legal claim in court against those co-shareholders for his withdrawal, requiring them to buy out his shares. In Swiss company law, Article 821(3) OR provides that any shareholder of a GmbH may apply to the court to dissolve the company for good cause, with case law recognizing continued abuse of power or trust as good cause.[154] Along the same lines, the German courts also recognize a withdrawal right as a mandatory and inalienable right in a GmbH if there is good cause ("wichtiger Grund").[155] The doctrinal source of this exit right can be found in §314 German Civil Code, which allows for the termination of contractual agreements without notice for good cause. The requirements for good cause are often satisfied in cases of majority abuse,[156] that is when the terminating party, in

---

[148] Mayson, French & Ryan, *supra* note 28, at 567 et seqq.

[149] Ragazzo & Fendler, *supra* note 126, at 627 et seqq.

[150] Id., at 639 et seqq.; see also §§ 226, 352, 353 DGCL.

[151] For further details, see Mette Neville, Conflicts in Small and Medium-Sized Enterprises, in Shareholder Conflicts 87, 102 et seqq. (Paul Krüger Andersen, Nis Jul Clausen, & Rolf Skog eds., 2006).

[152] Mette Neville, Shareholder Conflicts in the European Private Company (SPE), in The European Private Company—Societas Privata Europaea (SPE) 193, 228 et seq. (Heribert Hirte & Christoph Teichmann eds., 2013).

[153] For more, see de Vries, *supra* note 144, at 253 et seqq.

[154] See Christoph Stäubli, in Basler Kommentar, OR II Art. 821 marg. n°. 19 (4th ed. 2012).

[155] Lutz Strohn, in Münchener Kommentar zum GmbH-Gesetz § 34 marg. n°. 178 and relevant notes (2d ed., Holger Fleischer & Wulf Goette eds., 2015).

[156] Strohn, *supra* note 155, § 34 GmbHG marg. n°. 186.

light of all the circumstances of the case at hand and weighing the interests of both parties, cannot reasonably be expected to continue the contractual relationship until its agreed end.[157] In addition to this individual right for any shareholder, §61 GmbHG grants (minority) shareholders holding at least 10% of the share capital the right to apply for a court-ordered dissolution for good cause.

6.1.3 *Appraisal Rights*

Moving on from oppressive actions to "no-fault situations," we enter the field of appraisal rights. These allow shareholders who voted against an extraordinary corporate action, such as a structural change to the company, the right to sell their shares back to the company at a judicially appraised value. Unlike oppression remedies, appraisal rights are not contingent on a demonstration of illegality, fraud against the minority, or breach of fiduciary duties. Appraisal rights play an important role in stock corporation law, most notably in the United States, Japan, France, Germany, and Italy.[158] Their scope in the law of close corporations is more limited, however, a matter not facilitated by their being scattered throughout different legal or legislative sources, instead of presented as one coherent system. One exception in this regard is Italy, which introduced an extensive list of appraisal rights in Article 2473(1) C.c. in 2004. This provision entitles a shareholder of an s.r.l. to leave the company if he is opposed to a change of the corporate purpose or structure, a merger, a division, a transfer of the registered office to another country or a transaction that leads to fundamental modification of the company's objects. Similar rules can be found in Spain and Portugal.[159] In Germany, the legal landscape is less clearly arranged for appraisal rights: according to the Reorganization of Companies Act (UmwG), a shareholder has a right to exit in case of a merger (§§29 et seqq., 36 UmwG), division (§125 UmwG), asset transfer (§§176, 177 UmwG) or change in company form (§§207 ff. UmwG). Moreover, the inalienable withdrawal right mentioned above may also be triggered by an alteration of the objects clause, or the integration of the GmbH as a subsidiary into a corporate group.[160] A final illustration comes to us from the original Draft Statute for a European Private Company (SPE) proposed by the European Commission, which combined appraisal rights and oppression remedies in Article 18. This provision, which was later deleted, would have allowed the shareholder to withdraw from the SPE if serious harm to the interests of the shareholder was caused by: (1) the SPE being deprived of a significant part of its assets; (2) the transfer of the registered office of the SPE to another Member State; (3) a substantial change of the activities of the SPE; or (4) failure to distribute dividends for at least three years, even though the SPE's financial position would have permitted it.

---

[157] BGHZ 116, 359, 369.
[158] For further details, see Reinier Kraakman et al., The Anatomy of Corporate Law 88 (3d ed., 2017).
[159] For Spain see Art. 346 LSC, for Portugal Art. 240 CSC.
[160] For further details, see Strohn, *supra* note 155, § 34 GmbHG marg. n°. 183 et seqq.

6.1.4 The Right to Exit "at Will"

A final question is whether the legislator should go even further and grant minority shareholders a right to exit "at will." This has recently been advocated by several scholars— albeit subject to certain conditions.[161] However, successful examples of this approach are scant in comparative company law practice. In 2009, the Russian law on limited liability companies abolished one of the rare examples which had allowed a shareholder to exit at any time.[162] Comparative support for a more liberal approach is thus confined to Italy, which introduced a right to exit "at will" (*diritto di recesso*) in Article 2473(2) C.c. for private limited liability companies established for an indefinite term. This right can be exercised at any time, with a notice period of 180 days. The articles of association may provide for a longer notice period, but no longer than one year. In contrast, the majority of common law and civil law jurisdictions oppose the idea of facilitating an exit from close corporations. In England and Wales, the Law Commission investigated the matter in 1997, before denying a case for reform, stating: "In our view, there are strong economic arguments against allowing shareholders to exit at will. Also as a matter of principle, such a right would fundamentally contravene the sanctity of contract, binding the members and the company."[163] Similar concerns have been expressed in Germany, where the prevailing doctrine strictly rejects the idea of an exit right "at will," arguing that it would infringe on the venerable principle of *pacta sunt servanda*, and may potentially pose a significant risk of abuse and endanger the financial stability of small businesses.[164]

6.2 Expulsion of a Shareholder

The plight of the oppressed minority shareholder is one story, the plague of the obstructive shareholder yet another. The latter raises the question as to whether the troublemaker whose behaviour is detrimental to the company can be expelled for good cause. A comparative analysis reveals two basic approaches to this problem.

A large number of jurisdictions provide for a statutory expulsion right for good cause, irrespective of any expulsion clause in the articles of association. This group includes Switzerland, Portugal, Spain, Belgium, and the Netherlands. Again, Dutch law stands out with its detailed rules for resolving shareholder disputes (*geschillenregeling*):[165] Its basic provision in Article 2:336 NBW permits one or more shareholders who solely or jointly hold at least one-third of the issued share capital to obtain a court order that another shareholder whose conduct has harmed the interests of the corporation, in such a way that a continued share ownership can no longer reasonably be tolerated, transfer his shares to the plaintiffs. Germany must be included here as well: Even though an expulsion right has not

---

[161] See Harm-Jan de Kluiver, "Private Ordering and Buy-Out Remedies within Private Company Law: Towards a New Balance between Fairness and Welfare?", 8 Eur. Bus. Org. L. Rev. 103, 111 ff. (2007); Neville, *supra* note 152, at 193, 233 et seqq.

[162] See Novak, Korporativniĭ ûrist 2009, n° 6, 24 et seq.

[163] Law Commission, Shareholder Remedies, 1997, Cmnd 3769, marg. n°. 3.66.

[164] For example, Hans-Friedrich Müller, Das Austrittsrecht des GmbH-Gesellschafters 41 et seqq. (1995).

[165] See de Vries, *supra* note 144, at 253 et seqq.

been provided for in the Limited Liability Companies Act of 1892, the courts have filled this gap by drawing an analogy to a provision in the law of general partnership[166]—a nice example of a popular strategy in Germany to resort to principles of partnership law in order to find appropriate solutions for incorporated partnerships.[167] As a last illustration, the EU Commission's Draft Statute for a European Private Company (SPE) also provided for an expulsion right: According to its Article 17, the competent court may, on the basis of a resolution of the shareholders and an application by the SPE, order the expulsion of a shareholder if he has caused serious harm to the SPE's interest or if the continuation of the shareholder as a member of the SPE is detrimental to its proper operation. The overall policy behind a statutory exclusion right is that the proper functioning of the business enjoys priority and that its value as a going concern should be preserved and not destroyed by a dissolution of the company.

A second group of countries acknowledges expulsion clauses in the articles of association, but contains no statutory provision to that end and refuses to supplement with judge-made law in the absence of a provision in the corporate charter. This is the case, for example, in the United Kingdom where the matter is neither covered by the CA 2006 nor by the Model Articles for private companies, although the articles of association or shareholder agreements may make provision for the termination of membership.[168] Typical grounds would include prejudicial behaviour on the part of the offending shareholder. Similarly, in Australia, a minority shareholder cannot ordinarily be expelled, whether for good cause or otherwise, unless the company's internal governance rules or a shareholder agreement so provide[169]—which is rare. However, a court may order a buy-out under the statutory oppression remedy in cases where the minority shareholder has acted in a manner contrary to the interests of the shareholders as a whole or in a way that is unfairly prejudicial to or unfairly discriminatory against individual shareholders. Italy and France follow a similar route, but do alert business founders to the option of an exclusion clause in their codifications: Article 2473-*bis* Italian C.c. stipulates that the articles of association of an s.r.l. may provide for expulsion for good cause in specific cases, and Article L. 227-16 French C. com. permits the articles of association of a simplified stock corporation (SAS) to specify the conditions for expelling a shareholder. Interestingly, a couple of years ago, the French Court of Cassation decided that the shareholder is entitled to vote on (and in all probability: against) his own exclusion,[170] while German courts reached exactly the opposite result in cases of expulsion for good cause.[171] The principal reason why all these countries do not provide a statutory mechanism for expelling shareholders from close corporations against their will is probably rooted in their perception of shareholdership: In the common law tradition, a share is a property right which cannot be expropriated, save where this is provided for in the constitution of the company.[172] This view corresponds with the venerable French

---

[166] See BGHZ 9, 157, 161 et seqq.

[167] See Holger Fleischer, "Zur Lückenfüllung des GmbH-Rechts durch das Recht der Personengesellschaften", GmbHR 1121 (2008).

[168] See Davies & Worthington, *supra* note 33, marg. n°. 19–11.

[169] For limitations on the power to alter the articles in order to expropriate the shares of the minority see Austin & Ramsey, *supra* note 103, marg. n°. 10.070.

[170] See Cass. com., 23.10.2007, JCP E 2007, 2433.   [171] See BGHZ 9, 157, 178.

[172] See *North West Transportation Co Ltd v. Beatty* (1887) 12 App Cas 589; from an Australian perspective *Gambotto v. WCP Ltd* (1995) 182 CLR 432.

company law principle that a shareholder has a fundamental right to remain a member of the company,[173] which shifts the emphasis from the proprietary towards the personal element of shareholdership.

In order to provide a truly complete picture, one should add that a few countries have also introduced squeeze-out rights which enable shareholders who own more than 90% of the share capital to redeem the shares of minority shareholders without any further requirements. This is the case, for instance, in Sweden and Austria.[174] By contrast, many other countries confine an unconditional squeeze-out right to public or listed corporations.[175]

7 SHAREHOLDER CONFLICTS

Shareholder conflicts pose possibly the greatest threat to the continued existence of a small firm, and they have, rightly, been called the Achilles heel of close corporations.[176] Case law in many countries abounds with graphic examples of feuding shareholders whose differences have resulted in disputes as bitter as between arguing spouses in an acrimonious divorce.[177]

7.1 Oppression by Majority Shareholder

The plight of the minority shareholder in a close corporation is a global phenomenon. Minority shareholders are often depicted as particularly vulnerable to exploitation, given the principle of majority voting and the lack of an effective exit option. Examples of squeeze-out techniques employed by the majority shareholder include excessive retention of profits,[178] inflated directors' remuneration,[179] and unbalanced transactions to the detriment of the company[180].

7.1.1 Opportunities for and Limits of Self-Protection

Forewarned is forearmed, or so one should think. A minority shareholder who is aware of the risk of opportunistic behaviour by the majority can seek to protect himself either through the articles of association or through a shareholder agreement. To this end, most

[173] See Cass. com., 12.3.1996, Rev. soc. 1996, 554.
[174] See Susanne Kalss & Johannes Zollner, Squeeze out § 1 GesAusG marg n°. 22 (2007).
[175] See Holger Fleischer in Großkommentar zum Aktiengesetz § 327a marg. n°. 8 with further references (4th ed. Klaus Hopt & Herbert Wiedemann eds., 2007).
[176] Expressly, Bachmann et al., *supra* note 10, at 31; Neville, *supra* note 152, at 87, 91.
[177] See Davies & Worthington, *supra* note 33, marg. n°. 20–11: "Small companies emulate marriages in the frequency and bitterness of their breakdown"; in detail Martha M. Ertman, "Marriage as a Trade: Bridging the Private/Private Distinction", 36 Harv. C.R.-C.L. L. Rev. 79 (2001).
[178] See OLG Brandenburg, ZIP 2009, 1955; Cass. com., Rev. sov. 2004, 337; *Re Mc Carthy Surfacing Ltd* [2009] 1 BCLC 622, 651 et seqq.; *Brodie v. Jordan*, 857 N.E.2d 1076 (Mass. 2006).
[179] See BGHZ 111, 224; Cass. com., Rev. soc. 2012, 38; *Irvine v. Irvine* [2007] 1 BCLC 349; *Carlson v. Hallinan*, 925 A.2d 506 (Del. Ch. 2006).
[180] See Bachmann et al., *supra* note 10, at 37 et seq.

jurisdictions permit a great variety of self-help measures, ranging from nomination rights and representation on the board to veto rights, supermajority requirements for certain transactions and buy-sell provisions or withdrawal rights.[181]

Despite the general availability of self-help measures, it is today widely acknowledged that supplementary minority protection by statutory or case law is indispensable. The oft lamented lack of preventative planning is due to several inter-related factors: Close corporation participants are often linked by family or other personal relationships, resulting in "overtrust" or an unwillingness to rock the boat in bargaining hard for protection.[182] Moreover, they may be subject to over-optimism at the outset of a common venture, thus underestimating the potential for future dissension.[183] Similarly, they may be unable to write a contract that covers all eventualities due to their inability to foresee the countless variations of oppressive conduct.[184] In addition, having complete contracts drawn up for protection may be too expensive or even prohibitive for small businesses, especially at their inception.[185] Finally, there may be no opportunity at all to bargain for protection for certain shareholders who received their stock via gift or inheritance.[186] Given these findings, which appear to be well founded in empirical research, a large majority of legislators and courts worldwide have crafted protections for oppressed shareholders in close corporations. However, not everyone has been persuaded so far. A notable exception is Delaware, which refuses outright to provide additional protection for minority shareholders. In the words of the Delaware Court of Chancery: "It would be inappropriate judicial legislation for this Court to fashion a special judicially created rule for minority investors [. . .] when there are no negotiated special provisions in the certificate of incorporation, bylaws, or stockholder agreements."[187]

7.1.2 *Standards of Conduct for Majority Shareholders*

The resolution of minority oppression cases depends crucially on the standards of conduct for majority shareholders which have evolved over time. Taking a global perspective, one can discern converging trajectories, but also gradual differences.

7.1.2.1 *Fiduciary Duty and Duty of Loyalty*

A number of jurisdictions use the concept of fiduciary duty or its civil law equivalent, the duty of loyalty, as the basis of their standards of conduct for majority shareholders. Two

---

[181] For a list of self-help measures available under Australian and British law, see Elizabeth Jane Boros, Minority Shareholders' Remedies 104 et seqq. (1995).

[182] See Bachmann et al., *supra* note 10, at 48.

[183] See Melvin Eisenberg, "The Limits of Cognition and the Limits of Contracts", 47 Stan. L. Rev. 211, 251 (1995).

[184] See Bachmann et al., *supra* note 10, at 48 et seq.; fundamentally, Thomas S. Ulen, "Cognitive Imperfections and the Economic Analysis of Law", 12 Hamline L. Rev. 385, 386 (1989).

[185] See Brian Cheffins, Company Law: Theory, Structure and Operation 273 (1997); similarly Davies & Worthington, *supra* note 33, marg. n°. 20–11; Robert A. Ragazzo, "Towards a Delaware Common Law of Closely Held Corporations", 77 Wash. U. L. Q. 1099, 1130 (1999): "One can simply not expect a two-person dry-cleaning operation to run with the same level of attorney supervision as a Fortune 500 company."

[186] See Douglas K. Moll, "Shareholder Oppression & Reasonable Expectations: Of Change, Gifts, and Inheritance in Close Corporation Disputes", 86 Minn. L. Rev. 717, 763 et seqq. (2002).

[187] *Nixon v. Blackwell*, 626 A.2d 1366 (Del. 1993).

decisions handed down independently, but at almost the same time by the highest courts of the United States and Germany promoted the idea of fiduciary duty between shareholders, finding that shareholders in a closed corporation owe a duty of loyalty to each other, as well as to the corporation. In a landmark decision that still holds today, the Massachusetts Supreme Judicial Court ruled: "We hold that stockholders in the close corporation owe one another substantially the same fiduciary duty in the operation of the enterprise that partners owe to one another."[188] Five weeks later, the German Federal Court of Justice ruled that "the corporate law fiduciary duty governs not only the relationship between shareholders and the GmbH, but also the relationship between shareholders themselves."[189] Swiss legislation recently codified the fiduciary duty between GmbH shareholders in Article 803(2) OR.[190] The Dutch legislator has established a similar standard of conduct, mandating in Article 2:8 (1) NBW that all legal persons and those who pursuant to the law and the articles of association are involved in its organization must behave towards each other in accordance with what is required by standards of reasonableness and fairness (*redelijkeid en billijkheid*).[191] Finally, Greek company law resorts to the principle of equal treatment as a functional equivalent of fiduciary duties.

7.1.2.2 Abuse of Rights

Other countries like France and those following the French tradition shy away from recognizing a duty of loyalty between majority and minority shareholder in a close corporation. However, they do not leave the oppressed minority shareholder without protection, drawing on the concept of *abus de majorité* transposed from civil law notions of *abus de droit*.[192] This is also the case in Italy where the courts tend to invoke the concept of *abuso di maggioranza*, especially in cases of shareholder voting,[193] while many scholars favour good faith and fair dealing (*correttezza e buona fede*) as a guiding principle in shareholder disputes.[194] Spain belongs to this group as well, applying the notion of *abuso de mayoria* to fight minority oppression.[195] Finally, the Nordic countries have included provisions in their respective Companies Acts, addressing an abuse of voting rights.[196] The Norwegian Private Limited Companies Act, for instance, does not recognize a general duty of loyalty between shareholders, but rather a specific provision on the "abuse of authority of the general meeting": According to §5-21, the general meeting of the company cannot adopt any resolution which may give individual shareholders or other parties an unreasonable advantage at the expense of other shareholders of the company.

---

[188] *Donahue v. Rodd Electrotype Co.*, 328 N.E.2d 505, 515 (Mass. 1975).   [189] BGHZ 65, 15, 18.

[190] See Amstutz & Chappuis, *supra* note 76, § 803 marg. n°. 6 et seqq.

[191] See Maarten J. Kroeze, in Asser Serie, Rechtspersonenrecht 206 et seqq. (2015).

[192] See Cozian, Viandier, & Deboissy, *supra* note 27, marg. n°. 402; recent monograph Anne-Laure Champetier de Ribes-Justeau, Les abus de majorité, de minorité et d'égalité (Dalloz 2010).

[193] See Mario Campobasso, Diritto delle società 345 with further references (8th ed. 2012).

[194] See Campobasso, *supra* note 193, at 344.

[195] See Javier Megías López, "Opresión y obstruccionismo en las sociedades de capital cerradas: abuso de mayoría y de minoría", 47 Anuario jurídico y económico escurialense 13 (2014).

[196] See Filip Truyen, Shareholder Conflicts in Small and Medium Sized Companies—Remedies for Shareholders' Abuse of Authority and Improper Retention of Dividends, in Shareholder Conflicts 131, 135 (Paul Krüger Andersen, Nis Jul Clausen, & Rolf Skog eds., 2006).

7.1.2.3 Unfair Prejudice and Minority Oppression

Under UK, Irish, and Australian law, a majority shareholder is not treated as a fiduciary, and does not owe fiduciary duties to the company or to minority shareholders.[197] Rather, the law begins with the principle that any shareholder is free to vote in his or her own self-interest.[198] However, special statutory provisions place some constraints on the majority shareholder's exercise of its voting rights and other relevant conduct. If an act or omission by or on behalf of the company or a resolution of the shareholders meeting is unfairly prejudicial or unfairly discriminatory against a minority shareholder, this shareholder may complain to a court under the unfair prejudice remedy in s. 994 UK CA 2006[199] or the oppression remedy in s. 232 Australian Corporations Act.[200]

7.1.2.4 Intensity of Judicial Review

Fiduciary duty, duty of loyalty, abuse of rights, unfair prejudice, and minority oppression: every jurisdiction has its own approach to combating overreach by the majority shareholder in close corporations. From a functional perspective, the crucial question is not which doctrinal label is attached to a particular legal instrument, but rather the intensity of judicial review. In this respect, there are differences in degree. The duty of loyalty under German case law demands that the majority shareholder consider the interests of the corporation and membership interests of co-shareholders.[201] This applies to the exercise and actual influence of rights and other entitlements within the close corporation, but does not completely prohibit the consideration of personal interests. UK courts define unfair prejudice as a breach of good faith:

> Unfairness for the purposes of s. 994 Companies Act 2006 is not to be judged by reference to subjective notions of fairness, but rather by testing whether, applying equitable principles, the majority has acted, or is proposing to act, in a manner which equity would regard as contrary to good faith.[202]

Applying this test, the courts tend to protect the legitimate expectations of (minority) shareholders underlying the formation of their association, even where these are not explicitly included in the contract.[203] In the US, courts are split on the issue as to what extent, if any, implied agreements between shareholders or unspoken expectations are protected by fiduciary duties.[204] In France, the classical definition of abuse of rights is provided in a leading case from 1961, according to which a resolution constitutes abuse when it is made

---

[197] See Paul Davies, Introduction to Company Law 231 (2002): "The common law does not perceive the controlling shareholders to be in a fiduciary position towards non-controlling shareholders, so that basis for the individual shareholder to restrain the power of the majority as it reveals itself in shareholder decision-making is not available."

[198] See *Carruth v. ICI Ltd* [1937] AC 707, 765.

[199] See Mayson, French, & Ryan, *supra* note 28, at 577 et seqq.

[200] See Austin and Ramsay, *supra* note 103, marg. n°. 10.430 et seq.

[201] See BGHZ 65, 15, 18 et seq.   [202] *Re Guidezone Ltd* [2000] 2 BCLC 321, 355.

[203] See *Re Saul D. Harrison & Sons Plc* [1995] 1 BCLC 14, 19.

[204] For further details, see Bauman, Palmiter, & Partnoy, *supra* note 84, at 385 et seq.

"contrary to the general interests of the corporation and with the sole purpose of benefiting the members of the majority to the detriment of the minority"[205].

7.1.3 Legal Remedies for Minority Shareholders

It's the enforcement, stupid! Standards of conduct for majority shareholders alone do not suffice, but must rather be supplemented by effective means of redress for minority shareholders. In this respect, civil and common law jurisdictions have crafted their own remedies.

7.1.3.1 Actions Challenging the Validity of Shareholders' Resolutions

In most continental European legal systems, as well as those of Argentina and Japan, outvoted minority shareholders may bring an action to set aside a resolution of the shareholder meeting that violates the law or the articles of association. Usually, violations of the law include violations of general company law principles such as abuse of rights, duty of loyalty, and equal treatment of shareholders. This rather broad scope makes actions to set aside shareholders' resolutions, or nullity suits as they are also referred to, potentially the most forceful weapon available to minority shareholders.

Technically, the regime of nullity suits is regulated differently from jurisdiction to jurisdiction.[206] The German GmbH Act does not contain specific provisions to deal with unlawful shareholder resolutions; to fill this gap, courts draw on §§241 et seq. Stock Corporation Act by analogy.[207] The Swiss Code of Obligations states in Article 808c that the provisions for setting aside shareholder resolutions in stock corporations also apply mutatis mutandis to private limited liability companies. Other countries, for example Austria (§§41–44 Austrian Act on Limited Liability Companies) or Italy (Article 2479-*ter* C.c.), have an independent regime for actions against shareholder resolutions in private limited liability companies. Still other jurisdictions, namely France (Article L. 235-1 C. com.), provide a single set of rules for nullification suits across all forms of commercial companies. By contrast, in UK law, the concept of a general shareholders' right of review for majority decisions is completely unknown. Litigation is only available for resolutions pertaining to the transformation of a public company into a private company, for variations in share capital, and the purchase of a company's own shares (ss. 98, 633, 721 CA 2006). For all other matters, the minority shareholder only has recourse to general legal principles and remedies, such as an unfair prejudice petition. Similar findings can be made in Ireland, Australia, and the US. Given this great divide between civil and common law jurisdictions, the European Commission's SPE proposal saw no room for successful harmonization, providing in Article 28(4) that the shareholders' right to challenge shareholders' resolutions is determined according to the law of the individual state.

---

[205] Cass. com., 18.4.1961, D. 1961, 661: "contrairement à l'intérêt général de la société et dans l'unique dessein de favoriser les membres de la majorité au détriment de la minorité."

[206] For a comparative overview, Holger Fleischer, "Das Beschlussmängelrecht in der GmbH: Rechtsdogmatik—Rechtsvergleichung—Rechtspolitik", GmbHR 1289 (2013).

[207] See RGZ 85, 311, 313 et seq.

7.1.3.2 *Claims for Compensation*

In almost all jurisdictions, minority shareholders' claims for compensation are divided into direct and derivative actions. Grounds for a direct action arise, for example, under German GmbH law when a shareholder suffers individual, direct loss over and above the indirect losses suffered due to damage to the corporation's assets.[208] In the UK, a shareholder whose rights have been affected by the company can seek to have these rights enforced by a personal action; however, the no reflective loss principle rules out the recovery of indirect loss.[209] In France, Article L. 223-22 C. com. allows shareholders of a SARL to file an action for the compensation of personal losses distinct from losses suffered by the corporation resulting from a breach of duty by corporation directors[210]; however, this kind of direct action is often extremely difficult to enforce in practice.

Derivative shareholder actions are recognized in German GmbH law as an extension of the *actio pro socio* found in the law of partnerships, although they are not codified.[211] They permit individual shareholders to bring an action against other shareholders on behalf of the corporation, to the extent that the corporation does not pursue this action itself. In the UK, this approach has been codified in s. 260 et seq. CA 2006, adopted from the famous decision in *Foss v. Harbottle*, allowing a shareholder to pursue a derivative action against directors of the corporation for actions that breach their fiduciary duty as illegal or *ultra vires*. The shareholder must apply to the court for leave to pursue this action, which must then pass a two-stage test to ensure the application is being made in good faith and to prevent frivolous actions against the corporation. However, the derivative action, despite being extended to include actions for simple negligence, continues to operate only on the legal periphery, as its practical application is extensively overshadowed by the remedy for unfair prejudice.[212] Shareholders of a French SARL can use the actions for compensation (*action sociale ut singuli*) afforded by Article L. 223-22 (3) C. com., if a director has breached his duty causing loss or damage to the corporation.[213] In Italy, Article 2476 (3) C.c. provides that any shareholder may file an action against the corporation's director.

Drawing a line between direct actions and derivative actions can lead to greater problems for closed corporations than for stock corporations.[214] Some jurisdictions in the US therefore tend to allow direct actions in all cases of breach of fiduciary duties to the detriment of minority shareholders,[215] while others do not differentiate between direct and derivative actions.[216]

---

[208] See BGHZ 95, 330, 340; Hanno Merkt, in Münchener Kommentar zum GmbH-Gesetz § 13 marg. n°. 310 (2d ed. Holger Fleischer & Wulf Goette eds., 2015).

[209] Davies & Worthington, *supra* note 33, marg. n°. 17–13.

[210] See Merle, *supra* note 52, marg. n°. 199.   [211] See BGH NJW 1990, 2627, 2628.

[212] See Arad Reisberg, "Shadows of the Past and Back to the Future: Part 11 of the UK Companies Act 2006 (in)action", 6 Eur. Company & Fin. L. Rev. 219, 231 (2009).

[213] See Merle, *supra* note 52, marg. n°. 199.

[214] See Bachmann et al., *supra* note 10, at 66.

[215] See *Crosby v. Beam*, 548 N.E.2d 217 (Ohio 1989).

[216] See *Bagdon v. Bridgestone/Firestone, Inc.*, 916 F.2d 379, 384 (7th Cir. 1990).

7.1.3.3 Exit Rights

Exit rights, whether withdrawal or appraisal rights, are an additional remedy for minority shareholders and have already been discussed in a separate section.[217]

7.1.3.4 Oppression Remedies

In common law jurisdictions, minority shareholders may seek a special remedy in cases of oppression. In the UK, the main remedial provision is found in s. 994 CA 2006, allowing a shareholder to apply to the court where membership interests have been unfairly prejudiced in the conduct of the company's affairs. If the court finds that there has been unfair prejudice, it can prescribe any remedy to rectify the situation, though the normal solution is to order the person responsible or the company itself to buy out the petitioner at fair value.[218] Similarly, many modern US corporation statutes give the courts power to dissolve a corporation in response to a suit from a minority shareholder if the majority shareholder is found guilty of fraud or oppression.[219] Likewise, s. 232 Australian Corporations Act allows a court to grant relief if it is of the opinion that a certain conduct was oppressive, prejudicial, or unfairly discriminatory against minority shareholders.[220]

7.2 Ex Post Opportunism by Minority Shareholders

A majority shareholder, in principle, does not need special protection, as his majority voting power usually carries the power to remedy any disadvantageous situations himself. There are, however, situations in which the majority shareholder is dependent on the cooperation of minority shareholders. This is often the case where legislation imposes a unanimous vote requirement for specific resolutions or where shareholders have a statutory right of veto. A similar situation arises where the majority shareholder does not possess a sufficient qualified majority to make changes to the articles of association.

7.2.1 Standards of Conduct for Minority Shareholders

There is widespread consensus worldwide that the majority shareholder is entitled to relief against various forms of ex-post opportunism by a minority shareholder. The doctrinal approaches differ, however, presenting a mirror image of the resolution of minority oppression cases discussed above. German courts have extended the duty of loyalty to minority shareholders with blocking power.[221] In the Netherlands, the standard of fairness and reasonableness set in Article 2:8 (1) NBW applies equally to minority shareholders. In France, the majority shareholder has increasingly called upon the court-based remedy of abuse of rights (*abus de minorité*) in recent years.[222] The same is true for Spain (*abuso de*

---

[217] See above, 6.1.   [218] See Mayson, French, & Ryan, *supra* note 28, at 577.
[219] See Ragazzo and Fendler, *supra* note 126, at 627 et seqq.
[220] See Austin and Ramsay, *supra* note 103, marg. n°. 10.430 et seq.
[221] See BGHZ 129, 136.
[222] See Anne-Laure Champetier de Ribes-Justeau, Les abus de majorité, de minorité et d'égalité (2010).

minoría)[223] and, albeit to a lesser degree, Italy (*abuso di minoranza*).[224] In Japan, majority shareholders may also invoke the general abuse of rights rule. In the UK and Australia, oppressive conduct of a minority shareholder may form the basis of an application to the court under the unfair prejudice or oppression remedy.[225] Likewise, US courts may apply the provisions on oppressive actions contained in individual state statutes.[226]

7.2.2 Enforcement Issues

The effective remedy of minority shareholder misconduct is more controversial. The oft-cited case of a minority shareholder who uses veto powers to block an urgently needed capital increase in order to extract private benefits, may serve as an illustration. There is a range of potential solutions to this scenario. A first solution is to simply disregard the votes of a minority shareholder who exercises his voting rights in a disloyal or abusive way. This approach finds some support in German case law and academic writing,[227] though it is far from being unanimously accepted. French and Belgian courts, by contrast, are hesitant to replace a resolution of a shareholders' meeting with a court order, since this would arguably violate the right of shareholders to vote. As an expedient compromise solution, the courts appoint an ad hoc agent (*mandataire* ad hoc) who is instructed to vote in place of and in the name of the recalcitrant minority shareholder[228]—a dogmatic construction derided as hypocritical by legal scholars.[229] Alternatively and more pragmatically, one may think of initiating an expulsion procedure against the recalcitrant minority shareholder, as has been proposed and successfully implemented in Greece and Portugal. Less complicated solutions are available in most common law jurisdictions where capital increases are generally a matter for the board of directors and do not require shareholder approval, unless otherwise specified by the articles of association or a shareholder agreement. In the latter case, a majority shareholder in the UK, Ireland, and Australia may apply to the courts for equitable relief under the unfair prejudice or oppression remedy. It is well settled that access to this remedy is not limited to minority shareholders.[230]

7.3 Shareholder Deadlocks

Shareholder conflicts in close corporations can also arise for reasons other than opportunistic behaviour by majority or minority shareholders. These involve deadlocks at the shareholder and director level, for which neither or both parties may be responsible, but which make continuing commercial operation difficult or even cast doubt on the capacity of the

---

[223]   See Javier Megías López, "Opresión y obstruccionismo en las sociedades de capital cerradas: abuso de mayoría y de minoría", 47 Anuario jurídico y económico escurialense 13 (2014).

[224]   See Campobasso, *supra* note 193, at 345.

[225]   See, for example, *Parkinson v. Eurofinance Group Ltd* [2001] BCC 551.

[226]   See Douglas Moll and Robert A. Ragazzo, The Law of Closely Held Corporations Chapter 7.101 [D] [e] under the heading "Oppression of the Majority by the Minority" (2009).

[227]   See Wolfgang Zöllner, in Baumbach/Hueck, GmbH-Gesetz § 47 marg. n°. 108 (20th ed. 2012).

[228]   See Cass. com., 9.3.1993, JCPE 1993, II, 448.

[229]   Cozian, Viandier, & Deboissy, *supra* note 27, marg. n°. 383.

[230]   See note 225.

corporation's organs to act. Legal practice shows that these deadlock situations most fre-quently occur in two-member corporations where each shareholder owns 50% of the shares.[231]

7.3.1 Contractual Safeguards

Company law experts worldwide recommend that special arrangements to resolve deadlocks be included in the articles of association or in shareholder agreements.[232] Their practical use, however, varies considerably and they have only become standard procedure in certain types of cases such as joint venture contracts. Voting deadlocks on specific matters may be overcome by provisions stipulating that one member, for example the (rotating) chairperson of the general shareholders' meeting, holds the casting vote, or that the resolution is referred to another corporate body, particularly the supervisory board or advisory board, or that the decision should be made by an arbitrator. In case of permanent deadlock, the shareholders can make provision for a right of exit for good cause, or a duty to transfer shares to the other shareholder(s). A typical arrangement is a buy-sell procedure: Shareholder A, the party wishing to leave or take over the company, initiates the procedures by making an offer, ei-ther to sell all his shares to Shareholder B, or to purchase all of B's shares for a specific price. Shareholder B can then freely decide to buy or sell.

7.3.2 Conflict Resolution through Statutory or Case Law

Where voluntary mechanisms are lacking, the Gordian knot may only be severed through recourse to legislation or case law.[233] This external intervention is justified by the fact that valuable resources would otherwise lie idle.[234] Most jurisdictions consider the *ultima ratio* to be compulsory dissolution of the corporation upon application to the court by one of the members. In Germany, case law has confirmed that irreconcilable differences between the members of a two-member GmbH or a deadlock at a shareholders meeting constitute good cause as defined in §61(1) GmbHG.[235] For these situations in the UK, courts have usually resorted to a winding up of the corporation in accordance with s. 124 IA 1986.[236] In France, the courts have spoken in favour of exceptional dissolution for disputes between shareholders in a corporation.[237] In the United States, s. 14.30(2) RMBCA provides a com-pulsory dissolution mechanism for deadlock situations, which has been adopted in different

---

[231] From a German perspective, Harald Knies, Das Patt zwischen den Gesellschaftern der zweigliedrigen GmbH (2005); from a French perspective Champetier de Ribes-Justeau, *supra* note 222, at 21.

[232] See Bachmann et al., *supra* note 10, at 76 et seq.

[233] Id., at 78.

[234] See Moll & Ragazzo, *supra* note 226, marg. n°. 7-149–7.150: "The conventional explanation for the harm of deadlock is that socially useful assets are unable to be productively deployed when disagreements between the corporation's decision-makers paralyse the company from taking action."

[235] See BGHZ 80, 346, 348; OLG München GmbHR 2005, 428.

[236] See *Ng Eng Hiam v. Ng Kee Wei* (1964) 31 MLJ 238, 240.

[237] See Cass. com., Rev. soc. 1982, 804.

forms in the corporate law legislation of various states[238]; in Kansas, for example, only corporations with two members may be dissolved.[239]

As compulsory dissolution often reduces the value of otherwise prosperous corporations to nothing, there is scope for courts and legislature to consider less drastic conflict resolution measures. This could include setting a higher duty to cooperate for both shareholders on the basis of the duty of loyalty or the replacement of a disputed resolution by a court decision.[240] This seems to have been the intent behind the newly introduced sentence to Article 821(1) Swiss OR, which states that the court is in a position to identify potential solutions that are appropriate and reasonable for the participants, rather than dissolving the corporation.

7.4 Role of Courts in Shareholder Disputes

Identifying the proper role for the courts in shareholder disputes[241] is possibly the most fascinating topic for future research. In this respect, we are witnessing a veritable "clash of civilisations," with the broad equitable remedies of common law jurisdictions on the one hand and the narrow approach of most civil law jurisdictions on the other.

7.4.1 *Equitable Remedies in Common Law Jurisdictions*

Broad equitable remedies for resolving shareholder disputes have long been a hallmark of common law jurisdictions. In fact, from the early days of modern company law, English courts were given the power to wind up the company compulsorily where they thought it "just and equitable" to do so. This power is now codified in s. 122(1)(g) IA 1986. It has been supplemented by a more flexible remedy, the unfair prejudice procedure, which has already been mentioned above.[242] At this point, attention should be drawn to the wide discretion of the court to shape an adequate remedy. If the court is satisfied that an unfair prejudice petition is well founded, it may, by virtue of s. 996(1) CA 2006, make such order as it thinks fit for giving relief in respect of the matters complained of. According to s. 996(2) CA 2006, while not being confined to doing so, the court's order may, (1) regulate the conduct of the company's affairs in the future; (2) require the company to refrain from doing or continuing an act complained of, or to do an act that the petitioner has complained it has omitted to do; (3) authorize civil proceedings to be brought in the name and on behalf of the company by such person or persons and on such terms as the court may direct; (4) require the company not to make any, or any specified, alterations in its articles without the leave of the court; (5) provide for the purchase of the shares of any members of the company by other members or by the company itself and, in the case of a purchase by the company itself, the reduction of the company's capital accordingly. Going even further, s. 999(2)(b) CA 2006

---

[238] For a good overview Cox and Hazen, *supra* note 124, § 14:12.

[239] See Kans. Stat. Ann. § 17-6804(d).   [240] See Bachmann et al., *supra* note 10, at 79.

[241] Generally, from the French perspective, Michel Jeantin, Le rôle du juge en droit des sociétés, in Mélanges Perrot 149 (1996); Jaques Mestre, "Réflexions sur les pouvoirs du juge dans la vie des sociétés", Rev. juris. com. 81 (1985); from a German perspective, Wedemann, *supra* note 14, at 564 et seqq.

[242] See above, 7.1.2.3.

indicates that the court can also order an amendment of the company's articles of association.[243] Comparable oppression remedies are available under Australian (s. 232 Companies Act)[244] and Irish company Law (s. 205 Companies Act 1963).

Similarly, many US state statutes provide for a wide array of possible remedies in oppression cases. Section 41(a) Model Statutory Close Corporation Supplement sets out nine types of relief: (1) the performance, prohibition, alteration, or setting aside of any action of the corporation or of its shareholders, directors, or officers of or any other party to the proceedings; (2) the cancellation or alteration of any provision in the company's articles of incorporation or bylaws; (3) the removal from office of any director or officer; (4) the appointment of any individual as a director or officer; (5) an accounting with respect to any matter in dispute; (6) the appointment of a custodian to manage the business and affairs of the corporation; (7) the appointment of a provisional director (who has all the rights, powers, and duties of a duly elected director) to serve for the term and under the conditions prescribed by the court; (8) the payment of dividends; (9) the award of damages to any aggrieved party. In practice, the most frequently used remedy is a court order requiring a buyout of the petitioner's shares.[245]

7.4.2 Moving Towards More Discretion in Civil Law Countries?

Traditionally, civil law jurisdictions do not, in principle, confer broad discretionary powers upon the courts. There are, however, at least two recent counter-examples in continental Europe.

7.4.2.1 Recent Examples in Continental Europe

The most prominent example can be found in Dutch company law, which dedicates a whole section to rules for resolving disputes between shareholders (Article 2:335–2:343c NBW) and adds an additional section on the right of inquiry (Article 2:344–2:359 NBW). These inquiry proceedings date back to 1928, but gained practical importance after a reform in 1971, to become the most important source of minority shareholder protection today.[246] Upon written request from a shareholder with at least 10% of votes, the Enterprise Chamber of the Amsterdam Court of Appeal may appoint one or more persons to conduct an investigation into the policy and the state of affairs of a legal person, either in full or with respect to a specific matter or period. If the investigation report indicates a mismanagement of affairs, then the Enterprise Chamber may order, by virtue of Article 2:355 NBW, that one or more of a statutory list of measures must be taken, depending on which of these measures it regards appropriate in view of the outcome of the investigation. According to Article 2:356 NBW, these measures are (1) a suspension or annulment (nullification) of a resolution (decision) of the directors, supervisory directors, the general meeting of shareholders or any other body

---

[243] See Victor Joffe, David Darke, Giles Richardson, Daniel Lightman, Timothy Collingwood, Minority Shareholders marg. n°. 7.239 (4th ed. 2011).

[244] See Austin & Ramsay, *supra* note 103, marg. n°. 10.430 et seq.

[245] See Ragazzo & Fendler, *supra* note 126, at 639 et seqq.

[246] See L. Timmerman and A. Doorman, Rights of Minority Shareholders in the Netherlands, in Rights of Minority Shareholders, XVIth Congress of the International Academy of Comparative Law (Evanghelos Perakis ed., 2004).

of the legal person; (2) a suspension or dismissal of one or more directors or supervisory directors; (3) a temporary appointment of one or more directors or supervisory directors; (4) a temporary derogation from those provisions in the articles of incorporation that are designed by the Enterprise Chamber for this purpose; (5) a temporary transfer of shares for administrative purposes only; (6) a dissolution of the legal person.

There is a less recognized comparable remedy in Swiss company law, the so-called action for dissolution. According to Article 821(3) OR, any shareholder may request the court to dissolve the company for good cause, although the court may opt for an alternative solution that is appropriate and reasonable for the persons concerned, for example the payment of a commensurate financial settlement to the shareholder requesting dissolution. This remedy was introduced for stock corporations (AG) in 1991 and extended to private limited liability companies (GmbH) in 2008.[247] Unlike the Dutch Enterprise Chamber, however, Swiss courts have not yet made extensive use of their new equitable powers.[248]

7.4.2.2 Pros and Cons of Equitable Remedies

Supporters of equitable remedies contend that they are ideally suited to resolving shareholder disputes. They provide courts with great flexibility to choose a remedial scheme that most appropriately responds to harm suffered by the aggrieved shareholder. This is particularly relevant for closely held firms where internal conflicts often involve an interwoven mesh of commercial and personal interests that is almost impossible to unravel.[249] Closely related to this is the forward-looking aspect of equitable remedies: it empowers the court to make orders enabling the proper running of the company into the future. By contrast, the action to set aside a shareholders' resolution traditional to civil law jurisdictions is retroactive. Moreover, it addresses only one particular issue, making it unsuitable for comprehensive conflict resolution.[250] In addition, it does not extend to board decisions; these must be challenged by a separate action. Finally, with respect to excessive retention of profits, courts in civil law jurisdictions struggle with the fact that "negative" shareholders' resolutions cannot be transformed into positive ones by means of a nullity suit.[251] Equitable remedies, on the contrary, can easily overcome these doctrinal obstacles.[252] They also benefit from the fact that court orders under an unfair prejudice or oppression remedy can respond to both board decisions and shareholders' resolutions.

On the other hand, there are a number of potential disadvantages or drawbacks associated with broad equitable relief. A first objection is that arbitration panels are, for a variety of reasons, in a better position to offer proactive solutions for shareholder disputes than state courts, and that mediation is a superior means of dispute resolution whenever a review of the whole "relationship history" in a close corporation is deemed necessary. Secondly, judges may feel uncomfortable with the task of fashioning an adequate remedy, due to a lack

---

[247] See Reto Sanwald, in Martin F. Nussbaum, Reto Sanwald, & Markus Scheidegger, Kurzkommentar zum neuen GmbH-Recht Art. 821 marg. n°. 26 (2007).

[248] See BGE 136 III 278; Lukas Beeler/Hans Casper von der Crone, Auflösungsklage nach Art. 736 Abs. 4 OR, SZW (2010) 329.

[249] Bachmann et al., *supra* note 10, at 70.   [250] See Wedemann, *supra* note 14, at 565.

[251] See Fleischer & Trinks, *supra* note 15, at 293 et seq.

[252] See Forest Hodge O'Neal, Robert Bruce Thompson, & Blake Thompson, Oppression of Minority Shareholders and LLC Members § 9:20 (2d ed. 2009): "Compelling declaration of dividends"; see also § 41(a)(8) Model Stat. Close Corp. Supp.

of expertise or business acumen.[253] Jurisdictions would be well advised to mitigate these circumstances by establishing specialized business courts to preside over such proceedings, as has been the case in Delaware and the Netherlands.[254] Thirdly, the breadth of equitable remedies is potentially dangerous, as too much discretion may destroy certainty and predictability in company law.[255] Fourthly, and on a more general note, conferring broad discretionary powers to courts may be incompatible with traditional notions of the role of judges in civil law jurisdictions with their strong aversion to a "gouvernement des juges."[256]

[253]   On the cautious line taken by the English courts after the introduction of the unfair prejduice remedy in 1948 and their more active role in recent years, Davies, *supra* note 197, at 233 et seq.

[254]   As to Delaware Symposium, "The Delaware Court of Chancery: Change and Continuity", Col. Bus. L. Rev. 387–798 (2012); as to the Netherlands, The Companies and Business Court from a Comparative Perspective (Josephus Jitta ed., 2004); Maarten J. Kroeze, The Dutch Companies and Business Court as a Specialized Court, in The Quality of Corporate Law and the Role of Corporate Law Judges 143 (Louis Bouchez, Marco Knubben, Joseph A. McCahery, & Levinus Timmerman eds., 2006).

[255]   In this sense, Sandra K. Miller, "Minority Shareholder Oppression in the Private Company in the European Community: A Comparative Analysis of the German, United Kingdom, and French Close Corporation Problem", 30 Cornell Int'l. L.J. 381, 415 (1997).

[256]   See with respect to company law, Giuseppe B. Portale, "Minoranze di blocco e abuso del voto nell'esperienza europea: dalla tutela risarcitoria al 'gouvernement des juges'?", Europa e dir. priv. 153 (1999); for a more general picture the national reports collected in Discretionary Power of the Judge: Limits and Control (Marcel Storme & Burkhard Hess eds., 2003).

PART III

NEW CHALLENGES IN CORPORATE GOVERNANCE

CHAPTER 26

......

WESTERN VERSUS ASIAN LAWS ON CORPORATE GOVERNANCE

The Role of Enforcement in International Convergence

......

HIDEKI KANDA[1]

1 INTRODUCTION

......

THE volume of academic research on corporate governance is immense. Not only corporate governance in Western countries but also that in emerging economies in Asia and other regions has been explored in recent years.

Developing countries often import laws and regulations from developed countries. However, today, we observe a variety of laws and regulations throughout the world. In this chapter, I will discuss when laws do and do not converge in the field of corporate governance by emphasizing the cost of enforcement. In general, there are three familiar questions: (1) when, how, and why legal rules change; (2) whether transplantation of legal rules from Western countries has been successful; and (3) how enforcement interacts with substantive legal rules. In this chapter, I will focus on the first and the third questions by looking at situations where Asian jurisdictions import laws on corporate governance from Western jurisdictions.[2] Because of my limited knowledge, I will mainly compare Japanese law with US law, but I hope the general discussion in this chapter will be more generally applicable in the broader context where Asian jurisdictions import laws from Western jurisdictions.

[1] Professor of Law, University of Tokyo (until 2016); Fellow, European Corporate Governance Institute. I thank Professor Wolf-Georg Ringe for his helpful comments and suggestions.
[2] For the second question, see, e.g., Hideki Kanda & Curtis J. Milhaupt, "Re-Examining Legal Transplants: The Director's Fiduciary Duty in Japanese Corporate Law", 51 Am. J. Comp. L. 887 (2003).

More generally, a companion to the three questions noted above is the well-known inquiry of whether legal rules are converging around the world. Indeed, very often, Asian countries import laws from Western countries. For instance, Japan imported corporate law from the US in 1950.[3] In the process of legal transplantation, we sometimes observe persistence or resistance.[4] However, in my view, one aspect that has not been considered seriously in the past research on legal transplantation is enforcement. Thus, in this chapter, I will discuss the enforcement aspect of legal transplantation regarding corporate governance. I will limit my discussion to large publicly held business corporations. In section 2, I will present the general theme that the cost of enforcement affects the convergence of substantive legal rules. In section 3, I will discuss a few examples. In section 4, I will briefly discuss the convergence of enforcement. In section 5, I will briefly address whether and how the cost of substantive legal rules affect the convergence of enforcement. Section 6 is the conclusion.

2 WHEN LAWS CHANGE: INTERACTIONS BETWEEN ENFORCEMENT AND SUBSTANTIVE LEGAL RULES

Every country has its own legal developments, and such developments are the result of cultural, social, political and historical contingencies. Thus, for instance, the legal rules regarding the liability of managers and directors (and regarding shareholder derivative actions) seem to be developing quite uniquely in Japan.[5] For instance, shareholder derivative actions were unknown to the original Japanese corporate law codified as the Commercial Code of 1899, and were transplanted from the US in the amendments to the Commercial Code in 1950. The Japanese system is structured similarly to the US counterpart. In both

---

[3] See, e.g., Mark D. West, "The Puzzling Divergence of Corporate Law: Evidence and Explanations from Japan and the United States", 150 U. Pa. L. Rev. 527 (2001).

[4] See papers in Convergence and Persistence in Corporate Governance (Jeffrey N. Gordon & Mark J. Roe eds., 2004) and Convergence of Corporate Governance: Promise and Prospects (Abdul Rasheed & Toru Yoshikawa eds., 2012). On the convergence of legal rules, the case for convergence of corporate law has been advocated in Henry Hansmann & Reinier Kraakman, "The End of History for Corporate Law", 89 Geo. L. J. 439 (2001). See also Henry Hansmann, "How Close Is the End of History?", 31 J. Corp. L. 745 (2006); Henry Hansmann & Reinier Kraakman, Convergence of Corporate Governance: Promise and Prospects, in Rasheed & Yoshikawa *supra*. For "functional" convergence, see Ronald J. Gilson, "Corporate Governance and Economic Efficiency: When Do Institutions Matter?", 74 Wash. U. L. Q. 327 (1996); Ronald J. Gilson, "Globalizing Corporate Governance: Convergence of Form or Function", 49 Am. J. Comp. L. 329 (2001). For inquiries into divergence, see, e.g., Lucian Bebchuk & Mark J. Roe, "A Theory of Path Dependence in Corporate Ownership and Governance", 52 Stan. L. Rev. 775 (1999). For a more recent study, see Bernard Black, Antonio Gledson de Carvalho, & Erica Gorga, "Corporate Governance in Brazil", 11 Emerging Markets Review 21 (2010). For the importance of ownership structure, see Lucian Bebchuk, "The Elusive Quest for Global Governance Standards", 157 U. Pa. L. Rev. 1263 (2009).

[5] See Hideki Kanda, "Understanding Recent Trends regarding the Liability of Managers and Directors in Japanese Corporate Law", 17 Zeitschrift fur Japanisches Recht 29 (2004).

countries, typically shareholders are entitled to sue directors who are liable for damages to the company. Historical developments after 1950, however, have made the rules in both countries quite different. Just to illustrate one point of difference, most states in the US have recognized the dismissal of a derivative action where a special litigation committee of disinterested directors is set up and decides that the action is not for the benefit of shareholders,[6] while in Japan that type of dismissal is unknown and the plaintiff shareholder is entitled to maintain the action no matter what decision is made by a litigation committee or the like, or even by majority shareholders.[7] There are mechanisms that have been developed in Japan to disallow strike suits, but it is noteworthy that a single shareholder is entitled to maintain a derivative action even where most shareholders do not want the action.

In this chapter, however, I am inclined to argue, generally, that unique developments are producing non-unique results, and that the state of Japanese corporate law today is more, rather than less, similar to that of other countries' corporate law. In shareholder derivative actions, I am inclined to think that cases where derivative actions would be dismissed in the US would very often result in court decisions holding that the defendant directors should not be held liable. In this chapter, I focus on the interactions between enforcement and substantive legal rules.[8]

2.1 Legal Rules as a Component of a System

Any social system can be viewed as consisting of components or sub-systems, and legal rules are an important example. Thus, for instance, a corporate governance system consists of a variety of components or sub-systems, such as the firm size, the ownership structure, the financial system, the capital market, the labor system, the culture, and the law.

Legal rules, as a component or sub-system, have several distinctive characteristics. First, they are brought into a system automatically without any action by the parties who are subject to them. Second, many such rules may be brought into a system even if the parties do not want them (although there must be a decision by a state adopting and implementing such legal rules). Third, legal rules often must be enforced by courts or through other institutional mechanisms, which means that many legal rules are not self-enforcing.

From an economic standpoint, it is interesting to see how the coexistence of a sub-system that has these characteristics and one that does not shapes and affects the system. It is also interesting to see how this affects the behavior of the parties who are subject to the legal rules in question.

Legal rules, like other sub-systems, change over time. In a perfect world, other things being equal, there must be pressure in the marketplace or politically to make an inefficient

---

[6] See William T. Allen, Reinier Kraakman and Guhan Subramanian, Commentaries and Cases on the Law of Business Corporations 392 (4th ed. 2012).

[7] See Tomotaka Fujita, Transformation of the Management Liability Regime in Japan in the Wake of the 1993 Revision, in Transforming Corporate Governance in East Asia 15 (Hideki Kanda, Kon-Sik Kim, & Curtis J. Milhaupt eds., 2008). For a recent study on shareholder derivative actions in Asia, see The Derivative Action in Asia: A Comparative and Functional Approach (Dan W. Puchniak, Harald Baum, & Michael Ewing-Chow eds., 2012).

[8] The following discussion draws on Gerard Hertig & Hideki Kanda, Rules, Enforcement, and Corporate Governance (unpublished draft 1998).

legal rule a more efficient one. A system with an inefficient rule as a component is of course less efficient than a system with an efficient rule as a component, because the overall value of the system is the sum of the values of each component; a system with an inefficient rule is at a competitive disadvantage and has to adjust. In reality, however, we observe different legal rules in different corporate governance systems, and legal rules sometimes converge and sometimes do not.

This is quite simply due to the fact that the world is not perfect and that other things are not equal. This also indicates that different components of a corporate governance system cannot be considered in isolation. In theory, there are at least two general explanations as to why the legal rules component of each corporate governance system differs from that of other corporate governance systems, and why they do not converge.

First, one theory providing an analytical tool to understand corporate governance more deeply is the idea of substitutabilities. This theory—though not uncommon in traditional legal scholarship—suggests that one component of the system often serves as a substitute for other components. For instance, where the market for corporate control is active, as is or has been the case in the US and the UK, there is less need for other monitoring mechanisms. Similarly, a country having less developed capital markets might have stronger bank monitoring or, if bank monitoring does not work, something else might supplement capital markets, such as a strong board of directors or a controlling shareholder (including state ownership). Thus, France and Italy, for instance, have histories of heavy monitoring by the government. Indeed, the state has been the controlling shareholder in many major corporations. It is also possible for various components to combine in substitution for another component. In Germany, both banks and families as controlling shareholders substitute for capital markets. The theory holds even if nothing seems strong in isolation, as appears to be the case in Japanese corporate governance. In this particular situation, one can still argue that each of the various components serves some monitoring role, even if not necessarily a strong one, so that in total the system functions.

Second, another interesting theory concerns complementarities.[9] The idea is that various components (or sub-systems) of a given system are complementary to one another in certain situations. Where complementarities exist, the value of the system is not equal to the simple sum of the standard values of individual components. The integrated value of each component may vary, depending on the degree to which the component, as a whole or in part, is complementary to another component of the system. Thus, any given legal rule might have a different effect on the value (and efficiency) of the system. A legal rule that would have to be considered inefficient on a stand-alone basis is not necessarily a bad thing as part of a system if there are complementarities with its other components. This suggests that the same mechanism—bank monitoring, for instance—can have different effects in different corporate governance systems, depending on the complementarities it has with other components of the given system. Where (as in Germany) most firms are small or medium sized, bank

---

[9] For the idea of complementarities, see Paul Milgrom & John Roberts, "Complementarities and Systems: Understanding Japanese Economic Organization", 1 Estudios Economicos 3 (1994). See also Masahiko Aoki, The Japanese Firm as a System of Attributes, in The Japanese Firm: The Sources of Competitive Strength 11 (Masahiko Aoki & Ronald Dore eds., 1994); Ronald J. Gilson, "Reflections in a Distant Mirror: Japanese Corporate Governance through American Eyes", 1998 Colum. Bus. L. Rev. 203 (1998).

monitoring is more effective and thus plays a more important role than where (as in the US) firms are mostly very large or very small. On the other hand, where (as in France) state influence pervades both lender and debtor decision making, bank monitoring is all but meaningless, despite the fact that loans are the major source of financing. Japan can serve as a further example, because in Japan, employees under the lifetime employment system are dominant in the firm's decision making, and managers (who are former employees) are relatively familiar with respect to daily business activities, and thus information provided by banks and other business partners might be more valuable to them, which increases the value of bank monitoring. Finally, where (as in the UK) managers who come from outside are relatively good at using valuable information supplied by banks and other business partners, as a relative matter, the value of monitoring by banks and other business partners diminishes when lifetime employees, as opposed to outsiders, become managers.

Thus, given the existence of substitutabilities or complementarities, the fact that different systems have different legal rules should not be a surprise. To date, however, little attention has been paid to the interaction between legal rules and enforcement; if so, there must be insufficient understanding of the role and function of legal rules in corporate governance. In the following discussion, I will focus on the third characteristic of legal rules noted at the outset, namely that legal rules must be enforced. My central argument is that substantive legal rules sometimes converge, but sometimes they do not, and that they can even diverge because of the cost of enforcement. Enforcement is thus an important variable in the convergence or divergence of substantive legal rules.

For instance, the value of monitoring by shareholders should increase in conjunction with the reduction in the cost of enforcing legal rules regulating capital markets. This suggests that monitoring by shareholders should function better in the US than elsewhere, because the US has the class action system and other law enforcement mechanisms that are more effective than those of other major countries. In addition, I propose that the linkage between substantive legal rules and enforcement can operate the other way. Namely, the degree of convergence in substantive rules can affect the level and cost of enforcement.

2.2 Enforcement Affects Convergence of Substantive Legal Rules

With differing historical, cultural, and legal peculiarities, mechanisms and levels of enforcement are expected to vary from country to country, especially because of differences in the cost of enforcement relative to its value to enforcers.

Although substantive legal rules must be enforced, variations in enforcement costs do not necessarily affect the value of the legal rules component of a corporate governance system, if the component has substitutabilities or complementarities with other non-legal components. Thus, in a given corporate governance system, a component such as the structure of ownership might substitute for the legal framework. In that case, difference in the cost of enforcement might not be relevant, so long as the structure of ownership does not change. Similarly, variations in enforcement cost might simply reflect different complementarities. For instance, bank monitoring might be improved by a lower level of enforcement of manager liability by shareholders.

On the other hand, within the legal framework component, enforcement necessarily interacts with substantive legal rules. Because substantive legal rules must be enforced, the cost of enforcement affects the value of any substantive legal rule. In this sense, enforcement has complementarities to substantive rules. This suggests, first, that other things being equal, substantive legal rules do not converge when the cost of enforcement is different among jurisdictions. Second, we can expect convergence in substantive legal rules where the cost of enforcement is low. In such a situation, courts and regulators will develop substantive legal rules without worrying about their enforceability. This also holds where substantive legal rules are self-enforcing. Third, I submit that rules do change when enforcement is too costly. Indeed, there is then reason to think that market and other forces might arise to make substantive legal rules change to those that are enforceable at lower costs.

Simple numerical examples might be helpful to illustrate these points. First, suppose that the cost of enforcement for Rule A in Country X is 50, that that for Rule B in Country Y is 80, and that their substantive legal rules, Rule A and Rule B, differ from one another. Assume that the value (defined as how efficient the rule is to the system concerned, aside from the cost of enforcement) of Rule A is 100 and that that of Rule B is 120. Disregarding complementarities and the like, other things being equal, the situation in Country Y is worse because the combined value of the legal rule (the value of Rule A or Rule B minus enforcement cost) is 50 in Country X and 40 in Country Y. If complementarities exist, however, this might not be so, because the combined value of the rule in Country Y might be more than 40: say, 50. If that is the case, both countries might well stay as they are by maintaining different rules and different enforcement situations.

Second, suppose that the cost of enforcement for each of Rule A and Rule B is zero. In this environment, Country X, if it knows Country Y's situation, might well change Rule A to Rule B. The value of Rule B is higher than that of Rule A.

Third, suppose that the cost of enforcement for Rule B in Country Y is 10,000. We then would hardly believe that complementarities would offset the disadvantage of Country Y having the too costly enforcement situation. In such situation, because enforcement of Rule B is too costly, Rule B might change. Similarly, if Country Z, having a different substantive legal rule, Rule C, with the value of 110, has an excessively costly enforcement situation—say, with an enforcement cost of 10,000—one might expect that Rule C would change too. Thus, since both Country Y and Country Z might change their rules to those that would be enforceable at lower costs, the rules of the two countries might well converge.

In the following discussion, I will briefly examine three areas relating to corporate governance and focus on these points: the regulation of insider trading, financial disclosure and accounting rules, and corporate law rules on governance.

3 EXAMPLES

3.1 Insider Trading

The regulation of insider trading is a good and straightforward example showing that substantive legal rules do not converge where the cost of enforcement differs. The basic purpose of the substantive legal rule on insider trading is similar in most jurisdictions (which is the prohibition of trading of stock based on material non-public information), but the exact rule varies from jurisdiction to jurisdiction. For instance, the exact rule in the US is different from that in Japan. In short, the Japanese rule is narrower, as insiders and inside information (known as "material facts") are both defined in the statute more restrictively than in the US.[10] For instance, a recipient of insider information from a corporate insider (such as an officer or director of the relevant firm) is subject to prohibition, but a further recipient of the information from the first recipient (known as a "tippee" in the US) is not.[11] Additionally, even if a certain fact materially affects the stock price, if that particular type of fact is not on the statutory list, then trading based on that information is not prohibited.[12] Additionally, because this Japanese rule was adopted as late as 1988, the indication is that rules are not converging between the two countries.

The rule in the US developed on the basis of court cases concerning civil remedies under the SEC's Rule 10b-5, which was promulgated under Section 10(b) of the Securities Exchange Act of 1934. While there are several criminal cases on this point, the dominance of civil cases produced by private litigation is noteworthy in the US and resulted in continuous expansion of the basic prohibition stated by Rule 10b-5.

By contrast, in Japan, there have been no civil cases on this point at all, and all existing cases involve criminal sanctions and administrative fines. In fact, when the rule was adopted in 1988, it was designed to be enforced via criminal sanction, not civil sanction. Given the general importance of private action for enforcement, this necessarily implied a lower level of enforcement in Japan than in the US. Japan introduced administrative fines in 2005, and since then several insider trading cases have been dealt with by this means.[13] Yet, today, the lack of civil enforcement in Japan still makes the US and Japan different.

Thus, the difference between the US and Japanese enforcement mechanisms somewhat neatly explains the difference in the substantive legal rule between the two countries.

I might add that certain securities regulation, such as the regulation of insider trading, needs a strong enforcement agency, such as the US Securities and Exchange Commission, in addition to courts. A study of the data on the budgets and staffing of public enforcers shows that public enforcement is not so bad.[14] This also suggests that the cost of enforcement is quite different among jurisdictions, and if so, it is no surprise from my argument here that the substantive legal rules are different in the US and Japan.

---

[10] See Arts. 166 and 167 of the Financial Instruments and Exchange Act in Japan (Act No. 25 of 1948, as amended) ("FIEA"). The FIEA was introduced in 1948 (then it was called the Securities and Exchange Act) as an import of the US Securities Act of 1933 and Securities and Exchange Act of 1934.

[11] See Art. 166(3) of the FIEA.

[12] See Art. 166(1)(2) of the FIEA. There are catch-all provisions for inside information (see Art. 166(2) (iv)(viii)(xiv), but they are not discussed here.

[13] Through March 31, 2014, the Securities and Exchange Surveillance Commission recommended to the Financial Services Agency that administrative fines be imposed in 172 cases of insider trading. See http://www.fsa.go.jp/sesc/actions/kan_joukyou_naibu.pdf (in Japanese).

[14] Howell E. Jackson & Mark J. Roe, "Public and Private Enforcement of Securities Laws: Resource-Based Evidence", 93 J. Fin. Econ. 207 (2009).

3.2 Financial Disclosure and Accounting

Financial disclosure and accounting rules, particularly those for "hard" information such as data in the firm's financial statements, are often enforceable at low cost. If a publicly held company keeps supplying false accounting numbers in its financial statements, it is most likely to be uncovered and penalized in the marketplace.

Thus, contrary to the rule on insider trading, legal rules on financial disclosure and accounting are often self-enforcing. This implies that it is the value of the substantive legal rule itself that matters, and not so much the cost or level of enforcement. In that situation, there is reason to expect that various jurisdictions' financial disclosure and accounting rules will converge in a more efficient direction.

This simple statement needs a few cautions. First, we have found some cases of accounting fraud all over the world. Enron in the US[15] and Olympus in Japan[16] are well-known examples. These cases may show that disclosure rules are not self-enforcing. However, for the purposes of this chapter, I submit that in both cases, the fraud was ultimately uncovered and dealt with by heavy legal sanctions, so that, overall, the cost of enforcement of disclosure rules is rather low compared to other regulations.

Second, over the decades, there have been efforts to develop an international accounting or financial reporting standard, called the International Financial Reporting Standards ("IFRS"), by an international body, called the International Accounting Standards Board,[17] yet, to date, accounting standards throughout the world have not completely converged into IFRS or any other uniform standards. This might be contradictory to the theme I present above. However, as substantive legal rules, what matters is not the detail of the contents of the accounting standards but the mandatory disclosure of financial statements, and basic accounting figures in financial statements are not drastically different among jurisdictions in the world. Indeed, it is fair to say that the detailed contents of the accounting standards throughout the world have been converging, rather than diverging, in the past. If so, overall, I am inclined to argue that in financial disclosure, the low cost of enforcement has been stimulating convergence of substantive legal rules in this field.

3.3 Corporate Law

Corporate law rules seem more complex than rules on insider trading or on financial disclosure. There is a wide variety of rules, from voting rules, to monitoring devices such as board systems, and to shareholder litigation. This diversity, coupled with differences in enforcement mechanisms across jurisdictions, implies that corporate law rules might and might not converge. As noted before, convergence is more likely to occur with respect to two categories of rules: rules whose value does not depend on enforcement (self-enforcing rules) and rules having no value because of the low level of enforcement in the relevant jurisdictions.

---

[15] See John C. Coffee, Jr., Gatekeepers: The Role of the Professions and Corporate Governance (2008).

[16] See Bruce E. Aronson, "The Olympus Scandal and Corporate Governance Reform: Can Japan Find a Middle Ground Between the Board Monitoring Model and Management Model?", 30 UCLA Pacific Basin L. J. 93 (2012).

[17] See the website of the IFRS at http://www.ifrs.org.

Convergence is less likely to occur with respect to the rules having a value determined by complementarities with the applicable enforcement mechanism.

For instance, rules regarding management duties have a value which varies depending upon rules regarding shareholder litigation, such as rules regarding shareholders' derivative actions. Consequently, there are complementarities with the enforcement mechanism, and if enforcement levels vary among jurisdictions, one should expect a lack of convergence in substantive rules about management duties. As far as Japan is concerned, the popularity of shareholder derivative actions today seems to suggest that the cost of enforcement in this area has changed in the past 20 years and that it is quite low today in Japan.[18] If so, my analysis suggests that substantive legal rules tend to converge toward those of other jurisdictions where such rules are enforced at low cost, as in the US.[19] By contrast, in transition or emerging economies where there is no solid judicial system and the level of enforcement is low, there might be pressure to adopt rules that have a value independent of enforcement (self-enforcing rules) or that are enforceable with little involvement of the courts. As a matter of fact, and quite unsurprisingly, we observe the dominance of voting rules and other more self-enforcing rules in these economies. In other words, the low level of enforcement makes substantive rules tend to converge.

My convergence proposition can be tested by considering two areas in which corporate law rules differ markedly among major industrialized jurisdictions. One is the area of corporate takeovers, and the other is that of board structures (one-tier versus two-tier board systems). Regarding rules on takeovers, the test is rather easy: such rules have more value in jurisdictions where there is both a well-developed capital market (inter-component complementarity) and a high level of enforcement (intra-component complementarity). Indeed, the value of substantive legal rules on corporate takeovers, including those on defensive measures by incumbent management, particularly depends on how the market for corporate control operates. In the US, the well-developed capital market and the well-functioning judicial system led to quite distinctive features of detailed substantive rules on corporate takeovers. This situation is unique, especially insofar as the level of enforcement is concerned. For this reason, one cannot expect a convergence of rules in the near future on corporate takeovers among major jurisdictions in Europe and the US. This conclusion might not, however, be relevant in the longer term. Indeed, substantive rules on corporate takeovers have changed in the US over the past decades, and the market for corporate control was sometimes strong and sometimes weak. As a vast quantity of scholarship suggests, the value of the US corporate governance system was probably maintained (or possibly improved) over time because of the emergence of substitutes: institutional investors served as substitutes for the market for corporate control. The same has been happening in Europe, which would make divergence in the legal framework component of little importance.

In Japan, laws on takeover defenses are complicated. Securities regulation, codified as the FIEA, regulates tender offer processes, while most of the defense measures raise legal issues under corporate law, codified as the Companies Act (effective from May 1, 2006 as a successor of the Commercial Code with respect to business corporations), and not the

---

[18] See, e.g., Mark D. West, "Why Shareholders Sue: The Evidence from Japan", 30 J. Leg. Stud. 351 (2001); Fujita, *supra* note 7. For the situation in Asian jurisdictions, see Puchniak et al., *supra* note 7.

[19] See generally Kanda, *supra* note 5.

FIEA. In this sense, the distinction between the FIEA and the Companies Act roughly corresponds to that between the federal (and state) securities law and state corporate law in the US. The validity of some of the defenses was challenged before the courts, and in those cases the relevant issues were the ones under the Companies Act, not the FIEA.[20] In fact, the current tender offer regulations under the FIEA permit the target company to adopt defensive actions even after the commencement of a tender offer by a hostile bidder. Thus, like in Delaware, case law under the Companies Act shapes the landscape, although the substance of the case law is not identical between Delaware and Japan.[21]

In Japan, the Companies Act is important for the critical issues in the area of hostile takeovers and defenses, and courts play an important role in applying the relevant rules under the Companies Act. The Tokyo Stock Exchange also plays an important role in shaping the landscape in this area, since such issues are not directly regulated by the FIEA.

The existing variety of substantive rules on board structures does not fit into my analysis very well. Enforcing substantive rules on board structures does not seem to be costly. Rather such rules seem to be self-enforcing. If this is true, then rules on board structures should converge. The fact is, however, that we observe quite different rules on board structures across jurisdictions.

One might be inclined to say that differences in rules on board structures might be explained by the existence of substitutes or other components of the system having complementarities. One might also try a different argument. For instance, apparent differences in substantive rules might not be important, because different rules can solve the same problem without perceptible effect; or more bluntly, having a one-tier or a two-tier board might not matter, as firms with one-tier boards need to institute executive boards to make operational decisions. This argument is supported by the fact that major jurisdictions seem to be converging on what is the most important of structural features: the existence of an independent committee or body. Major jurisdictions tend to require the establishment of an independent monitoring body, such as an audit committee, for each publicly held firm, regardless of whether such firm has a one-tier or two-tier board system.

Japan imported the board of directors system from the US in the amendments to the Commercial Code in 1950, but did not abolish the statutory auditor system noted below. Since the amendments in 2002, a choice is permitted between a two-board company and a one-board and three-committee company. In the former, a board of directors and a board of statutory auditors are required, while in the latter, there are no statutory auditors and the board of directors is required to have three committees: a nominating committee, an audit committee, and a compensation committee. This latter form was introduced by the amendments to the Commercial Code in 2002 (effective from April 1, 2003), and more

---

[20] See, e.g., Hideki Kanda, Takeover Defenses and the Role of Law: A Japanese Perspective, in Perspectives in Company Law and Financial Regulation 413 (Michel Tison et al. eds., 2009).

[21] See Curtis J. Milhaupt, "In the Shadow of Delaware? The Rise of Hostile Takeovers in Japan", 105 Colum. L. Rev. 2171 (2005); Jack B. Jacobs, "Implementing Japan's New Anti-Takeover Defense Guidelines, Part II: The Role of Courts as Expositor and Monitor of the Rules of the Takeover Game", 3 U. Tokyo J. L. & Pol. 102 (2006). See also John Armour, Jack B. Jacobs, & Curtis J. Milhaupt, "The Evolution of Hostile Takeover Regimes in Developed and Emerging Markets: An Analytical Framework", 52 Harv. Int'l. L. J. 219 (2011).

than half of each of the committees' members must be "outside" directors. For two-board companies, at least half of the members of the board of statutory auditors must be "outside" statutory auditors, but the board of directors does not have to have outside directors. In practice, one-board and three-committee companies are not popular given the number of firms that have adopted that form. Only 2.2% of the listed firms on the Tokyo Stock Exchange (TSE), as of September 10, 2012, are one-board and three-committee companies.[22]

A brief further note on two-board companies may be worthwhile, because statutory auditors are not well known outside Japan. For a two-board company, there must be at least three directors. Directors are elected at the shareholders' meeting, and form the board of directors. The board elects representative directors, the Japanese counterpart of US officers or executives. There must be at least one representative director. Representative directors are the management, and they run the company. The Companies Act requires that the board of directors make important corporate decisions and supervise the management. Each director, as a member of the board, owes a duty of care and loyalty to the company.

A two-board company must have a "kansayaku," often (somewhat misleadingly) translated as a statutory auditor. Statutory auditors are elected at the shareholders' meeting, and do not have to be accountants or other professionals. A "large company," which is defined under the Companies Act as a joint-stock company having either legal capital in the amount of 500 million yen or more, or total debt (on the balance sheet) in the amount of 20 billion yen or more, must have at least three statutory auditors, and at least half of them must be "outside" statutory auditors. An auditor is "outside" where he or she does not, and did not in the past, serve as a director or employee of the company or its subsidiary. In a large company, there must be at least one full-time auditor.

In addition, a large company must have an accounting auditor, who must be a certified public accountant or certified auditing firm. An accounting auditor is elected at the shareholders' meeting, and is responsible for auditing the company's financial statements annually before they are submitted to the annual shareholders' meeting, where the audit opinion is also submitted. In contrast, a statutory auditor is responsible for overseeing the activities of management. This is understood to mean confirming the legality of management's activities. The Companies Act requires collaboration between accounting auditors and statutory auditors, providing complex rules, the details of which are beyond the scope of this article.

A two-board company may elect an outside director, although this election is not mandatory. If the company has an outside director, the Companies Act permits some special treatment. For instance, decision making on certain important matters may be delegated from the board of directors to a smaller special board. A director is "outside" where he or she is not, and was not, an executive director or employee of the company or its subsidiary.

There are two recent trends in this area. First, the Tokyo Stock Exchange today requires listed firms to have at least one "independent" director or statutory auditor, and

---

[22] See Tokyo Stock Exchange, "White Paper on Corporate Governance 2013", TSE-Listed Companies (February 2013), available at http://www.tse.or.jp/rules/cg/white-paper/b7gje60000050b1-att/b7gje6000003ukm8.pdf. See also Ronald J. Gilson and Curtis J. Milhaupt, "Choice as Regulatory Reform: The Case of Japanese Corporate Governance", 53 Am. J. Comp. L. 343 (2005).

the TSE has adopted a policy that encourages all listed firms to have independent directors. Second, as noted below, the Companies Act was amended in June 2014 (the amendments went into effect in May 2015). Under the 2014 amendments to the Companies Act, the definition of "outside" is stricter in two respects.[23] In addition to the requirement of lack of an employment relationship with the company or its subsidiaries, lack of an employment relationship with the company's parent firms will be required. Also, lack of a family relationship will be required. Note, however, that lack of a business or trade relationship, required by the current TSE rule for independence, will not be required under the new regime of the Companies Act. Aside from this, having an outside director is encouraged by a "comply or explain" rule. Specifically, two-board companies are to be subject to a rule where they must explain the reason why they do not have an outside director, if they do not have one, at the annual shareholders' meeting.[24]

In addition, under the 2014 amendments, a new type of company will be introduced allowing for a type with a one-board and one-committee structure (where there are no statutory auditors and the majority of the committee members must be outside directors).[25] As a result, listed firms will have the choice of three board structures: (1) two boards; (2) one board and three committees; and (3) one board and one committee. This one-board and one-committee structure is intended to encourage listed firms with a two-board structure to move to that structure and thereby have outside directors.

At any rate, it is noteworthy that enforcement alone does not seem to explain the non-convergence of substantive rules on board structure.

4 Convergence of Enforcement

My discussion thus far has assumed that enforcement mechanisms do not converge. This assumption, however, is not plausible, at least in theory. Like a legal rule, an inefficient enforcement mechanism must face pressure to change.

In this line of thinking, one important point must be made. Unlike substantive rules, the value (or cost) of enforcement can be defined in a straightforward way. That is, it is most efficient when the enforcement cost is zero. Viewed this way, talking about convergence of enforcement appears misleading because as far as the cost of enforcement alone is concerned, the lower the better. However, one could still discuss the level of enforcement. A rule is enforced up to the point where the cost of enforcement outweighs the cost of non-enforcement. Thus, a certain institutional mechanism, say, the court system, might be better or worse than another mechanism, say, the arbitration system, so that one could discuss convergence or divergence of enforcement mechanisms in this vein. Similarly, one could argue that if the number of judges and private attorneys is decreasing in one country and increasing in another country, the enforcement systems are converging. However, insofar as the area of corporate governance is concerned, I am inclined to make an empirical assumption that

---

[23] See Art. 2(xv) and Art. 2(xvi) of the Companies Act (amended in 2014).
[24] See Art. 327-2 of the Companies Act (added in 2014).
[25] See Art. 399-2 through Art. 399-14 of the Companies Act (added in 2014).

enforcement mechanisms have too many hurdles to converge, and will leave the discussion on convergence of enforcement to further research in the future.

5 Convergence of Substantive Legal Rules Affects Enforcement

My discussion thus far has examined how enforcement affects substantive rules. In theory, one can think of the reverse linkage between enforcement and substantive rules: how convergence of substantive rules affects enforcement. For instance, if certain substantive rules are similar in two jurisdictions, judges in one jurisdiction might borrow precedents from the other jurisdiction, so that similar substantive rules might result in quicker and cheaper court decisions. If so, convergence of substantive rules affects the level of enforcement. Similarly, when a jurisdiction prepares a new enforcement mechanism, if a similar substantive rule is adopted, the jurisdiction might be able to prepare a new enforcement mechanism rather quickly and easily by importing it from elsewhere. I believe that this phenomenon is in fact observed in the areas of consumer protection and environmental law. In corporate governance, this can happen where a large-scale law reform is considered in any given jurisdiction; for instance, where Asian jurisdictions attempt a large-scale law reform on corporate governance by introducing a new monitoring mechanism.

Indeed, when European countries introduced or strengthened the regulation of insider trading, there was pressure to adopt a US style of substantive rule, which operated as pressure for enforcement mechanisms to converge. Ultimately, the path to establish an enforcement agency like a US Securities and Exchange Commission was not imposed on the EU Member States, but to date, the discussion on the enforcement mechanism has continued.[26] Additionally, convergence of financial disclosure and accounting rules toward a more stringent standard has forced jurisdictions to give a higher legal profile to professional accountants and auditors as an additional monitoring body to facilitate the self-enforcing character of the relevant financial disclosure and accounting rules.

6 Preliminary Conclusion

In this chapter, I have examined the interrelationship between substantive legal rules and enforcement. I have shown that the cost of enforcement affects convergence or divergence of substantive legal rules in corporate governance. I have submitted a hypothesis that where enforcement costs are very low or too high, there is reason to expect that substantive rules will converge. Otherwise, differences in enforcement predict differences or divergence in substantive rules. As the cost of enforcement becomes lower in certain jurisdictions, there

---

[26] The European Securities and Markets Authority is not given much power of enforcement. See its website at http://www.esma.europa.eu/.

is more chance that their substantive legal rules will converge. I have also touched briefly upon the reverse linkage between rules and enforcement: convergence of substantive rules may affect enforcement. In my view, enforcement should be paid more serious attention in the research on comparative corporate governance. A proper focus on enforcement would shed new light on the issue and justify revisiting the familiar debate on convergence or divergence of substantive legal rules in world corporate governance systems. I hope the framework presented in this chapter will provide for a better understanding of the situations in which Asian jurisdictions import laws on corporate governance from Western jurisdictions.

....

CHAPTER 27

CORPORATE GOVERNANCE IN EMERGING MARKETS

....

MARIANA PARGENDLER[1]

1 INTRODUCTION

....

THE corporate governance movement, as well as the vast literature and industry to which it gave rise, is predicated on the premise that the structure, practices, and balance of power within the corporation matter for economic outcomes. The movement as we know it today first emerged in the United States in the late 1970s and early 1980s—a context of economic malaise and fear of imminent decline in view of the then booming economic performance of Germany and Japan.[2] In an era marked by growing skepticism of government intervention, the cure for economic woes had to lie in the private sector. As a result, governance substituted for government.[3] Adopted in 1977, the New York Stock Exchange listing rule requiring audit committees to be composed of outside directors was a first step in this direction.[4] Subsequently, the far more active role of private shareholders as corporate monitors in Germany and Japan would provide an attractive model for the revitalization and increased competitiveness of US firms.[5]

While comparisons between foreign models of corporate ownership and control have been a staple of the corporate governance movement since its early days, the first such studies centered on a handful of mature economies—most conspicuously the United States,

---

[1] Professor of Law, Fundação Getulio Vargas School of Law at São Paulo (FGV Direito SP); Global Professor of Law, New York University School of Law. The author is grateful to Luca Enriques, Merritt Fox, George Georgiev, Jed Kroncke, Bruno Salama, Erik Vermeulen, and Chuck Whitehead for helpful comments on an earlier version of this chapter.

[2] For an excellent description of the history of the corporate governance movement, see Brian R. Cheffins, The History of Corporate Governance, in Oxford Handbook of Corporate Governance (Mike Wright, Donald Siegel, Kevin Keasey, & Igor Filatotchev eds., Oxford University Press, 2013).

[3] Mariana Pargendler, "The Corporate Governance Obsession", 42 J. Corp. L. 359 (2016).

[4] Jeffrey N. Gordon, "The Rise of Independent Directors in the United States, 1950–2005: Of Shareholder Value and Stock Market Prices", 59 Stan. L. Rev. 1465, 1465 (2007).

[5] See, e.g., Louis Lowenstein & Ira M. Millstein, "The American Corporation and the Institutional Investor: Are There Lessons from Abroad?", 1988 Colum. Bus. L. Rev. 739 (1988).

the United Kingdom, Germany, and Japan. It was not until the 1990s and 2000s that the focus expanded to cover a larger array of jurisdictions. A number of economic and political factors help explain why corporate governance in emerging markets became an increasingly prominent theme in business, academic, and policy circles alike.

First, the fall of the Berlin Wall and the spread of the Washington consensus reinforced the wave of privatizations around the globe, and especially in the state-heavy economies of the old Second and Third World. A new system of corporate governance and financing was needed to replace the existing one based on state ownership of enterprise. It soon became apparent that privatization alone was unlikely to produce the desired improvements in economic performance in the absence of accompanying legal reforms that ensured a well-functioning corporate governance regime.[6]

Second, the 1990s witnessed the publication of several academic studies pointing to the existence of a causal relationship between financial development and economic growth.[7] Concurrently, a series of highly influential, albeit controversial, works on "law and finance" suggested that corporate governance institutions and practices—in particular, the level of legal investor protection afforded to minority shareholders—helped explain the variation in the ownership structures of business corporations and the level of financial development observed around the world.[8] In a period where the ascent of institutional economics persuaded international development agencies such as the World Bank to shift their strategy from the financing of physical infrastructure to the financing of improvements in institutional infrastructure, promoting corporate governance reform in emerging markets became a top policy priority.[9] This concern was only reinforced as commentators blamed the Asian financial crisis of the late 1990s on sub-par corporate governance practices.[10] Corporate governance improvements in emerging markets thus became a main area of concern at both domestic and international levels as an integral part of a developmental agenda.

Third, the growing attention to corporate governance in emerging markets is also attributable to strictly financial considerations. The spread of globalization, international trade, and financial liberalization worldwide in the last decades dramatically amplified cross-border investments. In 2012, for the first time in history, developing countries absorbed the lion's share of global flows in foreign direct investment.[11] Domestic equity markets in emerging economies also flourished, with firms from non-OECD countries raising a staggering 60%

[6] See Bernard Black, Reinier Kraakman, & Anna Tarassova, "Russian Privatization and Corporate Governance: What Went Wrong?", 52 Stan. L. Rev. 1731 (2000).

[7] See, e.g., Robert G. King & Ross Levine, "Finance and Growth: Schumpeter Might Be Right", 108 Q. J. Econ. 717 (1993); Ross Levine & Sara Zervos, "Stock Markets, Banks, and Economic Growth", 88 Am. Econ. Rev. 537 (1998); Raghuram G. Rajan & Luigi Zingales, "Financial Dependence and Growth", 88 Am. Econ. Rev. 559 (1998).

[8] See, for a review of this voluminous literature, Rafael La Porta et al., "The Economic Consequences of Legal Origins", 46 J. Econ. Lit. 285 (2008).

[9] The establishment of the Global Corporate Governance Forum in 1999, an organization co-founded by the World Bank and the Organization for Economic Co-operation and Development (OECD) to "[support] corporate governance reform in emerging markets and developing countries," illustrates this trend. See http://www.gcgf.org.

[10] Simon Johnson, Peter Boone, Alasdair Breach, & Eric Friedman, "Corporate Governance in the Asian Financial Crisis", 58 J. Fin. Econ. 141–86 (2000).

[11] United Nations Conference on Trade and Development (UNCTAD), World Investment Report 2013, at iii (2013), http://unctad.org/en/publicationslibrary/wir2013_en.pdf.

of the world's total IPO proceeds between 2008 and 2012.[12] In this context, foreign investors exploring emerging market opportunities had a keen interest both in better understanding their existing corporate governance structures and in ascertaining the extent to which the introduction of superior practices could boost firm value.

This is especially so given the increasing appreciation of the economic importance of the so-called "BRICs"—an acronym devised by Goldman Sachs in 2001 to designate the giant emerging markets of Brazil, Russia, India, and China.[13] According to estimates by the UN Development Program, the joint economic output of Brazil, India, and China alone is expected to exceed the combined production of the United States, Canada, France, Germany, Italy, and the United Kingdom by 2020.[14] Growth rates in the BRICs significantly outperformed those of developed economies in the 2000s, and played a key role in sustaining global demand in the immediate aftermath of the 2008 financial crisis.

For all these reasons, there has been a noticeable increase in the number of country-level corporate governance studies in different emerging economies,[15] even if they still lag far behind the immense literature covering developed countries. Nevertheless, devising a common framework to examine the state of corporate law and governance in emerging markets remains challenging, for the simple reason that these countries are a diverse bunch. The very label "emerging markets" was first crafted in the 1980s, not as a scholarly category, but simply as a marketing tool for a new index of foreign stocks—as a substitute for the then prevailing, but evidently unappealing, designation of "Third World" countries. Since then, the tag has also come to encompass certain ex-communist economies of the Second World, hence rendering the group even more heterogeneous.

Yet the shared trait of underdevelopment is evidently insufficient as a signal of underlying commonalities. Emerging markets are arguably even more diverse than developed economies, even though the latter's corporate governance systems are seldom grouped and studied as a unitary category. Indeed, countries such as Brazil, Russia, India, China, South Korea, and Turkey—to list only a few prominent examples—have deeply diverse histories, political systems, legal regimes, and economic structures. It should therefore come as no surprise that their corporate governance practices too look significantly different. Consequently, most sweeping generalizations about corporate governance in emerging markets—even if illuminating at a high level of abstraction—are unlikely to provide an accurate depiction of individual countries' realities.

With this caveat in mind, the remainder of this chapter explores some of the key characteristics shared by corporate governance systems in emerging markets, examines the degree of convergence to international standards in the recent past, and identifies promising avenues for future research. Although the exposition will concentrate on the BRICs—the giant countries that achieved notably high levels of economic growth in the 2000s—it will

---

[12] Mats Isaksson & Serdar Çelik, "Who Cares? Corporate Governance in Today's Equity Markets", OECD Corporate Governance Working Papers No. 8, at 12 (2013).

[13] For a critique of the concept, see Ruchir Sharma, "Broken BRICS: Why the Rest Stopped Rising", 91 Foreign Aff. 2 (2012).

[14] United Nations Development Programme, Human Development Report 2013, at iv (2013), http://www.undp.org/content/dam/india/docs/human-development/HDR/HDR2013-Report-English.pdf.

[15] See, for a review of this literature, Stijn Claessens & B. Burcin Yurtoglu, "Corporate Governance in Emerging Markets: A Survey", 15 Emerging Mkts. Rev. 1 (2013).

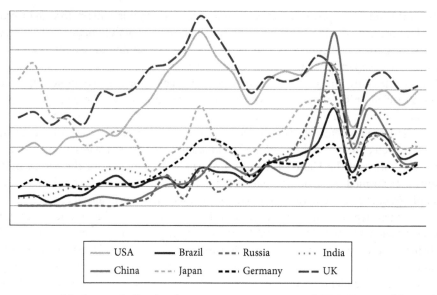

| USA | Brazil | Russia | India |
| China | Japan | Germany | UK |

FIGURE 27.1 Market capitalization by year as a percentage of GDP. Prepared by author based on World Bank data available at http://data.worldbank.org/indicator/CM.MKT. LCAP.GD.ZS.

also incidentally address the experience of other emerging markets as appropriate. The analysis will focus, in particular, on the driving forces, extent, and contours of corporate governance change in the last decades.

Despite their differences, emerging market economies are all latecomers in terms of capital market development, at least in recent history. But if the "emergence" of their capital markets was once a prophecy, it has since turned into reality, especially for the BRICs. As depicted in Figure 27.1, their stock markets have experienced significant growth since the 1990s—and along the way they have also shown a tendency to rise and fall in tandem. Apart from the intrinsic interest in these systems, the examination of the changing structures of corporate governance in emerging markets helps illuminate the variety of institutional arrangements that make capitalism viable around the world.

2 OWNERSHIP STRUCTURES

Most, if not all, emerging market economies operate in a taxing institutional environment that fails both to fully protect property rights and to expediently enforce commercial agreements. These institutional shortcomings, in turn, require different adaptations to the way of doing business. For instance, a lack of property rights protection may concentrate ownership in the hands of the state itself or of otherwise powerful cronies, hence discouraging investment by outsiders. Likewise, difficulties in obtaining timely and impartial court enforcement of commercial agreements may lead firms to rely on extra-contractual commitment mechanisms—such as family relationships and longstanding reputation—or resort to vertical integration.[16]

2.1 Ownership Concentration and Business Groups

In contrast to the model of dispersed ownership of publicly traded companies often observed in the United States and the United Kingdom, but similarly to the developed economies of continental Europe, emerging markets boast a system of mostly concentrated corporate ownership in the hands of wealthy families or the state. Accordingly, the average free float of listed companies in India and Russia does not exceed 35%, compared to over 90% in the United States and the United Kingdom.[17] The presence of a powerful controlling shareholder affords political influence and reputational bonding that compensates for a lack of formal property rights protection and contract enforcement. This, in turn, entails that the primary agency costs in listed firms concern the divergent interests of controlling shareholders and minority shareholders—and not of managers and dispersed shareholders, as is the case in the widely held corporations that populate Anglo-Saxon markets.

In addition, emerging markets tend to offer lower levels of legal protection to outside investors, a feature which, according to the large literature on "law and finance,"[18] also encourages ownership concentration and stifles capital market development, for at least two reasons. First, where minority shareholders are not adequately protected, entrepreneurs will be unwilling to give away control for fear of subsequent expropriation. Second, dispersed ownership—if it were to emerge—would be inherently unstable, since a corporate raider would have much to gain by acquiring a controlling stake in the market so as to extract hefty private benefits to the detriment of vulnerable minority investors.[19] Conversely, concentrated ownership can be self-perpetuating, as existing controlling shareholders will have every incentive to lobby against corporate reforms that enhance minority shareholder rights, hence decreasing their wealth and power.[20]

It is particularly common for controlling shareholders in emerging markets to exert uncontested control over the firm without holding a majority of the voting stock. This is made possible through the use of control-enhancing devices that dissociate cash-flow rights and voting rights—a strategy that induces large shareholders to monitor management, albeit at the risk of significantly increasing their incentives to extract private benefits of control to the detriment of minority investors.[21] Brazil, for instance, had the world's largest incidence of dual-class firms, with voting shares held by mostly corporate insiders and nonvoting shares

---

[16] Ronald J. Gilson, "Controlling Family Shareholders in Developing Countries: Anchoring Relational Exchange", 60 Stan. L. Rev. 663 (2007).

[17] Goldman Sachs, EM Equity in Two Decades: A Changing Landscape, Global Economics Paper No. 204, at 18 (2010).

[18] See *supra* note 8 and accompanying text.

[19] See, e.g., Lucian Bebchuk & Mark Roe, "A Theory of Path Dependence in Corporate Ownership and Governance", 52 Stan. L. Rev. 127 (1999).

[20] Id.

[21] George G. Triantis, Lucian A. Bebchuk, & Reinier H. Kraakman, Stock Pyramids, Cross-Ownership, and Dual Class Equity: The Creation and Agency Costs of Separating Control from Cash Flow Rights, in Concentrated Corporate Ownership (Randall Morck ed., 2000).

by outside investors.[22] In other jurisdictions, such as Chile and South Korea, corporate pyramids are the preferred method through which shareholders control the firm without holding a commensurate equity stake.[23]

Controlling shareholders in emerging markets often control not a single corporation, but rather an entire group of formally independent firms. Business groups play such a pivotal role in different emerging market economies that commentators have questioned the use of the term corporate governance, suggesting that, in such an environment, the group, not the individual firm, is the proper unit of analysis.[24] The economic implications of business groups, however, remain the subject of debate. While the pyramidal structures adopted by some groups can be particularly conducive to expropriation of minority investors, the literature suggests that, in allowing for vertical integration, internal capital markets, and relational contracting, business groups may serve as a valuable adaptation to a weak institutional environment.[25] More recently, commentators have come to underscore the strategic advantages of emerging market business groups in promoting long-term performance, suggesting that their conglomerate structure provides a useful model for developed markets as well.[26]

But if business groups are pervasive in most emerging markets, their precise contours vary from context to context. Diversification across different industries is the norm in some countries, such as Chile and South Korea, but less common in others, most conspicuously China.[27] Their recent trajectory following economic liberalization in the 1990s has not been uniform either. Business groups became ever more connected and centralized in "small-world" fashion in Mexico and Brazil during this period, but more decentralized and fragmented in South Korea.[28]

2.2 State Ownership and Influence

Even after the wave of privatizations in the 1980s and 1990s, state ownership remains alive and well in most emerging markets. All of the BRIC countries continue to exhibit high levels of state ownership. By 2011, companies under direct government control comprised 80% of

[22] Andre Carvalhal da Silva & Avanidhar Subrahmanyam, "Dual-Class Premium, Corporate Governance, and the Mandatory Bid Rule: Evidence from the Brazilian Stock Market", 13 J. Corp. Fin. 1, 4 (2007).

[23] Fernando Lefort, Business Groups in Chile, in Oxford Handbook of Business Groups (Asli M. Colpan, Takashi Hikino, & James R. Lincoln eds., 2010); Kon-Sik Kim, The Role of Judges in Corporate Governance: The Korean Experience, in Transforming Corporate Governance in East Asia 122 (Hideki Kanda, Kon-Sik Kim, & Curtis J. Milhaupt eds., 2008).

[24] Randall Morck, "Finance and Governance in Developing Countries", 3 Annual Rev. Fin. Econ. 375 (2011).

[25] For a review of the economic literature on business groups, see Tarun Khanna & Yishay Yafeh, "Business Groups in Emerging Markets: Paragons or Parasytes?", 45 J. Econ. Lit. 331 (2007).

[26] J. Ramachandran, K.S. Manikandan & Anirvan Pant, "Why Conglomerates Thrive (Outside the US)", 91 Harv. Bus. Rev. (2013).

[27] Khanna & Yafeh, *supra* note 25, at 333; Li-Wen Lin & Curtis J. Milhaupt, "We Are the (National) Champions: Understanding the Mechanisms of State Capitalism in China", 65 Stan. L. Rev. 697, 711 (2013).

[28] Jon Brookfield et al., The Small World of Business Groups: Liberalization and Network Dynamics, in The Small Worlds of Corporate Governance (Bruce Kogut ed., 2012).

the market capitalization in China, 60% in Russia, and 35% in Brazil.[29] In fact, the relevance of state ownership for the corporate governance debate has arguably increased in recent decades, as a number of former governmental divisions came to assume the corporate form.

China has famously pursued a strategy of "corporatization, not privatization," which resulted in the massive floating of minority stakes in its newly created stock exchanges in the last two decades.[30] Despite subsequent reforms decreasing the number of non-tradable shares held by the state and the increase in private sector activity, SOEs remain dominant in the Chinese economy.[31] Moreover, some of the earlier key privatizations in developing countries' natural resource sector have been reversed—either indirectly, as in Russia's re-nationalization of Yukos following inflated tax charges levied against the company, or directly, as in Argentina's outright expropriation of the controlling stake held by Spanish company Repsol in oil company YPF. In Brazil, privatizations often changed the form, but kept the substance, of government control. For instance, following privatization the federal government's majority stake in Brazilian mining giant Vale was replaced by a controlling coalition made of state-controlled institutional investors and members of business groups tied by a shareholders' agreement.[32]

State ownership, in turn, can be both a product of, and a contributing factor to, the weak institutional environment in emerging markets. In laggard economies, capital market failures prevent the financing of large-scale projects by the private sector and hence prompt the state to assume an entrepreneurial function.[33] Yet, once established, there is the risk that SOEs may crowd out, rather than crowd in, private sector firms.

State ownership may also help perpetuate low levels of legal investor protection through a more subtle mechanism: the political role of the state as a shareholder in corporate law reforms. In the 1990s, the Brazilian government, desirous of obtaining a larger control premium for itself in privatization sales, sponsored a series of statutory amendments explicitly aimed at eliminating various minority shareholder rights, to the detriment of outside investors.[34] In China, the interests of the government as controlling shareholder have shaped the development of different areas of the law, from the structure of its first corporations' statute, to the availability of securities class actions and the doctrine of veil piercing.[35]

The government's sway over corporate governance in emerging markets far exceeds its direct influence as a controlling shareholder of large SOEs. In Brazil, the state has also resorted to minority shareholdings—in the form of captive public pension funds and equity

---

[29] The Company that Ruled the Waves, Economist, Dec. 17, 2011, at 109.

[30] Donald C. Clarke, "Corporatisation, Not Privatisation", 7 China Econ. Quart. 27 (2003).

[31] Lin & Milhaupt, *supra* note 27.

[32] Aldo Musacchio & Sérgio G. Lazzarini, "Leviathan in Business: Varieties of State Capitalism and their Implications for Economic Performance" 16–17 (Working Paper, 2012), http://ssrn.com/abstract=2070942.

[33] Alexander Gerschenkron, Economic Backwardness in Historical Perspective (1962).

[34] Mariana Pargendler, "State Ownership and Corporate Governance", 80 Fordham L. Rev. 2917 (2012); Mariana Pargendler, "The Unintended Consequences of State Ownership: The Brazilian Experience", 13 Theoretical. Inq. L. 503 (2012).

[35] Donald C. Clarke, "Corporate Governance in China: An Overview", 14 China Econ. Rev. 494, 495 (2003); Zhiwu Chen, "Capital Markets and Legal Development: The China Case", 14 China Econ. Rev. 451, 453 (2003); Hui Huang, "Piercing the Corporate Veil in China: Where Is It Now and Where Is It Heading?", 60 Am. J. Comp. L. 743 (2012).

investments by its Development Bank (Banco Nacional de Desenvolvimento Econômico e Social—BNDES)—to shape corporate policy.[36] These state-controlled actors exercise influence not only through their regular statutory voting rights in the shareholders' meetings, but also by explicit control-sharing arrangements as parties to shareholders agreements, which habitually grant the state-controlled institutional investors both board representation and veto rights over key corporate decisions.[37] In China, the government's sway over, and support to, private sector corporations has effectively blurred the distinction between public and private modes of ownership.[38]

Still another avenue for state intervention in corporate governance in emerging markets comes from the provision of subsidized debt financing to selected private firms. The loan volume extended by Brazil's BNDES alone in 2012 reached nearly four times that of the World Bank.[39] Development economists have also long attributed the rapid catch-up process in Asia to the export requirements inserted in governmental loan agreements to business groups.[40] The Korean government has never been a major shareholder in Korean chaebols, but was nevertheless able to direct industrial policy through its grip on the financial sector.[41]

3 REFORM EFFORTS

Capital markets in BRIC countries underwent major developments in the last two decades. As depicted in Figure 27.1, these countries transitioned from having meager or virtually non-existent stock markets in the early 1990s to boasting sizable market capitalizations in the mid-2000s, even if they faced a substantial retreat thereafter as underlying economic conditions worsened. At the height of the bubble in 2007, China and Brazil, together with the United States, placed as the top three IPO destinations worldwide.[42]

Nevertheless, the precise makeup of stock markets in emerging markets continues to vary widely. With only a few hundred listed companies (most of which of relatively large size), Brazil has struggled to induced medium-sized firms to access public markets. At the other end of the spectrum, India boasts the largest number of publicly-traded companies in the world. Whereas most Latin American countries exhibit low ratios of market capitalizations to GDP, Chile stands out as an exception, displaying ratios comparable to the robust equity markets of the United States and the United Kingdom in recent years.[43]

---

[36] Musacchio & Lazzarini, *supra* note 32.

[37] Mariana Pargendler, Governing State Capitalism: The Case of Brazil, in Chinese State Capitalism and Institutional Change: Domestic and Global Implications (Benjamin Liebman & Curtis J. Milhaupt eds., 2015).

[38] Curtis Milhaupt & Wentong Zheng, "Beyond Ownership: State Capitalism and the Chinese Firm", 103 Geo. L. J. 665 (2015).

[39] Samantha Pearson, A Bank Too Big to Be Beautiful, Fin. Times, Sept. 23, 2012.

[40] Alice H. Amsden, The Rise of "The Rest": Challenges to the West from Late-Industrializing Economies 148 et seq. (2001).

[41] Curtis J. Milhaupt & Katharina Pistor, Law and Capitalism 118 (2008).

[42] Ernst & Young, Growth During Economic Uncertainty: Global IPO Trends Report (2008).

[43] World Bank data available at http://data.worldbank.org/indicator/CM.MKT.LCAP.GD.ZS.

The expansion of equity markets in emerging economies paralleled both economic and legal reforms. On the economic side, full and partial privatizations induced the private sector to assume the role of entrepreneur and financier that had been relinquished by the state. The elimination of barriers to trade and financial flows, in turn, encouraged foreign investors to jump in. On the legal side, the BRICs witnessed both the implementation of legal reforms and the adoption of superior corporate governance practices on a voluntary basis, with varying degrees of success.

3.1 The Tortuous Path of Legislative Change

Russia's experience is emblematic of the challenges inherent in large-scale reform. In the 1990s, prominent US legal scholars conceived its new corporate statute, which was deliberately based on a model of "self-enforcing" corporate law designed to compensate for the country's otherwise fragile legal system.[44] Nevertheless, the good intentions and the attentiveness to local circumstances were insufficient to make the new law effective, as it notoriously failed to constrain subsequent instances of self-dealing.[45]

Adopted in 1994 as the legal framework for China's corporatization strategy, its company law mixed standard Western elements with local idiosyncrasies. Molded by the vision of a state-dominated economy, the Chinese corporate statute imposed a rigid mandatory framework that, while arguably suitable for SOEs, was woefully inadequate for private sector enterprise.[46] The law was also reticent on the fiduciary duties of corporate managers and the means of enforcement, with no provision for derivative suits.[47]

In 2005, China's corporations and securities statutes underwent a major overhaul that was strongly acclaimed by local scholars as an improvement to the existing statute that changed it "almost beyond recognition."[48] The new regime imposed fiduciary duties on managers and controlling shareholders, required listed firms to have independent directors, permitted derivative suits, and recommended (though it did not compel) cumulative voting in director elections.[49] Nevertheless, a gap remains between the "law in the books" and the "law in action." For instance, the prominent role of the state has prompted a double standard in terms of legal enforcement, with SOEs appearing to face more lenient regulatory scrutiny than private sector firms.[50]

Brazil's 1976 Corporations Law—an innovative statute that borrowed freely from US and European sources to address local challenges—remains largely untouched, as subsequent legal reforms turned out to be modest in scope. A 1997 amendment to the statute eliminated

---

[44] Bernard Black & Reinier Kraakman, "A Self-Enforcing Model of Corporate Law", 109 Harv. L. Rev. 1911 (1996).

[45] Black et al., *supra* note 6.   [46] Clarke, *supra* note 35.   [47] Id. at 502.

[48] Xin Tang, Protecting Minority Shareholders in China: A Task for both Legislation and Enforcement in Transforming Corporate Governance in East Asia 143 (Hideki Kanda, Kon-Sik Kim, & Curtis J. Milhaupt eds., 2008).

[49] Id.

[50] Henk Berkman, Rebel A. Cole, & Lawrence J. Fu, "Political Connections and Minority-Shareholder Protection: Evidence from Securities-Market Regulation in China", 45 J. Fin. Quant. Anal. 1391 (2011); William T. Allen & Han Shen, Assessing China's Top-Down Securities Markets, in Capitalizing China 171 (Joseph P.H. Fan & Randall Morck eds., 2012).

the requirement of a mandatory bid for minority shares in sale-of-control transactions with the purpose of allowing the state to appropriate the entire premium control to itself in privatization sales. These legal changes—which applied to firms under both state and private control—facilitated a series of abusive going-private transactions, thereby destroying investor confidence in Brazil's capital markets. After the bulk of privatization sales, a legal reform in 2001 reinstated some of the minority protections that had been previously abrogated, but was otherwise timid, as political opposition from controlling shareholders frustrated attempts at more transformational change.[51]

Major legislative change was also slow to come by in India. Subject to several amendments primarily designed to relax governmental controls and increase governance flexibility, India's Companies Act of 1956 remained in force until the significant overhaul by the Companies Act of 2013.[52] Some of the changes introduced by the new statute were designed to incorporate US-inspired mechanisms (such as class actions) into Indian law, while others clearly surpassed prevailing international standards, as in the new requirement of a maximum term limit of ten years for independent directors.[53]

3.2 The Role of Government and Private Regulation

Most of the progress in Brazil's corporate governance practices did not stem from sweeping statutory changes, but rather from a combination of private regulation and the increasingly activist stance by the Securities Commission (Comissão de Valores Mobiliários—CVM). Brazil's experience with the Novo Mercado—a premium voluntary listing segment of the São Paulo Stock Exchange (BM&FBovespa)—was instrumental in the revitalization of the country's equity markets in the 2000s. By leaving the existing legal regime intact, this strategy of "regulatory dualism" successfully circumvented the powerful political opposition to reforms by existing corporate elites.[54] Firms opting for a Novo Mercado listing are subject to strictures such as a ban on nonvoting shares, a mandatory bid rule in sales of control, and director independence requirements.

Modeled after the US Securities and Exchange Commission, CVM was established in the 1970s as the sheriff of Brazil's capital markets. Subsequent statutory amendments in 1997 and 2001 increased its autonomy vis-à-vis the executive and expanded the scope of its regulatory oversight and disciplinary authority. Since capital markets boomed following a series of IPOs on the Novo Mercado, CVM has advanced the investor protection agenda in various fronts.[55]

---

[51] Ronald J. Gilson, Henry Hansmann & Mariana Pargendler, "Regulatory Dualism as a Development Strategy: Corporate Reform in Brazil, the United States, and the European Union", 63 Stan. L. Rev. 475 (2013).

[52] John Armour & Pryia Lele, "Law, Finance, and Politics: The Case of India", 43 Law & Soc'y Rev. 491, 501 (2009).

[53] Akshaya Kamalnath, "Corporate Governance Reform in India: Accommodating Local Culture along with the Drive for Global Convergence", 30 KLRI Journal of Law and Legislation 137 (2013).

[54] Gilson et al., *supra* note 51.

[55] For an overview of the enforcement authority of CVM and its recent developments, see Maria Helena Santana, Brazil: The Corporate Governance Framework and Practices relating to Supervision and Enforcement, in Supervision and Enforcement in Corporate Governance (OECD 2013).

First, the Commission made progress with respect to enforcement, culminating, for instance, in Brazil's celebrated first criminal conviction for insider trading in 2011.[56] Second, CVM came to embrace more protectionist interpretations of existing law, as in the famous Tractebel decision. By preventing controlling shareholders from voting to approve interested transactions, the Commission's new interpretation effectively implemented a "majority-of-the-minority" approval requirement at shareholders' meetings. Third, CVM improved the existing regulatory landscape through a variety of channels: it published a series of stringent advisory opinions on matters ranging from fiduciary duties to the scope of antitakeover defenses, instituted more expansive disclosure regulations that are stricter than the original Novo Mercado standards, and innovated in permitting proxy access (or conferring reimbursement of expenses incurred in proxy solicitations) to shareholders holding more than 0.5% of the company's stock. And, finally, CVM has effectively exercised its statutory authority to punish unlawful actions by company managers, as exemplified by the imposition of fines to the CFO and directors of listed firm Sadia. The Commission concluded that their failure to abide by the company's risk own management policies with respect to exchange rate derivatives, which resulted in hefty financial losses following the 2008 financial crisis, constituted a violation of their fiduciary duty of care under Brazilian law.

Similarly, until very recently corporate governance reform in India proceeded more quickly via the regulatory agency than the legislature.[57] Established and strengthened as an oversight body between 1988 and 1992, the Securities and Exchange Board of India (SEBI) provided the regulatory framework for the country's expanding capital markets. Like CVM, SEBI's aggressive posture has at times led to accusations that it was overstepping its regulatory authority.[58]

Among the innovations embraced by SEBI is the watershed "Clause 49" of stock exchange listing agreements. First enacted in 2001 and revised in 2005, Clause 49 reflects a set of corporate governance standards following the voluntary Corporate Governance Code sponsored by the Confederation of Indian Industry (CII)—which, in contrast to the business establishment in Brazil, played a prominent role in sponsoring, rather than opposing, corporate governance reforms. The requirements described in Clause 49, which came to apply to all listed firms in India, ranged from a minimum percentage of independent directors to the institution of an audit committee and the requisite of chief executive certification of financial statements. Empirical studies documented a positive stock market reaction to the announcement of Clause 49, as well as a positive effect of stricter enforcement of these standards on firm value,[59] even though actual compliance remained far from universal.[60]

---

[56] Admittedly, given the lax treatment of white-collar crimes under Brazilian law, the convictions resulted in no jail sentences; defendants were sanctioned to mandatory community service, a monetary fine, and a temporary ban from serving as executives of publicly traded companies.

[57] Armour & Lele, *supra* note 52.

[58] Afra Afsharipour, "Corporate Governance Convergence: Lessons from the Indian Experience", 29 Nw. J. Int'l. L. & Bus. 335, 376 (2009).

[59] Bernard S. Black & Vikramaditya S. Khanna, "Can Corporate Governance Reforms Increase Firm Market Values? Event Study Evidence from India", 4 J. Emp. Legal Stud. 749 (2007); Dhammika Dharmapala & Vikramaditya Khanna, "Corporate Governance, Enforcement, and Firm Value: Evidence from India", 29 J. L. Econ. & Org. 1056 (2013).

[60] Kamalnath, *supra* note 53, at 7.

3.3 The Role of Courts

Courts have generally played at best a modest and at worst a positively detrimental role in the transformation of corporate governance in emerging markets. The disadvantages of relying on the judiciary for investor protection include unreasonable delays, lack of technical sophistication, and even outright corruption. In most emerging market economies, corporate and securities litigation is a comparatively less significant means to rein in abuses by managers and controlling shareholders compared to more developed economies, and especially the United States.

There is a paucity of derivative lawsuits involving public company shareholders in both Brazil and India, even though these jurisdictions experience distinctively high levels of litigiousness in other areas of law.[61] China's more recent recognition of derivative actions "on the books" did little to encourage their filing.[62] Corporate litigation was also virtually nonexistent in South Korea before the East Asian crisis of the late 1990s (with actual derivative lawsuits being unheard of until 1997), but it has since soared.[63] At another extreme, Russia's highly dysfunctional judicial system allows for the filing of lawsuits that are frivolous—but potentially successful, considering the specter of corruption—to be used as a takeover strategy.[64]

Resistance to legal change is still another issue plaguing courts' role in emerging markets governance. In both Brazil and India the judiciary has been receptive to the use of constitutional law arguments to thwart reform efforts. In an attempt to cure the deficiencies of Brazilian laws on executive compensation disclosure, CVM issued new regulations in 2009 requiring companies to reveal the aggregate amounts paid to executives, as well as the highest, lowest, and average compensation packages of directors and officers. Executives have so far successfully challenged the rule by contending that—in view of the privacy rights guaranteed by the Brazilian constitution and the country's particularly high levels of violence—CVM rules were unconstitutional as a violation of their fundamental rights to privacy and personal security.

In India, too, several constitutional challenges to new laws on insolvency and secured credit have delayed the implementation of important reforms for the development of India's credit market.[65] A 2002 legal attempt to circumvent India's notoriously slow courts by creating a separate judicial body to enforce the provisions of the Companies Act was likewise

---

[61] Vikramaditya Khanna & Umakanth Varottil, The Rarity of Derivative Actions in India: Reasons and Consequences, in The Derivative Action in Asia: A Comparative and Functional Approach 369 et seq. (Dan W. Puchniak, Harald Baum & Michael Ewing-Chow eds., 2012); Gilson et al., *supra* note 51, at 494.

[62] See Donald C. Clarke & Nicholas H. Howson, Pathway to Minority Shareholder Protection: Derivative Actions in the People's Republic of China, in The Derivative Action in Asia: A Comparative and Functional Approach 243, 244 (D. Puchniak et al. eds., 2012).

[63] Kon-Sik Kim, The Role of Judges in Corporate Governance: The Korean Experience, in Transforming Corporate Governance in East Asia 104 (Hideki Kanda, Kon-Sik Kim, & Curtis J. Milhaupt eds., 2008).

[64] Alexander Settles, "Evolving Corruption: Hostile Takeovers, Corporate Raiding, and Company Capture in Russia, Center for International Private Enterprise" (Aug. 31, 2009), http://www.cipe.org/publications/detail/evolving-corruption-hostile-takeovers-corporate-raiding-and-company-capture.

[65] Armour & Lele, *supra* note 52, at 506.

frustrated by constitutional challenges.[66] The Korean judiciary, in turn, has unduly oscillated between formalistic and liberal methods of statutory interpretation in reaching conservative opinions that favored the interests of chaebols over those of outside shareholders.[67]

The few exceptional instances of judicial innovation in corporate law prove the rule. Despite their notorious subordination to the Communist Party's wishes, Chinese courts played a surprisingly activist part in imposing American-style fiduciary duties notwithstanding the lack of explicit statutory provision under the 1994 Corporations Law.[68] In recent years, Brazilian courts have come to consistently grant minority shareholders' requests for partial dissolution of closely held corporations, even though such a remedy is not available under the Corporations Law. One might be tempted to interpret this newly recognized right as a creative solution to protect minority shareholders from abuse in situations where they would otherwise be unable to prove the existence of wrongdoing by controlling shareholders and managers.[69] Such innovation, however, is not without costs, for it carries the risk of undermining the company's ability to "lock in" capital, a distinguishing—and economically crucial—feature of the corporate form.[70]

3.4 Alternative Institutional Arrangements

Substitute mechanisms compensate for the difficulties in judicial enforcement. Given the substantive and procedural legal hurdles to derivative actions in Brazil and India, aggrieved shareholders have typically turned to the securities regulator instead—CVM or SEBI—for more expedient and effective redress.[71] In some countries—such as Chile, Brazil and, to some extent, China—listed firms have often attempted to circumvent the judicial route altogether by embracing arbitration as the preferred method of dispute resolution.[72]

Whereas in Italy and the United States public company arbitration is either outlawed or frowned upon as a scheme for potential investor abuse; in emerging markets arbitration may operate as a second-best solution given the deficiencies of the court system.[73] Novo

---

[66] Afsharipour, *supra* note 58, at 397.

[67] Kim, *supra* note 63, at 104.

[68] Nicholas Calcina Howson, The Doctrine that Dared Not Speak its Name: Anglo-American Fiduciary Duties in China's 2005 Company Law and Case Law Intimations of Prior Convergence, in Transforming Corporate Governance in East Asia (Hideki Kanda, Kon-Sik Kim, & Curtis J. Milhaupt eds., 2008).

[69] On the practical difficulties of proving corporate wrongdoing in Brazil, see Érica Gorga & Michael Halberstam, "Litigation Discovery and Corporate Governance: The Missing Story about the 'Genius of American Corporate Law' ", 63 Emory L.J. 1382 (2014).

[70] Lynn Stout, "On the Nature of Corporations", U. Ill. L. Rev. 256 (2005) (for a an articulation of the concept of capital lock in); Edward B. Rock & Michael L. Wachter, "Waiting for the Omelet to Set: Match-Specific Assets and Minority Oppression in the Close Corporation", 24 J. Corp. L. 913 (1999) (describing the economic benefits of capital lock-in).

[71] Khanna & Varottil, *supra* note 61, at 389 (India); Paulo Cezar Aragão, "A CVM em Juízo: Limites e Possibilidades", 34 Revista de Direito Bancário e do Mercado de Capitais 38, 42 (2006).

[72] Christos A. Ravanides, "Arbitration Clauses in Public Company Charters: An Expansion of the ADR Elysian Fields or a Descent Into Hades?", 18 Am. Rev. Int'l. Arb. 371 (2007).

[73] Id.

Mercado, the premium corporate governance segment of the São Paulo Stock Exchange (BM&FBovespa), in fact mandates the arbitration of all internal affairs and securities law disputes, operating on the assumption that this is the most investor-friendly method of resolving corporate conflicts. Moreover, numerous other companies have voluntarily inserted arbitration clauses in their charters and shareholder agreements.[74] Nevertheless, the choice for arbitration brings about challenges of its own, especially where, as in Brazil, the proceedings are confidential, thus hindering the development of case law and contributing to the opaqueness of the institutional environment.

At any rate, changes in formal statutes, regulations, and enforcement at the national level are insufficient to account for the extent of the transformation in emerging markets' corporate governance practices. Brazil's positive experience with the Novo Mercado shows that self-regulation through stock exchange listing requirements may play a crucial role in kick-starting much-needed reform. Scholars have argued that, in China, reputational sanctions through public criticism by the Shanghai and Shenzen stock exchanges help deter corporate wrongdoing in the absence of formal public enforcement.[75] Individual emerging market companies are also free to adopt sensible corporate governance practices, which empirical studies have found to be associated with improvements in firm performance.[76]

Finally, international (and especially US) cross-listings by emerging market corporations have been another engine of corporate governance change. The existing literature has posited two different theories to explain firms' decisions to list their shares on a foreign exchange. According to the market segmentation (and liquidity) hypothesis, the benefits of cross-listings lie in permitting foreign issuers to expand and diversify their investment base. Proponents of the competing bonding hypothesis, by contrast, interpret overseas listings as a mechanism by which firms can make a credible commitment to the higher standards of corporate governance and transparency prevailing in the host jurisdiction.[77] But whether or not bonding considerations are determinative, overseas listings certainly play a role in corporate governance convergence.

4   CONVERGENCE AND PERSISTENCE IN EMERGING MARKETS GOVERNANCE

If the recent transformation of corporate governance practices in emerging markets is evident, the extent and direction of change remains contested. A main theme of the academic literature in the last decades concerns the impact of globalization on corporate structures and practices. Specifically, the question is whether corporate governance systems around the

---

[74] Mariana Pargendler et al., "Cláusulas Arbitrais no Mercado de Capitais Brasileiro: Alguns Dados Empíricos", 40 Revista de Arbitragem e Mediação 105 (2014).

[75] Benjamin L. Liebman & Curtis J. Milhaupt, "Reputational Sanctions in China's Securities Market", 108 Colum. L. Rev. 929 (2008).

[76] See Claessens & Yurtoglu, *supra* note 15.

[77] See, for a review of this literature, G. Andrew Karolyi, "Corporate Governance, Agency Problems and International Cross-Listings: A Defense of the Bonding Hypothesis", 13 Emerging Mkts. Rev. 516 (2012).

world have become increasingly uniform (the "convergence thesis"), or if, instead, path dependence significantly constrained the course of subsequent developments (the "persistence thesis").[78] While this debate focused primarily on the usual mature economies, it is easily replicated with respect to emerging markets.[79]

On the one hand, rising globalization, foreign competition, and international investment flows all militate in favor of some form of convergence. Mounting competitive pressures increase domestic firms' need for outside financing, which, in turn, creates demand for stronger forms of investor protection. As foreign investors flock into emerging market economies, they bring with them the corporate governance practices, structures, and norms of their home country, even if not always with due regard to local specificities.

On the other hand, the theoretical arguments favoring persistence in corporate governance structures are also strong. The political economy of corporate lawmaking is tilted toward existing structures, as controlling shareholders, dispersed investors, managers, and workers engage in lobbying efforts to maintain their status and privileges. And, perhaps more importantly, there are significant institutional complementarities between the corporate governance regime and other political and economic dimensions, such as the form of industrial organization, the flexibility of labor markets, the characteristics of the educational system, and the structure of political representation, which, taken together, engender different "varieties of capitalism."[80] As a result, particular corporate governance systems may be less amenable to change than a closer focus on corporate dimensions alone would suggest.

4.1 Forms, Functions, and Idiosyncrasies

The corporate structure has long become universal. Irrespective of their origin, corporations around the world today share certain core attributes, such as legal personality, tradable shares, limited liability, delegated management, and investor ownership.[81] These features, in turn, are increasingly relevant in emerging markets, as state-owned enterprises previously operating as governmental divisions in countries such as China and Russia, among many others, came to adopt the corporate form. But beyond the spread of corporate organization itself, there has been a visible tendency toward the implementation of the wide array of corporate law and governance features prevailing in developed, and especially Anglo-Saxon, markets—ranging from independent directors and fiduciary duties to insider trading bans and securities agency enforcement—to emerging market economies. Still, the intensity of such convergence, as well as the precise mix of best practices, can vary dramatically from one jurisdiction to another.

---

[78] For a collection of prominent works on this theme, see Convergence and Persistence in Corporate Governance (Jeffrey N. Gordon & Mark J. Roe eds., 2004).

[79] See, e.g., Henry Hansmann & Reinier Kraakman, Convergence of Corporate Governance: Promise and Prospects, in Convergence of Corporate Governance: Promise and Prospects (Abdul Rasheed & Toru Yoshikawa eds., 2012).

[80] See Mark J. Roe, "Rents and their Corporate Consequences", 53 Stan. L. Rev. 1463 (2001); Varieties of Capitalism: The Institutional Foundations of Comparative Advantage (Peter Hall & David Soskice eds., 2001).

[81] John Armour et al., What is Corporate Law?, in The Anatomy of Corporate Law: A Comparative And Functional Approach 1 (Reinier Kraakman et al., 2017).

Focusing only on the adoption of identical corporate governance practices prevailing in developed countries would certainly understate the degree of actual convergence. Functional, rather than formal, convergence is often the norm.[82] Diverse arrangements such as public company arbitration, stiff reputational sanctions, and governmental oversight of firm performance all operate as institutional substitutes that further the goal of investor protection without conforming to international "best practices."

Yet it would be both naïve and misguided to overstate the convergence thesis in its strong form. Just as functional convergence is feasible without accompanying formal convergence, the reverse is also true, as formally identical practices can have disparate significance in different underlying environments. Scholars have duly admonished the "elusive quest" for universal corporate governance standards, recognizing that identical practices can have diverse consequences depending on the prevailing ownership structures.[83]

Take, for instance, a longstanding policy prescription of the US corporate governance movement: the separation of the roles of board chair and CEO. By providing the board with independent leadership, the split of roles is designed to ensure that directors are in a position to effectively monitor the company's management. However, despite major strides, this recommendation remains highly contested in the US context of powerful CEOs, as independent chairs are still far from universal. In Brazil, where political opposition to corporate governance changes is particularly fierce, companies have refrained from vetoing the inclusion of a mandatory split of positions as a listing requirement for all premium corporate governance listing segments on the BM&FBovespa.

The greater receptivity to independent board leadership by Brazilian firms is less due to their especially strong commitment to best practices of corporate governance than to its different contextual significance. In a system of highly concentrated corporate control, the primary source of agency costs is not managerial omnipotence but rather the potential of abuse by controlling shareholders. While controlling shareholders typically seek to keep management on a tight leash, they do not always covet the consuming office of chief executive. And, even when they do, having an independent board chair may not be exactly threatening when she is elected by the controlling shareholder himself. In fact, a substantial number of Brazilian companies already had a split in place—with the controlling shareholder serving as board chair and delegating everyday managerial decisions to a professional CEO—before the advent of the listing requirement, which makes it far less consequential in the Brazilian context of concentrated ownership than in the US system of dispersed ownership.

Similarly, while the United States has only recently embraced an advisory shareholder vote on executive compensation ("say on pay") at least every three years, Brazilian corporate law has long required shareholders to approve executives' overall pay packages on an annual basis. In a context of concentrated ownership, however, the rule has different implications: it provides controlling shareholders with yet another opportunity to supervise management as well as to approve their own salaries as board members. In some Brazilian

---

[82] See Ronald J. Gilson, "Globalizing Corporate Governance: Convergence of Form or Function", 49 Am. J. Comp. L. 329 (2001).

[83] Lucian A. Bebchuk & Assaf Hamdani, "The Elusive Quest for Global Governance Standards", 157 U. Pa. L. Rev. 1263–17 (2009).

firms, director compensation to members of the controlling family even exceeds the pay of the professional CEO.

As a general matter, the recent transformation in emerging markets' governance has combined the influence of prevailing practices in mature markets with indigenously designed improvements. More recently, the origins of institutional transplants from foreign sources have also begun to change. Rather than invariably looking to developed countries for model norms and practices, emerging market economies have increasingly learned from each other's experiences. The apparent success of Brazil's Novo Mercado has invited similar initiatives in India and the Philippines.[84] After taking over traditional US firms such as Heinz and Burger King, Brazil's 3G Capital fund has exported its ruthless efficiency-oriented management style. In the future, one can expect the cross-fertilization in corporate law to become ever more multidirectional, with mature economies receiving the influence of emerging markets' norms and practices—not least due to the rising levels of foreign direct investment by multinationals and national champions from China, India, Brazil, and the like.

4.2 Evolving Ownership Structures

Changes in ownership structure have proceeded at a somewhat slower pace. Given the continued predominance of concentrated ownership in the BRICs, hostile takeovers either remain exceedingly rare, or assume a very different meaning. In Russia, a "hostile takeover" is not, as one might expect, the acquisition of a controlling stake from public shareholders against managers' will—a strategy which is hardly feasible given the presence of a controlling shareholder in most companies. Instead, it refers to the relatively common, if extreme, practice of gaining control over a firm through dubious practices ranging from fraud and corrupt law enforcement to outright violence.[85]

In Brazil, the failure of the hostile bid by meat-processing firm Sadia for its chief competitor Perdigão—the first and only hostile takeover attempt in recent history—illustrates how the apparent increase in ownership dispersion in recent years may be illusory.[86] Despite the absence of a single controlling shareholder, the target's several blockholders were party to a shareholders' agreement, and acted swiftly to reject the offer notwithstanding its sizable premium. Even in India, where a non-trivial minority of firms is widely held, hostile takeovers have faced practical difficulties thanks to hefty regulatory hurdles to control changes as well as the presence of founder-friendly financial institutions. Past hostile bids have failed for reasons ranging from the outright refusal of the target companies to register the acquired shares to strong political opposition leading to the enactment of regulatory impediments.[87]

---

[84] Inspiration from the East: Encouraged by the Novo Mercado's Success, the Philippines and India Create Special Listing Tiers in Their Own Stock Exchanges, 72 Capital Aberto (Aug. 2009).

[85] Settles, *supra* note 64.

[86] For a description of the recent evolution of ownership structures in Brazil, see Érica Gorga, "Changing the Paradigm of Stock Ownership from Concentrated Towards Dispersed Ownership? Evidence from Brazil and Consequences for Emerging Countries", 29 Nw. J. Int'l. L. & Bus. 439 (2008).

[87] Armour & Lele, *supra* note 52, at 506.

A notable exception is Korea, where reforms following the Asian crisis left local firms vulnerable to foreign threats.[88]

When it comes to ownership structures, convergence came mostly from the opposite direction: while dispersed ownership remains rare in emerging markets, there has been a visible trend toward concentrated corporate control in the United States. Dual-class shares, once banned by the New York Stock Exchange (NYSE) listing standards until 1984, used to be commonplace only in the South and continental Europe. In the 2000s, however, they experienced a revival in the US market, as founders of highly prominent technology firms, such as Google and Facebook, resorted to multiple voting shares to lock in control of the company before going public.[89] Ironically, the US market might become a refuge for foreign firms seeking entrenched management structures. In 2013, Chinese internet giant Alibaba announced that it would pursue a NYSE listing after the Hong Kong Stock Exchange—its initially preferred venue—refused to exempt it from the listing rules prohibiting dual-class stocks.

4.3 Stakeholders and Corporate Governance

Through the effect of concentrated ownership structures and accompanying legal institutions, the interests of (controlling) shareholders often take center-stage in emerging market firms.[90] Yet—at least on the books—consideration of stakeholder interests is also particularly salient in their governance. Even though the spurt in economic growth in the 2000s ameliorated social conditions for many, poverty and inequality—not to mention human rights violations—remain a major challenge in emerging market economies.[91] In this context, issues of distribution assume particular significance in shaping different doctrines of corporate law.

In assessing the distributive effects of corporate governance policies, the degree of equity ownership by the general population plays a fundamental role. In a "society of shareholders," the norm of shareholder primacy assumes greater legitimacy compared to contexts in which only a small fraction of the citizenry has a direct stake in stock market outcomes[92]—as is generally the case in emerging markets, where the recent capital market boom was mostly

---

[88]   Hwa-Jin Kim, A Tale of Three Companies: The Emerging Market for Corporate Control in Korea, in Transforming Corporate Governance in East Asia 122 (Hideki Kanda, Kon-Sik Kim, & Curtis J. Milhaupt eds., 2008).

[89]   See Joseph A. McCahery & Erik P.M. Vermeulen, "Six Components of Corporate Governance That Cannot Be Ignored", 11 Eur. Comp. & Fin. L. Rev. 160 (2014) (regarding the re-emergence of dual-class firms in the United States as consistent with long-term value creation).

[90]   In Brazil, for instance, there is widespread use of shareholder agreements that legally bind the votes of corporate directors, to the despair of corporate governance advocates. Érica Gorga, Corporate Control & Governance after a Decade from "Novo Mercado": Changes in Ownership Structures and Shareholder Power in Brazil, in Research Handbook on Shareholder Power 479 (Jennifer G. Hill & Randall S. Thomas eds., 2015).

[91]   Although absolute poverty has decreased in the last decades, emerging markets (with the notable exception of Brazil) have witnessed a concomitant increase in income inequality.

[92]   For data on stock ownership levels around the world, see Paul A. Grout, William L. Megginson, & Anna Zalewska, "One Half-Billion Shareholders and Counting: Determinants of Individual Share Ownership around the World" (Working Paper, 2009), available at http://ssrn.com/abstract=1457482.

fueled by foreign investors. While on average 40% of the population in developed countries is invested in stock markets, the proportion falls to 5% in emerging economies (ranging, in turn, from a minuscule 0.3% in Brazil to approximately 10% in China).[93]

Consequently, in an environment where stockholders are few and far between (and mostly well-off to begin with), the conflict between the interests of shareholders and non-shareholder constituencies assumes special significance. Distributional concerns aside, the norm of shareholder primacy might also fail to generate efficient outcomes if product markets are uncompetitive,[94] a still common feature of developing countries.

Perhaps unsurprisingly, emerging markets have not fully embraced the pursuit of shareholder value as the exclusive normative goal of corporate law. Under Brazil's corporations statute "the controlling shareholder must use its influence so as to make the company fulfill its purpose and its social function, and has duties and responsibilities to the other shareholders, employees and the community in which it operates, whose rights and interests he must loyally abide by and respect."[95] The statutory concept of abuse by controlling shareholders is broad enough to explicitly encompass actions that harm not only the company or its minority shareholders, but also the "national economy."

Social concerns have impinged on other facets of corporate law as well. Brazil, for instance, has embraced a particularly extensive version of the veil-piercing doctrine, thereby mitigating the attribute of limited shareholder liability in critical areas of law. Whenever the creditor is an employee or a consumer (as defined by consumer protection legislation), shareholders may be—and recurrently are—held liable whenever legal personality poses an obstacle to the discharge of the companies' obligations, despite the absence of fraud or other forms of abuse.

Rules addressing stakeholder interests appear in Chinese corporate governance as well. The main such interests are, of course, those of the state as run by the Communist Party. But the formally communist regime also pays considerable lip service to workers.

China has implemented employee board representation since its first modern Company Law of 1994. The 2006 legal reforms gave the prior requirement teeth by fixing the minimum participation of workers at one-third of the supervisory board.[96] The same statute provides that "[i]n the course of doing business, a company must comply with laws and administrative regulations, conform to social morality and business ethics, act in good faith, subject itself to the government and the public supervision, and undertake social responsibility."[97] Moreover, concerns about pay disparities and internal pay equity have led the Chinese government to cap executive compensation at 20 times average employee salary in all SOEs overseen by the State-Owned Asset Supervision and Administrative Commission of the State Council (SASAC), the governmental agency that serves as the controlling shareholder for China's largest SOEs.[98]

---

[93] PAC-PME, Sumário das Propostas do Brasil + Competitivo, sl. 30 (Oct. 2013).

[94] For this argument, see Mark J. Roe, "The Shareholder Wealth Maximization Norm and Industrial Organization", 149 U. Pa. L. Rev. 2063 (2001).

[95] Art. 116, Lei No. 6.404, art. 26, de 15 de Dezembro de 1976, Diário Oficial da União [D.O.U.] de 17.12.1976 (Braz.).

[96] Li-Wen Lin, "Corporate Social Responsibility in China: Window Dressing or Structural Change", 28 Berkeley J. Int'l. L. 64 (2010).

[97] Id. at 71.

[98] Milhaupt & Zheng, *supra* note 38 (noting that the widespread practice of "on duty consumption" of perquisites has nevertheless undermined the rule's efficacy).

While instances of human rights abuses, environmental degradation, and hazardous consumer products are still recurrent, China, at least on paper, has made formal progress when it comes to the embrace of Western-style corporate social responsibility (CSR) with "Chinese characteristics."[99] Chinese stock exchanges have required listed companies to disclose their CSR policy. The State-Owned Asset Supervision and Administrative Commission of the State Council (SASAC)—the governmental agency that serves as the controlling shareholder for China's largest SOEs—has issued a Guide Opinion on CSR.[100] While labor rights and environmental obligations figure prominently in the CSR movement in China, the promotion of human rights remains conspicuously absent.[101]

India's Companies Act of 2013 is particularly innovative in its approach to social considerations. Although reasonable minds may differ on its merits, the statute breaks new ground in requiring companies to spend at least 2% of average net profits to promote their corporate social responsibility policy, preferably in local areas, or to otherwise explain the reasons for noncompliance. Moreover, the Act requires directors to "act in good faith to promote the objects of the company for the benefit of its members as a whole, and in the best interests of the company, its employees, the shareholders, the community and for the protection of the environment."[102] It also seeks to promote female participation on corporate boards, albeit timidly, by conditioning the increase in the number of directors beyond fifteen to the presence of at least one female board member.

Yet emerging markets are not alone in the trend (however meritorious) of internalizing social issues in corporate governance. In the last decade, a number of European countries, such as Norway, France, and Italy have mandated minimum quotas for female directors on boards. Under the UK Companies Act of 2006, directors are under a duty to promote the success of the company for the benefit of shareholders, but must pay due regard to other interests such as those of employees, customers, and the community. In the United States, too, social concerns have recently made a reappearance, even if mostly in the form of new disclosure requirements on subjects such as the consideration of diversity in director appointments, the pay gap between chief executives and their employees, and even in the use of "conflict minerals" from the Democratic Republic of the Congo.

5 CONCLUSION

Today's emerging markets comprise a historical category rooted in the early promise, and later success, of capital market development. The rapid stock market growth in the last decades was associated with a deep transformation in the underlying institutional infrastructure, even if not always through the adoption of the same mechanisms prevailing in developed markets. Instances of formal convergence to international (and especially US) corporate governance best practices abound. The significance and practical consequences of these transplanted practices in this new context may, however, be quite different from what

---

[99] Lin, *supra* note 96, at 84.   [100] Id. at 74.   [101] Id. at 66.

[102] For a discussion of recent CSR developments in India and China, see Afra Afshariopu & Shruti Rana, "The Emergence of New Corporate Social Responsibility Regimes in India and China", 14 UC Davis Bus. L. J. 175, 209–10 (2014).

would be expected in their original environment. Critically, emerging markets governance is far from uniform, and the degree of internal diversity might even increase in the future, as the great variation in their political, economic, and legal conditions will likely continue to impact the performance of their economies and stock markets going forward.

Finally, the very category of emerging markets itself is unlikely to remain stable over time. As the BRIC economies seemed to falter in the second decade of the twenty-first century, new acronyms surfaced to describe then popular investment destinations. Irrespective of the precise mix of jurisdictions, attention to the corporate laws and governance structures in a broader array of jurisdictions beyond the traditional few of the wealthy West is likely here to stay—to the great benefit of those interested in the role of legal institutions in shaping capitalism's different incarnations.

CHAPTER 28

....

THE GOVERNANCE ECOLOGY OF CHINA'S STATE-OWNED ENTERPRISES

....

CURTIS J. MILHAUPT[1]

1 INTRODUCTION

....

CHINA's emergence as a global economic power poses enormous explanatory challenges for scholars of comparative corporate governance. While China appears to present a new variety of capitalism, frequently labeled "state capitalism," the features and implications of this system are still poorly understood.[2] Particularly since China's economic system may be in its early stages of development, understanding the mechanisms by which state capitalism currently operates and how they may change as Chinese enterprises globalize is a pressing task for researchers.

One highly distinctive characteristic of state capitalism in China is the central role of about 100 large, state-owned enterprises (SOEs) controlled by organs of the national government in critical industries such as steel, telecom, and transportation. Although only a handful of these firms, such as Sinopec and China Mobile, have become household names in the West, the state sector dominates major industries in China and is increasingly active in global markets. As The Economist noted, "as the economy grows at double-digit rates year after year, vast state-owned enterprises are climbing the world's league tables in every industry from oil to banking."[3] China now has the world's second largest concentration of

---

[1] This chapter is an abridged version of Li-Wen Lin & Curtis J. Milhaupt, "We Are the (National) Champions: Understanding the Mechanisms of State Capitalism in China", 65 Stan. L. Rev. 697 (2013).

[2] As one commentator puts it, "[H]aving co-opted Western capitalism and mirrored many of its surface features, China today poses an unprecedented and profound challenge to Western capitalism that scholars and policymakers have only begun to grasp." Marshall W. Meyer, "Is it Capitalism?", 7 Mgmt. & Org. Rev. 5, 8 (2010).

[3] Let a Million Flowers Bloom, Economist, Mar. 12, 2011, at 79.

Fortune Global 500 companies (73),[4] and the number of Chinese companies on the list has increased at an annual rate of 25% since 2005. These are China's national champions.

More than two-thirds of Chinese companies in the Global Fortune 500 are SOEs. Excluding banks and insurance companies,[5] controlling stakes in the largest and most important of the firms are owned ostensibly on behalf of the Chinese people by a central holding company known as the State-Owned Assets Supervision and Administration Commission (SASAC), which has been described as "the world's largest controlling shareholder."[6] In many respects the concept of state capitalism in China—particularly the organizational structure and broad governance regime surrounding these national champions—remains a black box. In part, this is due to scarcity of reliable data, but it is also a result of the way scholars have approached the subject.[7] Most corporate governance scholars working on China, for example, have taken the individual firm—the publicly listed company—as the unit of analysis, even though corporate groups are pervasive in China's state-owned sector and the listed firm is just one part of a complex web of corporate entities and relationships that characterize Chinese state capitalism. Moreover, scholars often begin and end their analyses by benchmarking the governance attributes of Chinese listed companies against global (which typically means US) corporate governance standards and institutions. This approach produces insights, to be sure, but it invariably focuses the analyst's attention on what the Chinese system lacks, as opposed to how it is constructed and actually functions. As was the case with scholarship on Japanese corporate governance in the 1990s, real headway in understanding China's variety of capitalism will come by analyzing the system on its own terms, rather than by reference to what it lacks.

This chapter explores the mechanisms of state capitalism in China by analyzing the distinctive system of industrial organization in which the country's largest SOEs were assembled and operate. To aid in the exploration, the focus is extended beyond the usual corporate governance concern with agency relationships in an attempt to understand the relational ecology that fosters production in a system where all roads eventually lead to the party-state. Two simple analytical constructs are introduced for this purpose: Networked hierarchy is the way top-down governance features within individual state-controlled corporate groups are coupled with extensive linkages to other state-controlled institutions. Institutional bridging is the pervasive use of personnel rotation systems, equity ownership structures, and strategic forms of cooperation such as joint ventures, which serve to unite separate components of the state sector. These mechanisms create networks among business and other organs of the party-state, promote information flow and provide high-powered incentives to actors in the system by linking corporate performance and political

---

[4] Behind the United States. China surpassed Japan on the list in 2012. Fortune 500 rankings are based on revenues.

[5] The banks are majority owned by other agencies of the state, and supervised by the Chinese Banking Regulatory Commission and the People's Bank of China.

[6] Boston Consulting Group, SASAC: China's Megashareholder (Dec. 1, 2007), available at http://www.bcgperspectives.com/content/articles/globalization_strategy_sasac_chinas_megashareholder/.

[7] This phenomenon is hardly unique to China. During Japan's economic ascendance, scholars working within the US tradition had theoretical "blinders" which obstructed their understanding of Japanese corporate structures and economic institutions. Ronald J. Gilson & Mark J. Roe, "Understanding the Japanese Keiretsu: Overlaps between Corporate Governance and Industrial Organization", 102 Yale L. J. 871 (1993).

advancement. Together, these features can be thought of as means to assemble what Mancur Olson called an "encompassing organization"—a coalition whose members "own so much of the society that they have an important incentive to be actively concerned about how productive it is."[8]

The chapter proceeds in six parts. Part 2 provides conceptual background for the study of Chinese SOEs. Analyzing the relational ecology in which large state-owned corporate groups operate provides a framework for understanding where Chinese corporate capitalism originated and how it is currently organized. Part 3 uses the conceptual frame to illuminate the key components and main organizational characteristics of the national business groups, contrasting certain features of the groups with those in Japan and Korea. Part 4 analyzes SASAC's behavior as a controlling shareholder within the larger institutions of the party-state. It explores the ways in which SASAC shares the role of controlling shareholder with the Party, and the institutional bridges linking the Party, the national champions, and the government in the management of state-owned enterprises. Part 5 discusses the implications of the analysis for comparative corporate governance scholarship. Part 6 concludes.

2 UNDERSTANDING CHINESE INDUSTRIAL ORGANIZATION

2.1 Introduction

Two decades of comparative corporate governance scholarship have shown that successful forms of corporate capitalism do not have identical features around the world. On the contrary, firms differ systematically in their ownership structures, sources of financing, and the surrounding set of national legal and market institutions in which they develop.[9] The spark for this insight, now so thoroughly explored as to seem prosaic in hindsight, was the striking economic ascendance of another East Asian country—Japan—in the 1980s. Two decades ago, observers recognized that while Japanese firms were globally competitive, their ownership structures, financing patterns, and governance norms bore little outward resemblance to those of US public firms, whose features had long been taken for granted as the natural end point of an evolutionary process in the formation of the "modern" corporation.[10]

Today, the world is once again confronted with a distinctive and globally important economic system in East Asia whose features appear opaque and even menacing to outsiders. Although China's economic system has received a label, much work remains to understand how "state capitalism" is organized. As in the case of Japan in the 1980s, most of the corporate governance literature on China is preoccupied with agency costs and monitoring in publicly listed firms. Indeed, Ronald Gilson and Mark Roe's 25-year old observation on the

---

[8] Mancur Olson, The Rise and Decline of Nations 48 (1982).

[9] This basic insight spawned a related literature on the "varieties of capitalism." The seminal work contrasts "liberal market economies" such as that of the United States with "coordinated market economies" such as those of Japan and Germany. See generally Varieties of Capitalism: The Institutional Foundations of Comparative Advantage (Peter A. Hall & David Soskice eds., 2001).

[10] Adolf A. Berle, Jr. & Gardiner C. Means, The Modern Corporation and Private Property (1932).

intellectual obstacle to understanding Japanese industrial organization remains apt in relation to China: "Viewing the Japanese system through Berle-Means blinders, in the belief that it reflects only an effort to bridge the separation of ownership and control, will cause us to misunderstand it and, as a result, to miss the lessons that comparative analysis can offer."[11]

Similar to the way in which the early literature on Japan sought to locate the "missing monitor" in the main bank system, many analysts of Chinese corporate capitalism have focused exclusively on agency problems in listed companies.[12] The search for solutions has taken most commentators down a path whose grooves were cut by US corporate governance logic, with a focus on independent directors, the market for corporate control, and robust securities regulation. This approach generates a lengthy list of (predominantly US-style) formal institutions whose development is deemed crucial to the future transformation and improvement of Chinese corporate governance. What it fails to do is confront a puzzle at the core of contemporary Chinese capitalism: how is a system without a plethora of formal institutions deemed important to Western firms producing a rapidly expanding list of Fortune 500 companies, and possibly supporting sustained levels of economic development in China?

Some commentators, recognizing but largely sidestepping the puzzle, claim that "relationships" are the key to success of the Chinese economy.[13] This is almost certainly an accurate observation. But analysis of the precise nature of these relationships and their role in the scheme of Chinese industrial organization is typically omitted in favor of references to cultural proclivities or historical influences.[14] As one of us has argued in joint work with Ronald Gilson, "governmentally encouraged commercial performance" under an authoritarian political regime attuned to incentives may be doing the work of formal legal institutions in the Chinese economy, allowing small-scale reputation-based trading to be scaled up to the point where entry into the global economy is possible.[15] And as we suggested there, business groups fostered by the political regime and deeply entwined with Chinese Communist Party leadership may be central to the developmental success of the regime.

This chapter represents an attempt to dig deeper into the structure and organizational ecology of the business groups at the center of China's system of state capitalism. The account attempts to unearth the mechanisms underlying the uniquely encompassing nature of Chinese industrial organization and its concern not only with corporate governance, but

---

[11] Gilson & Roe, *supra* note 7, at 881.

[12] An example of this approach is Chi-Wei Huang, "Worldwide Corporate Convergence within a Pluralistic Legal Order: Company Law and the Independent Director System in Contemporary China", 31 Hastings Int'l. & Comp. L. Rev. 361 (2008). A small number of Western scholars have focused on Chinese corporate groups. See, e.g., Lisa A. Keister, "Interfirm Relations in China: Group Structure and Firm Performance in Business Groups", 52 Am. Behavioral Scientist 1709 (2009); Lisa A. Keister, "Engineering Growth: Business Group Structure and Firm Performance in China's Transition Economy", 104 Am. J. Soc. 404 (1998).

[13] See, e.g., Franklin Allen et al., "Law, Finance, and Economic Growth in China", 77 J. Fin. Econ. 57 (2005).

[14] See id. (attributing success of Chinese economy in absence of sound legal institutions to Confucian belief system).

[15] Ronald J. Gilson & Curtis J. Milhaupt, "Economically Benevolent Dictators: Lessons for Developing Democracies", 59 Am. J. Comp. L. 227 (2011).

also with production, the transmission and implementation of industrial policy, and the maximization of state welfare, at least as interpreted by elite actors within the system.

2.2 Chinese Industrial Organization as a Networked Hierarchy

State capitalism as practiced in China has a remarkably complex architecture. To help make sense of it, this section develops a simple stylized model of Chinese industrial organization as it relates to nationally important firms and the corporate groups in which they are nested.

2.2.1 A Simple Analytical Construct

The organizational structure of state capitalism as practiced in China can be thought of as a networked hierarchy. This term captures a chief characteristic of the scheme of industrial organization: vertically integrated corporate groups organized under SASAC, the state-affiliated controlling shareholder, with strategic linkages to other business groups as well as to governmental organs and state institutions such as universities, enmeshed in a helix-like personnel appointment process of rotations managed jointly by the Communist Party and SASAC.

The hierarchical aspects of Chinese industrial organization are readily apparent. They range from the vertical integration of firms along the production chain to the top-down character of industrial policy formulation and transmission in an authoritarian political regime.[16] But the Chinese system is not simply one in which vertically integrated groups transmit commands from state economic planners to SASAC and down through a chain of vertically integrated firms. These hierarchical structures are embedded in dense networks—not only of other firms, but also of party and government organs. These networks appear to facilitate information flow from the bottom up as well as from the top down. They foster relational exchange and collaboration on many levels of the production and policy implementation processes. And they provide high-powered incentives to leaders within the system because success in business leads to promotion and accompanying rewards in the political realm, and vice versa. This combination of authoritarian hierarchy and collaboration within high-powered incentive structures is reminiscent of another mechanism of economic transitions—private equity investments.[17]

As discussed below in detail, these dense networks are the result of numerous pathways that link individual components of the system. Some are engineered through formal legal means, such as by contract or through shareholding relationships. Others are the result of personnel practices followed by the Communist Party and SASAC. Still others are incorporated into the distinctive notion of "representation" in Chinese governmental organs, which

---

[16] The vertical authority structure in Chinese SOEs is a reflection of the siloed, hierarchical governmental structure (known as xitong, or "system") for economic management from which they were created. The xitong are "a group of bureaucracies that together deal with a broad task the top political leaders want performed." Kenneth Lieberthal, Governing China: From Revolution through Reform 218 (2d ed. 2004).

[17] Gilson & Milhaupt, *supra* note 15, at 233.

assigns seats to select business leaders. The term institutional bridging is used to describe this practice.

One helpful way to view these constructed networks at the center of Chinese state capitalism is through the lens of Mancur Olson's concept of an "encompassing coalition." For Olson, this is a group representing a large enough segment of the population that it has incentives to grow the pie, as opposed to a "distributional coalition" representing a narrow segment of society, which tries to get a bigger slice for its members.[18] Olson focused on group size as the key distinguishing characteristic between encompassing and distributional coalitions, but in addition to size, it seems important that the encompassing coalition includes all members whose participation can have a major impact on development—a broad cross-section of political and business elites in society. The networked hierarchy resulting from institutional bridges is a means of creating precisely this type of large managerial coalition with control over developmental policy formulation and implementation.

The aim in introducing these concepts is descriptive, not normative. These features of Chinese industrial organization do not necessarily lead to production efficiency. Olson himself noted that encompassing organizations will not necessarily lead to efficiency under all circumstances. The networks described here likely produce countervailing effects: They enhance efficiency by fostering information sharing, reducing opportunism through repeat play, providing high-powered incentives, and reducing frictions in policy implementation. But they also reduce competition and transparency, multiply agency relationships, and soften budget constraints. The interesting question for purposes of this chapter is not whether the state sector is more efficient than the private sector, but how the state sector has produced globally important firms and supported economic growth in the absence of formal infrastructure deemed essential in the standard theories on the relationship between institutions and development.

2.2.2 A Stylized Model

The networked hierarchy and institutional bridging concepts bring into focus the main organizational features of, and linkages among, the corporate group structures in which the national champions are nested. Figure 28.1 is a stylized picture of a national champion group.

Four features of this structure are highlighted here, as they will be the focus of attention in the succeeding parts of the chapter. First, in contrast to the main postwar Japanese keiretsu and Korean chaebol corporate groups, Chinese business groups are vertically integrated firms focused on a particular industry or sector, not diversified groups involved in a wide range of industries. In complementary fashion, and again in contrast to keiretsu and chaebol structures, shareholding is hierarchical: firms higher in the structure own downstream subsidiaries, but there is very little upstream or cross-ownership among group firms. Second, most of the national business groups in China contain four main components: (1) the core (parent holding) company, whose shares are wholly owned by a government agency in the form of SASAC; (2) one or more publicly traded subsidiaries—the global face of the national champion—a majority of whose shares are held by the core company; (3) a finance

---

[18] Olson, *supra* note 8. These ideas were developed further in Olson, Power and Prosperity (2000), in which he introduced the notion of the "stationary bandit."

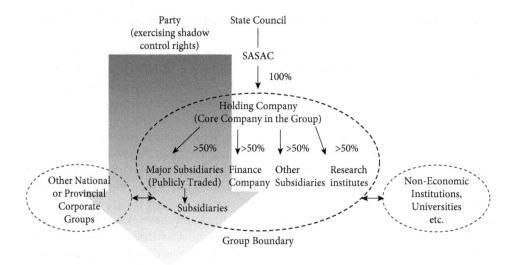

FIGURE 28.1 National Champions as Networked Hierarchy.

company, which serves many important financing needs of the group, and has certain parallels with the Japanese main bank; and (4) a research institute that coordinates innovative processes of the group. Third, monitoring is carried out within two parallel structures, a familiar one provided by the corporate law, with SASAC as controlling shareholder, and a party-based structure that shadows the corporate hierarchy, especially as to high-level managerial appointments.

Crucially, however, these group components, as well as their top individual managers, are extensively networked to the larger system of industrial organization. Although the various corporate groups are distinct from each other both legally and functionally, complementary groups are linked in important ways. Inter-group joint ventures, strategic alliances, and equity holdings are the corporate mechanisms providing such linkages. But the party-state, acting through SASAC and the Organization Department of the Party, provides another, probably more crucial, means of uniting the groups into a complementary whole. Finally, the economic aspects of this structure are linked through institutionalized personnel channels and political practices to governmental organs such as the National People's Congress, to important party organs, and to non-economic state institutions such as universities. These are the institutional bridges that unite separate components of the system.

2.3 Background

After an unsuccessful experiment with the formation of contract-based business alliances in the initial economic reform period, the Chinese central government took more control over the creation of business groups in the 1990s. The State Council formed 120 groups concentrated in critical industries, such as automobiles, machinery, electronics, steel, and transportation. The groups benefited from a range of preferential policies in areas ranging from taxation to government contracts and eligibility for stock exchange listing. The stated purpose of the government in forming these groups was to achieve economies of scale, facilitate inter-firm collaboration, and enhance international competitiveness. Formation of vertically integrated groups also had the administrative advantage of streamlining control over the economy: a small number of major firms would serve as conduits through which policy could be transmitted to vast numbers of enterprises organized under the core firms. By the mid-1990s, creation of national champions was explicitly recognized as a goal of the central government.

After years of experimentation with organizational structure, in 1998 a relatively clear concept of the business group emerged with the promulgation of Provisional Rules on Business Group Registration. Though "provisional," these rules are still in effect. Subject to various threshold qualifications, a business group is defined as a group of entities comprised of four layers: (1) a parent company and (2) its controlled subsidiaries (the two required layers), along with (3) non-controlled subsidiaries and (4) other firms which collaborate with the core company or its subsidiaries (two optional layers). In order to be registered, group members must enter into an agreement (Articles of Grouping) specifying the group's boundaries and internal governance rules. Only registered business groups qualify for important benefits, such as eligibility to establish a finance company.

This group formation process, together with the more basic step of "corporatization" of state enterprises—that is, the transformation of state agencies involved in economic activity into joint stock corporations—raised a variety of well-documented agency problems, including the most vexing: When a corporate asset is theoretically owned by "the people," who is the principal? In recognition of this problem, several attempts were made to create a controlling shareholder, leading to the establishment of SASAC in 2003. In theory, SASAC represents the state as "owner" and exercises shareholder's rights on its behalf. SASAC's distinctive role as a controlling shareholder within the context of the party-state will be examined in Part 4 below.

3 National Business Groups

The networked hierarchy and institutional bridging concepts are now used to examine the key members, networked structure, and internal governance mechanisms of the groups.

3.1 Components

3.1.1 Core (Parent) Company

As noted, Chinese corporate groups have a multi-tiered hierarchical structure. At the top of the group is the core company. Core companies were typically formed by "corporatizing" a government ministry with jurisdiction over a particular industry. For example, each of the core companies in the national petroleum groups was hived off from the former oil ministry and transformed into a corporate entity. The core company acts as a holding company, serving as an intermediary between SASAC and group firms that engage in actual production. The core company coordinates information flow and resource allocation within the

group. It transmits policy downward from the state to group members, and provides information and advice upward from the group to state economic strategists and planners. As
Chinese commentators explain, "The key sectors and backbone industries are still controlled
by the state through wholly state-owned or state-invested enterprises. . . In reality, the state
can control the nationally important industries and key areas to lead the economy simply by
grasping a few hundred large state-owned holding companies or business groups."[19]

3.1.2 Listed Company

The external face of the national champion is not a group of companies but a single firm,
whose shares are publicly traded on the Chinese or Hong Kong stock exchanges and often
on other major exchanges as well. For example, PetroChina, one of the largest oil companies
in the world, whose shares are listed on the Shanghai and New York stock exchanges, is the
external face of the CNPC Group, whose core company is the China National Petroleum
Corporation. SASAC's strategy in managing groups under its supervision has been to consolidate high-quality assets in specific companies and to seek public listing for those firms.
These listed firms are the focus of most scholarship on Chinese corporate governance to date.

3.1.3 Finance Company

One of the key benefits of registration as a group is eligibility to establish a finance company—a nonbank financial institution that provides services to group members.[20] Finance
companies are exempt from the general prohibition on inter-company lending.[21] Under
the current legal framework, a finance company provides services on behalf of group
members similar to those of commercial and investment banks. Subject to approval by
banking regulators, they are authorized to engage in a wide range of activities, including
accepting deposits from and making loans to member companies, providing payment,
insurance, and foreign exchange services to members, and underwriting the securities
of member firms. They also engage in consumer finance related to the products of group
members, and invest in securities issued by financial institutions.[22] Deposits from group
member companies comprise their main source of funds. Almost all finance companies
are members of state-owned groups, either at the national or provincial level, and many are
formidable in size.

In its role as the hub of group financial transactions, the Chinese finance company is a
partial analogue to the Japanese main bank, at least as it operated in the heyday of postwar
Japanese corporate finance and governance. However, there are several key differences. In

---

[19] Haihang Zheng et al., Guoyou Zichan Guanli Tizhi yu Guoyou Konggu Gongsi Yanjiu 2
[Management of State-Owned Assets and State-Controlled Companies] (2009).

[20] See Administrative Measures on Finance Companies in Business Groups, Art. 2, issued by China
Banking Regulatory Commission on July 27, 2004, revised Oct. 28, 2006. Authorization is not automatic.
Aside from various threshold capital and profitability requirements, bank regulators require that the
business group's functions be consistent with the government's industrial policies. Administrative
Measures on Finance Companies in Business Groups, Art. 7, item 1.

[21] General Provisions on Lending, Art. 61.

[22] Administrative Measures on Finance Companies in Business Groups, Arts. 28–29.

contrast to widespread, if low-level, cross-shareholding ties between Japanese main banks and their most important borrowers, the Chinese finance company holds virtually no equity in other group member firms, and few or no firms other than the core company own shares in the finance company. While the finance company can be utilized by the core company to help monitor group members, there is no evidence that finance companies perform an independent monitoring function, particularly with respect to the core company or listed companies in the group.

The Japanese banking system, particularly its perceived corporate governance benefits, was attractive to Chinese observers during the formative period of China's process of economic transition in the early 1990s.[23] In this period, legal and economic scholars widely argued that equity ownership by the main bank in its borrowers had important governance benefits,[24] and that the main bank served as a "delegated" or "contingent" monitor on behalf of other lenders to group firms.[25] It was even argued that the main bank substituted for the market for corporate control in Japan by displacing managers of financially troubled firms.[26] Yet China's finance companies bear only weak resemblance to the main bank system, serving primarily as an instrument of the core company for the purposes of internal group capital allocation. Moreover, unlike the situation in Japan, at this stage there is relatively little equity ownership of banks by the corporate sector, although this may be changing.

Given China's attraction to the Japanese model during a formative period in the formation of business groups, why did the country's economic strategists not pursue a financial and governance structure for its business groups that bore closer resemblance to the Japanese system circa the late 1980s? Two complementary explanations, closely linked to China's overall system of economic governance, might be offered. The first is that dispersion of governance rights in member firms to nonbank financial institutions would potentially dilute and complicate the hierarchical structure of economic management made possible by group formation under centralized state supervision. Second, the creation of nonbank finance companies within business groups—what one commentator has called "outside the plan financial intermediaries"[27]—poses an obvious competitive threat to the (largely state-owned) commercial banking sector. As such, Chinese regulators have been vigilant about not expanding the scope of finance company activities to the point that they constitute a complete substitute for Chinese commercial banks.

[23] See, e.g., Yingyi Qian, Financial System Reform in China: Lessons from Japan's Main Bank System, in The Japanese Main Bank System: Its Relevance to Developing and Transforming Economies 552, 577, 585 (Masahiko Aoki & Hugh Patrick eds., 1994). ("The historical similarities suggest that China may benefit more from adopting features of the Japanese financial model than from other [arm's-length financial] models in achieving its objective of restructuring the corporate sector while stabilizing its economy.")

[24] See, e.g., Gilson & Roe, *supra* note 7; Qian, *supra* note 23.

[25] See, e.g., Masahiko Aoki, et al., The Main Bank System: An Introductory Overview, in The Japanese Main Bank System: Its Relevance to Developing and Transforming Economies 552, 577, 585 (Masahiko Aoki & Hugh Patrick eds., 1994).

[26] Paul Sheard, "The Main Bank System and Corporate Monitoring and Control in Japan", 11 J. Econ. Behav. & Org. 399 (1989).

[27] Qian, *supra* note 23, at 569.

3.1.4 Research Institutes

Chinese policy makers have encouraged business groups to include research institutes as members in order to promote high-technology development and increase international competitiveness. Most of the national business groups contain one or more research institutes. The research institutes conduct R&D, particularly applied research in areas related to the group's products and production processes. Often, the research institutes collaborate with universities on particular projects to derive complementarities between the applied focus of business R&D programs and the theoretical approach of academic researchers.

Typically established as not-for-profit institutions, the research institutes receive funding from the core company in the group. Research institutes in groups with a diverse range of products may be multi-layered, with a chief institute affiliated with the core company and second-tier institutes established under particular operating subsidiaries. Intellectual property arising out of the research activities is typically owned by the core company, or allocated by contract in joint projects with outside institutes.

3.2 Membership and Internal Governance

Membership in most business groups is based on equity ownership of member firms by the core company. Although membership based on purely contractual relations among firms is permitted under the regulations on business groups, it is not common. The predominance of equity ties is a reflection of governance concerns by both the core company and the state. For the core company, equity ownership provides a more direct and flexible form of control than contract. For the state, the objectives of group formation are more effectively advanced through corporate ownership than loose affiliations of business partners.

In considerable contrast to business groups in Japan and Korea, equity ownership in Chinese business groups typically runs only in one direction: from the core company to downstream subsidiaries. Very little cross-share ownership is found in Chinese business groups. Again, governance concerns—both corporate and political—appear to be the primary reason. The core company, as the dominant player in the group with ultimate group-wide decision-making authority over personnel and strategic issues, has little use for upstream share ownership; top-down stock holdings reflect and reinforce the hierarchical structure of the group. For the government, the core company's role as delegated manager and monitor of group firms would not be enhanced—indeed it may be complicated—by cross-shareholding linkages among group firms. Moreover, to the extent that cross-shareholding is used to promote enhanced monitoring of, or risk sharing among, group members in countries such as Japan, this function may not be complementary to Chinese corporate group structures given pervasive party involvement in group firms and other forms of party-state monitoring outside the confines of corporate law norms.

Internal group governance structures are specified in a legally binding agreement called Articles of Grouping, which is adopted by all members. The Articles are state-supplied standard form contracts required of all registered business groups, but their specific provisions are largely composed of default rules. In reality, the core company dictates the terms of the Articles, and the internal governance rules grant it veto rights and other enhanced governance rights with respect to the group. Many Articles provide for plenary or management bodies to facilitate group or delegated decision making, respectively, but these organs typically either have only advisory power or are structured so that the core company effectively controls their decision-making processes. In short, governance in a Chinese business group is a largely top-down process, but one that is open to information and participation from below.

3.3 Networks

The foregoing are the main components of the corporate groups and the mechanisms by which member firms are linked. But the mechanisms of Chinese state capitalism operate by joining the corporate groups into a much larger network of organizations affiliated with the party-state. It is this aspect of Chinese state capitalism that generates its most distinctive features and raises the thorniest questions for competitors and regulators abroad. The larger networks in which individual corporate groups are embedded are examined below.

3.3.1 *Inter-Group Networks*

While groups in the same industry do sometimes compete domestically, SASAC has encouraged collaboration among the national groups in overseas projects to increase their global competitiveness. These linkages, often among groups in complementary industries, are designed to facilitate technological development, as well as a host of other objectives, such as information sharing, marketing, and pooling of capital for capital-intensive projects. These linkages typically take two forms: equity joint ventures and contractual alliances. We illustrate a few of the inter-group networks in the national steel groups by way of example. The number of relationships involving companies in these groups is actually much greater than is pictured here.[28] Figure 28.2 illustrates the use of both ownership and contract to construct inter-group networks. It also shows how networks are constructed among both complementary groups and groups of erstwhile direct competitors.

3.3.2 *Central–Local Inter-Group Networks*

National groups under SASAC control are sometimes linked to business groups under the control of local governments. (Figure 28.2 provides an example from the steel industry: provincial group Hebei Iron & Steel has an equity ownership interest in national champion BaoSteel.) These linkages are the result of an evolving dynamic between the central and local governments. Initially, local governments sought investment from the national groups to rescue moribund local SOEs. As the national groups expanded, local governments began to view them as a competitive threat to local business. Local protectionism increased, and a push was made to create "provincial champions." The relationship between national and local groups changed again as a result of the global financial crisis, which prompted renewed cooperation. The local governments came to view the national champions as sources of

---

[28] Figure 28.2 is based on data from SDC Platinum. This database focuses on international deals, so purely domestic linkages may be significantly under-reported.

Joint Ventures (Equity Linkages) Across Steel National Groups, 2000–2010

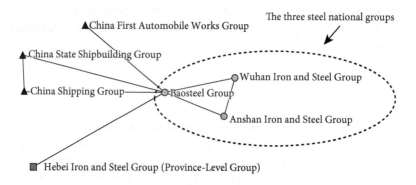

Note: triangle nodes indicate other national business groups supervised by SASAC.

Strategic Alliances (Contractual Linkages) Across Steel National Groups, 2000–2010

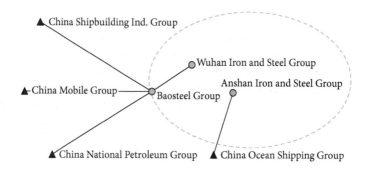

Note: triangle nodes indicate other national business groups supervised by SASAC.

FIGURE 28.2 Inter-Group Networks: An Illustration.

support for small and medium-sized enterprises, which suffered when they lost the backing of foreign and private companies. For the national groups, which are under pressure from their governmental supervisors to grow, tie-ups with local groups are an avenue of expansion.

3.3.3 Business Group–Government/Party Networks

Of course, as "state-owned" enterprises supervised by SASAC, all national champions are connected to the central government. But this simple syllogism masks the density of the networks which tie the leading business groups to institutions of the central government and the Communist Party. Multiple institutional bridges facilitate the network. The first is the China Group Companies Association, which is formally designed as an intermediary between the national business groups and the central government. It is overseen by both

SASAC and the Ministry of Commerce. The Association's board of directors is composed of senior government officials from these and other economic ministries, as well as top managers of the most important national business groups. The Association functions as a vehicle for airing issues of concern to the central SOEs and reporting to the State Council. Recent issues discussed by the Association include streamlining the government approval process for foreign investments and improving internal risk controls in connection with foreign investments. The Association also lobbied, against strong resistance from banking regulators, for the establishment of the finance companies within corporate groups.

A second bridge is the practice, with roots dating to the period prior to the establishment of SASAC, of granting substantive management rights in a nationally important SOE to the ministry with supervisory authority over the industry in which it operates. For example, the Ministry of Industry and Information Technology retains important management rights over China Mobile, including the power to nominate its top managers, even though China Mobile is part of a national business group whose core company is 100% owned by SASAC. In some industries, high-level two-way personnel exchanges between ministries and national groups reinforce this link.

A third institutional bridge is the routine exchange of personnel between SASAC and the central SOEs it supervises. In a policy designed to promote "mutual adaptation in political and professional qualities,"[29] 50 to 60 SOE managers are seconded to SASAC annually for one-year periods, and vice versa. Available data on this practice suggest that the corporate managers seconded to SASAC are fairly senior and are sent from leading enterprises. The SASAC officials are relatively junior. This suggests that the practice is not primarily designed to facilitate SASAC's monitoring of the SOEs, but rather to build SASAC capacity and promote cooperation between the SOE sector and the government.

A fourth institutional bridge between the national champions and the government is the practice of reserving a number of positions in several elite (if functionally obscure) government and party bodies for leaders of the national SOEs. Chief among these are the National People's Congress—the central government's symbolic legislative body—the National People's Political Consultative Conference, an advisory body composed of representatives of different social and political groups, and the National Congress of the Chinese Communist Party, the Party's general assembly. For example, based on a pool of candidates recommended by the party committees of the 120 central enterprises extant at the time, SASAC nominated 22 managers as representatives to the 11th National People's Congress, and 99 managers to the 11th National People's Political Consultative Conference, both of which ran from 2008 to 2013. In 2007, the Party Committee of SASAC and the party committees of the 120 central enterprises selected 47 members to the 17th National Congress of the Chinese Communist Party. The composition of the selected members was determined on instructions from the Central Organization Department of the Party, which specified that no more than 70% of the positions should go to top managers of the core companies, and no less than 30% to middle managers of core companies and top managers of their subsidiaries.[30]

---

[29] Statement by Mr. Xiping Shi (Head of Bureau of Personnel of SASAC). Press Release by the Bureau of Personnel of SASAC, June 21, 2007.

[30] China's State-Owned Assets Supervision and Administration Yearbook (2008), at 81 and 93. Guanyu Zuohao Zhongyang Qiye Xitong (Zaijing) Shiqida Daibiao Houxuanren Tuijian Gongzuo de Tongzhi [Notice on the Work of Nominating the Party's 17th National Congress Members

The Party also plays a major role in personnel appointments in the national business groups. One-third of the employees in the national SOEs are members of the Party,[31] and party organizations exist within each level of the business group hierarchy. At one time, there may have been ideological reasons for the Party's pervasive role in SOEs. But a compelling political economy explanation for the practice is also apparent. The party constitutes a massive interest group that maintained extensive ties to economic enterprises in the central planning era. Indeed, in this era there was often little separation between governmental, economic, and social organizations, with party involvement pervasive across all three spheres of activity. Corporatization and other economic reforms could have posed a major threat to important dimensions of party rule. Institutionalized party involvement in the post-reform state-owned sector can be seen as a way of buying the support of the party for reforms that it may have otherwise blocked. The Party is also functionally well situated to monitor personnel in the SOEs. As one commentator notes, "[t]he Party's control over personnel was at the heart of its ability to overhaul state companies, without losing leverage over them at the same time . . .. The party body with ultimate power over personnel, the Central Organization Department, is without doubt the largest and most powerful human resources department in the world."[32]

4 THE PARTY-STATE AS CONTROLLING SHAREHOLDER

Atop the national groups is SASAC, ostensibly "the world's largest controlling shareholder."[33] Controlling shareholder regimes are prevalent throughout the world, and in this sense, China's variety of capitalism shares an important trait with corporate capitalism in many other developing and recently developed countries, including, for example, Brazil, India, and Korea. Although, in contrast to state control in China, in other countries the controlling shareholder is typically the founding heir or members of his family, as one scholar has recently argued, "it is easy to overstate the extent to which the interests of the government as a controlling shareholder differ from those of private controlling shareholders."[34] This is because, regardless of identity, all controlling shareholders face similar incentives. On the one hand, the size of their ownership stakes provides incentives to monitor managerial performance more closely than do shareholders in dispersed ownership systems. But controlling shareholders also have unique incentives to maximize "private benefits of control" by engaging in transactions that expropriate wealth from minority shareholders.

Representing the Central Enterprise System (Beijing-Based)], issued by the Party Committee of SASAC, December 2006.

[31] As of the end of 2009, 3.03 million of the 9.36 million employees of the central SOEs were party members. China's State-Owned Assets Supervision and Administration Yearbook (2010).

[32] Richard Mcgregor, The Party: The Secret World of China's Communist Rulers 69 (2010).

[33] See *supra* note 6.

[34] Mariana Pargendler, "State Ownership and Corporate Governance", 80 Fordham L. Rev., 2917, 2923 (2012).

Macro-level generalizations and comparisons with other controlling shareholder regimes, however, are likely to mislead, because several aspects of China's regime make it highly distinctive. For one, it is uniquely encompassing in scope. In no other developed or developing country is a single shareholder—private or public—so pervasively invested in the leading firms in the national economy. More importantly, as explained below, it is misleading to attribute to SASAC the same bundle of control rights associated with controlling shareholders in other regimes.

4.1 SASAC as Ostensible Controller

The complex nature of SASAC's control rights in the national champions cannot be understood without at least a thumbnail sketch of its origins. The national SOEs were carved out of central government ministries in the "corporatization" process, which transformed governmental organs into joint stock companies. Initially, control shares in the SOEs were held by the ministries from which they had been created, with predictably negative results, such as lack of central coordination and weak oversight. In 1988, the State Council established the Bureau of State Assets Management, an agency supervised by the Ministry of Finance. Despite its name, the bureau did not actually centralize management rights over the SOEs; in reality, control remained dispersed among a range of ministries with jurisdiction over separate corporate activities such as investment and trade, as well the Communist Party, which was involved in labor and wage issues. The bureau was eventually absorbed by the Ministry of Finance, effectively abolishing it, and control rights remained dispersed.

SASAC, established under the State Council in 2003, represents a second attempt to consolidate control rights over the national SOEs. But SASAC is a work in progress, and the legacy of shared control rights was not overcome by its mere establishment. This is particularly true given its location in the government organizational chart: although SASAC is a ministerial level agency, so are 53 of the most important SOEs under its supervision. SASAC faces potential resistance not only from the firms it supervises but from the competing agendas being pursued by other important ministries such as the Ministry of Finance.[35] As one commentator notes, "In practice, SASAC has faced an uphill struggle to establish its authority over the SOEs that it supposedly controls as a representative of the state owner."[36]

Until recently, there was no overarching legal authority governing SASAC in its role as controlling shareholder. In 2008 a Law of the PRC on State-Owned Assets of Enterprises (SOE Asset Law) was enacted to "safeguard[] the basic economic system of China . . . , giving full play to the leading role of the State-owned economy in the national economy."[37] In essence, the law formally recognizes SASAC as an investor—a shareholder in the national SOEs, with the ordinary rights and duties of a shareholder. Ostensibly, the law confines SASAC to this role[38]

---

[35] See Barry Naughton, SASAC and Rising Corporate Power in China, China Leadership Monitor 24 (2008).

[36] Mikael Martin, Whose Money? The Tug-of-War over Chinese State Enterprise Profits, FIIA Briefing Paper No. 79 (Apr. 2011).

[37] SOE Asset Law, Art. 1.   [38] SOE Asset Law, Arts. 11–14.

and governs the agency's performance of its functions as an investor.[39] But there are no formal mechanisms in the law to enforce SASAC's responsibilities, and in reality, the law grants SASAC powers greater than those available to it as a shareholder under China's Corporate Law. In short, SASAC has both less and more power as a controlling shareholder than meets the eye.

4.1.1 Control Rights in Management

As with controlling shareholders everywhere, one of SASAC's main powers with respect to the national champions is the selection and compensation of top managers. But SASAC exercises this power in the shadow of party control. As just noted, various party organs held appointment power in the central SOEs prior to the establishment of SASAC, and this practice was retained even after its establishment. "Political qualities," including party membership, are one of the major criteria against which managerial performance in the national champions is evaluated.[40]

There are two parallel personnel systems in all Chinese SOEs: the regular corporate management system and the party system. In the corporate management system, positions are similar to those commonly found in firms elsewhere, such as CEO, vice CEO, chief accountant, and if the company has a board of directors, a chairman and independent board members. A leadership team in the party system includes the Secretary of the Party Committee, several Deputy Secretaries, and a Secretary of the Discipline Inspection Commission (an anti-corruption office), along with other members of the Party Committee. Institutionalizing party penetration of corporate roles is formal policy, and overlaps between the two systems appear rather uniform, such that a corporate manager of a given rank typically holds a position of equivalent rank in the party system.

Party and corporate leadership appointments take place in a highly institutionalized sharing arrangement between the party and SASAC. The top positions in 53 central enterprises, including board chairmen, CEOs, and Party Secretaries, are appointed and evaluated by the Organization Department of the CPC. This is a legacy of appointments practice prior to the establishment of SASAC. Some of these positions hold ministerial rank equivalent to provincial governors and members of the State Council; others hold vice-ministerial rank. Deputy positions in these enterprises are appointed by the Party Building Bureau of SASAC (the Party's organization department within SASAC). A separate division of SASAC, the First Bureau for the Administration of Corporate Executives, assists in this appointment process. Appointments and evaluations of top executives in the remaining central enterprises are made by yet another division of SASAC, the Second Bureau for the Administration of Corporate Executives. While appointment power formally resides with SASAC, appointment decisions are made with inputs from various party organs and ministries supervising relevant business operations, and are subject to approval by the State Council.

---

[39] See e.g., SOE Asset Law, Art. 69 provides for unspecified disciplinary measures against SASAC staff who neglect their duties as investor. Art. 70 subjects a shareholder representative appointed by SASAC to personal liability for loss caused by failure to carry out SASAC's instructions.

[40] Measures Concerning the Integrated Evaluation of the Top Management Teams and Managers of the Central Enterprises (Provisional), CPC Organization Dept. Doc. No. 17 (2009).

The appointment and evaluation process for top managers of the national SOEs is supported in two ways: ministry recommendations and party leadership training. The Party's Organization Department and SASAC compensate for information asymmetries about talent and suitability of individual SOE managers by obtaining input from the ministries that supervise the industry in which a national SOE operates. Moreover, SOE managers are trained in the party school system, which serves as a think-tank and mid-career training center for cadres. The Central Party School in Beijing, the most important and prestigious of these schools, offers specialized training classes for SOE managers.[41] While little information is available about the content of this training, the party school system would appear to provide an excellent opportunity for party leadership to evaluate the intelligence, skills, and commitment of those who pass through its programs.

Note that the standard corporate mechanism for the appointment and evaluation of senior executives—the board of directors—is missing entirely from this process. Indeed, many of the core companies of the national business groups still lack boards of directors. Although SASAC and the Party have begun taking steps to bring boards of directors into the appointment process and to create boards for those core companies which do not yet have them, the steps taken thus far leave little doubt that the party does not intend to relinquish appointment authority with respect to the most important enterprises and the highest-level appointments.

In order to understand how the party-state manages executives in the national champions, Table 28.1 reports hand-collected data on appointments and removals of "leaders" of the enterprises under SASAC supervision from 2003 to 2009. The term "leaders" is used by SASAC to refer to holders of top positions in both corporations and the party. These data include a limited number of high-level corporate appointments for which SASAC runs a public recruitment process.

Table 28.1 shows that from one-third to three-quarters of the national SOEs experienced at least one appointment or removal of a leader by SASAC in the covered years. SASAC does not explain why the number of appointments systematically exceeds the number of removals. But the most likely explanations are that (1) some appointments are actually reappointments of incumbents without any corresponding removal, and (2) some enterprises established a board of directors during the covered period, creating new positions for appointment.

SASAC also rotates senior corporate and party leaders among business groups. Table 28.2 shows that rotations are fairly common. Analysis of the data suggests that most of the corporate rotations reflected in the table are of directors or vice CEOs, and the party rotations are for positions below Secretary of the Party Committee. However, from time to time SASAC has rotated top executives in key industries. For example, in April 2011, SASAC rotated CEOs of the three central petroleum enterprises, each of which is a Fortune Global 500 Company. SASAC made similar rotations among top executives in the energy sector in 2008 and telecom in 2007 and 2004. Such rotations obviously ignore the separate identity of the corporate groups and flout standard corporate law concepts. But the practice is less jarring conceptually if all the national SOEs are viewed as one diversified meta-group under common (if somewhat attenuated) control of SASAC. The rotations are viewed, or at least explained, by Chinese

---

[41] See David Shambaugh, "Training China's Political Elite: The Party School System", 196 China Q. 827, 837 (2008).

Table 28.1 Appointments and Removals of the Leaders of the Chinese Central Enterprises*

Year	Number of Central Enterprises	Number of Central Enterprises with Appointments or Removals	Percentage of Central Enterprises with Appointments or Removals	Number of Appointments	Number of Removals
2003	196	65	33.16%	150	79
2004	178	77	43.26%	224	155
2005	169	113	66.86%	237	158
2006	159	101	63.52%	323	136
2007	155	90	58.06%	317	113
2008	148	95	64.19%	358	146
2009	129	97	75.19%	312	145

* Leaders include members of board of directors, CEOs, vice CEOs, chief accountants, secretaries of Party Committee, deputy secretaries of Party Committee, and secretaries of the Party's Discipline Inspection Committee.
Data Source: CHINA'S STATE-OWNED ASSETS SUPERVISION AND ADMINISTRATION YEARBOOKS 2004, 2005, 2006, 2007, 2008, 2009, 2010.

actors within the system as a monitoring device in groups without boards of directors. Rotations are said to reduce concentration of authority in a single individual in firms where institutionalized corporate oversight organs have yet to be developed.

As Table 28.2 shows, leaders are also rotated across the spheres of business, government, and the Party. These data, together with the data on appointment of business leaders to various government and party positions presented above, are another powerful illustration of institutional bridging at work in China's system of state capitalism.

Unfortunately, available data on appointments/removals and rotations do not permit more fine-grained assessments about a number of important issues such as the specific enterprises involved, the reasons for removals (e.g. firings versus promotions), and distinctions between corporate and party personnel management. But, taken as a whole, the available data suggest that SASAC exercises fairly extensive control rights over top managers in the central SOEs (or at least that SASAC is the mechanism through which the Party exercises such control rights), albeit in ways that pay little obeisance to ordinary corporate law norms.

Concomitant to its appointment power, SASAC also supervises executive compensation at the central SOEs. Prior to SASAC's establishment, managerial compensation was determined by the SOEs themselves, which led to a series of problems as well as major inequalities in pay across firms. In 2004, SASAC introduced a system to supervise compensation at the central enterprises. Under this system, the basic structure of managerial compensation consists of base salary, performance bonuses, and mid to long-term incentive

Table 28.2 Leader Rotations in the Chinese Central Enterprises*

Year	Leader Rotations				
	Between Central Enterprises	From Central Enterprises to Government/ Party	From Government/ Party to Central Enterprises	From Local SOEs to Central SOEs	Total Rotations
2004	27	6	13	0	46
2005	27	5	14	0	46
2006	20	3	10	1	34
2007	33	7	16	0	56
2008	NA	NA	NA	NA	50
2009	NA	NA	NA	NA	27

* Leaders include members of board of directors, CEOs, vice CEOs, chief accountants, secretaries of Party Committee, deputy secretaries of Party Committee, and secretaries of the Party's Discipline Inspection Committee.
Data Source: CHINA'S STATE-OWNED ASSETS SUPERVISION AND ADMINISTRATION YEARBOOKS 2005, 2006, 2007, 2008, 2009, 2010.

compensation.[42] Again, note that the standard corporate law organ for determining executive compensation—the board, or perhaps the board in cooperation with the shareholders—is bypassed by this process. Indeed, there is evidence that the compensation paid to executives of listed national champions which has been approved by the board and disclosed to shareholders is something of a fiction—the actual compensation received by the executive is the one set by SASAC.

4.1.2 *Control Rights in State Enterprise Assets*

SASAC's central mission is to preserve and increase the value of state assets while transforming SOEs into public companies. Since its establishment, SASAC has pursued a policy of building several large enterprises in each key industry. In recent years, SASAC has consolidated smaller and weaker SOEs into larger business groups. In the process, the number of SOEs under SASAC supervision declined to 121 in 2010, from 198 in 2003. SASAC's goal is to bring the number under one hundred. Simultaneously, as the Fortune Global 500 list attests, SASAC has successfully pursued a goal of building globally competitive conglomerates.

[42] SASAC employs complex personnel evaluation systems in order to determine managerial compensation and appointments/removals. Top managers enter into binding annual performance agreements with SASAC specifying evaluation criteria and benchmarks, and applicable rewards and punishments.

This central mission makes SASAC a gatekeeper with respect to transfers of state enterprise assets. With passage of the SOE Asset Law, SASAC now has solid legal backing for this role. Under the SOE Asset Law, share transfers involving national SOEs require SASAC's approval, even with respect to transactions over which it does not have veto power as a shareholder under the Company Law.[43] Some Chinese courts have upheld SASAC's superior control rights under the SOE Asset Law, holding that contracts for transfer of shares entered into without SASAC's approval are unenforceable or invalid, even where they are consistent with the Company Law.[44] SASAC has super-control rights in the transfer of SOEs.

4.1.3 Cash Flow Rights

As a large amount of corporate governance literature attests, the separation of cash-flow rights from control rights is a central problem in controlling shareholder regimes. Where a shareholder's control rights exceed its rights to cash flows, the agency problem between the controller and minority shareholders is magnified, with the scale of the problem growing as the wedge increases.

In controlling shareholder regimes outside the SOE context, the separation of control rights from cash-flow rights, and the ensuing potential to extract private benefits, arises because controllers are able to magnify equity's voting power through pyramiding and circular stock ownership arrangements among corporations in the group. In the SOE context, regulators and politicians acting as "owners" on behalf of the state may reap private benefits of control not shared with ordinary financial investors, in the form of political influence, opportunities for patronage or corruption, and national prestige. These types of pecuniary and nonpecuniary private benefits of control over the national champions are clearly available to the Chinese party-state managerial elite, and SASAC is a major vehicle through which such control is exercised. Beyond its role as a vehicle for party-state governance of the central SOE sector, the organizational incentives of SASAC as the formal "owner" of the national SOEs are affected by a peculiar historical circumstance: its control rights exceed its right to cash flows because until recently, the state collected no dividends from wholly state-owned enterprises.[45] This decision was reversed in 2007, with the wholly owned subsidiaries of SASAC—the core companies—now paying dividends to the state, but still at rates below those of the publicly traded SOEs. Moreover, SASAC receives only a portion of the dividends collected by the state, which it uses for asset acquisitions, restructurings, and emergency support for failing enterprises.[46] Thus, SASAC does not

---

[43] For example, SASAC's approval is required to transfer shares of a subsidiary of a company under its supervision. Under corporate law principles, only the board of directors of the company directly under its control has authority to approve such a transaction.

[44] See e.g., *Zhang Buo v. Beijing Jing Gong Garments Group Co. Ltd.*, Civil Case No. [2985] (Beijing Intermediate People's Court, May 20, 2009); *Hunan Zheqin Group Co. Ltd. v. Chendu Yinghua Investment Co. Ltd.*, Civil Case No. [6] (Huaihua City Intermediate Court People's Court, May 27, 2009).

[45] Publicly listed subsidiaries paid dividends to their parent (core) companies, but the core companies paid no dividends to the state.

[46] See Barry Naughton, SASAC and Rising Corporate Power in China, China Leadership Monitor No. 14, available at http://www.chinaleadershipmonitor.org/20052/bn.pdf.

fully internalize the financial consequences of its control rights over the national champion groups, and it cross-subsidizes the firms under its supervision with the cash-flow rights that it does hold.

These realities suggest that the central SOE sector collectively, rather than individual firms, are of greatest concern to SASAC in carrying out its governance responsibilities, and they may account for several outwardly puzzling aspects of national champion governance in China. For example, the practice of rotating top management among firms in the same industry makes a good deal of sense if maximizing shareholder wealth at individual firms is less important to the controlling shareholder than building up a number of globally competitive firms in critical industries. Another example is SASAC's heavy emphasis on the "corporate social responsibility" (CSR) of the enterprises under its supervision.[47] CSR is a theme typically trumpeted by non-shareholder corporate constituencies or NGOs, not large investors. But the CSR campaign by SASAC might be a means of building support for state capitalism domestically, improving its image abroad, and justifying management of the SOEs in ways that are not explicable solely from the standpoint of profitability and efficiency of individual firms.

4.2 Consequences

SASAC is not only the largest controlling shareholder in the world, at least in formal terms; it is also quite possibly the most idiosyncratic. Deconstructing SASAC's control rights in the firms it ostensibly owns reveals that it is simultaneously weaker and more powerful than a typical controlling shareholder in other regimes. It is weaker, because it lacks exclusive appointments power with respect to top management of the most important enterprises whose shares it owns, and it defers to other agencies—and even to the SOEs themselves— on substantive issues outside its realm of expertise. It is more powerful, due to the vast scope of its holdings over the most important firms in the national economy, and as a result of its super-control rights in state enterprise assets, which trump standard corporate law norms. SASAC appears, by design, to be yet another institutional bridge in the networked hierarchy—a high-level link between the national SOEs and other major components of the party-state. To be sure, many questions remain about SASAC's internal operations, relationships with the firms it ostensibly controls, and its oversight by party and governmental organs.

One major consequence of this arrangement is clear, even if all of its implications are not: the national champions represent much more than a purely financial investment for the party-state. SASAC, as the organizational manifestation of the party-state in its role as controlling shareholder, seeks to maximize a range of benefits extending from state revenues to technological prowess, and from soft power abroad to regime survival at home.

---

[47] Li-Wen Lin, "Corporate Social Responsibility in China: Window Dressing or Structural Change?", 28 Berkeley J. Int'l. L. 64 (2010).

5 Implications for Comparative Corporate Governance Scholarship

The last decade of comparative corporate governance scholarship has been dominated by two big, related questions: whether and how law influences corporate ownership structures around the world, and whether global systems of corporate governance are converging, particularly on a shareholder-centered, market-oriented model. In these debates, particularly the seminal works that set the terms of the inquiry, China is conspicuous by its absence, raising something of a "China Problem" for both bodies of literature.

5.1 Law and Finance

The familiar "law and finance" literature asserts that the quality of legal protections for investors determines the degree to which share ownership in a given country is dispersed. "Bad" law, which protects investors poorly, leads to concentration of corporate ownership; "good" law results in dispersed ownership. Legal systems of common law "origin" appear to systematically provide superior protections than systems of civil law origin, explaining pronounced differences in ownership structures around the world.[48]

Critiques of this literature are legion; suffice it to note that China's experience, like that of many other countries, seems consistent with the hypothesis on a surface level but far less so upon careful examination. At first blush, China's experience comfortably fits the hypothesis. China's legal system, ostensibly of civil law origin, is weak in the formal protections it provides to investors. The stock market is underdeveloped, corporate ownership structures are highly concentrated, and the economy is populated by corporate groups. But as this chapter has shown, large elements of the structure of contemporary Chinese corporate capitalism are products of conscious policy design, or at least governmentally structured experimentation. Corporate groupism may have partially been a response to institutional voids in the early reform period, but production concerns and the desire to transmit industrial policy played major roles in motivating the assembly of business groups. Where the state chose to use corporate law and other legal concepts such as contract-based alliances and business group registration in assembling its firms, it had the required capacity. Thus, it is hard to identify specific corporate law defects, let alone any negative effects that could be generally attributed to China's civil law "origin," that promoted formation of corporate groups under the control of the party-state.

Rather than asking whether China's experience supports the predictions of the law and finance literature, the discussion that follows uses the big questions in that body of work to motivate inquiries about the role of law and legalism in the growth of large, globally active Chinese firms, and, at least by plausible extension, the development of the Chinese economy.

The law and finance literature emphasizes the sticky effects of a country's "legal origin" on the structure of firms. Putting aside the thorny question of how to properly code

---

[48]   See, e.g., Rafael La Porta et al., "Law and Finance", 106 J. Pol. Econ. 1113 (1998).

legal families, which bedevils attempts to support this assertion empirically, let's consider whether the approach of Chinese economic strategists in building national champions has been heavily influenced (or bounded) by a particular tradition of legalism inherited from the civil law system. The Chinese approach certainly shares with the French civil law tradition a high degree of comfort with state involvement in the economy and regulatory paternalism. Moreover, contrary to the distrust of bigness that has animated US corporate law, governance, and institutional design over the course of the past century, bigness has not only been tolerated but celebrated in the Chinese economic reform period. Generalizing to a high degree, it is thus possible to say that China's approach to corporate law and governance resonates with attitudes prevalent in the civil law tradition.

But ending with this generalization would not capture the full story of how the legal order has influenced China's approach to corporate governance. Chinese institutional designers have been highly eclectic in the foreign models they have used in building the state sector. In early phases, Japanese and Korean corporate groupism held a high degree of attraction. More recently, the rights-based, shareholder-oriented approach of the US, with its emphasis (if less than perfect track record) on accountability and transparency has held sway on the drafters of Chinese corporate law, policy makers, and regulators. SASAC's rather schizophrenic role in national champion governance may result from the amalgam of these two sentiments— the quest for size and state control alongside an emphasis on independent accountability mechanisms and at least outward adherence to global corporate governance standards. Importantly, the absence of a firmly developed and entrenched legal order in reform-era China may have freed the hands of economic strategists to select forms of organization that were believed to best promote Chinese corporate development at a given moment in time.

The law and finance literature also raises the important question of precisely what matters in corporate law—which of its features are key to the growth of firms? For the authors of this literature, of course, the answer is legally enforceable investor protections. The law and finance literature emphasizes investor protections because capital is scarce, so that governance rights should be allocated to attract investment. But China's experience (along with those of Korea and Japan during their formative periods of development) suggests that where capital is available, at least to firms favored by the state, investor protections are not a first-order priority.[49]

Yet China's experience appears to confirm the importance of the corporate form to firm growth and, perhaps by extension, economic development. We have seen how central the corporatization process has been to the hydraulics of industrial organization in China's state sector: separating the regulatory from the operational aspects of enterprise in the corporatization process was a crucial first step in the development of a functional SOE sector. Corporatization alone, of course, did not complete the separation, and to a significant extent the line between regulation and operation remains blurred in China's SOEs today. But use of the corporate form is a powerful channel for organizational behavior, and it has provided a template for the structure of the state sector. Throughout the reform period, Chinese economic strategists have selectively chosen from among the menu of corporate attributes, making extensive use of the corporation's hierarchical governance structure and

---

[49] External constraints, such as competitive product markets, may be a necessary condition for the success of this model.

separate legal existence in building networks of firms responsive to direction from the party-state in its ostensible role as controlling shareholder. At the same time, the corporation's key decision-making and oversight organ, the board of directors, has been largely sidelined, and shareholder rights enforcement mechanisms have been downplayed. We have also seen how important the rearrangement of assets within, and creation of linkages among, corporate entities has been to the formation of industries deemed critical by the party-state. Unlike the early contractual business alliances, the corporate form has proven to be extraordinarily useful in providing the Chinese state with an enduring, highly adaptable, and to some extent anonymous vehicle for investment and economic activity. China's state capitalism is thus powerful confirmation of the genius of the corporate form as a vehicle for promoting investment and productive enterprise. Corporate law, however, in the narrow sense of an effective menu of readily enforceable legal protections for investors, has played little role in the emergence of large Chinese firms.

Indirectly, the law and finance literature raises an existential question about the linkage between corporate ownership structures and economic growth. The unstated assumption in the literature is that such a linkage does exist, and that dispersed ownership structures produce better economic outcomes than concentrated ones. Yet business groups which are the form of corporate structure prevalent in "bad" law jurisdictions around the world,[50] have been the engine of development in countries pursuing a diverse range of economic strategies over the past half century. These countries now prominently include China, pursuing a strategy of state capitalism. Thus, while the genius of the corporate form is present in all economic miracles, "good" corporate law (again in the narrow sense) is not an essential contributor to its genius; and dispersed corporate ownership is not a necessary condition for transformative economic development.[51] In this respect, China's recent history confirms the lessons provided by the experience of the United States in the late nineteenth and early twentieth centuries.

5.2 Convergence

Law and finance scholarship added fuel to the convergence debate, which considers whether corporate governance systems around the world are converging on a single shareholder-centered, market-oriented model. In the decade since the debate flowered and then promptly reached a theoretical stalemate,[52] China has emerged as one of the world's major economic powers. With the benefit of hindsight, the turn-of-the-century convergence debate now

[50] And some "good" law jurisdictions as well. See Ronald J. Gilson, "Controlling Shareholders and Corporate Governance: Complicating the Comparative Taxonomy", 119 Harv. L. Rev. 1641 (2006).

[51] A "law first" approach to investment and development might be preferable on the grounds of predictability, transparency, and accountability. But it may simply be too time consuming—and thus politically impossible—for countries at early stages of development to pursue this approach. An authoritarian state, and developing democracies displaying imaginative pragmatism in institutional design, can credibly commit to development and encourage investment without resort to frictionless legal enforcement. See Gilson & Milhaupt, *supra* note 15.

[52] The stalemate is between path dependence theories predicting persistence of national institutions which protect vested interests versus market imperative theories predicting global internalization of shareholder wealth maximization norms.

seems rather quaint. Scholars never seriously considered the possibility that domestic political legitimacy and international influence could be a major goal of a corporate governance regime. The concept of "nonpecuniary private benefits of control" was developed to help explain the persistence of controlling shareholder regimes, but this concept was used to describe social standing and influence of private founding entrepreneurs within the domestic political economy.[53] State capitalism as practiced in China blurs the distinction between pecuniary and nonpecuniary benefits of corporate control, and highlights major international soft-power ramifications of corporate governance structures, at least in a world where "state capitalism" is posing challenges to "market capitalism."

It was previously noted that Chinese corporate governance is often defined by what it lacks in comparison to other systems, and hopefully this chapter has made some headway in understanding its features other than by reference to negative space. In regard to the convergence debate, however, it bears emphasizing that, regardless of where the Chinese system may be headed, it presently does not fit neatly into any of the standard taxonomies. Chinese corporate governance for the national champions is not bank-based or stock-market-based. It is not shareholder-oriented or stakeholder-oriented, unless the concept of a corporate "stakeholder" is stretched to include the ruling political party and the government in its policy making, regulatory, and enforcement capacities. Nor is it a liberal market economy (LME) or a coordinated market economy (CME) per the "varieties of capitalism" literature. None of these taxonomies provides much analytical leverage on a system of national champion capitalism in which a party-state is residual claimant, controlling shareholder, financier, and chief engineer of an Olsonian encompassing coalition that ties the economic and political fortunes of a vast array of actors to national economic growth.

Of course, each country's governance structures are unique. The point is that the map used by comparative corporate governance scholars in recent decades to understand the world may lead observers of China astray, or at least cause them to overlook fertile areas for further investigation. To take an example relevant to the convergence question, most scholars have assumed that state capitalism in China is transitional, with the speed of the transition a function of state capacity and political will to make improvements in the formal institutional environment. Relatedly, many observers have emphasized the vast divergence between formal law and actual practice in Chinese corporate governance.[54] The gulf, some commentators imply, will close up when China becomes more "law abiding."[55]

The analysis here points in a different direction. There is certainly a yawning gap between law and practice in Chinese state capitalism if one focuses on the corporate law and related institutions. Direct involvement of the Communist Party in high-level executive appointments, SASAC's practice of bypassing the board of directors in the appointments and remuneration processes, and its veto power over downstream corporate transactions are all inconsistent with basic corporate law principles. (They also violate soft-law norms

---

[53] See Gilson, *supra* note 50.

[54] Donald C. Clarke, " 'Nothing but Wind'? The Past and Future of Comparative Corporate Governance", 59 Am. J. Comp. L. 75, 101–102 (2010) ("the reality of corporate governance in China remains very different from what appears in the statute books, and indeed is so opaque that it is difficult to measure reliably where it is, let alone to know in what direction it is moving").

[55] See Michael A. Witt, "China: What Variety of Capitalism?", INSEAD Working Paper 2010/88/ EPS, at 12.

on SOE governance promoted by international organizations such as the OECD.) But if one focuses on the regulations governing business group formation and governance, and the SOE Asset Law governing SASAC in its formal role as controlling shareholder over the national champions, the gap between law and practice in China's SOE sector narrows substantially. The existing legal environment is actually quite complementary to the current economic system, in which the state sector continues to play a major role in the government's economic and political policies.

Whatever its disadvantages, and they are likely substantial, state capitalism as it has evolved in China over the past 30 years represents a form of industrial organization that produces substantial benefits to members of the encompassing coalition—the managerial elite within the party-state system. The national champions themselves are now forceful players in the Chinese political economy. We need look no further than the US historical experience to see that large corporations—even ones not linked to the state—can exert tremendous influence on the design of national institutions and the nature of social relations. It is therefore quite possible that China's formal legal institutions may "improve" in ways that reinforce the current system of industrial organization rather than prompt a transition to different forms of corporate organization. State capitalism may prove to be a durable institutional arrangement as a result of interest group politics, public policy, and path dependence.

Thus, for the convergence debate, China raises the possibility of a new, durable, and possibly influential variety of capitalism. The Chinese system has already garnered attention as a model of political intervention in the economy among countries with authoritarian political traditions such as Russia, and interventionist tendencies, such as Brazil. Of course, imitating the Chinese model may prove difficult for a host of reasons. But as we have seen, Chinese firms have entered the global economy through a path that bears almost no resemblance to the standard institutionalist account of how firms grow and large-scale commercial economies develop. Thus, even short of replication elsewhere, China's variety of capitalism may prove influential to countries lacking the formal institutional foundations of growth. Quite apart from these forms of influence, it is apparent that China's rise is a significant disruptive force in global capitalism. It has disrupted previously settled notions about the nature of capitalism,[56] and sparked a predictable backlash in some realms.[57] The competitive challenges posed by an economic system in which, for the largest and most globally active firms, the country is the unit of maximization are profound. At a minimum, China's global economic rise, like that of Japan two decades ago, will likely encourage reconsideration of cooperative links between the state and the private sector, and refocus attention on networked varieties of corporate capitalism. In corporate governance, as in politics, the "End of History" is nowhere in sight.

---

[56] For insightful commentary, see the series of articles in 7 Org. & Mgmt. Rev. (2010).

[57] See, e.g., Jason Dean et al., China's "State Capitalism" Sparks a Global Backlash, Wall St. J., Nov. 16, 2010, at 1; Ian Bremmer, The End of the Free Market: Who Wins the War between States and Corporations? (2010).

6 CONCLUSION

This chapter has begun the task of unpacking the black box of "state capitalism" in China by examining business group ownership structures within the national state-owned enterprises and exposing the mechanisms connecting the national champions to organs of the party-state. Shifting the focus from agency problems in individual listed firms to networks of firms enmeshed in the party-state has provided a richer understanding of China's state sector and the architecture supporting a central component of the state's economic development model. It has also brought the organizational dimension of China's developmental experience to bear on important recent debates in the comparative corporate governance literature.

CHAPTER 29

THE RISE OF FOREIGN OWNERSHIP AND CORPORATE GOVERNANCE

MERRITT B. FOX

1 INTRODUCTION

ONE of the most striking changes in the world's capitalist economies has been the rise of cross-border share ownership over the last two decades. This chapter is devoted to understanding the relationship between this rise and corporate governance.

The chapter begins by documenting this rise statistically. Then, in order to situate the subject under study within its larger context, it explores the factors independent of corporate-governance considerations that favor a global market for securities and those that impede it. It will be shown that the rise in foreign ownership globally can be explained in significant part by the weakening of these impeding factors. The remainder of the chapter is devoted to the interaction between the rise in foreign ownership and corporate governance.

The underlying theme of the chapter is as follows. The demand outside a country for the shares of its issuers is determined both by how much the forces impeding a global market for securities have weakened and by the corporate governance of the country's issuers. This observation suggests pathways of causation between increased foreign ownership and improved corporate governance that run in both directions. For each, the weakening of the forces independent of corporate governance that impede a global market for securities acts as a catalyst. As they weaken, foreign ownership increases, leading to improved corporate governance, which in turn leads to increased foreign ownership. More specifically, we will consider the role of the weakening of these impeding forces in the following three regards.

First, a weakening of the forces impeding a global market for securities leads to a greater potential increase in foreign ownership for issuers in a poor governance jurisdiction if these issuers then in fact credibly improve their governance. This increased opportunity to tap the large global pool of capital abroad creates incentives for any country with a poor corporate-governance regime to make improvements. It also creates incentives for individual issuers within the country to improve their own governance above and beyond whatever floor is set by the country's overall regime. To the extent that countries and firms respond to these incentives, foreign ownership increases.

Second, some countries with poor corporate-governance regimes improve their regimes for reasons independent of the weakening of the forces impeding global share investing. With a weakening of the impeding forces, however, the improvement in corporate governance leads to a greater increase in foreign holdings of the shares of their issuers than would have been the case without the weakening.

Third, a weakening of the forces impeding a global market for equities leads to more foreign investors purchasing shares in issuers from countries with poor corporate governance even if, at the time, there is no improvement in their corporate governance. As the foreign investors acquire a larger portion of the outstanding shares of these issuers, they generate new pressure for governance improvement.

2 Documenting the Rise in Foreign Ownership

The dramatic rise in foreign ownership is illustrated in Tables 29.1 and 29.2, which compare 1993 and 2015 in terms of the proportion of US investor holdings in foreign issuers and of the proportion of foreign issuer holdings of US issuers. Comparing Table 29.1 with Table 29.2, we can see that over these 22 years, the proportion of non-US equities in US investor stock portfolios, and the proportion of US equities in the portfolios of non-US investors, have each more than quadrupled.

Table 29.1 Proportion of US investor holdings in foreign issuers and the proportion of foreign issuer holdings of US issuers, 1993

	US Issuer Equity	Non-US Issuer Equity	Total
Equity market capitalization	$5.2 trillion (37%)	$8.9 trillion (63%)	$14.1 trillion
Holdings by US investors	$4.9 trillion (94%)	$.3 trillion (6%)	$5.2 trillion
Holdings by non-US investors	$.3 trillion (3%)	$8.6 trillion (97%)	$8.9 trillion

Note: Figures in the 1993 table come from the following sources: US equity market capitalization in 1993 = $5.2 trillion, Securities & Exchange Commission, Annual Report, 28 (1994) available at: https://www.sec.gov/about/annual_report/1994.pdf; worldwide equity market capitalization in 1993 = $14.1 trillion (non-US equity market capitalization = $14.1 trillion−$5.2 trillion), id.; holdings by non-US investors of US equity securities in 1993 = $340.0 billion, Russel B. Scholl, The International Investment Position of the United States in 1994, Survey of Current Business, June 1995, at 52; holdings by US investors of non-US equity securities in 1993 = $297.7 billion, id.; holdings by US investors of US equity securities in 1993 = $5.2 trillion – $340 billion = $4.9 trillion; holdings by non-US investors of non-US equity securities = $8.9 trillion – $297.7 billion = $8.6 trillion.

Table 29.2 Proportion of US investor holdings in foreign issuers and the proportion of foreign issuer holdings of US issuers, 2015

	US Issuer Equity	Non-US Issuer Equity	Total
Equity market capitalization	$25.1 trillion (41%)	$36.7 trillion (59%)	$61.8 trillion
Holdings by US investors	$20.5 trillion (75%)	$6.8 trillion (25%)	$27.3 trillion
Holdings by non-US investors	$4.6 trillion (13%)	$29.9 trillion (87%)	$34.5 trillion

Note: Total market capitalization figures for US issuers and foreign issuers are derived from World Bank, Market Capitalization of Listed Companies, http://data.worldbank.org/indicator/CM.MKT.LCAP. CD. The cross-border holdings of both US and foreign investors come from Int'l. Monetary Fund, Coordinated Portfolio Investment Survey (2015) Table 11.1, available at http://cpis.imf.

The same pattern can be observed at the more granular country-to-country level. For example, in 1989, Japanese investors on average held only 0.3% of their portfolios in US issuer stocks and US investors on average held only 1.3% in Japanese issuer stocks.[1] In 2015, Japanese investors on average held 8.2% of their portfolios in US issuer stocks, a twenty-seven-fold increase in the proportion held, and US investors on average held 2.5% in Japanese issuer stocks, an almost twofold increase in the proportion held[2] (a much more significant increase than it appears because the market capitalization of Japanese stocks as a proportion of the total capitalization of all the world's publicly traded issuers dropped from 28% in 1995[3] to 8% in 2015[4]).

While starting from a much lower base, similar trends can be observed in the case of various emerging economies. US investors on average held only 0.02% of their portfolios in Indian stocks in 1994, but by 2015 the figure was up to 0.44%, a twenty-two-fold increase; for South Korea, the comparable figures are only 0.09% for 1994 and 0.51% for 2015, a more than fivefold increase.[5]

Finally, and importantly for our later discussion of the influence of foreign ownership on corporate governance in such countries, there has been a sharp increase in the proportion of the shares of issuers from countries with less well regarded corporate-governance regimes

---

[1] Kenneth R. French & James M. Poterba, "Investor Diversification and International Equity Markets", 81 Am. Econ. Rev. Papers and Proceedings 222 (1991).

[2] These figures were calculated using the same methods and same sources as the 2015 figures in Table 29.2. See note in Table 29.2.

[3] James L. Cochrane, James E. Shapiro, & Jean E. Tobin, "Foreign Equities and US Investors: Breaking Down the Barriers Separating Supply and Demand", 1 New York Stock Exchange Working Papers 95–04 (1995).

[4] This figure calculated using the same methods and same sources as the 2015 figures in Table 29.2. See note in Table 29.2.

[5] Total cross-border holding figures come from the US Holdings of Foreign Securities Treasury Report (2015) available at www.treasury.gov/ticdata/Publish/shchistdat.html. From these figures, US investor total worldwide holders in 1994 were calculated as follows (in millions): $5,067,016 (US Issuer Market Cap) – $397,703 (Foreign Holdings of US Equity) + $566,554 (US Holdings of Foreign Equity) = $5,235,867 (Total Equity Held by US Investors).

held by investors from countries with more well regarded regimes. Between 1994 and 2015, the proportion of Japanese issuer stocks held by US investors increased from 2.7% to 14.1%, a more than fivefold increase; for South Korea, the comparable figures increased from 2.3% to 11.3%, a more than fourfold increase; for India, the comparable figures increased from 0.9% to 7.9%, an almost ninefold increase; and for Brazil, the comparable figures increased from 4.5% to 13.5%, a three fold increase.[6]

All in all, at year end 2012, 38% of the capitalized value of all the world's publicly traded issuers was held by investors from a country different from that of the issuer.[7]

3 Trends in Non-Corporate-governance Factors Affecting the Extent of Foreign Ownership

As will be developed below, under ideal conditions, the typical passive portfolio investor around the world, to maximize her utility, should hold an equity portfolio containing shares of issuers of different countries roughly in proportion to the countries' respective total market capitalizations.[8] Thus, for example, a US and a Japanese passive investor should each have a portfolio with about 8% invested in Japanese corporations and 41% in US ones. This is because the market capitalization of Japanese public companies represents 8% of the total market capitalization of the world's publicly traded issuers and that of US corporations represents 41%.[9]

If all investors around the world followed this rule, all corporations would be predominantly foreign owned. Keeping with our examples, as the figures in Table 29.2 reveal for 2015, US investors held about 44% of the equity wealth in the world and non-US investors hold the remaining 56%, including 8.0% that is held by Japanese investors.[10] So the typical US corporation would have 56% of its shares owned by non-US investors, compared with 13% today.[11] Japanese investors hold about 8% of the equity wealth in the world and non-Japanese hold the remaining 92%, including the 44% that is held by US investors.[12] Therefore the typical

---

[6] Total cross-border holding figures come from the US Holdings of Foreign Securities Treasury Report (2015) available at http://ticdata.treasury.gov/Publish/shchistdat.html. Total market capitalization figures for US issuers and foreign issuers are derived from The World Bank, Market Capitalization of Listed Companies, http://data.worldbank.org/indicator/CM.MKT.LCAP.CD.

[7] The total cross border holdings of both U.S. and foreign investors come from International Monetary Fund, Coordinated Portfolio Investment Survey (2015) Table 11, available at http://cpis.imf.org.

[8] Jung-Koo Kang & Rene M. Stulz, "Why is There Home Bias? An Analysis of Foreign Portfolio Equity Ownership in Japan", 46 J. Fin. Econ. 3 (1997).

[9] See World Bank, Market Capitalization of Listed Companies, available at: http://data.worldbank.org/indicator/CM.MKT.LCAP.CD.

[10] International Monetary Fund, Coordinated Portfolio Investment Survey (2012) Table 11.1, available at: http://cpis.imf.org.

[11] See Table 29.2 and the national ownership figures in the text.

[12] These figures were calculated using the same methods and same sources as the 2012 figures in Table 29.2. See note in Table 29.2.

Japanese corporation would have 92% foreign ownership (compared to 18% today) including 44% of the ownership coming from US investors (compared with only 9% today).[13] These figures show that while there has been a striking increase in cross-border ownership of equity over the last two decades, there would be potential for much more if the remaining impediments to a global market for securities disappeared. This would have possibly profound corporate-governance implications.

In sum, the world of 20 years ago fell far short of the extent of cross-border holdings that would be welfare maximizing for passive portfolio investors. Today, with a severalfold increase in the foreign ownership of the typical, large established corporations around the world, it still falls well short, but not by as far. The distance that could still be traveled would represent a yet much greater amount of foreign ownership. This section considers trends in the factors that favor globalization and in the counter-factors that resist it. An examination of these factors and their trends both helps to explain the increase in foreign ownership that has occurred so far and predicts a substantial further increase in the future.

3.1 Factors Favoring Greater Foreign Ownership

Two factors push investors to hold shares of foreign issuers. First, when investors from a country rich in savings relative to its real investment opportunities are net positive purchasers of securities sold by issuers or persons from a country poorer in savings relative to such opportunities, savings are reallocated from the savings-rich country to the savings-poor one. This profits the residents of both countries. Second, when an investor holds a portfolio that is diversified across issuers of multiple countries, instead of across just the issuers of her own country, she can reduce the risk of the portfolio relative to its expected return and thereby increase the expected utility from her investment activities.

3.1.1 Returns to a Reallocation of Savings

One factor working in favor of foreign ownership is the existence of differences among nations in their amounts of domestically generated savings relative to the quality of the available opportunities for domestic real investment.[14] Real investment opportunities in each nation display diminishing marginal returns in the sense that the proposed projects that constitute any given nation's set of domestic real investment opportunities are bound to have differing earnings prospects and, if the projects are implemented down the list in rank order of their prospects, the more of a nation's projects that are implemented—i.e. the greater the amount of total domestic real investment—the lower the expected return on the marginal project.

---

[13] Id.

[14] Real (as opposed to financial) investment is the use of resources such as skilled labor, machinery, bricks, and mortar to create new capacity in a nation's economy to produce a particular good or service in the future. Financial investment is the acquisition of rights to receive future cash returns: for example, the purchase of a share or bond, the lending of money, or the deposit of money in an interest bearing savings account.

The amounts of available domestic savings and the sets of domestically available real investment projects have not historically been, and are not likely in the future to be, distributed among nations exactly in the same proportions. In other words, if there were no transnational investment, so that each nation simply took all of its savings and invested them in just its projects, the expected return on the marginal project of each nation would be unlikely to be exactly the same. For example, if Country A's marginal project would have, in the absence of transnational investment, an expected rate of return (say 8%) that is lower than Country B's marginal project would have been (say 10%), Country A can be said to have more savings relative to the quality of its investment opportunities than Country B. A reallocation of savings for investment from A to B will reduce the number of projects implemented in A and increase the number of projects implemented in B. This reallocation enhances global economic efficiency because the projects that are now left unimplemented in A have a lower expected return than the resulting additional ones that are implemented in B. Until such point that any further a shift of funds from A to B will no longer have this result, there will be incentives for persons with savings in A to invest them in B rather than A because they can get a higher expected return.

One of the ways that such a transnational reallocation of savings can occur is when an investor in one country purchases shares in a primary offering of shares issued by an issuer in another country. Further, when, on a net basis, investors in one country make secondary market purchases of securities from investors in a second country, this will have the same effect, and often the securities so purchased will be of issuers from the second country. There are other ways through which such savings reallocations occur, such as internal financial flows of multinational corporations engaging in direct investments, bank lending, private block purchases of securities, and even purchases of government debt. However, the purchase of shares that will be, or already are, publicly traded has the advantages of being an investment that is liquid and that facilitates diversification.

3.1.2 *Greater Diversification*

A share's future return is probabilistic, not certain, and so each stock has a certain riskiness associated with it. Global investing offers investors a more effective way of reducing the negative impact of this riskiness on their welfare than does exclusively domestic investing. To understand why requires a brief diversion into the theory of portfolio choice, which is a pillar of the modern approach to finance.

Portfolio choice theory teaches the investor to focus on what the acquisition of a given security does to the returns on his whole portfolio of securities, not on the security's characteristics in isolation.[15] The critical lesson of portfolio choice theory is that holding a

---

[15] Theories of individual investment behavior assume that the purpose of saving and investment is to consume the results of the investments at the end of the investment period. Since funds are fungible, whatever the combination of gains and losses on the investments in individual securities that make up the total return, all that counts is the total. Portfolio choice theory tells the investor how to compose a portfolio at the beginning of the investment period that will maximize the expected utility he will derive from the end of period value of this invested wealth (the means of his consumption at that time). If we assume that an investor is a rational maximizer of his expected utility, we can also use the theory to predict his behavior.

diversified set of risky securities results in lower risk for any given level of expected return.[16] The expected return of a portfolio is the aggregate of the expected returns of its individual securities. The variance of a portfolio is not, however, the aggregate of the variances of its individual securities. This is because of the likelihood that the actual returns of some of the securities will exceed their expected returns and the actual returns of others will fall short of their expected returns. Consequently, the deviations of the two groups will, to one extent or another, cancel each other out, which reduces the amount by which the actual return of the portfolio as a whole deviates from its expected return. By diversifying in accordance with the dictates of portfolio theory, the investor maximizes, for any given level of portfolio expected return, the extent to which this type of canceling out is likely to occur.

There are limits, however, to the effectiveness of diversification for lowering risk. This is most easily seen in terms of a simplified model of portfolio choice theory that focuses on the correlation between the return on each individual risky security and the return on the market of securities as a whole (rather than with each other individual security).[17] Each security has two kinds of riskiness associated with it: unsystematic risk (the portion of the security's variance that has a 0 correlation with the market) and systematic risk (the portion of its variance that is perfectly correlated with the market). Unsystematic risk is due to factors specific in their effects to the issuer or its industry, for example, uncertainty concerning the quality of an issuer's management. Systematic risk is due to factors affecting all issuers whose securities are traded in the market, for example, uncertainty concerning future interest rates. The contribution of the unsystematic risk of individual securities to a portfolio's overall risk can essentially be fully eliminated by sufficient diversification. This is because the deviations of the individual securities are unrelated to each other and will cancel each other out. The systematic risk of the individual securities, however, cannot be eliminated by diversification. To the extent that individual securities deviate from their expected returns due to factors causing systematic risk, generally all securities deviate in the same direction.

With this background, one can easily see why global investing offers an investor an opportunity to construct a portfolio with lower risk for any given level of expected return. The extent to which diversification can eliminate overall portfolio risk depends on the proportion of each security's total variance that results from unsystematic risk. This again is because unsystematic risk can be diversified away, but systematic risk cannot. The less each issuer in a market shares in common with the others, the smaller the proportion of systematic risk and the higher the proportion of unsystematic risk. Issuers worldwide share less in common with each other on average than issuers of a given country share in common with each other. Thus, if the relevant securities market is global rather than merely domestic, a

---

[16] Investors are typically assumed to be "risk averse," i.e., they like expected return and dislike risk. Thus, for any given level of expected return, the lower a portfolio's risk is, the better. The assumption of risk aversion is in turn derived from an assumption that the investor will derive declining marginal utility from consuming his end-of-period wealth, i.e., compared to the utility he gains from any given level of wealth, one dollar more adds less to his total utility than one dollar less subtracts from his total utility. This leads to risk aversion because, compared to the expected utility from a given level of end of period wealth known with certainty, the chance of one dollar over that level does not compensate for an equal chance of one dollar under that level. Thus, in a choice between two portfolios with differing risk, the investor will choose the riskier one only if it has a sufficiently higher expected return to compensate her for the disutility she associates with the greater risk.

[17] See, William F. Sharpe, "A Simplified Model for Portfolio Analysis", 9 Mgmt. Sci. 277 (1963).

larger proportion of each issuer's variance will constitute unsystematic risk and diversification will reduce portfolio risk more.

The concern with diversification highlights the fact that capital markets not only decide which proposed real investment projects should be implemented, but also who will bear the risk resulting from uncertainty concerning projects' future returns. This observation suggests two modifications of the simple model that views transnational investment simply as reallocation of savings. First, the desirability of a given project now depends not only on its expected return but also on its risk characteristics. Second, if all investors were to diversify globally sufficiently to achieve the maximum reduction in risk, the level of each investor's cross-border holdings as a proportion of all her holdings would be determined, not by the amount of savings reallocated transnationally, but by the investor's desire to eliminate unnecessary risk through diversification. If one nation consistently has more savings relative to its real investment opportunities than another, its investors would accumulate a larger absolute share of the joint pool of securities of the two nations.[18] But for investors in each country, the proportions of the securities of the two countries held in their portfolios would be the same and would depend on the respective total market capitalization of the issuers of each.[19]

3.2 Non-Corporate-governance Factors Impeding Global Securities Markets

We will now consider the factors independent of corporate governance that play major roles in why investors in fact fall so far short of being fully diversified globally.

3.2.1 *Specialized Information Concentrated Nationally*

Finance theorists often assume that all investors share identical beliefs concerning the probability distribution of the future returns of the available securities. This assumption is useful for understanding certain aspects of investor behavior. For example, it permits the demonstration that a totally passive investor, who in fact has no specific information concerning the future prospects of the available securities, can minimize risk for any given expected return by simply randomly choosing a sufficiently large number of different securities from all the securities available in the market.

In reality, however, investors in different countries still possess significantly different bodies of information. The assumption of identical beliefs in the face of this obvious reality obscures two other aspects of investor behavior that have been important contributors to a strong home bias in the holdings of securities. First, for the totally passive investor to be willing to undertake the strategy of randomly choosing securities, she needs a basic faith in the market pricing of the securities from which she makes her selection. This faith arises

---

[18] The larger absolute amount of transnational investment by the investors of the nation with relatively greater savings will be counterbalanced by the smaller absolute amount of such investment by investors in the other nation. If there were a safe asset available and one country's investor were less risk averse than the other, its investors would hold a larger absolute amount of transnational investment relative to if the investors in the two countries were equally risk averse, but again the proportions would be the same.

[19] See note 8 *supra*.

from a level of familiarity which, for many investors, is today still attained only for their particular domestic market.[20] Second, some investors ("speculators") choose their portfolios on the basis of their own beliefs, not randomly, and these beliefs in turn are based on specialized information not possessed by all participants.[21] Speculators are likely to do better concentrating their buying and selling in equities of issuers about which they and their advisers start with natural information advantages.[22] These are likely to be domestic issuers,

[20] John R. Graham, Campbell R. Harvey, & Hai Huang, "Investor Competence, Trading Frequency, and Home Bias", 55 Mgmt. Sci., INFORMS 1094 (2005) (investors tend to shy away from investing in foreign securities if their perceptions are that they lack an understanding in the attendant benefits and risks); French & Poterba, *supra* note 1, at 225 (investors, due to lack of knowledge about foreign markets, institutions, and firms, regard investments in foreign stocks as "unfamiliar gambles" and, even when they assign to a foreign and domestic stock identical probability distributions, impute to the foreign stock a special kind of extra (apparently undiversifiable) "risk," behavior explainable by certain theories of behavioral economics).

[21] This use of the term "speculator" thus covers both (1) persons who buy or sell for the short run on the basis of information (or evidence of the existence of information) that they believe will soon become more widely known, and (2) investors who purchase for the longer run on the basis of what they believe to be their superior analysis of the "fundamentals."

[22] This statement may appear inconsistent with the efficient market hypothesis (EMH). The EMH, most broadly stated, is that the market price of a security "fully reflects" all information publicly available at the time in question. See Richard Brealey, Stewart Meyers, & Franklin Allen, Principles of Corporate Finance 317–18 (10th ed. 2010) (the prices of established issuers trading in liquid markets reflect all publicly available information). While one of the implications of the EMH is that the ordinary investor is wasting her time trying to pick "winners" on the basis of information she gleans from public sources, a subset of all investors is the persons who initially obtain newly public information and whose trades cause the price to reflect it. Ronald Gilson & Reinier Kraakman, "The Mechanisms of Market Efficiency", 70 Va. L. Rev. 549, 569–70 (1984). This subset may be responsible for a substantial percentage of all transactions and would as a result create a home bias in the pattern of holdings. There are sound theoretical reasons for thinking that speculative investors tend to invest in the securities about which they know the most. See, e.g., Robert C. Merton, "A Simple Model of Capital Market Equilibrium", 42 J. Fin. 483 (1987) (formal model that shows how segmentation occurs when different groups of investors have different information sets, with each group preferring to trade in the securities about which they have the most information). Geographic proximity to the issuer has been shown empirically to be important even within the US market. Joshua D. Coval & Tobias J. Moskowitz, "Home Bias at Home: Local Equity Preference in Domestic Portfolios", 54 J. Fin. 2045 (1999). Prominent financial economists have been suggesting for a long time that this "home country bias" is related at least in part to differences between the information investors possess concerning home country issuers and that concerning foreign issuers. See, e.g., Martin Feldstein & Charles Horioka, "Domestic Savings and International Capital Flows", 90 Econ. J. 314, 316 (1980) (finding a high correlation between marginal increases in domestic savings and in domestic investment and attributing these in part to investors' greater uncertainty concerning foreign issuers due to less information); Martin Feldstein, "Domestic Saving and International Capital Movements in the Long Run and the Short Run", 21 Eur. Econ. Rev. 129, 130–31 and 148 (1983) (finding substantial imperfections in the international capital market and attributing them in part to investors having a higher subjective variance on foreign returns due to less information); Robert E. Lucas, Jr., "Interest Rates and Currency Prices in a Two-Country World", 10 J. Monetary Econ. 335, 357 (1983) (explaining home bias as the result of the local nature of information, but noting the lack of models that even begin to give an understanding of the relationship); Ian Cooper & Evi Kaplanis, "Home Bias in Equity Portfolios, Inflation Hedging, and International Capital Market Equilibrium", 7 Rev. Fin. Stud. 45 (1994) (taxes and extra costs of foreign investing cannot fully explain the extent of home bias and attributing a substantial portion of it to investor lack of knowledge concerning foreign issuers); Jung-Koo Kang & Rene M. Stulz, "Why is There a Home Bias? An Analysis

because the futures of most issuers are determined more by forces occurring within the borders of their own respective countries than by forces occurring outside.

For several reasons, historically, residents of a given nation have had advantages over foreigners in gaining specialized information about forces acting within their own nation. To start, the costs of simply acquiring bits of local information have been lower for a resident, whether that be through timely purchasing of published materials (in, or translated into, a language readable by the recipient) or computerized data, engaging in telephone conversations, or traveling in order to engage in face-to-face conversations or to make on-site physical observations. Thus it has traditionally been far easier for residents to gather a larger number of bits of information at a reasonable expenditure.

More importantly, these same economies that have permitted residents to receive large numbers of such bits of, permit them as well to develop refined rules for evaluating these bits of information: to choose which bits to analyze seriously and by which to be influenced.[23] This evaluation must be based both on the source of the information as well as on its content. The concern with the source goes to the accuracy of the information. It asks the questions, "How trustworthy is the source?" and, assuming that the information has an interpretative element, "How competent is the source?" The concern with content asks the question, "How much does the bit, even assuming the information conveyed is accurate, tell the recipient about whether a particular security is underpriced or overpriced?"

Moreover, the resident recipient, through his education and his continuous absorption of general information concerning his nation, has started with a much richer context in which to make these evaluations. He has also obtain, cheaply, much more concerning both the structure of the source's motivations and the reputation of the source (i.e., the experience of others with the source concerning his trustworthiness and competence). Since the source has been less expensive to acquire information from generally, the resident recipient is also more likely to have had prior personal experience with the source and hence to have had more feedback on the quality of information the source provides.[24] The resident recipient is, for the same reasons, more likely to have had prior experience with the usefulness of bits with any particular content when the information involved relates to local forces. For many of the same reasons, he is also more familiar with the institutions involved in the process of price formation for his own nation's issuers.

Technological change, of course, has been a game changer in this story. It can help explain the severalfold increases in the proportion of cross-border holdings in investor portfolios. It also forecasts further increases to come. Over the last 20 years, technological change has

---

of Foreign Portfolio Equity Ownership in Japan", 46 J. Fin. Econ. 3 (1997) (similar conclusion based on an examination of the Japanese firms in which foreign investors choose to invest).

[23] The questions being addressed here apply to the information processing by a whole network of persons—the participants in the "finance process"—whose decisions ultimately determine which real investment projects are implemented. The role played by these different participants—project proponents, firm managers, financial intermediaries, investment advisers and individual investors—and the nature of the rules by which these participants process information is considered in more detail in Merritt B. Fox, Finance and Industrial Performance in a Dynamic Economy: Theory, Practice and Policy 92–232 (1987).

[24] For an example in the legal literature of the use of this kind of "reputation theory," see, e.g., Ronald J. Gilson & Robert H. Mnookin, "Coming of Age in a Corporate Law Firm: The Economics of Associate Career Patterns", 41 Stan. L. Rev. 567, 578–79 (1989).

substantially narrowed, and in many cases eliminated, the differences in the respective costs of timely acquisition of information from foreign and domestic sources. Consider email, transmission of documents by email attachment, the web, links to computerized databases, all of which have no cost sensitivity to distance, and international telephone calls and travel for face-to-face meetings and on-site inspections, each of which has declined greatly in cost. This reduction in the difference between acquiring information domestically and from abroad applies with respect to both information directly relevant to predicting the prospects of issuers and information about the motivations and reputation of the sources of such directly relevant information. These same technological changes have also contributed to the development of truly transnational securities firms with the trust and control advantages of communications within a single organization. Finally, these technological changes, through their effect on mass media, marketing, education, scholarly research and direct personal interaction, are working toward creating a more uniform social and economic culture among the capitalist nations of the world and the coalescence around English as the international language. This greater uniformity of culture and language assists the speculative investor in evaluating the information he receives from abroad and gives the passive investor more faith in how stocks of foreign issuers are priced. Moreover, the rules by which investors and their advisers evaluate information have a "learning by doing" aspect and improve with experience, so that even the decline in information costs to date has not yet had anywhere near its full impact on reducing the impediment to global securities markets traditionally arising from the cost advantages of local information.

3.2.2 *Currency Exchange Risks*

If the resident of one nation, for example the United States, purchases a security of an issuer of another nation, for example the United Kingdom, the investor must consider the possibility that when he converts the return back into dollars, the rate of exchange may be different than at the time of the purchase. Thus, to the United States investor, the UK security has an additional element of risk—an additional source of variability of return—that would not be present with an otherwise identical United States security. With holdings of foreign securities from a diversified set of nations, the variations in return of individual securities caused by exchange rate fluctuations would tend to cancel each other out. There is still remaining risk, however, that comes from the extent to which the investor's home currency's value has changed relative to a basket made up of the currencies of the other nations of the world. This is a risk that will discourage cross-border stock holdings.

Two factors moderate this risk, changes in each of which have contributed at least slightly to the increase in cross-border holdings over the past two decades. One factor comes from the fact that an increasing portion of the goods and services consumed by the typical investor comes from abroad. For example, from 1993 to 2012, the percentage of goods and services imported from abroad increased from 10% to 17% for the United States, from 16% to 24% for China, from 7% to 17% for Japan, and from 26% to 34% for the United Kingdom.[25] Future fluctuations in currency exchange rates create risks concerning how much of these foreign

---

[25] World Bank, Imports of Goods and Services (% of GDP), available at http://data.worldbank.org/indicator/NE.IMP.GNFS.ZS.

goods and services the investor will be able to consume when, in the future, she liquidates her investments to consume. Holding foreign issuer securities is a hedge against this risk. In domestic currency terms, exchange rate fluctuation will affect the return on foreign securities and the cost of imported goods in the same direction. Since one is income and the other expenditure, the effects tend to compensate for each other. With the increase in international trade, there is more room for holdings of foreign securities to act as a hedge, thereby reducing an investor's overall risk from exchange rate fluctuations, rather than adding to it.

The other factor is the ability to use currency futures to hedge against the effect of future exchange rate changes on the returns of foreign securities. Futures markets for securities have become less expensive to use and allow for longer-term hedges than was the case a few decades ago.

3.2.3 Government Impediments to Transnational Investments

Governments can impede transnational securities transactions through currency controls and taxes and through securities regulation.

3.2.3.1 Currency Controls and Taxes

Consider a potential transnational transaction involving an issuer or secondary seller of one nation and an investor of another. The government of either nation can have tax or currency exchange regulations that create sufficient disincentives such that the transaction does not take place. The government of the investor, for example, may make it difficult or impossible to obtain the foreign currency with which to purchase the security, may tax the returns on foreign securities at a higher rate than it taxes the returns on domestic securities, or may refuse to grant the domestic holder of a foreign security a tax credit for taxes withheld from the returns by the government of the issuer. The government of the issuer may make it difficult or impossible for a foreign investor to turn returns paid in the local currency of the issuer's nation into the investor's domestic currency. Alternatively, it may impose a withholding tax on the returns which, for a number of possible reasons, may not reduce the investor's home tax obligations by a commensurate amount. Transnational transactions can be discouraged not only by currently existing regulations of these sorts, but also by the fear that they might be imposed at any point in the future during the life of the security.

The period after World War II witnessed a variety of such currency control and tax measures imposed by many of the world's most advanced economies. These measures tended to reinforce segmentation of securities markets along national lines. The countries involved had largely dismantled these measures by the end of the 1980s, however. A return of such measures in these advanced economies is unlikely because such nations compete with each other to provide environments congenial to the financial services industry, which regards such taxes and regulations as anathema.

Because of the rise of the emerging market countries as significant players in the world economy, however, such measures still play an important role impeding cross-border equity ownership. Many of these countries, most notably China, continue to impose such controls. There is much talk of liberalization concerning these countries, which would lead to a further weakening of this impediment to foreign ownership. For many of these countries, it is unclear, however, whether this talk will materialize into action. Among other reasons, they may hesitate because of the experiences of some emerging countries that have lifted such controls, which have then been subject to fluctuating capital flows. These fluctuations have accentuated upswings and downswings in their overall economies, leading to cycles of boom and bust. While equities, which have no fixed repayments, presumably contribute less to this boom-and-bust problem than do short-term fixed repayment securities, they may still play some role and in any event may still be subject to the same blanket restrictions that apply to all other capital market instruments.

3.2.3.2 *Securities Regulation*

There cannot be foreign ownership without transnational transactions. These transnational transactions in turn inevitably give rise to potential regulatory claims by multiple countries. When more than one country in fact imposes its regulations on an activity associated with a transnational securities transaction, the transaction becomes more expensive to undertake, thereby creating an impediment to a global market for the issuer's shares.

To see how such impediments can arise, we will review some US regulations and legal actions and consider their application to the shares of established foreign firms that are efficiently priced in trading markets abroad. Section 5 of the Securities Act of 1933 (the "Securities Act") prohibits the offer or sale of any security by any person unless the security is registered under the Act. Such registration requires a complex process of disclosure. The SEC has always been clear that it interprets Section 5 as covering public offerings made in the United States by foreign issuers. Further, any foreign issuer wishing its securities to be listed on a US stock exchange must, just like a US issuer, register these securities with the SEC pursuant to Section 13 of the Securities Exchange Act of 1934 (the "Exchange Act"), which again involves a complex process of disclosure. This registration automatically makes the issuer subject to the Exchange Act's periodic disclosure regime,[26] as does the registration of a public offering under the Securities Act.[27] This disclosure regime is generally regarded to be as strict as that of any country in the world.

Listing on a US exchange can also create the potential for a foreign issuer to be liable for large damages payments as the result of a fraud-on-the-market class action.[28] This kind of private action allows secondary market purchasers, who suffer losses because the price they paid was inflated by an issuer's misstatement made in violation of Exchange Act §10(b) and Rule 10b-5, to recover as a group their total damages. These actions give rise to the bulk of all the damages paid out in settlements and judgments pursuant to private litigation under the US securities laws and are what gives the United States the reputation in the rest of the world of being the securities damage action "Wild West."[29] No other country has a civil liability provision that regularly imposes a similar level of damages on issuers.

---

[26] Exchange Act Section 12(a) prohibits any member, broker, or dealer from effecting on a national securities exchange any transaction in "any security" not registered on such an exchange in accordance with the provisions of the Act. Section 13 sets out the registration procedure and provides the statutory basis for the SEC's system of ongoing periodic disclosure by issuers whose securities are registered under the Act.

[27] Exchange Act Section 15(d). The overall structure of the reach of the US disclosure regime with respect to primary offerings and secondary trading involving the shares of foreign issuers is discussed in detail in Merritt B. Fox, "The Political Economy of Statutory Reach: US Disclosure Rules in a Globalizing Market for Securities", 97 Mich. L. Rev. 696, 705–17 (1998).

[28] *Morrison v. Nat'l Austl. Bank*, 130 S. Ct. 2869, 2828 (2010).

[29] Merritt B. Fox, "Securities Class Actions Against Foreign Issuers", 64 Stan. L. Rev. 1173, 1176 (2010).

As discussed above, technological advances have substantially reduced the costs for US investors to acquire information about, and to evaluate, foreign issuers relative to the costs they face doing the same with respect to comparable US issuers, especially large established foreign issuers trading in efficient markets abroad. The US decision to apply these regulations and causes of action to foreign issuers creates costs on an expected basis that would not be present if the issuer were subject only to its home country's laws with respect to the activities involved. These expected costs lead some foreign issuers to avoid offering, or promoting the trading of, their shares in the United States. As a result, there are situations in which a public offering to US residents would provide a foreign issuer with the lowest cost of capital, but the offer is not made. Similarly, there are situations where a United States trading venue would offer the best liquidity services, relative to cost, for the trading of the issuer's shares but the issuer does not list or otherwise promote trading there. US investors suffer from these lost transactions as well. Because the issuer's securities are not conveniently available in the US primary or secondary trading markets, US investors face barriers to enjoying the risk-reduction benefits from full international diversification.[30]

The traditional rationale of the US decision to apply these regulations and causes of action to foreign issuers has been to protect US investors and markets.[31] I have argued elsewhere that in the case of foreign issuers trading in efficient markets abroad, such US application is not necessary to protect US investors against investing at unfair prices. This is because, if these US laws and causes of action were not applied to these foreign issuers, prices would be appropriately discounted to reflect this fact.[32] Rather, regulations and causes of actions of this type serve corporate governance and liquidity enhancement functions. These regulations have costs and benefits that depend on their intensity. The optimal level of regulatory intensity varies from one country's issuers to those of another. The benefits of getting the level of regulatory intensity right redound mostly to the issuer's home country, which thus has the greatest incentive to do so. Accordingly, the impediments to global trading arising from the US application of these regulations and causes of action to foreign issuers are needless from both a US and a global economic welfare point of view.

Perhaps in growing recognition of the costs associated with impeding global trading, the United States has in recent decades been pulling back. Since the early 1980s, foreign issuers have not been required to disclose as much in either their public offering or in their ongoing periodic reports as US issuers are required to disclose, whereas previously they were.[33]

---

[30] One might think that an easy solution to this problem arises because, with modern technology, it is no more costly in resource use terms for US investor orders to be sent to a foreign exchange than to be sent to a US exchange. US investors can simply purchase their foreign issuer shares in foreign markets. See section 3.2.3 *infra*. The problem is more complicated than this, however. For reasons inherent in the way that even the most advanced exchanges currently work, most traders, whether individual or institutional, must place their orders through a broker-dealer who is a member of the exchange to which the order is sent. Under current US law, foreign broker-dealers, the ones that would be members of the foreign exchanges, face legal difficulties dealing with US investors located in the United States. US broker-dealer rules could be liberalized so that it becomes easier for foreign broker-dealers to deal with US resident investors, but then US investors will not receive the consumer protection that the regulation of US broker-dealers and the regulation of US exchanges provide.

[31] Fox, *supra* note 29, at 1205–06, 1254–1255; Fox, *supra* note 27, at 706–08.

[32] Fox, *supra* note 29, at 1191–1204; Fox, *supra* note 27, at 730–44.

[33] Fox, *supra* note 27, at 706 n.21, 714.

More recently, the SEC decided to permit foreign issuers to report their financials in their US filings in accordance with International Financial Reporting Standards ("IFRS"), which many foreign issuers use to satisfy their home country requirements, whereas previously such financials needed to be reconciled with US GAAP.[34] Finally, in *Morrison v. Nat'l Austl. Bank*,[35] the US Supreme Court concluded in 2010 that Exchange Act §10(b)—and hence fraud-on-the-market actions—reached only situations where the securities were listed on a US exchange or where their purchase or sale was effected in the United States.[36] For most foreign issuers, this means that any need to pay fraud-on-the-market damages or settlements would be confined to only the portion of the foreign firm's shares that are purchased in US trading, whereas previous lower-court decisions created possible liability to purchasers worldwide.[37]

There are likely to be further reductions in these US impediments in the future. Consider what would happen if the United States were to maintain them at their current level. The global integration of equity markets outside the United States would continue to progress. This integrating market outside the United States would improve the non-US options available to foreign issuers. Fewer and fewer foreign issuers would find that the benefits of offering their shares in the United States, or promoting US trading of their shares, would be worth the costs. US capital markets would be left mostly with only US issuers,[38] while competing markets abroad would have the opportunity to be the trading venues for all the rest of the world's issuers. Thus, the level of activity in the US capital markets would fall further and further short of what it could be, and with it the skill-based rents earned by the US residents employed by enterprises associated with these markets. This prospect is likely to lead to increasing political pressure to reduce these US impediments, an effort that is particularly likely to succeed given, in my view, their lack of any real value in protecting US investors or markets.

3.2.4 *Transaction Costs of Acquiring Foreign Securities*

A final factor impeding foreign ownership of a corporation's shares are the extra costs associated with the transactions by which foreign investors acquire its shares. Two kinds of transactions can result in share ownership by foreign investors. One is a purchase by the foreign investor on an exchange in the issuer's home country, or in an offering being conducted in the issuer's country. Such a transnational transaction involves the additional costs associated with international communications, currency exchange, and clearances and settlements that are not present with transactions occurring at home. The other kind of transaction is a purchase by the foreign investor on an exchange in the investor's home country, or in an

---

[34] Acceptance from Foreign Private Issuers, Securities Act Release No. 8879, Exchange Act Release No. 57,026, 73 FR 986 (Jan. 4, 2008); see especially 17 C.F.R. 230.701(e)(4) and Form 20-F(G)(h)(2) referenced in 17 C.F.R. 249.220f.

[35] *Morrison v. Nat'l Austl. Bank*, 130 S. Ct. 2869 (2010).   [36] Id. at 2888.

[37] For a general discussion of fraud-on-the-market suits against foreign issuers and the impact of *Morrison*, see Fox, *supra* note 29, at 1199–1203, 1243–63.

[38] The exception would be foreign issuers that in fact find it beneficial to impose on themselves, as a form of bonding, the strict US disclosure regime. See section 4.2.4. The attraction of a US listing to these issuers can be maintained, however, by making being subject to the US disclosure regime optional, rather than a required part of an offering or cross listing.

offering being conducted in that country. This avoids the costs to the investor of a transnational transaction, but it imposes on the issuer the additional costs of maintaining an exchange listing in the investor's home country or conducting an offering there.

The same technological changes that have been narrowing the cost differential of obtaining information from foreign and from domestic sources have been greatly reducing differences in real resource costs between executing a purchase on a domestic exchange, or in a domestic offering, and making these purchases abroad. This is particularly true of secondary trading. It also has become much more practical for the major exchanges around the world to compete for listings from foreign issuers and orders from foreign traders. Share-trading venues in the advanced economies have all become electronic limit-order books, where a computer matches electronically posted limit orders with electronically submitted incoming marketable orders. It is essentially as easy and inexpensive to post a limit order or submit a marketable order from a country distant from the venue as from within the same city as the venue. The only remaining impediment to each of these venues serving a truly global market (other than that, as discussed above, posed by national securities regulation systems) is the need to perfect a seamless transnational system of clearance and settlement.

4 THE INTERACTION OF FOREIGN OWNERSHIP AND CORPORATE GOVERNANCE

As many of the other chapters in this book make clear, what constitutes good corporate governance is a matter of considerable contention. This chapter will not wade deeply into this fight. Rather it focuses on one dimension of an issuer's corporate governance: its capacity to support portfolio investment, i.e., to support a shareholding base that includes a substantial portion of the issuers shares held by persons who individually do not hold enough to exert control and who are numerous enough that it would be difficult to form a group to exercise control.

This choice to focus on portfolio supportive corporate governance is made for positive, not normative, reasons. Most publicly traded firms outside the United States and the United Kingdom have control shareholders. Control shareholders in turn are most often of the same nationality as the issuer. These control shareholders might sell a block of shares to a foreign holder, but the relationship thereafter between the control shareholders and the foreign block holder is likely to be governed by a contract specific to the particular transaction. Thus, for there to be some kind of more general relationship between foreign share ownership and corporate governance, this will arise out of a situation where the foreign holders are portfolio investors, i.e., holders of freely trading non-control shares. A firm's potential for having foreign portfolio investors depends on its potential for having portfolio investors more generally, which, in turn, depends on the portfolio supportiveness of its corporate governance.

This section begins with an elaboration of the concept of portfolio-supportive corporate governance and its implications. Subsequently, we review the literature suggesting that improved corporate governance in fact does lead to greater foreign ownership. Finally, we review the literature suggesting that increased foreign ownership leads to improved corporate governance. In each case, the review will consider the catalytic role played by the weakening of the non-corporate-governance impediments to foreign ownership discussed in section 3.

4.1 Portfolio-Supportive Corporate Governance

In an efficient market, the market price for an issuer's shares reflects an unbiased prediction of the cash flows to be received by the holder. Thus, the price of a stock trading in such a market should fully discount for the extent to which some feature of an issuer's corporate governance reduces this expected cash flow. At first take, this observation would appear to suggest an issuer's corporate governance should have no effect on the extent of foreign ownership. For an issuer with poor corporate governance, the market would expect the portfolio holder of its shares to receive a lower future cash flow discounted to present value than would be expected of an issuer with good governance. Thus the share price of the poor governance issuer would be commensurately less than that of the good governance issuer. As a consequence, this reasoning would go, the share of the poor governance issuer is an equally attractive purchase: the lower price would make up for its lower value.

This first take on the problem, however, ignores a fundamental precondition. A firm will never have portfolio investors of any kind—foreign or domestic—unless these initial control shareholders decide to sell some of their shares to such investors, or to direct the firm to issue and sell shares to such investors. Someone has to start a firm and so all firms inevitably start out their existence with only control shareholders and no portfolio shareholders. The control shareholders will not make the decision to effect a transaction that results in portfolio shareholders unless the portfolio investors are willing to pay a share price sufficiently high that controlling shareholders find the transaction to be worthwhile. Thus, to determine a firm's potential for having portfolio shareholders, we need to examine what portfolio investors are willing to pay and how this interacts with what control shareholders would think is a sufficiently high price to make a sale to the portfolio investors worthwhile.

4.1.1 The Problem of Information Asymmetries

As just noted, the value of an issuer's shares to portfolio investors is determined by the discounted present value of the distributions, including dividends, that the portfolio holder of each such share can expect to receive in the future. The value of these distributions in turn depends in important part on the extent to which the issuer's future discounted-to-present-value net cash flow is expected to be diverted to benefit just the control shareholders. Such a diversion can occur in either of two ways. In one, the firm's assets are deployed in a way that would maximize the value of their expected future cash flow, but the control shareholders give to themselves a greater than pro rata distribution of cash, or obtain the equivalent amount of cash by directly or indirectly entering into a contract with the firm on terms more favorable to them than market terms. The other way involves the control shareholders operating the firm in a way that benefits them, but does not maximize the discounted-to-present-value expected future cash flows of the firm.[39]

---

[39] Where the number of shares sold to portfolio shareholders is sufficiently large that, after the sale, the shareholders who had control until then no longer possess enough shares to retain control,

A sale to portfolio investors by a firm's control shareholders, or by the firm they control, will only be worthwhile to the control shareholders if the price that the portfolio investors are willing to pay is greater than the control shareholders believe, based on what they know, to be the value to them of simply retaining their ownership position as it is. The prospect of diversions by a firm's control shareholders would not affect this calculation, however, if, unlike the real world, the control shareholders and portfolio investors were equally well informed as to what size the diversions will be. Larger expected diversions would mean that control shareholders would enjoy more in the way of the private benefits of control in the future, but they would pay for this benefit now in terms of a commensurately lower price for the shares sold to portfolio investors. The fundamental problem is that control shareholders are in fact better informed about the expected size of these future diversions than portfolio investors.

This asymmetry of information creates a classic "lemons" situation. Consider two types of issuers. The first type has "high-quality" shares. Based on the better information possessed by the controlling shareholders of these high-quality issuers, the expected value of the distributions of these shares is high because they plan to engage in little or no diversion. The second type of issuer has "low-quality" shares. Based on the better information possessed by the controlling shareholders of these low quality issuers, the expected value of the distributions of these shares is low because the planned diversions by these issuers' control shareholders are large. Because the portfolio investors have less information, they are unable to distinguish between the two types of shares.

As George Akerlof showed in his classic 1970 article concerning adverse selection, if nothing alters this asymmetric information situation, the low-quality version of any item of sale can drive the high-quality version out of the market.[40] Suppose, in our example, that potentially there were an equal number of high-quality and low-quality shares offered in the market. Given that buyers cannot distinguish between what in fact are the high-quality shares and the low-quality ones, the price they rationally will be willing to pay will be the same for all the shares: the average of the expected values of the high-quality shares and the low-quality shares. This is because there would be a 50% chance a purchased share was

---

these former control shareholders are no longer capable of effecting diversions to themselves. This determinant of the value of the cash flows available to portfolio investors drops out. It is replaced, however, by the agency costs associated with the managers of a dispersed ownership corporation. As discussed in the seminal article by Jensen and Meckling, these agency costs consist of the sum of the costs of management decisions that diverge from what would be in the portfolio investors' best interests and the monitoring and bonding costs incurred to keep these divergences to a minimum. Michael C. Jensen & William H. Meckling, "Theory of the Firm: Managerial Behavior, Agency Costs and Ownership Structure", 3 J. Fin. Econ. 305, 308 (1976). Because firms outside of the United States and the United Kingdom predominantly have control shareholders, the discussion that follows in the rest of this chapter assumes, for the convenience of exposition, that the foreign issuers involved each have always had, and will continue to have, controlling shareholders. For firms where at some point this assumption is no longer correct, the focus of corporate-governance shifts from constraining control shareholder diversions to constraining agency costs, but, if the reader makes this substitution, most of the discussion is as applicable to management-controlled firms as ones with controlling shareholders.

[40] See George A. Akerlof, "The Market for Lemons: Quality Uncertainty and the Market Mechanism", 84 Q. J. Econ. 488 (1970). The classic article applying this kind of asymmetric information model to the issuance of securities is Stewart C. Myers & Nicholas S. Majluf, "Corporate Financing and Investment Decisions When Firms Have Information that Investors Do Not Have", 13 J. Fin. Econ. 187 (1984).

from a high-quality issuer and a 50% chance that it is from a low-quality issuer. This result would not be an equilibrium solution, however. The blended price that portfolio investors are willing to pay may well not make a sale worthwhile for the controlling shareholders of the high-quality share issuers. If so, the controlling shareholders of the high-quality issuers would decide not to offer their shares at all. The potential portfolio investors would then know that only the low-quality shares would be available and the shares would be priced in the market accordingly.

Now imagine a range of issuers in terms of their share qualities, with the worst, because of some mix of poor expected underlying cash flow and diversions by control shareholders, that are worth nothing. The highest-quality issuers, as just described, would not enter the market in the first place. Now the next-highest-quality issuers would be in the same position as the highest-quality issuers would have been if they had stayed in the market. This is because the price offered to them would be an average of the expected value of these next-highest-quality shares and the values of the shares of all the lower-quality issuers. So now these next-highest-quality issuers would not enter the market. Moving down the list in terms of the quality of an issuer's shares, this story can be repeated again and again. In the end, the market unravels completely and there are no share offerings to portfolio investors.

4.1.2 *The Incentives for Control Shareholders to Create Portfolio Holders*

If this information asymmetry problem can be solved, however, the control shareholders of a firm have a number of motives for selling to, or causing the firm to sell to, portfolio investors. To start, when the control shareholders are the sellers, they are able to diversify their investment portfolios by taking the cash received from the sales and investing it elsewhere. By doing so, they can have a reduced level of risk for any given level of expected return, as discussed earlier. Further, the existence of an active trading market in the shares of the firm makes the remainder of their holdings more liquid, especially when sold in small chunks. Finally, the prices of the firm's shares in an efficient secondary trading market can serve as useful guides to the firm's management. A firm's managers ordinarily know more about what is going on within the firm than does anyone else, but they are not so expert relative to others with respect to many features of the outside environment within which the firm operates. Prices in an efficient market very usefully incorporate all publicly available public information concerning these features of the outside environment. Thus market prices incorporate better predictions of the effects of these features of the outside environment on the firm's future cash flows than the parallel predictions of the managers.

4.1.3 *Overcoming Information Asymmetry Problems and the Role of Corporate Governance*

A number of market-based antidotes to the information asymmetry problem allow some sales to portfolio investors to occur that would otherwise be blocked by the asymmetry problems described above.[41] Each of these market-based antidotes to the information

---

[41] For a more extended discussion of these antidotes, see Merritt B. Fox, "Due Diligence with Residential Mortgage Backed Securities" (hereinafter Due Diligence) available at http://ssrn.com/abstract=235679.

asymmetry problem has significant limitations, however.[42] Mandatory disclosure law can supplement these market-based antidotes and allow more such sales to occur. So too can improved corporate governance, which is key to the theoretical story of how corporate governance can affect the level of foreign ownership.

4.1.3.1 Market-Based Antidotes to the Information Asymmetry Problem

The high-quality issuers, in our example above, may be able to credibly "signal" facts demonstrating their quality. This is so, however, only if making a false claim as to quality would not be worthwhile to the controlling shareholders of any issuer that is not high quality because of legal liability or loss of reputation. To avoid these costs, the low-quality issuers would remain silent rather than falsely claiming facts suggesting that they are high quality. The market then would infer from their silence that they are low quality.[43]

A high-quality issuer can also sell its shares to an investment bank that then resells them to portfolio investors at a premium that investors are willing to pay because of the bank's involvement. The bank will be able to sell the shares at this premium price if the bank has the capacity to distinguish between high- and low-quality issuers and has a reputation for honesty that the bank, as a repeat player, finds it worthwhile to retain.[44]

To the extent that the quality of an issuer can be demonstrated by accounting information concerning assets, liabilities, and financial performance to date, a high-quality issuer can also distinguish itself by having its accounts certified by an outside accounting firm with a reputation worth preserving.[45]

4.1.3.2 Mandatory Issuer Disclosure at the Time of an Offering to Portfolio Investors

Effective mandatory disclosure at the time of a public offering of shares can address aspects of the asymmetry directly and, because each of the market-based solutions has limitations, allows additional sales to portfolio investors that the asymmetry problem would otherwise block if only the market-based antidotes were available. Truthful information about an issuer's prior history of diversions, and about the histories of the control shareholders in connection with other business ventures, will narrow the gap between control shareholders and portfolio investors in terms of their respective abilities to predict the level of future diversions.[46]

---

[42] These limitations are discussed in Fox, Due Diligence at note 41 *supra*.

[43] The seminal articles in signaling theory are Michael Spence, "Job Market Signaling", 87 Q. J. Econ. 355 (1973); Steven A. Ross, Disclosure Regulation in Financial Markets: Implications of Modern Finance Theory and Signaling Theory, in Issues in Financial Regulation (Franklin Edwards ed., 1979).

[44] The theory that an intermediating merchant can serve this role can be traced back to Akerlof's seminal article on asymmetric information. See Akerlof, *supra* note 40, at 496. The theory has been applied specifically to the use of the investment bank in the offering of securities. See James R. Booth & Richard L. Smith, II, "Capital Raising, Underwriting and the Certification Hypothesis", 15 J. Fin. Econ. 261 (1986); Ann E. Sherman, "Underwriter Certification and the Effect of Shelf Registration on Due Diligence", 28 Fin. Management J. 5 (1999).

[45] See Linda D. DeAngelo, "Auditor Independence, 'Low Balling,' and Disclosure Regulation", 3 J. Acc'ting and Econ. 113 (1981).

[46] For a discussion of the superiority of a mandatory disclosure regime over a voluntary choice of a disclosure regime offered by a stock exchange or through a choice of jurisdiction, see Merritt B. Fox, "Retaining Mandatory Securities Disclosure: Why Issuer Choice is Not Investor Empowerment", 85 Va. L. Rev. 1335 (1999).

4.1.3.3 Corporate Governance

In this information asymmetry story, corporate governance is also relevant to the level of portfolio investor ownership and hence the possibility of foreign portfolio investor ownership. A principal focus of corporate law is the prevention of diversions. Much of modern corporate law has been built around this goal. The goal is reflected not only in rules requiring that dividends and distributions be made pro rata, but also in the basic fiduciary rules policing non-arm's-length transactions involving insiders and the corporation.[47] The more limited the possible extent of such diversions, the less important is the existence of information asymmetry between the controlling shareholders and portfolio investors concerning what the actual expected level of diversion will be. The information advantages of the controlling shareholders as to the expected extent of diversions will matter less since the maximum possible amount of diversion is less. The less important the asymmetry, the fewer stock sales are blocked that would have occurred absent the asymmetry.

The prospect that an issuer will be subject to an effective ongoing mandatory issuer disclosure regime—a regime that requires an issuer to regularly update its disclosures—can also reinforce the constraints that corporate law and reputational concerns put on diversions. Diversions are less likely to occur if control shareholders know that the diversions will subsequently become publicly known.[48] There is a general recognition that transparency is necessary for good corporate governance.[49]

These restraints on diversions arising from corporate law and from an effective ongoing periodic disclosure regime are especially important in the case of an issuer with no existing portfolio investors and whose controlling shareholders do not have significant involvement in prior business ventures. With such an issuer, disclosure at the time of the offering will do little to reduce the information asymmetry between the control shareholders and potential investors concerning the expected extent of future diversions. The conclusion that these diversion constraints are especially important for IPOs of first-time entrepreneurs should be highlighted because a public market for issuers of this kind is important for the dynamism of an economy,[50] which can contribute to economic growth even for emerging countries.

---

[47] Easterbrook and Fischel slightly refine this statement of basic norms in corporate law. Unequal divisions of gains from corporate activity will be tolerated, they suggest, provided that the transaction makes no shareholder worse off. Frank H. Easterbrook & Daniel R. Fischel, The Economic Structure of Corporate Law 143–44 (1991).

[48] At least as importantly, disclosure can reveal failures by an issuer to follow the procedures, such as an informed independent director or shareholder vote, for approving transactions in which the controlling shareholders have an interest. These procedures are designed to prevent diversions. For an elaboration of this point, see Merritt B. Fox, "Civil Liability and Mandatory Disclosure", 109 Colum. L. Rev. 237, 258–59 (2009).

[49] See, e.g., OECD Principles of Corporate Governance (2004); Mark J. Roe, "Corporate Law's Limits", 31 J. Leg. Stud. 233 (2002) (corporate law is ineffective without transparency).

[50] The possibility of an IPO gives venture capitalists an option to exit successful start-ups in a way that allows the founders to retain control. In so doing, this possibility permits a kind of implicit contracting that allows promising innovative projects to move forward that otherwise would not move forward and adds to the incentives for engaging in entrepreneurial activity. See Bernard Black & Ronald Gilson, "Venture Capital and the Structure of Capital Markets: Banks versus Stock Markets", 47 J. Fin. Econ. 243 (1999).

4.1.4 Conclusion and Some Terminology

In sum, corporations inevitably start their lives with control shareholders. For most countries of the world, control shareholding is the preponderant ownership structure even for their older, larger firms.[51] In many such firms, the control shareholders would enter into, or direct their firms to enter into, transactions that would result in a larger portion of the firm's shares being held by portfolio investors if it were not for adverse selection's negative effect on what potential offerees would be willing to pay. Subjecting the firm to more effective corporate law constraints on diversions by control shareholders reduces this impediment to greater portfolio holdings. So does subjecting the firm to a more effective ongoing periodic disclosure regime. Thus, where one or both of these diversion reduction constraints are mandatorily imposed on the firm pursuant to its home country's legal system, or where a firm is otherwise individually subjected to one or both of these constraints, we would expect, all else equal, that a greater portion of the firm's shares would be held by portfolio investors.

The remainder of this chapter will refer to both corporate law constraints on diversions and obligations to provide ongoing disclosure as "diversion constraints." This terminology will be used whether the constraint or obligation is imposed by a firm's home country's laws or by the firm's individual actions. The expression "more effective diversion constraints" will be applied to the situation where the rules constituting a diversion constraint stay the same but are enforced in such a way that the frequency of compliance is increased. It will also be applied to the situation where the rules constituting a diversion constraint are tightened but the frequency of compliance with new rules is not any greater than the frequency of compliance had been with the old, laxer rules.

4.2 More Effective Diversion Constraints Leading to Greater Foreign Ownership

There is a strong argument, based on a growing empirical literature, that being subject to more effective diversion constraints leads on average to a greater portion of a firm's shares being held by foreign investors. As elaborated below, this argument suggests that the continued lessening of the non-corporate-governance impediments to global shareholding is acting as a catalyst that is resulting both in increasing foreign ownership and in firms around the world being subject to increasingly effective diversion constraints.

4.2.1 Implications from the Discussion of Portfolio Supportive Corporate Governance

In the preceding discussion, we concluded that firms with more effective diversion constraints can be expected to have a higher proportion of their shares on average held by portfolio investors. This conclusion gives rise to two important implications.

---

[51] Rafael La Porta, Florencio Lopez-De-Silanes, & Andrei Shleifer, "Corporate Ownership around the World", 54 J. Fin. 471 (1999); Stuart L. Gillan & Laura T. Starks, "Corporate Governance, Corporate Ownership and the Role of Institutional Investors: A Global Perspective" (John L. Weinberg Center for Corp. Gov., U. Del., Lerner College of Bus. & Econ., Working Paper No. 2003-01, 2003), at 28.

First, the weakening of the non-corporate-governance impediments to foreign ownership discussed in section 3 increases the pool of the firm's potential portfolio investors. As a result, more situations arise where, absent the impediments created by adverse selection, both the firm's control shareholders and portfolio investors would find advantageous a transaction that increases the portion of the firm's shares held by portfolio investors. For any firm where this is the case, its control shareholders would, with the weakening of these impediments, have the incentive to adopt more effective diversion constraints. Using the same logic, a country with a relatively poor-quality corporate law or mandatory ongoing securities disclosure regime would have incentives to strengthen each. Individual firms, and countries as a whole, tend to respond to incentives.[52] When they respond to these incentives for more effective diversion constraints, the portions of firms' shares held by portfolio investors, including in particular those of foreign portfolio investors, should increase.

Second, some countries that start with a relatively ineffective corporate law or manda-tory ongoing periodic disclosure regime will decide to strengthen their corporate law or disclosure rules for reasons independent of the weakening of the non-corporate-governance-related factors impeding global markets that is discussed in section 3.[53] With the weakening of these impediments, however, this strengthening of the country's corporate or securities disclosure laws will lead to a greater increase in the proportion of shares held by foreigners in the country's firms than would have occurred otherwise.

[52] A country, of course, is a collection of individuals and may not have collective decision making that maximizes the aggregate wealth of the individuals composing it. Improved corporate governance creates losers as well as winners and the losers may be able to block the change. See Mancur Olsen, The Logic of Collective Action (1971). Professors Rajan and Zingales hypothesize that the losers to the strengthening of corporate governance and disclosure have a good chance of succeeding unless an economy is open to both international capital flows and trade. They argue that this hypothesis explains the decline in financial development after World War I and its rise, even after controlling for the level of economic development, in recent decades. It also explains the substantial differences at any given time in the level of financial development across countries with the same level of economic development. Raghuram G. Rajan & Luigi Zingales, "The Great Reversals: The Politics of Financial Development in the Twentieth Century", 69 J. Fin. Econ. 5 (2003).

[53] Professors Hansmann and Kraakman, for example, suggest that there has been an ideological convergence around the world centering on a "shareholder-oriented" model of corporate law based on a belief that it has efficiency benefits that will increase the wealth of each jurisdiction that adopts it. Henry Hansmann & Reinier Kraakman, "The End of History for Corporate Law", 89 Geo. LJ. 439, 443–49 (2001). To the extent that this is the case, the growth of this ideology would be an independent driver of stronger corporate governance and mandatory disclosure regimes. It has also been suggested that because of the efficiency benefits of this model, firms that are not subject to it will be disadvantaged in competition with those that are. Id. at 449–52, Ronald J. Gilson, "Globalizing Corporate Governance: Convergence of Form or Function", 49 Am. J. Corp. L. 329, 336 (2001). The competitive pressures on the nonconforming firms would thus be another driver for such change, which is accentuated by the increase in international trade. Another independent driver is the growing number of portfolio shareholders in each country resulting from increased wealth and privately based pensions. Hansmann & Kraakman at 451–53. A final possible independent factor is the risk that corporate assets will be expropriated by the government. If this risk is high, concentrated ownership may seem a necessity in order to have sufficient political power to fend the government off. When the risk lowers, less concentrated ownership is safer from an expropriation. So there are more situations where greater portfolio ownership would be advantageous to both a firm's control shareholders and portfolio investors if the problem of expected diversions could be solved. See Rene M. Stulz, "The Limits of Financial Globalization", 60 J. Fin. 1595 (2005). This in turn could lead to domestic political pressures to improve a country's corporate governance and disclosure laws.

Keeping in mind these two implications, we can now move on to consider what the existing empirical literature suggests about whether more effective diversion constraints in fact lead to increased foreign ownership and the role played in this process by the weakening of the non-corporate-governance-based impediments to the global markets for equities.

4.2.2 Strong Effective Domestic Corporation and Securities Disclosure Laws and the Size and Depth of Capital Markets

There is evidence that countries with stronger corporate-governance rules and enforcement have substantially larger equity markets as a proportion of their GDPs and more listed firms.[54] A large, deep capital market relative to a country's GDP suggests that more of its economy is composed of firms with a significant portion of their shares held by portfolio investors. Thus, this evidence suggests a link between the effectiveness of a country's diversion constraints and the proportion of its firms' shares held by portfolio investors. Even more to the point, there is also evidence that countries with stronger corporate governance have a lower concentration of ownership.[55] These two kinds of evidence are relevant to the issue under examination—whether more effective diversion constraints lead to greater foreign ownership—because, as we have seen, for a firm to have a significant portion of its shares held by foreign portfolio investors, a precondition is that a significant portion of its shares be held by portfolio investors more generally.

4.2.3 Strong Effective Domestic Corporation and Securities Disclosure Laws and the Extent of Foreign Ownership

Evidence that laws imposing more effective diversion constraints lead to larger, deeper domestic capital markets logically suggests that such laws facilitate greater foreign, as well as domestic, portfolio ownership of a country's firms. There is, however, more direct evidence. The starting point is a substantial body of scholarship showing a correlation between indicators of the effective strength of a country's corporate and securities laws and the extent of foreign ownership of its corporations, a correlation that holds even after controlling for

It should be noted that not everyone agrees that these independent drivers actually have much effect on the quality of corporate governance. Lucian Bebchuk & Mark J. Roe, "A Theory of Path Dependence in Corporate Ownership and Governance", 52 Stan. L. Rev. 127 (1999) (path dependence creates sharp resistance to these drivers); Tarun Khanna, Joe Kogan, & Krishna Palepu, "Globalization and Similarities in Corporate Governance: A Cross-Country Analysis", 44 Eur. Econ. Rev. 748 (2002) (using de facto measures of corporate governance, no evidence that countries that are more integrated in terms of product trade and labor mobility have more similar corporate governance than ones less integrated in these ways).

[54] See, e.g., Rafael La Porta, Florencio Lopez-De-Silanes, Andrei Shleifer, & Robert W. Vishny, "Legal Determinants of External Finance", 52 J. Fin. 1131 (1997).

[55] See European Corporate Governance Network (ECGN), The Separation of Ownership and Control: A Survey of 7 European Countries Preliminary Report to the European Commission (1997); Stijn Claessens, Simeon Djankov, & Larry Lang, "Expropriation of Minority Shareholders in East Asia", 57 J. Fin. 81 (2001); Charles P. Himmelberg, R. Glenn Hubbard, & Inessa Love, "Investor Protection, Ownership and Investment" (2000), available at http://www.nber.org/china/ghubbard.pdf.

the level of a country's economic development.[56] Concluding that this correlation is the result of effective laws leading to more foreign ownership, however, requires ruling out that the correlation is instead primarily the result of the reverse causal pathway, i.e., that a larger percentage of foreign shareholders in a country's firms leads to the country adopting more effective diversion-constraining laws. There is a good case for ruling out this possible alternative explanation, however.

As the data at the beginning of this chapter suggests, for most firms in the world, home bias means that at most only a minority of the shareholders of a country's firms are foreign. These foreign shareholders are unlikely on their own initiative to push through legal reforms abroad. As foreigners, they do not tend to wield much influence within the political systems of a firm's home country. Moreover, their stakes tend to be smaller and more disorganized than those of the opposing control shareholders. Thus, it seems unlikely that the correlation between more effective laws constraining diversions and foreign ownership is explained by the foreign owners prompting the legal changes.[57]

4.2.4 *The Effectiveness of Individual Firm Diversion Constraints and the Extent of Foreign Ownership*

Earlier discussion suggested that being subject to effective home-country corporate and securities laws is only one way for a firm to persuade investors that future diversions will be limited, and thereby resolve the adverse selection problem that impedes ownership of its shares by portfolio investors.[58] One alternative way would be for the firm to subject itself to one or more of a variety of ongoing transparency enhancing devices. These devices include credibly pledging to comply with a private disclosure code or to obtain certified financials on a periodic basis. They would also include listing on a stock exchange that requires certain ongoing disclosures or that requires registration with a foreign securities

---

[56] Reena Aggarwal, Leora Klapper, & Peter D. Wysocki, "Portfolio Preferences of Foreign Institutional Investors", 29 J. Banking & Fin. 2919 (2005) (finding that US mutual funds tend to invest more in countries with stronger shareholder rights and legal frameworks, even after controlling for the country's economic development). Khanna, Palepu, & Srinivasan find a positive relationship between a non-US firm's transparency measure and the equity owned by US investors in the firm's home country firms as a percentage of their total capitalization. While this result could be explained by US investors preferring investments in firms from countries with laws imposing more effective diversion constraints on its issuers, consistent with Aggarwal, Klapper, & Wysocki, it also could be explained by a higher percentage of firms willing to individually impose on themselves effective diversion constraints in some countries than others. Tarun Khanna, Krishna Palepu, & Suraj Srinivasan, "Disclosure Practices of Foreign Companies Interacting with US Markets", 42 J. Acct. Research 475, 499–500 (2004).

[57] It is true that the governments of some of the wealthiest countries, in particular the United States, advocate good governance, both directly and through their roles in the international financial institutions, and that wealthy countries are the source of most foreign investors in the firms of the countries of the rest of the world. The motivation for this kind of advocacy, however, appears to be to promote economic development in poorer countries and perhaps to expand a financial system in which some of the wealthy country's citizens earn rents. It is unlikely that the intensity of this advocacy applied by any one wealthy country is strongly positively correlated with the percentage of shares already held by the wealthy country's investors in the firms of the particular country being lobbied. Such a strong positive correlation would be needed for advocacy by wealthy countries to drive a causal link running from greater foreign ownership to stronger, more effective governance laws.

[58] See section 4.1.3.

disclosure regime that imposes such disclosure requirements on the firm. Another alternative would be to include provisions in the corporate charter that would reduce the chance of diversions.

There is considerable empirical evidence that there is a correlation between such individual firm efforts at good governance and greater foreign ownership.[59] Again the question arises as to whether this correlation is at least in part the result of good individual firm corporate governance leading to more foreign ownership, or instead is primarily the result of the reverse causal pathway, i.e., that a higher proportion of foreign shareholders leads a firm to adopt better corporate governance. Here we cannot rule out so easily this second reverse causation explanation. The fact that shareholders are foreign puts them at no particular disadvantage in the individual firm's governance process, unlike their situation with respect to the national political processes of a firm's home country. As discussed below, there is empirical evidence that foreign shareholders do in fact have at least some influence on firm governance.[60]

Theory, however, suggests that the correlation would be due at least in part to more effective diversion constraints at the individual firm level leading to greater portfolio share ownership, which presumably would include increased foreign ownership.[61] Fortunately, also, the much

[59]   Aggarwal, Klapper, &Wysocki, *supra* note 56 (positive correlation between firms that score well on good governance measures with extent of foreign ownership); Reena Aggarwal, Isil Erel, Miguel Ferreira, & Pedro Matos, "Does Governance Travel Around the World? Evidence from Institutional Investors", 100 J. Fin. Econ. 154, 161–164, 171–72 (2011) (same); Magnus Dahlquist & Goran Robertson, "Direct Foreign Ownership, Institutional Investors, and Firm Characteristics", 59 J. Fin. Econ. 413 (2001) (correlation between foreign ownership and low concentration of ownership); Christian Leuz, Karl Lins, & Francis Warnock, "Do Foreigners Invest Less in Poorly Governed Firms", 22 Rev. Fin. Stud. 3245 (2009) (US investors hold substantially smaller equity positions in non-US firms with poor scores on a transparency measure); Vicentiu M. Covrig, Mark L. Defond, & Mingyi Hung, "Home Bias, Foreign Mutual Fund Holdings, and the Voluntary Adoption of International Accounting Standards", 45 J. Acct. Research 41 (2007) (correlation between firms that voluntarily adopt international accounting standards and foreign ownership); Jia-Weng Liang, Mei-Feng Lin, & Chen-Lung Chin, "Does Foreign Institutional Ownership Motivate Firms in an Emerging Market to Increase Voluntary Disclosure", 39 Rev Quant. Fin. Acct. 55 (2012) (positive relationship between percentage of foreign ownership of Taiwanese firms and voluntary disclosure as measured by conference calls, which are shown to be informative by the fact that they are followed by greater institutional ownership turnover); Miguel A. Ferreira & Pedro Matos, "The Color of Investors' Money: The Role of Institutional Investors around the World", 88 J. Fin. Econ. 499 (2008) (for non-US firms, correlation between the extent of US institutional ownership and higher market to book value (Tobin's Q), which arguably is an indicator of better governance); Kimberly A. Webb, Steven F. Cahan, & Jerry Sun, "The Effect of Globalization and Legal Environment on Voluntary Disclosure", 43 Int'l. J. Accounting 219 (2008) (correlation between a measure of a firm's voluntary disclosure and a measure of its country's integration into the global economy including global capital markets, with the effect being stronger for firms from countries with weaker legal environments).

[60]   See section 4.3.1.

[61]   See section 4.1; Hansmann & Kraakman, *supra* note 53, at 451 (participants in international equity markets "understandably prefer shareholder-oriented governance"). As discussed further in section 4.3.1, Aggarwal et al. using fixed effects regressions, find a statistically significant positive relationship between a change in foreign ownership and a subsequent change in measures of good corporate governance, which suggests that foreign ownership leads to better corporate governance. In contrast, interestingly, they find no statistically significant relationship between a change in measures of good corporate governance and a later change in foreign ownership. Aggarwal, Erel, Ferreira, & Matos, *supra* note 59, at 167–70. This latter result, of course, is not an affirmative finding that good governance does not lead to more foreign ownership. The test may simply have not been powerful enough to pick up evidence of

larger number of observations allowed by using firm-level data, as compared to using country-level data, permits the use of econometric techniques that can help disentangle the question of causal direction. For example, Covrig, Defond, and Hung, using fixed effects regression techniques, show that foreign ownership increases after a firm switches from local to international accounting standards ("IAS").[62] Khanna and Palepu reach a similar conclusion in an investigation of the relationship between foreign ownership and measures of transparency of publicly traded firms that are affiliated with business groups.[63] Because the affiliated firms in a business group are all controlled by the same owners, they are particularly vulnerable to diversions. These common owners can use their control to have one affiliate, for below-market consideration, enter into a transaction with another affiliate in which the owners have a larger interest, thereby benefiting the owners at the expense of the portfolio shareholders of the first affiliate. Further, due to the possibility of highly frequent non-arm's-length transactions among a group's affiliates, they have a particularly high potential of being non-transparent in their accounts. As evidence that more transparency attracts foreign investors, Khanna and Palepu find that after India, in the early 1990s, lifted a number of provisions that had been preventing or discouraging foreign ownership of shares in Indian corporations, affiliates of business groups that were more transparent displayed a larger gain in their percentages of foreign ownership.[64]

4.2.5 *Bonding to Better Governance by an Offering Abroad or Cross-Listing on a Foreign Exchange*

A number of scholars have suggested that one way that an individual firm from a country with weak or ineffective corporate-governance laws can impose on itself a stricter regime is to conduct a public offering in, or cross-list on an exchange located in, a country that imposes on the firm the host country's own stricter regime.[65] Most of this "bonding" literature refers specifically to a public offering or cross-listing in the United States, which is generally believed to have as strict securities disclosure laws as any country. The discussion above suggests that firms that impose on themselves more effective diversion constraints will attract more foreign investors. So, to the extent that such a US offering or cross-listing by a foreign firm really does result in the firm being subject to more effective diversion constraints, the availability of these tools has played a role in the rise in foreign ownership.

How effective, though, is a US public offering or cross-listing as a bonding technique? Answering this question requires both an examination of the theory as to how these actions might work as bonds and a review of the related empirical literature.

such a causal relationship. One possibility is that such a causal relationship does exist, but that the lag structure between a governance change and any changes in foreign ownership may be more complicated than the lag structure going the other way and that this makes the relationship harder to test for.

[62] Covrig, Defond, & Hung, *supra* note 59.

[63] Tarun Khanna & Krishna Palepu, "Emerging Market Business Groups, Foreign Investors, and Corporate Governance" (Nat'l Bureau of Econ. Research, Working Paper No 6955, 1999).

[64] Id.

[65] See, e.g., John C. Coffee, Jr., "Racing Towards the Top? The Impact of Cross-Listings and Stock Market Competition on International Corporate Governance", 102 Colum. L. Rev. 1757 (2002); Rene Stulz, "Globalization, Corporate Finance, and the Cost of Capital", 26 J. Appl. Corp. Fin. 3 (1999).

4.2.5.1 *How Bonding Might Work and its Limitations*

As discussed above,[66] any foreign issuer that does a first public offering in the United States or cross-lists its shares on a US exchange is required to file an initial disclosure statement, after which the issuer becomes subject to the Exchange Act's ongoing periodic disclosure obligations.

Several things should be noted at the outset about a US public offering or cross-listing as a bonding device. First, the applicable US securities laws do not impose any obligations on the controlling shareholders of the issuer undertaking the offering or cross-listing to refrain from engaging in diversions. Rather, these acts of bonding work, to extent that they are effective, by the threat of US legal sanctions if the bonding firm misstates facts in its disclosure filings or omits required information. Thus, a controlling shareholder contemplating a diversion would know that if it were to go ahead, it either would need to comply with the disclosure rules intended to reveal such a diversion or face the threat of legal sanctions for non-compliance with these rules.

Second, whether a firm does a public offering in the United States or just cross-lists there, it is the periodic-disclosure obligation that does the main bonding work. The initial Securities Act or Exchange Act filing may help disclose the existence of past diversions and hence, by revealing the character of the control shareholders, help investors predict the level of future diversions. However, it does nothing to deter future diversions other than to provide baseline information that makes the subsequent periodic disclosures more meaningful.

Third, a US public offering or cross-listing is only effective as a bonding device to the extent that the control shareholders reasonably expect to be hurt if they violate their disclosure obligations. For a number of reasons, most foreign issuers and their managers and control shareholders have considerably less to fear from a violation than do their US counterparts. Many foreign issuers and their managers and control shareholders have little or no presence in the United States and hence, relative to their US counterparts, face much less exposure to the criminal, and even the civil, sanctions arising from a violation of their US disclosure obligations. In addition, there is some evidence that the SEC is unwilling to devote as much in resources to prosecuting cases involving foreign issuers.[67] Moreover, even the control shareholders of foreign issuers that fully comply with their SEC mandates have less to fear from these mandates because they are not required to disclose as much, or as frequently, as their US counterparts.[68]

Finally, the SEC and the US Supreme Court have each taken actions in recent years to reduce the effectiveness of foreign-issuer bonding. In 2007, the SEC promulgated Rule 12h-6, whereby the SEC has provided a means of exiting the periodic disclosure obligations for any foreign issuer whose average trading volume in the United States was less than 5% of its worldwide trading

---

[66] Section 3.2.3.

[67] See, e.g., Jordan Siegel, "Can Foreign Firms Bond Themselves Effectively by Submitting to US Law", 75 J. Fin. Econ. 319 (2005); Mark Lang, Jana Smith Ready, & Wendy Wilson, "Earnings Management and Cross Listing: Are Reconciled Earnings Comparable to US Earnings", 42 J. Acc'ting and Econ. 285 (2006).

[68] Traditionally, foreign issuers were required to disclose just as much as US issuers making a public offering, Harold Bloomenthal, 1980 Securities Handbook, 354–57 (1980), but in 1982, the SEC adopted registration forms exclusively for foreign issuers. Securities Act Release 6437 (Nov. 19, 1982).

volume.[69] A large portion of the world's publicly traded issuers would not have this large a US trading volume if they did a US public offering or cross-listed on a US exchange, in which case neither of these acts would constitute any real kind of bond since exit would be easily available soon thereafter. Even where the US trading volume would be greater than 5% immediately after the offering or cross-listing, investors in many cases could not be confident that they would not fall below 5% in the future.

In 2010, in *Morrison v. Nat'l Austl. Bank,*[70] the Supreme Court concluded that §10(b) reached only situations where the securities were listed on a US exchange or where their purchase or sale was effected in the United States.[71] As discussed, this ruling had a major impact on fraud-on-the-market class actions against foreign issuers.[72] Under *Morrison*, at least for foreign issuers that do their US equity listing in the form of American Depository Receipts (ADRs), which is the predominant approach, any damages or settlement payments arising from such an action are confined to only the portion of the foreign firm's equity that is purchased in US trading, often only a small fraction of the total, whereas previous lower-court decisions suggested that a firm could sometimes be liable to all purchasers worldwide.[73] US issuers, in comparison, continue to be liable to all purchasers who suffer these losses from their purchases. Thus, for the typical foreign firm listed on a US exchange, this civil damages cause of action has a smaller, often much smaller, capacity to deter misstatements.

4.2.5.2 *Empirical Evidence that a US Offering or Cross-Listing Constitutes an Effective Bond*

A number of studies document that when a foreign firm cross-lists in the United States, its stock price experiences a jump up in price.[74] Moreover, the weaker the disclosure regime of the firm's home country, the bigger the jump.[75]

What, though, causes this price jump? Theory suggests three possibilities, none mutually exclusive. First, cross-listing may lower the rate at which the market discounts the future cash flows expected to be received by shareholders. The discount rate decreases in part because the cross-listing reduces the segmentation between the market of the firm's home country and the US market, enlarging the number of investors that can conveniently trade

---

[69] SEC Release No. 34-55540 (2007) available at http://www.sec.gov/rules/final/2007/34-55540.pdf.

[70] *Morrison v. Nat'l Austl. Bank*, 130 S. Ct. 2869 (2010).   [71] Id. at 2888.

[72] Section 3.2.3.

[73] For a general discussion of fraud-on-the-market suits against foreign issuers and the impact of *Morrison*, see Merritt B. Fox, "Securities Class Actions Against Foreign Issuers", 64 Stan. L. Rev. 1173, 1176, 1199–1203, 1243–63 (2012).

[74] S. Foerster & G.A. Karolyi, "The Effects of Market Segmentation and Investor Recognition on Asset Prices: Evidence from Foreign Stocks Listing in the US", 54 J. Fin. 981 (1999); Darius Miller, "The Market Reaction to International Cross-Listings: Evidence from Depositary Receipts", 51 J. Fin. Econ. 103 (1999); Craig Doidge, "US Cross-Listings and Private Benefits of Control", 72 J. Fin. Econ. 592 (2004); Craig Doidge, G.A. Karolyi, & Rene Stulz, "Why Are Foreign Firms Listed in the US Worth More?", 71 J. Fin. Econ. 205 (2004) (hereinafter Worth More); Craig Doidge, G.A. Karolyi, & Rene Stulz, "Has New York Become Less Competitive Than London in Global Markets? Evaluating Foreign Listing Choices Over Time", 91 J. Fin. Econ. 253 (2009).

See, e.g., Luzi Hail & Christian Leuz, "Cost of Capital and Cash Flow Effect of US Cross Listings", 93 J. Fin. Econ. 428 (2009).

[75] Doidge, Karolyi, & Stulz, Worth More, *supra* note 74.

in its shares with the portfolio risk reduction that transnational investing allows. It also decreases in part because the improved disclosure resulting from the imposition of the US disclosure regime increases the stock's liquidity by reducing market maker's adverse selection concerns. Discounting expected future cash flows at a lower rate increases the present value of the right to receive these cash flows and hence the stock will trade today at a higher price. This is so even if the cross-listing is not expected to change the future behavior of the firm and its control shareholders and hence not expected to increase future cash flows received by the portfolio shareholders.

Second, the price jump may occur because the cross-listing leads the market to expect that the future cash flows received by the firm's portfolio holders will be greater than previously expected because the cross-listing shows the firm's willingness to submit to greater scrutiny its claims of a bright future. In other words, the decision of the control shareholders to cross-list is a signal that makes these claims more credible and hence leads to an increase in the outside market's perception of the expected level of the firm's future cash flows to portfolio holders. Thus, again, the price would increase even if those who are most knowledgeable do not expect the cross-listing to change the future behavior of the firm and its control shareholders, and hence do not expect an increase in actual cash flows to the portfolio shareholders.

A third possible reason for the price jump is the focus of the larger discussion here, i.e., bonding. This would be the idea that the greater scrutiny of the firm permitted by improved disclosure is expected by the market to change firm and control shareholder behavior in a way that will increase actual future cash flows to the firm's portfolio shareholders.

We can label these three potential explanations, respectively, the discount rate, signaling, and bonding explanations. The prospect of a price jump, whatever the explanation, is presumably an important motivation for a firm to cross-list. Determining, however, whether bonding is playing a significant role in this price jump is tricky because each of three explanations shares with the others either the same driving factors or ones that are at least highly correlated with each other. Disclosure improvement is the driving factor behind both the bonding and signaling explanations as well as behind the liquidity improvement part of the discount-rate explanation. The weaker the home country's disclosure regime, the greater will be the disclosure improvement from cross-listing. The driving factor behind the other part of the discount rate explanation is that the access to the US capital market helps make up for shortcomings in the size and functional quality of the home country's capital market and its lack of integration into the larger global capital market. The greater these home country shortcomings, the more cross-listing can help. The extent to which cross-listing can help in this way is likely highly correlated with the extent to which it improves disclosure. This is because home countries with smaller, more poorly functioning domestic capital markets that are more distinctly separate from the larger global capital market tend also to have weaker disclosure regimes. Thus the driver of this second part of the discount-rate explanation, though not the same as the driver of the other explanations, is highly correlated with it.

Some studies suggest that there is at least more at work in the price jump than the capital market improvement part of the discount-rate explanation. Reese and Weisbach, for example, find that firms from weak diversion-constraint countries are more likely to engage in equity offerings after cross-listing in the United States than firms from stronger diversion-constraint countries, yet the offerings tend to occur outside the United States.[76] This suggests that the price gain from the cross-listing carries over to these offerings in markets without the size and functional quality of those in the United States. Hail and Leuz use changes in analysts' predictions of future cash flows to isolate the typical foreign issuer's US cross-listing's effect on the discount rate from the market's expectations of the firm's future cash flows (which could be the result of the signaling effect, the bonding effect, or both). They find that on average a change in cash flow expectations explains about half the price jump.[77]

While these studies show that there is some effect from the bonding or the signaling effect, they do not allow us to distinguish between the two effects in order to see if the bonding effect in fact plays a role. There is at least some indirect evidence that bonding does play a role, however. Studies by Doidge[78] and by Bris, Cantale, and Nishiotis[79] each focus on firms with two classes of stock, where both classes have the same cash flow rights per share, but one class has higher voting rights per share and, as a result, trades at a higher price. Each study finds that the price ratio of the high voting stock to the low voting stock decreases significantly after a US cross-listing.[80] In each study, the authors attribute the high voting stock's premium at least in part to the ability of the control to engage in diversions and interpret the decline in this premium to the cross-listing imposing new constraints on such diversions.[81] It should be noted that the price for the high voting shares used in the study is of course the price at which the publicly held ones trade. The holders of these shares are not part of a control group that can steer diversions in their direction. However, if the current control group does not have a majority of the share votes, the publicly held high voting shares still have extra value that is related to the ability of control to extract diversions. This is because their holders can sell to someone who is trying to assemble a new control group or who is trying to reinforce the power of an existing one. Lel and Miller focus on the effect of cross-listing on the likelihood that a CEO would be fired in the face of disappointing financial results.[82] They find that cross-listing increases this likelihood more for firms from weak diversion-constraint countries than from strong ones, suggesting that cross-listing leads to better governance.[83]

4.2.5.3 *Effects of Cross-Listing Independent of its Bonding Effect*

A US cross-listing, independent of its effectiveness as a bonding device, will tend to promote foreign ownership because it reduces the cost, inconvenience, and regulatory hurdles associated with the purchase by US investors in the cross-listed foreign issuer. As discussed earlier, the availability of US cross-listings could play a larger role in promoting foreign ownership if the United States gave the issuer the option of imposing on itself the Exchange Act's

---

[76] William A. Reese Jr. & Michael S. Weisbach, "Protection of Minority Shareholder Interests, Cross-Listing in the United States, and Subsequent Equity Offerings", 66 J. Fin. Econ. 65 (2002).

[77] Hail & Leuz, *supra* note 74.

[78] Doidge, *supra* note 74.

[79] Arturo Bris, Salvatore Cantale, & George P. Nishiotis, 13 Eur. Fin. Mgmt. 498 (2007).

[80] Id.; Doidge, *supra* note 74.   [81] Id.; Bris, Cantale & Nishiotis, *supra* note 79.

[82] Urgur Lel & Darius P. Miller, "International Cross-Listing, Firm Performance, and Top Management Turnover: A Test of the Bonding Hypothesis", 63 J. Fin. 1897 (2008).

[83] Id.

ongoing periodic disclosure obligations, but did not require the issuer to do so. This optional approach would continue to allow firms to use these obligations as a bonding device, but would reduce the cost of cross-listing for firms that do not wish to bond.

4.3 Greater Foreign Ownership Leading to More Effective Diversion Constraints

There is also considerable evidence that a larger portion of a firm's shares being held by foreigners leads to the firm being subject to more effective diversion constraints. This evidence suggests that the continued lessening of the non-corporate-governance impediments to global shareholding is acting as a catalyst in a second way that is resulting in both increasing foreign ownership and better governance around the world.

4.3.1 How Greater Foreign Ownership Could Lead to More Effective Diversion Constraints

As discussed above, it is unlikely that if a country's firms have a larger proportion of foreign owners, there will be pressure on its government to enact and enforce stricter corporate and securities disclosure laws.[84] The idea that foreign owners might lead individual firms to adopt more effective diversion constraints is much more plausible, however. So is the idea that the presence of foreign owners can be a diversion constraining force in and of itself.

4.3.1.1 The Extent of Foreign Ownership

It is worth noting at the start that many of the larger corporations from countries not having the most effective constraints on diversions have a considerable portion of their shares held by investors from countries that do. Even more than a decade ago, Anglo-Saxon institutions held an average of 35% of the shares of the largest 40 firms listed on the Paris Bourse and 41% of large Dutch companies.[85] Foreign investors more generally held over 30% of shares of companies listed on Mexico's stock markets.[86] However, even where foreign holders have smaller percentages than these, as would be the case with smaller firms in continental Europe and most firms in the developing countries, there are still reasons, as discussed below, why they might have an influence on corporate governance.

4.3.1.2 The Special Role of Foreign Investors

Foreign shareholders and domestic non-control shareholders have the same interest in preventing diversions by a firm's control shareholders because, on per share basis, they each lose equally from such diversions. Foreign holders are more likely to act on this interest, however. To start, the foreign holders from strong corporate-governance countries may bring with them a greater familiarity and experience with the kinds of diversion constraints that

---

[84] Section 4.2.2.   [85] Gilson, *supra* note 53, at 346.
[86] Stuart L. Gillan & Laura T. Starks, "Corporate Governance, Corporate Ownership and the Role of Institutional Investors: A Global Perspective", John L. Weinberg Center for Corp. Gov., U. Del., Lerner College of Bus. & Econ., Working Paper No. 2003-01, 2003, at 29.

firms can impose on themselves, and a greater sense that diversions by control shareholders are an improper way of doing business. They and their agents are also less likely than domestic shareholders and their agents to be enmeshed in direct or indirect relationships with a firm's control shareholders that dissuade them from acting to prevent diversions.

The concentration of a country's equity holdings in the hands of institutional investors, characteristic of such wealthy good-governance jurisdictions as the United States and the United Kingdom, also makes holders from these countries more prone to act. This is because larger holders get proportionally greater gains for their efforts, while small holders rationally tend to freeride.

There is evidence that foreign shareholders from strong corporate-governance countries do in fact attempt to cause the adoption of stronger diversion constraints by the foreign firms in which they invest that are from countries with weaker corporate-governance legal regimes and traditions. For example, the California Public Employees Retirement System ("CalPERs") adopted a variety of corporate-governance standards that it urges upon foreign issuers in which it has invested,[87] and Fidelity has been reported as more aggressive on governance issues in Europe than in the United States.[88] There is also significant evidence of interventions by hedge funds from the United States and the United Kingdom in the governance of firms from continental Europe.[89]

4.3.1.3 Methods of Influence

Willingness to act and having influence are two different things. The range of available tools for influence depend on whether the control shareholders have over 50% of the share votes. If they do have more than 50%, it is impossible for foreign shareholders to affect the firm's corporate governance or behavior directly through the way they cast, or threaten to cast, their own votes. They can nevertheless still exercise influence through the threat that if the controlling shareholders fail to heed the foreign shareholders' desires, the foreign shareholders will sell their shares, with a resulting price drop. The reason that the control shareholders may respond to this threat goes back in part to the reasons that the control shareholders wanted the firm to have public shareholders in the first place. All else being equal, they prefer the firm's shares to trade at a higher than a lower price.[90] The sale of a significant number of shares, even as little as 5–10%, is likely to prompt a lower price, particularly if the market becomes aware that foreign institutional investors, who are likely to be particularly informed about the corporate-governance situation at the firm, have decided

---

[87] Gilson, *supra* note 53, at 346–47.   [88] Aggarwal et al., *supra* note 59, at 155.

[89] Marco Becht, Julian Franks, & Jeremy Grant, "Hedge Fund Activism in Europe", ECGI Working Paper 283/2010 (2010) (study of 305 activist interventions in UK and continental European corporations, more than half of which involved a US or UK firm intervening in the governance of a continental European corporation).

[90] Reasons why a majority control shareholder would care about the firm's share price may include its ability to sell some of its own shares at a higher price, the ability of domestic individuals and institutions that hold firm shares and with which the control shareholder has relationships to sell their shares at a higher price, a desire for these domestic persons or institutions to use whatever political influence they have in support of government policies favoring the firm, the ability of the firm itself to obtain new equity financing at favorable terms, and the simple prestige and social benefits arising from being the control shareholder of a firm with higher priced shares. See, generally, Sang Yop Kang, "Re-Envisioning the Controlling Shareholder Regime: Why Controlling and Minority Shareholders Often Embrace", 16 U. Pa. J. Bus. L. 843 (2014).

to get out. Indeed, because foreign institutional investors are particularly informed, just the public knowledge that control shareholders refused to make changes after one or more such institutions expressed dissatisfaction may result in a share-price drop.

The range of tools of influence expand if the control shareholders have less than 50% of the votes. Then the foreign shareholders have the possibility of providing, at least at the margin, the votes needed to force a change in governance or the elimination of the managers subservient to the control shareholders. Foreign institutional investors, by leading a movement that threatens such a vote, may be able to persuade the controlling shareholders to adopt stronger diversion constraints or simply to divert less without the necessity of a vote actually taking place.

If the control shareholders have less than 50% of the votes, there is also always the possibility of a hostile takeover. Again, the foreign shareholders can be, at the margin, the deciding factor in whether such a takeover occurs. Moreover a foreign institutional investor may be in a better position than any other shareholder credibly to communicate to a potential foreign acquirer the financial gain that could be attained from such a takeover in situations where the network of relationships in the firm's home country makes unlikely a domestic acquirer coming forward. In most situations, the chances are probably relatively small that a foreign institutional investor could help instigate a successful hostile takeover. A domestically instigated takeover attempt that succeeds because of the votes of foreign investors is probably also infrequent. Even so, the stakes for control shareholders in avoiding such a disaster are so high that they may well give some weight to the preferences of the foreign institutions and other foreign investors in order to avoid the risk.

4.3.2 *Empirical Evidence*

A number of studies provide empirical evidence that greater foreign ownership in fact leads a firm to being subject to more effective diversion constraints. Perhaps the most thorough is the 2011 study by Aggarwal, Erel, Ferreira and Matos ("AEFM").[91] Their starting point is their finding of a strong positive relation between foreign institutional ownership and a measure of a firm's quality of governance.[92] AEFM conclude that there is in fact a causal pathway leading from greater foreign institutional ownership to improvements in corporate governance.[93] They base this conclusion on the use of fixed effects regressions showing a statistically significant positive relationship between a change in foreign ownership and a subsequent change in measures of good corporate governance.[94] Use of these fixed-effects techniques also rules out the possibility that there is not some other characteristic of the sampled firms—one that correlates with both the extent of foreign ownership and the measure of firm corporate governance—that is the real driver of the observed relation between the two.[95]

AEFM's conclusion that foreign institutional ownership leads to better governance is reinforced by a few of their other findings. To start with, the relationship between foreign institutional ownership and the good governance measure is more intense for firms whose home

---

[91] Aggarwal et al., *supra* note 59.   [92] Id. at 161.   [93] Id. at 167–70.   [94] Id.
[95] This conclusion is subject to the caveat that these fixed-effect results would not rule out the existence of an alternative driver of the observed relationship if the alternative driver itself tended to change from one period to the next.

countries do more poorly on a measure of a good corporate-governance legal regime.[96] This is exactly what one would expect to see if greater foreign institutional ownership does in fact affect governance: such ownership has more room to make a difference where other constraints on control shareholders are weaker. Two other of their findings relate to governance outcomes, as opposed to constraints. One is that where foreign ownership is greater, the firm is more likely to replace its CEO if it has recently experienced poor market-adjusted stock returns.[97] The other is their conclusion that there is a causal pathway leading from greater foreign institutional ownership in a firm to a higher Tobin's Q, i.e., the ratio of a firm's stock market valuation to the book value of its assets.[98] Tobin's Q is considered a measure of how much management has been able to accomplish for the benefit of portfolio shareholders given the resources that shareholders have provided management to work with. AEFM base this Tobin's Q conclusion on the results of fixed-effects regressions showing a statistically significant positive relationship between a change in foreign ownership and a subsequent change in Tobin's Q.[99]

A number of other studies are, in one way or another, supportive of the idea that greater foreign ownership leads to better governance. Khanna and Palepu, for example, find that in 1994, following India's early-1990s removal of its very substantial barriers to foreign ownership, Tobin's Q had risen more for firms that had achieved higher foreign ownership than it had for firms that had only achieved low foreign ownership.[100] Liang, Lin, and Chin find that in Taiwan, greater foreign ownership is associated with greater voluntary disclosure as measured by frequency of management conference calls.[101] They in turn find that these calls contained meaningful information, as measured by the increase in trading activity immediately after.[102] Using an instrumental variable approach, they conclude that the direction of causation is from foreign ownership to more conference calls.[103] Ferreira, Massa, and Matos find that the greater the percentage of foreign institutional ownership, the more likely it is that the firm will be involved in a cross-border merger and that this effect is stronger when

---

[96] Id. at 164–167.

[97] Id. at 172 (table 9) (showing a statistically significant mean interaction effect between foreign institutional ownership and the previous period's market-adjusted return).

[98] Id. at 173.

[99] Id. A caveat is necessary with respect to these two governance-outcome-related reinforcing findings. AEFM have similar findings with respect to the effect of domestic institutional holdings on the sensitivity of CEO turnover to poor stock returns and the effect of changes in domestic institutional holdings on subsequent periods' Tobin's Q. Thus, to the extent that foreign and domestic institutional ownership, or changes in each, is correlated, it may not be the foreignness of the holdings that matters, but their institutional nature. This concern is significantly alleviated, however, by a study by Ferreira and Matos ("FM"). FM find a strong statistically significant positive relation between foreign institutional ownership and non-US firms' Tobin's Qs, and between "independent" institutional ownership (mutual funds, both foreign and domestic) and non-US firms' Tobin's Qs, but not between "grey" institutions (bank trusts and insurance companies) and non-US firms' Tobin's Qs, nor between domestic institutional ownership and non-US firms' Tobin's Qs. Miguel A. Ferreira & Pedro Matos, "The Color of Investors' Money: The role of Institutional Investors Around the World", 88 J. Fin. Econ. 499, 500–01, 517 (2008) Using an instrumental variable technique, they find the direction of causation is from the ownership factor to Tobin's Q, not the other way around. Id. at 517.

[100] Tarun Khanna & Krishna Palepu, "Is Group Affiliation Profitable in Emerging Markets? An Analysis of Diversified Indian Business Groups", 55 J. Fin. 867 (2000) at Table 3.

[101] Liang, Lin & Chin, *supra* note 59, at 66.   [102] Id. at 70–71.   [103] Id. at 72–73.

the firm's home country corporate-governance legal regime is weaker.[104] Using an instrumental variable approach, they conclude that the direction of causation runs from foreign institutional ownership to the propensity to be involved in a cross-border merger.[105] Thus, to the extent that the potential of being subject to a cross-border merger has a disciplining effect on the control shareholders (either as an incentive or as a threat), greater foreign ownership will lead to more such discipline by enlarging the likely pool of merger partners.[106] Finally, Iliev et al., in a study of the votes of US institutional investors in non-US firms, find that the larger the percentage of shares held by control shareholders, the more likely these institutions will be to vote against the recommendations of management.[107] Again, this effect is stronger when the firm's home country corporate-governance legal regime is weaker.[108]

5 CONCLUSION

Foreign ownership of publicly traded corporations around the world has increased dramatically in the last few decades. In substantial part, this has been due to the technological and legal changes that have made acquiring and trading shares of issuers from abroad much easier and less expensive. Even more important has been the reduction in the cost of obtaining information about the prospects of issuers abroad. Corporate governance has also been involved in this story with the reduction in impediments acting as a catalyst for both the process by which better corporate governance leads to more foreign ownership and the one by which more foreign ownership leads to better corporate governance.

There is considerable evidence that a firm that displays better corporate governance attracts more foreign investors, whether the better governance is the result of being subject to stronger, more effective corporate and disclosure laws imposed by its home country or the result of the firm's individual actions. This evidence suggests that as the pool of potential foreign investors grows with the reduction in the impediments to global share investing, countries with weak corporate and securities laws will have incentives to strengthen them and make them more effective. It also suggests that many firms whose home countries have weak corporate and securities laws will have incentives to undertake their own individual efforts to improve their own governance and disclosure. Thus the reduction in impediments acts as a catalyst that results in both better corporate governance and more foreign ownership. Countries and individual firms may also improve their corporate governance for reasons independent of the incentives created by the reduction in impediments, but the reduction

---

[104] Miguel A. Ferreira, Massimo Massa, & Pedro Matos, "Shareholders at the Gate? Institutional Investors and Cross-Border Mergers and Acquisitions", 23 Rev. Fin. Stud. 601, 617 (2010).

[105] Id. at 622–25.

[106] In addition, if the dominant party in the takeover is the foreign firm and it is from a country with better governance, the assets of the acquired company will become utilized in an enterprise with better governance.

[107] Peter Iliev, Karl Lins, Darius Miller, & Lukas Roth, "Shareholder Voting and Corporate Governance Around the World", 28 Rev. Fin. Studies 8 (2015).

[108] Id.

in impediments still means that these improvements will lead to greater foreign ownership than would have been the case without impediments reduction.

There is also considerable evidence that greater foreign ownership in firms from weak corporate-governance jurisdictions leads to better corporate governance. Here too, the reduction in the impediments to a global market for equities appears to have played a catalytic role. Such a reduction leads to more foreign investors purchasing shares in issuers from countries with poor corporate governance even if at the time there has been no improvement in the firms' corporate governance. As the foreign investors acquire a larger portion of the outstanding shares of these issuers, they generate new pressure for governance improvement, both through their share votes and through the threat to sell.

An interesting next step in the study of the relationship between foreign ownership and corporate governance would be to consider what developments in the past few decades can tell us about the future. Even if there were no further advances in information technology, there is substantial room for more "learning by doing" in taking advantage of the recent large decline in the cost differences in acquiring information from abroad versus acquiring information domestically. Thus the trends of the past may indeed be prologue.

CHAPTER 30

GOVERNANCE BY INSTITUTIONAL INVESTORS IN A STAKEHOLDER WORLD

GERARD HERTIG[1]

1 INTRODUCTION

FOR institutional investors, one thing is apparently clear: from a *long-term* perspective, the corporate objective must be the generation of sustainable shareholder value.[2] To the extent that this means the pursuit of overall social efficiency, one can expect little or no objection from most economists, lawyers, or even politicians.[3] In the same vein, it is generally accepted that no important constituency should be mistreated if a firm aims at maximizing its value in the long term.[4]

Controversies start when it comes to defining the *shorter-term* policies that facilitate the realization of the long-term sustainability objective. In the US, lawyers were already debating in the 1930s whether non-shareholders could also be the beneficiaries of corporate transactions. Adolf Berle reasoned that only shareholders had a claim over residual corporate income, whereas Merrick Dodd argued that changes in the attitude of courts and public opinion allowed for the taking into account of stakeholder interests.[5] Economists then joined the fray. Milton Friedman famously stated that the only social responsibility of corporations

[1] I thank Lawrence Cunningham, Paul Davies, Guido Ferrarini, Merritt Fox, Roberta Romano, Georg Ringe, and Ed Rock for their very helpful comments on an earlier draft.
[2] See International Corporate Governance Network (ICGN), ICGN Global Corporate Governance Principles 1.0 (Revised 2009).
[3] On the role of political pressures for the evolution of corporate governance systems, see Mark Roe, Strong Managers, Weak Owners: The Political Roots of American Corporate Governance (1994); Andrei Shleifer & Robert Vishny, "Politicians and Firms", 109 Q. J. Econ. 995 (1994).
[4] Michael Jensen, "Value Maximization, Stakeholder Theory, and the Corporate Objective Function", 12 Bus. Ethics Q. 235 (2002).
[5] Adolf A. Berle, "Corporate Powers as Powers in Trust", 44 Harv. L. Rev. 1049 (1931); E. Merrick Dodd, "For Whom Are Corporate Managers Trustees", 45 Harv. L. Rev. 1145 (1932).

is to make money and Edward Freeman responded that profits are only an outcome, the purpose of a corporation being to be well managed.[6]

Clearly, these debates are not merely about the law, economic theory, or business practices: they also reflect diverging political or philosophical opinions. This is a context where one can get lost unless one focuses on what is really at stake. For example, the rather rich Berle-Dood debate becomes easy to understand when one realizes it is essentially about the respective lawmakers' and courts' powers to take stakeholder interests into account. Similarly, the Friedman–Freeman discussion gains in clarity once established that it is about whether we should look at markets or at individuals when trying to understand how firms work.[7]

In the same vein, it is also useful to clarify what the terms "stakeholder" and "corporate social responsibility" generally mean. When mentioning stakeholders, one normally refers to a firm's employees, suppliers, and customers as well as to third parties effectively or potentially affected by the firm's activities.[8] For this contribution, the stakeholder category will comprise creditors at large, i.e., any contractual counterparty or person having a claim against the firm under torts or other externality-related legislation. In other words, the discussion will not be limited to persons owed fiduciary duties under corporate law, as is often the case in the US corporate governance literature. On the other hand, the discussion will not encompass persons who merely have an economic, reputational, social, or political relationship with the firm.

When one talks about "corporate social responsibility" (CSR) it is commonly recognized that he or she refers to a firm's responsibility to avoid harming stakeholders and to contribute to social welfare. What a firm is precisely expected to do or not to do varies over time and across countries.[9] Nowadays, however, demands for corporate social responsibility can largely be understood as demands for an alternative response to market and (state-led) redistribution failures.[10]

While focusing on what is at stake and referring to generally accepted terminology has analytical value, it can prove difficult to identify whether a given firm is of the *shareholder value* type or of the *stakeholder interest* type. Let's start with the big picture. While CSR efforts are not limited to improving the situation of stakeholders as defined above, we would expect the "stakeholder"-type group to comprise all firms that favor CSR and other investments also benefiting creditors at large and the "shareholder"-type group to include all high equity performance firms. Yet, there is evidence of (1) firms that undertake "social" investments also improving their financial performance and (2) firm performance also attracting socially

[6] Milton Friedman, The Social Responsibility of Business is to Increase its Profits, N. Y. Times Mag. 122 (1970); R. Edward Freeman, Strategic Management: A Stakeholder Approach (1984).

[7] R. Edward Freeman, "Ending the so-called 'Friedman-Freeman' Debate", 18 Bus. Ethics Q. 153, 162 (2008).

[8] See also the often-mentioned 1963 Stanford Research Institute Memorandum, according to which "stakeholders are those groups without whose support the organization would cease to exist."

[9] Stefen J. Brammer & Stephen Pamelin, Corporate Governance and Corporate Social Responsibility, in *The Oxford Handbook of Corporate Governance* 719, 721 (Mike Wright, Donald S. Siegel, Kevin Keasey, & Igor Filatotchev eds., 2013).

[10] See Roland Benabou & Jean Tirole, "Individual and Corporate Social Responsibility", 77 Economica 1 (2010).

oriented investors.[11] Similar results can be observed when looking more specifically at employee satisfaction. The classical prediction is that it comes at the price of shareholder value, but here too there is evidence of employee satisfaction being positively correlated with shareholder returns.[12]

This definitely does not imply that stakeholder-oriented firms are necessarily more valuable than their shareholder-oriented brethren. However, it has become clear that this can be the case in various circumstances.[13] As a result, the pro-shareholder versus pro-stakeholder debate has become less polarized.[14] For example, the suggestion made by stakeholder value advocates[15] to reduce the focus on short-term results by amending disclosure requirements and getting board members elected for longer terms is not radically different from what a shareholder value advocate may propose. More generally, the claim that pursuing stakeholder value will result in managers behaving opportunistically has become less persuasive in the face of mounting evidence of opportunistic behavior also occurring in shareholder value environments.[16] In addition, recent research finds no evidence of socially responsible activities being driven by managerial opportunism.[17]

Ongoing legislative developments are in line with this evolution, with corporate lawmakers paying increasing attention to stakeholder interests. Interestingly, this evolution is not only perceptible in jurisdictions like Germany, where corporate law has traditionally taken into account stakeholder interests. Even more shareholder-centric jurisdictions, such as the UK, are fostering strategies that focus on the interests of the "ultimate" beneficiaries of capital market investments.

In this new environment, corporate governance reformers have paid special attention to institutional investors. One reason for singling them out is that they are the prototypical stakeholder. On the asset side, they often hold equity as well as debt instruments, whereas on the debt side their counterparts have variable as well as fixed income claims. In other words, their corporate governance interventions should be more *balanced* than interventions by shareholders, employees, trade creditors or customers. Another reason is that institutional investors are perceived as having insufficiently monitored their investments during the period leading up to the credit crisis. In other words, institutional investors have allegedly *failed* to discharge their combined equity and debt holder responsibilities. Finally, and most importantly, shareholders as well as stakeholders increasingly depend upon institutional investors for their post-retirement income as private firms and governments gradually outsource their pension obligations.

---

[11] See Gordon L. Clark & Michael Viehs, "The Implications of Corporate Social Responsibility for Investors" (Working Paper 2014); Abagail McWilliams & Donald S. Siegel, "Corporate Social Responsibility: A Theory of the Firm Perspective", 26 Acad. Mgmt. Rev. 117 (2001).

[12] Alex Edmans, "Does the Stock Market Fully Value Intangibles? Employee Satisfaction and Equity Prices", 101 J. Fin. Econ. 621 (2011).

[13] Franklin Allen, Elena Carletti & Robert Marquez, "Stakeholder Governance, Competition and Firm Value" 19 Rev. Fin. 1315 (2015).

[14] See also Freeman, *supra* note 7.

[15] Lawrence E. Mitchell, Corporate Irresponsibility: America's Newest Export 129–34 (2001).

[16] Robert Phillips, Stakeholder Theory and Organizational Ethics 19–22 (2003); Lynn Stout, The Shareholder Value Myth: How Putting Shareholders First Harms Investors, Corporations and the Public (2012).

[17] See Allen Ferrell, Hao Liang, & Luc Renneboog, "Socially Responsible Firms", 122 J. Fin. Econ. 585 (2016).

In this context, corporate governance reformers have nudged institutional investors toward assuming bigger so-called "stewardship" responsibilities. The basic idea is relatively simple: it boils down to getting institutional investors to adopt policies that are more stakeholder or "socially" oriented. For implementation purposes, reformers have relied upon a transparency plus voice approach. On the one hand, they are encouraging industrial corporations and financial intermediaries to provide information on their self-proclaimed 'CSR' approach whereas institutional investors are expected to disclose how they intend to discharge the stewardship responsibilities they owe to their ultimate beneficiaries. On the other hand, reformers have signaled to institutional investors that they should take a more active corporate governance role, in particular by effectively using their voice options.

Markets have not been taken by surprise. Industrial firms that adopted CSR policies over the past decades have generally informed market participants accordingly. Institutional investors, for their part, are increasingly considering the adoption of socially responsible investment (CSI) principles as a (positive) future performance indicator. There is also evidence of institutional investors going a step further and actively encouraging firms to adopt stakeholder-oriented policies in addition to their traditional financial result driven policies. To be sure, one can still observe significant differences in ownership engagement levels[18]; overall, however, institutional investors have become more active over the past decade.[19]

These developments raise two fundamental questions. One is whether the increased (but not new) attention paid to stakeholders issues has had a positive economic or, at least, societal impact. The other issue is whether institutional investors are acting in the interest of their "ultimate" beneficiaries (defined here as the individuals who personally consume the investment returns) to the extent they foster the interests of stakeholders or society at large. This chapter will address these issues from two angles. First, it will assess the attention currently paid to stakeholder interests and the extent to which it justifies giving a new or stronger voice to stakeholders. Second, it will evaluate whether institutional investors are well placed to represent stakeholder interests and, if so, the extent to which their ultimate beneficiaries can contribute to institutional investor governance.

The remainder of this contribution is organized as follows. Section 2 describes recent stakeholder-oriented reforms and assess their impact. This allows for a preliminary assessment on the merits of giving stakeholders a new or reinforced governance voice.

Section 3 builds upon this assessment by discussing the hypothesis of having institutional investors act as stakeholder representatives. It shows that various institutional investors, in particular religious organizations, union managed pension funds, and ethical mutual funds already play such a role. But it also provides evidence of these interventions being biased toward special interests or having a limited impact. Therefore, section 3 also explores whether the ultimate beneficiaries of pension funds can be given the option to choose between shareholder and stakeholder-oriented investment strategies.

---

[18] Serdar Çelik & Mats Isaakson, "Institutional Investors as Owners, Who Are They and What Do They Do?" (OECD Corporate Governance Working Paper 11/2013).

[19] See, e.g., Robin Greenwood & Michael Schor, "Investor Activism and Takeovers", 92 J. Fin. Econ. 362 (2009); Alon Brav, Wei Jiang, & Hyunseob Kim, "Hedge Fund Activism: A Review", 4 Foundations and Trends in Finance 185 (2010); Maria Goranova & Lori Verstegen Ryan, "Shareholder Activism: A Multidisciplinary Review", 40 J. Mgmt. 1230 (2014).

2 Focusing on Stakeholder Interests

Institutional investor activism has had an impact on the inter-shareholder agency problem. Conflicts of interests between smaller and controlling shareholders used to be pervasive in larger continental European and East Asian corporations.[20] In recent decades, however, direct household share ownership has decreased by 20% to 50% in Canada, France, Germany, Japan, and Sweden due to portfolio diversification and tax optimization prompting households to favor mutual funds and retirement plans.[21] As a result, smaller owners have largely been substituted by pension funds, investment funds, and insurance companies. While one cannot expect these new owners to necessarily favor voice over exit,[22] their presence makes it more difficult for controlling owners to act opportunistically and to the detriment of minority shareholders.

In this context, increased attention is paid to the shareholder-creditor/stakeholder conflict of interests.[23] From a theoretical perspective, this novel environment is potentially detrimental to employees, suppliers and customers, and other creditor interests, especially when equity-based compensation incentivizes managers to undertake risky projects.[24] Real-world creditors see it the same way, with bond prices falling when executive stock option plans are adopted.[25]

To be sure, shareholders do not necessarily benefit from the new equilibrium as it may lead to risk-taking levels that are (directly or indirectly) detrimental to both creditors and shareholders.[26] This is especially likely to happen when shareholder demand for higher returns is not accompanied by an increase in creditor monitoring or creditor protection. Here too, real-world reactions confirm the theoretical prediction. In recent years, jurisdictions with weaker creditor protection regimes experienced higher declines in stock market index than jurisdictions with stronger creditor protection regimes.[27]

---

[20] See Rafael La Porta, Florencio López-de-Silanes, Andrei Shleifer, & Robert Vishny, "Corporate Ownership around the World", 54 J. Fin. 471 (1999); Mara Faccio & Larry H.P. Lang, "The Ultimate Ownership of Western European Corporations", 65 J. Fin. Econ. 365 (2002); Stijn Claessens, Simon Djankov, & Larry H.P. Lang, "The Separation of Ownership and Control in East Asian Corporations", 58 J. Fin. Econ. 81 (2000).

[21] Kristian Rydqvist, Joshua Spizman, & Ilya Strebulaev, "Government Policy and Ownership of Equity Securities", 111 J. Fin. Econ. 70 (2014).

[22] See Albert O. Hirschman, Exit, Voice and Loyalty 46 (1970).

[23] See Edward B. Rock, "Adapting to the New Shareholder-Centric Reality", 161 U. Pa. L. Rev. 1907 (2013); Barry Adler & Marcel Kahan, "The Technology of Creditor Protection", 161 U. Pa. L. Rev. 1773 (2013).

[24] See Theresa A. John & Kose John, "Top-Management Compensation and Capital Structure", 48 J. Fin. 949 (1993).

[25] See Richard A. DeFusco, Robert R. Johnson, & Thomas S. Zorn, "The Effect of Executive Stock Option Plans on Stockholders and Bondholders", 45 J. Fin. 617 (1990).

[26] On (efficient) risk taking in the financial sector imposing negative externalities on the real economy, see Anton Korinek & Jonathan Kreamer, "The Redistributive Effects of Financial Deregulation", 68 J. Monetary Econ. (Suppl.) S55 (2014).

[27] Galina Hale, Assaf Razin, & Hui Tong, "The Impact of Creditor Protection on Stock Prices in the Presence of Credit Crunches" (CESifo Working Paper 3440/2011).

2.1 Recent Stakeholder-Oriented Reforms

This evolution and the emergence of related creditor protection concerns have gone hand in hand with the adoption of a number of stakeholder-oriented corporate governance initiatives. Various international organizations have taken steps to make managerial compensation less dependent upon shareholder value, to improve risk-taking disclosure and to generally reinforce creditor protection.[28] At the national level, industrial corporations and financial intermediaries are encouraged to provide information on their CSR policies whereas institutional investors are expected to take a more active corporate governance role. German and UK code-makers, in particular, have emphasized the importance of long-term sustainability as well as focused on stakeholder involvement or representation.

In its original version, the German Corporate Governance Code stated in its foreword that its aim was to clarify "the needs of shareholders, who provide the company with the required equity capital and who carry the entrepreneurial risk." The foreword was amended in 2009 and now underlines the obligation of the board "to ensure the continued existence of the enterprise and its *sustainable creation* of value in conformity with the principle of the social market economy (*interest of the enterprise*)." This evolution is back in line with the German corporate law tradition of taking into account stakeholder interests, most famously by imposing employee representation in boards of large companies (so-called codetermination).[29]

In the UK, the 2009 Walker Review emphasized that governance failures had led to excessive risk taking and underlined the responsibility of institutional investors to encourage *long-term* improvements in performance.[30] Accordingly, the 2012 UK Stewardship Code has subjected UK pension funds, insurance companies, investment trusts, and other collective investment vehicles to explicit stewardship responsibilities.[31] According to the Financial Reporting Council,[32] the Code's aim is to enhance the quality of engagement between asset managers and companies and the value that accrues to *ultimate beneficiaries*. The UK's stewardship efforts are in line with theoretical work devoted to revamping the relationship between owners and managers,[33] in particular by getting institutional investors to focus on managers' intrinsic rather than extrinsic motivation.[34]

The German Code appears to be more stakeholder-oriented than the UK Code and its scope could be broader.[35] However, both codes aim at going beyond immediate shareholder

---

[28] See European Commission Recommendation complementing Recommendations 2004/913/EC and 2005/162/EC as regards the regime for the remuneration of directors of listed companies, C(2009) 3177; International Organization of Securities Commissions (IOSCO), *Objective and Principles of Securities Regulation* (June 2010).

[29] See e.g. Thomas Raiser & Rüdiger Veil, Mitbestimmungsgesetz (5th ed., de Gruyter 2009).

[30] A Review of Corporate Governance in UK Banks and Other Financial Industry Entities, July 16, 2009 at 8–9 (http://www.icaew.com/en/library/subject-gateways/corporate-governance/codes-and-reports/walker-report).

[31] Principle 1, Guidance (https://www.frc.org.uk/getattachment/e2db042e-120b-4e4e-bdc7-d540923533a6/UK-Stewardship-Code-September-2012.aspx).

[32] www.frc.org.uk.

[33] L. Donaldson & J.H. Davis, "Stewardship Theory or Agency Theory: CEO Governance and Shareholder Returns", 16 Austl. J. Mngmt 49 (1991).

[34] David Pastoriza, & Miguel A. Ariño, "When Agents Become Stewards: Introducing Learning in the Stewardship Theory", 2 Adv. Bus. Mngmt 113 (2011).

[35] See Brian R. Cheffins, "The Stewardship Code's Achilles' Heel", 73 Mod. L. Rev. 1004 (2010).

value so as to protect the interest of the firms' ultimate beneficiaries. From this perspective, one can expect institutional investors to adopt similar strategies in both jurisdictions.[36]

2.2 Assessing Regulatory Reforms

As already mentioned, the hard (and controversial) task is to identify the *shorter-term* policies that facilitate the realization of the long-term sustainability objective.

Lawyers have continued to this day the theoretical shareholder/non-shareholder orientation debate started by Berle and Dodd.[37] The original Friedman–Freeman controversy is also still alive. Financial economists have generally made theirs the claim that, in the long run, what is good for shareholders in the short term is also good for stakeholders in the long term.[38] Business management and industrial organization scholars, for their part, seem to favor a more stakeholder-oriented approach. Some justify it in terms of economic value creation.[39] Others broaden the approach by proposing to let stakeholders appropriate a bigger share of value creation.[40] Last but not least, some scholars favor psychological and sociological over *homo economicus* approaches.[41] In other words, human beings operating in or interacting with the firm are not merely self-interested actors; one has to take into account that they often bond with the firm and behave like its psychological owners.

In practice, there is evidence of firms trying to optimize their relations with *all* stakeholders. Empirical investigations show that board members often consider themselves accountable to stakeholders, with some directors having preferences that favor shareholder primacy and others being inclined to adopt a more balanced attitude.[42] More generally, CSR approaches have become increasingly relevant within the business community.[43]

This could be related to CSR being profitable by itself. Social investments may generate innovations and CSR-oriented managers can contribute to firm performance when their approach increases employee motivation.[44] In fact, there is empirical evidence of superior CSR performance going hand in hand with better access to finance.[45] Similarly,

---

[36] See Assaf Hamdani & Yishay Yafeh, "Institutional Investors as Minority Shareholders", 17 Rev. Fin. 691 (2013).

[37] See Robert C. Clark, "Agency Costs versus Fiduciary Duties", in Principals and Agents: The Structure of Business 55 (John W. Pratt and Richard J. Zeckhauser eds., 1985); Frank H. Easterbrook & Daniel R. Fischel, "The Corporate Contract", 89 Colum. L. Rev. 1416 (1989); and Margaret M. Blair & Lynn A. Stout, "A Team Production Theory of Corporate Law", 85 Va. L. Rev. 247 (1999).

[38] Michael C. Jensen, "Value Maximization, Stakeholder Theory and the Corporate Objective Function", 7 Eur. Fin. Mgmt. 297 (2001).

[39] Jeffrey S. Harrison, Douglas A. Bosse, & Robert A. Philipps, "Managing for Stakeholders, Stakeholder Utility Function, and Competitive Advantage", 31 Strat. Mgmt J. 58 (2010).

[40] Antonio Argandoña, "Stakeholder Theory and Value Creation" (IESE Working Paper 922/2011).

[41] James H. Davis, F. David Schoorman, & Lex Donaldson, "Toward a Stewardship Theory of Management", 22 Acad. Mgmt. Rev. 20 (1997).

[42] J. W. Lorsch & E. MacIver, Pawns or Potentat: The Reality of America's Corporate Boards (1989).

[43] Suzanne Benn & Dianne Bolton, Key Concepts in Corporate Social Responsibility 59 (2011).

[44] Michael E. Porter & Claas van der Linde, "Toward a New Conception of the Environment-Competitiveness Relationship", 9 J. Econ. Perspect. 97 (1995); Luigi Guiso, Paola Sapienza, & Luigi Zingales, "The Value of Corporate Culture", 117 J. Fin. Econ. 60 (2015).

[45] Beiting Cheng, Ioannis Ioannou, & George Serafeim, "Corporate Social Responsibility and Access to Finance", 35 Strat. Mgmt. J. 1 (2014). See also *supra* note 9.

there is increasing evidence of CSR investments being associated with financial performance improvements[46] and contributing to merger performance.[47] More generally, CSR investments can have positive reputation effects, which in turns may permit to increase output or charge higher prices.[48]

At the same time, CSR developments may essentially reflect institutional, political, or ethical factors.[49] In particular, there is empirical evidence of firms governed by Scandinavian law scoring the highest CSR scores and of firms governed by English common law scoring the lowest CSR scores—firms governed by German and French law being in the middle.[50] Similarly, it has been shown that companies that generate higher social costs or are subject to greater public attention also carry out higher social investments.[51]

Overall, it remains unclear why we observe a corporate social responsibility trend. CSR policies may contribute to the firm's bottom line even though the social responsibility debate is often fueled by public goods considerations. Alternatively, managers may invest in CSR projects simply because they are philanthropy-oriented managers[52] or are financially unconstrained.[53] In short, the value of CSR activities may be circumstance-dependent, for example contingent upon CSR activities having a real impact on stakeholder behavior.[54]

---

[46] Marc Orlitzky, Frank L. Schmidt, & Sara L. Reynes, "Corporate Social and Financial Performance: A Meta-Analysis", 24 Org. Stud. 403 (2003); Pieter van Beurden & Tobias Gossling, "The Worth of Values—A Literature Review on the Relation Between Corporate Social and Financial Performance", 82 J. Bus. Ethics 407 (2008); Michael L. Barnett & Robert M. Salomon, "Does it Pay to be 'Really' Good? Addressing the Shape of the Relationship between Social and Financial Performance", 33 Strat. Mgmt. J. 1304 (2012); Mark Blodgett, Rani Hoitash & Ariel J. Markelevich, "Sustaining the Financial Value of Global CSR: Reconciling Corporate and Stakeholder Interests in a Less Regulated Environment", 119 Bus. & Soc'y Rev. 95 (2014).

[47] Xin Deng, Jun-Koo Kang, & Buen Sin Low, "Corporate Social Responsibility and Stakeholder Value Maximization: Evidence from Mergers", 110 J. Fin. Econ. 87 (2013).

[48] See Abagail McWilliams & Donald S. Siegel, "Corporate Social Responsibility and Financial Performance: Correlation or Misspecification?", 21 Strat. Mgmt J. 603 (2000); David P. Baron, "Private Politics, Corporate Social Responsibility and Integrated Strategy", 10 J. Econ. & Mgmt. Strat. 7 (2001); Mark Bagnoli & Susan G. Watts, "Selling to Socially Responsible Consumers: Competition and the Private Provision of Public Goods", 12 J. Econ. & Mgmt Strat. 419 (2003).

[49] Markus Kitzmueller & Jay Shimshack, "Economic Perspectives on Corporate Social Responsibility", 50 J. Econ. Lit. 51 (2012). Interestingly, past returns seem to be driven by ethical investors' decisions: see Luc Renneboog, Jenke Ter Horst, & Chendi Zhang, "Is Ethical Money Financially Smart? Nonfinancial Attributes and Money Flows of Socially Responsible Investment Funds", 20 J. Fin. Intermediation 562 (2011).

[50] Hao Liang & Luc Renneboog, "On the Foundations of Corporate Social Responsibility", 72 J. Fin. 853 (2017).

[51] Matthew J. Kotchen & Jon J. Moon, "Corporate Social Responsibility for Irresponsibility", 12 The B.E. Journal of Economic Analysis & Policy, Article 55 (online).

[52] P.A. Hall & D. Soskice, Varieties of Capitalism: The Institutional Foundations of Comparative Advantage (2001).

[53] Harrison G. Hong, Jeffrey D. Kubik, & Jose A. Scheinkman, "Financial Constraints and Corporate Goodness", NBER Working Paper 18476/2012.

[54] See Henri Servaes and Ane Tamayo, "The Impact of Corporate Social Responsibility on Firm Value: The Role of Customer Awareness", 59 Mgmt Sci. 1045 (2013). Note that customer awareness may also be desirable from a shareholder value maximization perspective.

2.3 Giving Stakeholders a New Voice

Clearly, more research is needed to assess the extent to which CSR policies benefit shareholders, creditors, and/or society in general. However, the available evidence allows for a preliminary assessment of recent, more stakeholder-oriented corporate governance reforms. They can rely on (some) theoretical support, they are in line with recent business practices, and they cannot be considered per se detrimental to either shareholders or stakeholders. This rather lukewarm assessment may be due to lawmakers having essentially relied upon boards and information flows to foster stakeholder interests.

Germany's codetermination approach exemplifies the difficulties one faces when trying to get *boards* more responsive to stakeholder interests: after decades of experimentations, the debate about the costs and benefits of mandatory employee board participation has yet to be settled.[55] To be sure, there is increasing evidence of boards around the world becoming more directly involved in social issues.[56] However, we do not know whether this development has anything to do with either board structure or board composition. For example, appointing a CSR director does not seem to make a difference.[57] The same is true when it comes to having employee representative directors, as they generally seem to take a shareholder view when there is a shareholder-stakeholder dilemma.[58]

On paper, improving corporate *transparency* seems a better approach toward fostering stakeholder interests. Better information flows could result in more socially balanced external interventions while letting managers keep the discretion necessary for the efficient conduct of corporate affairs. In practice, however, the presence of presentation effects continues to cast doubt on the utility of CSR reports.[59] More importantly, the empirical evidence remains sketchy when it comes to accounting standards' contribution to the assessment of a firm's social investments.[60] On the one hand, financial accounting valuation usefulness seems negatively related to a firm's stewardship orientation.[61] On the other hand, it has been shown that socially responsible firms tend to produce higher-quality financial reports.[62] More generally, there is an ongoing debate about the compatibility of valuation

---

[55] See Gary Gorton & Frank A. Schmid, "Capital, Labor and the Firm: A Study of German Codetermination", 2 J. Eur. Econ Ass'n 863 (2004); Larry Fauver and Michael E. Fuerst, "Does Good Corporate Governance Include Employee Representation? Evidence from German Corporate Boards", 82 J. Fin. Econ. 673 (2006).

[56] Heiko Spitzeck, "The Development of Governance Structures for Corporate Responsibility", 9 Corp. Governance 495 (2009).

[57] See Brammer & Pamelin, *supra* note 9.

[58] Renée B. Adams, Amir N. Licht, & Lilach Sagiv, "Shareholders and Stakeholders: How Do Directors Decide?", 32 Strat. Mgmt J. 1331 (2011).

[59] W. Brooke Elliott, Stephanie M. Grant, & Kristina M. Rennekamp, "How Disclosure Features of Corporate Social Responsibility Reports Interact with Investor Numeracy to Influence Investor Judgments", 34 Contemporary Accounting Research 1596 (2017).

[60] See also Donald V. Moser & Patrick R. Martin, "A Broader Perspective on Corporate Social Responsibility Research in Accounting", 87 Acc. Rev. 797 (2012).

[61] Joachim Gassen, Are Stewardship and Valuation Usefulness Compatible or Alternative Objectives of Financial Accounting?, SFB 649 Discussion Paper 028/2008.

[62] Yongtae Kim, Myung Seok Park, & Benson Wier, "Is Earning Quality Associated with Corporate Social Responsibility", 87 Acc. Rev. 761 (2012).

and stewardship accounting.[63] This probably explains why securities regulators still focus on valuation issues, whereas accounting standard setters have yet to agree on how to approach stewardship.[64]

Going forward, the question is whether more could be done to foster stakeholder interests. This is not, as often in the past, a primarily continental European reflection. The adoption of the UK Stewardship Code and recent contributions by US academics show that the debate has reached the Anglo-Saxon world.[65] Many reformers still follow a "more of the same" approach and continue to focus on boards and corporate disclosure requirements. Nevertheless, as shown by the UK example, increasing attention is given to institutional investor activism.

From the latter perspective, it is worth noting that institutional investors have been filing an increasing number of "social" resolutions over the past decade.[66] The practice may or may not be in the interests of their ultimate beneficiaries, in particular when it comes to their stakeholder interests. It is therefore justified to investigate in more depth whether institutional investor are acting or should be required to act like stakeholder representatives.

3 INSTITUTIONAL INVESTORS AS STAKEHOLDER REPRESENTATIVES

Stakeholder issues have originally been put on the corporate governance agenda by societally oriented institutional investors such as mutual funds catering to clients who favored investments made according to ethical criteria, union-managed pension funds, and, especially, religious organizations.[67] However, this does not mean that societally-oriented institutional investors have necessarily aligned their corporate governance interventions with stakeholders' interests—nor, a fortiori, that other institutional investors have given priority to the societal or long-term interests of their ultimate beneficiaries.

For example, mutual fund managers understand that while some of their clients are prepared to pay a significant price for high ethical performance, other clients are less willing to sacrifice financial returns.[68] As a result, their corporate governance interventions may also reflect (short term) shareholder-oriented considerations. Similarly, labor unions that manage public pension funds are known for having their corporate governance

---

[63] See Vincent O'Connell, "Reflections on Stewardship Reporting", 21 Acct. Horizons 215 (2007).

[64] For a summary of recent disclosure initiatives, see Kevin Davis, Regulatory Reform Post the Global Financial Crisis: An Overview (May 2011).

[65] See Kenneth G. Dau-Schmidt, "Promoting Employee Voice in the American Economy: A Call for Comprehensive Reform", 94 Marq. L. Rev. 765 (2011); Aditi Bagchi, "Who Should Talk? What Counts as Employee Voice and Who Stands to Gain", 94 Marq. L. Rev. 839 (2011).

[66] See W. T. Proffitt & A. Spicer, "Shaping the Shareholder Activism Agenda: Institutional Investors and Global Issues", 4 Strat. Org. 165 (2006); Stuart L. Gillan & Laura T. Starks, "The Evolution of Shareholder Activism in the United States", 19 J. Appl. Corp. Fin. 55 (2007).

[67] Paula Tkac, "One Proxy at a Time: Pursuing Social Change through Shareholder Proposals", 91 Fed. Reserve Bank of Atlanta Econ. Rev. 1 (2006).

[68] R. H. Berry & F. Yeung, "Are Investors Willing to Sacrifice Cash for Morality", 117 J. Bus. Ethics 477 (2013).

interventions reflect union of member interests rather than the interests of pension funds' ultimate beneficiaries. Hence, there is evidence of union-managed pension funds focusing upon occupational health and safety, fair wages, or equal opportunity issues.[69] Likewise, religious organizations often target what they consider "unjust" corporate policies or try to promote peace and economic justice, which does not necessarily reflect the stakeholder interests of their constituencies.

Moreover, societally-oriented activism has not necessarily translated into corporations adopting societally-oriented policies. In particular, the available evidence points toward very limited success in terms of activists getting a majority of fellow investors voting in favor of stakeholder-oriented resolutions. That being said, it has not been uncommon for targeted firms to amend their policies on the basis of informal discussions or in view of a resolution getting a significant number of (minority) votes. This may actually have been activist investors' original intent, as there is often a difference between what they ask and what they want.

Regardless of how one assesses the results of these stakeholder-oriented governance efforts, the fact is that they have become more significant in recent years, with mutual funds and non-union pension funds joining the activist fray. In particular, there is evidence of US public pension funds promoting social diversity not only via conventional proxy voting efforts but also by favoring the use of asset managers owned or operated by women and minorities.[70] Overall, pension fund activism currently seems more stakeholder-oriented than mutual fund activism. Differences in investment strategies and client bases are likely to explain this result.

Firms targeted by mutual funds are very diverse and mutual fund beneficiaries have divergent expectations. Consequently, mutual funds have incentives to adopt a cautious and diversified approach to social issues and stakeholder interests. To be sure, we have seen that the ethical mutual fund industry has an established stakeholder activism record. But this is not necessarily the case for the mutual fund industry at large (partly because of regulatory constraints)[71] or for all ethical mutual funds (due to heterogeneous client preferences).

By contrast, pension funds tend to have more homogeneous investment strategies and client bases. In particular, they must take into account their ultimate beneficiaries' common expectations regarding the adoption of prudent investment strategies that secure their future financial security.[72] This environment obviously favors the adoptions of long-term oriented investment strategies. Clearly, this does not automatically mean that pension fund originated governance interventions reflect social concerns rather than mere long term financial value considerations.[73] Nevertheless, pension funds are generally considered active social issues advocates.[74] Two factors may explain this perception.

[69] Emma Sjöström, "Shareholder Activism for Corporate Social Responsibility: What Do We Know", 16 Sustainable Dev. 141 (2008)

[70] Angela Cai, "US Public Pension Fund Diversity Initiatives: Practices, Rationales, and Constitutionality", 13 DePaul Bus. & Commercial L. J. 107 (2014).

[71] Mutual funds may face restrictions in the taking of concentrated equity positions. See, for the US, Margaret M. Blair, Ownership and Control 153–55 (1995).

[72] Diane Del Guercio & Tracie Woidtke, "Do the Interests of Public Pension Fund and Labor Union Activists Align with Other Shareholders? Evidence from the Market for Directors" (Working Paper 2014).

[73] David Hess, "Public Pensions and the Promise of Shareholder Activism for the Next Frontier of Corporate Governance: Sustainable Economic Development", 2 Va. L. & Bus. Rev. 221 (2007).

[74] See e.g. Georgeson, 2012 Annual Corporate Governance Review at 6.

One is the increase in life expectancy and related changes in retiree expectations, which have put the limelight onto pension funds "trustee" responsibilities. Pension funds are nowadays expected to behave like good "stewards," i.e., to understand and take into account the *overall* interests of their ultimate beneficiaries.[75] To be sure, the latter are not necessarily interested in corporate social responsibility. However, the increase in life expectancy makes it likely that pension fund beneficiaries will have to work longer and bear a higher risk of suffering from the consequences of ongoing environmental and social changes. One can expect younger beneficiaries to be aware of these risks and support pension fund CSR activism as one way to protect their future retiree interests.

The other factor is related to concerns about the externalities that go hand in hand with a disproportionate focus on short-term profits. The 2008 credit crisis and related bank bailouts have made the beneficiaries of public pension funds aware of the relationship between immediate profit strategies and their taxpayer exposure. Bank bailouts have also (or possibly therefore) prompted policy makers to adopt corporate governance reforms aiming at constraining risk taking by getting asset managers to better take into account sustainable performance. We have seen that the 2012 UK Stewardship Code is nudging institutional investors toward adopting a longer-term stewardship approach.[76] Asset managers in Canada, France, and the Netherlands have similarly been encouraged to act like stewards.[77] The basic idea is to foster the longer-term interests of ultimate beneficiaries, in particular by having pension funds pay more attention to societal issues.

Reformers have, until now, refrained from prescribing ways to do so. As already mentioned, state intervention is generally limited to getting pension funds to disclose their governance policies and interventions, so as to make stewardship more transparent and to encourage more effective investor engagement. This regulatory approach has been considered futile by some commentators, the argument being that it fails to provide a clear and constraining legal framework.[78]

Clearly, it would be a mistake to assume that market forces automatically provide optimal stewardship levels. "Natural" stakeholder activism is not only likely to vary across institutional investor types, but also among those institutional investors generally considered stakeholder-oriented, such as pension funds.[79] Conversely, it would also be erroneous to require all institutional investors to engage in stakeholder activism. Activism capability or adequacy is similarly likely to vary across or among institutional investor types. What must be clarified here is whether some institutional investors are (1) better placed to pursue a stakeholder-oriented agenda that is in line with their ultimate beneficiaries' interests and,

[75] See Arleta A.A. Majoch, Andreas J.F. Hoepner, & Tessa Hebb, "Sources of Stakeholder Salience in the Responsible Investment Movement: Why do Investor Sign the Principles for Responsible Investment?", 140 J. Bus. Ethics 723 (2017).

[76] See also Konstantinos Sergakis, "The UK Stewardship Report: Bridging the Gap Between Companies and Institutional Investors", 47 Rev. Jur. Themis 109 (2013).

[77] Simon C.Y. Wong, "Why Stewardship is Proving Elusive for Institutional Investors", 2010 Butterworths J. Int. Banking & Fin. L. 406 (2010).

[78] Lorraine E. Talbot, The Coming of Shareholder Stewardship, Warwick School of Law Research Paper 22/2010.

[79] Diane Del Guercio & Jennifer Hawkins, "The Motivation and Impact of Pension Fund Activism", 52 J. Fin. Econ. 293 (1999); Stephen J. Choi & Jill E. Fisch, "On Beyond CalPERS: Survey Evidence on the Developing Role of Public Pension Funds in Corporate Governance", 61 Vand. L. Rev. 315 (2008).

if so, (2) to identify the governance mechanism that ensures the effectiveness, efficiency, and representativeness of their intervention.

3.1 Best-Placed Stakeholder Representatives

Whether an institutional investor can adequately represent stakeholders ultimately depends upon the respective interests of its managers and ultimate beneficiaries.

Let us start with business angels and venture capitalists. These are institutional investors with rather short-term objectives, i.e., they take stakes in *early-stage* firms with the objective of getting them to mature as rapidly as possible. Once this occurs, the firm type changes and becomes attractive for outside investors or suitable for public listing. Business angels and venture capitalists, respectively their funders, can then cash in and reinvest in another early stage firm. Stakeholder interests are not irrelevant in this context, but they are only taken into account if doing so contributes to increasing shareholder value. One could, of course, require (or incentivize) business angels and venture capitalists to foster stakeholder value as such. However, this is likely to be inefficient as it probably would constrain entrepreneurship at a critical firm development stage. More importantly, regulatory interference would also adversely affect the beneficiaries of pension funds and other funders of business angels and venture capitalists, which would be odd considering the importance stakeholder advocates give to the interest of ultimate beneficiaries.[80]

Private equity firms resemble business angels and venture capitalists in various respects. They have similar financial backers, as they are prototypically funded by investment banks, insurance companies, pension funds, and wealthy individuals.[81] They also take an active part in the management of the targeted firms and their main objective is to cash in on exit values. On the other hand, private equity firms usually target *mature* firms they consider to be underperforming, not emerging firms or firms that need to access capital markets to complete their development.

Stakeholder interests may prove more important for private equity firms than for business angels and venture capitalists for two reasons. First, as just mentioned, they generally invest in larger and often publicly traded firms. Second, private equity firms may themselves be publicly traded.[82] Overall, however, it is also likely to be contrary to the interests of ultimate beneficiaries to contrive private equity firms into taking stakeholder interests into account. In particular, getting an underperforming firm back into shape often requires the adoption of restructuring measures that can be disadvantageous for employees and suppliers. Such measures, which are controversial even in an ideal business environment, would be much harder to implement if private equity firms were forced to specifically consider their impact upon stakeholder interests.

---

[80] On pension funds as investors in the venture capital sector, see Paul Gompers & Josh Lerner, The Venture Capital Cycle 7–8 (1999).

[81] Mike Wright, Donald S. Siegel, Miguel Meuleman, & Kevin Amess, Private Equity, Leveraged Buyouts and Corporate Governance, in The Oxford Handbook of Corporate Governance *supra* note 9, at 539, 541.

[82] Brian Cheffins and John Armour, "The Eclipse of Private Equity", 33 Del. J. Corp. L. 1 (2008).

That leaves us with mutual funds, hedge funds, and pension funds. Mutual funds provide diversification advantages and, therefore, count not only institutional investors but also a significant number of households among their immediate funders.[83] Possibly but not necessarily for this reason, the mutual fund industry has paid increasing attention to socially responsible investments in recent years, both in terms of investment volume and investment value.[84] On the other hand, there is evidence of so-called social funds being more likely to support shareholder proposals than other funds.[85]

The implications in terms of performance are not easy to assess. As already indicated, mutual fund managers understand that while some of their clients are prepared to pay a significant price for high ethical performance, other clients are less willing to sacrifice financial returns. This may explain why various studies have found no significant difference in performance between conventional mutual funds and socially responsible funds.[86] At the same time, one cannot exclude that pursuing socially responsible investments may constrain portfolio diversification and, therefore, affect fund performance.[87] This theoretical prediction is supported by recent real-world evidence showing that socially responsible mutual funds have inferior reward-to-risk performance.[88]

It follows that there is no compelling reason to adopt measures prompting mutual funds to take into account stakeholder interests. Stakeholder-oriented investors can invest in social funds if they wish to do so. However, this can prove costly in terms of risk-adjusted returns and incentivizing mutual funds to increase socially responsible investments is likely to make things worse for their beneficiaries without obvious benefits for stakeholders as a class.

Turning to hedge funds, it is well known that they are normally open only to a limited number of institutional or wealthy investors. This does not prevent future retirees to be their ultimate beneficiaries: of the $3 trillion managed by hedge funds across the world, more than a third is provided by retirement funds.[89] Moreover, hedge funds often invest in industrial and financial firms. It could thus make sense to require (or incentivize) them to take into account stakeholder interests. However, when hedge funds undertake corporate investments, they essentially target badly managed firms—in particular those with free cash or excessive costs.[90] To make the most of the business opportunities these deficiencies provide, hedge fund managers actively use their shareholder powers. In particular, they regularly use their voting rights to create shareholder value by forcing the targeted firm into a

---

[83] Robert C. Pozen, The Mutual Fund Industry 61 (1998).

[84] See Eurosif 2010, *European SRI Study*, Paris (2010) (with data from eight European countries).

[85] Angela Morgan, Annette Poulsen, Jack Wolf, & Tina Yang, "Mutual Funds as Monitors: Evidence from Mutual Fund Voting", 17 J. Corp. Fin. 914 (2011).

[86] For the US, see Zakri Y. Bello, "Socially Responsible Investing and Portfolio Diversification", 28 J. Fin. Res. 41 (2005); for Europe, see Cristiana Albuquerque Torres, António Cerqueira, & Elisio Brandao, "Are European Socially Responsible Mutual Funds Rewarding and Profitable" (Working Paper 2013).

[87] H. M. Markowitz, "Portfolio Selection", 7 J. Fin. 77 (1952).

[88] C. Edward Chang & H. Doug Witte, "Performance Evaluation of US Socially Responsible Mutual Funds: Revisiting Doing Good and Doing Well", 25 Am. J. Bus. 9 (2010).

[89] See Miles Johnson, Calpers Exit Has Sent Hedge Funds Managers a Public Health Warning, Fin. Times, Sept. 23, 2014 at 24.

[90] William W. Bratton, "Hedge Funds and Governance Targets", 95 Geo. L. J. 1375 (2007); John Armour & Brian Cheffins, "The Rise and Fall (?) of Hedge Fund Activism", 14 J. Alternative Investments 17 (2012).

merger or to otherwise restructure.[91] Here again, this strategy can prove disadvantageous for the firm's employees and suppliers and would become much harder to implement (and less advantageous for ultimate beneficiaries) if the hedge fund had to specifically consider their impact upon stakeholder interests.

This leaves us with pension funds. They prototypically have individuals as beneficiaries. Private pension funds generally operate under a contribution-defined retirement scheme. Public pension funds traditionally operated under a defined benefits retirement scheme, but public finance constraints have recently resulted in an overall trend toward contribution-defined approaches.

As indicated, there is evidence of union-managed pension funds favoring union or union member interests over the interests of other stakeholders. However, it remains unclear whether labor union activism has any specific wealth impact, in particular on long-run beneficiary wealth.[92]

Non-union-managed pension funds are less likely to favor some beneficiaries over others, but they may nevertheless be conflicted. Private pension funds may not want to rock the boat when investing in firms that do business with their corporate sponsor.[93] More generally and importantly, their managers are likely to favor the immediate accumulation of pension assets over the longer-term interests of their beneficiaries.[94] Public pension funds, for their part, may have managers whose activism is tainted by political ambitions[95] or influenced by public debt financing considerations. When public pension funds operate under a benefit-defined scheme, self-interested managerial activism is unlikely to affect beneficiaries as any resulting asset shortfall will be funded by taxpayers. On the other hand, when public pension funds operate contribution-defined schemes or are not backed by taxpayers, beneficiaries are likely to bear the costs of misguided managerial activism.

It thus appears that pension fund beneficiaries face two specific longer-term risks. One is the so-called pension risk, i.e., the risk of not getting adequate retirement income. The other is what can be called the stakeholder risk, i.e., the risk of retiring in a world where asset misallocations have caused significant social costs. From this perspective, it is definitely worth analyzing more in depth if and how pension funds could be required or incentivized to take stakeholder interests into account. Our analysis will focus on defined-contribution pension plans, to avoid the insurance-related moral hazard issues that may affect benefit-defined pension plans.

Summing-up, business angels, venture capitalists, private equity, or hedge funds are not well-placed to act as stakeholder representatives due to their business plans often requiring

[91] Paul H. Edelman, Randall S. Thomas, & Robert B. Thompson, "Shareholder Voting in an Age of Intermediary Capitalism", 87 S. Cal. L. Rev. 1359 (2014).

[92] Andrew K. Prevost, Ramesh P. Rao, & Melissa A. Williams, "Labor Unions as Shareholder Activists: Champions or Detractors?", 47 Fin. Rev. 327 (2012).

[93] J. Brickley, R. Lease, & C. Smith, "Ownership Structure and Voting on Antitakeover Amendments", 20 J. Fin. Econ. 267 (1988); id., "Corporate Voting: Evidence from Charter Amendment Proposals", 1 J. Corp. Fin. 5 (1994).

[94] Fiona Stewart, "Providing Incentives for Long-Term Investments by Pension Funds", World Bank Policy Research Working Paper 6885/2014.

[95] See Roberta Romano, "Public Pension Fund Activism in Corporate Governance Reconsidered", 93 Colum. L. Rev. 795 (1993); Tracie Woidtke, "Agents Watching Agents? Evidence from Pension Fund Ownership and Firm Value", 63 J. Fin. Econ. 99 (2002).

them to take actions that are contrary to the (short-term) interests of major stakeholder constituencies. Mutual funds, for their part, are paying increasing attention to stakeholder value, but there is evidence of their socially responsible investments being costly for their beneficiaries without matching benefits for stakeholders at large.

Things look more promising when it comes to pension funds. The trend toward contribution-defined schemes and the longer-term risks associated with this evolution have generated a convergence of pension fund beneficiary and stakeholder interests. The remaining issue is to determine how pension funds managers, and more specifically managers of pension funds with *contribution-defined* schemes,[96] can be required or incentivized to better take these interests into account.

3.2   Investor Voice and Stakeholder Interests

Pension fund reforms are highly political exercises.[97] No proposal aiming at getting pension fund managers to take into account stakeholder interests is viable if it significantly affects the institutional status quo or can be perceived as jeopardizing "adequate" retirement income.

Two basic regulatory strategies, disclosure and voice, are best suited to such an environment. More specifically, pension funds could be asked to gather and disclose more information about the stakeholder value of their investments. On the voice side, pension fund beneficiaries could be given the possibility to individually choose among several investment plans, some being more stakeholder-oriented than others. In other words, the currently prevalent *collective* decision-making and investment mandates would be supplemented by *individual* decision-making and investment options.

Like other institutional investors, pension funds are increasingly gathering and disclosing information about the social value of their investments. However, the information provided to beneficiaries is often not very explicit, which obviously makes it more difficult to assess the market value of pension fund investments. More surprisingly, this lack of transparency could also prompt affective reactions and lead pension fund beneficiaries to over or underestimate the social value of their investment.[98]

Improving transparency is always a risky exercise. Simply requiring more or better disclosure may prove insufficient or even counterproductive. In particular, getting more information may overwhelm rather than help investors, especially if the goal is to improve individual decision making by pension fund beneficiaries. In the latter context, improving information quality is likely to be a better strategy. For example, pension funds could be required to

---

[96]   The proposals made in the next section could also be applied to benefit-defined schemes, given that benefits are increasingly subject to adjustments when fund returns are insufficient to allow for paying out the originally defined benefits. However, the proposals would have to be amended to take into account that such adjustments are still exceptional. This requires a more complex approach, which will be discussed in a future contribution.

[97]   See Enrico Perotti & Armin Schwienbacher, "The Political Origin of Pension Funding", 18 J. Fin. Intermediation 384 (2009).

[98]   W. Brooke Elliott, Kevin E. Jackson, & Mark E. Peecher, "The Unintended Effect of Corporate Social Responsibility Performance on Investors' Estimates of Fundamental Value", 89 Acc. Rev. 275 (2014).

provide information on the comparative shareholder and stakeholder values of a diverse set of portfolios.

More specifically, pension fund beneficiaries could be provided with tables comparing the value of three portfolios: (1) a portfolio mimicking the portfolio currently managed by the pension fund on a discretionary basis; (2) a portfolio mimicking the "managerial" portfolio for 80% of its value, but with the remaining 20% being invested in socially responsible investments; (3) a portfolio mimicking the "managerial" portfolio for 80% of its value, but with the remaining 20% being invested in shareholder value maximization.

In theory, this approach has four advantages: it reduces the impact of cognitive biases; it makes it easier to grasp the pension risk impact of undertaking of socially responsible investments; it facilitates a comparison between the stakeholder value allocation preferences of the pension fund beneficiary and the pension fund's effective stakeholder value allocation; it permits evaluation of the financial implications of an increase or decrease in stakeholder risk.

To be sure, the suggested approach requires the use of standardized shareholder and stakeholder value assessments. This could prove difficult, especially if one also aims at getting standardized shareholder and stakeholder value assessments that are comparable. However, given that shareholder value and stakeholder value are already commonly used to assess investment allocation and returns, these difficulties cannot justify the rejection of the proposed transparency improvement: they simply reflect the imperfect nature of current (and presumably future) disclosure practices.

Moreover, getting pension funds to compare three sets of asset allocations is not an end by itself. The aim is to give pension fund beneficiaries a choice when it comes to their respective pension and stakeholder risks. Up to now, pension fund beneficiaries often had limited or non-existent powers when it comes to influencing investment strategies. This not only provides pension fund managers with room to engage in opportunistic activism.[99] It also prevents the (many) pension fund beneficiaries whose main financial asset is a claim against their pension fund from effectively expressing their stakeholder preferences.

The standard way to address this governance issue would be to provide beneficiaries with monitoring and election rights. One could deem it naïve to expect beneficiaries to actively exercise such rights. Yet there is recent evidence of underperformance by unionized multi-employer plans disappearing when the pension is controlled by individual employers.[100] From that perspective, it seems conceivable to give pension fund beneficiaries an effective voice without having to rely on third-party activists that may have their own agenda (or whose interventions make good fund managers reluctant to work for pension funds).

Nevertheless, getting pension funds to change their overall investment strategy to reflect their beneficiaries' stakeholder preference is likely to prove very difficult. First, pension fund beneficiaries are unlikely to have identical stakeholder value preferences. Some may want the pension fund to be more "social" than it currently is, and others may want it to be less "social." Second, getting pension fund beneficiaries to demand and engage into collective decision making is likely to prove very difficult, especially because it will be unclear whether the final result will improve or worsen the status quo. Third, pension fund beneficiaries may

---

[99] See *supra* notes 90–95.
[100] William E. Even & David A. MacPherson, "What do Unions Do to Pension Performance?", 52 Econ. Inquiry 1173 (2014).

have stakeholder value preferences that are strong enough to make them favor an asset allocation that results in excessive pension risks.

These difficulties can be addressed by limiting beneficiary choice to a set of diverse but still comparable investment plans. More specifically, beneficiaries could be allowed to voice their preferences by opting for a diversified plan, a targeted shareholder value plan or a targeted stakeholder value plan. These plans could provide significant stakeholder choice without having radically different performance objectives. Indeed, the empirical evidence shows that shareholder value and stakeholder value approaches often result in relatively similar performances. Moreover, the risk of excessive performance difference could be minimized by constraining beneficiary choice in two ways. One would be to have beneficiary choice limited to a fraction of managed assets—for example the 20% mentioned for transparency purposes. The second way would be to require any given choice to be made for at least five years, so as to insure for any change of mind to be based on an effective track record rather than on emotional responses to short term performance or recent economic or social events.

This restriction is related to the more general issue of whether beneficiaries could be allowed to switch from one investment plan to another as they get older. To the extent beneficiaries are allowed to exit their firm's pension plan when to leave to work for another firm or to operate as independent contractors, there is no reason to forbid moving from one investment plan to another. Here again, it may prove necessary to impose a waiting period so as to avoid liquidity issues or significant investment losses. However, mutual funds regularly deal with such issues and there is no reason to believe that pension fund managers will not prove capable of managing them.

4 Conclusion

While changes in investor activism and compensation policies have reduced the shareholder–manager conflict of interests, the benefits of shareholder profit maximization strategies have been increasingly questioned over the past decade. This debate has generated a number of stakeholder-oriented corporate governance initiatives and put institutional investors under pressure to better take into account the overall interests of their constituencies.

As a result, institutional investors have gathered and disclosed more information about the social value of their investments. This has been criticized as too small a departure from the shareholder profit maximization approach. The point is well taken, but does not sufficiently take into account institutional investor diversity. It is not obvious why business angels, venture capitalists, private equity firms, or mutual funds should be required to take into account stakeholder interests. By contrast, it can make sense to give pension fund beneficiaries a voice regarding stakeholder investments by providing them with a choice among investment options.

CHAPTER 31

NEW METRICS FOR CORPORATE GOVERNANCE
Shifting Strategies in an Aging IPO Market

ERIK P.M. VERMEULEN

1 INTRODUCTION

SEVERAL questions are currently being debated by policy makers and regulators in an increasingly integrated and globalized capital market,[1] regarding the listings and governance structures of high-tech companies. Should policy makers and regulators stimulate initial public offerings (IPOs) of high-tech companies? Is the IPO market dying? If fast-growing companies are subject to less stringent listing and governance requirements, would this result in more listings and an increase in high-tech companies? If the number of IPOs increases, will it lead us towards another bubble?

There is a general consensus that over-regulatory approaches have led to an IPO crisis around the world, and there is evidence to support this.[2] Not only do we observe a number of high-tech companies rethinking their intentions to pursue an IPO, but we also witness more and more listed companies considering delisting. Countries that maintain strict rules, or have recently introduced more stringent listing or governance requirements in order to boost market liquidity, are currently experiencing a decrease in IPO activity and an increase in back-door listings.[3] Marc Andreessen, the reputed venture capitalist and cofounder of

---

[1] See European Commission, Green Paper: Building a Capital Markets Union, COM (2015) 63 Final, Brussels, Feb. 18, 2015.

[2] See Mats Isaksson and Serdar Celik, "Who Cares? Corporate Governance in Today's Equity Markets", OECD Corporate Governance Working Papers No. 8 (2013).

[3] See Erik P.M. Vermeulen, "Rules on Backdoor Listings: A Global Survey", Indonesia-OECD Corporate Governance Policy Dialogue (2014), http://www.oecd.org/daf/ca/OECDBackgroundReportBackdoorListingsIndonesia2014.pdf; Erik P.M. Vermeulen, "Going Public: On the JOBS Act and Backdoor Listings in the High Tech Industry", Lex Research Topic in Corporate Law & Economics 2015-2 Working Paper (2015).

Netscape, went so far as to say that the IPO market is dying,[4] and that he largely blames overregulation for this.[5]

In response to the overregulatory trends, new stock markets or stock market segments have been launched. These new listing venues are an attempt to bridge the funding gap that emerged after a number of uncoordinated, corporate governance reforms introduced numerous mandatory and stringent legal requirements which significantly increased the costs of being a public company on various main markets around the world. Another regulatory answer to stimulate IPO activity has been the introduction of more flexible governance rules and regulations for growth companies. An example of this took place in the US on April 5, 2012 when the Jumpstart Our Business Startups Act (JOBS Act) introduced "Emerging Growth Company" (EGC) status.[6] Companies that avail themselves of EGC status are offered a transition, or on-ramp, period during which they are exempt from a number of regulatory requirements associated with both going and being public.

Inspired by the JOBS Act, similar initiatives are being introduced in Europe actively to promote the listing of high-tech companies and other small and medium-sized enterprises (SMEs). For example, in February 2015 the European Commission started a consultation process expected to evolve into an EU-wide Capital Markets Union.[7] The idea is that a small company's access to financing would be significantly improved in a more harmonized capital market.[8] This initiative is in line with the NYSE Euronext's establishment of EnterNext—the new pan-European marketplace designed to encourage SMEs to go public, to raise growth capital, and offer liquidity to their shareholders.[9] Policy makers in the UK see the relaxation of listing rules, particularly lower free float requirements, as the key to reversing the trend of high-tech companies being reluctant to enter the bureaucratic and overregulated world of listed companies.

This renewed focus on listings of high-tech companies is not limited to the US and Europe. In 2013 South Korea launched a third stock exchange with the aim of helping promising startup companies to raise money from institutional investors and wealthy individuals. The exchange—dubbed "Korea New Exchange" or KONEX—is considered a stepping-stone to either the more regulated main board, KOSPI, or Korea's venue for high-tech companies, KOSDAQ.[10] KONEX is Korea's response to the JOBS Act, with any companies that want to list on KONEX facing less stringent listing requirements and more flexible corporate governance rules.[11]

But is the introduction of new alternative listing venues and deregulatory measures all that is needed to reverse the decline in the number of listed companies, and thereby boost long-term economic and employment growth? Proponents of this argue that the dream of

[4] Timothy B. Lee, The IPO is Dying. Marc Andreessen Explains Why, Vox, June 26, 2014.
[5] Peter Coy, IPOs Get Bigger but Leave Less for Public Investors, Bloomberg Businessweek, July 24, 2014.
[6] See H.R. 3606.
[7] See European Commission, Green Paper, Building a Capital Markets Union, COM(2015) 63 final, Brussels, Feb. 18, 2015.
[8] See Marion Dakers, Europe Launches Blueprint for Capital Markets Union, Telegraph, Feb. 18, 2015.
[9] See Eric Forest, WFE Interview with Eric Forest, Chairman and Chief Executive Officer of Enternext (NYSE Euronext Group), (http://www.world-exchanges.org/insight/views/wfe-interview-eric-forest-chairman-and-chief-executive-officer-enternext-nyse-euronext).
[10] See Kwanwoo Jun, Korea to Launch Third Stock Exchange, Wall St. J., May 31, 2013.
[11] See Simon Mundy, South Korea Launches Third Stock Market, Fin. Times, July 1, 2013.

a successful IPO is still one of the most important drivers for innovative entrepreneurs.[12] A strong and accessible IPO market is important as it attracts venture capital and other startup and growth capital investors, who provide early-stage investors with the opportunity to exit their ventures and realize strong positive returns. IPOs are thus considered essential to sustaining a robust venture capital industry, which is necessary to accelerate innovation and entrepreneurship.

However, there is another side to the story which argues that regulatory complexity and cost alone do not explain the decline in IPOs.[13] Modifying legal and institutional measures to encourage technology companies to float is not a new phenomenon. Over the past two decades, several alternative market venues have been introduced to support the fundraising of fast-growing companies. Unfortunately, most of these have failed to deliver the success they were designed to facilitate. Furthermore, of those venues still in existence, they have been experiencing a steep and slippery downward slope with respect to the number of listed companies, their quality, or both.

Further, recent trends and developments in the venture capital industry have called into question the primacy of the IPO as an exit strategy. It has been found that in a sluggish IPO market, venture capitalists and entrepreneurs are able successfully to employ other exit routes, most notably through a lucrative trade sale to a strategic party.[14] These trade sales (as well as secondary sales) have even become the preferred exit option for many investors in growth companies. In contrast to an IPO exit, a trade sale offers immediate liquidity without onerous lockup periods, disclosure requirements, and obligations for venture capitalists to maintain board seats.

Perhaps the most important factor in the decline of IPOs is that an increasing number of technology companies believe that it is in their best interest to remain private as long as possible. It is no longer necessary to go public to get access to large investments, high profiles, and liquidity. For example, Uber, the Internet/app-based transportation/taxi network, was able to close a financing round of $1.2 billion at a $17 billion pre-money valuation in June 2014. Amongst its investors are not only reputable venture capitalists and private equity funds, but also institutional investors (such as mutual funds and hedge funds) that usually limit their investment scope to public companies.[15] These privately held technology companies, such as Uber, usually provide liquidity to shareholders (employees and early investors) by offering regular access to buyback/liquidity programs. However, it should be noted here that these programs are typically viewed as a second-best "liquidity" solution due to nontransparent valuation practices.[16]

[12] See Jose Miguel Mendoza & Erik P.M. Vermeulen, Towards a New Financial Market Segment for High Tech Companies in Europe, in European Financial Market in Transition, 383–420 (Hanne S. Birkmose, Mette Neville & Karsten Engsig Sørensen eds., 2011).

[13] See Jay R. Ritter, Re-Energizing the IPO Market, in Restructuring to Speed Economic Recovery (Martin Bailey & Richard Herring, 2013).

[14] See Joseph A. McCahery & Erik P.M. Vermeulen, "Venture Capital, IPOs and Corporate Innovation", 15 fsrforum 6 (2013).

[15] See Steve Kovach, Uber Raises $1.2 Billion at $17 Billion Valuation, BusinessInsider, June 6, 2014.

[16] Michael Carney, DFJ Led a $30M Shareholder Liquidity Round that Valued SpaceX Between $4–5 Billion, Pandodaily, Mar. 20, 2013; Dan Primack, Uber Plays Hardball with Early Shareholders, Fortune, June 20, 2014.

There is a more critical issue with the increasing VC investments in high-growth private companies. Companies that attract enormous investments tend to have more excessive spending behavior. This trend has led prominent investors to believe that we are heading towards yet another tech bubble, worse than the dot.com bubble of the late 1990s.[17] One interesting and possible solution to this is to make IPO markets more accessible to growth companies by implementing flexible listing and governance rules. However, besides the question of whether more flexibility will eventually show the desired results, corporate governance experts argue that introducing more flexible rules is a "corporate governance" scandal waiting to happen. Although it is difficult to predict the timing of the bubble, the first signs may already be visible in the biotech market.

How can we solve this vicious circle? With the recent globalization trends in the financing and organization of high-growth (including high-tech) companies, now is a good time to take stock of the inner workings of IPOs as funding rounds and exit strategies, as well as the rules and regulations that apply to listed companies that are in the growth stages of their development. This chapter addresses these issues by offering a glimpse into the past, present, and future listings of high-growth companies. It shows that although the first empirical results indicated that the special IPO rules and regulations were not persuasive enough to lure a large number of high-tech companies to the stock market, as occurred in the late 1990s, prior to the burst of the dot.com bubble in 1999 to 2001, the policy makers' efforts were not completely in vain.

The deregulatory efforts have not only made the public market more accessible to high-tech companies, they can also be viewed as a first step towards redirecting corporate governance discussions away from merely focussing on increasing shareholders' short-term value to a more collaborative focus on stimulating "long-term" entrepreneurship, innovation, and value creation inside both nonlisted and listed companies. This view is supported by the emergence of a new establishment of active investors, such as venture capitalists, private equity funds, or hedge funds that see themselves as allies of corporate management and executives. They have an increasing willingness to downplay stringent corporate governance norms and practices that have only created an apparently "unbridgeable divide" between shareholders and management.[18] They believe that the future of corporate governance is about sharing nonfinancial and financial information and having open discussions with the companies' stakeholders. We call this trend: collaborative corporate governance.

2 THE PAST: THE EMERGENCE OF ALTERNATIVE STOCK MARKETS

Discussions about the design of stock markets that are ideally suited to high-tech growth companies are not new. Under substantial pressure to create a robust entrepreneurial climate, policy makers and regulators put a significant focus on increasing the financing opportunities for these companies while at the same time offering liquidity to investors. This has led to a

---

[17] See Marc Cuban, Why This Tech Bubble is Worse than the Tech Bubble of 2000, Blog Maverick, Mar. 4, 2015.

[18] See Guhan Subramanian, "Corporate Governance 2.0", 93 Harv. Bus. Rev. 96 (2015).

global increase in market venues designed to facilitate and stimulate venture-capital-backed IPOs over the past two decades. These markets initially sought to attract high-tech firms in their jurisdictions by mimicking the success of the NASDAQ model in the US. In an attempt to replicate NASDAQ's success, several stock exchanges in Europe launched high-tech market segments during the 1990s. EASDAQ, initially established as a pan-European stock market in 1996, was among one of the first venues to emerge in Europe. The NASDAQ model also inspired a number of national initiatives, such as the Neuer Markt sponsored by the Deutsche Börse, the Paris Stock Exchange's Nouveau Marché, the Italian Nuovo Mercato, and the Euro NM Brussels.

These "NASDAQ clones" proved not to be sustainable and were only able temporarily to support European high-tech companies. There were a few reasons for this. First, since these "new" markets mainly focused on Internet companies, the burst of the dot.com bubble logically ushered in their demise. Second, with a lack of institutional investments these markets were extremely vulnerable to economic downturns. There was one exception: the Alternative Investment Market (AIM), a listing segment operated by the London Stock Exchange in the UK.[19] The survival of AIM can be attributed to a series of factors that range from London's prominence as a financial center to changes in the IPO market in the US.

The most important factor behind AIM's good fortune is perhaps its regulatory model, which strikes a balance between the level of protection afforded to investors and the costs borne by the listed high-tech companies. Companies that trade their shares on AIM benefit from flexible rules that set low hurdles for listings and fewer ongoing principle-based obligations compared to other stock exchanges. In the absence of mandatory and stringent requirements, AIM introduced the Nominated Advisers (NOMADs), typically registered investment banks, assisting companies with the listing process and performing the role of "regulators," overseeing the admission process. This principle-based scheme contributed largely to the venue's reputation and continued success in the years leading up to the most recent financial crisis (Figure 31.1).

Unsurprisingly, US high-tech companies also started to use AIM to offer an exit mechanism for their investors. The migration of US firms gained momentum after the promulgation of strict and stringent corporate governance regulations and mandates, such as the Sarbanes–Oxley Act (SOX) in 2002, which imposed stiff legal requirements on listed companies, particularly with regard to their auditing and internal control processes. A study published in 2008 included compelling evidence showing that SOX had disproportionately affected small US publicly held firms.[20] Because, as already mentioned, significant costs were imposed on companies that intended to float their shares on NASDAQ, AIM quickly became an attractive IPO alternative. With US firms increasingly getting quoted on AIM, the reputation of the venue enhanced rapidly and it wasn't long before policy makers around the world started to adopt the AIM model.[21] Tokyo AIM (currently a Tokyo Pro Market), AIM

---

[19] See Jose Miguel Mendoza, "Securities Regulation in Low-Tier Listing Venues: The Rise of the Alternative Investment Market", 13 Fordham J. Corp. & Fin. L. 257 (2008).

[20] See Ehud Kamar, Pinar Karaca-Mandic & Eric L. Talley, "Going-Private Decisions and the Sarbanes–Oxley Act of 2002: A Cross-Country Analysis", 25 J. L. Econ. & Org. 107 (2009).

[21] AIM's thriving success and distinctive features inspired the creation of the Irish Enterprise Exchange in April 2005, with Euronext and Deutsche Börse quickly following suit by launching the Alternext market and the Entry Standard segment, respectively.

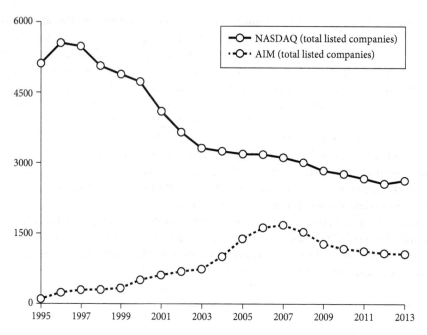

FIGURE 31.1 Listed Companies at NASDAQ (US) and AIM (UK) 1995–2013.

Source: NASDAQ, London Stock Exchange.

Italia, First North in Scandinavia, NYSE-Alternext in Belgium, France, the Netherlands, and Portugal, and Entry Standard in Germany are all examples of this.

So far, the performance of the AIM-type stock markets has fallen short of expectations, which is hardly surprising in light of the financial crisis that hit the global economy at the end of the previous decade. However, a closer look at the empirical evidence of the AIM-type stock market initiatives raises questions as to whether the mere introduction of flexible and accessible listing venues is sufficient to stimulate IPO activity. Looking at venture-backed listings in Europe, from 2009 to 2014, we can see that some countries attract far more venture capital-backed IPOs than other countries even though they offer similar regulatory regimes. Why is that? One credible explanation is that specific stock markets attract more companies because special "IPO ecosystems" (i.e., networks of underwriters, lawyers, and other advisors) have evolved around them. For instance, NYSE Alternext, an alternative stock market for high-tech companies in Europe, has venues in Amsterdam, Brussels, Lisbon, and Paris. NYSE Alternext is able to attract and retain issuers, with admissions outweighing de-listings year on year. In October 2014 alone, 205 companies were listed on NYSE Alternext. The differences in IPO ecosystems explain why 94% of the firms that enter NYSE Alternext are listed in Paris, with only 5% in Brussels and 1% in Amsterdam and Lisbon.

Clearly, regulatory and network advantages do not offer a guarantee for continuing success. The AIM market recently witnessed an exodus of companies. From its peak of 1694 companies in 2007, AIM has shrunk to 1087 companies in December 2013. There are several reasons for this. First, since it is generally paramount for companies that recently floated their shares to generate trading volume, it is not surprising that high-tech companies increasingly prefer to list on a main market (instead of AIM-type markets) (see Figure 31.2).

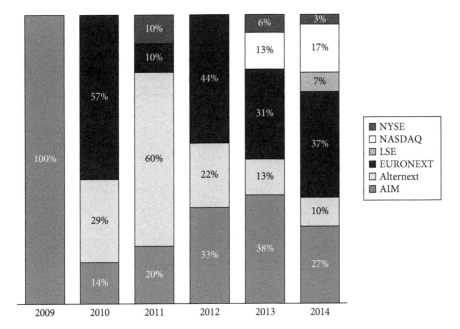

FIGURE 31.2 Venture Capital Backed IPOs on Alternative versus Main Markets in Europe (2009–2014).

Source: PitchBook.

These companies usually lack a track record; they trade less often and in smaller volume.[22] This entails that their stock price is particularly responsive to buying and selling pressures, which, in turn, increases the cost of capital. Low trading volume is often the explanation for a depressed stock price and negative IPO performance. Thus, there are strong incentives for "young" IPO companies to list on the main board of a capital market, which increases the chances of generating trading volume and attracting the interest of equity research analysts.

The second reason for shrinking markets is that the best performing high-tech companies prefer to extend their "private company" status for as long as possible before making the "irreversible" decision to go public. The staying private trend is apparent in both the US and Europe. Figure 31.3 shows that the time that elapses between the inception of a firm, the first involvement of venture capital funds, and their eventual exit has significantly increased in recent years in the US. The median time between the initial equity funding and the IPO in 2000 was approximately three years, compared with the seven years for companies pursuing an IPO in 2014.

3 THE PRESENT: THE AGING IPO MARKET

We ended the previous section with the observation that investors and entrepreneurs generally believe that IPOs are not in their best interest. In 2012, the Economist even proclaimed

---

[22] See Silvio Vismara, Stefano Paleari & Jay R. Ritter, "Europe's Second Markets for Small Companies", 18 Eur. Fin. Mgmt. 352 (2012).

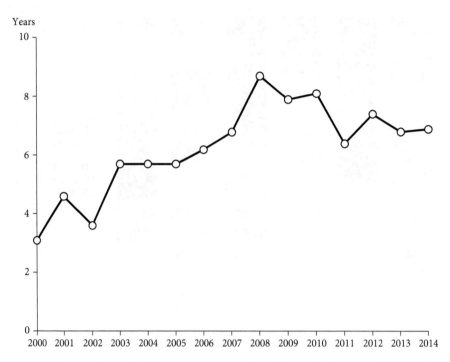

FIGURE 31.3 Median Time from Initial Equity Funding to IPO in the US (2000–2014).

Source: Dow Jones VentureSource.

that since high-tech companies remain private as long as possible, "going public" has lost its glamour, resulting in the public corporation becoming an endangered species.[23] The article refers to Michael Jensen's study of 1989, "The Eclipse of the Public Corporation," which supports the view that privately owned companies actually outperform their publicly listed counterparts.[24] However, in the same issue of the Economist, Schumpeter's column recognized that there is a symbiotic relationship between "being private" and "going public," suggesting that public companies will not be extinct in the near future. The argument is simple and straightforward: An IPO enables the entrepreneurs and investors to realize the gains in market value related to the growth that the best performing companies have realized in their "private" phase.

We have already mentioned that it is widely believed that entrepreneurs would not put so much effort into the establishment and development of their startups if they did not dream of a successful IPO. The IPO is allegedly also crucial for venture capitalists that invest in these entrepreneurs. To see this, it is important to understand the traditional venture capital model.[25] It typically starts with the creation of funds that raise capital from both institutional and private investors that are interested in backing innovative, often high-tech, companies. The venture capital funds select promising startups, which they nurture and support by

---

[23] See The Endangered Public Company. The Big Engine that Couldn't, Economist, May 19, 2012.
[24] See Michael C. Jensen, Eclipse of the Public Corporation, Harv. Bus. Rev. Sept.–Oct. (1989).
[25] See Paul Gompers & Josh Lerner, The Venture Capital Cycle (1999).

contributing money and services that these companies need to reach the next stage in their development. Ideally, this continues until the moment that the venture capital investors decide to exit their portfolio companies and reap the fruits of their investments. A significant part of the returns are then distributed back to the initial investors.

It is here that entrepreneurs and investors encounter some serious implications in the current IPO markets. When the best performing companies "finally" decide to pursue an IPO to find capital that is needed successfully to grow the company, most of the gains in the companies' market value have already been allocated to pre-IPO investors.[26] Consider the mere 0.6% first-day "pop" (or first-day increase in stock price) that Facebook realized during its IPO. Clearly, investors expected a "healthy" pop in the range of 20–30%,[27] which would have been in line with the average first-day increase of 27.9% (based on an empirical analysis of 2634 venture-capital-backed IPOs from 1980 to 2010).[28] The significant decrease in the first-day pop could largely be attributed to high-tech companies' decisions to remain private longer, allowing pre-IPO investors to appropriate most of the gains from the increase in the value of the company. This is of course different when a company's IPO is intentionally priced under market value, as was allegedly the case in the Alibaba IPO in 2014.[29] This strategy resulted in a 38% gain after the first day of trading.

When discussing this issue with investors, it is increasingly emphasized that much bigger cash on cash and IRR return can be realized while investing in early-stage and later-stage private opportunities than in the public markets. Investors mention several reasons for this. For instance, the supply–demand dynamics are much better for investors in private companies. That is to say, in public markets investors often have the feeling that the entire globe is their competitor when it comes to investing in a good deal. Private investors practically have a "monopoly," allowing them to select and invest in the best opportunities. Andrew Romans of Rubicon Ventures and author of the Entrepreneurial Bible to Venture Capital made an interesting observation:

> At a high level consider this. Most publicly traded companies have many bulge bracket investment banking analyst teams tracking them. Information is disseminated in real time via Bloomberg terminals, the Internet and mobile phones. By the time I meet a CEO and learn some new information that same information is available to the global market of traders and any arbitrage opportunity exists for less than a second.

Investors in the pre-IPO market can thus capitalize on "inside information".

Perhaps more importantly, making "hands-on" investments in private companies gives the investors more control over their own destiny. Simply put, they usually track approximately 1000 deals in their deal flow funnel each month, but invest in for instance "only" 10 new companies per year. This allows them to divert their time and resources to the very best ones. First, they use their proprietary networks for due diligence and

[26] See Peter Coy, IPOs Get Bigger but Leave Less for Public Investors, Bloomberg Businessweek, July 24, 2014.

[27] See Shayndi Raice, Ryan Dezember & Jacob Bunge, Facebook's IPO Sputters, Wall St. J., May 18, 2012.

[28] See Jay R. Ritter, Initial Public Offerings: Updated Statistics, 1 Sept. 2014. See also Jeremy Ashkenas, Matthew Bloch, Shan Carter & Amanda Cox, The Facebook Offering: How it Compares, N.Y. Times, May 17, 2012.

[29] See John Kell, Alibaba Shares End First Day of Trading with 38% Gain, Fortune, Sept. 19, 2014.

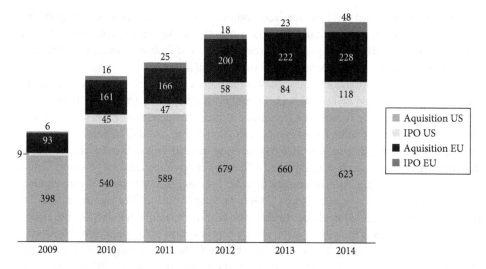

FIGURE 31.4 Venture-Capital-Backed Exits in the US and Europe.

Source: PitchBook.

separating the good investments from the bad. They then mobilize their proprietary network to add value to their portfolio companies. The deal selection process based on private information together with the personal "magic" touch and "value add" explains why the better investors are able to achieve growth in private companies that can never be realized in publicly traded equities (where they cannot wave their magic wand over the deal).[30]

The changing nature of the IPO market has also changed the way high-tech companies, and their founders and investors, deal with funding and liquidity strategies. For instance, even though Figure 31.4 shows a revival of the global IPO market starting in 2010, it seems hard to believe that "going public" will recover its traditional allure. Figure 31.4 also shows that venture capitalists tend to induce entrepreneurs to sell their companies to strategic investors.[31] They have good reasons to do this. In order to increase the track record of their funds and attract the interest of institutional and other investors, venture capitalists realized that a focus on an acquisition by a strategic corporate investor would significantly increase the probability of a successful exit. It is thus not surprising that the ratio of IPOs to trade sales increased from approximately 1:1 in 1997 to 1:7 in 2013 in the US. In Europe, this ratio was 1:10 in 2013.

There are other advantages to pursuing a trade sale. The median time to liquidity is shorter in the event of a trade sale (compared to an IPO), which took six years in 2014 (compared to seven years in the event of an IPO). The timing advantage may be significant for well-established venture capitalists and perhaps even the founders of startup companies. Employees (who are usually awarded with restricted shares and stock

---

[30] Interview with Andrew Romans, partner of Rubicon Ventures.

[31] See Brian J. Broughman & Jesse M. Fried, "Carrots & Sticks: How VCs Induce Entrepreneurial Teams to Sell Startups", 98 Cornell L. Rev. 1319 (2013).

options) and early-stage investors (particularly family, friends, and other early-stage risk capital providers) may have short-term views when it comes to liquidity issues. For them, the extended exit—and its delayed cash-out event—arguably creates a liquidity gap that could potentially discourage them to work for and with high-tech startup companies. The availability of an exit strategy is of such importance that it can make or break the commitment of prospective employees to contribute human capital resources to a fledgling enterprise. In 2008 when there was such a lack of liquidity options for holders of private shares, a former Facebook employee approached SecondMarket, a company that offered a marketplace for classes of stock in private companies and assets of defunct companies that could not be sold on the public market, to assist him in selling his stock options.[32]

There is, of course, little doubt that the best performing and most promising companies, as well as companies in highly capital-intensive sectors, will eventually pursue an IPO to find the capital needed to achieve stellar growth and success. What is remarkable, however, is that even if venture capitalists and high-tech entrepreneurs decide to float the company's shares on a stock exchange, the IPO can be completed with a relatively low median free float of 23% in the US and 27% in Europe, indicating that they can gradually give up their "private company" status (this is also due to onerous lock-up provisions which prevent venture capitalists from pursuing an immediate exit).[33] More generally, the pace with which the companies are willing to give up this status depends on the hype surrounding the IPO. If the IPO has attracted significant media and (retail) investors' attention, the technology entrepreneurs/founders in consultation with their lead venture capitalists tend to structure their future listed companies in such a way that investors and board members are not able to unseat them (see Figure 31.5).[34]

One example is LinkedIn, which went public on May 18, 2011 in the US. Similar to other social media companies, LinkedIn introduced dual class shares. Following its IPO, co-founder Reid Hoffman, together with the key venture capital investors, held Class B shares, which gave them 10 votes per share. Class A shares, with one vote a piece, were offered to the public. The outcome of this was that Hoffman, who is also the chairman of LinkedIn's board (and part-time partner in a venture capital firm in Silicon Valley), held (directly or indirectly) a minority stake of approximately 16.3% of the outstanding Class A and Class B shares, but controlled approximately 61.5% of the voting power on December 31, 2012. Indeed, Reid Hoffman's Class B shares, which gave him controlling voting power in excess of the cashflow rights attached to the minority stake, allowed him to resist immediate pressures from public market investors to produce short-term results and forgo investments in new products and services.

---

[32] See Kevin Kelleher, The SEC's Challenge in the Secondary Market, CNNMoney.com, Jan. 4, 2011.

[33] See Joseph A. McCahery, Erik P.M. Vermeulen & Masato Hisatake, "The Present and Future of Corporate Governance: Re-Examining the Role of the Board of Directors and Investor Relations in Listed Companies", 10 Eur. Comp. & Fin. L. Rev. 117 (2013).

[34] Joseph A. McCahery & Erik P.M. Vermeulen, "Business Growth and Firm Value Creation: The Ignored Third Dimension of Corporate Governance", 2 Journal of Self-Governance and Management Economics 69 (2014).

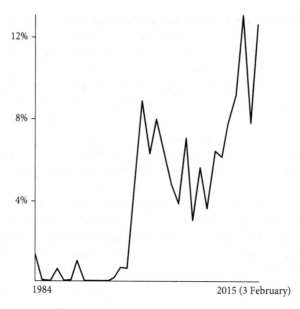

FIGURE 31.5 Percentage of US Companies that Went Public with Dual Class Shares.

Source: Bloomberg.

3.1 The Emergence of Robust pre-IPO (Private Secondary) Markets

It did not take long for clever entrepreneurs in the US to create and further develop on-line platforms to better facilitate pre-IPO trading in the shares of nonlisted venture-capital-backed firms. They were able to avoid compliance with strict securities rules and regulations by limiting access to trading to "accredited investors" or those deemed sufficiently wealthy. Unsurprisingly, these trading platforms fast became a critical component of the venture capital ecosystem, as they helped bridge the liquidity gap in the venture capital model. Perhaps the most well known online platform for shares in private firms was the New York-based SecondMarket, which rose to prominence after becoming the main platform for "trading" shares in Facebook. The sellers of shares traded through SecondMarket were mainly the former and current employees of firms, with founders also unloading their stock from time to time. The main competitor of SecondMarket was California-based SharesPost. In close resemblance to SecondMarket, SharesPost started operations in 2009 with the specific aim of dealing with "the lack of market liquidity for private company shares."[35]

The online platforms as an outlet for trading shares in private companies have never been free from controversy.[36] Concerns have been raised about the lack of sufficient

---

[35] See Jose Miguel Mendoza & Erik P.M. Vermeulen, "The New Venture Capital Cycle (part I): The Importance of Private Secondary Market Liquidity", Lex Research Topics in Corporate Law & Economics Working Paper No. 1/2011.

[36] See Elizabeth Pollman, "Information Issues on Wall Street 2.0", 161 U. Pa. L. Rev. 179 (2012); Adam Pritchard, "Revisiting 'Truth in Securities' Revisited: Abolishing IPOs and Harnessing Private Markets in the Public Good", 36 Seattle U. L. Rev. 999 (2013).

information regarding the companies whose stock "traded" through these platforms. As private firms have generally no obligation to make public disclosures, there has always been some doubt about the accuracy of the valuations used to determine the price of transactions in SecondMarket and SharesPost. Looking again at Facebook, in January 2010 their shares initially traded on SecondMarket at an implied valuation of $14.70 billion (and a share price of $6.39). By December 2010, following transactions carried out on SharesPost, Facebook's value reached $56 billion. SecondMarket transactions, executed just prior to the IPO, implied a valuation of $90.13 billion (and a share price of $36.05) in March 2012, an increase of more than six times in a little more than two years.

The IPO was priced at $38 per share, at which price Facebook raised an amount of $16 billion. The disappointing first-day pop and deteriorating "IPO performances" (Facebook's 30-day, 60-day, and six-month IPO performances were 21%, 26%, and 38%, respectively) fueled the general perception that Facebook was overvalued at the time of its decision to go public. The fact that the trading community was growing and started to include more and more investors (such as the "DLD"—doctors, lawyers, and dentists investors) without the necessary knowledge and expertise correctly to interpret the available information about the valuation of fast-growing startup companies has arguably created upward price pressures that significantly inflated the valuations of the private companies "listed" on these platforms.[37]

Naturally, the post-IPO fall in the price of Facebook shares quickly dampened the excitement for the private startup stock platforms. That is not to say that we have witnessed the end of these platforms, as was predicted in the wake of the Facebook IPO.[38] In fact, online platforms, such as SecondMarket and SharesPost, continue to play an important role in offering employees and investors a possibility to cash out of their "illiquid" positions in VC-backed companies that could still be years away from a trade sale or exit—but the model has changed. Prior to Facebook's IPO, the shareholders auctioned their securities directly to any buyer, under terms that were acceptable to both parties, and sometimes without the company's involvement and/or approval. The difference with the current post-Facebook IPO model is that the companies themselves employ SecondMarket-type platforms to give existing shareholders the possibility of exit. The companies are thus largely in control of the transactions—they select the buyers and set the price of the securities.

Over the years, trading in stock of private companies has grown rapidly and is currently doubling the volume of trades that took place in the pre-Facebook IPO period of 2011/2012, according to private equity research firm NYPPEX.[39] This shouldn't be all that unexpected for those attuned to the venture capital industry. Hedge funds, mutual funds, and other institutional investors are increasingly pushed to make later stage investments in the venture capital asset class since, as we have seen, the timing of the "IPO pop" has slowly but surely shifted to before the IPO, leaving less capital on the table for the investors in public markets.[40] Thus it makes sense for these institutional investors to buy into high-tech companies by acquiring

[37] See Tomio Geron, Secondary Chances: Is There Any Life Left in Pre-IPO Shares?, Forbes, Oct. 22, 2012.

[38] See Evelyn M. Rusli & Peter Lattman, Losing a Goose that Laid the Golden Egg, N.Y. Times, Feb. 2, 2012.

[39] See Jen Wieczner, Investing in Private Startups Is A Hot Trend. But, Sorry, You're Not Invited, Fortune, Aug. 14, 2014.

[40] See Hedge Funds and Mutual Funds Increase Investment Pace to Private Tech Companies, CBInsights, Jan. 7, 2014.

shares held by founders, early investors, and employees on the pre-IPO (secondary) market.[41]

With hedge funds and mutual funds gaining steam in the industry, there is however, sufficient evidence to suggest that venture capitalists do not plan on ignoring the new investors. Venture capitalists have more capital reserved for their pro-rata investment opportunities in the later financing rounds. The additional capital creates the opportunity to continue financing winners into later rounds (without running the risk of being significantly diluted when hedge funds and mutual funds bring out the big guns). We see "early-stage" or "life-cycle" venture capitalists setting up separate later-stage funds to "capture the pro-rata," as it was so clearly dubbed by Mark Susters of venture capital firm Upfront Ventures. The $225 million Foundry Group Select Fund and the $200 million Greycroft Growth fund are recent examples of special later stage funds.[42]

As public market investors are entering the private market and venture capitalists are being pushed to later rounds of financing, high-tech companies have even more reason to stay private longer. The result is larger investments in bigger and more mature companies with higher valuations. Indeed, the Wall Street Journal, in collaboration with data provider Dow Jones VentureSource, found that more and more venture-capital-backed companies with a valuation of $1 billion or more decide to remain private. This trend is not only happening in the US, but also in other parts of the world. As reflected in Figure 31.6, at least 73 private companies were valued at $1 billion or more in February 2015. In January 2014, this number was 41. The number of "exceptional" startup companies that were still private in 2013 was 28. During the dot.com boom in 2000, "only" 10 companies with a valuation of $1 billion or more had the status of being "privately-owned," the record number before the 2007–2008 financial crises.[43]

Dow Jones VentureSource data also reveal that the median amount that was raised prior to going public increased from $57.3 million in 2006 to $89.6 million in 2014. Another data provider, PitchBook, shows that the median late stage (series D) valuations jumped from $67.9 in 2005 to $190.6 in the first 6 months of 2014. What is even more remarkable is that the 10 largest amounts of venture capital in high-tech companies in 2014 are higher than the capital raised in the 10 largest IPOs in the US (see Figure 31.7). This will become more imminent as US venture capital investors are taking a more global view as they seek to benefit from global investment opportunities.[44] So what is the impact of these venture capital mega rounds and valuations on the IPO market? There are two possible answers: (1) Mega rounds will eventually make the IPO market irrelevant or (2) mega rounds still need an active IPO market in order to enable later-stage investors to realize the required liquidity multiples (and provide companies with a realistic option to go public). The latter answer appears to be correct (as was previously stated by the Economist in 2012),[45] which brings us to the introduction of the JOBS Act in the US.

---

[41] See Yuliya Chernova, Secondary Market Jumps for Shares in Billion-Dollar Startups, Wall St. J., Oct. 31, 2014.

[42] See Brian Park, "We Know the Savior . . . and It Is Them: The Future Face(s) of Venture Capital", Working Paper (2015).

[43] See Yuliya Chernova, More Big Venture-Backed Companies Shun IPOs, for Now, Wall St. J., Oct. 8, 2014.

[44] See Toshiyuki Kono, Brian Park & Erik P.M. Vermeulen, " 'Virtual Ecosystems': Unlocking Meaningful Innovation and Entrepreneurship in Your Community", Working Paper (2015).

[45] See Tomasz Tunguz, Are Tech IPOs Dying?, tomtunguz.com, Aug. 15, 2014.

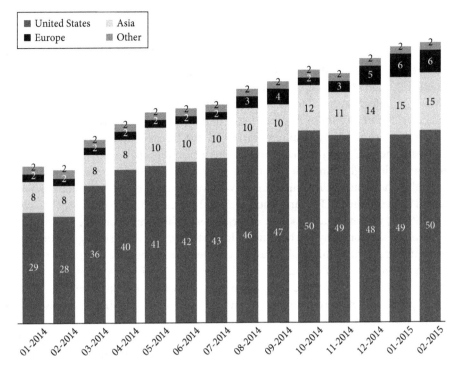

FIGURE 31.6 Private Companies Valued at $1 Billion or More.

Source: Wall Street Journal, Dow Jones VentureSource.

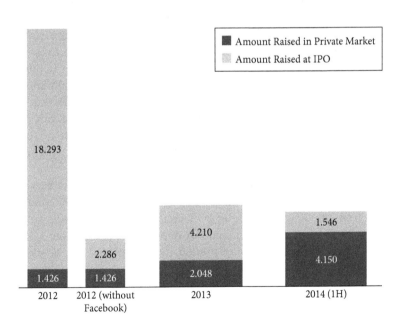

FIGURE 31.7 Top 10 Capital Raisings by High-Tech Companies in Public and Private Markets.

Source: qz.com, Deutsche Bank, Factset, Crunchbase.

3.2 The JOBS Act

The JOBS Act, viewed by some as a mishmash of several different initiatives,[46] illustrates the potential of a combined focus on both pre-IPO and IPO markets in successfully accommodating high-tech companies at different stages of their respective life cycles. The JOBS Act offers several benefits to high-tech companies in the pre-IPO and post-IPO periods. Before the JOBS Act was enacted, once a private company in the US had surpassed a threshold of $10 million assets and 500 shareholders of record, it had to register with the SEC and produce periodic disclosure reports under the US Securities Regulations. Although companies that had reached that threshold were not required to go public, the costs of disseminating private information about their activities were presumed to be significant. Preparing quarterly and annual reports requires the assistance of accountants, external auditors, and other professionals, whose service fees will have to be borne by the company. Perhaps more importantly, revealing strategic information about the firm's activities might also benefit competitors or increase transaction costs in the context of the company's relations with third parties. The JOBS Act has expanded the number of shareholders a private company may have from 500 to 2000, making it easier (and cheaper) for them to remain private, and thus extend the pre-IPO stage, as most of them currently prefer.

The JOBS Act also offers the possibility of a company to qualify as an "emerging growth company" (EGC) if its total annual gross revenues are less than $1 billion for the most recently ended fiscal year. The EGC label offers several benefits to high-growth companies in the pre-IPO and post-IPO stages. In the pre-IPO stage, an EGC will only be required to include two years—instead of the usually required three years—of audited statements in its IPO registration. An EGC can also elect to provide the market with reduced executive compensation disclosures (i.e., EGCs are allowed to disclose compensation statements for only the Chief Executive Officer and the two other highest-paid executives, while non-EGCs must provide five executive compensation disclosures). More importantly, the JOBS Act provides these companies with the possibility to confidentially submit a draft of its IPO registration statement for review to the SEC. The special status thus introduces "testing-the-waters" provisions, which also allow EGCs to communicate with professional investors (qualified institutional buyers or institutional accredited investors) to determine investors' interest in the company prior to or following the date of the IPO registration statement.[47]

The JOBS Act's "on-ramp" provisions grant temporary (five years or less if certain growth conditions are met) but important reliefs in the post-IPO period. For example, EGCs are exempted from the obligations under SOX Section 404(b) to provide an auditor attestation of internal control. Furthermore, the Act excludes EGCs from (1) complying with the full range of executive compensation disclosures and (2) say-on-pay votes

---

[46] See Dan Primack, JOBS Act: The Good, The Bad, The Irrelevant, Fortune, Mar. 22, 2012.

[47] See Mike Evans, What's in an IPO? My Experiences Through Grubhub's Offering from Start to Finish, mevans314.com, Feb. 9, 2015.

on executive compensation. Finally, EGCs need not comply with any new or revised accounting standards until the date on which private companies are required to apply these standards to their organization.

The JOBS Act is working. As we discussed in the previous section, venture-capital-backed companies do prefer to stay private longer, but the JOBS Act has contributed to a surge in IPOs within the US.[48] In 2014, 118 venture-capital-backed companies floated their shares, compared to 84 companies in 2013. In particular, a number of companies active in either the biotechnology or the medical sector completed their IPOs as an "emerging growth company."[49] This trend is reflected in Figure 31.8. The JOBS Act is also (at least partly) responsible for the increase in foreign companies "going public" on a stock exchange in the US.[50]

To see the success of the JOBS Act, consider the significant increase in the number of EGCs that have pursued a listing after having used the option confidentially to file their registration statements. It has already been argued that confidential filings have become the new normal for companies that consider going public.[51] According to data provider Renaissance Capital, approximately 70-80% of the 131 IPO companies (including non-venture-capital-backed companies) in 2013 availed themselves of the JOBS Act's confidential filing provision. Accounting firm Ernst & Young estimates that approximately 85% of the EGCs that have filed IPO registration statements in the period April 2012 to June 2014 submitted the statements confidentially.[52]

These observations are not surprising since high-tech companies value having control over the timing of the IPO (provided by a confidential filing) more than a possible discount in the stock price due to the reduced disclosure and reporting requirements of EGCs.[53] Corporate governance experts, however, have a different view. They acknowledge that the drawbacks may not be immediately apparent, but when something goes wrong (and they argue that it always does in business)[54] "then the investors are going to complain that the regulators screwed it up."[55] So who is right?

---

[48] See Catherine Clifford & Steve Case: JOBS Act Is Working, But D.C. Still Needs to Do More for Entrepreneurs, Entrepreneur, Apr. 4, 2014.

[49] See Michael Dambra, Laura Casares Field & Matthew T. Gustafson, "The JOBS Act and IPO Volume: Evidence that Disclosure Costs Affect the IPO Decision", 116 J. Fin. Econ. 121 (2015).

[50] See Ze'-ev Eiger, The Rise of Foreign Issuer IPOs, MoFo Jumpstarter, Aug. 29, 2014.

[51] See David Gelles & Michael J. De La Merced, "The New Normal" for Tech Companies and Others: The Stealth I.P.O., N.Y. Times, Feb. 9, 2014.

[52] See Ernst & Young, The JOBS Act: 2014 Mid-Year Update, An Overview of Implementation and An Analysis of Emerging Growth Company Trends (2014).

[53] See Michael Rapoport, Investment Bankers See JOBS Act Helping, and Hurting, IPOs, Wall St. J., July 10, 2012. See also Mariah Summers, How Confidential Filing and the JOBS Act Is Changing the IPO Game, BuzzFeedNEWS, Sept. 27, 2013.

[54] See Jeffrey Green & Carol Hymowitz, Let Them Eat Burgers: Investors Said They Wanted Good Governance. Then Sake Shack Came Along, Bloomberg Businessweek, Feb. 5, 2015.

[55] See Neil Amato, Lawmakers Reflect on Sarbanes–Oxley's Effect on Corporate Culture, Journal of Accountancy, July 30, 2012 (citing former US Sen. Paul Sarbanes and former US Rep. Michael Oxley).

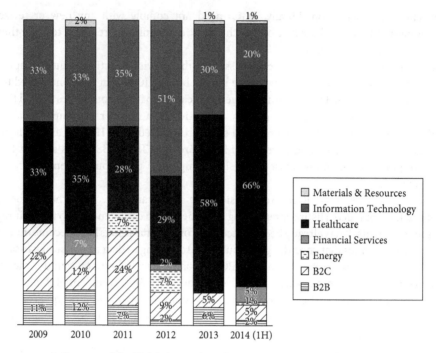

FIGURE 31.8 Impact of the JOBS Act in the US.

Source: PitchBook.

4 THE FUTURE: COLLABORATIVE CORPORATE GOVERNANCE

4.1 Another Bubble?

The National Venture Capital Association, the Biotechnology Industry Organization, the New York Stock Exchange, NASDAQ, and the US Chamber of Commerce all welcomed the JOBS Act.[56] However, not everyone was convinced of the potential benefits of the Act.[57] When the JOBS act was introduced in 2012, 55% of the investment bank executives who participated in a survey conducted by accounting and consulting firm BDO USA LLP believed that the JOBS Act was likely to produce accounting scandals, market manipulation, and fraud.[58] In particular, the relaxed accounting standards under the JOBS Act raised concerns among academics and practitioners.[59]

---

[56] See Sarah Johnson, Same Bump, Different Year, CFO Magazine, May 15, 2012.
[57] See Travis Waldron, Former SEC Official Slams House JOBS Act: "It Won't Create Jobs, But It Will Simplify Fraud", ThinkProgress, Mar. 15, 2012.
[58] See Olivia Oran, Bankers Fear Jobs Act Could Spur Scandals—Study, Reuters, July 10, 2012.
[59] See Justin P. Grant, JOBS Act Would Ease Sarbox Standard, but Might Pave Way for Fraud, CFO, Mar. 26, 2012.

In the two years since the enactment of the JOBS Act, concerns have changed. The benefits of the Act for the "lower valued" companies (those that had no or relatively little media attention before their IPOs) are now widely accepted. Current concerns focus on the billion-dollar companies that are also allowed to use the reduced disclosure requirements for EGCs for when they, eventually, decide to go public. In the media, Twitter's high-profile IPO is an example of the cost and problems of allowing prominent companies to test the water, buy time, and, most worrisomely, show less paperwork before they float their shares to the public.[60] Twitter's exceptional first-day pop of 73% (trading at $44.90 per share from its $26 IPO price) was among the 20 highest of any listing in the US in 2013.[61] The share price gradually increased 92% during the first three months of trading, but then tumbled to $50.05 per share (dropping 24%) after their first earnings report was disclosed.[62]

Twitter's sharp fall in the stock exchange worked exactly as the critics of the JOBS Act had predicted.[63] They argue that less disclosure and less transparency had the perverse effect of increasing speculation about Twitter's performance. They allocated most of the blame for the drop in share price following the disclosure of the earnings report on the JOBS Act.[64] High valuations of late-stage private companies involving public market investors and the subsequent hype building up to the eventual IPO arguably contributed to Twitter's stock price decline. Certainly, there is anecdotal evidence that suggests that the increase in IPOs, the massive valuations (compared to the revenues) of pre-IPO-stage high-tech companies and the confidential filing process under the JOBS Act (which allegedly explains some of the Twitter-like first-day IPO pops) would eventually lead to a bubble and a subsequent burst, similar to the dot.com bubble of the late 1990s.[65]

It is questionable whether or not full compliance with non-EGC disclosure standards and requirements would have completely avoided Twitter's shaky stock price. The giant sums of capital that private companies are able to raise, however, are a concern that both the opponents and proponents of the JOBS Act appear to share. As we have seen, approximately $4.2 billion was raised in the 10 biggest "venture capital" rounds in the first half of 2014, compared to $2 billion in 2013 and $1.4 billion in 2012.[66] The issue with the increasing venture capital investments is that there is usually some sort of correlation between the amounts raised and the burn rate (defined as the amount of money spent by a company in excess of its revenues per month).[67] Human capital-based high-tech companies that have raised huge piles of cash, usually increase

[60] See Jose Pagliery, Explaining Twitter's "Secret" IPO, CNNMoney, Sept. 12, 2013.

[61] See Yuval Rosenberg, How Twitter's First-Day Pop Compares to Other Tech IPOs, Fiscal Times, Nov. 8, 2013.

[62] See Vindu Goel, Twitter's Stock Crashes Back to Reality, N.Y. Times, Feb. 6, 2014.

[63] See John Wasik, JOBS Act Will Open Door to Investment Scams, Forbes, Mar. 14, 2012.

[64] See Emily Chasan, Relaxed Rules for Small-Company IPOs Raise Concerns, Wall St. J., Sept. 16, 2014.

[65] See We're Definitely in a Tech Bubble . . . Maybe, CBInsights, Jan. 12, 2014. See also Think We're in a Tech Bubble? 10 Charts That Will Help You Make Your Case, CBInsights, May 11, 2014.

[66] See Mark DeCambre, To See Tech's Biggest Capital Raises, You Have to Look Beyond the IPO Market, Quartz, Aug. 12, 2014.

[67] See Jay Yarow, One of the Smartest VCs of All Time Has an Ominous Warning for the Tech Industry, Business Insider, Sept. 15, 2014.

their monthly burn, according to several reputable venture capitalists that started to voice their worries about the increasing burn rates.[68]

Their worries appear to be supported by empirical research: the high-tech startup's average burn rate is at an all-time high since the burst of the Internet bubble. Data provider PitchBook calculated the burn rate at venture-capital-backed software companies in the US by dividing the capital raised by the time between the financing rounds. Their research also confirms that burn rates at later-stage companies are rising.[69] Danielle Morrill, founder CEO of business intelligence company Mattermark, analyzed the percentage of expenses covered by revenues at high-tech companies at the time of their IPOs.[70] Her data, which is included in Figure 31.9, shows that profitable IPOs made up a smaller portion of the IPOs in the first quarter of 2014 than they did before. It is however nearly impossible to predict the timing of a bubble based on the available data.

Since unprofitable IPOs are nowhere near to the numbers we saw before the Internet bubble burst, it could be argued that another bubble is not likely to happen in the IPO market in the near future. Unfortunately, this cannot be said about the pre-IPO private market. Bill Gurley, a partner at the Silicon Valley venture capital firm Benchmark, refers to the example of Fab.com, a private online retail company that sells designer-influenced products, including clothing, accessories, furniture, food, and pet products.[71] He argues that the later-stage investors that poured $150 million into the company at a $1 billion valuation should have been more wary about investing in a company that would most likely not have passed the immense scrutiny that is part of the IPO process. Companies that did not pursue an IPO in 2014 stayed private for a reason.

If we accept this line of reasoning, the Fab.com case suggests that there still remains a dilemma for the companies and their investors and a conundrum for policy makers and regulators. Arguably, the review of financial statements by auditors, bankers, lawyers, and the Securities and Exchange Commission is needed to reduce the information asymmetries between the investors and a company's executives during the IPO.[72] However, it is far from clear whether the disclosure of financial figures is truly material to any evaluation of a company's prospects for sustainable growth and value creation. Mindful of this, an analysis of Fab.com suggests that new metrics should be developed in order to measure the future performance of both private and public high-tech companies.[73] The focus of the remainder

[68]   See Mark Suster, What is the Right Burn Rate at a Startup Company?, BothSidesofTheTable.com, Sept. 28, 2014; Connie Loizos, Don't Panic: On VCs and Bubble Trouble, StrictlyVC, Sept. 26, 2014; Dominic Rushe, Leading Tech Investors Warn of Bubble Risk "Unprecedented Since 1999", Guardian, Sept. 16, 2014.

[69]   See Adley Bowden, Has the Canary Sung or Are the Pros Crying Wolf over Burn Rates?, Pitchbook, Sept. 26, 2014.

[70]   See Danielle Morrill, A Data-Driven Exploration of Tech IPOs from 1997 to Present, Mattermark, May 12, 2014; Danielle Morrill, Is My Startup Burn Rate Normal?, Medium.com, Sept. 28, 2014; Danielle Morrill, Putting the Hortonworks and New Relic IPO Filings in Context, Mattermark, Nov. 11, 2014.

[71]   See Bill Gurley, The Billion-Dollar Companies Silicon Valley Investors Ought to Fear, Fin. Times, Feb. 20, 2015.

[72]   See Bill Gurley, Investors Beware: Today's $100M+ Late-Stage Private Rounds Are Very Different from an IPO, Above the Crowd, Feb. 25, 2015.

[73]   See Dominic Barton & Mark Wiseman, Focusing Capital on the Long Term, Harv. Bus. Rev., Jan. (2014).

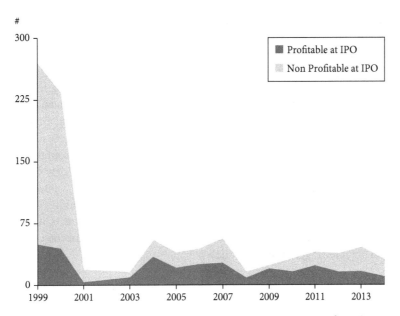

FIGURE 31.9 Profitable versus Nonprofitable Tech IPO Companies in the US.

Source: Mattermark.

of this chapter is on long-term metrics and the processes that we have already observed in practice.

4.2 The Emergence of a New Normal in Corporate Governance

There is something odd about the fear of another bubble in the venture capital industry. Surely, the most prominent and reputable venture capitalists acknowledge that the burn rate and spending plans of their own portfolio companies have increasingly made them grumpy.[74] It could be argued, however, that the ones who are able to prevent the next bubble are none other than the venture capitalists themselves.[75] When venture capitalists invest, they tend to hold preferred stock instead of common stock.[76] The precise scope of the provisions and restrictions attached to the preferred stock is established by the terms of the contractual arrangements. These typically protect the venture capitalists extensively against shirking, opportunism, and incompetence and, obviously, limit information asymmetries and agency issues which characterize the relationship between venture capitalists and the founders of high-tech companies. The provisions usually attached to the preferred stock are: preference on dividends, the proceeds of a liquidation event (including a sale of the company), and pre-emptive rights. The preferred shareholders are also entitled to elect a set

[74] See Fred Wilson, Burn Baby Burn, AVC, Sept. 16, 2014.
[75] See David Landau, Founder Manifesto, Medium.com, Sept. 15, 2014.
[76] See Josh Lerner, Boulevard of Broken Dreams, Why Public Efforts to Boost Entrepreneurship and Venture Capital Have Failed—and What to Do about It (2009).

number of representatives on the board of directors. Moreover (and most importantly in the current climate), they usually have the opportunity to replace the CEO, even if he or she is the founder, in the event of burn rates being excessive and irresponsible.

This was probably true under the traditional model of venture capital that has widely been discussed in the academic literature.[77] Lawyers tend to introduce more and more stringent agency-based contractual provisions, such as senior liquidation preferences, participating preferred shares, high liquidation preference multipliers, and anti-dilution provisions to ensure that self-interested managers will not act in ways that conflict with shareholder value creation or to offer downside-protection when venture capitalists were about to lose money. This all sounds great in theory; however, people nowadays are increasingly debating how well these provisions truly protect the venture capitalists and other risk capital providers.[78] Speaking from personal experience, when you are on the ground working with venture-capital-backed companies, you immediately recognize that there are other overriding considerations that should take precedence. Fred Wilson, co-founder of Union Square Ventures and notable blogger, puts it as follows:[79]

> One thing I know for sure is that those who advise and invest in startups cannot and should not meddle in the day to day decision making. It's harmful and hurtful to the startup and those that lead it. So operating at a higher level, helping to set the framework for decision making and then sitting down and watching the game being played, is certainly the way to go.

There is more and more evidence that venture capitalists are returning to the venture capital model in its most traditional form as risk takers and most importantly as real partners to the founders of high-tech companies. Mark Susters of Upfront Ventures summed it up perfectly:[80] "In my view the best VCs are merely your guides. They are your sparring partners. They are there to help you correct your course when you want to make decisions that their history and wisdom tells them might lead you into a dark alley." He continues as follows:

> That's not to say that we as VCs are without strong opinions. I'm no wallflower. And I cherish my role of being difficult to persuade about strategic moves without strong data or logic or conviction on your part. It's my job to help you find your True North. To know that while acquiring a business in China will help you globalize faster it most certainly will take you off of your most immediate problems at home and that dominating your national opportunity first is far better than being spread thinly across two complex opportunities. You want to do that early in your company's existing? Bring it on. You're going to have to run over me like a Mack Truck to get that decision approved. But I would never say "no" 100%.

The best venture capitalists are in essence bringing retro back to the forefront, where it was once fashionable to be bold, but with a modern twist that takes advantage of new-age (social media) platforms and creative as well as disruptive mechanisms to differentiate themselves from the herd. For instance, Fred Wilson, whom we mentioned earlier, shares the

---

[77] See for an extensive overview of the literature, Erik P.M. Vermeulen, "Towards a New 'Company' Structure for High-tech Start-Ups in Europe", 8 Maastricht Journal of European and Comparative Law 233 (2001).

[78] See Ciarán O'Leary, Downside Protection Doesn't Matter, BerlinVC, June 26, 2014.

[79] See Fred Wilson, Basketball, Startups, and Life, AVC, Feb. 16, 2015.

[80] See Mark Suster, You Can't Rely on a VC to Make Your Hardest Decisions, BothSidesofTheTable, Feb. 1, 2015.

three "must-have" terms (board representation, liquidation preferences, and pro-rata rights) to cover in a term sheet on his blog back in 2009.[81] These types of posts have positively impacted the industry on a variety of matters including terms negotiated.[82] In fact, we see that investor-favorable terms are being exchanged for more founder favorable clauses in term sheets. The very people that deal with this the most at Wilson Sonsini Goodrich & Rosati, Cooley, and Fenwick & West indicate in their quarterly reports on the industry that agency-based provisions continue to decline at a steady rate.

Consider the example of the liquidation preference, which traditionally entitles venture capitalists to get their money out first when an exit opportunity emerges and the company's valuation has gone down (also known as a down round). Liquidation preferences, however, are currently viewed less as stringent "down round risk protection" and more as a necessary provision to align the interests of the investors and the founders. To see this, contemplate a venture capitalist who decides to invest without any liquidation preference protection. He or she would receive their "ownership percentage" from the proceeds of the exit, but this may be significantly lower than their initial investment. Clearly, this could disadvantage the venture capitalist, as the founder may disproportionally monetize his stake in the company at the venture capitalist's expense. This different perception of the liquidation preference explains why the investor-favorable senior liquidation preference is used less often (see Figure 31.10), and additional participation in the remaining proceeds was infrequently used in 2013 (see Figure 31.11).

This is certainly not a call to remove all protections and agency-based provisions, but more to do with removing those that are purely unnecessary and uncalled for and can only destroy the founders' incentives to be prepared to go at any lengths to make their startup companies a long-term success. In this light, it is not surprising that not everyone in the venture capital industry is excited by the involvement of hedge funds and mutual funds in startup companies.[83] Venture capitalists generally believe that the typical characteristics of these investors do not match well with the objectives of venture capital to make patient medium- to long-term equity investments in early-stage companies. The companies' founders, however, are usually more positive about the new breeds of private investors.[84] In their view, institutional investors, particularly hedge funds, are able to add exceptional and unique value to later-stage companies (besides loads of cash). For instance, their knowledge and expertise with listed companies are invaluable for companies that are eventually considering an IPO. Startups that are looking for ways to expand to foreign markets also benefit more and more from hedge funds' broad international networks and experiences.

The founders are right. A new establishment of hedge funds (similar to the modern venture capitalists mentioned above) is emerging, with the hedge funds realizing that when they conceptualize the relationship between managers and investors as one of hierarchy, they create a short-term mentality within the company that usually leads to corporate

---

[81] See Fred Wilson, The Three Terms You Must Have in a Venture Investment, AVC, Apr. 10, 2009; Brad Feld, VC Rights: Up, Down, and Know What the Fuck is Going On, FeldThought, May 7, 2012; Brad Feld & Jason Mendelson, Venture Deals: Be Smarter than Your Lawyer and Venture Capitalist (2011).

[82] See Brian Park & Erik P.M. Vermeulen, "We Know the Savior . . . and It Is Them: The Future Face(s) of Venture Capital", Working Paper (2015).

[83] See Spencer E. Ante, Hedge-Fund Investors Scout Out Web Firms, Wall St. J., July 12, 2011.

[84] See Glenn Solomon, Hedge Fund Rising, TechCrunch, Feb. 22, 2014.

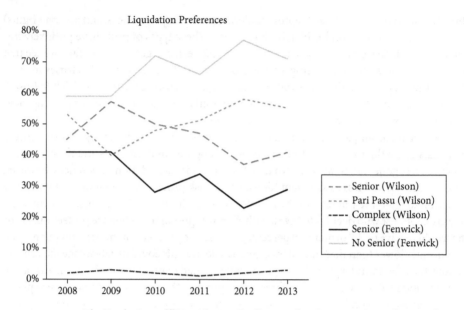

FIGURE 31.10 The Evolution of "Liquidation Preferences" in Venture Capital Term Sheets.

Source: Park and Vermeulen, "We Know the Savior . . . and It Is Them: The Future Face(s) of Venture Capital", Working Paper (2015).

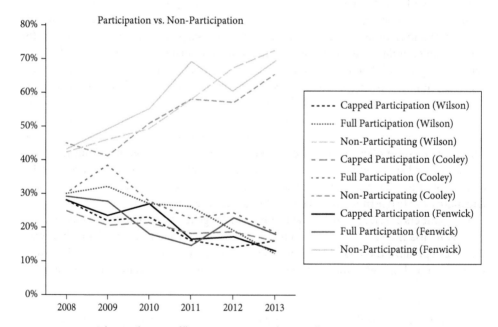

FIGURE 31.11 The Evolution of "Participation Preferences" in Venture Capital Term Sheets.

Source: Park and Vermeulen, "We Know the Savior . . . and It Is Them: The Future Face(s) of Venture Capital", Working Paper (2015).

reorganizations, and demands for increased dividends and stock buybacks. This makes it extremely difficult for companies to recapture the focus on innovation, growth, and wealth[85] Consider Nokia and Blackberry, once viewed as tech champions until they became share buyback heavyweights.[86] It is this disconnect that is slowly but surely causing a shift in corporate governance thinking amongst activist investors. They appear to be more interested in the question of what it is that causes companies to thrive and stay ahead of their competitors. As they ask themselves how to structure and design their private and public "portfolio" companies, they focus on certain common themes, such as board representation, M&A transactions, and business/growth strategy issues (see Figure 31.12). Consider ValueAct Capital's board seat at Microsoft. Undoubtedly, ValueAct was behind Satya Nadella's appointment as the new CEO of Microsoft on February 4, 2014.

It is exciting to see that the focus on helping business executives is starting to become the norm of what is expected of venture capitalists and active investors in both private and public companies. It is up to the founder/CEO and the board of directors, however, to make the investors work for the company (independently of the stage in the life cycle of a company).[87] The best way to engage the investors is frequently to share information and communicate with them.[88] This is also true for companies with a relatively small investor base, such as an early-stage startup.[89] Clearly, the information is not so much about quarterly financial statements that focus on the past. As we all know, past performance is not always indicative of future success. It is more effective to use metrics that are forward looking and complement some of the more historical data that is available in the market. Attributes that are critical for future performance are customer satisfaction, employee engagement, and community connections, collaborations, and co-creation activities, but also the introduction of new products, product innovations, and/or entering new markets.

As mentioned, it is not just the mere sharing of information, but the interactive discussion between executive management, investors, and also the board of directors that may prove to have a significant effect on the future performance of companies. There are generally three potential benefits for companies. First, the most important aspect of engagement may be in connecting with other leading investors across the globe to explain and discuss growth strategies (and invite input). These discussions assist the founder/CEO in making better decisions and avoiding tunnel vision. Second, a similar focus is on identifying opportunities and getting a better sense of their peers and competitors that often attract the same investors. Third, (pro-)active engagement helps the founders/CEOs in identifying expertise gaps on the board of directors and executive teams. It is in this collaborative context that investors may have the most impact on the spending plans of the CEOs of their portfolio companies.

---

[85] See An Investor Calls, Economist, Feb. 7, 2015.

[86] See Eric Reguly, Backback Boondoggle: Are Share Buybacks Killing Companies?, The Globe and Mail, Oct. 24, 2013.

[87] See Bryan Stolle, How to Make Your Investors Work for You, Forbes, July 31, 2014.

[88] See Joseph A. McCahery & Erik P.M. Vermeulen, "Six Components of Corporate Governance that Cannot Be Ignored", 11 Eur. Comp. & Fin. L. Rev. 160 (2014).

[89] See Jason Calacanis, Why Investor Updates Are Really, Really Important, Medium.com, Jan. 24, 2015; Jason Calacanis, What Should I Include in My Monthly Investment Update, Medium.com, Jan. 25, 2015.

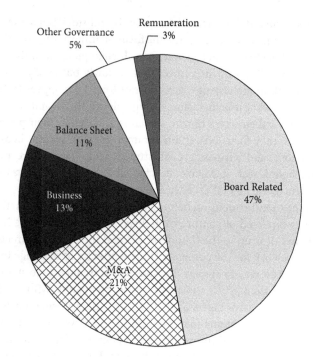

FIGURE 31.12   Activist Strategies in 344 Companies in 2014.

Source: Activist Insight 2015.

5 WHAT'S NEXT? THE BLURRING LINE BETWEEN PRIVATE AND PUBLIC COMPANIES

This chapter started with the observation that policy makers and regulators are convinced that an active IPO market is an indispensable component in an environment that fosters long-term economic growth and job creation.[90] Their efforts have mainly focused on nurturing alternative stock markets with low entry barriers and few ongoing requirements for listed firms. The discussion in this chapter, however, suggests that governments and policy makers may have to reconsider some of the policies designed to foster the growth and development of high-tech companies. For instance, the Korean KONEX was able to attract a "disappointing" 35 companies within its first year. Choi Kyung-soo, Chairman of Korea Stock Exchange, acknowledged that further steps are needed to deal with KONEX's low brand image and low trading volumes.[91]

---

[90] See the IPO Task Force, Rebuilding the IPO On-Ramp, Putting Emerging Companies and the Job Market Back on the Road to Growth, Report Presented to the US Department of the Treasury, Oct. 20, 2011.

[91] See Kim Eun-jung, South Korea's Third Bourse Expecting about 100 Firms by Year-End, Yonhap News Agency, July 1, 2014.

We can draw several lessons from the developments in the aging IPO market as discussed in the previous sections of this chapter. A first lesson is that there is a growing need to develop a pre-IPO market for high-tech companies. Pre-IPO platforms (such as SecondMarket) have emerged to satisfy the liquidity needs of founders, early-stage investors, and employees. The list of "new" players in the pre-IPO phase of venture-capital-backed-companies also includes public market investors such as hedge funds and mutual funds. Indeed, participating in later stage (pre-IPO) financing rounds of venture capital-backed companies (that offer unique investment opportunities and quick turnarounds) becomes more and more a must for institutional investors in order to maintain performance standards.[92]

It is thus important for policy makers and regulators to remove the regulatory uncertainty that creates barriers to the emergence of pre-IPO trading platforms and the involvement of institutional investors in the venture capital industry.[93] For instance, it is only waiting for stock exchanges to integrate platforms for pre-IPO (secondary) trading in shares of nonlisted companies into their existing venues in order to gain an edge in the increasingly fierce competition to dominate the market for IPOs of high-growth firms. A segmented venue of this nature would allow stock exchanges to create bonds with these firms early on in their life cycles. This may make it more likely for firms with high growth potential to undergo their IPOs in the same venue that supplied their investors with pre-IPO liquidity, rather than in competing exchanges. The launch of NASDAQ Private Market, which evolved from the joint venture with SharesPost, is one of the first examples of a stock exchange offering a 'pre-IPO' segment.[94]

In this context, the introduction of the JOBS Act makes perfect sense. It allows high-growth companies to stay private longer. But there is more. The JOBS Act also offers high-growth companies a legitimate basis to deviate from the "one-size-fits-all" agency-based rules and regulations that usually apply as soon as they decide to go public. Under the JOBS Act the focus on financial statements and past performance has become less important. This should be heralded as a first breakthrough in corporate governance thinking. As we have seen in section 4, it is preferable if both the companies and their investors focus on metrics and information that are material to their growth potential and competitive position. It is therefore only to be expected that connections, collaborations, and co-creation activities will emerge as leading-edge items on the agenda of the investor-management meetings and conversations.

Lastly, I would like to conclude with what I call "collaborative corporate governance". It is the process of developing new strategies with the aim of contributing to a culture that fosters valuable communications and conversations between a company's management, board of directors, and its investors that is likely to have real effects. A collaborative view on this considers corporate governance as the interface between what a company is today and

---

[92] See Arsham Memarzadeh, Bursting the Bubble Talk: The Difference between More Tech Funding and Overfunding, Openview Blog, Aug. 5, 2014.

[93] See, for instance, Erik P.M. Vermeulen & Diogo Pereira Dias Nunes, The Evolution and Regulation of Venture Capital Funds in Europe, 2 EUIJ-Kyushu Review (2012).

[94] Eric Blattberg, Nasdaq Launches Private Market for Trading Pre-IPO Shares, VentureBeat, Mar. 5, 2014; Kim-Mai Cutler, NASDAQ Finally Launches Its Market for Privately-Held Companies, TechCrunch, Mar. 5, 2014.

what it attempts to achieve in the medium-term or long-term future rather than focusing upon the conflict between investors and managers. Fortunately, more and more founders, CEOs, and investors have already successfully applied this collaborative corporate governance approach to maximize efficiency, performance, value creation, and innovation within the company.

PART IV

ENFORCEMENT

CHAPTER 32

CORPORATE LAW AND SELF-REGULATION

DAVID KERSHAW[1]

1 INTRODUCTION

TYPICALLY when we think about the regulation of corporate and business life we ask two questions: why should we regulate, and how should we regulate? The first question invokes justifications for interfering with the free contracting process amongst corporate actors, both within and outside of the corporation. The second question explores whether we should insist on corporations following a particular form of behavior through mandatory rules, or merely provide weighted guidance on rule choice through default rules that can be opted-out of. A third question relating to corporate regulation is less prominent and is the subject of this chapter: *who* should do the regulating? Traditionally, we have thought about this question through the dichotomy of state versus market. Not "the market" as a mechanism which generates regulatory benefits, but the market as a collection of actors capable of coordinating to produce and enforce rules regulating their activities. Through this lens we ask: in what, if any, circumstances should market actors regulate corporate activity themselves by endogenously generating and enforcing regulation without *overt* state involvement; and in what, if any, circumstances is such endogenous self-regulation likely to occur in practice?

Of course the rigid dichotomy of the state as regulator versus the market as self-regulator does not do justice to the different ways in which the state and the market interact to produce corporate law and regulation. In some sense both the state and the market are always involved in the production of regulation: the state's deference to self-regulation is inimical to its formation; the market forms state regulation through consultation processes, repeat player activity, and lobbying. However, in this chapter we are interested not in the ways in which the market molds and influences regulation but the circumstances in which it actually controls the production and enforcement of that regulation. Endogenous self-regulation

[1] Professor of Law, London School of Economics and Political Science. My thanks to the participants at the Columbia Law School conference on the Oxford Handbook of Corporate Law and Governance, with particular thanks to John Armour, Paul Davies, Michael Klausner, Georg Ringe, and Edmund Schuster.

is the ideal type of such regulation, but it is not the only one. Where there are regulatory benefits for the state to defer to the market to generate and enforce rules, the state, cognizant of these benefits, may command the market, collectively or individually, to generate regulation or to engage in practices that lead to targeted norm formation. We might view this type of regulation as *forced* self-regulation. We refer to this form of regulation in the chapter as *market-controlled* regulation and distinguish it from *self-regulation*, which the chapter will view as the (quasi-)endogenous production of regulation in the absence of legal instruction.

The purpose of this Chapter is first to explore the conditions in which self- and market controlled regulation arise in the field of corporate law. To do so, the chapter analyzes the dominant real-world examples of self- and market-controlled regulation in the field of corporate law; examples which are often lauded by regulators and commentators alike as model examples of these forms of regulation. They are: the UK Takeover Code and the Takeover Panel created in 1968; and the 'comply or explain' approach to the regulation of board structure and composition, pioneered in the UK in the early 1990s. However, the chapter is not only concerned with the pre-conditions to the creation of these regulatory forms. The chapter also explores the distinctive regulatory biases generated by these different modes of self-regulation and shows that they are more multi-faceted than, and often inconsistent with, the standard account that self-regulation is likely to generate rules that favour the regulated.

2 Forms and Pre-conditions

2.1 Endogenous Self-Regulation of Corporate Activity?

Self-regulation as an ideal theoretical type is said to generate several benefits. Self-regulation is cheap and imposes no direct cost on the state treasury: the marketplace pays for its own regulation.[2] In addition to such direct cost benefits, self-regulation has clear *potential* regulatory benefits. First and foremost, it is a means of addressing often acute knowledge and information asymmetries afflicting the relationship between the regulator and the regulated constituency. Market actors live the regulated activity and, accordingly, both understand the problems and issues that are generated by such activity and understand the means for most efficiently counteracting such problems through regulation. In contrast, state regulators, even ones with revolving doors from and back into practice, have partial vision and understanding of such activity and are more likely therefore to craft suboptimal regulation that neither deals with the actual problems and, worse, imposes unnecessary costs on such activity. This is compounded by the *them against us* lens generated by state regulation which disincentivizes information sharing as a result, inter alia, of the unpredictability of how a state regulator might respond to shared information about market practices. In contrast, the market's "ownership" of the regulatory space both promotes information sharing with the self-regulator and, in theory, promotes behavioral norms which foster compliance. The

---

[2] Of course this may be viewed simply as a form of indirect taxation as the costs of the regulation will be passed through to the consumers in the marketplace. Furthermore, there is no reason why state regulation cannot impose the costs directly on market players through a regulatory levy—which again would be passed through to end users.

second, well traversed,[3] benefit of self-regulation is that it is able to respond more quickly to new forms of activity that require regulation. Not only, for the reasons set forth above, is the self-regulator likely to be aware of the problem earlier, it is also not constrained by the procedures, checks, and balances associated with state action through primary or secondary legislation or through an authorized regulator.

Clearly, however, one needs to be wary of such broad-brush claims about the benefits of self-regulation. State regulatory forms, particularly regulatory bodies with rulemaking authority have the capacity to move relatively quickly. Self-regulatory bodies also typically provide for time-consuming procedures to effect rule changes. This is because public expectations of due process and consultation typically inform nonstate as well as state bodies. And not all forms of corporate activity generate acute information asymmetries between the regulator and the regulated. Corporate and audit scandals in the last two decades, as well as the global financial crisis, have illuminated areas of corporate activity where such asymmetries clearly exist, such as the accounting for off-balance sheet transactions or complex derivative instruments such as collateralized debt obligations. However, in many areas of corporate life, although we find market innovation and smart structuring, the conflict surrounding such activity typically renders it visible and comprehensible. For example, innovative activity in the market for corporate control has typically been transparent because of the conflict it has generated. Consider, for example, takeover defenses in the 1960s, 1970s, and 1980s or the conflicts over the use of equity swaps in the 2000s. In these areas claims that self-regulation addresses asymmetries of knowledge and information are overstated because the asymmetries are insignificant.

As with the benefits of self-regulation, its potential costs have been thoroughly explored. Most important in this regard is the concern that the self-regulator will abuse its position and its knowledge and information advantage to craft rules that enhance its welfare position at the expense of other affected parties that have no control or influence over the rulemaking and enforcement process. State regulators are, of course, not immune from rent seeking but are thought—certainly in the eyes of the state regulators themselves!—more able to resist pressures from market constituents and more likely to be able to craft rules that are not biased in favor of any particular constituency. The extent to which a self-regulator is able to bias the rules in favor of market actors is a function of several factors. First, whether or not other non-participating parties are thought to be affected by the activity in question. Where the activity is thought only to affect the direct parties involved (or where such third-party effects although real are very opaque) then the independence concern will be (or will be seen to be) less pressing so long as all affected market participants have a voice in such self-regulation. It is in such areas in particular that the welfare case for self-regulation is a strong one. Second, the extent to which bias is a concern is dependent on the alignment, or lack thereof, of the interests of the self-regulatory rulemaker and the perceived interests of society. If, for example, institutional shareholder groups exercise self-regulatory authority and the prevailing political and social norms view the advancement of shareholder interests as congruent with social welfare, then any such rule bias is unproblematic. Third, the extent of this bias problem is, paradoxically, connected to one of the purported key benefits of

---

[3] See, e.g., Robert Baldwin, Martin Cave, & Martin Lodge, Understanding Regulation: Theory, Strategy and Practice (2011).

self-regulation: the knowledge and information asymmetries of market actors. Where such asymmetries are significant, self-regulatory actors have more room to deploy self-interest, as the ability of the state and other nonstate actors, such as the financial press, to assess and monitor whether the rules are biased is much diminished. This means that where we think about the welfare implications of self- versus state-regulation we find that both the benefits and the costs are higher where knowledge and information asymmetries are high.

The second consensus drawback with self-regulation is the concern that the self-regulator is unlikely to enforce the rules against its own. There are two reasons given for this: the absence of the enforcement apparatus of the state and the lack of distance between the regulator and the regulated which undermines the willingness of the regulator to impose available sanctions for breach. Of course, these enforcement problems may be counterbalanced to some degree by both the positive compliance effects, mentioned above, of "owning" the regulatory space as well as the precarious nature of self-regulation—if rules are too pro market actor and are not enforced, the likelihood increases that the market will lose the regulatory franchise.

2.2 Theorizing the Preconditions for Self-Regulation

We might think about the probability that the market will elect to regulate itself through the lens of the costs (or lost benefits) of failing to do so. Clearly for many market actors there are significant benefits of remaining unregulated. However, market actors will collectively realize that where their actions are generating public and political disquiet there is a distinct likelihood of state regulatory intervention. Self-regulation in such a context may impose costs on market actors but will be viewed as the lesser of two evils and as way of deflecting political pressures to introduce more costly state regulation. Where $C_{SR} < C_S$ then the market actors will enter the "contracting zone"[4] to produce self-regulation, where *compared to a state of the world without regulation* C_{SR} equals the costs[5] for market participants of a self-regulatory regime which they control and enforce plus the transaction costs—the costs of coordination—of agreeing on and maintaining the terms of self-regulation; where C_S is the costs of state regulation to the market actors; and where C_S is discounted for the probability of state intervention. The costs of coordination will vary as a function of the homogeneity and proximity of the actors in question. Such homogeneity and proximity are also likely to foster coordination cost reducing norms, such as a sense of responsibility for the space within which the activity takes place.

C_{SR} and C_S are individual variables for each player—or category of player—in the marketplace. Where there are multiple categories of player it is possible that whereas $C_{SR} < C_S$ for some categories, $C_{SR} > C_S$ for others. In such circumstances all parties will not be brought into the "contracting zone" in the absence of either some differential power weighting for key actors for whom $C_{SR} < C_S$ or a coordinating mechanism that ensures a response where in aggregate $C_{SR} < C_S$. A similar calculus operates where market actors' concern is not the cost implications of state regulation but the cost implications of the failure to regulate due to, for example, the political failures of the executive or legislative authorities that are deadlocked or for other reasons incapable of acting. Here participants will optimally enter the contracting zone where the aggregate benefits of

[4] I am grateful to Michael Klausner for encouraging me to present this analysis through the lens of the contracting zone.

[5] If C represents benefits and not costs then the inequality is reversed for market participants to enter the contracting zone: $C_{SR} > C_S$.

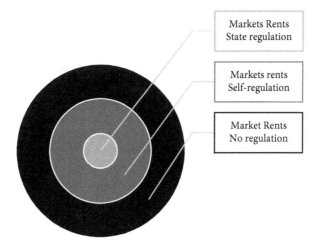

Markets Rents
State regulation

Markets rents
Self-regulation

Market Rents
No regulation

FIGURE 32.1 Contracting Zone Open.

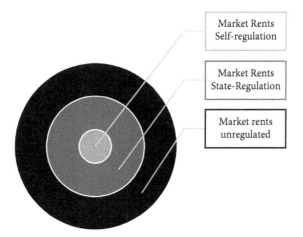

Market Rents
Self-regulation

Market Rents
State-Regulation

Market rents
unregulated

FIGURE 32.2 Contracting Zone Closed.

self-regulation, B_{SR}, exceed the transaction costs of coordination. Again, however, individual variation in B_{SR} may impede parties entering the contracting zone (Figures 32.1 and 32.2).[6]

It is plausible that such a cost calculus is an important component of the drivers of the real-world examples of self-regulation. However, it is most certainly a secondary driver. Whether actors can enter the contracting zone is a function of whether the state will countenance self-regulation. In an idealized world if the state acts as a rational actor, whether it would permit self-regulation would be a function of the costs and benefits of self- and state-regulation, discussed above, as applied to the particular regulatory context. Where the social welfare benefits of self-regulation exceed those of state regulation one would expect a rational state to permit or to facilitate self-regulation and where they do not to preempt self-regulatory contracting (Figures 32.3 and 32.4).

[6] These diagrams address $C_{SR} > < C_S$ not $B_{SR} < > 0$.

Clearly, however, the willingness of the state to open the contracting zone is a function of more than such a calculus. Of central importance in this regard is the regulatory conception of state and whether such a conception countenances or encourages self-regulation. By regulatory conception of the state I mean the shared understanding—amongst politicians, market actors and citizens more broadly—about the extent to which it is legitimate or illegitimate for the state to exercise power to identify and address problems generated by interactions within civil society; or, put differently, the extent to which it is legitimate or illegitimate for nonstate actors to perform regulatory, state-like functions. Where this regulatory conception of the state does not countenance self-regulation, even where Figures 32.1 and 32.3 apply, there is no scope for the marketplace to legitimately occupy the regulatory space policed by the state and therefore no scope for there to be a "contracting zone" within which the market actors' cost calculus could operate. In such a context market actors are left to try and coordinate improved behavior in the hope of dampening

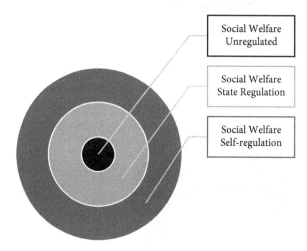

FIGURE 32.3 Contracting Zone Open.

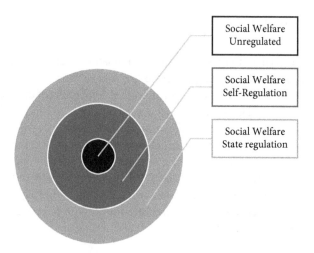

FIGURE 32.4 Contracting Zone Closed.

political concern, or, where the problem is the failure of the state to act, to lobby for state action. Where the conception of the state is open to, or favorable to, market-based action the contracting zone comes into play. For this reason it is unsurprising that we find that many of the examples of corporate self-regulation—some of which are discussed in this chapter—are produced in the UK, a jurisdiction that for several centuries following the Enlightenment actively promoted local and market-based solutions to identified problems—an approach that resulted from a longstanding and deeply held "wariness towards the central state apparatus."[7]

There is a significant body of scholarship on the passive conception of the UK state which we can only touch on here. Jenks, for example, contrasts the prevailing political style in nineteenth- and twentieth-century Britain with the "imaginative conception of politics" associated with the utilitarianism of Bentham and John Stuart Mill.[8] For Jenks, this utilitarian conception of politics involved an active form of government: "a conception of problem solving and exploration of opportunities for innovation as the very stuff of politics." The British political style and the conception of the state that underpinned it was the antithesis of such an active and interventionist style. For Jenks, the British approach is characterized by sobriety, neutrality, and a resistance to problem solving, almost a willed passivity in the face of identified problems until there is no alternative but to act. In his seminal work on the history of industrial relations in the UK Alan Fox observes that as "it was not part of the state's duty to anticipate and meet needs which seemed likely to grow"; the problem would have to grow "to a major size before the government decided to step in." But as the great labour lawyer Otto Kahn-Freund observed, the resistance to proactive intervention and directed control clearly should not be mistaken for the absence of any form of intervention or role for law. For Kahn-Freund, in the UK there was widespread support for the "social institution" of "organized persuasion" where the state's, and law's, role was to facilitate parties in creating order, reaching agreement, and resolving conflict.[9] At most, the government's role was to take steps—from cajoling actors to respond, to the creation of institutional structures—that would facilitate actors in addressing the problem themselves. The bedfellow of this political outlook was an expectation, and a sense of entitlement, that market actors themselves should be given an opportunity to address identified problems. For politicians, an electoral minefield awaited those who proactively disturbed those expectations, and accordingly "crisis dimensions" were required to drive government to (directly) intervene.[10]

For this reason until the latter part of the twentieth century in the UK there was no form of what today we would recognize as capital market or banking regulation, responsibility for which was left to the City of London and the City's "Pope,"[11] the Governor of the Bank

---

[7] See generally, Alan Fox, History and Heritage: The Social Origins of the British Industrial Relations System (1988). I am very grateful to Paul Davies for recommending to me that I consider the theory of state set forth in this wonderful text.

[8] C. Jenks, T. H. Green, "The Oxford Philosophy of Duty and the English Middle Class" 28 British Journal of Sociology 481, 494 (1977).

[9] Otto Kahn-Freund, "Industrial Relations and the Law—retrospect and prospect", 7 British Journal of Industrial Relations 301 (1969).

[10] Fox *supra* note 7, at 374.

[11] Sir Leslie warns on the Takeover Code, Guardian, Aug. 16, 1968. A different metaphor used in relation to the Bank of England was the Bank as "parent." Harry Siepmann of Lazards referred to the "faith in the Bank as the Leader and Parent of the City . . ."; David Kynaston, The City of London: A Club No More 57 (2002).

of England, a non-state body itself until 1947. This approach led Louis Loss in his treatise on US Securities Regulation to observe that it was paradoxical that the US "the arch apostles of private enterprise should have resorted to public control while socialist Britain . . . should have left so wide a field free from state control."[12] For this same reason, the UK did not have a developed system of industrial relations or labor law until well into the 1970s—a regulatory lacuna that was viewed as a mark of success not state failure. Alan Fox observes in this regard that as late as the early 1960s: "The industrial relations systems of less 'mature' capitalisms such as the United States and Germany were thought to reveal their immaturity by their heavy dependence on legal definitions and sanctions and on their being more consciously and deliberately designed by the state."[13]

Whilst one can chart a retreat from, or the disintegration of, this conception during the post-World War II period and in a more pronounced way in the past 40 years, many of the classic examples of corporate and non-corporate self-regulation in the UK are in large part a product of this conception and, as we shall see below, its mark is still impressed on contemporary self- and market-controlled UK approaches to the regulation of the corporation. In other jurisdictions, including twentieth-century US and other European jurisdictions, where the conception of the regulatory state more closely approximates Jenk's utilitarian conception of politics,[14] the scope for market players to take control of the regulatory space and enter the contracting zone has been much more attenuated. Unsurprisingly, in such jurisdictions examples of self-regulation are much less prevalent.

Where the conception of the state does enable self-regulation, the activity that takes place within the "contracting zone" must be framed through a continuing relationship of the state to the contracting market actors. We have already noted the role of possible state intervention in incentivizing actors to enter the contracting zone—the threat to act if the market fails to do so. Moreover, the long-term success and stability of any self-regulatory response is dependent upon it maintaining its (democratic) legitimacy in the eyes of the public and the state. In particular, as the self-regulator usurps the regulatory function of the state it must be seen to do so in an unbiased and even-handed way. Arguably, this need to maintain legitimacy renders self-regulation unstable, if not unworkable, in the long run in contexts where due to knowledge and information asymmetries it is difficult for the state to assess whether or not the self-regulator is acting in a neutral or unbiased fashion. Visible failures in that marketplace are likely to lead to the inference of self-regulatory failure. Even if such an inference is inaccurate, the knowledge and information asymmetries make it very difficult to explain to the regulator, or the public, why it is inaccurate. In these contexts, such failures may themselves irretrievably delegitimize the self-regulator regardless of any failing or fault on its part. By way of contrast, where asymmetries of information and knowledge are limited,

---

[12]   See L. C. B. Gower, "Investor Protection in the USA", 15 Mod. L. Rev. 446, 447 (1952).

[13]   Fox, *supra* note 7.

[14]   Clearly this chapter cannot undertake a broad-ranging comparative analysis of the conceptions of the regulatory state in US and European jurisdictions. But in support of this claim consider, and compare, for example, the mid-twentieth-century UK approach to the regulation of financial markers, corporate law, antitrust, and labor law with the evolution of US federal securities regulation (Gower, *supra* note 12), antitrust regulation, corporate law (see David Kershaw, "The Path of Corporate Fiduciary Law", 8 NYU J. L. & Bus. 395 (2012)), and labor law (see generally Fox, *supra* note 7).

a self-regulator can more easily explain its rules and actions and thereby maintain its legitimacy in the eyes of the state and the public.

2.3 Market-Controlled Regulation

Everyone wants the best of both worlds. But invariably the real world consists of second-best solutions that make inevitable trade-offs between the "bests" of each world. The above analysis of endogenous self-regulation has identified several advantages of this mode of regulation but also several bias, availability, and stability problems. Would it be possible to devise a system of corporate regulation that gets the knowledge and flexibility benefits of self-regulation but minimizes the downside rule and enforcement biases and stability problems; a system of regulation that guarantees a market response to the regulatory problem without having to rely on a panglossian alignment of private and public economic interests as well as the availability of co-ordination mechanisms?

In such a system of regulation the state would demarcate the contours of regulation and then command the market to fill in the substantive content of that regulation. We might describe this approach to corporate regulation as forced self-regulation or "market-controlled regulation." This typically takes place through a legal or regulatory requirement to comply with or to take account of rules produced by market actors. Corporate governance codes provide perhaps the best example of this approach, where legislation or regulation in several jurisdictions provides that publicly traded companies must comply or explain their failure to comply with the rules produced by a designated governance body or commission.[15] Typically this body is a hybrid state/market regulator staffed by market participants but with some formal connections to the state. We explore this form of market-controlled regulation together with the enforcement effects and regulatory biases that it generates in section 4 of this chapter.

3 "Endogenous" Self-Regulation: A Takeover Case Study in the UK and Brazil

Examples of successful self-regulatory regimes that regulate significant parts of corporate activity and that have no formal connection to the state are rare. The most notable

---

[15] The German Corporate Governance Code is not part of the German Stock Corporation Act but the requirement for publicly traded German stock corporations to comply with or to explain the failure to comply with its provisions are set forth in section 161 of the German Stock Corporation Law. The Code is produced by a government-appointed commission. Similarly, the UK Corporate Governance Code, although maintained by a quasi-state body, the FRC, benefits from a mandatory requirement in the UK Financial Conduct Authority's Listing Rules to comply or explain non-compliance with the Governance Code (LR 9.8.6(5)). Across the Atlantic, the governance rules set forth in the New York Stock Exchange are the product of a self-regulatory organization, but SROs are authorized by the SEC and its rules, including the governance rules, are subject to SEC oversight and approval (see section 19 Securities and Exchange Act of 1934).

example is the UK's Takeover Code and the Takeover Panel that enforces and maintains the Code. The Code provides a comprehensive body of rules regulating all aspects of the take-over process for publicly traded companies. The Takeover Panel is globally recognized as one of the most powerful and effective command and control regulators. Yet between 1968 and 2005—when it became a state regulator as a result of the implementation of the EU's Takeover Directive[16]—this was achieved without direct instruction from, or empowerment by, the state.

The first attempt to regulate the UK takeover market followed political and media dis-quiet which arose in the 1950s as a result of target companies using early takeover defenses, including a crown jewel defense in the battle for the Savoy Hotel and a white squire share issue defense in the battle for British Aluminium.[17] These actions generated multi-faceted political and public concerns from which one would be hard pressed to identify a dom-inant concern.[18] The concerns included: disapproval of hostile bids as an inappropriate interference in the "corporate bastion";[19] concern about the ethics of the takeover market-place;[20] anxiety about the effects of hostile activity on economic policy commitments to restrict income inflation;[21] and concerns about illegitimate board interference in share-holder sovereignty.[22] In July 1959 this led the Bank of England, which at the time was solely responsible for "regulating"[23] banking and capital markets in the UK, to form a working group consisting of participants in the UK capital markets in order to produce a Code of Conduct to regulate hostile and competitive bids. Importantly, UK merchant (investment) banks—through their trade association the Issuing Houses Association—took control of the production of this Code of Conduct. They produced their own working party which was tasked with producing an initial draft code.[24] Other market constituencies clearly had input into this process although it was reported that there was "general agreement about the principles involved."[25] The resulting Code of Conduct, which came into force in 1959, was

---

[16] EU Directive 2004/25/EC.

[17] The two key events were the attempted takeover of the Savoy Hotel which involved a lock-up of its key asset, the Berkley Hotel, and the battle for British Aluminium. In relation to which see Richard Roberts, "Regulatory Responses to the Rise of the Market for Corporate Control in Britain in the 1950s", 34 Business History 183, 187 (1992).

[18] See David Kershaw, Principles of Takeover Regulation (2016), chapter 3.

[19] Kynaston in his magisterial history of the City of London notes in relation the British Aluminium takeover battle discussed below the "entrenched belief that within its citadel, the board knew best," Kynaston, *supra* note 11, at 6.

[20] A note by Maudling, Economic Secretary to the Treasury, for the Prime Minister (Winston Churchill), observed that, although nothing could be done, "the process is distasteful and politically embarrassing" Pro, PREM/656, Letter from the Economic Secretary to the Treasury to the Prime Minister, 13 Nov, 1953 (quoted in Roberts, *supra* note 17, at 183, 187).

[21] See Roberts, *supra* note 17.   [22] See Directors Duties, Fin. Times, Dec. 8, 1953.

[23] Regulation in this context would be a misnomer as banks and capital markets actors were regulated by the Bank of England through direct supervision and what is sometimes referred to as a regime of nods and winks—see Kynaston, *supra* note 11.

[24] See City Views on Take-Over Bids, Fin. Times, Oct. 31, 1959, observing that the Notes were "prepared by the Issuing Houses Association *in co-operation with* the other working group members" (emphasis added). Roberts reports that the original draft of the Code was produced by its Chairman J. S. French who was a director of the Issuing House London and Yorkshire Trust (*supra* note 17).

[25] Id.

cumbersomely named the "Notes on the Amalgamation of British Business." However, the Code was wholly unsuccessful and did not generate behavioral constraint in the UK take-over market. From the moment it was published it was clear that it would not constrain be-havior when an actor's interest diverged from the rules. There was no body responsible for updating and enforcing the Notes and although the Notes contained the structural and sub-stantive seeds of modern takeover regulation, in many instances they were comically am-biguous: "Every effort" should be made to avoid market disturbance; shareholders should be given "adequate time (say three weeks) for accepting" the offer; and it was "desirable that the offer is for the whole share capital." It was, therefore, unsurprising that the mar-ketplace ignored the Notes in multiple ways,[26] including the replication of the very events that led to the Notes on the Amalgamation of Business. For example, in the 1967 battle for Cook & Watts Ltd. the target board locked up a deal with its preferred bidder by agreeing to issue a majority of the company's ordinary shares in exchange for the sale of one of the pre-ferred bidder's subsidiaries.[27] Similarly, later in the same year in relation to a hostile bid for Metal Industries, the target again agreed to issue a block of shares in exchange for the sale of the preferred bidder's subsidiary.[28] These events generated renewed political and media clamor for regulatory intervention and again resulted in the Bank of England bringing market participants together to put their own house in order.[29] For the first time the group included representatives of management. Again the merchant banks through the Issuing Houses Association took the lead in revising the Code. A sub-committee was created to revise the Notes, which "did most of the work and the drafting of the code" and consisted only of Issuing House Association representatives from four merchant banks, one of whom, Robert Clark, had previously been a partner at Slaughter and May, the leading City law firm.[30] The result was the newly named Takeover Code which, building on the Notes, provided a pro-shareholder code that directly responded to the problematic events that generated pressure for action and, of some contextual importance, was wholly in keeping with the pro-shareholder orientation of UK company law. Furthermore, the City provided for a self-regulatory body, staffed by representatives of market participants to administer the Code.

Today's Takeover Code provides for a set of extremely demanding rules as well as a feared and uncompromisingly independent regulator. Compared to the Takeover Code—which today amounts to 300 pages of rules and rule guidance—other jurisdictions' takeover rules,

---

[26] See, for example, Phillips' takeover of Pye in January of 1967, Explanation of Share Transactions, Fin. Times, Jan. 26, 1967, and the battle for Wilkinson & Ridell (Behind the Scenes of the Wilkinson & Ridell Battle), Fin. Times, June 29, 1967, both involving favorable treatment of institutional shareholders.

[27] Courtaulds wins Cook, Guardian, Apr. 28, 1967.

[28] "Outrageous" and Sir Jules Puts Thorn Back in the Battle, Guardian, July 17, 1967.

[29] See John Armour and David Skeel's careful documentation of this process and the resulting creation, at the end of the 1960s, of the City Code on Takeovers and Mergers and its enforcer, the Takeover Panel (John Armour & David Skeel, "Who Writes the Rules for Hostile Takeovers and Why?—Peculiar Divergence of US and UK Takeover Regulation", 95 Geo. L. J. 1727 (2007)).

[30] The members of the subcommittee were: Michael Bucks (Chairman) (Rothchilds); Robert Clark (Hill Samuel); Ken Barrington (Morgan Grenfell); Peter Cannon (Minster Trust—"an upstart finance house")—The Men behind the Code, Fin. Times, Mar. 27, 1968.

for example the US's Williams Act, appear rather insubstantial, perhaps incomplete,[31] and are much more deferential to the parties' freedom to contract. In addition to the well-known non-frustration rule preventing any target board frustrating action,[32] and the mandatory bid rules triggered when crossing the 30% threshold or further purchases within the 30–50% ownership range,[33] the Code provides many other highly interventionist and controlling rules. For example, the Code requires announcements of possible offers when there is any untoward movement in the share price[34]—what amounts to untoward is determined by the Panel. In contrast to the Williams Act[35] in the United States—which provides for an all-holders-best-price rule in relation to one class of shares and in relation to purchases during the offer period—the Takeover Code requires bids for all share classes and convertibles[36] and provides for an equal pricing rule both during the bid and between three to 12 months prior to the bid.[37] The Code provides for what is known as a "put up or shut up" rule requiring the bidder to make an announcement of a firm offer 28 days following an announcement of a *possible* offer.[38] An announcement of a firm offer as well as the offer itself may only be subject to limited conditionality which is controlled by the Panel.[39] It is the Panel, not the parties or a court, that, for example, determines whether a material adverse change clause can be called pursuant to the contractual agreement. Finally, and perhaps most surprising for a US audience, the Code has long placed significant constraints on the use of deal protections including break fees. Until 2011 a break fee could not exceed 1% of deal value. After 2011, save in limited circumstances, they are prohibited altogether.[40]

The Takeover Panel today is a state body. Pursuant to the Companies Act 2006, which implemented the European Takeover Directive, the Panel is a "recognised supervisory authority."[41] As a state body the Takeover Panel now has clear access to the power of the state to sanction Code transgressions.[42] It is noteworthy, however, that from the 1980s the Takeover Panel had theoretical access to the enforcement powers of the UK capital market regulators. And from its inception it had access to licensing sanctions in relation to certain market participants that were regulated by the Board of Trade, a government department. But these trappings of state power are of no relevance to the success of this endogenous self-regulatory body. They have never been and are highly unlikely ever to be used. If the probability of Code compliance were a function of the probability of the use of some form of state power to enforce the Code, then there would be no compliance with the Code because the probability of the use of state power is zero. Yet there is close to total compliance with the Code; and incontrovertible deference to the views and instructions of the Panel. What then explains the success of this self-regulatory mechanism and what are the preconditions to replicating its success? These are important questions of contemporary relevance both generally to the question of in what circumstances, if any, self-regulation can be effectively deployed within corporate law, but also of specific importance to takeover regulation in other jurisdictions,

---

[31] Of course in considering the completeness of US takeover process regulation, one needs to take account of the indirect process effects of the availability of takeover defenses subject to state corporate law.

[32] Rule 21 Takeover Code.   [33] Rule 9 Takeover Code.   [34] Rules 2.4 Takeover Code.

[35] Regulation 14D, Rule 14D-10.   [36] Rules 14–15 Takeover Code.

[37] See Rules 6, 9, and 11 Takeover Code.   [38] Rule 2.6 Takeover Code.

[39] Rules 12 and 13 Takeover Code.   [40] Rule 21.2 Takeover Code.

[41] Section 942 Companies Act 2006.   [42] See ss. 952–956 Companies Act 2006.

such as for example Brazil, who are currently experimenting with similar forms of self-regulation often because vested interests or governance failures are thought to prevent the state from regulating directly and effectively.[43]

Based on the experience of the Takeover Panel and Code, below I suggest five key drivers to the successful self-regulation of the market for corporate control. This set of drivers suggests that the Takeover Panel's existence and success is sui generis and that successful replication in other jurisdictions is improbable.

3.1 The Deferential State

The Takeover Code and the Takeover Panel are the product of the mid-twentieth-century conception of the British state which, as detailed in section 1, contained an inbuilt assumption of state passivity. This lens generated a regulatory logic which viewed the UK state's role as one of facilitating and organizing self-regulatory solutions. This conception did not merely generate space for the "contracting zone," it actively encouraged entry by market participants. Consider, for example, the UK government's sense of powerlessness in relation to the Battle for British Aluminium. Kynaston notes in this regard that the prime minister's (Harold Macmillan's) view was that "it would be a grave political error to interfere now . . . Let the rival forces fight it out . . . It's the only safe course."[44]

Self-regulation of the takeover market in the UK is often presented as political disarmament: the powerful state threatens to act which leads market actors to self-regulate their activity in order to deflect intervention. This is invariably a key factor in driving what appear to be self-regulatory solutions. And this lens certainly animated many actors and commentators around the time of the formation of the Code and the Panel.[45] But this lens must be placed within the context of this then prevailing conception of the British state which created a presumption and an expectation—firmly held within government, the City of London, and the Bank of England—that market participants should address and resolve the problems of their own making. State intervention in the market for corporate control in the UK at the end of the 1950s and 1960s would have represented a regulatory paradigm fissure. Publicly stated fears and threats of intervention must accordingly be discounted to take cognizance of this conception. Consider in this regard the Financial Times's (FT) LEX column of July 1967 that called both for more precise rules and a means of enforcement in light of the multiple high-profile takeover "scandals" of that year. It noted the concern that if the issues were not addressed by the City then government would be forced to step in.[46] This concern was repeated in the press and crystalized around the idea of the threat of a British Securities and Exchange Commission (SEC).[47] In spite of this perceived looming "threat," in fact consistent with the longstanding British regulatory style, the government, the media, and the City were all of the view that the takeover problem was presumptively a problem for the City to solve. Less than a week later in his Mansion House speech Prime

---

[43] See generally, Ronald J. Gilson, Henry Hansmann, Ronald J. Gilson, & Mariana Pargendler, "Regulatory Dualism as Development Strategy: Corporate Reform in Brazil, the US and the EU", 63 Stan. L. Rev. 475 (2011).

[44] Kynaston, *supra* note 11, at 114.

[45] "What the New Bid Panel Needs To Do, LEX", Fin. Times, Sept. 21, 1967.

[46] Id.   [47] Id.

Minister Harold Wilson echoed the FT's sentiments but observed that "it is for the City to ensure that these processes are and are seen to be, carried through in accordance with clearly formulated rules." Of course, if the City failed to act there remained a threat of government intervention, and certainly by the late 1960s this threat was increasing as more commentators called for a break with tradition and greater state involvement in the regulation of business.[48] However, given the continuing weight of presumption associated with the British approach to governance, the probability of intervention at this point was still extremely low. Historically situated, governmental concerns and media attention were communicative triggers to tell the City to organize itself to address the concerns that had arisen in relation to takeovers.

The centrality of this conception of the state to the UK takeover regulation story suggests that this form of corporate self-regulation is sui generis. In the absence of a similar conception, the contracting zone may be locked as self-regulation is viewed as an illegitimate intrusion into the role of the state; an anti-democratic grab for state authority. Moreover, this sense of illegitimate intrusion is likely to be compounded in more modern regulatory settings for capital markets, which typically already provide for a capital markets regulator who would be viewed as the natural regulator for such a new regulatory venture and who is likely to make a territorial claim thereover. In the United States context, for example, at the time of the introduction of the Williams Act the preexistence of the SEC generated a path-dependent preference to address takeovers through an expanded SEC jurisdiction.[49] This factor is of particular concern in relation to modern attempts to replicate the Takeover Code's self-regulatory success. Brazil has been much lauded for its regulatory dualism which involves the introduction of alternative regulatory regimes designed to offer companies and shareholders, at their election, protections that the state has failed to offer.[50] In this vein of regulatory dualism, a body of market constituents has come together in Brazil to produce a self-designated Committee on Mergers and Acquisitions (CAF).[51] The CAF Code describes the body as "a non-statutory independent body created by representatives from the main Brazilian capital market players to operate on the basis of a voluntary self-regulation model."[52] It provides takeover regulation to companies that *elect* to be bound by

---

[48] In 1969 (see *supra* note 9) Otto Kahn-Freund argued in the context of industrial relations that the law "should be called upon to play a much increased role in the moulding of industrial relations, and this in a manner that is contrary to a long established tradition, a tradition, however, that is beginning to fade." Although beginning to fade, it remained a forceful lens. Consider, for example, that the Royal Commission on Trade Unions and Employee Associations, the Donovan Commission, was set up in the mid-1960s to consider labor relations and collective bargaining problems. Several of the recommendations involved direct legal intervention. However, importantly, the primary innovation recommended by the Donovan Commission, and subsequently adopted by the Labour Government in its 1969 White Paper, In Place of Strife, involved the setting up of a Commission on Industrial Relations, a body staffed with non-governmental members from unions, business, and academia. The Commission was designed to facilitate the voluntary reform of the collective bargaining system; this was "organized persuasion" par excellence.

[49] Armour & Skeel, *supra* note 29, at 1776–85, detailing the centrality of the SEC to the US regulatory response to takeover concerns in the 1960s.

[50] See Gilson et al. *supra* note 43.

[51] CAF stands for Comitê de Aquisições e Fusões. See http://www.cafbrasil.org.br/eng/index.html.

[52] CAF Code, Introduction, 1.

its rules.[53] Although this author is in no position to provide any account of the contemporary conception of the Brazilian state, and whether or not it is similarly open to endogenous self-regulatory initiatives, it is clear that attempts to generate space for this regulatory solution have generated difficulties in traversing the territorial authority of the existing Brazilian Capital Markets regulator, CVM. In this regard, it is noteworthy that the Code itself observes that it "should not be regarded as a substitute" for either law or CVM.[54] That is, there is a pre-existing occupant of this regulatory space, even if—to carry the occupation metaphor further—they have been neglecting their property.

3.2 All for One and One for All: Rules, Trade-Offs, and Coordinating Mechanisms

Provided the contracting zone is open, it is necessary to get the affected market actors to the contracting table. The first UK Takeover Code acknowledged the importance of buy-in from all parties. In a statement issued shortly after its formation the Panel referred to the importance that the "voluntary system should function effectively and command the respect of all."[55] If key players opt out, there can be no self-regulatory solution. As noted above, the cost calculus for market actors will vary for different parties with both $C_{SR} <$ and $> C_S$ and $B_{SR} <$ and > 0 for different participants. There are two key considerations for successfully getting parties into the contracting zone. First, as B_{SR} and C_{SR} will be, inter alia, a function of the selected self-regulatory rule choices, compromises will have to be made to ensure that rule choices are not made that render $B_{SR} < 0$ or $C_{SR} > C_S$ for key players. In addition, but also as a substitute for such rule trade-offs, contracting is more likely to take place where there are coordinating mechanisms in place that either force contracting or reduce the coordination costs of contracting.

Let us consider first the relationship between rule choice and variation in relation B_{SR}. If the rulemakers reject the basic economic logic that key players will not contract if $B_{SR} < 0$, the self-regulatory venture is likely to fail. This logic and lesson does not bode well for Brazil's attempt to generate self-regulatory dualism in the takeover field. CAF has the support of several constituents of the Brazilian Capital Market including: the Brazilian Securities Exchange (BM&FBOVESPA S.A.—Bolsa de Valores, Mercadorias e Futuros, "BVMF"); the Association of Capital Markets Investors (Associação de Investidores no Mercado de Capitais; "AMEC"); the Brazilian Association of Entities of the Financial and Capital Markets (Associação Brasileira das Entidades dos Mercados Financeiro e de Capitais, "ANBIMA"); and the Brazilian Institute of Corporate Governance (Instituto Brasileiro de Governança Corporativa, "IBGC"). However, the Brazilian Association of Publicly Held Corporations (Associação Brasileira das Companhias Abertas, "ABRASCA") did not join the group after a long period of negotiation. The reason for their opt-out is thought to be the mandatory bid pricing rule contained in the Code.[56] A mandatory bid is triggered by

---

[53] See CAF Code, Introduction, 3. Companies sign up by amending the subject company's bylaws to provide that they are subject to the Code. In addition directors, officers, and controlling shareholders sign "statements of adherence" to the Code.

[54] CAF Code, Introduction, 1(iii).

[55] Panel on Takeovers and Mergers, Policy Statement, Apr. 28, 1969.

[56] See CAF Code, Section VI on Material Ownership Tender Offers.

a purchase of between 20–30% of the target's shares (the precise percentage determined by the applicable company's bylaws).[57] The mandatory bidder must offer to all shareholders the highest price paid for the shares in the previous 12 months.[58] The rule is understood to further the key takeover regulatory goal of equality of treatment of shareholders.[59] However, for many large Brazilian companies which are subject to blockholder control, such a rule would prevent a controller from receiving any payment for its private benefits of control as any premium paid to the blockholder within a 12-month look-back period must be offered to all shareholders. It is a forced sharing rule which, given the consensual nature of Code application, means that blockholder-owned public companies are unlikely to sign up, and the same goes for their trade association, ABRASCA. Alternative rules would have enabled sign-up by this key constituency: for example, no or a short look-back period would enable premium block purchases which would not be subject to the highest price rule; or a weighted pricing rule taking a percentage of the highest price paid. Of course even in the absence of widespread sign-up by public companies, from a regulatory dualism perspective the Code still offers benefits to existing widely held companies—as well as companies that intend to effect an IPO where there will be no post-IPO controller—allowing them to elect to lock in[60] the sharing rule. Nevertheless, rule integrity here appears to jeopardize generating momentum for the project. What is driving this counterproductive rule choice is difficult to parse. But it seems plausible that a possible driver is a classic translation problem: the desire of cosmopolitan legal elites to replicate, and to find authority for legal change in, foreign "best practice" regulation[61]—here in relation to the perceived importance of the equality of treatment of shareholders—at the expense of pragmatic adaptation to the conditions of the local marketplace. It is noteworthy in this regard that by the time the UK adopted a 12-month sharing rule for the mandatory bid rule in the mid-1970s there had been a significant reduction in the number of controlling shareholders in publicly traded companies and a concomitant increase in institutional holdings.[62]

Where parties refuse to enter or reach agreement within the contracting zone, optimal welfare-enhancing solutions—for the state and aggregate market actors—may be left on the table. In such circumstances coordination mechanisms are required to enable self-regulation. The story of the Takeover Code in this regard directs us to the importance of the financial incentives of pivotal players for coordinating self-regulatory contracting. Most important in this regard were the financial incentives of merchant (investment) banks. Prior to the Battle for British Aluminium, UK merchants banks were almost exclusively pro-management.[63] The seismic cultural shock which resulted from the failure of the target to succeed in this case led bankers to realize that their business model had to adapt to take account of the fact that there was money to be made in hostile activity. "Overnight," Roberts observes, City attitudes to takeovers changed and "financial advisors added hostile bids to

---

[57] See definition of "Material Ownership" in CAF Code.   [58] Article 65(1) CAF Code.

[59] Article 29(1) CAF Code.

[60] Lock in here is somewhat limited given to option of exit from the Code following a one year notice period. See CAF Code, Articles 23–25.

[61] See generally William Ewald, "Comparative Legal Jurisprudence (II): The Logic of Legal Transplants", 43 Am. J. Comp. Law 489 (1995) discussing the work of Alan Watson on legal transplants.

[62] See Brian R. Cheffins, Corporate Ownership and Control 301–77 (2008).

[63] Kynaston, *supra* note 11.

their repertoire of merger and acquisition techniques."[64] Bankers came to realize that there was money to be made in an active takeover market and in regulation that wedded takeover activity to the financial advisory role. These investment bankers were at the center of a network of advisory services, many of which were essential components in making a takeover bid. Accordingly, once the marketplace incentivized bankers to come into the contracting zone many others had no choice but to follow.

Plausibly, such an investment-banker-driven coordinating mechanism could act as a substitute for the absence of state or quasi-state drivers, as is the case in Brazil. However, for two reasons such replication is improbable. First, such an option is only available where hostile activity levels are sufficient to encourage bankers to take a more neutral stance between targets and acquirers. Where controlling ownership structures block a significant increase in such activity levels, as they do in Brazil, investment banker buy-in is likely to be difficult. Second, although investment bankers coordinated self-regulation in the UK, it was not an endogenous market response. Though coordinated action was in the bankers' interests and coordination costs for bankers were low—given pre-existing structures for collective action[65] and the close, geographically proximate and relatively homogeneous environment which was the Squire Mile of the City of London at this point in time[66]—bankers faced a prisoner's dilemma coordination problem between 1959—the introduction of the Notes— and the creation of the Code and Panel. Although it was in the long term financial interests of bankers (individually and collectively) to control a regulatory system that put them at the heart of the process, in the immediate term, in the absence of such a system, it was in the individual bankers' interests to serve their client's needs by facilitating creative (non-)compliance with the Notes. This they did in multiple high-profile events.[67] What was required— and what was in the bankers' individual and collective long-term interests—was forced coordination, which arose indirectly from state expectation in response to these events and directly from the Bank of England, who during this period remained the self-styled "Pope"[68] of the City.[69] In other jurisdictions, in the absence of such direct or indirect state pressure— which is necessarily the case where self-regulation responds to state governance failures— this financial advisor coordinating mechanism is unlikely to be triggered.[70]

Of course other market actors could also be incentivized to perform the coordinating role, even if no other constituency is as central to the deal process as the financial advisor. In an important article addressing the UK takeover context, Professors Armour and Skeel

---

[64] Roberts *supra* note 17. See also Armour & Skeel, *supra* note 29, at 1775 also observing that "there was plenty of money to be made on advising on acquisitions."

[65] The Issuing Houses Association and the Accepting Houses Association.

[66] See generally Armour & Skeel, *supra* note 29.   [67] See *supra* notes 25–27 and *infra* note 76.

[68] Sir Leslie warns on the Takeover Code, Guardian, Aug. 16, 1968. A different metaphor used in relation to the Bank of England was the Bank as "parent." Harry Siepmann of Lazards: "faith in the Bank as the Leader and Parent of the City . . ." (Kynaston, *supra* note 11, at 57).

[69] Importantly, the Bank of England was also strongly incentivized to ensure City coordination as any state interference in this zone would have represented a significant loss of authority at a time when its authority was increasingly being questioned. See, generally, Kynaston *supra* note 11.

[70] For a more detailed account of how state expectation and the Bank of England resolved this investment banking compliance prisoners' dilemma in the post-Notes period as well as a more detailed analysis of the substantive responses and how such responses connected to existing corporate law, and the interests of varying constituencies see Kershaw, *supra* note 18.

identify institutional shareholders as a coordinating mechanism. For Armour and Skeel, the increasing presence of institutional shareholders in the UK marketplace in the 1950s and 1960s[71] meant that it was in their interests to coordinate the market's response in order to exert influence over rule choice even where it may not have been in individual institutions' interests to coordinate to monitor individual companies.[72] In theory, with their increasing presence and power it seems very plausible that institutions could perform the role of self-regulatory coordinator in order to generate rules that favor their long-term interests. It would follow that the increasing institutionalization of corporate ownership in a jurisdiction may lead to an increase in the probability that self-regulatory solutions to corporate problems will arise, at least where the regulatory space has not already been occupied by the state. In this regard, Armour and Skeel suggest that: "It is not surprising that the emergence of a pro-shareholder approach to takeover regulation coincided with the emergence of institutional investors as a significant force in British share ownership."

With regard to the UK, Armour and Skeel are clearly correct that the "emergence of institutional investors" played a key role in creating the conditions within which the self-regulation of takeovers could arise. However, in my view this is not because the institutions themselves coordinated to claim the regulatory space. In the rule production process their role is better characterized as the interested observer rather than the coordinator. Several considerations point in this direction. First, it is not clear that either at the end of the 1950s or 1960s intra-institution coordinating mechanisms were in place.[73] Second, while it is correct that institutions expressed dissatisfaction at some pre-Takeover-Code events,[74] in relation to several others they were the beneficiaries of practices—at the expense of retail investors—that appeared to be in breach of the Notes.[75] Although, as is the case with merchant bankers, one could make a case that regulation was in the long-term interests of institutions even if they were tempted to take the low-hanging value fruit associated with preferential non-compliance. Third, and most importantly, it seems clear from the historical record that merchant banks controlled the drafting of both the Notes and the Code[76] through the Issuing Houses Association, producing a Code that responded to the high-profile takeover events

---

[71] Armour & Skeel, *supra* note 29.

[72] They view the Takeover Code as a "good example" of "the observed strategy . . . of coordinated lobbying for rules that were expected to maximise the joint welfare of institutional shareholders," id. at 1771.

[73] Welcome for a new initiative, The Times, July 20, 1967, observing that "It might be a useful long stop if the insurance companies, investments trusts, pension funds and unit trusts all formed a protection committee to look after those interests which they have in common. Such body would have a formidable influence."

[74] For example, Edwin Herbert of the Industrial and General Trust, and later a representative on the Notes Working Group, observed in the wake of British Aluminium that "where a change of control of a company is envisaged, or where the nature of the company's business is to be changed, shareholders should first be consulted"—Watney Sears Silence, Fin. Times, June 12, 1959.

[75] Several bids that contributed to the view that regulatory action was necessary gave institutional investors preferential price treatment. See, for example: RTB wins control of Whiteheads, Fin. Times, Feb. 2, 1963, noting that "the dealings in Whitehead shares aroused criticism in the Stock Exchange because different treatment was being accorded to different sellers"; Behind the Scenes of the Wilkinson & Riddell Battle, Fin. Times, June 29, 1967; Aberdare Wins MI Battle: Call for Inquiry, Fin. Times, July 13, 1967.

[76] See The Men behind the Code, *supra* note 30. See further, Kershaw, *supra* note 18.

that led to the Code whilst bonding the takeover process to a financial advisory role.[77] It is submitted that the more significant contribution of the institutionalization of share ownership to takeover regulation in the UK was then an indirect one: its demand-side contribution to the diffusion of share ownership created the conditions for the proliferation of hostile activity which, as observed above, altered the business model for investment bankers and generated strong incentives for them to take control of the regulatory process when action was coordinated by the Bank of England.

3.3 Enforcement

In the UK, unanimous constituency sign-up for the project was not only necessary for the project's momentum, it was central to its mode of enforcement. During the lifetime of the Code the Takeover Panel has acquired several state enforcement supports through the capital markets regulator prior to 2005 and after 2005, when the Takeover Panel became a state supervisory authority, through the courts.[78] But it has never, and is unlikely ever, to use them. It continues to rely on the enforcement tools introduced at its inception which involve neither injunctions nor fines but the corporate law equivalent of the naughty step and being sent to your bedroom.

There are three tiers of Panel sanction that ensure compliance with the Code and the Panel's instructions. Such instructions could include a direction to comply with the Code or, much more rarely, to compensate parties who are injured as a result of non-compliance. The sanction regime provides for a pyramid of increasingly onerous sanctions which fall clearly within the responsive regulation umbrella:[79] failing to comply with the Code could result in a private censure, a public censure, or a "cold shoulder." The censures are really precursors/warning signs for cold shouldering and involve either a private or public dressing down. If parties continue to offend or the first offense is an egregious one then the Panel may issue a cold shoulder statement. The effect of a cold-shoulder statement is to inform all market participants that they cannot work with this person for the specified period of time in relation to a UK takeover. In the early years following the Panel's formation, all the trade associations, together with the Board of Trade in relation to licensed dealers, agreed that any of their members who dealt with such a cold shouldered person would be subject to trade association sanctions which could result, in theory, in an effective loss of license for many of these participants. Today, the cold shoulder statement benefits directly from state support through the Financial Conduct Authority's Market Conduct Rules that provide that any person authorized to provide financial services business by the FCA must cease to work with the specified person in relation to takeovers and if they fail to do so may be sanctioned by the FCA, which again risks loss of license.[80] However, given the widespread compliance with the Code prior to this state support, it appears that the sanction worked effectively without it.

It is noteworthy that although this enforcement approach is widely considered to be highly effective, there are few public examples of sanctions being deployed. Although public censures do occur, they are relatively rare. There has only been one in the past five years.[81]

---

[77] See section 2.2.4 detailing this bonding.   [78] Sections 952–956 Companies Act 2006.
[79] See Baldwin et al., *supra* note 3.   [80] FCA Handbook, Market Conduct Rule 4.
[81] For a more detailed analysis of the number of public censures see Kershaw, *supra* note 18, chapter 4.

And cold shouldering orders are extremely rare. In the history of the Panel there have only been two. The last one was issued in 2010[82] but this was the first one for almost 20 years.[83] It is common, and sensible, in corporate governance scholarship to draw conclusions about the probability of enforcement from evidence about the number of enforcement actions brought against market participants. Through the lens of the regularity of enforcement action by the Panel one might conclude that the probability of Code enforcement is low. This would be a serious error of judgment for any market participant. However, it is only a mistake that an outsider would make. The Panel signals a high probability of enforcement for breach through its close engagement with the bid. For every deal the Panel appoints a case officer who is, purportedly, available in real time 24/7. This provides an unrivalled level of inter-action with, and oversight and control of, each deal.[84] The Panel's approach is not unfairly characterized as a surveillance culture, with deal participants aware of the Panel's presence and oversight throughout the deal.

Empirical evidence to support this account of such a surveillance culture is not avail-able. However, a recent case provides some more than anecdotal support for this position. *Re Expro International Group Plc*[85] involved an idiosyncratic UK deal structure known as a scheme of arrangement.[86] A scheme is a court-controlled deal structure that can be used to effect a merger or the functional equivalent of a tender offer.[87] To effect a scheme the parties must obtain the required approvals from shareholders, but also court approval that the scheme is fair and reasonable. This case involved a deal between Expro and a bidder called Umbrellastream. The parties agreed terms and obtained the scheme approvals. However, at the same time there was what UK M&A lawyers would call a virtual bid. In the shadows, Halliburton was lurking indicating that it might make an offer but never quite doing so. In such circumstances, the UK Takeover Code provides for a "put up or shut up" rule that requires such virtual bidders to either make a bid (put up) or announce that it will not make one (shut up).[88] If the bidder elects not to make a bid it cannot make an offer for the company in the following six months.[89] However, when a bidder elects to "shut up" it can condition its election on certain events which if they occur will allow it to re-enter the fray.[90] In this case Halliburton elected to "shut up" subject to the condition that if the court did not approve of the Umbrellastream scheme it would be able to make a bid. The possibility of a bidding war for the target incentivized several hedge funds to oppose the application for the court's ap-proval of the scheme. Halliburton instructed counsel to attend the scheme hearing. More interestingly, for our purposes, so did the Takeover Panel. What the Panel was doing at the

[82] Hearing Committee Decision in the case of Principal Capital Investment Trust Plc, 164. The order was made for a three-year period.

[83] The first cold shoulder was made in 1992 and arose in relation to purchases of shares in Dundee Football Club Plc. This cold-shoulder order was made for an unlimited duration.

[84] For empirical detail on the number of companies with whom the Panel engages each year see John Armour et al., "Private Enforcement of Corporate Law: An Empirical Comparison of the United Kingdom and the United States", 6 J. Emp. Legal Stud. 687, 717–18 (2009).

[85] [2010] 2 BCLC 514.   [86] Part 26 Companies Act 2006.

[87] A reduction and cancellation scheme involves the cancellation of existing shares in exchange for the deal consideration and then an issue of new shares to the bidder. See, Jennifer Payne, Schemes of Arrangement: Theory, Structure and Operation (2014).

[88] Rule 2.6 Takeover Code.   [89] Rule 2.8 Takeover Code.

[90] note 2 to Rule 2.8 Takeover Code.

hearing is at first blush rather unclear. Although the Takeover Code applies to schemes of arrangement, it had no role in the court's determination of whether or not to approve the scheme. The Code was not relevant to the outcome of the scheme. Nor was there any scope for the court to opine on Code rules; and its judgment would not affect the application of the Code to the scheme. What then was the Panel doing instructing expensive counsel to attend the meeting? It was there to make Halliburton aware that it was there. To ensure that Halliburton did not say anything at all that could be in breach of its shut-up election. Any indication of a particular price or encouragement to create space for a bid would have been, in the Panel's view, a breach of the Code. The Panel's presence was designed to ensure that Halliburton was aware of this.

The nature of this command and control compliance culture is difficult to describe and, as noted, has not been empirically documented. The above example merely provides a flavor of it. Moreover, how the culture came into being is also undocumented and illusive. It clearly cannot be accounted for by the mere existence of a powerful self-regulatory enforcement tool that has rarely been used. For a body attempting to replicate the Panel's success, such self-regulatory enforcement arrangements would, and should, appear hopelessly utopian. The Brazilian self-regulatory takeover code does not attempt any such replication. Indeed, it falls far short in this regard with no enforcement mechanism of any note.[91] Yet in close attention to the Panel's success there is a key replication lesson, although not one that will necessarily be available in the Brazilian context. The lesson is that a significant compliance dividend can be obtained, and a culture of self-regulatory compliance generated, if key (and coordinating) market actors can be given a financial stake in the rules and their enforcement. Put differently, and discussed in detail below, the key to self-regulatory enforcement success is, *through the rules and process*, to bribe the quarter-back.

3.4 Bribing the Quarterback: Creating Significant Financial Stakes in Compliance

For lawyers who encounter the Takeover Code in action for the first time it often involves a sense of surprise, if not disappointment. The reason for this is that the lawyers are not in charge of what is a very law-like and detailed rules-based[92] document. As the Code makes clear, it is the company's financial advisors that bear "a particular responsibility" for ensuring that their clients comply with the Code.[93] As a consequence of this, it is financial advisors (as well as lawyers) that perform a legal function for their clients. In meetings to discuss deal structure and compliance with the Code clients more often than not turn to their bankers to understand how the Code works and to understand the Panel's likely response to any requests that are made. Of course, given the central role that bankers played in the drafting of the Code and the creation of the Panel, this is unsurprising.

---

[91] The CAF Code provides for private censure, public censure, and then "withdrawal of the Panel seal," i.e., no longer being part of the CAF system (after a one-year exit period)—Art. 136 CAF Code.

[92] Although the Code purports to be a form of principle-based regulation, in addition to six General Principles, there are 300 pages of rules and sub-rules.

[93] Introduction, 3(f) Takoever Code.

Accordingly, UK investment bankers have valuable human capital wrapped up in their ability to interpret the Code and to predict Panel judgments. Such individual and firm investments are enhanced by the secondee case officer system that the Panel deploys. According to this system, the Panel staffs itself, in addition to its limited full-time staff, with secondees from financial advisors (including investment banks and financial consulting firms) and other members of the City establishment (including lawyers). In addition, at several junctures in the Code the role of financial advisor is hardwired into the takeover process. For example, a bidder cannot announce his intention to make a firm offer that will include a cash component without a "cash confirmation statement" from the financial advisor confirming that the cash resources needed to close the deal are available to the bidder.[94] Other, of the many, examples in which the Code builds in a role for the financial advisor include: the determination of whether or not to make a "possible offer announcement";[95] the requirement for certifications from financial advisors in relation to profit forecasts;[96] and target management's post-bid remuneration.[97] As each of these roles and functions generates fee income, the Code becomes a source of revenue.

As compliance with the Code is very clearly in the significant financial interests of financial advisors it is in the financial interests of the brokers, accountants, the lawyers whom they instruct and the companies, private equity houses, hedge funds that rely on their services. The lesson for effective enforcement of self-regulation from the Takeover Code is not only the hands-on involvement of the Panel and the innovative informal sanction of the cold-shoulder mechanism, but also a more straightforward incentive story: self-regulation will work if you make sure that strict compliance is in the financial interests of the most important player in the marketplace.

By providing one market player with such a key role in the regulatory space we might have legitimate public choice concerns that the rules will quickly become skewed toward the interests of the advisors and of their clients. A strong case can be made that multiple specific examples of such bias, referred to above, can be found, as well as a case that the exponential proliferation in the rule book is connected to financial advisor interests as it increases the scope for advice on Code interpretation and thereby solidifies a central role in the takeover process for bankers. However, with regard to the core of the Code that regulates bidder and target behavior it seems unlikely that any particular interests would be more forcefully transmitted to the Panel than others. Advisors typically work with bidders and targets and, therefore, see the advantages and disadvantages of the rules from both sides on a regular basis. The investment bank is therefore unlikely to become an effective conduit for the interests of a particular constituency in any regulatory reform or enforcement process. Of course, if advisors specialize in working for particular repeat-player clients such as private equity firms then their views may become weighted towards their client's regulatory preferences. But from the Panel's perspective, for every advisor putting forward a pro-bidder

---

[94] Rule 2.7 Takeover Code.

[95] Practice Statement No 20: Rule 2–Secrecy, possible offer announcement and pre-announcement responsibilities (2008) refers to the "particular responsibility of financial advisors for ensuring compliance with Rule 2" and that the financial advisors should be in control of drafting the announcement.

[96] Rule 28 Takeover Code.   [97] Rule 16.2 Takeover Code.

view there is an advisor putting forward the target's perspective. Accordingly, this problem is of limited concern.

This is different, of course, than saying that the Takeover Code provides a neutral system of rules as between shareholders and managers. It does not. It clearly provides a pro-shareholder rule book. But this rule book is not the product of shareholder control over or bias in the rulemaking process; rather the product of the deeper shareholder rights bias in British business culture and company law. A bias that generated the different strands of public and political outrage from the takeover events in the 1960s, relating to both shareholder sovereignty and equality of treatment, to which the original banker drafters of the Code directly responded.[98]

3.5 Demarcating the Regulatory Space

To operate effectively and ensure compliance with its rules, a self-regulator must "own" the regulatory space within which it operates. If it does not do so, market participants may attempt to subvert its rules by attempting to leverage the role of other lawmakers that may lay claim to the regulatory space. A self-regulator therefore requires either a regulatory space in which there is no other regulator or deference from such regulator. As detailed above, the Takeover Panel when it came into being benefited from both.[99] The Takeover Code also teaches us that the ability of an effective self-regulator to control the regulatory space is not only a function of the absence or deference of other regulators and adjudicators, but also a function of certain "keystone" rules that carve out that regulatory space. In the case of the Takeover Code there are two such rules: the non-frustration rule and the mandatory bid rule. The non-frustration rule is a rule that provides that where a bid has commenced or is imminent, target management cannot take any action that could prevent the shareholders from deciding on the merits of the bid without shareholder approval. This applies regardless of whether or not the board has any defensive motivation vis-à-vis the intended corporate action. As I have argued elsewhere,[100] the actual substantive effect of the non-frustration rule is overstated as the existing UK corporate law requires similar, although not identical, protection through the proper purpose doctrine.[101] However, the non-frustration rule's

---

[98] See notes 25, 26, and 27. Elaborating this claim, see further Kershaw, *supra* note 18, Chapter 3.

[99] Note also that when actions were brought in the courts for judicial review of Panel decisions the courts adopted an explicit and extremely deferential stance. They made it clear that although that they had the power to intervene—because the Panel, although a self-regulatory body, was performing state functions—it would only be in the most egregious of circumstances in which they would intervene. Furthermore, the courts clarified that in the very rare event in which they deemed intervention to be necessary, if the matter related to an ongoing takeover the court's ruling would be historic and not contemporaneous. This meant the court's ruling would only apply to future action by the Panel and would not alter the Panel's decision in the immediate case—*R. v. Panel on Takeovers and Mergers ex p Datafin Plc* [1987] QB 815 and *R. v. Panel on Takeovers and Mergers, ex p Guinness plc* [1989] 1 All ER 509.

[100] David Kershaw, "The Illusion of Importance: Reconsidering the UK's Takeover Defence Prohibition", 56 Int'l. & Comp. L. Q. 267–308 (2007).

[101] The proper purpose doctrine now set forth in section 171(b) of the Companies Act 2006 as the duty to use powers for proper purposes prohibits (without ex ante or ex post shareholder approval) the use of corporate power to interfere with the fundamental shareholder rights to vote and to decide on whether to accept or reject a takeover offer.

limited substantive impact should not be mistaken for its lack of importance to the Takeover Panel. In its absence, the question of the availability of defenses and the effects they could have on bid timing and process would not be in the hands of the Takeover Panel but in the hands of the courts interpreting the scope of application of the proper purpose doctrine. The Takeover Panel would often be forced to play second fiddle to the courts, undermining both its autonomy and the perception that it controls the rules of the game in the UK takeover market.

The second "keystone rule" is the mandatory bid rule. There is of course no such thing as a mandatory bid. All mandatory bids under the Takeover Code are voluntary bids because the bidder decides voluntarily to cross the mandatory bid threshold. It might do so to enhance its ownership position in the target prior to the offer if the bidder expects resistance from the target. The rules that apply to mandatory bids are more onerous than those that apply to voluntary bids. For example, the pricing look-back period for a mandatory bid is 12 months rather than three months,[102] and there is virtually no scope for any conditionality beyond a simple majority acceptance threshold.[103] Accordingly, most bidders opt for voluntary bids. However, without the mandatory bid rule the Panel would not be able to maintain its stringent regulation of voluntary bids as the costs of the incremental acquisition of control of the target over time would in many cases be lower than a Code-controlled voluntary bid. This would force the Panel to reduce the costs of voluntary bids by relaxing many of the rules.

Although both of these rules are contentious there are many valid arguments in their favor.[104] However, aside from the arguments for and against the rules, it is interesting to observe that the centrality of these rules to the creation and operation of self-regulation of the market for corporate control gives the regulator a distinct vested interest in those rules that may not be aligned with the interests of the companies it regulates or the economy in which those companies operate. Accordingly, in relation to such keystone rules the technique of self-regulation may bias substantive outcomes in an unexpected way, independently of the rule bias sought by constituency interests. It follows that where events problematize such keystone rules we cannot rely on the self-regulator—even one that is truly independent of constituency interests—to be a neutral arbiter of their suitability and efficiency.

Recent events in the UK lend support to this view. The high-profile, initially hostile, takeover of Cadbury Plc. by the US corporation Kraft Inc. raised the question in political, business, and media circles as to whether UK companies were too exposed to hostile deals and too easily taken over. At a speech at the Said Business School the outgoing Chairman of Cadbury, Roger Carr, asked whether the prevailing takeover rules "were fair and helpful to the long-term success of Britain's future."[105] As possible reform responses Mr Carr considered both the disenfranchisement of short-term shareholders in hostile bid contexts and an increase in the minimum acceptance condition from a simple to a super majority. We cannot explore the merits of these proposals here, but what should be noted is that both ideas explored ways in which boards could be directly or indirectly empowered and supported over the long term. An alternative means of altering the balance of power would be to provide boards with greater defensive capability which, inter alia, would involve reform to the

---

[102] Rule 9 Takeover Code.   [103] Rule 9 Takeover Code.
[104] See Edmund Schuster, "The Mandatory Bid Rule: Efficient, after All?", 76 Mod. L. Rev. 529–63 (2013); Kershaw, *supra* note 18, chapter 1.
[105] Speech available at http://podcasts.ox.ac.uk/roger-carr-cadbury-hostile-bids-and-takeovers.

non-frustration rule. Following Carr's comments, political and media attention on the role of the Code's rules was heightened and the Takeover Panel responded with a consultation process and rule changes that, at the margin, may have dampened takeover activity.[106] For our purposes, what matters here is not whether Carr was right or wrong; what matters is that there was no serious engagement in the consultation process regarding the merits of the non-frustration rule,[107] and no attempt to gather empirical evidence on the effects that this rule may have had on UK companies and the UK economy. This key issue was not placed in play at all, and the debate was ultimately channeled into marginal, if useful, reforms. The keystone rule remained untouched.

4 Market Controlled Regulation: Comply or Explain

It is clear that there are regulatory benefits of a regulator being able to access market knowledge and information about market practices and how those practices are likely to interact with regulation. However, unsurprisingly the regulated may be less than forthcoming to the regulator with that knowledge. Endogenous self-regulation may be one means of accessing that knowledge, but as we have seen the probability of generating effective self-regulation is low. A close analysis of the Takeover Code and Panel reveals several sui generis factors upon which its success it built. This analysis suggests that a regulatory strategy built upon encouraging or supporting self-regulation will often involve a considerable pinch of wishful thinking. The need to find alternative ways of harnessing market knowledge within regulation points us to another "light" version of self-regulation, referred to in this chapter as "market controlled regulation". Through market-controlled regulation the state does not wait for or encourage the market to regulate itself; rather it commands its direct involvement in rule production. It seeks to achieve its regulatory objectives by co-opting the market actors to form and tailor the rules. In doing so it takes the risk that control of the rules may bias the rules in favor of market actors, in order to obtain the substantive benefits of informed and tailored business regulation and the compliance and norm-formation benefits that may flow from market ownership of the regulatory space.

The main example of such market controlled regulation in the corporate sphere is the introduction during the last 20 years of market-controlled corporate governance codes designed to guide companies towards best practice in the composition and structure of boards. These Codes invariably address the number of non-executive directors and their role and independence of management, and board committee structure and the staffing of these

---

[106] Including a tightening up of the put up or shut up rule to commence automatically from the first announcement (Rule 2.6 Takeover Code) and the prohibition of deal protections (Rule 21.2 Takeover Code). See Consultation Paper Issued By the Code Committee of the Panel: Review of Certain Aspects of the Regulation of Takeover Bids (PCP 2010/2).

[107] As I have argued elsewhere, a strong case can be made that in fact the non-frustration rule does not make a significant difference to exposure levels for UK targets (see Kershaw, *supra* note 100); however, before one could consider altering UK company law to make it more board friendly the non-frustration rule would have to be addressed.

committees. They may also cover separation of the roles of chairman and chief executive officer, remuneration guidance, and internal controls. These Codes are typically—although as the US experience shows not always[108]—"comply or explain" codes. "Comply or explain" means that companies are required to comply with the recommendations set forth within the code or to explain to their shareholders why they do not comply. The underlying idea of such codes is to set forth guidance on governance best practice that one would expect most companies to follow but to leave companies the freedom to adapt governance rules and structures to their own conditions and circumstances: one size does not fit all, therefore one size is not imposed on all. However, departures from the code must be justified to shareholders who can assess and respond to the non-compliance explanation either through voice or exit. Although the code rules are typically produced by representatives of market actors who are the members of the code committee or commission who produce the rules, such commissions invariably have been formed by or are connected to the State, members are often appointed by the state or the state at least has a say in the broader membership, and typically the obligation to comply or explain is set forth in mandatory law.

4.1 Foundations

The first comply and explain corporate governance code was the UK's Code of Best Practice issued in 1992, which formed the basis of what today is known as the UK Corporate Governance Code. The first iteration of this Code resulted from Sir Adrian Cadbury's investigation into the "Financial Aspects of Corporate Governance." The "Cadbury Committee" was—like the Takeover Code and Panel—the product of the combination of a deferential conception of the British State, pressure generated by public outrage in relation to several corporate and accounting scandals,[109] and the coordination and forced entry of market participants into the "contracting zone" by the London Stock Exchange and the quasi-state body, the Financial Reporting Council (FRC), who commissioned the Report.[110] The FRC itself was then a recently formed response to the failed self-regulation of accounting standards.[111] After the Cadbury Committee's recommendations were delivered, the FRC became responsible for the maintenance and revision of the Code. The FRC is a quasi state body with certain formally designated state functions[112] and its Chairman and CEO are appointed by the secretary of state for business. Nevertheless, this is a body controlled by market constituents, with a majority of FRC appointed board members from the business and accounting worlds, and with no delegated representatives from other regulators or government.[113]

---

[108]   Although some composition rules are set forth in the Securities Exchange Act of 1934, as amended by the Sarbanes–Oxley Act, most composition and structure rules are set forth in the governance rules of the trading platform, for example, in Section 3.03A of the NYSE Listing Manual.

[109]   See, e.g., Mr Maxwell's costly legacy, Fin. Times, Dec. 5, 1991.

[110]   DTI Will Back In-Depth Review of Companies, Fin. Times, May 31, 1991.

[111]   Sir Ron's tough package sets standard, Fin. Times, Nov. 10, 1988.

[112]   Part 42 Companies Act 2006.

[113]   For current board membership see https://www.frc.org.uk/About-the-FRC/FRC-structure/FRC-Board/Members.aspx.

From its inception the Code has been a "comply or explain" Code. However, for companies subject to the Code the requirement either to "comply or explain" is mandatory. Pursuant to the FCA's listing rules, premium listed companies[114] must provide a statement in their annual reports setting forth whether they comply with the Code's provisions or explaining their failure to comply.[115] The Code itself recommends that explanations provide background to, the rational for, and risks associated with the departure for the Code.[116] However, there are no clear guidelines in the FCA's rules on the level of detail that must be provided in company's explanations of non-compliance. A statement providing that "the provision is unsuitable for our company" would appear to suffice for the purposes of compliance with the explain obligation. It is noteworthy that in this regard the FRC has no sanctioning powers, and that to date there has been no action by the FCA or its predecessor, the Financial Services Authority, in relation to companies' failure either to explain or in relation to the quality and detail of the explanation.

Worldwide at the beginning of this century there was an exponential increase in the production of Corporate Governance Commissions and Codes following multiple high-profile corporate and audit failures, particularly in the US.[117] Although the governance response in the US generated mandatory rules imposed through exchanges and trading platforms,[118] most other jurisdictions elected for the less intrusive "comply or explain" approach. In Germany, for example, a Corporate Governance Commission was appointed by the federal government in 2001 and a Code introduced in 2002.[119] Publicly traded companies are required either to comply or to explain non-compliance pursuant to section 161 of the German Stock Corporation Law. Although the German state provided for its formation, the Commission is staffed (by government appointment) with shareholder and management representatives as well as auditors and academics. The Austrian and Dutch Corporate Governance Codes adopt a similar approach of state authorized commissions and statutory "comply and explain" obligations coupled with Commissions staffed by market participants.[120]

4.2 Compliance Levels

The typical expectation of students who encounter the "comply or explain" idea for the first time, is that compliance levels will be low. We tend to think of regulation, particularly

---

[114] Companies listed on the Main Market of the London Stock exchange may elect to have a premium or standard listing. Premium listed companies are subject to more onerous listing and governance requirements.

[115] Listing Rule 9.8.6(5).   [116] UK Corporate Governance Code, 3.

[117] Including, most notably, the failures of Enron, WorldCom, and Tyco.

[118] See, e.g., Section 3.03A of the NYSE Listing Manual for corporations listed on the NYSE.

[119] Note that the stimulus to create a Corporate Governance Code was pre-Enron with a Code generated by academics in 1999 and the Commission appointed prior to Enron's collapse in September 2000—see Eddy Wymeersch, Corporate Governance Codes and their Implementation (http://papers. ssrn.com/sol3/papers.cfm?abstract_id=931100).

[120] In Austria the "comply or explain" obligation was made mandatory pursuant to the Austrian Business Code Amendment Act 2008. Pursuant to the Netherlands Civil Code, Dutch companies must comply or explain non-compliance with the Dutch Corporate Governance Code.

regulation that represents a response to failings, as directing participants to take actions contrary to their preferences. It follows that if you give the regulated a choice about compliance they will elect not to comply. This concern was acknowledged by the Cadbury Committee, which warned market participants that if they did not take the recommendations seriously, "it is probable that legislation and external regulation will be sought to deal with some of the underlying problems."[121] Yet contrary to this expectation, compliance levels for "comply and explain" codes are high, and very high amongst large, publicly traded companies. In the UK, Arcot and Bruno[122] report compliance levels of between 85% to 95% of companies in relation to a subset of key—arguably the most important—Code provisions.[123] Arcot and Bruno did note, however, that where there was non-compliance, the relevant explanation was often very brief and uninformative.[124] Over the course of the Code's lifespan Arcot and Bruno's results confirm that the UK Code is driving profound structural governance changes, even where those changes are contentious. Consider, for example, the recommendation to separate the roles of chairman and CEO,[125] an issue which continues to divide opinion both within the UK and across jurisdictions. Between 1991 and 1993 Conyon documents an increase in separation rates of 48%–64%.[126] Arcot and Bruno found that by 2003 the compliance rate had increased to 92%. Another example of how the Code appears to be driving change is in relation to the length of senior management's service contracts. As of 2003 Arcot and Bruno found weak compliance levels in relation to the Code provision recommending maximum one-year service contracts. Several years after their study, one would struggle today to find any companies that do not comply with this provision. In a later study, with a smaller sample but a broader assessment of compliance with all (at the time) 48 Code provisions, Seidl, Sanderson, and Roberts found that approximately 63% of the top 80 companies (by market capitalization) were fully compliant with the Code, whereas only 34% of the bottom companies were fully compliant.[127] The top 80 companies had an average of 0.96 deviations and the bottom 50 an average of 1.49 deviations. If one turns to continental European "comply or explain" Codes compliance levels are high, although again the quality of explanations where there is non-compliance is considered to be poorly informative.[128] The German Code makes a distinction between recommendation and suggestions. Compliance rates for DAX 30 companies in relation to recommendations are in the high 90s percentile and for suggestions in the high 80s.[129] This represents a notable increase on 2006

---

[121] Report of the Committee on the Financial Aspects of Corporate Governance (1992), 1.10.

[122] Sridhar Arcot and Valentina Bruno, "In Letter but not in Spirit: An Analysis of Corporate Governance", available at SSRN: http://ssrn.com/abstract=819784.

[123] The eight Code provisions: Chairman/CEO separation, appointment of a SID, number NEDS, percentage of NEDs, service contract terms, nominations committee, remuneration committee, and audit committee.

[124] Arcot & Bruno, *supra* note 122, at 18–22.   [125] UK Corporate Governance Code, A2.

[126] Martin Conyon & Chris Mallin, "A Review of Compliance with Cadbury", 22 Journal of General Management 14 (1997).

[127] David Seidl, Paul Sanderson, & John Roberts, "Applying "Comply or Explain": Conformance with Codes of Corporate Governance in the UK and Germany" (http://www.cbr.cam.ac.uk/pdf/WP389.pdf).

[128] This latter concern has led the European Commission to encourage companies to improve the quality of explanations. See European Commission Recommendation on the quality of corporate governance reporting (2014/208/EU).

[129] See Axel Weder & Jenny Bartz, Corporate Governance Report 2013: "Abweichungskultur und Unabhaengigkeit im Lichte der Akzeptance und Anwendung des Aktuellen DCGK" (available at http://

when only 40% of DAX companies were fully compliant and only 10% of MDAX (mid-cap) companies were in full compliance with the Code.[130] Dutch compliance rates are high 90s percentile for large caps, although compliance rates drop for mid and small caps (89%, 88%, respectively).[131]

Care needs to be taken, however, not to assume that the existence of a "comply or explain" governance code coupled with high rates of compliance necessarily represents a new and distinctive contribution to governance. Many corporate governance codes have extensive sections that merely replicate the existing legal position as set forth in the applicable Corporate Code. The Austrian Corporate Code, for example, explicitly acknowledges that the Code is based on Austrian corporate and securities law, as well as OECD Principles.[132] The German Code contains many provisions that again merely replicate corporate law and practice. For example, the German Code contains provisions referring to the unavailability of multiple voting rights, which for most companies are unavailable under German law.[133] Its section on the management board (*Vorstand*) involves in large part a replication of existing mandatory corporate law.[134] Furthermore, many of the provisions in the Code would not be viewed by many corporate governance scholars as governance terms at all, but merely as good process guidelines. For example in Provision 2.2.4 of the Code there is a suggestion that the general meeting last for four to six hours. Provision 2.3.3 suggests that the general meeting should be followed by modern communication. Of course, these Codes do take important steps to alter certain existing practices. Most important in relation to the German Code is the recommendation to limit the longstanding practice of management board members retiring to the supervisory board[135] or the provision recommending that supervisory board members do not take more than three supervisory board directorships.[136] The Code provides both a recommended limit on the number of supervisory board members who are former management board members and for a cooling off period for managers of two years before they are eligible for supervisory board membership. As of 2013, these provisions attracted between low 70s and high 90s percentile compliance, with larger companies more likely to comply.[137] The point here is not that these Codes do not, or do not have the potential to, make a governance difference, but that we must parse often lengthy codes for provisions that are different from applicable corporate law or are of real governance significance. This in turn means that we also need to be wary of overall compliance data which details partial compliance and percentage deviation from the Code provisions. There is a risk with this data that identified

www.bccg.tu-berlin.de/main/publikationen.htm). See also Paul Davies at al., Corporate Boards in European Law: A Comparative Analysis (2013).

[130] See id.

[131] Rapport Monitoring Commissie Corporate Governance Code (2012) available at http://www.commissiecorporategovernance.nl/rapport-2012.

[132] See Preamble, Austrian Corporate Governance Code, available at http://www.wienerborse.at/corporate/pdf/CG%20Codex%202012_v5_englisch.pdf.

[133] Provision 2.1.2 German Corporate Governance Code, available at www.dcgk.de/en/code.html. "Multiple voting rights are now generally prohibited for the stock corporation in the Stock Corporation Act", s. 12(2), and voting caps for public companies in s. 134(1).

[134] See id. For example, section 4.   [135] See id. 5.4.   [136] See id. 5.4.5.

[137] See Weder & Bartz, *supra* note 129, at 890.

partial compliance merely represents compliance with existing mandatory law or non-governance provisions.[138]

These caveats aside it remains clear that in relation to a substantial body of companies "comply or explain" governance codes alter the governance rules and practices of those companies even though there is no requirement to actually comply. In Germany, the UK, and the Netherlands, for example, high 80s and 90s percentile of the largest publicly traded companies comply fully with the Codes. Indeed, in some jurisdictions, for example the UK, excessive compliance is viewed as the primary enforcement problem. The FRC has become concerned that companies do not take seriously enough the idea that they can explain non-compliance. Recent amendments to the Code attempt to foreground this option to companies.[139] The UK's post-crisis Walker Review into the Governance of Banks and Financial Institutions lamented the fact that many of the UK Corporate Governance Code's rules may be inapt for banks, yet banks did not opt out and explain non-compliance.[140] Walker was particular concerned in this regard that the Code's focus on the independence of non-executive directors resulted in boards of banks staffed with directors who did not understand modern banking and financial services.[141] Whether or not this was the case across all UK banks is debatable,[142] but Walker was surely correct that UK banks did not consider that they had space to explain non-compliance. This has led some commentators (unsuccessfully) to propose changing the terminology to "apply and explain."[143] The idea being that companies need to distance themselves from a "compliance culture" and that using "apply" instead of "comply" will enable this.[144]

4.3 Enforcement Drivers

These Codes make recommendations many of which are not in the senior managers' interests. Separation of Chairman and CEO in the UK and management board cooling-off periods in Germany are good examples of such managerially unfriendly rules. Such rules are not enforced by regulators. There are no direct financial consequences of non-compliance. Yet the compliance levels are very high. What explains this? Where do we find the compliance pressures?

---

[138] See, for example, Seidl et al., *supra* note 127. See Weder & Bartz, *supra* note 129, separating out the existing mandatory law but not the non-governance like/business practice provisions from the overall compliance levels—but importantly providing provision-level compliance information.

[139] UK Corporate Governance Code, Comply or Explain, 4.

[140] A Review of Corporate Governance in UK Banks and other Financial Industry Entities (2009) Observing at 2.16 that some shareholders "appear to have interpreted [comply or explain] in a somewhat minatory way as 'comply or else.'"

[141] A Review of Corporate Governance in UK Banks and other Financial Industry Entities: Consultation Document 3.08–3.12 (2009).

[142] Compare the Board of HBOS in 2006 (little to no knowledge of banking and financial services) with the board of the Royal Bank of Scotland (significant financial services experience). See HBOS Annual Report and Accounts 2006, available at http://www.lloydsbankinggroup.com/globalassets/documents/investors/2006/2006_hbos_ra.pdf, at 90, with RBS's Annual Report and Accounts 2006, available at: http://www.annualreportowl.com/RBS/2006/Annual%20Report, at 101.

[143] See Call for More Flexibility on Code, Fin. Times, June 25, 2009.

[144] Note that the King Code of Governance for South Africa adopts an "apply or explain" approach.

It seems clear that the compliance pressure arises through a combination of market/investor expectation about good governance as benchmarked by the applicable Code coupled with reputational capital concerns for managers but also, more importantly, for non-executive directors whose rents are a function of their ability to obtain other (parallel or subsequent) non-executive positions. This reputational capital is, inter alia, a function of directors' association with companies that are known for good and not bad governance practices. The potential reputational downside of non-compliance for directors is a function of the likelihood that investors (fund managers) will reject the explanation and put their head above the parapet to complain about non-compliance and "bad governance." The question of importance here is: what factors determine an investor's response to explained non-compliance?

Ideally, such a response is a function of the arguments about the benefits and downsides of the provision itself and the provision's application to the company in question. It may be the case that compliance levels are high because attempts to explain non-compliance have met with careful consideration by institutional investors and their fund managers, but ultimately their rejection of the non-compliance and subsequent direct and indirect pressure to comply. However, there are several factors which may distort such an "ideal" shareholder assessment of non-compliance. First, consider the costs associated with that analysis for the fund manager. Although the economic benefits for the investor of the company complying or not complying with the provision are likely to be very uncertain, opaque, and distant, the opportunity costs of the governance conversation are clear and immediate. It may be cheaper in such circumstances to have a pro-compliance bias across all portfolio companies which resists detailed investigation, engagement, and conversation, and relies on the best practice recommendation of the expert market regulators. Of course, investors can also rely on, and pay for, the advice of governance specialists;[145] however, such specialists have a deep vested interest in a strong compliance culture that keeps governance relevant. This surely gives such advisors a pro-compliance bias. Second, compliance pressure may arise from the fact that many passive fund managers may themselves be subject to external pressure to be seen to be acting in order to be seen to be doing their job. Such pressure could come from the ultimate investors—for example, pension trustees, but could also come from government. In the UK, for several decades the monitoring and activism of shareholders has been on the regulatory agenda. Government ministers who have decried the role of shareholders prior to the crisis have described them as "absentee landlords."[146] Most recently this resulted in the introduction of a "comply or explain" Stewardship Code for investors.[147] Notably, this pressure and criticism rarely takes account of the fact that, due to limited share holdings as well as the practicalities and compensation structures of long UK fund management, shareholder activism may not be in the economic interests of the fund manager or the investor. However, fund managers sensitive to these pressures and criticisms are aware that they need to be seen to be acting, even when they are of the opinion that it is not in their, or their

---

[145] See generally, for example, Stephen Choi, Jill Fisch, & Marcel Kahan, "The Power of Proxy Advisors: Myth or Reality", 59 Emory L. J. 870 (2010).

[146] Different Kinds of Company Ownership Are Gaining in Popularity, Fin. Times, Oct. 10, 2011.

[147] UK Stewardship Code available at https://frc.org.uk/Our-Work/Codes-Standards/Corporate-governance.aspx.

ultimate investors', economic interests to invest resources in being more attentive and active. Opposing non-compliance with the Corporate Governance Code is arguably a very cheap way of being responsive to such external pressures.

As Ed Rock and Marcel Kahan have recently taught us,[148] in each jurisdiction, we need to understand the symbolism of investor activism which may reveal that the reason for acting is very different than the reason given for acting. It seems likely in the UK that compliance pressure comes *in part* from the symbolic capital investors can earn by opposing—loudly—non-compliance, regardless of explanations. High-profile examples of shareholder dissatisfaction with Code non-compliance would appear to fit with such an understanding. Consider, for example, the decision in 2008 by Marks & Spencer Plc., a household name in British retail, not to comply with the Code provision recommending separation of the chairman and CEO roles. Investors treated the separation rule as a mandatory provision, accusing the company of being "in breach" of the Code, leading one City commentator to observe that "apparently the English word 'or' in comply or explain has lost its meaning."[149] If this correctly describes investor motivation some of the time in objecting to non-compliance, then directors of companies cannot expect a fair hearing for their explanations. Furthermore, it seems probable that as soon as one investor publicly complains, other investors will line up to drink at the trough of symbolic capital, and directors will suffer reputational damage regardless of the strength of the justification for non-compliance. The larger and more high-profile the company the more likely it will be to trigger a knee jerk "object and shout loudly" response from the investment community. And the more likely the directors will be to comply rather than bother to explain why non-compliance makes sense, even when it does.

4.4 The effects of regulatory technique on rule choice

As noted in the Introduction to this chapter, one of the concerns about delegating regulatory authority to the marketplace is that the regulation will have a pro-market bias. Is it then surprising that the UK's market-controlled "comply or explain" Code is much more detailed and demanding, and much more pro-shareholder than mandatory governance regimes subject to state regulatory oversight such as those found in the US?[150] Two familiar explanations offer themselves for this variation, but neither are satisfactory. First, that the market-controlled rulemaking process has been captured by the interests of institutional shareholders which have pushed the Code's shareholder orientation. Indeed, it is clearly the case that for the past two decades institutional investors themselves, and via their trade associations, have exerted a strong public governance voice in the UK. However, a case for the overweighting of such direct influence is difficult to make when one considers the background of the key players of the members of the Cadbury Committee, the membership of the FRC, or the leading players in governance reform such as Sir Adrian Cadbury and Sir

---

[148]   Marcel Kahan & Edward B. Rock, "Symbolic Corporate Governance Politics" 94 B.U. L. Rev. 1997 (2014).

[149]   Why M&S Shareholders Should Think before We Speak, Fin. Times, Apr. 8, 2008.

[150]   S.19(b)(1) Securities Exchange Act of 1934 requiring SEC approval of self-regulatory organization rule changes following a SEC controlled consultation process.

Derek Higgs.[151] Second, that the Code's shareholder primacy bias may be an extension of, or a reflection of, UK company law's established shareholder rights orientation.[152] Whilst a pro-shareholder legal environment is surely an important contextual factor, given the absence of these type of rules until the 1990s, it is clearly only an ancillary driver.

The primary driver of this rule detail and rule orientation, it is submitted, is the effect of the "comply or explain" technique itself on the market-controlled regulator's outlook. The market-controlled regulatory bodies charged with drafting and amending a "comply or explain code" will approach their task very differently from a body tasked with drafting a set of mandatory governance rules. The latter is aware that the rules it selects must be adopted by the subject companies. It is, therefore, likely to be highly attuned to the authority/accountability[153] trade-offs associated with different rule choices and much more wary of changing the rules in the face of governance scandals. In contrast, a "comply or explain" regulator may feel that she has more room to ignore, or at least be less concerned about, the trade-offs and can "aim high" by providing truly best practice rules. This is because in such a regulator's mind's eye the trade-off, if it needs to be made, can be made by the company itself. That is, built into the "comply or explain" approach is the safety value that if the regulator gets it wrong for the company in question the company may simply ignore the rule and explain why. Such an outlook would also make a "comply or explain" regulator more receptive to calls for reviews of, and changes to, the rules in the face of public and political pressure to address governance scandals. Where "comply or explain" works as it is designed to, such responsiveness to accountability pressures and best practice outlook are not problematic. However, if "comply or explain" malfunctions for the reasons discussed above and in effect turns an optional regime into a mandatory regime, when combined with such a regulatory outlook, there is a strong case that "comply or explain" is a suboptimal regulatory technique likely to result in a regulatory overweighting of accountability concerns.

Take, for example, governance rules that determine whether a director is independent or not. Very demanding independence rules that provide for no business relations with the company or long employee cooling-off periods will exclude many individuals with the right skills and knowledge from performing the directorial role effectively: to exercise the managerial function and to bring industry-relevant experience, contacts, and networks to bear. There is a trade-off between tight independence rules and the pool of knowledgeable directors: the tighter the rules, the shallower the available pool of directors. This trade-off has been brought to light by the financial crisis. A "comply or explain" regulator may be more likely to select demanding rules that take independence seriously because she knows that if the rules are not suitable, the company can elect not to comply with the independent non-executive recommendation and appoint a non-independent but knowledgeable director. In an optional "comply or explain" environment there is, in theory, no demarcated pool of talent because companies can dip into the non-independent pool. In contrast, in a mandatory rule environment, as is the case for example with corporations listed on the New York Stock Exchange,[154] there is no option not to comply with the 50% independent non-executive director requirement and appoint the non-independent knowledgeable

[151] Both of whom played major roles in UK companies.
[152] See generally, David Kershaw, Company Law in Context: Text and Materials (2d ed. 2012).
[153] K. Arrow, The Limits of Organization (1974), Fels Lectures on Public Policy Analysis 77.
[154] NYSE Listing Manual, 303A.01 and A.02.

director. In such a mandatory environment the regulator will be acutely aware of the need to ensure that the definition of independence does not cut off the supply to the talent pool. However, if in a "comply or explain" environment companies experience the rules as mandatory rules, they are then faced with the same predicament as companies in the mandatory regime but with a regulator who thinks that the regime's non-compliance flexibility gives it more room to set rules that represent ideal standards. Of course a regulator could adjust its approach to rulemaking to take account of an over-compliance culture. However, such over-compliance with a rule may equally be viewed by the regulator as the broad affirmation of its rulemaking choices. When faced with interpretations of empirical facts that challenge or affirm our identities and roles, invariably people select the interpretation which defensively affirms their identity and their prior actions.[155] It is, therefore, improbable that one would see such an adjustment by a "comply or explain" regulator to its rulemaking outlook.

It is problematic to attribute jurisdictional variation to any particular driver. There are likely to be many drivers of variation. It is submitted, however, that a comparison of the UK corporate Governance Code with the US rules as set forth, for example, in the NYSE Listing Rules, raises concerns that the above suboptimality problem is present in the UK. Both jurisdictions have a 50% independent non-executive director requirement.[156] However, the independence definition is much more demanding in the UK than in the US. The UK has, for example, a cooling-off period of five rather than three years under the NYSE rules.[157] In the UK any performance-based pay for independent directors renders them presumptively non-independent,[158] as does nine years' continuous service; the NYSE rules contain no such limitations.[159] It is of course empirically very difficult/impossible to assess whether such rules are resulting in the staffing of UK boards with independent but unknowledgeable directors. The consequences of this being the case are reason enough to consider whether the UK should step back from governance leadership. It may also be a salient lesson that there is always a darker side to every governance innovation and that in practice we may find that regulatory theory—such as the probable bias associated with delegating regulatory power to the regulated—may be significantly wide of the mark.

4.5 Cultural governance beyond the ticked box

A traditional view of self-regulation focuses on the creation of law-like rules produced by market actors. More contemporary ideas of how to get the market to self-regulate focus less on enabling market actors to create and enforce rules applicable to all market actors, and more on facilitating pro-regulation norm formation within the players themselves: within the cultures of the firms and within the heads and identities of their managers and employees. If successful, this is true *self-regulation* in the literal meaning of the term and

---

[155] See generally, C. M. Steele, The Psychology of Self-Affirmation: Sustaining the Integrity of the Self, in Advances in Experimental Social Psychology 261 (L. Berkowitz ed., 1988); G. L. Cohen & D. K. Sherman, "The Psychology of Change: Self-Affirmation and Social Psychological Intervention", 65 Ann. Rev. Psychol. 333 (2014).

[156] NYSE Listing Manual, 303A.01; UK Corporate Governance Code, B.1.2.

[157] UK Corporate Governance Code, B.1.1; NYSE Listing Manual, 303A.02(b)(i).

[158] UK Corporate Governance Code, B.1.1.   [159] UK Corporate Governance Code, B.1.1.

external rules, whether state- or market-controlled, become far less important as internal firm norms ensure targeted behaviors. This approach to regulation has multiple academic labels, including meta-regulation,[160] principles-based regulation,[161] and process-based regulation.[162] The idea is that the regulator sets forth broad objectives and then requires the regulated firms to explore processes and procedures to enable those goals to be realized.[163] This both utilizes local knowledge to provide tailored firm-level regulation but also creates conversations and processes that bias local norm formation.[164] Several factors contribute to the likely success of this regulatory strategy that we cannot explore in detail here. First, and most importantly, clear and credible buy-in by senior management and the board must drive internal (firm-level) enforcement of failures to engage with the processes.[165] Secondly, the subject firms' incentives, in particular, but not only, those of senior management, must not be demonstrably non-aligned with the regulatory objectives.[166]

While increasingly this strategy is being used in the regulation of corporate activity, it has not featured significantly in corporate law. One area in which it is deployed is in relation to board performance. Again we see the UK as market leader in the use of this innovation. Whether this is connected to a traditional deference to market-solutions which remains embedded in the UK's regulatory psyche is clearly plausible, although speculative. The FRC has become increasingly aware that ticking several board composition and structure boxes provided by "comply or explain" codes may not necessarily drive improved performance in the boardroom. In this regard a key, if innocuous, change in the UK Corporate Governance Code in 2010 provided that boards must undertake a "formal and rigorous" annual evaluation of their performance. As per the process-based regulation tool-kit, the FRC also provides a non-binding set of objectives and guidance on both board effectiveness and the effectiveness of the different directors including the CEO and CFO, the chairman of the board, the lead independent non-executive director (known as a *senior independent director*), and more generally in relation to executive and non-executive directors. This guidance states, for example, that "effective boards" provide direction for management, demonstrate ethical

---

[160] Christine Parker, Meta-Regulation: Legal Accountability for Corporate Social Responsibility, in The New Corporate Accountability: Corporate Social Responsibility and the Law 33 (D. McBarnet et al. eds., 2007).

[161] Julia Black, "Forms and Paradoxes of Principles-Based Regulation", 3 Cap. Markets L. J. 425 (2008) (identifying cultural change as one of the potential advantages of this type of regulation (which she labels principles-based regulation)).

[162] Dan Awrey, William Blair, & David Kershaw, "Between Law and Markets: Is there a Role for Culture and Ethics in Financial Regulation", 38 Del. J. Corp. L. 191 (2013).

[163] See, e.g., the UK Financial Services Authority's "Treating Customers Fairly" initiative, available at http://www.fsa.gov.uk/doing/regulated/tcf.

[164] This view finds support in both organizational and sociological theory. See, e.g., Silbey et al., " 'The Sociological Citizen': Relational Independence in Law and Organizations", 59 L'Annee Sociologique 201, 218 (2009) (describing a case study in which project engagement resulted in a "perceptual and moral transformation"); see also Clifford Geertz, Thick Description: Toward an Interpretative Theory of Culture, in Interpretation of Cultures: Selected Essays 3 (1975) (observing that "it is through the flow of behavior—or more precisely social action—that cultural forms find articulation").

[165] Sharon Gilad, "Institutionalising Fairness in Financial Markets: Overcoming Resistance", 5 Regulation & Governance 309 (2011).

[166] Awrey et al., *supra* note 162.

leadership, and make well informed and high-quality decisions.[167] Importantly, the Code both builds in senior board responsibility for this evaluation—by requiring the chairman of the board to act on the results—and provides the means of imposing discipline on this evaluation process through: an annual report to shareholders on the evaluation; performance evaluation of the chairman led by the senior independent director; and a tri-annual facilitation of this performance review through an external facilitator.[168]

The effects of this process-based approach remain invisible to external scrutiny, which renders it unstable in the face of high-profile failure. However, in contrast to other areas of regulation where this technique is deployed[169] there are good reasons to be optimistic about its effects. The board, and in particular, the non-executive directors and the chairman have strong incentives to take, and to be seen to be taking, board performance and evaluation seriously. Failure to do so puts at risk their reputational capital.

5 CONCLUSION

A typical caricature of self- or market-controlled regulation is that it serves the needs only of the regulated constituencies by producing rules that purport but fail to really address the problems that require regulatory attention and which are rarely enforced against their "brethren." We see from the market-leading examples of self- and market-controlled regulation in the UK discussed in this chapter that, paradoxically, this is palpably not the case in corporate law. In the context of both takeover regulation and corporate governance codes, we find rule overload and rigorous enforcement. Do these examples then provide model approaches to regulation that other jurisdictions would be well advised to emulate? Has corporate law missed a trick in failing to employ more broadly such regulatory devices? The analysis in this chapter suggests that there is significant doubt that this is the case. The rule-content and enforcement overload in both the context of takeovers and "comply or explain" codes appear in part to be the product of regulatory malfunction. In relation to takeovers such overload may be a function of rent seeking itself—the investment banking role, which in the context of enforcement generates a positive regulatory dividend but may be a factor in the production of what is now a 300-page Code. In the context of "comply or explain" codes, over-enforcement generates a best practice, accountability driven code from which opt-outs are in many instances impracticable even though such a best practice outlook is premised on the possibility of opt-out.

The diffusion of market-controlled "comply or explain" codes shows that such innovations are clearly replicable. Any state can direct market actors to produce rules and can deploy the process-based tool-kit which we see used in the UK Corporate Governance Code's board evaluation requirement. But in relation to endogenous self-regulation where the state does not have a direct role, the analysis in this chapter does not hold out significant hope for effective replication where market actors—in jurisdictions such as in Brazil today in the

---

[167] FRC, "Guidance on Board Effectiveness" (2011), 2, available at: https://www.frc.org.uk/Our-Work/Publications/Corporate-Governance/Guidance-on-Board-Effectiveness.pdf.

[168] UK Corporate Governance Code, B.6.2.

[169] For example, in the context of retail financial regulation. See generally, Awrey et al., *supra* note 162.

takeover context—attempt to provide welfare-enhancing regulatory solutions where the state has failed to do so. The UK Takeover Panel and Code is in multiple respects a sui generis regulatory product. That said, the analysis in this chapter suggests that if there is one lesson which it offers in the hope of making it work it is "bribe your quarterback": bond the investment banking community to your regulatory product by showing them that it can generate income. If successful, it may be that you end up with a 300-page code! *Maybe* the trade-off is worth the candle.

CHAPTER 33

....

THE EVOLUTION IN THE U.S. OF PRIVATE ENFORCEMENT VIA LITIGATION AND MONITORING TECHNIQUES
Are There Lessons for Germany?

....

JAMES D. COX[1] AND RANDALL S. THOMAS[2]

1 INTRODUCTION

....

Two decades ago, it was generally agreed that US public companies had dispersed owner-ship structures, whereas almost all German public companies had a controlling shareholder, generally supported by a house bank.[3] Financial capital markets have changed dramatically since then so that today, in the US there is an increasing level of ownership consolidation,[4] whereas in Germany at public companies there has been a marked reduction in block holder size and a reduced governance role for banks.[5] If these trends continue, the two systems may

---

[1] Brainerd Currie Professor of Law, Duke University School of Law.
[2] John Beasley Professor of Law and Business, Vanderbilt University School of Law. We would like to thank the participants of the Columbia Law School's Authors' Conference for the Oxford Handbook of Corporate Law and Governance, March 20–21, 2014 for their helpful comments.
[3] Marco Becht & Ekkehart Boehmer, Ownership and Voting Power in Germany, in The Control of Corporate Europe (Fabrizio Barca & Marco Becht eds., 2001).
[4] Clifford G. Holderness, "The Myth of Diffuse Ownership in the United States", 22 Rev. Fin. Stud. 1377 (2009).
[5] Wolf-Georg Ringe, Changing Law and Ownership Patterns in Germany: Corporate Governance and the Erosion of Deutschland AG, in The Research Handbook of Shareholder Power (Jennifer Hill & Randall Thomas eds., 2015).

wind up having very similar public company ownership structures.[6] As ownership patterns in the US and Germany move toward one another, in this chapter we explore whether each country may learn from the other's past.

Historically, in the US dispersed ownership system, the central corporate governance problem was the agency costs arising out of the separation of ownership and control.[7] To police these costs, shareholders employed a variety of monitoring methods—corporate voting, the threat of a change of control transaction, and representative litigation—by which managers were disciplined if they were poor stewards and failed to create shareholder value. Over time, the value of these different devices for disciplining managers ebbed and flowed as capital markets evolved and legal rules changed. This was especially true for private representative shareholder litigation.

During the past 70 years, shareholder representative litigation has acted as an important policing mechanism of managerial abuses at US public companies.[8] Different types of representative litigation have had their moment in the sun—derivative suits early on, followed by federal securities class actions and most recently merger litigation—often producing benefits for shareholders but posing difficult challenges as well. In the last few years, new developments have placed pressure on representative shareholder litigation in each of its forms and cast doubt on the continuing ability of such suits to act as an effective monitoring device to constrain managerial agency costs.

Concurrently with, and perhaps causally related to, this development, a number of relatively new policing mechanisms for managerial agency costs have sprung up in the US. Most prominently, activist hedge funds that control large pools of unregulated capital have assumed a role of "governance intermediaries," as they develop and present choices to more docile institutional holders who can become supporters but rarely initiators.[9] Institutions are informed by their proxy advisors on initiatives teed up by the activist hedge fund.[10] These proxy advisors play a key role in this movement as they help to solve the collective action problems faced by investors. The passage of the Dodd–Frank Act further armed institutional investors by mandating that public companies hold a non-binding Say on Pay vote.[11]

We also consider the rising role of the appraisal remedy against the backdrop of developments in shareholder litigation focused on acquisitions. As we will see, the appraisal proceeding, an old, and previously largely defunct, form of litigation has been spruced up by a few intrepid investment groups, who have begun filing these actions in an effort to

---

[6] We do not take a position on the continuing debate about whether corporate law will converge across nations over time. See Henry Hansmann & Reinier Kraakman, "The End of History for Corporate Law", 89 Geo. L. J. 439 (2001) with Convergence and Persistence in Corporate Governance (Jeffrey N. Gordon & Mark J. Roe eds., 2004).

[7] Michael C. Jensen & William H. Meckling, "Theory of the Firm: Managerial Behavior, Agency Costs and Ownership Structure", 3 J. Fin. Econ. 305 (1976).

[8] Robert B. Thompson & Randall S. Thomas, "The New Look of Shareholder Litigation: Acquisition-Oriented Class Actions", 57 Vand. L. Rev. 133, 141–45 (2004).

[9] Ronald Gilson & Jeffrey Gordon, "The Agency Costs of Agency Capitalism, Activist Investors and Revaluation of Governance Rights", 113 Colum. L. Rev. 863 (2013); Paul H. Edelman, Randall S. Thomas, & Robert B. Thompson, "Shareholder Voting in an Age of Intermediary Capitalism", 87 So. Cal. L. Rev. 1359 (2014).

[10] Edelman, Thomas, & Thompson, *supra* note 9.

[11] Randall S. Thomas, Alan R. Palmiter, & James F. Cotter, "Dodd–Frank's Say on Pay: Will It Lead to a Greater Role for Shareholders in Corporate Governance?", 97 Cornell L. Rev. 1213 (2012).

engage in what some have called "appraisal arbitrage."[12] Each one of these new, or revived, monitoring techniques may be able to stand in for representative shareholder litigation during its hour of need to insure that managerial agency costs do not get out of line.

We finish by attempting to draw lessons from the evolution of monitoring devices in the US and apply them in Germany, and vice versa. As mentioned above, Germany has long been viewed as a control shareholder dominated system.[13] Such systems face a different type of agency cost problem than dispersed ownership systems: instead of constantly worrying about constraining managers' interests, they are more concerned with minimizing the conflict between the interests of controlling shareholders and those of minority investors.[14]

But things are changing rapidly in Germany. Control blocks are shrinking with time at German public companies.[15] The resulting increased dispersion of ownership has been accompanied by a decline in traditional bank monitoring at German public firms and a vast increase in foreign equity ownership. Germany's ongoing transition toward greater dispersed ownership has led commentators to argue in favor of greater shareholder protections to combat the rising managerial agency costs associated with shareholder dispersion.[16]

2 THE CONTRACTING SPACE FOR SHAREHOLDER LITIGATION

While there have been many shifts between forms of representative litigation over the past 70 years, its place within our corporate governance system has been secure, at least until recently. At present, there is a broad-based attack being mounted on all forms of representative shareholder litigation on the grounds that it creates excessive litigation agency costs. In this section, we outline the parameters of that assault.

2.1 Shareholder Merger and Acquisition Suits

Delaware jurisprudence has for some time placed a litigation bullseye on merger and acquisition transactions. Delaware's heightened judicial scrutiny for change of control transactions, control shareholder squeeze-outs, and defensive tactics in hostile litigation led plaintiffs to file numerous cases challenging mergers and acquisition deals.[17]

---

[12] See section 3.3 for further discussion.

[13] Wolfgang Streeck & Martin Höpner, Alle Macht dem Markt? Fallstudien zur Abwicklung der Deutschland AG 118 (Martin Höpner ed., 2003).

[14] Luca Enriques & Paolo Volpin, "Corporate Governance Reforms in Continental Europe", 21 J. Econ. Persp. 117, 117 (2007); Reinier Kraakman, John Armour, Paul Davies, Luca Enriques, Henry B. Hansmann et al., The Anatomy of Corporate Law 30 (3rd ed., 2017).

[15] Christoph Van der Elst, "The Influence of Shareholder Rights on Shareholder Behavior", 1 Corp. Fin. & Cap. Markets L. Rev. 56 (2010); Randall S. Thomas, International Executive Pay: Current Practices and Future Trends, in Labor & Employment Law & Economics 198 (Kenneth G. Dau-Schmidt, Seth D. Harris & Orly Lobel eds., 2009).

[16] Ringe, *supra* note 5, at 34–37.

[17] See generally Thompson & Thomas, The New Look of Shareholder Litigation, *supra* note 8 for a discussion of these developments.

Litigation against publicly held companies that are engaged in deals overwhelmingly arises in the form of class actions, as opposed to derivative suits.[18] Generally, multiple suits are filed very quickly after the announcement of a transaction, by law firms who are repeat players in such litigation.[19] Early data indicated that suits challenging deals in which managers had a conflict of interest in the proposed deal were the most likely to produce cash settlements and that these suits did not exhibit the same degree of litigation agency costs as suggested for other representative suits.[20] Thus, during 1999–2000, only 12% of deals had litigation and most of the deal litigation related to Delaware firms was in Delaware. [21] Furthermore, this litigation decreased the likelihood of a deal closing, but also increased return on the deals that closed, so that overall it was associated with an increased return for the deals.[22]

This has since changed dramatically with most deals attracting suits.[23] Cain et al. report that in 2013 96% of deals over $100 million in value experienced deal litigation.[24] Roughly 61% of these deals also resulted in litigation in more than one jurisdiction.[25] While several commentators have opined on the underlying causes for these developments,[26] we observe that it has occurred while, as seen later in section 2.3, the number of securities class actions and their lawyers has declined. Although causal relationship of observed social events is always a difficult challenge, we do surmise that the rapid rise in transaction-oriented litigation may, at least in part, be reflective of many plaintiff-oriented law firms redirecting their foci.

Just as too much fudge can be a problem, the warm invitation that Delaware substantive law extends to challenge commonly engaged in transactions also has its list of problems. When all the suits were in Delaware, this was a manageable problem. For example, simplifying rules such as "first to file," while crude, had the benefit of quickly whittling multiple nettlesome complaints down to a more easily managed consolidated case. However, with multiple suits involving the same transaction outside of Delaware, a problem of a very different order of magnitude arises. In addition to the higher administrative costs, a real fear existed that this could feed a reverse auction whereby a cooperative plaintiff would collaborate with the defendant corporation to bring all challenges to a swift resolution by a court-approved low-ball settlement that yields a quick return to the lawyers but fails to protect the interest of the shareholders.[27]

The antidote followed by many companies has been forum selection bylaws, approved solely by directors, which mandate most forms of shareholder suits can only be maintained in a particular forum; Delaware is generally the designated forum. In 2013, the Delaware

---

[18] Thompson and Thomas, The New Look of Shareholder Litigation, *supra* note 8, at 137.

[19] Id. at 138.   [20] Id. at 172 tbl.4.

[21] C. N. V. Krishnan et al., "Shareholder Litigation in Mergers and Acquisitions", 18 J. Corp. Fin. 1248, 1249–50 (2012).

[22] Id.

[23] Randall S. Thomas & Robert B. Thompson, "A Theory of Representative Suits and Its Application to Multijurisdictional Litigation", 106 Nw. U. L. Rev. 1753 (2012).

[24] Matthew D. Cain, Jill E. Fisch & Steven Davidoff Solomon, "The Shifting Tides of Merger Litigation", forthcoming Vand. L. Rev. (2018), at 21.

[25] Id.

[26] Thomas & Thompson, *supra* note 23; John Armour et al., "Is Delaware Losing its Cases?", 9 J. Emp. Legal Stud. 605 (2012); Sean J. Griffith & Alexandra D. Lahav, "The Market for Preclusion in Merger Litigation", 66 Vand. L. Rev. 1053 (2013).

[27] See, e.g., Transcript of Courtroom Status Conference, *Scully v. Nighthawk Radiology Holdings, Inc.*, No. 5890-VCL (Del. Ch. Dec. 17, 2010) (Laster, V.C.).

Chancery Court upheld a unilaterally adopted forum selection bylaw, reasoning that the bylaws, including the board's authority to adopt bylaws, were an extension of the shareholders' contractual rights to the corporation.[28] More recently, the Delaware Supreme Court similarly reasoned that a bylaw by a non-profit corporation could impose a "loser pays" standard on shareholder litigation.[29] The Delaware legislature has since divided the judicial baby, authorizing forum selection bylaws but prohibiting bylaws that would assign fees to the losing party. The ultimate step in a board of directors' resort to the bylaws to address feared shareholder suits will be mandated arbitration; this step remains to be adjudicated in Delaware but is clearly at hand elsewhere.[30]

We therefore see colliding developments in Delaware. On the one hand, the Delaware courts have developed substantive doctrines inviting shareholders to head to court to challenge the conduct of the board of directors in mergers and acquisitions. On the other hand, the Delaware courts have approved boards adopting bylaws that channel those challenges to Delaware, that discourage such suits' maintenance by shifting costs to the losing party, and that portend sweeping all such disputes behind the veil of arbitration. While there is no reason to believe that forum selection bylaws inevitably lead to less accountability on the part of managers and their boards, the other two developments most likely will.

2.2 Shareholder Derivative Suits

Traditional derivative cases raise state law breach of fiduciary duty claims by directors and officers. Typically, these claims allege breach of the duties of loyalty (including good faith) and care, as well as other state law issues. They are commonly used to attack directors or officers engaging in conflict of interest transactions with the corporation or taking a corporate opportunity belonging to the corporation. The options backdating scandal, in which a number of large corporations were found to have provided their executives with options to buy stock on dates and terms that were backdated, is a good example of such predilection.[31] These cases arose after a scandal sparked by academic research and news stories led to government regulatory investigations that revealed wide-ranging misbehavior. In the aftermath of these events, shareholders filed a series of derivative suits to recover benefits that insiders unjustly obtained from the corporation.[32]

---

[28] *Boilermakers Local 154 Retirement Fund v. Chevron Corp.*, 73 A.3d 934 (Del. Ch. 2013).

[29] *ATP Tour, Inc. v. Deutscher Tennis Bund*, 91 A. 3d 554 (Del. 2014).

[30] *Cent. Laborers' Pension Fund v. Portnoy*, Case No. 24-C-13-1996 (Baltimore Circuit Court, Maryland 2013).

[31] See John Armour, Bernard S. Black, & Brian R. Cheffins, "Delaware's Balancing Act", 87 Indiana L. J. 1345 (2012) (discussing data relating to option backdating cases).

[32] See C. Forelle & J. Bandler, The Perfect Payday: Some CEOs Reap Millions by Landing Stock Options when They Are Most Valuable: Luck or Something Else?, Wall St. J. A1 at c. 6 (March 18, 2006); *Ryan v. Gifford*, 918 A.2d 341, 360 n.60 (Del. Ch. 2007) (detailing scholarly research on the backdating controversy); Shannon German, "What They Don't Know Can Hurt Them: Corporate Officers' Duty of Candor to Directors", 34 Del. J. Corp. L. 221, 235 (2009) (explaining how a Wall Street Journal piece led to the investigation of 130 companies for backdating).

This category of shareholder suits is probably the most stable set of cases of all of the representative litigation groups. There has been little change in the underlying set of legal and procedural rules for derivative litigation in the past 20 years. In prior research, one of the authors studied all derivative litigation filed in Delaware during 1999 and 2000.[33] That article found that Delaware public companies were hit with about 30 cases per year with about 30% of them yielding relief to the corporation or its shareholders, and the remainder being quickly dismissed with little litigation activity.[34] Private Delaware firms were targeted with a dozen lawsuits annually, typically raising claims of minority oppression.[35]

This research showed that a careful distinction must be made between public and private corporations when discussing the role of shareholder derivative suits. Derivative suits are very much alive and well in the private company setting; in this context they perform their historical function of remedying breaches of duty of loyalty, customarily in the form of acts in bad faith and more particularly self-dealing practices. In the close corporation context they are better seen as remedying opportunistic behavior by those in control. While opportunistic grabs for assets and business are not foreign to public companies, in the non-private context the malefactor is more likely to enjoy the insulation provided by the demand requirement. That is, a major feature of the derivative suit is the requirement that the suit's plaintiff must either make a demand on the board of directors or establish a basis why such a demand would be futile. The ultimate outcome in either case depends on whether the board, or a subcommittee of the board, is believed to be sufficiently independent of the suit so that the board or committee's opinion that the suit fails to serve a corporate interest will be upheld by the reviewing court. As a consequence, the robust derivative suit boneyard for public companies is predominantly the handiwork of the demand requirement. In the case of the private corporation, because those disputes are largely between the "ins" and the "outs," the demand requirement is much less lethal as the alleged wrongdoing at the heart of the suit frequently can be more easily linked to a majority of the board. In addition, shaping the contours of such suits is the wide adoption of immunity shields whereby a provision in the firm's articles of incorporation insulates directors from liability for misconduct that is not illegal, in bad faith, or a knowing violation of the law.[36] Immunity shields thus limit suits focused on alleged managerial failures to those involving knowing and systematic breaches on the part of the board.

Failure to oversee claims finds its source in former Chancellor Allen's path-breaking Caremark decision holding that the directors' duty of good faith was breached when there is evidence of a "sustained or systematic failure of a director to exercise reasonable oversight." A dramatic instance of such a suit is *In re Massey Energy Company Derivative and Class Action Litigation*,[37] where the complaint withstood defendants' motions to dismiss by alleging facts reflecting that the board repeatedly ignored reports and sanctions of mine safety violations in the years preceding the explosion in its Upper Big Branch mine which killed 29 miners—the deadliest mine accident in 40 years. But, absent such dramatic pre-disaster warnings as occurred in *Massey*, there is generally insufficient evidence on which to conclude that the board has engaged in more than negligent oversight for which the ubiquitous

---

[33] Robert B. Thompson & Randall S. Thomas, "The Public and Private Faces of Derivative Lawsuits", 57 Vand. L. Rev. 1747 (2004).

[34] Id. at 1749–1750.   [35] Id.   [36] 8 Del. Code §102(b)7.

[37] *In re Massey Energy Company Derivative and Class Action Litigation*, 2011 Del. Ch. LEXIS 83.

immunity shield, discussed above, protects it from being accountable in the derivative suit. Indeed, the Delaware judiciary may well conclude that ignoring red flags may not even rise to director negligence. To illustrate, consider *In re Citigroup Inc. Shareholder Derivative Litigation*,[38] holding that the business judgment rule insulated the directors against charges that they failed to take precautions to avoid the ensuing financial losses arising from Citigroup's large exposure to the subprime lending markets. The suit alleged various red flags such as an economist's forecast that a speculative bubble was nearing its end, a leading subprime lender closing its 229 offices, another lender filing bankruptcy, analysts downgrading subprime mortgages, and a warning of increasing subprime delinquencies by another lender. The court reasoned:

> [The "red flags"] amount to little more than portions of public documents that reflected the worsening conditions in the subprime mortgage market and in the economy generally. Plaintiffs fail to plead particularized facts suggesting that the Board was presented with "red flags" alerting it to potential misconduct . . . [The plaintiffs] repeatedly make the conclusory allegation that the defendants have breached their duty of oversight, but nowhere do [they] adequately explain what the director defendants actually did or failed to do that would constitute a violation. Even while admitting that Citigroup had a risk monitoring system in place, plaintiffs seem to conclude that, because the director defendants were charged with monitoring Citigroup's risk, then they must be found liable because Citigroup experienced losses as a result of exposure to the subprime mortgage market. The only factual support plaintiffs provide for this conclusion are "red flags" that actually amount to nothing more than signs of continuing deterioration in the subprime mortgage market. These types of conclusory allegations are exactly the kinds of allegation that do not state a claim for relief under Caremark.[39]

The above reasoning appears consistent with observation made in a widely noted earlier Delaware Supreme Court decision that conduct that offends good corporate governance practices nonetheless is not inherently negligent conduct.[40] Thus, not only the immunity shield but more importantly the high standard of fault required to constitute an actionable breach on the part of the directors severely restrict the scope of duty to monitor suits.[41]

One type of derivative suits that has increased is the questionable "tag-along" derivative suits that parallel securities class actions. Erickson finds that in 75% of the derivative cases, there were also 10b-5 securities class actions.[42] She discovered that most of these

---

[38] *In re Citigroup Inc. Shareholder Derivative Litigation*, 964 A.2d 106 (Del. Ch. 2009).

[39] Id. at 128–130.

[40] *In re Walt Disney Company Derivative Litigation*, 906 A.2d 27 (Del. 2006).

[41] We raise here a comparative conundrum, namely that scholars are divided whether, in Germany, the business judgment rule carries as high a presumption as the US, in light of the fact that objectives are not isolated to shareholders but cover a range of stakeholders. Compare Franklin A. Gevurtz, "Disney in a Comparative Light", 55 Am. J. Comp. L. 452 (2007) (lower presumption of propriety attaches to decisions of a German supervisory board than a US board) with Theodor Baums & Kenneth E. Scott, "Taking Shareholder Protection Seriously? Comparative Governance in the United States and Germany", 53 Am. J. Comp. L. 31 (2005) (duty owed to multiple and diverse constituencies "tends to broaden the likelihood of upholding management actions that are contrary to the interests of the shareholders").

[42] Jessica M. Erickson, "Overlitigating Corporate Fraud: An Empirical Examination", 97 Iowa L. Rev. 49, 62 (2011).

cases produced nothing in the way of specific monetary recovery for the company.[43] Non-monetary relief was more common, and often came in the form of corporate governance changes, such as more independent directors, or splitting the chief executive officer and chair of the board positions.[44] However, such suits likely are corrosive in that they too frequently appear driven by the rewards they garner for their attorneys rather than the shareholders.

2.3   Federal Securities Class Actions

The story of the few trials and many tribulations of securities class actions is well known. Faced with the obstacles to derivative litigation, plaintiff shareholders moved to federal court and filed actions under Rule 10b-5 of the federal securities laws. Investors benefited from temporarily favorable interpretations of federal securities laws for such claims.[45] This led to a surge of federal securities class action filings, which was ultimately followed by a negative shift in judicial and legislative perceptions. Just as with derivative suits, legislatures and courts heard arguments that hasty, frivolous cases were being filed. These trends led to the passage of the PSLRA in 1995 in an effort to reform the field.

Since the mid-1990s the trend line for the number of filed and settled securities class actions has been downward; at the same time, the trend line for total settlements and the average amount of settlements has risen.[46] Thus, we might conclude that the good life of the securities class action lawyer persists; what is new is that today the good life is enjoyed by fewer than before.[47]

---

[43] Jessica M. Erickson, "Corporate Governance in the Courtroom: An Empirical Analysis", 51 Wm. & Mary L. Rev. 1749, 1803 (2010).

[44] These corporate governance changes in some cases bear little relation to the wrong alleged, but they do count as a benefit to the corporation which can support an award of attorneys' fees.

[45] See *Basic Inc. v. Levinson*, 485 U.S. 224, 245–46 (1988) (applying a presumption of reliance in a fraud on the market context, facilitating filings of class action suits in a Rule 10b-5 context).

[46] Securities Class Action Filings: 2013 Year in Review, Cornerstone Research (2014) available at http://www.cornerstone.com/Publications/Reports/Securities-Class-Action-Filings-2013-Year-in-Review.

[47] The cost curve for private suits has been greatly impacted by multiple developments over the last few decades with the consequential effect of reducing not just the areas where antifraud suits might be successful but the frequency of suits under the antifraud provision. For example, the Private Securities Litigation Reform Act of 1995 burdens the plaintiff with a heightened pleading requirement as well as barring discovery until all motions to dismiss have been resolved. This effectively requires plaintiff firms to be more resourceful prior to filing suit so that the complaint's factual allegations meet the "strong inference" of fraud demanded by the PSLRA. Such resourcefulness demands plaintiff firms to invest non-trivial sums in investigating possible cases so as to marshal the facts to meet the pleading requirement. The Supreme Court has also worked its transformative magic. The most dramatic effects on the conduct of securities class actions has been the Supreme Court's sweeping limitations on who is subject to liability under the antifraud provision. For example, *Janus Capital Group, Inc. v. First Derivative Traders*, 131 S. Ct. 2296 (2011) limits liability to individuals who had "ultimate authority over the statement, including its content and whether and how to communicate it." Thus, many individuals whose involvement was indispensable to the disclosure violation, such as the outside lawyer who schemes with managers to fabricate a series of transactions to conceal the firm's financial position, are beyond the reach of private litigants and therefore weaken the deterrence effect of antifraud provision. Moreover, Congress's enactment of the Securities Litigation Uniform Standards Act provides further

The seeds of eviscerating the antifraud provision potential to address agency costs were sown much earlier. The mantra invoked in the 1960s and 1970s to justify curbing the then ever-expanding scope of Rule 10b-5 was that it could not address "acts of corporate mismanagement." This phrase arose from *Birnbaum v. Newport Steel Corp.*,[48] where the gravamen of the complaint was that the controlling stockholder thwarted an ongoing acquisition of the company at a premium so that he could garner the entire control premium for himself. Later, the Supreme Court in *Santa Fe Industries, Inc. v. Green*[49] would take a similar position in holding that alleged unfairness, absent deception, in connection with a forced sale of securities held by minority holders was outside the scope of the antifraud provision. Thus, the *sine qua non* for a violation of the securities laws is a material deception; an egregious breach of fiduciary obligation absent deception is not within the reach of antifraud provisions.

Despite the legislative and judicial restrictions that have been imposed on 10b-5 private suits, we do see one form of antifraud suit that at its heart is addressed to managerial misconduct, not just misconduct by managers. As seen earlier, state fiduciary duty claims that the directors and officers were poor stewards must confront not only the business judgment rule's strong presumption of propriety but more importantly that at least with respect to directors the claim is likely insulated by the immunity shield that limits damage actions against directors to breaches of duty of loyalty. Suits focused on failure to disclose practices constituting poor to unlawful business practices are now being filed under the antifraud provision. The Supreme Court's recent *Omnicare* decision can be expected to encourage federal securities law suits based on generalized claims by companies that they operate legally; *Omnicare* holds that claims of legal compliance are to be evaluated with regard to whether facts known to the speaker regarding the illegality of operations needed to be disclosed to prevent what was represented from being materially misleading.[50] A purely state fiduciary suit on such a claim would not only confront the problems described above, but also would be a derivative claim for which the necessity of a demand on the board or a committee of the board greatly weakens the suit's possibilities.

We therefore find that disclosure-oriented federal securities suits can address errant stewardship provided the managers proffer bold claims of their compliance with the law, that their business strategies are yielding great returns, or that existing contracts will add immensely to future profits, when behind each assertion is an ongoing violation of federal or state law that upon detection and compliance will prove immensely unrewarding to the firm. However, outside this realm, the most significant contribution of private and public enforcement of the securities laws is the culture of compliance they compel. Complaints abound that suits, or most suits, are frivolous and drive up the cost of business transactions. Regardless of the accuracy of this claim, it nonetheless supports a healthy awareness of the

---

insulation as SLUSA has the effect of imposing the same narrow standard for state law class actions premised on securities violations. The Supreme Court has been equally restrictive in the realm of causality with the consequential effect of driving litigants to commission expensive econometric studies to address a range of causation issues that arise in the pre-trial period. See e.g., *Dura Pharmaceuticals Inc. v. Broudo*, 544 U.S. 336 (2005) (complaint must set forth facts supporting the claim that the alleged material misrepresentation caused the plaintiff to suffer a material loss); *Halliburton Co. v. Erica John Fund, Inc.*, 134 S. Ct. 2398 (2014) (defendants can challenge class certification by econometric evidence that alleged omission or misstatement did not distort the security's price).

[48] *Birnbaum v. Newport Steel Corp.*, 193 F.2d 461 (1952).
[49] *Santa Fe Industries, Inc. v. Green*, 430 U.S. 462 (1977).
[50] *Omnicare, Inc. v. Laborers Dist. Council Constr. Indus. Pension Fund*, 135 S. Ct. 1318 (2015).

perils of nondisclosure of material information in securities transactions, which includes periodic reports and other announcements that reach investors. Enforcement, public and private, of the securities laws shines a bright light on managers with not only the therapeutic effect of warding some from misbehavior, but also by alerting investors and regulators of facts warranting inquiry and perhaps enforcement.

3 EVOLVING US NON-LITIGATION MONITORING SUBSTITUTES

To summarize, all of this evidence suggests that shareholder litigation has a lessening role in addressing managerial agency costs. Managerial underperformance is insulated by the business judgment rule, the demand requirement in derivative suits, and the immunity shield. Finally, although it remains early in the life cycle of forum selection and fee shifting bylaws, they each portend weakening whatever force shareholder suits have had in protecting shareholders in acquisitions.

Coterminous with the constriction of shareholder litigation, a number of alternative monitoring techniques have developed that address, to some extent, the voids created by its contraction. While each of these methods has its advocates and critics, collectively they have brought about significant changes in the relationship between management and shareholders at American public corporations. In this section, we explore each one of these areas to explain how they are affecting corporate governance today as well as their limits as monitoring devices.

3.1 Hedge Funds as Effective Monitors

Hedge funds have been actively engaged in shareholder monitoring in recent years, both on their own and also by providing leadership to quieter institutional investors.[51] Hedge funds target firms that are undervalued by the market, perhaps because of poor management.[52] The stock market appears to recognize the hedge fund's potential impact on these firms as the filing of an activist hedge fund's Schedule 13D filing creates positive average abnormal returns from 7% to 8%.[53] These benefits appear to last: firms targeted by activists see a 1.22% increase in operating efficiency one year after acquisition.[54]

---

[51] Gilson & Gordon, *supra* note 9; Edelman, Thomas, & Thompson, *supra* note 9.

[52] Hedge funds often seek to get a company to use "excess" cash to pay out dividends, buy back shares, spin off less inefficient divisions or assets, or even force the sale of an entire company. Alon Brav et al., "Hedge Fund Activism, Corporate Governance, and Firm Performance", 63 J. Fin. 1729 (2008).

[53] Brav et al., *supra* note 52, at 1731. In contrast, Greenwood & Schor find that while activist hedge funds do produce these abnormal returns, the returns are produced by takeover premiums, not improvements in management. Robin Greenwood & Michael Schor, "Investor Activism and Takeovers", 92 J. Fin. Econ. 362, 363 (2009). The authors find that activist targets which do not result in a takeover have abnormal returns statistically indistinguishable from zero.

[54] Christopher Clifford, "Value Creation or Destruction? Hedge Funds as Shareholder Activists", 14 J. Corp. Fin. 323, 324 (2008).

Despite these apparent benefits, hedge funds have their detractors, being referred to as "villains,"[55] who pursue short-term profits at the expense of the long-term value of their portfolio companies.[56] Such charges have raised interest in whether fiduciary duties ought to be reformed to include the actions of hedge funds.[57] The data is inconsistent with the view that hedge fund activism is short-term oriented.[58] First, hedge funds seem to have little trouble recruiting long-term investors to support their activist goals.[59] If a hedge fund's plans actually only produced a short-term gain at the expense of long-term profitability, one would think that long-term investors would be reluctant to support them.[60] Second, hedge fund activism seems to improve a firm's long-term prospects.[61] Third, activist hedge fund holding periods are not that short, with one study finding they have an average holding period of 31 months.[62] Finally, one study of hedge fund interventions from 1994 to 2007 found that the initial stock price gains resulting from the initial announcement of a hedge fund's activism were sustained over a five-year period as were improvements in other measures of returns.[63] All of this evidence supports the claim that hedge fund activism is not generally a short-term strategy and generates valuable monitoring of corporate management.[64]

[55] David A. Katz & Laura A. McIntosh, Corporate Governance: Advice on Coping with Hedge Fund Activism, Wachtell, Lipton, Rosen & Katz (May 25, 2006) (activist hedge funds are the villains of the 2000s).

[56] Martin Lipton, Deconstructing American Business II, Wachtell, Lipton, Rosen, & Katz, Nov. 1, 2006 (The most important problem that causes concern about American business in the future is "[p]ressure on boards from activist investors to manage for short-term share price performance rather than long-term value creation"); Steven M. Davidoff, Deal Book, A Standard Criticism of Activist Investors that No Longer Holds Up, N.Y. Times, July 10, 2013, at B5 (describing and rejecting claim that hedge funds are short-term shareholders); Mark J. Roe, "Corporate Short-Termism: In the Boardroom and in the Courtroom", 68 Bus. Law. 977, 980 (2013) (reporting that managerial and boardroom autonomy have been justified recently by claims that activist hedge funds shareholders are focused on short-term gains); Lucian A. Bebchuk, "The Myth that Insulating Boards Serves Short-Term Value", 113 Colum. L. Rev. 1637, 1637 (2013) (arguing against claims that activist investors take profitable short-term actions that are long-term value decreasing).

[57] Iman Anabtawi & Lynn Stout, "Fiduciary Duties for Activist Shareholders", 60 Stan. L. Rev. 1255 (2008).

[58] Roe, *supra* note 56 contains an extensive discussion of the evidence pro and con claims that investors have a short-term perspective that is harming corporations and ultimately rejects these arguments.

[59] Thomas Briggs, "Corporate Governance and the New Hedge Fund Activism: An Empirical Analysis", 32 J. Corp. L. 681, 702 (2007).

[60] See Marcel Kahan & Edward Rock, "Hedge Funds in Corporate Governance and Corporate Control", 155 U. Pa. L. Rev. 1021, 1088 (2007).

[61] Brav et al., *supra* note 52, at 1731.

[62] William Bratton, "Hedge Funds and Governance Targets: Long-Term Results", 95 Geo. L. J. 1375 (2007).

[63] Lucian Bebchuk, Alon Brav, & Wei Jiang, "The Long Term Effects of Hedge Fund Activism", 115 Colum. L. Rev. 1085 (2015); see also, Nicole M. Boyson & Robert M. Mooradian, "Experienced Hedge Fund Activists" (Working Paper, Apr. 3, 2012) (finding that hedge fund activism "can lead to superior long-term target firm and hedge fund performance").

[64] Davidoff, *supra* note 56; see also, Dionysia Katelouzou, "Myths and Realities of Hedge Fund Activism: Some Empirical Evidence", 7 Va. L. & Bus. Rev. 459 (2012) (finding that hedge funds are not short-term in their focus).

3.2 Say on Pay: The New Conversation between Boards and Shareholders

In the US, derivative suits have proven impotent to either redress or retard excessive executive compensation.[65] In search of alternative monitoring mechanism, Congress passed the Dodd–Frank Act, which, among other things, required public companies to hold an advisory shareholder vote on the compensation of their top executives.[66] Why would such a vote, one that is merely advisory, be expected to produce tangible benefits to the firm?

Say on Pay may affect governance and compensation at firms for a variety of reasons. First, if a CEO is powerful enough to extract rents from his or her firm, then Say on Pay may provide the board of directors with additional leverage to negotiate a better deal for the firm.[67] Second, if directors are worried about being re-elected to the board, they may attach great importance to the level of shareholder support in a Say on Pay vote, and may therefore be more willing to reduce compensation levels or eliminate abusive pay practices.[68] Finally, Say on Pay may improve communication between shareholders and managers on compensation issues, which could result in a general improvement of corporate governance.[69]

We now have several proxy seasons' experience with Say on Pay. Generally speaking, shareholders strongly support existing pay practices at most firms with Say on Pay votes with only 1–2% of firms (40 to 60 firms of the Russell 3000) receiving less than 50% shareholder support during these same years.[70]

Despite the hopes of some proponents, Say on Pay has not led to lower executive pay levels or changes in its composition in the US.[71] Research on the UK has also found that overall CEO pay levels do not seem to have changed as a result of the Say on Pay vote.[72] However,

---

[65] Randall S. Thomas & Harwell Wells, "Executive Compensation in the Courts: Board Capture, Optimal Contracting, and Officers' Fiduciary Duties", 95 Minn. L. Rev. 846 (2011). For specific examples, see e.g., *Aronson v. Lewis*, 473 A.2d 805 (Del. 1984) (dismissing suit for failure to excuse demand where six-figure annual compensation was payable to a 70% stockholder regardless of his ability to serve as executive); *Marx v. Akers*, 88 N.Y.2d 189, 644 N.Y.S.2d 121, 666 N.E.2d 1034 (1996) (dismissing suit challenging CEO compensation for failure to excuse a demand where board not shown to have egregiously approved a lucrative compensation package.)

[66] Dodd–Frank Wall Street Reform and Consumer Protection Act, Pub. L. No. 111-203, § 951, 124 Stat. 1375, 1899 (2010) (adding new section 14A to the Securities Exchange Act of 1934).

[67] Examining the Improvement of Corporate Governance for the Protection of Shareholders and the Enhancement of Public Confidence: Hearing before the Subcommittee on Securities, Insurance and Investment of the S. Committee on Banking, Housing and Urban Affairs, 111th Cong. (July 29, 2009) (statement of John Coates), available at http://www.access.gpo.gov/congress/senate/senate05sh.html.

[68] Fabrizio Ferri & David A. Maber, "Say on Pay Votes and CEO Compensation: Evidence from the U.K.", 17 Rev. Fin. 527 (2013).

[69] Id.

[70] James F. Cotter, Alan R. Palmiter, & Randall S. Thomas, "The First Year of Say-on-Pay under Dodd–Frank: An Empirical Analysis and Look Forward", 81 Geo. Wash. L. Rev. 967, 979–80 (2013).

[71] Vincente Cuñat, Mireia Gene, & Maria Guadalupe, "The Vote is Cast: The Effect of Corporate Governance on Shareholder Value", 67 J. Fin. 1943 (2012).

[72] Martin Conyon & G. Sadler, "Shareholders Voting and Directors' Remuneration Report legislation: Say on Pay in the U.K.", 18 Corp. Gov.: An Int'l. Rev. 296 (2010) (finding no change in the overall level of executive pay or its rate of growth subsequent to Say on Pay votes); see also Ferri &

Correa and Lel find that executive pay growth rates are lower in countries that have adopted Say on Pay legislation.[73] If their results are correct, it is hard to know whether the relative decline in CEO pay levels reflects additional leverage for directors in negotiations with CEOs, or greater willingness of directors to stand up to CEOs because of their fear of losing their jobs.

Say on Pay's introduction did have a significant effect on American corporate governance though.[74] Dodd–Frank's mandated shareholder votes focused directors on shareholders' concerns about executive pay, increased shareholder participation in corporate governance, and opened lines of communication between management and shareholders (and proxy advisory firms) regarding executive compensation.[75] Management at many companies made changes to the substance and disclosure of their pay programs in an attempt to more clearly align pay to performance.[76] Other companies improved the compensation disclosures contained in their annual meeting proxy materials. At companies whose pay programs received negative Say on Pay recommendations by proxy advisory firms, management at some firms initiated discussions with shareholders following an "against" recommendation.[77]

3.3 A New Role for Appraisal Actions

Merger litigation has played a significant monitoring role of abusive corporate transactions in the past.[78] However, as we discussed in section 2.1 above, merger litigation's future has been placed in jeopardy by the board-adopted forum selection bylaws and fee shifting bylaws. If this is true, is there another form of litigation that could take its place?

One possible candidate is appraisal litigation. Traditionally, appraisal has been viewed as an ineffective remedy for shareholders that is cumbersome and very limited in its scope. It has three disadvantages that commentators have focused on:[79] difficult procedural steps that must be followed in precise order to preserve one's right to the remedy; the lack of a class action procedure that would permit easy joinder of all dissenting shareholders so that the costs of bringing an action could be more widely shared; and the narrow limits of the remedy, particularly in Delaware, where it is limited to mergers or consolidations and further restricted by the market out provision.[80]

Maber, *supra* note 68 (finding that firms did adjust contractual features and increase sensitivity to pay for performance in response to negative vote outcomes).

[73] Ricardo Correa & Ugur Lel, "Say on Pay Laws, Executive Compensation, CEO Pay Slice, and Firm Value Around the World" (Working Paper, June 2013), available at http://papers.ssrn.com/sol3/papers.cfm?abstract_id=2243921.

[74] See Thomas et al., *supra* note 11, at 1227.

[75] Luis A. Aguilar, Comm'r, U.S. Sec. & Exch. Comm'n, Speech to Social Investment Forum (June 10, 2011).

[76] Michael Littenberg, Farzad Damania, & Justin Neidig, "A Closer Look at Negative Say-on-Pay Votes During the 2011 Proxy Season, Director Notes" (Conference Bd.) 2 (July 2011), available at http://www.srz.com/A-Closer-Look-at-Negative-Say-on-Pay-Votes-During-the-2011-Proxy-Season-07-26-2011/.

[77] Cotter et al., *supra* note 70.   [78] Krishnan et al., *supra* note 21, at 1262.

[79] Charles Korsmo & Minor Myers, "Appraisal Arbitrage and the Future of Public Company M&A", 92 Wash. U. L. Rev. 1551 (2015).

[80] The market out provision eliminates appraisal rights for mergers and consolidations where there is a liquid market for their securities. 8 Del. C. §262(b) (1). The right to appraisal is restored if the target

Since appraisal is not a class action, a shareholder bringing such an action can only spread the costs across the group of shareholders that actually file complaints seeking such relief.[81] For small shareholders, this effectively means that seeking appraisal is almost never cost-justified. Perhaps as a result, in the past, few appraisal actions were filed and even fewer were actively litigated.[82]

However, Professors Kahan and Rock have recently observed that hedge funds may be adapting appraisal litigation to a new role.[83] After noting that hedge funds had been successful in blocking several proposed mergers when they believed that the price offered was too low, they noted that:

> [w]hen hedge funds are dissatisfied with the terms of an acquisition and unable to obtain better terms, they also resort to litigation. In particular, hedge funds have filed statutory appraisal actions, in which shareholders receive a court-determined fair value instead of merger consideration.[84]

Professor Geis[85] and Professors Korsmo and Myers[86] have advanced this idea and debated the appropriate role of appraisal litigation as a monitor of M&A deals.

Professor Geis focused on a relatively obscure Delaware Chancery Court appraisal decision involving a company called Transkaryotic Therapies.[87] The net effect of the decision was to facilitate hedge funds accumulating large stakes in target companies in order to file appraisal actions in the hopes of making large profits on their investments. Using this decision as a springboard, Geis argued that, "it is certainly possible that a robust after-market for appraisal rights will develop, analogous to the market for corporate control that allegedly disciplines otherwise entrenched managers with the threat of an external takeover." [88] After reciting the many limitations of appraisal as a remedy, he concludes that "corporate law might play a meaningful role in enhancing firm value by policing freeze out mergers in a more nuanced and creative manner."[89] In the end though, Geis equivocates about whether this is beneficial to target company shareholders because of concerns that opening up the appraisal remedy will lead to more strike suits, and therefore suggests further restrictions on shareholders' (already quite limited) ability to bring these cases.[90]

Professors Korsmo and Myers are much more enthusiastic about appraisal's current and future role as a managerial agency cost monitor. Using a data set on appraisal cases from 2004 to 2013, they find that the dollar value of dissenting shares in appraisal actions spiked

---

company's shareholders are required to take consideration different from the shares they formerly held, such as cash. Randall S. Thomas, "Revising the Delaware Appraisal Statute", 3 Del. L. Rev. 1, 11–12 (2000).

[81] Id. at 27–29.

[82] Id. at 22–23 (finding an average of less than 14 appraisal actions filed per year from 1977 to 1997).

[83] Kahan & Rock, *supra* note 60, at 1038–1039.

[84] Id. at 1038.

[85] George Geis, "An Appraisal Puzzle", 105 Nw. L. Rev. 1635 (2011).

[86] Korsmo & Myers, *supra* note 79. See also, Charles Korsmo & Minor Myers, "The Structure of Stockholder Litigation: When Do the Merits Matter?", 75 Ohio St. L. J. 829 (2014).

[87] *In re Appraisal of Transkaryotic Therapies, Inc.*, 2007 WL 1378345 (Del. Ch. 2007).

[88] Geis, *supra* note 85, at 1638.   [89] Id. at 1658.   [90] Id. at 1676.

sharply in 2013.[91] They document the rise of a small, but growing, group of investors filing multiple appraisal actions arising out of different transactions. These "repeat petitioners [are] increasingly dominating appraisal activity."[92] They go on to find that these repeat petitioners "target deals where the merger premium is low and where controlling shareholders are taking the company private."[93] Based on these findings, Korsmo and Myers argue that a robust appraisal remedy could be working in a socially responsible way as a "back-end check on abuses by corporate managers, controlling shareholders, or other insiders in merger transactions."[94]

We are much more cautious about this potential trend and its effects on the market for corporate control. First, any monitoring effects on M&A activity that will arise out of appraisal litigation will be limited to a relatively small set of deals where appraisal is available. Moreover, Korsmo and Myers find that only slightly more than 15% of the transactions that are covered have appraisal actions filed challenging the consideration paid in the deal.[95]

To the extent that appraisal is effective within this narrow class of deals, we would expect to see controlling shareholders and other acquirers revising existing deal structures to avoid appraisal's reach. Delaware's equal dignity doctrine will insulate other forms of acquisition from claims that appraisal ought to be available to shareholders in the event of changes of the form of the transaction. This suggests a need to expand the class of transactions covered by appraisal rights in order to offset such manipulations.

Another important limitation of appraisal is that it is realistically limited to big shareholders that own substantial dollar amounts of the stock. Smaller shareholders will not find appraisal to be cost effective and so their only real choices are either to take the merger consideration or sell to a hedge fund that is planning on seeking appraisal.

Indeed, small investors will benefit, if at all, from this appraisal litigation only if there is an ex ante effect on acquirers' original pricing of the deal because recent amendments to 8 Del. Code §§102(f) and 115 bar appraisal actions by shareholders whose holdings sum to less than $1 million. An acquirer might take into account the likelihood of subsequent appraisal litigation and, in an effort to stop such cases from being filed, choose to pay an acquisition price that is closer to the actual fair market value of the stock as it would be determined by a court in an appraisal proceeding. In this case, smaller investors might get a higher deal price. But note that, even if this is true, a rational acquirer will still offer less than fair market value in the deal because even if an appraisal action was filed and won, the acquirer would only pay fair market value of those shares covered in the appraisal action, which are still a small minority of the total number of shares outstanding. Furthermore, even if all of the dissenting shares seek appraisal, a majority of the stock must have voted in favor of the deal or it would not have closed, so that at most the acquirer will need to pay off the minority of investors. It is only in situations where shareholders accurately anticipate that they will win an appraisal action, and therefore threaten to block a deal, plus have the power to block a deal, that the ex ante effect of appraisal litigation would lead acquirers to pay close to fair market value for the target's stock.

---

[91] Korsmo and Myers, *supra* note 79, at 17, Figure 3.   [92] Id. at 18.
[93] Id. at 28.   [94] Id. at 42.   [95] Id. at 16, Figure 2.

Appraisal litigation may have a limited, but valuable role, to play as a monitor of managerial agency costs in mergers. For that to happen though, we agree with Professors Korsmo and Myers that the market-out exception must be eliminated.[96] As numerous critics have pointed out, it makes no sense to say that shareholders who receive marketable securities for their shares in a merger do not need appraisal: if they sell those shares in the market after the merger, then they will suffer an uncompensated loss. We would also go further and expand the number of transactions that qualify for appraisal, especially in Delaware, to limit acquirers' ability to recast the form of their acquisition to avoid appraisal's reach. Finally, we would note that the Delaware courts have the power to change, or reinterpret, the rules surrounding appraisal in ways that would greatly reduce its attractiveness to hedge fund and other appraisal seekers.[97] If that were to happen, this form of shareholder monitoring of M&A transactions could come to a screeching halt.

3.4 The Limits of Governance

Say on Pay and the revived appraisal remedy are unlikely to have strong immediate effects on managerial agency costs. First, it remains to be seen whether the American experience with Say on Pay votes will be more than a ritualistic blessing of the status quo or what the impact of hedge funds' opportunistic use of the appraisal remedy will be. If their promise fades over time, then established corporate doctrines that interface strongly with governance will likely remain the major bulwark to protect shareholder value. To this end, the antidote for the present epidemic of suits in multiple jurisdictions is a well-crafted forum selection bylaw, not the dilution of substantive doctrine that invites such suits. What remains to be seen is whether, just as the plaintiffs' bar overreacted to permissive substantive doctrines, there will be an overreaction by the defense bar drafting director-adopted bylaws that are more sweeping than necessary to centralize suits in an appropriate forum. One example would be director-approved bylaws that lodge shareholder suits behind the impenetrable veil of arbitration or eviscerate such suits by adopting a loser pays standard.

By far the most significant force addressing agency costs has been shareholder activism by hedge funds. Their effect is broader than the lash of change of control that has long been championed as a mechanism to address significant agency costs. But as significant as hedge funds have been, their impact does not reach abuses targeted in shareholder failure to monitor suits. Simply put, hedge funds are not likely to find the rewards of changing the mine safety in Massey or risk management at Citigroup at all sufficient to attract their attention. In contrast, vigorous application of Caremark obligations on the part of directors can be expected to promote better oversight by outside directors. Thus, hedge fund activism complements, but does not supplement, shareholder suits in this area, and likely other forms of agency costs.

---

[96] Id. at 50.

[97] Steven Davidoff Solomon, Fine Legal Point Poses Challenge to Appraisal Rights, N.Y. Times, May 30, 2014, available at <http://dealbook.nytimes.com/2014/05/30/fine-legal-point-poses-challenge-to-appraisal-rights/?_r=0> (discussing pending Delaware Chancery Court case where standing of beneficial owner to bring appraisal action has been raised).

4 IMPLICATIONS FOR AND FROM GERMANY

As we noted earlier, Germany is evolving into a more dispersed ownership system.[98] This will lead managerial agency costs to rise, and Germany will need to develop techniques to reduce them. While Germany already has some legal rules and institutions in place that facilitate minority shareholder monitoring,[99] the decline in bank monitoring, the increased levels of equity securities held by foreign investors, and the rapid drop in block holder ownership levels, in combination emphasize the need for it to carefully evaluate new options.[100]

Any such reform for shareholder litigation must overcome substantial inertial forces as for some time Germany has been skeptical of it, in large part because of concerns about litigation agency costs.

4.1 Representative Shareholder Litigation

Historically, German public company shareholders have not used litigation much as a device to discipline managers. This difference from the US is explained by the dominating role of the control block holder within the typical German public company. Even with the weakening of the role of banks and block holders generally in Germany, today derivative suits remain virtually non-existent. Moreover, the two-tiered board structure for German companies itself provides a governance structure to manage agency costs. Although the supervisory board has the statutory authority and requirement to initiate suit against misbehaving managers, there is a recognized bias on the part of the supervisory board not to go after managers since this may suggest weaknesses in oversight by the supervisory board that enabled the misbehavior.[101]

To be sure, there is express statutory authority for derivative-like suits in Germany to step in where the supervisory board has been reluctant to act. One means for such shareholder suits is upon the approval of a majority of the shareholders.[102] Alternatively, a shareholder or group of owners holding 1% of the firm's capital (or €100,000) can initiate suits for violations of the articles of incorporation or serious violations of law.[103] The board can nonetheless scuttle the suit, but to do so must show that the overriding interest of the company calls for the suit to be dismissed.

Few such suits occur, most likely due to Germany having, like most of continental Europe, a loser pays system so that representative shareholder litigation rarely makes sense and even less so in the absence of class action procedures.[104] However, the plaintiff can escape

---

[98] See notes 8–12 *supra* and accompanying text.

[99] Pierre-Henri Conac, Luca Enriques, & Martin Gelter, "Constraining Dominant Shareholders' Self-Dealing: The Legal Framework in France, Germany and Italy", 4 Eur. Comp. & Fin. L. Rev. 491 (2007) (discussing existing legal rules in named countries that constrain controlling shareholder misconduct).

[100] Enriques and Volpin, *supra* note 14, at 132 (listing recent shareholder empowerment reforms enacted in Germany).

[101] Baums & Scott, *supra* note 41.   [102] AktG § 147.   [103] AktG § 148.

[104] Martin Gelter, "Why Do Shareholder Derivative Suits Remain Rare in Continental Europe?", 37 Brook. J. Int'l. L. 843 (2012).

the clutches of loser pays upon the courts' preliminary determination that the suit should proceed and this outcome is not affected if the suit ultimately rules in favor of the manager defendants. Once the suit survives the preliminary determination, the court has the power to appoint a neutral party to prosecute the suit on behalf of the shareholders. Moreover, in making this preliminary determination, the court accords much less deference to the conclusions reached by the supervisory board than an American court customarily assigns to the business judgment rule.

The leading decision on supervisory boards' responsibility to address misconduct by managers is ARAG/Garmenbeck.[105] It involved two members of a supervisory board who sought review of that body's decision not to pursue the firm's CEO in connection with losses suffered by the corporation when it became the victim of a Ponzi scheme. Twice the supervisory board refused to authorize an investigation into the CEO's possible culpability in connection with the corporation's losses. The BGH held that in light of the supervisory board's affirmative duty to monitor the managing board that the supervisory board has a duty to determine whether members of the managing board have engaged in misconduct. If so, the supervisory board must evaluate the litigation risk and the burdens of the suit; if these weigh in favor of prosecuting the suit, then the supervisory board must, except in extraordinary circumstances, proceed with a suit against the offending manager.[106] Accordingly, the BGH overruled the decision of the supervisory board not to investigate the CEO.

Germany does have another species of lawsuit, the rescission, or contesting action. The German statute confers the power to shareholders who oppose either in person or by proxy resolutions at a stockholders' meeting, to challenge the action approved in a shareholder resolution.[107] The strength of such suits is that the corporation cannot complete the challenged transaction so long as the challenge is outstanding. These suits have over time grown in popularity. An empirical study by Vermeulen and Zetzsche make the case that the German contesting suits are fraught by unprofessional conduct by their lawyers and suggests they produce hardly any substantive relief to the corporation or its stockholders.[108] We can see that the German experience with contesting actions compares with the multi-forum litigation that thrives in the US with respect to mergers and acquisitions. Of interest is that Professors Vermeulen and Zetzsche, while marshaling a good deal of evidence of abuse with the German contesting action, find that the Dutch process whereby such shareholder claims must first pass through a neutral body before being initiated frequently leads to positive outcomes. Their finding underscores the virtues of a neutral screening mechanism for shareholder suits and lifting the blunt instrument of loser pays as the governor on shareholder suits.

Despite the infrequency of German derivative suits and the likely abuses of the more prevalent contesting actions, the German procedure whereby an external auditor can be appointed shows a good deal of promise.[109] A dramatic illustration of the special auditor was in IKB,[110] where the court granted the request for a special auditor to be appointed, holding that

---

[105] Bundesgerichtshof (BGH), 04/21/1997, II ZR 175/95.

[106] The holding in ARAG/Garmenbeck in 2005 was codified in § 93 I 2 AktG.

[107] AktG §§ 243 & 249.

[108] Erik P. M. Vermeulen & Dirk A. Zetzsche, "The Use and Abuse of Investor Suits", 7 Eur. Company and Fin. L. Rev. 1 (2010).

[109] AktG § 142.

[110] Higher regional Court (OLG) Düsseldorf, decision of 12/09/2009, 6 W 45/09, ZIP 2010, 28.

the petitioner had pleaded sufficient facts of gross breach of duty. IKB had invested 46% of its assets in collateral debt obligations (CDOs) where the underlying assets were subprime US home mortgages. Its articles of incorporation provided that IKB was to promote "trade and industry, in particular through the provision of mid- and long-term financing" and thereby meet the "financial needs of medium-sized enterprises." The appellate court stressed that it was the role of the auditor, if appointed, to determine whether a breach had occurred such that the role of the reviewing court was to determine if sufficient facts were pled to begin that inquiry, not to resolve the truthfulness or accuracy of the pled facts. The business judgment rule was held not to be a defense to violating a provision of the articles of incorporation. Furthermore, the court concluded that the petition alleged that the directors had acted in total reliance on the ratings provided by rating agencies which the IKB directors must have known were subject to a conflict of interest that rendered them less than independent. Notwithstanding not being fully informed, the petition set forth sufficient facts that the directors' action exposed the firm to excessive risk of loss. The court emphasized that the CDO holdings were not just risky themselves but given their magnitude relative to the firm's size thereby jeopardized the solvency of the IKB.

As seen in *IKB*, the procedure introduces a neutral party to the dynamics, rids the process of agency costs by the initiating lawyers, as occurs in the contesting action, and should with the auditor's independence accepted weaken the claim for further restraints such as automatic fee shifting as is the case in other forms of shareholder litigation. The outcome in *IKB* stands in stark contrast to the more deferential and less skeptical approach in *Citigroup*. discussed earlier. To be sure, *IKB* involved the distinguishing factor of involving, albeit only partly, the board acting inconsistently with the clear strictures of the company's bylaws; however, the focus of the *IKB* court was not this factor but rather the failure of the board to act reasonably in assessing the firm's substantial purchase of CDOs.

4.2 Evolving Monitoring Devices

Besides litigation, Germany does have a number of other shareholder monitoring mechanisms for protecting minority shareholders' rights. These are of varying strength, but include the duty of loyalty, German "group" law, and the equality principle.[111] But these devices are imperfect and seem insufficient to address the rising level of managerial agency costs that will accompany the shift from control shareholder ownership to dispersed ownership. As discussed in section 3, several new forms of shareholder monitoring have evolved in the US in recent years that could be considered for deployment in Germany.

While the market for corporate control in Germany has long been dormant, commentators have been pushing for it to open up to take the place of control block holder monitoring.[112] Hedge fund activism has become a powerful monitoring force that could be harnessed in Germany to free up the market for corporate control.[113] Hedge funds have had some success in raising shareholder value in Europe, including in Germany, although the levels of activism

---

[111]   Ringe, *supra* note 5, at 12–14.

[112]   Ringe, *supra* note 5, at 37 ("German lawmakers should consider strengthening the takeover market by removing obstacles to it").

[113]   See section 3.1 for further discussion of the US experience.

are much lower than in the US.[114] While international studies of hedge fund activism have found that the cumulative abnormal returns to activism in Europe are lower than in the US and Japan, they are still positive and significant.[115] European returns are especially high for hedge fund interventions that lead to restructurings or takeovers.[116]

However, Germany makes life very difficult for many hedge fund activists.[117] For example, German shareholders cannot gain access to the corporation's stock list in order to communicate with their fellow shareholders, making proxy solicitation very difficult.[118] Importantly, markets are also illiquid for many German companies, making it more difficult for hedge funds to accumulate large positions and to exit at the end of an engagement.[119] Given the significant monitoring potential of hedge fund activism, Germany might do well to consider making legal and structural changes that make it more feasible.

The Germans should also consider providing shareholders with an alternative device for monitoring abuse friendly transactions along the lines of appraisal arbitrage discussed above; indeed, this may be seen as a response to the overuse of contesting actions, described above. There is presently a limited appraisal remedy for minority shareholders in German firms.[120] In the event of a friendly change of control transaction at an unfair price, minority shareholders would benefit from having a stronger version of the appraisal remedy, particularly in management-financed transactions such as private equity management buyouts.

Shareholder monitoring of executive compensation is a third promising area for development. In the past, there was concentrated ownership by banks, which, all other things being equal, was associated with lower levels of CEO compensation at German companies.[121] Now, as ownership concentration has become more dispersed, we are seeing much higher levels of executive compensation. For example, the mean compensation of a member of the

---

[114] Marco Becht, J. R. Franks, G. Grant, & H. F. Wagner, "The Returns to Hedge Fund Activism: An International Study", 30 Rev. Fin. Stud. 2933 (2017), Table 4 (showing activist events per 1000 listed firms in Europe were 3.52 versus 12.18 in the US). For studies studying activism solely related to German firms, see Wolfgang Bessler, Wolfgang Drobetz, & Jullian Holler, "The Returns to Hedge Fund Activism in Germany", 21 Eur. Fin. Mgmt. 106 (2015); Mark Mietzner & Denis Schweizer, "Hedge Funds versus Private Equity Funds as Shareholder Activists in Germany: Differences in Value Creation", 38 J. Econ. & Fin. 181 (2014) (both finding positive cumulative abnormal returns to hedge fund activism at German companies).

[115] Becht et al., *supra* note 114, at Table 5A (showing positive abnormal returns in window around engagement disclosure).

[116] Id. at Table 5C (breaking out different levels of abnormal returns for five different types of outcomes).

[117] Id. at Appendix 2, Tables A1 and A2.   [118] Id.

[119] Brav et al., *supra* note 52, find that hedge funds prefer to invest in companies that have highly liquid trading markets for both of the reasons given in the text.

[120] Kraakman et al., *supra* note 14, at 186 ("Appraisal may be made available expressly where the merger involves a revolution in legal form or some other unusual restriction on shareholder rights," citing Unwandlungsgesetz §29.)

[121] Alfred Haid & B. Burcin Yurtoglu, "Ownership Structure and Executive Compensation in Germany" 15, 19 (Working Paper 2006), available at http://ssrn.com/abstract=948926. Interestingly, family ownership of German firms increases compensation, perhaps because families use it as a mechanism for diverting value to themselves. Id.

management board of a DAX company soared from €1.2 million in 2001 to over €2.8 million in 2011, an increase of over 240%.[122]

One potential pay-monitoring device is mandating a Say on Pay advisory shareholder vote. The Germans have made some tentative movements in this direction. The Law on the Appropriateness of Director Compensation states that the general meeting of shareholders may be provided an advisory vote of the remuneration system of the management board of listed companies.[123] While not mandatory, all DAX companies nonetheless have had their management board remuneration system approved at least once by their general meeting of shareholders since 2010.[124] While most such proposals are strongly supported by shareholders,[125] institutional investors make use of the advisory Say on Pay to signal their worries over pay increases.[126]

There is room to strengthen the German Say on Pay voting system. First, we would urge the Germans to adopt a mandatory vote on the top executives' pay level, such as the one in the US, rather than on the remuneration system of the management board.[127] Second, Germany should give serious consideration to making this vote binding, as it is in the UK and Australia, perhaps going so far as to implement the Australian "two strikes" rule.[128] The combination of a mandatory and binding vote might significantly improve shareholders' monitoring power over executive pay at German public companies.

We believe there are lessons for America to draw from the German experience. First, we believe that when evaluating a board's rejection of a demand in derivative suits that American courts would be better advised to accord, as German courts have, less deference to the board's determination on matters not germane to matters directly related to the conduct of the company's business. Just as the business of business is business, which supports the deference embodied in the business judgment rule, we believe courts have greater experience than the board or a committee of the board with matters related to the likely strengths of a derivative suit. Second, we believe that if this approach were taken that bylaws mandating fee shifting could more readily be seen as striking the right balance between fostering the meaningful therapeutic of the derivative suit and curtailing abusive litigation. However, once the demand is excused under the less deferential treatment of the board or committee

---

[122] OECD.StatExtracts, Organization for Economic Co-operation & Development (2013), http://stats.oecd.org/# (last visited May 28, 2013).

[123] Aktiengesetz [AktG] [Stock Corporation Act], at § 120, ¶ 4. The law only facilitates that the company allows the general meeting to vote on the remuneration system of the management board, there is no mandatory requirement.

[124] Randall S. Thomas & Christoph Van der Elst, "Say on Pay Around the World", 92 Wash. U. L. Rev. 653 (2015), at 692.

[125] Thomas & Van der Elst, *supra* note 124, at 693.

[126] Madison Marriage, Hermes Attacks Deutsche Pay Levels, Fin. Times, May 27, 2013, at 1.

[127] Such a system has already been proposed at the EU level and is likely to be adopted. Thomas and Van der Elst, *supra* note 124, at 709.

[128] Thomas and Van der Elst, *supra* note 124, at 664–75 (describing the UK and Australian systems).

rejection of a demand, this should lead to the same result as in Germany so that loser pays abates regardless of the ultimate outcome of the suit. We believe this balance approach could reflect moderation so that courts can be somewhat more welcoming to limited fee shifting via bylaw provisions.

5 Conclusions

Shifting ownership structures lead to changes in corporate governance systems as those systems evolve to address new problems. In the US, ownership structures have moved from largely dispersed to more concentrated in the past few decades, while in Germany the old control-shareholder-dominated, house-bank-driven ownership arrangements are slowly dissolving. For Germany, these changes will ultimately result in higher levels of managerial agency costs as control shareholders become less capable of engaging in close monitoring of managers.

In this chapter, we have closely examined shareholder monitoring devices created in the US and asked whether they might be of some service to (more) dispersed shareholders in Germany. We proposed that representative litigation, despite its flaws, may be useful to shareholders in their quest to monitor managements. We also suggested that Germany consider loosening the barriers to hedge fund activism and shareholder Say on Pay voting. Finally, we recommended that Germany consider adopting an appraisal-type remedy for minority shareholders to address potential unfair friendly transactions, especially when they benefit corporate managers.

CHAPTER 34

··

PRIVATE AND PUBLIC ENFORCEMENT OF SECURITIES REGULATION

··

HOWELL E. JACKSON[1] AND JEFFERY Y. ZHANG[2]

1 INTRODUCTION

··

IN a widely influential article published in the Journal of Political Economy in 1998, La Porta, Lopez-de-Silanes, Shleifer, and Vishny ("LLSV") pioneered the quantitative coding of legal rules to explore the relationship between the rule of law and the development of capital markets.[3] Their analysis produced the now well-familiar finding that common law countries have greater investor protection than civil law countries and that greater shareholder protection is associated with a lower level of ownership concentration. LLSV also inspired numerous sub-fields related to the theme of law and finance. In this chapter, we review one of them—the empirical relationship between actual enforcement of the law and the robustness of capital markets.

Research on the significance of enforcement intensity, especially the importance of private versus public enforcement, has provided a healthy debate with valuable insights. In a 2006 paper published in the Journal of Finance, La Porta, Lopez-de-Silanes, and Shleifer ("LLS") examined capital market development in 49 countries and concluded that private enforcement through liability rules positively affected capital market development while public enforcement had negligible consequences.[4] Jackson and Roe ("JR") revisited this issue a few years later, arguing that real resources in the form of a regulator's budget or staff,

[1] James S. Reid, Jr., Professor of Law, Harvard Law School.
[2] Economist, Board of Governors of the Federal Reserve System. The views expressed in this article are the author's alone and do not necessarily represent the views of the Federal Reserve or the United States government.
[3] See Rafael La Porta, Florencio Lopez-de-Silanes, Andrei Shleifer, & Robert W. Vishny, "Law and Finance", 106 J. Pol. Econ. 1113 (1998).
[4] See Rafael La Porta, Florencio Lopez-de-Silanes, & Andrei Shleifer, "What Works in Securities Laws?", 61 J. Fin. 1 (2006).

as opposed to formal legal indices, would better proxy public enforcement intensity.[5] Using resource-based measures of enforcement, the authors concluded that public enforcement was consistently associated with several measures of robust capital markets, most notably market capitalization, the number of publicly traded firms, initial public offerings, and overall trading levels. Moreover, for these measures, the authors claimed that public enforcement performed at least as well as the measures of private enforcement identified as important to capital market development in earlier research.

Although the debate between private and public enforcement is ongoing, at least two subsequent empirical studies have indirectly confirmed significant relationships between enforcement and robust capital markets found in JR and LLS. In a 2010 working paper, Echeverri-Gent and Bloom focused their attention on the relationship between politics and financial development.[6] In a model that incorporates controls for electoral competitiveness, federalism, and checks on executive power, the authors conceptualized regulatory budgets and staffing as reflections of political choices and thus also included the JR resource-based variables in the analysis. Using measures of robust financial markets similar to those used in JR, they concluded: "[W]e find support for those who argue that the well-endowed government regulators play an important role in promoting financial market development."[7]

In a recent publication, Cumming, Knill, and Richardson explored the influence of public and private enforcement on securities issuances using a research strategy that distinguishes between the size of issuers.[8] Their paper exploits a newly assembled data set of over 45,000 firms across 46 countries and spanning the years 1996 to 2007, thus generating considerably more statistical power than the country cross-sectional sample upon which the JR and LLS results were based. Utilizing various measures of enforcement intensity, the authors reported two main results:

> First, counter to what has been previously found in the literature, public enforcement, as measured by legal statute (i.e., LLS, 2006) and resources (JR, 2009), is influential in firm access to capital and seems to level the playing field for small firms who struggle for adequate access to equity capital . . . . Second, private enforcement is not found to be unilaterally beneficial as previously suggested in LLS; laws regulating private transaction exacerbate preferential access to equity markets for large firms. The disparate effects of private enforcement likely have to do with the marginal benefits versus the costs of additional regulation for firms of different sizes.[9]

Specifically with respect to the JR staffing variable, the authors reported that a one standard deviation increase in the resource-based proxy raised the probability of equity issuance of small firms by nearly 4%.[10] While documenting the beneficial impacts of greater public

---

[5] See Howell E. Jackson & Mark J. Roe, "Public and Private Enforcement of Securities Laws: Resource-Based Evidence", 93 J. Fin. Econ. 207 (2009).

[6] See John Echeverri-Gent & Benjamin Bloom, "Do Competitive Politics Produce Competitive Markets? Politics of Financial Market Development" (APSA Annual Meeting, 2010), available at http://ssrn.com/abstract=1644631.

[7] Id. at 1 (quoting abstract). See also id. at 23 ("Using measures of resources available to regulators, we found a positive and significant association between two of four dimensions of financial market development and standardized measures of regulatory budgets and staff").

[8] See Douglas Cumming, April Knill, & Nela Richardson, "Firm Size and the Impact of Securities Regulation", 43 J. Comp. Econ. 417 (2015).

[9] Id. at 425–27.

[10] Id. at 433. Using the LLS measure of public enforcement, the increase was almost 2%.

enforcement, the paper also presents a more nuanced view of private enforcement by showing that, once small firms gained access to equity markets, greater private enforcement intensity allowed them to raise significantly more capital.[11]

The papers by Echeverri-Gent and Bloom and by Cumming et al. are closest to directly addressing the JR conjectures, but they are only part of the growing literature in support of the view that enforcement, particularly public enforcement, plays an integral role in the development of robust capital markets. Our main analysis in this chapter appears in section 2, which summarizes the literature exploring the relationship between enforcement and other measures of robust capital markets, between enforcement and capital flows, valuations, and cross-listing decisions, and between enforcement and the success of regulatory reform efforts. At the end of that section, we offer a cursory review of some of the emerging literature surrounding the global financial crisis and discuss potential implications for public enforcement. Section 3 deals with issues of causation in the existing literature and presents papers which utilize data and methods capable of overcoming those obstacles. Finally, section 4 concludes and offers some tentative suggestions for future research.

2 Empirical Research

This section focuses exclusively on empirical findings related to private and public enforcement as measured by formal indices and resources. Many of the papers reviewed do not themselves have enforcement as their primary focus. Rather, each of these papers investigates a distinctive hypothesis and, as part of that analysis, utilizes one of the JR resource-based measures, the LLS measures, or some variant thereon to determine whether enforcement intensity has a bearing on the variables of interest. Oftentimes, the enforcement aspect of the analysis is a relatively minor piece of the overall paper. The goal of this section is to bring together these disparate lines of research to present a larger picture of the extent to which enforcement has been found to have a consistent and significant association with important indicia of financial market performance.

2.1 Financial Market Performance

We first turn to the association between enforcement intensity and technical measures of financial market performance (as opposed to the broader measures of capital market development explored in the original JR and LLS papers). In a 2012 working paper, Amiram and Owens studied the relationship between income smoothing in financial statements to the cost of firm debt.[12] Using 1,817 facility-level debt observations for 639 non-US borrowers across 20 countries from 1996 to 2009, the authors concluded that income smoothing was associated with lower costs of debt in countries where it was more difficult for managers

---

[11] Id. at 436.
[12] See Dan Amiram & Edward Owens, "Private Benefits Extraction and the Opposing Effects of Income Smoothing on Private Debt Contracts" (Jul. 18, 2012), available at http://papers.ssrn.com/abstract=1710122.

to extract private benefits of firm value and was associated with higher costs of debt in jurisdictions where it was easier to extract private benefits. In deriving the main results, the authors captured the threat of private benefits extraction using the anti-self-dealing index created by Djankov et al., which was based on private enforcement mechanisms available to minority shareholders related to disclosure, approval, and litigation in 2003.[13] In alternative specifications, the authors segmented jurisdictions by substituting the JR enforcement variables as a proxy for restraints on private benefits and reported "qualitatively consistent" results.[14] Accordingly, the paper offers evidence that increased levels of both public and private enforcement can be associated with lower costs of capital.

Another paper investigating technical measures of performance is Kerl and Ohlert's 2014 working paper on the accuracy of forecasts by star analysts.[15] Using over 30,000 analyst reports from 2005 to 2010, the authors tested a number of hypotheses, including the question of whether the quality of corporate governance affects the accuracy of analysts' forecasts. In distinguishing among corporate governance regimes, they used several different proxies, including the Djankov et al. anti-self-dealing index, the Leuz et al. public enforcement index,[16] and the JR staffing variable. In jurisdictions with higher levels of enforcement capabilities, the forecasts of all analysts were more accurate and the relative merits of star analyst forecasts were especially pronounced.[17] The paper concludes: "[B]etter corporate governance and stronger investor protection have a positive effect on forecast accuracy of star-analysts."[18]

In a similar vein, Arand, Kerl, and Walter undertook a study into the informativeness of nearly 700,000 sell-side analyst reports in eight leading capital markets.[19] The authors explored whether the regulatory environment of both issuers and institutional investors influenced the informativeness of analyst reports, measured by both short-term market reactions and an ex post assessment of report accuracy. They experimented with several different measures of the quality of the regulatory environment, including three mentioned previously (the Djankov et al. anti-self-dealing index, the Leuz et al. enforcement proxy, and the JR staffing variable). In all of these cases, the authors found that "the information value of target price and earnings forecast revisions, as proxied by the level of market reaction, increases with the level of investor protection."[20] Moreover, with the exception of the Leuz et al. measure of public enforcement, the other enforcement proxies generated results

---

[13] See Simeon Djankov, Rafael La Porta, Florencio Lopez-de-Silances, & Andrei Shleifer, "The Law and Economics of Self-Dealing", 88 J. Fin. Econ. 430 (2008).

[14] Id. at 23.

[15] See Alexander Kerl & Martin Ohlert, "Star-Analysts' Forecast Accuracy and the Role of Corporate Governance", 38 J. Fin. Research 93 (2015).

[16] This proxy is defined as the mean of the following three indices from LLSV: the efficiency of the judicial system, the rule of law, and the level of corruption. See Christian Leuz, Dhananjay Nanada, & Peter D. Wysocki, "Earnings Management and Investor Protection: An International Comparison", 69 J. Fin. Econ. 505 (2003).

[17] See id. at 38, Table 5, Panel D. The authors also use the LSS public enforcement index as a separate measure of corporate governance and find similarly positive though somewhat less consistent effects. See id. at Panel C.

[18] Id. at 16.

[19] See Daniel Arand, Alexander G. Kerl, & Andreas Walter, "When Do Sell-Side Analyst Reports Really Matter? Shareholder Protection, Institutional Investors and the Informativeness of Equity Research", 21 Eur. Fin. Mgmt. 524 (2015).

[20] Id. at 539.

showing that "forecast errors are negatively associated with the respective investor protection measure and highly significant at the 1% level."[21]

To be sure, not all intervening studies have reported robust effects of private or public enforcement on capital market performance. In a 2012 working paper, Cumming, Imad'Eddine, and Schwienbacher analyzed various law and enforcement proxies in connection with the degree of spread of UCITS equity funds and bond funds to other countries.[22] While the authors found a statistically significant correlation between the level of spread and host countries with better anti-director rights or with better creditor rights, they failed to indicate any association between enforcement measures (namely, the JR regulatory budget and staffing levels and the LLSV and LLS legal indices of law enforcement) of host countries and the spread of UCITS funds.[23] Similarly, in a 2009 working paper, Frijns, Gilbert, and Tourani-Rad developed a data set containing the scope, sanctions, and enforcement of insider trading laws for a sample of 1,432 firms from 30 countries to examine their efficacy in decreasing informational asymmetry and the incidence of insider trading.[24] In their analysis, they found private and public enforcement variables to be insignificant in the deterrence of insider trading; their empirical tests included the resource-based proxies of enforcement as well.[25]

At least one working paper identifies an association between enforcement and reform outcomes that might be viewed as having negative implications. In a study exploring the speed with which national authorities adopted International Financial Reporting Standards (IFRS), Pownall and Wieczynska concluded that a higher level of the JR regulatory budget variable was negatively associated with the likelihood that a firm in the European Union adopted IFRS.[26] However, when assessing their results involving other proxies for enforcement, the authors reported: "We find little evidence that cross-country enforcement conditions or mechanisms are associated with IFRS adoption during our period."[27]

In sum, it appears that private and public enforcement play significant roles in improving essential aspects of capital markets, notably with regards to the private cost of capital and the value of information, but these benefits do not seem to extend to areas such as insider trading and the speed of regulatory adoption. The negative results are not too surprising given that enforcement is only a piece of the regulatory framework, but the mixed results reported above are important to note as they highlight the importance of multiple channels of supervisory impact.

---

[21] Id. at 547.

[22] See Douglas J. Cumming, Gael Imad'Eddine, & Armin Schwienbacher, "Legality and the Spread of Voluntary Investor Protection" 34(3) Finance 31 (2013).

[23] Id. at 53.

[24] See Bart Frijns, Aaron B. Gilbert, & Alireza Tourani-Rad, "Elements of Effective Insider Trading" (Finance and Corporate Governance Conference 2010 Paper, Aug. 3, 2009), available at http://ssrn.com/abstract=1443597.

[25] Cf. Laura N. Beny, "Do Insider Trading Laws Matter? Some Preliminary Comparative Evidence", 7 Am. L. & Econ. Rev. 144 (2005). The paper concludes that public enforcement, as measured by the ability to impose criminal sanctions, is more important than private enforcement of insider trading laws.

[26] See Grace Pownall & Maria Wieczynska, "Deviations from the Mandatory Adoption of IFRS in the European Union: Implementation, Enforcement, Incentives, and Compliance" (Sept. 16, 2012), available at http://papers.ssrn.com/abstract=1919805.

[27] Id. at 34.

2.2 Capital Flows, Valuations, and Cross-Listing Decisions

A separate strand of research investigates the impact of cross-border flows of capital, valuation effects, and cross-listing decisions by corporate issuers. While some of the studies find statistically significant correlations with enforcement variables, the results again are mixed. On balance, however, the evidence available to date suggests a possible impact of public and private enforcement activities on cross-border capital flows and valuations.

In a 2012 paper published in the Journal of International Money and Finance, Eichler examined a data set measuring the equity home bias of US investors toward 38 countries from 2003 to 2008 with the goal of exploring the influence of the quality of corporate disclosure in each county on mitigating the equity home bias of US investors—a bias which generally leads investors to overinvest in the United States at the expense of what is thought to be more desirable levels of international diversification.[28] After first determining that the quality of corporate disclosure in foreign jurisdictions was associated with a statistically significant reduction in home country bias on the part of US investors,[29] the author expanded the analysis to the marginal impact of supervisory intensity, using the liability standards index from LLS to proxy for private enforcement and the JR staffing variable to proxy for public enforcement. Significant results were found using both variables. Specifically, investors preferred stocks from countries with more comprehensive corporate disclosure only if enforcement levels in those countries were sufficiently high.[30] In comparing private and public enforcement, the authors noted that "fewer countries have sufficient public enforcement to ensure that more comprehensive corporate disclosure yields significantly less home bias," thus implying that the relatively "lax public enforcement of securities laws may be a more probable cause of US investors' equity home bias than low liability standards."[31] Overall, the analysis corroborates a hypothesis advanced in JR that one of the channels through which public enforcement benefits capital markets is through its interaction with disclosure standards.[32]

In a further exploration of the relationship between disclosure and public enforcement in cross-border context, Loureiro and Taboada presented a 2012 working paper exploring the relationship between stock market informativeness and the adoption of IFRS of nearly 4,000 firms across 30 countries from 1999 through 2010.[33] While their primary investigation concerned the positive effect on stock market informativeness of voluntary adoptions, they also investigated whether higher public enforcement levels were associated with greater informativeness where issuers were mandated to adopt IFRS. Using both the public enforcement index from Djankov et al. and the JR budget variable, the authors concluded that "mandatory adopters in countries with better enforcement exhibit a more significant increase in stock price informativeness following IFRS adoption. These results are both statistically and economically significant."[34] The authors interpreted these results to suggest that, when an issuer

---

[28] Stefan Eichler, "Equity Home Bias and Corporate Disclosure", 31 J. Int'l. Money & Fin. 1008 (2012).

[29] Interestingly, the paper finds this effect only when using a measure of de facto disclosure and not when using the LLS disclosure index based on formal legal requirements. Id. at 1021.

[30] Id. at 1023–24.   [31] Id. at 1025.   [32] See Jackson & Roe, *supra* note 5, at 236.

[33] Gilberto R. Loureiro & Alvaro G. Taboada, "The Impact of IFRS Adoption on Stock Price Informativeness" (Apr. 2012), available at http://www.efmaefm.org/0EFMAMEETINGS/EFMA%20 ANNUAL%20MEETINGS/2012-Barcelona/papers/IFRS-Adoption_and_Stock_Price_Informativeness-5-7-2012.pdf.

[34] Id. at 18.

is forced to adopt IFRS as the result of a government mandate, stock market pricing rewards that adoption only when the jurisdiction maintains robust systems of supervisory oversight: the authors reasoned that mandatory IFRS adoption does not send a credible market signal in lax jurisdictions.[35]

Studies regarding the cross-listing of securities are more mixed in their findings with respect to enforcement intensity. In a 2012 paper published in the Journal of Banking & Finance, Sarkissian and Schill explored the importance of law enforcement in explaining foreign listing premiums in 2,838 listings on 32 foreign stock exchanges from 69 home markets during the period 1985–2006.[36] The authors used the JR budgetary and staffing variables to compare enforcement levels between countries, but failed to find any statistically significant correlation between the intensity of public enforcement and foreign listing premium, other than in a small positive effect in the cases of US firms listed overseas.[37]

Researchers have also utilized the Supreme Court's 2010 decision in *Morrison v. National Australia Bank Ltd.* to test the consequences of private enforcement on cross-listing decisions.[38] Previously, private lawsuits under Rule 10b-5 of the Securities Exchange Act of 1934 could be filed against non-US issuers if the alleged fraud occurred in the United States or had substantial consequences for the United States. In *Morrison*, however, the Court ruled that 10b-5 would only apply to securities transacted upon a US stock exchange or otherwise sold through US domestic transactions. According to a forthcoming article by Bartlett, institutional investors claimed that such a decision would bias investments toward securities listed on US exchanges.[39] Because the ruling was unexpected, it provided a natural experiment to test the influence of private enforcement on cross-listing decisions. Using proprietary trading data from over 300 institutional investors, Bartlett found:

> [N]o significant change in investor trading in the thirty month period surrounding Morrison. Nor did investors appear to be allocating more narrowly to US exchanges after Morrison in those cross-listed issuers where preserving the right to bring a 10b-5 action might be especially desirable. Most notably, an investor's level of US trading after Morrison appears to have had no demonstrable relation to a trade's investment risk, trading cost, or the condition of a local market's investor protection regime. Similarly, even though Morrison made it considerably easier to determine which foreign issuers were subject to the risk of a private 10b-5 action, investors showed no evidence of reallocating toward these "bonded" issuers within their non-US equity portfolios.[40]

---

[35] Id. at 22.

[36] See Sergei Sarkissian & Michael J. Schill, "The Nature of the Foreign Listing Premium: A Cross-Country Examination", 36 J. Banking & Fin. 2494 (2012).

[37] Id. at 2504.

[38] See Amir N. Licht, Christopher Poliquin, Jordan I. Siegel, & Xi Li, "What Makes the Bonding Stick? A Natural Experiment Involving the US Supreme Court and Cross-Listed Firms" (Aug. 27, 2013), available at http://papers.ssrn.com/abstract=1744905 (finding that investors responded with indifference, or even positively, following *Morrison*); see also SEC, "Study on the Cross-Border Scope of the Private Right of Action Under Section 10(b) of the Securities Exchange Act of 1934" (Apr. 2012), available at http://www.sec.gov/news/studies/2012/929y-study-cross-border-private-rights.pdf (finding no statistically significant changes in abnormal returns following the ruling).

[39] See Robert P. Bartlett, III, "Do Institutional Investors Value the 10b-5 Private Right of Action? Evidence from Investor Trading Behavior Following Morrison v. National Australia Bank Ltd. (2010)" (Dec. 5, 2014), available at http://papers.ssrn.com/abstract=2171006 (forthcoming J. Leg. Stud.).

[40] Id. at 22.

It should be noted that, following the Morrison ruling, Congress added Section 929P to the then-pending Dodd–Frank Wall Street Reform and Consumer Protection Act in order to allow the SEC "to bring public enforcement actions against non-US firms under the conduct and effects test."[41] This could partially explain the insignificant results, assuming that investors expected increased involvement from public regulators. However, the Bartlett findings do pose a question of whether market participants actually value the benefits of private enforcement provided by 10b-5.

The Bartlett article includes evidence suggesting that some measures of enforcement did seem to affect trading practices before the Morrison case was decided. In particular, the author found that, prior to the Morrison ruling, there was a significant negative relationship between the JR resource-based proxies of public enforcement and US trading of cross-listed issuers, which is consistent with the JR results. Regarding private enforcement, a significant negative association was found with respect to the anti-self-dealing index created by Djankov et al. (2008) but not the LLSV anti-director rights index.[42] In other words, investors were "more likely to purchase cross-listed shares in the US when an issuer's local market was characterized by low measures of investor rights protections."[43]

In a separate investigation of cross-border listings, Samarasekera, Chang, and Tarca presented a study of the accounting quality of 495 UK listed firms who implemented IFRS, including 246 cross-listed firms (mostly from Germany and the United States).[44] Finding that accounting quality improves for only cross-listed firms, the authors reported that changes in regulatory scrutiny (by cross-listed countries) had a material effect on the quality of accounting reporting, reasoning that the additional scrutiny imposed on firms listed in multiple jurisdictions contributed to these improvements. While the authors did not utilize the JR variables in their analysis, they concluded: "Consistent with the view of Jackson and Roe (2009) that public enforcement is a key mechanism for promoting protection of investors and growth of securities markets, our evidence shows benefits from activity by public bodies to promote the quality of audit and compliance with accounting standards."[45]

The affirmative results in this subsection are consistent with the previous analysis on technical measures of capital market performance. On the other hand, the mixed cross-listing results, especially the ones derived from the Morrison ruling, are somewhat surprising. The Supreme Court's unexpected decision in that case provided an opportunity to examine the benefits of private enforcement, but a negative investor reaction was simply not present in the empirical results. Perhaps the available data were not of sufficient quality to construct a valid counterfactual or perhaps the Dodd–Frank Act mitigated the potential fallout of weaker private enforcement. Regardless, the results presented here suggest that readers should carefully consider seemingly intuitive assumptions about the efficacy of private enforcement.

---

[41] Id. at 1.   [42] See id. at 29 (Table 4).   [43] Id. at 15.

[44] See Nelly Samarasekera, Millicent Chang & Ann Tarca, "IFRS and Accounting Quality: The Impact of Enforcement" (Dec. 1, 2012), available at http://papers.ssrn.com/sol3/papers.cfm?abstract_id=2183061.

[45] Id. at 8.

2.3 Success of Reform Efforts

Another group of studies utilize measures of enforcement to examine whether countries that dedicate more resources to regulatory reform behave differently in some areas of market activities. While the results of these studies are again not entirely uniform in their findings, in many contexts, greater public enforcement intensity has been found to have a statistically significant association with the market variable of interest.

For example, in a 2013 working paper, Christensen, Hail, and Leuz conducted an empirical study of the changes in the market liquidity and the cost of capital to firms in each of the countries in the European Union as the countries implemented Market Abuse Directive and Transparency Directive on a staggered basis between 2001 and 2011.[46] The paper shows that the implementation of the two directives was significantly correlated with the increase of market liquidity, as measured by bid-ask spreads and percentage of zero-return days, and the decrease of cost of capital, as measured by implied cost of capital and dividend yields. Of particular interest here, the authors' examination of liquidity effects partitioned countries based on various implementation and enforcement variables. They concluded that the "liquidity effects of the two directives are stronger in countries with a history of higher regulatory quality. Stricter implementation and enforcement of the two directives also result in larger liquidity effects, but these effects exist primarily in countries with strong prior regulatory quality."[47]

The Christensen, Hail, and Leuz results are informative on multiple dimensions. First, they provided evidence of a positive relationship between supervisory resources and a technical measure of market performance (bid-ask spreads), which might reasonably be thought to contribute to robust capital markets. Second, at least in this context, they isolated the source of this improvement as coming largely from countries that already had substantial supervisory staffing as measured by the growth in the number of full-time supervisory employees from 2004 to 2009. In other words, the gains did not come from traditionally low-supervisory jurisdictions that contemporaneously increased supervisory resources. The authors concluded with the following interpretation:

> In sum, our findings support a causal link between stricter securities regulation and market liquidity. They also support the notion that the success of regulation depends critically on how regulation is implemented and enforced. Thus, policy debates should pay close attention to implementation and enforcement issues if regulation is to have the intended effects. Our finding that countries with weaker securities regulation do not catch up with stronger countries illustrates the difficulty of harmonizing capital markets through regulatory reforms. It highlights that prior regulatory conditions matter and that imposing the same regulation on countries with disparate initial conditions can have the (unintended) effect of making countries diverge more, not less.[48]

---

[46] See Hans B. Christensen, Luzi Hail, & Christian Leuz, "Capital-Market Effects of Securities Regulation: Prior Conditions, Implementation, and Enforcement" (Dec. 31, 2013), available at http://papers.ssrn.com/abstract=1745105.

[47] Id. at 37. As discussed below, causality between enforcement and robust capital markets is potentially bi-directional. Findings such as the Christensen, Hail, & Leuz results, which establish links between regulatory intensity and improvements in technical measures of market quality, offer additional evidence that causation runs from resources to robustness.

[48] Id. at 37.

In a subsequent paper published in the Review of Finance, Dubois, Fresard, and Dumontier also explored the effects of adoption of the EU Market Abuse Directive (MAD) by documenting changes in other technical measures of stock market performance: biased research advice from the sell-side equity research industries in 15 European countries between 1997 and 2007.[49] Utilizing the JR budgetary and staffing variables as well as the LLS public enforcement index, the authors partitioned countries into "weak" and "strong" enforcement countries and found that optimism bias was significantly diminished after MAD in strong enforcement countries while it was not as effective in reducing bias in weak enforcement countries. The authors also included proxies for actual legal sanctions and found further positive effects. They concluded: "[U]sing the heterogeneity that exists in legal sanctions and enforcement practices across European countries, we find that the curbing effect of MAD largely depends on countries' institutional traits. The impact of MAD is significantly stronger in countries where the sanctions applicable in cases of violations of MAD's rules are severe."[50]

2.4 Financial Stability

Although our primary focus in this chapter is on the enforcement intensity of securities regulation, it is worth briefly discussing a few notable strands of research on the enforcement of banking regulation and its relationship to financial stability. The global financial crisis of 2008 caused a tremendous loss of economic output, employment opportunities, and social welfare. Since then, considerable academic work has attempted to identify its root causes, with many emphasizing banking supervision and regulation. Identifying the relationships between the type or degree of regulation and the incidence or severity of the crises is difficult not only because of the paucity of relevant data available to researchers, but also because of the complexity of the financial system and the inherent confounding factors in cross-country analyses. For instance, the United States and the United Kingdom both dedicated high levels of resources to supervisory functions but both were at the epicenter of the crisis. Australia and Canada, on the other hand, also invested high levels of resources into supervision and both are regarded as having weathered the crisis particularly well.[51] Nevertheless, the growing body of empirical investigation into regulation and financial stability offers intriguing insights into the study of public enforcement. We focus the following discussion on the consequences of the regulatory structure and content on stability, and conclude with some potentially undesirable effects of robust capital markets on stability.

---

[49] See Michel Dubois, Laurent Fresard, & Pascal Dumontier, "Regulating Conflicts of Interest: The Effect of Sanctions and Enforcement", 18 Rev. Fin. 489 (2014).

[50] Id. at 523.

[51] See Andrew K. Rose & Mark M. Spiegel, "Cross-Country Causes and Consequences of the Crisis: An Update", 55 Eur. Econ. Rev. 309, 324 (2011). See also Jennifer G. Hill, Why Did Australia Fare So Well in the Global Financial Crisis, in Eilis Ferran et al., The Regulatory Aftermath of the Global Financial Crisis 203 (2012); Donald J.S. Brean, Lawrence Kryzanowski, & Gordon S. Roberts, "Canada and the United States: Different Roots, Different Routes to Financial Sector Regulation", 53 Bus. Hist. 249 (2011).

2.4.1 Regulatory Structure

In a 2011 IMF working paper, Masciandaro, Pansini, and Quintyn investigated the association between the macroeconomic performance of 102 countries during the financial crisis in 2008–2009 and their supervisory unification, degree of central bank involvement in supervision, and supervisory governance (in terms of independence and accountability) in 2007.[52] The authors proxied macroeconomic performance using the average real output growth in the years 2008 and 2009. Possibly because of misaligned incentives of supervisors, their result suggests that the high levels of supervisory governance, as well as supervisory consolidation, were negatively associated with economic resilience, with central bank involvement in supervision having little effect on outcomes.[53]

In another recent paper studying the relationship between regulatory structure and crisis incidence, authors Amri and Kocher reviewed 124 banking crises from 65 advanced and developing countries during the period 1976–2005.[54] Their results depend on the specific measure of regulation used for analysis. With a measure that combined the scope and legal framework for banking regulators' ability to conduct on- and off-site examinations, compliance with Basel capital requirements, and independence of supervisory bodies, the authors found a significantly negative relationship with the probability of the incurrence of banking crises.[55] Interestingly, the authors found no significant relationship when using a private monitoring index, which proxied for the extent to which market or private monitoring exists; the authors noted that the latter result may be due to data limitations since certain index variables were available only for 1999.[56]

2.4.2 Content of Regulation

In a 2011 article, Ahrend, Arnold, and Murtin examined various indicators of on-the-book banking regulation, as collected by the World Bank, and their associations with the damage to each country during the crisis, as measured either by the degree of equity value destruction in the banking sector or by the fiscal cost of financial sector rescue.[57] The results reveal that moderately stronger prudential regulation, stricter regulatory requirements with respect to accounting and provisioning, and stricter restrictions on entry rules and ownership structures were associated with better stock prices and a lower expected rescue cost. Stricter

---

[52] See Donato Masciandaro, Rosaria Vega Pansini, & Marc Quintyn, "The Economic Crisis: Did Financial Supervision Matter?" (Nov. 2011), available at http://ssrn.com/abstract=1961908.

[53] Cf. Andrea Beltratti & René M. Stulz, "Why Did Some Banks Perform Better During the Credit Crisis? A Cross-Country Study of the Impact of Governance and Regulation" (July 2009), available at http://www.nber.org/papers/w15180 (finding a negative correlation between power of supervisory authorities and financial performance of banks in 2008, but suggesting that some of the effect may be the product of supervisory orders to raise capital and dilute existing shareholders). See also K.J. Hopt, "Corporate Governance of Banks and Other Financial Institutions After the Financial Crisis", 13 J. Corp. L. Stud. 219, 241–43 (Oct. 2013) (discussing role of shareholder control over bank risk taking).

[54] See Puspa Delima Amri & Brett Matthew Kocher, "The Political Economy of Financial Sector Supervision and Banking Crises: A Cross-Country Analysis", 18 Eur. L. J. 24 (2012).

[55] Id. at 35.   [56] Id. at 37.

[57] See Rüdiger Ahrend, Jens M. Arnold, & Fabrice Murtin, "Have More Strictly Regulated Banking Systems Fared Better During the Recent Financial Crisis?", 18 Applied Econ. Letters 399 (2011).

requirements for capital were also found to be correlated with a lower expected cost for the financial crisis.[58]

In the same mold, Čihák and co-authors highlighted findings from the World Bank's 2011–2012 Bank Regulation and Supervision Survey, which was distributed to 143 countries during the period 2008–2010.[59] First, the authors noted that countries affected by a systemic banking crisis imposed less stringent definitions of capital on their banks, allowed them to have more discretion in calculating capital requirements, and, not surprisingly, had lower actual capital ratios.[60] Second, crisis-hit countries had fewer restrictions on nonbank activities such as insurance, investment banking, and real estate. Third, regulations concerning the treatment of bad loans and loan losses were less strict in crisis countries. Fourth, regulators in crisis countries were less able to demand banks to put up more equity. Last, but not least, there were weaker incentives for the private sector to monitor bank risks in crisis countries because of a proliferation of credit rating for bonds and deposit insurance.[61] These findings provide systematic evidence of regulatory differences between countries which experienced a crisis and those that did not, and the evidence points toward regulatory leniency in crisis countries.[62]

While the beneficial effects of regulatory structure seem mixed and those of regulatory content more robust, it should be noted that all of these studies are conducted across countries, which inherently involves confounding factors. To prove a causal relationship, one would have to take country-level details and the specific type of supervision into account.[63] Having said that, the research presented in the previous two subsections

---

[58] Id. at 402; see also Gerard Caprio Jr., Vincenzo D'Apice, Giovanni Ferri, & Giovanni Walter Puopolo, Macro Financial Determinants of the Great Financial Crisis: Implications for Financial Regulation (Oct. 21, 2010), available at http://ssrn.com/abstract=1695335 (drawing on data sets on 83 countries over the period 1998–2006, this study documents that the incidence of the financial crisis was lower for countries with higher levels of restrictions to bank activities and private monitoring structures, but higher for those countries having higher levels of credit deposit ratio).

[59] See Martin Čihák, Asli Demirgüç-Kunt, Maria Soledad Martínez Pería, & Amin Mohseni-Cherghlou, Bank Regulation and Supervision Around the World: A Crisis Update? (Dec. 2012), available at http://www.asbaweb.org/E-News/enews-32/SUPER/3%20SUPER.pdf.

[60] The authors defined a crisis country as one that experienced a systemic banking crisis or a borderline systemic banking crisis from 2007–2009. The definitions and data of systemic or borderline systemic crises are taken from Luc Laeven & Fabian Valencia, Resolution of Banking Crises: The Good, the Bad, and the Ugly (Jun. 2010), available at http://www.imf.org/external/pubs/ft/wp/2010/wp10146.pdf.

[61] Id. at 7–10.

[62] See also Vighneswara Swamy, Bank Regulation, Supervision and Efficiency during the Global Financial Crisis (Sept. 4, 2014), available at http://papers.ssrn.com/abstract=2491413 (confirming that crisis-hit countries had weaker regulatory frameworks than non-crisis hit countries and differentiating the regulatory framework of the BRICS countries from those two groups).

[63] Consider the question of supervisory unification and economic resiliency. In a recent paper, Agarwal et al. exploit a legal setup in US banking rules in which federal and state supervisors take turns examining the same bank at predetermined time intervals. See Sumit Agarwal, David Lucca, Amit Seru, & Francesco Trebbi, "Inconsistent Regulators: Evidence from Banking", 129 Q. J. Econ. 889 (2014). The authors discovered that federal regulators were consistently tougher when it came to assigning bank ratings. Moreover, this relative leniency of the state regulator came at a real cost—namely, higher bank failure rates and lower repayment rates of government assistance funds. This type of natural experiment approach provides a more precise method to identifying the result. Of course, the trade-off results in a more narrow question.

suggests that financial stability and the ability to withstand global financial distress are variables of interest and should be part of future work on the effects of regulation and supervision.

2.4.3 Robust Capital Markets

When we analyzed the effect of enforcement on various indicators of capital markets in previous subsections—for example, market capitalization and trading volumes—we implicitly assumed that higher levels of those indicators were an unambiguously desirable outcome since they made capital markets more "robust" in a sense. A somewhat more troubling strain of empirical research into financial crises concerns the potentially destabilizing relationship between robust capital markets in ordinary times with the performance of national economies in times of financial stress. Several studies have drawn a connection between bank reliance on short-term credit and the severity of the financial crisis.[64] Particularly to the extent that banks moved away from deposit funding to reliance on short-term capital market funding, those institutions and their surrounding system appear to have been more vulnerable in times of financial turmoil.[65] Strong reliance on depository funding is one of the factors that researchers have cited as explaining the relatively strong performance of Canadian[66] and Australian[67] banks in the financial crisis.

A negative correlation between capital market funding for banks and poor results in financial crises is relevant to the study of enforcement and the law and finance approach more generally in that it suggests some potentially undesirable consequences of robust capital markets. Even if more robust capital markets lead to greater economic growth on average, a higher probability of experiencing financial crises may still result in an outcome that is suboptimal for social welfare. The possibility that some capital market expansions might have negative ramifications in times of financial distress suggests that a more nuanced analysis may be needed in the future.[68]

---

[64] See, e.g., Rudiger Ahrend & Antoine Goujard, Drivers of Systemic Banking Crises: The Role of Bank-Balance-Sheet Contagion and Financial Account Structure (June 5, 2012), available at http:// papers.ssrn.com/abstract=2113095.

[65] See, e.g., Gary Gorton & Andrew Metrick, "Securitized Banking and the Run on Repo", 104 J. Fin. Econ. 425 (2012).

[66] See Lev Ratnovski & Rocco Huang, "Why Are Canadian Banks More Resilient?" (IMF Working Paper No. 09/152, July 2009), available at http://ssrn.com/abstract=1442254 (a higher share of depository funding in liabilities was identified as a strong indicator of resilience to the financial crisis of Canadian banks).

[67] See Alison Lui, Macro and Micro Prudential Regulatory Failures amongst Financial Institutions in the United Kingdom: Lessons from Australia (Apr. 27, 2011), available at http://ssrn.com/ abstract=1716264 (noting that, among other things. Australian banks had better loans-to-deposits ratios than the UK banks).

[68] See also Beltratti and Stulz, *supra* note 53 (noting that banks located in share holder friendly regimes may have been encouraged to take on excessive risks before the financial crisis and therefore suffered greater losses when the crisis occurred).

3 CRITIQUES

A weakness of some earlier papers in the literature is their use of cross-sectional analysis (i.e., analysis using data from only a certain point in time), which is poorly suited to deciphering causality. Such data limitations in the time dimension cannot guard against causation running in the opposite direction. Many authors, including some of those cited above, have utilized longitudinal data (i.e., analysis using data across time) to address this issue.[69]

Armour et al. expanded the time dimension to overcome the obstacles presented by attempting to uncover causation. They pooled together time series from multiple countries during 1995–2005 to see whether common law or civil law countries had better shareholder protection, which was one of the main findings by LLSV.[70] Using this panel data approach, the authors found that common law countries did have better shareholder protection but that civil law countries were catching up to common law countries during the period studied. Importantly, they also found no positive relationship between changes in shareholder protection and stock market development, contrary to the proposition that better shareholder protection causes more rapid financial development.[71]

A second potential problem of many earlier papers in this line of research is their reliance on cross-country analysis (i.e., using data where the unit of observation is a country). It is understandable why authors would take such an approach since certain questions are specifically about the adoption of regulations across countries. However, this approach is often too coarse to establish causation because there are numerous confounding factors within each country that could affect the relationship of interest. Controlling for those factors can help to clarify the analysis but oftentimes does not completely resolve the issue.

Cheffins and co-authors revisited the law and finance relationship by focusing on the United States from 1930 to 1970.[72] As a first step, the authors presented various measures of stock market performance (e.g., SEC data on the value of publicly traded stocks, normalized by GDP) to show that they were more or less flat from the early 1930s through the early 1950s.

---

[69] In addition to causation, there are concerns in this literature related to data quality. In an influential 2010 paper, Spamann revisited a key legal indicator developed in the 1998 law and finance paper by La Porta et al. See Holger Spamann, "The 'Antidirector Rights Index' Revisited", 23 Rev. Fin. Stud. 467 (2010). The question posed by the author is straightforward: How accurate is the original antidirector rights index (ADRI)? Teaming up with local lawyers from 46 out of the 49 countries documented in the original La Porta et al. project and using primary sources instead of secondary ones, Spamann discovered that 33 of the 46 countries required revisions. In some cases, the extent of the revision was significant. The correlation between the 46 revised ADRI values and those of the original 46 was only 0.53. Not surprisingly, the revised ADRI values no longer support a couple of the well-known La Porta et al. findings: (1) shareholder protection is higher in common law than in civil law countries and (2) greater shareholder protection is associated with larger stock market size and lower ownership dispersion.

[70] John Armour, Simon Deakin, Prabirjit Sarkar, Mathias Siems, & Ajit Singh, "Shareholder Protection and Stock Market Development: An Empirical Test of the Legal Origins Hypothesis", 6 J. Emp. Legal Stud. 343 (2009).

[71] Id. at 371.

[72] Brian R. Cheffins, Steven A. Bank, & Harwell Wells, "Questioning 'Law and Finance': US Stock Market Development, 1930–1970", 55 Bus. Hist. 601 (2013).

Subsequently, the authors created a time series version of the anti-director index for the United States and demonstrated that the index was practically the same during the doldrums (1930s–1950s) as it was in the boom times, and thus inferring that this lack of correlation did not bode well for the law and finance argument with respect to anti-director rights.[73] The authors also considered the development of federal securities law, which is not captured by the anti-director index, but saw no convincing connection there either. Although no sophisticated statistical methods are used in the paper, it still shows that expanding the time horizon of the analysis (from a slice of time to decades) and internalizing country-specific details can potentially yield mixed results.

Articles such as the ones by Cheffins et al. and Armour et al. highlight issues with the causal element of law and finance analysis. We should note that the vast majority, if not all, of those articles discussed above do not claim to establish a causal mechanism. Moreover, some of the papers cited above actually take care to address both concerns. However, it is still the case that strong correlations can be misinterpreted by researchers and policy makers. In the next subsection, we focus on a growing body of enforcement related research that is well poised to disentangle causation by exploiting the wealth of data on the budget and enforcement actions of the US Securities and Exchange Commission. The reader will notice that, by taking a more rigorous approach to tackling the relationship between enforcement and market outcomes, researchers have sacrificed breadth. They are no longer able to address the grand questions on law and finance across national jurisdictional boundaries.

3.1 Resources Allocated to Enforcement

We start with a discussion of indirect, resource-based evidence on the efficacy of SEC enforcement actions. Lohse, Pascalau, and Thomann assembled a data set of SEC funding and enforcement between 1946 and 2010 in order to investigate whether increases in SEC resources improved compliance with securities market rules.[74] Following the resource-based approach taken by JR, the authors used SEC budgets as a proxy for public enforcement. The authors summarized their findings as follows:

> In a theoretical model, we characterize a corporation's compliance decision with the securities laws under the SEC's supervision. The model predicts, first, that increases in the regulator's resources deter firms from misbehaving (compliance hypothesis). Second, the model predicts that an increase in the SEC's budget leads to a (temporary) decrease of observed compliance. Given that the SEC may even police past misbehavior, this decrease reflects the delayed adjustment of corporations' compliance behavior (adjustment hypothesis). We test these hypotheses by using data on the SEC's funding and the reported cases of current noncompliance (injunctions). We find supportive evidence for our theory: Our empirical results show that the increases in the SEC's budget lead to a higher compliance by financial market participants. First, using Granger-causality tests we establish that there is a significant link between the SEC's resources and corporations' contemporaneous misbehavior. Second, we show that an

---

[73] Id. at 607–11.

[74] Tim Lohse, Razvan Pascalau, & Christian Thomann, "Public Enforcement of Securities Market Rules: Resource-based evidence from the Securities Exchange Commission", 106 J. Econ. Behav. & Org. 197 (2014).

increase in the SEC's budget leads to a (temporary) decrease of observed compliance. This is reflected in a temporary increase in the number of injunctions that the SEC brings against the securities industry. Third, the longer-term effect of an increase in the SEC's resources is a decrease in (reported) ongoing misbehavior. The results from the VAR analysis suggest that a positive budget shock leads to an aggregate decrease in the number of ongoing misbehavior, reflected by a decrease in the number of injunctions by 10% within five years and by 18% within ten years, respectively. This is clear evidence for higher firm compliance.[75]

Though limited to the United States, the analysis offers perhaps the most compelling evidence to date of the causal relationship between public enforcement and capital market behavior. In addition, the study documents the impact of real resources on an intermediate outcome: firm compliance. As the authors explained:

> In practice, before enforcement can lead to better financial markets, i.e., markets where investors demand a relatively low return on their capital as they do not have to be afraid of being defrauded, it must initially influence firms' decisions to comply with securities market rules. By analyzing the incentives for firms' disclosure provided by the SEC's enforcement, our study closes this gap. It is those changes in compliance that—over time—can lead to improved financial markets.[76]

Thus, the paper presents additional evidence of a channel through which real resources could lead to more robust capital markets.

A similar type of study was undertaken by Blackburne, who focused on the link between industry-level political activity and the SEC's regional budgetary allocation, and on the link between regulatory intensity (proxied by the budgetary allocation) and managers' reporting incentives.[77] The data used in the exercise were quite extensive. The author received proprietary SEC data on staffing and salary levels in each of the 12 disclosure review offices of the Division of Corporation Finance and the annual budgetary resources for the Division as a whole for fiscal years 2003 to 2012. The author then collected data for over 4,000 firms over the period 2003–2011 and matched each firm to the SEC office that reviews its disclosure filings. Notably, Blackburne first discovered that a 1% increase in industry-level political contributions was associated with a 0.12 to 0.31% decrease in the following year's SEC office-level budget allocation.[78] Since the SEC's budget is known to managers in advance (because it's allocated by Congress for an upcoming fiscal year), the author also tested whether the resource allocation caused managers' reporting behaviors to change. Again, the author used resource allocation as a proxy for enforcement intensity, finding that when SEC oversight was stronger, company managers reported lower discretionary accruals and were less likely to issue financial reports that were subsequently restated. On top of that, a 1% increase in the resource proxy resulted in a 0.3% decrease in firms' bid-ask spreads, which is a sizable market consequence. The results of this paper tell a story similar to that of Lohse et al., namely, that

---

[75] Id. at 6.   [76] Id. at 3.

[77] Terrence Blackburne, Regulatory Oversight and Reporting Incentives: Evidence from SEC Budget Allocations, (Jan. 2014), available at http://public-prod-acquia.gsb.stanford.edu/sites/default/files/documents/ACCT_TerrenceBlackburne_JTP.pdf.

[78] Cf. Tim Lohse & Christian Thomann, "Are Bad Times Good News for the Securities and Exchange Commission?", 40 Eur. J. L. & Econ. 33 (2015) (using over 60 years of time series data, the authors showed that the SEC's funding increased when the stock market was weak and decreased when the market was strong).

SEC enforcement as measured by real resources allocated to the institution can have real and sizable effects on capital markets.

3.2 Direct Enforcement Actions

Recent research has also tried to quantify the market effect of direct regulatory actions undertaken by the SEC. Using a before-and-after event study approach, Bengtsson and co-authors looked at the market reaction after the SEC enforcement actions on the structure of the PIPEs markets in 2002.[79] Using PIPE transactions data from 1999 to 2006, the authors demonstrated the existence of significant changes in the structure of PIPE transactions after the SEC's 2002 enforcement. Specifically, PIPE transactions after the SEC action were less likely to include the contractual element that the SEC was targeting.[80] While the authors reserved judgment on whether the effects served to enhance shareholder value, their work offers further empirical validation of the impact of supervisory actions on market behavior.[81]

Besides intervening in specific market activities, the SEC has a more routine task of reviewing company filings and sending comment letters should those filings be deemed lacking in any way. Johnston and Petacchi analyzed the effect of these comment letters on the abnormal returns and trading volume corresponding to a recipient firm around subsequent earnings report.[82] To conduct this experiment, the authors collected all the SEC comment letters regarding annual (10K) and quarterly (10Q) filings for the period 2004–2006. The sample consisted of over 6,000 letters from 2,374 cases for 2,256 firms and most of the letters' contents were about accounting, financial reporting, and disclosure issues. By looking at a letter recipient firm's subsequent eight earnings announcements, and comparing them to the previous eight earnings announcements, the authors found that absolute abnormal returns and trading volume around those earning announcements declined and that analyst forecast accuracy improved.[83] These results led the authors to conclude that the SEC's supervisory action (in the form of comment letters) had positive informational effects on the market.

The articles cited above all employ data and techniques better suited to establishing a causal link between enforcement and market outcomes than analyzing cross-sectional data or country-level data, and the results are striking. They show that the SEC's enforcement actions caused a real market effect, which strongly suggests that public enforcement intensity matters in the United States. If the data exist for other countries, it would be important to know whether this is a general empirical phenomenon or if there is something unique about the regulatory environment in the United States.

---

[79] See Ola Bengtsson, Na Dai, & Clifford Chad Henson, "SEC Enforcement in the PIPE Market: Actions and Consequences", 42 J. Banking & Fin. 213 (2014).

[80] Id. at 227.

[81] See also Dhammika Dharmapala & Vikramaditya S. Khanna, "Corporate Governance, Enforcement, and Firm Value: Evidence from India", 29 J. L. Econ. & Org. 1056 (2013) (finding increased levels of sanctioning to be associated with higher firm value in Indian companies).

[82] See Rick Johnston & Reining Petacchi, Regulatory Oversight of Financial Reporting: Securities and Exchange Commission Comment Letters (June 4, 2014), available at http://papers.ssrn.com/abstract=1291345.

[83] Id. at 32.

4 CONCLUSION

Building upon the work of LLS and JR, researchers have tested various hypotheses related to the link between enforcement intensity and capital markets. The work in this field has done much to support the theory that higher enforcement intensity can have positive effects on capital market outcomes. For instance, private and public enforcement are significantly associated with essential elements of capital markets like the private cost of capital and the accuracy of information. In addition, studies show that greater public enforcement intensity is significantly associated with market variables of interest in countries that dedicate more resources to regulatory reform.

Recent work using higher-quality data and more sophisticated statistical methods has also been carried out to establish that causality runs from enforcement to market outcomes and not in the opposite direction, especially with respect to public enforcement. Several articles focusing on the enforcement actions of the SEC show that the agency's actions have caused real market effects, which strongly suggests that public enforcement matters in the United States. Although much work remains—and the global financial crisis suggests ways in which future work might be refined—the intervening body of work confirms that greater levels of private and public enforcement are associated with key measures of robust capital markets.

Another lesson of the large and growing body of subsequent work is the appetite that the academic community has for data on enforcement beyond legal rules. The global financial crisis has demonstrated the necessity of maintaining effective supervision of financial markets and financial institutions. With more data on key variables of enforcement, researchers can tackle a myriad of questions and, just as importantly, provide more convincing answers.

CHAPTER 35

....

PUBLIC ENFORCEMENT
Criminal versus Civil

....

AMANDA M. ROSE

1 INTRODUCTION

PRIOR chapters have explored the distinction between private and public enforcement of corporate laws and standards. Whereas private enforcement mechanisms are necessarily civil, public enforcement may be civil or criminal in nature. What theories animate the choice between civil and criminal enforcement? How well do these theories explain the public enforcement choices we see in practice in the United States, the United Kingdom, and continental Europe? It is to these questions that this chapter turns.

2 THE CIVIL–CRIMINAL DIVIDE: THEORETICAL FOUNDATIONS

If asked what distinguishes criminal and civil cases, a lay person would likely recite the traditional markers: criminal cases require a showing of *mens rea* or "guilty mind," whereas negligence or strict liability may prevail in a civil case; criminal prosecutions seek to punish defendants for violations of community norms, through fines or imprisonment, whereas civil cases seek to compensate victims through money damages; criminal defendants enjoy heightened procedural protections relative to their civil counterparts; and so on. These traditional markers fail, however, to provide a coherent theoretical account of the civil–criminal divide. Moreover, they are increasingly inaccurate even as a descriptive matter. Consider the United States. Public civil enforcement has taken on a variety of traditionally "criminal" characteristics. Civil public enforcers like the Securities & Exchange Commission (SEC) do not limit themselves to seeking compensatory relief on behalf of victims, for example. Rather, their goal is often expressly to punish defendants through the imposition of severe fines.[1] Criminal prosecutions have also become more characteristically "civil," most notably through a loosening of the *mens rea* requirement. This is evident not only in criminal prosecutions of regulatory offenses, but also in the imposition of vicarious criminal liability on corporations.[2] In order to evaluate the wisdom of these changes, as well as to appreciate the significance of cross-border differences in public enforcement patterns, a normative theory of the civil–criminal divide is necessary. This part provides an overview of the competing alternatives.

The oldest normative theory of the civil–criminal divide is rooted in deontological ethics. It posits that the criminal label should be reserved for misconduct that is morally blameworthy. This view, shared by Blackstone, traces its roots to ancient Greek philosophers as well as natural law proponents like St. Thomas Aquinas.[3] Modern supporters include Henry Hart, who wrote in his seminal 1958 article "The Aims of the Criminal Law":

> [A crime] is not simply anything which a legislature chooses to call a "crime." It is not simply antisocial conduct which public officers are given a responsibility to suppress. It is not simply any conduct to which a legislature chooses to attach a "criminal" penalty. It is conduct which, if duly shown to have taken place, will incur a formal and solemn pronouncement of the moral condemnation of the community.[4]

Hart viewed the criminal label, when appropriately limited to morally repugnant conduct, as an important part of a free society's effort to develop a shared sense of conscience. Not surprisingly, he objected to the imposition of criminal sanctions for strict liability or negligence-based offenses, noting the "shocking damage that is done to social morale by open and official admission that crime can be respectable and criminality a matter of ill chance, rather than blameworthy choice."[5] Jerome Hall similarly believed that criminal punishment is just only when imposed on "those who have knowingly committed moral wrongs."[6]

A utilitarian challenge to this view of the civil–criminal divide was mounted by Jeremy Bentham and Cesare Beccaria in the eighteenth century,[7] and again by Oliver Wendell Holmes in the nineteenth,[8] but did not gain traction until Gary Becker's 1968 article "Crime and Punishment: An Economic Approach."[9] Becker argued that the civil and criminal law

---

[1] See generally Kenneth Mann, "Punitive Civil Sanctions: The Middleground Between Criminal and Civil Law", 101 Yale L. J. 1795 (1992) (discussing the increased use of punitive civil sanctions); Miriam H. Baer, "Choosing Punishment", 92 B.U. L. Rev. 577, 621–24 (2012).

[2] For a discussion of these trends, see Sanford Kadish, "Some Observations on the Use of Criminal Sanctions in Enforcing Economic Regulations", 30 U. Chi. L. Rev. 423 (1963), and John C. Coffee, "Does 'Unlawful' Mean 'Criminal'? Reflections on the Disappearing Tort/Crime Distinction in American Law", 71 B. U. L. Rev. 193 (1991).

[3] Jerome Hall, "Interrelations of Criminal Law and Torts: I", 43 Colum. L. Rev. 753, 756 (1943).

[4] Henry M. Hart, "The Aims of the Criminal Law", 23 L. & Contemp. Probs. 401, 405 (1958).

[5] Id. at 423.

[6] Hall, *supra* note 3, at 776; see also Richard A. Epstein, Crime and Tort: Old Wine in Old Bottles, in Assessing the Criminal: Restitution, Retribution and the Legal Process 231, 248 (R. Barnett & J. Hagel eds., 1977) (agreeing with Hart and Hall that "the criminal law works best when it deals with conduct of the defendant that the law thinks worthy of moral condemnation").

[7] Cesare Beccaria, An Essay on Crimes and Punishments (1764); Jeremy Bentham, An Introduction to the Principles of Morals and Legislation (1789).

[8] Oliver Wendell Holmes, The Common Law 39–76 (1881).

[9] Gary S. Becker, "Crime and Punishment: An Economic Approach", 76 J. Pol. Econ. 169 (1968).

should be viewed as serving the same goal: social welfare maximization. This goal is advanced when threatened legal sanctions—whether civil or criminal—cause individuals to internalize the costs their activities impose on third parties. In Becker's view, the criminal label derives its importance not because it targets "immoral" conduct, as Hart believed, but rather by virtue of the sanction it uniquely makes available: imprisonment. Imprisonment is more socially costly than monetary sanctions, but is better able to deter judgment-proof individuals. Becker therefore argued that conduct should be pursued criminally only if a defendant lacks sufficient assets to satisfy an optimal monetary sanction, warranting imprisonment; otherwise, civil remedies are preferred.[10]

Becker's article spawned tremendous interest in the economic analysis of criminal law.[11] It also attracted its share of critics.[12] For example, many objected to the notion that only judgment-proof defendants should face imprisonment as unfairly privileging the rich.[13] Others attacked the assumption that potential criminals behave as rational economic actors, weighing their anticipated gain from engaging in criminal conduct against the threatened criminal sanction.[14] Still others took offense at the idea that sanctions should invite such weighing in the first place. In Becker's framework, sanctions should cause a potential defendant to internalize the harm his actions will impose on society; if the benefit of a crime to the perpetrator exceeds this expected sanction, the socially efficient result is for the perpetrator to commit it. But such a notion is at odds with the traditional deontological account of the criminal law, as well as with common sense. Criminal sanctions should be designed to deter unconditionally, it is generally thought, not to price criminal behavior in the Pigouvian sense.

Subsequent writers in the law and economics tradition have attempted to deal with the last critique.[15] For example, in an influential article Steven Shavell assumed that the social benefits from crime are zero, regardless of the private benefits perpetrators

---

[10] Id. at 198 (explaining that, under his approach, "[m]uch of traditional criminal law would become a branch of the law of torts, say 'social torts,' in which the public would collectively sue for 'public' harm," and that a criminal action "would be defined fundamentally not by the nature of the action, but by the inability of a person to compensate for the 'harm' that he caused").

[11] For an excellent, though dated, overview of this literature, see Alvin K. Klevorick, On the Economic Theory of Crime, in NOMOS XXVII: Criminal Justice 290–97 (J. Pennock & J. Chapman eds., 1985). For updated references, see Murat C. Mungan, "The Law and Economics of Fluctuating Criminal Tendencies and Incapacitation", 72 Md. L. Rev. 156, 159 n.2 (2012).

[12] For a survey of the main critiques, see id. at 169–75.

[13] Becker anticipated this critique, explaining that "[w]hether a punishment like imprisonment in lieu of a full fine for offenders lacking sufficient resources is 'fair' depends, of course, on the length of the prison term compared to the fine." Becker, *supra* note 9, at 197. He observed that people "are often imprisoned at rates of exchange with fines that place a low value on time in prison," which "may explain why imprisonment in lieu of fines is considered unfair to poor offenders, who often must 'chose' the prison alternative." Id. at 197–98.

[14] Becker did observe that the sensitivity of criminal behavior to changes in expected sanctions may vary by type of crime, with crimes of passion being less responsive than calculated economic crimes. Id. at 205. See also Richard A. Posner, Economic Analysis of Law 279 & n.2 (8th ed. 2011) (defending the notion of the criminal as a rational actor).

[15] See Kenneth G. Dau-Schmidt, "An Economic Analysis of the Criminal Law as a Preference Shaping Policy", 1990 Duke L. J. 1, 12 & n.55 (1990) (noting that "[e]ven among economists, there is a growing consensus that criminal benefits should carry no weight in the social welfare function" and citing references).

derive.[16] "Allowing for a divergence between social and private benefits gives the analyst greater freedom to describe society's values," Shavell explained.[17] This approach calls for setting expected criminal sanctions so that they exceed the private gain the perpetrator would obtain from committing the crime, resulting in unconditional deterrence.[18] Richard Posner has similarly observed that criminal sanctions "are not really prices designed to ration the activity," as Becker's model suggests; rather their "purpose so far as possible is to extirpate it."[19] While this approach may comport better with our sensibilities than Becker's, it fails to provide a normative justification for the civil–criminal divide. When exactly should conduct be deterred unconditionally, thus warranting a criminal sanction, and when should it merely be priced? Are answers available that do not fall back on concepts of morality?

Guido Calabresi and Douglas Melamed provide one in their famous article "Property Rules, Liability Rules, and Inalienability: One View of the Cathedral."[20] According to Calabresi and Melamed, the first issue which must be faced by any legal system is the allocation of entitlements—for example, "the entitlement to make noise versus the entitlement to have silence, the entitlement to pollute versus the entitlement to breathe clean air, the entitlement to have children versus the entitlement to forbid them."[21] The second issue a legal system must confront is how to protect the entitlements it has decided to grant, whether by property, liability, or inalienability rules. Property rules require "someone who wishes to remove the entitlement from its holder [to] buy it from him in a voluntary transaction."[22] A liability rule, by contrast, allows someone to destroy the initial entitlement so long as they are willing to pay an objectively determined value for it, and inalienability rules forbid the transfer of the entitlement entirely, even if the holder consents.[23] Property rules are an appropriate way to protect entitlements when the transaction costs associated with voluntary negotiation are low, Calabresi and Melamed explained; liability rules, by contrast, are to be preferred when high transaction costs make a collective determination of value preferable, and inalienability rules when society wishes to bar transfer of the entitlement altogether.[24] Within this framework, Calabresi and Melamed view criminal punishment (which they understand as seeking to deter unconditionally) as a mechanism for preventing people from essentially converting property and inalienability rules into liability rules through fiat.[25]

---

[16] Steven Shavell, "Criminal Law and the Optimal Use of Nonmonetary Sanctions as a Deterrent", 85 Colum. L. Rev. 1232 (1985).

[17] Id. at 1234.

[18] This does not imply that the optimal level of crime will be zero, however, because society must expend resources on enforcement—something it should do up until the point the marginal cost of enforcement exceeds the marginal savings in social costs achieved thereby.

[19] Richard A. Posner, "An Economic Theory of the Criminal Law", 85 Colum. L. Rev. 1193, 1215 (1985). The distinction between the criminal sanctions Becker envisioned and those envisioned by Shavell and Posner bears a strong resemblance to the distinction Robert Cooter has drawn between "prices" and "sanctions," though Cooter did not view sanctions as within the exclusive domain of the criminal law. See Robert Cooter, "Prices and Sanctions", 84 Colum. L. Rev. 1523 (1984).

[20] 85 Harv. L. Rev. 1089 (1972).   [21] Id. at 1090.   [22] Id. at 1092.   [23] Id.

[24] Id. at 1105–15.

[25] See id. at 1126 & n. 70. Cooter expresses his normative theory for choosing between prices and sanctions somewhat differently than Calabresi and Melamed. Cooter argues that sanctions should be used when it is easier for lawmakers to identify socially optimal behavior than it is to determine the external costs created by that behavior, and that prices should be used when the opposite is true. Because "the information requirements for pricing crimes are prohibitive, while the information requirements

Like the deontological account discussed at the outset, Calabresi and Melamed's approach assumes that the criminal category includes only intentional misconduct. They explain that the thief or rapist must be treated differently from the negligent driver:

> The only level at which, before the accident, the driver can negotiate for the value of what he might take from his potential victim is one at which transactions are too costly. The thief or rapist, on the other hand, could have negotiated without undue expense (at least if the good was one which we allowed to be sold at all) because we assume he knew what he was going to do and to whom he would do it.[26]

Richard Posner, who has similarly argued that the "major function of criminal law in a capitalist society is to prevent people from bypassing the system of voluntary, compensated exchange,"[27] offers an additional reason for limiting the criminal law to intentional misconduct: a requirement of intent limits the unique over-deterrence potential of criminal sanctions.[28] Without an intent requirement, which allows one to avoid criminal liability with some degree of confidence, the severity of criminal sanctions might chill socially productive activities.[29] The same over-deterrence concern dictates clarity in the scope of the criminal prohibition.[30]

Expanding on Posner's work, Keith Hylton has addressed in more detail "when penalties should be set to internalize social harms and when they should be set to completely deter offensive conduct."[31] According to his model, sanctions designed to deter unconditionally (i.e., criminal sanctions) are appropriate in two situations: (1) when the offender's gain is never greater than the victim's loss (as one might presume is the case with respect to violent crimes) and (2) when the conduct is market-bypassing. If the transaction costs associated with bargaining over the entitlement are low, Hylton explains, "then the optimal punishment policy is to set the penalty at the full deterrence or gain-eliminating level" so as to "force potential offenders to use the market."[32] By contrast, if transaction costs are high, and the offender's gain may exceed the victim's loss, "then the optimal policy is to set the penalty at a level that internalizes society's losses."[33] Hylton proceeds to explain how the doctrine of criminal

---

for sanctioning crimes are relatively low," he posits that crimes should be sanctioned rather than priced. Cooter, *supra* note 19, at 1550.

[26] Calabresi & Melamed, *supra* note 20, at 1127.

[27] Posner, *supra* note 19, at 1195. Posner's analysis differs from Calabresi and Melamed's by focusing exclusively on efficiency considerations; Calabresi and Melamed, by contrast, recognize that distributional considerations may inform a society's choice between property and liability rules. See Calabresi & Melamed, *supra* note 20, at 1110.

[28] Posner, *supra* note 19, at 1221–22.

[29] Id. Of course, to the extent there is legal error the intent requirement does not wholly guard against the risk of over-deterrence. See Shavell, *supra* note 16, at 1243–46 (discussing, inter alia, the risk of over-deterrence as a reason why criminal sanctions should not be made arbitrarily high).

[30] See Coffee, *supra* note 2, at 208 (discussing the need for the criminal law to speak with greater precision than tort law due to the exemplary penalties it threatens); see also Cooter, *supra* note 19, at 1532 (explaining that "lawmakers who create an obligation backed by a sanction must be certain that the partition between permitted and forbidden zones is in the right place").

[31] Keith N. Hylton, "The Theory of Penalties and the Economics of Criminal Law", 2 Rev. L. & Econ. 175 (2005), at 176.

[32] Id. at 181–82.   [33] Id. at 181.

intent "serves a channeling function that permits us to distinguish the different sorts of conduct" in order to allocate civil and criminal penalties appropriately.[34]

The theories advanced by Posner and Calabresi and Melamed have, like the Beckerian model, been subject to critique. Alvin Klevorick, for example, has faulted them for being too restrictive.[35] To illustrate, he points out that buying votes may be deemed a crime even though it is not market-bypassing (to use Posner's lexicon) and even though it represents the conversion of an inalienability rule into a property rule rather than a liability rule (to use Calabresi and Melamed's).[36] He offers a similar but more generalized formulation of the civil–criminal divide: "An act is a crime because the actor behaves in a way that is contrary to [] the transaction structure that society has established."[37] This structure, he explains, "sets out the terms or conditions under which particular transactions or exchanges are to take place under different circumstances."[38] He emphasizes that the criminal category therefore ultimately depends on the transaction structure a society has chosen to adopt—something that is informed by moral and political considerations that disciplines other than economics are best suited to explore.[39]

All of the economic accounts of the civil–criminal divide discussed thus far treat individual preferences as exogenous to the criminal law. In "An Economic Analysis of the Criminal Law as a Preference-Shaping Policy," Kenneth Dau-Schmidt questions this assumption.[40] He suggests that the criminal law, in addition to shaping opportunities, should be viewed as a mechanism for shaping preferences. In other words, in addition to making crime unprofitable through the imposition of sanctions, Dau-Schmidt posits that the criminal law also has the capacity to make crime less desirable by shaping attitudes. He argues that the criminal label should apply to conduct only when the social benefits of changing individual preferences through the criminal law outweigh the social costs. This condition is most likely to be met, he explains, with respect to preferences "whose realization is assigned no value in the social welfare function and which interfere with preferences whose realization is highly valued in the social welfare function."[41] Dau-Schmidt fails to explain how a society should pick which preferences to ignore or exalt in the social welfare function, however, referring such questions to philosophers, theologians, and other non-economists.[42] Dau-Schmidt's analysis thus essentially recasts in economic terms the deontological theory of the civil–criminal divide discussed at the outset. As he himself explains, "[u]nder the preference-shaping theory, criminal punishment is not merely the price of crime, but is also an expression of society's condemnation of the criminal act and an effort to discourage preferences for such activity."[43] Social preferences, he writes, "can be understood as the economic description of morality."[44]

---

[34] Id. at 184.

[35] See Klevorick, *supra* note 11; Alvin K. Klevorick, "Legal Theory and the Economic Analysis of Torts and Crimes", 85 Colum. L. Rev. 905 (1985).

[36] Id. at 907.   [37] Id. at 907–08.   [38] Id. at 908.

[39] Klevorick, *supra* note 11, at 909. For a critique of Klevorick's theory, see George P. Fletcher, "A Transaction Theory of Crime?", 85 Colum. L. Rev. 921 (1985).

[40] See Dau-Schmidt, *supra* note 15.

[41] Id. at 21. Changing such preferences, he explains, would yield the greatest net social benefit "because society highly values the realization of the preferences that are saved from frustration, and there is no countervailing social cost from the loss of the realization of the preferences that are changed." Id.

[42] Id. at 37.   [43] Id.   [44] Id. at 19.

Like the deontological theory, Dau-Schmidt's preference-shaping account implies that the criminal category should be limited to intentional conduct: "If the person does not intend the proscribed harm but rather causes it out of negligence or mistake, the person's acts do not indicate deviant preferences" that require shaping.[45]

3 THEORETICAL IMPLICATIONS FOR CORPORATE LAW

From these diverse theories of the civil–criminal divide flow some common implications regarding the public enforcement of corporate laws and standards. It is worthwhile to briefly survey these implications before turning, in the next part, to review actual public enforcement patterns in the United States and abroad.

With the possible exception of Becker's pricing model of the criminal law, which I will not consider further, each of the approaches discussed above would support imposing criminal sanctions on corporate managers who intentionally defraud or steal from shareholders.[46] The same can be said for intentional derelictions of duty—"bad faith" conduct, in the language of the Delaware courts. This sort of behavior is widely perceived as morally blameworthy or, if you would rather, as reflecting deviant preferences. Moreover, it is an affront to a capitalist society's "transaction structure": shareholders are entitled to the residual value of their firms; if managers want to appropriate part of that value for themselves, or intentionally put it at risk through their recklessness, they are required to bargain for the right[47]— something a pricing system of civil liability would not encourage them to do.

Conversely, none of the theories would support imposing criminal sanctions on corporate managers who merely breach their duty of care, as none consider negligence an appropriate basis for criminal sanctions. If it were difficult to distinguish fraud or bad faith from mere negligent management or bad luck (in other words, if legal error were a significant

---

[45] Id. at 26–27. John Coffee, who has similarly argued that the "factor that most distinguishes the criminal law is its operation as a system of moral education and socialization," agrees that "the existence or non-existence of criminal intent. . . furnishes the most practical breakpoint at which to shift from pricing to prohibiting." Coffee, *supra* note 2, at 239. He warns that expanding the criminal law to cover strict liability and negligence-based offenses risks diluting the power of the criminal law, pointing out that "stigma is a scarce resource." Id. at 238. See also Paul H. Robinson, "The Criminal-Civil Distinction and the Utility of Desert", 76 B. U. L. Rev. 201 (1996) (warning that applying the criminal label to conduct that is not morally blameworthy will weaken the power of the criminal law).

[46] Recall that Becker argued that criminal sanctions, which he equated with imprisonment, are warranted only when asset insufficiency undermines the effect of civil monetary sanctions. Although corporate managers tend to be affluent, they may expect to be "judgment proof" in precisely the situations in which they are likely to defraud shareholders. See Jennifer H. Arlen & William J. Carney, "Vicarious Liability for Fraud on Securities Markets: Theory and Evidence", U. Ill. L. Rev. 691 (1992) (explaining why corporate officers may be under-deterred by monetary sanctions in "last period" situations, when telling the truth will cost them their job and most of their wealth). Thus, criminal sanctions for securities fraud may be warranted even under Becker's approach. Because Becker's model has fallen into disfavor (see *supra* note 15), I will not consider it in subsequent analysis.

[47] Failure to do so represents the conversion of a property rule into a liability rule and is market-bypassing.

risk), these theories would also uniformly urge caution in imposing criminal sanctions: imposing criminal sanctions on undeserving defendants would both be unjust and could lead to significant over-deterrence.

Each of these approaches also casts doubt on the use of vicarious corporate criminal liability—the imposition of criminal sanctions on a corporation (and, ultimately, its shareholders) for the crimes of its employees undertaken in the scope of their employment. Those who take a deontological view of the civil–criminal divide have traditionally rejected vicarious corporate criminal liability on the ground that it is divorced from personal guilt and moral agency.[48] Vicarious corporate liability has also been attacked as inefficient in the criminal context.[49] This is because the economic justification for vicarious liability presumes the underlying offense is "priced," rather than criminally sanctioned. When this is in fact the case, vicarious liability can have the laudable effect of incentivizing shareholders to prod their firms to invest socially optimal amounts of corporate resources in deterrence efforts.[50] When the conduct is sanctioned, by contrast, vicarious liability threatens to over-deter by causing shareholders to internalize more than the social harm employees cause.[51] Framed differently, the failure of shareholders to prevent employee misconduct is not itself an affront to society's "transaction structure" warranting criminal sanctions—at least absent evidence of shareholder complicity in, or willful blindness to, the employee misconduct (which would support direct, fault-based liability).

To be sure, attempts have been made to defend corporate-level criminal sanctions, on both moral and instrumental grounds. For example, theories of organizational guilt have been advanced to justify the practice.[52] It has also been argued that corporate-level criminal sanctions may serve a valuable "preference-shaping" or "expressive" function.[53] I cannot do

---

[48] See, e.g., Michael S. Moore, The Moral and Metaphysical Sources of the Criminal Law, in NOMOS XXVII: Criminal Justice 12–13 (J. Pennock & J. Chapman eds., 1985); Albert Alschuler, 71 B. U. L. Rev. 307 (1991).

[49] See, e.g., Daniel R. Fischel & Alan O. Sykes, "Corporate Crime", 25 J. Leg. Stud. 319 (1996) (making the case that the civil liability system is better suited to calculate appropriate fines for organizational defendants than the criminal system); Vikramaditya S. Khanna, "Corporate Criminal Liability: What Purpose Does It Serve?", 109 Harv. L. Rev. 1477 (1996) (arguing that, except in the rarest of circumstances, corporate civil liability is more socially desirable than criminal liability); see also Posner, supra note 14, at 578 (questioning whether criminal as opposed to civil corporate liability makes sense).

[50] For a summary of the traditional deterrence argument for vicarious employer liability, as well as its limitations, see Amanda M. Rose & Richard Squire, "Intraportfolio Litigation", 105 Nw. U. L. Rev. 1679, 1683–85 (2011).

[51] See Fischel & Sykes, supra note 49, at 324 (explaining that "the corporation should bear no more than the social cost of harm caused by crime, adjusted for the chance of nondetection," otherwise shareholders will expend socially excessive amounts on monitoring); see also Coffee, supra note 2, at 196 ("to the extent that the role of corporate criminal liability is to encourage the principal to monitor its agents, the criminal law is inevitably caught up in the problem of pricing").

[52] See, e.g., Lawrence Friedman, "In Defense of Corporate Criminal Liability", 23 Harv. J. L. & Pub. Pol'y 833 (2000); William S. Laufer, "Corporate Bodies and Guilty Minds", 43 Emory L.J. 647, 665–68 (1994); William S. Laufer & Alan Strudler, "Corporate Intentionality, Desert, and Variants of Vicarious Liability", 37 Am. Crim. L. Rev. 1285 (2000); Pamela H. Bucy, "Corporate Ethos: A Standard for Imposing Corporate Criminal Liability", 75 Minn. L. Rev. 1095 (1991).

[53] See, e.g., Dan M. Kahan, "Social Meaning and the Economic Analysis", 27 J. Leg. Stud. 610 (1998); Samuel W. Buell, "The Blaming Function of Entity Criminal Liability", 81 Ind. L. J. 473 (2006); Gregory M. Gilchrist, "The Expressive Cost of Corporate Immunity", 64 Hastings L. J. 1 (2012).

these arguments justice in the space afforded here,[54] but will simply note that they rarely go so far as to support true vicarious liability; rather, most require as a predicate to corporate liability a showing of fault that is either pervasive throughout the organization or traceable to the top management level.[55]

Vicarious corporate liability, whether imposed criminally or civilly, suffers from a more fundamental weakness when it comes to the public enforcement of laws that are meant, first and foremost, to protect shareholders from managerial opportunism. Imposing liability for misconduct on the victims of that misconduct is rarely just or efficient, and that is precisely what occurs when vicarious corporate liability is imposed for managerial violations of corporate laws and standards.[56]

The theories of the civil–criminal divide discussed in the last part also help illuminate the private–public divide discussed earlier in this book. If a polity took a pure approach to the civil–criminal divide, limiting civil enforcement to "pricing" with the task of "sanctioning" reserved for criminal enforcers, it would follow that public civil enforcement should properly be viewed as filling private enforcement gaps. After all, if shareholder suits were brought every time corporate managers breached their duties, and resulted in the offending managers paying damage awards that fully compensated for all the harm inflicted, there would be no pricing work left for public enforcers to do. Thus, an inquiry into the ways in which private enforcement fails would help elucidate the desired contours of public civil enforcement.[57]

Of course, the label a polity has chosen to assign a public enforcer may not correlate with the nature of the sanctions they actually impose. Lines can be blurred, with "civil" enforcers sometimes seeking "criminal" sanctions (in the sense of sanctions designed to deter unconditionally) and "criminal" enforcers sometimes seeking "civil" sanctions (in the sense of sanctions designed merely to price). The theories discussed above suggest this may be undesirable. Such blurring may make it more difficult for the populace to absorb messages about

[54] For a broad compilation of English language literature on the topic of corporate criminal liability, see Joseph F.C. DiMento, et al., "Corporate Criminal Liability: A Bibliography", 28 W. St. U. L. Rev. 1 (2000).

[55] See Buell, *supra* note 53, at 520 (explaining that "people simply do not blame entities for their agents' crimes across the board" and that "almost no one" has defended strict vicarious liability as the right liability rule). These modifications do not, however, fully alleviate the traditional deontological and utilitarian concerns with corporate-level criminal sanctions. See Alschuler, *supra* note 48, at 312 ("To suppose that minor variations on the theme of threatening to punish blameless shareholders can infuse the criminal law with its moral mission is once again unreal"); Fischel & Sykes, *supra* note 49, at 324–25 (explaining that the involvement of the board in the misconduct does not render corporate criminal liability efficient because "[w]hatever level of authority at which the decision is taken, there will always be opportunities for shareholders to utilize additional auditors, independent directors, consultants, and the like to economize on any attendant liability," such that imposing sanctions in excess of social cost will lead to excessive monitoring).

[56] A stronger case can be made for granting private enforcers the right to pursue vicarious corporate liability for managerial misconduct directed at shareholders, though this too has its drawbacks. See Amanda M. Rose, "Better Bounty Hunting: How the SEC's New Whistleblower Program Changes the Securities Fraud Class Action Debate", 108 Nw. L. Rev. 1235 (2014) (explaining that shareholders might benefit from corporate liability to the extent that it funds fraud detection efforts by the plaintiffs' bar that help shareholders monitor management); Rose & Squire, *supra* note 50, at 1693–98 (discussing the potential informational benefits to shareholders of vicarious liability in private litigation).

[57] See, e.g., Fischel & Sykes, *supra* note 49, at 330 (describing some scenarios in which private enforcement is likely to fail to adequately deter).

morality (or, if you would rather, social preferences) that criminal sanctions are hoped to deliver.[58] It also raises efficiency concerns. For example, if civil and criminal enforcers sought to sanction the same misconduct, it would create the prospect of wasteful redundancies; if both sought to price the same offense, it might lead to over-deterrence.[59] Furthermore, the involvement of multiple enforcers risks distorting litigation dynamics in unpredictable ways,[60] and overlapping authority can undermine accountability and in turn the performance of public enforcers.[61] This is not to say that a blurred civil–criminal divide is always undesirable: overlapping enforcement authority can, under the right circumstances, have laudable effects on regulatory incentives, for example.[62] It is to say, though, that a careful assessment of the institutional dynamics and political economy of a jurisdiction is necessary in order to determine whether shared responsibility is truly social welfare enhancing.[63]

4 Theory versus Reality in the United States and Abroad

How closely do countries hew to the theoretical ideal when allocating public enforcement efforts between criminal and civil enforcers in the corporate law sphere? As one might expect, the answer varies depending on the particular area of corporate law being examined, as well as the country of interest.

The nearly universal treatment of negligent corporate mismanagement as a civil offense tracks well with theory. In the United States, duty of care violations are primarily litigated in private derivative suits brought under state law, as discussed in the chapter by James Cox and Randall Thomas, this volume.[64] But in other countries with less robust private enforcement mechanisms, such as the United Kingdom, civil public enforcement plays a greater role.[65]

[58] See Robinson, *supra* note 45, at 208 (arguing that without a distinct criminal system, it would be more difficult for criminal sanctions to signal condemnation to the average person).

[59] See, e.g., Amanda M. Rose, "The Multienforcer Approach to Securities Fraud Deterrence: A Critical Analysis", 158 U. Pa. L. Rev. 2173, 2204–05 (2010).

[60] See, e.g., Jennifer Arlen, Evolution of Corporate Criminal Liability, in Leadership and Governance from the Inside Out (2004).

[61] See, e.g., Amanda M. Rose, "State Enforcement of National Policy: A Contextual Approach" (with Evidence from the Securities Realm), 97 Minn. L. Rev. 1343, 1354 (2013); Miriam H. Baer, "Choosing Punishment", 92 B. U. L. Rev. 577, 637–39 (2012).

[62] See Rose, *supra* note 59, at 1357.[63] See Rose, *supra* note 59, at 2210–27.

[64] Without allegations of disloyalty, however, derivative litigation is unlikely to succeed, due to the protection afforded defendants by Delaware's business judgment rule and the prevalence of charter provisions insulating directors of American public companies from liability for breaches of the duty of care. See Del. Code § 102(b)(7) (permitting waivers of director liability). To the extent that there is public civil enforcement related to corporate mismanagement in the United States, it tends to come in the form of SEC enforcement of federal securities law provisions. See, e.g., 15 U.S.C. § 78m(b)(2) (mandating that reporting companies adopt reasonable recordkeeping and internal control provisions); 15 U.S.C. § 7243 (requiring forfeiture of CEO and CFO incentive compensation when issuer misconduct leads to a restatement); 15 U.S.C. § 78j-4(b) (permitting clawback of officer incentive compensation when a restatement is required due to material noncompliance with reporting requirements).

[65] The relative lack of derivative litigation in the UK is due in part to differences in procedural rules (see, e.g., John Armour et al., "Private Enforcement of Corporate Law: An Empirical Comparison of the

In the wake of the financial crisis, there have been calls for more *criminal* prosecutions of the individuals and institutions whose risk taking contributed to the crisis.[66] Others have cautioned against criminalizing risk taking (or the failure to adopt adequate internal controls to regulate risk taking), and criticize recent prosecutions that they contend do so under the guise of criminal fraud.[67] As a matter of theory, the latter have the better argument. Imposing criminal sanctions for poor business decisions threatens to dilute the moral force of the criminal law, and risks over-deterring socially desirable behavior. Under no theory of the civil–criminal divide is it advisable.

True fraud presents a very different case, of course, as do other intentional violations of managers' fiduciary duties. These sorts of offenses do warrant criminal sanctions as a matter of theory, and in reality most jurisdictions treat this behavior as criminal. That is not to say that all jurisdictions pursue corporate fraud and disloyalty with the same level of intensity. As discussed in the chapter by Howell Jackson and Jeffery Zhang, this volume, there is significant variation in the level of public resources that countries invest in public enforcement efforts, whether civil or criminal.

One important dimension along which countries vary significantly concerns the use of corporate criminal liability. At one end of the spectrum stands the United States, which authorizes criminal sanctions against corporations for any employee's crime, so long as it is committed in the course of employment and the employee intended to benefit the company (with both conditions interpreted loosely by courts).[68] This may be referred to as the "agency" or "*respondeat superior*" approach to corporate criminal liability. At the other end of the spectrum stands Germany, which does not impose criminal liability on corporations at all, limiting corporate liability for employee misconduct to

---

United Kingdom and the United States", 6 J. Emp. Legal Stud. 687, 693, Table 1 (2009) (cataloguing the differences in US and UK civil litigation procedure that may explain the higher rates of private enforcement in the US)), as well as a tradition of informal enforcement activities by UK institutional investors (see John Armour, "Enforcement Strategies in UK Corporate Governance: A Roadmap and Empirical Assessment", 36–45, European Corporate Governance Inst., Working Paper No. 106 (2008), available at http://papers.ssrn.com/sol3/papers.cfm?abstract_id=1133542). Derivative suits are also a rarity in continental Europe, although shareholder suits seeking to rescind or nullify decisions made in the shareholder meeting play a comparable role. See Martin Gelter, "Why Do Shareholder Derivative Suits Remain Rare in Continental Europe?", 37 Brook. J. Int'l. L. 843, 881–87 (2012). Like US-style derivative suits, nullification suits provoke controversy. See id. at 884–85 (describing allegations of abuse and legislative responses). Dutch law provides a hybrid private-public model of civil enforcement to challenge problems with company management: a privately instituted judicial investigation. See id. at 889–891.

[66] See, e.g., Matt Taibbi, Why Isn't Wall Street in Jail?, Rolling Stone (Mar. 3, 2011); Jonathan Fisher, et al., "The Global Financial Crisis: The Case for a Stronger Criminal Response", 7 L. & Fin. Markets Rev. 159 (2013).

[67] See, e.g., Kent Hoover, Criminalizing Failure, Upstart Business Journal (Nov. 17, 2009); see also Zachary Kedgley-Foot, Criminalising Breaches of Directors' Duties: What is Wrong with Clause 4 of the Companies and Limited partnerships Amendment Bill? (Oct. 2012) (unpublished dissertation, University of Otago) (on file with author). The German criminal prosecution of Josef Ackermann and his fellow directors at Mannesmann over executive pay decisions made in the midst of Mannesmann's takeover battle with Vodafone provoked a similar debate. See, e.g., Peter Kolla, "The Mannesmann Trial and the Role of the Courts", 5 German L. J. 829 (2004).

[68] See Baer, *supra* note 1, at 620 & n.199.

administrative fines and only then for wrongs committed by certain corporate officers.[69] Taking an intermediate position is the UK, which holds corporations criminally liable, but only for crimes by persons who control and direct the activities of the corporation.[70] This is sometimes referred to as the "identification" or "alter ego" approach to corporate criminal liability.

Only the German approach is consistent with traditional theoretical accounts of the civil–criminal divide. The UK approach deviates from these, but finds some modern normative support given its restriction to crimes by high-level corporate officers.[71] The approach taken by the United States, however, finds no support in any extant theory of the civil–criminal divide.[72] What might then explain it? A full treatment of this interesting question is beyond the scope of this chapter, but a few preliminary observations may help to set it in context. The first is that criminal prosecutions of corporations in the United States may sometimes be driven by political or strategic, rather than theoretical, concerns. Billion-dollar settlements to resolve allegations of "corporate crime" play well in the headlines, after all, especially when populist sentiment runs high. It is also the case that criminal prosecutors can leverage the threat of corporate criminal liability (which can impose devastating collateral consequences on a firm) to obtain assistance in prosecuting individuals within the firm who might be difficult to convict without board cooperation.[73] The threat of corporate criminal prosecution may also be used to pursue non-criminal remedial objectives, like corporate governance reforms (which are often featured in so-called deferred prosecution agreements ("DPAs") entered into between companies and the United States Department of Justice[74]). While theory suggests that the pursuit of such objectives is better left to civil enforcers, path dependency and other frictions may give the edge to criminal enforcers in the United States. Finally, the United States may not be as different from the UK as it first appears. It may be that criminal enforcers in the United States use their prosecutorial discretion to target their enforcement efforts at firms with serious problems at high levels of the corporate hierarchy.[75] Moreover, the United States Sentencing Guidelines instruct courts to consider a corporation's internal control structure when making sentencing determinations.[76]

[69]   See Martin Böse, Corporate Criminal Liability in Germany, in Corporate Criminal Liability: Emergence, Convergence, and Risk 227 (Mark Pieth & Radha Ivory, eds., 2011).

[70]   See Celia Wells, Corporate Criminal Liability in England and Wales, in Corporate Criminal Liability: Emergence, Convergence, and Risk 91 (Mark Pieth & Radha Ivory, eds., 2011).

[71]   See *supra* note 55 and accompanying text.

[72]   It has therefore been subject to intense criticism. See, e.g., Miriam Baer, "Organizational Liability and the Tension Between Corporate and Criminal Law", 19 Brook. J. L. & Pol'y 1 (2010).

[73]   This practice has been the subject of critique. For background, see American Bar Association, Protecting the Attorney–Client Privilege, the Work Product Doctrine and Employee Legal Rights: Comprehensive Reform Still Critically Needed, available at http://www.americanbar.org.

[74]   See Wulf A. Kaal & Timothy A. Lacine, "The Effect of Deferred and Non-Prosecution Agreements on Corporate Governance: Evidence from 1993–2003", 70 Bus. L. 61 (2014). The use of DPAs to achieve governance reforms is controversial in the United States. See Lawrence A. Cunningham, "Deferred Prosecutions and Corporate Governance: An Integrated Approach to Investigation and Reform", 66 Fla. L. Rev. 1, 2–3 (2014).

[75]   See, e.g., Sara Sun Beale, "The Development and Evolution of the US Law of Corporate Criminal Liability", 126 Zeitschrift für die Gesamte Strafrechtswissenschaft 27–54 (2014).

[76]   Id. at 25–29.

5 Conclusion

A variety of theoretical and practical considerations may inform a polity's choice between civil and criminal public enforcement of corporate law violations. This chapter has identified the main normative arguments relevant to the choice between civil and criminal enforcement, both generally and as applied to the corporate law context specifically, and has examined actual corporate law enforcement patterns in the United States and abroad. While enforcement patterns vis-à-vis individual defendants hew closely to the theoretical ideal, there is substantial variation in countries' use of corporate criminal liability, with some countries (most notably the United States) pursuing policies that are difficult to defend theoretically.

CHAPTER 36

CORPORATE LITIGATION IN SPECIALIZED BUSINESS COURTS

JOSEPH A. MCCAHERY AND ALEXANDER DE ROODE

1 INTRODUCTION

CORPORATE litigation is a topic of much interest due to its potential effect on firm value. Prior literature shows that the cost and likelihood of litigation may have a negative impact on shareholder value.[1] Romano, for example, assumes that derivative cases are frivolous and add little shareholder value due to the size of the awards.[2] Supporting this view, Coffee focuses on the large fee awards that the plaintiff's attorneys expect to receive in a court settlement.[3] While prior research has attempted to disentangle the effects of attorney fees and case merits, the analysis of derivative litigation in the absence of externalities has largely been overlooked.

One common feature of the recent literature is the suggestion that the increase of independent board directors has made it more difficult to launch a derivative action since independent directors are unlikely to excuse the demand requirement.[4] Better legal protections and corporate governance have also been reported to lead plaintiffs to file higher-quality suits that increase the probability of success. Supporting this view is the growing role of M&A-related litigation that has prompted attorneys to file cases in multiple jurisdictions, causing diminishing effects on shareholder wealth.[5] Armour, Black, and Cheffins further

---

[1] Adam B. Badawi & Daniel Chen, "The Shareholder Wealth Effects of Delaware Litigation", 19 Am. L. & Econ. Rev. 287 (2017).

[2] Roberta Romano, "Shareholder Suit: Litigation Without Foundation", 7 J. L. Econ. & Org. 55 (1991).

[3] John C. Coffee, Jr., "Understanding the Plaintiff's Attorney: The Implications of Economic Theory for Private Enforcement of Law through Class and Derivative Actions", 86 Colum. L. Rev. 669 (1986).

[4] Robert B. Thompson & Randall S. Thomas, "Public and Private Faces of Derivative Lawsuits", 57 Vand. L. Rev. 619 (2004).

[5] Matthew D. Cain & Steven M. Davidoff, "Takeover Litigation in 2011" (2012), Working Paper, available at: http://papers.ssrn.com/sol3/papers.cfm?abstract_id=1998482.

show that a "high-quality" filing is consistent with a pattern of negative effects due to the percentage of high damage and attorney fees awards.[6] Additionally, Curtis and Myers report that the merit-related factors play a role in the initiation and disposition of derivative litigation, showing that plaintiffs' attorneys are selective in cases where both the underlying legal merits and backdating of options are more egregious, since they are more likely to bring larger settlements.[7] The focus of the current literature is to find the control forms to determine if these cases add value.

In this chapter, we use a natural experiment provided by the absence of attorney fees and monetary awards to examine whether derivative litigation impacts shareholder wealth negatively. Though the literature suggests that attorney fees and monetary awards stimulate the filing of derivative cases, we conjecture that the absence of such incentives has the potential to result in filings that may be associated with gains for shareholders. This is because when conflict resolution is speedy and effective it is likely to have an important impact on a variety of the corporate finance issues the firm faces. Moreover, if filings result in settlements that involve corporate governance reforms, the market's reaction to a perception of better post-litigation outcome might also materially benefit shareholders. The intuition is that shareholder wealth effects should be observable since conflict resolution improves the alignment of management's interests with shareholders' and provides new information to the market.

We select a sample of shareholder suits from a country that has a well-developed corporate litigation market that does not provide incentives for lawyers and private litigants: the Netherlands. We carry out our analysis using 589 filings that have been collected through multiple databases from the beginning of 2002 through the end of 2013. Corporate litigation in the Netherlands is comparable to the US derivative suit since litigation costs are borne by shareholders. Moreover, shareholder litigation in the Dutch Enterprise Chamber focuses mostly on providing nonpecuniary remedies to resolving deadlocks or other intrafirm disputes. In contrast to the US, a filing in the Enterprise Chamber involves a two-step procedure in which the court first investigates the complaint and produces an independent report on the correctness of the management's decision. In the second step, the court determines if there has been mismanagement and then may take appropriate measures to remedy them.

We examine corporate litigation in two ways. First, we empirically analyze filings of listed and non-listed firms at the Enterprise Chamber. Since most plaintiffs are non-listed firms that have different governance structures and economic resources than listed firms, we conjecture a different demand for corporate litigation. In contrast, listed firms typically have better governance mechanisms, and therefore shareholders are more likely to rely on public enforcement.[8] To evaluate the characteristics of listed firms, we split our sample and analyze these cases. Second, we focus on filings and resolutions to determine whether

---

[6] J. Armour, B. Black, & B. Cheffins, "Delaware's Balancing Act", 87 Ind. L. J. 1345 (2012).

[7] Q. Curtis & M. Myers, "Do the Merits Matter? Empirical Evidence on Shareholder Suits from Options Backdating Litigation", 164 U. Pa. L. Rev. 291 (2016).

[8] Organization for Economic Co-operation & Development (OECD), Supervision and Enforcement in Corporate Governance (2013), available at http://www.oecd.org/daf/ca/SupervisionandEnforcementinCorporateGovernance2013.pdf.

acquisition-related lawsuits have an effect on firm value. To our knowledge, we provide the first empirical evidence on the effect of acquisition-related litigation on the firm value of Dutch firms.

We first begin our investigation of these questions by examining the differences in the case filings of non-listed and listed firms. We find that most plaintiffs are non-listed firms seeking to obtain injunctions or resolve intra-firm conflicts, whereas listed firms are usually involved in merger and acquisition related corporate litigation. To proxy for the effect of corporate litigation on firm value in non-listed, we focus on the effectiveness of court mechanisms to resolve conflicts between shareholders. In this way, we consider the court's functioning in removing deadlock situations in small firms. While we cannot measure the wealth effects as is possible with listed firms, we nevertheless conjecture that, using our empirical evidence, litigation adds value for small, non-listed firms. In fact, our findings strongly support the view that where the threat of litigation is high, the withdrawal effect of a case filing may add value.

Second, we examine how a selection of acquisition-related filings could generate positive abnormal returns. First, similarly to Cain and Davidoff,[9] we focus on the relationship between M&A litigation and shareholder value. We collect data on the share prices and perform an event study for the impact of case filings and court resolutions. Using event windows of varying lengths to estimate the short- and longer-term effects, we find an abnormal return of 0.5% for firms that are subject to merger-related litigation between 2002 and 2013. Our findings imply, taking the abnormal returns on the day of the filing, that shareholders do significantly better. Our results highlight that the market responds positively to a filing since it may remove asymmetrical information and a deadlock situation between shareholders. In terms of resolution, we find a negative effect over the short-term period near the resolution. This indicates that shareholders incur actual costs from the proceedings in the Enterprise Chamber. However, over the long term, we find that resolutions have little impact on the stock price. The result of this analysis is consistent with previous literature.

Overall, our research contributes to prior literature in three distinct aspects. First, this study is most clearly related to work by Kroeze that shows the Dutch model of corporate litigation has similar features to the Delaware Court of Chancery even though it is much smaller and provides few, if any, incentives to overcome lawyers' collective action problems.[10] Second, while there are empirical studies on the effect of merit-based M&A litigation on firm value,[11] we believe that our findings are novel in this literature. To our knowledge, we are the first to show that M&A-related litigation is associated with positive shareholder wealth effects. Third, our work adds to the literature on the corporate litigation of publicly listed firms. Prior studies have often assumed that private conflict resolution is rarely launched by private parties against directors of publicly listed companies. The results of this study are consistent with other related studies on entrepreneurial firm litigation and venture capital[12]

---

[9] M. D. Cain & S. M. Davidoff, "A Great Game: The Dynamics of State Competition and Litigation" 100 Iowa L. Rev. 465 (2015).

[10] M. Kroeze, The Companies and Business Court as a Specialized Court, in The Quality of Corporate Law and the Role of Corporate Law Judges (L. Bouche, M. Knubben, J. A. McCahery, & L. Timmerman eds., 2006).

[11] See e.g., Badawi & Chen, *supra* note 1.

[12] D. J. Cumming, B. Haslem, & A. M. Knill, "Entrepreneurial Litigation and Venture Capital Finance", 52 J. Fin. Quant. Anal. 2217 (2017).

whose findings suggest that non-listed firms are more likely to rely on private enforcement to resolve conflicts.

This chapter proceeds as follows. Section 2 provides a review of the trends of corporate litigation in the US and provides summary statistics of the pattern of shareholder litigation in the Dutch Enterprise Chamber. Section 3 presents the empirical analysis of the effectiveness of the Dutch conflict resolution model. Section 4 examines the market impact of M&A-related litigation on firm value. Section 5 concludes.

2 CORPORATE LITIGATION IN THE UNITED STATES

In this section, we review recent trends in corporate litigation in the United States. We organize the theoretical discussion into the factors that can lead to externalities in derivative lawsuits. We also discuss the related empirical literature on multi-jurisdictional litigation. We continue by looking at how corporate litigation can, from a theoretical perspective, lower agency costs in a public firm. Finally, we describe the structure and characteristics of shareholder litigation in the Dutch Enterprise Chamber during the period 2002–2013.

2.1 Trends in American Corporate Litigation

The Delaware Court has been widely recognized as the main forum of corporate litigation.[13] Recent studies have identified two major trends in corporate litigation that complicate the analysis of shareholder wealth effects. The first trend reveals the number of acquisition-related cases strongly dropped in the period before 2009.[14] Since acquisition-related litigation is the predominant source of lawsuits filed in Delaware, this sharply reduces the court influence on corporate litigation. As Thompson and Thomas report, the majority of cases filed in the years 1999–2000 against public firms were acquisition-oriented class actions.[15] A second trend indicates an increase of multi-jurisdiction lawsuits between 2005 and 2010. In addition to identifying the increased role for foreign jurisdictions in adjudicating leveraged buyout and merger transactions, empirical evidence lends support to the view that litigation in Delaware appears to have contracted earlier in the decade due to a variety of factors. Thus, in an increasingly competitive and transparent litigation environment, it becomes harder for any jurisdiction to maintain the competitive advantage while providing the same quality and fairness in litigation.

Several theories have been put forward for the shift out of Delaware. The first theory reflects the pro-defendant orientation of the Delaware Chancery. Armour et al. argue that the sentiment has turned away plaintiffs to more favorable jurisdictions.[16] While Armour

---

[13] For an overview of the role of Delaware in corporate litigation see, e.g., R. Romano, Foundations of Corporate Law (2010).

[14] Armour, Black, & Cheffins, *supra* note 6.   [15] Thompson & Thomas, *supra* note 4.

[16] J. Armour, B. Black, & B. Cheffins, "Is Delaware Losing its Cases?", 9 J. Emp. Legal Stud. 605 (2012).

et al. report the Vice Chancellor's quotes that capture the sentiment against plaintiffs, they are unable to locate a shift in Delaware law that would lead to precedents favoring defendants.[17] Conversely, a second theory holds that plaintiffs' attorneys have a direct financial incentive to file cases outside Delaware. The implication is that factors, such as attorney fee cuts by the Delaware court in agreed settlements, create strong incentive to file cases outside Delaware. As attorneys seek out more profitable fees outside Delaware, state courts accelerate this trend by competing for acquisition-related cases. Cain and Davidoff show that states compete on attorneys' fees and settlement rate.[18] As such, to compensate for the loss of market share of cases, courts adjust these factors to account for their losses.

Filing cases in multiple jurisdictions allows for additional strategic advantages. First, attorneys can press for expedited proceedings. Second, filing cases in other jurisdiction can support objections made in previous filed cases. These advantages increase the pressure for the defendants to settle and increase the leverage of the plaintiffs. Collectively, these factors will accelerate the move out of Delaware and affect the results of measuring the shareholder wealth effect.

However, Delaware remains an important corporate litigation forum as it signals the determination of the plaintiff. Armour et al. report that plaintiffs' counsel still favors Delaware as the leading forum for acquisition-related and derivative litigation.[19] Given the stature of the court, plaintiffs filing cases in Delaware over competing jurisdictions still have credibility. In fact, over the period 2009–2011, the number of cases strongly increased. It is likely, moreover, that this trend will continue, particularly in light of the Delaware State Legislature's recent approval of amendments to the Delaware General Corporation Law authorizing forum selection clauses in the charters and bylaws that designate Delaware as the sole forum for litigation.

2.2 Measuring Wealth Effects of Corporate Litigation

This section examines the factors motivating corporate litigation and the effect of litigation on shareholder value. Absent externalities, corporate litigation is a mechanism that can improve the alignment of interests between shareholders and management. This alignment is typically conjectured to play an important role in generating value for shareholders. Two important factors influence shareholder value as lawsuits tend to limit the negative effect of principal–agent problems between shareholders and management.[20] First, as the early literature has established, asymmetric information may prevent an efficient outcome. In typical shareholder lawsuits, such as mergers and acquisitions (M&A), information known to the board, but unknown to shareholders, may prevent the shareholders from fully valuing and assessing a bidder's offer. Litigation can theoretically add value by removing the information asymmetry between parties. Second, inequality in bargaining power between the two parties may lead to inefficient outcomes. Hence, corporate litigation works to protect minority shareholder rights and improve shareholder value by limiting externalities in settlement procedures.

---

[17] Id.
[18] Cain & Davidoff, *supra* note 5.   [19] Armour, Black, & Cheffins, *supra* note 16.
[20] M. C. Jensen & W. H. Meckling, "Theory of the Firm: Managerial Behavior, Agency Costs and Ownership Structure", 3 J. Fin. Econ. 305 (1976).

Empirically, the relationship between corporate litigation and generating shareholder value is less well established. Early literature has moved from a focus on case studies of corporate litigation[21] to measuring wealth effects of intra-firm litigation.[22] One important strand of recent empirical evidence stems from studies that have focused on lawsuits related to M&A. An observation of M&A transactions is that most deals lead to litigation. Cain and Davidoff report that in 2005 only 38.7% of significant-sized deals were subject to litigation, whereas in 2011 this rose to 94.2%.[23] There is also evidence that, during the same period, the cases filed in multiple jurisdictions increased from 8.6% to 47.4%. Overall, the growing role of M&A-derivative litigation has led to the heavy use of fee-shifting and minimum-stake-to-sue provisions, as well as attorneys filing cases in multiple jurisdictions, which is consistent with diminishing effects on shareholder wealth.

Some writers argue that the optimal strategy of plaintiffs' law firms is to settle claims rather than pursue strong lawsuits.[24] There is also evidence that top plaintiffs' law firms are more likely to gain success in M&A lawsuits, suggesting the value-enhancing mechanism of filing plaintiff's lawsuits.[25] The implication of this study is that litigation offsets the fall in probability of deal completion with an increase in expected takeover premiums generating economic value for target shareholders.

On the other hand, target stock price reactions to bid announcements do not fully anticipate the positive effect from the potential ligation. One strand of the literature focuses on how settlements appear to have negative effects on share prices, whereas court rulings have a positive effect.[26] Typically, firms with weak corporate governance structures are willing to settle, signaling to investors they are vulnerable due to high agency costs. Thompson and Thomas find evidence that M&A lawsuits suits have high levels of litigation agency costs.[27] As a consequence, we would expect to see a weak response of the share price. Since litigation may remove asymmetric information, Thompson and Thomas argue that in 1999–2000 merger litigation had a role in reducing managerial agency costs.[28]

Another strand of literature offers insight on the shareholder wealth effect of corporate litigation via derivative lawsuits. Theoretically, derivative lawsuits can increase shareholder value through the protection of shareholder rights. As noted, early empirical studies find that the filing of a derivative lawsuit does not significantly affect the stock price.[29] This work is in line with prior findings that a negative effect can be expected with dismissals of a derivative suit and no market reaction to court decisions that overrule proposals to dismiss a case.[30] More recent literature, however, indicates a negative effect on shareholder value for

---

[21] D. M. Cutler & L. H. Summers, "The Costs of Conflict Resolution and Financial Distress: Evidence from the Texaco–Pennzoil litigation", 19 RAND J. Econ. 157 (1987).

[22] S. Bhagat, J. A. Brickley, & J. L. Coles, "The Wealth Effects of Interfirm Lawsuits", 35 J. Fin. Econ. 221 (1994).

[23] Cain & Davidoff, *supra* note 5.

[24] R. S. Thomas & R. B. Thompson, "A Theory of Representative Shareholder Suits and its Application to Multijurisdictional Litigation", 106 Nw. U. L. Rev. 1753 (2012).

[25] C. N. V. Krishnan, R. W. Masulis, R. Thomas, & R. B. Thompson, "Litigation in Mergers and Acquisitions", 18 J. Corp. Fin. 1248 (2012).

[26] B. Haslem, "Managerial Opportunism During Corporate Litigation", 60 J. Fin. 2013 (2005).

[27] Thompson & Thomas, *supra* note 4.   [28] Id.   [29] Romano, *supra* note 2.

[30] D. R. Fischel & M. Bradley, "The Role of Liability Rules and the Derivative Suit in Corporate Law: A Theoretical and Empirical Analysis", 71 Cornell L. Rev. 261 (1986).

the filing of derivative cases, and this effect increases with case quality.[31] One explanation for the decrease in shareholder wealth is that markets respond to increased uncertainty regarding the impact of the litigation on business continuity. The filing of a derivative suit signals unexpected corporate governance or management issues and information disclosed at the trial may harm future firm revenues.

An interesting recent suggestion is that shareholder litigation can increase shareholder value.[32] In fact, the $279 million settlement of a derivative suit involving Activision Blizzard in 2014, and a $130 million derivative settlement of the Freeport–McMoRan action in 2015 seems to reinforce the suggestion that settlements of derivative litigation will lead to direct dividend payments to shareholders, resulting in shareholder gains.

Other studies have investigated the wealth effects of corporate litigation in the pricing mechanism of IPOs. Underpricing at the IPO provides insurance for firms with high litigation risk and can lower the expected litigation costs.[33] In order to defend against corporate litigation, firms with high litigation risk might increase their cash holdings. Shareholders, on the other hand, would prefer higher payouts as excess cash might increase damage payments.[34] These findings suggest that while the size and impact of litigation risk is well known, the resulting effect on shareholder wealth is not entirely known due to the possible impact of externalities.

2.3 The Dutch Enterprise Chamber

In this section, we describe the development of the Dutch Enterprise Chamber from the perspective of its long-standing role in the enforcement of corporate governance. We then provide summary statistics about trends in cases filed and withdrawn and verdicts rendered over the last decade. The data shows that while there was a decline in cases from 2004 to 2007, there has been a steady increase in new cases after 2010.

For years, the Netherlands ranked consistently behind the United States and United Kingdom, with respect to corporate governance. This is reflected in much lower firm performance and increased cost of capital. In terms of the legal regime, the Netherlands ranked low in investor protection and, in the context of listed companies, Dutch firms were seen to make takeovers very difficult to achieve. The Netherlands has taken steps, over the last decade, to provide better legal protections for minority shareholders, and mechanisms to monitor management's actions. Starting with the introduction of the Dutch Corporate Governance Code in 2003, and amendments to the Dutch Civil Code in 2004, Dutch firms have been committed to the implementation of higher standards of governance. The perceived payoff of better corporate governance standards was also influenced, in some cases, by firms' calculation of potential costs associated with the "Dutch discount," which refers to the fact that firms trade lower than their competitors abroad due to the lower standards of governance

---

[31] Badawi & Chen, *supra* note 1.

[32] A. Frankel, Ugly Duckling Shareholder Derivative Suits are Poised for Swandom (Jan. 1, 2015), Reuters, available at: http://blogs.reuters.com/alison-frankel/2015/01/02/ugly-duckling-shareholder-derivative-suits-are-poised-for-swandom/.

[33] M. Lowry & S. Shu, "Litigation Risk and IPO Underpricing", 65 J. Fin. Econ. 309 (2002).

[34] T. A. Gormley & D. A. Matsa, "Growing Out of Trouble? Corporate Responses to Liability Risk", 24 Rev. Fin. Stud. 2781 (2011).

in the Netherlands. According to this theory, managers have tended to focus on lowering the "Dutch discount" as a motivation for their strongly held commitment to the enforcement of the Dutch corporate governance code. One of the results of the amendments to the Dutch law is the renewed focus of the Enterprise Chamber. The Dutch Enterprise Chamber has been labeled as the European counterpart of Delaware.[35] While there are similarities between Delaware and the Enterprise Chamber, a closer look at the Dutch statute and procedure suggests that there may be some differences. For example, derivative lawsuits are not possible in the Netherlands. Under Dutch law, the Enterprise Chamber has jurisdiction when: (1) doubts arise as to whether a company is properly managed (the inquiry procedure)[36]; (2) there are conflicts regarding the removal of a firm's Supervisory Board organized under the Structure Regime[37]; (3) shareholders are dissatisfied with financial reporting and challenge the annual account[38]; (4) a shareholder that owns at least 95% of the outstanding share capital seeks to freeze out the remaining shareholders[39]; or (5) conflicts arise between shareholders and harm the existence of the corporation, allowing for a forced buyout of shareholders.[40] Also, in the absence of contingency fees, Dutch lawyers do not have the same incentives as US lawyers.[41] Hence, plaintiffs' attorneys working under a fixed fee system in the Netherlands will no doubt have incentives to settle cases.[42]

The court, which includes three justices and two lay members with financial experience, has arguably exerted most influence on the development of Dutch corporate law and the protection of minority shareholders through the inquiry procedure.[43] Upon request, the court has the ability to initiate an inquiry into the policy, management, and conduct of business in a company when there are well-founded reasons to believe that a company is or has been managed improperly and incorrectly. The inquiry procedure was first introduced in 1928 to strengthen the position of minority shareholders in Dutch listed firms, although it had no practical use until 1971, when an overhaul of Dutch company law laid the foundation for a popular dispute resolution mechanism.

Over the years from 1996, the demand for the court in conflict resolution has increased substantially. Figure 36.1 shows that the arrival of new cases has mostly increased from the period 1996–2001. In this period, the number of new cases grew 165%, from 68 cases in 1996

---

[35] J. B. Jacobs, The Role of Specialized Courts in Resolving Corporate Governance Disputes in the United States and the EU: An American Judge's Perspective, in The Quality of Corporate Law and the Role of Corporate Law Judges (L. Bouche, M. Knubben, & J. A. McCahery eds., 2006).

[36] See Arts. 344–359 of Book 2 of the Dutch Civil Code.

[37] See Arts. 158 and 161a of Book 2 of the Dutch Civil Code. The Structure Regime applies to large firms in the Netherlands (roughly those with more than 100 employees and 16 million euros in capital). These firms are required to have a two-tier board structure. The directors are appointed by the supervisory board. The shareholders are only able to dismiss the entire supervisory board.

[38] See Arts. 447–453 of Book 2 of the Dutch Civil Code.

[39] See Art. 92a of Book 2 of the Dutch Civil Code.

[40] See Art. 336 of Book 2 of the Dutch Civil Code for the exclusion procedure of shareholders and Art. 343 of Book 2 of the Dutch Civil Code for relinquishment procedure of shareholders.

[41] M. W. J. Jitta, Dispute Resolution in the Netherlands: Recent Decisions of the Enterprise Chamber and Their Impact on the Corporate Governance of Dutch Companies, in The Quality of Corporate Law and the Role of Corporate Law Judges (L. Bouche, M. Knubben, & J. A. McCahery eds., 2006).

[42] M. Gelter, "Why Do Shareholder Derivative Suits Remain Rare in Continental Europe?", 37 Brook. J. Int'l. L. 843 (2012).

[43] Kroeze, supra note 10.

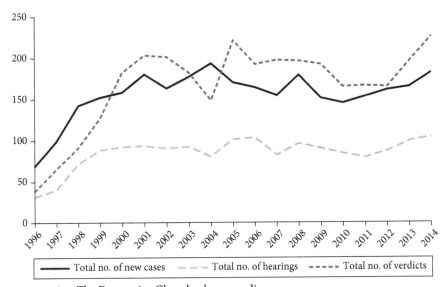

FIGURE 36.1 The Enterprise Chamber's proceedings.

Source: Data from the Enterprise Chamber.

to 180 in 2001. The large increase in these cases can be attributed to changes in the law. In the subsequent period, the number of cases started to decline. Several theories have been put forward to explain this trend. First, changes in the law and the appointment of a new president of the court may be one of the contributing factors.[44] Other factors contributing to the decline include the rapid and transparent proceedings of the Enterprise Chamber itself. Recent media accounts indicate that plaintiffs that prefer less transparent proceedings typically will lodge actions in Dutch civil courts to prevent negative publicity following from a lawsuit with the Enterprise Chamber.[45]

The two periods of decline in new cases seem to imply that the improved incentives to bring litigation in the first period may have had the unintended effect of increasing the costs of this style of litigation for some parties. Our evidence suggests that the Enterprise Chamber's highly public exposure of the details of the litigation, often involving weak cases and corporate governance practices, may have triggered the migration of cases away from the Enterprise Chamber to civil courts. The "reputation theory" holds that some shareholders tend to pursue claims in civil court to avoid the impact of negative publicity on firm value.

We also find some evidence that the pickup in new cases after 2010 is consistent with the corporate governance hypothesis that shareholders have incentives to litigate code violations to influence the quality of the firm's internal governance regime. This data is also consistent with Figure 36.3, which shows the increase in inquiry procedure requests from 2010 to 2014.

---

[44] R. G. J. Nowak, Corporate Boards in the Netherlands, in Corporate Boards in Law and Practice: A Comparative Analysis in Europe (2013).

[45] F. Schreurs, Ook bij Ondernemingskamer valt veel winst te behalen met aanstelling "stille bewindvoerder", Het Financieele Dagblad, Nov. 1, 2013.

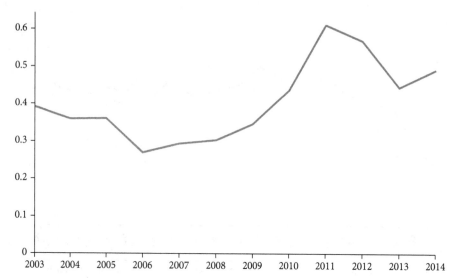

FIGURE 36.2 The number of cases withdrawn in the Enterprise Chamber.

Source: Data from the Enterprise Chamber.

We also ask whether the Enterprise Chamber, like Delaware, is delivering settlements between shareholders, and decreasing the costs of litigation to all parties. To understand the role of the Dutch Enterprise Chamber in facilitating agreements, Figure 36.2 shows the number of withdrawn cases. Over the period from 2003 to 2014, an average of 40.4% of new cases were withdrawn. There are various ways to interpret the increasing trend of settlements. First, it is quite possible that the economic downturn of 2008 and the following crisis may have triggered an increase in the number of settlements. Since most plaintiffs are unlikely to have recovered economic damages or costs, it is more likely that parties would focus on the potential to resolve conflicts through other channels. Similarly, since attorney fees are typically proportional to the length of procedure, plaintiffs clearly had an incentive to settle. To be sure, there is another possibility: that plaintiffs simply filed claims as a threat, which had lost its effectiveness during the financial crisis, to induce a settlement.

3 THE DUTCH ENTERPRISE CHAMBER AND THE CONFLICT-RESOLUTION MODEL

This section examines the two stages of the inquiry procedure and the injunction relief, which are the two main functions of the Dutch corporate court mostly sought after by firms. We analyze the number of inquiry procedure requests and measures that have been brought to the Enterprise Chamber by listed and non-listed companies.[46] Finally, we investigate the impact of the court on the Dutch governance model.

---

[46] Parts of this section are adapted from J. A. McCahery & E. P. M. Vermeulen, Conflict Resolution and the Role of Courts: An Empirical Study, in Company Law and SMEs (M. Neville & K. E. Sørensen eds., 2010).

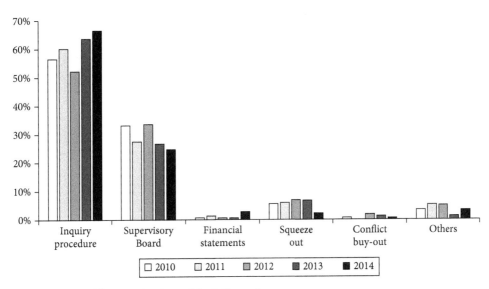

FIGURE 36.3 Characterization of the inflow of new cases.

Source: Data from the Enterprise Chamber.

3.1 Stage One: The Inquiry Procedure

As we have noted, the inquiry procedure is one of the most important mechanisms of the Dutch Enterprise Chamber. It is generally recognized that the certainty, speed, and predictability of the Enterprise Chamber increased as precedent expanded. Figure 36.3 shows that over the period 2010–2014 about 60% of the new cases were seeking conflict resolution within the scope of the inquiry procedure. The bulk of the remaining actions involve conflicts about the supervisory board, financial statements, squeeze-outs, and buyouts. As we might expect, Table 36.1 shows that while the length of these procedures can vary, the Enterprise Chamber is able to deliver fast-track conflict resolution.

Dutch corporate law provides that only a narrow range of individuals are entitled to request an inquiry procedure.[47] Besides the public prosecutor (for reasons of public interest) and labor unions (for employees' interests), the most important constituency allowed to request an inquiry procedure is shareholders (or depository receipt holders) alone or collectively owning at least 10% of the outstanding shares (or depository receipts, respectively) of a company or shares with a nominal value of €225,000, or a lesser amount as provided by the articles of association. The inquiry procedure contains two stages. In the first stage, parties may request an inquiry into the affairs of the corporation to determine whether the firm has been mismanaged. If the Enterprise Chamber shares the applicant's concerns, it will appoint one or more individuals, who will conduct an investigation and file a report with the court.[48] In the second stage, the Enterprise Chamber may

---

[47] Arts. 345, 346, and 347 of Book 2 of the Dutch Civil Code.
[48] See Art. 350 of Book 2 of the Dutch Civil Code.

Table 36.1 Average length of procedures

Period	Inquiry procedure stage 1	Inquiry procedure stage 2	Supervisory Board	Squeeze out	Conflict buy-out
2012	25	232	26	108	125
2013	37	245	43	103	125
2014	64	108	46	132	–

The average length of the main procedures in the Enterprise Chamber in days. The length is measured between the filing of the case and a court ruling.

Source: Data from the Enterprise Chamber.

be requested to take certain measures, provided that improper conduct and mismanagement follows from the report.[49] These measures include: (1) the suspension or dismissal of board members; (2) the nullification or suspension of board or shareholder resolutions; (3) the appointment of temporary board members; (4) the temporary transfer of shares; (5) the temporary deviation of provisions of the articles of association; and (6) the dissolution of the company.[50] The firm or the applicants may appeal to the Supreme Court on legal grounds.[51] On appeal, the Supreme Court will not review the factual findings and background of the case.

Table 36.2 summarizes the number of inquiry procedure requests and measures that have been brought by listed and non-listed companies to the Enterprise Chamber. Judging from the number of cases in the period 1971–1994, the inquiry procedure initially played a modest role in the development of company law and the reduction of managerial agency costs. First, the lengthy and formalistic two-stage procedure rendered immediate responses to practical needs in a dynamic and ever-changing business environment impossible. Second, the limitation on the number of measures that the Enterprise Chamber could order constituted another reason for initial caution in employing the inquiry procedure. If, for instance, a conflict between shareholders caused the mismanagement of a company, the court's discretion was limited to ordering the temporary transfer of shares to a nominee. This prevented the court from effectively resolving the dispute. Finally, the uncertainty about the application of the open "improper management" standard tempered the initial success rate of the inquiry

---

[49] Each case could generate several decisions, such as a preliminary measure, a final measure, the appointment of one or more persons to undertake an inquiry into the policy and conduct of the company, or the determination of the maximum amount of the costs of the inquiry.

[50] See Art. 356 of Book 2 of the Dutch Civil Code. Table 36.1 shows that only 6% of the requests in the context of listed companies (this is 13% in the context of non-listed companies) will result in a final measure. If we analyze our dataset for the period 2002–2008, we find that the appointment of temporary board members is the most popular measure (28%), followed by the suspension or dismissal of board members (23%), the temporary transfer of shares (18%), the nullification or suspension of board or shareholder resolutions (17%), the temporary deviation of provisions of the articles of association (11%), and the dissolution of the company (3%).

[51] See Art. 359 of Book 2 of the Dutch Civil Code.

Table 36.2 Inquiry requests and measures

	First stage	Second stage			
	Written request	Request sustained	Request to rule on mismanagement	Mismanagement found by court	Final injunction relief sustained
Listed companies	31	22	15	9	6
Non-listed companies	479	294	92	71	61

Source: Adapted from K. Cools, P. G. F. A. Geerts, M. J. Kroeze, & A. C. W. Pijls, Het recht van enquête, een empirisch onderzoek (2009).

Table 36.3 Length of the inquiry procedure

Period	Non-listed firms		Listed firms	
	Number	Length	Number	Length
1971–1994	99	–	4	–
1994–1999	80	mean 704 median 490	4	mean 1858 median 2024
2000–2007	300	mean 440 median 265	23	mean 564 median 447

The number of cases involving the inquiry procedure and the length of the procedure (days) for different time periods. The cases are split into non-listed and listed firms.

Source: Adapted from K. Cools, P. G. F. A. Geerts, M. J. Kroeze, and A. C. W. Pijls, Het recht van enquête, een empirisch onderzoek (2009).

procedure. Interestingly, as case law expanded, the certainty, predictability, and speed of the inquiry procedures increased (see Table 36.3). Table 36.1 shows that the length of the inquiry procedure has been considerably shorter in the recent period 2012–2014. The results highlighted here may partly explain the spur for new case demands in the same period, as shown in Figure 36.1.

An analysis of the decisions into the inquiry procedures shows that the Enterprise Chamber defined a number of situations in which there are reasonable doubts whether a company is properly managed. A large percentage of these actions involve conflicts with minority shareholders in non-listed firms. Most actions arising in the Enterprise Chamber involve the following conflicts: (1) a deadlock in the decision-making process of the company; (2) management has failed to disclose vital information to the minority shareholders; (3) conflicts of interest between managers and shareholders have arisen or have not been properly countered by the company; (4) the company does not comply with the disclosure and accounting requirements; (5) the company has no, or an unfair, dividend policy; (6) assets are being removed or reallocated to the detriment of the shareholders or other stakeholders of the company; or (7) decisions of management are challenged as being inconsistent with the rules of the Dutch Corporate Governance Code.

3.2 Stage Two: Injunctive Relief

Thus far we have looked at the number of inquiry procedure requests and measures that have been brought by listed and non-listed firms in the two-stage proceedings of the Enterprise Chamber. In this section we analyze requests for injunctive relief covering the period 2000–2008, and examine the factors contributing to the high settlement rate of these actions.

In 1994, the implementation of injunctive relief in Art. 349a (2) BW gave rise to the current popularity of the Enterprise Chamber (see Figure 36.4). Pursuant to Art. 349a (2) BW:

> where an immediate remedy is required in connection with the condition of the company or in the interest of the inquiry, the Enterprise Chamber may at any stage of the proceedings, upon the application of the persons that requested the inquiry, order preliminary injunctions for the duration of the proceedings at most.

Since then, an application for injunctive relief was the rule rather than the exception. In the period 2000–2007, out of 23 inquiry requests with respect to public firms, injunctive relief was requested in 21 of these cases; a preliminary remedy was granted in 57% of these cases. In the context of closely held firms, the number reached 234 requests for injunctive relief in 300 cases with a "success rate" of 47%.

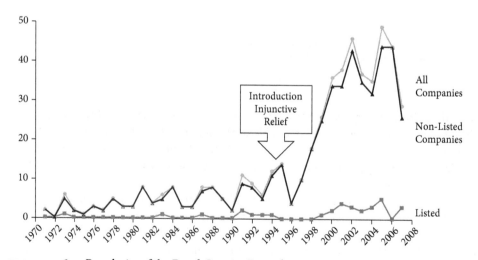

FIGURE 36.4 Popularity of the Dutch Inquiry Procedure.

Source: Adapted from K. Cools, P. G. F. A. Geerts, M. J. Kroeze, & A. C. W. Pijls, Het recht van enquête, een empirisch onderzoek (2009).

Table 36.4 Injunctive relief

	Mean	Median
Listed companies	5 days	4 days
Non-listed companies	72 days	65 days

The time length (day) before injunctive relief is granted by the Enterprise Chamber. These statistics are calculated over the period 2002–2008.

Source: Adapted from K. Cools, P. G. F. A. Geerts, M. J. Kroeze, & A. C. W. Pijls, Het recht van enquête, een empirisch onderzoek (2009).

Recall that the "fast-track" procedure, under Art. 349a (2) BW, is characterized by speed and informality. Even though the formalistic two-stage inquiry continues after the court has granted an injunctive relief, the preliminary nature of the decision furthers the judiciary's ability to assist in resolving the issues caused by the alleged improper management of the firm. Data on the number of days before an injunctive relief bears this out. During the period of 2002–2008, the average number of days before injunctive relief was granted was five days for listed and 72 for non-listed companies (see Table 36.4). On both counts, the procedure offered is clearly efficient for shareholders. Additionally, the process of injunctive relief is much quicker for publicly listed companies due to the amount of media attention and greater pressure that can be exerted by institutional investors involved in the litigation.

In terms of relief, the Enterprise Chamber has full discretion to order any preliminary remedy as it sees fit. The most popular remedies for publicly listed firms are: (1) the appointment of independent board members; (2) the prohibition of voting on particular agenda items; and (3) deviation from the articles of association.[52] Conversely, the preliminary remedies that are most popular for non-listed companies include: (1) suspending directors; and (2) suspending shareholder resolutions.[53] These results confirm our hypothesis that the inquiry procedure is not limited to mere after-the-fact adjudication. The evidence, moreover, indicates that the Enterprise Chamber procedure assists the parties in overcoming their differences by promoting informal and supposedly efficient solutions. These nonformalistic remedies offer parties an additional round of after-the-fact bargaining either by themselves or under the supervision of independent observers. The principle of

[52] The list is derived from our dataset including both listed and non-listed firms that were not involved in bankruptcy proceedings. In the period 2002–2008, the Enterprise Chamber granted more than 130 preliminary reliefs.

[53] Since the inquiry proceeding is often used in non-listed firms to resolve deadlock situations and minority squeeze-outs, the majority of resolutions that are either withdrawn or suspended include shareholder resolutions.

fast, informal, and what we call judge-initiated "mediation" or "conciliation" appears to be very attractive to minority shareholders.[54] In many cases, after the injunctive relief, the firm and its shareholders tend to follow the preliminary relief or settle their disputes amicably under the "supervision" of the Enterprise Chamber. In the context of non-listed firms, 120 out of 309 disputes in the period 2002–2008 were settled and published by the Enterprise Chamber.

3.3 The Chamber's Impact on the Governance Model in the Netherlands

In this section we document the dramatic differences in case characteristics of listed and non-listed firms. We use hand-collected data from lawsuits of the Dutch Enterprise Chamber. Our data set consists of all the 589 cases for the period 2002–2013. Most of the cases consist of non-listed companies that seek to obtain injunctions or resolve conflicts through an effective and efficient conflict-resolution process. Recall that listed firms typically have better governance mechanisms and shareholders are more likely to rely on public enforcement.[55] To explore the different dynamics of listed and non-listed firms, we split our sample and analyze the case characteristics.

Table 36.5 highlights the differences in litigation characteristics between listed and non-listed firms. Almost 90% of the cases filed in our sample are from non-listed companies. We find that proceedings on merits and Supreme Court rulings are substantially more frequently invoked in lawsuits with listed firms. For example, 55% of the cases for listed firms proceed on the merits, while only 40% for the non-listed firms. Supreme Court rulings are more frequently invoked for listed firms, about 28% for listed firms whereas only 2% of the cases for the non-listed firms. These findings support the size effect of the firm characteristics in our sample. Again, listed firms, because of their economic resources, are considerably more involved in complex litigation proceedings. Conversely, non-listed firms are typically smaller firms with fewer economic resources compared to listed firms.

In several lawsuit characteristics non-listed firms do not differ from listed firms. Surprisingly, we find no differences for interim measures taken by the court and recognition of mismanagement in lawsuits. Theory suggests that listed firms are more likely to establish good governance mechanisms than non-listed firms. As a result, mismanagement and court intervention would naturally be deemed less likely to be filed. On the other hand, listed firms may be considered mismanaged by self-interested managers in a struggle for corporate control. Indeed, it is possible to conceive of a firm as mismanaged not only if a potential conflict of interest existed, but also if it failed to take protection against such a conflict. Our data suggest, however, that listed firms are equally likely to face such matters in corporate litigation.

The data shows that, together with a decrease in rulings, the duration of the cases has strongly increased from 61 business days in 2002 to 95 business days in 2013. This result is

---

[54] This is true for both listed and non-listed companies. It appears that the inquiry proceeding is a very attractive mechanism for resolving deadlock situations in closely held firms.

[55] OECD, *supra* note 8.

Table 36.5 Summary characteristics of our sample of lawsuits from 2002 to 2013

	Listed	Non-listed
General characteristics		
Total cases 2002–2013	47	542
Average business days between filing and resolution	106	99
Mismanagement found by court	4	31
Proceeding on the merits	26	215
Supreme court ruling	13	9
Type of conflict		
Takeover	5	16
Restructuring	33	6
Merger	0	1
Conflict	8	276
Unknown	0	243
Interim measures		
Changes in statutes	6	46
Appointment of director	3	57
Appointment member of the board	4	25
Appointment member of the board with Veto	1	15

also in line with our previous conclusion from Table 36.1 on the average length of the inquiry procedure. While the average durations of court cases through the years have varied, the trend seems to be that these are increasing. This leads to a lower efficiency level in the Dutch model of corporate litigation.

Overall, these findings raise questions about the current levels of litigation and the impact of the quality of the Enterprise Chamber as a platform for conflict resolution in the Netherlands. On the other hand, the data may be explained by the fact that mediation or negotiation may have been more effective in recent years. As highlighted earlier, this would explain the notable decrease. One might expect that the Enterprise Chamber would facilitate more efficient conflict resolution outside the courtroom. Such an explanation is consistent with the evidence of longer case duration.

While efficiency reductions in conflict resolution for non-listed firms have a strong and direct effect on the Dutch economy, lower efficiency for listed firms will have a negative impact on international reputation and the possible establishment of international firms in the Netherlands. Table 36.6 shows the strong reliance of non-listed firms on the court resolution mechanism. The volume of cases involving non-listed firms has actually increased over time, while case characteristics remained relatively unchanged.

Table 36.6 Case characteristics of non–listed firms

	Total cases	Duration	Proc. merits	Interim measures	Mismanagement
2002	71	61	39	17	3
2003	73	109	30	12	6
2004	49	68	14	9	1
2005	84	108	39	21	5
2006	83	88	39	19	5
2007	82	97	27	9	4
2008	66	100	22	16	5
2009	17	131	4	3	1
2010	9	683	1	1	1
2011	2	41	0	1	0
2012	2	357	0	0	0
2013	4	95	0	2	0

The case characteristics of our sample of lawsuits for non-listed firms from 2002 to 2013. The duration of the case is measured in business days.

However, a reduction in these trends can lower the conflict resolution efficiency of the Dutch model.

Table 36.7 confirms a similarly negative effect for listed firms. While we have established differences in the characteristics of conflicts brought to court, the data show a similar time trend to that of non-listed firms. In absolute terms, the number of cases for non-listed firms have decreased over the time period, and the duration of some cases remains extensive and is unlikely to change.

Overall, this evidence suggests that the increased duration of corporate litigation will have an effect on the market. Given the great uncertainty about interim measures, the market may respond negatively to filings of cases. On the other hand, this pattern of filings may suggest improved efficiency obtained through litigation. Given the evidence, we cannot fully exclude the hypothesis that shareholders are more likely to settle through the litigation phase without a final court ruling. Note that as out-of-court settlements are typically conducted outside the public scope, empirical evidence is hard to obtain.

In this section, we have provided evidence on the important relationship between a specialized company law court and improving the quality of corporate governance at the firm level. The data indicate the important role that the Enterprise Chamber plays in the enforcement of the Dutch Corporate Governance Code and in limiting the asymmetric information problems for non-listed companies in governance conflicts. The evidence also reveals that the popularity of the Enterprise Chamber's unique two-stage inquiry procedure is linked to the success of its proceedings in balancing power in conflict-of-interest cases, and influencing the outcome of financial problems between parties. To some extent, the data presented here shows the extent to which lawmakers' commitment to the introduction and enforcement of efficient corporate-governance rules may make it possible eventually to eliminate the Dutch discount.

Table 36.7 Case characteristics of listed firms

	Total cases	Duration	Proc. merits	Interim measures	Mismanagement
2002	8	18	3	1	2
2003	5	110	3	1	0
2004	2	163	1	0	0
2005	8	48	5	3	0
2006	6	77	3	2	0
2007	3	6	3	2	0
2008	9	15	5	1	0
2009	–	–	–	–	–
2010	4	114	2	0	0
2011	1	679	0	0	1
2012	1	877	1	0	1
2013	–	–	–	–	–

The case characteristics of our sample of lawsuits for listed firms from 2002 to 2013. The symbol "–" denotes that data was not available in our sample.

4 Shareholder Wealth Effects

In Section 2, we discussed how corporate litigation could affect shareholder wealth through market reactions on firm value. Indeed, recent studies have focused on the filings effects of M&A-related lawsuits in Delaware on equity prices.[56] In this section, we present evidence of the cumulative abnormal common stock returns around the initial announcement and the final outcome of M&A-related cases in the Enterprise Chamber.

4.1 Measuring the Shareholder Wealth Effects in the Netherlands

Three central hypotheses are routinely discussed to explain the effect of acquisition-related litigation on equity prices. One explanation why derivative litigation has no impact on equity prices is that investors do not believe litigation will motivate management and deter misconduct.[57] A second explanation suggests that the market's reaction is an indication that a lawsuit will be used to negotiate a higher control premium, which should have a positive impact on share prices.[58] A third explanation documents how filings negatively impact the market's perception of the firm, leading to lower shareholder value.[59] This research suggests

[56] Krishnan, Masulis, Thomas, & Thompson, *supra* note 25; Badawi & Chen, *supra* note 1.
[57] Romano, *supra* note 2.   [58] Fischel & Bradley, *supra* note 30; Badawi & Chen, *supra* note 1.
[59] M. B. Billings, A. Klein, & E. Zur, "Shareholder Class Action Suits and the Bond Market" (2011), Working Paper, available at: http://papers.ssrn.com/sol3/papers.cfm?abstract_id=1838582.

that the market's reaction to the filing of M&A-related litigation can provide us with an indication of the litigation's impact on the firm value.

Our focus of analysis concerns two important events in the litigation process. The first event is the filing of the case at the Enterprise Chamber, which allows us to verify the effect of the market on the presence of a conflict between shareholders. The second event is the resolution of the matter in the Enterprise Chamber in which the conflict is settled by court intervention.

To measure the impact on shareholders' wealth for both events, we employ an event study for all the cases for the listed firms in our sample.[60] We collect the share prices[61] for each individual firm and regress the stock performance on the market index,[62] using the following equation

$$Return_t^i = \alpha_i + \beta_i Return_t^{Market} + \varepsilon_{t,}$$

where $Return_{t,i}$ denotes the daily stock returns of firm i at time t. The parameters α_i and β_i are estimated over a period of 200 days that ends ten days prior to the court filing. In this way, our abnormal returns derived from our estimates are not influenced by the events. Next, we determine the abnormal returns of the stock, which is the difference between the predicted return using the estimated parameters and the observed return. To analyze the effect of the events, we select a number of event windows and determine the cumulative absolute return over these periods.

Table 36.8 presents the cumulative abnormal returns (CARs) on the day of the filing of the litigation in the Enterprise Chamber and the final outcome of the litigation, as well as during the interval in between. These results are consistent with previous studies on general corporate litigation that find an average positive market response to the filing of litigation even though the firm has lost the lawsuit.[63] The data indicate that the day after the filing, the market reacts with a slight decrease in value, lowering its expectation.

The findings also confirm our hypothesis that a filing in the Dutch Enterprise Chamber may lead to a positive increase in the stock price, and therefore the conflict-resolution mechanism of the Dutch Enterprise Chamber might ultimately add value for shareholders. This impression is confirmed because the CAR over the event window [−2, 2] days is positive and significant.

We also find, on the longer horizon, a CAR that has a negative effect on the filing. On the one hand, this might indicate that case filing might lower the shareholder value. However, the event window with a longer horizon is based on a sample with only cases that have not yet been resolved. One explanation could be that over longer periods, the results suggest that these cases signal complexity to the market, causing additional uncertainty. The result is consistent with the view that after the filing, it is more likely that shareholder wealth will

---

[60] See e.g., J. Campbell, A. Lo, & A. C. MacKinlay, The Econometrics of Financial Markets (1997).

[61] All share prices are obtained using Datastream.

[62] For each individual firm we select the associated market, which is in our sample the AEX Index. As a robustness check for the market impact, we also use the MSCI World Index.

[63] Haslem, *supra* note 26.

Table 36.8 The impact of litigation on shareholder value

Window	Event	
	Filing	Resolution
[0]	0.48%*** (0.16%)	0.65%*** (0.15%)
[−2, 0]	0.25% (0.15%)	−0.05% (0.10%)
[−1, 0]	0.29%** (0.10%)	0.00% (0.13%)
[0, +1]	−0.30%** (0.11%)	0.26%*** (0.09%)
[−1, +1]	−0.22%* (0.10%)	−0.05% (0.11%)
[−2, +2]	0.21%* (0.11%)	−0.28%** (0.11%)
[−1, +10]	−0.14%* (0.06%)	−0.09% (0.08%)

The cumulative abnormal returns for the events of filing a case at the Enterprise Chamber and of a resolution by the court. Event window 0 is the abnormal return for the day of the event. Subsequent periods denote the cumulative abnormal returns and are either days before or after the events. The standard error of the coefficients are reported between brackets and significance at a level of 0.10, 0.05, 0.01 with respectively *,**,***. The total amount of companies used is 43 and varies across periods to avoid overlaps between filling and resolution events.

decrease, as uncertainty about the settlement increases. This interpretation is consistent with our view that speedy court procedures can add value for shareholders. Accordingly, if the time to settlement increases, the odds are that the market will react by lowering its expectation of the firm's value.

On the other hand, Table 36.8 shows that if the court announces a resolution, the market will respond positively. Over a period of two days before the resolution and two days after, we find a negative CAR, indicating that the resolution is costly in terms of the shareholders. However, over a longer horizon there is no significant impact on the share price. This suggests that the market has already priced the resolution at the times of the filing, which is consistent with prior US literature that the resolution of cases has little market impact.[64]

From the above analysis, it appears that the Dutch Enterprise Chamber has a reasonably similar conflict-resolution process to the Delaware court. Note, however, that while

---

[64] Romano, *supra* note 2.

Badawi and Chen find empirical evidence for the negative impact of filing a derivative suit in Delaware,[65] we show, in contrast, a positive effect associated with the filing of merger-related litigation in Amsterdam. Importantly, while cases at the Enterprise Chamber can be compared to derivative suits, as previously explained, the crucial difference is that the Enterprise Chamber is able to pursue an inquiry into management using the two-stage inquiry procedure. Yet, due to the special setting and inquiry methods, the court is able thoroughly to investigate claims in a transparent and low-cost fashion. For these and possibly other reasons, this procedure could in principle help out other countries with specialized courts to litigate mergers efficiently.

Overall, our results are consistent with the shareholder wealth effects hypothesis of litigation filings, suggesting that positive abnormal returns reflect the possibility that the case will lead to an increase in shareholder wealth. Our results are robust and suggest that the Enterprise Chamber could, over time, attract more plaintiffs in acquisition-related cases. Further, our results indicate that speed is an important factor for the Enterprise Chamber to prevent erosion of shareholder wealth.

5 CONCLUSION

The main purpose of this chapter is to examine if, absent attorney fees and monetary awards, the filing of a derivative case will add value for shareholders. Using Dutch data from the Enterprise Chamber, we show that a filing in an acquisition-related suit can have positive shareholder effects. This chapter finds that, in contrast with US literature, M&A-related litigation in the Netherland's Enterprise Chamber is associated with an abnormal return for target firms on a shorter horizon. We also show that the conflict-resolution procedure of the Enterprise Chamber appears to be very effective because of its speed and reliability. We find that the data reveal a negative effect for prolonging resolutions. However, as the US evidence shows,[66] resolutions do not necessarily improve shareholder value over a long horizon. These results support the view that markets may not fully account for how a case is resolved or the importance of complexity for interpreting the impact of the decision.

The findings of our chapter should be of interest to lawmakers and regulators who are interested in examining derivative litigation mechanisms. Our results suggest that a more effective derivative-suit mechanism can be obtained by prohibiting the use of incentives and improving speed to settlement. These findings also add further evidence as to the importance of the Dutch Enterprise Chamber's model of corporate litigation, which has significantly better outcomes in promoting shareholder wealth by relying on the impact of the proposed litigation on attorney reputations, and the prevalence of nonpecuniary settlements.

---

[65] Badawi & Chen, *supra* note 1.   [66] Haslem, *supra* note 26.

CHAPTER 37

....

THE COMPLIANCE FUNCTION
An Overview

....

GEOFFREY PARSONS MILLER

1 INTRODUCTION

....

THE compliance function consists of efforts organizations undertake to ensure that employees and others associated with the firm do not violate applicable rules, regulations, or norms. It is a form of internalized law enforcement which, if it functions effectively, can substitute for much (although not all) of the enforcement activities provided by the state. The importance of compliance and the extent of liability for its failure have greatly increased over the past decades in countries around the world. Together with its close cousins, governance and risk management, compliance is an essential internal control activity at corporations and other complex organizations.[1]

The compliance function is embodied, in part, in the fiduciary duty of directors, whose obligation to direct the management of corporations includes the responsibility to guard against illegal activities. The corporate law of compliance, however, extends beyond fiduciary duties traditionally understood. It also includes substantive regulatory statutes, criminal laws, guidance from administrative agencies, codes of best practices, internal corporate rules, and other governing norms.

This chapter will examine the following topics: the analysis of compliance within a general theory of enforcement; the development of the compliance function; the concept of internal control; the distribution of the compliance function among control personnel;

---

[1] Legal scholarship on the law of compliance is as yet underdeveloped. Important early contributions include Jennifer Arlen & Reinier Kraakman, "Controlling Corporate Misconduct: an Analysis of Corporate Liability Regimes", 72 N.Y.U. L. Rev. 687 (1997); Donald C. Langevoort, "Monitoring: The Behavioral Economics of Corporate Compliance with Law", 2002 Colum. Bus. L. Rev. 71 (2002). For recent work, see, e.g., Geoffrey Miller, The Law of Governance, Risk Management and Compliance (2014); Miriam Baer, "Governing Corporate Compliance", 50 B. C. L. Rev. 949 (2009); James Fanto, "Advising Compliance in Financial Firms: A New Mission for the Legal Academy", 8 Brook. J. Corp. Fin. & Com. L. 1 (2013).

oversight obligations of directors and executives; compliance programs and policies; internal investigations; whistleblowers; criminal enforcement; compliance outside the firm; and business ethics beyond formal compliance.

2 COMPLIANCE IN A THEORY OF ENFORCEMENT

At the most general level, compliance involves a trade-off of costs and benefits. On the one hand, compliance can be a cheaper and more effective means to ensure that complex organizations obey applicable norms. The reason is that an external norm enforcer may not have the resources or the ability either to detect violations or to devise an effective system of sanctions. The organization has the knowledge and the ability more effectively to perform these tasks. It therefore makes sense for institutions to police themselves—to carry out a compliance operation.

On the other hand, because compliance delegates responsibility for norm enforcement to the organization, the external enforcer (regulator, prosecutor, etc.) loses some degree of control over the situation: It may be perilous to rely on an institution to police itself when the institution wants to flout the norm or to cover up violations. Accordingly, the external enforcer needs to monitor the compliance function to ensure that it is faithfully and effectively carried out—adding to aggregate social costs.

There is also a problem of incentives. When the external enforcer operates directly, rather than through a compliance program, the enforcer bears most of the costs of the enforcement activity. It has an incentive to perform in a cost-effective way. When, however, the external enforcer relies on internal compliance to enforce norms, the enforcer does not bear the costs of enforcement; these are imposed on the organization. Since the external enforcer doesn't internalize the costs of compliance, it may demand that the organization implement compliance operations which are costly but not particularly effective or necessary.

The job of policy makers is to devise a system which minimizes total costs of norm enforcement and norm violations. This task cannot be performed scientifically. Lawmakers are not structural engineers. When it comes to designing a compliance system much is done by intuition and guesswork. Nevertheless, in examining any given compliance system, we can still ask the basic questions: Does it draw the right line between internal and external enforcement; are the requirements appropriate, insufficient, or excessive; are there sufficient backup lines of defense; and overall, does the chosen structure represent a reasonable trade-off of costs and benefits.

3 DEVELOPMENT OF THE COMPLIANCE FUNCTION

The history of the compliance function across the world remains to be written. Every country has a different history of compliance reflecting its unique legal, historical, and political circumstances. It appears, however, that two elements play a principal role.

First, compliance is a function of the enormous growth of the administrative state. This chapter will discuss developments in the United States; similar developments occurred in many countries around the world. In the case of the US, the compliance function might be said to have started in the Interstate Commerce Act of 1887, which created a federal administrative agency, the Interstate Commerce Commission, to regulate the railroads. The Progressive Movement of the 1890s through 1920s, another important step in the development of compliance, reflected concern for eliminating corruption and enhancing the efficiency of government. Among its achievements were the Pure Food and Drug Act (1906), the Federal Reserve Act (1913), and the Clayton antitrust law (1914). The collapse of financial markets and the Depression of the 1930s led to the Banking Act of 1933, the Securities Acts of 1933 and 1934, and other regulatory enactments. More generally, this period witnessed a change in attitude on the Supreme Court, from one that resisted regulation of business to one that enthusiastically embraced it.

In more recent times, the rise of environmental concerns in the 1960s sparked a series of important federal statutes, including the Clean Water Act and the Clean Air Act, as well as the birth of a new federal administrative body, the Environmental Protection Agency. In the mid-1970s, revelations of American companies bribing foreign officials led to the Foreign Corrupt Practices Act in 1977. In the 1980s, the collapse of savings and loan institutions shook America's confidence in the integrity of the financial system and sparked legislation that upgraded banking regulation in many respects. The corporate scandals of the early 2000s, including spectacular failures of Enron and other firms, led to the enactment of the Sarbanes–Oxley Act (2002). The terror attacks of September 2001 focussed attention on new threats to national security and triggered enhanced obligations to report suspicious activities and combat terror financing. Finally, the financial crisis of 2007–2009 undermined public confidence in banks and financial markets and led to a host of new regulations, including the Dodd–Frank Act of 2010.

These and other events punctuated what has been a broader and more "tectonic" change in American law. In the nineteenth century, relations between corporations and the state followed a judicial model in which the government was required to prove its case in court like any other litigant. Due to changes in constitutional doctrine and administrative law, the judicial model no longer accurately describes the government's relationship with regulated firms. Governments today possess awesome powers of enforcement and authority to impose devastating penalties, often with only minimal judicial involvement.[2]

The contemporary law of compliance in the US is profoundly influenced by these developments. Corporations faced with compliance problems are sometimes better described as supplicants seeking mercy from their regulators rather than as equal adversaries. Facing severe penalties for violations and significantly reduced powers to defend themselves in court, organizations have a strong incentive to internalize the law enforcement function by instituting procedures to guard against misconduct by their employees.

The second key factor that influences the growth of compliance is the globalization of enterprise and the parallel growth of service providers in the areas of internal control that have played a major role in standardizing the compliance activities of multinational firms. A global enterprise with operations in dozens of countries cannot, as a practical matter, operate independent compliance operations in every country where it does business. Even if

---

[2] For skeptical analysis of the rise of the administrative state, see Richard Epstein, Design for Liberty: Private Property, Public Administration, and the Rule of Law (2011); Gary Lawson, "The Rise and Rise of the Administrative State", 107 Harv. L. Rev. 1221 (1994).

it wished to operate in this fashion, doing so would not be wise because the activities of the enterprise cannot be hermetically sealed within national silos. Further, international organizations utilize consultants and other service providers, and look to models developed in similar institutions as prototypes for their open operations. These institutions operate in a world corporate culture in which developments that occur in one country or in one institution or one industry quickly transmit themselves to many others.

4 The Concept of Internal Control

Compliance is a form of internal control. The concept of internal control suggests that a well-managed organization is one in which assets and resources are effectively deployed to serve the purposes of the corporation. At one time in corporate history, a function of internal control was assigned to the corporate charter which would specify the purposes for which the firm was established and enumerate the powers it could exercise. Actions by a corporation that went beyond the purposes or powers so defined were ultra vires and wholly or partly unenforceable. In the modern corporation, however, purposes and powers restrictions have been all but nullified. The resulting gap has been filled by contemporary notions of internal control.

The leading statement of internal control in the modern business enterprise is set forth by the Committee of Sponsoring Organizations of the Treadway Commission (COSO), an umbrella of groups in the fields of accounting, auditing, and financial management.[3] COSO's *Integrated Framework* is the standard most public company auditors employ to evaluate management's assessment of the company's internal controls. COSO describes internal control as "a process, effected by an entity's board of directors, management and other personnel, designed to provide reasonable assurance regarding the achievement of objectives relating to operations, reporting, and compliance."[4] Internal control, so defined, consists of the following components: control environment, risk assessment, control activities, information and communication, and monitoring activities.

As implemented within firms, the concept of internal control is embodied in the metaphor of the "Three Lines of Defense." The metaphor associates internal control with the process of defending territory from an external threat. It stresses the gravity of breakdowns in the internal control function; defines the threat as external to the organization; and offers reassurance that if control functions are properly designed and maintained, the threat of a breakdown can be kept within tolerable limits.

The first line of defense is the operating units and the heads of the entities, offices, or divisions that carry out business activities. These people are named first because if they do not transgress applicable norms, the organization will not commit violations. But the metaphor also recognizes that the operating units cannot be relied on fully as a bulwark against violations, both because the line employees are not compliance professionals and

---

[3] See http://www.coso.org/. The principal author of the 2013 COSO framework is the global accounting and auditing firm PricewaterhouseCoopers.

[4] Committee of Sponsoring Organizations of the Treadway Commission, Internal Control—Integrated Framework (2013).

because they may experience incentives to test limits in order to enhance their status or compensation.

The second line of defense consists of persons or offices charged with carrying out monitoring and control activities. Two second-line offices are most important: the senior official responsible for preventing and/or detecting violations of legal norms (chief compliance officer or general counsel); and the chief risk officer, whose job is to ensure that the risks undertaken by the line employees are consistent with the risk appetite established by the board of directors.

The third line of defense, which is supposed to catch problems that filter through the first two, is internal audit. The internal audit department is responsible for checking on the entire organization, including senior managers, in order to ensure that policies and procedures are being observed and shortcomings in the organization's internal controls are identified and promptly fixed.

The metaphor of the three lines of defense is useful, but also incomplete and inaccurate. It omits to mention other important controls that serve to catch and correct problems that get past internal audit: the board of directors (especially the audit committee), the external auditor, and, for regulated firms, the government supervisor. Even more broadly, the concept of control includes figures such as activist shareholders, proxy advisory firms, takeover bidders, and the financial press, all of whom, to one degree or another, monitor the behavior of the organization's managers. The metaphor of the three lines of defense also fails to capture the ambiguous role of the second and third lines, which are supposed to operate as independent checks on the business lines, but at the same are themselves part of the management team.

5 Distribution of the Compliance Function

As suggested in the concept of the three lines of defense, the compliance function is distributed across institutions rather than being centralized in any single person or office. The distribution of responsibility is often unclear and varies from organization to organization.

To address the lack of clarity as to role responsibilities, a United Kingdom reform proposed in 2014 would require banks to maintain and disclose a "management responsibilities map" describing how control functions are allocated across the firm, outlining reporting lines and lines of responsibility, and providing detailed information about senior managers and their responsibilities.[5]

In the US, the Volcker Rule, which restricts proprietary trading by banks, requires large depository institutions to implement a framework that clearly delineates responsibility and accountability for compliance.[6] As yet, however, the US has not implemented more general requirements for disclosing the allocation of compliance responsibilities.

---

[5] See Bank of England Prudential Regulation Authority, Strengthening Accountability in Banking: a New Regulatory Framework (July 2014).

[6] Office of the Comptroller of the Currency, Board of Governors of the Federal Reserve System, Federal Deposit Insurance Corporation, and Securities and Exchange Commission, Prohibitions and Restrictions on Proprietary Trading and Certain Interests in, and Relationships with, Hedge Funds and Private Equity Funds (January 31, 2014), Subpart D.

5.1 The Board of Directors

It has always been clear that the board's responsibility for directing the management of a corporation includes a duty to oversee the activities of employees to ensure that they do not break rules.[7] The contours of this fiduciary duty of oversight, however, have evolved over time.

In the US, the business judgment rule, which protects directors against personal liability for actions undertaken in good faith, long appeared to provide a shield that protected directors in compliance cases. It is true that if a director failed to act as a director *at all*, the business judgment rule would not protect against liability.[8] But if a director carried out even minimal responsibilities and did not willfully ignore evidence of illegal conduct, corporate law provided substantial immunity.

This shielding of directors was problematic from the standpoint of public policy. The discretion afforded to directors under the business judgment rule is appropriate for ordinary business decisions because the incentives of shareholders align with the interests of society. In the case of compliance violations, however, illegal behavior might increase rather than reduce profits (an example is bribery to obtain lucrative contracts). In such cases, the business judgment rule threatened to immunize conduct inimical to the public interest. The problem became even more acute after Delaware authorized charter provisions that shield directors from monetary liability in duty of care cases.[9]

Delaware courts have attempted to remediate this problem. The theory, endorsed in *Stone v. Ritter*,[10] is that the director's duty of compliance is an aspect of the duty of loyalty, and therefore cannot be shielded by the business judgment rule or exculpated by charter amendment.[11] This duty requires directors to implement a "reporting or information system or controls"; and to "monitor or oversee" the operation of the system once implemented.[12] The meaningfulness of these duties is undercut, however, by the leniency of the standard of care: directors are liable only if they utterly fail to implement a compliance program or consciously fail to monitor its operations.[13] Delaware's approach to compliance thus has a curiously ambivalent quality: directors are subject to significant obligations, but are held liable only if they fail to manifest even minimal efforts.[14] Although Delaware might be criticized as ineffectual, the state's approach arguably influences attitudes within the boardroom and empowers lawyers to encourage clients to upgrade compliance efforts.

---

[7] E.g., Del. Gen. Corp. Law § 144(a).   [8] *Francis v. Jersey Bank*, 432 A.2d 814 (1981).

[9] Del. Gen. Corp. Law § 102(b)(7).

[10] *Stone v. Ritter*, 911 A.2d 362 (Del. 2006). The original and still most important explanation of the board's oversight liability is *In re Caremark International Inc. Derivative Litigation*, 698 A.2d 959 (Del. Ch. 1996).

[11] See Claire A. Hill & Brett H. McDonnell, "Stone v. Ritter and the Expanding Duty of Loyalty", 76 Fordham L. Rev. 1769 (2007).

[12] *Stone v. Ritter*, 911 A.2d at 370.   [13] Id.

[14] Cases that generate liability tend to involve egregious facts and companies operated out of countries with poor reputations for corporate governance. See, e.g., *Rich ex rel. Fuqi Intern., Inc. v. Yu Kwai Chong*, 66 A.3d 693 (Del. Ch. 2013).

In addition to liability for breach of fiduciary duty, directors may face exposure under regulatory statutes for failure to exercise oversight over compliance.[15] As yet the scope of this more general oversight liability is unclear. Future cases may clarify which regulatory statutes can support oversight liability, whether oversight liability can be based on negligence, and in what circumstances members of boards of directors face liability for money damages under this theory.

While the full board is charged with assuring compliance, primary responsibility is often allocated to committees. The audit committee is most important. Often the audit committee charter includes a specific reference to compliance, and key officers in the second and third lines may have substantive reports to the audit committee rather than to a senior executive. Other committees also play a role in compliance. Some firms have established committees with responsibility for compliance matters. The compensation committee can become involved because of the link between the incentives created by compensation arrangements and the propensity of managers to test the limits of legality. The nominating and governance committee may play a role, especially in cases where a member of the board or a senior manager is accused of wrongdoing.

5.2 The Management Team

Some compliance obligations are imposed on senior managers as a team. Section 404(a) of the US Sarbanes–Oxley Act requires that a reporting company's annual report must contain an "internal control report" which states "the responsibility of management for establishing and maintaining an adequate internal control structure and procedures for financial reporting."[16] The report must also contain management's assessment of the effectiveness of these procedures.[17] SEC regulations require reporting firms to "maintain disclosure controls and procedures" and "internal control over financial reporting."[18] "Disclosure controls or procedures" are designed to ensure that the necessary information "is accumulated and communicated to the issuer's management, including its principal executive and principal financial officers, or persons performing similar functions, as appropriate to allow timely decisions regarding required disclosure."[19]

5.3 The CEO

The chief executive officer (CEO) is the public face of a firm—the living embodiment and symbol of the institution in the eyes of the public and its regulators. She is ultimately responsible for decisions the organization makes (subject to oversight by the board). Most importantly, from the standpoint of compliance, the CEO is responsible for setting the "tone at the top"—a culture, flowing from the highest management level, which endorses scrupulous adherence to applicable rules and norms. For this reason, even if only a relatively small

---

[15] See *In the Matter of Steven A. Cohen*, S.E.C. Administrative Proceeding No. 3-15382 (2013). Although this action was not brought against a senior executive, the legal arguments would appear to carry over to proceedings against directors.

[16] Sarbanes–Oxley Act § 404, 15 U.S.C. § 7262.   [17] Id.   [18] See 17 CFR 240.13a–15(a).

[19] Id. § 240.13a–15(e).

percentage of her time is spent on compliance matters, the CEO is in a real sense the most important compliance officer in the organization.

Aside from the responsibility to establish a healthy tone at the top, CEOs have more specific compliance obligations. Section 302 of the Sarbanes–Oxley Act requires the CEO and chief financial officer (CFO) to certify that a public company's annual and quarterly reports are not misleading and that the information included in the reports fairly presents the financial condition and results of operations of the issuer.[20] In addition, the CEO and CFO must certify that they "are responsible for establishing and maintaining internal controls"; have "designed such internal controls to ensure that material information relating to the issuer and its consolidated subsidiaries is made known to such officers by others within those entities"; have "evaluated the effectiveness of the issuer's internal controls"; and have "presented in the report their conclusions about the effectiveness of their internal controls." [21]

The CEO and CFO must also certify that they have disclosed to the issuer's auditors and the board audit committee: "all significant deficiencies in the design or operation of internal controls which could adversely affect the issuer's ability to record, process, summarize, and report financial data and have identified for the issuer's auditors any material weaknesses in internal controls;" as well as "any fraud, whether or not material, that involves management or other employees who have a significant role in the issuer's internal controls."[22] The signing officers must indicate "whether or not there were significant changes in internal controls or in other factors that could significantly affect internal controls subsequent to the date of their evaluation, including any corrective actions with regard to significant deficiencies and material weaknesses."[23]

A related provision, § 906 of the Sarbanes–Oxley Act, requires that an issuer's periodic reports to the SEC be accompanied by a written statement of the CEO and CFO certifying that the information contained in the reports "fairly presents, in all material respects, the financial condition and results of operations of the issuer."[24] Anyone who certifies a financial statement that does not comport with this requirement is subject to criminal penalties: up to 10 years' imprisonment if the officer acted "knowing that the periodic report accompanying the statement does not comport with all the requirements," and up to twenty years if the officer acted "willfully."[25]

5.4 The Chief Compliance/Chief Legal Officer

Many organizations active in international business employ a senior officer who has explicit authority for compliance. Traditionally, that officer was the in-house general counsel (GC). Many organizations continue to assign compliance to general counsels, but others have vested the responsibility in a chief compliance officer (CCO), who is usually but not always an attorney. The rationale for creating the CCO position is the inherent tension in the GC's role: Is the person charged with overseeing compliance supposed to be a zealous advocate for the organization's interests in regulatory matters, or does she owe professional duties to a broader public? By separating the roles, organizations allow the GC to act with undivided

---

[20] Sarbanes–Oxley Act § 302, 15 U.S.C. § 7241(a)(4).   [21] Id.   [22] 15 U.S.C. § 1782(a)(4).
[23] 15 U.S.C. § 1782(a)(6).   [24] 18 U.S.C. § 1350(b).   [25] 18 U.S.C. § 1350(c).

loyalty to the client without being subject to potentially countervailing obligations to the public.[26]

To what extent should the CCO act independently of the CEO and other senior executives? There are advantages and disadvantages to any arrangement. Requiring the CCO to report to another executive officer—the CEO, the CFO, the GC, or perhaps the chief risk officer (CRO)—has the virtue of centralizing management and bringing an advocate for compliance into the senior management team. On the other hand, making the CCO subordinate to other executive officials can be dangerous when the boss might herself be involved in a violation. Considerations such as these suggest that the CCO should be given a direct reporting line to the board of directors or to the audit or compliance committee, and that the CCO may also be given a degree of budgetary independence. One common solution is for the CCO to report substantively to the audit committee and administratively to an executive such as the CFO or CEO.

The CCO can perform her job effectively only if she has unfettered access to information about the firm. Organizations thus need to empower CCOs to expect full cooperation from others in the organization. In the case of US mutual funds, such an expectation is guaranteed by law. SEC Rule 38a-1(c) prohibits an officer, director, or employee of a mutual fund or its investment advisor from taking any action to coerce, manipulate, mislead, or fraudulently influence the fund's chief compliance officer in the performance of her duties.[27]

Even in the absence of a statute, the power and independence of compliance officers has increased as a result of judicial decisions. An example is *UBS v. Communale Wasserwerke Leipzig*, [2014] EWHC 3615 (Comm), a 2014 decision of the Commercial Court of the British High Court of Justice holding a bank responsible for contracts procured through bribery; even though bank officials were not shown to have any direct culpability in the misconduct. An important fact that appeared to have influenced the decision is the finding that senior bank officials interested in obtaining large profits had overruled the bank's compliance department's objections to the deal.

The activities and powers of the CCO are generally defined in internal documents. In some cases, however, the law imposes non-delegable duties on these officials. In the US, for example, the Dodd–Frank Act's rules regulating swap dealers require the CCO to review and ensure the registrant's compliance with the Commodities Exchange Act (CEA), to resolve conflicts of interest, and to establish procedures for remediation of noncompliance. The CCO must prepare and sign an annual report describing the registrant's compliance with the CEA, the code of ethics, and the internal conflict of interest policy.[28]

What happens if the CCO doesn't perform effectively? In ordinary business settings, an officer who falls down on the job will face pay cuts, demotion, transfer, or dismissal. But these measures may not be effective in the case of the CCO, since that officer must monitor senior officials who determine the CCO's compensation and authority. Addressing this problem, the US SEC imposes supervisory liability on broker dealer CCOs who fail to prevent or detect wrongdoing. A difficulty here is an allegedly ineffective CCO may defend on the ground that they were not a supervisor of the culpable employee.[29]

---

[26] For an argument for the continuing importance of the general counsel, see Norman Veasey & Christine T. Di Guglielmo, The Indispensable Counsel: The Chief Legal Officer in the New Reality (2012).

[27] 17 CFR 270.38a–1(c).   [28] 7 U.S.C. §§ 6d(d), 6s(k).

[29] See *In the Matter of Theodore W. Urban*, SEC Administrative Proceeding File No. 3-13655 (2010), available at https://www.sec.gov/litigation/aljdec/2010/id402bpm.pdf; SEC Division of Trading and

5.5 The Chief Audit Executive

The internal audit function is carried out by a department within a firm. Internal audit departments are led by people with titles such as "Chief Audit Executive." The head of internal audit often has a direct reporting line to the chief executive officer—a formal acknowledgment that the audit function is not subject to the control of any other department and a recognition that the head of internal audit has rights of access to the senior leadership. At the board level, the head of internal audit reports principally to the board audit committee.

What is the relationship between internal audit and the external auditor? On the one hand, the two operate at arm's length. The external auditor reviews all aspects of financial controls, including internal audit. In this respect, the external auditor is an independent and potentially exacting critic. On the other hand, internal audit typically cooperates in the external audit, reducing the independence of the two functions to some extent. External audit may also help empower internal audit in cases where others in the organization are impeding the latter's work. In such cases, internal audit may find a way to get its needs met through the (more powerful) voice of the external auditor.

5.6 The Chief Risk Officer

Many financial institutions and an increasing number of other organizations have created specialized risk management offices headed by a CRO. The CRO has an important, although indirect, role in compliance. Compliance risk is one of the most important threats facing an organization, and therefore a matter falling within the natural purview of the CRO. Accordingly, when an organization hosts both a CRO and a CCO, the two offices must operate according to a border treaty that establishes the boundary between their respective responsibilities.

6 COMPLIANCE PROGRAMS, POLICIES, AND CONTRACTS

The compliance function is implemented through compliance policies, programs, and contracts. A compliance policy is a statement of an organization's approach to ensuring adherence to its normative obligations, approved by the board of directors or other managing body, and announced internally and externally as representing the organization's approach to carrying out this responsibility. A compliance program is a detailed statement of how

Markets, Frequently Asked Questions about Liability of Compliance and Legal Personnel at Broker Dealers under Sections 15(b)(4) and 15(b)6) of the Exchange Act, available at www.sec.gov/divisions/marketreg/faq-cco-supervision-093013.htm (opining that compliance and legal personnel are not per se supervisors, but that this status "depends on whether, under the facts and circumstances of a particular case, that person has the requisite degree of responsibility, ability or authority to affect the conduct of the employee whose behavior is in issue").

the organization intends to carry out the obligations that it has recognized in its compliance policy. In addition to these internal documents, the compliance function increasingly involves a host of representations, commitments, rights, and obligations contained in contractual agreements with counterparties, in areas as diverse as vendor risk management and supply chain due diligence.[30]

Most large organizations have adopted compliance policies and compliance programs. There are many reasons for doing so. Such activities reduce board members' potential liability under *Stone v. Ritter*. Implementing a robust compliance program can also shield managers from regulatory oversight liability. For example, the US Securities and Exchange Act of 1934 contains a safe harbor protecting against supervisory liability if "there have been established procedures, and a system for applying such procedures, which would reasonably be expected to prevent and detect [violations]."[31]

Organizations have other reasons to adopt compliance programs. In some cases, the law directly requires regulated industries to do so. An example is the US Bank Secrecy Act, a law which seeks to combat money laundering and the financing of illegal activities. This statute requires banks to establish anti-money-laundering programs with explicit compliance requirements.[32] Similarly, the SEC has adopted regulations under the Investment Advisors Act and the Investment Company Act, which require regulated investment companies and their advisors to create and maintain compliance programs.[33] The Dodd–Frank Act, likewise, requires swap dealers and major swap participants to designate a chief compliance officer who reports to the board of directors or CEO.[34]

Corporations also establish or upgrade compliance programs as a result of regulatory enforcement actions. Settlements of regulatory enforcement actions often include undertakings to enhance compliance activities. A similar pattern is observed in criminal cases: prosecutors demand that targets upgrade compliance programs as a condition to deferred prosecution or non-prosecution agreements.[35] These programs, adopted in the shadow of enforcement proceedings, will not necessarily be the same as the ones that the firms would have chosen in the absence of an enforcement action. Among other things, settlement agreements often provide for the retention of a third party monitor to verify that the target fulfills its commitments.

Compliance programs are affected by private litigation. Shareholders' derivative lawsuits challenging misconduct sometimes terminate in a settlement under which the company commits to implement "prophylactic" reforms to internal governance, often including reforms to processes of internal control. Compliance obligations may also be included in settlements of *qui tam* litigation brought by private parties in the name of the government.

---

[30] For valuable discussion, see Scott Killingsworth, The Privatization of Compliance, RAND Center for Corporate Ethics and Governance Symposium White Paper Series, Symposium on Transforming Compliance: Emerging Paradigms for Boards, Management, Compliance Officers, and Government (2014).

[31] 15 U.S.C. § 78o(b)(4)(E).   [32] 31 U.S.C. 5318(h).

[33] SEC Rule 206(4)-7; SEC Rule 38a-1.   [34] 7 U.S.C. §§ 6d(d), 6s(k).

[35] For a skeptical evaluation of the role of prosecutors in corporate governance, see Jennifer Arlen, Removing Prosecutors from the Boardroom; Deterring Crime without Prosecutor Interference in Corporate Governance, in Prosecutors in the Boardroom 267 (Anthony Barkow & Rachel Barkow eds., 2011).

Less commonly, compliance-related settlements are negotiated in class action litigation challenging allegedly illegal conduct.

Firms also implement compliance programs in order to mitigate the severity of enforcement. Regulators consider an organization's commitment to compliance when they decide whether to initiate enforcement actions. Federal prosecutors undertake a similar analysis: if a potential defendant has operated a compliance program and has cooperated wholeheartedly with the investigation, these factors will count in the decision whether or not to charge the entity.

An organization's compliance-related conduct is also taken into account at the penalty stage. Among civil regulators, the US Environmental Protection Agency is a leader in promising to mitigate the severity of sanctions if the defendant demonstrates sufficient cooperation and evidences a commitment to compliant behavior.[36] As for criminal conduct, the US Sentencing Guidelines provide for credit in sentencing to organizations that operate effective compliance programs, even if the program in question failed to deter or detect the criminal conduct.[37]

Conversely, an organization that implements a compliance program but then fails to administer it in an effective manner can suffer enhanced penalties. In 2011 the US SEC rolled out a policy applicable to firms that are warned about deficiencies in their compliance programs, fail to correct the problem, and subsequently commit violations. The program encourages firms to adopt robust compliance programs because if they do not do so and are warned about the problem, they will receive especially harsh treatment in the event of a violation.[38]

7 ELEMENTS OF A ROBUST COMPLIANCE PROGRAM

It is obvious that the mere creation of a compliance program will not ensure results. The program must also be effective.[39]

Perhaps the earliest statement of the requirements for a robust compliance program in the US is contained in the Federal Sentencing Guidelines, promulgated in 1991.[40] To qualify for potential reductions in sentencing, an organization must "exercise due diligence to prevent and detect criminal conduct; and otherwise promote an organizational culture that encourages ethical conduct and a commitment to compliance with the law." The organization must establish standards and procedures to prevent and detect criminal conduct; ensure that its governing authority understands the content and operation of the program and exercises reasonable oversight over its implementation; conduct effective training programs;

---

[36] See Environmental Protection Agency, "Incentives for Self-Policing: Discovery, Disclosure, Correction and Prevention of Violations", 65 Fed. Reg. 19,618 (Apr. 11, 2000).

[37] Federal Sentencing Guideline §8B2.1; §8C2.5(f).

[38] See, e.g., *In re: Modern Portfolio Management, Inc.*, SEC File No. 3-15583 (2013), available at http://www.sec.gov/litigation/admin/2013/ia-3702.pdf.

[39] See Geoffrey Miller, An Economic Analysis of Effective Compliance Programs, in Research Handbook on Corporate Crime and Financial Misdealing (Jennifer Arlen ed., 2018).

[40] Federal Sentencing Guideline §8B2.1, Effective Compliance and Ethics Program.

establish incentives to comply and disciplinary sanctions for noncompliance; and take reasonable steps to respond to the criminal conduct and to prevent repeat violations.

Other official pronouncements identify somewhat different ingredients of a robust compliance program. The Bank Secrecy Act specifies four elements: internal policies, procedures, and controls; a compliance officer; an employee training program; and an independent audit function.[41] The US Department of Justice notes 10 features: high-level commitment to compliance; written policies; peer-based review; oversight and independence of compliance officers; training and guidance for employees; internal reporting; investigation; enforcement and discipline; oversight of agents and business partners; and monitoring and testing.[42] The SEC and Department of Justice, in joint guidance on foreign corrupt practices, identify the following factors: commitment from senior management; code of conduct and compliance policies and procedures; oversight, autonomy, and resources; risk assessment; training and advice; incentives and disciplinary measures; third-party due diligence; confidential reporting and internal investigation; testing and review; and pre-acquisition due diligence and post-acquisition integration in mergers and acquisitions.[43]

The Volcker Rule, jointly promulgated by federal banking agencies, requires that the compliance programs of mid-sized banks satisfy the following six elements: written policies and procedures; a system of internal controls; a management framework that clearly delineates responsibility and accountability for compliance; independent testing and audit of the effectiveness of the compliance program; training for trading personnel and managers; and making and keeping records sufficient to demonstrate compliance.[44] In the case of megabanks, the rule mandates enhanced programs with more detailed policies, limits, governance processes, independent testing and reporting, and CEO attestation.[45]

Several features of robust compliance discussions warrant further discussion. One is the idea of "tone at the top." The concept is vague and indefinite, and it is all too easy for an unscrupulous CEO to mouth the right words while secretly subverting performance. Nevertheless, many government officials and compliance professionals view tone at the top as essential.[46] Part of the challenge of an effective compliance program is to signal the credibility of senior managers' commitment to compliant behavior.

Another key feature is controls over hiring. If an organization hires only employees of outstanding character, it is unlikely to run into compliance problems down the line. The problem is how to sort between good and bad candidates. People do not show up at the job interview bearing signs signaling the quality of their character. Human resources departments have developed a number of techniques to overcome this information asymmetry. The organization

---

[41] 31 U.S.C. 5318(h).

[42] Remarks by Assistant Attorney General for the Criminal Division Leslie R. Caldwell (October 1, 2014).

[43] U.S. Department of Justice and Securities and Exchange Commission, A Resource Guide to the U.S. Foreign Corrupt Practices Act (November 2012).

[44] Office of the Comptroller of the Currency, Board of Governors of the Federal Reserve System, Federal Deposit Insurance Corporation, and Securities and Exchange Commission, Prohibitions and Restrictions on Proprietary Trading and Certain Interests in, and Relationships with, Hedge Funds and Private Equity Funds (January 31, 2014), Subpart D.

[45] Id.

[46] On the relationship between institutional values and compliance, see Tom R. Tyler, "Reducing Corporate Criminality: The Role of Values", 51 Am. Crim. L. Rev. 267 (2014).

may investigate a job candidate's arrests, convictions, bankruptcies, credit scores, and employment history. The HR department may administer psychological assessments and may require employees and candidates to undergo drug or alcohol tests. These investigative techniques can be effective, but also pose legal risks. The organization must be careful not to cross the line into employment discrimination or illegal intrusions on privacy.

Yet another key feature of a robust compliance program is employee training. A robust program should inform traders, salespeople, and other employees about their obligations and—if possible—encourage them to internalize an ethical norm against shady dealing. Organizations devote considerable ingenuity to finding ways to ensure that the lessons conveyed during employee training have a real impact on behavior. Barclays, a large British bank, may have gone as far as any institution in this regard. In addition to making ethics training available to approximately 140,000 of its employees, Barclays has established a "Compliance Career Academy," a joint effort with the Cambridge Judge Business School, to deliver compliance training in Cambridge, Johannesburg, New York, and Singapore.[47]

Compliance programs may also include controls such as record keeping, reporting, data analysis, and sign-off requirements. Record keeping creates an audit trail that internal audit or other investigators can use to check on potential violations. Compliance officers can use the power of "big data" to identify red flags of potential misconduct; a host of vendors offer software, systems, and services to assist firms in implementing such analytic methods. Sign-off requirements call a supervisor's attention to decisions that might implicate compliance concerns, and operate as a check against uninformed or unethical behavior by junior staff.

Merely undertaking the steps described above is no guarantee that the program will function well. It is possible to establish a "paper program" that includes state-of-the-art compliance procedures but still operates ineffectively. Enron's cutting-edge compliance program failed to prevent one of the largest frauds in American history (although, in fairness, it should be noted that Sherron Watkins, the Enron whistleblower, did take advantage of one feature of Enron's program when she elevated concerns about the organization's financial shenanigans to the highest management level).

Regulators are taking an increasingly active interest in the compliance programs operated by firms they oversee. This interest involves not only obtaining extensive information about the nature and operations of the program,[48] but also substantive involvement in assessing whether the program is adequate to meet the regulators' expectations.

---

[47] See Joe Mont, "Amid Regulatory Woes, Barclays Launches Compliance Career Academy", Compliance Week, July 7, 2014, available at http://www.complianceweek.com/blogs/the-filing-cabinet/amid-regulatory-woes-barclays-launches-compliance-career-academy-0#.VOpJoHzF8mo.

[48] In the UK, for example, the Financial Conduct Authority requires certain applicants for authorization to offer consumer credit to provide information about their compliance monitoring programs, including factors such as what checks will take place, how often checks will take place, who will carry out the checks, what records the firm will keep of the checks to confirm they have been undertaken, the applicant's complaints procedures, training and competence procedures, and staff disciplinary processes. See http://www.fca.org.uk/firms/firm-types/consumer-credit/authorisation/prepare/terms-explained.

8 INVESTIGATIONS

Once an organization has received evidence of a violation, it must determine what to do. In many cases, the next step is an investigation which seeks to ferret out the underlying facts. Some companies have spent millions or tens of millions of dollars a year in an effort to get to the bottom of potential violations.

Compliance investigations come in two general types. One concerns the routine violations that occur at any workforce. Typically, organizations have a set procedure for such cases. Investigations of minor misconduct are almost always conducted in-house, and may be undertaken by the human resources department under the direction of in-house counsel. The other type of internal investigation is the large-scale inquiry associated with violations that are serious, systematic, or likely to result in government enforcement actions. These investigations are often outsourced to law firms which specialize in the practice area; the reasons are that the organization may not have the resources in-house for such a major undertaking and that enlisting the aid of an independent attorney may induce leniency by the regulators. A downside of outside investigations is that organizations lose control of costs: having assigned a third party to perform the inquiry, they cannot afford to be seen as denying the investigators the resources needed to pursue their inquiry wherever it may lead.

A notable feature of internal investigations is the fact that employees enjoy few of the rights that would be afforded to them if the investigation were being carried out by the government. Private employers are not bound by constitutional norms. Further, because employees generally lack an expectation of privacy in the workplace, there are few limits on what the employer may scrutinize: the employer can read the target's emails, monitor her web-browsing habits, listen to her voicemails, train video cameras on her (in public spaces), confiscate her hard drive, interview her without disclosing that she is under suspicion, and deny her the right to counsel during such interrogations. Even worse, from the employee's point of view, information obtained by the employer during such an investigation may be turned over to the government, and can even be used by the organization as a strategy for obtaining leniency for itself.[49]

Employees found to have committed a compliance violation will often be summarily terminated under circumstances that are hard to explain to other employers. They may lose their professional reputations. The emotional strains of investigation and punishment are likely to be high. They may experience a loss of benefits or a claw-back of compensation previously advanced. And while many who suffer these consequences have committed infractions that merit punishment, some who are innocent may find it difficult to clear their reputations.

9 WHISTLEBLOWERS

Whistleblowers are key to compliance because they come forward with private information about violations. The potential advantage offered by such informants, however, is

---

[49] For a critical analysis of internal corporate investigations, see Bruce A. Green & Ellen S. Podgor, "Unregulated Internal Investigations: Achieving Fairness for Corporate Constituents", 54 B.C. L. Rev. 73 (2013).

threatened by the powerful social norm against "snitching."[50] No one likes a tattle-tale, and people who report compliance violations face retribution, not only from the people they expose, but also from others who enforce the social code. To counteract this problem, compliance programs typically provide an anonymous means for whistleblowers to communicate with senior officers, potentially including the CEO or the board audit committee chair, and also offer guarantees against retaliation. Some organizations have gone further and defined whistleblowing not only as a right but also as an obligation: all employees are required to come forward and report when they observe evidence of misconduct.

Whistleblowing is now protected by law in many countries. The UK's Public Interest Disclosure Act of 1998 provided a degree of protection against retaliation for employees who report their employer's unlawful practices by making a "protected disclosure." In 2013 the UK substantially expanded these protections by, among other things, imposing vicarious liability on employers for retaliatory actions by employees as well as individual liability on co-workers who engage in such retaliation.[51] Most other Western European countries provide similar protections. Spanish case law protects employees from employer retaliation in response to acts undertaken to protect the employee's rights; this general rule can cover acts of whistleblowing as well as other conduct.[52] French law provides that employees may not be sanctioned by their employers for reporting facts of corruption which they learned in the course of their duties.[53] European firms, for their part, appear to have been somewhat slower to adopt whistleblower policies than their American counterparts, but by now a large majority of firms chartered in Western Europe have such policies in place.[54]

In the US, the phenomenon of whistleblowing is regulated by federal and state law. Typically, these laws offer protections against retaliation as well as compensation if retaliation occurs.[55] Several regulatory schemes also provide bounties for people who come forward with evidence leading to enforcement actions. The SEC's program authorizes payments to qualifying individuals who provide original information that leads to an enforcement action generating more than $1 million in sanctions; qualifying individuals receive between 10% and 30% of the penalty.[56] The Internal Revenue Service operates a similar program for persons who come forward with information about tax violations.[57] In the banking law area, the Federal Financial Institution Reform, Recovery and Enforcement Act of 1988 provides that private individuals may submit confidential claims of violations to the Department of Justice, which has 12 months to investigate. If the government responds by initiating enforcement proceedings, the whistleblower is entitled to between 20% and 30% of the first million recovered, 10% to 20% of the next $4 million, and 5% to 10% of the next $5 million.[58]

Also important are *qui tam* actions. The False Claims Act, the most important *qui tam* statute, sets forth a procedure under which a private party (a "relator") can file a lawsuit on behalf of the government, charging that a person has made a false claim on the government.[59] The relator

---

[50] See Ethan Brown, Snitch: Informants, Cooperators, and the Corruption of Justice (2007).

[51] See Helena J. Derbyshire, "Whistleblower Protection in the UK," June 25, 2013, available at http://www.skadden.com/insights/whistleblower-protection-uk.

[52] See Linklaters, Whistleblowing: the European Landscape (n.d.), available at http://www.linklaters.com/Insights/ThoughtLeadership/Whistleblowing/Pages/Index.aspx.

[53] Id.   [54] Id.   [55] See, e.g., 18 U.S.C. § 1514A; 15 U.S.C. § 78u–6(h)(1)(A).

[56] Securities and Exchange Commission Regulation 21F, 17 C.F.R. 240.21F-2.

[57] 26 U.S.C. § 7632; 26 C.F.R. 301.7623-1.

[58] 12 U.S.C. § 4205.   [59] 31 U.S.C. § 3730.

must deliver a copy of the complaint plus supporting evidence to the government, which has 60 days to decide whether to intervene. If the government intervenes, it takes responsibility for the litigation although the relator retains the right to participate. If the government doesn't intervene, the relator may continue the case on her own. Relators receive a bonus if the litigation generates a settlement or judgment on the merits, ranging from 15% to 25% if the government intervenes to 25% to 30% if it does not. The relator is also entitled to attorneys' fees and costs.

10 CRIMINAL ENFORCEMENT

Criminal enforcement of regulatory norms is problematic. Organizations are not human beings; they cannot feel remorse or act with evil intent. They cannot be imprisoned or executed (other than by being put out of business). The most effective sanction against an offending organization is a fine; but fines can be obtained in civil enforcement actions without the high burden of proof and constitutional protections required in criminal cases. Why prosecute organizations, moreover, when prosecutions against individuals appear to be effective? And prosecutors have responsibilities other than enforcing compliance obligations—they need to deal with murderers, drug kingpins, and terrorists. Since civil authorities are available to enforce regulatory norms, would a prosecutor's resources be better directed elsewhere? Notwithstanding these objections, criminal prosecution is now well entrenched as one of the government's arsenal of weapons arrayed against regulatory violations.[60] So active are prosecutors, in fact, that commentators debate whether regulatory enforcement has become "over-criminalized."[61]

A key issue in criminal cases is whether to initiate a prosecution. The Department of Justice's *Principles of Federal Prosecution of Business Organizations*[62] identifies factors that play a role in the charging decision. These include the nature and seriousness of the offense; the pervasiveness of wrongdoing; the organization's past history of offenses; the value of cooperation and voluntary disclosure; the existence of a pre-existing compliance program; remedial actions undertaken by the organization; collateral consequences to third parties; the adequacy of prosecution against the individual offenders; and the availability of remedies such as civil or regulatory enforcement actions.

Criminal cases only rarely result in a verdict after trial. More often, prosecutors and the regulated party settle the dispute. Traditionally, settlements took the form of plea bargains in which the defendant pleaded guilty to a lesser offense. A problem with plea bargains is that the offender is generally required to admit its guilt.[63] Organizational defendants don't want

---

[60] For a justification of corporate criminal responsibility, see Samuel W. Buell, "The Blaming Function of Entity Criminal Liability", 81 Ind. L. J. 473 (2006).

[61] See Lucian E. Dervan, "White Collar Overcriminalization: Deterrence, Plea Bargaining, and the Loss of Innocence", 101 Ky. L. J. 543 (2013); Ellen S. Podgor, "Overcriminalization: The Politics of Crime", 54 Am. U. L. Rev. 541 (2005); Sara Sun Beale, "The Many Faces of Overcriminalization: From Morals and Mattress Tags to Overfederalization", 54 Am. U. L. Rev. 747 (2005).

[62] US Department of Justice, *Principles of Federal Prosecution of Business Organizations* (2013).

[63] Pleas of *nolo contendere* which do not admit guilt are permitted by courts but disfavored by the Department of Justice.

to admit to criminal behavior for a number of reasons. Admitting guilt will likely damage their reputations, may result in their being debarred from providing services to government entities, and may be used against them in subsequent civil litigation. In many cases, therefore, the need to admit guilt in a plea bargain will be a stumbling block to settlement.

To avoid this problem, the US government has devised alternative remedies: deferred prosecution agreements (DPAs) and non-prosecution agreements (NPAs).[64] Because they are private agreements without a formal finding of liability, DPAs and NPAs do not involve judicial oversight and thus do not insert the court as an independent check on prosecutorial behavior. DPAs and NPAs may contain an agreed statement of facts but don't require an admission of guilt. Key to these agreements is the organization's commitment to cooperate with the government and to rectify control deficiencies. Often the agreement will set forth detailed obligations to establish or enhance compliance programs, policies, and procedures.[65]

11 COMPLIANCE BEYOND THE FIRM

Traditionally, the law of compliance has focused on a firm's internal norm enforcement activities. In recent years, however, law enforcement agencies and others have sought to enlist organizations to enforce norms against third parties. These cases of "compliance beyond the firm" can cause problems for the administration of compliance programs.

Consider the requirement under the US Bank Secrecy Act for financial institutions to file Suspicious Activity Reports (SARs) with FinCEN, an agency of the Department of the Treasury. These reports are required whenever a transaction involves at least $5,000 and the bank knows, suspects, or has reason to suspect that the transaction involves funds derived from illegal activities or is intended or conducted in order to hide or disguise funds or assets derived from illegal activities.[66] The SAR filing requirement is an example of compliance beyond the firm because the bank is asked to facilitate the government's efforts to combat money laundering and terror financing.

Another example of compliance beyond the firm is the UK Bribery Act, enacted in 2010, one of the most comprehensive and far-reaching anti-corruption measures in the world. This statute imposes penalties of fines and up to 10 years' imprisonment, and also provides for disqualification of directors found responsible for violations. The jurisdictional scope of this statute is exceptionally broad.

In the US, the Foreign Corrupt Practices Act (FCPA) prohibits firms with US connections from bribing foreign officials.[67] While the statute is directed at corrupt activity by employees or agents of US firms, it also has the obvious function of deterring corruption in foreign governments—a form of outsourced compliance.

---

[64] See Lawrence A. Cunningham, "Deferred Prosecutions and Corporate Governance: An Integrated Approach to Investigation and Reform", 66 Fla. L. Rev. 1 (2014).

[65] See Christopher J. Christie & Robert M. Hanna, "A Push Down the Road of Good Corporate Citizenship: The Deferred Prosecution Agreement Between the U.S. Attorney for the District of New Jersey and Bristol-Myers Squibb Co", 43 Am. Crim. L. Rev. 1042 (2006).

[66] 31 U.S.C. § 5318(g) (2006); 31 C.F.R. § 103.18(a)(2) (2006).

[67] 15 U.S.C. §§ 78dd-1 et seq.

Compliance beyond the firm has also become an issue in US securities law. The SEC's "conflict minerals" rule requires companies that use "conflict minerals"—tantalum, tin, tungsten, and gold—to disclose to the Commission whether those minerals originated in the Democratic Republic of the Congo or an adjoining country.[68] If such materials did originate in the defined area, then companies must also submit an additional report to the Commission containing a "description of the measures taken . . . to exercise due diligence on the source and chain of custody of such minerals," and "a description of the products manufactured or contracted to be manufactured that are not DRC conflict free."[69] An important purpose of this rule is to discourage companies from activities that could indirectly contribute to human rights abuses in the affected region.

12   ETHICS BEYOND COMPLIANCE

Organizations often include the term "ethics" in their compliance programs, promulgate codes of "ethics" that include a compliance component, and create positions such as "chief ethics officer" that include responsibility for compliance. As illustrated by these and other governance features, the law of compliance shares an uneasy boundary with a broader set of issues that might loosely be termed "ethics beyond compliance."

Several factors explain the ambiguity in topic definition. First, the notions of a culture of compliance and tone at the topic cannot be strictly limited to formal legal requirements; otherwise the task of compliance could become synonymous with skirting legal regulations. Second, it may be advisable for an organization to place a "fence" around legal norms, thus helping to ensure that even if employees make mistakes they are unlikely to break the law. Third, the norms enforced by the compliance function include not only external rules but also internal norms. Self-imposed rules are often thought of as matters of ethics rather than law (consider bar association ethics codes). Finally, organizations can benefit from the "good guy" image that ethical behavior beyond compliance can promote, either because the organization's constituents obtain psychological benefits from doing the "right thing" or because a favorable public image may enhance sales, attract investment, deflect criticism, or deter enforcement actions.

Issues of ethics beyond compliance were problematic in an earlier era. Corporations were conceived of as exclusively profit-seeking enterprises that existed to serve the financial interests of shareholders. Such a firm could not make substantial gifts to charity without raising concerns that the donations were *ultra vires*. Early decisions on charitable gifts gave credence to this idea, at least when the gift was unusually large or general in scope.[70] More recently, corporate law has evolved to a point where gifts to charitable causes are clearly authorized.[71] Nevertheless there probably are limits beyond which a firm's charitable activities could be called into question—either because the gift is large relative to profits or because an insider is seen as obtaining some special benefit.

---

[68] 15 U.S.C. § 78m(p); 17 C.F.R. §§ 240, 249b.   [69] Id. § 78m(p)(1)(A)(i)-(ii).
[70] *Dodge v. Ford Motor Co* 204 Mich. 459, 170 N.W. 668.
[71] *Shlensky v. Wrigley* 237 NE 2d 776, *A.P. Smith Co. v. Barlow* 98 A.2d 581.

Ethics beyond compliance has expanded beyond its initial grounding in charitable gifts. Permitted public interest goals include matters such as social responsibility, community empowerment, respect for human rights, sustainable environmental policies, labor rights, and other objectives.[72] Open any company website and you are likely to find a description of the various activities the firm is supporting to serve the public interest. State legislatures have also taken an active role. Many states now authorize "public benefit corporations" which serve the public interest as well as private profit.[73] A potential advantage of these companies is that they inform investors of their public interest goals; shareholders cannot claim unfairness or surprise when the company goes about seeking those goals at the expense of profits. It is too early to tell if public benefit corporations will have an important impact or to assess whether they will be subject to the same compliance obligations as apply to traditional profit-oriented firms.[74]

ACKNOWLEDGMENT

I thank James Fanto for helpful comments.

[72] For discussion of some of these objectives, see Judd F. Sneirson, "Green is Good: Sustainability, Profitability, and a New Paradigm for Corporate Governance", 94 Iowa L. Rev. 987 (2009); Faith Stevelman, "Global Finance, Multinationals and Human Rights: With Commentary on Backer's Critique of the 2008 Report by John Ruggie", 9 Santa Clara J. Int'l. L. 101 (2011). For a somewhat more skeptical view, see Donald J. Kochan, "Corporate Social Responsibility in a Remedy-Seeking Society: A Public Choice Perspective", 17 Chap. L. Rev. 413 (2014).

[73] See J. Haskell Murray, "Social Enterprise Innovation: Delaware's Public Benefit Corporation Law", 4 Harv. Bus. L. Rev. 345 (2014); Lyman Johnson, "Pluralism in Corporate Form: Corporate Law and Benefit Corporationss", 25 Regent U. L. Rev. 269 (2012–2013).

[74] For discussion, see Joseph W. Yockey, The Compliance Case for Social Enterprise, University of Iowa College of Law Legal Studies Research Paper 14–23 (2014).

PART V

ADJACENT AREAS

CHAPTER 38

COMPARATIVE CORPORATE INSOLVENCY LAW

HORST EIDENMÜLLER

1 INTRODUCTION

CORPORATE law and governance on the one hand and insolvency/bankruptcy[1] law on the other have long been viewed as distinct disciplines: whereas the former deal with legal issues associated with the organization and operation of a solvent corporation, the latter is meant to address a new set of legal problems arising once a corporation finds itself in severe financial distress. Agency conflicts between shareholders and management and between majority and minority shareholders figure prominently in corporate law and governance.[2] Agency conflicts between the corporation and its creditors and within the creditor community are at the center of insolvency law.[3]

The divide between these two spheres of law and academic discipline becomes less clear, however, once one conceives of insolvency law as "corporate governance under financial distress." Indeed, "insolvency governance" can be characterized as a special form (or case) of "corporate governance."[4] The conceptual/analytical apparatus to understand the regulatory problems and develop potential policy responses is the same; it is only the framework conditions which change, and possibly only to a small degree: laws on the (financial) restructuring of businesses pre-insolvency are gaining increasing importance, in the European Union and elsewhere.[5]

---

[1] "Bankruptcy law" is the term more commonly used in the US, "insolvency law" is more common elsewhere in the world, especially in the UK.

[2] Reinier Kraakman et al., The Anatomy of Corporate Law: A Comparative and Functional Approach (2009), chapter 2; Gregor Bachmann et al., Regulating the Closed Corporation 8–13 (2014).

[3] Kraakman et al., *supra* note 2, at 115 et seq.; Horst Eidenmüller, Unternehmenssanierung zwischen Markt und Gesetz (1999).

[4] While "insolvency governance" probably is a new term, the interaction of corporate law and corporate bankruptcy was noted decades ago by scholars such as Whitford, LoPucki, and Skeel. See David Skeel, "Rediscovering Corporate Governance in Bankruptcy", 87 Temple L. Rev. 1021 (2015).

[5] In 2014, for example, the EU Commission published a Recommendation on a new approach to business failure and insolvency (2014/135/EU, OJ of the EU of 14 March 2014, L 74/65) that asks the Member States to bring their domestic pre-insolvency restructuring regimes into line with the principles set out in the recommendation (see Horst Eidenmüller & Kristin van Zwieten, "Restructuring the European Business Enterprise: the European Commission's Recommendation on a New Approach to

Hence, it appears sensible to include a chapter on corporate insolvency law in a handbook on corporate governance. Such a chapter should of course be comparative in nature, i.e., it should consider the regulatory approaches of different jurisdictions with respect to corporate insolvency law issues and compare their respective merits. Adopting a comparative perspective enlarges the "solution set" for legal problems and also helps evaluate domestic regulatory approaches against an international benchmark ("best practice"). This chapter focuses on the corporate insolvency laws of the US, England, France, and Germany. It does so because these jurisdictions are representative of diverse legal traditions and because they can rightfully be characterized as leading the international search for optimal insolvency and/or restructuring regimes with respect to corporate entities that find themselves in or near financial distress. Harmonization efforts worldwide are, or have been, heavily influenced by Chapter 11 of the US Bankruptcy Code, the English Scheme of Arrangement, the French *sauveguarde* proceedings, and German proposals to regulate insolvencies of members of a group of companies—to name just a few examples.[6]

Interest in comparative corporate insolvency law has grown considerably in the last years, driven by various factors. It is increasingly recognized that (corporate) insolvency laws have a significant impact on entrepreneurship and economic growth.[7] Hence, jurisdictions attempt to identify best practices that allow them to boost their domestic economies. At the same time, the number of transnational insolvencies is clearly on the rise. Given the growth in international commerce, today even the insolvency of small or medium-sized (closed) corporations usually will exhibit some transnational aspect such as foreign creditors, subsidiaries/branches/offices in other jurisdictions, or assets that are located abroad. However, scholarly work in the field of comparative corporate insolvency law up till now has been rather scarce.[8]

This chapter will start out with an introduction to the comparative approach as applied to corporate insolvency law (section 2). It will then provide a taxonomy of insolvency laws and identify objectives that these pursue (section 3). Substantive issues covered will be the

Business Failure and Insolvency", 16 Eur. Bus. Org. L. Rev. 625 (2015)). The Commission has presented a legislative proposal in 2016; see Commission Proposal for a Directive of the European Parliament and of the Council on preventive restructuring frameworks, second chance and measures to increase the efficiency of restructuring, insolvency and discharge procedures and amending Directive 2012/30/EU, COM (2016) 723 final (22 November 2016). On the proposal see Horst Eidenmüller, "Contracting for a European Insolvency Regime", 18 Eur. Bus. Org. L. Rev. 273 (2017). See also section 11 *infra*.

[6] As for the last example, the recast European Insolvency Regulation (Regulation (EU) 2015/848 of 20 May 2015) contains a new Chapter V on insolvency proceedings of members of a group of companies (Arts. 56 et seq.). The conceptual approach underlying this chapter was first proposed by the German government in its legislative proposal for new domestic rules on insolvency proceedings of members of groups of companies. See Entwurf eines Gesetzes zur Erleichterung der Bewältigung von Konzerninsolvenzen, Bundestag-Drucksache 18/407 of 30 January 2014.

[7] See, for example, John Armour & Douglas Cumming, "Bankruptcy Law and Entrepreneurship", 10 Am. L. & Econ. Rev. 303 (2008); Kenneth M. Ayotte, "Bankruptcy and Entrepreneurship: The Value of a Fresh Start", 23 J. L. & Econ. 161 (2007).

[8] Gerard McCormack, Corporate Rescue Law: An Anglo-American Perspective (2008), focuses exclusively on the UK and the US. Philip R. Wood, Principles of International Insolvency (2007), is characterized by an enormous breadth of coverage and detail in the analysis but less by consideration of conceptual issues. Lawrence Westbrook et al., A Global View of Business Insolvency Systems (2010), are quite selective with respect to the issues studied. A book like Kraakman et al., *supra* note 2, for corporate insolvency law is missing.

opening (section 4) and governance (section 5) of insolvency proceedings, the ranking of claims, and, in particular, the position of secured creditors (section 6), contracting for assets of the debtor (section 7), rescue proceedings (section 8), and the contractual resolution of financial distress (section 9). The chapter concludes with some thoughts on the reasons for the identified jurisdictional divergences (section 10) and an outlook on the worldwide efforts toward harmonization of insolvency laws (section 11). It goes without saying that the level of detailed analysis that can be reached in a book chapter on these many important issues is limited. The emphasis will be on those issues that are more closely related to questions of corporate governance.

2 THE COMPARATIVE APPROACH

The comparative approach is characterized by a functional perspective. It starts with a particular regulatory problem, and it seeks to understand, describe, and evaluate how that problem is "solved" in a particular jurisdiction. This implies that the comparative approach needs to abstract from jurisdiction-specific categorizations and doctrinal classifications. To illustrate: one important issue in comparative insolvency law is the "initiation problem":[9] What triggers insolvency proceedings? How do they get started? Jurisdictions worldwide approach this issue very differently. Some use liability rules—in corporate and/or insolvency law—that penalize managers for filing too late. Some reward managers for initiating insolvency proceedings in time by, for example, rights and/or privileges such as the "debtor in possession" (no insolvency administrator is appointed and management stays in charge of running the bankrupt firm) or an "exclusivity period" during which only the debtor may propose a restructuring plan (see in detail section 4 *infra*). Comparative analysis must be open to very different regulatory approaches and techniques in order not to lose sight of the wealth of rules and mechanisms that attempt to address a particular regulatory problem.

Another recurrent and important issue in comparative law is the problem of the appropriate measuring rod. Once different regulatory approaches and techniques have been identified, their operation in legal practice and their effects in reality must be studied in closer detail. The former task involves, in particular, an in-depth analysis of the relevant case law and contract practice; the latter social-scientific studies of causal consequences of legal rules. It is against this background that the important normative question must be put: Which regulatory approach/technique is or works best, given the regulatory background? This question can only be answered, if it can be answered at all,[10] on the basis of a clearly specified measuring rod. For a long time, "conventional" comparative private law scholarship has not been very convincing in this respect. To characterize a specific jurisdiction's rule or regime as "better" or "more appropriate"[11] rather begs the question: Why? The analytical

---

[9] Douglas G. Baird, "The Initiation Problem in Bankruptcy", 11 Int'l. Rev. L. & Econ. 223 (1991).

[10] Apart from the regulatory background (complementarities in other areas of the law etc.), business realities (type of economy etc.) and the strength of different types of stakeholders of firms play an important role, to name just a few relevant factors. The point in the text is simply this: Without a precise normative measuring rod, no proper evaluative comparison of different approaches in different jurisdictions is feasible.

[11] Konrad Zweigert & Hein Kötz, An Introduction to Comparative Law 15 (1998).

landscape has changed considerably with the advent of the economic analysis of law in the 1970s. "Positive Law and Economics" offers tools to predict the effects of laws in reality, and "Normative Law and Economics" uses welfare economics to evaluate these effects, judging the underlying laws to be more or less efficient.[12] To be sure, both branches of the economic analysis of law are subject to severe criticisms.[13] The analytical apparatus of economics has been refined to respond to these criticisms, leading inter alia to new sub-disciplines such as "Behavioural Law and Economics."[14] For this reason and because (1) the economic analysis of legal rules often generates relatively precise answers (compared to more fuzzy measuring rods) and (2) efficiency has a relatively high appeal as a normative criterion especially in the field of commercial and corporate activities, this standard will be used in this chapter. However, shortcomings and/or limitations of the economic analysis will be mentioned where necessary.

3 TAXONOMY AND OBJECTIVES OF INSOLVENCY LAWS

As a starting point for comparative corporate insolvency law scholarship, it seems helpful to take stock of existing corporate insolvency law systems in select jurisdictions, identify the objectives these pursue, and compare them. A particular issue in this context is whether there is a need for a special insolvency regime for systemically important financial institutions. This issue has assumed a significant importance in the regulatory aftermath of the most recent global financial and economic crisis.

3.1 Taxonomy of Insolvency Laws: Different Systems

Corporate insolvency law systems in various jurisdictions differ formally especially in that some jurisdictions have a multiplicity of proceedings that are regulated in different statutes or at least different chapters in one statute, whereas others are less "rich" in the choices they offer for corporate debtors that find themselves in or near financial distress.[15] A broad distinction can be drawn between proceedings that aim at a restructuring of corporate debtors and those that are directed toward liquidation. In its simplest form, this distinction is reflected in two well-known Chapters of the US Bankruptcy Code: Chapter 7 on liquidations and Chapter 11 on reorganizations. Germany modeled its own *Insolvenzordnung* (in force

---

[12] Pioneering work in the field was done by Richard Posner. His book on Economic Analysis of Law was published in its first edition in 1972. It is now in its 9th edition (2014). "Law and Economics" has had and continues to have a significant influence on bankruptcy scholarship. See, for example, Mark J. Roe, Corporate Reorganization and Bankruptcy (2000); Douglas G. Baird, Elements of Bankruptcy (2006); Barry E. Adler, Foundations of Bankruptcy Law (2005).

[13] Horst Eidenmüller, Effizienz als Rechtsprinzip (2015).

[14] See, for example, Behavioral Law & Economics (Cass Sunstein ed., 2000).

[15] For reorganization in the US and in European bankruptcy law, see Maria Brouwer, "Reorganization in US and European Bankruptcy Law", 22 Eur. J. L. Econ. 5 (2006).

since 1999) against the background of these two Chapters: the statute contains liquidations in its initial parts and a Chapter-11-type debtor in possession restructuring proceeding in Parts 6 and 7.

With the increasing importance of corporate restructurings and the need for legal regimes to facilitate these, especially pre-insolvency, some jurisdictions now offer not just one restructuring regime but a multifaceted set of restructuring laws. This is true, for example, with respect to England: the Insolvency Act 1986 contains the Winding Up procedure in Part IV, a liquidation proceeding, but also the Administration (Schedule B1) and the Company Voluntary Arrangement [CVA] (Part I), which can be used as a restructuring framework. These are complemented by the Scheme of Arrangement (SoA) (sections 895–901 of the Companies Act 2006), another restructuring tool that can be employed both before and after insolvency (Solvent and Insolvent Schemes of Arrangement). The French insolvency landscape is even more diverse. Book 6 of the *Code de commerce* contains different types of court-supervised proceedings (*Redressement judiciaire, Liquidation judiciaire*), but also many different forms of restructuring proceedings with minimal or no court intervention: *Procédure de conciliation, Procédure de sauvegarde,*[16] *Procédure de sauvegarde financière accélérée,* and *Procédure de sauvegarde accélérée.*

A crucial distinguishing feature with respect to these various "modern" restructuring proceedings is whether they offer tools to discipline holdouts such as, for example, an automatic stay and/or the possibility of majority voting with respect to a restructuring plan.[17] Without these devices, the proceeding is purely voluntary in the sense that creditors cannot be forced to participate. This allows for strategic maneuvering and free riding. At the same time, introducing a stay or majority voting comes at a cost: it increases court involvement and (public) visibility and, as a consequence, direct and indirect bankruptcy costs.[18] The English Scheme, for example, does not impose a stay but allows majority voting, the French Procédure de sauvegarde and the Procédure de sauvegarde accélérée impose a (universal) stay but do not allow all dissenting creditors to be bound by a plan agreed by a majority of creditors, and the Procédure de conciliation exhibits neither of these "collectivizing" devices.[19]

Whether or not liquidations and (various forms of) restructurings are or should be regulated in different chapters of the same statute or in different statutes is more a formal

---

[16] This procedure was used, for example, in the Eurotunnel restructuring (2006), https:// www.nouvelobs.com/economie/20060801.OBS6977/procedure-de-sauvegarde-pour -eurotunnel.html, and in the Thomson case (2009), http://www.lefigaro.fr/societes/2009/12/01 /04015-20091201ARTFIG00013-thomson-tente-un-plan-de-sauvegarde-express-.php.

[17] See Sarah Paterson, "Rethinking the Role of the Law of Corporate Distress in the Twenty-First Century", 35 Oxford J. Leg. Stud. 1 (2015). Paterson distinguishes between "insolvency law" and "restructuring law." Whereas the former, in her view, is geared toward liquidation with the creditors facing a prisoners' dilemma justifying a stay, the latter is concerned with providing a deadlock resolution procedure that can discipline hold-outs but does not necessarily need a stay. Paterson does not, I believe, sufficiently appreciate that the strategic problem faced by creditors in a liquidation and in a restructuring is very much the same (prisoners' dilemma), and a stay is no less justified in a restructuring than it is in a liquidation.

[18] On bankruptcy costs see *infra* note 32 and accompanying text.

[19] In the case of the procédure de conciliation, there is no general stay affecting all creditors. However, where a creditor seeks to enforce his or her rights, the debtor can apply to the court for a moratorium (specific to that creditor) lasting a maximum of two years: Art. L.611-7 of the French Code de commerce, Art. 1343-5 Code civil.

than an important substantive question. Putting them in the same statute might generate certain cost advantages because an initial general chapter can be used to stipulate certain rules that apply to all types of proceedings. On the other hand, clarity and marketability of the proceeding for potential users might be said to argue in favor of a separate statute. Furthermore, including a chapter on restructurings in legislation entitled "Insolvenzordnung" (Insolvency Code)—as in Germany—might be said to be particularly bad in this respect, as "Insolvency Code" tends to be associated with liquidations.

A more important substantive issue is whether firms worldwide have access to efficient restructuring proceedings that can be initiated pre-insolvency. A lack of efficient local proceedings is not so much a problem for multinational corporations as they are usually able to forum shop for the best or most suitable restructuring regime. However, given the costs involved with forum shopping, this is not a viable alternative, especially for many SMEs. Hence, a case can be made for "minimum harmonization" with respect to jurisdictions' provisions of pre-insolvency restructuring regimes. Such harmonization efforts are currently being undertaken in the European Union, for example (see in detail section 11).

3.2 Bank Insolvency and Resolution

Before the most recent global financial and economic crisis, very few jurisdictions worldwide had special bank insolvency and restructuring/resolution regimes in their statute books. It is true that banks were mostly subject to distinctive supervisory regimes. But once it came to insolvency, regular insolvency proceedings were applied, usually with certain exceptions—to account for the banks' unique corporate features—such as, for example, filing rights and pick of insolvency administrators.

This all changed with the global financial and economic crisis, starting in the UK with the bank run on Northern Rock (2007) and involving the bankruptcy of Lehman and a bailout of American International Group (AIG)—both within a couple of days of each other in September 2008. The policy shift followed rapidly. The evidence supporting the shift was not very strong though: if one compared the reaction of certain capital market indices to the Lehman Chapter 11 filing on the one hand and to the AIG bailout on the other, it appears that it was not the bankruptcy procedure itself that was the problem—the TED spread, for example, increased more after the AIG bailout.[20] Nevertheless and very soon, a worldwide near-consensus amongst policy makers and regulators emerged that the default, in particular, of a systemically important financial institution demands a special regime that kicks in earlier, is more flexible, and also much speedier than an ordinary bankruptcy proceeding.[21] Further, depositors should not have to fear that their claims would be reduced in a bankruptcy proceeding. After the 2007 collapse of Northern Rock, the UK was

---

[20] See Kenneth M. Ayotte & David Skeel, "Bankruptcy or Bailouts?", 35 J. Corp. L. 469, 490 et seq. (2010); Horst Eidenmüller, Finanzkrise, Wirtschaftskrise und das deutsche Insolvenzrecht 51 et seq. (2009).

[21] See Horst Eidenmüller, Restrukturierung systemrelevanter Finanzinstitute, in Festschrift für Klaus J. Hopt zum 70. Geburtstag am 24. August 2010, 1713, 1716 et seq., 1718 et seq. (Stefan Grundmann et al. eds., 2010); Anat Admati & Martin Hellwig, The Bankers' New Clothes 35–38 (2013).

the first jurisdiction to enact a "modern" bank resolution and recovery regime (Banking Act 2009).[22] Other jurisdictions followed suit: the US with Title II of the Dodd–Frank Wall Street Reform and Consumer Protection Act (2010)[23] and Germany with the Kreditinstitute-Reorganisationsgesetz (2010).[24]

Experimenting with different types of bank resolution and recovery regimes might be viewed as a potential regulatory option—let the market decide which rule systems work (best). However, at least in the banking field, a consensus amongst policy makers and regulators soon again emerged that this was no real option and that, wherever feasible, harmonization along the lines of best practice should be achieved. One can, of course, ask critical questions as to the existence of a best practice in a regulatory field so new and untested as bank resolution and recovery, and point to the dangers of harmonizing along the lines of principles that are potentially fundamentally flawed.[25] Nevertheless, the European Union (EU), for one, pushed forward and enacted the "Bank Recovery and Resolution Directive (BRRD)" in 2014.[26] Member States only had until January 1, 2015 to adjust their domestic regimes to the rules stipulated in the Directive.

Simply put, it provides for a unitary system of bank resolution and recovery throughout the EU. The BRRD provides authorities with comprehensive and effective arrangements to deal with failing banks at national level, as well as cooperation arrangements to tackle cross-border banking failures. It sets out the rules for the resolution of banks and large investment firms in all EU Member States. Banks will be required to prepare recovery plans to overcome financial distress. Authorities are also granted a set of powers to intervene in the operations of banks to avoid them failing. If they do face failure, authorities are equipped with comprehensive powers and tools to restructure them, allocating losses to shareholders and creditors following a clearly defined hierarchy. They have the power to implement plans to resolve failed banks in a way that preserves their most critical functions and avoids taxpayers having to bail them out (bail-in versus bail-out). Precise arrangements are set out for how home and host authorities of banking groups should cooperate in all stages of cross-border resolution, from resolution planning to resolution itself, with a strong role for the European Banking Authority to coordinate and mediate in case of disagreements. National resolution funds are

---

[22] On this, see Peter Brierley, "The UK Special Resolution Regime for Failing Banks in an International Context", Bank of England Financial Stability Paper No. 5, July 2009, available at https://www.bankofengland.co.uk/-/media/boe/files/financial-stability-paper/2009/the-uk-special-resolution-regime-for-failing-banks-in-an-international-context.

[23] On the interaction of bank regulation and bankruptcy after Dodd–Frank see David Skeel, "The New Synthesis of Bank Regulation and Bankruptcy in the Dodd–Frank Era", ECGI Working Paper No. 308/2016, available at http://www.ecgi.org/wp/wp_id.php?id=771.

[24] For a comparison of the US, the English and the German system, see Matej Marinč & Razvan Vlahu, The Economics of Bank Bankruptcy Law 97 et seq. (2012). See also John Armour et al., Principles of Financial Regulation 340 et seq. (2016) with further references.

[25] Roberta Romano, "For Diversity in the International Regulation of Financial Institutions: Critiquing and Recalibrating the Basel Architecture", 31 Yale J. Reg. 1 (2014).

[26] Directive 2014/59/EU of the European Parliament and of the Council of 15 May 2014 establishing a framework for the recovery and resolution of credit institutions and investment firms and amending Council Directive 82/891/EEC, and Directives 2001/24/EC, 2002/47/EC, 2004/25/EC, 2005/56/EC, 2007/36/EC, 2011/35/EU, 2012/30/EU, and 2013/36/EU, and Regulations (EU) No 1093/2010 and (EU) No 648/2012, of the European Parliament and of the Council, OJ of the EU of 12 June 2014, L 173/190.

also being established. In the case of Member States within the Eurozone, these funds were replaced by the Single Resolution Fund as of 2016.

3.3 Economic versus Non-Economic Goals

What are the proper goals of a corporate insolvency procedure? The normative importance of the answer to this question cannot be overestimated. It defines the architecture of an insolvency proceeding and is also important with respect to most specific regulatory issues in corporate insolvency law. As with many other areas of the law, an economic perspective on insolvency laws has become very influential—both in the scholarly literature and in law-making. Hence, it is indispensable to understand and study this perspective in order to be able to follow the conceptual debates about most insolvency law issues. However, jurisdictions differ markedly regarding the extent to which they design corporate insolvency law systems according to economic principles. This difference is also reflected in another distinction, namely whether a country's corporate insolvency regime is more creditor or more debtor oriented.

3.3.1 *The Economic Perspective of Insolvency Laws*

The economic perspective clearly distinguishes between an ex post and an ex ante view of insolvency laws. The former view is the one usually adopted by lawyers and legal scholars. With respect to corporate insolvency law, it focuses on the question of what to do with the assets of a corporation and the corporation itself in a situation in which it finds itself in financial distress, i.e., unable to pay all its debts as they fall due.[27] The economic maxim to address this question is simple: maximize the net company value. The larger the pie, the more is available for distribution to the company's creditors. This goal (function) implies at least three important sub-goals: (1) First, prevention of an asset race, i.e., a solution to the common pool problem.[28] Creditors of a financially distressed corporation find themselves in a multi-party prisoners' dilemma.[29] Each creditor has a dominant strategy to seize assets as fast as possible—with potentially disastrous consequences for the group. (2) Second, restructuring of the firm only if the restructuring value exceeds its liquidation value, i.e., if the firm is economically viable.[30] On the basis of this test, the great majority of insolvent corporations in legal practice should be liquidated because they suffer from financial *and* economic failure.[31] (3) Third, minimization of the direct and indirect costs of insolvency proceedings.

---

[27] In insolvency law and scholarship, usually two different tests for financial distress are used: cash-flow insolvency and balance-sheet insolvency. According to the former (used in the text above), a firm is insolvent if it cannot fully meet its financial obligations as they fall due. According to the latter, a firm is insolvent if its liabilities exceed its assets, measured by the applicable accounting rules. On the opening of insolvency proceedings see in detail section 4 *infra*.

[28] Thomas H. Jackson, The Logic and Limits of Bankruptcy Law 7 et seq. (1986).

[29] Eidenmüller, *supra* note 3, at 19 et seq.

[30] To put it differently, if a firm is not only financially but also economically distressed, it should be liquidated. It should also be liquidated if it is economically distressed but not financially distressed. This scenario would lead to a liquidation outside bankruptcy/insolvency, however.

[31] In Germany, for example, businesses are reorganized in an *Insolvenzplanverfahren* according to sections 217 et seq. of the German Insolvenzordnung in no more than 1% of all business insolvencies; see

Direct costs comprise the transactions costs triggered by the procedure such as, for example, administrators' or court fees. Indirect costs are economic losses caused by the procedure such as, for example, the reputational damage to the firm associated with the mere fact of an insolvency procedure. Indirect bankruptcy costs are usually much higher than direct bankruptcy costs and tend to consume approximately 10–20% of the remaining firm value.[32] Given the creditors' interest in as large a pie as possible in bankruptcy, minimizing direct and indirect bankruptcy costs is an economic imperative.

Economic analysis complements the ex post view of insolvency laws with an ex ante perspective. The message is as clear-cut and simple as the maxim from an ex post perspective. Ex ante is about setting the appropriate, i.e., welfare-maximizing, incentives for shareholders and managers of a corporation that might find itself in financial distress (with a non-trivial probability). This goal (function) implies at least two important sub-goals: (1) First, agency costs of debt must be reduced. As is well known, shareholders of a near-insolvent corporation have an incentive to undertake risky projects that might even have a negative net present value ("betting the bank's money").[33] Managers have similar incentives to the extent that they can be assumed to act according to the shareholders' preferences.[34] Hence, in closed corporations, where shareholders are usually able to directly control managers' actions, the "risk shifting incentive" of managers will be stronger than in public corporations where management enjoys more freedom in business decisions. (2) Second, restructuring efforts of a firm that faces serious business problems should be initiated sooner rather than later. Experience teaches us that the timely triggering of restructuring initiatives is a crucial success factor for these initiatives.[35] Indeed, it is never too early to think about the competitiveness of one's business, and there is no clear-cut line between keeping a business on a competitive track—by appropriate measures—and restructuring it to avert a decline in financial and/or economic performance.

How do different jurisdictions' insolvency laws worldwide fare against these criteria for ex post and ex ante efficient insolvency regimes? There are no overall empirical analyses of the relevant cost/benefit effects available, and the methodological hurdles for such studies do

the analysis of Schultze & Braun based on all business insolvencies from 1999–2011, available at http://www.schubra.de/de/presseservice/pressemitteilungen/sb/InsolvenzplanIndex1999bis2011.pdf. Data from other jurisdictions point in the same direction with respect to the ratio between reorganizations and liquidations. Clearly these data are no more than a proxy for the statement in the text: businesses may be liquidated even though they should have been reorganized or vice versa. But even if the former is more likely than the latter (which is unclear), the ratio is not going to change much in absolute terms.

[32] See Michelle J. White, The corporate bankruptcy decision, in Corporate Bankruptcy: Economic and Legal Perspectives 207, 226 et seq. (Jagdeep S. Bhandari & Lawrence A. Weiss eds., 1996), with further references. A rough proxy for indirect bankruptcy costs with respect to listed firms is the loss in market capitalization triggered by an insolvency filing.

[33] Bachmann et al., *supra* note 2, at 11 et seq.

[34] Paul Davies, "Directors' Creditor-Regarding Duties in Respect of Trading Decisions Taken in the Vicinity of Insolvency", 7 Eur. Bus. Org. L. Rev. 301, 306–07 (2006); Horst Eidenmüller, "Trading in Times of Crisis: Formal Insolvency Proceedings, Workouts and the Incentives for Shareholders/Managers", 7 Eur. Bus. Org. L. Rev. 239, 243 (2006).

[35] For this reason, leverage has a positive influence on the likelihood and success rate of a restructuring: it triggers insolvency at an earlier point in time. See Michael C. Jensen, "Active Investors, LBOs, and the Privatization of Bankruptcy", 2 J. Appl. Corp. Fin. 35, 41 et seq. (1989).

seem insurmountable: recovery rates for creditors in bankruptcy tell only part of the story,[36] and how would one even start to identify and measure accurately all relevant cost/benefit factors that go into an overall calculus of the efficiency effects of a particular insolvency regime? What probably can be said, though, is that the ex ante effects are more important than the ex post effects: the former relate to all firms, whereas the latter are important only with a subset of firms, namely those that find themselves in financial distress.[37] To put it differently: maintaining the health of all firms is more important than getting it right with respect to the subset of firms that find themselves in the emergency room. Hence, the fixation of lawyers and legal scholars with ex post efficiency is misplaced—at least from an economic standpoint.

3.3.2 *Diversity of Bankruptcy Philosophies*

As already stated in the introduction to this section, jurisdictions worldwide differ markedly with respect to the "bankruptcy philosophies" that they pursue.[38] On the one hand, there are jurisdictions that view insolvency law primarily or even exclusively as debt collection law, i.e., as an instrument to best satisfy creditors' interests when the debtor is in a situation of financial distress. These jurisdictions tend clearly to prioritize economic efficiency vis-à-vis any other potential goal to be pursued by insolvency laws. On the other hand, there are jurisdictions that entertain a policy according to which insolvency law should serve not only creditors' but also other stakeholders' interests, for example those of the debtor, workers, and the (local) community.[39] Under this policy, environmental concerns are a legitimate factor in a corporate insolvency as well as are, potentially, redistributive aims: insolvency is not just about enforcing pre-existing entitlements under conditions of scarcity; it is also about redefining entitlements and shifting rents.[40]

---

[36] Recovery rates measure the return for creditors on the nominal value of their claim in a bankruptcy proceeding. They vary depending on various factors such as whether the company is liquidated or restructured, whether the claim is secured or unsecured, the claim ranking order in a specific jurisdiction, etc. For comparisons between France, Germany, and the UK see, for example, Régis Blazy, Joël Petey & Laurent Weill, "Can Bankruptcy Codes Create Value? Evidence from Creditors' Recoveries in France, Germany, and the United Kingdom", 2014, available at https://ssrn.com/abstract=2447296.

[37] Michelle J. White, The Costs of Corporate Bankruptcy: A U.S.–European Comparison, in Corporate Bankruptcy: Economic and Legal Perspectives, *supra* note 32, at 467–500. On the economics of English insolvency proceedings, see Julian Franks & Oren Sussman, The Economics of English Insolvency: Some Recent Developments, in Company Charges: Spectrum and Beyond 253–66 (Joshua Getzler & Jennifer Payne eds., 2006).

[38] For different perspectives in the US see, for example, Jackson, *supra* note 28, Introduction and Chapters 1 and 2; Douglas G. Baird, "Bankruptcy's Uncontested Axioms", 108 Yale L. J. 573 (1998); Elizabeth Warren, "Bankruptcy Policy", 54 U. Chi. L. Rev. 775 (1987); for the UK, see Roy Goode, Principles of Corporate Insolvency Law (1997), Chapters 2 and 3; for the EU, see Federico Mucciarelli, "Not Just Efficiency: Insolvency Law in the EU and Its Political Dimension", 14 Eur. Bus. Org. L. Rev. 175 (2013).

[39] See Vanessa Finch, Corporate Insolvency Law 38 et seq. (2009).

[40] Finch, *supra* note 39, at 40 et seq.

The current German insolvency regime for corporate debtors clearly falls in the first group, i.e. it is debt collection law and nothing else. Section 1 of the Insolvenzordnung reads as follows:

> The insolvency proceedings shall serve the purpose of collective satisfaction of a debtor's creditors by liquidation of the debtor's assets and by distribution of the proceeds, or by reaching an arrangement in an insolvency plan, particularly in order to maintain the enterprise. Honest debtors shall be given the opportunity to achieve discharge of residual debt.

The discharge mentioned in the second sentence is irrelevant for corporate debtors: it applies only to natural persons (see sections 286 et seq. Insolvenzordnung). On the other end of the spectrum, we find the current French insolvency laws. With respect to a Redressement judiciaire, the Code de commerce sets out the following objectives: "The purpose of the judicial restructuring is to allow the continuation of the business's operations, the maintenance of employment and the settlement of its liabilities."[41] Hence, considerations of maintaining employment (in the short run) or "local business structures" may well trump economic logic. The "middle ground," so to speak, is firmly occupied by the US and the English insolvency regimes. Traditionally, US Chapter 11 has a very strong debtor orientation: despite some changes in more recent times,[42] the fresh start philosophy and giving the debtor a second chance is still characteristic of Chapter 11 proceedings. Of course, discharge can be advocated both on economic and on redistributive grounds, and the US version of discharge as a tool to promote entrepreneurship probably falls more in the first than in the second category (whether it is successful in that regard is another matter[43]). English insolvency law used to be and still is fairly creditor rights oriented. For example, the holder of a qualifying floating charge may appoint an administrator or an administrative receiver under the Insolvency Act 1986 without the need for an order of the court.[44] However, as early as 1982, the "Cork Report" (commissioned by a Labour government in 1977) had suggested that insolvency laws should pursue a multiplicity of aims and that the effects of insolvency are not limited to the private interests involved.[45] This view was reflected in later reforms, especially in those introduced by the Enterprise Act 2002. The Act made substantial amendments to the administration procedure for failing companies. The purpose was to enhance the policy of creating a "rescue culture," so that insolvent companies should so far as possible be saved, before their assets are stripped and distributed to creditors.[46]

Against the background of even this small sample of insolvency policy debates and law-making in select countries, it clearly emerges how markedly jurisdictions worldwide differ with respect to the "bankruptcy philosophies" that they pursue. The extent to which economic reasoning should appropriately inspire corporate insolvency law reform certainly is one of the features of this ongoing discussion. At the same time, the marked differences also

---

[41] See Art. L.631-1 of the French Code de commerce.

[42] Most of these changes were introduced by the Bankruptcy Abuse Prevention and Consumer Protection Act of 2005, available at https://www.gpo.gov/fdsys/pkg/BILLS-109s256enr/pdf/BILLS-109s256enr.pdf.

[43] Armour & Cumming, *supra* note 7, provide evidence that it is.

[44] Paragraph 14 of Schedule B1 to the Insolvency Act 1986, introduced by the Enterprise Act 2002.

[45] Report of the Review Committee on Insolvency Law and Practice (1982) Cmnd 8558, 54–55.

[46] See Vanessa Finch, "Re-invigorating corporate rescue", J.B.L. 527, 530 et seq. (2003).

indicate how difficult harmonization efforts with respect to corporate insolvency lawmaking are and will be (on this, see section 11 *infra*).

3.3.3 Creditor versus Debtor Orientation

The significant differences between various jurisdictions with respect to the degree to which their insolvency systems attempt to achieve economic efficiency is also reflected in another distinction, namely whether a country's corporate insolvency regime is more creditor or more debtor oriented. There are at least two reasons why one might want to undertake such a categorization or classification: first, it serves a heuristic purpose in the sense of informing scholars or policy makers of the principal direction of a jurisdiction's bankruptcy philosophy; second, it might be used as a basis for undertaking econometric analysis, for example with respect to the level and/or structure of debt financing in a particular jurisdiction. One could hypothesize, for example, that more creditor orientation will lead to more credit being extended and at terms more favorable to the debtors—a hypothesis that has indeed been confirmed by econometric studies.[47]

Various features of an insolvency regime can be singled out to signal more or less creditor or debtor orientation: the appointment of a trustee to safeguard creditors' interests versus the "debtor in possession" (DIP), the imposition of an automatic (and complete) stay with respect to creditors' enforcement actions (less creditor protection), or the so-called absolute priority rule, i.e., the rule that lower-ranking creditors or, more generally, claim-holders are allowed to receive any value only if higher-ranking claim-holders have been paid in full (more creditor protection). Other criteria that have been suggested are the existence of a set-off in insolvency, the protection of security interests, the existence of the trust as a legal device, the marketability of contracts, and the tracing of tainted money[48]—every single one of these criteria is meant to indicate a stronger creditor orientation. While most of these criteria make intuitive sense, others appear to be more idiosyncratic such as the existence of the trust, which is unknown in civil law jurisdictions without it being obvious that these jurisdictions therefore necessarily are less creditor oriented. Clearly for econometric studies such as those mentioned above, a less heterogeneous proxy needs to be constructed, and in fact it was constructed ("creditor rights index"),[49] without doing away with the controversies about the appropriateness of the chosen index for its specific purpose.[50]

As with a categorization of jurisdictions as being more or less inclined to follow economic logic in the design of their insolvency laws, one can also categorize jurisdictions as being more or less creditor or debtor oriented (based on any of the metrics mentioned above). This would lead to Germany and England being representative of a fairly strong creditor-orientation policy, whereas France counts as strongly debtor oriented, with the US being positioned somewhere in the middle. The above-mentioned heuristic value of such a categorization or classification exists, but it is limited.[51] To begin with, it obviously

---

[47]   See, for example, Rainer Haselmann, Katharina Pistor & Vikrant Vig, "How Law Affects Lending", 23 Rev. Fin. Stud. 549 (2010).

[48]   Wood, *supra* note 8, at 56.

[49]   Rafael La Porta et al., "Law and Finance", 106 J. Pol. Econ. 1113, 1134 et seq. (1998).

[50]   See, for example, Matthias Siems, "What Does Not work in Comparing Securities Laws: A Critique on La Porta et al.'s Methodology", 16 ICCLR 300 (2005).

[51]   For a critique, see Kraakman et al., *supra* note 2, at 147–51.

makes a significant difference whether creditor orientation is about the interests and rights of secured creditors or whether one is talking about the interests and rights of unsecured creditors. Most metrics or schemes simply assume that, in principle, secured credit should receive priority in insolvency—an assumption that is far from uncontroversial (see section 6 *infra*). Moreover, a classification or categorization of an insolvency regime as creditor or debtor oriented neglects the importance of ownership, debt, and governance structures in a particular jurisdiction for the design of its insolvency laws.[52] For example, concentrated debt structures—such as exist in jurisdictions where the majority of debt is held by a few large commercial banks—facilitate workouts, i.e., out-of-court restructurings: the free-rider problem associated with holdouts is less acute in such jurisdictions, and negotiations amongst creditors proceed with greater ease and efficiency compared to jurisdictions in which most corporate debt is held by dispersed bondholders. Hence, in a jurisdiction with concentrated debt structures, there is less need for a debtor-friendly reorganization procedure. By contrast, fragmented and dispersed debt ownership calls for a statutory and debtor-friendly reorganization procedure that supports ex post efficiency in the restructuring of a financially distressed corporate debtor. To conclude, statements with respect to the creditor or debtor orientation of a particular jurisdiction need to be put in context, i.e., adjusted for the ownership, debt, and governance structures in the respective jurisdiction.

4 OPENING OF INSOLVENCY PROCEEDINGS

When should statutory insolvency proceedings with respect to a corporate debtor be opened? "The Initiation Problem in Bankruptcy"[53] is certainly one of the most important insolvency policy questions that every jurisdiction has to answer in one way or another. Based on economic reasoning, the answer to this question seems straightforward: insolvency proceedings should be opened in case of financial failure of a company. More formally, the test is $V = max(Vgc, Vl) < L$, where V stands for the greater of the going concern value and the liquidation value of the company and L for its liabilities. In essence this means that insolvency proceedings should be initiated once whatever value is left in the firm is less than the firm's liabilities to its creditors. This does not mean that the firm should be shut down. The latter question, i.e., economic failure, is defined by the following condition: $Vgc < Vl$. A firm should be shut down if its going concern value is lower than its liquidation value.

In reality, it can be very difficult to determine whether $V = max(Vgc, Vl) < L$ holds. Whereas it usually will be relatively straightforward to determine L, both the liquidation value of the firm (Vl) and especially its going concern value (Vgc) may be hard to estimate, let alone to quantify precisely. Hence, for practical purposes, a proxy for financial failure as defined above is needed. Most jurisdictions worldwide use some form of liquidity test: a firm that is not able to pay all its debts as they fall due must file for insolvency. Usually, illiquidity in this sense will occur after a firm fails financially based on the $V < L$ test. This is so because

[52] See Kraakman et al., *supra* note 2, at 147–51; Sefa Franken, "Creditor- and Debtor-Oriented Corporate Bankruptcy Regimes Revisited", 5 Eur. Bus. Org. L. Rev. 645 (2004).

[53] Baird, *supra* note 9. See also Bachmann et al., *supra* note 2, at 149 et seq.

even firms whose asset value is lower than its debts may still be able to obtain credit, given information asymmetries, and hence still be liquid.

Initiating insolvency proceedings only once a firm fails financially (on either test) may be too late for two reasons. First, it ignores the effect of backward induction and the incentives thereby created for the firm's creditors.[54] If creditors anticipate that a firm will fail financially the day after tomorrow, they all have an incentive to enforce their claims tomorrow, and they all know this. If they all know that everybody will take enforcement action tomorrow, they all have an incentive to do this today, and that is what is going to happen. So backward induction "backdates" the common pool problem. Second, creditors' interests are already endangered before financial failure of a corporation. Once the equity position of a corporation deteriorates, shareholders and managers have an incentive to engage in risk shifting, i.e., in initiating risky projects that might even have a negative net present value (see section 3.3.1 *supra*). It is difficult to draw a precise lesson from these two complicating factors for the design of laws on the initiation of corporate insolvency proceedings. The only thing that can be said with certainty is that both backward induction by creditors and risk shifting by shareholders/managers may need to be addressed by insolvency-type rules that apply before a firm is technically financially insolvent.

Different jurisdictions approach the "Initiation Problem" very differently. In the US, for example, the regulatory strategy was, and still is, primarily based on rewarding shareholders/managers for filing early. Central features of (the practice of) Chapter 11, such as the "debtor in possession," the "exclusivity period" for the debtor to propose a reorganization plan, the automatic stay, and violations of the absolute priority rule,[55] are best explained as carrots for the incumbent shareholders/managers to use the statutory reorganization procedure as a tool to get a distressed company back on track. The English and the French approaches differ significantly. Both jurisdictions rely on sticks rather than carrots to secure a timely filing. In England, section 214 of the Insolvency Act 1986 imposes unlimited personal liability ("make such contribution (if any) to the company's assets as the court thinks proper") for "wrongful trading" on a director of a company that went into insolvent liquidation, if he or she "knew or ought to have concluded that there was no reasonable prospect that the company would avoid going into insolvent liquidation" and did not take "every step with a view to minimizing the potential loss to the company's creditors."[56] This statutory liability is flanked by a similar liability at common law.[57] In addition, "misbehaving" directors face potentially stiff sanctions under

---

[54] Eidenmüller, *supra* note 34, at 242 et seq.

[55] Eidenmüller, *supra* note 34, at 246 note 13 with further references.

[56] However, directors will not be held liable despite having failed to take every step to minimize losses to creditors if the company does not suffer a net deficiency as a result of the wrongful trading, *Grant & Anor v. Ralls & Ors (re Ralls Builders Ltd)* [2016] EWHC 243 (Ch), Snowden J. 16 February 2016.

[57] *West Mercia Safetywear Ltd v. Dodd* [1988] BCLC 250. For fiduciary duties of managers vis-à-vis the firm's creditors in the vicinity of insolvency in the US, see *Credit Lyonnais Bank Nederland, N.V. v. Pathe Communications Corp.*, 1991 WL 277613 (Del. Ch. 1991); *Production Resources Group, L.L.C. v. NCT Group, Inc.*, 863 A.2d 772 (Del. Ch. 2004); *Trenwick America Litig. Trust v. Ernst & Young, L.L.P.*, 906 A.2d 168 (Del. Ch. 2006); *Big Lots Stores, Inc. v. Bain Capital Fund VII, LLC*, 922 A.2d 1169 (Del. Ch. 2006); *North American Catholic Educational Programming Foundation, Inc. v. Gheewalla*, 930 A. 2d 92 (Del. 2007).

disqualification rules.[58] The French liability regime is similar to the English one. Art. L.651-2, sentence 1 of the Code de commerce ("action en comblement de l'insuffisance d'actif") reads as follows:

> Where the judicial liquidation proceedings of a legal entity reveals an excess of liabilities over assets, the court may, in instances where management fault has contributed to the excess of liabilities over assets, decide that the debts of the legal entity will be borne, in whole or in part, by all or some of the de jure or de facto managers, or by some of them who have contributed to the management fault.[59]

In Germany, neither effective sticks nor sufficiently attractive carrots are currently in place to secure a timely filing. Managers face criminal and tort liability if they fail to file within three weeks *after* cash flow or balance sheet insolvency of a corporation (section 15a Insolvenzordnung, section 823 Bürgerliches Gesetzbuch). They are also liable vis-à-vis the corporation for payments made after that point in time (sections 64 GmbH-Gesetz, 92 para. 2 Aktiengesetz). Hence, it is only upon acute financial distress of a corporation that managers are required to take action.[60] In 2012, the German lawmaker tried to improve the situation by introducing a reformed DIP procedure which provides the debtor with a "protective regime" of three months during which creditors' enforcement action is stayed and the debtor is able to conceptualize and propose a reorganization plan (sections 270, 270a, 270b, 270c Insolvenzordnung). However, unlike in the US, the debtor may resort to this regime only after the firm is already balance sheet insolvent or there is a serious threat (likelihood > 50%) of a cash flow insolvency within the foreseeable future, i.e., the next months. This may be too late for the initiation of a successful restructuring operation.

The significant diversity of rules that seek to secure a timely initiation of insolvency proceedings in Europe and beyond gives rise to the question of whether some form of harmonization might be beneficial. The case for such harmonization rests on forum shopping by firms in the vicinity of insolvency. Imagine an English company whose directors would face liability under section 214 of the Insolvency Act 1986 were they to put the company in an English insolvency proceeding. They decide to move the "Centre of Main Interests"[61] (COMI) of the company from England to Germany and file for insolvency in Germany. Moving a firm's COMI from one jurisdiction to another is costly, but it can be done (it is less costly within Europe than, say, from England to the US).[62] Under German insolvency

---

[58] Pursuant to section 6 of the Company Directors Disqualification Act 1986, directors of insolvent companies who are deemed "unfit" to act as directors can be disqualified for a minimum of two, and a maximum of 15, years.

[59] The English translation is taken from https://www.legifrance.gouv.fr/Traductions/en-English/Legifrance-translations (last visited February 23, 2018).

[60] According to sections 64 GmbH-Gesetz, 92 para. 2 Aktiengesetz, managers also face a fault-based liability for payments to shareholders that directly caused the insolvency of the corporation. However, these provisions have only a very limited practical relevance as the insolvency administrator will usually find it extremely difficult to prove such an effect of a payment that was made.

[61] Under the European Insolvency Regulation (EIR), this is the criterion for jurisdiction to open a "main insolvency proceeding" which has, in principle, worldwide effect (Article 3 EIR).

[62] The recast EIR does not change this. It only tries to limit opportunistic COMI moves on the eve of bankruptcy by limiting the scope of the presumption that the COMI is where the place of the registered office of the company is. Article 3(1) EIR now reads as follows: "In the case of a company or legal person, the place of the registered office shall be presumed to be the centre of its main interests in the absence of

laws, they are free from liability as long as they stay within the three-week period mentioned above.[63] Hence, they can escape liability in England by shifting the firm's COMI to Germany. Against this background, a uniform European wrongful trading rule appears to be sensible, and it would also be within the competence of the EU to enact it.[64]

5 GOVERNANCE OF INSOLVENCY PROCEEDINGS

Once corporate insolvency proceedings are initiated, a governance mechanism must be put in place—"insolvency governance" substitutes "corporate governance." However, as mentioned in section 1, the divide between these two spheres of law and academic discipline is less pronounced once one conceives of insolvency law as "corporate governance under financial distress." To some extent, corporate law already caters for creditors. Just think about the European rules on legal capital, i.e., the regime established by the second company law directive on minimum capital (for certain corporations), capital maintenance, and actions to be taken upon a serious loss of capital.[65] Agency theory can be used to understand the regulatory problems and develop potential policy responses both with respect to financially healthy and financially distressed corporations. What is true, though, is that insolvency does not only exacerbate existing agency conflicts. The conflicts of interests also change, and new actors and interested parties come on to the stage: in addition to the debtor (shareholders/managers) and its creditors, insolvency courts—alongside general private law courts or specialized corporate courts—insolvency practitioners, and new institutions or agencies of the state/government—looking into, for example, tax, welfare, or environmental matters—become relevant actors, performing specific roles.

Who sits "in the driver's seat" in various jurisdictions? Again, jurisdictions worldwide differ significantly in the governance mechanisms employed.[66] Mirroring an earlier categorization or classification of different jurisdictions being more or less creditor or debtor

---

proof to the contrary. That presumption shall only apply if the registered office has not been moved to another Member State within the three-month period prior to the request for the opening of insolvency proceedings." Moreover, this provision does not affect the most "dangerous" of all COMI shifts, namely those that are factual only and not accompanied by a move of the registered office. These are detrimental to the company's creditors in particular because moving the registered office usually is done under the regime set up by the tenth company law directive on cross-border mergers (Directive 2005/56/EC of 26 October 2005) which contains safeguards for creditors and employees.

[63] On the issue of characterizing which laws are insolvency laws for the purposes of Article 4 EIR see CJEU, Case C-594/14 (*Kornhaas*), Judgment of 10 December 2015.

[64] See Eidenmüller, *supra* note 34, at 251 et seq. This proposal was suggested originally by the High Level Group of Company Law Experts, A Modern Regulatory Framework for Company Law in Europe, 2002, 68–69, available at http://www.ecgi.org/publications/documents/report_en.pdf.

[65] Directive 2012/30/EU of the European Parliament and of the Council of 25 October 2012 (recast), OJ of the EU of 14 November 2012, L 315/74.

[66] See, for example, Westbrook et al., *supra* note 8, at 74–83, 203–25; Douglas G. Baird & Robert K. Rasmussen, "Antibankruptcy", 119 Yale L. J. 648 (2010). On the importance of corporate ownership structures for issues of bankruptcy governance see John Armour, Brian Cheffins & David Skeel, "Corporate Ownership Structure and the Evolution of Bankruptcy Law: Lessons from the United Kingdom", 55 Vand. L. Rev. 1699 (2002).

oriented, creditors enjoy a very strong position both in England and in Germany. This holds true for the various (insolvency) proceedings in England, especially for the CVA and the SoA, which do not involve an insolvency administrator/receiver, but also, albeit to a somewhat lesser degree, for the German Insolvenzordnung under which the appointment of at least a supervisor is mandatory if no insolvency administrator is installed. Such a supervisor functions as a controller for significant transactions but also as a mediator between the interests of all other stakeholders. Both in England and in Germany, the insolvency courts are of course in the picture, too. However, they don't actively "manage" the case but rather function as an arbiter that makes sure that fundamental procedural rules and rights are observed.

By contrast in the US, the debtor typically sits "in the driver's seat." This was certainly the case before the Bankruptcy Abuse Prevention and Consumer Protection Act of 2005 curbed some of the debtor's rights and privileges in Chapter 11,[67] but it is still true today, albeit to a somewhat lesser degree. In France, it is the bankruptcy courts that hold a strong governance position. It was already mentioned that in a Redressement judiciaire, for example, the competent court can always decide on the closure or sale of distressed business—regardless of the business' economic viability (section 3.3.2 *supra*).

As a matter of first principles, there is much to be said in favor of a strong governance role of the firm's creditors in an insolvency proceeding. As the new residual claimants to the firm's assets, their money is at stake, so they have appropriate incentives to take economically rational decisions. However, not all creditors are alike, of course. Fully secured creditors may press for a premature liquidation even in cases where the company is not economically distressed, i.e., its going concern value exceeds its liquidation value. Conversely, creditors who are completely out of the money will push for a continuation of the business even where this would be unjustified economically. Hence, designing an appropriate "creditor governance mechanism" must ensure that creditors' control and decision rights are channeled toward value-maximizing decisions—by establishing appropriate procedural controls (by the competent courts), for example.

Putting creditors in the driver's seat does not imply that the debtor should be completely disempowered. The debtor's managers and, with respect to closed corporations, its shareholders will usually have a significant comparative informational advantage with respect to the debtor's economic and financial health. This can best be "exploited" for the timely initiation of insolvency proceedings if the debtor's managers and its shareholders are rewarded by retaining some control over the firm's management by a debtor in possession-like proceeding, and possibly also can expect to receive some equity value in the firm that is to be restructured. However, here again biases need to be controlled: as with out-of-the-money creditors, shareholders have a strong continuation bias even where a financially distressed firm should be liquidated because it suffers from economic failure.

Do courts have the information, expertise and incentives to play an active governance role that goes beyond arbitrating between competing stakeholders' interests and making sure that fundamental (procedural) rights are observed? Most scholars would probably doubt the courts' competence to perform such a role on all three counts mentioned (information,

---

[67] For example, the 2005 Act imposes mandatory plan filing and confirmation deadlines on small business debtors, see McCormack, *supra* note 8, at 109.

expertise, and incentives) and hence be very critical of the very active, managerial role assumed by the French courts in a Redressement judiciaire, for example. However, there is some evidence that courts may do a better governance job than one could and would expect. In a study on Chapter 11 bankruptcies, it appeared that judges do not suffer from a continuation bias and that they are able and competent to filter correctly economically distressed from healthy firms and to do so quickly.[68] One probably needs to distinguish between judges in various jurisdictions, their training, expertise and also powers and "goal function" as established by the insolvency rules in place.

An illustrative example of the governance problems raised in insolvency proceedings is offered by going concern sales as a substitute for restructuring proceedings. Such going concern sales seem to offer the possibility of preserving a viable business as a going concern while avoiding the duration and costs involved with developing, negotiating, and confirming a restructuring plan. At the same time, markets for distressed firms often are thin—if they exist at all—and insiders have a strong interest to acquire whatever value is left in the firm at as low a price as possible (see in detail section 8.5.1 *infra*).

6 RANKING OF CLAIMS AND POSITION OF SECURED CREDITORS

One of the most important questions in the design of (corporate) insolvency procedures is the ranking of claims in general and the position of secured creditors in particular.[69] Jurisdictions worldwide differ significantly in their approach to this question, not least because it is perceived to involve highly "political" judgments, and the scholarly work, if it exists, does not provide clear guidance. It is not surprising, then, that harmonization efforts in this area face significant challenges.

6.1 Approaches of Different Jurisdictions

If one makes a very stylized distinction between different types of claims, one can differentiate between administrative expenses (AE), secured creditors (SC), and unsecured creditors (UNSC). The latter include tax claims, wages and pensions, and shareholder loans. Based on these three categories, the ranking of different types of claims in England, the US, France, and Germany is remarkably different (see Table 38.1).[70]

The simplest ranking system appears to be the German one: secured creditors come first, followed by administrative expenses and all unsecured creditors. The English system varies this ordering in two important respects: first, floating charges have a lower

---

[68] Edward R. Morrison, "Bankruptcy Decision Making: An Empirical Study of Continuation Bias in Small-Business Bankruptcies", 50 J. L. & Econ. 381 (2007).

[69] For a general analysis see Douglas G. Baird, "The Importance of Priority", 82 Cornell L. Rev. 1420 (1997).

[70] The following representation is based on Wood, *supra* note 8, at 253 et seq. It takes account of later changes in the law.

Table 38.1 Ranking of Different Types of Claims

	England	US	France	Germany
1	SC (fixed charges)	SC (but see § 364 BC for post-commencement financing)	Pref. UNSC (certain taxes, wages/benefits)	SC
2	AE	AE	AE	AE
3	Pref. UNSC (including certain wages, unpaid pension contributions)	Pref. UNSC (including certain wages, unpaid pension contributions, taxes)	SC	UNSC
4	Up to £600,000 for General UNSC	General UNSC	General UNSC	
5	SC (floating charges)			
6	General UNSC (including taxes)			

ranking compared to fixed charges; second, certain unsecured creditors, including wage claims and unpaid pension contributions, receive a preferential treatment compared to general unsecured creditors. The differentiation between various types of unsecured creditors is also reflected in the US and the French system, with preferred unsecured creditors ranking highest in France—they top all other types of claims, even secured creditors.

6.2 Secured Creditors

The treatment of secured creditors in insolvency proceedings has a significant effect on lending practice. One would assume that the higher the ranking of secured creditors in insolvency proceedings is, the cheaper credit will be for debtors, and the higher debt levels/lending volume will be in a particular jurisdiction. This is exactly what is confirmed by the available evidence: Using a sample of small firms that defaulted on their bank debt in France, Germany, and the UK, Davydenko and Franks found that large differences in creditors' rights across countries lead banks to adjust their lending and reorganization practices to mitigate costly aspects of bankruptcy law. In particular, they found that French banks respond to a code that is "unfriendly" to secured creditors by requiring more collateral than lenders elsewhere, and by relying on forms of collateral that minimize the statutory dilution of their claims in bankruptcy.[71]

These effects say something about the empirical importance of how secured creditors in particular are treated in insolvency proceedings. A very different matter is whether

[71] Sergei A. Davydenko & Julian R. Franks, "Do Bankruptcy Codes Matter? A Study of Defaults in France, Germany and the U.K.", 63 J. Fin. 565 (2008).

according secured creditors full priority in insolvency proceedings is a defendable policy choice. This is a normative question, and it is one of the most controversial ones in the scholarly and political debate about the design of (corporate) insolvency proceedings. LoPucki once put the problem succinctly by stating that "Security is an agreement between A and B that C take nothing."[72] As between A (creditor) and B (debtor), security clearly has efficiency benefits: it lowers A's monitoring, enforcement, and risk costs, and it protects A against opportunistic business policies that would require B to use the pledged collateral. However, these efficiency benefits come at a cost to C if C cannot adjust to the transaction between A and B: the total asset pool available for the other creditors shrinks, and correspondingly their expected recovery prospects are reduced as well. C might not be able to adjust to the transaction between A and B either because C is an involuntary creditor such as a tort creditor, because C finds it not worth the effort given the size of his claim, or because he lacks the skill or bargaining power to push B to agree to a contractual regime that would effectively protect his interest.[73] Do the efficiency benefits of secured credit in the relationship between A and B outweigh the costs imposed on C? This is an empirical question, and some evidence suggests that in fact they do.[74] Hence, according secured creditors (full) priority in insolvency proceedings appears to be a defendable policy choice in principle.[75]

Even if, in principle, secured creditors are given this priority position, the question arises of whether certain limits may be justified vis-à-vis all other creditors and the debtor. It is easy to see that the immediate realization of a secured claim upon the opening of an insolvency proceeding may have detrimental effects on the going concern value of a distressed firm. Consider, for example, a machine that is crucial for running a production process in a business. If the financing bank were allowed to take it away and sell it on the market to realize its claim, restructuring prospects for the firm would be greatly reduced or even eliminated. Hence, imposing a stay on enforcement actions also with respect to secured creditors, as many jurisdictions do,[76] makes sense. However, jurisdictions differ in the protection granted to secured creditors on whom such a stay is imposed. The US Supreme Court once held that § 362(d)(1) of the Bankruptcy Code does not afford protection in the form of interest for the deferred realization of the encumbered asset with respect to undersecured creditors.[77] The converse holds true under section 169 of the German Insolvenzordnung.

---

[72] Lynn M. LoPucki, "The Unsecured Creditor's Bargain", 80 Va. L. Rev. 1887, 1899 (1994).

[73] Using the terminology of Bebchuk and Fried, in the latter two alternatives C can be called a "non-adjusting" creditor. See Lucian A. Bebchuk & Jesse M. Fried, "The Uneasy Case for the Priority of Secured Claims in Bankruptcy", 105 Yale L. J. 857 (1996); Lucian A. Bebchuk & Jesse M. Fried, "The Uneasy Case for the Priority of Secured Claims in Bankruptcy: Further Thoughts and a Reply to Critics", 82 Cornell L. Rev. 1279 (1997).

[74] See John Armour, "The Law and Economics Debate About Secured Lending: Lessons for European Lawmaking?", 5 Eur. Comp. & Fin. L. Rev. 3 (2008); Yair Listokin, "Is Secured Debt Used to Redistribute Value from Tort Claimants in Bankruptcy? An Empirical Analysis", 57 Duke L. J. 1037 (2008) ("high-tort firms" have unusually low amounts of secured debt).

[75] See Horst Eidenmüller, Secured Creditors in Insolvency Proceedings, in The Future of Secured Credit in Europe 273–83 (Horst Eidenmüller & Eva-Maria Kieninger eds., 2008), for a summary of the debate.

[76] See 11 U.S.C. § 362 in the US; Insolvency Act 1986 Schedule B1 para. 43 in England; Art. L.622-21 of the French Code de commerce, and sections 107 and 166 of the German Insolvenzordnung.

[77] *United Savings Association of Texas v. Timbers of Inwood Forest Associates, Ltd.*, 484 US 365.

6.3 Administrative Expenses

The rationale for putting administrative expenses—such as court fees or fees for an insolvency administrator—before general unsecured creditors is straightforward: as a collective proceeding that aims to solve a multi-party prisoners' dilemma, an insolvency proceeding is run for the benefit of the unsecured creditors' collective. A more difficult question is whether contributions of the secured creditors to the administrative expenses are justified as well. A case can be made for such contributions if it can be shown that secured creditors, too, benefit from a collective proceeding or that certain costs can be attributed to them, for example costs of identifying collateral and realizing its value. Section 171 of the German Insolvenzordnung, for example, forces secured creditors to contribute as much as 4% of the collateral value as sorting costs, 5% as realization costs, and, if applicable, 19% VAT, i.e., a total of 28% of the collateral value. Based on the above-stated considerations, this appears to be justifiable. Against this background, secured creditors have an incentive to "oversecure" their claim, and German law allows them to do this within certain limits.[78]

6.4 Unsecured Creditors

No apparent efficiency rationale exists why certain unsecured creditors, for example tax, wage, and pension claims, should be given priority over the claims of other, general unsecured creditors. It is rather fairness or distributional concerns that are instrumental in this regard, as with the wage or pension claims of workers, or the clout that certain stakeholders have in the political process, as with claims of tax authorities, i.e., the state.

An interesting and important case for the design of corporate insolvency laws in particular is the ranking of shareholder loans vis-à-vis other unsecured creditors. Debt finance by shareholders is an important source of financing for closed corporations or in group structures in particular. It is driven primarily by tax considerations. Some jurisdictions subordinate shareholder loans relative to the claims of other unsecured creditors. This is the case, for example, according to section 39 para. 1 no. 5 of the German Insolvenzordnung. In the US, 11 U.S.C. § 510(c)(1) gives the bankruptcy court discretion to subordinate claims (equitable subordination).[79] By contrast, English law treats claims arising from shareholder loans *pari passu* with other unsecured claims, as does French law.[80]

It is relatively easy to come up with a justification for provisions that subject payments on shareholder loans to the avoidance provisions of an insolvency code (within certain time limits): shareholders are insiders, and they may enrich themselves to the detriment of other creditors by such payments in the vicinity of insolvency.[81] However, it is much more difficult

---

[78] See Christian Tetzlaff, Commentary on section 170 Insolvenzordnung, in Münchener Kommentar zur Insolvenzordnung Band 2 section 170 margin nos. 35 et seq. (Hans-Peter Kirchhof, Horst Eidenmüller & Rolf Stürner eds., 2013).

[79] On this discretionary power see, for example, Charles Tabb, The Law of Bankruptcy 527 et seq. (1997).

[80] See Horst Eidenmüller, Gesellschafterdarlehen in der Insolvenz, in Festschrift für Claus-Wilhelm Canaris zum 70. Geburtstag Band II 49, 53 et seq. (Andreas Heldrich et al. eds., 2007).

[81] Eidenmüller, *supra* note 80, at 61 et seq.

to identify a convincing rationale for subordination rules if no such payments have taken place. Clearly, a subordination rule discourages debt financing by shareholders if the company is in financial distress, and the shareholders may be the only available financing source in such a setting. As a consequence, the prospects for a restructuring of the firm might be greatly reduced. On the other hand, one can argue that distressed firms might (ab)use funds made available by shareholder loans to "gamble for resurrection," further diluting existing claims of outside creditors. This is a serious concern. At the same time, it would appear that a liability rule for wrongful trading addresses this concern more directly and efficiently than a rule that subordinates all shareholder loans—whatever their purpose. The one remaining advantage of such a subordination rule might then lie in the lower-risk costs imposed on shareholders/managers compared to a liability regime: the loss from the shareholders' perspective is limited to the amount of the loan under a subordination regime, whereas they face a potentially unlimited personal liability under a liability regime.

7 Contracting for Assets of the Debtor

Given the statutory ranking of claims in an insolvency proceeding, creditors have an incentive to try and contract for a better position than that accorded to them by the statutory ranking. In principle, such contractual arrangements appear problematic as they are aimed at upsetting the statutory order. At the same time, creditors can legitimately contract for security and, hence, improve their ranking compared to having an unsecured position. So why not allow them to modify their statutory ranking in other ways?

A good illustration of the problem is the so-called "flip clause" that was the subject of litigation in the US and the UK in the aftermaths of the latest financial and economic crisis. The issue arose in the context of the Lehman bankruptcy. In essence, the flip clause stipulates that upon A's bankruptcy, a charge held by A over certain of B's assets would flip to certain of A's creditors. This results in these creditors gaining an advantage over A's other creditors: an asset that would have been available to *all* of A's creditors has now been carved out of the asset pool and is available only to *some* of them.

In the US, 11 U.S.C. § 365(e)(1) stipulates that executory contracts may not be terminated or modified as a result of a contractual provision which purports to permit such termination or modification conditioned on the insolvency of the debtor. According to § 541(c)(1)(B), an interest of the debtor in property becomes property of the estate notwithstanding any provision in an agreement, transfer instrument, or applicable non-bankruptcy law that is conditioned on the insolvency or financial condition of the debtor and that effects or gives an option to effect a forfeiture, modification, or termination of the debtor's interest in property. These provisions invalidate so-called ipso facto clauses,[82] and it has been held that the flip clause amounted to just that.[83] Further, the clause was judged to violate the automatic stay.[84]

---

[82] Ipso facto clauses are clauses which purport to set out the consequences of bankruptcy on an agreement (e.g., automatic termination of a lease).

[83] *In re Lehman Bros. Holdings Inc.*, 422 B.R. 407 (Bankr. S.D.N.Y. 2010).   [84] Id.

The English courts came to a different conclusion. The litigation in the UK centered around the common law "anti-deprivation principle," which aims to prevent arrangements—operating upon bankruptcy—which withdraw from the insolvent estate assets which would be otherwise available to the debtor's creditors.[85] The rationale of the principle originally was to prevent "false" ownership of assets and a deception of creditors.[86] Later on, the policy of preventing contracting out of bankruptcy became an issue as well, but there are other ways to contract out of bankruptcy not affected by the principle, such as creating a charge or contractually subordinating a claim.[87]

In *Belmont Park*, the UK Supreme Court held that a good faith transaction without the purpose of circumventing bankruptcy rules does not violate the anti-deprivation principle.[88] So the crucial test appears to be whether there is a "valid commercial reason" for the transaction or whether the only ("real") purpose is to circumvent bankruptcy rules.[89] Such a valid commercial reason was found to be present in *Belmont Park* and, accordingly, the transaction was upheld.

However, distinguishing cases based on the (non-)existence of valid commercial reasons for the transaction in question appears to obfuscate the real issue. If an insolvency system creates a mandatory statutory order with respect to the ranking of claims, *any* private arrangement that has the *effect* of upsetting or modifying the order must be judged to be impermissible. It simply does not matter whether it is a good faith transaction that was undertaken with other (legitimate) motives (also) in mind. The policy underlying the mandatory statutory ordering system overrides any "legitimate" commercial goal that the parties to the transaction wish to pursue. The only permissible contractual arrangement is for parties to agree to a priority position as defined by the statute, for example by creating a security right.[90]

8 RESCUE PROCEEDINGS

A central feature of modern corporate insolvency systems are rescue proceedings. These are proceedings that aim at restructuring the financially (and possibly also economically) distressed firm and putting it back on track financially (and possibly also economically). Various types of rescue proceedings exist in the US, England, France, and Germany.

---

[85] See *Belmont Park Investments Pty Ltd and others v. BNY Corporate Trustee Services Ltd and another*, [2011] UKSC 38 at [1] and at [2]–[3] for references to further authorities.

[86] See Gabriel Moss, "Should British Eagle Be Extinct?", 24 Insolv. Int. 49 (2011).   [87] Id.

[88] *Belmont Park*, *supra* note 85, at [102] et seq.

[89] See *Belmont Park*, *supra* note 85, at [74]–[83] and [108]–[109].

[90] The flip clause did not give rise to litigation in Germany. If it had, there is little doubt that according to section 81 para. 1 of the Insolvenzordnung, the clause would have been held to be invalid. According to this provision, rights in objects forming part of the insolvency estate cannot be acquired with legal effect after the opening of the insolvency proceedings even if such acquisition of rights is not based on the debtor's transfer or effected by way of execution. For a comparison of section 81 para. 1 of the Insolvenzordnung and the anti-deprivation principle see Reinhard Bork & Martin Voelker, "§ 91 InsO und die Anti-Deprivation Rule—ein Rechtsvergleich", 74 KTS 235 (2013).

8.1 Types of Proceedings

One way to classify or categorize these proceedings is to distinguish between "structured bargaining" procedures that involve negotiations over a restructuring plan and procedures that do not involve such negotiations.[91] Another differentiating feature is whether the procedure allows dissenting creditors to be bound by a restructuring plan or not. Chapter 11 of the Bankruptcy Code in the US, Company Voluntary Arrangements and Schemes of Arrangements under English law, the French Procédure de sauvegarde, and the Insolvenzplanverfahren according to sections 217 et seq. of the German Insolvenzordnung are structured bargaining procedures, and they also allow dissenting creditors to be bound. The French Redressement judiciaire allows dissenting creditors to be bound (but is not a structured bargaining procedure), the French Procédure de conciliation is a structured bargaining procedure (but does not allow dissenting creditors to be bound), and the English Administration is neither a structured bargaining procedure nor does it allow dissenting creditors to be bound (but it may be used as a restructuring tool).

Within the category of structured bargaining procedures, a further distinction can be drawn between systems that provide for a segmentation of creditors into classes with each class voting on the restructuring plan (followed by court approval)—this is the case, for example, with respect to Chapter 11, the Scheme of Arrangement, and the Insolvenzplanverfahren—and systems that do not provide for such a segmentation as, for example, the Company Voluntary Arrangement. Conducting bargaining and voting within classes enhances the legitimacy of the process as the likelihood of voting results that reflect the interests of similarly situated creditors increases. At the same time, the process becomes more cumbersome, and therefore costly. If time is of the essence, as it is with respect to the restructuring of financial institutions, for example, one would rather not want to use a structured bargaining process with creditors voting in classes (if one wanted to use an "ordinary" bankruptcy procedure at all).

8.2 The Position of Shareholders

Structured bargaining procedures with voting by classes often provide that the incumbent shareholders of the corporation form one or more of the various classes, i.e., they are "part of the plan," and their interests can be affected by it. This makes sense conceptually, as a corporation's shareholders, in a situation of financial distress, have the lowest ranking claim on the corporation's assets, i.e., they are "sub-subordinated."[92] This is how shareholders are treated, for example, in a Chapter 11 process (11 U.S.C. § 1123(a)(1)) and in

---

[91] On the former see, for example, Baird, *supra* note 12, chapter 11; Jennifer Payne, "Debt Restructuring in English Law: Lessons from the US and the Need for Reform", 120 Law Quarterly Review 282 (2014); McCormack, *supra* note 8, chapter 8; Westbrook et al., *supra* note 8, at 121–64.

[92] Horst Eidenmüller & Andreas Engert, "Reformperspektiven einer Umwandlung von Fremd- in Eigenkapital (Debt-Equity Swap) im Insolvenzplanverfahren", 30 Zeitschrift für Wirtschaftsrecht (ZIP) 541 (2009).

an Insolvenzplanverfahren according to the German Insolvenzordnung (sections 217, 225a) since 2002.[93]

Integrating the shareholders into the structured bargaining and voting process allows debt to equity swaps to be part of a restructuring plan. Such swaps are an important element of restructuring practice. They reduce debt levels and interest payments, improving the balance sheet and liquidity position of a distressed firm. If they could not be implemented in a restructuring plan against the will of the incumbent shareholders as well, these shareholders could use their legal position to extract rents from the creditors—which is not justified. However, the prospect of being "expropriated" in an insolvency procedure by virtue of a debt to equity swap might lead the shareholders to delay the filing of an insolvency petition—which is not in the interest of the creditors. On the other hand, debt to equity swaps are a tool that is usually employed more with respect to large public corporations, and in these managers enjoy more independence vis-à-vis the shareholders—also with respect to the filing decision—than in small closed corporations.

8.3 Cram Down Power of Courts

Structured bargaining procedures with class-wise voting differ with respect to the majority requirements that must be met if the plan is to be approved by the competent court. In the US, for example, a plan must, in principle, be accepted by each impaired class (11 U.S.C. § 1129(a)(8)). However, the competent court may "cram down" the plan on a non-accepting class if the members of this class do not fare worse than in a liquidation, and lower-ranking classes receive nothing under the plan ("absolute priority rule"). A similar provision can be found in the Insolvenzplanverfahren of the German Insolvenzordnung (section 245).

One of the critical questions relating to this cram-down power centers around a potential equity stake in the reorganized enterprise for the incumbent shareholders. Sometimes it appears commercially sensible to give them such a stake, for example in order to incentivize an early filing or to make them contribute productively to the restructuring process. US courts, therefore, have recognized a "new value" exception to the absolute priority rule. If the incumbent shareholders contribute "money or money's worth" to the restructured firm, they may retain an equity stake.[94] The German rule in section 245 of the Insolvenzordnung is stricter than its US counterpart and does not allow for a similar exception.

8.4 Financing Rescue Proceedings

Critically important for the success of a rescue proceeding is the issue of financing.[95] The firm entering an insolvency proceeding will usually be (extremely) cash short, making

---

[93] See Horst Eidenmüller, Commentary on section 225a Insolvenzordnung, in Münchener Kommentar zur Insolvenzordnung Band 3 section 225a margin nos. 1 et seq. (Hans-Peter Kirchhof, Horst Eidenmüller & Rolf Stürner eds., 2014).

[94] The promise of future labor was held not to be "money or money's worth," *Norwest Bank Worthington v. Ahlers*, 485 US 197 (1988).

[95] See McCormack, *supra* note 8, chapter 6; David Skeel, "The Past, Present and Future of Debtor-in-Possession Financing", 25 Cardozo L. Rev. 1905 (2004).

continuation and restructuring of the enterprise a difficult task that requires "fresh money." If no further security is available for a potential lender, no loan might be forthcoming and restructuring may be made impossible. Hence, many jurisdictions have provisions granting "superpriority" to financiers of restructuring proceedings under certain circumstances. This is the case, for example, with respect to a Chapter 11 proceeding. 11 U.S.C. § 364(d) permits the use of already encumbered assets as security for new loans provided that adequate protection is given to existing (secured) lenders. Superpriority loans are also possible in France[96] (but not vis-à-vis employee claims) but not in England[97] or in Germany.[98]

It is clear that superpriority provisions not only facilitate the financing of rescue proceedings. They also have a significant governance impact. The debtor in possession financier usually will condition lending on being granted important "governance rights"—for example, via loan covenants—on top of a superpriority before providing "fresh money." Baird and Rasmussen once put it succinctly as follows: "The board may be in the saddle, but the whip is in the creditors' hands."[99] The clout exercised by dominant lenders is potentially problematic for various reasons: the managers negotiating the financing agreement on behalf of the firm may not have the best incentives to do so if they (are forced to) leave the firm and a new crisis management team comes in; firms might take too little risk in the restructuring process, and the dominant lenders might divert value from outside creditors with less clout but who are still in the money. The applicable insolvency regime needs to make sure that the benefits of superpriority are not outweighed by these costs.

8.5 Reform Proposals

Rescue proceedings for corporate debtors are a vibrant field for law reforms worldwide. Jurisdictions experiment with new proceedings (such as, for example, France with the Procédure de sauvegarde accélérée), or they try to improve on existing ones (such as, for example, the US with reforms of Chapter 11[100]).[101] Two "radical" proposals for corporate insolvency law reform deserve to be singled out: going concern sales as a substitute for restructuring proceedings, and "full" debt to equity swaps as a specific form of such proceedings.

---

[96] Arts. L.611-11 and L.622-17 II of the French Code de commerce.

[97] Gerard McCormack, "Super-priority new financing and corporate rescue", J.B.L 701 (2007), notes that the Enterprise Act 2002 did not provide a legislative "superpriority" due to risk that it would grant a superpriority to all lenders irrespective of prospects of success of rescue proposals. He suggests that DIP financing will normally end up with a priority, however, if it is classed as an expense of the administration (section 19 Insolvency Act 1986 and para. 99 to Schedule B1 to the Insolvency Act 1986)—which are generally paid out of the pot of money available to the floating charge holders, as the fixed chargeholders are paid out of proceeds of realization of the assets to which they relate.

[98] Josef Parzinger, Fortführungsfinanzierung in der Insolvenz (2013), has convincingly argued that the legal position in Germany should be changed.

[99] Douglas G. Baird & Robert K. Rasmussen, "Reply: Chapter 11 at Twilight", 56 Stan. L. Rev. 673, 699 (2003).

[100] See, for example, ABI Commission to Study the Reform of Chapter 11, 2012-2014, Final Report and Recommendations, https://abiworld.app.box.com/s/vvircv5xv83aavl4dp4h.

[101] On various alternatives to corporate bankruptcy see Adler, *supra* note 12, at 264 et seq.

8.5.1 *Going Concern Sales*

Restructuring proceedings are often lengthy and costly. This is especially so with respect to structured bargaining procedures with class-based voting. Hence, instead of restructuring a firm in the hands of an existing legal entity by creating a new financial structure, one can also try to salvage its going concern value by selling all its assets to another legal entity (an investor). This entity would implement the necessary reforms of the business, having paid a purchase price for the assets out of which the firm's creditors can be paid. In order to maximize the returns to the creditors, an auction might be set up under which the investor who puts up the highest bid gets the firm's assets.

Such going concern sales were already suggested many decades ago as a viable alternative to Chapter 11,[102] and they are used by many jurisdictions' corporate insolvency regimes as one form of restructuring of a distressed firm.[103] At the same time, there are limits to this approach which reconfirm the need for a statutory restructuring proceeding directed toward the legal entity that faces financial distress. First, markets for firms do not always exist, and if they exist, they may not be very competitive and/or informationally efficient. In crisis-ridden industries, usually only a few potential buyers will be interested. These buyers will often be insiders (managers, shareholders) or competitors of the distressed firms because these are, given their industry knowledge and experience, best positioned to assess its economic prospects. At the same time, they have a strong incentive to acquire the firm as cheaply as possible, possibly at a price much lower than the value of the firm were it to be restructured in the hands of the existing legal entity. Second, asset sales sometimes do not allow the transfer of "dedicated assets" which make up a significant part of the firm's value. Such dedicated assets can come in the form of IP rights, (public) permits, or leases at favorable conditions—to give just three examples. Again, to capture the full going concern value, the firm should be restructured in the hands of the existing legal entity in such circumstances.[104]

If a jurisdiction permits or even promotes going concern sales in insolvency proceedings, it must address the intricate governance problems raised thereby. The most fundamental of these problems is the pricing issue. More specifically, precautions must be taken to avoid sales to insiders at fire sale prices. Jurisdictions differ significantly in their approach to this problem. Under the German Insolvenzordnung, for example, creditors are involved in the sale decision (sections 160 et seq. Insolvenzordnung). A sale to insiders requires the assent (by majority decision) of the whole creditors' assembly (section 162 Insolvenzordnung). By contrast, in England and Wales, administrators have the power to carry out a pre-packaged

---

[102] See, in particular, Douglas G. Baird, "The Uneasy Case for Corporate Reorganizations", 15 J. Leg. Stud. 127 (1986); Douglas G. Baird, "Revisiting Auctions in Chapter 11", 36 J. L. & Econ. 633 (1993). Roe has suggested to sell a 10% stake in the company as a basis to extrapolate the value of the reorganized firm, see Mark J. Roe, "Bankruptcy and Debt: A New Model for Corporate Reorganization", 83 Colum. L. Rev. 527 (1983).

[103] In Germany, for example, going concern sales can be achieved under the Insolvenzordnung either on the initiative of the insolvency administrator or as part of an Insolvenzplan.

[104] It may be true, as Baird and Rasmussen argue (Douglas G. Baird & Robert K. Rasmussen, "The End of Bankruptcy", 55 Stan. L. Rev. 751 (2002)), that the nature of modern firms, in particular the rise of the service sector, has reduced "dedicated assets" with respect to many (distressed) firms. However, there are still many cases where such assets play an important role with respect to firm value.

sale without the prior approval of the creditors or the permission of the court under certain conditions, including extensive disclosure obligations (Statements of Insolvency Practice (SIP) 16). In addition, section 129 of the Small Business, Enterprise and Employment Act 2015 provides the UK Government with the power to enact legislation restricting, or imposing conditions on, administrators' powers to sell or otherwise dispose of assets to "connected persons" (such as directors of the company) in the event that the insolvency industry fails to comply with SIP 16. In comparison, the German approach places greater emphasis on ex ante controls and safeguards, and the UK approach on procedural efficiency.[105] Alternatively, or in addition to these measures, one could contemplate a fault-based liability of administrators who fail to effect a sale that is in the interest of all creditors. Data on recovery rates for creditors that could help assess the merits of the respective regulatory approaches are missing.

8.5.2 Full Debt to Equity Swaps

It has already been mentioned that debt to equity swaps are an important element of modern restructuring practice (see section 8.2 *supra*). The good thing about such swaps is that they put creditors in a position in which they then all have the "correct" economic incentive to implement whatever measures maximize firm value. As creditors, they do not always have this incentive: fully secured creditors may push to liquidate the firm even if restructuring would be value-maximizing, and creditors who are out of the money will push toward a restructuring even if the firm is economically distressed and should be liquidated. It is hard to design rules on class formation and voting that make sure that such "skewed" incentives are not decisive for the outcome of the process.

As early as 1988, Lucian Bebchuk suggested a radically different reorganization procedure based on a "full debt to equity swap" that would "solve" this problem and also be in line with the absolute priority rule.[106] Assume that a firm has two creditors with a claim of US$1 million each: a fully secured creditor (SC) and an unsecured creditor (UNSC). The firm has one (sole) shareholder (SH). Under Bebchuk's scheme, SC would become the sole shareholder. UNSC would get an option to acquire SC's shares at an exercise price of US$1 million. SH would get an option to acquire UNSC's option and SC's shares at an exercise price of US$2 million. This scheme preserves absolute priority. Each stakeholder would get exactly what she can claim under the absolute priority rule. Whoever ends up as the sole shareholder of the firm will implement the restructuring plan that maximizes firm value.

Bebchuk's scheme is elegant and in line with fundamental principles of corporate insolvency law. At the same time, to date it has not been implemented in the real world of restructuring. The simple reason is probably that policy makers worldwide stay clear of

---

[105] For a balanced assessment of different reform proposals see John Armour, The Rise of the "Pre-Pack": Corporate Restructuring in the UK and Proposals for Reform, in Restructuring Companies in Troubled Times: Director and Creditor Perspectives 43–78 (Robert P. Austin & Fady Aoun eds., 2012).

[106] Lucian A. Bebchuk, "A New Approach to Corporate Reorganizations", 101 Harv. L. Rev. 775 (1988). Bebchuk's scheme was adopted by Philippe Aghion, Oliver Hart & John Moore, "The Economics of Bankruptcy Reform", 8 J. L. Econ. Org. 523 (1992). See also Oliver Hart, Firms, Contracts, and Financial Structure (1995), chapter 7.

all proposals that force all creditors to exchange their debt against an equity position. In many jurisdictions, such an involuntary swap would violate fundamental constitutional guarantees. In others, political lobbying by banks in particular prevents legislatures from moving to implement Bebchuk's scheme. If it were implemented, creditors would need to expect to find themselves in the position of a shareholder of a distressed firm whenever they extend credit to a firm with a non-trivial prospect of insolvency. This would potentially have a serious impact on their business model, and many creditors are not comfortable with that prospect. That said, however, Bebchuck's model is useful for restructuring practice because it highlights important features (and benefits) of debt for equity swaps.

9 Contractual Resolution of Financial Distress

Statutory insolvency proceedings are associated with significant direct and indirect bankruptcy costs (see section 3.3.1 *supra*). Hence, stakeholders of a financially distressed firm have a strong incentive to avoid these costs and attempt a private resolution of financial distress: the "privatization of bankruptcy" promises flexible, tailor-made, and fast solutions that come with significantly reduced bankruptcy costs.[107] Two forms of such a privatization must be distinguished: ex ante contracting about bankruptcy, and an ex post renegotiation of the firm's debt structure ("workouts").

9.1 Ex ante Contracting about Bankruptcy

There would be no need for a statutory bankruptcy procedure if all of the firm's creditors and the firm were able to contractually agree ex ante on the procedure that would be applicable if the firm entered a—contractually specified—condition of financial distress. In reality, this is not feasible as some creditors, for example those who have a claim based on tort, do not have a contractual relationship with the firm at all. Nevertheless, scholars have designed schemes that would give contracts with individual lenders an *erga omnes* effect vis-à-vis the whole creditor community.[108] Instead of a full-blown statutory insolvency procedure, the statutory rules would then operate as a backup to legitimize certain private schemes under specified conditions.

Another, probably more realistic form of ex ante contracting about bankruptcy would be to allow firms to choose the applicable bankruptcy regime in their charter.[109] This could be

---

[107] For a critical view see Elizabeth Warren & Jay Lawrence Westbrook, "Contracting Out of Bankruptcy: An Empirical Intervention", 118 Harv. L. Rev. 1197 (2005).

[108] Alan Schwartz, "A Contract Theory Approach to Business Bankruptcy", 107 Yale L. J. 1807 (1998).

[109] Pioneering work in this field has been undertaken by Rasmussen, see Robert K. Rasmussen, "Debtor's Choice: A Menu Approach to Corporate Bankruptcy", 71 Tex. L. Rev. 51 (1992); Robert K. Rasmussen, "A New Approach to Transnational Insolvencies", 19 Mich. J. Int'l. L. 1 (1997); Robert K. Rasmussen, "Resolving Transnational Insolvencies through Private Ordering", 98 Mich. L. Rev. 2252 (2000). See also Horst Eidenmüller, "Free Choice in International Company Insolvency Law in Europe", 6 Eur. Bus. Org. L. Rev. 423 (2005).

done by either allowing firms to choose the bankruptcy forum—with the applicable bank-ruptcy law being that of the forum—or by giving firms the option to directly pick a particular bankruptcy regime out of a "menu" of different regimes provided for by the competent lawmaker. The former regime would be easier to implement—no need to agree (as between states) on the "menu" —and it also has the advantage that it directly incentivizes states to improve their domestic bankruptcy procedures and make them more competitive. Moreover, in contrast to ex post forum shopping by COMI manipulations in times of crisis, picking the forum ex ante in the corporate charter makes the choice visible to all creditors, allowing them to adjust. A critical issue with respect to this form of contracting for bankruptcy is charter amendments. These would need to be subject to a super-majority requirement. To further reduce the danger of opportunistic maneuvers on the eve of bankruptcy, a "waiting period" of a couple of months before the amendment takes effect probably also makes sense.

9.2 Ex post Renegotiation of Debt Structure

Ex ante contracting for bankruptcy regimes is still very much a scholarly enterprise, not a real-life phenomenon. By contrast, ex post renegotiation of the debt structure of a firm that finds itself in financial distress is an important fact of restructuring practice worldwide.[110] Such "workouts" face many challenges, of which the free-rider (or hold-out) problem probably is the most important one: all creditors have a common interest in a success of the restructuring process, but each individual creditor of course wants to maximize her economic benefit, i.e., reduce her contribution to the common good. This strategic incentive problem of a multi-party prisoners' dilemma is "solved" by statutory insolvency procedures that impose a stay on creditors' enforcement actions. Out of court, no such general statutory regime exists. No legal duty forces creditors and/or shareholders to cooperate in a workout.[111] Hence, workout negotiations are destabilized by the free-rider problem.

Creditors can address this issue by putting "majority voting clauses" in common debt instruments such as syndicated loans or bond indentures. Such clauses allow a majority of the creditors—based on voting rights—to agree on debt reductions even if a minority objects. Some jurisdictions are more accommodating of these clauses than others. For example, US law does not allow a reduction of the principal claim by majority decision in a bond indenture (15 U.S.C. § 77ppp),[112] but section 5 of the German *Schuldverschreibungsgesetz* (2009) does.

In any event, such clauses are helpful only with strategic/opportunistic actions of certain creditors that are part of a specific debt instrument. They do not address the free rider problem as between the creditor community as a whole, i.e., regarding creditors of different debt instruments. Various attempts have been made to ameliorate this problem by "soft law" tools. One of these is the so-called London Approach to out-of-court restructurings, which achieved a certain prominence with respect to the restructuring of City firms in the

---

[110] See, in general, Westbrook et al., *supra* note 8, at 165–81; Finch, *supra* note 39, chapter 7.

[111] Eidenmüller, *supra* note 34, at 254 et seq.

[112] For a critical view, see Mark J. Roe, "The Voting Prohibition in Bond Workouts", 97 Yale L. J. 232–79 (1987).

1980s and 1990s.[113] Another soft regulatory instrument is the INSOL Principles for a global approach to multi-creditor workouts (2000).[114]

These instruments are helpful especially in settings with a relatively homogeneous and stable creditor community such as, for example, in cases where a firm is financed primarily by bank debt. However, debt structures worldwide have changed significantly compared to what they looked like in the City of London two or three decades ago. Bond financing has become much more widespread, also with respect to smaller firms. Debt is traded on secondary markets, and new activist investors have entered the scene, especially hedge funds and private equity funds. Credit default swaps (CDS) are available to protect against insolvency risks, changing the incentives of insured creditors or other holders of these instruments. Hence, firms today face workout scenarios where the creditors are extremely heterogeneous and deeply fragmented, have very different interests (effects of CDS, hedge funds as active investors ["loan to own"], etc.), and the composition of the creditors is permanently changing (due to debt trading). Workouts have become more difficult than a couple of decades ago.[115]

If a workout fails because of strategic maneuvers of hold-outs, one way to save at least some of the benefits of an out-of-court restructuring is a "slim statutory reorganization" procedure that is initiated only to get a restructuring plan passed by a majority vote. These types of procedures are often termed "pre-packaged bankruptcies" because most of the issues except the acceptance of the pre-negotiated plan have already been resolved before the bankruptcy petition is filed.[116] The technique of pre-packaged bankruptcies is most advanced in the US where the vote on the plan can also be taken out of court—only plan confirmation requires initiation of a bankruptcy procedure and court approval ("pre-voted pre-packaged bankruptcy").[117] If this is not feasible, the drafted and pre-negotiated plan will be subject to a vote after the bankruptcy petition has been filed ("post-voted pre-packaged bankruptcy").[118] If a full-blown "pre-packaged bankruptcy" is not feasible, the Chapter 11 process can at least be streamlined by so-called restructuring support agreements. These are usually concluded between the debtor and other key players, often senior secured lenders.[119]

---

[113] See Eidenmüller, *supra* note 3, at 236 et seq.; John Armour & Simon Deakin, "Norms in Private Insolvency: The London Approach to the Resolution of Financial Distress", 1 J. Corp. L. Stud. 21 (2001).

[114] https://www.insol.org/pdf/Lenders.pdf. INSOL is the International Association of Restructuring, Insolvency & Bankruptcy Professionals.

[115] See Douglas G. Baird & Robert K. Rasmussen, "Antibankruptcy", 119 Yale L. J. 648 (2010); Horst Eidenmüller, "Privatisierung der Insolvenzabwicklung: Workouts, Covenants, Mediation—Modelle für den Insolvenzstandort Deutschland?", 121 Zeitschrift für Zivilprozess (ZZP) 273, 280 et seq. (2008).

[116] On pre-packaged bankruptcies see, for example, John J. McConnell & Henri Servaes, "The Economics of Pre-Packaged Bankruptcy", 4 J. Appl. Corp. Fin. 93 (1991); Douglas G. Baird & Robert K. Rasmussen, "Beyond Recidivism", 54 Buff. L. Rev. 343 (2006); Eidenmüller, *supra* note 3, at 437 et seq.

[117] See 11 U.S.C. § 1126(b); Eidenmüller, *supra* note 3, at 438.

[118] See Eidenmüller, *supra* note 3, at 438 et seq. For an overview of pre-packaged administrations in England, see the Graham review into pre-pack administration (June 2014), available at https://www.gov.uk/government/publications/graham-review-into-pre-pack-administration.

[119] See Douglas G. Baird, "Bankruptcy's Quiet Revolution", 91 Am. Bankr. L. J. 593 (2017) (advocating a process control by bankruptcy judges that focuses on the flow of information needed to apply Chapter 11's substantive rules).

10 REASONS FOR THE JURISDICTIONAL DIVERGENCES

Insolvency laws worldwide differ significantly—as should be apparent by now. This is true both with respect to corporate and individual insolvencies. Crucial issues of corporate insolvency law, such as the opening and governance of insolvency proceedings, the ranking of claims, the position of secured creditors, and the type and structure of rescue proceedings, are regulated very differently in the jurisdictions that are the focus of this chapter (US, England, France, and Germany). What are the reasons for these jurisdictional divergences? Answering this question can inform projects that aim at harmonizing (corporate) insolvency laws (see section 11 *infra*). If, for example, competitive pressures (regulatory competition) gradually push jurisdictions to adopt particular "solutions" to corporate insolvency law problems, harmonization might not be necessary. And if certain divergences are rooted in different regulatory philosophies or even in differences between the "deep normative structures" of particular societies, then harmonization might be positively harmful—at least from the perspective of those jurisdictions whose regimes are replaced by harmonization.

The reasons for jurisdictional divergences with respect to important corporate insolvency law issues have yet to be studied (empirically) in detail. It is probably true that competitive pressures are influencing corporate insolvency lawmaking, but their intensity is far from clear. The latest major reform of the German Insolvenzordnung was explicitly motivated, for example, by the fact that some German firms "forum shopped" to England, seeking access to a more attractive restructuring regime than that in place in Germany before the reform.[120] At the same time, it would be a gross overstatement to say that market pressures (in Europe) are so strong that we can identify a clear trend toward certain uniform procedures.

Forces that hinder further convergence are, for example, strong lobbying by well-organized stakeholder groups, different regulatory or insolvency philosophies, and "functional" reasons such as differences in financing structures. There are probably many other causes influencing the degree of jurisdictional divergences, and their explanatory force will always be a function of the specific regulatory problem and jurisdiction(s) studied. Insolvency administrators, for example, are a very powerful lobby group in a country like Germany that, for a long time, did not recognize debtor in possession-like proceedings. Hence, it does not come as a surprise that it took Germany so long to introduce such proceedings and that, in practice, they are still a very rare phenomenon. By contrast, the fresh-start philosophy is characteristic for insolvency policy and practice in the US (see section 3.3.2 *supra*). It would require a paradigm shift to move to a regime that starts from the premise that, in the great majority of cases, insolvency is not an "accident" but the consequence of

---

[120] See Entwurf eines Gesetzes zur weiteren Erleichterung der Sanierung von Unternehmen, Bundestag-Drucksache 17/5712 of 4 May 2011, p. 17: "In der Vergangenheit haben einige Unternehmen deshalb ihren Sitz nach England verlegt, da der Geschäftsleitung und den maßgeblichen Gläubigern die Eröffnung eines Insolvenzverfahrens nach englischem Recht zur Sanierung des Unternehmens vorteilhafter erschien. Auch wenn dies Einzelfälle geblieben sind, so haben sie doch Anstoß zu einer umfassenden Diskussion in der Fachöffentlichkeit über den Sanierungsstandort Deutschland gegeben und den Blick für die Schwächen des geltenden deutschen Rechts geschärft."

negligent if not fraudulent management actions. Finally, concentrated debt structures reduce the need for a debtor-friendly restructuring procedure, as has already been pointed out (see section 3.3.3 *supra*). Whether this really *explains* the existence of such procedures in jurisdictions with fragmented and dispersed debt ownership is another question.

If anything, the absence of empirical evidence for dysfunctional regulatory diversity cautions against too much zeal in pursuing harmonization projects in the field of corporate insolvency law. Regulatory competition with respect to corporate insolvency law systems has certain benefits of its own, and what appears "dysfunctional" may be an expression of completely different (but legitimate) insolvency philosophies, as will be seen in the concluding section of this chapter.

11 OUTLOOK: HARMONIZATION OF INSOLVENCY LAWS

The great diversity of (corporate) insolvency systems worldwide has benefits: it creates an "international laboratory" for better solutions, spurring regulatory competition between states for the best "insolvency product." At the same time, last-minute forum shopping by firms—possibly initiated by dominant lenders—can create problems, especially for outside creditors whose interests might be compromised by the move.[121] Further, not all firms have the knowledge and money to engage in sophisticated regulatory arbitrage and, as a consequence, might not have access to an efficient domestic insolvency or restructuring regime. Hence, a case can be made for harmonization of insolvency laws, at least in the form of "minimum harmonization" that allows states to go beyond the required minimum.

Even then, however, harmonizing substantive insolvency laws will always be an exceedingly difficult enterprise, given the heterogeneity of bankruptcy philosophies (objectives of insolvency laws, governance of proceedings, ranking of claims, etc.) and the legitimate resistance of states to harmonization if it is felt directly or indirectly to impact negatively on their respective autonomous regulatory policy. It is not surprising, therefore, that "early" harmonization efforts focused rather on jurisdictional and private international law rules and not on issues of substantive law as a first step. The guiding philosophy with respect to these projects was and is that, as a start, predictable and stable jurisdictional rules should be established and cases should be decided on the basis of the same or at least similar rules, regardless of the forum in which the insolvency procedure takes place. In Europe, the outcome of these efforts was the European Insolvency Regulation of 2002, which was recast in 2015.[122]

---

[121] For a very critical view on forum shopping (on the eve of bankruptcy) see Lynn LoPucki, Courting Failure (2005).

[122] Regulation (EU) 2015/848 of the European Parliament and of the Council of 20 May 2015 on insolvency proceedings (recast), OJ of the EU of 5 June 2015, L 141/19. For an overview see Kristin van Zwieten, An introduction to the European Insolvency Regulation, as made and as recast, in Commentary on the European Insolvency Regulation (Reinhard Bork & Kristin van Zwieten eds., 2016); Gerard McCormack, "Something Old, Something New: Recasting the European Insolvency Regulation", 79 Mod. L. Rev. 121–46 (2016).

The UNCITRAL Model Law on Cross-Border Insolvency (1997) attempted to provide a blueprint for states to harmonize their cross-border insolvency regimes on a global scale.[123]

More recently, efforts to also harmonize substantive insolvency laws have gained greater momentum. Early on, it was again UNCITRAL that moved first with the "Legislative Guide on Insolvency Law" (2004)[124] and its special provisions on "Group Insolvencies" (2010).[125] However, these are, like the 1997 Model Law, not binding legal instruments but merely blueprints for states who wish to reform their domestic regimes based on what might be considered international best practice. The European Union, as with the European Insolvency Regulation, plans to move one step further: in 2014, the European Commission issued a "Recommendation on a New Approach to Business Failure and Insolvency",[126] and it has proposed, in 2016, a binding legal instrument (a Directive) as part of its plan to complete the capital markets union.[127] The driving force behind this initiative is the idea of giving firms in all Member States of the EU access to efficient pre-insolvency restructuring proceedings.[128] By and large, the substantive insolvency regimes of the Member States would be left intact, potentially reducing the political resistance that is to be expected. However, important elements of the proposed restructuring regime are subject to criticism. The draft directive is flawed because it (i) creates a refuge for failing firms that should be liquidated; (ii) rules out going-concern sales for viable firms; (iii) is, in essence, a twisted and truncated insolvency proceeding but without strong court involvement from the beginning and without the tools needed for the court to guarantee a fair outcome of the process.[129] Further, there would be a stifling effect on regulatory competition between the Member States and on the benefits that could bring ("laboratory for the best solutions").

---

[123] http://www.uncitral.org/uncitral/en/uncitral_texts/insolvency/1997Model.html. The Model Law was supplemented in 2011 by rules on the "Judicial Perspective" when applying the Model Law, http://www.uncitral.org/uncitral/uncitral_texts/insolvency/2011Judicial_Perspective.html.

[124] https://www.uncitral.org/pdf/english/texts/insolven/05-80722_Ebook.pdf.

[125] http://www.uncitral.org/pdf/english/texts/insolven/Leg-Guide-Insol-Part3-ebook-E.pdf.

[126] 2014/135/EU, OJ of the EU of 14 March 2014, L 74/65.

[127] Commission Proposal for a Directive of the European Parliament and of the Council on preventive restructuring frameworks, second chance and measures to increase the efficiency of restructuring, insolvency and discharge procedures and amending Directive 2012/30/EU, COM (2016) 723 final (22 November 2016).

[128] See Recital (1) of the draft directive (*supra* note 127): The directive aims at "[...] ensuring that viable enterprises in financial difficulties have access to effective national preventive restructuring frameworks which enable them to continue operating; that honest over indebted entrepreneurs have a second chance after a full discharge of debt after a reasonable period of time; and that the effectiveness of restructuring, insolvency and discharge procedures is improved, in particular with a view to shortening their length."

[129] For a detailed discussion, see Horst Eidenmüller, "Contracting for a European Insolvency Regime", 18 Eur. Bus. Org. L. Rev. 273 (2017).

CHAPTER 39

CORPORATE GOVERNANCE AND EMPLOYMENT RELATIONS

ZOE ADAMS AND SIMON DEAKIN[1]

1 INTRODUCTION

WHY does capital hire labor, rather than the reverse? Why are employee-owned enterprises so rare? Modern institutional economics has answers to these questions, which stress the efficiency properties of shareholder-based monitoring of managers.[2] Following this lead, the corporate governance literature evolved during the 1980s and 1990s to arrive at a consensus around the salience, in both positive and normative terms, of the norm of shareholder primacy.[3] Alternative approaches, such as the "stakeholder" or "team production" model,[4] did not win general acceptance in the field. In the 2000s, policy makers around the world followed this consensus, adopting numerous laws and corporate governance codes which set out to strengthen the rights of shareholders to hold managers to account.[5]

The debate over the role of employees within corporate governance never entirely went away. Transaction cost economics models the employment relationship as an incomplete contract which does not in itself guarantee the conditions for cooperation between workers and management.[6] Thus even allowing for the predominant role given to shareholders in the governance structure of the business enterprise, laws mandating

---

[1] The authors are at the Centre for Business Research, University of Cambridge (www.cbr.cam. ac.uk).

[2] E. Fama & M. Jensen, "The Separation of Ownership and Control", 26 J. L. & Econ. 301 (1983).

[3] H. Hansmann & R. Kraakman, "The End of History for Corporate Law", 89 Geo. L. J. 439 (2001).

[4] M. Blair, Ownership and Control: Rethinking Corporate Governance for the Twenty-First Century (1995); M. Blair & L. Stout, "A Team Production Theory of Corporate Law", 85 Va. L. Rev. 247 (1999).

[5] R. Aguilera & A. Cuervo-Cazurra, "Codes of Good Governance", 17 Corp. Governance 376 (2009).

[6] R.H. Coase, "The Nature of the Firm", 16 Economica (NS) 386 (1937); H. Simon, "A Formal Theory of the Employment Relation", 19 Econometrica 293 (1951); O. Williamson, M. Wachter, & J. Harris, "Understanding the Employment Relation: The Economics of Idiosyncratic Exchange", 6 Bell J. Econ. 250

job security and worker voice may increase the value of individual firms and enhance the societal surplus (or minimize the social costs) that they create.[7] In line with this suggestion, a growing body of empirical work finds that worker-protective labor and employment laws are positively correlated with productivity and innovation at firm level.[8]

By contrast, the empirical literature on shareholder rights is much more equivocal: it seems that there is a tenuous relationship, at best, between corporate governance practices associated with the shareholder primacy norm, in particular independent boards, and enhanced firm performance.[9] Laws mandating or encouraging higher levels of shareholder protection, by tilting the balance of corporate power away from workers and toward investors, may limit the ability of managers to make credible commitments of job security and worker voice. Empowerment of shareholders may also impact negatively on the innovative capacity of firms.[10]

To assess the relationship between corporate governance and employment relations requires a dual approach: investigating, on the one hand, the impact of the worldwide move to enhanced legal protection of shareholder rights beyond those provided by the basic framework of corporate law, and, on the other, the implications for the firm and for the wider economy of laws and regulations affecting the employment relationship. This chapter will provide an overview of relevant theoretical perspectives (section 2), a consideration of research methods (section 3) and an analysis of recent empirical findings, starting with evidence on long-run trends in laws relating to shareholder and employee protection (section 4), and then going on to review studies on the relationship between corporate governance, employment protection and innovation across a range of different country contexts (section 5). This empirical overview will cover recent research using "leximetric" data sets in the course of a wider review of the research field. Section 6 concludes.

(1975); B. Bartling, E. Fehr, & K. Schmidt, "Use and Abuse of Authority: A Behavioral Foundation of the Employment Relation", 11 J. Eur. Econ. Ass'n 711 (2013).

[7] S. Deakin & A. Rebérioux, Corporate Governance, Labour Relations and Human Resource Management in Britain and France: Convergence or Divergence?, in Does Corporate Ownership Matter? 125 (J.-P. Touffut ed., 2009).

[8] S. Storm & C. Nastepaad, "Labour Market Regulation and Productivity Growth: Evidence for 20 OECD Countries (1984–2004)", 48 Industrial Relations 629 (2009); S. Deakin & P. Sarkar, "Assessing the Long-Run Economic Impact of Labour Law Systems: A Theoretical Reappraisal and Analysis of New Time Series Data", 39 Industrial Relations Journal 453 (2008); H. Zhou, R. Decker, & A. Kleinknecht, "Flexible Labor and Innovation Performance: Evidence from Longitudinal Firm-Level Data", 20 Industrial and Corporate Change 941 (2011); V. Acharya, R. Baghai-Wadji, & K. Subramanian, "Wrongful discharge laws and innovation", 27 Rev. Fin. Stud. 301 (2014); V. Acharya, R. Baghai-Wadji, & K. Subramanian, "Labor Laws and Innovation", 56 J. L. & Econ. 997 (2013); F. Belloc, "Law, Finance and Innovation: The Dark Side of Shareholder Protection", 37 Cambridge J. Econ. 863 (2013).

[9] R. Adams, B. Hermalin, & M. Weisbach, "The Role of Boards of Directors in Corporate Governance: A Conceptual Framework and Survey", 48 J. Econ. Lit. 58 (2010).

[10] Belloc *supra* note 8.

2 EMPLOYMENT RELATIONS AND CORPORATE GOVERNANCE: THEORETICAL PERSPECTIVES

Among the first tasks of corporate governance theory is to explain the incentive structures which arise from different configurations of ownership within the firm.[11] "Governance" in a narrow sense is concerned with how residual income and control rights are partitioned between the different corporate constituencies. Once shareholders are identified as the firm's residual owners, an arrangement which corporate governance theory tends to regard as efficient,[12] the claims of other groups fall to be determined by contract, supplemented by regulation. Thus how employees are positioned in relation to the firm could be seen as falling outside the scope of "corporate governance," understood both as an organizational and institutional practice, and as a field of study.

The boundary between "governance," on the one hand, and "contract," on the other, may not be so clearly fixed. On one view, it is because the contract between investors and the firm is too difficult to write that it is necessary to allocate residual income and control rights to shareholders rather than to workers or customers.[13] If that is so, it is the comparative costs of contracting under different ownership regimes which determine the governance structure of the firm in the first place. Putting the point slightly differently, and without ascribing causal priority to one over the other, we might say that "ownership" and "contract" are interrelated mechanisms for the governance of the business firm.

When corporate governance scholarship has addressed the role of employees within the firm it has done so largely in order to explain why it is that they are so rarely constituted as its residual owners.[14] Given the rarity in industrialized market economies of "employee-owned" firms such as producer cooperatives, this is certainly a legitimate question, but it is not the only one of interest. Another approach is to take the near-ubiquity of the "shareholder-owned" firm (referring to the standard legal model of the company limited by share capital) as a given, and to explore its consequences for employment relations and, more generally, for firm performance.

A starting point in this analysis is to consider the distinct features of the employment contract when viewed from a transaction cost perspective. The sum total of the norms governing employment—legal, contractual, and customary—can be thought of as providing a framework for repeated exchange in a setting characterized by uncertainty. Ex ante, the worker sells to the employer his or her labor power or capacity to work in return for an agreed wage. Ex post, residual income and control rights are vested in the employer. What juridical language refers to as the worker's "subordination" can be described in economic terminology as contractual incompleteness.[15] Because the precise terms of the bargain between employer and worker cannot be specified in advance, their formal agreement is supplemented by other norms, many of which have a fairness dimension in the sense of specifying distributions which the parties regard as legitimate. Behavioral studies show that fairness norms help

---

[11] H. Hansmann, The Ownership of Enterprise (1996).   [12] Fama & Jensen, *supra* note 2.
[13] Hansmann, *supra* note 11, ch. 2.   [14] Hansmann, *supra* note 11, ch. 5.
[15] S. Deakin & F. Wilkinson, Labour Law and Economic Theory: A Reappraisal, in Law and Economics and the Labour Market (G. De Geest, J. Siegers, & R. van den Bergh eds., 1999).

build trust between the parties to the employment contract, thereby reconciling equity and efficiency.[16]

That it may be in the enlightened self-interest of employers to offer job security and worker voice in order to improve contractual outcomes is not surprising; this observation is recognized in some well-established economic concepts such as those associated with efficiency wage theory, for example.[17] It is less obvious that labor law should mandate particular forms of worker protection. It could be argued that if employers would adopt these norms anyway, the law should not impose them; and if they would not, the law would be interfering with autonomous contractual choices. However, this view neglects the presence, in practice, of constraints on the spontaneous emergence of worker-protective rules. Adverse selection effects may deter employers from offering job security to prospective employees,[18] while the threat of free-riding by other employers may lead to under-provision of training by firms.[19] Labor laws setting standards for termination in employment and requiring employers to train are essentially means of overcoming collective action problems associated with the inability of employers to coordinate on efficient rules. Laws of this kind have often had the support of employer groups and have been legislated for by political parties with a broadly pro-employer leaning.[20]

The economic case for employment regulation applies particularly to innovative firms. Innovation entails the transformation of productive inputs into saleable outputs in the form of goods and services which are more desirable and/or affordable to consumers than those previously available. The innovative enterprise must assess the quantity and quality of the productive resources that it has to invest to develop such goods and services, in the light of what it knows of its competitors' strategies.[21] In this context, value creation is a developmental process, which turns on the capacity of the firm to utilize the human knowledge at its disposal.[22] Innovative firms are characterized by decentralized decision making, alignment of risks and rewards over the medium to longer term, and toleration of failure.[23] The firm's dependence on specific knowledge may mean that internal, peer-based monitoring is more

[16] B. Bartling, E. Fehr, & K. Schmidt, "Use and Abuse of Authority: A Behavioral Foundation of the Employment Relation", 11 J. Eur. Econ. Association 711 (2013).

[17] J. Bulow & L. Summers, "A Theory of Dual Labour Markets with Application to Industrial Policy, Discrimination and Keynesian Unemployment", 4 J. Lab. Econ. 376 (1986).

[18] D. Levine, "Just-Cause Employment Policies in the Presence of Worker Adverse Selection", 9 J. Lab. Econ. 294 (1991).

[19] D. Acemoglu & J. Pischke, "Beyond Becker: Training in Imperfect Labour Markets", 109 Econ. J. 112 (1999).

[20] M. Barry, M. Michelotti, & C. Nyland, Protectionism, Common Advocacy and Employer Interests: Business Contribution to Labour Market Regulation in Australia, in Labour Law and Labour Market Regulation: Essays on the Construction, Constitution and Regulation of Labour Markets (C. Arup, P. Gahan, J. Howe, R. Johnstone, R. Mitchell, & A. O'Donnell eds., 2006).

[21] W. Lazonick & M. O'Sullivan, "Organization, Finance and International Competition", 1 Industrial and Corporate Change 1 (1996); W. Lazonick & M. O'Sullivan, "Maximizing Shareholder Value: A New Ideology of Corporate Governance", 29 Economy and Society 13 (2000); M. O'Sullivan, "The Innovative Enterprise and Corporate Governance", 24 Cambridge J. Econ. 393 (2000).

[22] B. Holmstrom, "Agency Costs and Innovation", 12 J. Econ. Behav. & Org. 305 (1989).

[23] G. Manso, "Motivating Innovation", 66 J. Fin. 1823 (2011).

efficient than external monitoring through outside investors.[24] However, decentralization of decision making and reliance on specific knowledge may make shareholders vulnerable to opportunism on the part of workers and managers. The innovative firm therefore faces a series of trade-offs.[25]

These trade-offs could be resolved contractually, but only up to a point. In highly liquid capital markets, the threat of shareholder exit through a takeover bid or related restructuring may make employees reluctant to commit to innovative projects in which returns will be realized over the longer term. Firms may therefore offer managers and senior employees incentives to innovate through long-term compensation plans, stock options, golden parachutes, and job security guarantees.[26] These strategies may, however, give rise to new opportunities for managerial rent extraction, particularly where performance-related pay can be manipulated by insiders.[27]

An alternative to contractual solutions of this kind is to alter the governance structure of the firm, so that residual control and income rights are shared between employees and investors. In principle these "hybrid" systems are unstable because of the high transaction costs associated with decision making within and across heterogeneous stakeholder groups.[28] However, they may be a feasible alternative to suboptimal contractual arrangements governing executive pay and performance. Although, as already noted, employee-owned firms in the form of cooperatives or worker-managed enterprises are rare, it is not uncommon to see workers being given voice rights within the firm via contract and regulation, in ways which may significantly qualify shareholders' control and income rights. Nor are shareholders' rights simply a function of ownership: the degree of control they exercise over management may also be affected by laws and regulations.

The literature on comparative capitalisms argues that corporate governance arrangements will be framed by nationally specific institutional factors, which may derive in varying degrees from legal origins,[29] political ideologies,[30] or technological complementarities.[31] In so-called "liberal market" systems, firms tend to be characterized by dispersed ownership and a high degree of director independence. These features may nevertheless be qualified in the context of the innovative firm by measures designed to lock shareholders in, including

[24] Acharya, Baghai-Wadji, & Subramanian (2013 and 2014) *supra* note 8.

[25] H. Shadab, "Innovation and Corporate Governance: The Impact of Sarbanes–Oxley", 10 U. Pa. J. Bus. & Emp. L. 955 (2007).

[26] H. Mehran, "Executive Compensation Structure, Ownership, and Firm Performance", 38 J. Fin. Econ. 163 (1995); H. Gospel & A. Pendleton, "Finance, Corporate Governance and the Management of Labour: A Conceptual and Comparative Analysis", 41 British Journal of Industrial Relations 557 (2003); H. Gospel & A. Pendleton, Corporate governance and labour management: an international comparison, in Corporate Governance and Labour Management: An International Comparison (H. Gospel and A. Pendleton eds., 2005); Manso, *supra* note 23.

[27] L. Bebchuk & J. Fried, Pay without Performance: The Unfulfilled Promise of Executive Compensation (2006).

[28] Hansmann, *supra* note 11.

[29] R. La Porta, F. Lopez-de-Silanes, & A. Shleifer, "The Economic Consequences of Legal Origins", 46 J. Econ. Lit. 285 (2008).

[30] M. Roe, Political Determinants of Corporate Governance (2003).

[31] P. Hall & D. Soskice, An Introduction to Varieties of Capitalism, in Varieties of Capitalism: The Institutional Foundations of Comparative Advantage (P. Hall and D. Soskice eds., 2001).

poison pills, weighted voting, and insider-dominated boards.[32] In "coordinated market" systems, the legal system itself may supply alternative governance mechanisms to the conventional model of shareholder-based control, in the form of dual-board structures and related mechanisms for employee participation in managerial decision making ("codetermination"[33]). In both cases, firms' governance choices are liable to be influenced by the state of the laws governing shareholder and worker protection.

3 Empirical Methods: Leximetrics and Time-Series Econometrics

How far the legal system actually drives corporate governance outcomes depends on a range of factors including the scope for firms to opt into or out of particular governance models and the leeway they have for customizing them. The tightness of the "fit" between legal norms and particular technological and organizational configurations may differ from one national and/or sectoral context to another. In this regard, it is helpful that the empirical turn in law and economics has seen the development of new data sources for analyzing cross-national differences in the legal framework for corporate governance and their economic effects. Attempts to measure legal institutions in a systematic way go back to the OECD's *Employment Protection Index* (EPI), first published in the mid-1990s,[34] and the World Bank *Doing Business Reports* (DBR) from the early 2000s,[35] which built on the methods used in the legal origins literature.[36] Although these indices are very widely used by social scientists, they suffer from numerous flaws including home-country bias, inconsistent coding, and a lack of transparency in the reporting of sources.[37]

A particular weakness of the OECD and World Bank data sets is that they each provide limited time-series. The OECD's EPI has recently been revised to incorporate a more consistent time series but there are still gaps in the coverage.[38] The legal origins studies on which

---

[32] H. Sapra, A. Subramanian, & K. Subramanian, "Corporate Governance and Innovation: Theory and Evidence", 49 J. Fin. Quant. Anal. 957 (2014).

[33] J. Rogers & W. Streeck, Works Councils: Consultation, Representation, Cooperation in Industrial Relations (1995).

[34] D. Grubb & W. Wells, "Employment Regulation and Patterns of Work in EC Countries", 21 OECD, Economic Studies 7 (1993); OECD, *OECD Jobs Study, Evidence and Explanations, Part I: Labour Market Trends and Underlying Forces of Change* (1994); see now OECD, *Employment Outlook* (2013).

[35] World Bank, *Doing Business Report* (various years).

[36] R. La Porta, F. Lopez-de-Silanes, A. Shleifer, & R. Vishny, "Law and Finance", 106 J. Pol. Econ. 1113 (1998); La Porta et al. *supra* note 29; J. Botero, S. Djankov, R. La Porta, F. Lopez-de-Silanes, & A. Shleifer, "The Regulation of Labor", 119 Q. J. Econ. 1340 (2004).

[37] M. Barenberg, *Literature Review and Bibliography for Research Project: Refining the NAS-ILAB Matrix, US Department of Labor, Bureau of International Affairs* (2011); Z. Adams & S. Deakin, "Quantitative Labour Law", in New Frontiers in Empirical Labour Law Research (A. Blackham and A. Ludlow eds., 2015).

[38] OECD (2013) *supra* note 34; discussed by Adams & Deakin, *supra* note 37.

the DBR indicators are based were mostly cross sectional. The later DBR studies have a limited time series, going back only to the early 2000s. By contrast, the data sets constructed at the Centre for Business Research in Cambridge provide several decades of continuous time series data.[39]

An empirically informed assessment of the effects of corporate and labor laws should take into account a number of features of legal rules. A first of these is their partial endogeneity: legal rules reflect economic conditions as well as shaping behavior. Legal systems co-evolve alongside developments in the economy and the political system.[40] Thus quantitative economic analysis should be able to take on board the possibility of reverse causation or of multi-directional causal flows between legal and economic variables. It further follows that econometric analysis of law should be longitudinal. Cross-sectional analyses can indicate correlation but not, normally, causation.

A second relevant feature of legal rules is their mutability. Legal rules rarely have a completely fixed meaning or unique interpretation. Thus the application of a legal rule is rarely a matter of "either/or." Binary variables, which purport to measure the presence or absence of a legal rule using a simple (0, 1) coding scheme, may well not be an appropriate way of conceptualizing the operation of regulatory norms.[41]

A third feature to consider is the gap between law in action and law in the books. The formal enactment of a legal rule may tell us something about its practical effects, but legal rules are not self-enforcing. If a given legal rule reflects an existing social consensus, it may well take effect without the need for regular enforcement. In other contexts, general respect for the law, the efficiency of the court system and the amount of resources devoted to enforcement may be critical variables to add into the analysis.[42]

"Leximetric" coding techniques attempt to address these issues.[43] Leximetric method involves breaking down the process of index construction into a series of stages, beginning with the identification of a *phenomenon* of interest ("corporate law," "employment law") that may be expressed as a conceptual *construct* ("regulation," from the viewpoint of the firm or employer, or "protection," from that of the shareholder or worker). Then one or more *indicators* or *variables* are identified which, singly or together, express the construct

---

[39] P. Lele & M. Siems, "Shareholder Protection: A Leximetric Approach", 7 J. Corp. L. Stud. 17 (2007); J. Armour, S. Deakin, P. Sarkar, M. Siems, & A. Singh, "Shareholder Protection and Stock Market Development: An Empirical Test of the Legal Origins Hypothesis", 6 J. Emp. Legal Stud. 343 (2009a); J. Armour, S. Deakin, P. Lele, & M. Siems, "How Legal Norms Evolve: Evidence from a Cross-Country Comparison of Shareholder, Creditor and Worker Protection", 57 Am. J. Comp. L. 579 (2009b); S. Deakin, P. Lele, & M. Siems, "The Evolution of Labour Law: Calibrating and Comparing Regulatory Regimes", 146 Int'l. Lab. Rev. 133 (2007).

[40] Armour et al. (2009b) *supra* note 39.   [41] Armour et al. (2009b) *supra* note 39.

[42] S. Fagernäs, "Labor Law, Judicial Efficiency and Informal Employment in India", 7 J. Emp. Legal Stud. 282 (2010).

[43] M. Siems & S. Deakin, "Comparative Law and Finance: Past, Present and Future Research", 166 J. Institutional & Theoretical Econ. 120 (2010); J. Buchanan, D.H. Chai, & S. Deakin, "Empirical Analysis of Legal Institutions and Institutional Change: Multiple Methods Approaches and their Application to Corporate Governance Research", 10 Journal of Institutional Economics 1 (2014).

in numerical terms. A *coding algorithm* is devised, setting out a series of steps to be taken in assigning numerical values to the primary source material. The algorithm incorporates a *measurement scale* of some kind. Finally, a decision must be taken on whether and/ or how to apply *weights* to the individual variables or indicators. The result is an *index* which provides a measure of the phenomenon of interest, which can be used in statistical analysis.

The CBR data set, which has been constructed according to these principles, can be put to use in time-series econometric analysis, to study the effects of legal change, and to iden- tify the direction of causality in the law–economy relation. If the law–economy relation is essentially one of co-evolution,[44] a statistical method capable of identifying two-way causal flows, and of indicating when a change in the law induces a long-run shift in the evolutionary path of the economy or just a temporary adjustment after which the economy resumes its previous path, is needed. Vector autoregression (VAR) and vector error correction (VEC) models, which can distinguish between the short-run and long-run effects of a change in legal rules,[45] are among the methods which can be used here.[46]

Leximetric datasets are a comparatively recent development, and the methods they employ are still being tested. Even with such data, there are limits to how far econo- metric testing can elucidate causal relationships. While VAR models can be used to test for short-run and long-run relationships between variables subject to a co-evolutionary dynamic, data and modelling constraints place limits on their use. In our current state of knowledge, they cannot be used to study the operation of informal institutions which are beyond the reach of quantitative data collection processes. To access these requires direct contact with actors who are in a position to explain to researchers what their perceptions of a particular institutional practice are. Qualitative research of this kind requires "a sub- stantial period of fieldwork, keen observational skills, thorough record keeping, and a high degree of self-awareness and ethical management of social relations" on the part of researchers, who should have "appropriate language skills and sufficient understanding of the local context to gain access, recognize informal institutions, and accurately in- terpret culturally coded observations."[47] Evidence from such studies may be essential in formulating questions for quantitative analysis and in filling in the gaps left by statistical studies.[48]

[44] S. Deakin & F. Carvalho, System and Evolution in Corporate Governance, in *Law, Economics and Evolutionary Theory* (G.-P. Calliess and P. Zumbansen eds., 2011).

[45] K. Juselius, The Cointegrated VAR Model: Methodology and Applications (2006).

[46] See Deakin & Sarkar *supra* note 8; S. Deakin, P. Sarkar, & A. Singh, An End to Consensus? The Selective Impact of Corporate Law Reform on Financial Development, in Complexity and Institutions: Markets, Norms and Organizations (M. Aoki, K. Binmore, S. Deakin, & H. Gintis eds., 2012); S. Deakin, J. Malmberg, & P. Sarkar, "How Do Labour Laws Affect Unemployment and the Labour Share of National Income? The Experience of Six OECD Countries, 1970–2010", 153 Int'l. Lab. Rev. 1 (2014); S. Deakin, C. Fenwick, & P. Sarkar, Labour Law and Inclusive Development: The Economic Effects of Industrial Relations Laws in Middle-Income Countries, in Institutional Competition between Common Law and Civil Law (M. Schmiegelow ed., 2014).

[47] A. Poteete, M. Janssen, & E. Ostrom, Working Together: Collective Action, the Commons, and Multiple Methods in Practice 16 (2010).

[48] Buchanan, Chai, & Deakin *supra* note 43.

4 Evidence on Long-Run Trends in Shareholder and Employee Protection

The Shareholder Protection Index (SPI) and Labor Regulation Index (LRI) are two of a number of databases developed at the Centre for Business Research in Cambridge since the mid-2000s which provide longitudinal data on changes in labor and company law. They are based on a "fine-grained" approach to the coding of primary legal sources which makes it possible to indicate not just the presence or absence of a shareholder/worker-protective law in a given country, but to estimate magnitudes concerning the degree of protection conferred by a given legal rule. These are represented using graduated scores between 0 (indicating little or no protection) and 1 (indicating high protection). Coding algorithms or protocols are used in an attempt to ensure consistency in the scoring of legal rules, and primary sources are reported in full alongside the scores for particular variables (see https://www.repository.cam.ac.uk/handle/1810/263766 (last accessed 4 April 2018).).

The SPI focuses on laws protecting shareholders against managerial control or power, using ten indicators which were intended to capture the core of what, despite its common-law origins, had become a "global consensus" on shareholder protection from the early 1990s onwards. The indicators were drawn from texts of global relevance for corporate governance standards at this time, in particular the OECD's *Principles of Corporate Governance* (1999, amended in 2004).[49]

The LRI contains 40 indicators in all, spread across five sub-indices, covering, respectively, the regulation of different forms of employment (self-employment, part-time work, fixed-term employment, and temporary agency work), working time (daily and weekly working time limits and rules governing overtime), dismissal (procedural and substantive rules on termination of employment), employee representation (rules on collective bargaining, the closed shop and codetermination), and the industrial action (the extent of legal support for the right to strike, including rules on secondary and political strikes). Not all labor law rules touch on corporate governance. For the purposes of this paper, a segment of the LRI is relevant, that is to say, the nine indicators in the dismissal law sub-index, and two additional indicators from the employee representation index, covering employee directors and code-termination respectively.[50]

Figure 39.1 to Figure 39.4 present data on trends in shareholder protection and employment protection in 30 countries since the early 1990s, using the CBR data sets. It can be seen that shareholder protection scores have risen steadily over this period, and that the increase has been particularly marked in civil law countries, which have now more or less converged with common law ones. When the sample of countries is broken down by level of development, developed countries are shown to have higher levels of shareholder protection over most of this period than either transition or developing countries, but here again there has been convergence, with transition systems in particular catching up with developed ones.

---

[49] For further details on the SPI data set, see D. Katelouzou & M. Siems, "Disappearing Paradigms in Shareholder Protection: Leximetric Evidence for 30 Countries, 1990–2013", 15 J. Corp. L. Stud. 127 (2015).

[50] For further details on the LRI data set, see Deakin, Lele, & Siems *supra* note 39.

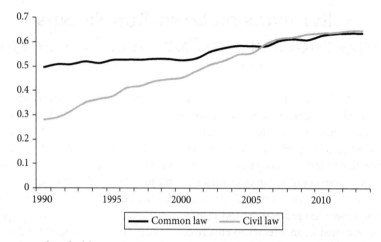

FIGURE 39.1 Shareholder protection in 30 countries, 1990–2014, comparing common law and civil law origin countries.

Note: The countries in the data set are Argentina, Austria, Belgium, Brazil, Canada, Chile, China, Czech Republic, Cyprus, Estonia, France, Germany, India, Italy, Japan, Latvia, Lithuania, Malaysia, Mexico, Netherlands, Pakistan, Poland, Russia, Slovenia, Sweden, South Africa, Spain, Switzerland, Turkey, UK, US.

Source: CBR Leximetric Database (https://www.repository.cam.ac.uk/handle/1810/263766).

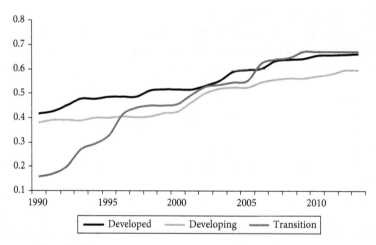

FIGURE 39.2 Shareholder protection in 30 countries, 1990–2014, comparing developed, developing and transition countries.

Source: CBR Leximetric Database (https://www.repository.cam.ac.uk/handle/1810/263766)

The story for employment protection is somewhat different: civil law countries have consistently higher scores than common law ones. There is little difference between developed and developing systems, and they follow similar trends, but transition systems show higher scores than the other two groups. There is no evidence of a general trend toward deregulation of employment protection laws, although a fall in the scores in some

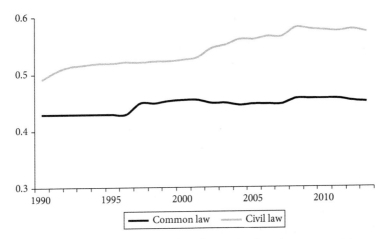

FIGURE 39.3 Dismissal protection and codetermination in 30 countries, 1990–2014, comparing common law and civil law origin countries.

Source: CBR Leximetric Database (https://www.repository.cam.ac.uk/handle/1810/263766)

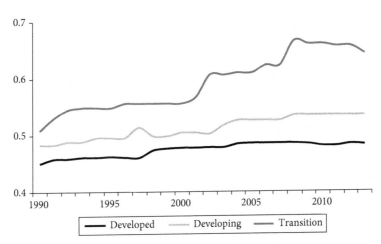

FIGURE 39.4 Dismissal protection and codetermination in 30 countries, 1990–2014, comparing developed, developing, and transition countries.

Source: CBR Leximetric Database (https://www.repository.cam.ac.uk/handle/1810/263766)

transition systems and developed countries reflects the impact of the economic crisis in Europe after 2010.

With both data sets, it should be borne in mind that these scores record the formal content of the law and do not take account of weaknesses in implementation or enforcement. These qualifications are important and are reflected in the use of additional data sets measuring the quality of legal institutions, such as the World Bank Rule of Law index, in econometric studies.[51]

---

[51] For discussion of this point, see Armour et al. (2009a) *supra* note 39.

5 Evidence on the Economic Effects of Corporate Governance and Employment Laws

5.1 Shareholder Rights and Economic Performance

One of the key empirical questions arising from the trend toward greater shareholder protection is whether the strengthening of shareholders' legal rights has had tangible effects on firm performance and, more generally, on economic growth. In principle, it should have led to improved managerial effectiveness and, via that route, to greater organizational efficiency and higher growth. These effects should be measurable in a number of ways: by reference to the value placed by shareholders on firms (share price movements around the "event window" of corporate announcement, and longer term share values relative to assets, or "Tobin's q"); the efficiency with which firms use their capital (return on equity); their profitability (return on assets); and their productivity performance.

Early research in this field was shaped by Gompers, Ishii, and Metrick's study[52] of the effects on firm values of the adoption by US listed companies of measures restricting shareholder decision making over changes of control, including takeovers and mergers, and entrenching boards against shareholder influence. Their so-called G-index of corporate governance provisions focused on poison pills, supermajority requirements, staggered board rules, golden parachutes, and similar measures adopted by US listed firms, mostly in the period during the 1980s when the effects of hostile takeover bids were highly contested. They found a consistently negative correlation between firm value (measured by Tobin's q) and a high score on the G-index (indicating weak shareholder rights). Subsequent studies have refined this analysis, and have suggested that the results derived from the G-index are mostly driven by the adoption by firms of poison pills and similar devices for restricting the role of shareholder decision making in change of control transactions.[53] The G-index and later variants based on it mostly focus on company bylaws and other internal corporate arrangements rather than legal regulation of corporate governance, although some account is taken of state-level laws on takeover bids. Because of its focus on poison pills and other features of corporate practice which are mostly specific to the American experience, this series of studies, although highly influential for both research and policy in the US, has limited relevance for the experience of other countries.

Another highly significant paper in the development of the field was the study by La Porta et al.[54] of the impact of cross-national differences in shareholder rights on financial development and growth. Their "anti-director rights index" measured shareholder rights by coding for laws affecting shareholders' voting, voice, and dividend rights. Higher scores on this

---

[52] P. Gompers, J. Ishii, & A. Metrick, "Corporate Governance and Equity Prices", 118 Q. J. Econ. 107 (2003).

[53] L. Bebchuk, A. Cohen, & A. Ferrell, "What Matters in Corporate Governance", 22 Rev. Fin. Stud. 783 (2009); M. Cremers & A. Ferrell, "Thirty Years of Shareholder Rights and Firm Value", 69 J. Fin. 1167 (2014); M. Cremers & A. Ferrell, "Thirty Years of Shareholder Rights and Stock Returns: Beta, not Alpha?" Working Paper, Yale School of Management/Harvard Law School (2013).

[54] *Supra* note 36.

index, indicating a higher degree of shareholder protection, were found to be correlated with more dispersed share ownership, and also with common law legal origin. This original index was limited in scope (it did not code for director independence or takeover regulation) and time invariant; later studies (reviewed below) have added further variables and incorporated a time-varying element to the process of legal index construction.

The first studies of the likely effects of legal encouragement for independent boards and related aspects of corporate governance were carried out in the context of US listed firms in the 1990s, when director independence was not a legal requirement, making it possible to compare the situation of companies with different board arrangements. In the most comprehensive such study, Bhagat and Black[55] found that there was no clear correlation between independent boards and corporate performance. While underperforming companies increased the proportion of non-independents on their boards, apparently in an attempt to improve performance, this strategy was largely unsuccessful.

Bhagat and Black's causal variable, board structure, was constructed from data on the proportion of "inside," "affiliated" (that is, non-executive but linked to the company) and "independent" directors, in a sample of around 1,000 large US public companies across a range of industries (including manufacturing sectors). Their outcome variables were Tobin's q, return on assets, sales over assets, and adjusted stock price returns. They controlled for firm-specific characteristics including pre-existing board structure, firm size, industry, and the presence of larger, "blockholder" shareholders (>5%). They found that there was a negative correlation between director independence and one or more of the performance variables in the period prior to the adoption of majority independent boards, suggesting that weaker firms were more likely to increase the proportion of independent directors on their boards. They also found that firms adopting independent boards did not subsequently outperform the market, and, for one of the variables (Tobin's q), did worse than comparable firms. They then looked at the impact on growth, using the percentage growth in assets, sales, and operating income over a period of years as the outcomes variables. Again, they found no positive impact of director independence on performance.

Bhagat and Black concluded from their study that the performance advantages of independent boards were most likely being overstated: insider directors were "conflicted" (that is, inclined to support management) but well informed, whereas independent directors, while likely to be more attuned to shareholder concerns, were also less knowledgeable on the underlying business of the firm. On this basis, they argued for corporate governance standards based on a model of a "mixed" board of insiders and outsiders, rather than the majority-independent boards that were then being widely advocated in both the US and the UK.

Notwithstanding these findings, which were replicated by a number of other studies at the time and since,[56] US corporate governance standards in the early 2000s moved in the direction of mandatory independent boards: the Sarbanes–Oxley Act of 2003 required a majority of independent directors on audit and remuneration committees, and listing rules on the NYSE and NASDAQ exchanges were tightened up to require main boards of quoted companies to have majority independent membership. Studies of the impact of the SOX provisions including those on board structure have generally found negative effects of its

---

[55] B. Bhagat & B. Black, "The Non-Correlation between Board Independence and Long-Term Firm Performance", 27 J. Corp. L. 231 (2002).

[56] See Adams, Hermalin, & Weisbach *supra* note 9 for a recent survey.

introduction, in particular for already well-governed firms, indicating high costs of compliance associated with this form of legislative intervention, and few if any performance-related benefits.[57]

In the UK, company law largely leaves companies free to structure boards as they wish. The issues of board composition and structure are governed by the flexible regulatory approach of corporate governance codes applying to listed companies (currently, the UK Corporate Governance Code). Under the principle of "comply or explain," listed companies have the option of either complying with the relevant corporate governance standard (such as rules on board structure), or of explaining why they do not comply. The thinking behind this approach is that companies are heterogeneous and should be allowed to match their corporate governance arrangements to their own needs. Thus the test of whether a given firm has adopted effective governance procedures is, in the final analysis, for the market to make; weak (or ill-matched) governance structures will be reflected in lower share prices.

The flexibility inherent in the UK approach makes it possible to test for the consequences for firm performance of companies' decisions on board structure and other corporate governance arrangements. The empirical literature for the UK broadly follows that for the US, in failing to find a clear correlation between the adoption of independent boards and separate CEO/Chair roles, on the one hand, and firm performance on the other. One of the few studies to examine in detail the effects on performance of companies' different approaches to disclosure (or "explanation" as an alternative to "compliance") is by Arcot and Bruno.[58] Using a sample of 245 non-financial listed UK firms, they studied the impact of corporate governance compliance and reporting on firms' return on assets, over a five-year period (1999–2004). They found some evidence of a positive correlation between compliance and performance, but also evidence that firms which did not comply with the standards set out in the Cadbury Code but offered effective explanations for non-compliance performed best of all. The worst performers were those which did not comply with corporate governance standards prior to the implementation of the Code, but did so after it was introduced.

The implication of the Arcot–Bruno study is that corporate governance standards may perform a useful function in enabling already well-run firms to signal this fact, in particular through their use of the "explanation" option. However, this potentially positive effect of corporate governance codes must be qualified by another of Arcot and Bruno's findings, namely that shareholders did not value this subset of firms as highly as they should have done given their higher profitability; rather, there was a bias, in the valuations placed on companies by the stock market, in favor of firms which formally complied with the provisions of the Cadbury Code. This result implies a degree of shareholder myopia which puts into question the assumption, implicit in the "comply or explain" approach, that the market can efficiently gauge the quality of explanatory disclosures.

There is evidence to suggest that the impact of the laws and corporate governance codes strengthening shareholder rights differs according to the national context that is being considered. A number of studies have found that changes to legislation and/or to listing

---

[57] K. Litvak, "The Effect of the Sarbanes–Oxley Act on foreign Companies Cross-Listed in the US", 13 J. Corp. Fin. 195 (2007).

[58] S. Arcot & V. Bruno, "One Size Does Not Fit All, After All: Evidence from Corporate Governance" (2007), available at SSRN: http://ssrn.com/abstract=887947.

rules, encouraging greater independence of boards and related corporate governance changes, have been reflected in improved firm performance in developing countries, as measured by Tobin's q[59] and abnormal share price returns around the "event window" of the announcement of legal changes.[60]

There are few studies directly comparing the experience of developed and developing countries. Deakin, Sarkar, and Singh[61] report findings from a study of the impact of legal reforms in a panel of 25 developed and developing countries over the period 1995–2005. Their causal variable consisted of the measure of legal adoption of pro-shareholder reforms in the CBR SPI. As we have seen, this index is focused on issues of board structure, shareholder voice and voting rights, and protection of minority shareholder interests in the context of takeover bids. The outcome variables in this study consisted of country-level measures of financial development, drawn from the IMF's Financial Structure Dataset. They used a VEC analysis and the GMM (generalized method of moments) technique to estimate the long-run impact of legal changes, and Granger causality techniques to test for the direction of causation. They found a positive impact of legal change on stock market values (stock market capitalization over GDP) for developing countries, as well as evidence, in the developing world, of reverse causation, suggesting that investor demand was, in part, driving legal change. For developed countries, they found a positive impact of reforms on stock market capitalization for common law countries only; there was no effect in civil law systems. This finding suggests that standards of the kind contained in corporate governance codes have had most impact in common law systems, such as the US and UK, which have dispersed share ownership, but a limited impact in civil law systems, which tend to have concentrated or blockholder ownership. In addition, the results from this study for developed common law countries indicated a possible "bubble" effect, with legal change associated with an increase in equity values but not in the underlying volume of shares traded (this was not the case with the developing country sample).

This study implies that corporate governance reforms encouraging or mandating protections for shareholders are most likely to have positive impacts in systems where equity markets are still in the process of emerging and where firm-level governance is weak. In developed country contexts, on the other hand, they can have negative implications, imposing regulatory costs on already well-governed firms, and contributing to overvaluation of shares during stock market bubbles. This effect is most marked in common law systems such as the UK and US.[62] In civil law countries, where ownership still tends to be concentrated in large blocks, reforms premised on the assumption of the US or UK-style separation of ownership and control run the risk of failing to bed down in practice.

One of a very small number of cross-country studies to address the interaction of corporate governance standards and employment laws is by Conway et al.[63] They used

[59] B. Black, H. Jang, & W. Kim, "Does Corporate Governance Predict Firms' Market Values? Evidence from Korea", 22 J. L. Econ. & Org. 366 (2006), for Korea.

[60] B. Black & V. Khanna, "Can Corporate Governance Reforms Increase Firm Market Values? Event Study Evidence from India", 4 J. Emp. Legal Stud. 749 (2007), for India.

[61] *Supra* note 46.

[62] Deakin, Sarkar, & Singh *supra* note 46.

[63] N. Conway, S. Deakin, S. Konzelmann, H. Petit, A. Rebérioux, & F. Wilkinson, "The Influence of Stock Market Listing on Human Resource Management: Evidence for France and Britain", 46 British Journal of Industrial Relations 631 (2008).

establishment-level data on workplace practices (the UK Workplace Employment Relations Survey and its French equivalent, REPONSE) to test for the significance of a stock-market listing on firm-level human resource management practices. They found that UK-listed companies were less likely to engage in high-commitment HRM practices than "stake-holder" firms (mutual, cooperatives, and public interest companies). In France, there was a somewhat different result: French listed companies were more likely to engage in formal HRM practices than non-listed firms, but reported lower levels of worker engagement than stakeholder firms. One interpretation of the different results for France and Britain is that French labor law, which is more worker-protective than that in the UK, mediated the impact of shareholder pressure on management, resulting in a more sustainable form of rent-sharing between investors and workers.

5.2 Board Structure and Managerial Strategy

One of the consequences of the move toward independent boards in both the UK and the US has been greater scrutiny of the hiring of senior executives, including CEOs, by board members, and the increased use of incentive payments and bonuses for CEOs based on share price performance and other performance criteria. The delegation of nomination and re-muneration decisions to board subcommittees with a majority of independent members is mandatory for US listed companies under the Sarbanes–Oxley Act and recommended prac-tice under the UK Corporate Governance Code. Although in principle these changes should bring about a closer alignment of managerial and shareholder interests, and hence increase firm value, there is evidence that firm value may be negatively affected by short-termism associated with the financial incentivization of CEOs. Antia, Pantzalis, and Chul[64] find that longer time horizons for CEOs of US listed companies, which they calculate in terms of current tenure plus age, are associated with higher firm value as measured by Tobin's q, while Brochet, Loumioti, and Serafeim,[65] who measure the short-term orientation of CEOs on the basis of transcripts of conference calls with investors, find that US firms with a short-term strategy attract short-term investors and have higher stock price volatility.

The nature of relationships in the investment chain between pension fund trustees (who have a fiduciary duty to maximize returns for the scheme members) and asset managers, and the resulting implications for the strategies pursued by investee companies, is the subject of a small but growing empirical literature. Del Guercio and Tkac[66] find, in the context of a US study, that pension funds are more likely than mutual funds to replace fund managers after poor performance over the short term (up to one year), and Heisler et al.[67] similarly find that US pension fund trustees' fiduciary duties and duty to monitor managers together make

---

[64] A. Antia, C. Pantzalis, & J. Chul, "CEO Decision Horizon and Firm Performance: An Empirical Investigation", 16 J. Corp. Fin. 288 (2010).

[65] F. Brochet, M. Loumioti, & G. Serafeim, "Short-Termism, Investor Clientele, and Firm Risk", Harvard Business School Accounting and Management Unit Working Paper No. 1999484 (2012).

[66] D. Del Guercio & P. Tkac, "The Determinants of the Flow of Funds of Managed Portfolios: Mutual Funds vs. Pension Funds", 37 J. Fin. Quant. Anal. 523 (2002).

[67] J. Heisler, C. Knittel, J. Neumann, & S. Stewart, "Why Do Institutional Plan Sponsors Hire and Fire their Investment Managers?", 13 Journal of Business and Economic Studies 88 (2007).

them prone to use short-term performance measures and to replace managers who fail to meet them.

In the case of the US and the UK, there is evidence of potentially negative effects of shareholder-orientated corporate governance rules on investment decisions. Graham, Harvey, and Rajgopal[68] report that US listed companies are becoming less willing to invest in R&D when they come under pressure to prioritize shareholder returns through share buy-backs and higher dividends. Asker, Farre-Mensa, and Ljungqvist[69] find that US listed firms invest less than comparable private firms and are less responsive to changes in investment opportunities, particularly in industries characterized by high sensitivity of stock prices to current earnings. Comparative studies also provide evidence of trade-offs between shareholder protection and stock market values, on the one hand, and innovation, on the other. Belloc reports the findings of a 48-country study which analyses the relationship between shareholder protection, as measured by the World Bank and CBR indices, and innovation, as measured by investments in R&D and patenting activity. Employing a panel data methodology, he finds that a high level of legal shareholder protection is correlated with a higher level of stock market capitalization, but a lower level of innovation activity.[70]

Lazonick and Prencipe's[71] case study of Rolls Royce points to tensions between corporate governance practices in the UK and the development of technological capabilities by manufacturing firms. The paper describes how Rolls Royce consolidated and then improved its position in the global market for aircraft engine production in the course of the 1990s through a strategy of building internal capabilities that was led by a largely engineering-focused team of managers. In this period, the development of the company's three-shaft turbofan engine enabled it to overtake its US rival Pratt and Witney to become the second-ranked commercial aviation engine producer after GE. In the early 1990s the company cut dividend payments, and its share price subsequently under-performed in the FTSE 100 index. Despite this, the company was able to raise capital through a rights issue in 1993, and it took on debt to fund a number of acquisitions. By the end of the decade it had largely paid off its debt through the revenues generated by increasing sales; its share of the global turbofan market increased from 8% in 1987 to 30% in 2002. Throughout this process, the company's management was effectively protected from negative investor opinion by the "golden share" retained by the UK government. The senior management team had virtually no ownership stake in the company, and the board members between them held less than 0.5% of the issued share capital. The authors of this study make the point that the success of Rolls Royce needs to be seen against the background of "the relative lack of success, more generally, of British companies in high-technology manufacturing industries over the past half century or so."[72]

[68] J. Graham, C. Harvey, & S. Rajgopal, "The Economic Implications of Corporate Financial Reporting", 40 J. Acct. & Econ. 3 (2005).

[69] J. Asker, J. Farre-Mensa, & A. Ljungqvist, "Comparing the Investment Behavior of Public and Private Firms", European Corporate Governance Institute Finance Working Paper 282/10 (2012).

[70] Belloc, *supra* note 8.

[71] W. Lazonick & A. Prencipe, "Dynamic Capabilities and Sustained Innovation: Strategic Control and Financial Commitment at Rolls-Royce plc", 14 Industrial and Corporate Change 501 (2005).

[72] Id., at 502.

5.3   Shareholder Rights, Product Market Competition, and Innovation

There is a growing literature examining the interaction between corporate governance standards and product market competition, which has implications for the relationship between governance and innovation. Giroud and Mueller[73] analyze the impact of firm-level governance practices on a number of performance measures (share price performance, Tobin's q, return on equity, return on assets, net profits) for a sample of over 3,000 US listed companies across a range of industries (including but not confined to manufacturing sectors). They then control for the competitive structure of industries, as measured by the Hirschman–Herfindahl index of concentration. They find that governance has only a small effect on firm performance in competitive industries and a more sizable positive impact on performance in non-competitive ones. They conclude that product market competition and corporate governance operate as substitutes: governance has little role to play in enhancing firm performance if product markets are already competitive.

Knyazeva and Knyazeva[74] reach an opposite result, although differences in their focus, which is on legal rules rather than firm-level practices, and in the scope of their study, which does not include the US or Canada, may partly explain the divergence. Rather than focusing on differences in firm-level governance practices in a single jurisdiction as Giroud and Mueller[75] did, they look at differences in country-level laws on shareholder protection, using, for this purpose, the time-invariant index developed by La Porta et al.[76] They use a very large sample of mostly manufacturing firms (regulated industries and financial firms are excluded) in 45 developed and developing countries, excluding US or Canadian incorporated firms. They find that shareholder rights have a positive impact on firm performance (both financial performance and profitability) in industries which are more competitive (using the HHI as the measure of competitive structure). They explain this result on the basis that shareholders are likely to monitor managers more effectively in competitive industries where it is easier to identify and remedy managerial under-performance.

Chai et al.[77] introduce innovation into the picture by using as a measure of product market competition the abnormal persistence of firm-level profits. If markets were perfectly competitive, abnormally high profits should be competed away over time. Persistence of profits can therefore be interpreted as indicating incomplete or imperfect competition in product markets. However, abnormal persistence can also be interpreted as evidence for the presence of innovative firms which are successful over time in capturing rents from product or process innovation. Using a very large sample of manufacturing firms in 18 developed and developing countries, Chai et al.[78] estimate the impact of laws governing shareholder rights on the persistence of firm-level profits. They use the CBR SPI as the measure of legal shareholder protection; as this

---

[73] X. Giroud & H. Mueller, "Corporate Governance, Product Market Competition and Equity Prices", 66 J. Fin. 563 (2010).

[74] A. Knyazeva & D. Knyazeva, "Product Market Competition and Shareholder Rights: International Evidence", 18 Eur. Fin. Mgmt. 1194 (2012).

[75] *Supra* note 73.   [76] *Supra* note 36.

[77] D. Chai, S. Deakin, P. Sarkar, & A. Singh, "Corporate Governance, Legal Origin and the Persistence of Profits", CBR WP series no. 465, December (2014).

[78] Id.

varies over time it provides an alternative (and potentially more revealing) measure to the time-invariant index of La Porta et al.[79] They find that higher shareholder protection reduces the persistence of profits in common law countries and increases it in civil law countries. This is consistent with the view that increases in legally mandated or encouraged shareholder protection during the 1990s and 2000s had a negative impact on firm-level innovation (proxied here by the abnormal persistence of profits) in common law systems. In civil law systems, which had a lower level of shareholder protection to begin with, the effect was positive, implying that there is a curvilinear (inverted U) relationship between shareholder rights and firm-level profitability based on innovation.

5.4 Employment Protection and Innovation

A body of work is beginning to look at the relationship between employment protection laws (EPL) and innovation. There are two possible routes by which they might be related. One possibility is that EPL, by raising dismissal costs, provides incentives for firms to move to, or remain on, a "high road" to competitive success, based on continuous product and process innovation, as the condition of being able to maintain a credible commitment to job security. This also implies a greater commitment by firms to training and upgrading of the labor force. A second possible route depends on the effect of EPL in reducing the downside costs to employees of risk taking of the kind associated with high-innovation practices. If employees are confident that their knowledge and know-how will not be appropriated ex post by the employer, through dismissal, they are more likely to contribute their skills and knowledge to the development of innovative products and processes.

There is some evidence to support both these sets of claims. With respect to the first, Koeniger[80] finds that a high level of EPL at country-level is associated with more innovation-related firm-level training. With respect to the second, Acharya, Baghai-Wadji, and Subramanian[81] use the dismissal protection variables in the CBR-LRI to examine the effects of changes in EPL over time on patenting activity and citations to patents in four industrialized countries (France, Germany, the UK, and the US). Using a difference-in-differences approach, they find a positive correlation which can be interpreted as a causal relationship, with greater employment protection laws stimulating higher innovation based on employee input into new products and processes.

These findings on the positive link between innovation and employment protection are being replicated in other studies. A cross-national study by Belloc reports evidence that a combination of low EPL and high shareholder protection is correlated with reduced innovation, measured in terms of patenting and patent citation rates.[82] Griffith and McCartney[83] report a correlation between high EPL and investments by multinational firms engaging in incremental innovation (involving the adaptation of existing technologies), although they

---

[79] *Supra* note 36.

[80] W. Koeniger, "Dismissal Costs and Innovation", 88 Economics Letters 79 (2005).

[81] Acharya, Baghai-Wadji, & Subramanian (2013 and 2014), *supra* note 8.

[82] Belloc, *supra* note 8.

[83] R. Griffith & G. McCartney, "Employment Protection Legislation, Multinational Firms and Innovation", 96 Rev. Econ. & Statistics 135 (2014).

also find that low EPL attracts cross-border investments by firms pursuing radical innovation (developing new technologies). Zhou, Decker, and Kleinknecht[84] find, in an econometric study of Dutch firms in a range of sectors including manufacturing, that firms
adopting "Rhineland"-style job security practices had stronger innovation performance
(measured in terms of sales of new or improved products) than those with "Anglo-Saxon"
hire-and-fire-type practices. Temporary contracts were positively correlated with "imi-
tative" (follower) strategies on the part of innovating firms, but negatively correlated with
strategies of market-leading firms. They interpret their findings as support for a theoretical model within which innovating firms offer "functional flexibility," combining job security with a high degree of firm-specific training and intra-organizational mobility on the
part of workers, rather than "numerical flexibility," which relies on temporary contracts
and redundancies to meet fluctuations in labor demand. On this basis they caution against
policies of labor market deregulation, arguing that they will reduce pressures on weaker
firms to upgrade their performance.

A particular subset of this literature has looked at the legal regime governing early-stage
finance and startups, which is a composite of the standard-form contracts which have
evolved over time to meet the needs of firms and investors, and elements of the legislative
framework drawn from each of the areas considered in this review (company law, insolvency
law, and employment law), as well as tax law. It has been argued that shareholder pressure
operates as a device for releasing capital from under-performing firms and ensuring its reallocation to more profitable and, in principle, innovative ones elsewhere in the economy,
including startups. Specifically, it is suggested that the availability of venture capital for
startups is linked to the ability of shareholders to extract value from companies in mature
sectors through takeover bids and direct engagement with companies to increase dividends
and engage in share buy-backs ("shareholder activism"). Once the capital is released in this
way, the capital market functions to redirect it to growing firms in developing sectors of the
economy.[85] More generally, it is argued that a liquid stock market is important for providing
venture capital firms with an exit strategy, via an IPO, which will enable them to cash out
their investments.[86]

In the same vein, a flexible labor market can be understood as complementing the corporate governance mechanisms which underpin early-stage finance. The ability of established firms to downsize at minimal cost is part of the process by which hostile takeovers
and shareholder activism work to free up capital for wider circulation in the economy.
While downsizing in response to shareholder pressure can be analyzed as a breach of implicit contracts between the firm and its core workforce,[87] agency-theoretical approaches see
advantages in labor law regimes which give employers the freedom to restructure the enterprise where to do so will enhance shareholder value.[88] This implies a regime of minimal
employment protection regulation and limited provision for collective employee voice in the

---

[84] *Supra* note 8.

[85] L. Summers, London Stock Exchange Bicentennial Lecture (2001).

[86] R. Gilson & B. Black, "Venture Capital and the Structure of Capital Markets: Banks versus Stock
Markets", 47 J. Fin. Econ. 242 (1997).

[87] A. Shleifer & L. Summers, Breach of Trust in Hostile Takeovers, in Corporate Takeovers: Causes
and Consequences (A. Auerbach ed., 1988).

[88] M. Jensen, "The Modern Industrial Revolution, Exit, and the Failure of Internal Control Systems",
48 J. Fin. 831 (1993).

event of redundancies. For startups, a low degree of employment protection could therefore be seen as providing an important source of flexibility in hiring and firing.

Acharya, Baghai-Wadji, and Subramanian[89] examine the effects of the erosion of the employment-at-will rule in California and a number of other US states from the 1970s onwards. Contrary to the predicted effects upon innovation of a strengthening of employment protection, they find that stricter controls over dismissal are found to be correlated with higher innovation, with the direction of causation running from the former to the latter. This study finds that the states with the greatest concentration of high-tech firms, namely California and Massachusetts, are among those with the most significant exceptions to the employment at will rule (the "implied good faith exception"), and that following the tightening of wrongful discharge laws in these states there was an increase not only in patenting activity but in the number of entrepreneurial startups and in the numbers employed in innovative firms. The study also reports positive effects on patenting activity in California following the adoption of the federal WARN law of 1988 on notice and severance pay. The authors ascribe these effects to the reduced risk of "hold-up" of innovative employees by firms following the adoption of stricter employment protection laws. The ability of employees to move between firms free of the constraints imposed by non-competition clauses or "restrictive covenants" may be a more important dimension than weak levels of employment protection in explaining the emergence of "high velocity" labor markets.[90]

5.5 Takeover Bids and Hedge Fund Activism

The way in which the potentially divergent interests of shareholders and workers are addressed in the context of takeover bids is an important indicator of cross-national differences in approaches to corporate governance. In principle, hostile takeover bids enable shareholders in systems with liquid capital markets to hold managers to account in circumstances where, thanks to diffused share ownership, they may not be in a position to exercise direct control over the board.[91] Hedge fund activism, in which takeover bids may be used as one of a number of tactics to put pressure on boards to enhance short-term financial returns to shareholders,[92] is a related phenomenon which may similarly tip the balance of power within the firm in favor of shareholders.[93] The potential downside in both cases is decreased investment by employees in firm-specific human capital, which is vulnerable to expropriation though a "breach of trust" if the firm is taken over or its strategic direction altered through a hedge fund intervention.[94]

---

[89] *Supra* note 8.

[90] A. Saxenian, Regional Advantage: Culture and Competition in Silicon Valley and Route 128 (1994); A. Hyde, "Silicon Valley's High Velocity Labour Market", 11 J. Appl. Corp. Fin. 28 (1998).

[91] Fama & Jensen, *supra* note 2.

[92] R. Greenwood & M. Schor, "Investor Activism and Takeovers", 92 J. Fin. Econ. 362 (2009).

[93] J. Macey, Corporate Governance: Promises Kept, Promises Broken (2008).

[94] Shleifer & Summers, *supra* note 87; S. Deakin & G. Slinger, "Hostile Takeovers, Corporate Law and the Theory of the Firm", 24 J.L. Soc'y 124 (1997).

Evidence on the incidence of takeover bids and on success rates suggests that they are associated with diffused ownership, as theory would suggest. Jackson and Miyajima[95] report nearly 200 hostile bids in the UK between the early 1990s and the mid-2000s and over 300 in the US, during which there were only 18 hostile bids in France and six each in Germany and Japan, while there were 176 in the UK and 332 in the US. The success rate for bids, indicating whether the target company was taken over, was 42% in the UK and 22% in the US. In France 12 out of 18 bids succeeded but in both Germany and Japan there was only one instance of a successful bid during this period.[96] Hedge fund activism, while growing after 2000 in Europe[97] and Japan,[98] is still largely a US phenomenon.[99]

There is also evidence to connect the scale of hostile takeover and hedge fund activity to differences in regulatory regimes. The UK's Takeover Code has since its inception been highly protective of the rights of minority shareholders during takeover bids, to the extent of effectively prohibiting poison pills and similar defences of the kind which are common among US-listed companies.[100] Cross-national analysis suggests that the incidence of adversarial hedge fund activism is correlated with higher scores for shareholder rights on the CBR's SPI.[101]

The efficiency and wealth effects of takeovers and activist interventions have been among the most intensively studied in the empirical corporate governance literature, and the field continues to evolve with a growing emphasis on comparative analysis. Recent cross-national studies suggest that hostile bids do not, on average, lead to improved firm performance, but also that a large proportion of bids do produce enhanced value for shareholders, and that there is considerable variance in the range of outcomes.[102] These findings do not rule out the possibility that pro-shareholder takeover regimes induce efficiency gains in firms which are never targeted for takeover, a result predicted by agency theory.[103] In the US context, firms

---

[95] G. Jackson & H. Miyajima, A Comparison of Mergers and Acquisitions in Japan, Europe and the United States, in Corporate Governance and International Business-Strategy, Performance and Institutional Change 186 (R. Strange and G. Jackson eds., 2008).

[96] Jackson & Miyajima, *supra* note 95.

[97] M. Becht, J. Franks, & J. Grant, "Hedge Fund Activism in Europe", ECGI Working Paper Series in Finance Working Paper N°. 283/2010 (2010).

[98] J. Buchanan, D.H. Chai, & S. Deakin, Hedge Fund Activism in Japan: The Limits of Shareholder Primacy (2012).

[99] A. Brav, W. Jiang, F. Partnoy, & R. Thomas, "Hedge Fund Activism, Corporate Governance and Firm Performance", 63 J. Fin. 1729 (2008); A. Brav, W. Jiang, & H. Kim, "The Real Effects of Hedge Fund Activism: Productivity, Asset Allocation, and Product Market Concentration" 28 Rev. Fin. Stud. 2723 (2015); L. Bebchuk, A. Brav, & W. Jiang, "The Long-Term Effects of Hedge Fund Activism" 115 Colum. L. Rev. 1085 (2015).

[100] Deakin & Slinger, *supra* note 94.

[101] D. Katelouzou, "Worldwide Hedge Fund Activism: Dimensions and Legal Determinants", 17 U. Pa. J. Bus. L. 789 (2015).

[102] M. Martynova, S. Oosting, & L. Renneboog, The Long-Term Operating Performance of European Mergers and Acquisitions, in International Mergers and Acquisitions Activity Since 1990—Recent Research and Quantitative Analysis (Greg N. Gregoriou & Luc Renneboog eds., 2007).

[103] Fama & Jensen, *supra* note 2.

without anti-takeover defences are more highly valued by shareholders,[104] which may be evidence for the negative effects of poison pills on managerial performance.[105]

There is evidence that corporate restructurings triggered by a change of control or by a hedge fund intervention may have negative effects for labor while producing value for shareholders. For the UK, studies suggest that takeovers which result in redundancies and downsizing also lead to improvements in firm value.[106] In the US, adversarial hedge fund activism tends to produce positive returns for shareholders of target firms around the period of the intervention, and while evidence of long-term improvements in firm performance is mixed, the consensus is that activism of this kind operates to reduce agency costs by aligning managerial strategy with shareholder interests.[107] Since there is also evidence that adversarial interventions involve losses for bondholders[108] and workers,[109] it is plausible to see hedge fund activism, whatever its wider implications for firm performance, as involving a trade-off between shareholder and worker interests.

5.6 Hybrid Forms of Governance: The Effects of Sharing Residual Income and Control Rights between Shareholders and Employees

There is a large literature on the effects of employee financial participation, but relatively little on the distinctive features of enterprises in which employees have residual income and/or control rights. The literature on employee share ownership suggest that while financial participation can induce heightened commitment and morale, it rarely has this effect on its own, but does so in conjunction with HRM practices which encourage employee engagement and the exercise of voice.[110] The practice of employee share ownership through ESOPs (in the US) and similar financial structures in other countries (in the UK, ETs and QUESTs) indicates that while they may provide employees with individualized residual income rights, they are rarely associated with worker control rights, in part because they cannot easily be used as a means of exercising collective worker voice.[111]

The codetermination model found in certain mainland European countries provides employees with a form of residual control rights, although these are best understood as structures within which shareholders and employees share supervisory responsibilities

---

[104] Gompers, Ishii, & Metrick, *supra* note 52; Cremers & Ferrell (2013, 2014) *supra* note 53.

[105] Bebchuk, Cohen, & Ferrell, *supra* note 53.

[106] M. Conyon, S. Girma, S. Thompson, & P. Wright, "The Impact of Mergers and Acquisitions on Company Employment in the United Kingdom", 46 Eur. Econ. Rev. 31 (2002).

[107] Brav, Jiang, Partnoy, & Thomas, *supra* note 99; Bebchuk, Brav, & Jiang, *supra* note 99; Brav, Jiang, & Kim, *supra* note 99.

[108] A. Klein & E. Zur, "Entrepreneurial Shareholder Activism: Hedge Funds and Other Private Investors", 64 J. Fin. 187 (2009); A. Klein & E. Zur, "The Impact of Hedge Fund Activism on the Target Firm's Existing Bondholders", 24 Rev. Fin. Stud. 1735 (2011).

[109] Brav, Jiang, & Kim, *supra* note 99.

[110] J. Cook, S. Deakin, J. Michie, & D. Nash, Trust Rewards: Realising the Mutual Advantage (2003).

[111] A. Bagchi, "Varieties of Employee Ownership: Some Unintended Consequences of Corporate Law and Labor Law", 10 U. Pa. J. Int'l., Bus. L. 305, 324 (2008).

in a way which is intended to encourage consensus between them over issues of corporate strategy. There is limited empirical evidence on the impact of two-tier boards on company performance. The German literature is mainly focused on the performance implications of works councils, which studies find to be positively correlated with innovation and productivity indicators.[112] The works council provides a basis for codetermination over matters of workplace organization, not corporate strategy. It is possible that the supervisory board and the works council complement each other in providing a framework for labor-management cooperation, but this has not been shown empirically. The informational benefits which a two-tier board structure is meant to confer on worker representatives are commonly offset in practice by the informality of supervisory board processes.[113] The Biedenkopf Commission which reviewed dual-board structures in Germany the early 1970s came to the view that worker directors had little impact on strategic or financial decision making, but did raise the profile of social aspects of firm performance.[114]

In Germany, the two-tier board structure is mandatory for larger companies, making direct comparisons with other structures problematic. In France, by contrast, the two-tier structure is optional. Rouyer[115] studies the impact of supervisory boards using a sample of the 250 largest non-financial French firms, around a third of which had moved to the two-tier structure. She finds that companies with a supervisory board have superior long-run financial performance, as measured by Tobin's q, and lower cash holdings, a result she attributes to the superior monitoring achieved by the two-tier model.

The Japanese firm offers another national variant, which in practice treats workers as if they had a share of the residual control rights, alongside shareholders, although in formal legal terms this is far from the case. Japanese company law is strongly pro-shareholder. The CBR-SPI index ranks Japan in the top quintile of countries for this type of shareholder protection, alongside countries such as Canada, the UK, and US.[116] Shareholders with a 1% holding can submit proposals to the annual general meeting and those with 3% can call for an extraordinary meeting. In most cases, a simple majority of participating shareholders is entitled to appoint the board and to dictate the level of dividend payouts, while a majority of two-thirds can vote to alter the company's capital structure. In the early 2000s Japanese company law was amended to permit firms to opt into a US-inspired "company with committees" model, with a more prominent role for external directors and a clearer demarcation between the managerial and monitoring functions of the board.[117]

However, very few firms took up this option, and those which did so used it to streamline executive decision-making structures, not to move to a different model of board-level

---

[112] F. FitzRoy & K. Kraft, "Co-Determination, Efficiency and Productivity", 43 British Journal of Industrial Relations 233 (2005); U. Jirjahn, J. Mohrenweiser, & U. Backes-Gellner, "Works Councils and Learning: On The Dynamic Dimension of Codetermination", 64 Kyklos 427 (2011).

[113] K. Pistor, Codetermination in Germany: A Socio-Political Model with Governance Consequences, in Employees and Corporate Governance (M. Blair & M. Roe eds., 1999).

[114] See Bagchi, *supra* note 111, at 327.

[115] E. Rouyer, "Company Performance and the Two-Tier Board Structure: Empirical Evidence from France", 12 International Journal of Business and Economics 45 (2013).

[116] M. Siems, "Shareholder Protection around the World ("Leximetric II")", 33 Del. J. Corp. L. 111 (2008).

[117] J. Buchanan & S. Deakin, "Japan's Paradoxical Response to the New Global Standard in Corporate Governance", 13 Zeitschrift für Japanisches Recht 59 (2008).

governance. External directors continue to have limited influence in Japanese firms and generally have an advisory rather than a monitoring role. The boards of large Japanese companies continue to be dominated by executive directors, and corporate governance practices more generally are "internally focused," with an emphasis on peer-based monitoring by informed insiders which is consistent with a broadly pro-stakeholder or "communitarian" conception of the firm. The strong and mostly effective resistance of listed Japanese companies to hedge fund activist campaigns in the mid-2000s testifies to the limited influence of minority shareholders in the Japanese system.[118]

In addition to their implications for firm-level performance, hybrid regulatory regimes have an impact on the relative wealth of shareholders and workers. Deakin, Malmberg, and Sarkar[119] use the CBR LRI to analyze the effects of worker-protective labor laws on the labor share, which measures the relative proportion of national output taken by wages and profits in six OECD countries. After controlling for differences in GDP, they find a correlation between legal support for employee representation through codetermination and collective bargaining, and an increased labor share. Conversely, there is evidence that a higher degree of protection for shareholders affects distribution. Sjöberg[120] finds that protection for minority shareholders, in conjunction with the incidence of takeover bids, is correlated with a higher degree of earnings inequality in OECD countries.

6 ASSESSMENT

The consensus position in corporate governance theory is that it is efficient to allocate residual income and monitoring rights to shareholders, leaving other stakeholders, including employees, to resolve their claims against the firm through contract. Because, however, the employment contract is inherently incomplete, some element of rent sharing between workers and investors is a necessity for the firm. Governance mechanisms which reflect this reality are commonly found in legal systems around the world: they include two-tier boards and codetermination systems of the kind that occur in parts of mainland Europe. While codetermination is relatively rare, laws making it costly for firms to dismiss workers and granting them voice rights in the firm are not, and may have similar effects in terms of enhancing employees' investments in firm-specific human capital, in particular in the context of innovative firms.

Systems in which employees play no role in governance and where regulation of the employment contract is minimal do not thereby escape the dilemmas posed by the need for rent sharing. In place of codetermination and job security clauses, firms compensate employees for the risk of dismissal by increasing their remuneration and linking it to stock price increases and other indicators of corporate performance. These solutions, supposedly

[118] Buchanan, Chai, & Deakin, *supra* note 98. J. Buchanan, D.H. Chai, & S. Deakin, "Agency Theory in Practice: A Qualitative Study of Hedge Fund Activism in Japan", 22 Corporate Governance: An International Review 296 (2014).

[119] *Supra* note 46.

[120] O. Sjöberg, "Corporate Governance and Earnings Inequality in OECD Countries 1979–2000", 25 European Sociological Review 519 (2009).

designed to align employee and shareholder interests, often do not work, since they invite new forms of opportunism and rent extraction on the part of strategically placed employees and managers, mostly to the detriment of shareholders. Meanwhile, laws adding to the rights shareholders already have to hold managers to account may tilt the balance of corporate power too far in favor of investor power, shortening managerial time horizons and leading to under-investment in firm-specific capabilities.

While the efficiency implications of a regime of high shareholder protection and low employee protection are equivocal, the distributional effects of such a regime are clear: they are regressive. Strong shareholder rights regimes are correlated with high earnings inequality, and worker-protective labor laws with an increased share of national production being taken in the form of wages rather than profits. At a time of growing concern over inequality, this may become an issue for corporate governance research and practice.

CHAPTER 40

....

CORPORATE GOVERNANCE, CAPITAL MARKETS, AND SECURITIES LAW

....

ADAM C. PRITCHARD

1 INTRODUCTION

....

AT first blush, the connection between corporate governance and capital markets might seem tenuous. Under the Efficient Capital Market Hypothesis (ECMH),[1] investors will incorporate their assessment of a firm's corporate governance into their valuation of the firm's future cash flows and the risk associated with those cash flows. Consequently, a company's stock price will reflect the quality of its corporate governance in limiting agency costs associated with the company's managers and/or controlling shareholders.[2] On this view, securities regulators' only concern is ensuring that corporate governance terms are accurately disclosed. If disclosure is effective, even unsophisticated investors will be protected. Poor corporate governance—if it is adequately disclosed—will not affect investors' expected returns because the price they pay for a security will be "fair," i.e., discounted to reflect any reduced returns that may result from poor corporate governance. Thus, one can think of securities markets as a grading mechanism for the efficacy of corporate governance.

From its beginnings, however, securities law has sought to do more than neutrally grade corporate governance. Securities law obviously needs to discourage fraud, with its obvious implications for the value of disclosure. (Fraud also has the potential to undermine the market's ability to grade firms' corporate governance provisions.) But securities law has also worried about other forms of overreaching by corporate insiders. Justice Louis Brandeis' oft-quoted phrase that "s[]unlight . . . is the best disinfectant; electric light the best

---

[1] See Eugene F. Fama, "Efficient Capital Markets: A Review of Theory and Empirical Work", 25 J. Fin. 383 (1970) (surveying theoretical implications of efficient markets and empirical testing of the efficient markets hypothesis).

[2] See Frank H. Easterbrook & Daniel R. Fischel, "The Corporate Contract", 89 Colum. L. Rev. 1416, 1432 (1989) ("Governance structures are known to anyone seeking the information, so the pricing mechanism will embody their effects for good or ill").

policeman" captures the attitude succinctly.[3] Disclosure has been justified, not simply as a means of promoting accurate pricing, but also as a means of exposing—and disinfecting—problematic behavior. Exposure would deter wrongdoing by managers and promoters.[4] Managers bent on self-dealing may restrain themselves if related-party transactions must be disclosed, at least if disclosure is backed by a plausible threat of enforcement. If investors (and perhaps, regulators) can see such activities clearly, then market participants (assuming either a modicum of shame or oversight) are less likely to engage in opportunistic behavior in the first place.[5]

What role should securities law play in encouraging corporate governance standards that hold managers and directors accountable to shareholders? Is disclosure, bolstered by market forces, sufficient to induce efficient corporate governance provisions, as the ECMH suggests? Or should securities law affirmatively seek to put a thumb on the scale of corporate governance outcomes, pushing companies toward "good" corporate governance? From the perspective of those who believe that governance has significant potential to limit agency costs, a disclosure regime—coupled with robust enforcement—that promoted good corporate governance might provide a signal that a company was well run, with structural provisions in place (e.g., independent directors) to keep agency costs in check. If investors value that signal, we have the groundwork for a virtuous circle, with an efficient and effective disclosure regime fueling a potential race to the top in corporate governance.

This argument blurs the line between corporate governance and the disclosure focus of securities law. But another question lurks: Does corporate governance influence the efficiency of securities markets? History suggests it might. Exchanges have long imposed corporate governance mandates on companies listing their shares for trading. Securities regulators, as they have gained greater authority over exchanges, have used listing standards as a tool for promoting more stringent corporate governance standards in the name of promoting "investor confidence," and at least implicitly, liquidity.

There may be limits, however, to the connection between liquidity and corporate governance. In the US, listing standards for public companies have become a favored tool by which the federal government imposes governance standards. Those standards, however, do not always have a clear connection to the efficiency of securities markets. Consequently, it is unclear whether the US model of securities law provides a useful lesson, or a cautionary tale, for other jurisdictions contemplating corporate governance reform.

This chapter explores the dividing line between corporate governance and securities law from both historical and institutional perspectives. Section 2 examines the origins of the dividing line between securities law and corporate governance in the United States, as well as the efforts of the SEC to push against that boundary. That history sets the stage for section 3, which broadens the inquiry by examining the institutional connections between capital markets and corporate governance. Are there practical limits to the connection between

---

[3] Louis D. Brandeis, Other People's Money 92 (1913).

[4] Troy A. Paredes, "Blinded by the Light: Information Overload and its Consequences for Securities Regulation", 81 Wash. U. L.Q. 417, 464 (2003) ("The strategy of shaming is premised on actively using disclosure to influence corporate conduct").

[5] See Paul G. Mahoney, "Mandatory Disclosure as a Solution to Agency Problems", 62 U. Chi. L. Rev. 1047 (1995) (contending that mandatory disclosure works to deter managers from engaging in opportunistic behavior at the expense of shareholders).

securities law and corporate governance? The US again illustrates the point, as Congress has increasingly crossed the traditional boundary between securities law and corporate governance. I conclude by speculating on the future of the dividing line between corporate governance and securities law.

2 A Brief History of the Dividing Line between Corporate Governance and the Securities Law in the United States

2.1 Corporate Law and Corporate Governance in the United States

The US treats corporate governance and securities law as separate spheres. Why not just "company law"? The answer is historical, not functional. Before there were federal securities laws in the US, there were state corporate laws. State corporate law not only gave corporations their legal existence, but also imposed corporate governance mandates for the protection of shareholders and creditors. State corporate law determines most questions of internal corporate governance—the role of boards of directors, the allocation of authority between directors, managers, and shareholders, etc.[6] The force of those mandates is constrained by the fact that, under US law, companies have unfettered discretion in choosing their state of incorporation. Moreover, the "internal affairs" doctrine requires courts to apply the law of the state of incorporation to corporate law disputes.[7]

The result of this combination has been an "issuer choice" regime in state corporate law in that US Corporations are free to choose the law of the state that best suits the needs of their directors, managers, and shareholders, without regard to where the corporation principally does business. States can compete to attract firms by offering the most attractive menu of corporate law rules and the best judges for resolving any disputes that may arise. Directors make that choice, subject to the risk that the market will sanction them if they pick a jurisdiction with overly lax standards. Thus, the stage was set early on for an "enabling" or "permissive" model of state corporate law, which progressively diluted a number of the regulatory mandates that were common in early state corporation statutes. First New Jersey, then Delaware, took the lead in attracting corporations headquartered in other jurisdictions, with the principal selling point being the elimination of restrictions on corporate directors and managers that earlier featured prominently in the corporate law of many states. [8] Defenders

---

[6] *Cort v. Ash, 422* U.S. 66, 84 ("Corporations are creatures of state law, and investors commit their funds to corporate directors on the understanding that, except where federal law expressly requires certain responsibilities of directors with respect to stockholders, state will govern the internal affairs of the corporation").

[7] On the history of the internal affairs doctrine, see Frederick Tung, "Before Competition: Origins of the Internal Affairs Doctrine", 32 J. Corp. L. 33 (2006).

[8] Curtis Alva, "Delaware and the Market for Corporate Charters: History and Agency", 15 Del. J. Corp. L. 885, 898 (1990).

of this trend contend that competition in the capital markets compels managers to offer shareholders corporate law rules that effectively constrain the agency costs inherent in the separation of ownership and control.[9]

Even before the adoption of the federal securities laws, there were counterweights to the influence of the states over corporate governance, primarily driven by capital markets. That market-driven response suggests there may be an inherent connection between corporate governance and capital markets. The New York Stock Exchange (NYSE)—the first truly national exchange in the US—provided a contractual version of a national securities law, at least for the US's largest public companies. Through its listing agreement, the NYSE played an important role in promoting both disclosure and improved corporate governance by allowing companies to pre-commit to best practices. Most conspicuously, the NYSE waged a long campaign against the traditional secrecy of corporate managers.[10] Despite a number of practical obstacles,[11] the NYSE eventually was able to require listed corporations to provide regular balance sheets and other financial data to stockholders.[12] The NYSE's requirement that those financial statements be audited also provided a substantial impediment to fraud.[13]

The NYSE's practice of imposing corporate governance and disclosure requirements through listing standards, although purely voluntary (no one could force a company to list its shares), did create a contractual certification mechanism that companies could use to signal their quality. The value of the NYSE's listing requirements is testified by the fact that Congress closely tracked the NYSE disclosure requirements when it drafted the Securities Exchange Act of 1934 (Exchange Act).[14] The difference, of course, is that the disclosure requirements for public companies became a legal mandate, backed up by SEC enforcement, rather than a contractual undertaking, backed up by the threat of delisting from the exchange. With the advent of that mandate, the stage was set for the dividing line between corporate governance and securities law to have significant consequences because securities law, unlike state corporate law or listing standards, could not be easily evaded.

---

[9] Ralph K. Winter, "State Law, Shareholder Protection, and the Theory of the Corporation", 6 J. Leg. Stud. 251 (1977).

[10] George L. Leffler, The Stock Market 428–29 (1951).

[11] The movement toward requiring greater disclosure by listing companies was prolonged by the fact that changes in listing agreements do not work retroactively. Leffler, *supra* note 10, at 433 ("Companies could be held only to agreements which they had signed; some of these were entered into a great many years ago. If new and additional agreements were formulated by the Exchange, old listed companies could not be compelled to comply except by Exchange persuasion, or if they applied for further listing of stock"); Michael E. Parrish, Securities Regulation and the New Deal 40 (1970) ("Recommendations by the listing committee were never retroactive"). Until 1939, companies paid a one-time listing fee which gave them the right to a listing in perpetuity. Leffler, *supra* note 10, at 427. Finally, other exchanges imposed substantially lower listing standards than did the NYSE, and the over-the-counter market imposed none at all. Leffler, *supra* note 10, at 433. The combination of these factors undoubtedly reduced the NYSE's bargaining leverage with companies in pushing for greater disclosure. More fundamentally, it also suggests that the demand for disclosure among investors was limited.

[12] Paul G. Mahoney, "The Exchange as Regulator", 83 Va. L. Rev. 1453, 1469–70 (1997).

[13] The policy was adopted in 1928; by 1931, 83% of listed companies were complying, and in 1932 the NYSE made the policy mandatory for all newly listed companies. See Leffler, *supra* note 10, at 430 (discussing NYSE's struggle to force companies to submit to independent audits).

[14] George J. Benston, "Required Disclosure and the Stock Market: An Evaluation of the Securities Exchange Act of 1934", 63 Am. Econ. Rev. 132, 133 (1973).

2.2 The Introduction of the Federal Securities Laws

The gradual relaxation of corporate governance mandates in state corporate law was not without its detractors, then or now. Critics of issuer choice argue that states were competing for charter fees—soliciting "tramp" corporations—by pandering to corporate managers. The incentive for the states to compete for charters is clear. Delaware, as the long-term winner of that competition for corporate charters,[15] currently funds roughly a quarter of its state budget from corporate charter fees.[16] Critics of issuer choice charge that states prevail in this competition by leaving shareholders vulnerable to overreaching by corporate managers. Exchange listing requirements are an insufficient counterweight, on this view, because exchanges are similarly beholden to corporate managers. The result, critics alleged, has been a "race to the bottom."[17]

The obvious answer to concerns raised by a potential "race to the bottom" was federal minimum standards, but at one time, the federal structure of the US government was thought to limit the federal government's power over corporate governance. As the US confronted the economic devastation wrought by the stock market crash of October 1929 and the ensuing Great Depression, corporate governance was seen as the province of the states, whose corporate laws gave corporations their very existence. Thus, the scope of the federal intervention was necessarily constrained, the policy levers available were limited.

There was some support among more radical New Deal reformers for a "federal corporate law." The interventions that Franklin Delano Roosevelt would ultimately pursue were more targeted, however, as his administration was reluctant to push constitutional limits. As we shall see, those limits were soon abandoned. By the end of the Second World War, the constitution was no longer a meaningful constraint on the power of the federal government to dictate corporate governance standards. The dividing line fostered by those now-discarded constitutional doubts, however, persists in the US as a matter of tradition and interpretive presumption. Even today, state corporate law determines most internal governance questions while federal securities law is generally limited to governing questions of disclosure to shareholders—annual reports, proxy statements, and periodic filings.

The push to enact federal securities law was one of the great political battlegrounds of the New Deal; 1933 to 1935 saw annual fights to enact the three laws that established the foundation of federal securities legislation. The first, the Securities Act of 1933 (Securities Act), brought the federal government into the regulation of the public offering of securities, curbing the investment bankers' prior domination of that process. The law required corporate issuers to make full disclosure when selling securities. The second, the Exchange Act, required disclosure of operations and results by companies listing on exchanges, as noted above. Although the Exchange Act targeted the NYSE, particularly in regulating broker-dealers, the NYSE did get one benefit from the law: The Exchange Act's mandate

---

[15] According to the Delaware Secretary of State, 83% of U.S. IPOs in 2013 were incorporated in Delaware, along with more than half of all public companies and 65% of the Fortune 500. Delaware is the Jurisdiction of Choice for U.S. IPOs, Delaware Corporate and Legal Services Blog (June 2, 2014), available at http://decals.delaware.gov/2014/06/02/delaware-is-the-jurisdiction-of-choice-for-u-s-ipos/.

[16] Delaware Division of Corporations, 2012 Annual Report, at 2 (reporting that division collected "$867.2 million dollars in fiscal year (FY) 2012 and accounted for 26% of the State's general fund").

[17] William Cary, "Federalism and Corporate Law: Reflections Upon Delaware", 83 Yale L. J. 663 (1974).

for disclosure by listed companies eliminated the ability of rival exchanges to undercut the NYSE's disclosure requirements. The NYSE's gold-plated standards would be mandated for all listed companies, although companies that traded in the over-the-counter market remained exempt for another 30 years. These two laws cemented disclosure as the foundational basis of the securities law.

The third foundational securities law, the Public Utility Holding Company Act of 1935 (PUHCA), departed from the disclosure model underpinning the Securities Act and the Exchange Act, making it the most controversial of the three securities laws from FDR's first term.[18] PUHCA targeted the holding companies that owned most of the public utilities in the US at the time. The public utility structure had long been a *bête noire* of reformers; the collapse of the Insull public utility holding company was the Enron of its day.[19] The demise of the Insull empire cemented the public utility holding company structure's reputation for abuse.

Given that the holding companies sprawled across multiple jurisdictions, no state could effectively control their corporate governance. Disclosure was not enough to correct the abuses. If regulatory oversight of these monopolies was to be effective, stronger medicine was required: The federal government needed to control corporate governance. The economic crisis provided Roosevelt with the opportunity to eliminate the holding companies. On January 4, 1935, Roosevelt called for the "abolition of the evil of holding companies" in his State of the Union address to Congress.[20] The public utilities industry was considerably less enthusiastic about being the subject of the federal government's experiments in corporate governance, predicting economic disaster if the bill were enacted.[21]

PUHCA went well beyond the disclosure mandates of the two earlier securities statutes. PUHCA's "death sentence" provision effectively limited utility holding companies to one geographic area; those that did not comply were to be broken up under the direction of the SEC.[22] The death sentence provision was a major departure from the disclosure paradigm

---

[18] Joel Seligman has characterized PUHCA as "the most radical reform measure of the Roosevelt administration." Joel Seligman, The Transformation of Wall Street 122 (3d ed. 2003); see also Morris L. Forer, "A Postscript to the Administration of the Public Utility Holding Company Act: The Hydro-Electric System Case", 45 Va. L. Rev. 1007, 1007–08 (1959) ("Probably the most dynamic piece of New Deal legislation, [PUHCA] was revolutionary in that it required not only the immediate eradication of specific and now all too familiar abuses, but also in that it provided for the minute supervision of actions and programs then conceived as being safely reposed in management. This statute aimed not only at the remedial, but, shooting at the escaping present, had also as its target a better economic future" (footnote omitted)).

[19] See David Skeel, Icarus in the Boardroom: The Fundamental Flaws in Corporate America and Where They Came From 8, 80–89 (2005) (discussing Insull); Richard D. Cudahy & William D. Henderson, "From Insull to Enron: Corporate (Re)Regulation After the Rise And Fall of Two Energy Icons", 26 Energy L. J. 35, 36 (2005).

[20] Quoted in Arthur M. Schlesinger, Jr., "The Age of Roosevelt: 1935–1936", The Politics of Upheaval 305 (1960).

[21] Wendell Willkie, the president of Commonwealth and Southern (and future Republican presidential nominee), warned that: "the utility industry would be thrown "into a chaos of liquidation and receiverships," holders of utility stocks would suffer "practically complete" losses, and a "great bureaucracy in Washington will be regulating the internal affairs of practically all utility operating companies in the United States." The backers of the death sentence, Willkie charged, were trying "to 'nationalize' the power business of this country." Id. at 310.

[22] Seligman, *supra* note 18, at 131.

of the earlier securities laws. The holding company legislation also required registration and disclosure, but it broke new ground in giving the SEC control over the utilities' capital structures and corporate governance as part of their reorganization. Thus, the legislation set a new high water mark for federal interference with business: "Except in wartime, the federal government never before had assumed such total control over any industry."[23] PUHCA's sweeping reforms would trigger a decade-long war in the courts, as the giant utilities resisted the efforts of the SEC to dismantle them. But it also set the stage for the SEC to play a key role in corporate governance, albeit for only a portion of American business.

For opponents of federal economic regulation, PUHCA looked like the constitutional test case for the federal control of corporate governance that liberals had long sought. The Roosevelt administration ultimately prevailed despite the industry's resistance, but only after an epic legal struggle, requiring three visits to the Supreme Court before it was finally resolved in the government's favor.[24] Only a decade after PUHCA's enactment did the Court resolve the constitutionality of the controversial death sentence provision.[25] When the *North American v. SEC* decision came down, it was an enthusiastic validation of the SEC's power to break up utility holding companies. The Court's opinion painted with a broad, moralistic brush: "The fact that an evil may involve a corporation's financial practices, its business structure or its security portfolio does not detract from the power of Congress under the commerce clause to promulgate rules in order to destroy that evil."[26] Under its new understanding of the Commerce Clause, the Court had validated the federal government's authority over corporate governance. Would Congress and the SEC exercise that authority?

The answer was no—at least in the short term. Having gained the power, the federal government lost the will. PUHCA, which in the 1940s allowed the SEC to dictate corporate governance standards to an industry vital to the economy, faded in significance after the nation's public utility holding companies were broken up by the 1950s. It did not prove to be the trial run for "federal corporation law" as liberals had hoped. A generation later, narrow interpretations and regulatory exemptions undid much of the work accomplished by the SEC in breaking up the holding companies. New utility conglomerates emerged, such as Enron, with diverse business interests and sprawling operations. PUHCA's purpose was largely repudiated, and the Act itself was repealed in 2005.[27] After PUHCA's repeal, the SEC was deprived of the role that gave the agency an important say in corporate governance, limiting the agency to overseeing the disclosure-focused regulation of the Securities Act and Exchange Act.

PUHCA's withering foreshadowed a broader retreat by Congress and the SEC in the realm of corporate governance, and indeed, securities law generally. Congress passed no significant securities legislation between 1940 and 1964. The SEC went from being an activist force in the 1930s, to being a backwater after its wartime move to Philadelphia. (It was not returned

---

[23] Schlesinger, *supra* note 20, at 306.

[24] The Court first addressed whether a host of individual challenges to the statute could be stayed pending Supreme Court consideration of a test case. *Landis v. North American Co.*, 299 U.S. 248, 249 (1936). The second case upheld only the constitutionality of the relatively uncontroversial registration and disclosure provisions of PUHCA. *Electric Bond & Share Co. v. SEC*, 303 U.S. 419, 442–443 (1938).

[25] See *N. Am. Co v. SEC*, 327 U.S. 686, 704 (1946).

[26] Id. at 706. Murphy similarly disposed of the due process clause claim. Id. at 708.

[27] Energy Policy Act of 2005, Pub. L. 109–158, 119 Stat. 594.

from exile until 1948.) Simply put, almost as soon as the constitutionality of PUHCA was es-tablished in *North American*, affirming the power of Congress over corporate governance, securities law stopped pushing those boundaries. Not until the 1960s would that push be revived, but that extension would come from the SEC and the courts, not Congress.

2.3 The 1960s Expansion

The 1960s witnessed a rapid expansion of the influence of the federal securities laws, in the form of broad interpretations of Rule 10b-5 of the Exchange Act.[28] Rule 10b-5, which the Commission had adopted two decades earlier under its § 10(b) authority as a general anti-fraud prohibition, threatened to become an overarching "federal corporation law."[29]

The development began with a topic squarely at the intersection of disclosure and cor-porate governance: insider trading. Informational advantages discourage stock market liquidity, so exchanges and securities regulators have an incentive to check information asymmetry if it is feasible to do so. For that reason, the NYSE and other exchanges have long had (spottily enforced) requirements that listed companies disclose information that was likely to move the market. The intersection with corporate governance arises because use of inside information can be thought of as a misappropriation by the insider of a corporate asset: material, confidential business information. That misappropriation has come to be seen as a breach of fiduciary duty under state corporate law.[30] The influence of inside infor-mation on the securities markets has also attracted the interest of the SEC, however, and that agency has played the starring role in developing the law of insider trading.

The SEC's first salvo came in 1961, when it pioneered prohibitions against insider trading with its *Cady, Roberts* decision.[31] The source of the prohibition was somewhat surprising. In *Cady, Roberts*, the Commission interpreted Rule 10b-5 to prohibit insider trading, de-spite the fact that neither Rule 10b-5 nor § 10(b) makes any mention of insider trading. Notwithstanding this omission, the SEC found in *Cady, Roberts* that a director of a public company violated Rule 10b-5 by tipping non-public information. The director had learned that the company was planning to cut the size of its dividend. The director, who happened to be the partner of a brokerage firm, provided the information to one of his partners at the bro-kerage house, who traded on it. In concluding that the director had violated Rule 10b-5, the SEC set out a broad fiduciary standard for the insider trading prohibition:

> The obligation rests on two principal elements; first, the existence of a relationship giving access, directly or indirectly, to information intended to be available only for a corporate pur-pose and not for the personal benefit of anyone, and second, the inherent unfairness involved where a party takes advantage of such information knowing it is unavailable to those with whom he is dealing.[32]

---

[28]   17 C.F.R. § 240.10b-5 (2002).

[29]   See generally Arthur Fleischer, Jr., " 'Federal Corporation Law': An Assessment", 78 Harv. L. Rev. 1146 (1965) (arguing that "the growth of federal law in the corporate area is sound," but noting the criticism "that federal law has invaded areas never contemplated by the Congress when adopting the securities acts").

[30]   *Brophy v. Cities Services Co.*, 31 Del. Ch. 241, 70 A.2d 5 (1949).

[31]   *In re Cady, Roberts & Co.*, 40 S.E.C. 907, 912–913 (1961).   [32]   *Id.* at 912 (footnote omitted).

This standard was not constrained by state law notions of fiduciary duty. Indeed, *Cady, Roberts* noted in passing that "the securities acts may be said to have generated a wholly new and far-reaching body of Federal corporation law."[33]

The SEC's interpretation is breathtaking in its assertiveness. The fiduciary obligation outlined by the agency finds no support in the text of either Rule 10b-5 or § 10(b). With the *Cady, Roberts* decision, the SEC gave notice that in interpreting "[the] elements [of § 10(b)] under the broad language of the anti-fraud provisions we are not to be circumscribed by fine distinctions and rigid classifications."[34] Thus, the SEC announced its intent to root out information asymmetries in the secondary markets to protect "the buying public" "from the misuse of special information."[35] The securities laws would be interpreted as needed to achieve that goal; the SEC developing its own body of fiduciary principles, unmoored from statutory text and untethered by state corporate law, to achieve that end.[36]

Three years later in *Securities and Exchange Commission v. Capital Gains Research Bureau, Inc.*,[37] the Supreme Court gave a green light to the SEC to extend the boundaries of its powers in fleshing out a new—federal—understanding of fiduciary obligation. The *Capital Gains* decision, although turning on an interpretation of the Investment Advisers Act of 1940,[38] suggested that the SEC could expand its power through agency and judicial interpretation of existing statutes and regulation. The agency would not need to resort to the cumbersome rulemaking process under the Administrative Procedure Act, or, still more daunting, seek legislation. According to the Court, "Congress intended the Investment Advisers Act of 1940 to be construed like other securities legislation enacted for the purpose of avoiding frauds, not technically and restrictively, but flexibly to effectuate its remedial purposes."[39] After its victory in *Capital Gains*, the SEC would push an aggressive interpretation of § 10(b) of the Exchange Act in the lower courts, particularly the Second Circuit, as its principal weapon in its bold new campaign against insider trading. Four years later, in *SEC v. Texas Gulf Sulphur*, the Second Circuit would validate the SEC's expansive reading of § 10(b) of the Exchange Act.[40] *Capital Gains* would be cited by the *Texas Gulf Sulphur* majority for the proposition that even negligent insider trading would be unlawful.[41] Post *Capital Gains*, the SEC and the lower courts could feel confident that their expansive interpretations would be upheld.

By the end of the 1960s the federal securities laws seemed poised to take over the law governing corporations entirely. In the words of Louis Loss, "the great Rule 10b-5 . . . seems to be taking over the universe gradually."[42] This usurpation of corporate governance standards was being accomplished by the SEC and the courts without any intervention from Congress.

---

[33] Id. at 910 (footnote omitted).   [34] Id. at 912.   [35] Id. at 913.

[36] David S. Ruder, "Pitfalls in the Development of a Federal Law of Corporations by Implication Through Rule 10b-5", 59 Nw. U. L. Rev. 185, 185 (1964) ("Despite Congressional unwillingness to enact a 'federal law of corporations', it now appears that such a law is arising by implication through interpretation of the various securities acts").

[37] 375 U.S. 180 (1963).   [38] 54 Stat. 847, as amended 15 U.S.C. § 80b-1 et seq.

[39] *Capital Gains*, 375 U.S. at 195 (citations and quotations omitted).

[40] 401 F.2d 833 (2d Cir. 1968) (en banc).   [41] Id. at 855.

[42] Louis L. Loss, "The American Law Institute's Federal Securities Code Project", 25 Bus. Law. 27, 34 (1969).

2.4 The 1970s and 1980s: Retrenchment

The era of 10b-5 expansionism came to an abrupt halt in the 1970s. The first salvo came in a pair of class actions from the mid-1970s—*Blue Chip Stamps*[43] and *Ernst & Ernst*[44]— in which the Supreme Court made plain its intention to rein in Rule 10b-5. *Blue Chip Stamps* holds that a private plaintiff must be a purchaser or seller of securities to state a claim under Rule 10b-5,[45] but the opinion is notable for its skepticism regarding securities fraud class actions, which were the lawsuits affording the Second Circuit the opportunity to push the boundaries of Rule 10b-5.[46] *Ernst & Ernst* signals a reading of Rule 10b-5 narrowly tethered to the text of § 10(b). In rejecting the argument that an allegation of negligence would establish a fraud claim under Rule 10b-5, the Court emphasized that the scope of Rule 10b-5 "cannot exceed the power granted the [SEC] by Congress under § 10(b)."[47] *Blue Chip* and *Ernst & Ernst* signaled that the Supreme Court had abandoned "flexible" construction of the sort seen in *Cady, Roberts* and *Capital Gains* to achieve "remedial purposes."

The nail in the coffin for the effort to push Rule 10b-5 into the realm of corporate governance arrived soon thereafter. *Santa Fe Industries v. Green*[48] is the Court's most sweeping defense of state corporate law. The Second Circuit held that a short form merger authorized by Delaware law,[49] which "froze out" the company's minority shareholders, violated Rule 10b-5.[50] That court held that "no allegation or proof of misrepresentation or nondisclosure [was] necessary" to state a violation of Rule 10b-5; a breach of fiduciary duty was sufficient.[51] Rule 10b-5 was completely divorced from disclosure. Moreover, that breach of fiduciary duty arose out of federal, rather than state, common law.[52]

In reversing the Second Circuit, Justice Byron White held for the Court that fraud requires a misrepresentation or nondisclosure.[53] That was sufficient to answer the question presented, but White went out of his way to defend the role of state corporate law:

> The reasoning behind a holding that the complaint in this case alleged fraud under Rule 10b-5 could not be easily contained . . . The result would be to bring within the Rule a wide variety of corporate conduct traditionally left to state regulation . . . this extension of the federal securities laws would overlap and quite possibly interfere with state corporate law. Federal courts applying a "federal fiduciary principle" under Rule 10b-5 could be expected to depart from state fiduciary standards at least to the extent necessary to ensure uniformity within the federal system. Absent a clear indication of congressional intent, we are reluctant to federalize the substantial portion of the law of corporations that deals with transactions in securities, particularly where established state policies of corporate regulation would be overridden.[54]

---

[43] *Blue Chip Stamps v. Manor Drug Stores*, 421 U.S. 723 (1975).
[44] *Ernst & Ernst v. Hochfelder*, 425 U.S. 185 (1976).   [45] *Blue Chip Stamps*, 421 U.S. at 754–755.
[46] *Blue Chip*, 421 U.S. at 739 ("litigation under Rule 10b-5 presents a danger of vexatiousness different in degree and in kind from that which accompanies litigation in general" and the risk that the threat of enormous discovery costs could produce "'in terrorem' settlements").
[47] *Ernst & Ernst*, 425 U.S. at 214.   [48] 430 U.S. 462 (1977).
[49] Del. Code Ann. tit. 8, § 253 (1974).
[50] *Green v. Santa Fe Indus., Inc.*, 533 F.2d 1283, 1299 (2d Cir. 1976).   [51] Id. at 1287.
[52] Id. at 1286.   [53] *Santa Fe Indus., Inc. v. Green*, 430 U.S. 462, 473–474 (1977).
[54] *Santa Fe*, 430 U.S. at 478–479 (citations and footnotes omitted).

Thus, the Supreme Court was emphatic in drawing a line in the sand to preserve state corporate law from lower federal courts developing their own "federal corporate law."

A decade later, the Court did not hesitate to reaffirm the line between state corporate law and federal securities law when a wave of hostile takeovers reached its zenith in the 1980s.[55] The states were taking the lead in discouraging takeovers. The SEC was in the opposing corner, attempting to use federal law to head off state efforts to restrict the market for corporate control.[56] Once again, the Supreme Court came down firmly on the side of states' control over corporate governance.

In *CTS Corp. v. Dynamics Corp. of America*,[57] the Indiana anti-takeover statute at issue required a potential acquirer (defined as anyone acquiring certain threshold percentages of the company's shares) to obtain the approval of a company's "disinterested" shares (defined as shares not owned by the acquirer or management) before it would be allowed to vote its own shares.[58] Thus, a hostile tender offeror could not use its voting power to remove incumbent management without the approval of the company's independent shareholders. The Indiana statute was limited to corporations organized under the law of Indiana, with their principal place of business and a substantial shareholder presence in that state.[59]

In upholding the statute against twin challenges based on the Dormant Commerce Clause and preemption under the federal securities law, the Court emphasized that state authority over voting rights was supported by tradition: "No principle of corporation law and practice is more firmly established than a State's authority to regulate domestic corps, including the voting rights of shareholders."[60] By implication, the SEC's authority in this area was doubtful absent explicit legislative authorization.[61] As far as the Supreme Court was concerned, corporate governance was a topic for the states, not the SEC.

In some tension with these decisions rebuffing "federal corporate law" is the Supreme Court's insider trading decision in *Chiarella v. United States*.[62] Justice Lewis Powell, writing for the Court, construed *Cady, Roberts* and *Texas Gulf Sulphur* and its progeny in the Second Circuit narrowly, fitting those decisions into a common law framework, but that

---

[55] Patrick A. Gaughan, Mergers, Acquisitions, and Corporate Restructurings 44–49 (3d ed. 2002) (collecting statistics on the incidence of hostile takeovers).

[56] Tender Offer Reform Act of 1984, H.R. 5693, 98th Cong. (1984) (proposing, at the SEC's urging, that the Williams Act be expanded to give the SEC jurisdiction over anti-takeover devices).

[57] 481 U.S. 69, 73–74 (1987).   [58] Id.

[59] Ind. Code § 23-1-42-4(a) (1986), quoted in *CTS*, 481 U.S. at 72–73.   [60] *CTS*, 481 U.S. at 89.

[61] The limits on the SEC's authority over corporate governance were reinforced by D.C. Circuit's resolution of the conflict over dual-class voting stock. For over fifty years the NYSE prohibited listed companies from issuing common stock without voting rights. See Stephen M. Bainbridge, "The Short Life and Resurrection of SEC Rule 19c-4", 69 Wash. U. L. Q. 565, 569 (1991) (discussing origins of NYSE rule against non-voting common). The Nasdaq did not impose similar restrictions in its listing agreement. Id. at 575. In the 1980s General Motors, an NYSE company, refused to comply with the rule prohibiting non-voting common stock, and the NYSE essentially ignored GM's defiance of the rule. Id. at 576–77 & n. 54. The NYSE was unwilling to enforce its rule unless the AMEX and Nasdaq prohibited the practice as well. Daniel R. Fischel, "Organized Exchanges and the Regulation of Dual Class Common Stock", 54 U. Chi. L. Rev. 119, 121 (1987). The SEC responded by adopting a rule of its own prohibiting non-voting common stock. That rule was struck down by the D.C. Circuit as beyond the Commission's statutory authority. *Business Roundtable v. SEC*, 905 F.2d 406 (D.C. Cir. 1990). Subsequently, the NYSE, AMEX, and Nasdaq agreed upon a rule limiting non-voting common stock. See "SEC Approves New Voting Rights Rule, Adopts Rule Streamlining SRO Regulation", 26 Sec. Reg. & L. Rep. (BNA) 1708 (Dec. 23, 1994).

[62] 445 U.S. 222 (1980).

framework rested on a *federal* common law.[63] Powell rejected a duty to the sellers because Chiarella owed them no fiduciary duty.[64] The common law of fraud required a duty to the person on the other side of the transaction.[65] Despite his reliance on common law principles, Powell was creating a federal fiduciary principle, not incorporating state law into federal law. Consequently, *Chiarella*'s approach is hard to square with Justice White's rejection of a federal fiduciary standard in *Santa Fe*. Powell's justification for relying on fiduciary duty? "Section 10(b) is aptly described as a catchall provision, but what it catches must be fraud."[66] Powell recognized that insider trading law would have implications for corporate governance, but he wanted to keep that body of law firmly rooted in disclosure, the province of federal law. Fiduciary duty provided him the doctrinal tool to confine insider trading to (somewhat) traditional notions of fraud.

3 CAPITAL MARKETS AND CORPORATE GOVERNANCE

3.1 An International Market for Corporate Governance?

We have seen the US market for corporate charters protected by the Supreme Court from incursions by the SEC. That market now has an international analogue. Capital markets are no longer parochial; technological changes have made the market for listings much deeper. Improvements in communication and related technologies have created an *international* market for stock exchange listings that resembles, in many respects, the longstanding *federal* market for corporate charters in the US.

Historically, issuers listed their stock for trading on one of the exchanges in the country where they principally did business. In an era when businesses are consolidating across national boundaries to create international conglomerates, the notion of a corporation having a "home" country seems increasingly archaic. Corporations, at least those of a certain size, are now citizens of the world, although they may identify for a time with the jurisdiction where their headquarters are located. Today, corporations around the world realistically can choose the location, or locations, where they want to raise capital. They can also choose where they want their common shares to trade. Corporations are not limited to their "home" country for financing and trading, and the capital-raising decision need not be linked to the listing decision.

Why not, then, list on an exchange that allowed a company to signal the quality of its corporate governance? There are obvious efficiency advantages. Disclosure of corporate governance terms will not only facilitate more accurate securities prices, but also allow investors to make better choices in allocating their investment dollars, funneling capital to better managed companies. If firms do not give credible assurances that they will not abuse their investors' trust, investors will not entrust them with their investment dollars. Companies

---

[63] A.C. Pritchard, "United States v. O'Hagan: Agency Law and Justice Powell's Legacy for the Law of Insider Trading", 78 B.U. L. Rev. 13 (1998).

[64] *Chiarella*, 445 U.S. at 232–233.   [65] Id. at 228.   [66] *Chiarella*, 445 U.S. at 234–235.

looking to maximize their returns when selling securities to the public will accordingly have a strong incentive to include corporate governance mechanisms valued by shareholders.

Exchanges have market incentives to promote the signal: "Self-interested stock exchange members will produce rules that investors want for the same reasons that self-interested bakers produce the kind of bread that consumers want."[67] Securities markets live or die with trading volume. Broker-dealers make a substantial portion of their revenues from trading commissions; another chunk comes from trading for their own accounts. More trading by customers obviously means more commissions, but more liquid markets also enhance the profitability of broker-dealers' own trading. Exchanges attract trading volume by encouraging companies to list their shares and by encouraging investors to trade in those listed shares. These two goals are largely consistent, as companies will want to list their shares on exchanges that provide the greatest liquidity because liquidity minimizes their cost of capital. The exchanges also have a quasi-property interest in the stock prices quoted in their market. This interest effectively makes the exchanges residual claimants in the integrity of those stock prices. Thus, exchanges might compete to attract trading volume by providing a "bonding" signal to companies seeking to attract investors, if investors are more willing to trade in the stock of companies with good corporate governance.

That story provides an optimistic scenario of corporate government and securities law complementing each other. What is the practical limit of legislators and securities regulators to impose corporate governance mandates through securities laws? If capital markets provide the critical connection between the two, the answer to that question may lie with liquidity. Greater disclosure of information is associated with higher levels of liquidity.[68] And there is evidence that fraud may have market-wide effects on liquidity.[69] So exchanges, and perhaps, securities regulators, will have incentives to regulate in areas where the connection to liquidity is clear.

Consider insider trading, one area where the SEC has had considerable success in imposing fiduciary standards on corporate insiders, with the blessing of both the Supreme Court and Congress. Economic theory and empirical evidence suggest that insider trading harms liquidity.[70] Insider traders hold information advantages over outsiders. Those information asymmetries lead to trading profits—insiders buy low and sell high. To avoid the corresponding trading losses, outsiders would prefer to trade only with other outsiders. Securities markets are anonymous, however, so outsiders have no way of knowing when they are trading with an insider, but they do know that they will systematically lose when they do so. Market makers who supply liquidity to the markets on an uninformed basis will increase their spreads to reflect the possibility of dealing with an insider, converting insider trading into a transaction cost of all trading. Uninformed shareholders will discount the amount that they are willing to pay for shares by their expected losses from trading with insiders;

---

[67] Mahoney, *supra* note 12, at 1459.

[68] Frank L. Heflin et al., "Disclosure Policy and Market Liquidity: Impact of Depth Quotes and Order Sizes", 22 Contemporary Accounting Research 829 (2005).

[69] Panjak K. Jain et al., "The Sarbanes–Oxley Act of 2002 and Market Liquidity", 43 Fin. Rev. 361–82 (2008) (showing that market liquidity deteriorated following Enron and related scandals, and improved after the adoption of Sarbanes–Oxley).

[70] See, e.g., Louis Cheng et al., "The Effects of Insider Trading on Liquidity", 14 Pacific-Basin Fin. J. 467 (2006).

they may attempt to avoid losses from trading with insiders by trading less frequently. Less trading means less liquidity, and less liquid securities markets raise the cost of trading. In this scenario, the SEC's effort to harness fiduciary principles in the service of promoting liquidity deftly walks the line where corporate governance and securities law intersect.

Policy makers recognize that encouraging liquid securities markets will facilitate capital formation, and thus, economic growth. Unfortunately, politicians are unlikely to worry about the details of promoting economic growth during a bull market. The capital markets are not crying out for government intervention when investors' primary focus is counting their gains. Bear markets, however, inevitably follow bull markets. Corporate mismanagement and corruption can be obscured by rising stock prices, but the dirty laundry has a way of surfacing in bear markets. The bad news produces dissatisfied investors who clamor for government intervention, and politicians shake off their apathy and suddenly become profoundly interested in securities law. This dynamic means that demands for regulation will arise in times of crisis, particularly if that crisis spills over into the real economy. Politicians will want to "do something," even if the proposed something has scant connection to the promotion of liquid securities markets. Corporate governance may fit the bill, providing a salient response to the scandals arising during the crisis.

3.2 The US Competes

The recent history of securities regulation in the US illustrates the phenomenon. For a time, proponents of the US securities law regime argued that its rigor gave US exchanges a competitive edge by allowing them to provide a bonding signal. Foreign companies could signal their integrity by exposing themselves to the demands of the US disclosure and enforcement regime, which proponents claimed was the best in the world.[71] That regime permitted foreign companies to credibly pre-commit to limit self-dealing transactions, a concern that might be particularly salient in jurisdictions where controlling shareholders are common, i.e., most jurisdictions other than the US and the UK. Companies headquartered in jurisdictions not known for the quality of their legal systems might be particularly interested in the possibility of buying a credible "bonding" signal; it might be difficult or impossible for such companies to duplicate such a signal on their own.[72] The power of contract goes only so far if enforcement mechanisms are dubious.

Critically, the mechanism for the precommitment signal was not a corporate governance-style ban on such transactions, which might have been unworkable for companies in countries where cross shareholdings are common. Instead, the tool of choice was disclosure requirements under exacting US standards, backed by the threat of SEC scrutiny. The US exchanges' computerized surveillance systems also promised real teeth for enforcing insider trading rules and other prohibitions against market manipulation. Other countries have followed the US lead in prohibiting insider trading, but enforcement of those

---

[71] See generally John C. Coffee, Jr., "Racing Towards the Top?: The Impact of Cross-Listings and Stock Market Competition on International Corporate Governance", 102 Colum. L. Rev. 1757 (2002).

[72] Edward Rock, "Securities Regulation as a Lobster Trap: A Credible Commitment Theory of Mandatory Disclosure", 23 Cardozo L. Rev. 675 (2002); see Michael Spence, "Job Market Signaling", 87 Q. J. Econ. 355 (1973) (outlining economic theory of signaling).

prohibitions pales in comparison to the SEC's vendetta against the abuse. Of equal significance for companies listing in the United States, misstatements about a company's fortunes
would be subject to the sting of SEC enforcement, generally regarded as a step above other
jurisdictions, both in the probability and size of sanctions.[73]

In response to lobbying by the exchanges, the SEC encouraged foreign companies to list in
the US by relaxing a number of potentially expensive requirements for listing.[74] The SEC did
not, however, go so far as to allow foreign companies to merely comply with the disclosure
requirements of their home jurisdictions (a "mutual recognition" regime). From the SEC's
perspective, US disclosure standards were superior; they could be tinkered with around
the edges, but wholesale waiver was not an option. Although the SEC was anxious to bring
foreign companies to US exchanges, it recognized that it bore a "significant political risk"
from financial scandals involving foreign firms if American retail investors incurred substantial losses.[75] Moreover, the SEC did not exempt foreign companies from the anti-fraud
rules, with their potential for both SEC enforcement, but also, the risk of private litigation,
unheard of in other jurisdictions until very recently. Companies willing to face this risk by
listing in the United States sent a strong signal of honesty and integrity.

The twin burdens of SEC disclosure requirements and exposure to securities class actions
made listing in the United States a costly proposition for foreign companies, notwithstanding
the SEC's efforts at accommodation. The fact that a significant number of companies were
willing to pay this price allowed the SEC to tell a happy story of a race to the top in the competition for international listings. The best companies—world-class companies—sought
to list in the United States because it had the best regulation, the story went. Evidence of a
listing premium for companies selling shares in the United States strongly supported the
SEC's account.[76]

3.3 The US Loses its Lead

The cheery equilibrium between corporate governance and listing in the US has since proved
to be fragile. The flow of foreign companies coming to the US stopped, and more worryingly,

---

[73] John C. Coffee, Jr., "Law and the Market: The Impact of Enforcement", 156 U. Pa. L. Rev. 229, 238 n.17
(2007) (summarizing LSE's treatment of foreign issuers). The probability of SEC enforcement against
foreign issuers cross-listing in the U.S. was probably overstated. See Jordan Siegel, "Can foreign firms
bond themselves effectively by renting U.S. securities laws?", 75 J. Fin. Econ. 319, 342 (2005) (finding that
the SEC averaged two enforcement actions per year against cross-listed firms).

[74] Most notably, the agency: (1) allowed foreign issuers to reconcile their accounts with U.S. generally
accepted accounting principles, rather than requiring a new set of financial statements prepared in
accordance with US standards (see SEC Form F-1); (2) relaxed certain reporting requirements (17 C.F.R.
§ 240.13a-13(b)(2) (2009) (exempting foreign issuers from quarterly reporting requirements); Id. §
243.101(b) (exempting foreign issuers from Regulation FD's equal access to disclosure requirements); and
(3) exempted foreign companies from the short-swing insider trading rule of Section 16 of the Exchange
Act and the proxy requirements (17 C.F.R. § 240.3a12-3).

[75] Ethiopis Tafara & Robert J. Peterson, "A Blueprint for Cross-Border Access to U.S. Investors: A New
International Framework", 48 Harv. Int'l. L. J. 31, 49 (2007).

[76] See Craig Doidge et al., "Why are Foreign Firms Listed in the U.S. Worth More?", 71 J. Fin. Econ.
205 (2004).

reversed. After the SEC relaxed standards for foreign companies wanting to delist,[77] a flood of companies headed for the doors.[78]

What derailed the US-led race to the top? The answer is politics, and more particularly, Congress. The dividing line between securities law and corporate governance drawn by the Supreme Court limits the SEC and the lower courts, but it does not constrain Congress. Nonetheless, for nearly fifty years after PUHCA had begun to dwindle, Congress generally respected that line. The securities laws were about disclosure.

The major exception to the disclosure focus of the securities laws was the enactment of the Foreign Corrupt Practices Act (FCPA) in 1977. The FCPA is a response to Watergate-era scandals involving the bribery of foreign officials by US companies, which came under the SEC's purview because companies were not recording the bribes and slush funds in their accounts (Surprise!). The FCPA includes a variety of books and records provisions intended to improve the accuracy of corporate disclosures, so some of its provisions are squarely within the bailiwick of the SEC. The FCPA, however, also includes a substantive provision outlawing payments by US companies to foreign officials, which can be enforced civilly by the SEC and criminally by the Justice Department. The provision sits oddly amidst the disclosure-oriented provisions of the securities laws, but its practical import has been limited until recent efforts to increase enforcement. Moreover, although it does contain a substantive provision that limits the conduct of corporations, it is not limited to *public* corporations, the traditional concern of the securities laws, but rather, US corporations generally. More importantly, the prohibition is outward directed. The law prohibits bribing foreign government officials. It says nothing about bribing company officers, which would be a classic corporate governance problem. Thus, the FCPA departs from the disclosure focus of the securities laws, but not in a direction that one could fairly criticize as an incursion into the state's domain of corporate governance.

More recently, however, Congress has made substantial inroads into corporate governance through amendments to the securities laws, blurring the line separating the two. Those forays by Congress into corporate governance correspond with the demise of the US as a listing destination. The first salvo of incursions into the field of corporate governance came with the Sarbanes–Oxley Act fueled by accounting scandals at Enron and WorldCom.[79] Collecting a hodge-podge of reforms, Congress (1) took over the regulation of accounting firms from the private sector;[80] (2) imposed expensive internal controls and certification requirements;[81] and (3) adopted an array of new sanctions.[82] The most expensive of these requirements were standards relating to internal accounting controls, requiring both review and certifications of those controls by the chief executive officer and chief financial officer.[83]

---

[77] Termination of a Foreign Private Issuer's Registration of a Class of Securities Under Section 12(g) and Duty to File Reports Under Section 13(a) or 15(d) of the Securities Exchange Act of 1934, Exchange Act Release No. 34-55540, 90 SEC Docket 860 (Mar. 27, 2007).

[78] Comm. on Capital Mkts. Regulation, Summary of Competitiveness Measures (2009) (noting that more than 12% of foreign firms listed on the NYSE delisted during the first 10 months of 2007); see also Craig Doidge et al., "Why Do Foreign Firms Leave U.S. Equity Markets?", 65 J. Fin. 1507 (2010) (finding that departing firms had lower growth prospects and capital requirements).

[79] Pub. L. No. 107-204, 116 Stat. 745 (codified in scattered sections of 11, 15, 18, 28, and 29 U.S.C.).

[80] Sarbanes–Oxley Act §§ 101–109, 15 U.S.C. §§ 7211–7219.   [81] Id. § 302, 15 U.S.C. § 7241.

[82] E.g., id. § 906, 18 U.S.C. § 1350.   [83] Id. § 404(a), 15 U.S.C. § 7262(a).

Foreign company executives proved less than enthusiastic about the spotlight afforded by those certifications, perhaps helping to speed the exodus that followed.

Not surprisingly, Congress also sought to improve corporate governance relating to the auditing function. Sarbanes–Oxley mandates that the retention, compensation, and oversight of the company's external auditor must be entrusted to an audit committee of the board of directors. The auditors must report to the audit committee "critical accounting policies and practices." The audit committee is also charged with establishing procedures for dealing with complaints relating to auditing and internal controls. These provisions are intended to set up audit committees as an independent power center within the governance structure of public corporations.

That independence is bolstered by additional mandates relating to the audit committee's composition. Audit committees must be made up exclusively of independent directors, meaning that the only compensation the director can receive from the company is the director's fee—no consulting or other employment arrangements are permitted.[84] The SEC has bolstered this independence requirement by requiring companies to disclose whether any member of the audit committee qualifies as a "financial expert," which requires either experience as an accountant or an accounting officer, or experience supervising an accounting officer or overseeing public accountants.[85] Listing requirements for the NYSE and Nasdaq now require financial literacy for all audit committee members.

These minor incursions into corporate governance in the Sarbanes–Oxley Act coincided with the exodus of foreign companies from US exchanges described above. Far from being chastened by that trend, Congress demonstrated even less restraint when it came to "do something" in response to the next financial crisis. This time, with the Dodd–Frank Act, the corporate governance mandates have no connection whatsoever to liquidity.[86] For example, the Dodd–Frank requires that companies disclose whether the same person holds both the CEO and Chairman of the Board positions, and explain why the position is combined or not.[87] This is a pure corporate governance provision, styled as a disclosure mandate, but with no possible connection to liquidity. It simply uses disclosure to put a thumb on the scale toward Congress's view of best corporate governance practices.

Other mandates are more explicitly driven by a political agenda. Most blatant is Dodd–Frank's mandate relating to conflict minerals. Concerned about violence in the Democratic Republic of Congo relating to a variety of resource extraction industries, Congress decided to use its leverage over corporate disclosure policies to deal with the problem.[88] The SEC adopted a new disclosure form, Form SD, requiring companies to disclose payments in excess of $100,000 made to governments for the purpose of commercial development of natural resources.[89] The target was armed groups that were profiting from extortion of mining operations. The teeth of the rule were provided by the requirement that firms investigate and disclose if their products used any "conflict minerals." The expense of the investigation was calculated to be enormous: the SEC estimated that the total costs of the final rule would be

[84]   Securities Exchange Act of 1934 § 10A(m), 15 U.S.C. § 78j-1(m) (2006).
[85]   Regulation S-K, Item 309.
[86]   Dodd–Frank Wall Street Reform and Consumer Protection Act, Pub. L. No. 111-203, 124 Stat. 1376 (relevant parts codified at 15 U.S.C. §§ 78m(p), 78m) (2010)).
[87]   Section 972, Dodd–Frank Act.   [88]   Section 1504, Dodd–Frank Act.
[89]   77 Fed. Reg. 56,274, 56,277–278 (Sept. 12, 2012) (codified at 17 C.F.R. §§ 240.13p-1, 249b.400).

$3 billion to $4 billion initially, and $207 million to $609 million annually thereafter.[90] The benefits of the rule? Hard to calculate, according to the SEC, because it was hard to quantify peace and stability in the Congo.[91] It is not hard to guess, however, the benefit to investors from these disclosures, which are presumably zero.

Somewhat more closely tied to corporate governance are Dodd–Frank's mandates relating to executive pay, an issue with apparently evergreen populist appeal. The political agenda is quite clear in Dodd–Frank's requirement that companies disclose the ratio of their CEO's pay to that of their median employee.[92] On the governance side, the Dodd–Frank Act requires the SEC to direct, by rule, the securities exchanges to prohibit the listing of any equity securities of public companies unless the compensation committees of the public companies' boards are made up exclusively of independent directors.[93] The independence requirement for the board compensation committee parallels the independence requirement for the board audit committee. Moreover, Dodd–Frank imposes a variety of responsibilities on compensation committees, such as the hiring and supervision of compensation consultants.

The Dodd–Frank Act also enhances shareholder power over executive compensation. Public companies are now required to conduct an advisory vote of shareholders on the pay packages of top executives at least once every three years.[94] "Golden parachute" payments made to executives displaced in connection with mergers and acquisitions also require an advisory vote of shareholders. In connection with these advisory votes, the SEC has enhanced the disclosure requirements for these executives in the Compensation Discussion and Analysis section of the proxy statement. That disclosure now must also address whether (and if so, how) the company has considered the results of the most recent say-on-pay vote in determining compensation policies and decisions. Shareholders are not allowed to dictate the pay packages of senior executives, but the new regime attempts to maximize the leverage implicit in embarrassment.[95]

The Dodd–Frank Act also attempted to shift power to shareholders by ensuring access to the company's proxy. Historically, outside insurgents could launch a full-blown contest with their own proxy statement to elect a competing slate to a company's board of directors, but such contests are costly and correspondingly rare. The Dodd–Frank Act authorized the SEC to allow shareholders to nominate candidates for director directly on the company's proxy without going to the trouble and expense of a proxy contest using a separate proxy statement.[96] The SEC attempted to implement proxy access through Rule 14a-11. Rule 14a-11

---

[90] Id. at 56,334   [91] Id. at 56,350.   [92] Section 953, Dodd–Frank Act.

[93] Section 952, Dodd–Frank Act. The SEC has implemented this requirement through Exchange Act Rule 10C-1.

[94] Exchange Act § 14A; Rule 14a-21(a).

[95] The initial results of the say on pay votes that occurred immediately after the enactment of the Dodd–Frank Act showed that shareholders were approving the compensation packages for 98.5% of the companies. Even though almost all say on pay votes to date have resulted in approval of executive compensation, the mere prospect of a say on pay vote may change the amount and form (e.g., base pay versus incentive pay) of pay presented to shareholders for a vote. A number of companies, moreover, were able to secure approval only after modifying their compensation packages. The relative lack of impact for this provision is consistent with experience in the UK, which provided the model for the provision. See Jeffrey N. Gordon, " 'Say on Pay': Cautionary Notes on the U.K. Experience and the Case for Shareholder Opt-in", 46 Harv. J. Legis. 323 (2009).

[96] Section 971, Dodd–Frank Act.

allowed shareholders (and shareholder groups) who have held at least 3% of the company's stock for three years the right to nominate directors and have those nominees included in the company's proxy statement and ballot. The rule did not provide an alternative to a full-fledged proxy contest, however, as shareholders were limited to nominating candidates for only 25% of the board. The SEC adopted Rule 14a-11 over the heated objections of corporate management. Groups representing management then challenged the rule in court, and in mid-2011, the D.C. Circuit vacated Rule 14a-11.[97] The SEC has not been stripped of its rulemaking authority, however, so it is a matter of time before it returns to the topic.

The net effect of the Sarbanes–Oxley and Dodd–Frank Acts has been to erode the traditional line between securities law and corporate governance in the US. The key word is "traditional"; there has not been any legal barrier to Congress taking over the governance of public corporations since the 1940s. Perhaps what is surprising is that the incursion took as long as it did. Perhaps less surprising is that Congress now appears completely indifferent to the status of the US as a listing destination. Competitiveness in financial services, once a hot topic, was swept aside as a concern in the rush to respond to accounting scandals and a financial crisis. Also swept aside has been the notion that there "should" be a dividing line between corporate governance and securities law.

4 CONCLUSION

The US maintained the dividing line between corporate law and securities law for nearly 70 years after the adoption of the federal securities law. Much of the work done protecting that line was done by the Supreme Court, which affirmed the role of the states in corporate law as a matter of tradition, rather than enforcing strict constitutional limits. The last 15 years, however, have seen that line beginning to erode as Congress has amended the federal securities laws to include corporate governance mandates with little or no connection to liquidity, the traditional focus of securities regulation. Those intrusions were responses to accounting scandals and financial crisis. Congress's interventions in corporate governance have coincided with a decline in the competitiveness of the US in the market for listings, but Congress has not responded to that decline, which is not salient enough to rise to "crisis" level.

To be sure, the US's decline as a listing destination cannot wholly be ascribed to Congress. Another factor fueling the trend has been the continuing development of trading technology and market liquidity that once promised to fuel the US's race to the top. The comparative advantage of US exchanges has now been substantially eroded. Stock exchanges around the world now offer similar speed in executing orders. Increasingly, securities trading has been reduced to the status of commodity. The best trading systems are no longer the monopoly of the exchanges, which are hemorrhaging market share to proprietary trading systems and dark pools.[98] Commodification of trading technology—along with greater access

---

[97] *Business Roundtable v. S.E.C.*, 647 F.3d 1144 (D.C. Cir. 2011).
[98] See generally Jerry W. Markham & Daniel J. Harty, "For Whom the Bell Tolls: The Demise of Exchange Trading Floors and the Growth of ECNs", 33 J. Corp. L. 865 (2008).

to information about companies in other jurisdictions—has greatly reduced the liquidity advantages historically enjoyed by the NYSE, which has cut fees in response.[99]

Of equal importance to the question of liquidity is the fact that companies no longer need to bring their shares in physical proximity to investors. Institutional investors can access virtually any market in the world.[100] As a result, ADRs have fallen out of favor, as investors invest directly abroad.[101] Moreover, Rule 144A allows issuers to access capital in the United States without a US listing.[102] Why should a company pay for an expensive listing in New York if a listing in their home country allows them easy access to capital from around the world? For regulators, this means that listing requirements are likely to offer little leverage as a regulatory tool. Draconian mandates, unrelated to liquidity, will be met by an exodus to jurisdictions with more lenient standards.

Another threat to the use of listing standards as a means of promoting corporate governance reform is private equity. The rise of private equity has demonstrated that firms in many industries with diverse business models can thrive without access to public capital markets. For these firms, corporate governance is purely a matter of contract. Firms that value liquidity are likely to tolerate disclosure mandates relating to liquidity, but if securities law and disclosure mandates drift toward corporate governance imperatives unrelated to liquidity, firms are likely to exit the public markets. If Congress continues to intervene in corporate governance, the number of US public companies could dwindle.

The US experience thus presents a cautionary tale for reformers contemplating the use of securities law to upgrade corporate governance standards. Countries may vary, however, in the relationship that corporate governance has to liquidity. Lessons from the US experience may have limited relevance for other parts of the world: US corporate governance is pretty good, so marginal improvements in any particular aspect may have limited real-world effects.[103]

The situation may be quite different in developing economies, where the baseline may not be as high. For example, there is evidence that degree of board independence and splitting the roles of Chair and CEO may correlate with greater liquidity post-IPO for Chinese firms.[104] These correlations may be explained by the prevalence of controlling shareholders in Chinese firms, and perhaps, relatively weak legal enforcement. The Chinese experience may be singular in another way—many governance reforms in that country are initiated by the country's securities regulator, which may be forced to act due to the absence of any

[99] Jacob Bunge, NYSE Adjusts Charges In Bid to Draw Traders, Wall St. J., Feb. 4, 2009, at C5 ("Incumbent stock exchanges are grappling with lower year-on-year trading volumes and tougher competition from newer entrants like BATS Exchange and Direct Edge in the U.S., and a host of trading platforms in Europe").

[100] Chris Brummer, "Stock Exchanges and the New Markets for Securities Laws", 75 U. Chi. L. Rev. 1435, 1459–66 (2008).

[101] See Eric J. Pan, "Why the World No Longer Puts Its Stock in Us" 8–11 (Benjamin N. Cardozo School of Law, Working Paper No. 176, 2006).

[102] 17 C.F.R. § 230.144A (2009). On the importance of Rule 144A in undermining the incentive of foreign issuers to list in the U.S., see Pan, *supra* note 101, at 7. See also William K. Sjostrom, Jr., "The Birth of Rule 144A Equity Offerings", 56 UCLA L. Rev. 409 (2008).

[103] Jeffrey N. Gordon, "The Rise of Independent Directors in the United States, 1950-2005: Of Shareholder Value and Stock Market Prices", 59 Stan. L. Rev. 1465, 1469 (2007).

[104] Junheng Zhu et al., "Ownership Structure, Corporate Governance and IPO Post-Listing Liquidity", Queensland University Working Paper, 2014.

alternative actor.[105] In countries such as China, where the rule of law is not as well established, the move toward mandating better corporate governance standards may substantially improve the operation of the capital markets, even absent an obvious connection between corporate governance and liquidity.

Another consideration for corporate governance reformers is that familiarity may breed liquidity. Standardization may be an important feature in corporate governance if information is incomplete and market participants are boundedly rational. If investors understand a common governance structure, making it mandatory may allow for easier comparability, which may be particularly important to firms seeking overseas investment. From the US perspective, the prevalence of Delaware as the choice of incorporation for most public companies in the US is sometimes attributed to investors' preference for Delaware incorporation—which may be based on Delaware's prevalence. Institutional investors are familiar with Delaware corporate law; they know what they are getting. Sometimes having a consistent standard is more important than having the best standard, or the standard best tailored for a particular firm.

On the other hand, a standardization strategy may have long-term consequences. Once standards become prevalent, if not universal, in the marketplace, politicians may be tempted to mandate the prevalent standard as "best practice." Once mandated, however, there may be costs imposed on firms that deviated from the norm for idiosyncratic, but perhaps legitimate reasons. In addition, the mandate may stifle experimentation and adaption to new conditions. Assessing the benefits and costs flowing from standardization is a daunting empirical task, particularly because the incidence of those benefits and costs is unlikely to be evenly distributed.

This chapter has focused on the connections between corporate governance, capital markets, and securities law. Looking at how the relation among these has developed over time in the US, it has identified liquidity as the key variable connecting the three. Corporate governance mandates with a clear connection to liquidity are more likely to be accepted and to last. When policy makers move beyond the promotion of liquidity, firms may choose to exit to avoid costly mandates.

---

[105] Nicholas Calcina Howson, " 'Quack Corporate Governance' as Traditional Chinese Medicine—the Securities Regulation Cannibalization of China's Corporate Law and a State Regulator's Battle Against Party State Political Economic Power", Working Paper, University of Michigan, 2014.

CHAPTER 41

VERTICAL AND HORIZONTAL PROBLEMS IN FINANCIAL REGULATION AND CORPORATE GOVERNANCE

JONATHAN R. MACEY AND MAUREEN O'HARA

1 INTRODUCTION

RECENT efforts to mitigate systemic risk and moral hazard in capital markets and financial institutions have run headlong into long-standing principles of corporate governance. This chapter discusses three contexts in which that is the case. The first issue relates to what we will describe as the "vertical" challenge between financial institutions and the separately incorporated holding companies that own and control them. The second issue relates to what we call the "horizontal" challenge, which concerns the regulatory arbitrage that occurs between the banking subsidiaries of complex holding companies and their less-regulated non-bank and shadow bank siblings. The final issue is the conflict between the conception of fiduciary duty in the federal law of insider trading and the different concept of fiduciary duty in state law.

2 FINANCIAL INSTITUTIONS AND THE COMPANIES THAT OWN THEM

That corporate governance problems are particularly acute in banks is well understood.[1] What may not be appreciated, however, is the degree to which certain unique features of

---

[1] See Ross Levine, "The Corporate Governance of Banks: A Concise Discussion of Concepts and Evidence", World Bank Policy Research Working Paper 3404 (2004); Lucian A. Bebchuk & Holger Spamann, "Regulating Bankers' Pay", 98 Geo. L. J. 247 (2010); Jakob de Haan & Razvan Vlahu, "Corporate

banking complicate both the role of financial institutions' boards of directors and the effectiveness of their governance.

In an earlier paper, we reviewed the different models of corporate governance, with a particular focus on the duties board members owe to different constituencies.[2] We argued that these unique features of banks dictated a heightened duty of care for bank directors. We discussed the various legal cases defining the duty of care for directors, and how the courts have vacillated in their application of these duties owed by directors. Since then a lot has changed with respect to banking structure and practice, but little has changed with respect to the duties and obligations of bank directors. This inertia with respect to bank directors is all the more puzzling given that the Dodd–Frank Wall Street Reform and Consumer Protection Act[3] (Dodd–Frank Act) explicitly addressed the externalities imposed by individual banks on the financial system—yet imposed no additional corporate governance requirements on bank directors to make them responsible for limiting such risks. Thus, while Dodd–Frank unleashed a plethora of changes for markets, with restrictions on what banks can do, who can regulate them, how they should be liquidated, mortgage and insurance reform, and consumer protection, the duties required of bank directors per se were not a focus of specific attention in the statute.

2.1 An Introduction to the Corporate Governance of Banks

Generally speaking, the problem of corporate governance stems from agency problems that emerge when the residual claims on a firm's income take the form of shares of stock that are mostly owned by people who are not involved in the management or operations of the company.[4] In order to ameliorate agency costs, over time corporate law has generated the general rule that fiduciary duties should be owed exclusively to shareholders.[5] The justifications for making shareholders the exclusive beneficiaries of the fiduciary duties owed by managers and directors are based on the fact that creditors, as fixed claimants, can safeguard their investments through a combination of pricing and the imposition of contractual protections such as conversion rights or put options.[6]

In our earlier paper on corporate governance problems in banks, we argued that banks are different from other firms and that the economic policies that justify making shareholders the

governance of banks: A survey", 30 J. Econ. Surveys 228 (2016); Renée B. Adams & Hamid Mehran, "Bank Board Structure and Performance: Evidence for Large Bank Holding Companies", 21 J. Fin. Intermediation 243 (2012); Charles W. Calomiris & Mark Carlson, "Corporate Governance and Risk Management at Unprotected Banks: National Banks in the 1890s", NBER Working Paper No. 19806 (2014).

  [2] See Jonathan R. Macey & Maureen O'Hara, "The Corporate Governance of Banks", 9 FRBNY Economic Policy Review 91 (2003).

  [3] Pub.L. 111–203, H.R. 4173.

  [4] See Adolf A. Berle & Gardiner Means, The Modern Corporation and Private Property (1932); Michael C. Jensen & William H. Meckling, "Theory of the Firm: Managerial Behavior, Agency Costs and Ownership Structure", 3 J. Fin. Econ. 305 (1976).

  [5] See Jonathan R. Macey, "Fiduciary Duties as Residual Claims: Obligations to Non-Shareholder Constituencies from a Theory of the Firm Perspective", 84 Cornell L. Rev. 1266 (1999).

  [6] See Jonathan R. Macey & Geoffrey P. Miller, "Corporate Stakeholders: A Contractual Perspective", 43 U. Toronto L. J. 401 (1993).

exclusive beneficiaries of fiduciary duties do not apply with the same force to banks as they do to other types of corporations, such as manufacturing companies or technology companies. We believe these difficulties have only increased in the past decade, with the result that banks in the post-crisis era face even greater corporate governance difficulties. Specifically, we believe there are a variety of unique features of banks relative to other firms that make them unusually risky, more fragile, and more difficult to monitor and control.[7]

First, banks' unusual capital structures give them a unique role in generating liquidity for the economy. It is well known that banks' balance sheets are highly leveraged,[8] with fixed-claim creditors supplying 90% or more of the funding banks require to operate. Moreover, these fixed-claim liabilities generally are available to creditors/depositors on demand, while on the asset side of the balance sheet, the bank's loans and other assets have longer maturities.

The development of increasingly robust secondary markets and banks' ability to securitize assets has enabled banks to move assets off their balance sheet, but this process has not led to a reduction in the size of banks' balance sheets: Banks tend to grow rather than shrink even as they securitize more of their assets. Because more transparent and liquid assets are the ones that tend to be sold either outright or as part of a pool of securitized financial assets, what is left on the bank's balance sheet tends to be the more opaque and idiosyncratic assets. Arguably, these evolutionary developments in capital markets have led to a secular deterioration, rather than to an improvement in the transparency and liquidity of bank assets.

The phenomenon of holding simultaneously transparent, liquid liabilities on the one hand, and illiquid, opaque assets on the other, enables banks to serve the vital economic role of creating liquidity.[9] However, to create liquidity, banks must lend the funds that they receive from deposits and other short-term liabilities, and consequently banks keep only a small fraction of funds as reserves to satisfy depositors' demands for liquidity. This asset transformation process results in a situation in which no bank has sufficient funds on hand to satisfy the demands of depositors if a significant number demand payment simultaneously.

The mismatch in the liquidity characteristics and term-structure of banks' assets leads to bank runs and other systemic problems in the financial system. With greater than a third of US bank liabilities uninsured, rational uninsured depositors (and claimants) will try to be among the first to withdraw before other, more nimble creditors deplete the banks' assets. Thus, bank depositors, unlike creditors in other companies, are in a situation closely akin to the classic prisoner's dilemma. This prisoner's dilemma can lead to failures in solvent banks because the need for liquidity in the event of a run or panic can lead to fire-sale liquidations of assets, thereby spreading problems to heretofore solvent banks. For bank directors, the need to manage such liquidity risks is fundamental to a bank's survival.

Second, the existence of federally sponsored deposit insurance means that banks can continue to attract liquidity to fund their operations even after they are insolvent. Thus, unlike other sorts of companies, it is virtually impossible for federally insured banks to

---

[7] Macey & O'Hara, *supra* note 2, at 97.

[8] See Bebchuk & Spamann, *supra* note 1; Mark J. Flannery, "Debt Maturity Structure and the Deadweight Cost of Leverage: Optimally Financing Banking Firms", 84 Am. Econ. Rev. 320 (1994).

[9] See Douglas W. Diamond & Philip H. Dybvig, "Banking Theory, Deposit Insurance, and Bank Regulation", 59 Journal of Business 55 (1986).

become insolvent in the "equitable" sense of being unable to pay their debts as they come due in the ordinary course of business.[10] Federal insurance eliminates the market forces that starve nonfinancial firms with poor prospects of cash. The federal government has attempted to replace these market forces with regulatory requirements such as capital requirements and requirements for the "prompt resolution" of financially distressed banks. Nevertheless, it seems clear that the well-established tenet of corporate finance that there is a conflict between fixed claimants and shareholders is, as we previously observed "raised to a new dimension in the banking context."[11] In banking, neither creditors nor capital markets have incentives either to negotiate for protections against risky, "bet-the-bank" investment strategies, or to demand compensation for such risk in the form of higher interest payments.

Bebchuk and Spamann argue that these agency conflicts manifest particularly in problems with bank executive compensation.[12] They make the intriguing point that governance reforms aimed at aligning compensation with shareholder interests—such as say-on-pay votes, use of restricted stock, and increased director independence—fail in banks because shareholders also benefit from bank management taking on excessive risk. This raises the disturbing specter that bank directors are in fact doing their job—but that their job does not include adequately recognizing the systemic risks that banks pose for the financial system.

Third, moral hazard caused by deposit insurance coupled with imperfections in the regulatory system also leads not only to suboptimally easy access to liquidity, but also to an industry-wide reduction in levels of monitoring within the firm, resulting in a higher incidence of large losses and bank failures due to fraud.[13] The high incidence of fraud is attributable both to the lack of monitoring by creditors and to the highly liquid form of banks' assets, which makes it easy to divert bank assets to private use relative to less liquid assets such as factories and equipment.

Shareholders' incentives to monitor to prevent fraud and self-dealing exist in banks as they do in other sorts of companies. As in these other sorts of companies, however, "such monitoring is notoriously ineffective in many cases because individual shareholders rarely have sufficient incentives to engage in monitoring because of collective-action problems."[14]

Perhaps no event illustrates the endemic monitoring and other corporate governance problems in the context of the banking industry more clearly than the London whale trading loss debacle, in which Mary Jo White, the new chair of the US Securities and Exchange Commission (SEC) deployed her marquee policy to require admissions

---

[10] In bankruptcy law and practice, there are two types of insolvency. Insolvency in the balance sheet sense means that the value of a company's liabilities is greater than the value of its assets. Insolvency in the equity sense means that the firm is unable to pay its debts as they come due in the ordinary course of business. J. Jurinsk, "Bankruptcy Step by Step", Barron's Educational Series, 2003.

[11] Macey & O'Hara, *supra* note 2, at 98.   [12] Bebchuk & Spamann, *supra* note 1.

[13] See Remarks of R. L. Clarke, Comptroller of the Currency News Release NR 88-5, The Exchequer Club, Washington, D.C., January 10, 1988, p. 6, noting that fraud and self-dealing were "apparent" in as many as one-third of the bank failures that occurred during the 1980s. See also Howell E. Jackson & Edward Symons, The Regulation of Financial Institutions 152 (1999), citing a study by the U.S. General Accounting Office of banks failures in 1990 and 1991 that reported that in slightly more than 60% of these failures (175 out of 286), insider lending was a "contributing factor."

[14] Macey & O'Hara, *supra* note 2, at 98.

of wrongdoing in certain "egregious" cases.[15] The SEC charged JPMorgan Chase with misstating financial results and lacking effective internal controls to detect and prevent its traders from fraudulently overvaluing investments to conceal hundreds of millions of dollars in trading losses.[16]

The SEC's lawsuit against JPMorgan charged the company with violating provisions of the Sarbanes–Oxley Act of 2002 (SOX) relating to corporate governance and disclosure. In particular, SOX requires public companies to maintain disclosure controls and procedures that ensure that important information flows to the appropriate persons so that timely decisions can be made regarding disclosure in public filings.[17] Also at issue were JPMorgan's alleged violations of SEC regulations requiring corporate managers to evaluate on a quarterly basis the effectiveness of the company's disclosure controls and procedures and to disclose management's conclusion regarding their effectiveness in its quarterly filings.[18] The SEC also alleged that even after having announced a trading loss of approximately $2 billion on May 10, 2012, the full extent of the trading losses that occurred during the first quarter of 2012 was not detected and reported. This failure was due, in part, to ineffectiveness of internal control functions within the bank's Chief Investment Office, which was known as the Valuation Control Group ("CIO-VCG").[19]

Within banks, valuation control units are a critical part of a company's internal controls because they monitor and control for accuracy of the valuations of the financial assets acquired and held by traders and other market professionals within the firm. From a corporate governance perspective it is obvious that a valuation control group must be independent of the trading desks it monitors in order to be effective. The consequences of a corporate governance failure in this respect are severe because such failures risk both the inaccurate valuation of the bank's assets as well as the material misstatement of the bank's financial condition in its public filings. In the case of JPMorgan, the SEC found that JPMorgan's CIO-VCG was "unequipped to cope with the size and complexity of the credit derivatives" that were the principal assets in the bank's Synthetic Credit Portfolio ("SCP").[20] As of March 31,

---

[15] Kevin LaCroix, "A Closer Look at JP Morgan's $920 Million "London Whale" Regulatory Settlements, The D&O Diary", September 20, 1013, available at http://www.dandodiary.com/2013/09/articles/securities-litigation/a-closer-look-at-jp-morgans-920-million-london-whale-regulatory-settlements/. The SEC's new policy was announced internally in an email sent to SEC staff this week. Co-Enforcement directors Andrew Ceresney and George Canellos announced that "cases in which the defendant engaged in 'egregious intentional misconduct' may justify requiring an admission, as would the obstruction of an SEC investigation or 'misconduct that harmed large numbers of investors.'" The traditional "neither-admit-nor-deny" settlements remain a "major, major tool" used by the SEC in the majority of cases, according to the SEC. Bruce Carton, "SEC to Require Admissions of Wrongdoing in Settlements of Most Egregious Cases, Compliance Week", June 19, 2013, available at https://www.complianceweek.com/blogs/enforcement-action/sec-to-require-admissions-of-wrongdoing-in-settlements-of-most-egregious.

[16] SEC, Order Instituting Cease-and-Desist Proceedings Pursuant to Section 21C of the Securities Exchange Act of 1934, "Making Findings, and Imposing a Cease-and-Desist Order", September 19, 2013, available at http://www.sec.gov/litigation/admin/2013/34-70458.pdf.

[17] Id. Such requirements on internal accounting controls are intended to "provide reasonable assurances that transactions are recorded as necessary to permit preparation of reliable financial statements."

[18] Id.   [19] Id.

[20] The SCP was invested in two primary index groups: CDX, a group of North American and Emerging Markets indices, and iTraxx, a group of European and Asian indices. Some indices referenced

2012, the SCP contained 132 trading positions with a net notional amount of approximately $157 billion.[21]

The SEC also found that the CIO-VCG "did not function as an effective internal control" during the relevant time period because the CIO-VCG was "understaffed, insufficiently supervised, and did not adequately document its actual price-testing policies."[22] Perhaps more disturbingly, it appeared to the SEC that the price-testing methodology used by CIO-VCG "was subjective and insufficiently independent from the SCP traders, which enabled the traders to improperly influence the VCG process."[23] In addition, during the first quarter of 2012, CIO-VCG failed to escalate to CIO and JPMorgan management significant information that management required in order to make informed decisions about disclosure of the firm's financial results for the first quarter of 2012. As a result, JPMorgan did not timely detect or effectively challenge questionable valuations by the SCP traders as the portfolio's losses accumulated in the first quarter of 2012, leading the bank to publicly misstate its financial results for that period.[24]

The internal problems were egregious. For example, when losses were incurred on the traditionally profitable SCP portfolio in the first quarter of 2012, the senior SCP trader instructed SCP traders to stop reporting losses to CIO management unless there was a market-moving event that could easily explain the losses. At least one SCP trader changed his daily marking methodology for the SCP and began assigning values at the point in the bid-offer spread that resulted in highest valuations of the SCP positions, a valuation technique inconsistent with Generally Accepted Accounted Principles (GAAP).[25] Things got much worse when this trader even began valuing assets at prices that were completely "outside every dealer's bid and offer received that day" and thereby "intentionally understated mark-to-market losses in the SCP."[26]

In JPMorgan's $200 million settlement of the SEC's enforcement action against it, the bank acknowledged significant corporate governance failures. For example, the bank admitted

---

companies considered to be investment grade and others referenced companies considered to be high-yield (which generally means that their credit risk is viewed as higher). Investors in CDX and iTraxx indices, including CIO, can be "long" risk, which is equivalent to being a seller of CDS protection, or "short" risk, which is equivalent to being a buyer of CDS protection. See SEC, *supra* note 16, Annex A.

[21] Id.   [22] SEC, *supra* note 16, at 2.

[23] Id.

[24] Another significant corporate governance failure was inadequate communication between JPMorgan's Senior Management and the Audit Committee of JPMorgan's Board of Directors (the "Audit Committee"). JPMorgan senior management initiated reviews of the CIO-VCG's work after learning of significant disputes between the bank and its counterparties about the value of the assets held in the SCP. From these reviews, the bank's management learned that there were problems with the CIO-VCG's price testing and "an undue amount of subjectivity" in its control function. Contrary to the requirements of SOX, however, JPMorgan's management did not inform the Audit Committee of the bank's board of directors that it was aware of significant deficiencies or material weaknesses in the firm's internal control over financial reporting. As the SEC observed in its Order, this information must be passed along to the board by management so that the Audit Committee can fulfill its oversight role and help to assure the integrity and accuracy of information.

[25] Under applicable accounting rules, the positions in the SCP had to be marked "within the bid-ask spread" at the point that is "most representative of fair value in the circumstances," with a particular emphasis on the price where the traders could reasonably expect to transact. GAAP also allows for the use of mid-market pricing "as a practical expedient for fair value measurements within a bid-ask spread."

[26] Id.

that significant facts learned in the course of the various internal reviews were not shared in meetings and calls among the participants in such reviews. As a result, these facts were not escalated to JPMorgan senior management or communicated to the Audit Committee of the board in a timely fashion.[27] However, it is not clear that the Bank's Audit Committee would have been able to handle the monitoring and internal control problems in the bank even if they had been better informed. Also apparently missing in action was the bank's risk committee which also was not kept informed of what was clearly a gaping hole in the bank's risk management process.

The Board of Governors of the Federal Reserve (Fed) joined the SEC in suing and settling with JPMorgan Chase & Co. (JPMC), the registered bank holding company that owns and controls the bank.[28] The Fed's Order did raise these deficiencies in risk management and oversight, as well as raising concerns with the governance, finance, and internal audit functions of the company.[29]

In earlier decades, the mismatch between the maturity and liquidity characteristics of banks' assets and liabilities, their unusually high leverage, and the moral hazard caused by such institutional features as the Fed discount window, deposit insurance, and the expectation of bailouts, largely defined the unique corporate governance problems experienced by banks.[30] These characteristics remain, but the JPMorgan whale debacle underscores some important new dimensions of bank corporate governance problems: the opacity of bank activities, combined with the complexity of risk-management activities involving the valuation and control of complex asset positions, create significant monitoring difficulties for directors.[31]

Thus, a large part of the problem with JPMorgan Chase appears to be that the firm's directors lacked the special expertise necessary to evaluate the nature and the quality of the information they were getting (or not getting) from managers.[32] JPMorgan Chase was not by any means the only financial institution whose board lacked sufficient industry and financial markets expertise. When Citibank teetered on the brink of insolvency, requiring a massive federal bailout, its board was:

> filled with luminaries from all walks of life.—It boasted directors from a chemical company, a telecom giant, and a liberal arts university, for example. Yet in early 2008 only one of the

---

[27] Id. Annex A at 31.

[28] In addition to the SEC's enforcement action, the Office of the Comptroller of the Currency, which regulates the national bank subsidiaries of the holding company, and the UK Financial Conduct Authority filed lawsuits against JPMorgan Chase, N.A., the bank subsidiary JPMorgan.

[29] Board of Governors of the Federal Reserve System, "Order of Assessment of a Civil Money Penalty Issued Upon Consent Pursuant to the Federal Deposit Insurance Act, as Amended", September 19, 2013, http://www.federalreserve.gov/newsevents/press/enforcement/enf20130919a.pdf.

[30] See Calomiris & Carlson, *supra* note 1, for a discussion of the factors leading to bank corporate governance issues in the era predating deposit insurance.

[31] See also Hamid Mehran, Alan Morrison, & Joel Shapiro, Corporate Governance and Banks: What Have We Learned from the Financial Crisis?, Federal Reserve Bank of New York Staff Reports, no. 502 (2011), who make similar complexity and opacity arguments in their analysis of governance problems in the financial crisis.

[32] Robert Pozen, "The Big Idea: The Case for Professional Boards", 88(12) Harv. Bus. Rev. 50 (2010).

independent directors had ever worked at a financial services firm—and that person was concurrently the CEO of a large entertainment firm.[33]

2.2 Vertical Corporate Governance: The Problem of Dual Boards

A significant corporate governance challenge for banks arises from their unique organizational structure in which banks, which are corporations with their own boards of directors,
tend to be entirely owned and controlled by holding companies, which are also corporations
but are generally publicly held. In the case of major commercial banks such as JPMorgan
Chase and Citibank, the holding companies are incorporated in Delaware, while the banks
are federally chartered and under the jurisdiction of the Comptroller of the Currency.
Delaware has strong, shareholder-centric corporate governance norms and rules oriented
toward profit maximization. In stark contrast, the Comptroller of the Currency has only a
remote interest in profit maximization. Its concern is on the safety and soundness of banks
and the financial system.

> Since Goldman Sachs[34] and Morgan Stanley[35] became bank holding companies and financial
> holding companies during the financial crisis, every major bank in the US is now organized as
> some form of bank holding company ("BHC"). A BHC is defined as
> > [a] company that owns and/or controls one or more U.S. banks or one that owns, or has con-
> > trolling interest in, one or more banks. A bank holding company may also own another bank
> > holding company, which in turn owns or controls a bank; the company at the top of the owner-
> > ship chain is called the top holder.[36]

Bank holding companies are, by definition, involved in the business of banking. In fact,
bank holding companies are limited by law to activities that are "so closely related to banking

---

[33] Id. at 53.

[34] Goldman Sachs Group, Inc., a Delaware corporation, is a bank holding company and a financial
holding company regulated by the Board of Governors of the Federal Reserve System (Federal Reserve
Board). Its US depository institution subsidiary, Goldman Sachs Bank USA (GS Bank USA), is a
New York State-chartered bank.

[35] Morgan Stanley has operated as a bank holding company and financial holding company under the
BHC Act since September 2008. Morgan Stanley is a financial holding company regulated by the Board
of Governors of the Federal Reserve System (the "Federal Reserve") under the Bank Holding Company
Act of 1956, as amended (the "BHC Act"), see http://www.morganstanley.com/about/press/articles/6933.
html.

[36] Under § 2020.1.3.1 of the Bank Holding Company Act of 1956, administered by the Federal Deposit
Insurance Corporation (FDIC), a bank holding company is defined as "any company which has control
over any bank or over any company that is or becomes a bank holding company by virtue of this Act.
  (2) Any company has control over a bank or over any company if—

a. the company directly or indirectly or acting through one or more other persons owns, controls, or
   has power to vote 25 per centum or more of any class of voting securities of the bank or company;

b. the company controls in any manner the election of a majority of the directors or trustees of the bank
   or company; or

c. the Board determines, after notice and opportunity for hearing, that the company directly or indirectly exercises a controlling influence over the management or policies of the bank or company."

as to be a proper incident thereto."[37] Because the BHC controls the bank, the monitoring and control of risk must take place at multiple levels. From a regulatory perspective, the Federal Reserve "is responsible for regulating and supervising bank holding companies, even if the bank owned by the holding company is under the primary supervision of a different federal agency (OCC or FDIC)."[38] When assessing a BHC, however, the Fed will "work cooperatively" with the functional regulator of the subsidiary bank "to address information gaps or indications of weakness or risk identified in a supervised BHC subsidiary that are material to the Federal Reserve's understanding or assessment" of the BHC.[39] This structure of supervision acknowledges that bank holding companies wield control over the banks they hold.

From a governance perspective, the holding company's board inevitably exerts control over the banks within the holding company structure, particularly where, as is often the case, the directors of the bank holding company also sit as officers and directors of the bank. As such, it is each holding company director's duty to control risk down to the level of the banks the BHC holds.[40] This means the directors of holding companies, like the directors of the banks themselves, must be involved in the governance, risk-management, and monitoring and oversight of the banks and bank affiliates within the holding company structure. The formal corporate separateness of BHCs and the banks they control does not absolve holding company directors from involvement with the activities of their subsidiary banks even if there are directors who are on the board of a BHC but not on the board of the bank.[41]

Howell Jackson has observed that holding companies and the banks they own and control are not truly separate as a practical matter:

> Within bank holding companies, there is a natural tendency of management to centralize decision making power and resources in the parent bank or BHC. It is doubtful that management would leave the bank and nonbank subsidiaries free to make the important business decisions as to activities, reinvestment of profits and new markets. It is more likely that there would be significant centralization of decision making at the parent company level, with management deciding what products and markets will be focused upon and how profits will be reallocated.[42]

Jackson also argues that this interrelatedness of banks and BHCs has increased over time:

> Until twenty years ago [i.e. until 20 years prior to the publication of this article by Professor Jackson in 1994], financial holding companies [. . .] had relatively few affirmative obligations with respect to their regulated subsidiaries [. . .]. Over the past two decades however, financial

---

[37] BHC Act, passim.

[38] National Information Center, All Institution Types Defined, http://www.ffiec.gov/nicpubweb/Content/HELP/Institution%20Type%20Description.htm.

[39] The Board of Governor's Division of Banking Supervision and Regulation, Bank Holding Company Supervision Manual, § 1050.1.4.1.1 (2011).

[40] For further discussion, see Gang Bai, Asset Opacity and CEO Compensation of Bank Holding Companies, 2011 Financial Management Association Annual Meeting, Session 099: Managerial Compensation and Financial Institutions (Jan. 12, 2011).

[41] See, e.g., Andrew Ellul & Vijay Yerramilli, "Stronger Risk Controls, Lower Risk: Evidence from U.S. Bank Holding Companies", 68 J. Fin. 1757 (2013) (for a discussion of bank holding companies' directors crucial role in risk management of the entire organization).

[42] Howell E. Jackson, "The Expanding Obligations of Financial Holding Companies", 107 Harv. L. Rev. 509, 510 (1994); see also Jackson & Symons, *supra* note 13, at 304.

holding companies have become increasingly embroiled in the regulatory supervision of subsidiary financial institutions.[43]

Jackson posits that this increased interrelatedness reflects a regulatory push to "transfer front-line supervisory responsibility from governmental agencies to financial holding companies." This is because:

> [n]ot only are financial holding companies apt to be more proficient than government officials in evaluating institutional behavior, but holding companies also can monitor risks at a lower cost than government agencies, because holding companies already have substantial information about their regulated subsidiaries as a result of ordinary managerial activities.[44]

The Fed evaluates bank holding companies' directors and senior executives based upon their ability to identify, measure, and control risk, which includes those posed by the underlying banks. Thus, the Fed essentially treats BHCs and their bank affiliates as so inextricably linked that, when evaluating BHCs, it analyzes the *consolidated* organization's financial strength and risks. Additionally, the Fed can examine a BHC's subsidiaries directly to "inform itself of the systems for monitoring and controlling risks to such depository institutions."[45]

Since both the holding company and the bank have boards of directors, a natural question is what role should each board play? Thomas C. Baxter, Jr., General Counsel and Executive Vice-President of the Federal Reserve Bank of New York addresses this point:

> We want the governing body of the holding company to perform two critical functions. First, we want it to understand the risks to the "enterprise," meaning the risks in all of the company's constituent parts. Second, we want the holding company to *take reasonable steps to manage* those risks and keep them within acceptable limits.[46]
>
> ...
>
> As I see it, the public interest in the bank subsidiary is protected by a panoply of prudential laws and regulations. The ownership interest of the holding company in the bank is protected by the holding company's ability to control the bank's board of directors.[47]

From both a regulatory perspective and a corporate governance perspective, bank safety and soundness is paramount. The well-known "source of strength" doctrine requires that bank holding companies provide financial assistance to support its banking subsidiaries. In particular, § 225.142 of the Bank Holding Company Act provides that "[i]n supervising the activities of bank holding companies, the Board has adopted and continues to follow the principle that bank holding companies should serve as a source of strength for their subsidiary banks." This notion pervades the BHC's corporate governance and directly impacts the relationship between the BHC and its subsidiaries.

[43] Id.   [44] Id. at 513.

[45] Richard Scott Carnell, Jonathan R. Macey, & Geoffrey P. Miller, The Law of Financial Institutions 458 (5th ed. 2011).

[46] Thomas C. Baxter, Jr., Governing the Financial or Bank Holding Company: How Legal Infrastructure Can Facilitate Consolidated Risk Management, presented at the Puerto Rico Bankers Association conference "Financial Transparency and Corporate Governance of Financial Institutions after the Sarbanes–Oxley Act of 2002" in San Juan, Puerto Rico, 9(3) Current Issues in Economics and Finance 1 (2003).

[47] Id.

It is our contention that the Fed's BHC regulations, the principles of corporate governance developed here, as well as basic concerns about systemic risk and bank safety all indicate that BHC officers and directors have fiduciary obligations that guide—and when necessary, trump—corporate form. Fiduciary duties flow not only to shareholders of the holding company but also to the corporate organization itself. Thus the responsibility for bank safety and soundness must be shouldered by both holding company directors and officers and the directors and officers of their subsidiaries, particularly their bank subsidiaries.

Less clear, however, is how the shared responsibility between the holding company board and the bank board should work in practice in the post-crisis environment. On the one hand, it clearly makes no sense to say that BHC officers and directors can ignore issues of safety and soundness that affect their subsidiary banks on the grounds that they are fiduciaries of a different corporate entity, namely the holding company. On the other hand, the notion that the duties and obligations of holding company officers and directors and bank officers and directors are identical and wholly duplicative also appears problematic. To see why, consider the perspective of the OCC (the Office of the Comptroller of the Currency), the main regulator of nationally chartered banks, on its expectation for the subsidiary bank's directors. The OCC argues "For its part, the primary duty of the subsidiary bank's directors is to protect the bank."[48] This may be the view of the OCC, but it is inconsistent with the duties of the directors of BHCs, which require that directors of holding companies—like directors of other firms—maximize value for shareholders.

Thus, there is a significant obstacle to making safety and soundness the primary duty of BHCs or BHC directors. And these holding companies determine who sits on the board of directors of the banks they own or control. BHCs are, from a state-law point of view, garden-variety corporations, with garden-variety fiduciary duties that are owed exclusively to shareholders. Unlike banks themselves, holding companies are not only subject to the same corporate governance rules as other companies, but, also unlike banks, which receive charters either from the Comptroller of the Currency (national banks) or state bank regulators (state banks), holding companies are chartered by the same state chartering authorities as any other nonbanks. For example, Citigroup, which owns a national bank, is charged in the state of Delaware,[49] as are Morgan Stanley[50] and Goldman Sachs.[51]

The problem is simple to describe. Because they are considered simply to be directors of garden-variety corporations, holding company directors (and bank directors too, for that matter), ostensibly have no obligation to mitigate risk, but rather are tasked with *maximizing* the value of the company on whose board they sit. This rule makes perfect sense in the context of non-financial corporations, whose failure poses no systemic risk and whose shareholders can eliminate the firm-specific risk of the company's business antics easily and cheaply through diversification.

---

[48] See Office of the Comptroller of the Currency, The Directors Book, October 2010 (reprinted October 2013), p. 26.

[49] See Certificate of Incorporation of Citigroup, available at http://www.citigroup.com/citi/investor/data/citigroup_rci.pdf.

[50] See Certificate of Incorporation of Morgan Stanley, available at http://www.morganstanley.com/about-us-governance/certcomp.

[51] See Certificate of Incorporation of Goldman Sachs, available at http://www.goldmansachs.com/investor-relations/corporate-governance/corporate-governance-documents/re-stated-certificate.pdf.

On the other hand, of course, the federal government, if not the state governments, wants banks and BHCs to refrain from engaging in excessive risk taking. Thus, BHC directors are pulled in two opposite directions by the legal rules that govern their behavior. On the one hand, as established in this section, it is the clear policy of federal banking regulators, particularly the Fed, that holding companies—and particularly large holding companies whose operations pose systemic risks—should focus primarily on issues of safety and soundness. On the other hand, the state laws that impose fiduciary duties on the directors of all corporations, both banks and nonbanks, require all such directors to maximize the value of the firm, even if doing so causes the company to assume considerable risk. And because of the low cost of leverage for federally insured banks and for companies designated as "systemically important financial institutions" (SIFIs),[52] these fiduciary duties will channel directors towards tolerating, if not actively encouraging, risky capital structures and risky investment practices. One way to reconcile the apparent deep inconsistency between bank and BHC directors' fiduciary obligation to maximize returns and their statutory and regulatory obligations to promote safety is to prioritize these conflicting dictates. The regulatory and

[52] SIFIs are firms whose failure the Board of Governors of the U.S. Federal Reserve System has determined would pose a serious risk to the economy. In theory (though not in practice) supervision and regulation by the Fed. and other regulators will prevent a financial company designated as a SIFI from becoming "too big to fail." In fact, designating a financial institution as a SIFI means that it is too big to fail, and SIFIs commonly are referred to as "too big to fail." See, e.g. Mary Williams Walsh, MetLife Sues Over Being Named Too Big To Fail, N.Y. Times, January 13, 2015, http://dealbook.nytimes.com/2015/01/13/metlife-to-fight-too-big-to-fail-status-in-court/?_r=0. Somewhat more rigorously, the credit rating agencies rate SIFIs more highly because they assume that they will receive government support. See Mark Labonte, Systemically Important or 'Too Big to Fail' Financial Institutions, Congressional Research Service, September 19, 2014.

The most reliable evidence of whether SIFIs are or are not too big to fail is funding (capital) costs. Firms that are too big to fail should have lower capital costs. A study for Bloomberg by Robert Litan and Christopher Payne found that "the funding advantage received by the eight designated U.S. global systemically important financial institutions (G-SIFIs) by virtue of being perceived as 'too-big-to-fail' may be as large as $34.4 billion in 2012." At least eight separate studies support this view. They are: Priyank Gandhi & Hanno Lustig, "Size Anomalies in U.S. Bank Stock Returns", 70 J. Fin. 733 (2015); Kenichi Ueda & Beatrice Weder di Mauro, "Quantifying Structural Subsidy Values for Systemically Important Financial Institutions", 37 J. Banking & Fin. 3830 (2013); Frederic Schweikhard & Zoe Tsesmelidakis, "The Impact of Government Interventions on CDS and Equity Markets", Nov. 2012, http://papers.ssrn.com/sol3/papers.cfm?abstract_id=1573377; Stefan Jacewitz & Jonathan Pogach, "Deposit Rate Advantages at the Largest Banks", FDIC CFR Working Paper 2014-02 (Feb. 2014), available at https://www.fdic.gov/bank/analytical/cfr/2014/wp2014/2014-02.pdf; María Fabiana Penas & Haluk Unal, "Gains in Bank Mergers: Evidence from the Bond Markets", 74 J. Fin. Econ. 149 (2004); Richard Davies & Belinda Tracey, "Too Big to Be Efficient? The Impact of Implicit Subsidies on Estimates of Scale Economies for Banks", 46 J. Money, Credit & Banking 219 (2014); Michel Araten & Christopher Turner, "Understanding the Funding Cost Differences Between Global Systemically Important Banks (GSIBs) and non-G-SIBs in the USA", 6 J. Risk Management in Fin. Institutions 387 (2013); Zan Li, Shisheng Qu, & Jing Zhang, Quantifying the Value of Implicit Government Guarantees for Large Financial Institutions, Moody's Analytics Quantitative Research Group, January 2011, available at https://www.moodysanalytics.com/-/media/whitepaper/2011/2011-14-01-quantifying-the-value-of-implicit-government-guarantees-for-large-financial-institutions-20110114.pdf. See also Marc Labonte, Systemically Important or "Too Big to Fail" Financial Institutions, Congressional Research Service Report, June 30, 2015, available at http://fas.org/sgp/crs/misc/R42150.pdf; Government Accountability Office, Large Bank Holding Companies—Expectations of Government Support, GAO-14-621, July 2014, p. 24 and Financial Stability Oversight Council, Annual Report, 2014, p. 117.

statutory obligations come first. Managers and directors can only maximize profits to the extent that doing so does not conflict with relevant legal rules and regulations. As the influential American Law Institute Principles of Corporate Governance make clear, a corporation "[i]s obliged, to the same extent as a natural person, to act within the boundaries set by law."[53] Or as Milton Friedman admonished, corporations are obligated "to make as much money as possible while conforming to the basic rules of the society, both those embodied in law and those embodied in ethical custom."[54]

In our view, the fact that banks and, their officers and directors, can only maximize profit within the limits of applicable law and regulations is an extremely important feature of the corporate governance landscape. Establishing and maintaining this hierarchy, however, does not resolve entirely the tension between profit maximization and the regulatory and social goals of achieving safer and sounder financial institutions. This is because, as we have seen over the past several decades, there is plenty of room for financial institutions to engage in excessive risk taking even after they have complied with the law.

For example, banks must, of course, comply with the relevant rules regarding the maintenance of certain capital levels. But even after complying with such rules, there is ample room to maneuver. Banks, for example, can, and do invest in the riskiest assets within a particular risk-weighting class. They also look for loopholes in regulations such as the Volcker rule in order to squeeze the highest returns they can for their shareholders: and, of course, this quest for the highest returns involves risk, which, in turn, is not something that regulators are interested in maximizing.

But the fiduciary duty to maximize profits is not the only obstacle to reaching the goal of incentivizing managers and directors of financial institutions to focus on keeping banks safe with the same intensity as directors of other companies focus on maximizing share prices. In addition to fiduciary duties, it also is the case that holding company directors, like the directors of all other corporations, are elected by the shareholders. Fixed and contingent claimants, such as depositors, non-depositor-creditors, and the US government lack voting power. In an election between a risk taker and a non-risk taker, the shareholders will vote for the risk taker. Thus, to the extent that directors survive in their jobs in the Darwinian environment that characterizes the democratic process, among the strongest characteristics for survival in the job of bank or BHC directors is a strong proclivity for risk taking.[55]

Outside of the US, bank directors have faced strictly higher burdens, with some jurisdictions viewing bank failures as a criminal offense on the part of directors. Brazil, for example, holds banks' executives and directors personally liable for the debts of failed institutions even when no fault is proven.[56] The UK government, following on the recommendation of the Parliamentary Commission on Banking Standards, has recently introduced a new criminal offense for reckless misconduct in the management of a bank. This criminal liability would apply to both executive and non-executive directors of a bank.[57] The maximum sentence for the offense is seven years in prison and/or an unlimited fine.

[53] A.L.I. Principles of Corporation Governance, Section 2.01(b).

[54] Milton Friedman, The Social Responsibility of Business is to Increase its Profits, N.Y. Times Magazine, September 13, 1970.

[55] This argument may explain Laeven and Levine's (2009) empirical finding that ownership by more institutional investors increases the riskiness of the bank. L. Laeven & Rose Levine, "Bank Governance, Regulation and Risk Taking", 93 J. Fin. Econ. 259 (August 2, 2009).

[56] See Prosecuting bankers: Blind Justice, Economist, May 4, 2013.

[57] See Financial Services (Banking Reform) Act 2013. HM Treasury, Financial Services (Banking Reform) Bill—Government Amendments: Criminal Sanctions (October 2013), available at https://

The notion that "reckless management" is a crime is rather alien to the US perspective that business failure is not a criminal offense, but rather a natural, albeit unfortunate, outcome of business judgment in an uncertain world. In our view, criminalizing bank failure is not a viable approach to resolving the difficulties of bank corporate governance. It does, however, change the calculus for bank directors with respect to the acceptable level of risk for a financial institution.

A similar change in calculus can arise from the concept found in Germany, Switzerland, and Austria called *Untreue*. This "breach of trust" is defined as "a derogation of duty that causes real harm to the institution,"[58] and it has been the basis for charges against bankers at West LB, Bayern LB, HSH Nordbank, and Sal. Oppenheim.[59] Indeed, the CEO of West LB paid a fine of EUR 150,000 to settle charges relating to breach of trust, and the former CEO of Bayern LB was convicted to a suspended prison sentence of 18 months in 2014 for bribery, although the court dismissed separate allegations of breach of trust against him.[60] More intriguing are the cases involving board members of these failed financial institutions. The entire management board of the German bank HSH Nordbank stood on trial for breach of trust due to risk management failures relating to a CDO and other off-balance-sheet activities that resulted in the bank having to be bailed out to the tune of EUR 30 billion, although the board was eventually acquitted.[61] Similarly, seven former directors of LBBW, Germany's largest public sector lender, were charged with breach of trust (and eventually settled) in connection with moving risky assets to special-purpose vehicles allegedly to hide the riskiness of the bank.[62]

In the US, bank directors and managers can be criminally prosecuted for fraud and for violating the federal securities laws or provisions of the securities laws, and this was the fate that befell more than 800 bankers jailed in the aftermath of the S&L crisis. But pursuing such cases, particularly against bank directors, is notoriously difficult due to the challenge of linking wrongdoing to those actually running the bank.[63] The rarity of this outcome means that bank director behavior is unlikely to be affected.

What is clear from this review is that corporate governance problems are remarkably resilient. While some approaches have been more successful than others, in general even the most extreme outside constraints have failed to resolve bank governance problems. In our view, this suggests using a new approach, one that explicitly recognizes the inherent difficulty of managing and controlling risk in the post-crisis era.

---

www.gov.uk/government/uploads/system/uploads/attachment_data/file/245758/HoL_Policy_Brief_-_Criminal_Sanctions.pdf.

[58] This duty of trust does not just attach to financial firms. Board members of the German firm Mannesmann were also charged with *Untreue* in connection with that firm's takeover by Vodafone. See Breach of Trust? German corporate governance is literally on trial, Economist, Feb. 20, 2013.

[59] Op. cit.

[60] Reuters, Former BayernLB CEO gets suspended sentence for bribery, Oct. 27, 2014, available at http://www.reuters.com/article/bayernlb-hldg-trial-idUSL5N0SM2CV20141027.

[61] HSH Nordbank executives acquitted for financial crisis wrongdoing, Deutsche Welle, July 9, 2014, available at http://www.dw.com/en/hsh-nordbank-executives-acquitted-for-financial-crisis-wrongdoing/a-17769276.

[62] German court closes LBBW bank case with settlement, Reuters, Apr. 24, 2014, available at http://uk.reuters.com/article/uk-lbbw-courts-idUKBREA3N15G20140424.

[63] Prosecuting Bankers: Blind Justice, Economist, May 4, 2013.

2.3 Bank Governance in the Post-Crisis World: A Proposal

Several factors suggest that it may be time to impose a more rigorous standard on the directors of certain financial institutions, particularly those deemed to be systemically important by regulatory authorities. The fact that an institution is systemically important seems to us reason enough to expect directors of such institutions to be able to perform their functions at the level of other directors at comparable financial institutions. The vast complexity not only of the businesses of banking and finance but also of the laws and regulations that govern financial institutions, particularly in the wake of Dodd–Frank, provide additional support for the argument that bank directors should be held to higher standards than the amateur standard that governs directors generally. Our proposal here is particularly relevant for directors of BHCs, who currently face no special requirements as to qualifications.[64]

While our proposal that bank directors have special expertise is new, the idea that corporate directors in general should have special expertise is not new, though the idea has not been well developed in the literature. Some scholars define the term "professional directors" simply as directors who serve on multiple boards, and adduce evidence that board membership of such professional directors correlates with improved performance for the companies on whose boards those directors serve.[65] Others use the term "professional" to refer to the particular, industry-specific expertise that certain directors have.[66] We use the term in the latter sense.

Among the earliest and most persuasive appeals to require that corporate directors have substantial industry-specific expertise was made by Yale law professor, later Supreme Court Justice William O. Douglas. Douglas argued that experts on the board "would be invaluable [. . .] in determining the course of conduct for the managers," and would be "better qualified to determine financial and commercial policy." For these reasons Douglas argued that outside experts on boards of directors "should have a position of dominance and power on the board" so that they can "make their directive influence effective" by means of their "real power over executive management."[67] In arguing for directors with sufficient industry expertise, Robert Pozen has observed,

> Lack of expertise among directors is a perennial problem. Most directors of large companies struggle to properly understand the business. Today's companies are engaged in wide-ranging operations, do business in far-flung locations with global partners, and operate within complex political and economic environments. Some businesses, retailing, for one, are relatively

---

[64] Interestingly, directors of subsidiary banks do face additional requirements. For example, the OCC notes "In addition to the citizenship and residency requirements contained in 12 USC 72, the qualifications of a candidate seeking to become a member of the board of directors of a national bank include (1) Basic knowledge of the banking industry, the financial regulatory system, and the laws and regulations that govern the operation of the institution: (2) Willingness to put the interests of the bank ahead of personal interests; (3) Willingness to avoid conflicts of interests; (4) Knowledge of the communities served by the bank; (5) Background, knowledge, and experience in business or another discipline to facilitate oversight of the bank; (6) Willingness and ability to commit the time necessary to prepare for and regularly attend board and committee meetings." See OCC, The Directors Book (2010, reprint 2013) at 4.

[65] Phyllis Y. Keys & Joanne Li, "Evidence on the Market for Professional Directors", 28 J. Fin. Res. 575 (2005).

[66] Pozen, *supra* note 32.

[67] William O. Douglas, "Directors Who Do Not Direct", 47 Harv. L. Rev. 1305 (1934).

easy to fathom, but others—aircraft manufacture, drug discovery, financial services, and telecommunications, for instance—are technically very challenging. I remember catching up with a friend who had served for many years as an independent director of a technology company. The CEO had suddenly resigned, and my friend was asked to step in. "I thought I knew a lot about the company, but boy, was I wrong," he told me. "The knowledge gaps between the directors and the executives are huge."[68]

Just as the idea that some directors should be held to higher standards is not alien to the academic literature, neither is it new to policy makers. As noted above, Dodd–Frank requires at least one of the members of the risk committees of BHCs and SIFIs to have risk-management experience commensurate with the firm's capital structure, risk profile, complexity, size, and activities. The Sarbanes–Oxley Act explicitly set higher requirements for qualified audit committees by requiring all members to be independent and at least one member to be a "financial expert" as defined by SEC rules.[69] Indeed, one of the motivations behind Sarbanes–Oxley was to strengthen audit committees to "avoid future auditing breakdowns" which were contributing to a loss of confidence in the integrity of US companies and markets.[70] Our argument here is that the failure of risk management at financial institutions, particularly systemically important ones, can lead to outcomes of even greater consequence, and that current steps are insufficient to address the magnitude of the problem of excessive risk taking by financial institutions.

How might such a system work? We suggest a two-part structure involving differential standards for both bank risk committee members and bank directors. With respect to risk committee members, we note that risk management of a complex financial institution is not something easily grasped by a typical corporate director but instead requires specialized expertise. Indeed, the shareholder advisory services ISS and Glass Lewis both recommended voting against the members of JPMorgan Chase's Risk Committee, citing their lack of risk-management experience. We believe that risk-management committees should be composed only of individuals who can demonstrate expertise in evaluating and monitoring the risk control systems of a bank. Allowing "amateur hour" in this oversight function at large complex financial institutions is simply irresponsible in post-crisis financial markets.

Such individuals, whom we will call "banking experts," would have acquired, either through experience or education, the skills needed to monitor the risk-management

---

[68] Pozen, *supra* note 32.

[69] An "audit committee financial expert" is defined as a person who has the following attributes: "(i) an understanding of generally accepted accounting principles and financial statements; (ii) the ability to assess the general application of such principles in connection with the accounting for estimates, accruals and reserves; (iii) experience preparing, auditing, analyzing or evaluating financial statements that present a breadth and level of complexity of accounting issues that are generally comparable to the breadth and complexity of issues that can reasonably be expected to be raised by the registrant's financial statements, or experience actively supervising one or more persons engaged in such activities; (iv) an understanding of internal controls and procedures for financial reporting; and (v) an understanding of audit committee functions." See Lawrence J. Trautman, "Who Qualifies as an Audit Committee Financial Expert Under SEC Regulations and NYSE Rules?", 11 DePaul Bus. & Comm. L.J. 205 (2013).

[70] See Senate Report No.107-205 as cited in Stephanie Tsacoumis, Stephanie R. Bess, & Bryn A. Sappington, The Sarbanes–Oxley Act: Rewriting Audit Committee Governance, BLI Issue 3, International Bar Association.

functions of the bank. For smaller financial institutions, this expertise may be more lim-ited, reflecting that risk management at such institutions generally involves less complex methodologies (such as gap analysis, liquidity monitoring, and the like). For large, complex financial institutions, the needed skill set will be larger, requiring familiarity with risk mod-eling, valuation of complex derivatives, synthetic asset replication, hedging strategies, etc. The specific qualifications for being a banking expert could be defined in much the way that audit committee financial experts are determined.

Second, we also propose higher professional standards for bank directors. As we have argued in this chapter, bank corporate governance issues pose an ongoing threat to the financial system. While heightened oversight of banks is surely called for, such oversight will be successful only to the extent that the directors of financial institutions have both the incentives, and the experience and skill required to be successful in carrying out their oversight responsibilities. At a minimum, we believe bank directors should be "banking literate," where such literacy is defined by an understanding of the basic functions of banking, the nature of risk in complex financial organizations, and the complex regulatory structure defining banking. Such literacy, which would be a prerequisite for becoming a director, could have been acquired through experience or through education.

We suspect that some may object to these proposals on the grounds that if having more qualified directors were valuable, then bank shareholders would demand this on their own. Alternatively, others may argue that if higher requirements are desirable for banks, then perhaps they should be required of firms more generally. We think the response to both objections is actually the same: banks are different from other firms. As we have argued, bank shareholders do not have properly aligned incentives to limit bank risk, so externally imposed requirements may be necessary. Other firms can adequately address corporate gov-ernance deficiencies internally, so requiring higher standards for all corporate directors is unnecessary.

Another objection to our proposal involves a more subtle point about bank risk taking. There is empirical research that indicates that banks with more knowledge-able directors are more likely to take on greater risk than other banks. One could argue that our proposal could actually exacerbate the risk taking problem at banks rather than ameliorate it because our proposal would place more knowledgeable directors on boards. We have two responses to this. First, ignorance is not a good strategy for risk control—relying on directors' lack of knowledge to restrain risk is surely not a for-mula for a safe and sound banking system. We completely agree, however, that knowl-edge alone is not sufficient to achieve the goal of safety and soundness in banking. In addition to knowledge and competence, there must also be a culture within banks that considers prudent banking to be a way of life rather than an oxymoron. Culture starts at the top, so efforts by regulators to highlight the importance of cultural issues within banks should be viewed as working hand in hand with our proposals to improve corporate governance in banking.

Finally, a legitimate concern is that our proposal would cause the demand for qualified bank directors to exceed the supply. We acknowledge that it will take time and effort to groom enough competent directors for all of the important financial firms in the economy. But if better directors result in creating better banks, then the returns to searching for, educating, and empowering those directors will pay off for all concerned.

3 Horizontal Governance Issues: Nonbank Subsidiaries versus Bank Subsidiaries

Another context in which financial regulation and corporate governance clash are the interactions among the bank and the nonbank subsidiaries of BHCs. The banks' subsidiaries operate as banks, while the nonbank subsidiaries often operate in the shadow banking sector as so-called "shadow banks." Shadow banking refers to traditional banking activities, particularly lending, that occur outside the regulated banking system and are effectuated by nonbank financial intermediaries as well. Claessens and Ratnovski define shadow banking as a nonbanking institution that engages in what, from an economic and functional point of view, is the business of banking.[71] In contrast, other researchers, including Paul McCulley and Mehrling et al., focus on the nature of the financial assets involved in the transactions.[72]

Shadow banking includes such important financial sectors as the repo market and the commercial paper market. Among the more important sorts of firms that operate as shadow banks are money market mutual funds, hedge funds, commercial and personal/finance companies, and broker-dealers firms. Because unregulated nonbanks are active in the shadow banking system, such institutions were able to engage in transactions featuring significantly higher credit risk, market risk, and liquidity risk, while holding much smaller capital cushions than their regulated bank competitors.

According to the IMF, in the US shadow-banking assets exceed those of the conventional banking system and have for some time.[73] Shadow banking amounts to between 15 and 25 trillion dollars in the United States, between 13.5 and 22.5 trillion in the euro area, and between 2.5 and 6 trillion in Japan—depending on the measure—and around 7 trillion in emerging markets. In emerging markets, its growth is outpacing that of the traditional banking system.[74] In the US, the UK, and the euro area, the value of assets in the shadow banking system is greater than the GDPs of each of the individual countries.

Subsequent to the subprime meltdown in 2008, the activities of the shadow banking system came under increasing scrutiny and regulation in Europe, Japan, and the United States. In particular, new rules cover money market funds (MMFs), securitization, and financial companies such as American International Group, General Electric Capital Corporation, MetLife, Inc., and Prudential Financial that have been designated as "systemically important financial institutions" (SIFIs) by the Financial Stability Oversight Council (FSOC). This is an entity created by Dodd–Frank that is empowered to determine that a

---

[71] Stijn Claessens & Lev Ratnovski, "What Is Shadow Banking?", IMF Working Paper 14/25, International Monetary Fund, Washington (2014).

[72] Paul A. McCulley, Teton Reflections, Pimco Global Central Bank Focus Series, August/September 2007, available at https://www.pimco.com/insights/economic-and-market-commentary/global-central-bank-focus/teton-reflections; Perry Mehrling, Zoltan Pozsar, James Sweeney, & Dan Neilson, "Bagehot was a Shadow Banker: Shadow Banking, Central Banking, and the Future of Global Finance", Working Paper, Shadow Banking Colloquium, a project of the Financial Stability Research Program of the Institute for New Economic Thinking (2013).

[73] See IMF, Global Financial Stability Report 66 (2014), available at http://www.imf.org/external/pubs/ft/gfsr/2014/02/pdf/c2.pdf.

[74] Id.

financial institution poses a threat to US financial stability and thereby is to be subjected to prudential regulation by the Board of Governors of the Federal Reserve System.[75] A threat exists if the material financial distress of an institution or the particular characteristics of the institution could cause systemic effects throughout the US economy.

Also pursuant to Dodd–Frank, in July 2014, the SEC issued final rules for the reform of MMFs. Certain MMFs known as "prime institutional" MMFs will be required to transact at a floating NAV and to maintain daily share prices that change according to changes in the value of the individual assets that constitute the portfolio.[76] MMFs whose customers are natural persons and government MMFs, which are MMFs that invest in government debt, may impose the practice of using constant NAV pricing. However, in times of stress, all MMFs may impose liquidity fees and redemption gates.[77]

Another point of entry for US regulators seeking to regulate the shadow banking systems is through the imposition of credit risk retention requirements in securitizations. Such requirements, known colloquially as "skin-in-the-game" provisions, are, strangely enough, coupled with prohibitions against hedging the retained credit risk portion of the securitization. These anti-hedging provisions are strange, of course, because they increase rather than decrease the risks of the firms that are subject to the credit risk retention rules. Anti-hedging provisions are necessary, because without them hedging would permit financial firms involved in securitizations to avoid having "skin in the game" by implementing hedging strategies that nullified the risks associated with the securitized financial assets retained by these financial firms.

From a corporate governance perspective, one particular facet of the shadow banking system is of particular concern. Bank and financial holding companies can conduct banking activities not only through the downstream banks that they own and control, but also through virtually unregulated nonbank subsidiaries such as mortgage companies:

> Mortgage companies were largely ignored (by both functional and institutional regulators), despite the fact that they had held a dominant market share (of mortgage originations) since the early 1990s. Mortgage companies were not funded by deposits, so no institutional regulator oversaw them, and their activities did not fall under the domain of any functional regulator. The Federal Trade Commission and the State Attorneys General did have the ability to bring punitive actions against mortgage companies, but only if they observed unfair and deceptive practices evidenced by a pattern of customer complaints. Before the 2007 crisis, this "repeat-complaint-oriented supervision" had little power to systematically affect mortgage company behavior, leaving them essentially free of regulatory oversight.[78]

In a recent article, Yuliya Demyanyk and Elena Loutskina observe that, while defaulted mortgages originated by bank subsidiaries weakened the balance sheets and income

---

[75] FSOC's designation authority is limited in Section 113(a)(2) of the Dodd–Frank Act to "U.S. nonbank financial compan[ies]." See also Section 102(a)(6).

[76] Institutional prime MMFs are marketed to institutional investors, who constitute over one-half of the market for MMFs. Generally speaking, institutional prime MMFs have portfolios that are riskier than other funds' portfolios and include certificates of deposit, commercial paper, and repurchase agreements. See IMF, *supra* note 73, at 99, footnote 60.

[77] IMF, *supra* note 73, at 99.

[78] Yuliya Demyanyk & Elena Loutskina, A Gap in Regulation and the Looser Lending Standards that Followed, Federal Reserve Bank of Cleveland Economic Commentary, No. 2014-20, October 9, 2014.

statements of their holding company parents by increasing their reported loan losses and reducing their profits (net income), the defaults on mortgages originated by their nonbank mortgage-company subsidiaries did not.[79] Thus, rather stunningly, loan losses from mortgage defaults from subprime mortgages "have an adverse effect on a BHC's reported loan losses and net income only if they were originated by a bank subsidiary, not a mortgage-company subsidiary."[80]

Unsurprisingly, the different consequences for a BHC of making loans through a mortgage company subsidiary rather than through a subsidiary bank had consequences. Demyanyk and Loutskina document the fact that "mortgage-company subsidiaries of BHCs originated more loans to borrowers with lower credit scores, higher loan-to-income ratios, and lower relative incomes than did their bank subsidiaries. Mortgage companies were also more likely to originate loans of riskier types, such as adjustable-rate and interest-only mortgages."[81]

The incentives for holding companies to shift their riskiest subprime lending activities out of banks and into nonbank mortgage companies were further heightened by the Gramm–Leach–Bliley Act of 1999, which, in an effort to control risk, isolated the activities of bank and nonbank subsidiaries by erecting "formal financial barriers between the BHCs' bank and their non-depository subsidiaries."[82] In particular, BHCs were required to erect "firewalls" between their bank subsidiaries and their nonbank subsidiaries. Gramm–Leach–Bliley explicitly prohibited BHCs from bailing out troubled nonbank subsidiaries, which meant that as a practical matter "BHCs' exposure to the limited liability mortgage-company subsidiaries was indeed limited to their equity investment."[83]

Gramm–Leach–Bliley had the stated policy objective of protecting FDIC-insured banks, the federal deposit insurance fund and taxpayers—from the costs associated with the failure of their nonbank/uninsured affiliate. The unintended consequence of Gramm–Leach–Bliley was that it increased systemic risk because risky activities were simply shunted from insured banks to their uninsured, unregulated nonbank affiliates within the same holding company. This shift not only led to weaker lending standards, but also led to the financial crisis.[84]

4 Regulatory Externalities

In previous joint work, we have observed another tension between the interests of the financial markets and the interests of individual market participants. In particular, we have shown that the SEC's order-handling rules for securities trading, the so-called "trade-through rules," tend to benefit the securities markets in general but tend to harm certain individual traders who bring liquidity to the markets by preventing them from attaining the most efficient execution of their orders.[85]

The trade-through rule requires that purchasers (sellers) buy (sell) securities at the best displayed offer (bid) price even if the offer (bid) is for fewer shares than the bidder (offeror) would like to buy (sell). The problem arises because traders with a large block to buy or sell

---

[79] Id.   [80] Id.   [81] Id.   [82] Id.   [83] Id.   [84] Id.
[85] Jonathan Macey & Maureen O'Hara, "From Orders to Markets", 28 Regulation 62–70 (2005).

may achieve better overall execution terms for their entire order by executing the entire order at an inferior price rather than splitting their entire order up into smaller blocks and taking offers or hitting bids seriatim at different, and usually constantly worsening, prices. As we have explained in earlier work:

> For example, if the best bid anywhere for a stock is $100, a large block seller (with 10,000 shares to sell) must, under the current incarnation of the trade-through rule, execute the trade at that price, even if the bid were for only 1,000 shares and the seller would prefer to sell the entire 100,000-share block at an inferior bid of $99.75. Of course, if the block trader were permitted to "trade-through" the superior bid as the SEC proposed in 2004 and consummate the transaction at $99.75, the retail trader who entered the $100 bid might not obtain best execution if the market moves higher before the trade can be executed.[86]

Here in contrast to having rules, the so-called firewall rules of Gramm–Leach–Bliley that cabin off the unregulated nonbank affiliates from their affiliate regulated banks, which make individual banks safer but may increase systemic risk by shifting risky activities from regulated banks to unregulated and relatively monitored subsidiaries.

Several provisions in 2010 Dodd–Frank Act provide regulators with the tools to deal with the problem just identified. But it is important that regulators understand this problem so that they can address it properly.

Dodd–Frank is an enormously complex and multifaceted statute. Here we focus as precisely as we can on the provisions that can be most useful as a tool for dealing with the negative externality problem just identified. These provisions call for establishing the Financial Stability Oversight Council (FSOC) to address systemic risks. The FSOC was established primarily to (1) identify risks to the financial stability of the United States that could arise from the material financial distress or failure, or ongoing activities, of large, interconnected bank holding companies or nonbank financial companies, or that could arise outside the financial services marketplace; (2) promote market discipline, by eliminating expectations on the part of shareholders, creditors, and counterparties of such companies that the US government will shield them from losses in the event of failure; and (3) to respond to emerging threats to the stability of the US financial system.[87]

In addition, Dodd–Frank requires the Federal Reserve to adopt enhanced prudential regulatory standards for the largest BHCs and designated nonbank financial companies. The stringency of these requirements increases with the size and complexity of the holding company subject to the rules.

Further, Dodd–Frank restricts banks, bank affiliates, and BHCs from proprietary trading or investing in a hedge fund or private equity fund, requires the Federal Reserve to impose a debt-to-equity limit on companies the Council has determined pose a grave threat to financial stability, and to establish enhanced prudential standards for large BHCs and foreign banking organizations (known as FBOs).

These rules have the potential to mitigate the risk-shifting problem that arises when insured and regulated depository institutions shift their riskiest activities to uninsured

---

[86] Id. at 64–67.

[87] See Financial Stability Oversight Council, 2014 Annual Report, at iii, available at https://www.treasury.gov/initiatives/fsoc/Documents/FSOC%202014%20Annual%20Report.pdf.

unregulated subsidiaries, at least for depository institutions that are designated as SIFIs. It appears to us, however, that the rules do not go far enough. They do not affect holding companies such as General Electric, which has many subsidiaries but only one (General Electric Credit Corporation) that is designated as a SIFI. The rules also do not affect non-SIFIs. SIFIs consist of BHCs with total consolidated assets of $50 billion or more as well as nonbank financial companies[88] designated as systemically important by the FSOC. The nonbank holding companies designated as SIFIs are American International Group (AIG), General Electric Capital Corporation (GECC), MetLife, Inc., and Prudential Financial Inc.[89]

Title I of Dodd–Frank gives the FSOC the authority to determine whether a non-bank financial company will be subject to the Fed's supervision and prudential standards. Specifically, the Fed's powers kick in if the company's size, complexity, interconnectedness, and mix of activities pose a threat to the US financial system, and also when a nonbank financial company is in "material financial distress," defined as being in imminent danger of default or insolvency, that poses a threat to the financial system of the US.

Under Dodd–Frank, the FSOC must apply 10 statutory considerations when it makes its determination.[90] In so doing, the FSOC will employ a three-stage process. In the first stage, it will analyze nonbank financial companies based on six quantitative measures (see Table 41.1). The companies that exceed the asset size threshold plus one or more of the remaining five quantitative measures "could move onto the second stage, during which the

---

[88] A Nonbank Financial Company is defined in Title I of Dodd–Frank as a company that is predominantly engaged in financial activities. Predominantly means that 85% of its consolidated gross revenues are derived from what are defined as financial activities by the Bank Holding Company Act of 1956.

[89] The Dodd–Frank Act also authorizes the FSOC to designate a Financial Market Utility (FMU) as "systemically important" if it determines that the failure of or a disruption to the functioning of the FMU could create or increase the risk of significant liquidity or credit problems spreading among financial institutions or markets and thereby threaten the stability of the U.S. financial system. Designated FMUs are subject to the heightened prudential and supervisory provisions of Title VIII of Dodd–Frank, which relate to risk management and safety and soundness issues such as requiring that FMUs conduct their operations in compliance with applicable risk-management standards; providing advance notice and review of changes to their rules, procedures, and operations that could materially affect the nature or level of their risks; and being subject to relevant examination and enforcement provisions.

At its July 18, 2012 meeting, the FSOC voted to designate eight FMUs as systemically important under Title VIII of the Dodd–Frank Act: (1) The Clearing House Payments Company L.L.C. (on the basis of its role as operator of the Clearing House Interbank Payments System); (2) CLS Bank International; (3) Chicago Mercantile Exchange, Inc.; (4) The Depository Trust Company; (5) Fixed Income Clearing Corporation; (6) ICE Clear Credit LLC; (7) National Securities Clearing Corporation; and (8) The Options Clearing Corporation. See Financial Stability Oversight Council, Designations, http://www.treasury.gov/initiatives/fsoc/designations/Pages/default.aspx.

[90] The statutory considerations are: (1) the extent of (financial) leverage; (2) the extent and nature of off-balance-sheet exposures; (3) the extent and nature of the company's transactions with other significant nonbank financial companies and bank holding companies; (4) the importance of the company as a source of credit for households, businesses, and municipalities, and as a source of liquidity for the U.S. financial system; (5) the importance of the company as a source of credit for low-income, minority, and underserved communities; (6) the extent to which assets are managed rather than owned by the company and the extent that ownership of AUM is diffused; (7) the nature, scope, size, scale, interconnectedness, and mix of the company's activities; (8) the degree to which the company is already regulated by one or more primary regulatory authorities; (9) the amount and nature of the financial assets; and (10) the amount and types of liabilities, including the reliance on short-term funding PLUS any other risk-related factors that the FSOC deems appropriate.

Table 41.1 Selected FSOC Stage 1 thresholds

Selected FSOC Stage 1 Thresholds*

	Total consolidated assets (GAAP) (mil. $)	Total debt outstanding (mil. $)	Leverage multiple (x)§	Short-term debt ratio (%)
FSOC Stage 1 thresholds	50,000	20,000	15	10
Asset Managers				
BlackRock Inc.	179,896	27,282	2.4	1.0
Finance companies				
SLM Corp.	193,345	183,966	36.8	15.3
Independent Brokers				
Charles Schwab Corp.	108,553	2,853	14.1	0.0
E*TRADE Financial Corp.	47,940	9,752	9.7	9.0
IBG LLC	30,404	2,880	6.5	0.4
Jefferies Group Inc.	34,564	17,551	9.5	0.7
Alternative Asset Managers (Hedge Funds And Private Equity Firms)				
Blackstone Group LP	21,909	10,396	2.5	0.1
Icahn Enterprises L.P.	25,136	6,473	3.2	0.4
KKR & Co. L.P.	40,378	1,565	1.1	0.5
Oaktree Capital Management L.P.	44,294	702	35.8	0.2

* This chart excludes the threshold "notional amount of credit default swaps on reference entity," because the threshold amount $30 billion is relevant only for GECC (with $96 billion in CDSs) and SLM Corp. (with $28 billion in CDSs).

Source: Standard and Poor's, New Regulatory Rules Likely Will Have A Limited Impact On U.S. Nonbank Financial Company Ratings, May 9, 2012,
<http://static.ow.ly/docs/5-9-12%20-%20New%20Regulatory%20Rules%20Likely%20Have%20 A%20Limited%20Impact%20On%20U%20S%20%20Nonbank%20Financial%20Company%20 Ratings_Clg.pdf>.

FSOC will evaluate their risk profiles using a wider variety of quantitative information that is available from public and regulatory resources." In the third stage, the FSOC will use quantitative and qualitative information it receives from the companies to determine whether they are potential threats to the financial stability of the US.[91]

As reflected in Table 41.1, several nonbank financial companies are not designated as SIFIs despite meeting the $50 billion asset threshold. For other such companies see Table 41.1.

---

[91] Standard and Poor's, "New Regulatory Rules Likely Will Have A Limited Impact On U.S. Nonbank Financial Company Ratings," May 9, 2012, http://static.ow.ly/docs/5-9-12%20-%20New%20 Regulatory%20Rules%20Likely%20Have%20A%20Limited%20Impact%20On%20U%20S%20%20 Nonbank%20Financial%20Company%20Ratings_Clg.pdf.

5 CONCLUSION

There is a fundamental and perhaps irreconcilable difference between the corporate governance goals of systemically important financial institutions and federally insured financial institutions on the one hand, and non-federally insured, non-systemically important companies on the other. Because all systemically important financial institutions and virtually all insured banks are controlled by holding company parents, this means that different subsidiaries of the same holding companies will be subjected to different corporate governance norms. This structure creates a conflict between the goal in financial regulation of reducing the incidence of failure of systemically important financial institutions and the goal in corporate law of maximizing the value of the corporation for shareholders.

The conflict between BHCs and their subsidiaries, discussed earlier in this chapter is a "vertical" corporate governance problem. The horizontal conflict is exacerbated by the size and complexity of large financial institutions. It can be mitigated by imposing higher professional standards on bank directors and on members of board risk committees.

The conflict between the bank and nonbank subsidiaries of BHCs discussed in the second part of this chapter is a "horizontal" corporate governance problem. The horizontal conflict exists among bank and nonbank subsidiaries, and is, if anything, even more difficult to resolve than the vertical governance problem. The extent of this challenge is reflected in the immense complexity of Dodd–Frank, and particularly in the designation and regulation of entities designated as systemically important. In light of the small number of institutions designated as SIFIs, however, it appears that more work is required to mitigate the horizontal challenge, particularly as the shadow banking system remains extremely robust.

CHAPTER 42

....

BANK GOVERNANCE

....

JOHN ARMOUR

1 INTRODUCTION

....

ACCORDING to a common narrative, the failure of banks during the financial crisis in part reflected poor corporate governance on their part, as well as failures in the prudential regulatory regime to which they were subject.[1] According to this view, bank failures reflected internal deficiencies stemming from the relation between those who financed the banks, as shareholders or creditors, and those who ran these firms, as managers. Yet empirical studies report that the banks with the "best" corporate governance practices, as measured by ordinary standards, were the ones that did worst during the financial crisis.

Reconciling these views requires a theory of what "good" corporate governance for banks should look like. Banks are materially different in their financing, business model and balance sheets from most non-financial firms. First, banks are extremely highly leveraged institutions. The core of a bank's business model is to transform short-term deposits into long-term loans, implying that most of its capital is raised through debt. With any leveraged firm, shareholders may gain at creditors' expense from an increase in risk and associated returns. If things go well, shareholders keep the higher returns; if things go badly, the creditors suffer. The potential for such risk-shifting rises with the level of leverage. It is consequently greater for banks than for most nonfinancial firms. At the same time, the financial assets held by a bank are distinguished from the assets of a non-financial firm by their opacity—that is, the difficulty outsiders have in determining their quality. This makes it more difficult for outsiders to monitor asset quality in a bank than in a non-financial firm.

So banks have greater potential for risk shifting, in ways that may be harder to detect, than non-financial firms. What is worse, their failure can impose enormous costs on society at large—negative externalities. The interconnection of the banking system means that the failure of a large bank can trigger contagion to other institutions, and the collapse of banks imposes costs on the real economy, not least through a reduced supply of capital for investment. To avoid this outcome, prudential regulation imposes capital and liquidity

---

[1] See e.g., OECD, Corporate Governance and the Financial Crisis: Key Findings and Main Messages 41 (2009); European Banking Authority, EBA Guidelines on Internal Governance 3 (2011).

requirements on banks so as to reduce their probability of failure. Deposit insurance mitigates the incentives of depositors to engage in a run. Moreover, as a last-ditch measure, bank bailouts prevent a failing bank from creating systemic costs.

Unfortunately, these policy measures have the effect of muting bank creditors' incentives to engage in monitoring of bank risk taking. If banks were companies like any other, depositors and other creditors would take notice of the risk of shareholder opportunism and either charge a higher interest rate (making financing through debt more expensive and therefore less predominant) or insist on having stronger governance and control rights.[2] Yet various factors stand in the way of creditors themselves playing an important part in disciplining bank shareholder opportunism. Depositors have no oversight rights, are dispersed, and are protected by deposit insurance. Banking regulation and supervision are there exactly to prevent shareholder opportunism of this kind, so that (at least unsophisticated) market participants may over-rely on their effectiveness. And perhaps most importantly, creditors of larger banks could (and perhaps still can) reasonably expect a state bailout that will avoid losses for them should the bank become insolvent.

In the period leading up to the financial crisis, the peculiarities of banks' balance sheets, their regulation, and the externalities they can create were thought not to necessitate any difference in the structure of bank governance from that of non-financial firms. It was believed that prudential regulation caused banks to internalize the full social costs of their activities, meaning that what maximized bank shareholders' returns would also be in the interests of society. On this view, which we might call the "assimilation" theory of bank governance, it was appropriate for banks to use the same governance tools as non-financial companies to minimize shareholder-management agency costs, namely independent boards, shareholder rights, the threat of takeovers, and equity-based executive compensation.

Unfortunately, tightening the linkage between shareholders and managers in banks had the adverse effect of encouraging bank managers to test the limits of regulatory controls. Given the opacity of bank assets, it is hard for regulators to ensure that bank risk taking is appropriately controlled. In the presence of less than complete regulatory controls, those running banks have incentives to take excessive risks. As described throughout this chapter, the banks that had the most "pro-shareholder" boards and the closest alignment between executive returns and the stock price were those that took the most risks prior to, and suffered the greatest losses during, the crisis.

As a result, a significant rethink about the way in which banks are governed is required. The revised perspective might be termed the "bank exceptionalism" theory of governance.[3] On this view, the structure and function of bank boards, the compensation of bank employees, and the function of risk management within organizations need careful differentiation from ordinary corporate governance if reforms are to address, and not exacerbate, bank failures.

---

[2] On the important role of creditors in the governance of listed companies even in a highly shareholder-focused corporate governance system such as the US, see Douglas G. Baird & Robert K. Rasmussen, "Private Debt and the Missing Lever of Corporate Governance", 154 U. Pa. L. Rev. 1209 (2006).

[3] To the extent that the concerns described above also apply to other, nonbank, financial firms, then the "banks are different" theory of governance would also apply mutatis mutandis.

The rest of this chapter is structured as follows. Section 2 reviews the conventional goals and mechanisms of corporate governance, and explains their limitations when applied to banks. Sections 3–6 then consider, respectively, the operation of boards of directors, executive pay, shareholder rights and directors' duties in relation to banks, reviewing empirical evidence, and describing regulatory initiatives. Section 7 offers a brief conclusion.

2 CORPORATE GOVERNANCE: HOW ARE BANKS DIFFERENT?

2.1 The Conventional Approach to Corporate Governance

The standard approach to corporate governance exhorts managers to run their firm in the interests of shareholders. This is because shareholders are "residual claimants": that is, they receive what is left after all fixed claimants have been paid. Focusing on maximizing the residual surplus gives incentives to maximize the overall value of the firm: that is, to run it as efficiently as possible. Moreover, amongst those who contract with the firm—investors, creditors, employees, customers, and suppliers—the shareholders have the most homogeneous interests in the financial performance of the firm.[4] Their interests relate simply to the maximization of the value of their claims, which, in the context of a publicly traded firm, is reflected in the firm's stock price. Consequently, maximizing the stock price should be management's objective.

To implement this, shareholders are given the right to appoint directors, who in turn select the managers.[5] The significance of the directors derives from the fact that ownership of shares in large public corporations is typically widely dispersed. As a consequence, shareholders face high coordination costs in exercising their rights. A number of mechanisms are relied upon to overcome this problem.

First, the board of directors has increasingly come to be viewed as performing the function of monitoring managerial performance on behalf of the shareholders. If the shareholders are too dispersed to be able to engage in effective monitoring themselves, then the elected board of directors can do so in their stead. The problem here is that the shareholders' very lack of coordination may undermine the process of election of effective monitors. The managers may influence the list of candidates and ensure that only their friends and associates are represented on the board. In response to this concern, directors are increasingly expected to be "independent" of the firm: that is, they should have no family, financial, or employment ties to the firm or its managers. Independent directors, it is thought, will make better delegated monitors on behalf of shareholders. The problem remains that in the absence of effective shareholder input, the "independence" of directors means simply the absence of a conflict of interest; it does nothing to ensure the presence of the necessary qualities to be an effective monitor.

---

[4] Henry Hansmann, The Ownership of Enterprise (1996).
[5] Reinier Kraakman et al., The Anatomy of Corporate Law 12 (3d ed. 2017).

Executive pay comprises a second mechanism, which has in recent years become the most important focus of governance activity in the US. Tying managerial compensation to the stock performance gives very direct incentives. A drawback with conditioning pay on financial performance is that it requires managers to bear the risk of the firm's underperformance, even for reasons beyond their control. This may result in managers adopting an unduly risk-averse approach to decision making, passing up valuable but risky opportunities in favor of safer, more conservative, strategies. One way to encourage managerial risk taking and stock price maximization at the same time is to pay managers by way of options. These have the potential to offer managers rewards for increasing the stock price, but with no associated loss if the share price falls. However, the incentives associated with options are highly sensitive to the way in which the strike price is set. These contracts are normally negotiated by the compensation committee of the board of directors. Their success, therefore, is a function of the quality of the board. Because of this, some influential scholars argue that the rise in option-based compensation is not so much a function of improved corporate governance, but of a combination of changes to the US tax code that made it cheaper for firms to grant options than cash compensation, and of thinly veiled managerial self-interest.[6]

Third, shareholder rights provide channels through which shareholders may exercise control, for example by voting on major business decisions or more generally by removing directors. The exercise of shareholder rights requires some concentration of ownership, so as to overcome coordination problems. It is sometimes suggested that takeovers are a mechanism by which external discipline is brought to bear on management even in the presence of dispersed shareholdings. Poorly performing management faces the threat of acquisition by another company, and the mere threat of this occurring may be sufficient to encourage management to pursue the interests of their shareholders vigorously.

The last few years have witnessed the emergence of a second mechanism by which external discipline is brought to bear on management in the presence of dispersed shareholders. Activist shareholders, and in particular hedge funds, have acquired significant but not necessarily controlling shareholdings in firms to effect changes in corporate policy and management. They frequently act in conjunction with other institutional investors in promoting change. The rise of institutional activists has had a profound impact on the conduct of management in dispersed ownership systems in the UK and US particularly.

Fourth, directors and officers are subject to legal duties to avoid conflicts of interest and to take appropriate care in the running of their company. These may be enforced by shareholders through derivative or class actions, which enable a single shareholder or group of shareholders to represent the rest in claims against errant directors. However, it is unlikely that the shareholders who initiate such an action, or the judges called upon to adjudicate them, will know as much about the business as the incumbent managers. This makes litigation a blunt instrument. To avoid over-zealous enforcement, there are typically checks on shareholder litigation in relation to good faith business decisions that grant considerable discretion to management in the running of their businesses, leaving shareholder plaintiffs to focus on more egregious cases of conflicts of interest.

---

[6] See Lucian A. Bebchuk & Jesse Fried, Pay Without Performance: The Unfulfilled Promise of Executive Compensation (2004); John C. Coffee, Jr., "A Theory of Corporate Scandals: Why the USA and Europe Differ", 21 Oxford Rev. Econ. Pol'y 198, 202 (2005).

2.2 How Are Banks Different?

As anticipated in the introduction, governance problems and mechanisms often play out differently in banks than in ordinary firms, reflecting how banks are special from this perspective in three important respects. The first difference is that banks are highly leveraged. The core of a bank's business model is to transform short-term deposits into long-term loans, implying that most of its capital is raised through debt. In addition to deposits, banks raise money via short-term and long-term debt, which, together with deposits, typically make up most of the liability side of their balance sheets. As a result, shareholders may stand to benefit at creditors' expense from changes in the bank's investment projects that increase risk and associated returns. If things go well, the shareholders keep the increased returns, whereas if things go badly, the creditors suffer losses. Perversely, mechanisms that succeed in tying executives to the interests of shareholders may actually exacerbate these financial agency costs. Creditors should therefore satisfy themselves that there are strong checks in place to ensure that the riskiness of the bank's activities is kept within acceptable limits. However, depositors are usually widely dispersed with only small amounts at stake, and do not wish to, or feel able to, monitor bank lending effectively.

The second difference is that bank failure imposes greater costs on society. A bank failure can trigger contagion in other parts of the financial system and, by impeding the operation of the financial system can harm the ability of businesses to obtain finance. Since losses are purely economic, they are not generally susceptible to compensation through the tort system.[7] Moreover, as the source of contagion is usually the failure of a financial firm, governments have incentives to throw money at troubled firms to avert such failure.[8] The more systemically important the bank, the more likely it will be able to rely on government support should it get into difficulties. This gives banks a perverse incentive to structure their operations such that they are systemically important and, in the eyes of policy makers, "too big to fail."[9] The implicit government guarantee means that such firms enjoy a lower cost of credit, and that creditors' incentives to monitor the firms' performance is weakened. What this does is to morph the creditors' problem described in the previous paragraph into a problem for society more generally, through the implicit subsidy that creditors receive.

Of course, bank shareholders will lose money if their bank fails, but, because of limited liability, the shareholders' maximum loss is set by the initial value of their shares. Consequently, other than the extent to which it affects creditors' willingness to lend, shareholders have no

---

[7] This is ordinarily justified on the basis that economic harms to one party often represent opportunities to someone else: a power outage closing firm A's factory for a week (and resulting in lost profits) represents an opportunity for A's competitors to earn extra profits by selling more products instead. However, if contagion is systemic in the sense that it affects the entire financial sector, competitors will not profit from a bank's difficulties, nor will competitors of manufacturing firms who are unable to raise finance be readily able to profit from their circumstances. And even if the economic losses caused by contagion were in principle recoverable, the way in which they are triggered ensures they will not be visited on shareholders. Banks trigger contagion through their financial distress and there would consequently be no assets to pay tort liabilities.

[8] This is distinct from other cases of catastrophic industrial accidents, where governments intervene to ameliorate the consequences but nevertheless are content to bankrupt the firm in the process.

[9] See Mark J. Roe, "Structural Corporate Degradation Due to Too-Big-To-Fail Finance", 162 U. Pa. L. Rev. 1419 (2014).

incentive to take precautions that might reduce the total losses consequent upon failure: as far as the shareholders are concerned, they have lost everything anyway by that point. There is even a Wall Street acronym used by market participants to reassure themselves they need not worry about marginal losses consequent upon failure: "IBG–YBG"—"I'll be gone, you'll be gone."[10]

The third difference is that certain types of financial assets are hard to observe and measure. The rationale for bank lending is that banks may be able to collect information on borrowers that is not available to others. Hence, the value of their loan portfolio may not readily be subject to external scrutiny by shareholders as well as potential hostile bidders and creditors themselves.[11]

As a result of the first and second of these differences, regulators—in lieu of creditors—are tasked with monitoring and controlling bank risk taking. However, the very difficulty of monitoring financial assets—the third of the differences described above—makes it particularly challenging for regulators, as well as investors, to perform this task effectively. And the efficacy of regulatory control is further compromised by very intense managerial incentives to maximize the share price. Managers may, therefore, seek to avoid regulation and to minimize the costs of regulation by influencing regulators, rather than taking desired actions and precautions to minimize risks of failure.

2.3   Bank Governance before the Crisis

For much of the postwar period, banks were treated as utilities subject to a form of rate regulation: both entry to the sector, and profits, were restricted. This gave shareholders a steady stream of returns, and no great incentive to push managers. Managers in turn had no great incentive to push to increase the firm's performance. From the 1980s onward, there was significant deregulation in banking in the US, the UK, and many other countries. This introduced greater competition to the sector and volatility to shareholder returns. Bank governance, therefore, became more intensely focused on share price maximization. To the extent that banks were different, it was thought that financial regulation could be relied upon to correct any problems. Consequently, policy makers and industry participants sought to apply ordinary "best practice" in corporate governance to banking firms. For example, guidance by the Basel Committee on Banking Supervision concerning corporate governance in banks emphasized the monitoring role of the board of directors.[12]

Of the governance mechanisms described in section 1, incentive pay was perhaps the most heavily relied upon to control bank executives. This tracked the rise of executive compensation as a governance mechanism generally. Moreover, variable pay has long been a feature

[10]   See e.g. Eric Dash, "What's Really Wrong with Wall Street Pay", N.Y. Times Economix Blog, Sept. 18, 2009, http://economix.blogs.nytimes.com/2009/09/18/whats-really-wrong-with-wall-street-pay/.

[11]   See e.g. Donald P. Morgan, "Rating Banks: Risk and Uncertainty in an Opaque Industry", 92 Am. Econ. Rev. 874 (2002) (reporting greater disagreement amongst ratings agencies about banks than about other industries, consistent with greater opacity).

[12]   Basel Committee on Banking Supervision (BCBS), Enhancing Corporate Governance for Banking Organisations 6–7 (1999); BCBS, Enhancing Corporate Governance for Banking Organisations 6–15 (2006).

of employment in the investment banking sector. When the major investment banks converted from partnerships to corporations in the 1990s, profit-sharing that had previously been effected through partnership status came to be managed through variable pay for risk takers instead. As investment banks merged with commercial banks, these pay practices were rationalized as promoting shareholder value and extended to the commercial banking divisions of the resulting financial conglomerates.

However, reliance on incentive compensation has a serious drawback in the context of financial institutions. Correctly calibrating incentive pay depends on assessments of the state of financial assets, which by definition are hard to observe. For example, consider a loan officer, who agrees loans on the bank's behalf. The number of loans she writes, and the interest charged, are easy to observe. But the quality of the borrowers she lends to is not. If the bank were to offer her "incentive" compensation, this should condition amongst other things on the quality of borrowers, but because borrower quality is hard to observe, the bank may only be able to make the contract conditional on loan size and interest rates, which will lead to predictably problematic results.

The failure to appreciate that the differences between banks and non-financial firms had implications for governance, and that these could not readily be solved by regulators, had unfortunate consequences. An emerging body of literature reports that the bank executives who had the strongest incentives to maximize the value of their shares—as reflected in stock-based compensation, oversight by independent directors, and shareholder power—worked at banks that took the greatest risks and suffered the greatest losses.[13] In other words, financial firms that had the "best" governance mechanisms, as conventionally understood before the crisis, actually did *worst* during the crisis.

We now review the application to financial institutions of each of the corporate governance mechanisms described in section 1. We begin with boards of directors, then consider compensation practices, then shareholder rights, and conclude with a discussion of legal duties. In each case, we consider first what we have learned from pre-crisis practices, and then review critically recent regulatory initiatives.

3 BANK BOARDS OF DIRECTORS

3.1 Before the Crisis

Historically, bank boards in the UK and US were typically larger, and had more independent directors, than non-financial firms.[14] However, the size of bank boards around the world had been shrinking during the decade prior to the financial crisis, making these boards

---

[13] See below, section 3.1, for references.

[14] Renée B. Adams & Hamid Mehran, "Bank Board Structure and Performance: Evidence for Large Bank Holding Companies", 21 J. Fin. Intermediation 243 (2012) (study of 35 bank holding companies over 1964–1999, reporting positive relationship between board size and shareholder returns, and no link between number of independent directors and shareholder returns); cf David Walker, A Review of Corporate Governance in UK Banks and other Financial Industry Entities 41 (2009); Renée B. Adams, "Governance and the Financial Crisis", 12 Int'l. Rev. Fin. 7, 27 (2012).

look more like those in non-financial firms.[15] Yet banks' compliance with general norms of "good" corporate governance was associated with their failure during the financial crisis.[16] Two studies of banks around the world report that those with more "shareholder-oriented" boards had greater levels of risk prior to the crisis and experienced greater losses subsequently.[17] There are at least two, likely complementary, explanations for these results. The first is that independent directors in banks may have assumed that regulators were exercising appropriate risk controls and consequently become less intensive in their own scrutiny. The second is that, because of the externalities associated with bank risk taking, shareholders would have wanted banks to take greater risks. In other words, since financial gains benefit shareholders and losses that are so large as to put to banks into bankruptcy are borne by others, shareholders benefit from the firm's pursuit of more risky investments.

3.2 Bank Internal Controls

An important role of the board of directors is to oversee internal controls within a firm. In most firms, these are primarily concerned with ensuring operational decisions are actually made in accordance with the firm's strategy. However, the business of financial institutions is principally concerned with the allocation of risk. As a result, these firms need to engage in risk management—that is, ensuring that the financial risks assumed by the organization are consistent with its objectives.[18] At the core of this is the need to assess whether (1) the risks are justified by the returns associated (for particular contracts), and whether (2) the portfolio of risks taken on by the firm as a whole is appropriately constructed.

Banks' risk management systems can be subdivided into four components:[19] (1) the assimilation and communication of information about exposures, in the form of standards and reports; (2) the application of rules governing limits on positions that employees with a given level of authority may enter into on the firm's behalf; (3) the development of strategies and guidelines governing investment; and (4) the design of employee compensation so as to generate appropriate incentives. Each component needs to be monitored and reviewed on a continuing basis, as does its relationship with the others.

---

[15] Marco Becht, Patrick Bolton & Ailsa Röell, "Why Bank Governance is Different", 27 Oxford Rev. Econ. Pol'y 437, 448 (2012). In contrast to non-financial companies, some studies report a positive association between bank board size and shareholder returns: see Adams & Mehran, *supra* note 14.

[16] For reviews, see Becht et al., *supra* note 15.

[17] Andrea Beltratti & René M. Stulz, "The Credit Crisis Around the Globe: Why Did Some Banks Perform Better?", 105 J. Fin. Econ. 1, 10–11, 14–15 (2012) (sample of 503 deposit-taking banks around the world; reporting positive association between index of "shareholder-friendliness" compiled from 25 ISS board variables and pre-crisis default risk, and a negative association with post-crisis performance); David H. Erkens, Mingyi Hung & Pedro Matos, "Corporate Governance in the 2007–2008 Financial Crisis: Evidence from Financial Institutions Worldwide", 18 J. Corp. Fin. 389 (2012) (panel of 296 financial firms worldwide; reporting positive association between proportion of independent directors and pre-crisis risk taking, and negative association with post-crisis performance).

[18] Anthony M. Santomero, "Commercial Bank Risk Management: An Analysis of the Process", 12 J. Fin. Services Research 83, 89–90 (1997); David H. Pyle, Bank Risk Management: Theory, in Risk Management and Regulation in Banking 7, 8 (Dan Galai, David Ruthenberg, Marshall Sarnat & Ben Z. Schreiber eds., 1999).

[19] Santomero, id., at 86.

A number of aspects of bank risk management are particularly problematic. First, the gross level of complexity. In addition to the inherent difficulty of observing financial assets, noted in section 2, bank risk management systems have evolved gradually over time, following different trajectories in relation to different categories of risk. Credit risk management differs from interest rate risk or liquidity risk, for example. The level of complexity involved in the management of each of these has evolved in accordance with the limit of the competence of the most highly skilled teams of experts. This makes it extremely difficult for senior management to synthesize and assess overall risks to the firm.[20]

Second, there is a particular conflict between risk management and high-powered financial incentives for employees. Employees with strongly incentive-based compensation will seek to maximize whatever performance benchmark has been set for them. The more intense the incentive to maximize a particular benchmark, the more single-minded the focus on that measure will be, which may be to the detriment of other business objectives. Worse still, intense incentives can lead employees to seek to "game" the performance benchmark through steps that are positively harmful to the business as a whole, or even fraudulent. Given the great difficulties in monitoring financial assets, the appropriate calibration of employee compensation schemes and the policing of the way in which employees meet their performance targets are extremely important for the successful operation of the business. They therefore demand significant levels of internal oversight. This needs to be effected not just at the level of individual compensation targets and behavior, but also at group- and firm-wide levels, ensuring that individual (group) targets are set in a way that are mutually consistent at the level of the firm as a whole.

Consistent with intuition, there is evidence that the level of resources devoted to risk management has a meaningful impact on bank overall returns. Ellul and Yerramilli constructed an index of risk management intended to capture the strength and independence of risk management functions at US bank holding companies. They report that bank holding companies with higher scores in this index were less risky prior to the crisis and enjoyed better returns during the crisis.[21]

3.3 EU Regulation of Bank Board Structure and Risk Management

The EU has, under the aegis of the Capital Requirements Directive IV ("CRD IV") and the accompanying Capital Requirements Regulation ("CRR"),[22] introduced a wide-ranging and prescriptive set of guidelines for bank governance, dealing inter alia with board structure

---

[20] Id., at 110–112.

[21] Andrew Ellul & Vijay Yerramilli, "Stronger Risk Controls, Lower Risk: Evidence from U.S. Bank Holding Companies", 68 J. Fin. 1757 (2013).

[22] Directive 2013/36/EU of the European Parliament and of the Council on Access to the Activity of Credit Institutions and the Prudential Supervision of Credit Institutions and Investment Firms, Amending Directive 2002/87/EC and Repealing Directives 2006/48/EC and 2006/49/EC [2013] OJ L 176/338; Regulation (EU) No 575/2013 on Prudential Requirements for Credit Institutions and Investment Firms and Amending Regulation (EU) No 648/2012 [2013] OJ L 176/1.

and risk management. In contrast, the US has steered clear of imposing prescriptive rules on bank boards, save as respects compensation committees (discussed in section 4) and for risk management, for which a board committee with oversight over risk management policies is required under Dodd-Frank and the implementing regulations, with heightened requirements for the largest firms.[23]

CRD IV, which applies to credit institutions and investment firms, emphasizes the obligations of the board to monitor the performance, risk controls, compensation strategy, and the integrity of disclosures of the firm.[24] It imposes regulatory duties of care and loyalty on board members.[25] It does not impose any minimum requirements for the proportion of independent directors, or the extent of their independence, save for separation of Chair and Chief Executive and the composition of the nomination, remuneration, and risk committees.[26] However, it does require that board members "commit sufficient time to perform their functions in the institution," and to encourage this, mandates that not more than two non-executive roles at other organizations may be combined with one executive role, and not more than four non-executive roles in total may be held by any individual director.[27] It also requires firms to promote diversity in the boardroom, on the theory that this will assist in "recruiting a broad set of qualities and competences."[28] To this end, nomination committees must specifically introduce targets for representation of women on the boards, although not as regards ethnicity.[29]

CRD IV also imposes both procedural and substantive requirements regarding risk management. Procedurally, it emphasizes the importance of overall risk management functions that are proportionate to the nature, scale, and complexity of the risks inherent in the firm's business model.[30] It also requires boards to "devote sufficient time to consideration of risks," and for large firms to establish a risk committee of the board comprised of non-executive directors.[31] Firms are also required to ensure that they have a "risk management function," which is independent of the operational decision makers, reports to the board, has sufficient stature and resources to ensure that "all material risks are identified, measured, and properly reported", and is capable of delivering a "complete view of the whole range of risks of the institution."[32] Turning to substantive requirements, the Directive requires regulators to specify guidelines regarding the management of various types of risk run by financial institutions.[33] Ironically, however, to the extent that these detailed guidelines adopt different measurement technologies for different types of risk, they may actually make it harder for boards and risk committees to comply with their procedural obligations.[34]

Institutions must also disclose their recruitment and diversity policies for the board and its members' relevant knowledge and expertise, whether or not the firm has a risk committee, and if so, how frequently it meets, and a description of the information flow on risk to the management body.[35]

---

[23] Dodd-Frank Act § 165(h); 12 CFR 252.22, 252.33.   [24] Art. 88(1).   [25] Art. 91(7)–(8).
[26] Arts. 88(2), 95.   [27] Art. 91.   [28] Art. 91(10).
[29] Arts. 88(2)(a), 91(10). For a critical overview of the measures described in this paragraph see Luca Enriques & Dirk Zetsche, "Quack Corporate Governance, Round III? Bank Board Regulation Under the New European Capital Requirement Directive", 16 Theoretical Inq. L. 211 (2015).
[30] Art. 74(2).   [31] Art. 76(2)–(3).   [32] Art. 76(5).   [33] Arts. 77–87.
[34] See *supra* text to notes 19–20.   [35] CRR, Art. 435(2).

4 Executive Pay in Banks

4.1 History and Problems

Prior to the crisis, the financial sector made enthusiastic use of performance-related pay.[36] In keeping with the pattern for non-financial firms, CEOs of US banks typically received far more variable pay than base salary.[37] For example, Fahlenbrach and Stulz ("F&S"), studying compensation of US bank CEOs in 2006, report a mean base salary of $760,000, which is less than a sixth of the mean variable pay (comprising cash bonus and equity compensation) of $5.3 million.[38] This heavy weighting towards variable pay—characterized as "performance-related"—was relatively recent. Historically, US bank executives received a greater fraction of fixed pay than was the norm in non-financial firms.[39] Following the deregulation of banking in the 1990s, the use of equity-based pay rose sharply in the sector, such that by the turn of the century, bank executive pay looked very similar to other sectors.[40]

Just as before the crisis no one questioned the application to banks of ordinary governance standards, it has now become an article of faith that high levels of variable pay for bank executives tend to encourage "excessive" risk taking. Yet such a generalization might be just as misleading as the pre-crisis complacency. We need to look carefully at the details in order to understand the mechanisms in play.

Did having "skin in the game" restrain risk taking? First, we should note that bank executives typically held significant holdings of stock in their firms. In F&S's sample, the mean value of the stock CEOs held in their own firm was $87.5 million, approximately 0.4% of the outstanding stock.[41] In part this would have been because stock awards were often "restricted" for five years, meaning that the CEO could not sell until five years after grant. However, these very large holdings also reflected a significant degree of voluntary exposure by executives—that is, not selling their stock holdings even when they were no longer restricted. As a result, bank CEOs suffered huge losses—averaging $31.5 million—over the

---

[36] Most is known about the compensation of US CEOs and "top five" executives, because US disclosure rules require the most detailed information to be made public about their compensation.

[37] Nevertheless, in comparison to non-financial firms, when controlling for firm characteristics (especially size), banks typically have less CEO total and incentive compensation, and less director compensation: Adams, *supra* note 14, at 27.

[38] Rüdiger Fahlenbrach & René M. Stulz, "Bank CEO Incentives and the Credit Crisis", 99 J. Fin. Econ. 11, 16 (2011).

[39] See Joel F. Houston & Christopher James, "CEO Compensation and Bank Risk: Is Compensation in Banking Structured to Promote Risk Taking?", 36 J. Monetary Econ. 405 (1995); Lazarus Angbazo & Ranga Narayanan, "Top Management Compensation and the Structure of the Board of Directors in Commercial Banks", 1 Eur. Fin. Rev. 239 (1997).

[40] David A. Becher, Terry L. Campbell II & Melissa B. Frye, "Incentive Compensation for Bank Directors: The Impact of Deregulation", 78 J. Bus. 1753 (2005); Vicente Cuñat & Maria Guadalupe, "Executive Compensation and Competition in the Banking and Financial Sectors", 33 J. Banking & Fin. 495 (2009); Robert DeYoung, Emma Y. Peng & Meng Yan, "Executive Compensation and Business Policy Choices at U.S. Commercial Banks", 48 J. Fin. Quant. Anal. 1 (2013).

[41] Fahlenbrach & Stulz, *supra* note 38.

period 2006–2008.[42] Should we conclude that because managers had such a substantial amount of "skin in the game," they did not have incentives to indulge in "excessive" risk taking?

Apparently not. While managers clearly had significant downside exposure, looking solely at their holdings of stock does not take account of cash already received from bonuses and stock sales. Bebchuk, Cohen, and Spamann report that the top five executives in Bear Stearns and Lehman Brothers received aggregate cash flows of $2.4 billion over the period 2000–2008.[43] Although these executives suffered losses of approximately $1.4 billion through their holdings of stock in their firms, taking cash flows into account showed they were still ahead by approximately $1 billion over these eight years.[44] In other words, even for the financial firms that failed outright, managers' payouts from good years had greatly exceeded their eventual losses when the firms failed. This asymmetry—upside returns exceeding downside—seems to generalize. Thus F&S report that, taking into account options and cash bonuses, the mean CEO in their sample would receive 2.4% of the value of any increase in the stock price.[45] However, their downside losses would only be 0.4% of any decrease, tracking their holdings of the firm's stock. In short, incentives on the upside were five times as strong as on the downside.

Moreover, this asymmetry of incentives appears linked to underperformance during the financial crisis. F&S report that the greater the managers' incentives to increase the stock price—as measured by the proportion of the increase in value they captured—the worse were bank shareholders' returns during the financial crisis.[46] This suggests that powerfully asymmetric financial incentives encouraged managers to pursue strategies that, at least ex post, turned out to be harmful to shareholders. We need to understand why this may have been the case.

One answer may be that stock options gave incentives to take risks in excess of what was optimal even from the shareholders' perspective. The basic rationale for using options is that—assuming they are correctly priced (that is, "out of the money")—they provide a powerful upside incentive to take actions that will increase the stock price. But might managers be pushed too far? Could options encourage them to pursue risky projects simply for the sake of it? An increase in the volatility of firm's stock price will increase the value of an out-of-the-money option on that stock[47] and if the incentive is sufficiently powerful then managers may be induced to select projects with lower net present values simply because they are more risky. F&S did not find any evidence of a link between the risk-sensitivity of

---

[42] Id., at 23. Note that the median was only $5.1m, however.

[43] Lucian A. Bebchuk, Alma Cohen, & Holger Spamann, "The Wages of Failure: Executive Compensation at Bear Stearns and Lehman 2000–2008", 27 Yale J. Reg. 257 (2010).

[44] Similarly, Bhagat and Bolton look at CEO payoffs in the largest 14 crisis institutions, and find that they took $1.77 bn in net stock sales plus $0.89 bn in cash compensation during the period 2000–2008, a total cashflow of $2.66 bn. In 2008, their equity holdings suffered an aggregate loss of $2.01 bn. Nevertheless, they were better off, on net, over the period by $0.65 bn. Sanjai Bhagat & Brian Bolton, "Financial Crisis and Bank Executive Incentive Compensation", 25 J. Corp. Fin. 313, 319–23 (2014).

[45] Fahlenbrach & Stulz, *supra* note 38, at 17.

[46] F&S gauge the incentive effect for managers by measuring the dollar value CEOs earn from a 1% increase in stock price. Id. This measure—the change in managerial pay associated with a change in the stock price—is known as the "delta" of the compensation package.

[47] This is because the increase in volatility implies an increase in the states of the world in which the option will be in the money. The extent to which an increase in the volatility of the share price results in an increase in the value of managerial compensation is known as the "vega" of the latter.

managers' portfolios and shareholder returns.[48] In other words, they found no evidence that option compensation led managers to select projects with lower expected values—thus harming even shareholders—simply because they are more risky. However, this does not imply that option contracts do not encourage a degree of risk taking that is detrimental to creditors or society more generally.

Were the risks excessive from a societal perspective? The costs of financial firm failure are not borne entirely by shareholders. Implicit or explicit government guarantees of creditors mean that these costs are only partially priced into credit agreements. As a result, shareholders as a group may stand to benefit from strategies that increase default risk but generate more positive cashflows in other states of the world. Consistently with this, Balachandran et al. report a positive relationship between managerial equity compensation and default risk.[49] That is, firms whose managers had the strongest incentives to maximize share price were also those most likely to fail. However, this cynical perspective fails to explain why managers did not reduce their holdings of shares in anticipation of the financial crisis. Had managers simply been ramping up risk in order to transfer losses to the state, it would make no sense for them to remain holding shares at the time the losses crystallized. Moreover, this perspective also overlooks the fact that—in the US and UK at least—most bank shareholders are diversified, meaning that they incur significant losses through their other portfolio firms should systemic harms materialize.[50] Such shareholders would not want bank managers to take socially excessive risks.

What about more junior employees? We have so far focused on the compensation of senior managers, primarily because these are the only group for whom detailed compensation information must be disclosed. Consequently, far less is known about the compensation of less senior employees. However, such literature as exists suggests that incentive problems stemming from miscalibrated "performance" pay may have been most egregious at the level of trading and sales staff, rather than senior executives. Shortly after the onset of the financial crisis, the (then) Financial Services Authority (FSA) carried out a study of bank employee compensation practices in the UK.[51] They found that cash bonuses accounted for a large proportion of employees' pay. However, these bonuses were typically not linked to the stock price, but to *net revenues* in that financial year. This seems an astonishingly poor way to motivate employees. Where a financial firm takes on a risk under a contract, it is functionally—albeit not legally—providing insurance to the counterparty in respect of that risk. We would expect the premium for providing this insurance to be reflected in the price of the contract. It is clearly a mistake to reward people for writing insurance based only on the size of the premium they earn, without taking into account the risks insured. This simply gives them incentives to commit their firm to the biggest risks they can find, because these will attract the highest premiums. But this is precisely the effect of rewarding employees in a financial firm on the basis of revenues, without any adjustment for risk.

---

[48] Id., at 18–19. But see Bhagat & Bolton, *supra* note 44.

[49] Sudhakar Balachandran, Bruce Kogut, & Hitesh Harnal, "Did Executive Compensation Encourage Extreme Risk-Taking in Financial Institutions?", Working Paper (2011).

[50] John Armour & Jeffrey N. Gordon, "Systemic Harms and Shareholder Value", 6 J. Legal Analysis 35 (2014).

[51] FSA, Reforming Remuneration Practices in Financial Services, Consultation Paper 09/10 (2009).

This disturbing picture is reinforced by Acharya et al.'s innovative study of the impact of employee incentive compensation.[52] These authors identify the aggregate compensation for sub-board-level employees by subtracting the (disclosed) compensation for "top five" executives from the (disclosed) aggregate total compensation paid by financial firms, and then determine how sensitive this total compensation is to the firm's revenues (not stock price). This gives a measure of the extent to which employees are incentivized to maximize revenues in a given year. The authors go on to report that greater revenue-sensitivity of aggregate employee cash pay was associated with greater default risk for the firm. This implies that incentive contracts of the type the FSA reported—linking pay to revenues—were associated with greater default risk.

In light of our discussion in section 4 about the deficiencies of internal monitoring, we can offer a conjecture about the ways in which senior management may have made mistakes about risk taking. Management with strong incentives to increase the stock price may have been more inclined to focus simply on revenues generated by employees and (mistakenly) reflected in the stock price, paying insufficient attention to appropriate risk adjustment of returns. That is, there was likely a negative synergy between the extent to which managers were encouraged to "manage the stock price" and the extent to which the stock price failed—owing to opacity—to take into account the true downside costs of firms' strategies.

4.2 The New Regulation of Executive Compensation in Banks

Bank executive compensation became an early target for regulatory reform. At the G20 summit in Pittsburgh in September 2009, member countries circulated a *Statement of Principles* regarding executive pay in the financial services sector.[53] This encompassed a programme of reform with the following three pillars: First, internal governance mechanisms were to be strengthened as regards the process of setting compensation. Second, the substance of compensation packages should be more closely aligned with "prudent risk taking." Third, there should be more disclosure, and effective supervisory oversight, of both the process and substance of compensation arrangements.

These principles were first implemented in Europe through CRD III,[54] and subsequently tightened considerably in CRD IV,[55] which goes significantly beyond what is envisaged by the Financial Stability Board's (FSB) *Statement of Principles*. In the US, the Dodd–Frank Act requires the appropriate Federal regulators to introduce rules in relation to internal governance,[56] disclosure of executive pay, and substantive regulation of compensation contracts.[57]

---

[52] Viral Acharya, Lubomir P. Litov, & Simone M. Sepe, "Seeking Alpha, Taking Risks: Evidence from Non-Executive Pay in U.S. Bank Holding Companies", Working Paper (2014).

[53] Financial Stability Forum, FSF Principles for Sound Compensation Practices (Apr. 2, 2009).

[54] Directive 2010/76/EU [2010] OJ L 329/3. In the UK specifically, this was implemented under the Financial Services Act 2010, ss 4–6, and amendments to the FSA's (now FCA's) Remuneration Code: FSA, Revising the Remuneration Code, Consultation Paper 10/19 (2010).

[55] Directive 2013/36/EU, OJ [2013] L176/338.

[56] §952, inserting new §10C into the Securities Exchange Act of 1934.

[57] §956 (enhanced disclosure and reporting of compensation arrangements at financial institutions and provision for prohibition of "types of incentive-based compensation arrangement, that the regulators determine encourages inappropriate risks by covered financial institutions").

Rules regarding internal governance, in particular the role of compensation committees, have been implemented by the SEC, and in 2016 there was a revised interagency rule proposal regarding enhanced disclosure of compensation in financial firms and substantive standards on compensation contracts.[58] However, it currently appears unlikely that this proposal will be implemented under the Trump administration. Table 42.1 sets out the firms and executives to which the regulations apply in the EU and US, respectively. We now turn to consider specific details of the rules that have emerged.

4.2.1 The Process of Setting Compensation

The FSB's first pillar proposed more active internal oversight of the setting of compensation.[59] At the center is the idea of a remuneration committee of the board with sufficient independence and expertise to exercise appropriate judgment on remuneration policies. The remuneration committee should work with the firm's risk committee to evaluate the incentives created by the firm's compensation arrangements so as to ensure that these are consistent with the risk committee's assessment of the firm's financial condition and prospects, and with regulatory guidelines. It should also oversee an annual review of compensation practices which should be produced for regulators. Employees working in the firm's risk and compliance function should have their remuneration set independently of the firm's performance, at a level sufficient to attract qualified and experienced staff, and their performance should be assessed on the basis of the achievement of the objectives of their functions (that is, risk management).

This was the least controversial aspect of the FSB's proposals, and—with the addition of a nod to greater involvement by risk management officials in the process—largely reflected existing best practice.[60]

4.2.2 Substantive Regulation of Executive Compensation Arrangements

Much more significant are the substantive guidelines regarding the content of executive compensation, which are to be overseen by regulators. At their heart is a commitment to continued use of performance-related pay, but in a manner better aligned with the long-term and risk-adjusted performance of the firm. There are two principal routes by which the guidelines seek to do this. First, variable compensation awards must be adjusted ex ante in accordance with the riskiness of the activities undertaken by the employee and/or the firm.[61] While this idea is easy to state in principle, it is harder to implement in practice, because it requires a benchmark of risk. Any such benchmark in turn creates incentives to game the system.

The second limb operates in part as a check against such gaming. It requires that performance-related pay should vary with ex post realizations of risk outcomes, over a

---

[58] U.S. Department of the Treasury et al., "Notice of Proposed Rulemaking and Request for Comment: Incentive-Based Compensation Arrangements", 81 Fed. Register 37670 (2016).

[59] Financial Stability Board, FSB Principles for Sound Compensation Practices: Implementation Standards 2 (Sept. 25, 2009).

[60] See, e.g., FSA, Revising the Remuneration Code, Consultation Paper 10/19, at 24–25 (2010).

[61] See CRD IV, Art. 92(a) and (g)(ii).

Table 42.1 To which financial firms does the regulation of executive compensation apply?

	EU	US
Which firms?	CRD IV Art 3, CRR Art 4(1). "*Credit institutions*" (firms taking both deposits and granting credit); "*Investment firms*" (firms providing investment services or engaging in investment activities, including brokers, dealers, investment managers, underwriters and market operators).	Dodd–Frank Act of 2010, § 956 "*Covered financial institutions*" (firms taking deposits or their holding companies, registered broker-dealers, credit unions, investment advisors, Fannie Mae and Freddie Mac, and any other financial institution that Federal regulators jointly determine should be treated as such) with assets > $1 billion.
Which employees?	CRD IV Art 92(2) and Delegated Regulation (EU) No 604/2014. "*Material risk-takers*" (categories of employee whose professional activities have a material impact on [the firm's] risk profile). Identification based on both internal criteria developed by the firm and qualitative (functions performed) and quantitative (compensation value) criteria applied by supervisors. *Qualitative criteria*: Board and senior management; staff with the authority to commit significant credit risk exposures. *Quantitative criteria*: (1) Total gross remuneration > €500 000; or (2) among firm's 0.3% most highly paid staff; or (3) remuneration equal to senior managers; or (4) variable pay could exceed €75 000 and 75% of fixed pay.	Dodd–Frank Act of 2010, § 956 and Proposed Rule "*Senior executive officers and significant risk-takers*": senior executive officers, and any other executive officer or employee who received total compensation in top 5% (for firms with assets >$250bn) or top 2% (for firms with assets >$50bn but <$250bn) of firm's payroll, or who can expose 0.5% or more of the firm's net worth.

sufficiently long period of time. The FSB consequently prescribes that for senior executives and other employees whose actions have a material impact on the firm's risk exposure ("material risk takers"), a "substantial proportion" of pay should be performance-related over time.[62] A large part of this variable pay (no less than 40%, rising to at least 60% for the most senior executives) should be deferred for a period of at least three years, but possibly longer depending on the risks associated with the business.[63] This is most easily done for equity-related pay (stock and options), by restricting the manager's ability to sell stock or exercise the options for a longer period. The FSB also suggests that at least half of variable pay should be awarded in equity. Some part of cash bonuses can also be deferred, with the possibility

---

[62] FSB, *supra* note 59, at 3.   [63] Id.

that it will not vest if negative performance is realized. This deferred compensation must then be subject to clawback—a so called "malus" award—if poor performance outcomes are realized within the vesting period.[64]

Although the EU first implemented these guidelines under CRD III, it then went significantly beyond them with CRD IV.[65] CRD IV imposes an outright cap on the amount of variable compensation that may be paid.[66] It may not exceed the amount of fixed pay for any individual, although with the approval of a supermajority of the shareholders, it may be up to twice the size of fixed pay. What is more, the rules regarding the identification of material risk takers (to whom the restrictions apply) are extensive in their coverage.[67] They apply to all employees of EU-based organizations, including, for example, those working in New York or Singapore.[68] Up to 25% of variable compensation may be discounted (for the purposes of the cap) at a supervisor-determined rate, provided that it is deferred for at least five years.[69] Moreover, up to 100% of variable compensation (not just that part which has been deferred) is subject to "malus" or clawback provisions.[70]

In the US, implementation of the FSB *Principles* has been proposed through an interagency rule made under the mandate conferred by section 956 of the Dodd–Frank Act. The current draft outlines standards as regards incentive-based compensation, such that it must not "encourage inappropriate risks" either by providing "excessive compensation, fees, or benefits," or "that could lead to a material financial loss."[71] Moreover, for institutions with assets in excess of $50 billion, there are detailed rules requiring deferral of 40–60% (depending on employee seniority and the size of the firm) of variable compensation for at least three years (or four years for firms with assets of more than $250 billion), and its adjustment downward to reflect losses realized during this period. However, it appears unlikely that these proposed rules will be implemented under the Trump administration.

The EU's step of capping the ratio of variable pay to fixed pay is likely to lead to an increase in base rates of pay, given an internationally competitive market for executive talent. It may also have a counter-intuitive impact on risk taking. This is because, according to some commentators, the base pay in a traditional investment banking compensation scheme was set below the competitive rate, such that the bonus already incorporated a significant amount of downside performance sensitivity. Increasing the proportion of fixed pay will reduce this. Decreasing the proportion of variable pay will also reduce the upside payoffs. As a result, executives will have less incentives to take risks with upside components, and more incentive to take risks with downside components.[72] Moreover, incentives to increase performance

---

[64] The FSB's guidelines also seek to ensure that the payment of variable compensation does not occur at times when the firm's capital is, or is likely to become, impaired, or when it is in receipt of government assistance.

[65] At least 50% of any variable compensation must be equity linked; at least 40% of variable compensation must be deferred for more than 3 years; at least 60% where it is "particularly high." And the deferral period must relate to the risks of the business: CRD IV, Art. 94(1)(l)–(m).

[66] CRD IV, Art. 94(1)(g).

[67] Commission Delegated Regulation (EU) No. 604/2014 supplementing Directive 2013/36/EU with regard to regulatory technical standards with respect to qualitative and appropriate quantitative criteria to identify categories of staff whose professional activities have a material impact on an institution's risk profile [2014] OJ L167/30.

[68] CRD IV, Art. 92(1).   [69] CRD IV, Art. 94(1)(g)(iii).   [70] CRD IV, Art. 94(1)(n).

[71] U.S. Proposed Rule, *supra* note 58, § _.4.

[72] Kevin J. Murphy, "Regulating Banking Bonuses in the European Union: A Case Study in Unintended Consequences", 19 Eur. Fin. Mgmt. 631 (2013).

will entirely dry up once the bonus has been "maxed out." Coupled with deferrals and realized performance contingencies, it will create incentives to "manage" performance into subsequent periods as well. There are also likely to be employment selection effects. Making pay less performance-sensitive will select away from highly talented individuals and in favor of less talented types.

4.2.3 *Disclosure and Supervision of Compensation Practices*

The FSB's third pillar exhorts that information about both the process of setting compensation and the quantum of pay for top executives should be disclosed publicly, at least annually.[73] Process information should include information about the composition and mandate of the remuneration committee; the most important criteria used in setting compensation (performance measurement, risk adjustment, pay-performance linkage, deferral policy and vesting criteria, and the parameters used for choosing between cash and other forms of compensation). As regards substantive pay, there should be aggregate disclosure of the total (and the breakdown into various components) paid to all senior executives and material risk takers. This level of disclosure was already largely in place in the US under existing rules for disclosure by public corporations of executive compensation arrangements. In the EU, the relevant disclosure obligations are found in the Capital Requirements Regulation accompanying CRD IV.[74]

The FSB also called for "rigorous and sustained" domestic supervisory engagement with the implementation of the FSB Principles.[75] In particular, compensation practices should be taken into account as part of supervisory risk review of financial service firms. Failure by firms to implement appropriate compensation policies should result in "prompt remedial action" to offset any associated risks. This would be implemented in the US through proposed rules made under section 956 of Dodd–Frank, which would require covered financial institutions to keep records for at least seven years of incentive-based compensation plans. In the EU, this will be implemented by Article 75 of CRD IV.

5 SHAREHOLDER RIGHTS

Early responses to the financial crisis suggested that lack of shareholder oversight was part of the problem in the governance of financial institutions. For example, the Walker Review, commissioned by the UK government in 2009, concluded that greater engagement by institutional shareholders with boards of financial institutions was desirable.[76] Similarly, the Dodd–Frank Act in the US introduced powers for the SEC to strengthen shareholders' rights, in particular their ability to put forward candidates for the board not supported by incumbent management and a right to vote to approve the compensation of senior executives.[77]

---

[73] FSB Principles, 2009, ¶3; Implementation Standards ¶15.
[74] CR Regulation, Art. 450.   [75] FSB Principles 2009 ¶3, Implementation Standards ¶16.
[76] David Walker, A Review of Corporate Governance in UK Banks and Other Financial Industry Entities: Final Recommendations 12, 68–89 (2009).
[77] Dodd–Frank Act of 2010 §§ 951, 971.

It is far from clear that such proposals are appropriate. As shareholders enjoy limited liability, then in the presence of imperfectly priced deposit insurance, or the expectation of a bail-out for "too big to fail" firms, we might think they would have incentives to encourage firms to take more risk than is socially desirable.[78] Consistently with this, Ferreira et al. report that US banks in which shareholders enjoy objectively greater power—in terms of shareholder rights and ability to control management—were more likely to be bailed out during the financial crisis.[79]

We might expect this concern to be ameliorated where investors hold shares in banks as part of a diversified portfolio. Such investors will internalize a large part of the costs to society of bank failure through losses to their other portfolio firms.[80] On the other hand, the problems will be exacerbated by the presence of controlling shareholders, who will be in a position to make more of a difference to the control of the firm than dispersed shareholders, and who will be less diversified and so care less about impacts on other firms. In a study of large banks from across 48 countries, Laeven and Levine report that the proportion of the cash flow rights enjoyed by large shareholders is positively correlated with bank risk taking.[81] To this end, many regimes require regulatory approval of the identity of major shareholders as a condition of bank licensing.[82] Similar restrictions apply to changes of control, with regulators reserving the right to refuse to approve such deals.[83] A key factor as regards such approval is the reputation of the controlling shareholder.[84]

6 LIABILITY RULES

Is it enough simply to moderate the "upside" returns that those running a bank receive, by altering the terms of executive compensation? Or should we also push for the imposition of more "downside" liability? The classic objections to liability for those controlling a business firm—at least for business decisions (as opposed to conflicts of interest)—are that judges lack the capacity to review such decisions effectively, and that fear of liability will induce undiversified managers to take less risk than diversified shareholders might want. In the case of firms whose activities have the propensity to create systemic risk, this logic might actually be reversed. Diversified shareholders may actually stand to lose proportionally more, in the case of default, than executives who have a stake in the firm through equity-based compensation. This is because systemic harms can impact negatively on their entire portfolios, not just on their holding in the bank. Consequently, for banks with diversified share ownership and managers with equity-based pay, fear of liability would not lead to undesirable risk-aversion on the part of managers. Rather, it might simply rein in undesirably risky activities such managers might otherwise take.[85]

---

[78] See *supra* text to notes 49–50.
[79] Daniel Ferreira, David Kershaw, Tom Kirchmaier, & Edmund-Philipp Schuster, "Shareholder Empowerment and Bank Bailouts", ECGI Finance Working Paper No. 345/2013.
[80] Armour & Gordon, *supra* note 50.
[81] Luc Laeven & Ross Levine, "Bank Governance, Regulation and Risk Taking", 93 J. Fin. Econ. 259 (2009).
[82] E.g. CRD IV, Art. 14.   [83] CRD IV, Arts. 22–23.   [84] CRD IV, Art. 23(1)(a).
[85] Armour & Gordon, *supra* note 50.

Such liability is in principle available in the US in the case of banks entering FDIC receivership proceedings.[86] However, for other banks, directors and officers are shielded from liability for errors and omissions in relation to business judgment and oversight, unless they are so egregious as to evince a lack of good faith.[87] In the UK and many other European countries, directors and officers do in principle owe a duty of care in relation to business decisions, but this is almost never enforced. Civil procedure rules make it costly for shareholder litigation to be commenced. Enforcement by public agencies seems a more worthwhile strategy in this case. Here, the problem has been that agencies lack standing to pursue private law obligations, but rather enforce a parallel regulatory regime. Within this, there has been a lack of clarity as to individual versus organizational responsibility.[88] Upon the input of the UK's Parliamentary Commission on Banking Standards, UK supervisory authorities have approved a new 'Senior Managers Regime' aimed at focusing regulatory responsibility onto specific individuals, who should then become natural targets for regulatory enforcement.[89] Moreover, a new criminal offense for bank senior managers whose reckless misconduct causes their firm to fail has been introduced.[90]

7 Conclusion

In this chapter, we have explored why the corporate governance framework that is applied for most businesses, in which managers are encouraged to focus on maximizing the stock price, is less well suited to the case of banks. Financial assets are particularly hard to monitor, and so managerial agency costs are unusually high. Banks' business model makes them unusually fragile, and their failure imposes costs on society beyond those borne by their investors. As a consequence, ordinary mechanisms of corporate governance, which rely on stock market prices to incentivize managers, are liable to yield perverse results. Managers may exploit the opacity of financial assets to game the measures, and regulators will face an uphill struggle to uncover this. Maximizing the stock price may not be the right approach in any event, as shareholders' interests may diverge from those of society. Reforms since the financial crisis have gone some way to address these problems. Two particularly beneficial steps have been the push toward greater resources being deployed in risk management and internal monitoring functions, and an attempt to better calibrate incentives in relation to executive pay. The latter task will be extremely challenging for regulators to get right, but the former seems more promising.

---

[86] See Financial Institutions Reform, Recovery, and Enforcement Act of 1989 ("FIRREA"), Pub. L. No. 101–173, Title II, § 212(k), 103 Stat. 243, codified at 12 U.S.C. § 1821(k).

[87] *Stone v. Ritter*, 911 A.2d 362, 370 (Del. Sup. 2006); *In re Citigroup Inc. Shareholder Derivative Litigation*, 964 A.2d 106 (Del. Ch. 2009).

[88] Parliamentary Commission on Banking Standards, Changing Banking for Good, Volume II 289–290 (2013).

[89] See Financial Conduct Authority, CP15/22 Strengthening accountability in banking: Final rules (including feedback on CP14/31 and CP15/5) and consultation on extending the Certification Regime to wholesale market activities (2015).

[90] Financial Services (Banking Reform) Act (2013), section 36.

CHAPTER 43

.....

TAX AND CORPORATE GOVERNANCE

The Influence of Tax on Managerial Agency Costs

.....

DAVID M. SCHIZER[1]

1 INTRODUCTION

.....

MOTIVATING managers to be faithful agents of shareholders is a foundational challenge of corporate governance. The tax system is regularly conscripted in this effort.[2] In addition, tax also can affect managerial agency costs in ways policy makers do not intend or even recognize. Yet although the tax system influences managerial agency costs in a number of ways, many of these effects have attracted only limited scholarly attention; tax experts rarely focus on agency costs, while corporate experts seldom have detailed knowledge of tax. To fill this gap, this chapter of the *Oxford Handbook on Corporate Law and Governance* canvasses a broad range of ways that tax influences managerial agency costs, focusing especially on the United States.

In doing so, this chapter has two goals. The first is to help corporate law experts target managerial agency costs more effectively. The analysis here flags when tax is likely to exacerbate agency costs, and when it is likely to mitigate them. Armed with this information, corporate law experts have a better sense of how vigorous a contractual or corporate law response they need. In some cases, a change in the tax law may also be justified. This chapter's second goal, then, is to enhance our understanding of tax rules, shedding light on a set of

[1] Dean Emeritus and the Harvey R. Miller Professor of Law & Economics, Columbia Law School. Copyright David M. Schizer. 2014–2015. All Rights Reserved. Helpful comments were received from John Coates, Michael Doran, Victor Fleischer, Michael Graetz, Robert Jackson, and Barbara Lester, as well as from participants at workshops at Columbia Law School and the Tax Club.
[2] Steven A. Bank, "Tax, Corporate Governance, and Norms", 61 Wash. & Lee L. Rev. 1159, 1162 (2004) (describing US tax as a "means to preempt the traditional state role in the regulation of corporations without actually establishing a system of federal incorporation").

welfare effects that are important but understudied. After all, tax policy is more likely to enhance welfare if policy makers weigh *all* possible welfare effects, including managerial agency costs.

Overall, the US tax system's record in influencing agency costs is not encouraging. After all, the system's priority is not to reduce agency costs, but to raise revenue efficiently and fairly. Government tax experts do not usually have the expertise or motivation to tackle corporate governance problems. Tax also is a poor fit because it typically applies mandatorily and uniformly, while responses to agency cost should be molded to the context. For example, promoting stock options or leverage will be valuable in some settings, but disastrous in others. There also are political hurdles to be overcome. Accordingly, when tax rules target agency costs, the results are often poorly tailored or even counterproductive. This is all the more true when tax influences agency costs by accident, instead of by design.

Fortunately, the effects are not all bad. On the positive side of the ledger, US tax rules encourage performance-based pay both intentionally and inadvertently, albeit in blunt ways.[3] In addition, by taxing intercompany dividends, the US keeps block-holders in one firm from indirectly controlling other firms. In so doing, tax discourages "pyramidal" ownership, which is a common source of agency costs in other jurisdictions.[4] US tax rules also encourage leverage, which usually (but not always) mitigates managerial agency costs.[5] Likewise, some tax rules favor long-term ownership,[6] which can motivate shareholders to monitor management more carefully. The need to disclose financial information on a corporate tax return can also discipline management.[7] Discouraging the use of offshore accounts and off-balance sheet entities, moreover, can keep managers from cheating shareholders, as well as the fisc.[8]

On the other side of the ledger, US tax rules can be a reason (or excuse) for flawed pay.[9] Managers also can use tax as a pretext to retain earnings, and also to oppose takeovers that put their jobs at risk. Tax also can be invoked to justify "empire building" acquisitions as well as hedging, each of which appeals more to undiversified managers than to diversified shareholders.[10] US tax rules also encourage firms to incorporate offshore or to use

---

[3] David M. Schizer, "Executives and Hedging: The Fragile Legal Foundation of Incentive Compatibility", 100 Colum. L. Rev. 440 (2000) (hereinafter "Executives and Hedging").

[4] Randall Morck, Daniel Wolfenzon, & Bernard Yeung, "Corporate Governance, Economic Entrenchment, and Growth", 43 J. Econ. Lit. 655 (2005).

[5] See generally John R. Graham, "Taxes and Corporate Finance: A Review", 16 Rev. Fin. Stud. 1075 (2003).

[6] See David M. Schizer, "Realization as Subsidy", 73 N.Y.U. L. Rev. 1549 (1998) (hereinafter "Realization as Subsidy").

[7] Marjorie E. Kornhauser, "Corporate Regulation and the Origins of the Corporate Income Tax", 66 Ind. L. J. 53, 133–34 (1990–1991).

[8] Mihir A. Desai & Dhammika Dharmapala, Tax and Corporate Governance: An Economic Approach 14–15, in Tax and Corporate Governance (Wolfgang Schön ed., 2008) (tax system and shareholders have a common interest in targeting "complexity and obfuscation" that can be used both for tax avoidance and for "earnings manipulation . . . the concealment of obligations . . . or outright diversion").

[9] David M. Schizer, "Tax Constraints on Indexed Options", 149 U. Pa. L. Rev. 1941 (2000–2001) (hereinafter "Indexed Options").

[10] See, e.g., John R. Graham & Daniel A. Rogers, "Do Firms Hedge in Response to Tax Incentives?", 57 J. Fin. 815 (2002).

pass-through entities, even though these steps can weaken shareholders' corporate law rights.[11]

This chapter concentrates on public companies, where the separation of ownership and control is especially pronounced. The focus is on "C-corporations," since pass-through entities (such as S-corporations, LLCs, and partnerships) are generally ineligible for public trading.

While the topic here is how tax can affect agency costs, causation also can run the other way: that is, agency costs can affect tax. For instance, a manager whose bonus is based on accounting earnings might reject a tax planning strategy that reduces book earnings. If so, agency costs (and accounting rules) are serving as non-tax constraints on tax planning (or "frictions"). Frictions are not the focus of this chapter, but a few are mentioned along the way.

After section 2 assesses why tax is an imperfect vehicle for mitigating managerial agency costs, section 3 assesses how tax influences the compensation of managers. Section 4 analyzes how tax affects management decisions about distributing and investing firm resources. Section 5 considers how the tax system influences the ability and incentives of shareholders to monitor management, as well as how the tax system *itself* monitors managers. Section 6 is the conclusion.

2 An Imperfect Vehicle for Mitigating Managerial Agency Costs

Although there is a plausible theoretical case for using tax to influence managerial agency costs, tax is likely to be an imperfect vehicle for a number of reasons.

2.1 Agency Costs, Free Riding, and Externalities

In theory, a tax rule that successfully enhances corporate governance is appealing, since poor governance leads to suboptimal allocations of capital, less innovation, inflated costs, and slower economic growth. Of course, a government role is unnecessary if shareholders are effective in monitoring management. Yet although monitoring is in their collective interest, individual shareholders would prefer to free ride on others. As a result, monitoring usually is undersupplied. By compensating for this free riding, the government can enhance welfare.

2.2 An Existing and Potentially Persuasive Mechanism to Influence Managers

Even though there is a plausible case for government intervention, is tax the right instrument? One advantage is that managers pay attention to tax. They want to reduce their own

---

[11] Mihir A. Desai & James R. Hines, Jr., "Expectations and Expatriations: Tracing the Causes and Consequences of Corporate Inversions", 55 Nat. T. J. 409 (2002).

tax liabilities as well as the firm's tax bill (as long as doing so isn't costly to them). Using this existing mechanism for communicating government policy to management avoids the costs of building another from scratch.

Of course, tax considerations are not always persuasive to managers. While executives want to reduce the firm's tax bill (and, of course, their own), they have other priorities as well, such as maximizing the firm's accounting earnings. Indeed, managers sometimes favor book over tax when these goals are in conflict.[12]

2.3 Mismatch in Institutional Focus and Expertise

Another limitation of using tax to constrain agency costs is the mismatch in institutional focus and expertise. Many government tax experts do not have deep experience with key corporate governance problems or potential solutions. Most do not view these issues as central to their mission. This lack of focus and expertise helps explain why some tax rules targeting agency costs pursue misguided goals, while others pursue sensible goals in poorly tailored ways.

2.4 Political Constraints and Symbolic Legislation

These deficiencies sometimes derive also from political dynamics. In enacting these rules, Congress often responds to critical media reports about a particular practice. At the same time, organized interest groups exert offsetting pressure to keep this response limited. A politically expedient reaction, then, is to target the abuse, while allowing an obscure way for it to continue. Since these rules and the targeted practices are usually complex, unsophisticated constituents are unlikely to know how narrow the response actually is. As a result, government officials can claim credit with these constituents without alienating affected interest groups.

2.5 Poorly Tailored Scope: The Drawbacks of Uniform and Mandatory Rules

These political constraints, combined with the mismatch in expertise and institutional focus, tend to breed poorly tailored rules. Some are easy to avoid. A modest tweak allows a

---

[12] See, e.g., John R. Graham, Michelle Hanlon, Terry Shevlin, & Nemit Shroff, "Incentives for Tax Planning and Avoidance: Evidence from the Field", 3 Acct. Rev. 991 (2014) (surveying 600 publicly traded firms and finding that top management at 84% care at least as much about the GAAP earnings as they do about taxes); Douglas A. Shackelford & Terry Shevlin, "Empirical Tax Research in Accounting", 31 J. Acct. & Econ. 321 (2001) (noting that negative effect on reported earnings serves as constraint on tax planning). But cf. Michelle Hanlon, Edward Maydew, & Terry Shevlin, "Book-Tax Conformity and the Information Content of Earnings", U. Mich. Working Paper (2005) (noting that firms responded to a change in US tax law, which enhanced book-tax conformity, by reporting lower earnings in order to reduce their tax bill).

firm or manager to dodge a well-deserved penalty or claim an unwarranted benefit. Other measures are too broad. A practice that compounds agency costs in one setting may mitigate them in another. The answer can vary by industry, firm size, dispersion of share ownership, overall market conditions, and so forth. The tax authorities may not be sensitive to these differences. In addition, unlike corporate law, whose default rules can be tailored to a firm's circumstances, tax rules usually are mandatory and uniform. In principle, tax rules could vary with the context or be waivable (e.g., by a board or shareholder vote), but this sort of tax rule is rare.

In navigating these tax rules, firms typically rely on the ingenuity of law firms, compensation consultants, and other professional advisors. Their services do not come cheap, and shareholders usually are footing the bill. These planning costs are regrettable even when the goal is to reduce agency costs—and all the more so when the opposite goal is pursued.

2.6 The Magnitude of the Penalty or Subsidy

In targeting agency costs, tax subsidies or penalties must have not only the right scope but also the right magnitude. In other words, the *amount* has to be calibrated to the relevant externality. Unfortunately, though, government tax experts are unlikely to have the expertise to pick the right level, especially if the externality varies with the context.

An additional problem is that the level varies with the taxpayer's marginal rate when a deduction or exclusion is used.[13] Yet marginal rates obviously are not set with managerial agency costs in mind. For example, a firm with substantial net operating losses, which would not pay taxes anyway, could be immune from the penalty. If anything, this seems backwards. Firms may be unprofitable *because of* agency costs, and these firms should not be left out. Moreover, to the extent that marginal rates otherwise vary with income—as is more true of LLCs (subject to individual rates) than corporations (subject to largely flat corporate rates) in the US—the penalty or subsidy is lower for less profitable firms. Credits and some excise taxes can avoid these problems, as can rules that affect the tax bill of the manager instead of the firm.

2.7 Imposition on the Wrong Party

There is another reason to target the manager instead of the firm: the manager is more likely to pay attention. After all, a manager who wastes the firm's money on lavish offices or travel accounts presumably will not mind inflating the firm's tax bill. Since tax is complex and esoteric, shareholders may not notice. In contrast, managers usually will know (and care) about their *own* tax liabilities. Admittedly, the latter incentive is neutralized if the firm grosses the manager up. But, at least in some cases, a gross-up could discourage the relevant practice by calling more attention to it.

---

[13] A deduction is worth the amount of tax that is avoided, which in turn depends on the taxpayer's marginal rate. If a firm has a 35% marginal rate, then a dollar of deductions avoids 35 cents of tax. If the marginal rate is 25%, a dollar of deductions is worth only 25 cents.

2.8 Accidental Effects

These issues arise not only when the government uses the tax law deliberately (so-called "Pigouvian" measures), but also when effects are unintended. For example, a goal pursued by the tax system, such as reducing compliance costs or blocking a form of tax planning, could end up affecting agency costs as well. In some cases, government tax experts may not even be *aware* of these accidental effects. When they are, they often won't consider them *their* problems to solve.

This mismatch in expertise and mission is a problem, then, not only because tax experts are unlikely to craft a successful Pigouvian measure, but also because they are unlikely to consider managerial agency costs when making run-of-the-mill tax policy decisions. Tax experts may overvalue a tax rule that fares well on traditional tax policy criteria, but has adverse corporate governance effects. Likewise, they may undervalue a rule that is weak on traditional criteria, but diminishes managerial agency costs. Of course, agency costs are not a trump that always should override these traditional tax policy considerations, but they should not be neglected either.

For parallel reasons, an interdisciplinary perspective is also valuable for corporate governance experts. For example, if a change in tax law exacerbates agency costs, corporate experts should consider an offsetting change in contracts, corporate law, or securities law. Admittedly, though, this sort of coordination is a delicate matter, which requires enough tax expertise to know of the change and its likely effect on agency costs.

There are good reasons, then, for the government to develop more interdisciplinary expertise, although it may be optimistic to expect them to do so. Practitioners and academic commentators can play a valuable role in identifying unintended effects and suggesting reforms to respond to them.

2.9 Randomness and Instability

Just as tax effects can be *enacted* unintentionally, they also can be *repealed* unintentionally. The tax rule can change for policy or political reasons having nothing to do with corporate governance. When this happens, the good news is that executives are unlikely to capture the process. The bad news is that changes are essentially random. They are as likely to exacerbate agency costs as to mitigate them.

3 COMPENSATION

To see how these dynamics play out, we turn to a key setting in which tax influences agency costs: executive compensation. In the US, a number of Pigouvian tax provisions regulate executive pay. Some pursue worthy goals in imperfect ways, while others are misguided. There also are unintended effects. In some cases, the tax system has its own reasons to target activity that could compound agency costs. In other cases, the effects are essentially an accident. Ironically, the unintended effects have a somewhat better track record, a reality that does not inspire confidence.

3.1 Pigouvian Provisions Encouraging Performance-Based Pay

3.1.1 Performance-Based Pay: A Standard Response to Agency Costs

In general, managers should earn more for doing good work, but this is easier said than done. If cash bonuses reward executives for meeting specified goals, the right goals must be set and progress must be measured in ways that are hard to manipulate. Alternatively, equity compensation can motivate executives to raise the stock price, but it has three familiar problems. First, equity compensation can tempt managers to use accounting gimmicks (or fraud) to raise the stock price. Second, this pay often rewards executives for general market increases. Third, stock and options create different incentives. Unlike stockholders, option-holders generally do not benefit from dividends, so option grants can exacerbate agency costs by discouraging dividends.[14] Option grants also encourage more risk taking than stock grants.[15] This incentive often is valuable, since managers tend to be more risk averse than shareholders. Yet options sometimes induce *too much* risk.

The right mix of stock, options, and bonuses, then, depends on a broad range of context-specific factors, including the business's maturity, its debt-equity ratio, general market conditions, the executive's overall portfolio and risk preferences, the extent of shareholder monitoring, and the type of industry (since risk taking at banks, for instance, creates unique concerns). One-size-fits-all answers will not be optimal, and sometimes are quite flawed.

3.1.2 Tax Deferral for Equity Compensation

Compared to cash compensation, US tax on equity compensation generally is deferred.[16] During this deferral period, the employer can invest the cash it otherwise would have used to pay cash compensation. When the firm pays tax on these investments, it in effect serves as a surrogate taxpayer for the employee.[17] This arrangement is tax-advantaged, as Daniel Halperin and Alvin Warren have shown, "if the employer earns an after-tax return on the deferred compensation that is higher than that available to the employee."[18] This can happen, for instance, if the firm uses this cash to buy back its stock (e.g., to hedge its obligation on the executive compensation), since (unlike executives) firms are not taxed on gains in their own stock.[19] In other cases, though, the firm cannot earn a higher after-tax return than the executive. For example, if the firm invests in stock of a third party, its tax rate could be *higher*

---

[14] Richard A. Lambert, William N. Lanen, & David F. Larcker, "Executive Stock Option Plans and Corporate Dividend Policy", 24 J. Fin. Quant. Anal. 409 (1989) (noting that executive stock options lose value when firms pay dividends and thus create incentives to retain earnings or repurchase shares).

[15] Wm. Gerard Sanders & Donald C. Hambrick, "Swinging for the Fences: The Effects of CEO Stock Options on Company Risk Taking and Performance", 50 Academy of Man. J. 1055 (2007).

[16] See 26 USC § 83(a) (tax on restricted stock grants generally is deferred until the shares vest, and tax on option grants is deferred until they are exercised). All references to sections are to the Internal Revenue Code of 1986, as amended.

[17] This is an example of what Professors Halperin and Warren call "counterparty deferral." Daniel I. Halperin & Alvin C. Warren, "Understanding Income Tax Deferral", 67 Tax L. Rev. 317 (2014).

[18] Id.   [19] Section 1032(a).

than the executive's tax rate on the same investment.[20] In this case, the arrangement is not tax advantaged, once all the parties' tax burdens are considered.[21]

3.1.3 *Favoring Bonuses and Stock Options: A Worthy Goal Sometimes, but Not Always*

Section 162(m) accords a clearer tax advantage to equity compensation (and other performance-based pay), but in a blunt way. It denies a deduction for pay above $1 million to certain senior executives.[22] The goal was to use tax to police abuses in managerial pay, a model that in principle can be used more generally.[23]

Yet Section 162(m) is not an encouraging precedent. When enacted in 1993, it was explained as a limit on the *amount* of pay. Nevertheless, its main effect has been on the *type* of pay, since it offers a widely used exception for "performance-based compensation."[24] To qualify, pay must be "solely on account of the attainment of . . . pre-established, objective performance goals," and attaining these must be "substantially uncertain."[25] In response, firms shifted from cash compensation to stock options and stock appreciation rights (SARs) in the 1990s,[26] something they were doing for other reasons anyway. Options and SARs qualify as long as they are not in-the-money when issued, as do earnings-based bonuses if the target is challenging enough.[27]

Section 162(m) has introduced potentially useful process requirements. A committee of independent directors must set performance-based targets and confirm that they have been met.[28] In addition, shareholders must vote to approve material terms.[29] These requirements could mitigate agency costs in some cases.

Yet Section 162(m) has also distorted compensation practices in unfortunate ways. For example, the formula for computing performance-based pay can provide discretion to *reduce* pay, but not to *increase* it.[30] This asymmetry can justify (or rationalize) a more generous

---

[20] Under current law, corporate capital gains generally are taxed at 35%, while the individual (long-term) capital gains rate is generally lower.

[21] See David I. Walker, "Is Equity Compensation Tax Advantaged?", 84 B.U. L. Rev. 695, 731 (2004) ("The fisc actually comes out ahead versus cash compensation, since the cost of the employee-level exemption . . . is more than offset by the tax on the employer-level investment").

[22] Section 162(m).

[23] See, e.g., David I. Walker, "A Tax Response to the Executive Pay Problem", 93 B.U. L. Rev. 325 (2013) (proposing surtax on executive pay combined with investor tax relief).

[24] Section 162(m)(4)(C).   [25] Treas. Reg. 1.162-27(e).

[26] Nancy L. Rose & Catherine Wolfram, "Regulating Executive Pay: Using the Tax Code to Influence Chief Executive Officer Compensation", 20 J. Labor Econ. 138 (2002) (finding decrease in rate of growth of cash compensation after 1993); Todd Perry & Marc Zenner, "Pay for Performance? Government Regulation and the Structure of Compensation Contracts", 62 J. Fin. Econ. 453 (2001) (enactment of 162(m) contributed to growth in equity compensation); Brian Hall & Jeffrey B. Liebman, The Taxation of Executive Compensation, in Tax Policy and the Economy 14 (James Poterba ed., 2000); M. Johnson, S. Nabar, & S. Porter, "Determinants of Corporate Response to Section 162(m)", U. of Mich. Working Paper (1999) (of 297 publicly held US firms that paid more than $1 million of compensation in 1992, 54% preserved deductibility; of these 78% did so through plan qualification).

[27] A further advantage of at- or out-of-the-money options and SARs is that they are generally exempt from the onerous requirements of Section 409A for deferred compensation.

[28] Treas. Reg. 1.162-27(e)(3) & (e)(5).   [29] Treas. Reg. 1.162-27(e)(4).

[30] Treas. Reg. 1.162-27(e)(2)(iii)(A).

formula, since the resulting number can be cut but not raised. If compensation committees then reduce the number, they can claim to be holding the line on pay—by offering less than was authorized—even as they award a substantial increase over the prior year.

Section 162(m) also creates a preference for options and SARs over stock, which is not always advisable. Restricted stock grants do not qualify as performance-based—and thus are not deductible—unless employees earn the stock grant only by satisfying a performance-based standard (e.g., an earnings-based bonus paid in stock). In deciding whether to compensate executives with stock or options, a key question is how much risk we want executives to take. Unfortunately Section 162(m) does not account for the context-specific factors bearing on this judgment. In addition, as noted above, option grants may discourage firms from paying dividends.[31]

Unfortunately, section 162(m) may even have motivated some firms to commit fraud. By favoring options that were at-the-money when granted, the rule creates a tax incentive to lie about the grant date. Many firms have "backdated" options to conceal that the options were in-the-money when granted.[32]

3.1.4 Conventional Options Instead of Indexed Options: Worthy Goal but Imperfect Means

Another problem with Section 162(m) is that it treats options as performance-based even when they are not—or, at least, when a significant source of their value is not. Assume XYZ stock is trading at $100, and executives are given options to buy shares at $100. Let's say that the market as a whole increases by 30%, while XYZ shares rise by only 10%. Even though XYZ has significantly underperformed the market, executives still earn $10 per share. In contrast, if the overall market declines by 30%, but XYZ declines by only 1%, XYZ has significantly outperformed the market. Nevertheless, executives earn nothing on these conventional options.

To avoid this problem, the exercise price should not be a fixed number. Instead, it should float with the overall market or with the performance of industry competitors.[33] For example, the exercise price on an "indexed" option can be 1/20th of the S&P 500 (e.g., if the S&P 500 is 2000 when the option is granted). Yet even though an indexed option is more performance-based, Section 162(m) does not distinguish between it and a conventional option.

On the contrary, Section 162(m) actually *favors* conventional options over indexed options in a range of ways. First, the process requirements for conventional options are more relaxed than for indexed options.[34] Second, conventional options offer pay that is not really

---

[31] See *supra* section 3.1.1.

[32] See Jesse M. Fried, "Option Backdating and its Implications", 65 Wash. & Lee L. Rev. 853, 854 (2008) ("Evidence has emerged that several thousand publicly traded firms used hindsight to secretly backdate stock option grants"). Before 2005, firms also had an accounting reason to avoid in-the-money grants. These had to be expensed, while at-the-money options did not. Since 2005, all option grants must be expensed. Id. at 859.

[33] Schizer, Indexed Options, *supra* note 9, at 1941.

[34] Conventional options comply with the so-called "performance goal requirement" if they are issued at-the-money or out-of-the-money, so that "the amount of compensation the employee could receive is based solely on an increase in the value of the stock after the date of the grant or award" 1.162-27(e)(2)(vi).

performance-based but is still deductible. These options offer two sources of value: a firm-specific bet, which is performance-based, and a general market bet, which is not. As a result, compensating executives with conventional options is like giving them indexed options along with extra cash that is invested in a diversified portfolio.[35]

Finally, there is even an argument that indexed options cannot qualify as "performance-based pay," although the better view is that they can. The concern derives from Section 162's legislative history, which suggests that stock options are performance-based only if they reward *increases* in the stock price.[36] If this is the rule, indexed options may not pass muster; they reward executives whose stock price *declines*, as long as it declines *less than the index*. Yet unlike the legislative history, the statute itself says nothing about this issue. Instead, it merely requires compensation to be "payable solely on account of the attainment of one or more performance goals."[37] Indexed options should satisfy this requirement. Their performance goal is that the stock price has to outperform the index.[38]

3.1.5 Incentive Stock Options: Worthy Goal but Imperfect Means

Another US tax rule favoring performance-based pay is Section 422, which offers capital gains tax treatment for so-called incentive stock options (ISOs). Under current rates, executives are taxed at 23.8% on ISOs (20% on capital gains and, in some cases, an additional 3.8% net investment tax), instead of the top bracket of 39.6%, as long as holding period and other requirements are satisfied.[39] Yet this tax advantage is offset—often, more than offset—by a tax disadvantage to the firm: ISOs are not deductible.[40] For each dollar, the firm gives

In contrast, this language—and the process shortcut it provides—does not apply to indexed options; rather, indexed options offer a return if the stock prices increases more (or decreases less) than the index, and not "solely" if the stock price increases. As a result, indexed options are subject to the more rigorous process requirements governing earnings based bonuses.

[35] Assuming this market exposure represents half of a conventional option's value, a package of $1 million in conventional options and $1 million in cash is roughly comparable to one of $500,000 in indexed options and $1.5 million of cash, of which $500,000 is invested in the stock market. A difference is that the executive loses the $50,000 stock market portfolio if the firm-specific bet is sufficiently unsuccessful. In other words, if the firm declines in value in a rising stock market, the executive gets no return. This is different from a package composed of an indexed option and a separate investment in the S&P, since the executive would still have the latter even if the former expires worthless.

[36] See H.R. Conf. Rep. No. 103–213, at 587 (1993) (treating stock options as performance-based if the return is "based solely on an increase in the corporation's stock price," but not performance-based "if the executive is otherwise protected from decreases in the value of the stock (such as through automatic repricing)").

[37] Section 162(m)(4)(C).

[38] If this interpretation is not fully reassuring, the option's terms can be adjusted to avoid rewarding executives whose stock price declines. A (partially) indexed option can reward executives if the firm outperforms the index, but only if the stock price also appreciates. For example, if the stock price is $100 and the S&P 500 is 2000 on the grant date, the exercise price can be the greater of: (a) 1/20th of the S&P 500; and (b) $100.

[39] For example, the taxpayer must satisfy a 12-month holding period for the option and another 12-month holding period for the stock, and the options must not be issued in-the-money.

[40] In contrast, non-qualified options (NQOs) allow the firm to deduct the same amount that employees include as ordinary income, which generally is the difference between the stock price and the exercise price when the option is exercised.

up 35 cents to save employees 15.8 cents. ISOs are not truly tax advantaged, then, unless the employer cannot use the deduction, as is the case with a tech startup that is not yet profitable.

Even so, ISOs are used beyond this narrow setting presumably because managers care more about *their* taxes than the *firm's* taxes. In theory, a firm could instead persuade shareholders to forgo capital gains treatment by "grossing them up" with a larger (but deductible) grant that is taxed as ordinary income.[41] But managers may be reluctant to accept this trade because the gross-up would be more visible to shareholders than the lost deduction. As a result, even though the tax law limits the size of ISO grants, executives often receive the largest allowable grant. Ironically, a form of pay that is supposed to target agency costs is probably overused for agency cost reasons.

3.1.6 Deferred Compensation: Worthy Goal but Imperfect Means

Managers are supposed to be faithful agents not only to shareholders but also to creditors. A familiar concern is that when insolvency is likely, executives take unwise risks hoping to save the company (and their jobs). If the bet doesn't pay off, creditors will be hurt, but the executive has little to lose.[42] In response, the interests of managers and creditors can be aligned by giving managers deferred compensation so they become unsecured credits.[43] A tax preference can promote deferred compensation by offering higher after-tax returns if pay is deferred.[44]

Even so, deferred compensation reduces agency costs only if structured properly. To expose this pay to the risks of bankruptcy, it should not be paid too soon after the executive retires.[45] Yet US executives can accelerate this pay by incurring a 20% penalty.[46] They will be willing to incur this cost if bankruptcy is imminent, which means acceleration is most likely when it is most problematic.[47] Deferred compensation also should be disclosed

---

[41] On an ISO grant of 100 shares, each dollar of share appreciation gives the executive $80, but it costs the firm a full $100 (because this cost is not deductible). If instead the executive receives a non-qualified grant of 140 shares, both the executive and the firm are better off: the executive has $84.56 ($140 minus $55.44 in tax), while the firm spends only $91 (since it can deduct $49).

[42] See also Chenyang Wei & David Yermack, "Investor Reactions to CEOs' Inside Debt Incentives", 24 Rev. Fin. Stud. 3813–40 (2011); Frederick Tung & Xue Wang, "Bank CEOs, Inside Debt Compensation, and the Global Financial Crisis" (Boston Univ. School of Law Working Paper No. 11-49) (December 11, 2012).

[43] Michael C. Jensen & William H. Meckling, "Theory of the Firm: Managerial Behavior, Agency Costs and Ownership Structure", 3 J. Fin. Econ. 305 (1976) (if a firm is capitalized with equity and debt, an optimal pay package provides both).

[44] In the US, for instance, non-qualified plans are taxed favorably if the employer's tax rate on investment earnings is lower than the employee's rate. Halperin & Warren, *supra* note 17, at 12–13 ("any benefit from nonqualified deferred compensation is due entirely to the difference between the employer's and the employee's after-tax rate of return on income earned by investing the deferred amount").

[45] Robert J. Jackson, Jr. & Colleen Honigsberg, "The Hidden Nature of Executive Retirement Pay", 100 Va. L. Rev. 479, 486 (2014) ("for retirement arrangements to serve as inside debt the executive must, in the event of bankruptcy, recover amounts comparable to those recovered by the company's other unsecured creditors").

[46] Section 409A(a)(1)(B).

[47] Jackson & Honigsberg, *supra* note 45, at 503 ("But the provision instead merely limits accelerations to cases in which executives are most certain that bankruptcy is coming").

clearly. It should not be performance-based, and it should not encourage executives to take risks.[48] However, according to Robert Jackson and Colleen Honigsberg, these conditions are often violated.[49]

3.1.7 Golden Parachutes: Misguided Goal

The US also imposes a Pigouvian tax on golden parachutes, or payments to managers when their employer is sold. Presumably, the concern is that parachutes make managers too willing to accept acquisitions.[50] Yet this provision neglects the strong management interest in resisting acquisitions, which can eliminate their jobs. In tempering this self-interested impulse, parachutes *align* shareholder and management interests in many cases, and should not be discouraged.[51]

Unfortunately, Section 4999 imposes a 20% excise tax on "excess parachute payments," which generally are the excess over three years' salary. This penalty applies not only to cash payments, but also to the accelerated vesting of stock and options. These grants appreciate if there is an acquisition premium, so this appreciation—a significant percentage of most parachutes[52]—increases the excise tax bill. Yet it makes no sense to penalize managers for a deal premium that benefits shareholders.[53]

The tax penalty on parachutes is misguided also in imposing costs on the firm, instead of on management. Experts must be retained to value this accelerated vesting, and this difficult and costly process is funded by shareholders. In addition, Section 280G disallows the firm's deduction for excess parachute payments (as well as payments "grossing up" managers for the excise tax). But if managers really put their own interests ahead of the firm, as this regime assumes, why would a tax penalty on *the firm* deter them?

---

[48] Id. at 486 ("Unlike bonuses or stock-based pay, which reward managers for taking risk, fixed payments encourage executives to avoid risks that might render the firm insolvent").

[49] Id. at 506 (estimating that $32,500 of annual compensation is hidden through deferred compensation for the average executive in their sample).

[50] David W. Leebron, "Games Corporations Play: A Theory of Tender Offers", 61 N.Y.U. L. Rev. 153, 183 n.105 (1986) (managers may not drive a hard enough bargain); Ronald J. Gilson, "Value Creation by Business Lawyers: Legal Skills and Asset Pricing", 94 Yale L. J. 239, 285 n.114 (1984) (noting perverse incentives in parachutes).

[51] Daniel R. Fischel, "Organized Exchanges and the Regulation of Dual Class Common Stock", 54 U. Chi. L. Rev. 119, 137 (1987) (parachutes are a way to protect managers for developing firm-specific skills; John C. Coffee, Jr., "Shareholders Versus Managers: The Strain in the Corporate Web", 85 Mich. L. Rev. 75–76 (1986) (parachutes can be a way to recruit quality management in active takeover environment).

[52] Jay C. Hartzell, Eli Ofek, & David Yermack, "What's In It For Me? CEOs Whose Firms Are Acquired", 17 Rev. Fin. Stud. 37, 45 (2004) (noting that "mean CEO's gains from stock and option appreciation are just under $5 million," median gains "are a little over $1.5 million," and "[t]hese sources of wealth represent the largest component of the overall gains obtained by sample CEOs").

[53] Id. ("CEOs obtain [equity appreciation] only because shareholders as a group receive a premium price from the buyer. Therefore, to the extent that a conflict of interest exists between CEOs and shareholders in connection with merger negotiations, the conflict must arise from" other components of parachutes).

3.2 Shared Interests: Hedging Stock Options and Suspicion of Hedged Positions

Although the focus so far has been on tax effects that are intentional, unintended effects can also be important. In fact, one of US tax law's main contributions to corporate governance—discouraging executives from hedging their stock options—arose essentially by accident. Options are supposed to reduce agency costs by rewarding executives when the firm's stock price rises, but in theory executives could thwart this goal by neutralizing this exposure with derivatives.[54] Although firms should have contractual bans on hedging, only some do. US securities laws can require reporting, but this reporting can be obscure and is required only in some cases.

Instead, US tax law plays an important but largely unintended role.[55] Executives are reluctant to hedge stock options because they can incur tax even when they have no economic gain. Although the relevant rules are technical, the executive's problem is that stock option gains are taxed as ordinary income, while (offsetting) hedging losses generally are treated as capital losses, which cannot shelter ordinary income.[56] For example, assume an executive's options appreciate by $1 million after she hedges them. She has an extra $1 million of ordinary income, which is matched by a $1 million capital loss on the hedge that cannot be deducted from ordinary income. As a result, she owes an extra $396,000 in tax, but without a corresponding economic gain. Of course, she still has $1 million of capital losses, but she cannot use them unless she has $1 million of capital gains elsewhere in her portfolio.[57] Unlike the Pigouvian measures discussed above, the relevant tax rules here are not meant to target managerial agency costs. Rather, tax systems have their own reasons to penalize offsetting positions. In a realization-based system, gains and losses can be timed in ways that reduce tax; in response, capital loss and other limitations are supposed to impede this tax planning. These rules were added by the tax system for its own reasons, but they end up playing a valuable corporate governance role.

Even so, these rules are incomplete and potentially unstable. They apply only if equity compensation is taxed as ordinary income, which is true of non-qualified options but not (always) of stock. Although stock grants usually are taxed as ordinary income when they vest, executives can elect to pay tax earlier, so that subsequent appreciation is capital gain.

---

[54] For instance, an executive who receives a compensatory option to buy 10,000 shares at $100 might sell a similar over-the-counter call option to a derivatives dealer so the two positions essentially cancel each other out.

[55] Schizer, Executives and Hedging, *supra* note 3, at 440.

[56] Only a modest amount of capital loss can be used to offset ordinary income each year. Some hedges generate ordinary losses, but involve comparable problems. See generally Schizer, Executives and Hedging, *supra* note 3.

[57] If the capital loss can be used currently, but offsets long-term capital gain, it reduces tax only by $238,000. (The tax rate is assumed here to be 23.8%, which includes the 20% capital gains rate and the 3.8% net investment tax of Section 1411.) As a result, the executive's tax bill still increases by $158,000. In theory, the executive could respond by adjusting the size of the hedge so the two positions are offsetting on an after-tax, instead of a pre-tax, basis. But another anti-abuse rule, the straddle rules of Section 1092, prevents this by subjecting hedging gains and losses to different rates. See Schizer, Executives and Hedging, *supra* note 3, at 481.

After this "83(b) election," executives can hedge stock without any tax mismatch.[58] Unlike option grants, then, stock grants sometimes can be hedged. This difference is all the more significant because stock grants have increasingly been replacing option grants in recent years.[59] Not only is this tax effect becoming less important, but it also is at risk of being repealed. A range of tweaks in US tax law could solve the executive's tax mismatch.[60] Since the tax authorities never intended to block hedging, they are unlikely to notice (or care) if they inadvertently stop doing so.

3.3 Accidental Byproducts

Accidental effects can arise not only because tax and corporate governance have partially overlapping goals, but also because of wholly unrelated choices made by the tax system. This Section offers two examples, which derive from the tax system's reluctance to require difficult valuations.

3.3.1 Venture Capital (VC) and Valuation

The first involves venture-capital-financed startups. Although this chapter focuses on public companies, privately owned high-tech startups also struggle with agency costs. When these firms fail, investors cannot always tell whether the idea was unworkable or managers were not working.

Equity compensation is a standard response, which the tax system enhances (inadvertently) by applying capital gains rates. Although the US tax system intentionally offers a preference for startups,[61] the focus here is on an unintended preference that helps executives who receive stock in early VC funding rounds. This stock is effectively salary—issued for "sweat equity," not capital—which otherwise would be taxed at ordinary rates. Assume, for instance, that VCs pay $100 per share for their stock, and the executive receives identical shares at the same time. Under the usual rules, the executive has $100 of ordinary income upon receiving the stock and is eligible for capital gains rates only on subsequent appreciation.[62] Nevertheless, executives prefer capital gains to ordinary income, and Silicon Valley

---

[58] Likewise, executives who received stock as investors (e.g., as founder of the company) also do not face this mismatch since their return also is taxed as capital gain. Also, once executives exercise their options, they can hedge the stock they receive. Yet they are also permitted to sell it, so hedging does not have the same agency costs implications, as long as it is disclosed.

[59] Emily Chasan, "Last Gasp for Stock Options", WSJ.Com, Aug. 26, 2013, http://blogs.wsj.com/cfo/2013/08/26/last-gasp-for-stock-options/ ("At their peak in 1999, stock options accounted for about 78% of the average executive's long-term incentive packages. Last year, they represented just 31%, and are expected to shrink to 25% in the next two years, based on grant values so far this year"); James F. Reda, David M. Schmidt & Kimberly A. Glass, "The Move Away from Stock Options Continues: Preview of 2012 Data", J. Comp. & Ben. 12, 14 (May/June 2013), http://www.jfreda.com/public/pdf/The%20Move%20Away%20from%20Stock%20Options.pdf (estimating that in 2015 stock options will represent just 25% of the typical award).

[60] For a discussion, see Schizer, Executives and Hedging, *supra* note 3.

[61] See Section 1202 (qualified small business stock).

[62] This assumes they make a Section 83(b) election. They also have the option of deferring the tax until the shares vest, but then all gain up to that point is taxed at ordinary rates. See Ronald J. Gilson & David

has a strategy to provide it. The key is for VCs to receive convertible preferred stock[63] so their shares are no longer the same as the executive's common shares. If the startup is liquidated, the VC is paid first. Although the value of this preference is unclear—since early stage startups typically have few assets[64]—the standard practice is to treat the VCs preferred as much more valuable than the executive's common. When executives pay tax on the common, then, they assign a low valuation for it (e.g., one dollar, instead of the $100 paid by the VC). When they sell later, proceeds above one dollar are reported as capital gain.[65]

The lynchpin of this strategy—aggressive valuation—has not been explicitly blessed by the US government. Even so, valuation is difficult to challenge, especially when the relevant assets are ideas (which might not work), and not hard assets. Once again, the tax system makes a choice for its own reasons—in this case, administrability—that inadvertently reduces agency costs. The resulting subsidy piggybacks on the judgments of VCs. Since the strategy works only when outside investors provide funding, it is limited to startups that attract outside investors.[66]

3.3.2 *Untaxed Perquisites and Valuation*

Administrability also explains why the tax system does not tax some perquisites and thus inadvertently encourages them. It is hard to tax the utility that managers derive from light hours, long lunches, lavish offices, and nepotistic hiring practices. Unfortunately, though, a manager may favor these benefits for a parallel reason: they are hard for shareholders to see. While tax is unlikely to motivate these practices, then, it may reinforce them. Unlike most issues in this chapter, this issue arises in all tax systems since the administrative cost challenge is universal.

Even so, different jurisdictions target work-related consumption in particular contexts. For example, US firms can deduct only half of work-related entertainment expenses.[67] Again, though, taxing the firm instead of the executive is a poor strategy. Managers who put their own interests ahead of the firm's worry less about a tax on the firm than one on them. Even a tax on managers will not have much effect, moreover, if it is too low. In the US, for example, executives are taxed on personal travel on corporate jets, but the tax is based on the taxpayer-friendly "standard industry fare level." The actual cost to the firm, then, significantly exceeds what the executive includes in income.[68]

M. Schizer, "Understanding Venture Capital Structure: A Tax Explanation for Convertible Preferred Securities", 116 Harv. L. Rev. 874 (2003).

[63] Id.

[64] Indeed, there is an extensive literature debating why VCs in the US always take convertible preferred, instead of common stock. Although signaling and other governance reasons are often invoked, tax is a central reason. Id.

[65] A cost of this favorable tax treatment is that the startup itself can deduct only one dollar per share instead of one hundred dollars. But early stage high tech startups often are not yet profitable, so they don't (yet) need the deduction. Id.

[66] Gilson & Schizer, *supra* note 62.   [67] Section 274(n).

[68] The firm's deduction is limited to this amount so that, again, much of the tax cost is imposed on the firm, instead of the executive. See, e.g., Cleary Gottlieb Alert Memo, New Personal Use of Corporate Aircraft Tax Rules: Notes for Tax and Executive Compensation Practitioners (Aug. 22, 2012), http://www.cgsh.com/files/News/90795eb3-eb05-43a8-9a3e-69ae66fcb5b6/Presentation/NewsAttachment/

Another tax strategy to constrain agency costs is to offer tax-free treatment only if a perquisite is available to all employees. Under these "nondiscrimination rules," executives can either offer the benefit broadly, which raises costs and can attract more attention, or pay tax on it. By raising a perquisite's visibility or imposing a tax on the executive, these rules discourage the proliferation of benefits, at least at the margin.

4 Management Decisions about Capital Structure, Hedging, and Acquisitions

Tax influences not only the pay executives receive, but also the choices they make. In a number of jurisdictions, for example, Pigouvian tax provisions discourage bribes and participation in international boycotts, while encouraging research and development, corporate charity, and various types of investments.[69] In addition to these deliberate uses of tax, unintended effects also can be quite important. In the US, for instance, tax influences management decisions about capital structure, hedging, and acquisitions. This section focuses on these (largely) unintended effects.[70]

4.1 Capital Structure

The US tax system has two (largely) positive effects on capital structure, and one that is less clear. First, US tax rules encourage leverage, which usually (but not always) reduces agency costs. Second, it discourages pyramidal ownership by taxing intercompany dividends. Third, the US tax system can distort payout policies, although the magnitude and direction of this effect varies with the context and over time.

4.1.1 Accidental Byproduct: Tax Advantages of Leverage

The US tax system favors leverage, and debt can reduce agency costs in three ways. First, debt ensures that some earnings are distributed as interest, leaving less for pet projects and perquisites. Second, the need to pay interest pressures managers to generate earnings. Third, bankruptcy can be even more costly for managers than shareholders. Senior executives are likely to lose their jobs and could have trouble finding another. This means debt—and thus

---

48406b2f-00b4-4baa-a071-6c9f97bdcd30/CGSH%20Alert%20-%20New%20Personal%20Use%20of%20 Corporate%20Aircraft%20Tax%20Rules.pdf.

[69] See, e.g., Section 162(c); IRC Section 908; see also, e.g., Jeffrey P. Owens, Good Corporate Governance: The Tax Dimension, in Tax and Corporate Governance 11 (Wolfgang Schön ed., 2008) (all OECD members disallow deduction for bribery, and Germany, the UK, and the US all allow deductions for corporate charity).

[70] In a frictionless world, capital structure does not affect firm value, as Modigliani and Miller famously showed, but the analysis obviously changes once we account for tax, information and transaction costs, and other frictions. See Franco Modigliana & Merton H. Miller, "The Cost of Capital, Corporation Finance and the Theory of Investment", 48 Am. Econ. Rev. (1958).

the prospect of bankruptcy—can motivate managers to perform better. These factors could help explain why share prices usually rise when firms issue debt to buy back equity.[71]

Context is also important since debt sometimes can *add* to agency costs. Managers and shareholders often have different risk appetites, and debt can increase these differences in two (competing) ways. On one hand, managers of levered firms might shy away from especially risky investments, since bankruptcy is costlier for them than for shareholders. On the other hand, once managers believe bankruptcy is likely, they have the incentive to take extra risk, even if it has negative expected value.[72] Managers "swing for the fences" if anything short of a home run would not prevent bankruptcy and save their jobs. In contrast, creditors and shareholders would prefer more modest returns with higher expected value, which would increase their recoveries in bankruptcy.

Given these competing effects, the net impact of debt on agency costs varies with general market conditions, the maturity of the business, the sector, the assets backing the loan,[73] and the negative externalities from insolvency. Bank failures, for example, are likely to pose greater systemic effects.

Just as debt usually (but not always) reduces agency costs, it also usually (but not always) has tax advantages. Unlike a dividend, interest is deductible in the US.[74] This means profits paid to creditors are taxed only once (at the creditor level), while profits paid to shareholders are taxed twice. Although this difference persuaded Franco Modigliani and Merton Miller that firms should be capitalized with 100% debt, it is not quite so simple.[75] The incentive to add debt is stronger when corporate tax rates are high.[76] At the same time, this incentive is weaker when the firm already has enough debt to shelter its profits[77]—or, for that matter, when it has other deductions to do so, such as depreciation, foreign tax credits, or stock option expenses.[78] There also is a competing effect for multinationals. Though the relevant

---

[71] See, e.g., Kshitij Shah, "The Nature of Information Conveyed by Pure Capital Structure Changes", 36 J. Fin. Econ. 89 (1994) (correlating exchange offers with information about reduced future cash flows for leverage-decreasing offers, and decreased risk for leverage increasing offers).

[72] Jensen & Meckling, *supra* note 43 (managers take excessive risk since they benefit from gains but do not share in losses).

[73] Stewart C. Myers & Nicholas S. Majluf, "Corporate Financing and Investment Decisions when Firms Have Information that Investors Do Not Have", 13 J. Fin. Econ. 187 (1984) (firms with more tangible assets borrow more, since it is easier to grant security interest); James H. Scott, Jr. "Bankruptcy, Secured Debt, and Optimal Capital Structure", 32 J. Fin. 1 (1977) (same).

[74] Section 163(a). Cf. Arne Friese, Simon Link, & Stefan Mayer, Taxation and Corporate Governance—The State of the Art, in Tax and Corporate Governance 392 (Wolfgang Schön ed., 2008) (noting that interest is 50% deductible in Germany).

[75] Franco Modigliani & Merton H. Miller, "Corporate Income Taxes and the Cost of Capital: A Correction", 53 Am. Econ. Rev. 433 (1963).

[76] Graham, *supra* note 5, at 1075 (the higher the corporate tax rate, the stronger this effect).

[77] E. Han Kim, Optimal Capital Structure in Miller's Equilibrium, in 2 Financial Markets and Incomplete Information: Frontiers of Modern Financial Theory 36–48 (Sudipto Bhattacharya & George M. Constantinides eds., 1989) (if firm is already using enough debt to shield likely profits, there is no tax advantage in using more debt).

[78] Harry DeAngelo & Ronald W. Masulis, "Optimal Capital Structure Under Corporate and Personal Taxation", 8 J. Fin. Econ. 3 (1980) (noting that other sources of deductions can reduce tax advantage of debt); Dan Dhaliwal, Robert Trezevant, & Shiing-Wu Wang, "Taxes, Investment-Related Tax Shields and Capital Structure", 14 J. Am. Tax'n. Ass'n. 1 (1992) (showing that firms with nondebt tax shield are less likely to use debt); John R. Graham, Mark H. Lang, & Douglas A. Shackelford, "Employee Stock Options, Corporate Taxes, and Debt Policy", 59 J. Fin. 1585 (2004) (option deductions are large enough

rules are technical, the upshot is that borrowing more can sometimes reduce a firm's foreign tax credits.[79]

Moreover, if we look only at the tax treatment of the firm, but not the investor, we are missing half the picture. In the US, (taxable) investors are taxed *less* favorably on debt than on equity: interest is ordinary income, while dividends and capital gains are eligible for reduced rates. The importance of this offsetting disadvantage depends on who the creditor is, and also on the rate structure.[80] If the creditor is tax exempt or foreign (and thus does not pay US tax), this disadvantage is irrelevant. As a result, these clienteles are especially likely to hold debt.[81] When they do, corporate cash flow funded by debt is, in effect, never taxed by the US.[82] However, if the creditor is taxable, the tax advantage of debt over equity depends on how the

to reduce the median marginal tax rate for sample of large firms from 34% to 26%); Robert Trezevant, "Debt Financing and Tax Status: Tests of the Substitution Effect and the Tax Exhaustion Hypothesis Using Firms' Responses to the Economic Recovery Tax Act of 1981", 47 J. Fin. 1557 (1992) (finding support for debt substitution and tax exhaustion hypotheses by examining 1981 legislation); Kathleen M. Kahle & Kuldeep Shastri, "Firm Performance, Capital Structure, and the Tax Benefits of Employee Stock Options", 40 J. Fin. Quant. Anal. 135 (2005) ("long- and short-term debt ratios are negatively related to the size of tax benefits from option exercise").

[79] In general, firms need foreign income in order to use foreign tax credits. Thus, if US interest expense shelters foreign income, it can reduce the credits a firm can claim. There is a formula for deciding whether US interest expense reduces overseas income, which is based on the percentage of assets abroad. The more assets held overseas, then, the more foreign tax credits a firm loses by taking on more US debt. Empirical evidence shows that firms respond to this incentive. Julie H. Collins & Douglas A. Shackelford, "Foreign Tax Credit Limitations and Preferred Stock Issuances", 30 J. Acct. Research (Supp.), 103 (1992) (multinationals respond to 1986 change by using preferred stock instead of commercial paper); Kenneth A. Froot & James R. Hines, Jr., Interest Allocation Rules, Financing Patterns, and the Operations of US Multinationals, in The Effects of Taxation on Multinationals (Martin Feldstein, James R. Hines, Jr., & R. Glenn Hubbard, eds., 1995) (excess credit firms reduce their use of debt, with greater reductions in firms with more foreign assets); Rosanne Altshuler & Jack M. Mintz, "US Interest-Allocation Rules: Effects and Policy", 2 Int'l. Tax and Pub. Fin. 7 (1995) (multinationals with more assets abroad have more foreign debt, presumably because domestic interest would be allocated abroad).

[80] This disadvantage obviously grows as the gap widens between ordinary and capital gains rates. Graham, *supra* note 5, at 1082 ("If the investor-level tax on interest income (τ_P) is large relative to tax rates on corporate and equity income (τ_C and τ_E), the net tax advantage of debt can be zero or even negative."); Jeffrey K. MacKie-Mason, "Do Taxes Affect Corporate Financing Decisions?", 45 J. Fin. 1471 (1990) (finding that firms slightly increased use of debt after 1986 tax reform, which reduced tax rates on interest income).

[81] It is not easy, though, to document this clientele effect empirically. See Graham, *supra* note 5, at 1096 ("The truth is that we know very little about the identity or tax status of the marginal investors").

[82] Not surprisingly, then, there is empirical evidence that share prices rise when firms announce they are replacing equity with debt. See, e.g., Ronald W. Masulis, "Stock Repurchase by Tender Offer: An Analysis of the Causes of Common Stock Price Changes", 35 J. Fin. 305 (1980) (leverage-increasing exchange offers increase equity value by 7.6%, and leverage-decreasing transactions decrease value by 5.4%). Moreover, the exchange offers with the largest increases in tax deductions (debt-for-common and debt-for-preferred) have the largest positive stock price reactions. Ellen Engel, Merle Erickson, & Edward Maydew, "Debt-Equity Hybrid Securities", 37 J. Acct. Research 249 (1999) (comparing MIPS yields to preferred yields and concluding that the tax benefit of MIPS are approximately .28 per dollar of face value, net of the aforementioned costs.); see also John R. Graham, Taxes and Corporate Finance in 2 Handbook Of Corporate Finance: Empirical Corporate Finance 73 (B. Espen Eckbo ed., 2008). ("If all firms lever up to operate at the kink in their benefit functions, they could add 10.5% to firm value over the 1995–1999 period.")

corporate tax rate (which firms avoid by using debt) compares with the extra tax investors must pay. This additional tax is the spread between the tax on interest (at ordinary rates) and dividends (at capital gains rates). Under current rates, debt has a significant advantage.

Yet the magnitude of this advantage can change over time, since ordinary and capital gains rates for individuals fluctuate. When Congress changes these rates, it usually is not focused on managerial agency costs. The same is true when government tax experts modify the interest deduction. So although the tax treatment of debt has an important influence on agency costs, it is a blunt instrument.

4.1.2 Pigouvian Effort to Discourage Pyramidal Ownership: Intercompany Dividends

US tax rules also reduce agency costs by discouraging "pyramidal ownership." As an example of a pyramid, assume A owns 10% of B (effectively controlling it), and B owns 10% of C (effectively controlling it). This means A effectively controls C, even though it (indirectly) owns only 1%. This sort of control, "assembled mainly with other people's money," can breed agency costs.[83]

Yet although pyramids are the norm in many developed economies,[84] they are much less common in the US. One reason is that the US taxes intercompany dividends (i.e., a 7% tax on dividends received by firms owning between 20% and 80% of the dividend-paying firm), while many other jurisdictions do not (e.g., the EU, Japan, Australia, Switzerland, Singapore, and Canada).[85] Commentators suggest that President Franklin Roosevelt proposed this tax in 1935 to address corporate governance problems with pyramids,[86] although others claim that pyramids were already becoming uncommon in the US for other reasons.[87]

4.1.3 An Earnings Trap?

Tax also can affect agency costs by influencing firm payout policies. In general, dividends mitigate agency costs by reducing the resources under management's control. When a project is funded with retained earnings instead of new debt or equity, managers are under less pressure to demonstrate the project's value, and thus are more likely to fund perquisites and pet projects.[88] Paying dividends also is a signal of a firm's good health.[89]

---

[83] See Randall Morck & Bernard Yeung, "Dividend Taxation and Corporate Governance", 19 J. Econ. Persp. 163, 177 (2005).

[84] See Rafael La Porta, Florencio Lopez-de-Silanes, & Andrei Shleifer, "Corporate Ownership Around the World", 54 J. Fin. 471 (1999).

[85] Morck & Yeung, *supra* note 83, at 176.   [86] Id.

[87] Steven A. Bank & Brian R. Cheffins, The Corporate Pyramid Fable, University of Cambridge Faculty of Law Legal Studies Research Paper Series 11/04 (January 2011) ("The introduction of the intercorporate dividend tax did not foster a rapid dismantling of corporate pyramids. Instead, pyramidal arrangements were already rare in the US").

[88] Michael C. Jensen, "Agency Costs of Free Cash Flow, Corporate Finance, and Takeovers", 76 Am. Econ. Rev. 323 (1986); Andrei Schleifer & Robert W. Vishny, "Management Entrenchment: The Case of Manager-Specific Investments", 25 J. Fin. Econ. 123, 123–24, 137 (1989) (retained earnings can fund irreversible investments that make firm less valuable but enhance management's value to firm); Nancy L. Rose & Andrea Shepard, "Firm Diversification and CEO Compensation: Managerial Ability or Executive Entrenchment", 28 Rand J. Econ. 489 (1997) (diversified firms are harder to manage and make skills more valuable).

[89] Sudipto Bhattacharya, "Imperfect Information, Dividend Policy, and 'The Bird in the Hand' Fallacy", 10 Bell J. Econ. 259 (1979). As a result, empirical evidence suggests a connection

As a result, if tax discourages dividends, it could exacerbate agency costs. But does the US tax system actually discourage dividends? The answer is somewhat complex and context-specific. By retaining earnings, a firm defers the shareholder's dividend tax, but this deferral does not necessarily reduce the shareholders' tax burden. Obviously, this deferral is irrelevant to tax exempt shareholders.[90] For less intuitive reasons, it may also not matter to taxable shareholders: if the firm reinvests these earnings at a profit, tax ultimately is levied on a larger base (the compounded earnings).[91] Therefore, a taxable shareholder has the same after-tax return—whether the dividend is paid now or later— as long as two conditions are satisfied: first, the dividend tax has to be paid eventually (at the same tax rate); second, earnings must grow at the same (after-tax) rate either inside or outside the firm.[92] When these conditions hold, there is no tax reason to retain earnings.

Yet the plausibility of these conditions can fluctuate over time, causing the US tax system to discourage dividends in some circumstances while favoring them in others. For instance, the first condition—that the dividend tax is inevitable and constant— does not hold if earnings can be bailed out another way that avoids this tax. Share repurchases are a familiar example.[93] For many years, they were taxed more favorably than

between dividends and good governance. Larry H.P. Lang & Robert H. Litzenberger, "Dividend Announcements: Cash Flow Signaling vs. Free Cash Flow Hypothesis?", 24 J. Fin. Econ. 181 (1989) (dividend increases raise share prices the most for firms with ample cash flows and few investment opportunities); Rafael La Porta, Florencio Lopez-de-Silanes, Andrei Shleifer, & Robert W. Vishny, "Agency Problems and Dividend Policies Around the World", 55 J. Fin. 1 (2000) (concluding that good governance causes higher dividends and that public investors demand dividends where free cash-flow problems are worst).

[90] It is hard to know how common tax-exempt shareholders are, but there is empirical evidence suggesting that taxable shareholders are the marginal holders. See, e.g., Edwin J. Elton, Martin J. Gruber, & Christopher R. Blake, "Marginal Stockholder Tax Effects and Ex-Dividend-Day Price Behavior: Evidence from Taxable Versus Nontaxable Closed-End Funds", 87 Rev. Econ. Stat. 579 (2005) (share values fall by after-tax value of dividend, not its full nominal value, on ex-dividend date); Trevor S. Harris, R. Glenn Hubbard, & Deen Kemsley, "The Share Price Effects of Dividend Taxes and Tax Imputation Credits", 79 J. Pub. Econ. 569 (2001) (taxable individuals are marginal equity investors, so dividend taxes are impounded in price).

[91] Daniel Halperin, "Will Integration Increase Efficiency? The Old and New View of Dividend Policy", 47 Tax L. Rev. 645, 648 (1992) ("The advantage of deferral would be offset by the fact that the tax base would be growing as the corporation continued to accumulate earnings").

[92] Id. at 648 ("if all distributions were taxed at the same rate, the corporate and individual rates were the same and the rate of return inside the corporate sector is no different than the rate of return outside the corporate sector, the tax burden on corporate distributions could not be reduced by deferral of distributions"); see also, e.g., Alan J. Auerbach, "Share Valuation and Corporate Equity Policy", 11 J. Pub. Econ. 291 (1979). For example, assume a firm has $100 of earnings, which it either can distribute immediately or reinvest for three years. Assume also that this money can be invested—either inside or outside corporate solution—to earn the same 6.5% after-tax return. Assume also that it is subject to a shareholder level tax of 23.8% when it is distributed (the 20% capital gains rate plus the 3.8% net investment tax). If the money is distributed now, the shareholder has $76.20. After three years, this amount grows to $92.05. Alternatively, if the firm invests the $100, it grows to $120.80 over three years and is distributed. After a 23.8% tax, the shareholder has the same $92.05.

[93] Fisher Black, "Dividend Puzzle", 2 J. Portf. Man. 215 (1976); Morck & Yeung, *supra* note 83, at 163, 168 ("Another option is for firms to make cash payments to shareholders by repurchasing their own shares").

dividends,[94] and often replaced them in the 1990s.[95] Like dividends, share repurchases can mitigate agency costs by reducing a firm's free cash flow. Yet if repurchases are more sporadic, so that scaling them back attracts less market attention, they impose somewhat less discipline on managers. In any event, the tax difference between repurchases and dividends was largely (but not entirely) eliminated in 2003.[96] This sort of tax change, moreover, is another reason why dividend timing can matter. If dividend tax rates are expected to decline, there is a tax advantage in retaining earnings, so they can be distributed after the rate cut. Conversely, an expected rate increase is a reason to *accelerate* dividends.

The second condition—that earnings grow at the same after-tax rate whether they are reinvested or distributed—also does not always hold. If shareholders can earn a better return elsewhere, they will want a dividend. In making this judgment, shareholders should account for tax treatment, as well as pre-tax returns. For instance, a dividend can fund an investment in an LLC (which avoids corporate tax) or a foreign corporation (which is taxed at a lower corporate rate). In contrast, a shareholder may want to *delay* a dividend if reinvested earnings would compound at a favorable tax rate. For example, US multinationals often do not want dividends from foreign subsidiaries, so these earnings can continue to earn tax-advantaged returns in low-tax jurisdictions.[97] Obviously, these choices about retaining or distributing earnings can affect agency costs. For example, if foreign firms are harder for shareholders to monitor, a tax incentive to keep (or shift) capital there can compound agency costs.[98]

---

[94] If structured properly, a share repurchase is taxed as capital gain. In contrast, dividends were taxed as ordinary income before 2003. See Graham, *supra* note 5, at 1105 ("All else being equal, tax effects imply that firm value is negatively related to 1) the portion of payout dedicated to dividends, and 2) dividend taxation relative to capital gains taxation"); see also Friese, Link, & Mayer, *supra* note 74, at 383 (noting an analogous effect in Germany and other imputation systems if the shareholder tax is higher than the corporate tax).

[95] Eugene F. Fama & Kenneth R. French, "Disappearing Dividends: Changing Firm Characteristics or Lower Propensity to Pay?", 60 J. Fin. Econ. 3 (2001) (declining dividend yields in recent years); Morck & Yeung, *supra* note 83, at 171 (ordinary dividends remain roughly proportional to permanent component of corporate income, and extraordinary dividends or share repurchases are used to disburse free cash flow); id at 168 ("Since firms can make cash payments to their investors without dividends, and do so in ways that avoid dividend taxes, cutting dividend taxes may have less effect now than several decades ago."); Erik Lie & Heidi J. Lie, "The Role of Personal Taxes in Corporate Decisions: An Empirical Analysis of Share Repurchases and Dividends", J. Fin. Quant. Anal. 34, 533–52 (1999) (firms with low-dividend payout (and presumably high-tax-rate investors) use self-tender-offer share repurchases more often than they use special dividends, and these firms also use open-market repurchases more often than they increase regular dividends).

[96] Since 2003, dividends (like share repurchases) have been taxed at capital gains rates. But a difference still remains: shareholders can use tax basis to reduce their tax on share repurchases, but not on dividends. For the firm itself, though, the tax burden is the same: deductions are not available for either dividends or share repurchases. See Section 162(k) (disallowing deduction for expenses associated with share repurchases).

[97] Alvin C. Warren, Jr., "Deferral and Exemption of the Income of Foreign Subsidiaries: A Review of the Basic Analytics", Harv. Pub. Law Working Paper 14–18, at 9 (Jan. 2014), http://papers.ssrn.com/sol3/papers.cfm?abstract_id=2390021 ("if the repatriation tax rate . . . does not go down, the advantage of delaying repatriation of foreign earnings under current law comes not from delaying the repatriation tax, but from the application of a foreign tax rate . . . on investment earnings during the period of deferral that is lower than the US tax rate . . . on such earnings").

[98] Cf. Mihir A. Desai, C. Fritz Foley, & James R. Hines, Jr., "Dividend Policy Inside the Multinational Firm", 36 Fin. Mgmt 5 (2007) (dividends of nonlisted foreign subs to US parents typically are steady or

This analysis is sufficiently complex that unsophisticated shareholders may not fully understand it. If so, managers could invoke tax as a pretext not to pay dividends, even if it is not (and could not be) the real reason. Yet whether the facts actually support this claim— that is, whether tax actually discourages dividends—can vary across firms and over time.[99] Indeed, during the Great Depression, an undistributed earnings tax was enacted to encourage dividends, but was soon repealed.[100] Instead of this stick, the US used a carrot in 2003, slashing the shareholder tax from 35% to 15%. Dividends increased in response,[101] especially where executives (or large taxable block-holders) owned relatively more stock.[102] Correspondingly, just before this tax cut was supposed to expire, firms accelerated dividends—paying one-time "special" dividends and shifting January dividends into December—so the lower rate would still apply.[103]

4.2 Hedging

In addition to influencing payout policy in some cases, tax also can affect the decision of firms to hedge. Corporations often use derivatives to hedge currency, interest rates, commodity prices, and other sources of revenue or costs. The pervasiveness of hedging is something of a puzzle since diversified shareholders are already insulated from these fluctuations. For instance, while a spike in fuel prices is bad for airlines, it is good for oil companies. Because diversified shareholders hold both, firm-level hedging seems wasteful to them.

rising, so that "dividend policies are largely driven by the need to control managers of foreign affiliates. Parent firms are more willing to incur tax penalties . . . when their foreign affiliates are partially owned, located far from the United States, or in jurisdictions in which property rights are weak."); C. Fritz Foley, Jay C. Hartzell, Sheridan Titman, & Garry Twite, "Why Do Firms Hold So Much Cash? A Tax-Based Explanation", 86 J. Fin. Econ. 579–607 (2007).

[99] Cf. Roger Gordon & Martin Dietz, Dividends and Taxes, in Institutional Foundations Of Public Finance: Economic And Legal Perspectives 220 (Alan J. Auerbach & Daniel N. Shaviro eds., 2008) (concluding that signaling offers only a partial explanation for why firms pay dividends).

[100] See Mark J. Roe, Strong Managers, Weak Owners: The Political Roots of American Corporate Finance 118 (1994) ("The tax on undistributed profits threatened managers; within a few years the tax was dead"); Bank, *supra* note 2, at 1204–06.

[101] Raj Chetty & Emmanuel Saez, "Dividend Taxes and Corporate Behavior: Evidence From the 2003 Dividend Tax Cut", 120 Q. J. Econ. 791, 828 (2005) ("The 2003 dividend tax cut induced a large set of firms to initiate regular dividend payments or raise the payments they were already making"); Brandon Julio & David L. Ikenberry, "Reappearing Dividends", 89 J. App. Corp. Fin. (2004) (tax reduction is consistent with the reappearance of dividend-paying firms, although trend to initiate dividends was already in motion before tax cut was announced); Jennifer L. Blouin, Jana Smith Raedy & Douglas A. Shackelford, "The Initial Impact of the 2003 Reduction in the Dividend Tax Rate", University of North Carolina, Working Paper (2004) (tax cuts also led to special dividends).

[102] Chetty & Saez, *supra* note 101, at 818–820, 823 (larger changes for firms with large taxable shareholder and bigger changes where senior executives have relatively more stock and fewer unexercised options; no change in dividends for firms where largest shareholder is not taxable).

[103] See Michelle Hanlon & Jeffrey L. Hoopes, "What Do Firms Do When Dividend Tax Rates Change?: An Examination of Alternative Payout Responses", 114 J. Fin. Econ. (estimating a $7 billion increase in special dividends paid in the end of 2010 and 2012, as well as significant shifting of January dividends into December).

Yet managers may take a different view because they are less diversified. Hedging protects their human capital by keeping the firm out of bankruptcy. It also can smooth earnings, increasing earnings-based bonuses. While agency costs may explain some hedging, there are other explanations as well. For example, hedging can protect retained earnings so the firm does not depend as heavily on the capital markets, with their associated information and transaction costs.

In addition, tax supplies two additional reasons (or excuses) to hedge. First, hedging can increase a firm's debt capacity by reducing the likelihood of financial distress.[104] This enables firms to take on more debt so they can shelter more profits with interest deductions. Second, hedging can smooth earnings, reducing the likelihood of net losses that firms cannot deduct.[105] While the first reason arises only when debt-financed profits are tax-favored, as in the US, the second reason applies in any tax system that limits net losses.

4.3 Acquisitions

Tax also can motivate and shape acquisitions. In some cases, tax is a key reason for the deal. For instance, a US firm may want to combine with a foreign firm in order to become a foreign firm for tax purposes, thereby reducing its tax bill.[106] Even if tax is not the deciding factor, it is still likely to shape the deal's structure.

4.3.1 Agency Cost Implications of Acquisitions: Entrenchment, Empire-Building, and Camouflage

Affecting the probability or structure of an acquisition is important, since wise acquisitions can advance shareholder interests for familiar reasons. They transfer a business to new owners who value it more, for instance, because of synergies in production, better management, and the like. In addition, the possibility of being replaced in an acquisition can discipline management.

For parallel reasons, managers may resist being acquired. They want to preserve their jobs, as well as private benefits from controlling the target business, such as higher pay for managing a larger firm. Managers may also worry about becoming less diversified, as discussed above. Just as *selling* is unappealing to management, *buying* can be correspondingly

---

[104] Graham & Rogers, *supra* note 10, at 815 (finding that hedging leads to greater debt usage, increases the debt ratio for the average firm by 3%, and adds tax shields equal to 1.1% of firm value).

[105] John R. Graham & Clifford W. Smith, Jr., "Tax Incentives to Hedge", 54 J. Fin. 2241 (1999) ("From our analysis of more than 80,000 COMPUSTAT firm-year observations, we find that in approximately 50% of the cases, corporations face convex effective tax functions and thus have tax-based incentives to hedge"); Georges Dionne & Martin Garand, "Risk Management Determinants Affecting Firms' Values in the Gold Mining Industry: New Empirical Results", 79 Economics Letters 43 (2003) (hedging among gold-mining firms is positively related to estimated convexity); Morton Pincus & Shivaram Rajgopal, "The Interaction between Accrual Management and Hedging: Evidence from Oil and Gas Firms", 77 Acct. R. 127 (2002) (profitable oil and gas firms use derivatives to smooth income in response to tax incentives). But see Graham & Rogers, *supra* note 10, at 815 (finding no evidence that firms hedge in response to tax function convexity).

[106] See *infra* section 5.1.1.

appealing, since "empire building" offers diversification and private benefits of control. In addition, the complexity of acquisitions can enable managers to negotiate self-interested terms that are obscure enough to escape shareholder notice.

4.3.2 Pigouvian Measures and Management Entrenchment: Parachutes and Greenmail

Since managers have self-interested reasons to resist being acquired, offering them special compensation in this scenario can reduce agency costs. As a result, Pigouvian taxes targeting golden parachutes are potentially counterproductive, as discussed above.[107]

Instead, it would be wiser to discourage the techniques managers use to *resist* acquisitions. In this spirit, the US has a Pigouvian tax on "greenmail," or payments to potential acquirers for ceasing efforts to acquire a firm. The concern about greenmail is that managers are using the firm's money to save their jobs[108] (although some defend the practice as a way of motivating outsiders to monitor management).[109] To discourage greenmail, Section 5881 imposes a 50% tax on greenmail gains. But it is a very blunt instrument. In addition to taxing a premium received only by greenmailers, it also taxes general market appreciation.[110]

4.3.3 Accidental Byproducts: Net Operating Losses and Lock-in as Reasons (or Excuses) for Management Entrenchment

A change in control sometimes triggers tax costs that managers can invoke as a reason (or excuse) not to sell. For instance, when a firm has accumulated tax losses that it cannot use currently ("net operating losses" or "NOLs"), tax is a powerful reason not to be acquired. NOLs are a silver lining of losing money, since a firm can use them to avoid tax in later years. Indeed, profitable acquirers used to buy unprofitable targets in order to access their NOLs. However, to prevent this "loss trafficking," the US enacted Section 382, which severely limits an acquirer's ability to use a target's tax losses. As a result, Section 382 offers firms with NOLs a compelling tax reason to avoid being acquired. Indeed, even an increase in a large shareholder's ownership stake can trigger draconian limits. In effect, NOLs become a poison pill of sorts, and also can prompt firms to adopt *actual* poison pills.[111] The

---

[107] See *supra* section 3.1.7.

[108] See John C. Coffee, Jr., "Regulating the Market for Corporate Control: A Critical Assessment of the Tender Offer's Role in Corporate Governance", 84 Colum. L. Rev. 1145, 1293 (1984); Jeffrey N. Gordon & Lewis A. Kornhauser, "Takeover Defense Tactics: A Comment on Two Models", 96 Yale L. J. 295, 297 (1986–1987) ("[T]arget stock buybacks are unlikely to increase shareholder wealth as a general matter and, on a shareholder wealth criterion, should not be permitted").

[109] Jonathan R. Macey & Fred S. McChesney, "A Theoretical Analysis of Corporate Greenmail", 95 Yale L. J. 13, 15 (1985) ("greenmail payments can be an efficient means of compensating those who supply valuable information to the market (or the firm) about the value of a firm's stock").

[110] For a critique, see generally Edward A. Zelinsky, "Greenmail, Golden Parachutes and the Internal Revenue Code: A Tax Policy Critique of Sections 280G, 4999 and 5881", 35 Vill. L. Rev. 131, 166–68 (1990) (fails to distinguish between good and bad greenmailing).

[111] Mark C. Van Deusen, A Primer on Protecting Tax Losses from a Section 382 Ownership Change, William & Mary Annual Tax Conference, Paper 20, at 18 (2010), http://scholarship.law.wm.edu/tax/20 ("Many public companies with significant NOLs and NCLs have recently adopted poison pill plans that

implications for agency costs are unfortunate. After all, a management team that has generated sizable NOLs usually should be replaced, not protected. Yet in seeking to defend the tax base, Section 382 inadvertently handed self-interested managers an argument for keeping their jobs, while also complicating the task of reviving struggling companies.[112] In approving NOL pills, moreover, Delaware courts have emboldened managers to implement other aggressive takeover defenses; NOL pills have especially low triggers—taking effect when a would-be-acquirer has acquired only 4.99% of the target—and are invoked to justify other low-trigger pills.[113]

In resisting a change of control, self-interested managers also can emphasize the tax bill that would come due. Unsophisticated observers might not realize that this tax problem could be solvable, for instance, with a "tax-free" reorganization (which defers the seller's tax) or a larger deal premium to offset the seller's tax. Again, the tax system's goal here is not to protect management. The relevant tax rule—the so-called "realization rule," which defers gain or loss until the asset is sold—is supposed to make the tax system more administrable, not to influence agency costs. At the same time, rules that allow "tax-free" acquisitions have governance advantages in facilitating a more vibrant market for corporate control.[114]

4.3.4 Accidental Byproducts: Depreciation, Tax Holidays, and Avoiding Net Losses as Reasons (or Excuses) for Empire Building

Managers can invoke tax not only as an obstacle to selling, but also as a justification for buying. Like many tax effects in this chapter, the tax advantages of acquisitions come and go. Before the 1986 tax reform, newly purchased assets offered very generous depreciation in the US, so the tax advantage to purchasers could outweigh the tax cost to sellers.[115] Yet

---

are intended to discourage an ownership change. In 2009, over 40 public companies adopted section 382 poison pills, including Citigroup Inc. and Ford Motor Company").

[112] Samuel J. Dimon, "Limit My Practice Instead! Thoughts on Reforming Section 382", Taxes—The Tax Magazine 65 (March 2010) ("Code Sec. 382 influences corporate decision-making more than it should. Stressed companies too often are inhibited by fear that otherwise rational economic decisions will precipitate an ownership change (or set up conditions where an ownership change could easily occur). As a consequence, stock-for-debt exchanges outside of bankruptcy may be avoided, or pared back, and so may stock offerings to raise needed cash").

[113] *Versant, Enters. v. Selectica, Inc.*, 5 A.3d 586 (Del Sup. Ct. 2010) (approving NOL pill with 4.99% trigger); Paul H. Edelman and Randall S. Thomas, "Selectica Resets the Trigger on the Poison Pill: Where Should the Delaware Courts Go Next?", 87 Ind. L. Rev. 1087, 1090 n. 27 (2012) ("Law firms are already claiming that Selectica validates 'acting in concert' poison pills with 4.99% triggers, which are designed to stop shareholders from engaging in coordinated activities").

[114] Friese, Link & Mayer, *supra* note 74.

[115] See Ronald J. Gilson, Myron S. Scholes, & Mark A. Wolfson, Taxation and the Dynamics of Corporate Control: The Uncertain Case for Tax-Motivated Acquisitions, in Knights, Raiders, And Targets: The Impact Of The Hostile Takeover (John C. Coffee, Jr., Louis Lowenstein, & Susan Rose-Ackerman eds., 1988) (describing this pre-86 strategy); Carla Hayn, "Tax Attributes as Determinants of Shareholder Gains in Corporate Acquisitions", 23 J. Fin. Econ. 121 (1989) (finding that target shareholder capital gains and tax benefit of stepped up basis affect returns of bidder and target after taxable acquisition is announced in pre-86 transactions).

this tax advantage was eliminated when the 1986 act raised corporate capital gains rates (increasing the tax cost to sellers) and lowered corporate ordinary rates (reducing the tax benefit to buyers).[116] Even so, the pendulum swung back (to an extent) after 1993 when the US enacted more generous depreciation for goodwill and other intangibles purchased in acquisitions.[117]

Likewise, the US offered a temporary tax cut in 2004 when US multinationals received dividends from foreign subsidiaries. To claim this "tax holiday," US firms had to invest the money instead of paying dividends or buying back their shares. As a result, many used this cash for acquisitions.[118]

There also is a more enduring tax justification for empire building. A firm with diversified businesses is less likely to have net losses, which cannot be deducted (currently).[119] This advantage flows from a pervasive feature of tax systems that is unlikely to change: taxpayers usually need income to use tax losses. This tax advantage of diversification can reinforce (or rationalize) a manager's personal desire for diversification (discussed above).

4.3.5 Accidental Side-Effects: Complexity as Camouflage

Agency costs arise not only in deciding *whether* to make an acquisition, but also *how* to make it. Various acquisition structures offer different tax consequences,[120] and faithful agents choose the structure that best serves shareholder interests. For example, US buyers are likely to prefer a taxable deal, which gives them a higher tax basis and thus more depreciation. In contrast, US sellers usually favor "tax-free" deals that defer their tax. To resolve this conflict, the parties should choose the structure that minimizes their combined tax liabilities (and advances their business objectives).[121] They can then share the resulting tax savings by

---

[116] Before 1986, corporate capital gains were taxed at 28%, while the maximum rate for ordinary income was 46%. Since 1986, the top rate for both has been 35%. See also Myron S. Scholes & Mark A. Wolfson, "The Effects of Changes in Tax Laws on Corporate Reorganization Activity", 63 J. Bus. S141 (1990).

[117] Section 197; see also Steven L. Henning & Wayne H. Shaw, "The Effect of the Tax Deductibility of Goodwill on Purchase Price Allocations", 22 J. Amer. Tax'n Assn. 18 (2000) (finding that enactment of Section 197 increased purchase price, as buyers shared tax savings with sellers); Connie D. Weaver, "Divestiture Structure and Tax Attributes: Evidence from the Omnibus Budget Reconciliation Act of 1993", 22 J. Amer. Tax'n. Assn. (Supp.) 54 (2000) (enactment of Section 197, which introduced deduction for goodwill, increased the probability of the taxable transaction being structured to obtain a step-up in basis and thus a deduction for goodwill; step-up is more likely when acquiring firm has higher marginal tax rate); Benjamin C. Ayers, Craig E. Lefanowicz, & John R. Robinson, "The Effects of Goodwill Tax Deductions on the Market for Corporate Acquisitions", 22 J. Amer. Tax'n Assn. 34 (Supp.) (2000) (enactment of 197 did not increase frequency of taxable transactions with basis step up, but did increase purchase price premium, so that target gets 75% of tax benefit).

[118] Thomas J. Brennan, Where the Money Really Went: A New Understanding of the AJCA Tax Holiday (March 6, 2014). Northwestern Law & Econ Research Paper No. 13-35.

[119] See, e.g., Randall Morck, Andrei Shleifer, & Robert W. Vishny, "Do Managerial Objectives Drive Bad Acquisitions?", 45 J. Fin. 31, 31–32 (1990).

[120] See generally Mergers, Acquisitions & Leveraged Buy-Outs (Martin Ginsburg & Jack S. Levin eds., 1989).

[121] Gilson, Scholes & Wolfson, *supra* note 115.

adjusting the purchase price.[122] In this way, managers can maximize the after-tax returns of shareholders.[123]

As in other responsibilities, however, managers are not always faithful agents in tax planning. Self-interested tax structuring is especially hard for shareholders to monitor, since tax rules are so esoteric. For example, assume managers have self-interested reasons to buy another company. To clinch the deal, they might accommodate the seller's desire for a tax-free structure, even if a taxable deal is more tax-efficient. This is a form of overpaying, but one that is well hidden from shareholders, who are unlikely to notice the firm's lost depreciation deductions. Alternatively, instead of neglecting the *firm's* tax position, managers can overemphasize their *own* taxes. For instance, in selling the company, managers may seek to minimize their own tax bills as selling shareholders.[124] They might accept a reduced sale price in return for a "tax-free" structure, even though tax exempt and foreign shareholders (who do not owe US tax anyway) would prefer a higher price. Managers who prioritize their own tax bills in this way are effectively taking money from these shareholders, but in a way that is hard to see.

Discerning the true motivation of managers is all the more difficult because deal structuring—such as the use of cash or stock as the acquisition currency—can be explained in other ways. For example, cash deals usually close more quickly and involve fewer hurdles than stock deals.[125] In addition, when an acquirer offers its own stock instead of cash, it may be signaling that its stock is overvalued.[126] Because there are competing considerations, it can be all the more difficult for shareholders to know if managers are making a value-maximizing structuring choice or a self-interested one.[127] To my knowledge, this influence of tax on corporate governance—tax structuring that camouflages self-interested deal terms—is new to the academic literature.

---

[122] Merle Erickson & Shiing-wu Wang, "The Effect of Transaction Structure on Price: Evidence from Subsidiary Sales", 30 J. Acct. & Econ. 59 (2000) (finding that when one firm buys another's sub, price depends on the seller's tax on gain); Benjamin C. Ayers, Craig E. Lefanowicz, & John R. Robinson, "Shareholder Taxes in Acquisition Premiums: The Effect of Capital Gains Taxation", 58 J. Fin. 2783 (2003) (finding that premium paid in taxable acquisitions increases with the capital gains taxes of the target shareholders).

[123] See, e.g., Edward L. Maydew, Katherine Schipper, & Linda Vincent, "The Impact of Taxes on the Choice of Divestiture Method", 28 J. Acct. & Econ. 117 (1999) (finding that the size of the tax differential between divestiture methods affects the form of divestiture; firms with the largest potential tax benefits from using a spin-off opt for spin-offs); William M. Gentry & David M. Schizer, "Frictions and Tax-Motivated Hedging: An Empirical Exploration of Publicly-Traded Exchangeable Securities", 56 Nat'l. Tax J. 167 (2003) (empirical study of use of contingent notes to simulate economics of sale without triggering tax).

[124] The assumption here is they received shares as equity compensation and made an 83(b) election, so they are eligible for "tax-free" treatment in selling these shares.

[125] See Isfandiyar Shaheen, Stock Market Reaction to Acquisition Announcements using an Event Study Approach, 2006, https://dspace.fandm.edu/bitstream/handle/11016/4167/Shaheen.pdf?sequence=1.

[126] Myers & Majluf, *supra* note 73, at 187.

[127] The market may well react to structuring choices; indeed, there is a literature showing that cash deals generate a more favorable market reaction than stock deals. See, e.g., Nickolaos G. Travlos, "Corporate Takeover Bids, Means of Payment, and Bidding Firms' Stock Returns", 42 J. Fin. 943 (1987) (cash bids generate more favorable market reaction for bidder than stock bids); Shaheen, *supra* note 125 (cash bids generate more favorable market reaction for both target and bidder). But in explaining this difference, commentators focus on signaling and the likelihood that the deal closes, and not on the tax difference in these structures or the possibility that managers are allocating tax costs as a less visible means of under- or over-paying. If sophisticated commentators do not focus on these issues, unsophisticated shareholders also are unlikely to do so.

5 Tax and Monitoring: Who is Watching Management?

Although shareholders can reduce agency costs by monitoring management, individual shareholders may not have enough at stake to do so. Their legal ability and economic incentive to monitor can be influenced by the tax system, at least to a degree. While some of these effects are intended, most are not. The tax system not only can encourage (or discourage) shareholder monitoring, but also can substitute for it (at least to a degree). After all, the government has its own revenue-related reasons to monitor management. Even so, this is a mixed blessing for shareholders.

5.1 Shareholder Monitoring

5.1.1 Accidental Byproduct: Inversions and Jurisdiction

Tax has perhaps the greatest impact on shareholder monitoring in influencing where a firm incorporates and, thus, what corporate law protections shareholders have. Under US tax rules, incorporating outside the US offers a notable advantage: avoiding US tax on overseas earnings. Although a Delaware firm owes US tax on profits earned abroad, a Cayman Islands firm does not. Yet this tax savings can come at a cost. Other jurisdictions may not offer comparable shareholder protections, especially tax havens like the Cayman Islands or Bermuda.[128] This means US tax rules offer a reason (or excuse) to incorporate in jurisdictions with weaker legal constraints on managerial agency costs.

A straightforward response to this tax incentive is to incorporate overseas when starting a business. Still, this practice is relatively rare.[129] It is cheaper and easier to organize in the US. Founders also are sometimes unsophisticated about tax planning or are unsure how much non-US profit they will earn. In addition, key investors may want US corporate law protections.

Even so, a US firm can become a non-US firm later. In a so-called "inversion," the US entity that has been the multinational's parent becomes a subsidiary of a new non-US parent.[130]

---

[128] Victor Fleischer, Despite Tax Rules, Companies Stick With US, N.Y. Times, June 6, 2013 ("Minority investors might be nervous about enforcing their contractual and shareholder rights in a court in Bermuda, British Virgin Islands or Ireland"), http://dealbook.nytimes.com/2013/06/06/despite-tax-rules-companies-stick-with-u-s/?_php=true&_type=blogs&_r=0.

[129] Susan C. Morse, "Startup Ltd: Tax Planning and Initial Incorporation Location", 14 Fla. Tax. Rev. 319, 320 (2013) (arguing that "startup firms generally organize as US corporations" because of "limited tax benefits of non-US incorporation, legal benefits of US incorporation, startups' liquidity and other resource constraints, and investor preferences"); Eric J. Allen & Susan C. Morse, "Tax Haven Incorporation for US-Headquartered Firms: No Exodus Yet", 66 Nat. Tax. J. 395 (2013) (finding that US-headquartered MNCs rarely have incorporated parent corporations in tax-haven jurisdictions; only 27 firms, or about 3%, of the 918 US-headquartered MNCs identified in their sample of IPOs have incorporated in tax havens).

[130] Desai & Hines, *supra* note 11, at 410 ("These national differences create opportunities for American companies with foreign income to reduce their tax obligations by expatriating, thereby shedding their American identities and becoming foreign corporations").

Yet after a number of high-profile inversions in the late 1990s and early 2000s,[131] Congress responded with Section 7874, which taxes the new non-US parent as a US firm when the relevant conditions are satisfied. Although Section 7874 shut down this "first wave" of inversions,[132] it does not reach a firm that has substantial business operations in its new sites of incorporation.[133] In addition, the rule does not apply when a US firm combines with a sufficiently large non-US firm. For this combined entity to avoid being taxed as a US firm, the former shareholders of the US firm must own less than 80% of it. Using this rule, a wave of US pharmaceutical companies have bought smaller foreign firms to become Irish, British, Dutch, or Swiss companies.[134] In these deals, shareholder protections can change, depending upon where the new firm is incorporated and what its new charter provides.[135]

While the goal of these tax rules is to have a broader tax base—not to influence corporate governance—the tax system can respond to inversions in various ways, each of which has agency cost implications. One possibility is to make the tax benefits from inversions harder to claim. If this goal is pursued successfully, the incentives to reincorporate overseas (and the associated governance risks) are diminished. Another approach is to stop using the site of incorporation to define tax residence. In the UK and Canada, for instance, tax residence does not turn on where the firm is incorporated, but on where it is *managed*. Under this approach, if senior management stays in the US, there is no US tax advantage to incorporating in the Cayman Islands. Finally, instead of trying *harder* to tax worldwide earnings, the US can stop trying. Most developed economies have territorial systems that tax firms only on domestic earnings, not on foreign earnings. If the US adopts a territorial system, Delaware firms—like Cayman Islands or Irish firms—would not owe US tax on overseas profits. There would no longer be a tax reason to leave Delaware.

5.1.2 *Accidental Byproduct: Choice of Entity*

In the US, tax and governance are in tension in deciding not only where to incorporate, but also what entity to use. A partnership or LLC has a familiar tax advantage over a

---

[131] Donald J. Marples & Jane C. Gravelle, "Congressional Research Services Report 7-5700: Corporate Expatriations, Inversions, and Mergers: Tax Issues", May 27, 2014, 4, http://fas.org/sgp/crs/misc/R43568. pdf ("Among the more high-profile inversions were Ingersoll-Rand, Tyco, the PXRE Group, Foster Wheeler, Nabors Industries, and Coopers Industries").

[132] See generally Jefferson P. Vanderwolk, "Inversions under Section 7874 of the Internal Revenue Code: Flawed Legislation, Flawed Guidance", 30 Nw. J. Int'l. L. & Bus. 699, 700 (2010) ("Section 7874 is widely believed to have had a severe chilling effect on inversions of publicly held corporations").

[133] To make it more difficult to avoid the statute by doing business in the new site of incorporation, the US Treasury increased the safe harbor for substantial business activities from 10% to 25%. This more demanding test makes it less likely this path will be used. Marples & Gravelle, *supra* note 131, at 6.

[134] Doug Gelles & Chad Bray, Drug Firms Make Haste to Elude Tax, N.Y. Times, July 14, 2014, http://dealbook.nytimes.com/2014/07/14/shire-and-abbvie-in-talks-over-53-billion-pharmaceutical-merger/?_php=true&_type=blogs&_r=0. ("It appears that health care companies are playing an expensive game of keeping up with the Joneses").

[135] See Orsolya Kun, "Corporate Inversions: The Interplay of Tax, Corporate, and Economic Implications", 29 Del. J. Corp. L. 313 (2004) (noting that fiduciary duties of managers can be different, and that courts are likely to have less corporate law experience and fewer reported precedents).

corporation: shareholders are taxed, but the entity is not.[136] Under current law, the max-imum US rate for a pass-through entity is 43.4%, compared with a combined 51.5% rate for a corporation.[137] Yet this tax advantage has a governance price, although probably a lower one than inversions: pass-through entities can have weaker investor protections be-cause corporate default rules do not automatically apply. This difference should not be overstated, since these protections can be added to the charter.[138] In addition, investors in a pass-through may not need as much legal protection. Because pass-through treatment is not available for public corporations,[139] there are fewer shareholders, so monitoring is more feasible.

5.1.3 Pigouvian and Unintended Incentives for Long-Term Ownership: Reduced Capital Gains Rates and Lock-in

Tax can affect monitoring also by encouraging long-term investment. To claim the US capital gains preference, for example, investors must hold for at least a year. Yet this pref-erence is an imperfect vehicle for enhancing monitoring. After all, monitoring is effective only if shareholders can influence management, something that is more plausible for large shareholders than small ones.

The analysis is similar for other ways the tax system (inadvertently) encourages long-term holding. The realization rule, in deferring tax until stock is sold, can reduce the present value of tax for those who keep it longer.[140] In the US, the step up in basis at death also discourages sales, since those who die with stock avoid income tax on appreciation.[141] Once again, how-ever, the incentive to hold longer may not translate into better monitoring. In addition, there is no longer an incentive to hold when a tax-free exit is available, for instance, through

---

[136] A further tax advantage of LLCs is that they allow losses to flow through to investors, so that net operating losses are not trapped inside a failed firm. Cf. Joseph Bankman, "The Structure of Silicon Valley Start-Ups", 41 UCLA L. Rev. 1737, 1738 (1994) (noting that Silicon Valley startups are usually C-corporations instead of pass-through entities, and that this structure is potentially tax-inefficient).

[137] A dollar of corporate profit is taxed at 35% at the corporate level and then at 23.8% at the shareholder level (a 20% capital gains tax plus the 3.8% net investment income tax). This leaves only 49.5 cents: 1(1-.35)(1-.238) = .495. In contrast, a dollar taxed once at the maximum individual rate of 39.6 (plus the 3.8% net investment income tax, assuming it applies) leaves 56.6 cents.

[138] For instance, although Delaware LLCs impose fiduciary duties, the case law is considerably less developed than Delaware corporations. Cf. Victor Fleischer, "The Rational Exuberance of Structuring Venture Capital Start-Ups", 57 Tax L. Rev. 137 (2003–2004). (why nontax business considerations often lead firms to organize as corporations instead of as partnerships). A business that wants both Delaware corporate law and pass-through treatment can use an S-Corporation. Yet S-Corporations are subject to various limits that do not apply to LLCs.

[139] Michael Doran, "Managers, Shareholders, and the Corporate Double Tax", 95 Va. L. Rev. 519, 528 (2009) ("Whether it makes policy sense or not, the corporate double tax serves as a toll charge imposed by the government on accessing capital through the securities markets").

[140] Schizer, Realization as Subsidy, supra note 6, at 1551–52.

[141] As James Repetti has observed, though, this rule can have adverse corporate governance effects by favoring retained earnings over distributions. James R. Repetti, "The Misuse of Tax Incentives to Align Management-Shareholder Interests", 19 Cardozo L. Rev. 697, 716–17 (1997).

hedging or a tax-free reorganization.[142] The same is true if stock prices decline; the incentive then is to sell in order to trigger tax losses.[143]

All these effects depend on tax details that vary over time and across jurisdictions. For example, tax effects reduced the concentration of share ownership in both the UK and Germany, but for different reasons. In the UK, estate taxes forced families to sell.[144] Germany, by contrast, was deliberately pursuing a corporate governance agenda, introducing an exemption from the corporate capital gains tax so banks and insurance companies would sell their cross-holdings.[145]

5.1.4 Accidental Byproduct: Tax Exempts, Institutional Investors, and Boards as Monitors

These lock-in effects obviously do not affect tax-exempt shareholders who have no tax liability to defer. In theory, this freedom from tax affords them extra resources for monitoring, as Randall Mork and Bernard Yeung have argued. Yet tax exempts still have the same reason as taxable shareholders not to monitor: they bear the full cost while reaping only part of the benefit.

US tax rules can also influence monitoring by institutional investors. On the one hand, individual investors secure favorable tax treatment by investing in tax deferred accounts; these often (though not always) are invested with an institution, which has more resources for monitoring than an individual investor.[146] On the other hand, US tax rules keep mutual funds from concentrating on a small number of companies, even though this strategy would be more conducive to monitoring.[147] Analogous diversification requirements apply to real estate holding companies (so-called REITS),[148] annuities, and segregated accounts.[149] The significance of these rules should not be overstated, however; institutional investors vary in their willingness to monitor, while the value of their monitoring is debated.

Tax rules can also weaken monitoring by the board. In Germany, director compensation is only partially deductible (as a way to keep it from serving as disguised, and thus untaxed, dividends). According to Wolfgang Schön, this rule discourages firms "from hiring and

---

[142] David M. Schizer, "Frictions as a Constraint on Tax Planning", 101 Colum. L. Rev. 1312 (2001). As noted above, "tax-free" reorganizations can reduce agency costs by enlivening the market for corporate control. See *supra* section 4.3.3.

[143] The price pressure from selling may have positive corporate governance effects but not through monitoring.

[144] Steven Bank & Brian R. Cheffins, Tax and the Separation of Ownership and Control, in Tax and Corporate Governance 111 (Wolfgang Schön ed., 2008).

[145] Courtney H. Edwards, Mark H. Lang, Edward L. Maydew, & Douglas A. Shackelford, "Germany's Repeal of the Corporate Capital Gains Tax: The Equity Market Response", 26 JATA 73 (Supp. 2004); Friese, Link & Mayer, *supra* note 74, at 375 (describing exemption as an effort "to unravel the close net of cross-holdings" in Germany).

[146] Andrei Shleifer & Robert W. Vishny, "Large Shareholders and Corporate Control", 94 J. Pol. Econ. 461 (1986) (Tax on dividends gives investors an incentive to hold stock through tax exempt organizations).

[147] To qualify for pass-through tax treatment, a mutual fund (or so-called "RIC") cannot hold more than 25% of its portfolio in a single company. Section 851(b)(3).

[148] Section 857.   [149] Treas. Reg. 1. 817-5(b).

paying high-class people" for the board,[150] although some firms avoid the constraint by also hiring directors as consultants.[151]

5.2 Shared Interests: Government Monitoring

In addition, the tax system has its own revenue-related reasons to verify a firm's profits, which sometimes have spillover benefits for shareholders.[152] After all, managers who cheat the government might be willing to steal from (or mislead) shareholders as well.[153] Both types of strategies use similar techniques, such as offshore accounts and off-balance sheet entities. As a result, rules protecting the fisc can (inadvertently) protect shareholders as well, as Mihir Desai and Dhammika Dharmapala have emphasized.[154] For example, when the Russian government began cracking down on offshore entities, the Russian stock market reacted favorably.[155] The (bizarre) implication is that managers were stealing more than the Russian government was seeking in taxes.

These spillover benefits are more obvious when book and tax accounting are conformed.[156] In these circumstances, when the tax system demands greater transparency, shareholders receive more informative financial statements. Yet the opposite can be true as well. If book-tax conformity induces firms to report *less* accurately (e.g., understating profits to minimize taxes), shareholders end up with less reliable information.[157]

Even without book-tax conformity, tax enforcement can generate useful information for shareholders in two ways. First, if returns are publicly available—as was briefly true when the US corporate tax was first enacted—they are an independent source of information; indeed, transparency was an early justification for the US corporate tax.[158] Second, even if returns are confidential, managers who have to track information for tax reasons (e.g., on corporate campaign contributions) cannot invoke administrative costs as a reason to withhold it from shareholders.

---

[150] Wolfgang Schön, Tax and Corporate Governance: A Legal Approach, in Tax and Corporate Governance 60 (Wolfgang Schön ed., 2008).

[151] Friese, Link, & Mayer, *supra* note 74, at 392.

[152] Mihir A. Desai, Alexander Dyck & Luigi Zingales, "Theft and Taxes", 84 J. Fin. Econ. 591 (2007).

[153] Michelle Hanlon & Joel Slemrod, "What Does Tax Aggressiveness Signal? Evidence from Stock Price Reactions to News About Tax Shelter Involvement", 93 J. Pub. Econ. 126, 128 (2009) (aggressive tax planning "may signal that the dishonesty extends to the financial accounting statements").

[154] Desai & Dharmapala, *supra* note 8, at 17–18.   [155] Desai, Dyck, & Zingales, *supra* note 152.

[156] In Germany, tax and financial accounting generally are aligned, whereas in the US, tax and financial accounting can diverge in significant ways. See Friese, Link, & Mayer, *supra* note 74, at 376–78, 380–381 (discussing corporate governance advantages and disadvantages of book-tax conformity).

[157] See Hanlon, Maydew, & Shevlin, *supra* note 12 (finding that quality of information to shareholders declined as a result of change in tax law requiring greater book-tax conformity, which induced firms to report more conservatively).

[158] Kornhauser, *supra* note 7, at 134–35 ("publicity" was important early rationale for corporate tax; as first enacted, corporate tax made publicly traded firms' returns available to the general public); Dave Hartnett, The Link Between Taxation and Corporate Governance, in Tax And Corporate Governance 4 (Wolfgang Schön ed., 2008) ("Some countries publish tax returns ... to produce ... transparency").

Needless to say, though, government and shareholder interests are only partially aligned. To shareholders, lowering the tax bill is likely to enhance returns[159] and raise stock prices.[160] As a result, rules requiring the disclosure of tax risks, such as FAS 48, may not advance shareholder interests; while tax risk may become easier to evaluate, it is magnified if the disclosure attracts government scrutiny.[161] In general, shareholders have reason to value tax planning even more than managers, since shareholders do not bear the same downside risks. If the firm is caught being too aggressive, shareholders are unlikely to bear reputational costs, while managers could lose their jobs and even go to jail.[162] This is an agency cost, but a socially useful one.

Just as shareholders may not think they share interests with the tax authorities, the reverse can also be true. The priority of tax authorities is to collect tax, not to protect shareholders. As long as a firm is paying its taxes, tax collectors may not care about earnings manipulation or diversion.[163] Indeed, in a high-profile German case, tax authorities did not intervene even though they knew managers were defrauding shareholders.[164]

6 Conclusion

The bottom line, then, is that tax affects managerial agency costs in a broad range of ways. In the US, tax influences how managers are paid, how they allocate the firm's resources, and

---

[159] See Hanlon & Slemrod, *supra* note 153, at 126 ("in order to maximize the value of the firm, shareholders would like to minimize corporate tax payments net of the private costs of doing so").

[160] See Hanlon & Slemrod, *supra* note 153, at 127 (noting that stock price declines associated with news that corporations are involved in tax shelters tend to be less severe for firms with high effective tax rates; suggesting the reason for this difference may be that shareholders value the fact that firms are "not as 'tax passive' as previously believed"); Katharine D. Drake, Stephen J. Lusch, & James M. Stekelberg, "Investor Valuation of Tax Avoidance and the Uncertainty of Tax Outcomes: Evidence from the pre- and post-FIN 48 periods", Working Paper, University of Arizona, Eller College of Management (March 2014) (investors generally value tax avoidance, although they discount it for tax risk); Michelle Hutchens & Sonja Rego, "Tax Risk and the Cost of Equity Capital", Working Paper, Indiana University (September 2013) (investors do take tax risk into account in valuing companies, especially now that there is an accounting requirement for increased disclosure of tax risk); Mihir A. Desai & Dhammika Dharmapala, "Corporate Tax Avoidance and Firm Value", 91 Rev. Econ. & Stat. 537 (2009) (tax avoidance is positively related to firm value in well governed firms, but negatively related in poorly governed firms).

[161] Schön, *supra* note 150, at 50.

[162] Incentives may vary among managers as well. Tax directors could have higher appetites for tax risk than other managers, for instance, since successful planning can enhance their reputations. See Schön, *supra* note 150, at 49. Yet the other side of the coin is that they have more to lose from unsuccessful planning.

[163] Merle Erickson, Michelle Hanlon, & Edward L. Maydew, "How Much Will Firms Pay for Earnings That Do Not Exist? Evidence of Taxes Paid on Allegedly Fraudulent Earnings", 79 Acc. Rev. 387 (2004) (firms paid significant tax on fraudulent earnings, presumably because they worried more about IRS monitoring than shareholder monitoring).

[164] Schön, *supra* note 150, at 60 (discussing the Baden-Wurteemberg decision, in which the court found for the state in a suit where shareholders sued because the state's tax authorities knew of fraud but did not intervene to stop it).

how effectively they are monitored by shareholders, as well as by the tax authorities themselves. The overall record is unimpressive, but not uniformly so.

Indeed, four effects are particularly useful in mitigating agency costs. First, tax rules discourage executives from hedging stock option grants, thereby backstopping the incentives these grants are supposed to create. Second, tax rules promote the use of equity compensation in venture-capital-backed startups. Third, the tax advantages of leverage pressure managers to issue debt, and thus to generate sufficient earnings to pay interest. Fourth, the tax on intercompany dividends discourages pyramidal ownership. Notably, only the last of these was (arguably) intended by Congress as a response to agency costs.

At the same time, three tax effects are especially pernicious. First, to the extent that tax offers a reason (or an excuse) not to pay dividends, managers have more control over retained earnings, which they can use in self-interested ways. Second, it is unfortunate that managers can invoke tax losses as an argument against being acquired, since these losses are often evidence of poor management. Third, governance can suffer when tax supplies a reason (or excuse) to reincorporate in jurisdictions with weaker corporate law protections.

The reality, though, is that tax authorities are unlikely to focus on these effects. Their institutional mission is to collect taxes, not to target managerial agency costs. It is not surprising, then, that virtually all the Pigouvian measures discussed here are imperfectly tailored or even misguided. Accidental effects do not give any more cause for optimism. Some will escape the notice of government tax experts, while others will not be considered a priority. Given this track record, Congress should use tax only sparingly, if at all, to target agency costs.

Even so, there is value in charting these effects. In some (rare) cases, the tax authorities may be willing and able to adjust tax rules in ways that reduce agency costs. A more promising avenue, though, is to educate corporate governance experts about these tax effects, so they can account for them when tailoring corporate and securities law responses to agency costs.

INDEX